PILOTING,
SEAMANSHIP

AND

SMALL BOAT HANDLING

Piloting, Seamanship

and

Small Boat Handling

---

*A Complete Illustrated Course on the Operation of Small
Boats Supplemented by Hundreds of Problems,
Questions and Answers*

1964-65 EDITION

by CHARLES F. CHAPMAN, M.E.
Publisher of MOTOR BOATING

Published by

959 Eighth Avenue
New York 19, N.Y.

VOLUME V—MOTOR BOATING'S IDEAL SERIES

Copyright
1963
by
THE HEARST CORPORATION
959 Eighth Avenue
New York 19, N. Y.

PRINTED IN THE UNITED STATES OF AMERICA

PREFACE TO 1964–65 EDITION

NOTE:—Page numbers in the 1964–65 edition of this book remain the same as in earlier editions. Additional new material is folioed by the use of letters, a, b, c, etc.

FOR many years *Piloting, Seamanship and Small Boat Handling* has been the most popular book published on subjects of vital interest to all who love or sail boats, either motor propelled or wind driven.

Often it has been necessary to print several editions each year to meet the demand. From its beginning, it has been a text for members of the United States Power Squadrons. Various branches of the Navy, Coast Guard and Army specify it a "must." Many nautical schools and colleges use it in their prescribed courses in Seamanship and Elementary Navigation. It serves members of the Coast Guard Auxiliary from coast to coast.

Although the first edition was published over forty years ago and was considered complete at that time, it was small compared to this latest 624-page edition. Subsequent editions from the first have increased in size, have had much new material added and the range of subjects covered greatly broadened. All data have been kept up-to-date and the provisions of the new laws enacted by Congress included.

FEATURES of special interest which have been added to the new 1964–65 edition include a new section on compass adjusting; a comprehensive discussion of the use of the maneuvering board; specimen questions asked by the Coast Guard when renewing deck officers' licenses; and additional computer-calculated tables to solve current problems by inspection without graphs.

Other features in recent editions deal with the nation-wide system of uniform buoyage on state waters; offshore light stations being built to replace lightships; new types of buoys on Federal waters; amendments to state numbering regulations; suggestions to promote safety at sea; yacht club commissioning ceremonies; and methods to simplify application of compass errors.

Full-color plates have been used for years to highlight significant features in *Chapman's*. In this edition, two color pages show in detail the flags and insignia adopted by the United States Power Squadrons, as well as the official insignia and pennants of the U. S. Coast Guard Auxiliary. These are, of course, in addition to the color plates illustrating flags flown on American craft; lights carried by all types of craft; characteristics of lights on aids to navigation; the buoyage system; and International code flags.

Special features which have proved of outstanding value in recent editions in the instruction classes where *Chapman's* is used as the text include the chapters on Outboard Seamanship, River Piloting, an expanded index and tables of references for specific class lessons.

MANY members of the armed forces and United States Power Squadrons have given the publishers suggestions which have been included in the contents of this edition. My associate on the editorial staff of MOTOR BOATING, William H. Koelbel, is responsible for many of the chapters and particularly for the material which appeared originally in MOTOR BOATING. To all who have contributed so generously toward making this book a success, the author expresses his sincere thanks and appreciation.

Much of the contents is a compilation of data collected from many sources but never before brought together in one volume. No originality is claimed for much of this. Neither is it claimed that seamanship or navigation can be mastered from the printed page alone. But it is felt that if those interested in becoming adept at small-boat seamanship will study the following pages and apply the information with a goodly amount of practice, they will learn to get a greater amount of enjoyment out of boating, promoting safety for themselves and others afloat.

—C.F.C.

Happy Piloting.

This book, now in its 43rd printing
and with each edition enlarged and brought
up to date, has for years been the "bible"
for well over a million boatmen.

It is hoped that those who have read
and studied its contents have been able to
handle their craft with greater skill
and have developed a keener love
of the sea.

—Charles F. Chapman

CONTENTS, 1964-65 EDITION

(See Complete Index, pages 495–504)

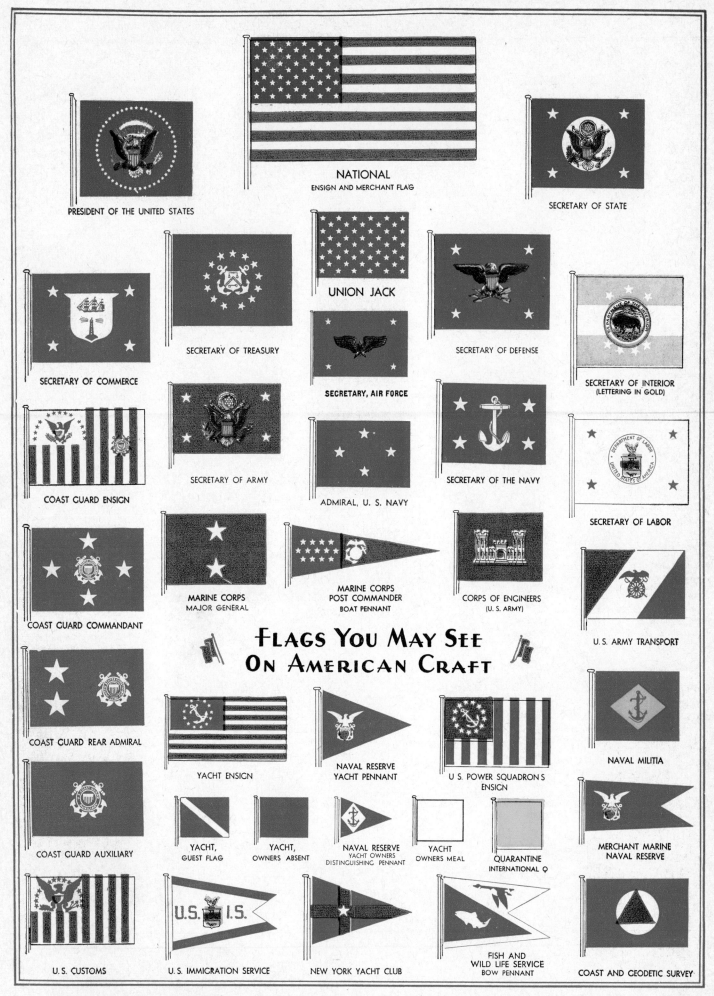

PRESIDENT OF THE UNITED STATES

NATIONAL
ENSIGN AND MERCHANT FLAG

SECRETARY OF STATE

SECRETARY OF COMMERCE

SECRETARY OF TREASURY

UNION JACK

SECRETARY OF DEFENSE

SECRETARY OF INTERIOR
(LETTERING IN GOLD)

COAST GUARD ENSIGN

SECRETARY OF ARMY

SECRETARY, AIR FORCE

ADMIRAL, U. S. NAVY

SECRETARY OF THE NAVY

SECRETARY OF LABOR

COAST GUARD COMMANDANT

MARINE CORPS
MAJOR GENERAL

MARINE CORPS
POST COMMANDER
BOAT PENNANT

CORPS OF ENGINEERS
(U. S. ARMY)

U. S. ARMY TRANSPORT

**FLAGS YOU MAY SEE
ON AMERICAN CRAFT**

COAST GUARD REAR ADMIRAL

YACHT ENSIGN

NAVAL RESERVE
YACHT PENNANT

U. S. POWER SQUADRONS
ENSIGN

NAVAL MILITIA

COAST GUARD AUXILIARY

YACHT,
GUEST FLAG

YACHT,
OWNERS ABSENT

NAVAL RESERVE
YACHT OWNERS
DISTINGUISHING PENNANT

YACHT
OWNERS MEAL

QUARANTINE
INTERNATIONAL Q

MERCHANT MARINE
NAVAL RESERVE

U. S. CUSTOMS

U.S. I.S.

U. S. IMMIGRATION SERVICE

NEW YORK YACHT CLUB

FISH AND
WILD LIFE SERVICE
BOW PENNANT

COAST AND GEODETIC SURVEY

(For U.S.P.S. officers' flags, see pages IX-a and IX-b. For U.S.C.G. Auxiliary pennants, see page X.)

U. S. POWER SQUADRONS' NEW FLAGS AND INSIGNIA

(NATIONAL OFFICERS)

	OFFICE	RANK	SLEEVE INSIGNIA	CAP INSIGNIA	SLEEVE BRAID	FLAG
1	Chief Commander	C/C	3 Gold Crossed Tridents (1¼ in.)	3 Gold Crossed Tridents (2 in.)	1-Two inch 3-Half inch (Spaced ¼ in. apart)	Blue Rectangular 3 Crossed White Tridents (12 inch)
2	Executive Officer	V/C	2 Gold Crossed Tridents (1¼ in.)	2 Gold Crossed Tridents (2 in.)	1-Two inch 2-Half inch (Spaced ½ in. apart)	Red Rectangular 2 Crossed White Tridents (12 inch)
2	Director of Education	V/C	Same as above	Same as above	Same as above	Same as above
2	Administrative Officer	V/C	Same as above	Same as above	Same as above	Same as above
2	Secretary	V/C	Same as above	Same as above	Same as above	Same as above
2	Treasurer	V/C	Same as above	Same as above	Same as above	Same as above
3	As Defined in By-Laws	R/C	One Gold Trident (1¼ in.)	One Gold Trident (2 inch)	1-Two inch 1-Half inch (½ in. Apart)	White Rectangular One Blue Trident (12 inch)
4	As Defined in By-Laws	Stf/C	One Gold Trident (1¼ in.) without Cross Bar and with Interposed Circle	Same as for Rear Commander but without Cross Bar	1-Two inch	White Rectangular One Blue Trident (12 inch) without Cross Bar but with Interposed Circle
5	Flag Lieutenant	F/Lt	Two Gold Crossed Speaking Trumpets ¾ inch long	Two Gold Crossed Speaking Trumpets ¾ inch long	1-Two inch	White Swallowtail Two Blue Crossed Speaking Trumpets (12 in.)
6	Chaplain and Aides to Chief Commander	Aides C/C	Gold Binocular ½ inch across	Gold Binocular ½ inch across	1-Two inch	White Swallowtail Blue Binocular 8 inches in length
	General Member of Governing Board		One Gold Scallop Shell, ½ inch wide with base down	One Gold Scallop Shell, ½ inch wide with base down		None

(DISTRICT OFFICERS)

	OFFICE	RANK	SLEEVE INSIGNIA	CAP INSIGNIA	BRAID	FLAG
7	District Commander	D/C	3 Gold Delta Tridents (1 inch) arranged as Squadron Cdr.	3 Gold Delta Tridents (5/8 in.) arranged same as Squadron Cdr.	1-One inch 3-Half inch (Spaced ¼ in. Apart)	Blue Rectangular 3 White Delta Tridents (10 inch) arranged same as Squadron Commander.
8	District Executive Officer	D/Lt/C	2 Gold Delta Tridents (1 inch) arranged same as Squadron Lt/C	2 Gold Delta Tridents (5/8 in.) arranged same as Squadron Lt/C	1-One inch 2-Half inch (Spaced ½ in. Apart)	Red Rectangular 2 White Delta Tridents (10 in.) arranged same as Squadron Lt. Commander
8	District Administrative Officer	D/Lt/C	Same as above	Same as above	Same as above	Same as above

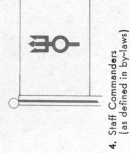

1. Chief Commander

2. Vice Commander—Executive Officer, Director of Education, Administrative Officer, National Secretary, National Treasurer

3. Rear Commanders (as defined in by-laws)

7. District Commander

4. Staff Commanders (as defined in by-laws)

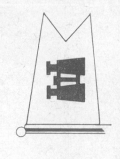

5. USPS Flag Lieutenant

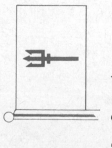

6. Aides to the Chief Commander, National Chaplain

10. District Lieutenants (appointed District Officers and appointed Committee Chairmen other than Chaplain and Aides to District Commander)

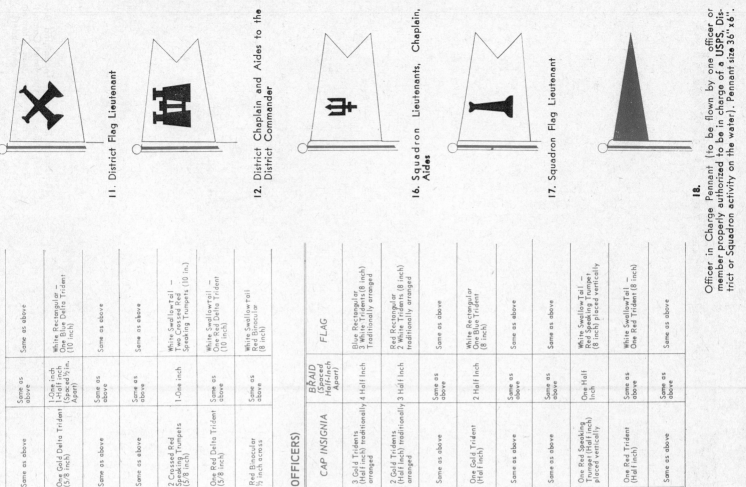

(SQUADRON OFFICERS)

	OFFICE	RANK	SLEEVE INSIGNIA	CAP INSIGNIA	BRAID (Spaced Half-Inch Apart)	FLAG
8	District Educational Officer	D/Lt/C	Same as above	Same as above	Same as above	Same as above
9	District Secretary	D/1st/Lt	One Gold Delta Trident (one inch)	One Gold Delta Trident (5/8 inch)	1-One inch 1-Half inch (Spaced ½ in. Apart)	White Rectangular – One Blue Delta Trident (10 inch)
9	District Treasurer	D/1st/Lt	Same as above	Same as above	Same as above	Same as above
9	Other elected Officers and/or Elected Committee Chairmen	D/1st/Lt	Same as above	Same as above	Same as above	Same as above
11	Flag Lieutenant	D/F/Lt	2 Crossed Red Speaking Trumpets (5/8 inch)	2 Crossed Red Speaking Trumpets (5/8 inch)	1-One inch	White Swallow Tail – Two Crossed Red Speaking Trumpets (10 in.)
10	Appointed Officers Other than Chaplain and Aides to D/C	D/Lt	One Red Delta Trident (One inch)	One Red Delta Trident (5/8 inch)	Same as above	White Swallow Tail – One Red Delta Trident (10 inch)
12	Chaplain and Aides to District Commander	Aide/D/C	Red Binocular ½ inch across	Red Binocular ½ inch across	Same as above	White Swallow Tail Red Binocular (8 inch)
13	Commander	Cdr.	3 Gold Tridents (¾ inch) placed at traditional angle)	3 Gold Tridents (Half inch) traditionally arranged	4 Half Inch	Blue Rectangular 3 White Tridents (8 inch) Traditionally arranged
14	Executive Officer	Lt/C	2 Gold Tridents (¾ inch) traditionally arranged	2 Gold Tridents (Half inch) traditionally arranged	3 Half Inch	Red Rectangular 2 White Tridents (8 inch) traditionally arranged
14	Educational Officer	Lt/C	Same as above	Same as above	Same as above	Same as above
15	Elected First Lieutenant	1st/Lt	One Gold Trident (¾ inch)	One Gold Trident (Half inch)	2 Half Inch	White Rectangular One Blue Trident (8 inch)
15	Secretary	1st/Lt	Same as above	Same as above	Same as above	Same as above
15	Treasurer	1st/Lt	Same as above	Same as above	Same as above	Same as above
17	Flag Lieutenant	F/Lt	One Red Speaking Trump. (Half inch) placed vertically	One Red Speaking Trumpet (Half inch) placed vertically	One Half Inch	White Swallow Tail – Red Speaking Trumpet (8 inch) placed vertically
16	Lieutenant	Lieut.	One Red Trident (¾ inch)	One Red Trident (Half inch)	Same as above	White Swallow Tail One Red Trident (8 inch)
16	Chaplain	Lieut.	Same as above	Same as above	Same as above	Same as above

11. District Flag Lieutenant

12. District Chaplain and Aides to the District Commander

16. Squadron Lieutenants, Chaplain, Aides

17. Squadron Flag Lieutenant

18.

Officer in Charge Pennant (to be flown by one officer or member properly authorized to be in charge of a USPS, District or Squadron activity on the water). Pennant size 36"x6".

8. District Lieutenant Commander (Executive, Administrative and Educational Officers)

9. District Secretary, District Treasurer, other District Elected Officers and/or District Elected Committee Chairmen

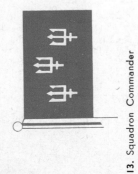

13. Squadron Commander

14. Squadron Lieutenant Commander, Squadron Executive Officer, Squadron Educational Officer

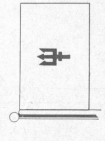

15. Squadron Elected First Lieutenant, Squadron Secretary, Squadron Treasurer

U. S. COAST GUARD AUXILIARY INSIGNIA

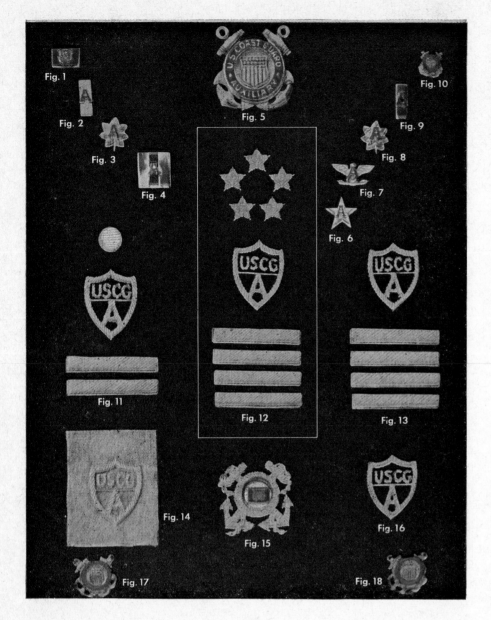

Fig. 1. Civilian lapel emblem.

Fig. 2. Right collar insignia, Flotilla Vice Commander.

Fig. 3. Right collar insignia, National Staff Officer, District Vice Commodore, District Rear Commodore, Division Captain.

Fig. 4. Right collar insignia. District Staff Officer, Division Vice Captain, Division Training Officer, Division Staff Officer, Flotilla Commander.

Fig. 5. Uniform cap device.

Fig. 6. Right collar insignia, National Commodore.

Fig. 7. Right collar insignia, National Vice Commodore.

Fig. 8. Right collar insignia, District Commodore.

Fig. 9. Right collar insignia, Flotilla Training Officer.

Fig. 10. Left collar emblem insignia.

Fig. 11. Right sleeve insignia, Division Staff Officer.

Fig. 12. Right sleeve insignia, National Commodore.

Fig. 13. Right sleeve insignia, Division Captain.

Fig. 14. Right sleeve Corps Device, khaki background, all members.

Fig. 15. Yachting cap device.

Fig. 16. Right sleeve Corps Device, blue background, all members.

Figs. 17 and 18. Garrison cap emblem insignia (women's style).

★ ★ ★

NOTE 1: District Vice Commodore same as Fig. 12 but with two stars. District Commodore same as Fig. 12 but with three stars. National Vice Commodore same as Fig. 12 but with four stars.

NOTE 2: Division Vice Captains same as Fig. 13 but with three bars. Flotilla Commander and Division Training Officer same as Fig. 13 but with two bars. Flotilla Vice Commander and Flotilla Training Officer same as Fig. 13 but with one bar.

NOTE 3: District Staff Officer same as Fig. 11, but with three bars. National Staff Officer same as Fig. 11 but with four bars.

NOTE 4: Collar insignia is worn on khaki uniform shirts only.

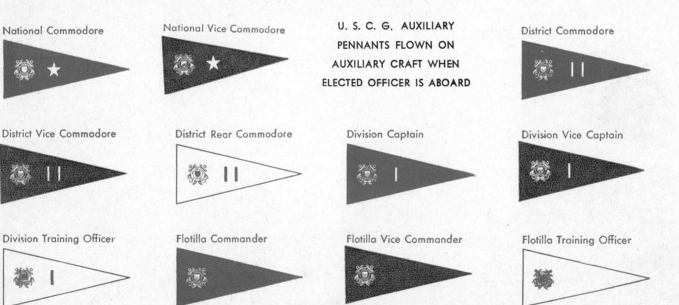

U. S. C. G. AUXILIARY PENNANTS FLOWN ON AUXILIARY CRAFT WHEN ELECTED OFFICER IS ABOARD

National Commodore · National Vice Commodore · District Commodore · District Vice Commodore · District Rear Commodore · Division Captain · Division Vice Captain · Division Training Officer · Flotilla Commander · Flotilla Vice Commander · Flotilla Training Officer

PAST OFFICER BURGEES—These have the same hoist as officers' pennants, with the fly one and one-half times the hoist. The apex of the swallow-tail shall be at a point one and one-sixth times the hoist from the hoist. Position of Auxiliary emblem and insignia of office shall be the same as pennants except for the past district officers' burgees where the two vertical bars shall be seven-tenths and nine-tenths of the hoist from the hoist. Colors of burgees shall be the same as the respective incumbent officers'. NOTE:—Coast Guard, when abbreviating "commodore", uses Como. (with period) or COMO (without period).

CHAPTER I

Equipment and Government Regulations

Equipment Required by The Motorboat Act; Other Equipment Which Should be Aboard; Requirements for a C.G.A. Decal; The Federal Boating Act of 1958; Documenting; Tonnage; Licensing; Inspection; Customs and Immigration Regulations; Report of Accidents; Digest of State Boating Laws; Equipment Carried by U.S.C.G.A. Facilities.

A COMPREHENSIVE knowledge of piloting, seamanship and the proper handling of small boats embraces many subjects. Perhaps the first and most important is an understanding of what constitutes the proper equipment of a motor boat. This includes not only the equipment required by the Motor Boat Act, which specifies what equipment *must* be carried, but also a consideration of other equipment without which the boat cannot be safely, properly and efficiently operated.

Logically considered with this is a study of those regulations which have been drafted to govern the operation of certain types of boats which require licensed operators, licensed officers and crew, and inspection of hull and machinery. As will be pointed out later in greater detail, the motor boat which is operated for pleasure only is primarily concerned with the equipment regulations alone, since she requires no licensed operator, officers or crew, nor is any inspection of her hull and machinery prescribed. She may, however, be boarded for inspection of the equipment required by law.

Division of Motor Boats Into Classes

Under the new Motor Boat Act of 1940, motor boats are divided into four classes according to length. Equipment prescribed by law varies somewhat according to the class. Class A includes boats less than 16 feet in length. Class 1 comprises those of 16 feet or over, but less than 26 feet. Class 2 takes in those from 26 to 40 feet. Class 3 includes motor boats of 40 to 65 feet in length.

Lights

The following few paragraphs relating to lights are only a brief resumé of the type of lighting equipment prescribed for the four classes of motor boats in the Motor Boat Act. Chapter II discusses in detail the lighting requirements for vessels of all classes, including motor boats.

Lights are required on all classes, to be displayed from sunset to sunrise. Motor boats under 26 feet (embracing Class A and Class 1) carry forward a combination red-and-green bow light arranged to show a red light on the port side and a green light on the starboard side. Each colored light shows through 10 points from dead ahead to two points abaft the beam on its respective side. Aft they carry a bright white light showing all around the horizon, arranged higher than the combination light forward.

Lights prescribed for motor boats from 26 to 65 feet (embracing Class 2 and Class 3) are different from those just described. Forward they carry a 20-point white bow light showing from dead ahead to two points abaft the beam on either side. On the port side a separate red 10-point light shows from dead ahead to two points abaft the port beam. On the starboard side a separate green 10-point light shows from dead ahead to two points abaft the starboard beam. Aft, a 32-point white light, higher than the white bow light, shows all around the horizon.

Lighting equipment is not required to be aboard in the daytime.

Other Lighting Requirements

On boats of Class 2 and Class 3 the colored side lights must be fitted with inboard screens of sufficient length and height or mounted on the cabin sides so as to prevent the lights from being seen across the bow.

For all classes, white lights prescribed by the act must be visible at least two miles. Colored lights must be visible at least one mile.

Motor boats of Class 2 and Class 3, when under motor and sail, show the same lights as when they are under motor only (white bow light, red and green side lights and white stern light). Under sail alone, they carry red and green side lights and 12 pt. white stern light.

Motor boats of Class A and Class 1, when under motor and sail, show the lights of their class as a motor boat (red and green combination light forward, and white light aft). Under sail alone, they carry the red and green combination light and 12 pt. white stern light.

Note, however, that under the new law, motor boats and auxiliaries not more than 65 feet in length, may, optionally, elect to carry lights prescribed for their respective classes on the high seas by International Rules. (*See pages 16, 32 and 40.*)

When at anchor, motor boats of all classes must show a white light less than 20 feet above the hull and visible around the horizon for at least one mile. The only exception is in areas specially designated by the Secretary of War as anchorages, where anchor lights are not required.

Since the regulations prescribe that lights must be shown "from sunset to sunrise", no penalty is incurred for failure to carry them by day between sunrise and sunset.

Whistle and Bell

Boats of Classes 1, 2 and 3 must carry an efficient whistle or horn. This is used to give both passing signals and fog signals. A fog horn is not required on motor boats and should not be used in place of a whistle.

On Class 1 the whistle or horn may be hand-, mouth-, or power-operated, and must be audible at least ½-mile. On Class 2, it must be hand- or power-operated, audible at least 1 mile. On Class 3, it must be power-operated, audible at least 1 mile.

In every case the whistle must be capable of producing a blast of 2 seconds or more duration.

The whistle is not required on Class A (less than 16 feet).

Boats of Class 2 and Class 3 must also carry an efficient bell, used when the boat is at anchor in a fog. When struck, it must produce a clear bell-like tone of full round characteristics.

Fire Extinguishers

All motor boats must carry the means for promptly and effectually extinguishing burning gasoline. The number, size and type of fire extinguishers necessary for each class of motor boat to cover this requirement has been prescribed by law. The law stipulates that they must be kept in condition for immediate and effective use and must be placed so as to be readily accessible.

Fire extinguishers are classified as to type and size and a minimum number is prescribed by the Coast Guard for each class of motorboat. The classification and requirements are shown in the tables below.

Fire Extinguisher Classification

Classification type-size	Foam, gallons	Carbon dioxide, pounds	Carbon tetrachloride	Dry chemical, pounds
B-I	1¼	4	Not approved	2
B-II	2½	15		10

Fire Extinguisher Requirements

Class of motor-boat	Length, feet	Minimum number of B-I hand portable fire extinguishers required [1]	
		No fixed fire extinguishing system in machinery space	Fixed fire extinguishing system in machinery space
A	Under 16	1	0
1	16 and over, but under 26	1	0
2	26 and over, but under 40	2	1
3	40 and over, but not over 65	3	2

[1] One B-II hand portable fire extinguisher may be substituted for two B-I hand portable fire extinguishers.

Outboard boats of open construction less than 26 feet in length, not carrying passengers for hire, are not required to carry fire extinguishers. However, if there is an enclosed space, however small, the outboard must carry prescribed fire extinguishing equipment.

Special regulations apply to motor vessels over 65 feet in length and to motor boats and motor vessels of more than 15 gross tons carrying freight or passengers for hire. Generally speaking, they are required to carry a minimum number, size and type of portable extinguishers plus additional protection for machinery spaces. Specific requirements vary with the tonnage of the vessel.

Approved types of fire extinguishers are identified by make and model number. When purchasing be sure to buy only approved equipment. Toxic vaporizing liquid type fire extinguishers (carbon tetrachloride and chlorobromethane types) are not approved.

Life Preservers

All motor boats are required to carry one life-saving device for every person on board, including children and babies. They must be readily accessible.

Motor boats up to 40 feet in length (Classes A, 1 and 2) may carry either regulation approved life preservers, buoyant vests, ring buoys or buoyant cushions.

On Class 3 boats, buoyant vests and cushions are not acceptable. Life-saving devices on Class 3 motor boats must be regulation approved life preservers or ring buoys.

Note that life preservers, buoyant vests and cushions, and ring buoys must all be of a type approved by the Coast Guard.

Approved lifesaving devices carry markings such as stamps of approval, tags, etc. to indicate that they meet Coast Guard requirements. Details concerning these markings for life preservers, buoyant cushions, ring buoys, and buoyant vests are contained in Coast Guard pamphlet CG-290 outlining all legal requirements for motorboats. (Extracts from this are given on page 16.)

On all motor boats which carry passengers *for hire* and on motor boats over 15 gross tons carrying freight *for hire,* each life-saving device must be an approved life preserver. Neither ring buoys nor buoyant vests or cushions are permitted on such craft. Motor boats and motor vessels, carrying passengers *for hire,* must also carry an additional number (10%) of approved life preservers suitable for children (unless children are never carried).

Commercial fishing motor boats may carry life-floats made of light buoyant wood provided they comply with regulations regarding dimensions, weight, construction, materials, etc.

Pneumatic devices or appliances filled with granulated cork are not acceptable.

Exemption of Racing Boats

Motor boats while competing in a race previously arranged or announced, or engaged in tuning up for such a race, are exempt from the need of carrying bells and whistles.

Below are shown some of the articles of equipment that should find a place on every properly equipped boat. The green starboard 10-point sidelight is mounted in the approved manner so that it will not be seen across the bow. A cowl ventilator is placed at the upper end of a duct which leads to the bilge, removing inflammable vapors. The bell, used at anchor in a fog, is conveniently mounted. Electric horns cover the requirement for a sound-producing appliance, used for passing and fog signals. Searchlights, though not required, are useful

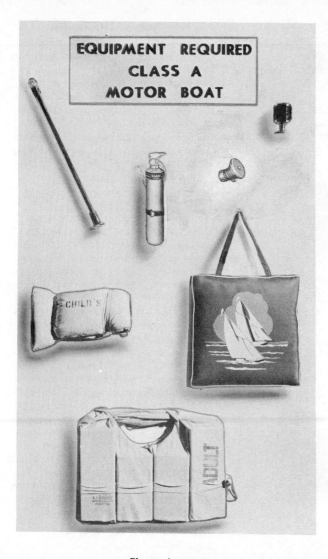

EQUIPMENT REQUIRED
CLASS A
MOTOR BOAT

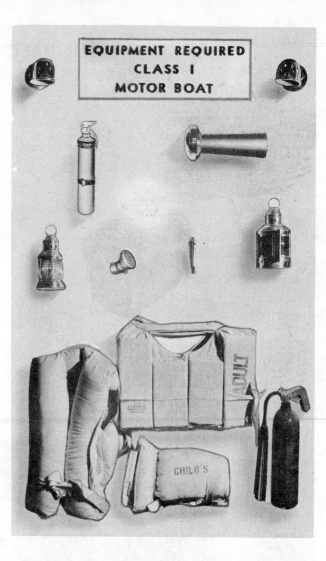

EQUIPMENT REQUIRED
CLASS I
MOTOR BOAT

Flame Arresters

The carburetors on motorboat engines (except outboards) must be fitted with an approved device for arresting backfire. Installations made before November 19, 1952, may be continued in use as long as they are in good condition.

Ventilation

Motor boats built or decked over since April 25, 1940, using gasoline or any other liquid fuel having a flash point of less than 110 degrees Fahrenheit must be equipped with provision for ventilating the bilges of every engine and fuel tank compartment.

The minimum requirement specifies at least two ventilators fitted with cowls or their equivalent, and they must be capable of properly and efficiently removing any inflammable or explosive gases from spaces mentioned.

If the greater part of the bilges under the engine and fuel tanks is open and exposed to the natural atmosphere at all times, ventilators are not required.

Equipment On Inland Lakes

Motor boats operating on other than federal waterways, that is, on inland lakes which do not form part of the boundary line between two states or between this country and Canada, are not required to carry the equipment required by the Federal Government. Boats operating on such inland lakes are under the jurisdiction of the various state governments, many of which require certain specified equipment to be carried on boats navigating the waterways of such states.

Amphibious Vehicles

Amphibious vehicles, when they leave the land and hit the water, are classed as motorboats and must com-

Equipment required by law on motor boats of Class A (under 16 feet) and Class 1 (16 to 26 feet). Note that a bell is not required and that a combination bow light is used instead of the separate bow and sidelights of the larger classes. One fire extinguisher of approved type covers the law on boats under 26 feet. (See p. 16)

ply with applicable Motorboat and Numbering Regulations.

Inspection of Equipment

The United States Coast Guard is charged with the duty of seeing whether the proper Government equipment is aboard every motor boat while under way. Inspectors or members of the U. S. Coast Guard or customs officials are authorized to make such inspections.

A boat must be operated or navigated without proper equipment to incur a penalty. A boat hauled out on shore therefore, is not subject to these requirements. However, a boat temporarily at anchor with persons aboard, which was navigated to the anchorage and will subsequently be operated, must have all required equipment. If tied to a wharf or at anchor with no persons aboard, no equipment is required if there is no intent to operate the craft (except where an anchor light might be required).

A boat of an inspection officer or having an inspection officer on board will fly the flag of the U. S. Coast Guard.

Motorboats Rented by Liveries

Motorboats (including outboards) rented by launch liveries must, of course, comply with the Motor Boat Act as to equipment, etc. On motor boats carrying passengers for hire, a penalty of $200 may be imposed on the owner, operator, or both, for violations having to do with life preservers, fire extinguishers, or licensed operators.

EQUIPMENT REQUIRED
CLASS II
MOTOR BOAT

Class 2 boats (26 to 40 feet) carry a separate white 20-point bow light, red and green 10-point side lights properly screened, 32-point white stern light, a bell, hand or power-operated whistle or horn, a life preserver for each person on board, at least two fire extinguishers and a flame arrester on the carburetor of each gasoline engine. At least two cowl ventilators and ducts to the bilges are required. Note that a box-type buoyant cushion is acceptable in lieu of a life preserver on boats up to 40 feet

How Tonnage Is Measured

Persons unfamiliar with the term tonnage as it is used in connection with the measurement of vessels are likely, in error, to think only of the common ton which is a measure of weight—either 2,000 or 2,240 pounds, depending on whether it is a short or a long ton.

The law repeatedly refers to vessels of a certain tonnage, as for example when it states that a yacht of 5 net tons or over may be documented. Gross tons are not measurements of weight, but of volume.

Gross and Net

Gross tonnage is the total enclosed space or internal capacity of a vessel, calculated in terms of tons of 100 cubic feet each. This has been agreed upon as an average space or volume required by a ton of general merchandise. Gross tonnage includes all spaces below the upper deck as well as permanently closed-in spaces on that deck.

Net (or registered) tonnage is a measurement of the earning power of a vessel when carrying cargo. Therefore, to arrive at a net tonnage figure it is necessary to deduct from the gross the volume of such spaces as would have no earning capacity or room for cargo. For example, from the gross would be deducted engine room, boiler and shaft alley spaces, also fuel compartments and the space required for the steering and working of a vessel, crew's quarters, etc. Many charges against vessels such as canal tolls, harbor dues, etc., are based on the net.

Displacement and Deadweight

Displacement tonnage is the actual weight in tons of 2,240 pounds which a vessel displaces when floating at any given draft. This naturally varies with the draft. The displacement is calculated by figuring the volume of the vessel under water in cubic feet and dividing by 35, since 35 cubic feet of sea water weigh one ton (2,240 pounds).

Deadweight tonnage is the carrying capacity of a vessel, figured by weight in terms of tons of 2,240 pounds. If her displacement were calculated when the vessel was light (but with fuel and stores aboard) and again when she was loaded (with the same fuel and stores aboard), the difference would express the deadweight tonnage.

Very roughly, considering a modern freighter as an example, the gross tonnage would be about 1½ times the net, the deadweight carrying capacity about 2½ times the net, and the loaded displacement about 2¼ times the gross.

Yachts Not Required To Be Inspected or Carry Licensed Officers

The Government does not require that the owner of a motor boat or yacht of any size whatever shall have any knowledge of his boat or navigation or the handling of his boat. Neither does the Government require that a motor boat or motor yacht

14

under 300 gross tons not engaged in trade or not carrying passengers for hire should have on board a licensed officer. Nor are boats of this kind subject to inspection.

No licensed officers are required on motor vessels documented as yachts except on those of 200 gross tons and over when navigating the high seas.

Licensed Officers and Crew

Motor vessels of above 15 gross tons carrying freight or passengers for hire, but not engaged in fishing as a regular business, and sea-going motor vessels of 300 gross tons and over, shall not be navigated unless there are on board such complement of licensed officers and crew as are required by the certificate of inspection.

In the case of such motor vessels, above 15 gross tons, but not more than 65 feet in length, the only licensed officer required by the certificate of inspection shall be a person duly licensed as described in the Motor Boat Law.

In the case of such motor vessels, of above 15 gross tons, and more than 65 feet in length, there will be required by the certificate of inspection at least one pilot and one licensed engineer.

The licensing of pilots and engineers for boats of over fifteen tons gross or over 65 feet in length engaged in trade should not be confused with the operator's license which is required for motor boats of under 65 feet in length or under sixteen tons carrying passengers for hire. On motor boats of this size carrying passengers for hire only an operator's license is required.

Fishing vessels and vessels propelled by machinery not more than 65 feet in length, except tugboats propelled by steam, will not be required to carry licensed officers, except a licensed operator on such vessels carrying passengers for hire.

Inspection of Hull and Machinery

All motor vessels of above 15 gross tons, carrying freight or passengers for hire, but not engaged in fishing as a regular business, and all sea-going motor vessels of 300 gross tons and over, are subject to inspection by the Officer in Charge, Marine Inspection, of the U. S. Coast Guard.

Such vessels may not be navigated without having on board, and posted in a conspicuous place in the vessel, framed under glass, where it will be most likely to be observed by passengers and others, an unexpired certificate of inspection.

The machinery of a motor boat over 40 feet in length, if propelled by steam, would be subject to inspection.

Under the provisions of the Ray Act (Public Law 519) which became effective May 10, 1956, inspection is required, at least every three years, of all vessels carrying more than six passengers. Types of vessels specifically affected include sailing vessels of 700 gross tons or less; barges of 100 gross tons or less; and mechanically-propelled vessels of 15 gross tons or less (thus affecting, for example, the usual types of charter fishing boats, etc.). For detailed regulations, which became effective June 1, 1958, consult the Officer in Charge, Marine Inspection, U. S. Coast Guard. (See also page 484.)

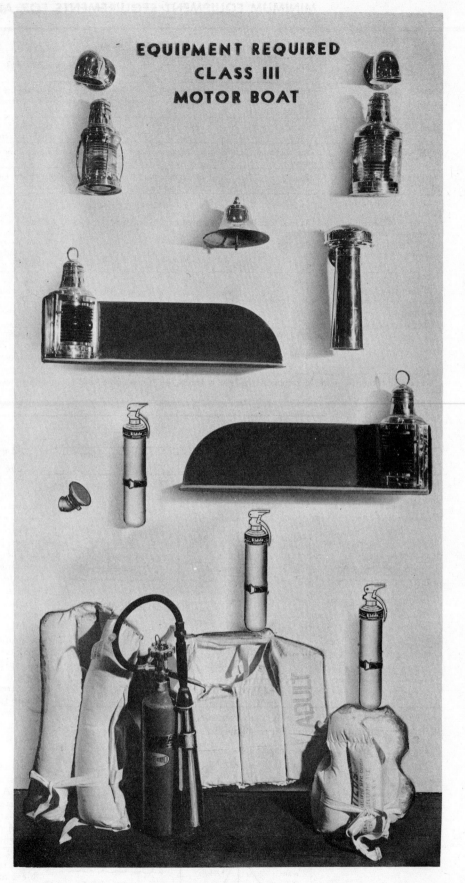

EQUIPMENT REQUIRED
CLASS III
MOTOR BOAT

Equipment for Class 3 (40 to 65 feet) is the same as that required for Class 2 motor boats with a few exceptions. The whistle or sound-producing device on Class 3 must be power-operated. Buoyant cushions are not allowed as life preservers on Class 3, although ring buoys (not shown) are. Not less than three fire extinguishers of approved type and capacity are required. Lights, bell, flame arresters and proper ventilation are also required, as on Class 2. The table on p. 16 summarizes differences in each class

MINIMUM EQUIPMENT REQUIREMENTS FOR ALL MOTORBOATS

EQUIPMENT	CLASS A (Less than 16 feet)	CLASS 1 (16 feet to less than 26 feet)	CLASS 2 (26 feet to less than 40 feet)	CLASS 3 (40 feet to not more than 65 feet)
BACK-FIRE FLAME ARRESTOR	One approved device on each carburetor of all gasoline engines installed after April 25, 1940, except outboard motors.			
VENTILATION	At least two ventilators fitted with cowls or their equivalent for the purpose of properly and efficiently ventilating the bilges of every engine and fuel-tank compartment of boats constructed or decked over after April 25, 1940, using gasoline or other fuel of a flashpoint less than 110° F.			
BELL	None.*	None.*	One, which when struck, produces a clear, bell-like tone of full round characteristics.	
LIFESAVING DEVICES	One approved life preserver, buoyant vest, ring buoy, or buoyant cushion for each person on board.			One approved life preserver or ring buoy for each person on board.
WHISTLE	None.*	One hand, mouth, or power operated, audible at least ½ mile.	One hand or power operated, audible at least 1 mile.	One power operated, audible at least 1 mile.
FIRE EXTINGUISHER— PORTABLE When NO fixed fire extinguishing system is installed in machinery space(s).	At least One B–I type approved hand portable fire extinguisher.		At least Two B–I type approved hand portable fire extinguishers; OR At least One B–II type approved hand portable fire extinguisher.	At least Three B–I type approved hand portable fire extinguishers; OR At least One B–I type *Plus* One B–II type approved hand portable fire extinguisher.
When fixed fire extinguishing system is installed in machinery space(s).	None.	None.	At least One B–I type approved hand portable fire extinguisher.	At least Two B–I type approved hand portable fire extinguishers; OR At least One B–II type approved hand portable fire extinguisher.

B–I Type Approved HAND PORTABLE FIRE EXTINGUISHERS contain: Foam, 1¼ up to 2½ gallons; or Carbon Dioxide, 4 up to 15 pounds; or Dry Chemical, 2 up to 10 pounds.

B–II Type Approved HAND PORTABLE FIRE EXTINGUISHERS contain: Foam, 2½ gallons; or Carbon Dioxide, 15 pounds; or Dry Chemical, 10 up to 20 pounds.

*NOTE.—Not required by the Motorboat Act of 1940; however, the "Rules of the Road" require these vessels to sound proper signals.

Under Power alone	Auxiliaries under Sail and Power	Auxiliaries under Sail alone

INLAND RULES.—These lights may be shown only on Inland Waters, Western Rivers, and Great Lakes.[1]

Under 26 Feet

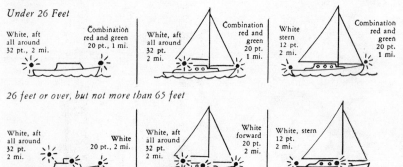

26 feet or over, but not more than 65 feet

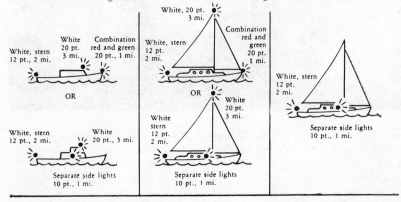

INTERNATIONAL RULES.—Lights under International Rules may be shown on Inland Waters, Western Rivers, and Great Lakes, and are required on the high seas.

Power vessel under 40 gross tons and sail vessels under 20 gross tons [2]

Lights Required—Inboards, Outboards, Auxiliaries

The tables on this page, taken from the *Recreational Boating Guide*, CG-340, U. S. Coast Guard, for sale by the Superintendent of Documents, U. S. Government Printing Office, Washington 25, D. C., at 40 cents per copy, are a brief resumé of equipment required on motorboats. For detailed information, see pages 11-15 and 28-46.

The lights shown in the table at the left are the running lights required on motorboats (including inboards, outboards and auxiliaries) between sunset and sunrise. Boats at anchor (except those not over 65 feet in length in special anchorage areas designated by the Secretary of the Army) must also display anchor lights.

A motorboat on the waters of the United States may carry the lights prescribed by the Motorboat Act of April 25, 1940, or it may carry the lights prescribed by the International Rules. In addition, there are requirements for special lights contained in the applicable Inland, Western Rivers, and Great Lakes Rules.

A motorboat on the high seas *must* carry the lights prescribed by the International Rules, and *only* these lights.

* * * *

NOTES:—The following notes apply to the table of lights at the left:

1. A motorboat under sail alone on the Great Lakes is not required to display a stern light. All motorboats under sail alone must on approach of another vessel display a white light in the direction of the approaching vessel.

2. Under International Rules powerboats of 40 gross tons or over must carry separate sidelights, visible 2 miles, and a 20-point white light visible 5 miles. Sailing boats of 20 gross tons or over must carry separate sidelights, visible 2 miles. Those less than 20 gross tons may use a combination lantern, if under sail alone.

BUOYANT CUSHIONS AND JACKETS—Buoyant material used in Coast Guard approved kapok and fibrous glass life jackets and cushions manufactured since 1960 is protected by plastic bags. Those not conforming to this approved standard were to have been outlawed July 1, 1963 but the deadline was extended to Jan. 1, 1965. If your jackets and cushions were purchased before 1960, you must request extension of the deadline from the Coast Guard inspection officer when he boards your craft. Older equipment must be in first-class condition to pass inspection.

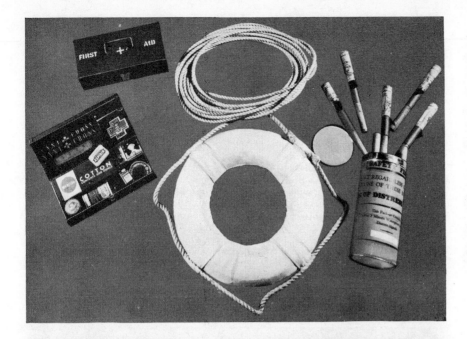

Left—To cover the law, a boat may carry regular life preservers or box type cushions for her life saving devices, but in addition, at least one ring buoy should be aboard. On boats not carrying passengers for hire it passes as a life preserver. Attached to it should be a length of strong light line and it should be so mounted that it can be thrown quickly to a person in the water. First aid essentials are packed in regular kits. With it there should be a good first aid manual. One of the most effective means of summoning aid is the use of flares which can be purchased in a small watertight container, convenient to stow. More elaborate equipment consists of a pistol that shoots a parachute type of flare

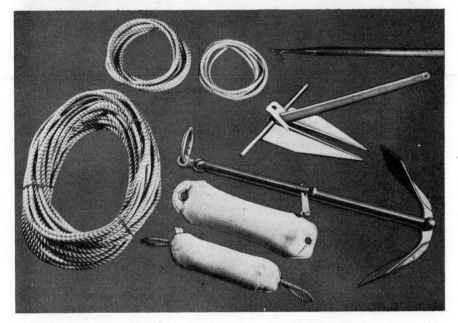

Left—Carry at least two anchors, preferably three. For brief stops, a light anchor is sufficient. Overnight stops and all-around service require one of greater holding power. A heavy spare should be aboard for emergencies. Anchors should be selected on the basis of holding power, not by weight alone. Anchor lines should be manila or nylon, generous in length, not necessarily thick in diameter, but strong. An extra long new unused line should be aboard for use with the spare anchor. Large craft often use chain. A couple of dock lines and a few extra lines for spring lines and general use should also be carried. For picking up mooring lines, the boat hook is useful. A number of fenders will be essential for the protection of the hull

complete and detailed inventory. Rather they emphasize some of the more important articles of equipment; others will suggest themselves to the boatman from time to time.

Illustrated are such items as anchors and lines, boat hook, fenders, bilge pump, tool kit, spare engine parts, piloting equipment, auxiliary lighting equipment, and such special safety equipment as ring buoys, flares, and a first aid kit.

In the same category with tools and spare parts we might include a few good carpenter's tools, extra pieces of line of several sizes, a ball of marlin, an assortment of nails, screws, bolts, washers, wire, caulking cotton, paint, etc. On boats equipped with sails a small repair kit should be added containing twine, wax, needles, palm, fid, and similar articles. All should be properly stowed to keep it accessible and in good condition.

Other miscellaneous items would be a deck mop, pail (some prefer a canvas bucket), a chamois for cleaning windows, brass polish, a supply of oil for engine, grease (both the regular and waterproof varieties as required), some light machine oil and penetrating oil for rusted parts, vaseline petroleum jelly, distilled water, a hydrometer, some clean rags and several rolls of paper towels. An emergency tiller is often carried.

Club burgee, ensign and owner's private signal or officer's flag are usually found aboard, together with any

OTHER ARTICLES OF EQUIPMENT WHICH

SHOULD BE ABOARD EVERY WELL-FOUND

BOAT, THOUGH NOT REQUIRED BY LAW

THE Motor Boat Act prescribes that motor boats must carry certain equipment for the safety of those aboard. This includes life preservers, lights, whistle, bell, fire extinguishers, flame arresters on carburetors, ventilating cowls and ducts for the bilges, and the certificate of registration. These requirements vary with the class of boat, and certain exceptions are made in some classes.

In addition to this required equipment, however, there are other things which should be aboard before a boat may be considered to be well-found. The extent of cruising the boat does will determine the amount and kind of equipment.

The items illustrated here should not be taken as a

Left—Every boat should be equipped with a good bilge pump, one that will really throw quantities of water without effort. Its intake should be screened to prevent its being clogged by chips and other matter in the bilge. Don't use a supply line from pump to strainer that may collapse with suction. A good set of mechanic's tools, though seldom required, should always be aboard. Some spare parts for the engine are desirable. An extra coil, a condenser, breaker points for the distributor, some spark plugs, extra wire, tape, gasket material, etc., are among the more important items

Below—Essentials of piloting equipment would include a good compass, parallel rules or course protractor, a timepiece, dividers, pencil and log book, lead line, charts, pelorus or bearing finder, and up-to-date charts. A barometer and good pair of binoculars are very useful. Certain publications are particularly valuable in piloting, such as Tide and Current Tables, Tidal Current Charts, Light Lists and the Coast Pilot. All should be kept up-to-date by means of corrections published in Notices to Mariners. For general information the Yachtsman's Guide is very helpful. The compass should be properly installed and with it should be a deviation card showing its error. Some boats have a patent log to record distance run, and a marine type of speedometer is excellent. A tachometer to record engine revolutions may be used to determine speed, from which distance may be computed

other flags that might be desired. A set of signal flags would be a good investment. Slickers or some other form of wet weather clothing will be required at times.

The gallery will be stocked with utensils of the owner's selection, together with the usual food supplies when cruising. Lay aside in a locker some canned foods and pilot biscuits in air-tight tins as an emergency reserve.

Modern radio equipment is a source of great satisfaction. A good receiving set for entertainment and weather reports is fine and the radiotelephone is becoming increasingly popular. The radio direction finder is a valuable adjunct to piloting equipment.

Right—Provide your boat with plenty of lighting equipment, entirely independent of the boat's electrical system. A waterproof hand flashlight would be a minimum. Some types of battery-operated portable flashlights can be carried like a lantern. A trouble light that can be clipped directly on the terminals of the boat's storage battery is a fine thing when working around an engine. A built-in searchlight is invaluable for picking up aids to navigation at night and when maneuvering around docks and moorings. The more powerful the better, but don't play it on other craft. Sailing craft and other boats without a storage battery may use a portable searchlight mounted directly on a battery. Another handy light is the portable searchlight which can be held in the hand but operated from the boat's regular battery. Spare bulbs should be carried for all of the boat's lighting equipment, and fuses as well

EQUIPMENT REQUIRED FOR AWARD OF A C.G. AUXILIARY SEAL OF SAFETY

Coast Guard Auxiliary decal displayed on a boat shows she meets high standards of safety, above minimum legal requirements. Free examinations of equipment, never compulsory, given by Auxiliary members on boat owner's request

Have you ever wondered about the significance of those attractive shield-shaped decalcomanias prominently displayed by some of the boats in your area? Perhaps you have guessed they were the symbol of membership in some boating club or organization. They're not, as such, but rather identify the owner as one who maintains his boat according to a relatively high standard outlined by the U. S. Coast Guard Auxiliary.

Practically everyone is, or should be, aware of the fact that all motorboats must meet certain minimum safety standards by complying with regulations outlined in the Motorboat Act, specifying the equipment each is to carry, according to its class. When a motorboat is inspected by the Coast Guard, these are the minimums which have been set to avoid citation for violation of this Act. These legal requirements have been discussed elsewhere, so we will not repeat here.

In the interest of a high degree of safety on the water, the Coast Guard Auxiliary has specified certain other additional conditions which, though not legally required, must be met if a boat is to earn the Coast Guard Auxiliary's Courtesy Examination decal.

Courtesy examinations—they are not "inspections"—are made by qualified members of the Coast Guard Auxiliary, a civilian group. They are performed strictly as a courtesy to the boat owner, upon his request, with a view toward making boating more enjoyable through safety, education and knowledge. Examinations are never forced on an owner.

The Shield of Safety

After a boat has been examined, the decal for the current year will be awarded if the boat meets all requirements. Display of the decal on a boat generally means that the Coast Guard will not board that boat for a formal inspection unless a violation in operation or required equipment is apparent. If the courtesy examination reveals any deficiencies, they are not reported as violations but are brought to the attention of the owner so he will have an opportunity to correct them.

Suppose, then, that we have equipped our boat so that she complies with every legal requirement of the Motorboat Act, as to life preservers, lights, fire extinguishers, whistles, bells, ventilation, flame arresters, etc. Just what more will the C.G.A. Courtesy Examiner expect before he considers that the boat rates a decal? Here's the gist of what the official Vessel Examiners Guide (CG-289) has to say about each point.

Amplification of Legal Requirements

LIGHTS—Though the Motorboat Act does not require lights to be aboard during daylight hours, the decal will not be awarded unless the boat is so equipped, the lights are operative, and visible through the required arc.

LIFESAVING EQUIPMENT—There must be at least as many approved devices on board as there are berths, with two as a minimum, even if there are less than two berths.

FIRE EXTINGUISHERS—Class A and 1 motorboats having a fixed CO-2 system in the engine room must also have at least one portable extinguisher. Outboard boats, of open construction, less than 26 feet in length not carrying passengers for hire, are not required by law to carry extinguishers, but class 1 outboards must have at least one hand portable extinguisher to qualify for the decal.

FLAME ARRESTERS—Carburetors must be equipped with flame arresters, regardless of when the engine was installed.

NUMBERS—Must be of correct size and style, properly applied.

Other Items Checked

The paragraphs above amplify the legal requirements. Other points the examiner will check are as follows.

GALLEY STOVES—These must be installed so they cannot shift, and located so no flammable material nearby can be ignited. Any of the common types of stove fuel may be used, except gasoline. Decals will not be awarded to boats equipped with gasoline stoves.

FUEL TANK FILLER PIPE—The fuel tank filler pipe must be connected to a filler plate on deck, outside the cockpit, to prevent vapors from getting inside the boat and to assure that overflow when fueling will run overboard. If the cockpit is self-bailing, filling pipes may connect to plates in the deck of such cockpits.

FUEL TANK VENTS—Vent pipes of fuel tanks must lead outboard, and never discharge into enclosed spaces.

CARBURETOR DRIP PAN—Downdraft carburetors, because of their construction, require no drip pan. Updraft carburetors, however, must have a drip pan installed beneath them, equipped with fine mesh wire screen to prevent gasoline in the pan from catching fire. Preferably, drip pans should be connected by thin copper tube to the intake manifold to empty them automatically. If not so equipped, the owner should empty the pan frequently to prevent accumulation of gasoline. Some updraft carburetors have a vacuum sump which prevents leakage; these do not require a drip pan.

General Condition of Boat

GENERAL CONDITION—Boats, to earn a decal, must be in good overall condition. Bilges must be clean and free from oil, grease and water. Fuel lines must be intact and preferably lead from the top of the fuel tanks. Electrical wiring and fittings must comply with good marine practice, be in good condition, and installed to minimize danger of short circuits. The hull must be generally sound. In fact, the boat as a whole must, in the examiner's opinion, be shipshape and seaworthy.

CLASS A BOATS—Class A boats (those under 16 feet in length), whether inboard or outboard, must meet the same basic requirements as outlined, but must in addition carry certain other equipment before a decal may be awarded. This includes a distress flare, one paddle or oar, anchor and line suitable to the locality, and an adequate pump or bailer.

RADIOTELEPHONE CHECK—While the presence or absence of a radiotelephone, or its condition, has no bearing on the award of a decal, a boat owner may request a check of his equipment. The examiner will do this as a further courtesy, and will not report any violations to enforcement officials, but merely bring them to the owner's attention for correction.

THE FEDERAL BOATING ACT OF 1958

First drastic revision of nation's small-boat registration system since 1918 provides new regulations for numbering undocumented vessels by states—requires report of accidents—and makes provision for civil penalties for violations, imposed by Coast Guard

THE intent of the Federal Boating Act of 1958 is defined by the subtitle of the document itself: "An act to promote boating safety on the navigable waters of the United States, its Territories, and the District of Columbia; to provide coordination and cooperation with the States in the interest of uniformity of boating laws; and for other purposes." That "coordination and cooperation" are key words for the law provides that the states were to have first crack at setting up its legislation. The limit to the provision is that the state-enacted legislation be within the federal framework.

States had to: (1) Institute a system of numbering in accordance with the Federal Act; (2) provide for the re-numbering of boats at least every three years; (3) agree to a reciprocity period of 90 days in recognizing numbers awarded by another state, and (4) require that reports be made to the state concerning accidents involving vessels numbered by the state under its numbering system. These four points are the principal requirements a state must have met to comply with the Act.

They are broad requirements, though, allowing plenty of room for modification. States were able, for instance, to lower or eliminate the 10-horsepower exemption (explained below) to include all types of pleasure craft, from dinghies to sailboats.

WHAT GETS NUMBERED: The Act calls for the numbering of every undocumented * vessel propelled by machinery of more than 10 horsepower, whether or not such machinery is the principal source of propulsion, using the navigable waters of the United States, its territories and the District of Columbia, and every such vessel owned in a state and using the high seas. Exceptions are:

(1) foreign vessels temporarily using the navigable waters of the U.S., its territories, etc.;

(2) public vessels of the U.S.;

(3) state and municipal vessels;

(4) ships' lifeboats;

(5) certain vessels specifically desig-

* "Undocumented Vessel" here means any vessel not required to have, and does not have, a valid Marine Document.

HIGHLIGHTS

In substance, this Act requires that the operator of any boat involved in an accident causing death, personal injury, or property damage, must stop, render aid, offer identification, notify authorities, and file a written report.

It provides for the publication by the Coast Guard of statistics based upon the accident reports.

It amends the Motorboat Act of April 25, 1940, to permit the imposition of a civil penalty by the Coast Guard for reckless or negligent operation, failure to obey the Rules of the Road, failure to comply with the regulations, etc. (Note: the new Law makes NO CHANGE IN THE REQUIREMENTS of the Motorboat Act of 1940 respecting lifesaving equipment, fire extinguishers, lights, or other equipment.)

It requires the numbering of all undocumented vessels on the navigable waters of the United States, propelled in whole or in part by machinery of more than 10 horsepower (in the aggregate), regardless of the vessel's length. Numbers issued under this act are for identification only and do not authorize any vessel to engage in trade.

Boats are numbered according to the state of principal use, and that state may, at any time, by the enactment of a suitable law, assume the numbering functions.

Until April 1, 1960, the Coast Guard continued to issue numbers in accordance with the Numbering Act of 1918 *except* in those states that assumed the numbering functions under the Federal Boating Act of 1958. This necessitated issuance as of April 1, 1960, of new numbers by the Coast Guard to all boats subject to this new act and principally used in states which, by that date, had not assumed the numbering functions.

---

nated by the Secretary [of the Treasury] as being exempt;

(6) Undocumented vessels used exclusively for racing; and

(7) Undocumented vessels operating under valid temporary certificates of number.

That "10 horsepower" terms as used here means the total of all propellant machinery on a vessel. In general, the Coast Guard will accept as evidence of the horsepower of the machinery in question, the manufacturer's rated horsepower at a stated maximum rpm as given on the nameplate attached to the engine, or as described in a "book of instructions" or other literature issued for the engine.

States administering their own system will probably do the same. If a state has not acted by April 1, 1960, the Coast Guard must administer the program, collect the fees ($3 for first numbering, $3 for renewal, $1 for re-issue of lost or destroyed certificate of number), and register the state's boats that come under the Act's provisions.

WHERE IT GOES: The Act says: "The number awarded shall be required to be painted on, or attached to, each side of the bow of the vessel for which it was issued, and shall be of such size, color, and type, as may be prescribed by the Secretary." And prescribed it has been. On March 10, 1959, the following regulation, one of several passed to implement the Federal Boating Act,* became effective:

"The numbers shall be placed on each side of the forward half of the vessel in such position as to provide clear legibility for identification. The numbers shall read from left to right and shall be in block characters of good proportion not less than 3 inches in height. The numbers shall be of a color which will contrast with the color of the background and so maintained as to be clearly legible; i.e., dark numbers on a light background, or light numbers on a dark background."

WHAT YOU GET: The actual certificate of number—and remember, we are talking about the Federal Government's system now—includes: name, address,

* See *Federal Register*, December 25, 1958.

date of birth, and present citizenship of owner; state in which the vessel is principally used; hull material (wood, steel, aluminum, plastic, other); length of vessel; make and year built (if known); type of propulsion; type of fuel; declaration as to use (pleasure, livery, dealer, manufacturer, commercial-passenger, commercial-fishing, commercial-other); ownership certification by the applicant; number awarded to vessel; expiration date of certificate; and the owner's signature.

Also included on the certificate of number, which, incidentally, is pocket size (approximately 2½" x 3½") and water resistant, is a notice to the owner that he (1) report within 15 days changes of ownership or address, and destruction or abandonment of vessel; (2) report every accident involving injury (personal injury causing incapacitation for more than 72 hours) or death to persons, or property damage over $100; (3) stop and give aid if involved in a boating accident; and (4) always carry this certificate on the vessel when it is in use.

NUMBERING MANUFACTURERS' BOATS: Provision has been made to meet the requirements of boats operated by manufacturers and dealers. The description of the boat will be omitted from the certificate of number because the numbers and the certificates of number awarded may be transferred from one boat to another. In place of the description, the word "manufacturer" or "dealer" will be inserted on each certificate.

The manufacturer or dealer may have the awarded number printed upon or attached to a removable sign or signs to be temporarily mounted upon or attached to the boat being demonstrated or tested so long as the display meets the requirements (see previous section "Where It Goes").

The certificate of number of livery boats will be marked "livery boat" and the description of the motor and type of fuel will be omitted where the motor is not rented with the boat.

One more point concerning the certificate of number needs clearing. If a vessel is to be principally used on the high seas, it will be assigned a number for the state in which the vessel is usually docked, moored or berthed.

ABOUT CHANGES: When the owner of a vessel numbered by the Coast Guard changes the state in which the vessel is principally used, he must within 90 days surrender the certificate of number to the Coast Guard, and apply for another original number to the office issuing numbers for that state.

If only the address is changed but not the state, the owner must within 15 days notify the Coast Guard of his new address.

It may be fruitful to remind the reader that most of the above is in effect only in states which have not enacted their own legislation under the Federal Boating Act. Even so, however, the requirements will be similar to those listed here. And regardless of whether the state or the Coast Guard is administering the system, one thing is certain: every inboard and outboard boat powered by an engine of more than 10 horsepower must carry an assigned number on its bows if it operates on waters under federal control (navigable waters).

ACCIDENT REPORTING: The new accident-reporting program *in force on all federal waters* throughout the nation stipulates that whenever a death results from a boating accident, a written report shall be submitted within 48 hours. For every other reportable boating accident a written report shall be submitted within five days after the accident.

The written reports must be submitted to the Coast Guard Officer in Charge, Marine Inspection, nearest the place where the accident occurred or nearest to the port of first arrival after the accident. If more than one boat is involved, a separate report must be submitted by the operator of each boat. If the operator is not physically capable of making the report it should be made by the boat owner or other person familiar with the facts of the accident. Every written report must give the following information:

(1) The numbers and names of vessels involved.

(2) The locality where the accident took place.

(3) The time and date of the accident.

(4) Weather and sea conditions at time of accident.

(5) The name, address, age, and boat operating experience of the operator of the reporting vessel.

(6) The names and addresses of operators of other vessels involved.

(7) The names and addresses of the owners of vessels or property involved.

(8) The names and addresses of any person or persons injured or killed.

(9) The nature and extent of injury to any person or persons involved.

(10) A description of damage to property (including vessels) and estimated cost of repairs.

(11) A description of the accident (including opinions as to the causes).

(12) The length, propulsion, horsepower, fuel and construction of the reporting vessel, and

(13) Names and addresses of known witnesses.

The Coast Guard Form CG-3865 (Boating Accident Report) may be used for the written accident report required.

Photograph by U. S. Coast Guard—UPI

Administration of the Federal Boating Act is under the jurisdiction of the U. S. Coast Guard. In the dramatic illustration above, the Coast Guard is shown engaged in one of its activities centered about the safeguarding of life and property at sea, as a patrol boat crosses an inlet bar against a breaker—no place for any but Coast Guard boats. (See Chapter XXVIII, pp. 439a-439t, Seamanship in Breaking Inlets.)

DOCUMENTATION
(See also page 474)

Not all vessels come within the provisions of the Numbering Act. For example, those vessels which are documented as vessels of the United States by the Bureau of Customs are not subject to the requirements for numbering as motorboats. The documents which are issued to vessels by that Bureau are of five forms, namely: register, enrollment and license, license, yacht enrollment and license, and yacht license.

Marine documents are also described as permanent, granted to vessels at their home ports; and temporary, granted to vessels at ports other than their home ports.

A vessel under a register which is not limited by a prohibitive endorsement on its face may engage in any trade, including the foreign trade, the coastwise trade, and the American fisheries. Registered vessels, however, may be subject to the requirement for payment of certain pilotage fees and other charges upon arrival in a port of the United States to which other documented vessels are not generally subject.

An enrollment and license may be issued to a vessel of 20 net tons or more and, if the vessel is entitled to be so documented, may authorize it to engage in the coasting trade, the mackerel fishery, the cod fishery, the whale fishery, or the coasting trade and mackerel fishery. A vessel so authorized to engage in the mackerel fishery may be used in the taking of fish of any description. Special enrollments and licenses are issued on the frontiers, authorizing vessels to engage in the foreign and coasting trades. Vessels of 5 net tons or more may be granted an enrollment and license for navigating the waters of the northern, northeastern, or northwestern frontiers.

A license may be issued to a vessel of 5 net tons or over but of less than 20 net tons and, if the vessel is entitled to be so documented, may authorize the vessel to engage in any one of the employments for which an enrollment and license may be issued.

A yacht enrollment and license may be issued to a vessel used exclusively for pleasure of more than 20 net tons and a yacht license may be issued to such a vessel of 5 net tons or over but of less than 20 net tons. Important privileges extended by documentation of vessels as yachts are: (1) authority to fly the yacht ensign, which authority is not granted other boats; (2) right to voyage to a foreign port without clearing the vessel through United States customs; (3) in the case of yachts of 15 gross tons or less, the right to return to a port of the United States from a foreign port or ports without entering * the vessel through United States customs; (4) the privilege of recording bills of sale, mortgages, and other instruments of title for the vessel in the office of the collector of customs at the vessel's home port, giving constructive notice to all of the effect of such instruments and permitting the attainment of the status of preferred mortgages by mortgage instruments which are so recorded, thus giving additional security to the mortgagee and facilitating financing and transfers of title for such vessels.

The master of a documented vessel, other than one under register, must renew the document annually and any changes of master (except in the case of a licensed ferryboat) must be reported to a collector of customs.

The name of every documented vessel, yachts excepted, is required to be marked in full upon each bow and upon the stern and the hailing port is required to be marked upon the stern. A yacht is required to have its name and hailing port marked on some conspicuous part of its hull.

However, the documentation of yachts is not mandatory and it is entirely discretionary with the owner as to whether he should document his craft as a yacht. If the vessel is not documented, however, as indicated above, it may become subject to the requirements for numbering.

On the other hand, vessels which are engaged in trade and which are of 5 net tons or over will become subject to penalties provided by law if not documented for the employment in which they are engaged.

Foreign-built vessels, except in special circumstances, may be documented only to engage in the foreign trade, in trade with certain island possessions of the United States, or as yachts when used exclusively for pleasure. Such vessels may not be documented for the coastwise trade nor the American fisheries. In addition, vessels sold foreign or placed under foreign flag cannot thereafter be documented, as a general proposition, for the coastwise trade but are otherwise unrestricted as to documentation.

Before a vessel may be issued a document, it must be admeasured by the office of the collector of customs in whose district the vessel is at the time to determine the gross and net tonnages of the vessel.

The license granted to a vessel by the Bureau of Customs should not be confused with any licenses required for the officers or operators of vessels, which are issued by the United States Coast Guard.

LICENSES TO OPERATE MOTORBOATS CARRYING PASSENGERS
(For recent legislation affecting vessels carrying more than six passengers, see page 484)

Since June 9, 1910, persons wishing to operate a motorboat carrying passengers *for hire* have required a license. This is not to be confused with those held by licensed pilots and engineers on vessels over 15 tons gross, or more than 65 feet in length, engaged in trade. Nor should it be implied that any license is required of a person who operates his motorboat for pleasure only. As a matter of fact licensed officers are required on yachts or other motor vessels used exclusively for pleasure *only* if they are seagoing and exceed 300 gross tons.

Motorboats under 65 feet in length carrying freight for hire are not required to have licensed pilots and engineers.

The terms of the Motor Boat Act of 1940 and Executive Order No. 9083 empower the Commandant, U. S. Coast Guard, to draft any regulations necessary to implement the Act and make it effective.

Section 7 of the Act itself exempts from the need of having a license operators of motorboats engaged in any fishing contest previously arranged and announced.

Licenses to operate motorboats for hire are not granted to anyone under 18 years of age.

The license is required regardless of whether passengers carried for hire are aboard the motorboat or are carried on another non-self-propelled vessel being towed or pushed.

Who Issues Licenses

Licenses are issued by the Officers in Charge, Marine Inspection, U. S. Coast Guard. These officers are located in the ports listed in Table I-B (p. 22).

The applicant must submit a sworn application on Form 866 to an Officer in Charge, Marine Inspection, who examines him concerning his character and fitness to hold the license. He investigates the proofs submitted concerning his character and ability and determines whether his "capacity, knowledge, experience, character and habits of life" qualify him to hold such a license.

The applicant must also submit documentary evidence of at least one year's experience in operating motorboats.

The oral examination is based upon subjects which any person operating a motorboat carrying passengers should

---

* *However, any vessel having dutiable merchandise aboard must report to customs.*

United States Coast Guard

License to
Operate or Navigate Motorboats Carrying Passengers for Hire

This is to certify that _____
has given satisfactory evidence to the undersigned Officer in Charge, Marine Inspection for the district of _____,
that he can safely be intrusted with the duties and responsibilities of operator of motorboats as defined in the Act of April 25, 1940, when carrying passengers for hire, on the navigable waters of the United States, and is hereby licensed to act as such operator for the term of five years from this date.

Given under my hand this _____ *day of* _____, 19__

OFFICER IN CHARGE, MARINE INSPECTION.

The form of license required by the Motor Boat Act of those who operate motorboats carrying not more than six passengers. A special license is provided for small vessels carrying more than six passengers. (See page 484.) A limited license may be issued to operators of tenders of less than 30 feet in length at marinas and yacht clubs. Applicants for licenses may get detailed information from the Officer in Charge, Marine Inspection, U.S. Coast Guard

know before being entrusted with its operation and navigation.

Questions deal generally with regulations governing motor boats, collision regulations on the waters the applicant operates in, fire protection, life-saving equipment, safe operation of gasoline engines, methods of operating and navigating boats carrying passengers for hire, and elementary first aid.

Collision regulations differ in various parts of the country. Consequently, if the holder of a license ever operates elsewhere than on the waters for which he was examined, it is his duty to familiarize himself with the collision regulations applicable to the new locality.

Physical Examination

Applicants must be physically fit. In the case of persons who have held a license prior to April 25, 1941, a physical examination may not be required, if it appears to the inspectors that the applicant's color sense, vision, hearing and physical fitness are not badly impaired.

Those who have not held a license prior to April 25, 1941, must be examined by a U. S. Public Health surgeon or reputable physician. Bad hearing or eye-sight, color blindness, use of narcotics, insanity or presence of certain diseases are grounds for rejection of the applicant. The applicant must be able to read and write.

The License

Licenses are issued and signed by Officers in Charge, Marine Inspection. Every license (or certificate of lost license) must be signed by the person to whom it is issued, who also places his fingerprint upon the back. It is good for five years, after which it can be renewed by application on form CG-3479. There is no charge.

To renew the license one must present it to an Officer in Charge, Marine Inspection, together with a certificate of color sense, within one year after the date of its expiration. If more than a year elapses after expiration, the operator will have to take another examination. Except under extraordinary circumstances, renewal cannot be made more than 90 days in advance of the date of expiration.

learns that a license has been lost or stolen, he in turn notifies the District Coast Guard Officer and supplies him with all available information concerning the case.

When License Is Lost

In case of loss, except where the license has been suspended or revoked, a certificate may be obtained from the Officer in Charge, Marine Inspection, on presentation of satisfactory evidence of loss. The certificate is then as valid as the license for the unexpired term.

When an Officer in Charge, Marine Inspection,

Suspension and Revocation

If any operator is found guilty of incompetency, misbehavior, negligence, unskillfulness, endangering life, or wilfully violating any provision of law or safety regulations, his license may be suspended or revoked. When revoked, it automatically expires. If revoked or suspended, the license must be surrendered to the hearing officer before whom the hearing was held. If an appeal is made to the hearing officer, a temporary certificate for the period of the appeal may be issued upon request.

Specimen Questions

The following sets of specimen examinations are not intended to present the exact questions which will be asked by the marine inspectors, but are given only to serve as a guide so that an applicant may have a general understanding of the type of questions he is likely to be asked.

I

1. What is the meaning of two short blasts of the whistle?
2. What signal would you display while at anchor during the night?
3. What is the rule concerning speed during foggy weather?
4. Suppose you see a red light on your starboard bow, what would you judge it to be and what would you do?
5. In keeping clear of another vessel what must you avoid doing?
6. What motor boats are included in Class 2?
7. What person must hold a motor boat operator's license? Under what conditions would a license as operator of a motor boat be subject to suspension or revocation?
8. Explain how a life preserver is worn and how it is adjusted.
9. Must fire extinguishers used on motor boats be approved?
10. Outline briefly the features of the fixed CO_2 system. What boats are required to be equipped with it?
11. What precaution would you take in regard to the bilges of the engine and fuel tank compartments of motorboats (except open boats) using as fuel any liquid of a volatile nature?
12. What should you do after refueling?
13. What precautions do you take with oily rags and waste?
14. What would you watch out for in regard to wiring?
15. When passengers are aboard how must you handle your motor boat with regard to their safety?
16. Suppose a person falls overboard and is recovered in an unconscious state, how would you go about reviving him?

II

1. You are anchored in a fairway in a fog. What signals must you give and how often?
2. What is the meaning of one short blast on the whistle?

3. You are navigating in foggy weather. What signals must you give? What duration and at what intervals?

4. Suppose you saw a red pennant displayed from a Coast Guard station, or a lighthouse, or yacht club, what would it mean to you?

5. In narrow channels, on which side shall vessels navigate, if safe and practicable?

6. What does the word "motorboat" include according to the Motor Boat Regulations?

7. Describe the lights carried on Class 3 motor boats.

8. What would you look for before purchasing a life preserver?

9. What type, size and number of fire extinguishers are accepted for use on motor boats? How are they operated?

10. If gasoline is spilled, what immediate steps should be taken?

11. What safety measures must be observed when refueling?

12. Before starting an engine, which is located in a cabin or other enclosed space, what would you do first?

13. Where should the vent from the gasoline tank terminate?

14. What precaution must be taken to prevent back-fire of the engines (except outboard motors) of motor boats, the construction of which, or the replacement of the engines of which was commenced subsequent to April 25, 1940?

15. When carrying passengers for hire, what provision must be made for one's safety?

16. Name the points of the compass.

*When a Motor Boat Is Carrying Passengers for Hire

There are many obvious cases where a motor boat, normally used for pleasure only, might carry passengers for hire. The owner, for example, might charge a group of persons a definite amount for taking them on a day's outing, fishing or cruising. It is clear that in cases of this kind the boat is carrying passengers for hire, and must be equipped in accordance with all the regulations for such boats, including a life preserver of approved type for every person on board. The operator of such a boat must have a license to carry passengers for hire.

However, there are other border-line cases where the status of the motor boat owner may be in doubt. For example, consider the following examples:

1. When he (the ordinary yachtsman) invites guests on his boat, and a guest brings a gift of food or liquor to be used on the trip.

2. When arranging a cruise with guests, and the guests agree to pay their proportionate part of the expenses, including gasoline and other supplies.

3. Or, in the extreme case, where the cruise guest takes the owner ashore for dinner and entertainment.

4. Supposing a yachtsman takes business associates on a cruise, perhaps with the intent of creating good will and friendship in negotiating business not relating to the yacht or the cruise.

According to a ruling of the former Bureau of Marine Inspection and Navigation, and reaffirmed by the Commandant, U. S. Coast Guard, a motor boatman would *not* be considered to be carrying passengers for hire in cases 1, 3, and 4.

When There Is An Agreement in Advance

However, in case 2 if there was a prearranged plan or agreement *in advance* that the guests agree to pay their proportionate part of the expenses of the cruise, then the boat would be considered to be carrying passengers for hire, the operator would have to be licensed, and the equipment as explained above would have to be in conformity with regulations for boats carrying passengers for hire.

If, on the other hand, the owner of a motor boat invites guests to accompany him on a cruise and while on the cruise one or more of the guests offers to pay for gasoline or food in return for the hospitality extended them, then the owner would not be regarded as carrying passengers for hire, would not require a license, and his ordinary equipment carried on a motor boat operated for pleasure only would be adequate.

In April 1953, the following clarification was made, in an opinion expressed by the Commandant of the Coast Guard: "It is possible, of course, for the owner of any vessel to operate on a share-the-expense basis if all guests are willing to enter into a written agreement that the voyage will be a joint venture and that all parties to the contract will share all liabilities as well as benefits. In this situation the owner would not be considered as transporting passengers for hire. Expenses could then be shared. In case of a casualty all parties to the contract would be jointly responsible in case of suit."

At the same time, the opinion was given that "In a case where the owner of a vessel competes in a regatta for cash prizes or trophies and has on board a paid driver or mechanic, this is not considered carrying passengers for hire as no passengers are being transported. The driver, mechanic or operator of the vessel is considered part of the crew necessary to man the boat . . ."

When An Owner Charters and Supplies the Crew

Subsequently the former Bureau was asked for a decision on the following:

5. In the event an owner of a motorboat, under 65 feet in length, which is in complete commission with a paid crew aboard, elects to charter this boat for a definite period of time for the exclusive use of another individual, the charter to include the furnishing by the owner of his crew to operate the vessel during the period of charter.

In such a case it was the former Bureau's opinion and reaffirmed by the Commandant, U. S. Coast Guard, that the boat would be regarded as carrying passengers for hire and accordingly would have to be in charge of a licensed operator.

6. Supposing the same situation as 5 (above) but with a vessel of more than 65 feet in length.

Here again the former Bureau's ruling, and reaffirmed by the Commandant, U. S. Coast Guard, was to the effect that the vessel is carrying passengers for hire and if she is over 15 gross tons, she must be in charge of the necessary complement of licensed engineers and pilots as prescribed by the Officer in Charge, Marine Inspection.

When the Owner Does Not Supply the Crew

7. In the event of an owner of a motor boat under 65 feet in length which has not as yet been commissioned and on which there is no crew elects to charter this boat for a period of time to another individual who will hire and place upon it his own crew at his own expense.

8. The same situation as 7 (above) but considering a motor boat over 65 feet in length.

In both cases 7 and 8, the former Bureau's ruling, and reaffirmed by the Commandant, U. S. Coast Guard, was that if such a vessel, regardless of its length, is used exclusively for pleasure, it would *not* be considered to be carrying passengers for hire. Therefore no licensed operators would be required.

Coast Guard in Charge of Licenses and Inspection

The U. S. Coast Guard has charge of the granting of all licenses and the inspection of hull and machinery of those motorboats where this is required. A list of the offices of the Officers in Charge, Marine Inspection, will be found below.

Application should be made to any of these for information relative to obtaining certificates, examinations, etc.

These local offices (ports) are grouped into districts under the direction of district Coast Guard commanders:

District No. 1. BOSTON—Portland, Me., Providence, R. I. 2. ST. LOUIS—Cairo, Dubuque, Cincinnati, Louisville, Memphis, Nashville, Pittsburgh, Pt. Pleasant. 3. NEW YORK—Bridgeport, Albany, Philadelphia. 5. NORFOLK—Baltimore. 7. MIAMI—Charleston, Savannah, Tampa, San Juan. 8. NEW ORLEANS—Mobile, Port Arthur, Galveston, Houston, Corpus Christi. 9. CLEVELAND—Buffalo, Oswego, Detroit, Duluth, Toledo, St. Ignace, Chicago, Ludington, Milwaukee. 11. LONG BEACH, CALIF. 12. SAN FRANCISCO. 13. SEATTLE—Portland, Ore., Ketchikan. 14. HONOLULU, T. H.

* NOTE: See page 484 for information on Ray Act affecting vessels carrying more than six passengers.

CUSTOMS AND IMMIGRATION REGULATIONS

When an American yacht crosses the national boundaries of the United States to visit a foreign port, or a foreign yacht visits an American port, certain customs and immigration regulations must be complied with. Due to various provisions and exemptions applying to yachts, not engaged in trade, the procedure has been made so easy that there is nothing in these legal requirements to deter a pleasure craft from enjoying a cruise outside the limits of United States waters. Severe penalties are provided for failure to observe regulations, however.

It should be noted that customs and immigration inspections are two separate functions even though, in some of the smaller ports, they may be administered by a single official or his office. Separate offices handle these duties where traffic across the border is heavy.

Clearing and Entering

The terms clearing and entering are commonly used in connection with a vessel's voyage to a foreign port. Clearing involves the obtaining of permission to sail by presenting the ship's papers to a customs official. Entering relates to arrival, when the owner or master enters his vessel by having his ship's papers accepted by customs authorities. Thus a vessel might be required to clear from an American port, enter at a Canadian or other foreign port, and then, on returning, clear from the foreign port and enter at the American port.

Under provisions of an Act of September 1, 1954, neither a licensed yacht nor an undocumented American pleasure vessel (not engaged in trade nor in any way violating the customs or navigation laws of the United States) is required to clear upon departure from the United States for a foreign port or place. Similarly, a licensed yacht of any size and an undocumented American pleasure vessel (not engaged in trade nor in any way violating the customs or navigation laws of the United States and not having visited any hovering vessel) are exempted from entry.

Foreign vessels are not only subject to the requirements of entry and clearance on foreign voyages but must also enter and clear when proceeding between U. S. ports.

If desired, bills of health may be secured free of charge before leaving for a foreign port. This is not compulsory and is used chiefly by vessels going to tropical countries, where epidemics are more prevalent.

Report on Arrival

On arrival at the foreign port the owner or captain of a yacht (any size) should report at once to the customs and immigration authorities. When reporting, crew and guests must remain aboard the boat until it has passed inspection. Any additional regulations to be complied with, including any details in connection with clearing from there, will be supplied by the customs and immigration authorities of the port.

Every vessel, whether documented or not, arriving in the United States from a foreign port or place must come into a port of entry and, within 24 hours, must report to the customhouse at that port. The crew and guests of all vessels arriving within the United States should remain aboard and no baggage or merchandise should be removed until the customs and immigration officials have made their inspection.

All boats regardless of size must report to the immigration authorities on return to a United States port. Any alien passengers aboard must be reported and a heavy penalty attaches to failure to detain passengers and crew, if ordered to do so by the authorities. A report giving names and other information concerning any paid hands aboard must be made on a crew manifest.

Charges

There is no charge for the documentation of a vessel, but nominal fees are charged for the recording of instruments of title presented to the collector of customs in connection with any application for documentation and, if the vessel is outside a port of entry or a customs station at

The navigation bridge of a modern 65' yacht. All engine controls are located at the steering position, with spherical compass directly ahead of the wheel. Automatic steering is provided and other electronic aids to piloting include (l. to r.) radiotelephone, loran, radar, and depth sounder. Another invaluable aid to piloting, not shown here, is the radio direction finder. Loran provides lines of position based on signals from pairs of transmitting stations. These are fixed with respect to the earth's surface and are not dependent upon any of the vessel's other instruments for accuracy

the time of admeasurement, certain charges are made to defray the cost of sending an admeasurer to the vessel.

Vessels of less than 100 net tons which are entered must pay an entry fee of $1.50. The fee for vessels of 100 net tons or over is $2.50. The same fees are charged upon the clearance of a vessel for a foreign port. Payment of entry and clearance fees is not required in the case of a vessel proceeding between Canada and the northern, northeastern or northwestern frontiers of the United States otherwise than by sea.

Free Permits

Yachts going into Canada may secure cruising permits with privileges of free entry and clearance for the period from May 1 to October 1. This is issued free of charge by the Canadian customs authorities at the Canadian port where the yacht first reports and must be surrendered to the issuing authority when leaving that country. Provided the yacht does not leave Canadian waters, she is then free to visit other Canadian ports until the permit is surrendered, though reports are to be made at any port called at where a customs officer is located.

Under special statute, qualified foreign yachts may receive from customs authorities in the United States a cruising license granting them special treatment in United States waters.

A documented yacht, belonging to a regularly organized and incorporated yacht club, may be issued a commission to sail for pleasure on a foreign voyage. Application therefor may be made to any collector of customs in the United States. The commission serves primarily as an identification of the owner and the vessel. It must be surrendered upon return from the foreign country.

Tonnage Tax

Regular tonnage tax is assessed upon the entry from a foreign port or place of a vessel engaged in trade. Special tonnage tax at the rate of 50 cents per net ton and light money at the same rate, or a total of $1 per net ton, are assessed upon the entry from a foreign port or place of an American or foreign undocumented vessel of 5 net tons or over which is engaged in trade. The rate of special tonnage tax is reduced to 30 cents per net ton if the undocumented foreign vessel was built in the United States. Undocumented American vessels which are documented as vessels of the United States prior to their departure from the first port of arrival are exempt from the payment of special tonnage tax and light money.

General

For detailed information with regard to customs requirements, see your nearest customs officer. (*See also* page 474.)

Log Books and Records May Be Inspected

Regulations provide that the owner, charterer, agent, master, or other licensed officer of any vessel involved in a marine casualty or accident shall retain the voyage records of the vessel, including both rough and smooth deck and engine room logs, bell books, navigation charts, navigators' work book, compass deviation cards, stowage diagrams, records of draft, aids to mariners, radiograms sent and received and the radio log and crews' and passengers' lists, which upon request shall be produced for the inspection of the U. S. Coast Guard Examiners whenever required.

The Shipping Act of 1916

Section 37 of the Shipping Act of 1916, as amended (46 U. S. C. 835), became effective upon Presidential Proclamation 2914, dated December 16, 1950 (15 F. R. 9029). Accordingly, this proclamation has brought into operation, among others, the statutory provisions prohibiting the transfer of any interest in an American owned vessel or shipbuilding plant to foreign ownership without prior Maritime Administration approval.* The prohibition extends to sales, charters, leases, and other transfers of interest in such vessels and plants; in agreements to effect such transfers; to agreements and understandings whereby the controlling interest or a majority of the stock of a corporation, organized in the United States and owning such vessels or facilities, would be vested in or for the benefit of a noncitizen; and to related activities. Accordingly, sales of undocumented and numbered vessels by American citizens to aliens without the consent of the Maritime Administration, U. S. Department of Commerce, *under such regulations as are prescribed by that agency cannot be consummated.*

[Ed. note: Undocumented vessels of less than 40 feet overall length and less than 50 horsepower are given blanket approval provided that the purchaser is not a citizen of any of the following nations: Soviet Union, Latvia, Lithuania, Estonia, Poland, Czechoslovakia, Hungary, Rumania, Bulgaria, Albania, North Korea, the Soviet Zone of Germany, Manchuria, or Communist China. Violations of any of the provisions of Section 37 of the Shipping Act of 1916, as amended (46 U. S. C. 835), are reported in the usual manner to the Maritime Administration, U. S. Department of Commerce through the Commandant, U. S. Coast Guard.]

* Approval was granted April 12, 1961 on undocumented pleasure boats of 65 feet in overall length and/or 500 rated horsepower, or less, sold to any Canadian citizen, living in Canada, and importing it for registration or license under Canadian law. Approval is required on undocumented pleasure boats of 40 feet overall length or more, and/or of 50 rated horsepower or more, to Canadian citizens living outside of Canada when the boat is neither imported into nor registered or licensed in Canada, nor intended to be imported into Canada or registered or licensed under Canadian law.

Right: A Coast Guard Auxiliary member, making a free courtesy examination of equipment, checks the Coast Guard approval stamped on a life preserver. Below: This boat has passed inspection and has a decal applied to the windshield

TEXT OF THE MOTORBOAT ACT OF APRIL 25, 1940

As Amended to June 15, 1959 (46 U.S.C. 526-526u)

An act to amend laws for preventing collisions of vessels, to regulate equipment of certain motorboats on the navigable waters of the United States, and for other purposes

Be it enacted by the Senate and House of Representatives of the United States of America in Congress assembled, That the word "motorboat" where used in this Act shall include every vessel propelled by machinery and not more than sixty-five feet in length except tugboats and towboats propelled by steam. The length* shall be measured from end to end over the deck, excluding sheer: *Provided,* That the engine, boiler, or other operating machinery shall be subject to inspection by the Coast Guard, and to its approval of the design thereof, on all said motorboats, which are more than forty feet in length, and which are propelled by machinery driven by steam. *(46 U.S.C. 526.)*

Classes of Motorboats

Sec. 2. Motorboats subject to the provisions of this Act shall be divided into four classes as follows:

Class A. Less than sixteen feet in length.

Class 1. Sixteen feet or over and less than twenty-six feet in length.

Class 2. Twenty-six feet or over and less than forty feet in length.

Class 3. Forty feet or over and not more than sixty-five feet in length. *(46 U.S.C. 526a.)*

Lights

Sec. 3. Every motorboat in all weathers from sunset to sunrise shall carry and exhibit the following lights when under way, and during such time no other lights which may be mistaken for those prescribed shall be exhibited:

(a) Every motorboat of classes A and 1 shall carry the following lights:

First. A bright white light aft to show all around the horizon.

Second. A combined lantern in the fore part of the vessel and lower than the white light aft, showing green to starboard and red to port, so fixed as to throw the light from right ahead to two points abaft the beam on their respective sides.

(b) Every motorboat of classes 2 and 3 shall carry the following lights:

First. A bright white light in the fore part of the vessel as near the stem as practicable, so constructed as to show an unbroken light over an arc of the horizon of twenty points of the compass, so fixed as to throw the light ten points on each side of the vessel; namely, from right ahead to two points abaft the beam on either side.

Second. A bright white light aft to show all around the horizon and higher than the white light forward.

Third. On the starboard side a green light so constructed as to show an unbroken light over an arc of the horizon of ten points of the compass, so fixed as to throw the light from right ahead to two points abaft the beam on the starboard side. On the port side a red light so constructed as to show an unbroken light over an arc of the horizon of ten points of the compass, so fixed as to throw the light from right ahead to two points abaft the beam on the port side. The said side lights shall be fitted with inboard screens of sufficient height so set as to prevent these lights from being seen across the bow.

(c) Motorboats of classes A and 1 when propelled by sail alone shall carry the combined lantern, but not the white light aft, prescribed by this section. Motorboats of classes 2 and 3, when so propelled, shall carry the colored side lights, suitably screened, but not the white lights, prescribed by this section. **Motorboats of all classes, when so propelled, shall carry, ready at hand, a lantern or flashlight showing a white light which shall be exhibited in sufficient time to avert collision.

(d) Every white light prescribed by this section shall be of such character as to be visible at a distance of at least two miles. Every colored light prescribed by this section shall be of such character as to be visible at a distance of at least one mile. The word "visible" in this Act, when applied to lights, shall mean visible on a dark night with clear atmosphere.

(e) When propelled by sail and machinery any motorboat shall carry the lights required by this section for a motorboat propelled by machinery only.

(f) Any motorboat may carry and exhibit the lights required by the Regulations for Preventing Collisions at Sea, 1948, Act of October 11, 1951 (65 Stat. 406–420; 33 U.S.C. 147–147d), as amended, in lieu of the lights required by this section. *(46 U.S.C. 526b.) (Amended by Act of June 4, 1956.)*

Whistle, Bell and Life Preservers

Sec. 4. Every motorboat of class 1, 2, or 3, shall be provided with an efficient whistle or other sound-producing mechanical appliance. *(46 U.S.C. 526c.)*

Sec. 5. Every motorboat of class 2 or 3 shall be provided with an efficient bell. *(46 U.S.C. 526d.)*

Sec. 6. Every motorboat subject to any of the provisions of this Act and also all vessels propelled by machinery other than by steam more than sixty-five feet in length shall carry at least one life preserver, or life belt, or ring buoy, or other device of the sort prescribed by the regulations of the Commandant of the Coast Guard, for each person on board, so placed as to be readily accessible: *Provided,* That every such motorboat and every such vessel propelled by machinery other than by steam more than sixty-five feet in length carrying passengers for hire shall carry so placed as to be readily accessible at least one life preserver of the sort prescribed by the regulations of the Commandant of the Coast Guard, for each person on board. *(46 U.S.C. 526e.)*

Licensed Operator

Sec. 7. No such motorboat, and no other vessel of fifteen gross tons or less propelled by machinery other than steam, while carrying passengers for hire, shall be operated or navigated except in charge of a person duly licensed for such service by the Secretary of the department in which the Coast Guard is operating. Whenever any person applies to be licensed as operator of any motorboat, or of any other vessel of fifteen gross tons or less propelled by machinery, carrying passengers for hire, the Secretary shall make diligent inquiry as to his character, and shall carefully examine the applicant orally as well as the proofs which he presents in support of his claim, and if the Secretary is satisfied that his capacity, experience, habits of living, and character are such to warrant the belief that he can safely be entrusted with the duties and responsibilities of the station for which he makes application, the Secretary shall grant him a license authorizing him to discharge such duties on any such motorboat, or on any other vessel of fifteen gross tons or less propelled by machinery, carrying passengers for hire, for the term of five years. Such license shall be subject to suspension or revocation on the same grounds and in the same manner with like procedure as is provided in the case of suspension or revocation of license of officers under the provisions of section 4450 of the Revised Statutes, as amended (U.S.C. 1952 edition, title 46, sec. 239): *Provided,* That motorboats and other vessels of fifteen gross tons or less propelled by machinery shall not be required to carry licensed officers except as required in this Act: *And provided further,* That licenses herein prescribed shall not be required of motorboats or of any other vessels of fifteen gross tons or less propelled by machinery engaged in fishing contests previously arranged and announced. *(46 U.S.C. 526f.) (Amended by Act of May 10, 1956.)*

Fire Extinguishers

Sec. 8. Every motorboat and also every vessel propelled by machinery other than by steam more than sixty-five feet in length shall be provided with such number, size, and type of fire extinguishers, capable of promptly and effectually extinguishing burning gasoline, as may be prescribed by the regulations of the Commandant of the Coast Guard, which fire extinguishers shall be at all times kept in condition for immediate and effective use and shall be so placed as to be readily accessible. *(46 U.S.C. 526g.)*

Racing Outboards Exempt

Sec. 9. The provisions of sections 4, 5, and 8 of this Act shall not apply to motorboats propelled by outboard motors while competing in any race previously arranged and announced or, if such boats be designed and intended solely for racing, while engaged in such navigation as is incidental to the tuning up of the boats and engines for the race. *(46 U.S.C. 526h.)*

Flame Arresters

Sec. 10. Every motorboat and also every vessel propelled by machinery other than by steam more than sixty-five feet in length shall have the carburetor or carburetors of every engine therein (except outboard motors) using gasoline as fuel, equipped with such efficient flame arrester, backfire trap, or other similar device

*NOTE—The expression "length shall be measured from end to end over the deck excluding sheer" has been interpreted to mean a straight line measurement of the overall length from the foremost part of the vessel to the aftermost part of the vessel. Bowsprits, boomkins, rudders, outboard motor brackets, and similar fittings or attachments are not to be included in the measurement. Length shall be stated in feet and inches.

** Now carry 12-pt. white light aft.

as may be prescribed by the regulations of the Commandant of the Coast Guard: *Provided,* That this section shall apply only to such motorboats or vessls, the construction of which or the replacement of the engine or engines of which is commenced subsequent to the passage of this Act.

Ventilation of Bilges

Sec. 11. Every such motorboat and every such vessel, except open boats, using as fuel any liquid of a volatile nature, shall be provided with such means as may be prescribed by regulations of the Commandant of the Coast Guard for properly and efficiently ventilating the bilges of the engine and fuel tank compartments so as to remove any explosive or inflammable gases: *Provided,* That this section shall apply only to such motorboats or vessels, the construction or decking over of which is commenced subsequent to the passage of this Act.

Pilot Rules Not Required

Sec. 12. Motorboats shall not be required to carry on board copies of the pilot rules.

Negligent Operation

Sec. 13. (a) No person shall operate any motorboat or any vessel in a reckless or negligent manner so as to endanger the life, limb, or property of any person. To "operate" means to navigate or otherwise use a motorboat or a vessel.

(b) In the case of collision, accident, or other casualty involving a motorboat or other vessel subject to this Act, it shall be the duty of the operator, if and so far as he can do so without serious danger to his own vessel, or persons aboard, to render such assistance as may be practicable and necessary to other persons affected by the collision, accident, or casualty in order to save them from danger caused by the collision, accident, or casualty. He shall also give his name, address, and identification of his vessel to any person injured and to the owner of any property damaged. The duties imposed by this subsection shall be in addition to any duties otherwise provided by law.

(c) In the case of collision, accident, or other casualty involving a motorboat or other vessel subject to this Act, the operator thereof, if the collision, accident, or other casualty results in death or injury to any person, or damage to property in excess of $100, shall file with the Secretary of the Department within which the Coast Guard is operating, unless such operator is required to file an accident report with the State under section 3 (c) (6) of the Federal Boating Act of 1958, a full description of the collision, accident, or other casualty, including such information as the Secretary may by regulation require.

(46 U.S.C. 526l.) (Amended by Act of September 2, 1958.)

Penalty for Negligent Operation

Sec. 14. Any person who shall operate any motorboat or any vessel in a reckless or negligent manner so as to endanger the life, limb, or property of any person shall be deemed guilty of a misdemeanor and on conviction thereof by any court of competent jurisdiction shall be punished by a fine not exceeding $2,000, or by imprisonment for a term of not exceeding one year, or by both such fine and imprisonment, at the discretion of the court. *(46 U.S.C. 526m.)*

Authority to Arrest

Sec. 15. Any officer of the United States authorized to enforce the navigation laws of the United States, shall have power and authority to swear out process and to arrest and take into custody, with or without process, any person who may commit any act or offense prohibited by section 13, or who may violate any provision of said section: *Provided,* That no person shall be arrested without process for any offense not committed in the presence of some one of the aforesaid officials: *Provided further,* That whenever an arrest is made under the provisions of this Act, the person so arrested shall be brought forthwith before a commissioner, judge, or court of the United States for examination of the offense alleged against him, and such commissioner, judge, or court shall proceed in respect thereto as authorized by law in cases of crimes against the United States. *(46 U.S.C. 526n.)*

Penalties for Other Violations

Sec. 16. If any motorboat or vessel subject to any of the provisions of this Act is operated or navigated in violation of this Act or any regulation issued thereunder, the owner or operator, either one or both of them, shall, in addition to any other penalty prescribed by law be liable to a penalty of $100: *Provided,* That in the case of motorboats or vessels subject to the provisions of this Act carrying passengers for hire, a penalty of $200 shall be imposed on the owner or operator, either one or both of them, thereof for any violation of section 6, 7, or 8 of this Act or of any regulations pertaining thereto. For any penalty incurred under this section the motorboat or vessel shall be liable and may be proceeded against by way of libel in the district court of any district in which said motorboat or vessel may be found. *(46 U.S.C. 526o.) (Amended by Act of September 2, 1958.)*

Regulations and Enforcement

Sec. 17. The Commandant of the Coast Guard shall establish all necessary regulations required to carry out in the most effective manner all of the provisions of this Act, and such regulations shall have the force of law. The Commandant of the Coast Guard or any officer of the Coast Guard authorized by the Commandant may, upon application therefor, remit or mitigate any fine, penalty, or forfeiture incurred under this Act or any regulation thereunder relating to motorboats or vessels, except the penalties provided for in section 14 hereunder. The Commandant of the Coast Guard shall establish such regulations as may be necessary to secure the enforcement of the provisions of this Act by any officer of the United States authorized to enforce the navigation laws of the United States. *(46 U.S.C. 526p.)*

Sec. 18. The proviso contained in the last paragraph of section 2 of the Act of May 11, 1918 (40 Stat. 549; 46 U.S.C. 223), shall apply also with like force and effect to motorboats as defined in this Act.

Motorboats as defined in this Act are hereby exempted from the provisions of Revised Statutes 4399, as amended (48 Stat. 125; 46 U.S.C. 361). *(46 U.S.C. 526q.)*

When Act Takes Effect

Sec. 19. This Act shall take effect upon its approval as to all of the sections hereof except sections 6, 7, and 8, which sections shall take effect one year from the date of said approval, and for a period of one year from the date of approval of this Act sections 5, 6, and 7 of the Motorboat Act of June 9, 1910 (Public, Numbered 201, Sixty-first Congress; 36 Stat. 462), shall continue in full force and effect, except that from and after the date of the approval of this Act the Secretary of Commerce shall have authority to remit or mitigate all fines or penalties heretofore or hereafter incurred or imposed under sections 5 and 6 of the Motorboat Act of June 9, 1910. Except as hereinabove expressly provided, the Motorboat Act of June 9, 1910, above referred to, is repealed upon the approval of this Act and as to sections 5, 6, and 7 of said Act hereinabove continued the said sections are hereby repealed effective one year from the date of approval of this Act. Nothing in this Act shall be deemed to alter or amend section 4417a of the Revised Statutes (U.S.C., 1934 edition, Supp. IV, title 46, sec. 391a), the Act of August 26, 1935 (U.S.C., 1934 edition, Supp. IV, ch. 7A, secs. 178 and 179), the Act of June 20, 1936 (U.S.C., 1934 edition, Supp. IV, title 46, sec. 367), or repeal Acts of Congress or treaties embodying or revising international rules for preventing collisions at sea. *(46 U.S.C. 526r.)*

Sec. 20. There are hereby authorized to be appropriated such sums as may be necessary to carry out the provisions of this Act. *(46 U.S.C. 526s.)*

Section 21 (Numbering Certificate) Repealed

(NOTE.—The following section 21 is repealed, effective April 1, 1960, by Act of September 2, 1958.)

Sec. 21. The provisions of section 210 of title II of the Anti-Smuggling Act, approved August 5, 1935 (49 Stat. 526; U.S.C., 1934 edition, Supp. IV, title 46, sec. 288), requiring a certificate of award of a number to be kept at all times on board of the vessel to which the number has been awarded shall not apply to any vessel not exceeding seventeen feet in length measured from end to end over the deck, excluding sheer, or to any vessel whose design of fittings are such that the carrying of the certificate of award of the number on such vessel would render such certificate imperfect, illegible, or would otherwise tend to destroy its usefulness as a means of ready identification. *(46 U.S.C. 526t.)*

Application of Act

Sec. 22. (a) This Act shall apply to every motorboat or vessel on the navigable waters of the United States, its Territories and the District of Columbia, and every motorboat or vessel owned in a State and using the high seas.

(b) As used in this Act—

The term 'State' means a State of the United States, a Territory of the United States, and the District of Columbia. *(46 U.S.C. 526u.) (Added by Act of September 2, 1958.)*

Approved: April 25, 1940 (as amended 1946 Reorganization Plan No. 3, July 16, 1946; 1950 Reorganization Plan No. 26, July 31, 1950; May 10, 1956, June 4, 1956, September 2, 1958).

TEXT OF THE FEDERAL BOATING ACT OF 1958

Public Law 85-911 85th Congress, H. R. 11078
September 2, 1958

An act to promote boating safety on the navigable waters of the United States, its Territories, and the District of Columbia; to provide coordination and cooperation with the States in the interest of uniformity of boating laws; and for other purposes.

Be it enacted by the Senate and House of Representatives of the United States of America in Congress assembled, That this Act may be cited as the "Federal Boating Act of 1958".

Definitions

SEC. 2. As used in sections 3 to 5, inclusive, and sections 7 to 13, inclusive, of this Act—

(1) The term "undocumented vessel" means any vessel which is not required to have, and does not have, a valid marine document issued by the Bureau of Customs.

(2) The word "vessel" includes every description of watercraft, other than a seaplane on the water, used or capable of being used as a means of transportation on water.

(3) The word "Secretary" means the Secretary of the Department in which the Coast Guard is operating.

(4) The word "owner" means the person who claims lawful possession of a vessel by virtue of legal title or equitable interest therein which entitles him to such possession.

(5) The term "State" means a State of the United States, a Territory of the United States, and the District of Columbia.

Numbering of Vessels

SEC. 3. (a) Every undocumented vessel propelled by machinery of more than 10 horsepower, whether or not such machinery is the principal source of propulsion, using the navigable water of the United States, its Territories and the District of Columbia, and every such vessel owned in a State and using the high seas, shall be numbered in accordance with this Act, except—

(1) foreign vessels temporarily using the navigable waters of the United States, its Territories and the District of Columbia;

(2) public vessels of the United States;

(3) State and municipal vessels;

(4) ships' lifeboats; and

(5) vessels designated by the Secretary under section 7 (b) of this Act.

(b) The owner of an undocumented vessel required to be numbered under subsection (a) of this section shall secure a number for such vessel in the State in which it is principally used, in accordance with the State numbering system approved by the Secretary in accordance with subsection (c) of this section, or if no such numbering system has been approved by the Secretary for the State where such vessel is principally used, shall secure a number for such vessel in accordance with subsection (d) of this section.

(c) The Secretary shall establish an overall numbering system for the numbering of vessels required to be numbered under subsection (a) of this section. He shall approve any State system for numbering vessels which is submitted to him which meets the standards set forth below:

(1) The system of numbering shall be in accordance with the overall system of numbering established by the Secretary.

(2) The certificate of number and the number awarded shall be valid for a period not exceeding three years, unless canceled or surrendered, and may be renewed for additional periods.

(3) The number awarded shall be required to be painted on, or attached to, each side of the bow of the vessel for which it was issued, and shall be of such size, color, and type, as may be prescribed by the Secretary. No other number shall be permitted to be carried on the bow of such vessel.

(4) The certificate of number shall be pocket size and shall be required to be at all times available for inspection on the vessel for which issued, whenever such vessel is in use.

(5) The owner shall be required to furnish to a designated State official, notice of the transfer of all or any part of his interest in any numbered vessel, and of the destruction or abandonment of such vessel, within a reasonable time thereof. The owner shall be required to notify a designated State official of any change in his address within a reasonable time of such change.

(6) The State shall require that reports be made to it of accidents involving vessels numbered by it under its numbering system, and shall compile and transmit to the Secretary such statistics on such accidents.

(7) The State shall recognize the validity of a number awarded to any vessel by another State under a numbering system approved by the Secretary under this Act, or awarded a number by the Secretary, for a period of at least ninety days.

(8) In the case of a State having its numbering system approved after April 1, 1960, such State shall accept and recognize any valid certificate of number awarded under subsection (d) of this section for so long as such certificate would otherwise be valid under such subsection (d), except that where such a certificate would remain valid for more than one year after the date when such State's numbering system was approved, the State may accept and recognize the validity of such certificate for a lesser period, but such period shall not end sooner than one year from the date of approval of such system.

(9) The State may exempt any vessel or class of vessels from the numbering provisions of its system if such vessel or class of vessels has been made exempt from the numbering provisions of section 3 (d) by the Secretary under section 7 (b) of this Act.

(10) The States may charge fees in connection with the award of certificates of number and renewals thereof.

(11) The States may require that the operator of a vessel required to be numbered hereunder shall hold a valid safety certificate to be issued under such terms and conditions as may be provided by State law.

(d) The owner of an undocumented vessel required to be numbered under subsection (a) of this section who uses his vessel principally in a State which does not have a numbering system approved by the Secretary under subsection (c) of this section, shall make application to the Secretary, and upon payment of the fee established under section 5, such owner shall be granted a certificate of number containing the number awarded such vessel by the Secretary.

Certificate Valid Three Years

(e) The certificate of number initially awarded to an owner under subsection (d) of this section shall be valid for three years from the date of the owner's birthday next occurring after the date the certificate of number is issued, unless surrendered or canceled pursuant to regulations of the Secretary. If at the end of such period such ownership has remained unchanged, such owner shall, upon application and payment of the fee established under section 5 of this Act, be granted a renewal of such certificate of number for an additional three-year period.

(f) The number awarded under subsection (c) or (d) of this section shall be painted on, or attached to, each side of the bow of the vessel for which it was issued, and shall be of such size, color, and type as may be prescribed by the Secretary. No other number shall be carried on the bow of such vessel.

(g) The certificate of number granted under subsection (c) or (d) of this section shall be pocket size and shall be required to be at all times available for inspection on the vessel for which issued whenever such vessel is in use, and shall constitute a document in lieu of a marine document that sets forth an official number issued by the Bureau of Customs.

(h) Whenever the Secretary determines that a State is not administering its approved system for numbering vessels in accordance with the standards set forth under subsection (c) of this section, he may withdraw such approval. The Secretary shall not withdraw his approval of a State system of numbering until he has given notice in writing to the State setting forth specifically wherein the State has failed to maintain such standards.

SEC. 4. The owner of any vessel numbered under section 3 (d) of this Act shall furnish to the Secretary notice of the transfer of all or any part of his interest in any numbered vessel, and of the destruction, or abandonment of such vessel, within a reasonable time thereof. The owner shall notify the Secretary of any change in his address within a reasonable time of such change.

Sec. 5. The Secretary may prescribe reasonable fees or charges for the numbering of a vessel, or renewal thereof, under subsections (d) and (e) of section 3 of this Act.

Motorboat Act Amended

Sec. 6. (a) Section 13 of the Act entitled "An Act to amend laws for preventing collisions of vessels, to regulate equipment of certain motorboats on the navigable waters of the United States, and for other purposes", approved April 25, 1940 (46 U. S. C. 526l), is amended to read as follows:

"Sec. 13. (a) No person shall operate any motorboat or any vessel in a reckless or negligent manner so as to endanger the life, limb, or property of any person. To 'operate' means to navigate or otherwise use a motorboat or a vessel.

"(b) In the case of collision, accident, or other casualty involving a motorboat or other vessel subject to this Act, it shall be the duty of the operator, if and so far as he can do so without serious danger to his own vessel, or persons aboard, to render such assistance as may be practicable and necessary to other persons affected by the collision, accident, or casualty in order to save them from danger caused by the collision, accident, or casualty. He shall also give his name, address, and identification of his vessel to any person injured and to the owner of any property damaged. The duties imposed by this subsection shall be in addition to any duties otherwise provided by law.

"(c) In the case of collision, accident, or other casualty involving a motorboat or other vessel subject to this Act, the operator thereof, if the collision, accident, or other casualty results in death or injury to any person, or damage to property in excess of $100, shall file with the Secretary of the Department within which the Coast Guard is operating, unless such operator is required to file an accident report with the State under section 3 (c) (6) of the Federal Boating Act of 1958, a full description of the collision, accident, or other casualty, including such information as the Secretary may by regulation require."

(b) Section 16 of such Act of April 25, 1940 (46 U. S. C. 526o), is amended by striking out "than that contained in section 14 of this Act".

(c) Such Act of April 25, 1940 (46 U. S. C. 526–526t), is further amended by adding at the end thereof the following new section:

"Sec. 22. (a) This Act shall apply to every motorboat or vessel on the navigable waters of the United States, its Territories and the District of Columbia, and every motorboat or vessel owned in a State and using the high seas.

"(b) As used in this Act—

"The term 'State' means a State of the United States, a Territory of the United States, and the District of Columbia."

Sec. 7. (a) The Secretary shall make such rules and regulations as may be necessary to carry out the provisions of this Act: *Provided*, That such rules and regulations shall be submitted to the Speaker of the House and the President of the Senate when Congress is in session, and shall not become effective until sixty days thereafter.

(b) The Secretary may, from time to time, and for such periods as he may prescribe, exempt any vessel or class of vessels from the numbering provisions of subsection (d) of section 3 of this Act.

Violations and Penalties

Sec. 8. (a) Whoever being the owner of a vessel required to be numbered under this Act, violates section 3 or 4 of this Act, or regulations established by the Secretary under section 7 of this Act, shall be liable to a penalty of $50 for each violation. Whoever operates a vessel in violation of section 3 of this Act, or regulations established by the Secretary under section 7 of this Act, shall be liable to a penalty of $50 for each violation.

(b) The Secretary may assess and collect any penalty incurred under this Act or any regulations prescribed pursuant to section 7 of this Act. The Secretary may, in his discretion, remit or mitigate any penalty imposed under this section, or discontinue prosecution therefor on such terms as he may deem proper.

(c) Commissioned, warrant, and petty officers of the Coast Guard may board any vessel required to be numbered under this Act at any time such vessel is found upon the navigable waters of the United States, its Territories and the District of Columbia, or on the high seas, address inquiries to those on board, require appropriate proof of identification therefrom, examine the certificate of number issued under this Act, or in the absence of such certificate require appropriate proof of identification of the owner of the vessel, and, in addition, examine such vessel for compliance with this Act, the Act of April 25, 1940, as amended, and the applicable rules of the road.

Sec. 9. It is hereby declared to be the policy of Congress to encourage uniformity of boating laws, rules, and regulations as among the several States and the Federal Government to the fullest extent practicable, subject to reasonable exceptions arising out of local conditions. In the interest of fostering the development, use, and enjoyment of all the waters of the United States it is further declared to be the policy of the Congress hereby to encourage the highest degree of reciprocity and comity among the several jurisdictions. The Secretary, acting under the authority of section 141 of title 14 of the United States Code, shall to the greatest possible extent enter into agreements and other arrangements with the States to insure that there shall be the fullest possible cooperation in the enforcement of both State and Federal statutes, rules, and regulations relating to recreational boating.

Publication of Accident Reports

Sec. 10. The Secretary is authorized and directed to compile, analyze, and publish, either in summary or detailed form, the information obtained by him from the accident reports transmitted to him under section 3 (c) (6) of this Act, and under section 13 (c) of the Act entitled "An Act to amend laws for preventing collisions of vessels, to regulate equipment of certain motorboats on the navigable waters of the United States, and for other purposes", approved April 25, 1940 (46 U. S. C. 526l), together with such findings concerning the causes of such accidents and such recommendations for their prevention as he may deem necessary. Such information shall be made available for public inspection in such manner as the Secretary may deem practicable.

Sec. 11. (a) Except section 3 (d), this Act shall take effect on the date of its enactment.

(b) Section 3 (d) of this Act shall take effect April 1, 1960.

Sec. 12. The Act entitled "An Act to require numbering and recording of undocumented vessels", approved June 7, 1918, as amended (46 U. S. C. 288), and section 21 of the Act entitled "An Act to amend laws for preventing collisions of vessels, to regulate equipment of certain motorboats on the navigable waters of the United States, and for other purposes", approved April 25, 1940, as amended (46 U. S. C. 526t), shall not be applicable in any State having a numbering system approved by the Secretary under section 3 (c) of this Act. Such Act of June 7, 1918, and such section 21 of the Act of April 25, 1940, are repealed effective April 1, 1960.

Law Enforcement

Sec. 13. The applicability and the jurisdiction for enforcement, upon the navigable waters of the United States, its Territories and the District of Columbia, of the laws of the United States and of any State which require the numbering and otherwise regulate the use of undocumented vessels, shall be as follows:

(1) Such laws of the United States shall be applicable and enforced on such waters by law enforcement officers of the United States.

(2) Such laws of any State in a State having a numbering system approved by the Secretary under section 3 (c) of this Act shall be applicable and enforced on such waters by law enforcement officers of the State or by law enforcement officers of the appropriate subdivisions of the State.

(3) Nothing herein shall preclude enforcement of State or Federal laws pursuant to agreements or other arrangements entered into between the Secretary and any State within the contemplation of section 9 of this Act.

(4) Nothing herein shall interfere with, abrogate or limit the jurisdiction of any State: *Provided, however,* That the Secretary shall not approve any State system for numbering which does not fully comply with the standards set forth in section 3 (c).

Approved September 2, 1958.

REGULATIONS DRAFTED BY THE UNITED STATES COAST GUARD
TO IMPLEMENT THE FEDERAL BOATING ACT OF 1958

(Effective March 10, 1959)

PART 170—GENERAL PROVISIONS
Authority and Purpose

§ 170.01–1 *Purpose of regulations.* The regulations in this subchapter provide:

(a) Standards for numbering under the Federal Boating Act of 1958.

(b) Requirements with respect to statistical information under the Federal Boating Act of 1958 and the Act of April 25, 1940, as amended.

(c) Requirements with respect to "Boating Accident Reports" and accident statistics.

§ 170.01–5 *Assignment of functions.* By virtue of the authority vested in the Commandant of the Coast Guard by the Secretary of the Treasury in Treasury Department Order No. 167–32, dated September 23, 1958 (23 F. R. 7605), the regulations in this subchapter are prescribed to carry out the intent and purpose of the Federal Boating Act of 1958, and the Act of April 25, 1940, as amended (46 U. S. C. 526–526t).

Application

§ 170.05–1 *Scope.* The regulations in this subchapter are applicable in the United States, its Territories, and the District of Columbia.

§ 170.05–5 *Vessels subject to the requirements of this subchapter.* Except as specifically noted, this subchapter shall be applicable to undocumented vessels.

Definitions of Terms

§ 170.10–1 *Commandant.* This term means the Commandant of the U. S. Coast Guard.

§ 170.10–5 *Coast Guard District Commander.* This term means an officer of the Coast Guard designated as such by the Commandant to command all Coast Guard activities within his district.

§ 170.10–10 *Horsepower.* This term means the rated horsepower of the machine at maximum operating RPM.

§ 170.10–15. *Length.* As set forth in section 1 of the Act of April 25, 1940, as amended (46 U. S. C. 526), this term means the length of the vessel "measured from end to end over the deck excluding sheer."

§ 170.10–20 *Machinery.* This term includes inboard and outboard engines and all other types of motors or mechanical devices capable of propelling vessels.

§ 170.10–25 *Officer in Charge, Marine Inspection.* This term means any person from the civilian or military branch of the Coast Guard designated as such by the Commandant and who, under the superintendence and direction of the Coast Guard District Commander, is in charge of an inspection zone.

§ 170.10–30 *Operate.* As set forth in subsection 13 (a) of the Act of April 25, 1940, as amended (46 U. S. C. 526 *l*), this term "means to navigate or otherwise use a motorboat or a vessel."

§ 170.10–35 *Operator.* This term means the person who operates or who has charge of the navigation or use of a motorboat or a vessel.

§ 170.10–40 *Owner.* As set forth in subsection 2 (4) of the Federal Boating Act of 1958, this term "means the person who claims lawful possession of a vessel by virtue of legal title or equitable interest therein which entitles him to such possession."

§ 170.10–45 *Ships' lifeboats.* This term means lifeboats used solely for life-saving purposes and does not include dinghies, tenders, speedboats, or other types of craft carried aboard a vessel and used for other than lifesaving purposes.

§ 170.10–50 *State.* As set forth in subsection 2 (5) of the Federal Boating Act of 1958, this term "means a State of the United States, a Territory of the United States, and the District of Columbia."

§ 170.10–55 *Ten horsepower.* As used in subsection 3 (a) of the Federal Boating Act of 1958, this term means the aggregate of all propellant machinery on a vessel.

§ 170.10–60 *Undocumented vessel.* As set forth in subsection 2 (1) of the Federal Boating Act of 1958, this term means "any vessel which is not required to have, and does not have, a valid marine document issued by the Bureau of Customs."

§ 170.10–65 *Vessel.* As set forth in subsection 2 (2) of the Federal Boating Act of 1958, this term "includes every description of water craft, other than a seaplane on the water, used or capable of being used as a means of transportation on water." This definition includes, but is not limited to, motorboats, sailboats, rowboats, canoes, ships, tugs, towboats, ferries, cargo vessels, passenger vessels, tank vessels, fishing vessels, charter boats, party boats, barges, scows, etc.

Appeals and Judicial Review

§ 170.15–1 *Judicial review or relief.* Nothing in this subchapter shall be so construed as to prevent any party from seeking a judicial review by, or relief in, an appropriate Court of law. This applies to any standard or regulation in this subchapter or to any decision or action taken pursuant thereto by the Coast Guard. If any provision of the regulations in this subchapter is held invalid, the validity of the remainder of this subchapter shall not be affected thereby.

§ 170.15–5 *Right of administrative appeal.* (a) Any person aggrieved by a decision or action taken by the Coast Guard under the regulations in this subchapter has a right to an administrative appeal therefrom. An appeal from a decision or action initially made or performed by an enforcing officer may be made to his commanding officer. Any decision or action of such commanding officer may be appealed to the Coast Guard District Commander of the district in which the action was taken or decision was made. A further appeal may be made to the Commandant, U. S. Coast Guard, from the decision of the District Commander.

(b) No special form is required, but such appeal shall set forth the decision or action appealed from and the reasons why it should be set aside or revised. Arrangements may be made for presenting an appeal in person.

§ 170.15–10 *Time limits.* (a) Any appeal to a Coast Guard District Commander shall be made in writing within 30 days after the decision or action appealed from shall have been rendered or taken.

(b) Any appeal to the Commandant shall be made in writing within 30 days after the decision or action appealed from shall have been rendered or taken.

§ 170.15–15 *Decision on appeal.* Pending the determination of an appeal, the decision or action appealed from shall remain in effect.

§ 170.15–20 *Initial decisions or actions of the Commandant.* Any person aggrieved by any decision or action initiated by the Commandant may request a review by writing to the Commandant within 30 days after the decision or action has been rendered or taken. Such a request shall set forth the decision or action desired to be reviewed and the reasons why it should be set aside or revised.

§ 170.15–25 *Reports and assessments of penalties for violations.* The reports of violations, assessment, collection, mitigation or remission of civil penalties shall be in accordance with §§ 2.50–20 to 2.50–30, inclusive, of Subchapter A (Procedures Applicable to the Public) of this chapter.

3. Subchapter S is amended by inserting a new Part 171, reading as follows:

PART 171—STANDARDS FOR NUMBERING

General

§ 171.01–1 *Vessels to be numbered.* (a) Certain undocumented vessels are required to be numbered by subsection 3 (a) of the Federal Boating Act of 1958, which reads as follows:

Every undocumented vessel propelled by machinery of more than 10 horsepower, whether or not such machinery is the principal source of propulsion, using the navigable waters of the United States, its Territories and the District of Columbia, and every such vessel owned in a State and using the high seas, shall be numbered in accordance with this Act, except—

(1) Foreign vessels temporarily using the navigable waters of the United States, its Territories and the District of Columbia;

(2) Public vessels of the United States;

(3) State and municipal vessels;

(4) Ships' lifeboats; and

(5) Vessels designated by the Secretary under section 7 (b) of this Act.

(b) Nothing in this section shall prohibit the numbering of any undocumented vessel, which may be propelled by machinery, upon request of the owner.

§ 171.01–5 *Exemptions.* Pursuant to subsections 3 (a) (5) and 7 (b) of the Federal Boating Act of 1958, the following are exempt from the requirement to be numbered:

(a) Undocumented vessels used exclusively for racing.

(b) Undocumented vessels operating under valid temporary certificates of number.

§ 171.01–10 *Determining horsepower of machinery.* (a) In general, for existing and new equipment, the manufacturer's rated horsepower at a stated maximum operating RPM as set forth on the nameplate attached to the engine, or as stamped on the engine, or as described in a "book of instructions" or other literature issued for such engine will be accepted as prima facie evidence of the horsepower of the machinery in question. In event the machinery does not have marked thereon or accompanying it any literature or tag setting forth the manufacturer's rated horsepower, or should the Coast Guard dispute the manufacturer's rated horsepower, then the Coast Guard's listing of horsepower will be accepted as prima facie evidence of the horsepower.

(b) In the event the owner or operator of a power propelled vessel disagrees with the findings of the Coast Guard as to horsepower, it shall be the responsibility of such owner or operator to prove to the satisfaction of the Coast Guard what is the actual horsepower of the propelling machinery.

Vessel Identification

§ 171.05–1 *Numbering pattern to be used.* (a) The numbers issued pursuant to the Federal Boating Act of 1958 shall be in accordance with the pattern described in this section.

(b) The number shall be divided into parts. The first part shall consist of the symbols identifying the State of principal use, followed by a combination of numerals and letters which furnish individual vessel identification. The group of digits appearing between letters shall be separated from those letters by hyphens or equivalent spaces. As examples: AL–001–AA, or AK 99 AZ.

(c) The first part of the number shall be an abbreviation in capital letters of the State. The abbreviations of the States are as follows:

Alabama—AL	North Carolina—NC
Alaska—AK	North Dakota—ND
Arizona—AZ	Nebraska—NB
Arkansas—AR	Nevada—NV
California—CF	New Hampshire—NH
Colorado—CL	New Jersey—NJ
Connecticut—CT	New Mexico—NM
Delaware—DL	New York—NY
Florida—FL	Ohio—OH
Georgia—GA	Oklahoma—OK
Hawaii—HA	Oregon—OR
Idaho—ID	Pennsylvania—PA
Illinois—IL	Rhode Island—RI
Indiana—IN	South Carolina—SC
Iowa—IA	South Dakota—SD
Kansas—KA	Tennessee—TN
Kentucky—KY	Texas—TX
Louisiana—LA	Utah—UT
Maine—ME	Virginia—VA
Massachusetts—MS	Vermont—VT
Maryland—MD	Washington—WN
Michigan—MC	West Virginia—WV
Minnesota—MN	Wyoming—WY
Mississippi—MI	Wisconsin—WS
Missouri—MO	District of Columbia—DC
Montana—MT	

(d) The remainder of the boat number shall consist of not more than four arabic numerals and two capital letters or not more than three arabic numerals and three capital letters, in sequence, separated by a hyphen or equivalent space, in accordance with the serials, numerically and alphabetically.

(1) As examples of the first alternative:

State designator	Maximum of 4 digits; numerical group	Maximum of 2 letters; alphabetical group
NY	1	A
NY	83	A B
NY	345	T R
NY	9999	Z Z

(2) As example of the second alternative:

State designator	Maximum of 3 digits; numerical group	Maximum of 3 letters; alphabetical group
NC	1	A
NC	83	A B
NC	345	P F
NC	999	Z Z Z

(e) Since the letters "I", "O" and "Q" may be mistaken for arabic numerals, all letter sequences using "I", "O" and "Q" shall be omitted. Objectionable words formed by the use of two or three letters will not be used.

(Sec. 3 (c), 72 Stat. 1754)

§ 171.05–5 *Display of number on vessel.* (a) Subsection 3 (f) of the Federal Boating Act of 1958 requires in part that "the number awarded * * * shall be painted on, or attached to, each side of the bow of the vessel for which it was issued * * *".

(b) The numbers shall be placed on each side of the forward half of the vessel in such position as to provide clear legibility for identification. The numbers shall read from left to right and shall be in block characters of good proportion not less than 3 inches in height. The numbers shall be of a color which will contrast with the color of the background and so maintained as to be clearly visible and legible; i. e., dark numbers on a light background, or light numbers on a dark background.

(Sec. 3 (c) (3), (f), 72 Stat. 1754, 1755)

(c) Subsection 3 (f) of the Federal Boating Act of 1958 also provides "no other number shall be carried on the bow of such vessel."

§ 171.05–10 *Numbering livery boats.* (a) The numbering requirement of this part shall apply to livery boats.

(b) The certificate of number of a livery boat shall be plainly marked, "livery boat."

(c) The description of the motor and type of fuel will be omitted from the certificate of number in any case where the motor is not rented with the boat.

§ 171.05–15 *Numbering of manufacturers' and dealers' boats.* (a) Numbering requirements of this part shall apply to boats operated by manufacturers and dealers.

(b) The description of the boat will be omitted from the certificate of number since the numbers and the certificates of number awarded may be transferred from one boat to another. In lieu of the description, the word "manufacturer" or "dealer,"

as appropriate, will be plainly marked on each certificate.

(c) The manufacturer or dealer may have the number awarded printed upon or attached to a removable sign or signs to be temporarily but firmly mounted upon or attached to the boat being demonstrated or tested so long as the display meets the requirements in § 171.05–5.

Application for Number

§ 171.10–1 *To whom made.* (a) On and after April 1, 1960, the owner of any vessel required to be numbered and principally used in a State which has not assumed the functions of numbering under the Federal Boating Act of 1958 shall prior to its use apply to the U. S. Coast Guard for a number for such vessel.

(b) An undocumented vessel principally used in a State which has assumed the functions of numbering under the Federal Boating Act of 1958 will not be numbered by the Coast Guard.

§ 171.10–2 An amendment (March 15, 1960) describes procedures for making application for a Coast Guard number. Applications (Forms CG–3876 and CG–3876A) are available at all First Class and Second Class Post Offices and at designated Third and Fourth Class Post Offices in those states in which undocumented vessels must be numbered by the Coast Guard.

§ 171.10–5 *Application requirements.* The application for a number shall include the following:

(a) Name and address of owner.

(b) Date of birth of owner.

(c) Present citizenship of owner.

(d) State in which the vessel is principally used.

(e) Present number (if any).

(f) Hull material (wood, steel, aluminum, plastic, other).

(g) Type of propulsion (outboard, inboard, other).

(h) Type of fuel (gas, diesel, other).

(i) Length of vessel.

(j) Make and year built (if known).

(k) Statement as to use (pleasure, livery, dealer, manufacturer, commercial-passenger, commercial-fishing, commercial-other).

(1) A certification of ownership by the applicant.

(m) Signature of owner.

§ 171.10–15 *State in which vessel is principally used.* (a) For the purposes of numbering, the statement of the owner with respect to the State in which the vessel is to be principally used, as set forth in the application for number, will be accepted, prima facie, as true.

(b) If the vessel is to be principally used on the high seas, then it shall be assigned a number for the State in which the vessel is usually docked, moored, housed, or garaged.

§ 171.10–20 *Application for renewal of number.* An application for renewal of a certificate of number shall be made by the owner on an application therefor which must be received by the Coast Guard within a period consisting of the last 90 days before the expiration date on the certificate of number and the same number will be issued upon renewal. Any application not so received shall be treated in the same manner as an original application except that the same number may be reissued if the application is received within one year from date of expiration.

§ 171.10-25 *Lost or destroyed certificate of number.* (a) If a certificate of number is lost or destroyed, the owner within 15 days shall notify the Commandant (MVI-10), U. S. Coast Guard, Washington 25, D. C. The notification shall be in writing and shall describe the circumstances of the loss or destruction.

(b) If an application for a duplicate certificate of number (Form CG-3919) (see § 171.10-30) is submitted without delay, it may also provide the written notification required by paragraph (a) of this section.

§ 171.10-30 *Duplicate certificate of number.* An amendment (March 15, 1960) describes procedure for making application for a duplicate certificate when the original is lost or destroyed. Two-part applications (Forms CG-3919 and CG-3919A) are available at post offices as described in § 171.10-2. Completed application forms are submitted to the post office, where a special fee stamp is bought and attached.

Ownership

§ 171.13-1 *Claim of ownership.* (a) The certified statement of ownership on the application for number shall be the minimum requirement for proof of ownership acceptable to the Coast Guard.

§ 171.13-5 *Liens.* Liens of all kinds, including reservations or transfers of title to secure debts or claims, will be disregarded in determining ownership under this subpart. A lienholder who acquires possession and title by virtue of default in the terms of the lien instrument, or any other person who acquires ownership through any such action of a lienholder, may apply for a number and shall attach to such application a signed statement explaining the fact in detail.

Certificate of Number

§ 171.15-1 *Information required on certificate.* The certificate of number shall include the following:

(a) Name and address of owner.

(b) Date of birth of owner.

(c) Present citizenship of owner.

(d) State in which the vessel is principally used.

(e) Present number (if any).

(f) Hull material (wood, steel aluminum, plastic, other).

(g) Type of propulsion (outboard, inboard, other).

(h) Type of fuel (gas, diesel, other).

(i) Length of vessel.

(j) Make and year built (if known).

(k) Statement as to use (pleasure, livery, dealer, manufacturer, commercial-passenger, commercial-fishing, commercial-other).

(l) A certification of ownership by the applicant.

(m) Signature of owner.

(n) Number awarded to vessel.

(o) Expiration date of certificate.

(p) Notice to the owner that he shall report within 15 days changes of ownership or address, and destruction or abandonment of vessel.

(q) Notice to the owner that the operator shall:

(1) Always carry this certificate on vessel when in use.

(2) Report every accident involving injury or death to persons, or property damage over $100.

(3) Stop and render aid or assistance if involved in boating accident.

§ 171.15-5 *Size and characteristics of certificate.* The certificate of number shall be pocket size (approximately 2½″ x 3½″) and water resistant.

§ 171.15-10 (a) *Temporary certificate.* Pending the issuance of the original certificate of number, the owner of the vessel will be furnished a temporary certificate of number valid for 60 days from date of issue. This temporary certificate shall be carried on board when the vessel is being operated.

Two amendments, paragraphs (b) and (c), (March 15, 1960) identify temporary certificates and require that they be postmarked to be valid.

§ 171.15-15 *Period of validity of certificate.* The original certificate of number initially awarded by the Coast Guard shall be valid for a period ending 3 years from the anniversary of the date of birth of the applicant next succeeding the issuance of the certificate. Each renewal shall be valid for a period ending 3 years from the date of expiration of the certificate so renewed. A certificate issued to other than an individual shall expire 3 years from date of issuance.

§ 171.15-20 *Notification of changes required.* (a) When the owner of a Coast Guard numbered vessel changes the State in which the vessel is principally used, he shall within 90 days surrender the certificate of number to the Coast Guard. The owner shall also apply for another original number to the office issuing numbers for that State.

(b) When the owner of a Coast Guard numbered vessel changes his address from that shown on his certificate, but does not change the State in which the vessel is principally used, he shall notify in writing the Commandant (MVI-10), U. S. Coast Guard, Washington 25, D. C., of his new address within a period not to exceed 15 days from such change. This written notification should be on Form CG-3920 (change of address notice), which is available upon request from any Post Office which handles applications for certificates of numbers (see § 171.10-2), or from any Coast Guard Marine Inspection Office.

(c) When a Coast Guard numbered vessel is lost, destroyed, abandoned, or transferred to another person, the certificate of number issued for the vessel shall be surrendered to the Commandant (MVI-10), U. S. Coast Guard, Washington 25, D. C., within a period not to exceed 15 days after such event. When the numbered vessel is lost, destroyed, abandoned, or transferred to another person, the owner shall within 15 days notify in writing the Commandant (MVI-10), U. S. Coast Guard, Washington 25, D. C., of the change in the status of the vessel. This written notification should be on Form CG-3921 (Notification of change in status of vessel), which is available upon request from any Post Office which handles applications for certificates of numbers (see § 171.10-2), or from any Coast Guard Marine Inspection Office. If the certificate of number is lost or destroyed, a description of such circumstances shall be reported as required by § 171.10-25.

(d) The application for number by a new owner of a vessel shall, for purposes of fee, be regarded as an original application for number, but where the vessel will continue in use in the same State of principal use, the new number shall be identical with the previous one, except where a lienholder acquires title and lawful possession by virtue of his lien, in which case a new number shall be issued.

(e) A change of motor is not required to be reported to the Coast Guard.

§ 171.15-25 *One certificate for each vessel.* The intent of this subpart is that the owner of an undocumented vessel shall not have more than one valid number or valid certificate of number for any one vessel at any time. Therefore, the owner will violate the regulations if he retains more than one valid certificate of number for any one vessel.

§ 171.15-30 *Cancellation of certificate and voiding of number.* (a) Subsection 3 (e) of the Federal Boating Act of 1958 authorizes the cancellation of certificates of number, thereby voiding the numbers issued. This means that a certificate may be canceled and number voided by proper authority even though such action occurs before the expiration date on the certificate and such certificate is not surrendered to the issuing office.

(b) Certain causes for cancellation of certificates and voiding of numbers are:

(1) Surrender of certificate for cancellation.

(2) Issuance of a new number for the same vessel.

(3) Issuance of a marine document by the Bureau of Customs for the same vessel.

(4) False or fraudulent certification in an application for number.

(c) In the absence of an application for renewal as provided in §171.10-20 a number is automatically void on the date of expiration as shown on the certificate of number.

Fees and Charges

§ 171.17-1 *Fees.* (a) The fees charged by the U. S. Coast Guard are based upon the estimated cost of the administration of the Coast Guard's numbering system.

(b) The fees are as follows:

(1) Original numbering—$3.00.

(2) Reissue of lost or destroyed certificate of number—$1.00.

(3) Renewal of number—$3.00.

§ 171.17-5 *Method of Payment.* (a) The fee for original numbering shall be paid by purchase of a special fee stamp from any Post Office which sells the special fee stamps. (See § 171.10-2)

(b) The fee for reissue of lost or destroyed certificate of number (duplicate certificate of number) shall be paid by purchase of a special fee stamp from any Post Office which sells the special fee stamps. (See § 171.10-30)

(c) No application for an original certificate of number or for a duplicate certificate of number will be processed without an appropriate special fee stamp attached thereto. No special fee stamps shall be sold prior to April 1, 1960.

(d) The fee for renewal of number is payable to the U. S. Coast Guard and shall accompany the application.

Availability of Records

§ 171.20-1 *Enforcement or assistance programs.* Upon request, information on ownership and identity of Coast Guard numbered vessels shall be available to Federal, State, and local officials, as needed, in any enforcement or assistance programs.

§ 171.20-5. *Disclosure of information.* (a) The records pertaining to the numbering of undocumented vessels pursuant to this part are considered to be public records.

(b) Information based on such Coast Guard records may be released upon oral or written inquiry, subject only to reasonable restrictions necessary to carry on the business of the office. The Coast Guard may permit excerpts to be made or the copying or reproduction thereof by a private individual or concern authorized by the Coast Guard. The fees and charges for copying, certifying, or searching of records for information shall be assessed in accordance with 33 CFR 1.25.

4. The title for Part 172 is amended to read:

PART 172
NUMBERING REQUIREMENTS UNDER ACT OF JUNE 7, 1918

5. Part 172 is amended by adding at the end thereof a new Subpart 172.25, reading as follows:

Termination Requirements

§ 172.25-1 *Effective termination dates of numbering laws.* Effective April 1, 1960, the Act of June 7, 1918, as amended, and section 21 of the Act of April 25, 1940, are repealed by section 12 of the Federal Boating Act of 1958. In addition, these laws shall cease to be applicable prior to April 1, 1960, in any State when such State has assumed the functions of numbering under the Federal Boating Act of 1958.

§ 172.25-5 *Effective termination dates for regulations in this part.* (a) No certificate of award of number will be issued nor numbers assigned to vessels pursuant to this part on and after April 1, 1960.

(b) The regulations prescribed under the Act of June 7, 1918, as amended, shall cease to be applicable in any State when such State has assumed the functions of numbering under the Federal Boating Act of 1958.

§ 172.25-10 *Interim use of certificates of award of number and numbers awarded.* Pending receipt of a certificate of number under the Federal Boating Act of 1958, for which application has been made and proof thereof retained, the owner of every vessel of more than 10 horsepower with a valid certificate of award of number on March 31, 1960, shall retain such number and certificate for temporary identification until renumbered pursuant to the Federal Boating Act of 1958.

6. Subchapter S is amended by inserting a new Part 173, reading as follows:

PART 173—BOATING ACCIDENTS, REPORTS, AND STATISTICAL INFORMATION

Boating Accidents

§ 173.01-1 *General.* (a) The provisions of this subpart shall apply (1) to all uninspected motorboats and (2) to all other uninspected vessels used for pleasure or recreational purposes. Uninspected vessels, other than motorboats, used for commercial purposes are not included.

(b) The provisions in this subpart are applicable in the United States, its Territories, and the District of Columbia, as well as to every such vessel which is owned in a State, Territory, or the District of Columbia and using the high seas.

§ 173.01-5 *Reportable boating accidents.* (a) Subsection 13 (c) of the Act of April 25, 1940, as amended (46 U. S. C. 526*l*, reads as follows:

In the case of collision, accident, or other casualty involving a motorboat or other vessel subject to this Act, the operator thereof, if the collision, accident, or other casualty results in death or injury to any person, or damage to property in excess of $100, shall file with the Secretary of the Department within which the Coast Guard is operating, unless such operator is required to file an accident report with the

State under section 3 (c) (6) of the Federal Boating Act of 1958, a full description of the collision, accident, or other casualty, including such information as the Secretary may by regulation require.

(b) For the purpose of this subpart a "boating accident" means a collision, accident or other casualty involving (1) an uninspected motorboat or (2) any other uninspected vessel used for pleasure or recreational purposes.

(c) A vessel subject to this subpart is considered to be involved in a "boating accident" whenever the occurrence results in damage by or to the vessel or its equipment; in injury or loss of life to any person, or in the disappearance of any person from on board under circumstances which indicate the possibility of death or injury. A "boating accident" includes, but is not limited to, capsizing, collision, foundering, flooding, fire, explosion and the disappearance of a vessel other than by theft.

(d) A report is required whenever a vessel subject to this subpart is involved in a "boating accident" which results in any one or more of the following:

(1) Loss of life.

(2) Injury causing any person to remain incapacitated for a period in excess of 72 hours.

(3) Actual physical damage to property (including vessels) in excess of $100.

§ 173.01-10 *Written report required.* (a) Whenever death results from a boating accident, a written report shall be submitted within 48 hours. For every other reportable boating accident a written report shall be submitted within five (5) days after such accident.

(b) The operator(s) of the boat(s) shall prepare and submit the written report(s) to the Coast Guard Officer in Charge, Marine Inspection, nearest to the place where such accident occurred or nearest to the port of first arrival after such accident, unless such operator is required to file an accident report with a State under subsection 3 (c) (6) of the Federal Boating Act of 1958.

(c) Every written report shall contain the following information:

(1) The numbers and/or names of vessels involved.

(2) The locality where the accident occurred.

(3) The time and date when the accident occurred.

(4) Weather and sea conditions at time of accident.

(5) The name, address, age, and boat operating experience of the operator of the reporting vessel.

(6) The names and addresses of operators of other vessels involved.

(7) The names and addresses of the owners of vessels or property involved.

(8) The names and addresses of any person or persons injured or killed.

(9) The nature and extent of injury to any person or persons.

(10) A description of damage to property (including vessels) and estimated cost of repairs.

(11) A description of the accident (including opinions as to the causes).

(12) The length, propulsion, horsepower, fuel and construction of the reporting vessel.

(13) Names and addresses of known witnesses.

(d) The Coast Guard Form CG-3865 (Boating Accident Report) may be used for the written report required by this section.

Statistics Required

§ 173.05-1 *Required reports.* The Coast Guard will obtain, compile, analyze, and publish periodic reports in a uniform manner with respect to vessels having currently valid certificates of number, and with respect to boating accidents.

§ 173.05-5 *Reports with respect to numbered vessels.* The Coast Guard will compile statistics on numbered vessels as of March 31, June 30, September 30, and December 31 of each year. This information includes as of the reporting date:

(a) The total number of all valid certificates of number outstanding.

(b) The total number of valid certificates of number held by vessels numbered under subsection 3 (a) of the Federal Boating Act of 1958.

(c) The total numbers of valid certificates of number held by vessels described by class, type, and construction.

§ 173.05-10 *Reports with respect to boating accidents.* The Coast Guard will compile statistics on boating accidents reported during each quarter, ending on March 31, June 30, September 30, and December 31 of each year. This information will include:

(a) The total number of boating accidents reported during each such period.

(b) The totals of boating accidents reported during each such period, grouped according to the cause, nature, and results and including the class, type, and construction of vessels involved.

(c) The totals of boating accidents reported during each such period by vessels required to be numbered under subsection 3 (a) of the Federal Boating Act of 1958 according to vessels described by class, type, and construction.

Availability of Information

§ 173.10-1 *"Boating Accident Reports".* (a) The "Boating Accident Reports" are intended to furnish the information necessary for the Coast Guard to make findings of causes of accidents and recommendations for their prevention, and to compile information for use in making statistical reports.

(b) Except as provided in paragraph (c), individual "Boating Accident Reports," or copies of or excerpts therefrom, will not be released.

(c) "Boating Accident Reports" may be available for additional statistical studies, on the condition that information from individual reports shall not be disclosed, and subject to prior arrangements and reasonable restrictions necessary in the carrying on of the business of the office.

§ 173.10-5 *Statistical records and statistical reports.* After information has been released or published, the statistical records and statistical reports obtained and compiled by the Coast Guard, as distinguished from the individual "Boating Accident Reports" described in § 173.10-1, shall be made available for inspection and use by the public during normal office hours subject to reasonable restrictions necessary in the carrying on of the business of the office.

Dated: December 19, 1958.

[SEAL]   J. A. HIRSHFIELD,
*Rear Admiral, U. S. Coast Guard,
Acting Commandant.*

[F. R. Doc. 58-10628; Filed, Dec. 24, 1958; 8:45 a. m.]

DIGEST OF STATE NUMBERING LAWS

The Federal Boating Act of 1958 called for the registration and numbering of all motorboats over a specified horsepower for identification, with a provision that the individual state should have jurisdiction in all cases where their state legislation would conform to the standard established by the federal act. Approval by the U. S. Coast Guard is required in each case.

By May 1963, the Coast Guard had officially approved the numbering systems of 43 states. Boats principally used in these states are numbered exclusively by the state; Coast Guard numbers are obsolete. In compliance with the Federal Act all of these state laws grant 90-day reciprocity to out-of-state boats awarded numbers pursuant to Federal law or a federally approved state numbering system.

As of May 1963, the states that had either failed or neglected to adopt state numbering systems in compliance with the Federal Boating (Bonner) Act of 1958 were: *Alaska, Hawaii, Maine, New Hampshire, Pennsylvania, Tennessee, and Washington.*

At that time, legislation was pending in some of these states and approval of several of these was probable. See page 27j for latest information at the time of going to press with this edition.

The Outboard Boating Club of America (307 No. Michigan Ave., Chicago 1, Ill.) has compiled all available information on state boating laws in handbooks for various regions of the country. These include not only the registration and numbering requirements, but also all related laws on equipment, operation, use of trailers, etc., which readers are urged to obtain.

Through the courtesy of the Outboard Boating Club of America, extracts from their handbooks and digests are published below, on pages 27f-27j.

NOTE: In the tabulation below, numbers in parentheses alongside state names refer to amendments since the list was compiled. Extracts from these amendments, keyed with the same numbers, are given on page 27j.

State	STATE NUMBERING LAWS Where to Apply for Certificate of Number	Special Motorboat Exemptions and Waters Not Covered by Numbering Law	Special Numbers for (a) Boat Mfrs. & Dlrs. (b) Boat Livery Operators —Unless otherwise indicated numbering fees are the same as for private pleasure craft	Agency Responsible for Administration and Enforcement of State Boating Act
ALABAMA	Div. of Water Safety, Dept. of Conservation, Administrative Building, Montgomery, Alabama or County Probate Judges' offices, or License Commissioners.	Boats 12' or less in length used on farm ponds of less than 50 acres exempt.	(a) YES. $10.00 for first license, $1 each additional.	Dept. of Conservation
ALASKA	Absent federally approved state numbering system, Coast Guard numbers motor boats over 10 horsepower principally operated upon navigable waters of the State.			
ARKANSAS	Office of County Clerk.	Boats with 10 HP. or less.	(a) YES. Available only to licensed manufacturers and dealers.	Game & Fish Comm.
ARIZONA	Motor Vehicle Div., Dept. of Hwys., 1739 W. Jackson Phoenix, Arizona.	Numbers issued by racing or other associations or recognized by federal law shall be recognized by Arizona provided the boat owner files a copy of such number with the State Motor Vehicle Department within 90 days after entering Arizona, or after obtaining such a number, on a form provided by the Motor Vehicle Division.	(a) YES. ($5.00 for each registration.)	Motor Veh. Div., Dept. of Hwys.
CALIFORNIA	Division of Small Craft Harbors Sacramento, California	Undocumented vessels propelled solely by oars, paddles, or electric motors of 10 HP. or less, and undocumented vessels 8 ft. or less propelled solely by sail.	(a) YES.	Small Craft Harbors Comm., Dept. of Natural Resources
COLORADO	State Park & Recreation Board 221 State Services Building Denver 3, Colorado	Boats with 10 HP. or less; boats propelled by air motor if operated upon waters of this State which are not navigable waters of the United States.	(a) YES. A motorboat belonging to a duly authorized and licensed dealer, exhibiting or demonstrating such boat, pursuant to business, shall in addition to the certificate of number and detachable number plates, have a flag bearing the conforming dealer number on display on bow of the boat.	State Park & Recreation Board
CONNECTICUT	Resident boat owners file application with Town Clerk in Town of Residence; Non-Residents with Town Clerk in Town where boat will be principally used.	(a) Motorboats with 5 HP. or less; undocumented vessels bearing a C.G. number issued after Apr. 1, 1960, until such number expires.	(a) YES.	Boating Safety Commission

State	Where to Apply for Certificate of Number	Special Motorboat Exemptions and Waters Not Covered by Numbering Law	Special Numbers for (a) Boat Mfrs. & Dlrs. (b) Boat Livery Operators —Unless otherwise indicated numbering fees are the same as for private pleasure craft	Agency Responsible for Administration and Enforcement of State Boating Act
DELAWARE	Commission of Shell Fisheries Dover, Delaware		(a) Dealers pay $5 for first number, and $3 for each additional one. (b) Livery owners shall pay standard numbering fee.	Delaware Commission of Shell Fisheries thru appointed Boat Safety Director
FLORIDA	Office of County Tax Collector, for Pleasure boats; Game & Fresh-Water Fish Comm. or State Board of Conservation, Tallahassee, Florida for commercial boats.	Boats with 10 HP. or less; motor boats used exclusively on private lakes; racing boats.	(a) YES.	State Board of Conservation
GEORGIA	State Game and Fish Commission, Motorboat Registration Unit 179 Washington St. Atlanta 3, Georgia	Any watercraft propelled by a motor of 10 HP. or less. Act does not apply on privately owned ponds or lakes not open to the general public.	(a) YES. (b) Owners of rental boat fleets may buy livery boat numbers for $1.25 each up to 20 boats, and 50¢ each for all over 20.	State Game and Fish Commission. During times when the Comm. is not in session, the Director of the State Game and Fish. Comm. shall have authority to take any action the Commission is authorized to take.
HAWAII	Absent federally approved state numbering system, Coast Guard numbers motor boats over 10 horsepower principally operated upon navigable waters of the State.			
IDAHO	Act approved 7/15/61. Motorboats registered with State Dept. of Law Enforcement. Fee $2. Mfrs. and dealers. $3.			
ILLINOIS	Dept. of Conservation Motorboat License Division 400 S. Spring St. Springfield, Illinois	Official racing boats, registered with a nationally recognized racing group and not used for pleasure at any time.	(a) YES. (b) YES.	Dept. of Conservation
INDIANA	Conservation Department 311 W. Washington St. Indianapolis, Indiana	———	(a) YES. (b) Numbers awarded to livery boat operators may be printed upon or attached to removable signs to be temporarily but firmly mounted on the boat being rented, since livery boat numbers may be transferred from one rental boat 'to another.	Conservation Dept.
IOWA	State Conservation Comm. East 7th and Court Des Moines, Iowa	Farm ponds of less than 10 surface acres, and privately owned lakes.	(a) YES.	State Conservation Comm.
KANSAS	Forestry, Fish & Game Comm., Pratt, Kansas	Boats propelled by machinery of less than 10 HP. Private lakes, owned or leased.	(a) YES. ($10.00 for each registration)	Forestry, Fish & Game Comm.
KENTUCKY	Circuit court clerk of the county in which a motorboat owner resides, except, if the motorboat is to be operated principally in a county other than the owner's place of residence the owner may apply to the circuit court clerk of the county of principal operation.		(a) YES. ($25.00 annually for original certificate of number, and $2.00 for each additional certificate of number desired.) (b) Annual registration fee for boats for hire from a boat livery, as follows: Less than 16' in length—$1.00; 16' to 26'—$2.50; 26' to 40'—$4.00; 40' and over and all inboard motorboats—$5.00	Div. of Boating, Dept. of Public Safety.
LOUISIANA	Louisiana Wildlife and Fisheries Commission Baton Rouge, Louisiana	Boats powered by motors of 10 HP. or less.	(a) YES. ($25.00 for a 3-year period.) (b) Boat livery owners shall be entitled to pay $5.00 per boat for their first three boats and $3.00 per boat for every one thereafter.	Louisiana Wildlife and Fisheries Commission
(1) MAINE	Absent federally approved state numbering system, Coast Guard numbers motor boats over 10 horsepower principally operated upon navigable waters of the State.			
MARYLAND	Dept. of Tidewater Fisheries State Office Building Annapolis, Maryland	Motorboats of 7½ HP. or less.	(a) YES. ($2.00 for each boat, and valid for a period of only one year.) (b) Special licenses granted to owners of fleets of boats for the same fee as for dealers and manufacturers.	Dept. of Tidewater Fisheries, upon tidal waters; Dept. of Game and Inland Fish, upon non-tidal waters.
MASSACHUSETTS	Director, Division of Motorboats, Registry of Motor Vehicles 100 Nashua Street Boston 14, Massachusetts	Motorboats with less than 5 HP. Act does not apply to private ponds of less than 10 acres owned by one person.	(a) YES.	Director of Division of Motorboats.
MICHIGAN	Secretary of State Capitol Building Lansing 19, Michigan, or sheriff's dept. of each county.	Watercraft participating in races, regattas and trials therefor sanctioned by Michigan State Waterways Commission.	(a) YES. ($5.00 for each registration.)	Enforcement by sheriff's dept. of each county.

State	Where to Apply for Certificate of Number	Special Motorboat Exemptions and Waters Not Covered by Numbering Law	Special Numbers for (a) Boat Mfrs. & Dlrs. (b) Boat Livery Operators —Unless otherwise indicated numbering fees are the same as for private pleasure craft	Agency Responsible for Administration and Enforcement of State Boating Act
MINNESOTA	County auditors or their agents.	Duck boats during duck hunting season, sailboats, canoes, rice boats during harvest season, seaplanes.	(a) YES.	Commission of Conservation
MISSISSIPPI	Sheriff of the county where vessel is usually moored, docked, housed or garaged.	Boats powered by motors of 10 HP. or less; racing boats Act does not apply to any private pond or lake, which is not used for boat rentals or the charging of fees for fishing.	(a) YES. An owner of more than one vessel with more than 10 HP. may obtain certificate of number for all such vessels upon payment of $1.00.	State Game and Fish Commission, with the advice and consent of a special five-man Water Safety Committee appointed by the Governor.
MISSOURI	Dept. of Revenue 100 E. Capitol Ave. Jefferson City, Missouri	Boats with 10 HP. or less. Farm ponds not commercially operated for boating purposes, municipally or privately-owned waters, public water supply impoundments and drainage ditches built by drainage districts.	(a) YES. ($10.00 for each registration.)	Missouri Boat Commission
MONTANA	Dept. of Fish & Game Water and Hunter Safety Section Helena, Montana	Boats with 10 HP. or less;	(a) YES.	Fish & Game Comm.
NEBRASKA	Game, Forestation & Parks Commission Lincoln 9, Nebraska	———	(a) YES. ($3.00 for each registration.)	Game, Forestation & Parks Comm.
NEVADA	County Assessor in county where owner resides, except in the counties of Washoe and Elko, where you apply at the branch offices of the Dept. of Motor Vehicles in Reno and Elko.	———	(a) YES. ($5.00 for first number.) No dealer will be assigned more than 3 dealer numbers. The second and third numbers are $1.00 each.	Dept. of Motor Vehicles
(2) NEW HAMPSHIRE	Absent federally approved state numbering system, Coast Guard numbers motor boats over 10 horsepower principally operated upon navigable waters of the State.			
NEW JERSEY	Dept. of Conservation and Economic Development Trenton 25, N. J.	Motorboats with 10 HP. or less on tidal waters; any power vessel used exclusively for racing while actually competing in an authorized race held under the auspices of an incorporated yacht club or racing association; undocumented vessels bearing a Coast Guard number issued after April 1, 1960, until such number expires.	(a) YES ($5 for each registration, good for a 1-year period). (b) Owners who rent boats for public use, $10 for 5 boats and $1 for each additional boat thereafter, good for a 1-year period.	Boat Regulation Committee (Commissioner of Dept. of Conservation & Economic Development plus 6 public members appointed by the Governor with the advice and consent of the Senate)
NEW MEXICO	State Park Commission P.O. Box 958 Santa Fe, New Mexico	Boats under 10 HP.	———	State Park Comm.
NEW YORK	Division of Motor Boats State Conservation Dept. Albany 1, New York	(b) Privately owned waters reserved solely for private use.	(a) YES ($10 for each certificate)	Conservation Commissioner
NORTH CAROLINA	Motorboat Registration Section Wildlife Resources Comm. P.O. Box 2919 Raleigh, North Carolina	Boats with 10 HP. or less.	(a) YES. ($15.00 for initial certificate of number, and $6.00 for each additional certificate.)	Wildlife Resources Comm.
NORTH DAKOTA	Game & Fish Department Bismarck, North Dakota	Boats under 10 HP.	———	Game & Fish Dept.
OHIO	Division of Watercraft Dept. of Natural Resources 1800 W. Fifth Ave. Columbus 15, Ohio	———	(a) YES. ($20.00 annually for a dealer license and certificate of number.) *In addition, person using outboard motor on a bailed or rented boat, must secure detachable outboard motor license.	Administrator, Div. of Watercraft, Dept. of Natural Resources.
OKLAHOMA	Planning & Resources Board 533 State Capitol Oklahoma City, Oklahoma (In addition, owner of any outboard motor of more than 10 HP. to be used on vessel required to be numbered in Okla. shall secure license and certificate of title for motor.)	A watercraft or motorboat used exclusively for racing; boat used solely on private lake or on any lake of 100 acres or less.	(a) Annual dealer's license, $10.00.	Planning & Resources Board
OREGON	State Marine Board 311 Capitol Building Salem, Oregon	Boats with motors under 3½ HP., and sailboats less than 12' long.	(a) YES. ($10.00 for first number applied for and $2.00 for each additional number applied for in any application.)	State Marine Director appointed by State Marine Board.
(3) PENNSYLVANIA	Absent federally approved state numbering system, Coast Guard numbers motor boats over 10 horsepower principally operated upon navigable waters of the State.			
RHODE ISLAND	Division of Harbors & Rivers Dept. of Public Works Boat Regulation Section Room 100, State Office Building Providence 3, Rhode Island	Motorboats used exclusively for racing.	(a) YES.	Div. of Harbors & Rivers, Dept. of Public Works.

State	Where to Apply for Certificate of Number	Special Motorboat Exemptions and Waters Not Covered by Numbering Law	Special Numbers for (a) Boat Mfrs. & Dlrs. (b) Boat Livery Operators —Unless otherwise indicated numbering fees are the same as for private pleasure craft	Agency Responsible for Administration and Enforcement of State Boating Act
SOUTH CAROLINA	Division of Boating, Wildlife Resources Dept. P.O. Box 360 Columbia, South Carolina	Boats under 10 HP.	(a) YES.	Div. of Boating, Wildlife Resources Dept.
SOUTH DAKOTA	Department of Game, Fish & Parks Pierre, South Dakota	Boats with 6 HP. or less; racing boats.	(a) YES. ($5.00 for each registration.)	Dept. of Game, Fish & Parks
(4) TENNESSEE	Absent federally approved state numbering system, Coast Guard numbers motor boats over 10 horsepower principally operated upon navigable waters of the State			
TEXAS	Motor Vehicle Division, Highway Department 40th and Jackson Ave. Austin 14, Texas	Boats with 10 HP. or less; racing boats, provided they are operated only in a regulated and supervised race or exhibition; commercial fishing boats required to be licensed by Texas Game and Fish Comm. to fish in salt waters of the state are exempt from numbering fees, but must display a Texas number on either side of their bow.	(a) YES. ($25.00 for each registration.)	Motor Vehicle Div., Highway Dept.
UTAH	Office of the Supervisor of Boating Administration and Development 19 W. South Temple Room 662 U P Annex Building Salt Lake City 1, Utah	Racing boats during the three twenty-four (24) hour periods prior to, during and following any race authorized by the Commission.	(a) YES.	State Park & Recreation Comm.
VERMONT	Public Safety Department Marine Division Montpelier, Vermont		(a) YES. ($25 for the first number, and $5 for each additional number applied for in the current registration period.)	Commissioner of the Dept. of Public Safety
VIRGINIA	Boat Section Virginia Game Commission P.O. Box 1642 Richmond 13, Virginia	Any vessel propelled by a motor of less than 10 HP.	(a) YES. ($15 for dealers for original certificate of number, and $25 for manufacturers. Additional dealer's or manufacturer's certificates of number cost $8 each.)	Commission of Game and Inland Fisheries
(5) WASHINGTON	Absent federally approved state numbering system, Coast Guard numbers motor boats over 10 horsepower principally operated upon navigable waters of the State.			
WEST VIRGINIA	Director, Dept. of Natural Resources State Office Bldg. No. 1 Washington St., East Charleston 5, W. Va.	Boats with 5 HP. or less; boats used exclusively for racing while preparing for and participating in authorized races.	(a) YES. ($5 for each certificate of number.)	Dept. of Natural Resources
WISCONSIN	Conservation Department Madison 1, Wisconsin	Racing boats present in the state for not more than 10 days for the express purpose of competing in a race authorized by official permit.	(a) YES. (b) Owners of 3 or more rental boats may, at their option, pay a flat fee of $5 plus 50¢ per boat for obtaining or renewing certificates of number.	Conservation Comm.
(6) WYOMING	Absent federally approved state numbering system, Coast Guard numbers motor boats over 10 horsepower principally operated upon navigable waters of the State.			

AMENDMENTS TO STATE NUMBERING LAWS

(The following are brief extracts only, based on data available in May 1963, affecting the tabulation on pages 27f-27i. For more detailed and latest information on numbering laws and amendments, and other state laws relating to equipment and operation, see latest digests and supplements published by the Outboard Boating Club of America, 307 North Michigan Avenue, Chicago 1, Illinois.)

	State	Where to Apply for Certificate of Number	(a) Special Motorboat Exemptions (b) Waters Excused from Numbering Law	Special Numbers for (a) Boat Mfrs. & Dlrs. (b) Boat Livery Operators —Unless otherwise indicated numbering fees are the same as for private pleasure craft	Agency Responsible for Administration and Enforcement of State Boating Act
(1) *	MAINE	Absent federally approved state numbering system, Coast Guard numbers motorboats over 10 HP. principally used on navigable waters of state.			
		On inland or non-tidal waters of state			
		Commissioner of Inland Fisheries & Game Augusta, Maine	(a) Private non-commercial motorboats with 10 HP. or less; motorboats already covered by C.G. numbers or a numbering system of another state of which the owners are resident.	(a) YES	Commissioner of Inland Fisheries & Game
(2) *	NEW HAMPSHIRE	Absent federally approved state numbering system, Coast Guard numbers motorboats over 10 HP. principally used on navigable waters of state.			
		On inland or non-tidal waters			
		Division of Motor Vehicles, Dept. of Safety Concord, N. H.	(a) Any boat or outboard motor brought into the state under special authorization to participate in a race, provided it does not remain within the state in excess of 10 days.	(a) Dealer Registration, $5 for first number plate, and $3 for each additional one. (b) Commercial boats, i.e., boats for hire carrying a lawful max. of not more than 10 persons, $6; not more than 25 persons, $12; not more than 150 persons, $18; over 150 persons, $30.	Division of Safety Services, Dept. of Safety
	PENNSYLVANIA	Absent federally approved state numbering system, Coast Guard numbers motorboats over 10 HP. principally used on navigable waters of state.			
		On inland waters of the state			
(3) *		Dept. of Revenue Harrisburg, Pa.		(a) YES ($5 for each license).	Fish Commission

(1) (2) (3) *As of May 1963, legislation had been proposed in MAINE, NEW HAMPSHIRE and PENNSYLVANIA which, if enacted into law, would qualify under the Federal Boating Act of 1958.

(4) *TENNESSEE.* Numbering bill to comply with Federal Boating Act of 1958 failed despite intensive interim legislative study. Consequently, Coast Guard continues numbering boats over 10 hp on Federal waters.

(5) *WASHINGTON.* As of May 1963, legislation had been proposed which would qualify under the Federal Boating Act of 1958.

(6) *WYOMING.* As of April 1963, was expected to be the 43rd state to pass legislation complying with the Federal Boating Act of 1958.

Lights   CHAPTER II

(See pages 36-46, and Chapter IV, pages 61-78)

NO matter how the subject is presented, there always seems to be some misunderstanding as to how certain classes of small vessels are to be lighted at night—particularly auxiliaries. Most of the confusion is caused by the fact that regulations governing lights are to be found both in the Pilot Rules, which cover all water craft on federal waters generally, and also in the Motor Boat Act, which is concerned *only* with boats up to 65 feet in length, "propelled by machinery."

More than one interpretation might reasonably be taken from that phrase "propelled by machinery" so a further element of doubt enters into the picture. Fortunately, a recent amendment (June 4, 1956) to the Motor Boat Act goes a long way toward making the rules more consistent and logical, particularly with respect to auxiliaries.

Therefore, in an attempt to clarify the subject, we will try to analyze the situation in a manner that can leave no possibility of misinterpretation.

The Pilot Rules

At the outset it is important to note that the Pilot Rules govern the navigation of vessels on harbors, rivers and "inland waters" of the United States, separate rules being provided for the Great Lakes and connecting and tributary waters as far East as Montreal, and other rules for the Red River of the North and certain rivers emptying into the Gulf of Mexico and their tributaries.

When the Pilot Rules say "inland waters" they do not mean inland lakes lying wholly within the boundaries of one state, as such waters are subject to state jurisdiction. Inland waters are all other waters lying inland and inshore of lines that have been laid down to separate them from the high seas, on which International Rules apply.

Left: While sailboats in general, without engines, are lighted according to the Pilot Rules, which require separate red and green side lights only, it has been held that open sailboats up to 18 feet in length should be regarded as rowboats under sail. Under Great Lakes and Mississippi River Rules, they may show a lantern having a green slide on one side and a red slide on the other. Under Inland Pilot Rules for other waters, they may simply show a white light. In both cases, the lights are not fixed but are kept at hand to be shown in time to avert collision

Right: An outboard motor boat, being "propelled by machinery", is a motor boat and at night must carry the lights prescribed for a motor boat. Under 26 feet in length, it would have a combination red-and-green bow light and a white stern light. White stern lights should be placed on the centerline to serve not only as identification but as a range with the bow light. However, the Coast Guard recognizes the difficulty of carrying the white stern light on the centerline of some small boats and has ruled that on classes A and I it may be carried off the centerline

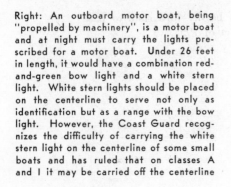

The Proper Lights to be Carried by All Classes of Boats

Disregarding, for the purposes of our discussion here, all special types such as pilot vessels, ferry boats and other classes for which specific lights are prescribed, the big, broad classifications of "vessels" i. the Pilot Rules would be—steam vessels and sailing vessels. So far as these rules are concerned, a steam vessel includes any vessel propelled in whole or in part by machinery. Furthermore a steam vessel under sail and not under steam is considered a sailing vessel. Every vessel under steam, whether under sail or not, is considered a steam vessel. This is explicit and easily interpreted.

The Motor Boat Act

Now, on "navigable" (Federal) waters of the United States, vessels propelled by machinery, not over 65 feet in length (except tug boats and tow boats propelled by steam) are classed as motor boats. They come within the provisions of the Motor Boat Act of 1940, which divides them into four classes (A, up to 16 feet; 1, 16 to 26 feet; 2, 26 to 40 feet; and 3, 40 to 65 feet) and contains provisions prescribing the equipment to be carried by each class. Included in this equipment are the lights which must be exhibited by every motor boat in all weathers from sunset to sunrise when under way. (A vessel is under way when not at anchor, aground or made fast to the shore.) The law does not require lights to be aboard during the day.

"Navigable" waters of the United States are those navigable to the sea or which cross state and international lines. Outside these waters (on the high seas) a motor boat would comply with International Law. On lakes and other waterways lying wholly within the boundaries of one state, motor boats would not be under Federal jurisdiction and would, therefore, comply with the motor boat law of that state, if any statutes have been passed. (About a dozen of the states do have some regulations regarding the lighting of motor boats on state waters.)

Below: An inboard motor boat of Class 1 (16 to 26 feet). Forward she carries a combination red-and-green light, each showing through 10 points, and aft a 32-point white light showing all around the horizon

When Is a Vessel "Propelled by Machinery"?

Now, in order to determine whether a certain vessel should be lighted in accordance with the Motor Boat Act or according to the Pilot Rules, it is necessary to determine whether she is "propelled by machinery" and whether she is under or over 65 feet.

According to an opinion given originally by the former Bureau of Marine Inspection and Navigation, when asked about the status of auxiliaries, a vessel (under 65 feet) is considered to be a motor boat when the motor is connected to the shaft and propeller, regardless of whether the engine is actually in operation or not. Thus, they say, in the case of a sailing vessel carrying an outboard motor, the vessel is an auxiliary (and would be classed as a

Above: Sailboats (without an engine) are not lighted according to the Motor Boat Act but as provided by the Pilot Rules, which require a 10-point red side light to port and a 10-point green side light to starboard. Under new regulations they must also carry a 12-pt. white stern light showing aft. Under the Inland Pilot Rules (excepting the Great Lakes and Mississippi River), vessels under 10 gross tons, in bad weather, when the side lights cannot be fixed, may keep their separate red and green side lights (properly screened) at hand ready to show to approaching vessels

motor boat) when the outboard motor is attached to the stern. A sailing vessel is also an auxiliary when it has an inboard motor aboard connected with the shaft and propeller. (This definition or ruling is also important from the angle of the Federal regulations which require undocumented "motor boats" to carry a number assigned by the Collector of Customs.)

In the light of this interpretation, any auxiliary—whether its engine is running or not—is subject to the light requirements specified in the Motor Boat Act of April 25, 1940 for motor boats under sail alone or under sail and power. A recent amendment to the act clarifies rules in respect to lights to be carried by auxiliaries, eliminating much confusion on the subject.

Left: This motor sailer, when running under sail only, carries separate red and green side lights. She must also carry a 12-pt. white stern light showing aft

Above: The same motor sailer, driven by her engine alone, or sail and engine both, carries, in addition to separate red and green side lights, a 20-point white bow light and a 32-point white stern light

Lights for the various types of boats under way differ and the remainder of this article is concerned entirely with the lights carried at night by boats *under way*.

Sailboats

Considering first the out-and-out sailboat that has no motive power of any kind aboard (or perhaps may have an outboard motor stowed away somewhere in a locker for emergency), since she is not "propelled by machinery" it makes no difference whether she is under or over 65 feet. She does not come under the definition of a motor boat and is not subject to the Motor Boat Act, but should carry the lights specified by the Pilot Rules. The vessel mentioned parenthetically above, with outboard stowed away, would be considered an auxiliary only when the outboard was attached to the hull in its propelling position.

Now the Pilot Rules specify, for sailing vessels, a red 10-point side light to port and a green 10-point side light to starboard. Formerly they carried no fixed white lights. Now, they must carry a 12-pt. fixed white stern light showing aft (except that small vessels in bad weather may, if necessary, show a lighted lantern or electric torch to overtaking vessels).

To provide for small craft where it might not be feasible to carry the separate red and green side lights (which are ordinarily attached to the standing rigging) it has been held, under the Pilot Rules for the Great Lakes and the Mississippi River, that an open sailboat not

At Anchor and Under Way

All boats under 150 feet in length at anchor are required to display one white 32-point light forward not more than 20 feet above the hull. This must be visible at least 1 mile. In special anchorage areas designated by the Secretary of the Army, however, no anchorage light is required on vessels under 65 feet in length.

Vessels over 150 feet in length at anchor show one white 32-point light forward, 20 to 40 feet above the hull. In addition, they also show another white 32-point light aft at least 15 feet lower than the forward light. These, too, must be visible at least 1 mile.

Mississippi River Rules formerly required only one white light for a vessel over 150 feet in length at anchor, but new rules now require the additional white light aft.

Above: This cruiser, in Class 2 (26 to 40 feet), carries a 20-point white bow light, 32-point white stern light, and separate red and green side lights, each showing through 10 points

Right: Here is an auxiliary. Having an engine, she is lighted according to the Motor Boat Act. When she is under sail only, she carries separate red and green side lights, and a 12-point white light aft. If her engine were running, whether or not her sails were up, she would carry side lights and the white bow and stern lights of a motor boat. If she were less than 26 feet in length, under sail alone, she would carry a combination red-and-green light forward and 12-point white light aft. With engine running, she would carry a combination light and a white 32-point light aft

over 18 feet in length is not required to carry the separate red and green side lights. However, if she does not, she must carry a lantern having a green slide on one side and a red slide on the other. This must be shown in time to avert collision, in a manner that will prevent the red slide from being seen across the starboard bow, and the green slide across the port bow.

Under the Inland Pilot Rules for other Federal waters, provision is also made for small craft. Whenever, as in the case of vessels of less than 10 gross tons under way *during bad weather,* the green and red side lights cannot be fixed, these lights must be kept at hand, lighted and ready for use. On the approach of or to other vessels, these are shown on their respective sides in time to prevent collision. Such lights should be screened and the lanterns painted outside with the color of the light.

Furthermore, the Pilot Rules for inland waters other than the Mississippi River and the Great Lakes also provide for open sailboats under 18 feet in length. It has been held (Art. 7, Sec. 1, Act of June 7, 1897—33 U.S.C. 176) that under the language of this article a small open sailboat of around 18 feet in length is, for the purpose of this particular article, a row boat under sail. They are not required to carry the regular separate red and green side lights, but should carry a white light to be exhibited in time to prevent collision.

The paragraph dealing with vessels under 10 gross tons applies to small vessels under way in bad weather only, whereas the ruling about open sailboats under 18 feet is generally applicable, even in clear weather.

Motor Boats—Not Under Sail

Now we turn to the out-and-out motor boat, having no sail. It is propelled by machinery and is, by definition, of necessity under 65 feet. It is lighted according to the Motor Boat Act, and the nature of the lights varies with the size of the boat. There are four classes: Class A, under 16 feet; Class 1, 16 to 26 feet; Class 2, 26 to 40 feet; Class 3, 40 to 65 feet.

Classes A and 1 (including all motor boats up to 26 feet) carry a combination lantern forward which shows red from dead ahead to two points abaft the port beam and green from dead ahead to two points abaft the starboard beam. Aft they carry a white 32-point light, higher than the red-and-green combination light forward.

Classes 2 and 3 (including all motor boats from 26 to 65 feet) carry a 20-point white light forward showing from dead ahead to two points abaft the beam on each side, and a white 32-point light aft, showing all around the horizon, higher than the white bow light. Separate red and green side lights are prescribed, the red showing 10 points from dead ahead to two points abaft the port beam, and green showing from dead ahead to two points abaft the starboard beam.

Motorboats—Under Sail Only
(See Fig. 4, page 37)

There are times when a motorboat may be driven by sail only, as for example when a motor sailer is sailing while her engine is not in operation.

In such cases motorboats of classes 2 and 3 (26 to 65 feet) carry the separate red and green side lights and, under a recent regulation, a 12-point white stern light, showing aft.

Motorboats of classes A and 1 (under 26 feet) under sail only, carry a red-and-green combination bow light and 12-point white stern light.

Small boats, in bad weather, may carry in lieu of the fixed white stern light a white lantern or flashlight which is shown in time to avert collision.

Auxiliaries—Under Sail Only

Like the motor sailer illustrated in Figure 4, page 37, the auxiliary subject to the Motor Boat Act (under 65 feet) shows colored side lights, when driven by sail alone.

This means that the auxiliary from 26 to 65 feet (classes 2 and 3) carries separate 10-point red and green side lights.

The auxiliary under 26 feet (classes A and 1) shows a combination red-and-green light forward.

Under sail only, they must now carry a fixed white 12-point stern light, showing aft, except that small boats in bad weather may have a white lantern or flashlight at hand to be shown in time to avert collision.

Auxiliaries—Under Motor Only or Motor and Sail
(See illustrations, pages 30 and 31)

Auxiliaries, when driven by motor only, or motor and sail both, are lighted like motorboats of their respective classes driven by motor only. Thus, auxiliaries of 26 to 65 feet (classes 2 and 3) carry their separate red and green 10-point side lights, a 20-point white bow light, and the 32-point white stern light.

Auxiliaries less than 26 feet in length (classes A and 1) carry the red-and-green combination light forward and white 32-point stern light aft.

Amendment to Motor Boat Act

From the foregoing sections, it will be seen that there is now a consistency in the provisions for lights, requiring the craft under sail to be lighted as a sailboat, and the craft driven by motor to be lighted as a motorboat, whether or not she is using sails. These provisions are contained in an amendment which became effective June 4, 1956 (Public Law 552).

Optional Lighting Under Motor Boat Act

Public Law 552 also provides a new optional arrangement of lights which eliminates the necessity of changing lights when motorboats of any class operate from inland waters to the high seas.

On Inland Waters, the Great Lakes, and Western Rivers, between sunset and sunrise, motorboats of classes A, 1, 2 and 3 may continue to carry the lights prescribed for their respective classes in the Motor Boat Act. However, they now have the option of carrying, instead, the lights prescribed in International Rules for the high seas.

According to the Coast Guard's interpretation (in "Motorboats," pamphlet CG–290) motorboats of 40 gross tons or more lighted under International Rules should carry the regular seagoing lights prescribed for power-driven vessels. (See item 31, page 40.) Motorboats under 40 gross tons they would classify as "small power-driven boats such as are carried by seagoing vessels" which may carry their white light forward at a height of less than 9 feet above the gunwale, but higher than their red and green sidelights or combination light. (See item 27, page 40.)

Caution in Night Piloting

At night good practice necessitates that no other lights outside of the specified navigation lights be shown anywhere on the deck of a vessel. Not only are extraneous lights disconcerting to the pilots of other vessels, but the glare of nearby lights on a boat will interfere with the vision of its own pilot. The visibility at night is at its best when the pilot is in absolute darkness.

Visibility Requirements

Every white light must be visible at least two miles. Every colored light must be visible at least one mile.

Lights installed on new boats or replacements on old ones must be of approved type. (See page 16.)

Basic Rules

Colors are used to differentiate one light from another; they have distinct and separate meanings. White, red and green lights are used and these are arranged to show in four different ways. There are 10, 12, 20 and 32-point lights indicating the arc of the compass through which they would be visible—the 32-point light being one visible from every point in the compass.

Red and green side lights show through 10 points for all classes of vessels. White lights which are designed to show only ahead are always made to show through 20 points. Lights which show through 32 points are naturally visible from ahead also.

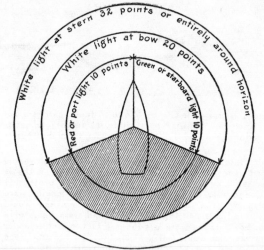

Diagram showing the arc covered by various lights. The 32-point white stern light shows all around the horizon, the white bow light ahead through 20 points (10 points each side) and the colored side lights 10 points on their respective sides

Side Lights Should Be Screened
(See illustrations, pages 14 and 15)

The regulations provide that the red and green side lights shall show from dead ahead to two points abaft the beam. The lens makers will generally provide a lens which will cover this angle.

It is necessary that screens be fitted so that these lights will not show across the bow. The light itself must necessarily be a small distance from the screen and the size of the lamp and reflected light all tend to make the light show across the bow. Care should be exercised and tests made to prevent this as much as possible.

Formerly the size of light lenses and light screens for Classes 2 and 3 was prescribed and lenses were also required to be of fresnel or fluted type. However, the new Motor Boat Act of 1940 did away with these requirements. Under the new law the side lights on boats of Class 2 and Class 3 must be fitted with inboard screens, but instead of a prescribed size the law merely mentions that they must be of sufficient length and height so as to prevent these lights from being seen across the bow. As an alternative they may be mounted on the cabin sides.

It is interesting to note that the Navy discovered, after World War II, that red and green paint on side light screens was not satisfactory, as it permitted, by diffuse reflection, the colored lights to be seen across the bow. Dull black was tested but, strangely, glossy black was found to be best. The Navy adopted the latter and subsequently the Coast Guard required it on merchant vessels.

Rowboats

Under Inland Rules a rowboat, under oars or sail, merely shows a white light at the approach of another vessel. This does not have to be permanently fixed. A lantern showing a white light may be kept at hand and displayed in sufficient time to avert collision. A similar provision is made for rowboats under the International Rules.

Inland Steamers

Inland steamers are lighted at night in exactly the same way as motor boats of Classes 2 or 3. Sizes are larger, but arrangement is identical.

A white light forward will show through 20 points of the horizon. The port and starboard lights will show over 10 points of the horizon, while the white range light aft will show through 32 points. The range light aft is arranged so as to be carried higher than the bow light.

Ocean-Going Power-Driven Vessels

(See Fig. 31, page 41)

The lights prescribed for power-driven vessels under International Rules are shown not only by ocean liners, but also by seagoing yachts and other vessels which navigate the high seas outside the limits delineated for inland waters.

They show a white 20-point bow light 20 to 40 feet above the hull, visible 5 miles. Their red and green 10-point side lights are visible 2 miles and are fitted with 36-inch screens.

The sea-going power-driven vessel carries a white 20-point range light at least 15 feet higher than the foremast light, visible 5 miles. The two white masthead lights must be in line with, and over, the keel. Horizontal distance between them must be at least 3 times the vertical distance. The range light is optional only on vessels under 150 feet and those engaged in towing.

A fixed white 12-point taffrail light is now mandatory, except on towing vessels which may use a small towing light.

Power-driven vessels under 40 gross tons (see Fig. 27, p. 41) may, optionally, carry a 20-point white light forward, 10-point red and green side lights, and 12-point white light aft.

Government Vessels

(See item 18, Table 1, page 38)

Vessels of the U. S. Government are required to display the same lights as other vessels. However, the exhibition of any light on board a vessel of war of the United States or on vessels of the U. S. Coast Guard may be suspended whenever, in the opinion of the Secretary of the Navy, the Commander-in-Chief of a Squadron, or the Commander of a vessel acting singly, the special character of the service may require it.

Similarly, special lights may be prescribed for use on Naval and other vessels of the Government when found necessary. Differences in the lighting of certain types of naval vessels are necessitated because of their military function or special construction. Aircraft carriers are one example. The special lights shown by some naval craft may be displayed in combination with navigational lights, and sometimes naval vessels will appear to have an unorthodox arrangement of lights.

The inland steamer shown above carries lights similar to a Class III motor boat, but larger. Note the 20-point white bow light, 32-point white stern light, and 10-point red and green side lights

Range Lights

(See illus. below, also Fig. 6, p. 37 and Fig. 31, p. 41)

When a vessel's lights are visible in the distance there may be reasonable doubt as to its course. The relative location of the range lights will be the key. Where only one of the side lights is seen it can be assumed that you are within the 10-point sector of the other boat's side light.

Whether the relative courses of the two vessels will bring them together or not will be determined by the location of the range lights. Should the lower forward range light be to the left or right of the after range light the distance between them will indicate the approximate angle of the other vessel with your line of sight.

Should the range lights be directly over one another then it can be assumed that the other vessel is approaching head on and danger of collision exists. When the course is changed the range lights will separate and a shift to starboard will show by the lower light moving to your left while a shift to port will show by the lower light moving to your right.

Of particular value when the port light of a vessel shows is the relative location of these range lights. It can be assumed that the other vessel is in your danger zone and has the right of way.

Naturally, the relative speeds of the two boats must be taken into consideration. Also, the angle of alignment of range lights of an approaching vessel off on the beam may change rapidly, closing together and then opening again, indicating that you are safely crossing ahead of her.

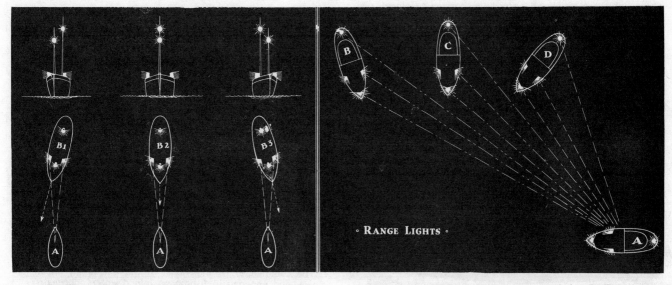

At the left, above, range lights one above the other indicate a vessel (B 2) approaching A head on. In B 1 and B 3 the position of the forward lower bow light to the left or right of the aft (upper) range light shows her course directed to port or starboard of A's course.

At right, above, A knows the other vessel (at B, C or D) is in her danger zone. Although the relative positions of range lights and side lights here are similar, they aid A in changing course to keep clear

Ferry Boats
(See Fig. 7, page 37)

Special provision has been made in the Inland Rules for the type of craft generally termed double-ended ferry boats. They are provided with two central white range lights at the same height above the water line and generally placed on top of the pilot houses on each end of the vessel. These show through 32 points.

A special light, which may be colored, carried amidships, designates the line to which the ferry belongs. Red and green 10-point side lights are of course also carried. Ferries not of the double-ended type carry the same lights as inland steamers.

Vessel Not Under Control
(See Fig. 38, page 41)

There are other cases which call for special lights. A vessel which is not under control, for example a steamer which may have lost a rudder, can operate to some extent by means of its twin screws. It would indicate the fact by showing two red lights vertically arranged and the customary red and green lights. If she is not making headway through the water the red and green lights are not used.

Cable-Laying Vessels

A cable-laying steamer, under International Rules, displays three 32-point lights, vertically arranged, 20 to 40 feet above the hull. They are spaced at least 6 feet apart and must be visible at least 2 miles. The upper and lower lights are red, the middle one white. She carries no side lights unless under way with way on, when the regular red and green 10-point side lights would be carried. (This now includes vessels working on navigation marks, surveying and underwater operations.)

Pilot Vessels

When operating on their station and not at anchor pilot vessels will indicate their character by carrying in addition to the red and green lights two other lights on their main mast showing completely around the horizon. Of these the upper one is white and the lower one is red.

When at anchor the pilot vessel continues to display the special distinguishing lights but extinguishes the red and green side lights. When not engaged in pilot service the vessel will carry the customary lights belonging to her class.

Fishing Boats

All fishing craft will show the regulation lights similar to other vessels except when engaged in operating at their nets or trawls. Under Inland Rules, boats over ten tons when engaged in fishing will exhibit two lights in some part of the boat where they can best be seen. The upper one of these is red and the lower one is white. The vertical distance between them shall not be less than six feet, nor more than 12 feet, and the horizontal distance, if any, shall not be more than ten feet. These lights are visible all around the horizon. Colored side lights are not carried when fishing.

Tugs (Inland Rules)
(See illustrations, pages 37, 39 and 44)

Tugboats, under Inland Rules, if they have *no tow*, are lighted the same as ordinary steam vessels. In addition to red and green 10-point side lights, they have a 20-point white light forward and a 32-point white range light at least 15 feet higher than the foremast light.

If the tug has a *tow alongside*, the tug carries her red and green side lights as usual, and if one side light should be obscured by the tow, it is transferred to the outside of the tow. The tug also carries two white towing lights, vertically arranged, at least 3 feet apart. Optionally these may be 20-point foremast lights or 32-point lights carried where her white range light would be if running without a tow. When the tow is *pushed ahead* she now carries at the stern two 12-point amber lights showing aft, vertically arranged, with two 20-point white towing lights forward, vertically arranged, and the usual red and green side lights.

Under Inland Rules if the tug's *tow is astern*, her lights are identical with those just described for the case where the tow is alongside except that she carries three white lights in vertical line instead of two. Red and green side lights are, of course, carried, as above.

Whether her tow is alongside or astern, if her towing lights are carried forward, she may carry a 32-point white light aft as a range. If the towing lights are carried aft, she may display a 20-point white light forward.

Ocean-Going Tugs
(See Fig. 41, page 41 and page 43)

The ocean-going tug is lighted according to International Rules. If she has *no tow*, she has a white 20-point light forward, 20 to 40 feet above the hull, visible 5 miles. Her red and green 10-point side lights, in 36-inch screens, must be visible 2 miles. Aft she carries a white 12-point light showing astern, visible 2 miles. A white 20-point range light is also carried, at least 15 feet higher than the foremast light, and visible 5 miles. When towing, the range light is optional. Horizontal distance between masthead lights must be at least 3 times the vertical.

An ocean-going tug with *one vessel in tow* carries, in addition to the red and green side lights, two white 20-point towing lights in a vertical line on the foremast, not less than 6 feet apart. Either a fixed 12-point stern light or a small white light is carried aft for the tow to steer by. This must not be visible forward of the beam.

When she has more than one vessel in tow, *if the tow exceeds 600 feet in length*, she carries the same lights as mentioned in the previous paragraph, except that she has three 20-point white towing lights, instead of two. The third light must be at least 14 feet above the hull.

Regardless of the length of her tow, authorities agree that she should carry the optional 20-point white range light aft.

Red 32 Points

White 32 Points

White
Red | 32 Points

Red &
Green

The pilot vessel above is under way on her station. In addition to her red and green side lights she shows a white 32-point light in vertical line above a red 32-point light. At anchor on station she extinguishes side lights

The commercial fishing vessel at the left, when under way and engaged in fishing on inland waters, carries a red 32-point light above a white 32-point light. (See Table II, page 40, for various lights prescribed for fishing vessels under International Rules)

Vessel Towing Submerged Object

Sometimes, when a vessel has a submerged or partly submerged object (such as wreckage, etc.) in tow, it is not feasible to display lights on the object towed. In such cases, under the Pilot Rules, the towing vessel carries her regular red and green 10-point side lights, but in lieu of the regular white towing lights she displays four lights in a vertical position not less than three feet nor more than six feet apart, the upper and lower of which are white, and the two middle lights red, all of the same character as prescribed for regular towing lights.

Inland rules permit the option of carrying these four special lights as 20-point lights forward, with a 32-point white light aft; or as 32-point lights aft, with a 20-point white light forward. The object of the extra white light, forward or aft, as the case may be, is to provide a range.

The vessel above at work on a wreck shows a white 32-point light at bow and stern, and two red 32-point lights in a vertical line. Steamers, derrick boats, lighters and any other vessels so engaged are lighted in this manner.

Vessels Working on a Wreck

Under the Pilot Rules steamers, derrick boats, lighters, or other vessels made fast to a wreck which is on the bottom or partly submerged or drifting, show a white 32-point light from the bow and stern of each outside vessel, not less than 6 feet above the deck. In addition, two red 32-point lights are displayed in a vertical line not less than 3 feet nor more than 6 feet apart, and not less than 15 feet above the deck.

Dredges

Lights for dredges which are held in position by moorings or spuds are also provided for in the Pilot Rules. They show a white light at each corner not less than 6 feet above the deck. In addition, they show two red 32-point lights in a vertical line not less than 3 feet nor more than 6 feet apart, and not less than 15 feet above the deck.

When scows are moored alongside such dredges they show a white light on each outboard corner, not less than 6 feet above the deck.

Canal Boats and Barges
(See illustrations, pages 37 and 39)

Canal boats and barges when operating on inland waters are provided with particular types of lights which will indicate their character. It is important to note that the general regulations for these types of craft for inland waters do not apply on the Hudson River and adjacent waters and on Lake Champlain. The Great Lakes, the Red River of the North, and certain rivers emptying into the Gulf of Mexico are also excepted. By recent amendment of the Inland Rules, tows on the Gulf Intracoastal Waterway are lighted according to Western River rules.

Inland Waters

Under the general Inland Rules, when barges and canal boats are towing singly or in tandem astern of steam vessels, each boat in tow carries a green light on the starboard side and a red light on the port side and a white light on the stern, except

that the last vessel of the tow must carry two white lights on the stern, athwartship, horizontally arranged, showing through 32 points. The colored lights are 10-point.

When two or more boats are towed abreast, the colored lights are carried at the outer sides of the bows of the outside boats. Each of the outside boats in the last tier of a hawser tow carries a white light on the stern.

The white stern lights carried by barges and canal boats which show red and green side lights are 12-point lights, showing right aft and 6 points on each side.

When barges, canal boats or scows are towed alongside a steam vessel, if the deck, deckhouse, or cargo of the towed boat should obscure the side lights of the towing boat, then the colored side light of the towing boat is carried on the outer side of the barge or canal boat. If there is more than one barge, canal boat or scow abreast alongside, the colored lights are displayed from the outer side of the outside boats.

Scows carry a white light at each end of each scow, except that when they are massed in tiers, astern, two or more abreast, each of the outside scows carries a white light on its outer bow, and the outside scows in the last tier carry in addition a white light on the outer part of the stern. White lights for scows are 32-point.

When scows, barges or canal boats are pushed ahead of the tug, the head boat carries red and green 10-point side lights on the outer bows. If there are more than one abreast, these colored lights are shown from the outer bow of outside boats.

Nondescript vessels, not otherwise provided for, are lighted like scows.

Hudson River and Lake Champlain

The following special regulations apply to barges and canal boats in tow of steam vessels on the Hudson River, its tributaries from Troy to the boundry lines of New York Harbor off Sandy Hook, the East River, and Long Island Sound (and the waters entering thereon, and to the Atlantic Ocean) to and including Narragansett Bay, Rhode Island, and Tributaries, and Lake Champlain.

On these waters barges and canal boats towing singly astern of steam vessels carry a white light on the bow and a white light on the stern. When towing in tandem, close up, each boat carries a white light on its stern, and the first or hawser boat carries in addition a white light on its bow. When towing in tandem with intermediate hawser between the separate boats of the tow, each boat carries a white light on the bow and a white light on the stern, except that the last vessel in the tow carries two white lights on her stern, athwartship, horizontally arranged. When towed at a hawser, two or more abreast in one tier, each carries a white light on the stern and a white light on the bow of each of the outside boats. When in more than one tier, each boat carries a white light on its stern and the outside boats in the hawser or head tier carry in addition a white light on the bow.

The white lights specified above are 32-point lights showing all around the horizon.

Nondescript vessels known as scows, car floats, lighters, barges, or canal boats and vessels of similar type when towed alongside the steam vessel show a white light at the outboard corners of the tow.

Garbage scows navigating on the Hudson or East River or tributary waters when towed in tandem carry, instead of the white lights previously required, red and green side lights in addition to the white lights shown by an overtaken vessel.

Seagoing Barges

Seagoing barges towed in tandem carry red and green side lights on each barge. The last one in the string also carries two white lights horizontally arranged to show all around the horizon, while the others show small white steering lights at the stern. When towed alongside they carry the red or green lights on the proper side if their height obscures the row boat's side light.

When seagoing barges come into the waters covered by the Hudson River rules they are not required to change their seagoing lights except that the last vessel of the tow must carry two white 32-point lights on her stern athwartship, horizontally arranged.

Note—Illustrations, tables and additional data on lights will be found on the following eleven pages.

LIGHTS FOR VARIOUS TYPES OF CRAFT—INLAND RULES
TABLE I

Note: Ocean-going vessels lighted according to the International Rules are not required to change their lights when navigating waters tributary to the High Seas.

		Bow (Foremast or Forward)	Side	Range	Remarks or Additional Lights
1	MOTOR BOATS Class A—under 16' Class 1—16' to 26'	None	Combination red and green each color showing 10 pts.*	White 32 pt.¹ Visible 2 mi.	¹Placed higher than combination *Visible 1 mi.
2	Class 2— 26' to 40'	White—20 pts. Visible 2 mi.	Red—10 pt. Green—10 pt. Screened so as not to show across bow.†	White 32 pt. ‡Visible 2 mi.	†Visible 1 mi. ‡Placed higher than bow light
3	Class 3— 40' to 65'	White—20 pts. Visible 2 mi.	Red—10 pt. Green—10 pt. Screened so as not to show across bow.†	White 32 pt. ‡Visible 2 mi.	†Visible 1 mi. ‡Placed higher than bow light

4 Motorboats and auxiliaries driven by *sail only*, as in illustration 4, show the colored side lights appropriate to their class, and are now required to carry a *fixed white 12 pt. stern light showing aft, visible 2 miles, carried as nearly as possible at the level of the side lights. Motorboats and auxiliaries, under *motor and sail*, are lighted as motorboats of their respective classes.

Note:—Under amended Motor Boat Act, motorboats of any class may, optionally, carry lights prescribed by International Rules. (See pages 32, 40 and 41.)

		Bow (Foremast or Forward)	Side	Range	Remarks or Additional Lights
5	Sailing vessel or vessel in tow (except barges, canal boats, scows, etc.)	None	Red—10 pt. Green—10 pt.	None	*12 pt. white showing aft, visible 2 mi., at level of side lights (See note bottom of page)
6	Steam or motor vessels over 65' in length (except those vessels falling in classifications noted below)	White 20 pt. vis. 5 mi.	Red—10 pt. Green—10 pt. Vis. 2 mi. 36 in. screens	White—32 pt.³	³At least 15 feet higher than foremast light
7	Double-ended³ ferry boat	White—32 pt.⁴	Red—10 pt. Green—10 pt. Vis. 2 mi. 36 in. screens	White—32 pt.⁴	³If not of double-ended type, carries same lights as inland steamer ⁴On both pilot houses at same height. Special light amidships designates line
8	Steam pilot vessel on station⁵ on pilotage duty and underway⁶	None	Red—10 pt. Green—10 pt.	None	White 32 pt. at masthead 8' above red 32 pt., each vis. 2 mi. Shows flares at intervals of not more than 15 min. ⁵If not on station, carries same lights as other steam vessels ⁶On station at anchor, side lights are extinguished
9	Fishing vessel underway engaged in commercial fishing⁷	None	None	None	Red 32 pt. 6' to 12' above white 32 pt. not more than 10' apart horizontally. White vis. 3 mi.; red 2 mi. ⁷If underway, but not fishing, carries usual lights of her class, except vessel under 10 gross tons may show combination red and green lantern to other vessels, in lieu of fixed side lights
10	Inland¹⁰ tug without tow⁸	White 20 pt.	Red—10 pt. Green—10 pt.	White 32 pt.⁹	⁸Lighted same as ordinary inland steam vessel ⁹At least 15' higher than foremast light ¹⁰For lights of ocean-going tug on inland waters, see International Rules, Table II
11	Inland tug with tow alongside or pushed ahead	Two white 20 pt. vertically arranged, at least 3' apart or lights mentioned in fourth column	Red—10 pt. Green—10 pt. If side light is obstructed by vessel towed, light is transferred to outside of tow	Two white 32 pt. vertically arranged, at least 3' apart or foremast lights mentioned in second column	With 20-pt. towing lights forward, may carry 32-pt. white range light aft. May carry small white light aft for tow to steer by, not visible forward of beam. With 32-pt. towing light aft, may carry 20-pt. white light forward. When pushing tow ahead and using 20 pt. white towing lights forward, carries two amber 12 pt. lights aft (vertically) not visible forward of beam.
12	Inland¹⁰ tug with tow astern	Three white 20 pt. vertically arranged, at least 3' apart or lights mentioned in fourth column	Red—10 pt. Green—10 pt.	Three white 32 pt. vertically arranged, at least 3' apart or foremast lights mentioned in second column	
13	Rowboat (under oars or sail)	None	None	None	White light shown on approach of another vessel
14	Vessels working on a wreck	White 32 pt.¹¹ (each outside vessel)	None	White 32 pt. stern light¹¹ (each outside vessel)	Two red 32 pt. in vertical line, 3' to 6' apart, at least 15' above decks ¹¹White lights at least 6' above decks

NOTE:—Small sailing vessels under 10 gross tons under way in bad weather, if they cannot keep their side lights fixed, may keep side lights at hand ready to show in time to avert collision. Also, under Inland Rules, open sailboats under 18 feet may carry, instead of separate red and green side lights, a white light to be shown in time to prevent collision. Under Great Lakes and Mississippi Rules, open sailboats under 18 feet may carry a lantern showing a red slide to port and green slide to starboard.
*In bad weather, small boats may, if necessary, show an electric torch or lighted lantern to overtaking vessels.

1 and 24

2

6

4

5

7

12 and 21

LIGHTS FOR VARIOUS TYPES OF CRAFT—INLAND RULES
TABLE I (Continued)

		Bow (Foremast or Forward)	Side	Range	Remarks or Additional Lights
15	Dredge (held in position by moorings or spuds)	None	None	None	White 32 pt. each corner at least 6' above deck. Two red 32 pt. in vertical line 3' to 6' apart, at least 15' above deck. Scows moored alongside show white 32 pt. on each outboard corner, at least 6' above deck
16	Dredge (self-propelling suction type, underway, with suction on bottom)	White 20 pt.	Red—10 pt. Green—10 pt.	White 32 pt.	Two red 20 pt. under the white 20 pt. foremast light, 3' to 6' apart. Upper red light 4' to 6' below white light. At stern two red 4 pt. showing aft, in vertical line 4' to 6' apart
17	Vessel towing wreck	Carries lights same as described for inland tug with tow astern (see No. 12) except that in lieu of the regular 3 white towing lights she shows 4 lights vertically arranged, 3' to 6' apart, upper and lower white, two middle lights red, 20-point if carried on the foremast, 32-point if carried aft			
18	Naval and other U.S. Government vessels[12]	[12]	[12]		[12]Both the Inland and International Rules provide, in Article 13, that these rules shall not interfere with special rules made by the Government of any nation with respect to additional station and signal lights for two or more ships of war or for vessels sailing under convoy, or with exhibition of recognition signals adopted by ship owners, properly authorized by their respective Governments
19	At anchor—vessel under 150' in length	One white 32 pt. forward, vis. 1 mi. not more than 20' above hull	None	None	In specially designated anchorage areas, vessels under 65' need no anchor light.
20	At anchor—vessel 150' in length or over	None	None	None	One white 32 pt. forward 20' to 40' above hull. One white 32 pt. aft, at least 15' lower than forward light. Vis. 1 mi.

LIGHTS FOR BARGES, CANAL BOATS AND SCOWS IN TOW ON INLAND WATERS
TABLE IA

Except Great Lakes, east to Montreal—Red River of the North—Mississippi River and tributaries above Huey P. Long Bridge—that part of the Atchafalaya River above its junction with the Plaquemine-Morgan City alternate waterway—Gulf Intracoastal Waterway and certain connecting waters, from the Rio Grande to Cape Sable—Hudson River (Troy to Sandy Hook)—East River and Long Island Sound—Narragansett Bay— Lake Champlain—and other tributaries.

		Bow	Side	Stern	Remarks or Additional Lights
21	One barge or canal boat towed astern of tug	None	Green—10 pt. Red—10 pt. Vis. 2 mi.	Two white 32 pt. athwartship horizontal. At least 5' apart and at least 4' above deckhouse	None
22	More than one barge or canal boat towed astern in tandem	None	Green—10 pt. Red—10 pt. Vis. 2 mi.	[13]One white—12 pt. Vis. 2 mi.	[13]Except last vessel of tow which carries instead, two 32 pt. white athwartship horizontal at least 5' apart and at least 4' above deckhouse
23	More than one barge or canal boat towed astern abreast (one tier)[14]	None	Green—10 pt. Red—10 pt. Vis. 2 mi. (carried at outer sides of bows of outside boats)	[14]One white—32 pt. on each outside boat.	[14]If more than one tier, white stern lights are placed on outside boats of last tier only
24	Barges, canal boats or scows towed alongside of tug	None	Colored side lights carried on outer side of outside barge if side lights of towing vessel are obstructed by barge	None	None
25	Scows towed singly or tandem	White 32 pt.	None	White 32 pt.	Lights to be carried at least 8' above surface of water. Vis. 5 mi.
26	Scows massed in tiers, two or more abreast, astern	White 32 pt. on outer side of all outside scows	None	White 32 pt. on outer side of outside scows in last tier only	Lights to be carried at least 8' above surface of water. Vis. 5 mi.

NOTE:—When barges, canal boats or scows are *pushed ahead* of the tug, head boat carries red 10-pt. and green 10-pt. side lights on outer bows, or if more than one abreast, they are shown from outer bow of outside boats.

12 and 22

10 PT. LT.
20 PT. LT.
32 PT. LT.

11 and 24

19

20

12 and 23

12 and 25

LIGHTS FOR VARIOUS TYPES OF CRAFT — INTERNATIONAL RULES
TABLE II

		Bow (Foremast or Forward)	Side	Range	Remarks or Additional Lights
27	Power - driven vessels of less than 40 gross tons[17] NOTE—In illustration 27, opposite page, bow light, often rigged as shown on inland craft, should be higher to comply with 9' minimum requirement. Small power-driven boats may carry white light forward at height less than 9 feet but it must be carried higher than side lights or combination red and green light.	White—20 pt. at least 9' above gunwale. Vis. 3 mi.	Red—10 pt. Green—10 pt. Vis. 1 mi. or combination red and green, each color showing 10 pts. At least 3' below foremast light	None	12 pt. white showing aft. [17]Optional to carry instead of lights indicated those regularly prescribed for larger power-driven vessels
28	Vessels under oars or sails under 20 gross tons	None	Combination red and green, each color showing 10 pts. shown to approaching vessels	None	If stern light is not fixed, shows electric torch or lighted lantern to overtaking vessels
29	Rowboats, under oars or sails	None	None	None	Shows electric torch or lighted lantern to approaching vessels
30	Sailing vessel or vessel in tow	None	Red—10 pt. Green—10 pt. Vis. 2 mi. 36 in. screens	None	12 pt. white light showing aft. Vis. 2 mi. Carried at level of side lights
31	Power-driven vessels (ocean liners, seagoing yachts, etc.)	White 20 pt. 20' to 40' above hull. Vis. 5 mi. Both 20-pt. white lights must be in line with, and over, the keel	Red—10 pt. Green—10 pt. Vis. 2 mi. 36 in. screens	White 20 pt. at least 15' higher than foremast light vis. 5 mi. Optional on vessels under 150 feet, and vessels towing. Horizontal distance between white lights at least 3 times the vertical	White 12 pt. showing astern. Vis. 2 miles. Carried at, or near, level of side lights
32	Pilot vessels (power-driven)	On station, under way, carry white 32-pt. masthead light and 8 feet below it a red 32-pt. light, both vis. 3 mi.			Show flare or intermittent 32-pt white light at 10-minute intervals
33	Fishing vessels trolling	[18]	[18]	[18]	[18]Show only lights appropriate for power-driven or sailing vessel
34	Fishing vessels using nets or lines extending less than 500 feet	None	None	None	One 32-pt. white light, and show another to approaching vessels in direction of outlying gear. (See note 34 below)
35	Power-driven trawler or dredger	Tri-colored lantern showing white ahead 4 pts., red from 2 pts. on port bow to 2 pts. abaft beam and green from 2 pts. on starboard bow to 2 pts. abaft beam	None	None	White 32 pt. 6' to 12' below tricolored foremast light 12-pt. white stern light showing aft
36	Vessels at anchor[19] (including fishing vessels)	None	None	None	[19]Same as prescribed under Inland Rules (except must be visible 2 mi. if under 150 feet, 3 mi. if over 150 feet)
37	Vessel aground in or near fairway	None	None	None	In addition to anchor lights, shows two red vertical 32 pt., indicating not under control
38	Vessel not under control	None	None, unless under way with way on, when side and stern lights are carried	None	Two red 32 pt. in vertical line at least 6' apart. Vis. 2 mi.
39	Cable-laying vessel	Three 32-pt. in vertical line at least 6' apart. Upper and lower red; middle white. Vis. 2 mi. 20' to 40' above hull	None, unless under way with way on, when side and stern lights are carried	None	Same rules now apply to vessels laying or picking up a navigation mark, or engaged in surveying or underwater operations
40	Ocean-going tug without tow	White 20 pt. 20' to 40' above hull, vis. 5 mi.	Red—10 pt. Green—10 pt. Vis. 2 mi. 36 in. screens	White 20 pt.	White 12 pt. showing astern. Vis. 2 mi.
41	Ocean-going tug with one vessel in tow, or more, if less than 600' in length	Two white 20 pt. in vertical line not less than 6' apart	Red—10 pt. Green—10 pt. Vis. 2 mi. 36 in. screens	White 20 pt. optional	Must show either the fixed white 12-pt. stern light, or small white light aft for tow to steer by, not visible forward of beam
42	Ocean-going tug with more than one vessel in tow if tow exceeds 600' in length	Three white 20 pt. in vertical line at least 6' apart. Third light may be not less than 14' above hull	Red—10 pt. Green—10 pt. Vis. 2 mi. 36 in. screens	White 20 pt. optional	Must show either the fixed white 12-pt. stern light, or small white light aft for tow to steer by, not visible forward of beam

Note 34:—If nets or lines (except trolling lines) extend more than 500 feet, fishing vessels show 3 white 32-pt. lights in a vertical triangle. Also show side lights if making way through the water.

27

37

30 and 41

35

38

31

CHARACTERISTICS OF LIGHTS
USED ON LIGHTHOUSES, LIGHTSHIPS, BUOYS AND OTHER AIDS TO NAVIGATION

CHARACTERISTIC	NAME OF LIGHT (Number in 1941 Light List)	CANDLEPOWER AND VISIBILITY	SYMBOLS AND PERIOD	DESCRIPTION OF CHARACTERISTIC
	TIME SCALE IN SECONDS 0 5 10 15 20 25 30 35 40 45 50 55 60			
Fixed White	SANDY HOOK, N. J. (740)	45,000 c.p., Vis. 15 mi.	F.W.	
Fixed Green	NEWBURYPORT HARBOR, MASS. (137)	4,000 c.p., Vis. 12 mi.	F.G.	
Fixed Red	THROGS NECK, N. Y. (531)	5,000 c.p., Vis. 14 mi.	F.R.	
Flashing White	CAPE COD, MASS. (249)	4,000,000 c.p., Vis. 20 mi.	Fl. W., 5 sec.	Flash 0.2 sec., eclipse 4.8 sec.
Flashing White	SAN FRANCISCO LIGHTSHIP, CALIF. (191)	13,000 c.p., Vis. 13 mi.	Fl.W., 15 sec.	Flash 5 sec., eclipse 10 sec.
Flashing Green	BRIDGEPORT BREAKWATER, CONN. (684)	130 c.p.	Fl. G., 3 sec.	Flash 1 sec.
Flashing Red	PENFIELD REEF, CONN. (505)	13,000 c.p., Vis. 13 mi.	Fl. R., 5 sec.	Flash 0.8 sec., eclipse 4.2 sec.
Alternating Flashing White and Red	CLEVELAND WEST PIERHEAD, OHIO (323)	W. 32,000 c.p., R. 9,600 c.p. Vis. 16 mi.	Alt. Fl. W. and R. 10 sec.	White flash 1 sec., eclipse 4 sec.; red flash 1 sec., eclipse 4 sec.
Alternating Flashing White and Green	FORT WADSWORTH, N. Y. (764)	W. 24,000 c.p., G. 7,200 c.p. Vis. 14 mi.	Alt. Fl. W. and G. 10 sec.	White flash 1.3 sec., eclipse 3.7 sec.; green flash 1.3 sec., eclipse 3.7 sec.
Alternating Flashing Red and Green	OLD FIELD POINT, N. Y. (504)	90,000 c.p., Vis. 14 mi.	Alt. Fl. R. and G., 30 sec. U. (Unwatched)	Red flash 0.5 sec., eclipse 14.5 sec.; green flash 0.5 sec., eclipse 14.5 sec.
Fixed and Flashing White	LITTLE RIVER, MAINE (7)	F. 2,900 c.p., Fl. 13,000 c.p. Vis. 13 mi.	F. Fl. W. 15 sec.	Fixed light with 0.6 sec. flash every 15 sec.
Fixed White Alternating Flashing Red	DEER ISLAND, MASS. (184)	W. 2,500 c.p., Fl. R. 10,000 c.p. F.R. 750 c.p., Vis. 13 mi.	F.W. Alt. Fl. R., 30 sec. R. sector	Fixed white light with red 1.2 sec. flash every 30 sec.
Group Flashing White	CAPE ARAGO, OREGON (592)	270,000 c.p., Vis. 16 mi.	Gp. Fl. W., 20 sec., 3 flashes	3 flashes 0.4 sec. each, 2 eclipses 3.6 sec. each, 1 eclipse 11.6 sec.
Group Flashing White	MATINICUS ROCK, MAINE (45)	43,000 c.p., Vis. 15 mi.	Gp. Fl. W., 15 sec., 1 flash, 2 flashes	Flash 0.5 sec., eclipse 5.5 sec.; flash 0.5 sec., eclipse 2.5 sec.; flash 0.5 sec., eclipse 5.5 sec.
Group Flashing White	MINOTS LEDGE, MASS. (200)	75,000 c.p., Vis. 15 mi.	Gp. Fl. W., 30 sec., Flashes "143"	Flashes "143" every 30 sec., 1 flash, eclipse 3 sec., 4 flashes, eclipse 4 sec., 3 flashes, eclipse 16 sec. Each flash 0.2 sec.
Group Flashing White Alternating Flashing Red	NEW LONDON LEDGE, CONN. (469)	24,000 c.p., Vis. 13 mi.	Gp. Fl. W. Alt. Fl. R. 30 sec., 3 W., 1 R. Flashes	3 white flashes 0.7 sec. each, eclipse 9 sec.; red flash 0.7 sec., eclipse 9 sec.
Fixed White Alternating Group Flashing Red	GREAT CAPTAIN ISLAND, CONN. (518)	W. 2,900 c.p., R. Fl. 7,200 c.p., Vis. 14 mi.	F.W. Alt. Gp. Fl. R., 10 sec. 2 flashes	Fixed white 6.7 sec., eclipse 0.7 sec.; red flash 0.2 sec., eclipse 1.5 sec.; red flash 0.2 sec., eclipse 0.7 sec.
Occulting White	BARNEGAT LIGHTSHIP, N. J. (1098)	15,000 c.p., Vis. 14 mi.	Occ. W., 10 sec.	Light 8 sec. eclipse 2 sec.
Group Occulting White	MANISTEE PIERHEAD, MICH. (1358)	5,000 c.p., Vis. 15 mi.	Gp. Occ. W., 30 sec. 3 eclipses	3 eclipses 2 sec. each, 2 light periods 2 sec. each, 1 light period 20 sec.
SLOW FLASHING (Red or Black Buoys)	If not fixed, lights on red buoys or black buoys are regularly flashing or occulting, light and dark periods remaining unchanged. Ordinarily, rate of light flashes is not more than 30 per min.			
	FIRE ISLAND INLET LIGHTED BUOY 1, N. Y. (823.2)	10 c.p.	Fl. G. 2.5 sec.	Flashing green every 2.5 seconds Flash 0.5 sec.
QUICK FLASHING (Caution)	On lights which have a distinct cautionary significance, as at sudden constrictions or sharp turns, the rate of light flashes is not less than 60 per minute			
	EAST ROCKAWAY INLET LIGHTED BUOY 2 ER, N. Y. (825)	70 c.p., Vis. 7 Mi.	Qk. Fl. W.	75 white flashes per minute
INTERRUPTED QUICK FLASHING (Red-and-black horizontally banded buoys)	Lights on red-and-black horizontally banded buoys, marking obstructions, middle grounds or junctions, are a series of quick flashes interrupted by eclipses about 8 times per minute			
	CAPE MAY HARBOR LIGHTED BUOY, N. J. (1118.6)	10 c.p.	I. Qk. Fl. R.	Red flashes interrupted by eclipse
SHORT-LONG FLASH (Black-and-white mid-channel buoys)	Lights on black-and-white vertically striped mid-channel buoys are group flashing white, a short flash and a long flash, recurring 6 to 8 times per minute			
	ROCKAWAY CHANNEL LIGHTED GONG BUOY, N.Y. (827)	390 c.p., Vis. 9 Mi.	S-L. Fl. W.	Short flash and a long flash (white)
SUMMARY OF BUOY LIGHTS	(R) RED lights used only on STARBOARD side of channel, proceeding from seaward; (G) GREEN lights used only on PORT side. (W) WHITE lights may be used on either side; always on black-and-white vertically striped mid-channel buoys. (W) WHITE, (R) RED, or (G) GREEN lights may be used on buoys marking junctions, middle grounds or obstructions, as follows: (W) WHITE unless desired to show a preferred channel; (R) RED, preferred channel to PORT; (G) GREEN, preferred channel to STARBOARD.			
	TIME SCALE IN SECONDS 0 5 10 15 20 25 30 35 40 45 50 55 60			

NOTE: The examples on this page are illustrative only. Characteristics, from the 1941 Light Lists, are subject to change. For navigational purposes, see Current Light List, supplemented by changes from Notices to Mariners.

See also pages 282-299

Lights for Steam Vessels, Towing

THE International, Inland and Pilot rules are none too explicit as to the white lights displayed by a towing vessel.

International and Inland Rules deal with range lights for steam vessels in Article 2e, and lights for steam vessels towing in Article 3.

Briefly, Article 3 (Inland Rules) states that a steam vessel towing shall, *in addition to her side lights, carry two or three bright white lights in a vertical line*, one over the other. These may be placed forward, in which case they are to be 20-point, or they may be carried aft (except by seagoing vessels), in which case they are to be 32-point.

If Article 3 of the Inland Rules is read alone, without reference to other articles, it would appear that the 2 or 3 vertically arranged white lights, in addition to the red and green side lights are all the lights to be carried by a towing vessel.

However, even though Article 3 is the only Article of the Inland Rules which refers specifically to lights for a towing vessel, yet as the Rules are enacted chiefly to prevent collisions, they should apply as a whole, rather than any specific part or article. Some authorities feel that lights provided by Article 3 alone do not provide sufficiently for the safety of navigation and therefore other Articles should be applied.

Article 2 of the Inland Rules, while it makes no mention of towing vessels, provides that a steam vessel underway shall carry red and green side lights, a white 20-point light forward and a seagoing vessel *may* carry a white 20-point light aft. Article 2 (f) provides that (except in case of seagoing vessels and ferry boats) the after light shall be a 32-point range light.

Consequently, when Articles 2 and 3 are read together, range lights would be required of the steam vessel towing. On this theory on the East Coast, most tugs carry both masthead and after towing lights.

Other authorities feel that Article 3 is complete in itself, so that the towing vessel should display only side lights and towing lights, without the range. Thus, in most West Coast ports, the masthead light forward is seldom seen in conjunction with after towing lights.

The Steamboat Inspection Service (functions of which are now discharged by the Coast Guard) for many years *required* th after range light with forward towing lights, and *permitted* the forward masthead light with after towing lights.

According to an opinion expressed in the Proceedings of the Merchant Marine Council of the U. S. Coast Guard, "it appears that range lights may be carried by steam vessels towing in inland waters . . . but that to make such lights compulsory an amendment to rule 3, Inland Rules, would be necessary."

If *both* the forward and aft range lights specified by Article 2 were added to the white towing lights specified by Article 3, one of the added white lights would be useless. Therefore, it appears that a practical solution would be that if the towing lights are carried forward, one of the towing lights is in lieu of the forward light required by Article 2 (a) and all are 20-point lights. If carried aft, one of the lights is in lieu of the range light required by Article 2 (f) and all are 32-point lights. Thus a range is established.

Where the Rules provide that the after range light *may* be carried, it is recommended that it should be.

As to whether two or three towing lights should be carried, the Inland and International Rules differ slightly. In the case of the latter, in order to carry three lights, two conditions must be fulfilled, namely, the total length of the tow must be over 600 feet *and* there must be more than one vessel in tow. If these two conditions are not met only two lights are required.

In the case of the Inland Rules when towing alongside or pushing ahead, only two towing lights are required regardless of the number of vessels towed. When towing astern, three towing lights are used regardless of the length of the tow or the number of vessels towed.

Of course in addition to the two or three towing lights and the forward light (if the towing lights are 32-point lights carried aft) and the after range light (if the towing lights are 20-point lights carried forward) the towing vessel must carry 10-point red and green side lights. In addition, the towing vessel may carry a small white light aft * for the towed vessels to steer by, but such light shall not show forward of the beam. On the high seas, she might, optionally, carry a fixed white 12-point stern light.

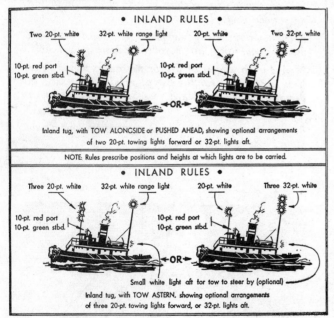

• INLAND RULES •

Two 20-pt. white   32-pt. white range light   20-pt. white   Two 32-pt. white

10-pt. red port
10-pt. green stbd.

10-pt. red port
10-pt. green stbd.

←OR→

Inland tug, with TOW ALONGSIDE or PUSHED AHEAD, showing optional arrangements of two 20-pt. towing lights forward or 32-pt. lights aft.

NOTE: Rules prescribe positions and heights at which lights are to be carried.

• INLAND RULES •

Three 20-pt. white   32-pt. white range light   20-pt. white   Three 32-pt. white

10-pt. red port
10-pt. green stbd.

10-pt. red port
10-pt. green stbd.

←OR→

Small white light aft for tow to steer by (optional)

Inland tug, with TOW ASTERN, showing optional arrangements of three 20-pt. towing lights forward, or 32-pt. lights aft.

• INTERNATIONAL RULES •

Two 20-pt. white   20-pt. white range light (optional)

10-pt. red port
10-pt. green stbd.

Small white light aft for tow to steer by or fixed 12-pt. white stern light

Seagoing tug with one vessel in tow, or more than one if tow does not exceed 600 feet in length.

NOTE: INLAND Rules permit the seagoing vessel to continue to carry her 20-pt. optional white range light, instead of the 32-pt. after range light prescribed by the Inland Rules.

• INTERNATIONAL RULES •

Three 20-pt. white   20-pt. white range light (optional)

10-pt. red port
10-pt. green stbd.

Small white light aft for tow to steer by or fixed 12-pt. white stern light

Seagoing tug with more than one vessel in tow, when tow exceeds 600 feet in length.

Illustrated above are possible arrangements of lights on a towing vessel, according to Inland Rules,* showing optional 20-point or 32-point towing lights, with range lights, in each case. Inland Rules are not explicit, so that in some localities the single white 32-point range light aft or the single 20-point white foremast light is not carried. It is usual to carry the towing lights aft

The seagoing tug, under International Rules, carries her 20-point white towing lights forward. Red and green side lights are required; the 20-point white range light aft is optional. White stern light may be fixed 12-point or small towing light

* NOTE:—*Under an amendment to Inland Rules, effective Aug. 14, 1958, when tow is pushed ahead and 20-pt. white towing lights are carried forward, the tug must carry two 12-pt. amber lights aft in vertical line, showing aft. In illustration, top left, they would be carried below the optional 32-pt. white range light. Amber lights are not required when 32-pt. white towing lights are carried aft. The small white light aft for tow to steer by, which formerly could be carried regardless of position of towing lights, may now be carried only when towing lights are carried forward.*

International Rules of the Road Revised

*New rules governing traffic on the high seas drafted
by International Safety at Sea Conference at London.
Revised regulations became effective January 1, 1954*

EVER since the International Rules of 1897 (based on a conference of 26 nations in 1889) were adopted by maritime nations to establish rules of the road governing traffic of vessels navigating the high seas (as distinguished from inland waters) there have been attempts made to revise them, with little success except for minor changes in 1910.

In 1948, however, an International Conference on Safety of Life at Sea was held in London, at which a proposed revision of the International Regulations for Preventing Collisions at Sea (commonly known as the International Rules of the Road) came up for consideration. When substantial unanimity had been reached among the nations concerned as to acceptance of the rules, January 1, 1954, was set as the date when the rules would become effective. In the meantime the 82nd Congress had adopted the revised regulations for the United States and with the issuance of Presidential Proclamation #3030, the new rules went into effect.

The revisions do not involve a complete new set of rules, but there have been significant changes with which all boatmen should be familiar. Bear in mind that whenever a boat, however small, leaves the so-called "inland waters," and crosses the limits defined as boundaries of the high seas, she becomes subject to International Rules. (Boundaries of the high seas are shown in Rules of the Road pamphlets available free of charge from offices of the U. S. Coast Guard.)

HIGHLIGHTS OF THE REVISION

Although the text throughout this book has been corrected to bring it into conformity with the new International Rules, the following three-page illustrated digest will be found helpful in visualizing most of the more important changes.

1. The formerly optional second white masthead light (i.e., range light) on "power-driven" (formerly "steam") vessels is now mandatory, except for vessels less than 150 feet in length and for vessels engaged in towing.

2. Lighting requirements for pilot vessels, fishing vessels, and vessels engaged in towing operations have been revised.

3. The formerly optional fixed stern light for vessels under way (with few exceptions) has been made mandatory, and its range of visibility increased to two miles.

4. The range of visibility of anchor lights has been increased for all vessels under 150 feet in length from 1 to 2 miles; for vessels over 150 feet from 1 to 3 miles.

5. Fog signals for certain vessels at anchor in fog have been revised.

6. A bend signal of one prolonged blast has been made mandatory for vessels navigating channels.

7. A danger signal of five or more short blasts has been authorized for the use of privileged vessels in doubt as to the burdened vessel's intentions and/or actions.

8. Distress signals have been regrouped, and a new signal has been provided.

Above: The new International Rules now include seaplanes on the water. In general, they are required to keep well clear of all vessels and avoid impeding their navigation. Where risk of collision exists, they must comply with the rules. Mariners are warned that seaplanes in the act of landing or taking off, or operating under adverse weather conditions, may be unable to change their intended action at the last moment

Right: A vessel under sail, when also propelled by machinery, must obey the rules for a "power-driven" vessel (formerly called a "steam vessel"). An entirely new day signal has been provided for her, consisting of a black conical shape, point upward, not less than 2 feet in diameter at the base. It is shown forward where it can best be seen. Under revised rules for the high seas, there is no provision for the "steam" (power-driven) vessel under sail alone, which formerly carried one black ball (now the day signal for a vessel at anchor)

Above: A power-driven vessel when towing carries the customary red and green 10-point (112½°) sidelights and two white 20-point foremast lights in vertical line (three if tow is over 600 feet in length). A second 20-point white masthead light (that is, a range light) is still optional on vessels towing (and power-driven vessels less than 150 feet in length) though now mandatory on other power-driven vessels under way. The towing vessel, under new rules, must carry either the 12-point fixed white stern light aft (used by power-driven vessels) or a small white light (not visible forward of the beam) for the tow to steer by. Vessels being towed carry red and green sidelights and the same 12-point white stern light. With more than one vessel in tow, all except the last may substitute for the 12-point fixed stern light a small white light not visible forward of the beam

Above: A new rule for the high seas (similar to existing rules in the Great Lakes and Inland Waters) provides for a power-driven vessel nearing a bend in a channel when another vessel approaching from the other direction cannot be seen. She is required to signal by one prolonged (4 to 6-second) blast on her whistle when she arrives within ½ mile of the bend, and this signal must be answered by approaching power-driven vessels within hearing, around the bend, though out of sight

Right: Vessels fishing (20 tons or over) continue to use a fog signal consisting of a blast (on the whistle, if power-driven) at intervals of not more than 1 minute, followed by ringing the bell. In lieu of this she may, under a new provision, use a special fog signal consisting of a series of several alternate notes of higher and lower pitch. The visual day signal for such craft is a basket. If they have their gear or nets out while at anchor, then they display the black ball of a vessel at anchor and the basket in the direction (from the anchor ball) of the net or gear

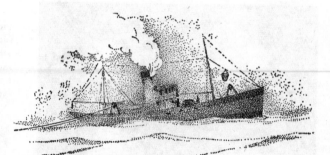

Left: Sailing vessels under way at night will continue to carry the red and green 10-point (112½°) sidelights (no white lights showing forward). Formerly they showed a white light or flare aft to over-taking vessels. Now they must carry the stern light provided in Rule 10—a 12-point (135°) white light, fixed so as to show the light 6 points (67½°) from right aft on each side of the vessel. It must be visible at least 2 miles and carried at the level of the sidelights. (Small vessels which cannot keep such a light fixed are permitted to have an electric torch or lighted lantern at hand to show at the approach of overtaking vessels.)

Right: In the revised rules, use of a rocket parachute flare showing a red light has been authorized as a distress signal. In addition to signals formerly provided, the new rules also list the Morse code . . . — — — . . . (SOS); the spoken radiotelephone signal "May-day"; and a radio signal (series of 12 dashes, sent in 1 minute, duration of each dash 4 seconds, duration of interval between 2 consecutive dashes 1 second) which actuates the auto-alarms of other vessels

Above: An entirely new signal (equivalent to the "danger" signal found in other rules) has been included. This provides for a signal consisting of at least five short and rapid blasts on the whistle or siren. It may be given by a power-driven vessel required under the rules to hold her course and speed if, when she is in sight of another vessel, she is in doubt whether that other vessel is taking sufficient action to avert collision

Left: Under the revised International Rules for the high seas, a second white 20-point (225°) masthead light is now mandatory for power-driven vessels 150 feet or more in length under way. Formerly it was optional. (Now it is optional only on vessels under 150 feet and vessels engaged in towing.) Masthead lights must be in line with and over the keel. One must still be at least 15 feet higher than the other, but now the horizontal distance between them must be at least three times the vertical distance. Other lights are the customary 20-point (225°) white foremast light, red and green 10-point (112½°) sidelights and white light aft (see below)

Right: A new rule makes the showing of a stern light mandatory on vessels (including seaplanes on the water) under way. It is white, 12-point (135°), showing aft, and carried at the level of the side-lights. Visibility has been increased from 1 to 2 miles. (Small vessels, in bad weather, may keep an electric torch or lighted lantern at hand, ready for use, to display to approaching vessels.) Other lights for power-driven vessels are as in the illustration above

Left: Vessels at anchor between sunset and sunrise continue to show a white all-around light forward. If over 150 feet, they carry such a light forward (at least 20 feet above the hull) and another aft (at least 15 feet lower than the other.) Lights are the same as before but the range of visibility has been increased from 1 to 2 miles for vessels under 150 feet, from 1 to 3 miles for vessels over 150 feet

Right: A new rule provides a day mark or identifying signal for the vessel at anchor by day. She carries a black ball (at least 2 feet in diameter) forward where it can best be seen. This brings the International Rule almost into conformity with all others (Inland, Great Lakes, and Western Rivers) where one black ball is required on vessels over 65 feet at anchor in a fairway or channel. Formerly on the high seas this signified a steam vessel under sail only

Left: Rules specifying lights and day signals for vessels working on a submarine cable have now been extended so as to apply also to vessels engaged in laying or picking up a navigation mark, or in surveying or underwater operations. The day signal consists of 3 shapes in vertical line (at least 6 feet apart)—a white diamond between two red balls. By night she would show a white light between two red lights in vertical line, visible all around

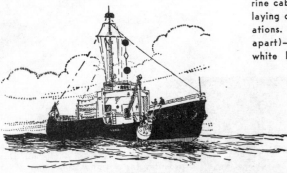

Right: A new provision authorizes a vessel at anchor in fog to give, in addition to the usual bell signals, a sound signal of 3 blasts—1 short, 1 prolonged, 1 short—to give an approaching vessel warning of its position. The customary bell signal, as before, is a rapid ringing of the bell for 5 seconds at intervals of not more than 1 minute and in the case of a vessel over 350 feet in length the bell signal forward is supplemented by sounding a gong aft. The vessel at anchor shows a black ball forward as a day mark

CHAPTER III
Rules of the Road, Right of Way, Whistle Signals

(See also pages 44-46, 60, and Chapter IV, pages 61-78)

ALL of us on land have had the experience upon walking down the street of meeting another pedestrian, turning to the right and having him turn to his left, then turning to the left and having him turn to his right and finally bumping him. To the pedestrian on the sidewalk, such action and such a collision is comical but between two boats on the water, it is serious, yet boats often behave like human beings and do that very thing.

Besides, in the case of pedestrians on the sidewalk and even in the case of automobiles in the street, it is a fairly simple matter to keep clear of such approaching danger as both pedestrians and motor cars follow fairly well defined paths or channels and by keeping to their own right, the danger of collision is eliminated. However, on water it is a far different matter. Except in a very limited number of cases, there are no narrow paths or channels to follow. Boats as a rule have a wide expanse of water on which to navigate, with their paths or courses constantly crossing those courses of many other craft which may be in the immediate vicinity. Therefore, the caution which must be observed on the water, even if the traffic may be much more limited than it is on land, is far more serious and important than on the sidewalks and streets.

To prevent such things and collisions, very carefully considered rules have been laid down so that the duty of the skipper in charge of any boat under any meeting, overtaking or crossing situation is pretty definitely prescribed. The rules which prescribe such duties and actions are of three general classes: First, there are the International Rules of the Road adopted at conventions among maritime nations. The second type is the Inland Rules of the Road. These rules are enacted by the Congress of the United States and are law. The Inland Rules authorize the Commandant, U. S. Coast Guard, to issue regulations based upon the Inland Rules and these regulations are issued in what is commonly known as the Pilot Rules.

The Pilot Rules are not necessarily laws but are more in the form of interpretations by the proper officials and regulations issued to make the Inland Rules of the Road effective. Such regulations can be upset in proper court proceedings and the courts have not hesitated to upset certain of the pilot rules as being unwarranted by the Inland Rules passed by the Congress of the United States.

Piloting

Piloting in the usual sense of the word might be defined as the art of conducting a boat or vessel through the channels and harbors and along the coasts, where landmarks and aids to navigation may be properly identified and are available for fixing one's position and where the depth of the water and the dangers to navigation are such as to require a constant watch to be kept upon the boat's course and frequent changes to be made therein.

Piloting is a most important part of navigation and perhaps the part requiring the most experience and best judgment. An error in position on the high seas may be subsequently corrected without serious result but an error in position while piloting usually results in disaster. Therefore, the boatman should make every effort to be a good pilot.

Requisites for a Good Pilot

It will be seen that a study of piloting embraces a knowledge of a wide range of subjects which are allied to the proper handling of one's boat. This includes a knowledge of the Rules of the Road, rights of way, whistle signals, lights for the various types of craft, fog signals, both under the Inland and International Rules and a study of where these are applicable, whether on the high seas, Great Lakes or inland waterways.

Other important subjects which should be included in the study of piloting are a knowledge of the buoyage and lighthouse system of the United States, the necessary equipment to have aboard, including both that equipment required by law and for one's own safety, the compass and the chart and the use of each, piloting instruments, and a knowledge of tides and currents, as well as many other lesser allied subjects. Good seamanship and particularly a knowledge of the regulations of safety at sea are most important. Weather sense and the fundamentals of ground tackle and anchoring are important requisites.

Only One Way to Learn Boat Handling

There is only one way for one to learn how to handle his boat correctly. That way is by practise alone. No amount of printed matter or rules can accomplish this. However, it is a fact that a knowledge of the basic principles which compose successful boat handling goes a long way, especially in conjunction with an equal amount of experience.

Perfection cannot be obtained unless the skipper becomes familiar with his duties upon the water. He must practise them. He should practise them upon every occasion whether his fellow boatman does or not.

Duty of Man at Wheel

It should be remembered as the first principle to learn, that the man at the wheel while he is on watch has but one duty in life—the safe guidance of his ship. Everything else should be absolutely out of his mind until his boat is brought to her destination or the command is turned over to another person.

A Captain or person in charge is absolute authority over the guidance of his ship as well as being responsible not only for her safety but for the safety of all on board. Under ordinary conditions the judgment, instructions and commands of the Captain must be complied with and may not be questioned.

Safety First

The Golden Rule for small boat handling is Safety First and Keep to the Right. Indecision of action or those actions having an obscure motive may mislead the other vessel and confusion may result. Time should never be considered wasted if safety is at stake. When there are alternate methods of avoiding danger, the safer of the two should be selected.

Rules of Road Applicable to All Types of Vessels

The rules of the road are applicable to all types of vessels when underway. Therefore, they apply with equal force whether a boat has headway or sternway. They apply to craft which are adrift or not under control. They apply to boats driven by steam, motor or sail power, ferry boats, pilot boats, tugs and tows, sailing vessels and, to some extent, to a vessel propelled by hand power and the current.

When Is a Vessel Underway?

A boat is considered underway when she is not at anchor, aground or made fast to the shore. Under all other conditions except these three, a boat is considered underway and the Rules of the Road are applicable.

Where Inland and International Rules Prevail

The Inland Rules are those applicable to the navigation of all vessels on all harbors, rivers and inland waters of the United States tributary to the sea, including coastal waters inshore of the lines established by Congress as dividing the inland waters from the high seas. Upon the high seas, that is, waters outside of these established boundary lines laid down, the International Rules apply. The inland rules also apply (generally speaking) at all buoyed entrances from seaward to bays, sounds, rivers etc. for which specific lines are not prescribed by the Pilot Rules, inshore of a line drawn approximately parallel with the general trend of the shore, drawn through the outermost buoy or other aid to navigation of any system of aids. The Pilot Rules list in detail the lines of demarcation which have been established between the inland waters and high seas.

Generally speaking, waters wholly within any one state are not federal waters but are under the jurisdiction of the State. For example, Lake Champlain located on the boundary between the states of New York and Vermont is Federal water and the Inland Rules of the Road prevail. However, Lake George, wholly within the State of New York, and Lake Hopatcong, wholly within the State of New Jersey, are not Federal waterways. The former is controlled by the navigation laws of the State of New York while Lake Hopatcong is under the jurisdiction of the State of New Jersey.

In some respects the state navigation laws are similar to those of the Federal government yet in other respects the laws of the states differ considerably among themselves and with the Inland Rules.

The International Rules prevail on waters outside the territorial waters of the United States. In many instances the Inland and International Rules are identical. In others they differ. (On pages 60 and 178 will be found tables giving comparisons of the International and Inland Rules. See also Chapter IV.)

A Vessel's Rights Not Altered by Whistle Signals

An unanswered signal creates a situation of doubt and demands great caution. The vessel must not conclude that any signal has been assented to by any omission on the part of the other vessel to answer. Signals should be repeated as often as is necessary to secure an answer. On the other hand, failure to respond to signals by a privileged vessel is not an abandonment of her right of way. Neither is the answering of a signal, whether it is as prescribed by the rules or not, by a privileged vessel an abandonment of her privileges. Signals which are required under the rules do not take away any rights from the privileged vessel, neither do they confer any benefits

upon the burdened ship. The vessel which first signals gains no advantage or disadvantage. Should the burdened vessel first whistle it does not relieve her of any burden even if she should attempt to secure a privilege from the privileged vessel.

The method of passing whether to starboard or to port as provided by the rules cannot be violated except by mutual consent by appropriate whistle signals given and answered. Notwithstanding any such agreement, the vessel which changes the method of passing prescribed by the rules, assumes all risk.

Fundamental Objects of Rules
(See Figs. 1 and 7)

The fundamental objects of the Rules of the Road whether they be the International, Inland or Pilot Rules are to prevent collisions at sea or on the water. Therefore, it may be assumed that the Rules of the Road are applicable only when danger of collision exists. Danger of collision may be deemed to exist also when there is uncertainty or doubt from any cause.

Boats Coming Out of Slip
(See Fig. 2)

In the case of boats coming out of a slip or moving from docks or piers the Rules of the Road do not apply nor do their rights become applicable until such vessels are entirely clear of the slip or pier. No rights of way prevail nor may passing whistle signals be given until such boats are entirely free and clear of the slip or pier. On the other hand, passing craft may not block the entrance to or exit from any pier or slip.

As a boat leaves her pier or slip, she should sound one long blast on her whistle but this signal should not be considered as a passing whistle signal. As soon as a boat is clear of such obstruction, the regular Rules of the Road and rights of way apply.

Overtaking
(See Figs. 3, 10 and 11)

A boat is considered to be overtaking another boat when she is approaching the course of the leading boat from more than two points abaft the beam of the leading boat. In such a case, the rights and privileges all rest with the leading boat, the overtaking vessel having no rights whatsoever.

Even though a sailing vessel, which under all other conditions has the right of way over motor vessels, may be overtaking a motor vessel, such sailing vessel has no rights. In all instances, an overtaking vessel must keep clear of an overtaken vessel.

In Case of Accident
(See Fig. 4)

In case of collision or other serious accident between vessels, it is the duty of the person in charge of each vessel to stand by the other vessel until he has ascertained that she is in no need of further assistance. He must render to the other vessel, her master, crew and passengers such assistance as may be practical and necessary so far as he can do so without danger to his own vessel. He must also give the name of his own vessel and her port when requested. (See also p. 24.)

When boats are involved in a marine casualty or accident either to hull or machinery, equipment, crew or any persons or when any persons are injured or any lives are lost, immediate notice thereof must be forwarded to the nearest Local or District Officer of the United States Coast Guard or to Coast Guard Headquarters, Washington, D. C.

Fig. 1. Above: Rules of the road are applicable only when danger of collision exists. Ordinarily in a situation like the one illustrated, a vessel in the position of the tug with the tow would have the right of way over the ship in the other position shown, as this latter vessel has the tug with the tow in her danger zone. However, in this particular case, the speed of the larger vessel is such that she will pass clear of the tug without danger of collision. Such action is proper although the tug with the tow has the right of way provided the ocean-going ship (the burdened vessel) uses caution to keep clear and sees to it that the disturbance caused by her wake and waves does no damage

Fig. 2. Above: Boats coming out of a slip must exercise particular caution. They should sound one long blast on their whistle as a warning. They may not sound passing whistle signals or exercise any rights of way until such vessels are entirely clear of the slip or pier. On the other hand, other boats must not block or prevent exit or entrance from or to slips or piers

Fig. 3. Below: A vessel overtaking another has no rights until she is free and clear of the overtaken vessel. The overtaking vessel may ask permission to pass to starboard by sounding one blast of her whistle or pass to port by sounding two blasts. If the leading vessel thinks it is expedient for the overtaking vessel to pass, she will answer with the same number of whistle signals. However, should the leading boat think it not expedient for the overtaking boat to pass, she should sound the danger signal of four or more blasts. The following boat must then stay astern until given permission to pass by exchange of proper signals

Fig. 4. Above: In case of collision or other serious accident between boats, it is the duty of each to stand by and give any necessary assistance. Boats shall not leave the scene of an accident until no further assistance to crew, passengers or boat is necessary. In assisting, one is not expected to endanger his craft or take unnecessary chances

SEE TABLE OF
WHISTLE SIGNALS, PAGE 60

Boats on Parallel Courses
(In Same Direction)
(See Fig. 5)

Neither the Inland Rules nor the Pilot Rules have anything to say about two boats on parallel courses, heading in the same direction, since no danger of collision is involved and no whistle signals are necessary.

Figure 5 illustrates a situation which might conceivably develop, as for example if two vessels were to leave adjacent docks at the same time. If their courses are parallel or if the courses are diverging, even slightly, there is no necessity to exchange signals.

However, their courses may have been laid so that they gradually converge, resulting in a crossing situation. On crossing courses, the vessel which has the other on her own starboard side must keep out of the way of the other. Thus the vessel on the starboard side may exercise her right of way, signal with one blast, and expect to receive a one-blast reply indicating that the boat to port will slow down and pass astern. An exchange of two blasts would indicate that the boat to starboard (the privileged vessel) intends to slow down and go astern of the other.

Boats on Opposite Parallel Courses
(See Fig. 14)

When two boats are on parallel courses heading in opposite directions but each course so far to the starboard of the other that no change of course is necessary in order to allow the boats to clear, two blasts of the whistle should then be given by one boat, which should then be acknowledged by two blasts from the other boat. Each boat will hold its course and speed and should pass clear of the other, starboard side to starboard side. This is the only meeting or crossing situation where it is allowable to use a two-whistle signal in passing.

Rights of Way of Fishing Vessels
(See Fig. 6)

Boats of all types while underway must keep out of the way of boats fishing, including fishing boats at anchor or with nets, lines and trawls. No vessel is permitted to engage in fishing in a channel or fairway nor to obstruct navigation in any way. The boats underway should give all boats fishing a wide berth in order not to disturb them by their wash.

Duties of Privileged and Burdened Vessels
(See Figs. 8, 13 and 17)

In the eyes of the Rules of the Road, that is, the laws to prevent collision between two vessels, one of the two vessels must necessarily be considered to have the right of way. This vessel is called the privileged vessel. The other, which is the vessel which must give way, is known as the burdened vessel. In all of the rules, no matter to what phase of boating they refer, the privileged vessel must hold her course and speed. The burdened vessel must adopt every means known to keep out of the way of the privileged vessel.

When a Departure from Rules Is Allowable

As the rules of the road are written to prevent collision rather than to cause it, it follows that situations might develop of such a naure that, if the rules were complied with, a collision would be inevitable. This has led Congress to adopt the following rules to prevent collisions, which become effective when special circumstances warrant:

"In obeying and construing these rules, due regard shall be had to all dangers of navigation and collision and to any special circumstances which may render a departure from the rules necessary in order to avoid immediate danger." Also the following rules: "When, in consequence of thick weather or other causes, the vessel which has the right of way finds herself so close that a collision cannot be avoided by the action of the giving way vessel alone, she also shall take such action as will best aid to avert collision."

Both Vessels May Be Responsible

By the above two rules, to a greater or lesser degree, the responsibility for an accident is up to the masters of both boats. If for any reason an accident cannot be prevented by one of two boats, namely the boat which is supposed to give way, then the other boat must do all in her power to prevent a collision. In the case of motor boats which are, or at least should be, able to stop within almost their own length as well as to maneuver readily there is little to relieve them of some of the responsibility for an accident, especially when a commercial or vessel of large size is the other party to the situation.

The Danger Zone
(See Figs. 9 and 15)

The area around one's boat located clockwise from dead ahead to two points abaft the starboard beam might well be called the Danger Zone. It is this area which should give the skipper the greatest concern. Other boats located in this Danger Zone which are approaching the course of your boat have the right of way over your boat. Consequently your boat must keep clear of boats in the Danger Zone.

Boats located outside of your Danger Zone which are approaching your course must give way to you. You have the right of way over all such boats.

The fact that the Danger Zone is located in the area from dead ahead to two points abaft the starboard beam is an excellent reason to locate the steering wheel on the starboard side of one's boat instead of on the port side if the wheel has to be located on one side or the other. With the steering being done where the best and an unobstructed view of the Danger Zone can be obtained, it works out for the greatest safety. Should the steering wheel be located to port, there would be danger that deck obstructions, persons on deck, etc., would hide, to a greater or lesser extent, this important Danger Zone.

At night, boats in your Danger Zone show you their red side light—the danger signal for you to give way. Boats outside the Danger Zone show their green side light—the clear signal to you that they must give way.

Meeting Obliquely or Crossing
(See Figs. 9, 10, 11 and 17)

If the courses of two motor vessels are such that the two are approaching each other at right angles or obliquely, so as to involve risk of collision (other than overtaking) the motor vessel which has the other on her own port side shall be the privileged vessel and shall hold her course and speed. The motor vessel which has the other on her own starboard side is the burdened vessel and shall keep out of the way of the other vessel, using whatever means are necessary to do so. They exchange one short blast of the whistle. Though the privileged vessel should blow first, either may.

Visual Signal

An amendment to the pilot rules for boats operating on Western Rivers requires that, after January 1, 1945, whistle signals must be further indicated by a visual signal consisting of an amber colored light visible one mile all around the horizon. The light must operate simultaneously and in conjunction with the whistle, and be visible during the same period as the whistle blast.

This rule does not apply to Class A and Class 1 motor boats. Class 2 and Class 3 motor boats are also exempt from this regulation if not engaged in trade or commerce.

Fig. 5. Above: In the illustration above it would appear that the ferry and tug were on parallel courses, a situation concerning which neither Inland Rules nor Pilot Rules have anything to say, since no danger of collision exists, and no whistle signals are required. If the courses in reality are diverging, there is still no risk of collision and no need for whistle signals. However, if the courses are actually converging, we have a crossing situation in which the tug (in the ferry's danger zone) has the right of way. Exchanging one blast of the whistle, the ferry would properly slow down and pass astern of the tug. If two blasts were exchanged, the tug would slow down and go astern of the ferry

Fig. 6. Below: The rights of fishing craft must be respected by other craft underway. Boats have a right to fish in all waters other than in channels and fairways and while they are not obstructing navigation. Passing craft should give fishermen a wide berth

Fig. 8. Left: As the motor vessel has the tug on her port bow, and the motor vessel is in the tug's danger zone, the motor vessel technically has the right of way and it would ordinarily be the tug's duty to keep clear. To exercise her rights as the privileged vessel, the motor vessel would sound one blast, hold her course and speed and pass ahead of the tug. However, even though the rules give no special rights to the tug, the motor vessel is so much easier to maneuver that good judgment in this case would dictate that she sound two blasts, slow down, and pass astern of the tow

Fig. 7. Below: Give whistle signals only when danger of collision exists. In the situation illustrated, both boats would pass clear, without either changing her course or speed; signals are unnecessary

Fig. 9. Right: The danger zone of the boat in the center of the illustration is shown by the shaded section. Therefore, she has the right of way over all other vessels except the one in the shaded zone which has the right of way over the boat in the center. Thus the boat at the lower right may pass ahead of the center craft. As will be seen in the illustration, the boat in the center has the right of way over the one which is crossing her stern and also over the small boat which is overtaking

When in Doubt as to Whether One or Two Blasts Should Be Given

As to the action called for by one or two blasts of the whistle, there is a very simple rule which if kept in mind will assist every skipper to remember whether he is to pass port or starboard, ahead or astern of the craft giving him the signal. The rule will also hold good when the man at the wheel of your boat wishes to indicate to the other craft what action you are to take, as well as the course you wish to follow, providing you are the right-of-way boat and have the right to dictate to him.

Keeping in mind the two sides of the boat—that is, port and starboard—we have the former word, port, of one syllable, and the other side of the boat indicated by a word of two syllables—namely, starboard. If one simply remembers that the word of *one* syllable is always associated with *one* blast of the whistle and the word of *two* syllables with *two* blasts of the whistle, he will have no difficulty in giving and obeying the passing whistle signals. If the oncoming boat gives you one blast of her whistle, it is your duty to answer with one blast of the whistle, provided all is well. The signal of one blast is an indication that the boats must pass port side to port side. If two whistles are given and answered, associate this signal with the word of two syllables, and the boats will then pass starboard side to starboard side. This rule holds good in all instances of meeting and crossing.

Cross Signals

Motor vessels are forbidden to use what is known as cross signals; that is, answering one whistle with two or answering two whistles with one. In cases where a whistle is correct according to the rules which it is deemed injudicious to comply with, instead of answering it with a cross signal, one should at once sound the danger signal of four or more short and rapid blasts. In such a case, both boats should be stopped or reversed and a boat should not proceed again until the proper whistles have been given, answered and understood and conditions have developed so that the boats can safely pass.

Method of Giving Signals

The method of giving the various signals, whistles and other kinds, by the various types of boats under different conditions of navigation are fully described in the rules. Whether the signal should be given by whistle, horn or other means is important. Promptness in giving signals is of the first importance. The navigator of any boat, big or small, whether it be the smallest motor boat or the largest ocean liner, who fails to promptly give and answer signals, is subject to a penalty and should be immediately reported to the nearest District Coast Guard Officer of the U. S. Coast Guard.

Differences Between International, Inland and Great Lakes Rules
(For a complete analysis, see pages 60-78)

As to when passing whistle signals should be given, the International Rules prescribe that they should be given only when (and always when) there is a change of course if any other vessel is in sight. The signals must be accompanied by a change of helm. Limits of risk of collision are the visibility limits in fair weather and this visibility limit also prevails in thick weather.

The Inland or Pilot Rules prescribe that in fog, mist, falling snow, or heavy rain storms when vessels cannot see each other, whistle signals must not be given but fog signals only must be used. Passing signals are to be given when proposing how to pass and are to be given whether or not accompanied by a change of helm, and always when risk of collision is involved.

The Great Lakes rules prescribe that passing whistle signals shall be given in all weathers regardless of weather or visibility and are to be sounded whether or not accompanied by a change of helm and are to be given when risk of collision is involved.

The signals of one short blast or two short blasts have practically identical significance in the International, Inland and Great Lakes Rules. Three short blasts indicate that "my engnes are going astern" by the International and Inland Rules, yet three short blasts are recognized officially by the Great Lakes Rules only as a steamer fog signal when underway. However, by common use, it is recognized as indicating sternway and as a request to a passing vessel to slow down.

The signal of four or more short blasts (five or more on the Great Lakes) is recognized as a danger signal in the Inland Rules. In general, this danger signal is used to indicate that the other vessel's course or intention is not understood, is an alarm signal in emergency, to indicate to an overtaking vessel that the overtaken vessel considers it unsafe to pass as requested and to indicate that conditions prevent immediate compliance with the signals. On the high seas, five or more short blasts may be used when a power-driven vessel, required to hold her course and speed, is in doubt that another vessel is taking sufficient action to avert collision. A whistle signal of one long blast is a signal specified in the Inland and Great Lakes Rules to be given by a vessel navigating a channel where visibility is less than $\frac{1}{2}$ mile because of a bend in the channel and high banks and to be given by a vessel leaving the dock or berth. In both of these instances, this one long blast is a warning (not passing) signal and should be answered by approaching vessels with the same signal. A new International Rule requires a power-driven vessel, when within $\frac{1}{2}$ mile of a bend, to give a "prolonged" (4- to 6-second) blast.

When Crossing and Overtaking Rules Conflict
(See Fig. 11)

When one vessel is both overtaking and crossing another, the overtaking rule prevails. Once an overtaking vessel, always an overtaking vessel, until free and clear.

A crossing vessel which has come up from more than two points abaft the beam of the leading vessel must keep clear even though she is on the starboard side of the leading boat. She is not free from this obligation even after she draws ahead on the beam and bow of the other vessel until she is free and clear of her.

Sailing Vessels Have Right of Way Over Motor Craft
(See Page 12)

A sailing vessel has the right of way over a motor craft in all situations except when the sailing vessel is overtaking the motor vessel, in which case the sailing vessel must keep clear. A sailing vessel is not required to stand in stays, tack or wear or jibe to allow another vessel to pass. A sailing vessel must observe the difficulties under which the burdened vessel may be and give due attention thereto. A motor vessel must observe any condition which would prevent a sailing vessel from finishing its tack and must be prepared for a sailing vessel accidently missing stays, jibing, etc. A sailing vessel must not endanger a motor vessel by tacking suddenly in a narrow channel or fairway, directly in the path of the motor vessel, without due warning, when an alternative action may be safely taken by the sailing vessel.

Whistle Signals as Salutes

Yachts should never exchange salutes by means of whistle signals. Commercial craft often salute by the whistle; those on the east coast by three long blasts and on the Great Lakes by three long followed by two short.

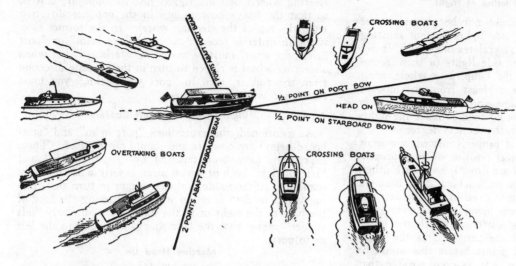

CROSSING BOATS

½ POINT ON PORT BOW

HEAD ON

½ POINT ON STARBOARD BOW

2 POINTS ABAFT PORT BEAM

OVERTAKING BOATS

2 POINTS ABAFT STARBOARD BEAM

CROSSING BOATS

Fig. 10. Above: The three situations—meeting head on, crossing and overtaking. Boats are considered meeting head on when their masts seem to be in line or nearly in line. They are overtaking when one boat is approaching the course of another from a point more than two points abaft the beam of the leading boat or when at night her side lights, if correctly placed, cannot be seen. In all other cases where the courses intersect either at right angles or obliquely, the situation is said to be crossing. Only those boats shown in the lower right-hand corner of the illustration should hold their course and speed relative to the boat in the center. All boats in the other positions must alter their courses and keep clear

Fig. 11. Below: A boat approaching the course of another from a position more than two points abaft the beam of the leading boat is considered the overtaking vessel and has no rights. An overtaking boat remains an overtaking boat until she is free and clear of the overtaken vessel

Fig. 12. Right: A sailing vessel, that is, one propelled by wind power alone without the assistance of any kind of motor or mechanical power, has the right of way over every form of motor or steam vessel in all situations except when a sailing vessel is overtaking a motor vessel. If the sailing vessel is using power also she then becomes a motor vessel and must abide by the rules for a motor vessel

Fig. 13. Left: The privileged vessel, that is, one having the right of way, must hold her course and speed. It is not permissible for the right of way vessel in crossing ahead or attempting to cross ahead, to steer a crooked course. The burdened vessel, that is, the one not having the right of way, must keep clear by any means she elects

Caution When Piloting at Night

Too much dependence should not be placed on the supposition that the colored side lights are not showing across the bow. There are several reasons which, if not taken care of, will cause the side lights to show across the bow. The position of the lamp, as a whole, must necessarily be several inches at least from the inboard screen, the width of the flame and the reflection from the after side of the light-box all tend to make the lights show across the bow to a greater or less degree.

The white range lights, if properly placed, are most useful in determining the exact position of an approaching vessel. When the lights are directly over each other, it is clear that the vessel is approaching dead head-on, but when her course is changed even in the slightest the range lights will open out, the lower one drawing away from the upper in the same direction which the boat's bow is changing. Without the range lights the ship's course might change several points before this would be evident from the side lights. It is even possible that the course of the approaching vessel is away from the course of one's own boat when the side lights are first sighted, and that she swings around toward your course without this being detected from the side lights as the boats draw closer together. This is a very dangerous position and requires great caution.

Rules Prohibit Excessive Speed

The rules of the road make very little specific mention of speed, except when navigating in the fog or heavy weather, when the rules state speed should be reduced to the safety limit. However, good seamanship as well as good ethics require that the speed of a boat be reasonable for the time, place and surrounding conditions. Court rulings have upheld these statements even though the laws are silent on these points. Excessive speed is a fundamental fault which may cause collision or accident. A speed reasonable in open waters, free from traffic, would be considered an unreasonable speed in crowded waters, harbors, narrow channels and particularly where yachts and motor boats are anchored. Excessive speed in the vicinity of fishing vessels, boats aground, tied to piers or floats should be avoided. A vessel is responsible for injury caused by her wash or suction.

Generally speaking, the speed of a boat should not be greater than would enable her to change from headway to sternway, when danger presents itself. The requirement of reasonable speed applies with even greater force to sailing vessels.

Excessive speed in anchorages or in the vicinity of docks or floats should be avoided at all costs. Speed must be reduced so that the wash can cause no discomfort or damage.

The Motor Boat Act of 1940 provides that anyone who shall operate any vessel in a reckless manner may be deemed guilty of a misdemeanor and upon conviction shall be punished by a fine not exceeding $2,000, or by imprisonment for not over one year, or both.

Port Helm and Starboard Helm

The orders of "port your helm" or "starboard your helm" are most confusing and should never be used.

The helm is not the boat's steering wheel nor is it the boat's rudder. It more closely refers to the tiller which was the method of steering boats in the days gone by. When the tiller was moved to port the boat's bow swung to starboard and when the tiller was put over to starboard the boat's bow went to port.

Most steering wheels on modern craft are rigged so that the boat's bow swings in the same direction that the top of the wheel moves. But it is not uncommon to find steering wheels that are rigged just the opposite, that is, so that the boat's bow swings in the opposite direction from the top of the steering wheel. In the former case, when an order is received to "port your helm" or "port helm" the wheel must be moved to "starboard" but when a steering wheel is rigged to turn in the opposite direction from the rudder, then to "port your helm," you must turn your wheel to port, etc.

Right Rudder and Left Rudder

As mentioned, the expressions "port helm" and "starboard helm" are obsolete and should not be used. These expressions have been replaced by "right rudder" and "left rudder," both of which mean exactly what the term implies. "Right rudder" always means to turn the steering wheel in that direction which will swing the bow of the boat to the right or to the starboard. Similarly "left rudder" means that the bow should be swung to the left or to port.

Meeting Head On
(See Fig. 14)

When two motor vessels are approaching each other head-on or nearly so, it is the duty of each skipper to swing the bow of his boat to starboard and thus pass port side to port side. It is the duty of each to give one short blast of a whistle.

Points on the Bow, Beam or Quarter
(See Fig. 15)

The directions Dead Ahead and Astern are too well known to require any explanation. Directions and bearings between dead ahead and astern are given names, first depending upon whether they are on the boat's starboard (right) or port (left) hand. Then the 180 degrees between dead ahead and astern on each side are divided into 16 equal parts ($11\frac{1}{4}$ degrees each) called points. The first point to the right of dead ahead is known as 1 point on the starboard bow; then 2 points on the starboard bow; 3 points on the starboard bow. The 45 degree direction is called 4 points or broad on the starboard bow. The next point aft is called 3 points forward of the starboard beam, then 2 points forward of the starboard beam; one point forward of the starboard beam. Then on the starboard beam.

Working further aft the points become, in order, 1 point abaft the starboard beam; 2 points abaft the starboard beam; 3 points abaft the starboard beam; then 4 points or broad on the starboard quarter. The next point aft is known as 3 points on the starboard quarter; 2 points on the starboard quarter; 1 point on the starboard quarter, and astern.

The similar points on the port side have corresponding names.

Rights of Way of Sailing Craft
(See Fig. 16)

Sailing vessels do not indicate their course or intended action in passing either another sailing vessel or a motor vessel by any whistle signal. The rights of way between two sailing vessels are determined solely by the direction of the wind in reference to the boats' sailing directions at the time. One which is running free must give way to a close-hauled sailing vessel. When both sailing vessels are close-hauled, the one on the port tack (having the wind over her port bow) must keep clear of the sailing vessel on the starboard tack. In the case when both sailing vessels are running free but with the wind on different sides, that one which has the wind on her port side must keep clear. If both are running free with the wind on the same side, the boat to windward shall keep clear of the vessel which is to leeward. A sailing vessel having the wind aft shall keep out of the way of other sailing craft.

Fig. 14. Above: When two vessels are meeting head on, it is the duty of the skipper, of each boat to give one blast on the whistle, and swing his bow to starboard, boats passing port side to port side

Fig. 15. Below: Diagram illustrating the proper way in which directions and bearings are named on shipboard. The unit is the "point" which is 1/32 of a complete circle or 1/16 of the angular distance from dead ahead to dead astern. Each point has a distinct name. These names are dependent upon the angular distance and the particular direction from the bow, the beam and the stern of the boat. The word starboard or port is always used with the name of the point to indicate to which partcular side of the boat it refers. The black zone of the illustration below, from dead ahead to two points abaft the starboard beam, is known as the danger zone. Boats in this zone of your boat have the right of way over you and you must keep clear. Boats approaching your course which are not in your danger zone must give way and keep clear of you

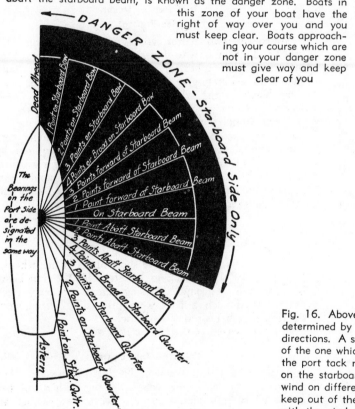

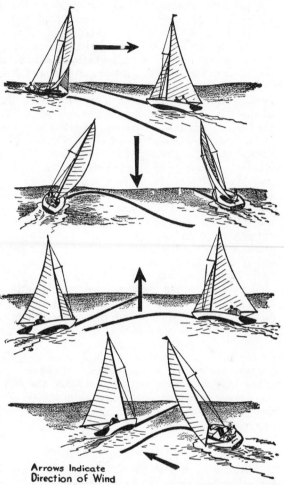

Arrows Indicate
Direction of Wind

Fig. 16. Above: The rights of way between two strictly sailing vessels is determined by the direction of the wind in reference to the boats' sailing directions. A sailing vessel which is running free must keep out of the way of the one which is close-hauled. A sailing vessel which is close-hauled on the port tack must keep out of the way of a vessel which is close-hauled on the starboard tack. If both sailing vessels are running free, with the wind on different sides, the one which has the wind on the port side shall keep out of the way of the other. If both sailing vessels are running free, with the wind on the same side, the vessel which is to windward shall keep out of the way of the vessel which is to leeward. A sailing vessel having the wind aft shall keep out of the way of other sailing craft

Fig. 17. Right: In the crossing situation, the boat having another on her own port bow has the right of way and is the privileged vessel. Her action is to give one blast on her whistle, maintain her course and speed and pass ahead of the other boat. The other craft, the burdened vessel, having the privileged vessel in her danger zone, must take any action to keep clear. The privileged vessel should blow first, but either may

55

Crossing Ahead

Every vessel which is directed by the rules to keep out of the way of the other vessel, if the circumstances of the case admit, must avoid crossing ahead of the other.

This is probably the rule which is most violated. However, it should be remembered that under no ordinary circumstances is it permissible for the vessel not having the right of way (the burdened vessel) to pass ahead of the vessel having the right of way (the privileged vessel) or to cause the privileged vessel to change her course or speed. It is also important that the burdened vessel shall not give whistle signals which would permit her to cross ahead of the privileged vessel. Even though such whistle signals be given by the burdened vessel, properly answered and assented to by the privileged vessel, yet the burdened vessel gains no rights by such actions nor does the privileged vessel relinquish any of her lawful rights.

Assuming that no whistle signals have been previously given, if for any reason the boat not having the right of way desires to, she may ask permission to pass ahead of the right-of-way boat by giving two blasts on the whistle. If the right-of-way boat is so inclined, she may grant this permission by answering with two short blasts of her whistle. However, in granting this permission by giving two blasts of the whistle, it is understood by the other (burdened vessel) that she may pass ahead at her own risk. Such a reply does not of itself change or modify the statutory obligation of the giving-way boat to keep out of the way as before, nor does it guarantee the success of the means she has adopted to do so. In other words, should an accident occur, the responsibility will rest entirely or partially with the boat which has not the right of way, even though the fault seems to lie entirely with the other craft. This is a situation which is very common on the waterways of our country. But motor craft should always be careful to avoid it as it is entirely illegal.

Should the boat not having the right of way request permission to pass ahead of the other boat by giving two blasts of her whistle, and should the right-of-way boat not desire to grant this request or permission, she will sound the danger signal, in which case both vessels must stop and be absolutely sure of the action of each other before proceeding.

Passing Starboard to Starboard

The law in this matter is clearly laid down in the following decision of the U. S. Courts:

"A steamer bound to keep out of the way of another steamer by going to the right, has no right, when under no stress of circumstances, but merely for her own convenience, to give the other steamer a signal of two whistles, imparting that she will go to the left unless she can do so safely by her own navigation, without aid from the other, and without requiring the other steamer to change her course or speed. Otherwise she would be imposing upon the latter steamer more or less of a burden and the duty of keeping out of the way which by statute is imposed on herself. When two blasts are given under such circumstances, the steamer bound to keep out of the way thereby says in effect to the other: 'I can keep out of your way by going ahead of you to the left and will do so if you do nothing to thwart me; do you assent?' A reply of two whistles to this means nothing more than an assent to this course, at the risk of the vessel proposing it. Such a reply does not of itself change or modify the statutory obligation of the former to keep out the way as before, nor does it guarantee the success of the means she has adopted to do so."

(See "The City of Hartford," Federal Reporter 23, page 650.)

Indicate Your Course
(See Fig. 18)

In addition to the sounding of the proper whistle signal, it is essential that the helmsman of each boat should indicate what his course is to be by the swinging of the bow of his boat sharply to port or starboard, as the case may be, for a moment, as in many instances the whistle signals of a small boat cannot be heard at a great distance. When the helmsman of an approaching boat sees its bow swing to one side or the other, he immediately recognizes what the action of this boat is to be, even if he has failed to hear or to understand the whistle signals.

When Does Danger of Collision Exist?

Danger of collision may be deemed to exist when the bearing between two vessels does not change. If there is no change of bearings as the boats proceed on their course and at a uniform speed, a collision will ultimately result. If the bearings change materially they will pass clear.

Whether there is a change of bearing may be easily determined by noting a range or bearing on some part of the boat's structure, such as a stanchion, or from the boat's compass to the other craft.

In Cases of Doubt
(See Fig. 19)

Whenever two motor vessels are approaching each other and either fails to understand the signals, course or intentions of the other for any reason, the vessel in doubt should immediately give the danger signal of four or more short blasts of the whistle (five or more on the Great Lakes).

Until January 1, 1954, no equivalent of the danger signal was provided for the high seas. Now, under new International Rules, a power-driven vessel required by the rules to hold her course and speed may use a warning signal of five or more short (1-second) and rapid blasts if she is in doubt that another vessel is taking sufficient action to avert collision.

Boats Backing
(See Fig. 21)

A boat backing sounds three short blasts of her whistle. In the case of a boat backing, her stern for the time being is considered her bow. Passing signals are exchanged exactly as if such a boat were proceeding ahead, considering that her stern is her bow.

Note: See exception on Great Lakes, page 60.

Rights of Tow Boats

A tug with a tow is responsible for her tow and they are to be regarded as one vessel. A tug with a tow has no special rights under the rules. Moreover, as such an outfit is unwieldy and hard to handle, a tug has increased responsibilities due to these facts and is not excused from obeying all the rules applicable to a vessel without a tow. Steam and motor vessels, upon passing a tow when there is a chance that their wash or waves will cause damage, must slow down. (*But see also caption, Fig. 8.*)

Rights of Way of Ferry Boats

While there is no special provision of the law giving special privileges to ferry boats yet the courts have repeatedly ruled that ferry boats are entitled to a reasonable freedom of entrance to and exit from their slips. The same is true in regard to other boats using slips or piers. Vessels navigating in a harbor should avoid passing close to piers, etc.

Fig. 19. Below: In all cases of doubt, **the danger** signal consisting of four or more short and rapid blasts of the whistle should be given. Whenever a whistle signal or the anticipated course of another vessel is not understood or recognized, then it is one's duty to blow the danger signal immediately. When the danger signal is blown, it is the duty of every vessel to stop immediately and reverse and not proceed until the situation has cleared itself or until the proper whistle signals have been given, answered and understood. In no case should cross signals be given, that is, answering one signal by two and vice versa. If such signals are given, it should be followed by the danger signal and both boats should stop (See p. 56 for proper signals on the high seas.)

Fig. 18. Above: It is very essential, especially in the case of small motor craft, that they indicate what their course is to be, not only by giving the correct whistle signal, but by swinging the boat's bow sharply in one direction as an indication of what course and action they intend to take. The chances are that this action will be much more readily recognized and understood than if reliance is placed solely on whistle signals for the proper execution of the law

LESTER FALANS

Fig. 20. Left: Perhaps, strictly speaking, war vessels or other government craft have no special rights, yet it is always best to keep clear of them

Fig. 21. Right: In case of a boat backing, she should sound three blasts on her whistle. When the vessel has sternway on, her stern must be considered as her bow for the time being, and crossing and passing whistle signals given accordingly. In the situation illustrated, the boat at the right is backing and therefore her stern is considered her bow, putting her in the danger zone of the boat at the left. Consequently the backing boat has the right of way and may back across the bow of the other boat. Her proper whistle signal would be one blast, this to be answered by one blast by the other boat

Definition of Motor Boat

Under the Motor Boat Act of 1940, which superseded the original act of 1910, any boat propelled by machinery and not more than 65 feet in length, with the exception of tugs propelled by steam, is designated as a motor boat. Motor craft of a greater length fall into the class of steamers.

The rules also provide that any such vessel (motor boat) propelled in whole or in part by machinery shall be considered a motor vessel—a very clear and concise statement, the meaning of which there can be no doubt.

Operating Under Both Sail and Power in Day Time
(See Fig. 23)

For a boat (motor) having a length of more than 65 feet, a special day mark is specified when the boat is under both sail and power. For a motorboat (less than 65 feet in length) there is no such provision. It will be realized that there are times when it is difficult if not impossible to determine from even a short distance even in the daytime whether a boat which has the outward appearance of a sailing vessel is using power in addition to her sails. Should she be a sailing craft her rights will be supreme over every other type of craft but should she be an auxiliary, providing her motor is running, such a boat will have no more rights than though she had no sails.

The situation just described may lead to very dangerous complications, as one will realize. A certain action and change of course may be planned on the assumption that the oncoming vessel is strictly a sailing vessel. Should she be an auxiliary (with motor running and sails up), which would call for action of an entirely different nature, her identity might not be discovered until the execution of the action based upon the first assumption was well under way. In the meantime, the crew of the vessel carrying sail, inasmuch as there is no reason for doubt to exist in their minds as to the proper action of the other (motor) vessel as well as their own, may have changed their own course (probably correctly) in a manner which will be exactly contrary to the expectations of those on the vessel carrying no sails. Both boats might give way in the same direction at the same instant, presumably to allow the (assumed) right-of-way boat to hold her course and speed. A collision under such circumstances is almost inevitable.

A common sense action in a situation where two boats are approaching each other in the daytime, one of which is operating under power alone and the other under both sail and power, is for the one which is likely to cause confusion as to her status of being a sailing or motor craft to be prompt and generous with her whistle signals and take whatever action is possible in order to communicate her status to the other craft. Strictly speaking, neither of such boats has the right of way if only the types of the boats are considered. The relative position of the two boats must decide which is to hold her course and speed and which boat is to keep clear. Both craft are motor boats under the law. However, the crew of the vessel carrying sail in addition to her power must be careful to take no action which will confuse the other craft.

Under Sail and Power by Night
(See Fig. 22)

Figure 22 illustrates a situation in which a sailboat and a motorboat are on crossing courses at night. The sailboat—if her engine is not running—has the right of way and the motorboat must keep clear.

The motorboat knows the other is under sail only, as she does not show a white light forward. If the sailboat were to start her engine and run under both sail and power, the rules require her to show the lights of a motorboat (that is, the white bow and stern lights, in addition to her colored side lights). With motor running, whether her sails were up or not, she would be subject to rules for motor vessels, and would become the burdened vessel in Figure 22, giving way to the motorboat in her danger zone.

The Pilot Rules all provide that every vessel under steam, whether under sail or not, is to be considered a steam vessel. These Pilot Rules define the term "steam vessel" as including any vessel propelled by machinery. Motorboats under sail and power thus fall within the definition of steam vessels in the Pilot Rules and are therefore subject to all the provisions of the Pilot Rules except as the Pilot Rules are modified by other statutes.

When Not to Give Passing Signals
(See Fig. 24)

Passing signals provided by Inland Rules are never to be given except when the vessels are in sight of each other and the course of each can be determined by the sight of the vessel itself or at night by seeing the sailing lights. In fog, mist, falling snow or heavy rainstorms, when vessels cannot actually see through, fog signals only must be given. Whistle signals are not to be given unless danger of collision exists. If there is doubt or uncertainty as to whether danger of collision does exist, then it should be assumed to exist. Whistle signals between a motor boat and sailing vessel or between two sailing vessels should never be given.

Meeting in Winding Channel
(See Fig. 25)

When two boats are approaching each other in a winding channel, they must be considered as meeting head on and not as meeting obliquely or crossing. Each boat should keep to the starboard side of the channel. Good judgment provides that when two boats are to meet at a narrow bend in the channel, the one which is navigating against the current shall stop until the boat navigating with the current has safely passed.

Rights of Way of Row Boats

Row boats should take into consideration their ability to maneuver promptly and more readily than motor or sailing craft, and when they can keep out of the way of motor or sailing craft by a few strokes they should do so. When row boats are in distress or where there is any uncertainty of their movements, a motor or sailing vessel should keep clear of them. Small boats capable of being handled by oars should be equipped with them even when their usual power is either sail or motor. Such boats should use oars in order to avoid collision whenever necessary.

Fig. 22. Left: A boat under sail has the right of way over a motorboat, both by night and day, except when the sailboat is an overtaking vessel. Until the Motor Boat Act was changed by an amendment in 1956, confusing and dangerous situations often developed when the sailboat was operating at night as an auxiliary, with sail up and engine running. Now, however, the auxiliary with engine running is lighted as a motorboat of her class. Consequently other craft can tell from her lights whether she is under sail only and has the right of way, or whether she has her engine running and must follow rules of the road prescribed for a motorboat in a similar situation

Fig. 23. Right: In the daytime, a vessel under both sail and power is considered a motor vessel and must observe only the rules of the road of motor vessels. The addition of sail power does not change her status over that of the motor vessel in any way. Confusion is likely to result unless the boat under both sail and power is very careful in her navigation and takes the necessary action to make it clear to other vessels that she is following the rules of a motor vessel. This is often not apparent from distant observation unless caution is observed

Fig. 24. Left: Whistle signals are to be given only when danger of collision exists and the boats are in actual sight of each other. When navigating in the fog, snow or at night or under any other conditions when the other boats or her lights cannot be seen or when her action or course is not clearly understood, then passing whistle signals should not be exchanged. Whistle signals between motor and sailing craft or between two sailing vessels should never be exchanged. It should also be kept in mind that the giving, exchanging and acknowledging of whistle signals in no way affects or alters a boat's rights. If a privileged vessel fails to respond to signals, it is not an abandonment of her rights of way. By signaling first, one does not gain or lose any advantage. Under Great Lakes rules, in certain rivers and narrow channels where there is a current, the down-bound vessel has right of way and signals first to indicate the side she will take

Fig. 25. Right: Boats approaching a bend in a river or channel where other approaching boats cannot be clearly seen, should give one long blast on their whistle. Ordinarily they should keep to the starboard side of the channel and should not depart from this rule either to escape unfavorable currents or to gain any tidal advantage. Boats approaching each other around such a bend should be considered as meeting head on and not as meeting obliquely or crossing. Passing signals are given accordingly. It has been ruled that passing signals should be given as soon as vessels sight each other

PASSING WHISTLE SIGNALS

How International, Inland and Great Lakes Rules Differ

	INTERNATIONAL RULES	INLAND OR PILOT RULES	GREAT LAKES RULES
WHEN passing signals are given	Only when (and always when) there is a change of course if any other vessel is in sight. Signals must be accompanied by change of helm. Limits of risk of collision are the visibility limits in fair weather, and the visibility limit also prevails in thick weather.	Prescribe that in fog, mist, falling snow, or heavy rain storms when vessels cannot see each other, *fog* signals only must be given. Passing signals to be given when proposing how to pass or in answer thereto. Signals given whether or not accompanied by change of helm. Signals given when risk of collision is involved. 3-blast signal (engine reversing) required when vessels are in sight of one another. Signals given when passing or meeting at a distance within ½ mile of each other.	*Passing signals* given in all weathers regardless of weather or visibility. Signals given when proposing to pass or in answer thereto. Signals given whether or not accompanied by change of helm. Signals given when risk of collision is involved. Signals given before vessels approach within ½ mile of each other.

SUMMARY of the above, as to WHEN passing signals are given:—

GREAT LAKES and INLAND rules similar, except when visibility is bad.
On the GREAT LAKES, passing signals are given not only in clear weather but even in a fog (or other conditions of low visibility) when the situation can be understood, and positions and intentions of vessels made clear, from sound alone, or by sight.
INTERNATIONAL and INLAND rules, on the other hand, provide for passing signals to be given when the other vessel can be seen.
GREAT LAKES and INLAND rules both differ from the INTERNATIONAL in that the latter prescribe passing signals only when (and always when) changing course within sight of another vessel. (*Exception*—At bends, with visibility restricted by banks, vessels may not be in sight of each other when they exchange passing signals, following the long warning blast.)

COMPARISON OF WHAT THE PASSING SIGNALS MEAN

	INTERNATIONAL	INLAND OR PILOT RULES	GREAT LAKES
One short blast (A "short" blast means about one second duration)	I am altering my course to STARBOARD	Used in any of the following situations:— 1. When changing course to starboard. 2. When maintaining a course to starboard which will allow a safe passing on parallel courses, port side to port side. 3. On crossing courses, privileged vessel signifies she will hold her course and speed. 4. On crossing courses, burdened vessel agrees and understands that privileged vessel will hold her course and speed. (This may require burdened vessel to stop, slow down, or change course, in order to give way.) 5. Request by overtaking vessel to pass another on overtaken vessel's starboard side. 6. Granting request by another vessel to overtake you and pass on your own starboard side, and indicating it may be done with safety. 7. If danger signal has previously been sounded to prohibit passing, one blast indicates that overtaken boat now considers it safe for overtaking boat to pass on the former's starboard side.	Same as INLAND (On Great Lakes, blasts are "distinct," not "short".)
Two short blasts	I am altering my course to PORT	Used in any of the following situations:— 1. When changing course to port. 2. When maintaining a course to port which will allow a safe passing on parallel courses, starboard side to starboard side. 3. Request by overtaking vessel to pass another on the overtaken vessel's port side. 4. Granting request by another vessel to overtake you and pass on your own port side, and indicating it may be done with safety. 5. If danger signal has previously been sounded to prohibit passing, two blasts indicate that overtaken boat now considers it safe for overtaking boat to pass on the former's port side.	Same as INLAND (On Great Lakes, blasts are "distinct," not "short".)
Three short blasts (International 1 second) (Inland—short) (Great Lakes—distinct)	My engines are going astern.	My engines are going at full speed astern.	Recognized officially only as a steamer *fog* signal when underway. However, by common use, it is recognized by seamen as indicating sternway and as a request to a passing vessel to slow down.*
Four, or more, short blasts (danger signal) See note †.	Five or more short blasts used by power-driven vessel required to hold course and speed if in doubt other vessel is taking sufficient action to avert collision.	Used in any of the following situations:— 1. To indicate that other vessel's course or intention is not understood. 2. An alarm signal in emergency (failure to understand other vessel's course or intention because of lack of time to effect agreement through exchange of proper signals). 3. To indicate to an overtaking vessel that the overtaken vessel considers it unsafe to pass as requested. 4. To indicate conditions prevent immediate compliance with signals.	Danger signal requires not less than five short blasts.
One long blast (A "long" blast means about 10 to 12 seconds duration)	One "prolonged" (4- to 6-second) blast given by power-driven vessel within ½ mile of bend in channel where approaching vessel cannot be seen	1. Given by vessel navigating a channel where visibility is less than ½ mile because of bend in channel and high banks. This is a *warning* (not passing) signal and should be answered by approaching vessels with the same signal. Passing signals given only after the exchange of such warning signals. 2. Given by vessel leaving a dock or berth. This is a *warning* (not passing) signal. Passing signals exchanged when vessel is clear of berth and fully in sight of approaching vessels.	Same as INLAND (On Great Lakes, blast is at least 8 seconds.)

* NOTE:—U. S. and Canadian Government patrol vessels on the Great Lakes signal a vessel to slow down with 3 long blasts of a whistle or horn; order her to stop until further orders are given by the patrol vessel, with 4 long blasts; indicate she may proceed, by 1 long blast followed by 4 short blasts.
† NOTE:—In many U. S. ports, a signal of five prolonged (4 to 6 second) blasts on the whistle or siren is sounded by ships when afire in port or in the harbor (except when under way) as a supplement to other means of sounding the alarm of fire aboard the vessel.

How Pilot Rules Differ

CHAPTER IV

INTERNATIONAL, INLAND, GREAT

LAKES, AND WESTERN RIVER RULES

VARY IN REGULATIONS PERTAINING

TO VARIOUS SITUATIONS AFLOAT

THE rules of the road governing traffic afloat have been drafted with the express purpose of preventing collision. And yet, there is a condition inherent in the rules themselves that undoubtedly contributes toward confusion—and therefore possibility of collision—on the part of those who may be earnestly trying to understand and obey the rules.

We refer, of course, to the obvious lack of uniformity that exists in the several sets of rules governing various waters. In justice to the rules it may be said that there is a certain uniformity of principle running through all, but the differences in detail are bewildering, to say the least.

Without going into detail as to how the complexity of rules has arisen in the United States, we should point out that a boat cruising along our coastal and inland waters may find herself successively under the jurisdiction of the following different sets of rules:

1. *The International Rules*—These apply on the high seas, outside of the limits specified for so-called "inland waters." Boundary lines have been prescribed outside of which the International Rules apply, connecting, in the main, offshore aids to navigation, points of the mainland, islands, etc. At buoyed entrances from seaward to bays, sounds, rivers, or other estuaries for which specific lines are not established, International Rules apply outside of a line roughly parallel with the trend of the shore, drawn through the outermost buoy or other aid to navigation of any system of aids.

2. *Inland Rules and Pilot Rules*—These apply on waters inside the above-mentioned boundary lines of the high seas, except (a) the Great Lakes and connecting and tributary waters, and the St. Lawrence River as far east as Montreal; (b) the Red River of the North; (c) the Mississippi River and its tributaries above Huey P. Long Bridge; and (d) that part of the Atchafalaya River above its junction with the Plaquemine—Morgan City alternate waterway.

3. *Great Lakes Rules and Pilot Rules for the Great Lakes*—These apply on the Great Lakes and connecting and tributary waters, and on the St. Lawrence River as far east as Montreal.

4. *Western River Rules and Pilot Rules for Western Rivers*—These apply on the Mississippi River and its tributaries above Huey P. Long Bridge, the Red River of the North, and that part of the Atchafalaya River above its junction with the Plaquemine—Morgan City alternate waterway.

5. *The Motorboat Act of 1940*—In addition to the rules outlined above for various waters, motorboats must also comply with provisions of the Motorboat Act. Rules in this act apply to motorboats on navigable inland waters of the United States, including the Great Lakes, and rivers emptying into the Gulf of Mexico. Requirements for lights and signals apply to all motorboats, in their respective classes and as defined by the act, when operating in these waters. They do not apply on the high seas, subject to International Rules. Motorboats, like other vessels, observe the rules of the road governing the particular waters in which they happen to be operating.

Comparison of the rules reveals that, in a given situation, International Rules might, for example, require one signal, Inland Rules another, and Great Lakes Rules and Western River Rules may omit the situation entirely. In other cases, rules to cover a given situation might be entirely different in each of the four jurisdictions.

The publications giving the full text of the rules and regulations include:— 1. CG-169 Rules of the Road—International-Inland; 2. CG-172 Rules of the Road—Great Lakes; and 3. CG-184 Rules of the Road—Western Rivers. (These formerly were commonly referred to as the "Pilot Rules" for these waters. The titles were changed in 1959.)

These are Coast Guard publications, available free from Coast Guard Headquarters, or the nearest Marine Inspection Office of the Coast Guard.

It would take a sizable volume to present in detail all the points of conflict between the various rules. However, a digest of some of the highlights is of considerable interest, emphasizing to all boatmen the existence of such discrepancies, and the necessity of understanding rules applicable to the body of water you happen to be navigating, if collision is to be avoided, and safety afloat assured.

Less than 1 percent of all collisions, reports the Coast Guard, have occurred with both vessels acting in compliance with the rules. They lay stress on certain fundamental ideas which should form the basis of any consideration of the rules. A collision approach, they point out, is not the time or place to study the rules; hence the importance of knowing them before an emergency arises. When a situation is met calling for application of the rules, they must be obeyed until the vessels are finally past and clear.

They cite five important points to be borne in mind: (1) the rules, as a whole, are not optional but mandatory; (2) they must be obeyed promptly; (3) they apply alike to all vessels; (4) court interpretations have modified many of the rules; and (5) vessels are governed by the particular rules which apply in the geographical location where they find themselves at the time of an approaching situation.

And here are four cardinal points in the prevention of collision. Motor boatmen will do well to heed them. (1) keep proper lookout; (2) take bearings to determine whether risk of collision exists; (3) carry proper lights; and (4) use the prescribed whistle signal. Failure to give whistle signals is one of the commonest causes of collision.

Reduced to simplest terms, there are eight general instances in which the various rules may be said to reflect uniformity in underlying principle:

(1) Approaching steam (power-driven) vessels, in good visibility, may be classified as meeting, overtaking, or crossing.

(2) Right of way as between approaching sailing vessels is determined by their courses relative to the wind direction.

(3) Vessels are said to be meeting when their courses

are opposite, or within a point or two of opposite. Vessels may meet at bends though they first sight each other at right angles. Vessels meeting should pass port to port, except where a starboard-to-starboard passing would be safe without changing course. Before passing port to port, change of course at a safe distance is required.

, (4) An overtaking vessel is one proceeding on a course within six points of the same direction as a slower vessel ahead. The overtaking vessel, under all rules, is burdened and must keep clear. The principle of privilege and burden is evident in all rules.

(5) Steam (power-driven) vessels are said to be crossing when one approaches the other on either side in the arc between meeting and overtaking—from a point or two on the bow to two points abaft the beam. All rules require the privileged crossing vessel (having the other on her own port hand) to keep her course and, in three out of the four jurisdictions, to hold her speed, until definite remedial action is imperative. The burdened vessel must keep clear, avoid crossing ahead and, if necessary, slow down, stop or reverse. When in dangerous proximity, both must take positive action to avert collision.

(6) Though differing radically in the fog signals themselves, rules agree that in thick weather signals must be given on the whistle, siren, or fog horn, and these signals must be given at frequent intervals. Speed in fog must be moderate, and collision averted by stopping, not

dodging. When fog signals are heard ahead, speed must be reduced.

(7) All rules recognize that there may be situations where conditions are such that departure from the rules is necessary. This is covered in the Rule of Special Circumstances, which authorizes departure from the rules, only to avoid imminent danger, and only to the extent that such departure is necessary.

(8) The rules are also uniform in requiring the exercise of good seamanship, covered in a general precautionary rule.

These, then, are the broad points of similarity in principle common to all the rules. What are some of the fundamental differences in detail, which give rise to confusion when passing from one jurisdiction to another? The most important differences are in the use of whistle signals (both clear weather and fog) and in lights and day signals prescribed for certain classes of vessels in the various jurisdictions.

WHAT WHISTLE SIGNALS MEAN (EXCEPT FOG SIGNALS)

Whistle equipment prescribed under International, Inland and Western River Rules consists of a whistle or siren for steam (power-driven) vessels; a fog horn for sailing vessels and vessels towed. On the Great Lakes, steam vessels require a whistle (steam or substitute); sailing vessels, a fog horn. On Western Rivers, a compara-

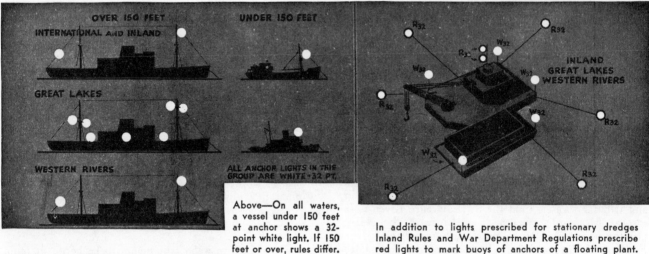

Above—On all waters, a vessel under 150 feet at anchor shows a 32-point white light. If 150 feet or over, rules differ. Under International and Inland Rules, they display another white light aft. On the Great Lakes, two white lights are carried horizontally, both fore and aft, plus white lights every 100 feet along the deck. Western River Rules, effective January 1, 1949, now require the second white light, as on the high seas and inland waters

In addition to lights prescribed for stationary dredges Inland Rules and War Department Regulations prescribe red lights to mark buoys of anchors of a floating plant. Or, the dredge may throw a light on buoys when vessels approach. This applies on all except the high seas and certain waters of New York Harbor. International Rules make no mention of this case, but a dredge could throw a searchlight on the mooring buoys as required

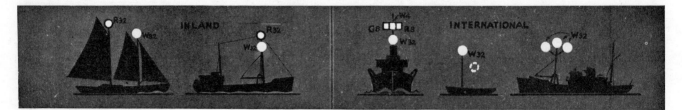

Above—On inland waters vessels trawling, dredging or fishing with nets or lines out show a red light 6 to 12 feet vertically above a white light. (At anchor, fishing vessels in all waters, with gear attached, display only white anchor lights, except that on the high seas extra white lights are shown, as indicated in the caption at the right.) When under way and not fishing, such vessels show the same lights as other vessels under way

Above—A power-driven trawler on the high seas carries a tri-colored (red-white-green) lantern forward, and below it a white light. Her 12-point white stern light, showing aft, is not visible in this view. Fishing boats, with lines or nets extending less than 500 feet, show one all-around white light. Another is shown, in the direction of their gear, to approaching vessels. When gear extends more than 500 feet they show three white lights in a vertical triangle

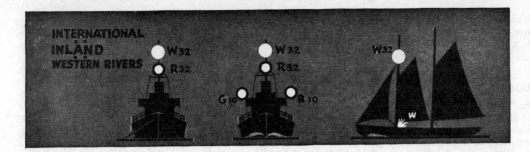

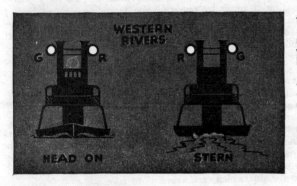

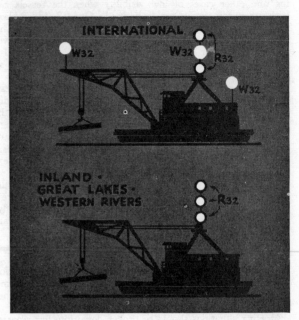

Left—Under International, Inland and Western River Rules, the steam (power-driven) pilot vessel on station shows a white light above a red light. When not at anchor, she also shows side lights. Sailing pilot vessels have a white masthead light and exhibit a flare-up at short intervals. Great Lakes Rules do not provide for pilot vessels. International Rules require all pilot vessels at anchor to show anchor lights also

Below—Western River rules make special provision for "river steamers", that is, a river-type steam vessel with two smokestacks in an athwartship line. They may carry, in lieu of the usual lights of a steam vessel underway, a red light on the outboard side of the port smokestack and a green light on the outboard side of the starboard smokestack. These lights show forward, aft and abeam on their respective sides. Under Western River rules, a seagoing steamer carries the lights required of her by International Rules, and steam vessels in general, other than those specially provided for, are lighted as under Inland Rules

Right — Except on the high seas, vessels moored or anchored, laying pipe or operating on submarine construction or excavation, show three red lights in vertical line. Under the new International Rules, three vertical lights (upper and lower red; middle one white) are shown by a vessel laying cable, working on aids to navigation, or on surveying or underwater operations. Appropriate anchor lights are also shown, when at anchor

tively new requirement (from which motor boats used for pleasure are exempt) is an amber visual signal synchronized with the whistle blasts. Motorboats, under the terms of the Motor Boat Act, carry a whistle, horn, or other sound-producing mechanical device. Class A (less than 16 feet) is exempt; regulations specify whether it must be mouth-, hand-, or power-operated in Classes 1, 2, and 3. The bell, when required, is used in fog.

Under the International Rules power-driven vessels, under way, when in sight of one another, must use prescribed signals of one, two, or three short (1 second) blasts to indicate their course when taking any action prescribed by the rules. Thus, a power-driven vessel will blow 1 short blast to indicate she is changing her course to starboard; 2 if she is directing her course to port; 3 if her engines are going astern. This applies in meeting, overtaking, and crossing situations, regardless of the bearing of the other vessel and whether or not the other is a power-driven or sailing vessel. One- and 2-blast signals thus are rudder signals to be used each time the vessel changes course. The 3-blast signal is required, not only when engines are going at full speed astern, but at any speed astern, or whenever the vessel is making sternway. As a warning signal, to attract attention, a vessel may use a flare-up light or detonating signal, such as a gun.

Under Inland Rules, steam vessels under way when in sight of one another, also blow the 3 short blasts when engines are going at any speed astern, or when the vessel is making sternway. On the other hand the 1 or 2 short blast signals must be given, and answered, when steam vessels approach from any direction within ½ mile of each other. Change of course in these cases is irrelevant. Proper signals for meeting, overtaking, and crossing are prescribed and these will be discussed later. Inland Rules

also provide for an optional warning signal (flare-up light or detonating signal) to attract attention.

The danger signal is now used on all waters in some form, both in clear weather and in fog. It consists of 4 or more short blasts (under Inland and Western River Rules) given when the course or intention of an approaching vessel is in doubt. On the Great Lakes, the danger signal is now 5 or more short and rapid blasts, and if vessels are within ½ mile of each other, both must reduce speed to bare steerageway and, if necessary, stop and reverse. On the high seas, a power-driven vessel required to hold her course and speed may give 5 short, rapid blasts on the whistle if in doubt as to whether an approaching vessel is taking necessary action to avert collision. All except International Rules have an express provision against cross signals (answering 1 blast with 2, and vice versa) and call for the danger signal in such cases.

No provision is made in Western River Rules for a "long" blast signal, found nearly alike in Inland and Great Lakes Rules. The long blast (8 to 10 seconds) is in the nature of a warning, sounded when nearing a bend or curve where an approaching vessel could not be seen at a distance of ½ mile. The long blast must be answered by any approaching steam vessel within hearing, after which the usual meeting and passing signals are exchanged, when vessels come in sight of each other. Inland and Lake Rules also prescribe the long blast as a warning signal when steam vessels are leaving a dock or berth. When clear of the berth, in sight of other vessels, passing whistle signals are exchanged. If backing out of a berth, the long blast is followed by 3 short blasts, as soon as another vessel is in sight. (On the Lakes, rules now specify not a "long" blast, but one of at least 8 seconds duration.)

On Western Rivers, the new signal for vessels within 600 yards of a bend, or leaving a dock, is three distinct blasts.

New International Rules provide a "prolonged" (4- to 6-second) blast when a vessel arrives within ½ mile of a bend, to be answered by other vessels within hearing.

WHEN TO GIVE PASSING SIGNALS

IT is important to note that passing whistle signals on the high seas are given only when (and always when) there is a change of course if any other vessel is in sight.

Inland Rules require passing whistle signals to be given only when vessels are in sight of each other, and there is risk of collision; in fog and other cases of low visibility when the vessels cannot see each other, fog signals are to be used. One-, 2- and 3-blast signals may be used in fog only after vessels sight each other. The danger signal, of course, may be used properly in fog or clear weather as necessary. Under Inland Rules, the 1- or 2-blast signal must be exchanged whenever steam vessels approach within ½ mile (or sooner), regardless of change of course.

On the Great Lakes, passing signals are given in all weathers regardless of visibility, before vessels meet or pass within a distance of ½ mile of each other, if risk of collision is involved. On the theory that a 1-second blast is considered too short for passing signals, Lakes rules now require "distinct" blasts, not "short." Three blasts on the Lakes is not a signal when reversing; it signifies a steam vessel under way in a fog. On the Lakes, signals must be exchanged whether or not either vessel changes her course.

On Western Rivers, as on the Lakes, the passing whistle signals are given in all weathers, regardless of visibility, and care must be used to sound the proper signal if a vessel is not distinctly visible. Where possible, signals must be exchanged before vessels are within ½ mile of each other.

WHEN STEAM (POWER-DRIVEN) VESSELS MEET

THE meeting, overtaking, and crossing situations have already been touched upon in respect to the meaning of the signals under the various sets of rules. Other aspects of each of these situations will now be discussed in turn.

Meeting situations should be broken down into five separate cases: (1) exactly head on (2) slightly port-to-port, but without safe clearance (3) port-to-port with course far enough apart for clearance without changing course (4) slightly starboard-to-starboard, but without safe clearance, and (5) starboard-to-starboard, with courses far enough apart for safe clearance without changing course. In the first four cases, all rules require a port-to-port passing. Only in the fifth case is a starboard-to-starboard passing permissible. In cases requiring a turn to starboard it is imperative that, long before any danger of collision exists, the pilot should decide, with the aid of bearings, on which side he is to pass, signal promptly accordingly, and change course at the same time. In open water this means a definite and ample change of course which cannot be misunderstood; in narrow channels it means moving promptly to the proper side of the channel as far as safety permits.

In meeting situations, vessels are not required to hold their course and speed. On the contrary, they are required to change course and reduce speed when safety demands. Danger signals should be blown if a signal is not agreed to, if a vessel repeatedly fails to answer or appears to be making the wrong maneuver, or if she is unable to obey the rule, as, for example, if her rudder jams.

We have previously indicated that short blast whistle signals on the high seas are basically rudder signals, evidencing change of course. When power-driven vessels meet end on, or nearly so, on the high seas, in such a manner as to involve risk of collision, each alters course to starboard and blows one short blast to indicate her change of course. If a second change of course were required, she would signal again. If courses were so far to starboard of each other that no course change was needed, no signal would be given.

Now, under Inland, Lake, and River Rules, the situation is different. Here rules prescribe that when two steam vessels meet head-and-head (end on or nearly so) they shall pass port side to port side and exchange one short blast. If the courses are so far to starboard of each other as not to be considered a head-and-head meeting, then they pass starboard-to-starboard and exchange two short whistle blasts. If they pass port-to-port, and do not change course, they still exchange one short blast. In short, except on the high seas, the signals are given, whether or not there is a change of course. (For simplicity, the "distinct" Lakes and River signal is here considered short, though not 1 second.)

Under Western River Rules, vessels pass on the side determined by the descending steam vessel.

Meeting in Narrow Channels

INTERNATIONAL and Inland Rules both contain a provision that in narrow channels steam (power-driven) vessels must, when safe and practicable, keep to the starboard side.

When steamers meet in narrow channels where there is a current, Great Lakes rules give right of way to the less-maneuverable descending steamer, and she is required to signal which side she elects to take, before they approach within ½ mile of each other.

On Western Rivers, the rules also give the right of way to the (privileged) descending steamer, but require the ascending (burdened) vessel to signal first, to be answered by the same signal from the descending steamer unless the latter regards passing, on the side indicated, as dangerous. In that case, she blows the danger signal of 4 or more short blasts, which the ascending steamer must answer in kind, after which both are stopped and backed if necessary, until signals for passing are given and answered. After the danger signal is exchanged, the descending steamer indicates on which side she wishes to pass and the pilot of the (burdened) ascending steamer must govern himself accordingly. Signals, where possible, must be exchanged before the vessels have approached within ½ mile of each other. Unless they do complete their understanding of intended action while still a great distance apart, a hazardous situation is created.

In narrow channels, River rules also provide for the right of way of descending steamers by requiring the ascending steamer to stop below the entrance of a narrow channel till a descending steamer has passed through. If they unavoidably meet in a narrow channel, the ascending steamer signals and then lies at the side of the channel with bare steerageway while the descending steamer is worked carefully by. When meeting near a bridge span, if the descending steamer deems it dangerous to pass between bridge piers, she sounds the danger signal, which the ascending steamer must answer in kind, slowing or stopping until the (privileged) descending steamer has passed through.

When two steam vessels meet at the confluence of two (Western) rivers, the steam vessel which has the other to port must give the first signal. In no case, however, may pilots of steam vessels attempt to pass each other until there has been a thorough understanding as to the side which each vessel is to take.

Passing Dredges, Vessels Aground, Etc.

RECENTLY the Pilot Rules for Inland Waters were amended, modifying regulations having to do with whistle signals required when passing floating plants, dredges, etc., working in navigable channels. Similar regulations of the Department of the Army make them effective also on the Great Lakes and Western Rivers.

Essence of the new regulations is to the effect that vessels intending to pass such floating plants, when within 1 mile, shall blow a long blast of the whistle. The dredge responds with the correct passing signal so as to direct the approaching vessel to the proper side for passing, which signal is returned by the approaching vessel. If the channel is not clear, the dredge blows a danger signal, whereupon the approaching vessel must slow down or stop, and await further signals from the dredge.

If the pipe line of a dredge obstructs the channel in such a way that it is not safe for an approaching vessel to pass around it, the dredge will sound the danger signal, open the pipe line and give the correct passing signal.

A special signal is also provided in Great Lakes Rules for St. Mary's River only, when a vessel is aground in a channel. Such a vessel sounds not less than 5 short and rapid blasts, upon the approach of another vessel bound up or down the channel. If the approaching vessel cannot pass with safety, she must stop and avoid fouling the grounded vessel, and sound the same signal to any vessel coming up astern of her. If additional vessels approach from the same direction, the last vessel in line sounds this signal. When visibility is low, fog signals are also sounded.

THE OVERTAKING SITUATION

THE overtaking situation differs from the meeting situation in that an overtaking vessel may pass on either side, if safe; and the overtaking vessel is burdened and must keep clear by slowing down, stopping, or reversing, while the overtaken vessel is privileged and must hold her course and speed (a privilege she exercises until the other vessel is finally past and clear.) In open water a wide berth should be allowed when overtaking; in narrow channels it should not be attempted unless safe, having due regard for the effect of a vessel's suction in shallow water.

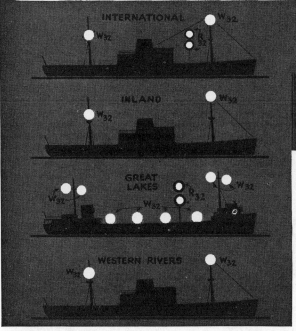

ALL WATERS

LOWER WHITE (BOW) LT. 20 PT.
UPPER WHITE (RANGE) LT.:
INTER. 20 PT. — INLAND 32 PT.
SIDE LIGHTS 10 PT.

Left—Five types of meeting situation: 1. Port to port, with clearance without change of course. 2. Port to port, without safe clearance. 3. Exactly head on. 4. Starboard to starboard, without safe clearance. 5. Starboard to starboard, with clearance without change of course. On all waters, in all cases except number 5, meeting vessels must pass port to port. Range lights indicate approaching vessel's heading. On the high seas, after range light is now mandatory on power-driven vessels, except for those under 150 feet, or vessels towing

Right—Head-on and port side views of a seagoing power-driven vessel under way. Ocean-going vessels lighted according to International Rules are not required to change lights when navigating waters tributary to the high seas. Thus, in any waters, the seagoing vessel would be lighted as shown. Her 12-point white stern light is not visible from abeam. On Great Lakes, 32-point white range light is required on vessels over 100 feet

ALL WATERS

INTERNATIONAL

INLAND

GREAT LAKES

WESTERN RIVERS

Above—A moored dredge, under International Rules, shows three lights in vertical line (one white between two red), also appropriate anchor lights. The scow alongside carries a similar white light. The two red lights, shown in other waters by the dredge, are used on the high seas by a vessel not under command

INLAND
GREAT LAKES
WESTERN RIVERS

Above—A dredge held stationary by moorings or spuds, on all waters except the high seas, displays two vertical red lights in addition to white lights at each corner and white lights at outboard corners of the scow alongside. The red lights are shown 3 to 6 feet apart, and not less than 15 feet above the deck, displayed where they may best be seen

Above—A steam (power-driven) vessel (over 150 feet) aground in various waters. She carries lights of a vessel at anchor except for two additional red lights required under International and Great Lakes Rules. All vessels aground use them on the St. Mary's River; vessels over 65 feet on the Lakes. On Western Rivers, lights would be same as in Inland Rules

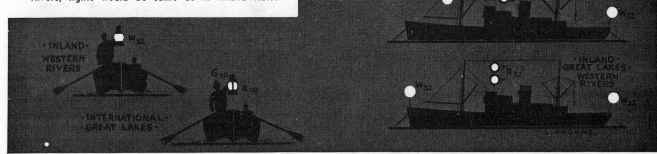

INLAND
WESTERN RIVERS

INTERNATIONAL
GREAT LAKES

INTERNATIONAL

INLAND
GREAT LAKES
WESTERN RIVERS

Above—Under International and Great Lakes Rules, a vessel of less than 20 tons, under oars, would keep at hand a lantern with green glass on one side and red glass on the other, showing it to avert collision. International Rules also provide for rowboats (as distinguished from a vessel of less than 20 tons under oars) which show a white light. Inland and Western River Rules require rowboats, under oars or sail, to show a white light

Above—Vessels on all waters except the high seas made fast alongside or moored over a wreck on the bottom, partly submerged or drifting, show a white light from bow and stern of each outside vessel (where several are at work) and two red lights in vertical line. On the high seas, she would display the lights of a vessel engaged in underwater operations—one white between two red, vertically arranged. If not drifting, anchor lights are shown also

A vessel is considered to be overtaking when she comes up from a direction more than 2 points abaft the beam of another, and if there is any doubt, the overtaking vessel should conduct herself as an overtaking vessel. Furthermore she must not alter course or speed in such a way as to embarrass the overtaken vessel, even after she has passed.

On the high seas, an overtaking vessel uses her 1- and 2-blast signals in accordance with the general rule which requires 1 blast when she alters her course to starboard, 2 blasts when she turns to port. She does this not only when she makes her initial change of course, but also when she turns to get back on course after passing. The overtaken vessel, holding course and speed, does not reply to the signals, and the overtaking vessel would also remain silent if no course change were required.

Under Inland Rules, when an overtaking vessel, approaching within ½ mile, wishes to pass, whether changing course or not, she sounds 1 short blast if she wishes to pass on the starboard side of the vessel ahead, or 2 short blasts if she wishes to pass on the port side of the vessel ahead. Rules require the overtaken vessel to answer with similar signals if she wishes to agree to the proposed passing. But if she does not think the passing safe, she must not blow a cross signal; instead she would use the danger signal which would keep the overtaking vessel astern until passing was safe, and proper signals had been exchanged. Should the overtaken vessel use a danger signal to indicate that she considers passing on the side first proposed unsafe, she may follow it with a contrary signal to indicate that passing on the opposite side is agreeable.

Assent to a passing signal never relieves the burdened overtaking vessel from keeping clear, and when she returns to her course she does not whistle as she would under International Rules.

Essentially, the rules for the overtaking situation are the same on the Great Lakes and Western Rivers as in the Inland Rules except, of course, that use of the danger signal would now require 5 short blasts on the Lakes. There is also a provision in Great Lakes rules which, in channels less than 500 feet wide, prevents a steam vessel from passing another going in the same direction unless the latter is disabled or signifies her assent to the passing.

STEAM (POWER-DRIVEN) VESSELS CROSSING

As an aid in analyzing the crossing situation with a view to understanding it, it is suggested that there are, in essence, only two types of crossing situation. First, where you look to starboard, in any direction from a few degrees on the bow to 2 points abaft the starboard beam, and see another steam (power-driven) vessel crossing your own course from right to left. At night, a red side light would be visible, accompanied by one or more white lights. No green light would be visible. Here you are burdened—you must keep clear; you must not cross the other vessel's bow; if necessary, you must slow down, stop, or reverse. Usually the best action is to swing to starboard and pass well astern of the other vessel; the other alternative would be to slow down so the other vessel may maintain her course across your bow. The burdened vessel must never cross the bow of the privileged vessel. The taking of continuous bearings in a situation like this is of the greatest importance. If the bearing does not change, collision is certain.

The other kind of crossing situation would be one in which you look to port, in any direction from a few degrees on the bow to 2 points abaft the port beam and see another power-driven vessel crossing your own course from left to right. At night, you would see a green light, and one or more white lights, but no red light.

Here you are the privileged vessel. You have the right of way. Under all rules you must hold your course and speed (except on Western Rivers where you must hold your course). It is only by adhering to this regulation that the burdened vessel will know how to act in keeping clear.

We have already explained how, under International Rules, a privileged vessel holding her course and speed has no duty to blow a whistle signal. However, if circumstances arise where a collision would be inevitable if she held on, then she must take action to avert collision. Under the new International Rules, a warning signal is now provided for a power-driven vessel required to hold her course and speed. If she is in doubt that the burdened vessel (which must be in sight) is taking sufficient action to avert collision, she may give at least 5 short (1-second) rapid blasts on the whistle. This calls attention of the burdened vessel to her obligations under the rules. The burdened vessel, in most normal crossing cases, would blow 1 short whistle blast as she altered her course to starboard when passing astern of the privileged vessel, but here too if she alters course a second time or reverses, it must be accompanied by the appropriate whistle signal blast (2 if she turns to port, 3 if she reverses).

In a crossing situation on inland waters, 1 short blast signifies that the (privileged) steam vessel to starboard of the burdened vessel, will hold her course and speed. Though the privileged vessel should blow first, either may. If signals are misunderstood, or if immediate compliance with the signals is not possible, the danger signal (4 or more short blasts) is blown and both vessels stop and back if necessary until proper signals are made and understood. Thus, though the privileged vessel would normally hold her course and speed, she is obliged to take remedial action if signals are misunderstood. When a burdened vessel receives the 1-blast signal in a crossing situation, she properly replies with 1 blast and keeps out of the way by passing astern of the privileged vessel, which may necessitate her changing her course to starboard, slacking speed, stopping, or reversing.

The necessity of exchanging 1-blast signals on inland waters is an aid to the privileged vessel in knowing when the burdened vessel is failing in her duty to give way.

Broadly, Great Lakes Rules are in agreement with Inland Rules on crossing situations. Formerly, on the Great Lakes, the privileged vessel was required to blow "one blast," to be answered by "one short blast" from the burdened vessel. By recent amendment, the signal is now one "distinct" blast. Again, on the Lakes, the danger signal, if used, would be 5 or more short blasts. Though whistle signals are required on the Lakes in fog as well as clear weather, there is no obligation to hold course and speed till vessels are in sight of each other. Rather the obligation is to reduce speed and proceed with caution.

On Western Rivers, either vessel may signal first with one "distinct" blast, which is to be answered with a similar blast. However, a steam vessel with tow descending a river has right of way over any steam vessel crossing the river, and gives, as a signal of her intention to hold on across the bow of the other vessel, 3 distinct blasts, to which the crossing vessel must immediately reply.

SPECIAL RULES—ST. MARYS RIVER

Special anchorage and navigation requirements for the St. Marys River, in Michigan, supplement the general rules and regulations applicable to vessels on the Great Lakes. These are set forth in a separate section of the Great Lakes Pilot Rules.

Right of Way; Distress Signals; Special Circumstances; Day Marks

RULES governing actions of vessels in fog concern themselves with the proper signals to be given both when under way and at anchor, and the subject of moderate speed. The common theory underlying rules in all jurisdictions is that vessels must run at moderate speed, and avoid collision by stopping, not dodging. Moderate speed, according to the courts, means bare steerageway when visibility ahead is little or nothing; when visibility is an appreciable distance, it means such a speed as will enable a vessel to stop in half the distance of visibility. On high seas and inland waters engines must be stopped on hearing a fog signal forward of the beam. On Great Lakes and Western Rivers speed must be reduced to bare steerageway (on the Lakes, if the signal appears to come from within 4 points of ahead.)

International and Inland Rules require as fog signal equipment on steam (power-driven) vessels a whistle or siren (sounded by steam or substitute for steam), a fog horn, and bell. Under International Rules the fog horn must be mechanically operated. Sailing vessels of 20 gross tons or over carry a fog horn and bell. Under Great Lakes Rules steam vessels carry a whistle (sounded by steam or substitute for steam) audible 2 miles, and a bell. Sailing vessels carry a fog horn and bell. On Western Rivers, steam vessels have a whistle or siren, and bell; sailing vessels a fog horn (and bell, if over 20 gross tons).

Motor boats (except Class A, under 16 feet) under the Motor Boat Act, carry an efficient whistle or other sound-producing mechanical appliance. This is used for fog signals as well as passing signals. Motor boats of Class 2 and Class 3 carry an efficient bell. The fog horn is not required on any motor boats.

Courts have ruled that fog signals are proper when

RULES IN FOG

visibility falls below two miles, the required visibility of side lights. Fog signals are proper not only in fog, but also in mist, falling snow, and heavy rain-storms, by day or night. Under International and Inland Rules, the "prolonged" blast called for in fog signals means from 4 to 6 seconds duration. With respect to motor boats, however, 2 seconds is considered prolonged. A sailing vessel may use either short or prolonged blasts in fog.

Courts have decided that the danger signal is a fog signal as well as a clear weather signal. In inland waters, therefore, it should be used whenever approaching signals of another vessel would indicate impending collision.

Steam Vessels Under Way

On the high seas, the fog signal for a power-driven vessel under way is 1 prolonged blast of the whistle or siren at intervals of not more than 2 minutes. Under Inland Rules she would sound 1 prolonged blast, but at intervals of not more than 1 minute. On the Great Lakes she sounds 3 distinct blasts

The square flag and ball (above or below the flag) are now (since recent amendments to Great Lakes rules) recognized as a daytime distress signal by all except Inland Rules. However, the International Code Signal NC—illustrated at the right—is not recognized under Great Lakes or Inland Rules, though specifically provided for under International and Western River Rules

Illustrating the difference in lighting of the last canal boat, scow or barge in tandem tows

INTERNATIONAL and GREAT LAKES (left)—Regardless of type, the last vessel towed carries colored side lights, and shows a white light to overtaking vessels. On the high seas, this white stern light must be fixed, 12 point

INLAND (left center)—Here the last canal boat and barge carry colored side lights and two 32-point white lights aft, horizontally arranged. The scow carries a white light at each end

WESTERN RIVERS (below)—In these waters, the last barge carries a white light forward and at each corner aft. So do canal boats and scows, being included in the definition of "barge"

NOTE:—For the Gulf Intracoastal Waterway and certain adjacent waters, provision is made for vessels in tow in a separate section of the Inland Rules.

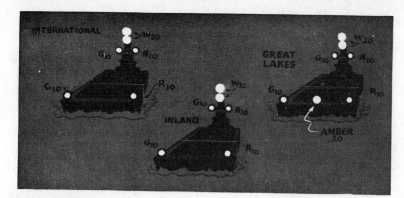

Above: Two tandem barges pushed ahead. Tugs display side lights and towing lights. On Western Rivers, lights of tug and tow are the same as shown for Great Lakes except that, instead of the 20-point white lights, the tug has two amber lights vertically arranged, visible from aft, not forward of the beam. The 20-point amber light at the head of the tow, in the centerline, is required on the Western Rivers and Gulf Intracostal Waterway, optional on the Lakes. Barges are lighted as one vessel. Instead of white 32-point towing lights aft, the inland tug might carry two 20-point white towing lights forward and two 12-point amber lights aft, vertically arranged, not visible forward of the beam

Right: A tug with steamship in tow. In every case, the ship towed shows her side lights and no white lights (except for the white light shown to overtaking vessels, or fixed stern light on the high seas). The ocean-going tug, in addition to side lights, has two towing lights because only one vessel is in tow. The inland tug has three towing lights because her tow is astern. (Optionally, these may be 32 or 20-point, and range lights also are optional.) Vessels towing may carry a small white light abaft the funnel or aftermast for the tow to steer by (not visible forward of the beam). On the high seas, they must carry the towing light or fixed 12-point white stern light

vessels under way. They prescribe, at intervals of not more than 1 minute, 1 blast on the fog horn when on the starboard tack; 2 blasts in succession when on the port tack; and 3 blasts in succession when the wind is abaft the beam. (Great Lakes Rules conform to the above only when the vessel is not in tow.) On Western Rivers sailing vessels give signals prescribed for steam vessels, but use the fog horn.

Vessels at Anchor

In all waters, the bell is used as a fog signal by vessels at anchor. Under International, Inland and Western River Rules, it is to be rung rapidly for 5 seconds, at intervals of 1 minute. On the Great Lakes it is rung rapidly for 3

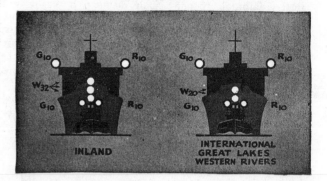

on her whistle at intervals of not more than 1 minute (except when she has a raft in tow). On Western Rivers her signal would be 3 distinct blasts every minute (2 of equal length, followed by a longer one).

International Rules (only) also provide for the power-driven vessel under way, but stopped, and having no way upon her. Here the signal is 2 prolonged blasts (with 1-second interval between)

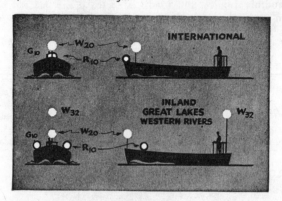

Left: A 40-foot motor launch. Except on the high seas, she carries the lights of a Class 3 motor boat. Being under 40 tons, under International Rules she may carry a combined red-and-green lantern and, above it, a 20-point white light. The fixed white 12-point stern light, now required by International Rules, is not visible from abeam

to 5 seconds at intervals of 2 minutes. In addition, a signal is sounded every 3 minutes on whistle or horn—1 short, 2 long, 1 short blasts in quick succession. (The same signal is used by vessels aground in or near a channel or fairway.) On the high seas, a vessel aground gives 3 strokes on the bell before and after the regular anchor signal.

On the high seas, a vessel at anchor in a fog, in order to give an approaching vessel more definite warning of her position, may give, in addition to the usual bell signals, a sound signal of three blasts—1 short, 1 prolonged, 1 short.

Vessels Towing or Towed

On the high seas, a vessel when towing, or when employed in laying or picking up a telegraph cable or navigation mark, and a vessel under way which is unable to get out of the way of an approaching vessel through being not under command, or unable to maneuver, would sound 1 prolonged blast on the whistle followed by 2 short blasts. A vessel towed gives 1 prolonged blast, followed by 3 short blasts—on the whistle or fog horn. (Despite the provision above for the vessel not under command, it is held that if the vessel broken down is a steam vessel she must use the

Above: Rules for all waters are fairly consistent in requiring sailing vessels under way to show colored side lights, and a white light aft. On the Great Lakes the stern light is a flare-up; on other waters it must be fixed, 12-pt.

at intervals of not more than 2 minutes. This signal must not be used except on the high seas. With respect to the interval between signals, this is a maximum interval; in heavy traffic they should be given more frequently.

Sailing Vessels Under Way

International, Inland, and Great Lakes Rules are fairly uniform with respect to fog signals for sailing

Except on the high seas, a single black ball is the day mark of a vessel over 65 feet in length anchored in a fairway or channel. On the high seas, it is used on all vessels at anchor, regardless of length. On inland waters it may be used by a steam vessel under sail only

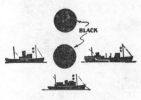

Two black balls, on the high seas, identify the vessel not under command. It is also used on the Lakes by vessels over 65 feet. On all waters other than the high seas, it is the day mark of a self-propelling suction dredge with suction on the bottom. Inland Rules also provide for this day mark for a Coast and Geodetic Survey vessel at anchor in a fairway. Three black balls, on the high seas, indicate a vessel aground (also used on Great Lakes, if over 65 feet in length)

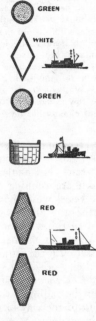

Inland Rules, only, provide a special day mark for the Coast and Geodetic survey vessel under way and engaged in hydrographic surveying. This is a white diamond, and above and below it a green ball

On the high seas (or any waters navigable by sea-going vessels) vessels fishing with nets, lines, trawls, or other gear, under way, display a basket in the rigging

Except on the high seas, steamers, derrick boats, lighters and other vessels made fast alongside, or moored over, a wreck display two red shapes, each double frustums of a cone, base to base

2 prolonged blast signal if she loses all headway at sea but does not come to anchor—that is, the signal for steam vessels under way, but having no way on.)

Under Inland Rules, a steam vessel towing also uses the signal of 1 prolonged blast followed by 2 short blasts, and the vessel towed may give the same signal on the fog horn. Analyzing these rules, it will be noticed that, on the high seas, the towing signal is used by either a steam or sailing vessel towing. In inland waters, a sailing vessel towing would give the customary signals of a sailboat without a tow.

On the Great Lakes a steamer towing a raft sounds at intervals of not more than 1 minute a screeching or Modoc whistle for from 3 to 5 seconds. Any vessel being towed sounds 4 bells at intervals of 1 minute (2 in quick succession, followed by 2 more after an interval, in the manner that 4 bells would be struck to indicate time).

On Western Rivers, a steam vessel towing sounds 3 distinct blasts of equal length, at intervals of not more than 1 minute.

Miscellaneous Craft

International Rules provide that sailing vessels, seaplanes, and boats of less than 20 gross tons are not obliged to give the regularly prescribed fog signals but, if they do not, they must make some other efficient sound signal at intervals of not more than 1 minute. Fishing vessels of 20 gross tons or more, with nets or lines out, sound a fog signal of 1 blast followed by ringing of

the bell. In the case of a steam vessel the blast is from her whistle or siren; if a sailing vessel, from her fog horn. They may also substitute a blast of a series of alternate notes of higher and lower pitch. Fishing vessels and boats of less than 20 tons need not make these signals but, if they do not, they must make some other efficient sound signal at intervals of not more than 1 minute.

Inland Rules contain a provision for rafts and other water craft navigating by hand power, horse power, or the current of a river. They sound a blast on a fog horn, or equivalent signal, at intervals of not more than 1 minute.

On the Great Lakes, vessels under 10 registered tons need not give prescribed signals but, if they do not, must make some other efficient sound signal at intervals of not more than 1 minute. Produce boats, fishing boats, rafts, and other craft navigating by hand power, horse power or by current of the river, or anchored or moored in or near a channel or fairway and not in any port, not otherwise provided for in the rules, sound a fog horn or other equivalent signal at intervals of not more than 1 minute.

An old regulation requiring miscellaneous nondescript craft on Western Rivers to sound a foghorn, "which shall make a sound equal to a steam whistle" has been omitted in new Rules.

On Western Rivers, steamers lying to during fog or thick weather, when another steamer is heard approaching, give 1 tap on the bell if lying on the right bank (facing downstream), 2 taps if lying on the left bank, at intervals of not more than 1 minute. The signals are continued until the approaching steamer has passed.

On the Great Lakes and Western Rivers, signals for meeting and passing are also used in foggy weather, in addition to the special fog signals prescribed.

Lower left: Day marks are not provided in the rules for minesweepers, but the naval services in all waters use three black balls, one each at the masthead and spreader ends

Right: Except on the high seas (and certain waters in and adjacent to New York Harbor) barrels or buoys are used to mark bow, stern, and breast anchors of floating plant moorings

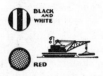

On all waters except the high seas, two red balls are the day mark of a dredge held stationary by moorings or spuds

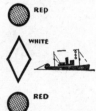

Except on the high seas, a vessel moored or anchored and engaged in laying pipe or operating on submarine construction or excavation displays two balls, the upper having black and white vertical stripes, the lower red

On the high seas, the day mark shown above (white diamond between red balls) is used by vessels laying or picking up telegraph cable, working on aids to navigation, or engaged in surveying or underwater operations

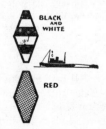

On waters other than the high seas, a vessel with submerged object in tow uses a day mark consisting of two shapes; these are double frustums of a cone, base to base. The upper has horizontal black and white stripes; the lower is red

RIGHT OF WAY

Rules of the road recognize the basic idea that risk of collision in any given situation will be minimized if one of two vessels is privileged and the other burdened, the privileged vessel being under obligation to continue exactly what she is doing until the vessels are past and clear, the burdened vessel to take positive action to keep out of the way. However, though a vessel may be "privileged," her obligation to hold course and speed is as definite as that of the burdened vessel to keep clear, reduce speed, and avoid crossing ahead.

Circumstances may sometimes arise, due to thick weather or other causes, when a collision would be inevitable if the privileged vessel continued to hold her course and speed too long. Consequently, when a privileged vessel finds herself in such a situation, she is required to take any other action

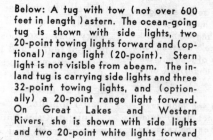

Below: A tug with tow (not over 600 feet in length) astern. The ocean-going tug is shown with side lights, two 20-point towing lights forward and (optional) range light (20-point). Stern light is not visible from abeam. The inland tug is carrying side lights and three 32-point towing lights, and (optionally) a 20-point range light forward. On Great Lakes and Western Rivers, she is shown with side lights and two 20-point white lights forward

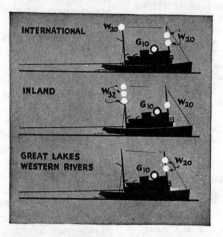

Above: A tug with more than one vessel in tow (length of tow over 600 feet). The ocean-going tug carries three towing lights in addition to her side lights. (Optional after range light is not showing here.) Stern light is not visible from abeam. The inland tug, since the tow is astern, is lighted the same as when her tow is under 600 feet. On Great Lakes and Western Rivers, too, the fact that her tow is over 600 feet in length does not change her lighting

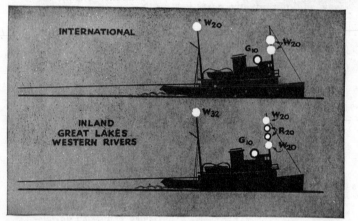

Above: A tug with submerged tow. On the high seas her lights are the same as though her tow were on the surface. Her 12-point white stern light or towing light is not visible from abeam. In other waters, she carries two red lights between two white lights in vertical line, in place of her usual towing lights, and also side lights. On inland waters, she may also carry the optional range light aft (shown)

that will best help to avert collision, and this action must be taken just as soon as she sees that the giving way of the burdened vessel alone will not of itself prevent collision. This is true in all waters.

In the matter of right of way, International and Inland Rules are identical in intent, if not exactly in terminology. Under both sets of rules, in any situation where one vessel is directed to keep out of the way, the privileged vessel must keep her course and speed, while the burdened vessel keeps clear by slackening speed, stopping, or reversing, not by crossing ahead.

On the high seas and inland waters alike, when steam (power-driven) vessels are on crossing courses, the vessel which has the other on her own starboard side is burdened and must keep clear. Overtaking vessels are burdened.

When sailing vessels approach one another, so as to involve risk of collision, right of way is determined as follows: (1) A vessel running free keeps out of the way of a vessel close-hauled. (2) A vessel close-hauled on the port tack keeps out of the way of a vessel close-hauled on the starboard tack. (3) When both are running free, with the wind on different sides, the vessel which has the wind on the port side keeps out of the way of the other. (4) When both are running free, with the wind on the same side, the vessel to windward keeps out of the way of the vessel to leeward. (5) A vessel with the wind aft keeps out of the way of the other vessel.

Sailing vessels invariably have right of way over steam vessels, except in the rare case when the sailing vessel is overtaking. All vessels must keep out of the way of fishing vessels, though fishing vessels have no right to obstruct fairways.

Seaplanes on the water are subject to International Rules, though it should be remembered that they may not be able to change their intended actions at the last moment. They must keep clear of all vessels, but when danger of collision exists, they must comply with the rules.

On the Lakes

On the Great Lakes, the rules governing right of way are substantially the same as those outlined above for both the high seas and inland waters. The privileged vessel holds her course and speed and the burdened vessel keeps out of the way, slackening speed, stopping or reversing as necessary. The special provision in Lakes rules, giving right of way to a descending steamer in narrow channels with a current, has already been discussed in connection with whistle signals.

With respect to right of way as between sailing vessels, Great Lakes Rules omit the fifth provision noted above which requires a vessel with the wind aft to keep out of the way of the other vessel.

On Western Rivers

Western River Rules differ from all others in that they require a privileged vessel to hold her course, but not her speed. In fact, every steam vessel approaching another vessel so as to involve risk of collision is obliged to slacken her speed or if necessary stop and reverse.

The provision granting right of way on Western Rivers to a descending steamer has also been mentioned in the discussion of whistle signals. In other than the cases just noted, River Rules are practically in agreement with the International with respect to the principle of right of way.

SPECIAL CIRCUMSTANCES

ONE point where all four sets of rules are in agreement is in the general prudential rule, or rule of special circumstances, which authorizes (in fact, requires) departure from the rules in order to (and only to) avoid immediate danger. The rule reads: "In obeying and construing these rules due regard shall be had to all dangers of navigation and collision, and to any special circumstances which may render a departure from the above rules necessary to avoid immediate danger.

Courts have laid emphasis on the words "immediate danger" in rendering their decisions, the principle being that rules must not be abandoned whenever perceptible risk of collision exists, but only when imperatively required by special circumstances in order to avoid immediate danger.

The courts have recognized five cases where the rule of special circumstances is properly invoked, as follows:

(1) Where vessels get so close that collision is inevitable unless preventive action is taken by both.

(2) When physical conditions prevent compliance with the rules. The example cited is that of a tug with tow astern running down a river in a swift current, meeting a free vessel crossing the river. The tug and tow, in such an unusual circumstance, would necessarily be granted the right of way, regardless of ordinary rules.

(3) When more than two vessels are involved in an approaching situation. In such a case, one or more of the vessels might be unable to obey the regular rules, as there may be a conflict between her duty to one vessel and her duty to another. Prompt, intelligent use of whistle signals is often a solution in such cases, with care that one vessel does not accept a signal intended for another. At the first evidence of confusion, every vessel must slow down and take any other action that will help to avert collision.

(4) Where a situation is not covered in the rules, as when one vessel is backing toward another. International and Inland Rules provide only for the 3 short blast whistle signal when a vessel is backing, and say nothing of passing signals for vessels going astern. In practice, the stern is usually regarded as the bow in such a case as it enables a vessel to determine what passing signals she should propose in inland waters. When one or both vessels approach on a collision course stern first, the rule of special circumstances replaces regular rules for meeting and passing.

(5) When one steam (power-driven) vessel proposes an action contrary to the rules and the other vessel agrees to the proposal. Examples of this would be a crossing situation where vessels exchanged 2 blasts and the burdened vessel attempted to hold her course across the bow of a privileged vessel, or a starboard-to-starboard passing when vessels meet head-and-head. Out of such cases have arisen the following decisions: A proposal to proceed contrary to law is not binding on the other vessel. Unless and until such a proposal is agreed to, both vessels must proceed in accordance with the regular rules. When such a proposal has been agreed to, neither vessel has right of way and both are equally bound to proceed with caution under the rule of special circumstances.

GOOD SEAMANSHIP

THE rule of good seamanship, binding on all vessels on all waters, states that "Nothing in these rules shall exonerate any vessel, or the owner or master or crew thereof, from the consequences of any neglect to carry lights or signals, or of any neglect to keep a proper lookout, or of the neglect of any precaution which may be required by the ordinary practice of seamen, or by the special circumstances of the case."

Good seamanship requires the exercise of any required precaution in addition to mere observance of the rules. With regard to the keeping of a proper lookout, courts have said that this means at all times when under way. The lookout must be an experienced seaman, alert and vigilant; he must have no conflicting duties; and he must be stationed as low down and as far forward as possible. If necessary, more than one lookout must be posted. Proper lookout, it is ruled, is a matter of good ears as well as good eyes. The Supreme Court has judged the duty of a lookout to be one of the highest importance.

DISTRESS SIGNALS

INTERNATIONAL Rules provide the following methods of indicating distress:

(1) A gun or other explosive signal at intervals of about 1 minute.

(2) Continuous sounding of any fog signal apparatus.

(3) Rockets or shells, throwing red stars fired one at a time at short intervals.

(4) Signal by radiotelegraphy, or other method, consisting of the group . . . — — — . . . in the Morse Code.

(5) Signal by radiotelephony consisting of spoken word "Mayday."

(6) The International Code signal NC.

(7) A signal consisting of a square flag and above or below it a ball, or something resembling a ball.

(8) Flames on the vessel (as from a burning oil or tar barrel).

(9) A rocket parachute flare showing a red light.

• NOTE: Radio signal (12 dashes sent in one minute—each dash 4 seconds, each interval 1 second) has been provided to actuate auto-alarms of other vessels.

Inland Rules combine (1) and (2) above in prescribing, as a daytime signal, the continuous sounding of any fog signal apparatus, or the firing of a gun. These two signals are also recognized in Inland Rules as acceptable by night, as well as flames on the vessel, as from a burning tar or oil barrel, as in International Rule (8) above.

Great Lakes Rules provide for (1), (2) and (7) of the International Rules (above) by day; and, at night, (1), (2), (3) and (8).

Western River Rules provide for (1), (3), (6) and (7) of the International Rules (above) by day; and, at night, (1), (3), and (8). In addition to the use of a fog signal apparatus, by day or night, Western River Rules include the continuous sounding of a steam whistle.

All except International Rules recognize a new signal: slowly and repeatedly raising and lowering arms outstretched to each side.

Special distress signals for airplanes down at sea and for submarines are used by the Navy both on the high seas and in inland waters. While these are not statutory, they should be understood, so that proper assistance may be rendered—by going immediately to the aid of an airplane, or by communicating at once with the nearest Coast Guard Air-Sea Rescue or Naval Station in the case of a submarine.

A submarine unable to surface fires a bomb which, at an altitude of 100 to 200 feet above the surface, explodes and releases a parachute with a red smoke bomb. A yellow smoke bomb (not a distress signal) warns surface vessels when a submarine is about to surface.

Very signals are used by airplanes forced down on navigable waters, with the following significances: White—"Slight damage, no assistance needed." White and green—"Stand by, may need assistance." Green alone—"Need mechanic and tools, stand by." Red—"Send assistance to save personnel."

MISCELLANEOUS RULES

THERE are a number of special rules which are specifically written into Inland, Great Lakes, and Western River Rules, and, though not expressly provided for in International Rules, vessels on the high seas would nevertheless observe them in following the rule of good seamanship. Among these are the following:

When passing floating plants, vessels are required to reduce speed to insure safety (not more than 5 m.p.h. when passing within 200 feet). Passing over lines of such plants, engines must be stopped, while light draft vessels are required to keep outside buoys marking the ends of mooring lines of a plant working in the channel.

Flashing the rays of a searchlight or other blinding light onto the bridge or into the pilot house of any vessel under way is prohibited. Lights not required by law, which would interfere with distinguishing the signal lights, must not be shown. Unnecessary whistling within any harbor limits of the United States is also prohibited. Violation of any of these rules may lead to revocation or suspension of a pilot's license or certificate.

Failure to have the required "Rules of the Road" pamphlet (which replaced old "Pilot Rules" as of May 1, 1959) on board and readily available (when practicable) on vessels and craft over 65 feet in length while on Inland Waters and Western Rivers, or two copies of the placard form CG-807 while on the Great Lakes, may be grounds for assessment of a $500 penalty.

In all waters, in case of collision, vessels must stand by to render assistance. Masters or persons in charge are required to give the vessel's name, her port, and ports from and to which she is bound.

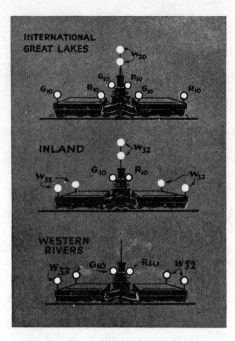

Lights displayed by a tug with one scow on each side. Note that each scow, on the high seas, carries both red and green lights, as distinguished from practice on Western Rivers. The fixed white stern lights on tug and tow are not visible from ahead. On inland waters, the scow's lights are white; the tug is shown with two 32-point white lights, the usual practice, though optionally the towing lights might be 20-point. Optionally, she might in the illustration also have a 20-point white range light forward, though it is neither required nor forbidden. Tows on the Gulf Intracoastal Waterway carry the same lights as they do under Western River rules. The tug, on Western Rivers, has two amber lights aft, vertically arranged, not visible forward of the beam

Lights for Vessels—
On the High Seas,
Inland Waters,
Great Lakes,
And Western Rivers

Steam (Power-driven) Vessels Under Way

Under International Rules, a power-driven vessel under way carries a white 20-point (225°) light forward (20 to 40 feet above the hull); red and green 10-point (112½°) side lights (with 36-inch screens); and a white 20-point (225°) range light aft (at least 15 feet higher than the foremast light). Horizontal distance between masthead lights (which must be in line with, and over, the keel) must be at least 3 times the vertical distance. A fixed 12-point (135°) stern light, showing aft, is now mandatory. (The 20-point white masthead light aft is optional on vessels under 150 feet, and vessels towing.)

Under Inland Rules, a steam or motor vessel under way (excepting seagoing vessels, ferry boats and motor boats) shows a 20-point white light forward; 10-point red and green side lights (with 36-inch screens); and a 32-point white range light aft at least 15 feet higher than the foremast light. Overtaken vessels, except steam vessels with 32-point after range light, show a white light or flare-up.

On the Great Lakes, a steam vessel under way carries the

Vessel at Anchor or Aground

WITH respect to the carrying of lights at night, rules are fairly uniform in requiring them to be carried in all weathers from sunset to sunrise. The word visible as applied to lights mentioned in the rules means visible on a dark night with a clear atmosphere. No other lights which can be mistaken for the prescribed lights may be exhibited.

In all waters, a vessel less than 150 feet in length displays forward, not more than 20 feet above the hull, one 32-point white light when at anchor, visible at least 1 mile (2 on Western Rivers and the high seas). Under International and Inland Rules, a vessel over 150 feet displays a 32-point white light forward (20 to 40 feet above the hull) and another 32-point white light aft (at least 15 feet lower than the forward light). On the high seas, these must be visible 3 miles. In anchorage areas specially designated by the Secretary of The Army vessels under 65 feet need not show anchor lights.

On the Great Lakes a vessel over 150 feet in length at anchor would carry two white 32-point lights forward (at the same heights as mentioned above) and two white 32-point lights aft. These are horizontally arranged athwartships (at least 10 feet apart) in such a manner that one or both will be visible from any direction at a distance of 1 mile. In addition, at intervals of 100 feet, she carries white 32-point deck lights not less than 2 feet above the deck.

On Western Rivers, vessels over 150 feet carry the white light forward where it can best be seen, and aft another white light, at least 15 feet lower, both visible at least 2 miles.

With a few exceptions, a vessel aground shows the lights prescribed for her when at anchor. Under International Rules, in addition to the anchor light (or lights) she would also show the two vertically arranged red 32-point lights of a vessel not under command. Great Lakes Rules provide that vessels aground, over 65 feet in length, must show the two red vertical lights, except on the St. Mary's River where they are shown regardless of length.

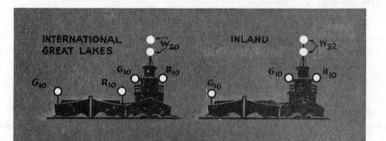

A tug with barge or canal boat alongside, her side light not obscured by the tow. Though Inland Rules do provide for white lights for scows alongside, no lights are specified for canal boats and barges alongside unless they obscure the tug's side light. It is held that, in such a case, it is proper for the tow to be lighted the same as though the tug's side light were obscured. On the Great Lakes, a canal boat shows only the outer side light, whereas a barge shows both. On Western Rivers, lights would be the same as shown for Inland Waters, except that the tug's white lights would be replaced by 12-pt. amber ones, not visible forward of the beam and tow would show white lights on outboard corners, as on the Intracostal Waterway

20-point white light forward, and 10-point red and green side lights (with 36-inch screens). The forward light is carried higher than the side lights. Steam vessels under 100 feet in length also carry a 32-point bright white light aft, in line with the keel and higher than the white light forward. Steamers over 100 feet carry a 32-point white range light (at least 15 feet higher than the bow light and at least 50 feet abaft it). Optionally, the range light may be replaced by two lights not more than 30 inches apart horizontally, "one on either side of the keel," arranged so that one or both will be visible from any angle.

Ocean-going steamers, when under way on Western Rivers, carry the lights required by International Rules.

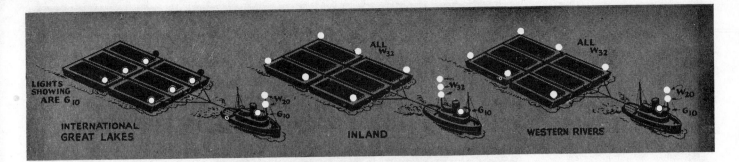

INTERNATIONAL GREAT LAKES

INLAND

WESTERN RIVERS

Above: A tug with scows astern, three abreast in two tiers. Note colored side lights on the tow on the high seas and Great Lakes, white lights on other waters. Three towing lights on the inland tug indicate tow is astern. (Optional range lights not shown)

Right: A tug with tow alongside, her side light obscured. On the high seas and Great Lakes, the tow is also carrying a 10-point red light on the port side, not visible here. In all waters, a side light must show on the outer side of the tow. Inland tug is showing optional range light. (White stern lights required on high seas not visible in these views.) On Western Rivers, white lights are carried on outboard corners of tow, side lights only if tug's colored side lights are obscured

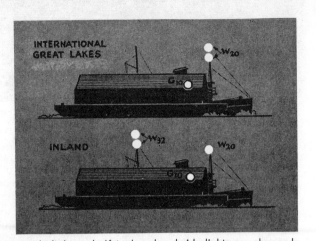

INTERNATIONAL GREAT LAKES

INLAND

INTERNATIONAL

INLAND · GREAT LAKES WESTERN RIVERS

Above: On Western Rivers, the tug carries side lights and, aft, two red lights, vertically arranged, not visible forward of the beam

Left: Except on the high seas, double-ended ferries carry a central range of two white 32-point lights at equal height fore and aft, in addition to side lights. On the high seas, they use a set of range and side lights each way, and 12-point stern light

larger craft. If they do not, then they are lighted as follows:—

Power-driven vessels under 40 tons carry forward (at least 9 feet above the gunwale) a 20-point white light and red and green side lights, or in lieu of separate red and green lights a combined red-and-green lantern, carried not less than 3 feet below the white light. Small motor craft, such as are carried aboard sea-going vessels, may carry the white light less than 9 feet above the gunwale, but in that case rules specify it must be above the combined red-and-green lantern.

Vessels under oars or sails of less than 20 tons carry ready at hand a lantern with green glass on one side and red glass on the other shown, with the colored lights on the proper sides, at the approach of other vessels.

Small craft on the high seas, if unable to carry a fixed white 12-point stern light showing aft, may show an electric torch or lighted lantern to approaching vessels. Rowboats on the high seas show a white lantern in time to prevent collision.

Great Lakes Rules also have a provision for open boats, which are permitted to carry, instead of regular side lights, a lantern with red and green slides, to be shown when other craft approach. They show a white light at anchor, and may use a flare-up if necessary.

Lights Required by Motor Boat Act

Motor boats (including auxiliaries) on the navigable waters of the United States must be lighted in accordance with the Motor Boat Act of 1940, rather than Pilot Rules pertaining to any one of the four geographical jurisdictions thus far discussed. "Navigable" waters, under Federal jurisdiction, are those navigable to the sea, or waterways crossing state or international boundaries.

Briefly, under the terms of the Act, motor boats (vessels propelled by machinery not more than 65 feet in length, excepting tugs and towboats driven by steam) are divided into four classes determining, among other things, how they are to be lighted. Classification is by length, as follows:

Class A, under 16 feet; Class 1, 16 to 26 feet; Class 2, 26 to 40 feet; and Class 3, 40 to 65 feet.

Classes A and 1, instead of a white bow light, carry a combination red-and-green light forward (each color showing through the customary 10 points), and a 32-point white light aft higher than the combination light.

Classes 2 and 3 carry a white 20-point bow light, screened separate 10-point red and green side lights, and 32-point white light aft higher than the bow light.

A motor boat under sail is lighted as a sailboat,

River steamers navigating waters subject to Western River Rules carry a red light on the outboard side of the port smoke pipe and a green light on the outboard side of the starboard smoke pipe, showing forward and abeam on their respective sides.

Steam vessels, other than those expressly provided for, are required under Western River Rules to carry lights similar to the usual lights of a steam vessel on inland waters.

There is no provision in Rules of the Road for the Great Lakes to permit seagoing vessels to display lights required by International Rules while navigating the Lakes.

International and Inland Rules both provide that a vessel may, if necessary to attract attention, show a flare-up or use any detonating signal that cannot be mistaken for a distress signal.

Small Vessels Under Way

All rules uniformly provide that on small vessels when, due to bad weather, it is impractical to keep side lights in their fixed positions, they may be kept lighted and at hand, ready to be displayed at the approach of other vessels.

Under International Rules, power-driven vessels under 40 gross tons, vessels under oars or sails under 20 tons gross, and rowboats need not carry the lights required of

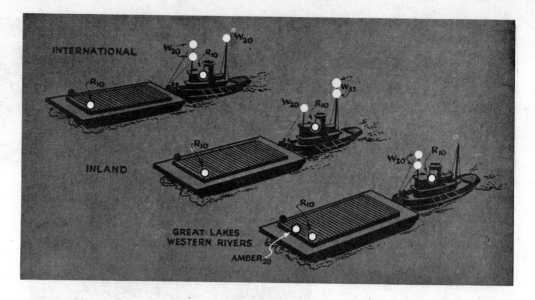

On inland waters, a tug pushing her tow ahead must now carry two white towing lights the same as if her tow were alongside. She is shown here with optional 20-point range light. The ocean-going tug is also shown carrying the optional 20-point range light, but her required white stern light is not visible in this view. In all cases, the tow displays colored side lights forward. The amber bow light is now required on Western Rivers and Gulf Intracoastal Waterway, and optional on the Great Lakes

showing colored side lights and she is now required to carry a 12-pt. white light aft. Motorboats under sail and power both are now lighted like motorboats of their respective classes. Under the amended Motor Boat Act, motorboats may, optionally, carry lights prescribed by International Rules.

White lights prescribed for motor boats must be visible at least 2 miles, colored lights at least 1 mile. Outboards are required to carry the appropriate lights of their class, depending on length. At anchor, motor boats show a single white 32-point light, the same as other vessels. On the high seas motor boats would be lighted according to International Rules.

Steam (Power-driven) Vessels Towing

A power-driven vessel towing, on the high seas, carries red and green side lights and two white 20-point towing lights forward in vertical line not less than 6 feet apart, the lower not less than 14 feet above the hull. She must carry either a small white light aft (not visible forward of the beam) for the tow to steer by, or a fixed 12-point

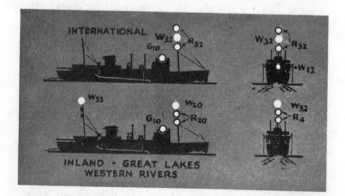

Above: On the high seas, a self-propelling suction dredge under way with suction on bottom would show in addition to side lights, three vertical lights (one white between two red), and a 12-point white stern light. On other waters, besides running lights, they have two red 20-point lights below the 20-point white masthead light, and two red 4-point lights showing astern

Right: The distinguishing lights of the minesweeper are the three green 32-point lights at the masthead and spreader ends. She also shows towing light. Optionally, she might show a range light

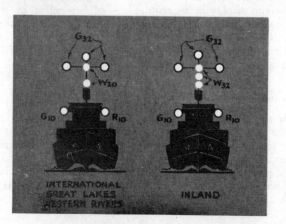

(135°) white stern light. She may also carry the 20-point after range light provided for a power-driven vessel under way. If carried, it should be high enough above the towing lights so as not to be mistaken for another towing light. If there is more than one vessel in tow and the length of tow from the stern of the tug to the stern of the last vessel exceeds 600 feet, she carries three white 20-point towing lights instead of two.

On inland waters vessels towing, in addition to side lights, carry two vertical white towing lights if the tow is alongside or ahead, and three if the tow is astern (regardless of the length of the tow or number of vessels composing it). The towing lights may be 20-point, carried forward, or 32-point, carried aft. Range lights are neither required nor forbidden, but when 20-point towing lights are carried forward, a 32-point range light aft is desirable, not only because it provides a range but because it is visible from aft. To prevent confusion, a range light (whether it is carried forward or aft) should be placed so that the vertical distance between it and the towing lights is at least twice as much as the interval between towing lights. Otherwise it might be mistaken (when seen from dead ahead) as a third towing light, when in fact only two are being carried.

Tugs showing a 32-point light aft (either towing lights or range light) are not required to show the white light or flare-up light usually required of overtaken vessels.

On the Great Lakes a steam vessel with a tow (other than a raft) carries, in addition to her side lights, two 20-point white towing lights forward in vertical line (at least 6 feet apart). Aft she carries a small white light (not visible forward of the beam) for the tow to steer by. On the Lakes she is similarly lighted when towing a raft, except that the two towing lights forward are 32-point, and are carried in a horizontal line athwartships (at least 8 feet apart).

On the Lakes, harbor tugs under 100 tons net register, when not towing, carry red and green side lights, and a 20-point white light at the foremast head or on top of the pilot house. When towing (except a raft) they carry an additional 20-point white light at least 3 feet vertically above or below the 20-point headlight. When towing a raft, the two headlights are 32-point instead of 20-point, horizontally arranged athwartships not less than 4 feet apart.

On Western Rivers, steam vessels towing one or more vessels on a hawser astern carry in addition to their sidelights two 20-point white lights on the foremast, vertically arranged. When the tow is alongside or ahead, they show, instead of the white lights, two amber lights aft, vertically arranged, not visible forward of the beam.

When the tow is submerged, towing vessels on the high seas are lighted the same as when their tow is on the surface. On all other waters, Inland Rules and War Department Regulations require her to substitute for the white towing lights four 32-point lights vertically arranged—the upper and lower white, the two middle ones red.

Sailing Vessels Under Way

ON all waters, sailing vessels under way carry the red and green side lights, and show a white light aft. Under new Inland and Western River Rules, this white light must be a fixed 12-point light showing aft except that small boats, in bad weather, may show an electric torch or lighted lantern to overtaking vessels. Under Great Lakes Rules sailing vessels under way show "a lighted torch on that point or quarter to which such steamer shall be approaching." On the high seas, a fixed white 12-point stern light is now mandatory.

Vessels Being Towed

WITH the exception of barges, scows, and canal boats (for which special lights are prescribed) vessels in tow are almost uniformly lighted like the sailing vessel—with side lights and the white light shown aft. The special lights for barges, scows, and canal boats are prescribed by the Commandant of the Coast Guard. Since these regulations are applicable only on inland waters, the Great Lakes and Western Rivers, it follows that on the high seas every vessel in a tow (whether she is steam, sail, or not self-propelled) must show red and green side lights. The last vessel in a tow, under new International Rules, must carry a fixed white 12-point light aft. Others may carry the fixed light or a small white towing light.

A special section of the Inland Rules is devoted to lights for barges, canal boats, scows and other vessels of nondescript type in tow on the Gulf Intracoastal Waterway.

Barges and Canal Boats, Towed Astern—Inland Waters (Except New York Harbor and Vicinity, Hudson River, Lake Champlain, East River, Long Island Sound, and Certain Gulf Intracoastal Waters)

ON inland waters, with the exceptions noted above, barges and canal boats, towed astern singly or in tandem, each carry red and green side lights and a 12-point white light on the stern. The last vessel in the tow (or the only one, if there is but one) carries, instead of the 12-point light, two white 32-point lights horizontally arranged athwartships. When two or more boats are abreast, the colored side lights are carried on the outboard bows of outside boats, and each outside boat in the last tier carries a 32-point white light on the stern. White stern lights for boats other than the last are 12-point.

Under Inland Rules, tows on the Gulf Intracoastal Waterway now carry the same lights as prescribed for Western Rivers.

Barges, Canal Boats, and Scows, Alongside (Obscuring Side Lights)

WHEN the side lights of a towing vessel are obscured by such a craft alongside, the towed vessel carries a green side light if towed on the starboard side, a red side light if on the port side. If there is more than one towed boat abreast, the colored side light is displayed from the outer side of the outside boat.

In this situation (towing alongside and obscuring the towboat's side lights) and also when pushed ahead of the towboat, barges, canal boats and scows are lighted alike. When the tow is astern, scows are lighted differently from barges and canal boats.

Barges, Canal Boats, and Scows, Pushed Ahead

WHEN pushed ahead of a towboat, barges, canal boats, and scows show a red light on the port bow and green light on the starboard bow of the head boat. If there is more than one abreast, the lights are displayed from the outer sides of the outside barges. A tow boat pushing her tow in inland waters now carries the same towing lights she would show with tow alongside.

Barges, Canal Boats, and Scows, in Tow (In New York Harbor and Vicinity, Hudson River, Lake Champlain, East River, Long Island Sound, and Narragansett Bay)

IN these waters, to which special rules apply, all nondescript vessels such as barges, canal boats, scows, car floats, lighters, etc. are lighted alike.

When towed astern, singly, they carry a white light on bow and stern. In tandem, close up, each boat carries a white light on the stern and the first boat also carries a white light on the bow. In tandem, with intermediate hawser between boats in tow, each carries a white light on bow and stern, except the last which carries two white lights on the stern, horizontally arranged.

Seagoing barges are not required to change their seagoing (red and green) lights on entering these waters except that the last vessel in tow must display two white lights on the stern, horizontally arranged athwartships.

When towed at a hawser, two or more abreast, in one tier, each boat has a white light on the stern, and each outside boat has a white light on the bow. In more than one tier, every boat carries a white light on the stern and the outside boats in the head tier also carry a white light on the bow.

(All the white lights mentioned above are 32 point.)

When towed alongside, a white light is displayed at each outboard corner of the tow. When pushed ahead, a 10-point red light is carried on the port bow and a 10-point green light on the starboard bow of the head barge or barges.

Dump scows carrying garbage from New York Harbor waters to the high seas when in tandem carry red and green side lights and show a white light to overtaking vessels.

Barges and canal boats in tow, correctly lighted according to the rules of waters in which they are usually employed, need not change their usual lights if merely passing through the waters governed by these Inland Rules.

Canal Boats in Tow—Great Lakes

CANAL boats towed astern on the Great Lakes, singly or in tandem, carry colored side lights and a small bright white light aft. At a hawser in one or more tiers, two or more abreast, the starboard boat in each tier carries a green light on her starboard side and the port boat in each tier carries a red light on her port side, and each outside boat in the last tier carries a small white light aft. Towed alongside, a canal boat on the starboard side of a steamer carries a green side light; towed on the port side, she carries a red side light. With one boat on each side, the starboard boat carries a green light, the port boat a red light. The side lights mentioned, of course, are 10-point; the white light must not be visible forward of the beam.

On the Great Lakes specific provision is made as above for canal boats, but not for barges, scows, lighters and other nondescript craft in tow. Thus, they would carry the lights provided generally for vessels in tow which means colored side lights and a small bright white light aft.

When a tow is pushed ahead on the Great Lakes, red and green side lights mark the maximum projections to port and starboard, and a 20-point amber light may be carried forward, in the center line.

Rafts in Tow or Drifting or at Anchor in a Fairway

UNDER Inland Rules, vessels propelled by hand power, horsepower, or river current (except rafts and rowboats) carry one white light forward. Rafts of one crib in width carry one white light at each end. Rafts of more than one crib in width carry 4 white lights, one at each outside corner. Unstable log rafts of one bag or boom in width carry 2 to 4 white lights in a fore-and-aft line, one of which is at each end. If more than one bag or boom in width, they carry a white light on each outside corner. The white lights are all 32-point, carried at least 8 feet above water.

Barges, Canal Boats and Scows—Western Rivers

IN the new Western River rules (effective January 1, 1949) a "barge" is taken to include not only barges, but canal boats, scows, and nondescript vessels not otherwise provided for. In a tow of one or more barges pushed ahead, a 20-point amber light must now be carried at the extreme forward end of the tow, at the centerline, visible 2 miles.

In addition to the amber light, barges towed ahead carry colored side lights—red on the port bow, green on the starboard bow—to mark the outermost projections of the tow. Towed alongside, barges carry white lights at outside corners of the tow, colored side lights only if the side lights of the tug are obscured by deckhouses, etc. A single barge, towed astern, has a white iight at each corner. With two or more astern, with intermediate hawsers, the first barge has a white light at each corner of the bow, and one at the stern, amidships. Intermediate barges carry a white light bow and stern, amidships. The last barge has a white light forward, amidships, and a white light at each corner of the stern. For tows astern in tandem, close up, the arrangement is much the same except that intermediate barges have a single light aft, amidships. When in tiers astern, each outside barge in each tier has a white light at the outboard corner of the bow; in addition, outside barges in the last tier carry white lights at the outboard corners of the stern.

Naval Vessels

RULES are, broadly, in agreement in providing that nothing shall interfere with the operation of special rules made by the government of any nation with respect to additional station and signal lights for war vessels and ships in convoy, or with the exhibition of recognition signals by shipowners, authorized by their respective governments. Compliance with them is proper on all waters navigable by seagoing vessels, in accordance with terms of the enacting clause of International Rules. Under the provisions of this rule special lights have been prescribed for such craft as minesweepers which carry, in addition to side lights and towing lights, three 32-point green lights, one at the foremasthead and one at each yardarm.

On PT boats, landing craft and other naval vessels of special construction, where it is impossible to carry lights in prescribed positions, they are displayed in accordance with regulations issued by the Secretary of the Navy. Under such provisions the masthead light of a PT may be located in the after part of the vessel rather than forward.

Under all rules except the International, a special provision permits suspension of the exhibition of lights aboard vessels of war or Coast Guard cutters whenever, in the opinion of the Secretary of the Navy, the commander-in-chief of a squadron, or the commander of a vessel acting singly, the special character of the service may require it.

Pilot Vessels

ALL except Great Lakes Rules provide special lights for pilot vessels. A steam (power-driven) pilot vessel under way on station on pilotage duty carries a 32-point white light at the masthead and, 8 feet below it, a 32-point red light. These are in addition to the red and green side lights. At anchor, or course, side lights are extinguished.

A sailing pilot vessel carries a 32-point white light at the masthead and shows a flare-up at short intervals. (On the high seas, instead of a flare, a bright intermittent white light may be used on power-driven pilot vessels.) Side lights, when under way, are shown at the approach of other vessels.

If the pilot boat is of a type designed to go alongside a vessel to put a pilot aboard she may show the white light instead of carrying it at the masthead and also have a red-and-green lantern at hand to be shown as necessary.

Pilot vessels not engaged on station on pilotage duty carry the same lights as other vessels of their tonnage.

Revised International Rules specifically provide that all pilot vessels on station on duty at anchor must carry anchor lights in addition to their special lights.

On the Great Lakes no special rule is provided, so pilot vessels are lighted the same as other vessels of their class.

Fishing Vessels

UNDER new International Rules, vessels engaged in line fishing or fishing with drift nets are separated into two classes. When nets or lines extend less than 500 feet into the seaway they show one all-around white light. On the approach of another vessel, a second white light is shown in the direction of the fishing gear.

When the lines or nets of fishing vessels extend more than 500 feet into the seaway, revised rules require them to exhibit three white lights in a vertical triangle.

Power-driven trawlers show a tri-colored (red, white and green) lantern forward, and 6 to 12 feet below it, an all-around white light. They are also required to carry a white 12-point stern light showing aft. When a fishing vessel gets her gear fast to a rock or other obstruction at night, she would carry the anchor lights appropriate for a vessel of her size.

Under Inland Rules, fishing vessels of less than 10 gross tons, under way with no lines, nets, trawls, or other gear out, need not carry side lights but may have ready at hand a lantern with red glass on one side and green glass on the other to show to approaching vessels. Such a vessel over 10 tons would carry the usual lights of a vessel of her class under way.

When trawling, dredging, or fishing with any kind of dragnets or lines, fishing boats on inland waters exhibit a red light over a white light (6 to 12 feet apart vertically, and the horizontal distance, if any, is less than 10 feet). These are 32-point lights.

On the Great Lakes and Western Rivers fishing boats navigating bays, harbors, or rivers by hand power, horsepower, or river current, or at anchor in a channel, carry one or more white lights.

Seaplanes

SEAPLANES on the water on the high seas are now subject to International Rules. Seaplanes under way on the water carry forward, amidships, a 220° white light showing 110° each side from right ahead (visible 3 miles); on the starboard wing tip a 110° green light and on the port wing tip a 110° red light, each showing from right ahead to 20° abaft the beam on its respective side (visible 2 miles); and at the stern a white 12-point (135°) light showing 6 points (67½°) each side from right aft (visible 2 miles), carried at the approximate level of the side lights.

Vessel Not Under Command

UNDER International Rules (and Great Lakes, if vessel is over 65 feet) a vessel not under command, that is, not maneuverable, carries two red 32-point lights vertically arranged. If making way through the water such a vessel would also carry side lights.

On other waters vessels not under command cannot show the same signal, as two red lights in Inland Rules and War Department Regulations are reserved for a different use.

Vessel Working on Telegraph Cable

VESSELS laying or picking up telegraph cable on the high seas carry three 32-point lights in vertical line (at least 6 feet apart)—the upper and lower red, and the middle white. When making way through the water they also carry side lights.

On other waters, they carry three red lights in vertical line, 3 to 6 feet apart, with the lowest light carried at a height of at least 15 feet above deck.

Vessels Working on Buoys, Underwater Operations, Etc.

IN the revision of the International Rules, effective January 1, 1954, provision was made for types of vessels engaged in operations which would prevent their getting out of the way of approaching vessels. Rule 4 not only provides for vessels not under command but enlarges the scope of the rule applicable to vessels working on submarine cables (see paragraphs above).

On the high seas, a vessel engaged in laying or in picking up a navigation mark, or a vessel engaged in surveying or underwater operations, when from the nature of her work she is unable to get out of the way of approaching vessels, carries the same lights as one working on a submarine cable, that is, 3 lights in vertical line, the upper and lower red, the middle one white. When making way through the water, they also carry side lights. At anchor, they carry appropriate anchor lights as well as the distinguishing lights.

On other waters, specific regulations in Inland Rules and War Department Regulations, not binding on the high seas, cover such special types of vessels as dredges, those working on wrecks, etc. These are discussed in the following paragraphs.

Fixed White Stern Lights Required

PRIOR to August 14, 1958 some vessels, like sailboats under sail alone, were permitted the choice of showing a flare-up light to overtaking vessels. Since that date, Inland Rules and Western River Rules both require all vessels not otherwise required to carry a light visible from aft, to carry when under way a fixed 12-point white stern light showing aft. It is carried as nearly as possible at the level of side lights. Only exception is in the case of small vessels unable to do so, as in bad weather. They may show an electric torch or lighted lantern to overtaking vessels.

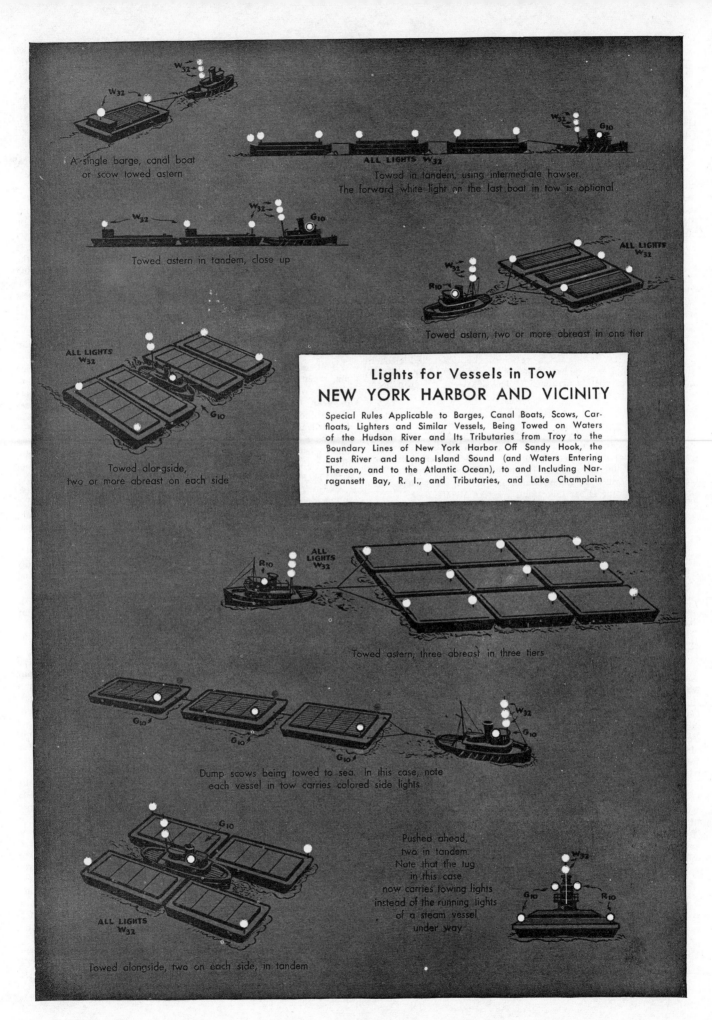

A single barge, canal boat or scow towed astern

Towed in tandem, using intermediate hawser. The forward white light on the last boat in tow is optional

Towed astern in tandem, close up

Towed astern, two or more abreast in one tier

Towed alongside, two or more abreast on each side

Lights for Vessels in Tow
NEW YORK HARBOR AND VICINITY

Special Rules Applicable to Barges, Canal Boats, Scows, Carfloats, Lighters and Similar Vessels, Being Towed on Waters of the Hudson River and Its Tributaries from Troy to the Boundary Lines of New York Harbor Off Sandy Hook, the East River and Long Island Sound (and Waters Entering Thereon, and to the Atlantic Ocean), to and Including Narragansett Bay, R. I., and Tributaries, and Lake Champlain

Towed astern, three abreast in three tiers

Dump scows being towed to sea. In this case, note each vessel in tow carries colored side lights

Pushed ahead, two in tandem. Note that the tug in this case now carries towing lights instead of the running lights of a steam vessel under way

Towed alongside, two on each side, in tandem

Moored Dredges

ON WATERS other than the high seas, by Inland Rules and War Department Regulations, dredges held stationary by moorings or spuds show a white 32-point light at each corner (at least 6 feet above deck) and in addition two vertical red lights (3 to 6 feet apart) not less than 15 feet above deck. Scows alongside would show a white light at each outboard corner (not less than 6 feet above deck).

Vessels Moored at Wrecks

INLAND RULES and War Department Regulations, binding on all except the high seas, require a vessel moored alongside or over a wreck (whether stationary or drifting) to show a white light from bow and stern of each outside vessel (not less than 6 feet above deck) and, where they can best be seen, two red lights vertically arranged (3 to 6 feet apart) not less than 15 feet above deck.

Vessels Engaged in Submarine Construction

EXCEPT on the high seas, vessels moored or anchored and engaged in laying pipe or cable, or operating on bank protection, submarine construction or excavation, show three red lights in vertical line (3 to 6 feet apart) not less than 15 feet above the deck.

Survey Vessels

ON INLAND WATERS a vessel of the Coast and Geodetic Survey at anchor in a fairway, engaged in surveying, would display two red lights vertically arranged (6 feet apart—or 3 feet, if necessary, on small craft).

Suction Dredges

SELF-PROPELLING suction dredges under way with suction on the bottom carry regular running lights. In addition, they carry two red 20-point lights vertically arranged under the 20-point white masthead light and aft two red 4-point lights to show astern. These are lights prescribed by Inland Rules, and also by War Department Regulations for the Great Lakes and Western Rivers.

Floating Plant Moorings

UNDER INLAND RULES, excepting certain waters in and adjacent to New York Harbor, anchors of a floating plant in navigable channels are marked by throwing a searchlight on their buoys when a vessel is passing, or the buoys may be lighted by red lights. Under War Department Regulations the same rule applies to the Great Lakes and Western Rivers. On the high seas, with no specific rule to cover the situation, white anchor lights on buoys would be proper and the searchlight may also be used, though not required.

Double-Ended Ferries

DOUBLE-ENDED FERRIES, on all except the high seas, carry a central range of two white 32-point lights at equal height fore and aft. In addition, they carry the usual red and green side lights. Amidships, 15 feet above the range lights, they may show an extra white or colored light designating the line. Single-ended ferries are lighted like other steam vessels. On the high seas a double-ended ferry would use one set of range and side lights each way, similar to the lights of other steam vessels under International Rules.

To Attract Attention

INTERNATIONAL and Inland Rules provide that any vessel may, to attract attention, show in addition to required lights a flare-up light or use any detonating signal that cannot be mistaken for a distress signal. This would be proper on any waters navigable by seagoing vessels.

DAY MARKS

JUST AS special lights characterize various types of vessels at night, so day marks prescribed by the rules indicate to other craft the nature of a vessel or the kind of work she is engaged in. There is a considerable difference in rules to be observed in waters under the various jurisdictions, the principal difference being between the International and all other rules.

Vessels over 65 feet in length, *anchored in a fairway* or channel, use a day mark consisting of one black ball or shape at least two feet in diameter. This is uniform on all waters except that on the high seas, this day signal is used by vessels at anchor regardless of length.

On inland waters, a *steam vessel under sail only* may use one black ball as a day mark.

On the high seas, a power-driven *vessel* when *propelled by both sail and machinery* carries forward a black conical shape, point upward.

On the high seas a *vessel not under command* carries, in vertical line, two black balls or shapes, each 2 feet in diameter. They are also carried on the Great Lakes but only by vessels over 65 feet.

On all waters except the high seas two black balls (at least 2 feet in diameter and 15 feet above the deckhouse) are the day mark of a self-propelling *suction dredge under way* with suction on the bottom.

Under Inland Rules only, two black balls (in vertical line 6 feet apart) are also used as a day mark by *survey vessels* of the Coast and Geodetic Survey at anchor in a fairway on surveying operations. If under way and engaged in hydrographic surveying they may carry three shapes in vertical line, the highest and lowest globular in shape and green in color, the middle one diamond in shape and white.

On the high seas, three black balls in vertical line are the day mark for a *vessel aground*. They are also shown on the Lakes, but only by vessels over 65 feet.

Boats or *vessels fishing* with nets, lines, trawls, or other gear out when under way on inland waters display a basket. If at anchor with gear out they show the basket toward the nets or gear. On the high seas, the basket is also used but in cases where lines or nets extend more than 500 feet, they show the basket forward and also a black conical shape, apex upward, where it can best be seen. When a fishing vessel gets her gear fast to a rock or other obstruction, revised International Rules require her to haul down the basket (day mark) and carry forward a black ball not less than 2 feet in diameter, the day mark of a vessel at anchor.

Steamers, derrick boats, lighters and other *vessels fast to a wreck,* alongside or moored over it, display two red shapes in vertical line, except when more than one vessel is at work, when the shapes are displayed from one vessel on each side of the wreck. These shapes are double frustums of a cone, base to base. The rules are uniform except on the high seas.

On all waters except the high seas *dredges held stationary* by moorings or spuds display two red balls in vertical line 3 to 6 feet apart, 15 feet above the deckhouse.

Under all rules except the International, a *vessel* moored or anchored and *engaged in laying pipe* or operating on submarine construction or excavation displays two balls in vertical line, the upper painted in black and white vertical stripes 6 inches wide, and the lower ball solid red.

A *vessel laying or picking up telegraph cable* on the high seas carries three shapes in vertical line, the highest and lowest globular in shape and red in color, the middle one diamond in shape and white. This International rule has been extended to apply to *vessels engaged in laying or picking up a navigation mark, or engaged in surveying or underwater operations.*

On waters other than the high seas, a Coast Guard vessel handling or *servicing aids to navigation* displays two orange and white vertically striped balls in vertical line.

Except on the high seas the day mark for a *vessel with submerged object in tow* is two shapes in vertical line. The shapes are in the form of double frustums of a cone, base to base. The upper is painted in alternate horizontal stripes of black and white 8 inches wide and the lower is solid red. Shapes are 2 feet in diameter (8 inches at the end of cones) and 4 feet from end to end. This case is not covered in International Rules.

Special provision is made for a *vessel towing a "dracone"* (a sausage-shaped envelope of strong woven nylon fabric coated with synthetic rubber). Strings of these dracones used as flexible "barges" to carry cargoes of petroleum products are towed astern on long hawsers, almost entirely submerged. The towing vessel uses a black flag as a daymark and the dracone tows a float also showing a black flag. At night the vessel towing carries ordinary towing lights and the dracone shows an all-around white light.

Bow, stern and breast anchors of *floating plant moorings* working in navigable channels (except on the high seas) are marked by barrels or buoys. Certain waters in and adjacent to New York Harbor are also excepted.

HOW many times have you heard a boatman, in describing his boat to a friend, remark that "she made 10 knots per hour on a measured mile," or perhaps, that his run from port to port was a distance of 12 knots? Often, no doubt.

As a matter of fact, a strict interpretation of his terms would be the equivalent of "she made 10 nautical miles per hour per hour." You see, the knot is a measure of speed, equal to one nautical mile per hour. Similarly, the second statement is not according to the best usage. The speaker should have said "12 nautical miles" because the knot isn't a measure of distance, in this sense.

Landsmen's terms grate hard sometimes on the ear of one trained to speak the language of the sea, who thinks naturally in nautical terms. When the guest who unnecessarily remarks that he doesn't know "the front from the back" of the boat, goes "downstairs" into what he is pleased to call the "kitchen" and adds insult to injury by calling the chart a "map," the boatman's re-action must be akin to that of the well-bred English professor who must listen to "ain'ts" and "he don'ts" hurled with reckless abandon into his learned conversation.

Landsmen are not the only offenders in the use of incorrect nautical terminology as our first reference to knots and miles shows. Few persons speak absolutely pure English—few are always precisely right in their seafaring language. The words carline and beam are often used interchangeably by men with a broad background of nautical knowledge, yet a distinction could be drawn in their meanings.

Within the limits of our space here, we hope to cover just as many as possible of the more common terms used aboard boats. We do not pretend to offer verbatim definitions as might be taken from a dictionary. Rather the sense will be condensed into the briefest possible terms for the benefit of those to whom sea language is still a jargon. This is done at the risk of being taken to task by hair-splitting "sea lawyers" who might feel that brevity leaves the explanation vague. Glossaries are available to those who wish precise, long-winded definitions.

The landsman guest previously referred to might have incurred less of his host's displeasure had he called the front and back of the boat, the *bow* and *stern,* respectively. *Port* and *starboard* (starb'd) are terms in constant use—port designating the left; starboard, the right side, facing the bow or, to express it otherwise, facing *forward.* Turning around and facing the stern, we look *aft.* The bow is the *fore* part of the boat, the stern the *after* part. When one point on the boat is further aft than another it is said to be *abaft.* Thus we might say that the deckhouse is abaft the main cabin. When an object lies on a line parallel to the keel we refer to it as *fore-and-aft,* as distinguished from *athwartships,* which is at right angles to the keel line. Planks in a deck run fore and aft; the beams supporting deck planks run athwartships.

The term *amidships* has a double meaning. In one sense, it refers to an object in the line of the keel, midway between the sides, as an engine is mounted amidships in the centerline over the keel. Often, however, it relates to something mid-way

CHAPTER V

Nautical Terms

(See also Nautical Dictionary, Pages 440x, 441–456)

between bow and stern. The galley, for example, might be located amidships, though off to the port or starboard side. The *midship section* would be the view of a boat presented by cutting it transversely through the middle.

To express the idea upward, overhead, or above the deck, one says *aloft.* *Below* means below deck. A seaman goes aloft in the rigging, below to his berth in the cabin.

We never say that a person is on or in a boat—rather, he is *aboard,* though *on board* is an alternate expression. *Inboard* and *outboard* draw a distinction between objects near or toward amidships and those which are out from the boat, away from the centerline. Inboard engines are those permanently installed within the hull; outboards being temporarily attached at the stern, outside the hull.

To convey the idea opposite or at right angles, we say *abreast.* An object at right angles to the centerline (keel) of the boat is *abeam.* If we draw ahead to a point where that object is midway between its position abeam and another directly astern, then it is *broad on the quarter,* starboard or port as the case may be. *Dead ahead,* of course, refers to any point which the boat is approaching directly on a straight course. Midway between dead ahead and a point abeam, an object is *broad on the bow* (port or starboard).

To express the direction of another vessel or any object relative to our position we say it *bears* so-and-so. Directions through 360 degrees around the horizon are divided into 32 *points.* Each point or direction is named. Thus a lighthouse might be said to bear two points *abaft the starboard beam, broad on the port bow,* etc.

Windward means toward the wind, the direction from which the wind blows; *leeward,* away from the wind, or

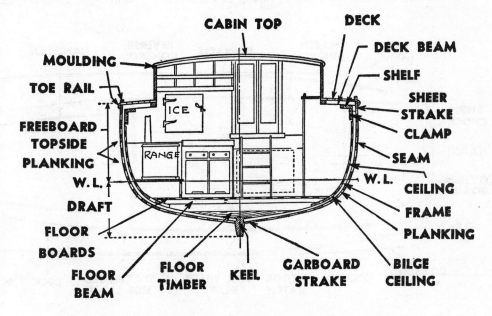

CABIN TOP   DECK

MOULDING   DECK BEAM

TOE RAIL   SHELF

ICE   SHEER STRAKE

CLAMP

FREEBOARD   SEAM
TOPSIDE
PLANKING   RANGE   W. L.

W. L.   CEILING

DRAFT   FRAME

FLOOR   PLANKING
BOARDS

FLOOR   BILGE
BEAM   FLOOR   KEEL   GARBOARD   CEILING
         TIMBER   STRAKE

the direction toward which the wind blows. The *lee* side of a boat or island is protected; the *windward* or *weather* side is exposed, unprotected. Note, however, that while one runs into the lee of an island or point for an anchorage protected from the wind, a *lee shore* refers to a shore line to leeward of a vessel, consequently a dangerous one exposed to the wind. While this may seem confusing at first, the logic of it is apparent with a little thought.

Some of the common terms by which the dimensions of a vessel and characteristics of her design are expressed are obvious in their meanings. Others baffle the tyro. The length of a boat is often given in two dimensions: on the *waterline* (W. L.), the meaning of which is apparent; and *over-all* (O.A.), measuring from the fore part of the stem to the after part of the stern. The breadth of a vessel is its *beam; draft,* the depth of water required to float it. This is not to be confused with the term *depth* as applied to larger vessels, which is measured vertically inside the hull from deck to bottom or floors. *Headroom,* in a small boat, is the vertical space between floor boards or deck and the cabin or canopy top, or other overhead structure.

Sheer is the term properly used to designate the curve or sweep of the deck of a vessel. The side planking of a boat between the waterline and deck or rail is called the *topsides.* If they are drawn in toward the centerline away from a perpendicular, as they often do at the stern of a boat, they are said to *tumble home.* Forward they are more likely to incline outward to make the bow more buoyant and keep the hull dry by throwing spray aside. This is *flare. Flam* is that part of the flare just below the deck. The height of a boat's topsides from waterline to deck is called the *freeboard.* The significance of the term *deadrise* can be appreciated by visualizing a section transversely across a hull. If the bottom planking were flat, extending horizontally from the keel, there would be no deadrise. In a round or vee bottom boat, when the bottom rises at an angle to such a horizontal line, the amount of rise is the deadrise.

The *bilge* is the turn of a boat's hull just below the waterline. *Bilge water* accumulates in the *bilges,* the deepest part of the hull inside along the keel. Aft where the lines converge toward the stern, under the overhang, is the *counter.* The lines converging toward the stern post are called the boat's *run.* The *buttock* is the rounding part of a boat's stern; *buttock lines,* drawn by the architect, may be visualized if one pictures longitudinal saw cuts vertically through a boat's planking at a distance

from the keel, parallel to the plane of stem and keel.

We have been talking about the *hull,* but haven't defined it. This term refers generally to the principal structure of the boat whereas cabins, deckhouses, etc., built above the deck are referred to as the *superstructure.* The main longitudinal timber in a hull, first laid in construction, is the *keel.* When another timber is fastened along the top of the keel to strengthen it, or as a necessary part of the construction, this is the *keelson,* sometimes *apron.* One-piece timbers running the full length of the keel are not always available. In this case, shorter pieces are bevelled and bolted together in a joint called a *scarph.* *Deadwood,* in small boats, is usually the solid timber above the keel at the stern. The *propeller post* stands vertically behind the deadwood, is joined to it and also to the keel.

The *frame* is the skeleton of a hull, comprising its principal structural members. The transverse members to which the planking is fastened are called *frames*—in some instances *ribs,* though some contend that a boat has frames, an animal ribs. The *stem* is one of the main frame members, at the bow. When the stern is shaped like the bow, drawing to a point as in a canoe, the boat is a *double-ender.* The *transom* type of stern is more common.

Knees reinforce the joints between members butting or intersecting at or near a right angle. *Clamps* and *shelves* are the longitudinal members joining the frames on which the deck beams rest. Misunderstanding often exists in connection with the use of the term *floor.* A *floor* in boat construction is one of the transverse frame members tying the lower ends of frames together at the keel. It has nothing to do with the decking. *Limber holes* are cut in the lower edge of frames to allow bilge water to flow into the deepest part of the hull from which point it can be pumped out.

Planks are applied to the outside of frames in constructing the hull, each continuous line of planks from bow to stern being called a *strake.* If short planks are used in one strake, the ends are *butted* and joined on *butt blocks.* The lowest strake, next to the keel, is called the *garboard.* Strakes between the bottom and topsides are called *wales,* and the *gunwale* (pronounced gun'l) is the upper part of the sheer strake or top plank of the *topsides.* When the topsides are carried above the deck, they are called *bulwarks;* the top of the bulwarks, the *rail.* The *taffrail* is the rail at the stern, furthest aft. Spaces between planks are called *seams;* to make them watertight, these are *caulked* by rolling or driving cotton

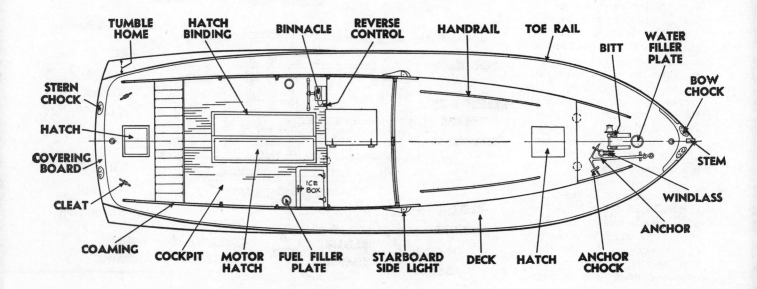

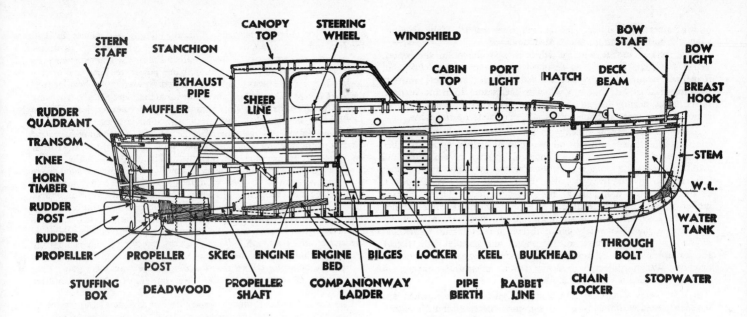

into them (*oakum* in large boats) after which the seams are *payed* (filled) with white lead or seam composition.

Frame members such as the keel and stem are *rabbetted* to receive the edges and ends of planks. This rabbet is merely a longitudinal recess or cut into the wood of proper size to take the plank. Plank ends at the stem and stern are the *hood ends*. We have already referred, in passing, to *beams* and *carlines*. *Deck beams* are the thwartship members which carry the decks; *carlines,* properly, are fore-and-aft timbers placed between the deck beams.

Vertical partitions, corresponding to the walls in a house, in a boat are called *bulkheads*. *Scuppers* are holes permitting water to drain overboard from decks and *cockpits,* the latter of course being the open space outside the cabins and deckhouses, not decked over flush. *Flush decks* are unbroken by either cockpits or deck erections such as the cabin or other houses.

Coamings (often misspelled combings, probably through confusion with the word *comber,* which is the name for a long curling wave) are vertical members around cockpits, hatches, etc., to prevent water on deck from running below. Deck openings are commonly referred to as *hatches*. *Companion ladders* are stairways or steps leading below from the deck. These are also referred to as *companionways*.

Another misunderstood term is *ceiling*. For this the landsman would be inclined to look overhead; as a matter of fact, this is actually a light sheathing of staving or planking applied to the inside of frames, for strength and interior finish.

On deck, lines are made fast to *cleats* or *bitts* (*samson posts*) and led through *chocks,* either open or closed, to reduce chafing. In larger craft *hawse pipes* are often provided in the bow through which the anchor chain runs, and into which the anchor is hauled.

The *forecastle* (pronounced fo'c's'l), if any small boat may properly be said to have one, is the compartment furthest forward, in the bow. In olden days, the forecastle head was an elevated structure forward, providing a platform from which men could fight. As construed today, it generally is considered to mean the crew's quarters forward.

Berths and *bunks* are the seagoing names for beds aboard a boat. *Lockers* are closets or chests to provide space for stowage. Afloat one does not pack or put away; he *stows*.

When a vessel is hauled out of the water she is *shored* up with supports to hold her upright. If she is not supported properly, so that she is held amidships while bow and stern settle, the boat will assume a shape described as *hogged*.

Helm is a term relating to the tiller, by which some sailboats are steered. More loosely, the term covers a wheel aboard a motor boat or any other method of steering. In the old days, the command *port your helm* meant put the tiller to port, thus throwing the rudder and the boat's head to starboard. Universal practise today dictates the command *right rudder* to carry the same meaning, *left rudder* the opposite. This eliminates much confusion.

Compasses are mounted near the helm, in boxes or other protective casings which are known as *binnacles*. Compasses are swung in *gimbals,* or pivoted rings, which permit the compass bowl and card to remain level regardless of the boat's motion. To enable the helmsman at the wheel to steer a compass course, a *lubber line* is painted on the inner side of the compass bowl to indicate the boat's bow.

We've spent considerable time getting familiar with the proper names for various parts of the boat and its construction, so let's pass to a consideration of more general terms dealing with the action and behavior of boats, the handling of lines and anchors, the action of water, navigational terms, etc.

When a boat moves through the water she is said to be *under way* (or *weigh*). According to the Pilot Rules she is under way when not aground, at anchor, or made fast to the shore. The direction in which she is moving may be made more specific by stating that she makes *headway* (when moving forward), *sternway* (backward), or *leeway* (when she is being set off her course by the wind). The track or disturbance which she leaves in the water as a result of her movement is called the *wake*. When she is not made fast to the bottom, shore, a dock

A GENERAL EXPLANATION OF THE MEANING OF

SOME OF THE MORE COMMON NAUTICAL TERMS

WHICH SHOULD BE FAMILIAR TO ALL BOATMEN

or any other fixed object, she is said to be *adrift*. She *grounds* when she touches bottom, and is then *aground*.

Trim relates to the way in which a boat floats in the water. When she floats properly as designed, she is on an *even keel,* but if inclined to port or starboard she *lists*. *Heel* (not keel) conveys the same idea as list, that is, a sidewise inclination from the vertical. If she is too heavily loaded forward, she trims *by the head,* whereas if her draft is greater than normal aft, she trims *by the stern*.

A *stiff vessel* returns quickly to her normal upright position; if she rolls in a seaway without quick action or sudden movement, her roll is *easy*. When a boat's center of gravity is too high and stability low, she is *tender; crank* conveys the same idea. Sidewise motion in a seaway is called *roll;* while the vertical motion as the head rises and falls in the waves is *pitch*. Quick upward motion in pitching is *scending*. She *yaws* when she runs off her course as a vessel might if she didn't steer properly in a following sea. If she yaws too widely and is thrown broadside into the *trough of the sea* (between crests of the waves and parallel with them) she *broaches to,* a situation which should always be carefully avoided. When subjected to heavy strains in working through a seaway, a vessel is said to *labor*.

A boat *scuds* when she runs before a gale; is *driven* when she is pressed hard with much sail. A ship may *capsize* without *foundering*—in the first instance she turns over; in the latter she is overwhelmed by a heavy sea, fills and sinks. Before she is reduced to such straits, the wise skipper *heaves to,* in order to enable a vessel to ride the seas more comfortably, generally head to the wind, or near it, with shortened sail and possibly lying to a *sea anchor* which prevents the head from falling off from the wind. The sea anchor does not go to the bottom, merely serves as a drag.

G ENERALLY speaking, the word *rope* is used but little aboard a boat, being referred to rather as *line*. *Hawsers* are heavy lines, in common use on larger vessels, but rarely aboard small pleasure craft. *Heaving lines* are light lines with a knot or weight at the end which helps to carry them when thrown from one boat to another or to a dock. *Heave* is the nautical term for throw. The knot which encloses the weight at the end of a heaving line is a *monkey's fist*. *Painters* are lines at the bow of the boat for the purpose of towing or making fast. Thus dinghies are usually equipped with painters. The line by which a boat is made fast to her mooring is called a *pennant*. *Spring lines* are among those used at docks, leading from the bow aft to the dock or from the stern forward to the dock, to prevent the boat from moving ahead or astern.

The *bitter end* of a line is the extreme end, the end made fast to a *bitt* when all line is paid out. *Belay* has a double meaning. A line is belayed when it is made fast; as a command it signifies stop, cease. Ends of lines are *whipped* when twine is wrapped about them to prevent the strands from untwisting. Ragged ends of lines are said to be *fagged*. When a line is made fast with light line or twine to another line or any other object, it is *seized*. Joining two ends to make one continuous line by tucking strands under without knotting is called *splicing*. When an end is worked back into the line itself to form a loop, it is called an *eye-splice*. One does not tie a line to another aboard a boat; he *bends* it on. Line is coiled down on deck, each complete turn being a *fake* or *flake*.

When a line is let out, one *pays* it out; it is *cast off* when let go. *Blocks* (pulleys) are provided with *sheaves*. These are the wheels or rollers of the block and the term is pronounced as though spelled shiv. When a line is passed through a block or hole it is *reeved; render* indicates that it passes freely through the block or hole. If a strain is put on a line heavy enough to break it, then it *parts*. Lines have *standing parts* and *hauling parts,* the standing part being the fixed part, that is, the one which is made fast; the hauling part, that part of a tackle which is hauled upon. A *bight* is any part within the ends of a line, that is to say, a bend. Lines are *foul* when tangled, *clear* when in order ready to run.

Ground tackle is a general term embracing anchors, lines, etc., used in anchoring. On small boats, the anchor line is a *rode*. *Moorings* are the permanent anchorages at which boats lie, consisting of a heavy anchor (usually *mushroom* type), chain, shackles, swivels, a mooring buoy, and pennant of manila or wire rope. Larger vessels are said to be moored when lying with two anchors down. They may also be moored to piers when made fast with stout mooring lines. *Grapnels* are light anchors with claw-like hooks or prongs. A *kedge* is a light anchor often used for getting off a shoal. The kedge is carried out in the dinghy and power to haul the boat off is then applied either by man power or *winch* (a device for raising the anchor). This is called *kedging*. *Warping* consists of turning a boat at a dock by applying power to lines fast to the dock. *Bowers* are heavy anchors carried forward; the heavier one, the *best bower*. Years ago *sheet anchors,* the heaviest aboard, were carried in the *waist* of a ship (amidships) for emergencies. *Stream anchors* are heavier than kedges, lighter than bowers.

Various terms are used to describe specific water movements or conditions of the surface. *Rips* are short, steep waves caused by the meeting or crossing of currents. The confused water action found at places where tidal currents meet is also called a *chop*. *Sea* is a general term often used to describe waves and water action on the surface but, properly, it should be applied only to waves produced by the wind. *Swell* is the long heavy undulation of the surface resulting from disturbances elsewhere on the sea. *Surf* is produced when waves leave deep water, breaking on the shore as the *crests* curl over. A *following sea* is one which comes up from astern, running in the same direction as the boat's course; a *head sea* is just the opposite, where the progress of the waves is against that of the boat, the boat meeting them bow on. *Cross* seas are confused and irregular.

The word *tide* has probably been misused as much as any nautical term, so much so that its misuse has come to be accepted without question as a matter of course. Commonly it has been used to describe the inflow and outflow of water caused by the gravitational influence of the moon and sun. Better usage would restrict the term to the vertical rise and fall of water produced by these causes. *Current* is the proper term for a horizontal flow of water. Thus a current resulting from tidal influences is a *tidal current*. It is better to say two-knot current than two-knot tide.

The incoming tidal current running toward shore is the *flood;* the retreating current flowing away from the land is the *ebb*. The direction in which the current flows is the *set; drift,* its velocity. (The amount of leeway a vessel makes is also called its drift.) *Slack* is the period between flood and ebb when the current is not flowing; *stand* the period with no rise or fall in tide level.

Reversing currents are those in rivers, straits, and channels which flow alternately in opposite directions. Offshore, where there is no restriction, the current may be *rotary,* flowing continually with no period of slack, but changing direction through all points of the compass during the tidal period. *Hydraulic* current is the type of reversing current in a strait resulting from a difference in the tidal head of water at the two ends of the passage.

Spring tides are those produced when the moon is new or full, and have a greater *range* (difference between the heights of high and low water) than average. *Neap* tides, caused when the positions of sun and moon relative to the earth are such as to offset each other in effect, have a smaller range than average. Too often every huge wave is referred to as a *tidal wave*. Generally, it is used in the wrong sense, as this term should be limited to waves resulting from tidal action, rather than indiscriminately applied to the great waves which build up as a result of wind storms.

R ANGE, mentioned above, is also a navigational term and is used when two or more objects are brought into line to indicate a safe course. The distinction between *knots* and *miles* has already been made. A *fathom* is six feet; this is a measure of depth. One *heaves a lead* to determine depth, the process being known as *sounding*. The lead (a weight at the end of the lead line) is *armed* by greasing the bottom with tallow or some other sticky substance to bring up a sample at the bottom. In navigation, one *plots* a course on the chart (never map), takes *bearings* to determine his *position* (*fix*), takes a *departure* to establish an exact point from which to commence his *dead reckoning* (calculation of courses and distances sailed), has an *offing* when he is well to seaward, though yet in sight of land.

Entries are made in a *log* (book) to record all events during a cruise; the *patent log* is an instrument to record distance travelled. One *raises* a light or landmark when it first becomes visible, makes a *landfall* when land is first sighted coming in from sea. *Passage* is generally construed to mean a run from port to port; *voyage* includes both the outward and homeward passage. *Watches* are four-hour periods of duty aboard ship; *dog watches* are two-hour periods between 4:00 and 8:00 P.M. A period of duty at the wheel is a *trick*.

When any part of the vessel's gear or equipment breaks or gives way, it *carries away;* an object goes *by the board* when it goes

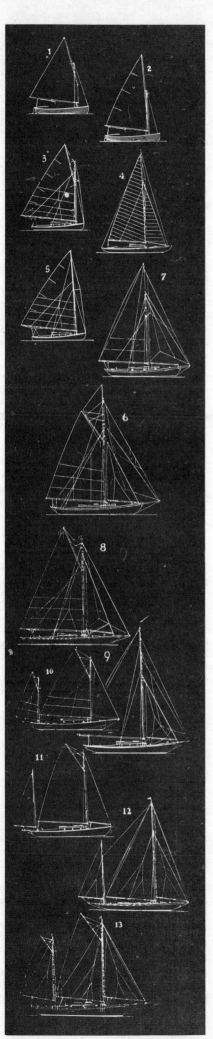

THE RIGS OF SAILING CRAFT

Here's a chance to test your knowledge of the rigs of various types of sailboats, or to learn them if you've never been able to distinguish a sloop from a cutter, or a yawl from a ketch. How many can you identify?

1—Standing lug rig—strictly small boat sail plan.
2—Sliding gunter—"gaff" fits snug against mast. Used on small boats.
3—Gaff cat rig.
4—Marconi-rigged knockabout—features are jib and mainsail and no bowsprit. Is also seen gaff-rigged, of course.
5—Marconi cat rig.
6—Gaff-rigged cutter. Usual definition of cutter is: single-masted yacht with mast placed about 2/5 of the waterline length abaft the forward termination of the waterline.
7—Marconi-rigged cutter.
8—Gaff-rigged sloop. The placing of the mast further forward distinguishes the sloop from the cutter. Otherwise, there is little difference.
9—Marconi-rigged sloop.
10—Gaff-rigged yawl. Usual distinction between yawl and ketch is that yawl's mizzen is stepped aft of the rudder post and mizzen is generally not over 20 percent of the total sail area in size.
11—Gaff yawl, with jib-headed or Marconi mizzen. Not usual rig.
12—Marconi-rigged yawl.
13—Gaff-rigged ketch.
14—Marconi-rigged ketch.
15—Staysail ketch, or "main trysail-rigged" ketch.
16—Staysail schooner. Main staysail (lower sail between spars) sets on boom.
17—Gaff-rigged schooner. Schooners can also have three or more masts, all fore-and-aft rigged.
18—Marconi mainsail and gaff foresail schooner (most usual schooner rig today).
19—Topsail schooner, or square topsail schooner.
20—Hermaphrodite brig, *not* brigantine, though often termed such. If vessel has three or more masts, square-rigged throughout on the foremast and schooner-rigged on all the rest, she is called a barkentine.
21—Ship. A ship-rigged vessel has three (or more) masts, all square-rigged.
22—Bark. This example is a four-masted bark (Hussar). Bark is a vessel with three or more masts, square-rigged on all but the aftermost mast.

Illustrations courtesy of Marine Facts, 1954, by Peirce & Kilburn Corp., New Bedford, Mass.

A brig (not illustrated) is two-masted, square-rigged on both fore and main. A brigantine is like a brig, but the mainsail (only) is fore-and-aft.

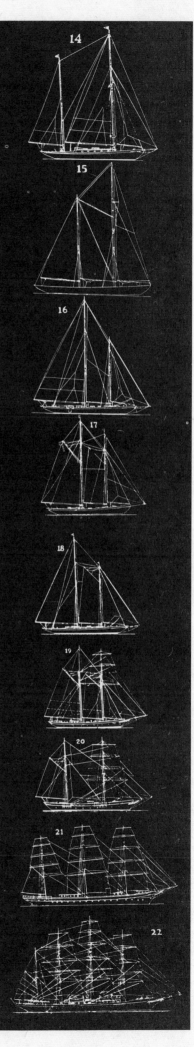

overboard. If a boat is *stove* (planking broken in from outside) the boat *springs a leak,* or *makes water.* When water is dipped out of a small boat, the process is called *bailing.*

By general usage, the term *Corinthian* has come to mean amateur sailor. A boat is *ship-shape* when everything is in good order, *well found* if well equipped. One *swabs* the deck when he washes it down with a mop (called a swab aboard ship). *Clean* is a term applied, not to a ship's condition, but rather to her lines. If the lines are *fine,* so that she slips through the water with little disturbance, the lines are clean.

The term *clear* has many meanings. Before leaving for a foreign port, a ship must be cleared through the Customs authorities. She clears the land when she leaves it, clears a shoal when she passes it safely. The bilges may be cleared of water by pumping it out. Tangled (*foul*) lines are cleared by straightening them out and getting them ready for use.

The meaning of the word *lay* also depends on its usage. One lays aft, when he goes to the stern of the boat; lays down the lines of a boat full size before building; lays up the boat when putting her out of commission. A vessel lays her course if, in sailing, she can make her objective without tacking. When an oarsman stops rowing, he lays on his oars. *Lay to* is synonymous with heave to, previously defined.

A boat *stands by* when she remains with another vessel prepared to give her assistance if necessary. When used as a command, stand by means to be prepared to carry out an order. A vessel is said to *hail* from her home port. One hails a vessel at sea to get her attention, *speaks* her when communicating with her.

SPACE does not permit a long discussion of sails, wind, and the rigs of vessels, but a few of the more common terms will be touched on briefly. Wind *veers* when it shifts, changing its direction clockwise; it *backs* when it shifts in a counter-clockwise direction. Wind changing from abeam forward, *hauls;* from abeam aft, *veers.* A vessel is sailing *off the wind* when her *sheets* (lines controlling the sail, not the sail itself) are slacked off (*eased*). She is *on the wind* when sailing *close-hauled,* as close to the wind as possible. When *before the wind,* the wind comes from aft and is called a *fair, free* or *leading* wind. A *following* wind blows in the direction of the ship's course. Sailing *down the wind,* a vessel sails to leeward. A *beam wind* obviously is one which blows athwart the boat's course. An *offshore* wind blows from the land; an *onshore* wind, toward it,

Canvas is a general term for a boat's sails. Sails *draw* when they fill with the wind providing power to drive the boat through the water. One *makes sail* when the sails are set; *shortens sail* when the amount of sail set is reduced; *reefs* by partly lowering the sail and securing it so that its area is reduced; *dowses* it when it is lowered quickly; *furls* it when it is rolled up and secured to a boom or yard.

A sailboat *tacks* by sailing in a zig-zag direction to make good a course directly into the wind. This is also called *beating.* If the wind comes from the starboard side, she is on the *starboard tack;* from the port side, the *port tack.* Tacking, she *goes about.* If she attempts to tack and the head does not fall off on the other tack she is *caught in* (or *misses*) *stays,* or is said to be *in irons.* When preparing to tack the order is given, *ready about;* then, as the helmsman puts the helm over to change the boat's course, *hard alee. Wearing ship* is another means of bringing a vessel on the other tack, but in this case she does it by changing course so that the wind is brought astern, from one side to the other. As the boom swings from one side to the other as the wind comes dead aft in this maneuver (sometimes it occurs accidentally when running before the wind) she *jibes.*

When the wind comes from abeam or forward of the beam, the boat is *reaching; running* when she is sailing dead before the wind. A vessel is *sailing free* when the wind is well aft; *full and by* or *close hauled* when all sails are drawing and her course is as close to the wind as she can sail. She is *pinched* when she is brought so close to the wind that the sails shiver. A vessel is *luffed* when she is brought up into the wind so as to spill some of it out of the sail, thus relieving the pressure and *easing* her. Sailing *before the wind,* sails are sometimes set on opposite sides of the boat; this is called *wing and wing.* One boat *blankets* another when, being just to windward, she takes the wind out of the other's sails. She *outfoots* another by sailing faster, *outpoints* her by sailing closer to the wind.

Catboats have a single mast and sail. *Sloops* have one mast but, in addition to the mainsail, have *headsails,* forward of the mast. Sometimes additional sails are set from *bowsprits,* projecting over the boat's bow. A sloop without a bowsprit, in which the jib sets from a stay at the stem, is a *knockabout.* A *cutter* is a sloop in which the

single mast is stepped further toward amidships than in the conventional sloop. *Yawls* have two masts, the after one of which is much the shorter and stepped abaft the rudder post. A *ketch* is rigged somewhat like a yawl, except that the short after mast is stepped forward of the rudder post instead of aft of it as in the case of the yawl. *Schooners* are *fore-and-aft* rigged (as distinguished from *square-rigged*) and have two or more masts. Unlike yawls and ketches, the after mast is never the shorter. *Rig* is the general term applying to the arrangement of a vessel's masts and sails. The term *slutter rig* (not in general use) is a British term used to distinguish a sailing craft that uses a masthead genoa, reaching jib or ballooner.

In *trunk cabin* cruisers (see Fig. 248, p. 355), the cabin is built up from the deck in such a manner as to provide a deck forward and at the sides of the cabin. The *raised deck* cruiser (see Fig. 253, p. 356) has its forward cabin provided by extending topsides upward from the normal sheer line and decking over the raised portion for the full width of the boat. It may have a small cockpit forward (see Fig. 263, p. 358). *Deckhouses* may be built up as superstructures on both the trunk cabin (Fig. 249, p. 355) and raised deck (Fig. 250, p. 356) types. On small boats, the trunk cabin may be modified to provide relatively larger areas of glass as in the *sedan* type (Fig. 259, p. 358.) Many small sea skiffs have a somewhat similar *shelter cabin* forward, consisting of a light permanent windshield, top and side wings, frequently open aft, or perhaps enclosed by canvas curtains.

Some confusion has arisen in use of the term *skiff.* It has been defined as a flat bottom, shallow draft open boat of simple construction, with sharp bow and square stern, propelled by motor, sail or oars, and used often as a pleasure boat in sheltered water. This is a general term, often loosely used. The *Seabright skiff,* native to the New Jersey beach, was originally a dory type, its flat tapered bottom merging into rounded lapstrake topsides, the garboards shaped aft into a boxed deadwood construction. Later, *sea skiffs* evolved from this type, retained the lapstrake construction (though they have been built smooth, or carvel, as well) but used a conventional keel instead of the flat keel. In recent years, many craft have been loosely referred to as "skiffs" or "sea skiffs" when referring to the modern fast fisherman-type of seaworthy design developed from the Jersey boats.

Motor sailers are a cross between the motor cruiser and the sailboat or auxiliary driven principally by her sails. Motor sailers perform well under power but generally do not carry sail enough to do as well under sail alone as the conventional sailboat. See illustrations, page 30.

THE term *spars* is used generally to cover masts, booms, gaffs, yards, etc. *Masts,* of course, are the principal vertical spars from which sails are set. They are *stepped* when set in position, *raked* when the mast is not plumb, but inclined aft at an angle. *Gaffs* are spars supporting the *head* (upper edge) of a fore-and-aft sail. Triangular sails requiring no gaff, in which the head of the sail is a point, are *Marconi* sails (jib-headed). *Yards* are the horizontal spars supporting the head of square sails. The *foot* (lower edge) of fore-and-aft sails is usually attached to a *boom.* If no boom is used, or if the sail is not laced or otherwise secured to it, the sail is *loose-footed.* The *luff* is the forward edge of a fore-and-aft sail; the *leach* the after edge. *Roach* in a sail is curvature of its edge. The *peak* is the upper aft corner of a gaff-rigged sail; the *tack,* the lower forward corner; the *clew,* the lower aft corner; the *throat,* the forward part of the head. *Bolt rope* is the rope sewed around the edge of a sail to reinforce it. *Battens* (thin, flat wooden strips) are placed in *pockets* along the leach of a sail to flatten the edge and give it shape.

Gear is the general term for miscellaneous lines, spars, sails and similar items. *Rigging* refers to all the lines aboard a boat, used in connection with setting and handling sail. Lines or wire staying the masts comprise the *standing rigging;* the lines used in setting and furling sails, the *running rigging.* *Halyards* are lines or tackles used to hoist sails; *shrouds* stay the mast at the sides. The wire ropes commonly used to support the mast from a point forward are called *stays.* Those supporting the mast from aft are *backstays.* When the slack in stays and shrouds is taken up, the rigging is said to be *set up.*

One could go on indefinitely defining a multitude of terms that constitute the vernacular of the sea, but space forbids. What has been covered here will serve as framework. As the novice gains experience in sailing and handling boats, his vocabulary will broaden proportionately and naturally. We hope, however, that his enthusiasm for the subject will not cause him to toss indiscriminate Avasts, Ahoys and Belays into every conceivable nook and corner of his conversation. The natural, proper use of correct terms is much to be desired; strained efforts to affect a salty lingo are conspicuously inappropriate.

conventional bow. The stem is a vertical member set up on the forward end of the keel. It is commonly of white oak in wooden construction and may be straight or curved, depending on the shape desired. It is *plumb* if set up perpendicular to the waterline, but is often *raked* at an angle for better appearance. *Ring bolts,* having a ring through the eye of the bolt, are fitted through the stems of many small boats, and often at the stern as well.

Deadwood is solid timber placed on the keel to connect

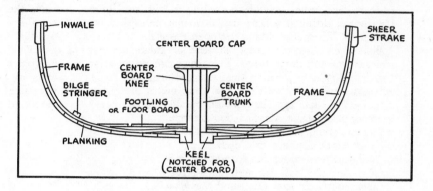

WHAT'S the difference between a sheer plank and the plank sheer? Do the terms carvel and clinker have any special significance to you? Do you know the distinction between a keel and a keelson?

In the first part of this chapter on nautical terms, we have explained the meaning of many of the more common nautical terms. In it special emphasis was laid on those which should be part of every motor boatman's vocabulary, including correct terminology applying to various parts of a motor boat.

Sailing and rowing craft, too, have their special nomenclature, some of the terms seldom being encountered by the motor boatman not concerned with sailing. The terms applicable to sailing and rowing craft are of particular interest to men going into the Navy, Coast Guard and other branches of the service. Knowledge of the correct technical terms to use in connection with the whaleboats, cutters, dinghies, wherries and other small craft they will handle will stand them in good stead.

There must of necessity be some overlapping in the terms discussed here and those covered in the foregoing pages. Certain parts are common to all types of boat, whether propelled by motor, sail or oars. In such cases some repetition is unavoidable.

To begin at the logical beginning, let's consider some of the terms identified with the boat's hull construction. The *keel* is the principal frame member of the boat, usually the first one laid when construction is begun. Almost invariably it is on the outside of the hull, though in cases (as in some P.T. boats) the keel is inside. Often an extra piece is fastened to the bottom of the main keel to protect it. This is a *false keel.*

Ordinarily a timber or stringer, bolted inside as a reinforcing member to the keel, is called a *keelson* (pronounced kelson). Between the keel and keelson, blocks are fitted *athwartship* (at right angles to the fore and aft centerline of the keel). These blocks are called *filling pieces.*

Keel blocks are used to support the keel of a boat during construction. When boats are stowed in *cradles* aboard a vessel, a *keel stop* is fitted at the after end of the keel to locate the boat in a fore and aft position on the cradle. The keel stop is a small metal fitting.

A *stem* is common to all boats with the conventional type of bow, whereas the square-nosed *pram* or *punt* type has a bow resembling its square stern. Flat planking across the stern is called the *transom,* but in a *double-ender* the stern construction is pointed, resembling the

the end timbers. Most of it is found at the stern of a boat, though it may also be used forward, in which case it may take the form of a *stem heel.* Timbers connecting the *stem knee* to the keel are often called *sole* pieces. An *apron* (sometimes called *stemson*) is an inner stem fitted abaft (behind) the stem to reinforce it. It gives added surface on which the *hood ends* of the planking can land, the hood ends being those ends which fit into the *rabbet,* cut into the stem to receive them.

Stem bands of metal are usually fitted on the forward edge of the stem for protection. The spars which project out over the bow on sailing craft to take the *stays* from which jibs and other *head sails* are set, are called *bowsprits.* *Breast hooks* are reinforcing knees set horizontally behind the stem.

Various kinds of *knees* are used throughout the hull construction to connect members joined at an angle to each other. They may be of metal, though often a natural growth of wood is selected—hackmatack, for example—in which the grain runs in the desired shape for maximum strength. There are *bosom* knees and *carling* knees, *dagger* knees and *hanging* knees, *lodging* knees, *panting* knees, *thwart* knees, etc., each designating the special part of construction in which it is employed, or its relative position.

Going *aft,* now to the *stern* of the boat, we have *horn timbers,* used to fasten the *shaft log* to the *transom knee.* The transom has already been defined. Shaft logs are timbers between keel and deadwood through which the propeller shaft (if the boat is motor driven) passes. At the stern the principal vertical member is called the *stern post,* set up on the after end of the keel or shaft log, to which it is attached by the *stern knee.* A *stern hook* is not a hook at all but, in a double-ended boat, is that reinforcing member which corresponds to the *breast hook* at the bow. Breast hooks at the stern are also called *crutches.* If the boat has a transom stern, she would have *quarter knees* at each side of the transom instead of the one stern hook.

Frames are the timbers set up on the keel, providing the skeleton over which the *planking* is laid. The frames may be curved as in a round bottom boat or straight as in certain types of V-bottom design. Sometimes they are *sawn* to shape; otherwise they are *steam bent.*

Floors, nautically speaking, are not laid as in a house to be walked upon. In a boat they are important transverse structural members, tying together the keel and the lower ends of the frames.

The *gunwale* (pronounced gun'l) of an open boat is the upper edge of the side. *Inwales* are the longitudinal members fastened inside a canoe or small boat along the gunwales. Sometimes they are referred to as *clamps.* The ends of *deck beams,* on which decking is laid, rest upon the clamps, although a horizontal *shelf* may be used above the clamp. Then deck beams rest upon the shelf.

Sometimes boatmen speak of deck or cabin *carlines* when they really mean beams. The beams run *thwartships* (at right angles to a center line passing through the keel) whereas carlines, or carlings, are short pieces of timber running *fore and aft* (lengthwise, parallel to the keel) between deck beams. Carlines, for example, would be found at the port and starboard sides of *hatch* openings in a deck.

Stringers are longitudinal members fastened inside the hull for additional structural strength. If they run along the *bilge* (the turn of the hull below the waterline) they are called *bilge stringers.* There are other types.

Open boats often have a finishing piece which runs along the gunwale, lying on top of the clamp or inwale and covering the top edge of the planking and heads of frames. This is a *capping.* In many small boats, capping is omitted, so that there is nothing to catch dirt and water when the boat is turned over to be emptied instead of *bailing.* Such a boat would be said to have *open gunwales.*

Planking, laid over the outside of frames in *strakes* (continuous narrow lengths from stem to stern), provides the outer shell of the *hull,* which is the general term describing the main structure of the boat. Planking is called *carvel* if the surface finishes smooth with *caulked seams* between the strakes to make the hull watertight. It is *clinker* or *lapstrake* if the successive strakes lap each other as the clapboards of a house are lapped. Hulls are sometimes *double planked,* in which case there is commonly an inner *skin* or layer of planking laid diagonal to the keel, and an outer skin fore and aft, with waterproof glue, or glue and fabric, between layers. Sometimes the two layers of planking are run diagonally at an angle of forty-five degrees from keel to gunwale, planks of the two layers being at right angles to each other. Frames are omitted in this type of construction.

The *sheer* line is the line, as seen in profile, along the hull defined by the gunwale or top edge of the topmost strake of planking, the *sheer strake.* Sheer strakes are sometimes thicker than other strakes of planking. When a second plank, next below the sheer strake, is fitted thicker than the others, it is called a *binding strake.*

Bilge strakes would be the heavier planks fitted at the turn of the bilge, though the term might be applied to ceiling inside in the bilge. *Ceiling* is not overhead, as ashore; it is planking laid inside the frames. The *garboard* (pronounced garb'd) strake is the lowest strake of planking, fitted next to the keel.

Strakes of planking between the bottom and *topsides* are called *wales.* Topsides refers to the portion of the hull between the waterline and the rail or gunwale. The term wales is also used to describe heavy strakes (*rubbing strakes*) below the gunwale. Longitudinal timbers, extending outside the exposed faces of planking, usually metal-shod to protect the topsides, are referred to as *side fenders* or *fender guards.* In pleasure boating, the term *fenders* commonly calls to mind the cork-filled canvas devices, or those of rope or rubber, suspended over the side to take shocks when lying against a dock or another boat.

We have already used the term *bilge* in speaking of the "turn of the bilge" and in its

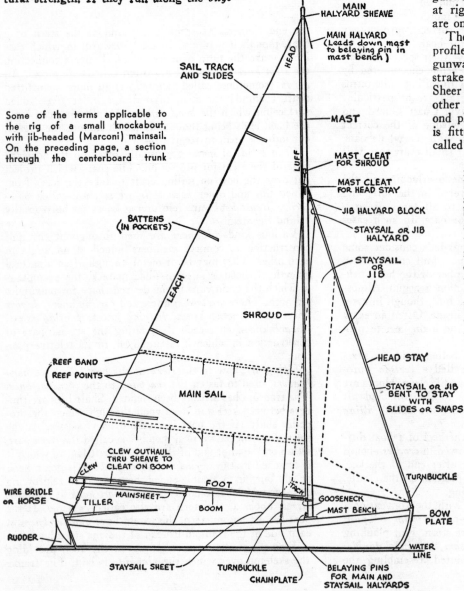

Some of the terms applicable to the rig of a small knockabout, with jib-headed (Marconi) mainsail. On the preceding page, a section through the centerboard trunk

MAST-HEAD

MAIN HALYARD SHEAVE

MAIN HALYARD (Leads down mast to belaying pin in mast bench)

SAIL TRACK AND SLIDES

HEAD

MAST

LUFF

MAST CLEAT FOR SHROUD

MAST CLEAT FOR HEAD STAY

JIB HALYARD BLOCK

STAYSAIL OR JIB HALYARD

STAYSAIL OR JIB

BATTENS (IN POCKETS)

LEACH

SHROUD

REEF BAND

REEF POINTS

HEAD STAY

MAIN SAIL

STAYSAIL OR JIB BENT TO STAY WITH SLIDES OR SNAPS

CLEW OUTHAUL THRU SHEAVE TO CLEAT ON BOOM

CLEW

FOOT

TURNBUCKLE

WIRE BRIDLE OR HORSE

TILLER

MAINSHEET

BOOM

TACK

GOOSENECK

MAST BENCH

BOW PLATE

RUDDER

WATER LINE

STAYSAIL SHEET

TURNBUCKLE

CHAINPLATE

BELAYING PINS FOR MAIN AND STAYSAIL HALYARDS

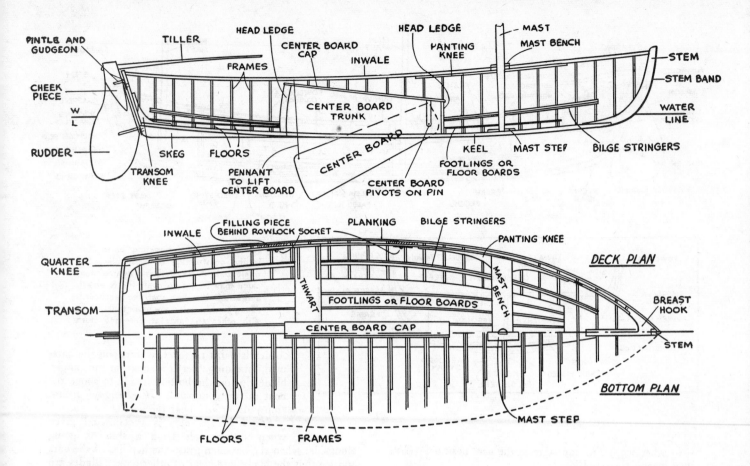

association with "bilge strakes." However the bilge is also the lowest part of the hull inside where *bilge water* accumulates. Boats carried out of water on larger craft must have *boat plugs,* usually of metal, which can be removed to drain water which might otherwise collect inside.

The sheer plank has been defined as the topmost strake along the hull where the deck joins the topsides. *Plank sheer,* on the other hand, means the outermost plank of the deck. Sometimes called a *covering board,* it covers the tops of frames and upper edge of the sheer strake in a decked boat, as capping does in an open boat. Covering boards are usually wider than any of the narrower deck planks.

Chain plates are strips of bronze or iron bolted to the side of a boat, to which rigging is attached, such as the shrouds or shroud whips (to be defined later). *Bottom boards* (sometimes *foot boards*) are those laid in the bottom of the boat to walk upon. In small boats they are often removable. Where there are no deep *floors,* previously defined, boards may be laid directly upon the inside of the frames to walk on. These are *footlings.*

The transverse seats in small craft are called *thwarts.* On them, oarsmen sit when rowing. When two men pull one oar, the oars are *double-banked,* but the boat is also double-banked if two men pull from one thwart. To support the thwart, a vertical piece is often fitted under it amidships, called a *thwart stanchion.* A man who is *sculling* would stand in the stern and propel the boat by working a single oar back and forth, using either one or two hands. The term sculling is also applied to the rowing of light racing *shells.*

Stretchers (also called *foot boards,* although this creates confusion with the alternate term for bottom boards) are sometimes fitted in small boats, athwartships, for the oarsmen to brace their feet against. The ends of thwarts land on *risers,* or *risings,* which are fore and aft pieces or stringers fastened to the inside of the frames.

Side benches, running fore and aft, are fitted at the sides of a boat over the air tanks which float the boat if capsized. The benches protect the tanks. Planking over tanks is also called *ceiling.* Instead of decks, some small boats have *platforms* at the level of the thwarts forward of the foremast. A *gang-board* runs down the centerline of the boat from the forward platform to the after thwart.

The terms *rowlock* and *oarlock* are synonomous. These are the fittings which hold the oars when rowing. In place of oarlocks, wooden *thole pins* are sometimes driven into holes or sockets. In certain types of boats, like surf boats and whaleboats, used in rough water where a rudder might be out of water so much as to destroy its effectiveness, a *steering oar* is used at the stern, *shipped* (put or held in place) in a swiveled *steering rowlock,* sometimes called a *crutch.* *Trailing lines* are attached to oars to keep them from going overboard. When oars are *muffled* to prevent noise, pieces of canvas with strands of rope yarn attached are placed between the oars and the oarlocks. These are *thrum mats.* *Sweeps* are long oars.

Oars are very simple in their construction, yet they have a special nomenclature to designate their respective parts. The *handle* of course is the part gripped in the hand when rowing. At the other end, in the water, is the flat *blade.* *Spoon* oars, for racing, have curved blades. The round part of an oar between handle and blade is usually called the *loom,* although the term loom may properly be applied to the part from handle to oarlock, in the boat when rowing. The loom tapers as it approaches the blade. Where loom and blade meet is the *neck;* at the end of the blade is the *tip,* sometimes protected with a strip of sheet copper.

Oars is a command given to oarsmen to order them to stop pulling, holding the oars horizontally with blades *feathered* (parallel with the water to reduce wind resistance.) *Out oars* is a preliminary command given when the oars are to be made ready in the oarlocks for pulling

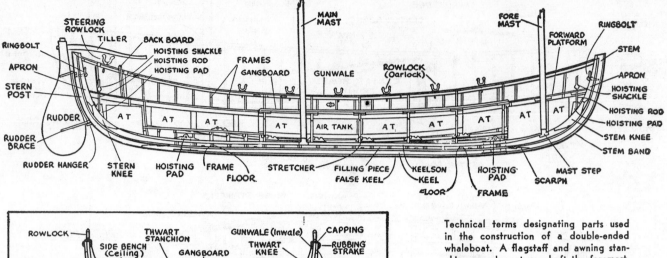

Technical terms designating parts used in the construction of a double-ended whaleboat. A flagstaff and awning stanchion may be set up abaft the foremast, and also in the stern abaft the backboard. Along each side is a row of air tanks (A T) with other air tanks at bow and stern

—in other words, to ship them in the *oars* position. *Give way* means start pulling.

Trail is an order to let go the oars while the boat is under way, allowing them to swing around in a fore and aft position, with blades trailing alongside. (Hence the term trailing line, defined above.) If there are no trailing lines, the handle of the oar is held in the hand to execute this order. To check the *way* (movement through the water) of a boat—either *headway* if going forward, or *sternway,* if going backward (some old salts might prefer to say *sternboard* instead of "backward")—the command is *hold water.* The command hold water is executed by holding the blades vertically in the water with oars at right angles to the keel.

To go astern, the command to oarsmen is *stern all,* whereupon they will *back water,* using the oars in a manner just opposite to that when pulling to give the boat headway. To make a turn the order is *back starboard* or *back port* depending on whether the turn is to be made to starboard or port. A quick turn to starboard can be made, provided the boat does not have too much headway, by ordering *back starboard, give way port.* *Back port, give way starboard* will result in a quick turn to port, as the port oarsmen are backing water while the starboard oarsmen are pulling ahead. *Stand by to give way* calls for the position at the beginning of a stroke as oarsmen, leaning forward, prepare to row.

When coming alongside a vessel, the command *toss oars* is given to order the the oarsmen to place their oars in a perpendicular position, blades fore and aft, handles resting on the footlings. Commonly the command is preceded by a cautionary *stand-by to toss.* Whenever a warning to the crew is desirable, before issuing any command, the expression is *stand by to. . . .* For example, a preparatory or warning command for the order or position *oars* is *stand by to lay on the oars.*

Boat the oars means place them in the boat on the thwarts, blades forward. When a boat has grounded, the order is *point the oars,* whereupon the oarsmen, standing, set the oars at an angle, blade tips on the bottom, ready to shove the boat off on command. *Way enough* means stop pulling and boat the oars.

Stand by the oars is a command given when shoving off from a ship or going alongside, when the oarsmen grasp the handles of the oars and see that the blades are clear of other oars. Blades are laid flat on the gunwale, handle over the thwart. At *up oars,* they are raised vertically, blades trimmed fore and aft, handles on the footlings. These commands make a boat ready for duty alongside a ship.

At the command *shove off* the bowman lets go the painter and shoves the bow off from a vessel's side with the boat hook while the *coxswain* aft, in charge of the boat, *sheers* the boat off with the tiller. The duty of various oarsmen in such a maneuver varies with their position in the boat. The order *let fall* is a command given when the boat is clear of a vessel's side. This is an intermediate order between *up oars* and *oars* as the blades are dropped outboard into the rowlocks. *In bows* is ordered as a landing is made to instruct bowman to toss oars at a forty-five degree angle, boat them, pick up boat books and stand holding them vertically in readiness for the landing or ready to receive lines.

The coxswain (pronounced cox'n), as explained, is the officer in charge of a boat. He stands aft at the *tiller* to steer and issues the orders. The tiller of course is the bar or handle on the *rudder head* by which the rudder is moved to steer the boat. Sometimes the tiller is not shipped. Instead a thwartship piece of wood or metal may be fitted on the rudder head. This is a *yoke.* Then the boat is steered by means of lines called *yoke ropes* or *lanyards* attached to the yoke. In order to provide sufficient thickness for a slot for the tiller to be shipped in, *cheek blocks* may be bolted on the sides of the rudder.

Pintles and *gudgeons* are commonly used to hang the rudder of small boats. The pintle is in the form of a hook or pin on the rudder, point downward. This fits into the gudgeon on the stern post, which has an eye to receive the pintle. In other boats, *rudder hangers* are used, providing a vertical rod of metal for attachment to the stern post with *rudder braces* to fit over the hanger.

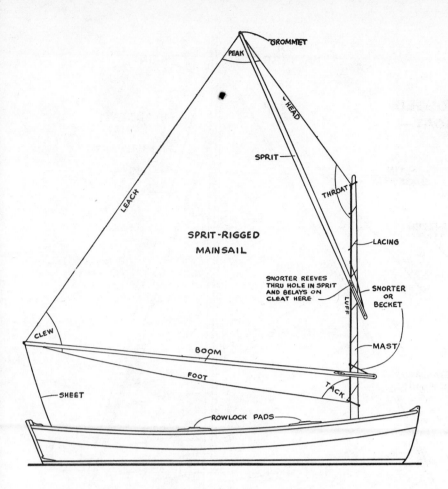

PEAK · GROMMET · HEAD · SPRIT · THROAT · LEACH · SPRIT-RIGGED MAINSAIL · LACING · SNORTER REEVES THRU HOLE IN SPRIT AND BELAYS ON CLEAT HERE · SNORTER OR BECKET · LUFF · CLEW · MAST · BOOM · FOOT · SHEET · TACK · ROWLOCK PADS

NAUTICAL TERMS USED IN CONNECTION WITH
THE RIGGING AND HANDLING OF SAILING
CRAFT. VARIOUS TYPES OF SAILS AND RIGS

WE have covered in the preceding pages many of the nautical terms relating to parts of the construction of rowing and sailing craft. Most of these terms are applicable alike to the whaleboats, cutters, and other small craft used by the Navy and Coast Guard, and to many types of small pleasure craft. Proceeding now to the terms used in the rigging and handling of sailing craft, we encounter a jargon quite unintelligible to the landsman.

For example, consider some of the *rigs* which distinguish various types of sailboats by the arrangement of their masts and sails. Simplest of all is the *catboat,* with its single heavy mast stepped well forward, and one sail. The original type of catboat had a *gaff-headed* mainsail and no *bowsprit* or *shrouds.* (These terms will be defined later.)

The *sloop* also has one mast, stepped further aft so that, in addition to its *mainsail* abaft the mast, there is room for *jibs* and other *headsails* forward of the mast. Properly, the sloop has a bowsprit. Without a bowsprit, the rig is described as a *knockabout* or *stem-head sloop.*

The *cutter,* like a sloop, has one mast but this is stepped more nearly amidship so that the total *sail area* is almost equally divided between mainsail and headsails. (A cutter is also a type of ship's boat.)

Ketches have two masts. Of these the taller (the *mainmast*) is forward. The *mizzen mast* (the after one) is stepped forward of the rudder post. *Yawls* resemble ketches, except that the mizzen mast or *jigger* is abaft the rudder post. Yawls have proportionately less of their total sail area in the mizzen, and the rig of the ketch is said to be *inboard* because it does not project much beyond the stern of the boat as in a yawl.

Schooners have two or more masts, with the *fore-and-aft* rig which distinguishes practically all modern sailing craft from the *square* rigs of the old windjammers. In the latter, the square sails were set from *yards* set horizontally across the mast. Unlike yawls and ketches, the after mast (mainmast) of a schooner is always as tall as, or taller than, the *foremast.*

Schooners are sometimes *staysail rigged* with triangular fore and aft *staysails* between the fore and mainmast, jib-headed triangular (*Marconi*) mainsail and the usual headsails. Schooners without *topmasts* above the lower masts are *baldheaded.*

A *sprit* rig is used on some dinghies and other small craft. In this type of rig the upper aft corner (*peak*) of the fore and aft sail is held *aloft* by a light *spar* called a sprit, inserted in an eye called a *grommet.* The sprit at its lower end is supported by a *snorter* or *becket* consisting of a light line about the mast with an eye in the lower end to take the sprit. Although the sail is quadrilateral, no *gaff* at the *head* of the sail or *boom* at the *foot* is required, though a boom is sometimes used, as in the illustration, its forward end held in a becket, the same as the sprit above it.

Lug rigs are of various types and their use is also confined to small craft. The *standing lug* has a yard which crosses the mast obliquely while the *tack* (forward lower corner) of the sail is made fast to the mast. If there is no boom, the sail is said to be *loose-footed.* The *balance lug* differs in that the boom projects somewhat forward of the mast. In a *dipping lug* the tack is made fast to the stem, or ahead of the mast, so that the yard must be *dipped* around the mast when tacking.

A *sliding gunter* has a triangular jib-headed sail, with topmast sliding aloft as an extension of the lower mast. This is popular on many small racing dinghies.

Whale-boats are double ended pulling lifeboats, 24 to 30 feet in length, used by the Navy. They often have a standing lug rig on two masts, but no jib. *Cutters* are double-banked ships' boats, with transom sterns, used for general duty. (See also previous definition of cutter rig.)

Wherries are a type of small pulling boat, 12 to 14 feet in length, used generally by officers of Navy craft. *Dinghies* are not only the small boats towed by pleasure craft, and propelled by oars, sails, or outboard motors. Dinghies used by the Navy are 16 to 20 feet in length, have four oars, single-banked, and a sprit rig for sailing. *Gigs* are ships' boats used by captains or commanding officers.

From bow to stern, the mast of a four-masted schooner would be named the *fore, main, mizzen,* and *jigger.* The principal (lower) sails set on these are the *foresail, mainsail, mizzensail* and *spanker,* the latter being the after sail of a schooner having more than three masts.

Topsails may be set above lower sails from *topmasts,* with names corresponding to the masts on which they are set. A *bowsprit* projects out from the stem and a jib-boom may be rigged out beyond the bowsprit.

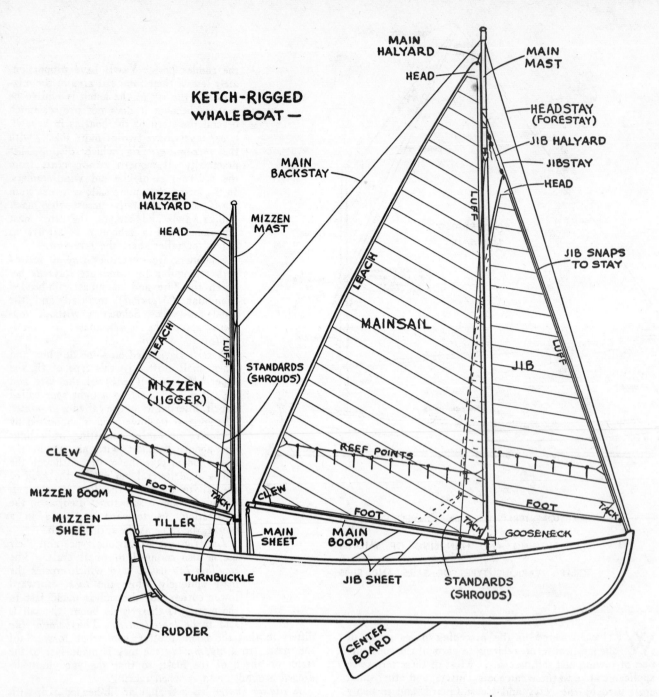

KETCH-RIGGED WHALEBOAT —

MAIN HALYARD
HEAD
MAIN MAST
MAIN BACKSTAY
HEADSTAY (FORESTAY)
JIB HALYARD
JIBSTAY
HEAD
JIB SNAPS TO STAY
MIZZEN HALYARD
HEAD
MIZZEN MAST
LUFF
LEACH
MAINSAIL
JIB
LEACH
LUFF
MIZZEN (JIGGER)
STANDARDS (SHROUDS)
REEF POINTS
LUFF
CLEW
FOOT
TACK
CLEW
FOOT
TACK
FOOT
MIZZEN BOOM
MIZZEN SHEET
TILLER
MAIN SHEET
MAIN BOOM
GOOSENECK
TURNBUCKLE
JIB SHEET
STANDARDS (SHROUDS)
RUDDER
CENTER BOARD

Jibs are usually triangular sails set before the foremast, although in recent years the *clew* (aft lower corner) has been cut off certain jibs, making them quadrilateral. Some jibs are large, like the *Genoa* and *balloon jib,* overlapping the mainsail.

If a schooner has four principal *headsails* before the foremast, they are, working aft, the *flying jib, outer jib, inner jib,* and *fore staysail.*

Staysails, as previously mentioned, are triangular jib-shaped sails set from the *stays* which support the masts. *Spinnakers* are large triangular sails set from booms called *spinnaker poles* on the opposite side of the main or fore boom when running before a *fair wind.*

Canvas is a term used in speaking about all sails in general. *Plain sails* are the ordinary *working* sails, not including the lighter jibs and staysails. *Storm canvas,* on the other hand, includes jibs, staysails, or *trysails* of extra heavy canvas for use in heavy weather.

The *head* of a quadrilateral sail is its upper side, *bent* (made fast or secured) to a *gaff;* in a jib-headed sail, the head is the upper corner. The *foot* is the lower edge, bent to a *boom.* The forward side of a fore-and-aft sail is the *luff,* bent to the mast by means of *hoops,* or the

more modern *sail track* and *slides.* In either case the method of bending the sail to the mast is such as to permit *hoisting* and *lowering.* The small pieces of manila used to secure mast hoops to the luff of a sail are called *robands.* The *leech* is the after side of a fore-and-aft sail.

In a gaff-rigged sail, the upper aft corner is the *peak;* the forward upper corner where gaff and mast meet, the *throat* (also called *nock.*) The lower corner forward where mast and boom meet is the *tack;* the lower corner aft, the *clew.*

Bolt rope is sewed to the edges of a sail to strengthen it. *Tabling* is the re-enforced part of the sail to which the bolt rope is sewed. The leech of a fore-and-aft sail (and the foot of a square sail) is usually cut with a curve called the *roach.* To support the roach and preserve its shape by flattening the leech, wooden *battens* (thin flat strips of wood) are inserted in *pockets* in the sail along the leech. *Brails* are lines running from the leech to the mast, used to aid in gathering sail in and securing it.

Sails today are usually *cross-cut*—that is, the cloths or strips which are seamed together to make the sail are laid out so that the seams are perpendicular to the leech.

(See illustration of ketch-rigged whaleboat.) Cross-cut sails allow a freer flow of wind across their surface. A variation of this practice is found in *mitered* sails. In loose-footed sails, the general practice is to run the cloth strips two ways, perpendicular to both leech and foot, joining at the *miter* which runs from the clew to a point on the luff.

When wind pressure is too great on a sail, sail area is reduced by *reefing,* which is accomplished by gathering in canvas along the boom as the sail is lowered part way. Parallel to the foot of the sail, strips of canvas called *reef bands* are sewed for reenforcement and short pieces of line are attached. These are *reef points,* passed around the foot of the sail and secured. A *reef cringle* is an eye in the leech or luff of a fore-and-aft sail in line with the reef points. *Reef earings* (or *pendants*) are short pieces of line spliced into the cringles to permit the latter to be secured to the boom.

The masts, gaffs, booms, yards, etc., from which sails are set are referred to generally as *spars.* The mast, of course, is the principal vertical spar, supporting the gaffs, booms, sails, etc. On larger craft there may be a *topmast* above the lower mast, and even *topgallant* masts above the topmast. A *jury* mast is any spar rigged temporarily as a mast in the event that the mast itself is carried away.

The *boom* has already been spoken of as the spar to which the foot of a fore-and-aft sail is bent; the *gaff,* the one to which the head is bent. At the mast end, *jaws* of the boom and gaff encircle the mast to keep these spars in place. *Goosenecks* (also called *Pacific irons*) are swiveled metal fittings used on many booms instead of jaws. Light spars used on a staysail or topsail or foot of the jib are not booms, but *clubs.*

Square sails are set from *yards,* a term applied also to the light spars used at the head of a lug rig sail. *Bowsprits* have been defined elsewhere as spars projecting from the stem. Short spars sometimes project from the stern, particularly on boats of the yawl type, where the mizzen boom overhangs the stern considerably. These are *boomkins.*

The foot of a mast—that is to say, its lower end—is called the *heel;* it fits in a *step* on the keel. Its topmost end is the *masthead,* often capped by a *truck,* a flat circular piece of wood. Hence the expression "from truck to keel," including everything in a ship from top to bottom. At the masthead, a *sheave,* the grooved wheel of a block, may be let into the mast to take *halyards* by which sails are hoisted.

Mast cleats of wood are sometimes attached to masts at the point where shrouds and stays (see definitions under rigging) are attached. Horizontal spars fitted on the mast to spread the shrouds and stays are *spreaders.* *Tangs* are metal plates attached to a mast where rigging is to be made fast. They distribute the strain over a considerable area.

A *mast hole* in a deck or the thwart of a small boat is the hole through which the mast is passed when stepped. When the primary function of a thwart is to serve as a support for the mast, rather than as a seat, it is often spoken of as a *mast bench.* Instead of a hole in the thwart, a semi-circular metal band is sometimes hinged at the edge of a thwart to hold the mast. This is called a *gate,* sometimes *mast clamp.*

All the various ropes of a vessel which secure masts and sails, taken together, are referred to as *rigging.* The *standing rigging* includes that part, like shrouds and stays, which is permanently secured, whereas the *running rigging* embraces the part which is movable, such as the sheets, halyards, etc., running through *blocks.*

Masts are supported by *stays* forward (*headstays, jibstays, forestays,* etc.), usually of wire rope, with *shrouds* at the sides, and *backstays* from aft. A *spring stay* is one running between a schooner's mastheads. *Turnbuckles,* as previously indicated, may be used in rigging to *set it up. Deadeyes* (round blocks of lignum vitae with holes through them and a groove around the edge) are used for the same purpose. They are found between the shrouds and chain plates on the vessel's side. *Lanyards* of rope *reeve* (pass) through the holes of the deadeyes and provide a method of adjusting tension in the shrouds. *Shroud whips* are also used to set up the shrouds.

While a mast is *stayed* in a vertical position, bowsprits are *guyed* horizontally (or at an angle) by *bowsprit shrouds* at the sides and a *bob-stay* from below. *Steeve* is the term that describes technically the angle the bowsprit makes with the horizontal.

Sheets are *not* sails. Sheets, of rope, are made fast to booms or the clew of loose-footed sails to control the angle at which the sail sets, relative to the wind directions.

While a simple single sheet is used on some small sailboats, on larger craft it is customary to provide additional power for handling the sails by reeving the sheet through blocks, constituting a *tackle (purchase).* A *gun tackle,* as used in shroud whips, is a purchase having

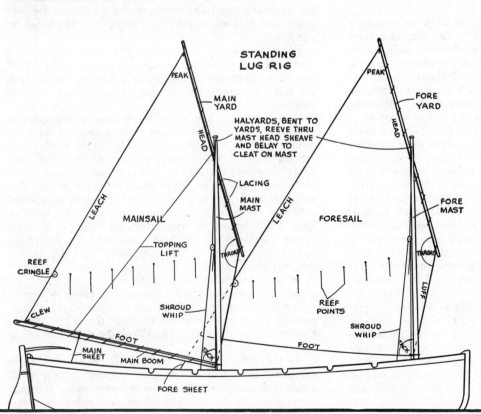

STANDING LUG RIG

PEAK

MAIN YARD

HALYARDS, BENT TO YARDS, REEVE THRU MAST HEAD SHEAVE AND BELAY TO CLEAT ON MAST

LACING

MAIN MAST

HEAD

LEACH

MAINSAIL

TOPPING LIFT

REEF CRINGLE

SHROUD WHIP

CLEW

FOOT

MAIN SHEET

MAIN BOOM

PEAK

FORE YARD

FORE MAST

HEAD

LEACH

FORESAIL

THROAT

REEF POINTS

SHROUD WHIP

LUFF

FOOT

FORE SHEET

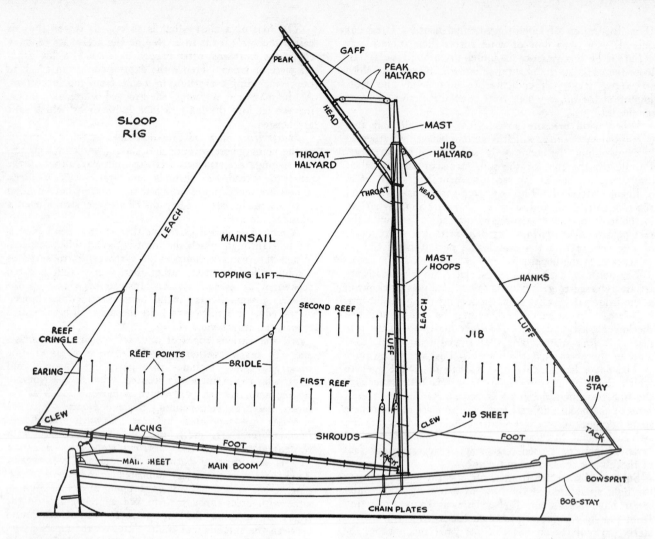

Figure labels: SLOOP RIG — PEAK — GAFF — PEAK HALYARD — HEAD — MAST — THROAT HALYARD — JIB HALYARD — LEACH — MAINSAIL — THROAT — HEAD — TOPPING LIFT — MAST HOOPS — HANKS — SECOND REEF — REEF CRINGLE — REEF POINTS — LEACH — LUFF — JIB — LUFF — BRIDLE — EARING — FIRST REEF — JIB STAY — CLEW — LACING — CLEW — JIB SHEET — TACK — FOOT — FOOT — MAIN SHEET — MAIN BOOM — SHROUDS — BOWSPRIT — CHAIN PLATES — BOB-STAY

two single blocks. There are *main sheets, jib sheets,* etc., depending upon what particular sail the sheet is used to control.

A metal rod called a *deck horse* or *boom horse* is commonly bolted to the deck and on it the ring of a *sheet block* can travel from side to side as the boom swings over. This is the *traveller.* On small boats, a wire bridle often takes the place of a deck horse. Ordinarily today one speaks of the deck fitting (horse) or wire bridle on which the sheet block runs, as the traveller. Running rigging is secured to *belaying pins* of metal or wood set in *pin rails* (*fife rails*) and is said to be *belayed,* when made fast. *Cleats* are also used on small craft in place of belaying pins. In small boats it is good judgment never to belay the sheets, as sudden squalls may make it necessary to let them go in a hurry, to prevent capsizing (turning over).

Halyards (also spelled halliards), another part of the running rigging, are the ropes or tackles used to hoist sails or yards, while the tackle or rope that hauls them down is called a *downhaul. Outhauls* haul the corner of a sail, the clew for example, out to the end of a spar. *Topping lifts* are lines used to support or hoist the outer end of a boom. Down from the topping lifts, light lines lead, in the form of bridles, to the boom. These are *lazy jacks,* which control the sail as it is taken in, preventing the sail from falling on deck.

Whereas a motor boat has only to lay her course, regardless of wind and weather, (except under unusual conditions), a sailboat's course is governed to a large extent by the wind direction. For example, a sailboat can never go *dead to windward* or into the *wind's eye* (in the direction from which the wind is blowing) but would be said to *point well* if she could sail within four or five points of the wind. Therefore, to reach an objective to windward, she must *tack* along a zig-zag

course, each leg of which is a *board.* Thus she goes alternately on the *starboard tack* (when the wind comes over the starboard bow) and the *port tack* (wind on the port bow) and is then said to be *beating* (or *working*) to windward.

When she is sailing as close to the wind as possible, a boat is *close-hauled, on the wind,* or *by the wind. Full and by* is a synonymous expression indicating that all sails are full (*drawing*) and the boat is *pointing* as *high* as possible.

Opposed to the idea of sailing as close to the wind as possible is the expression *sailing free,* associated with the condition when the wind is aft. Or, under similar conditions, if she is sailing with sheets well *eased off* (not hauled in close) she may be said to be *sailing large* or *off the wind.* She *runs before the wind* when sailing free with the wind well aft, that is, over the stern or quarter.

Sheets taken in as much as possible are *hauled flat.* Sails are *trimmed in* when they are brought in more nearly parallel with the boat's fore and aft centerline, but to allow the sails to swing off away from that centerline, the sheets are *started.*

In changing from one tack to another the boat *goes about* or *comes about.* To prepare his crew to execute such a maneuver, the coxwain orders *Ready about!* Then, putting the tiller *down* (away from the wind, toward the *lee* side of the boat), he calls *Hard alee!* and brings her about.

As the sails belly out, catching the wind as it shifts across the bow, they *fill away,* or the boat is said to fill away as it gathers headway on the new tack. To *miss stays* is to attempt to come about and fail to complete the maneuver. Then if the boat is caught in a position where she will not fill away on either tack, she is *in irons.* Should the wind catch the sails on the wrong side while she is in irons and start to drive the boat astern, sails are said to be *aback.*

One *fetches* a given objective if he is running a course to windward and reaches the mark without tacking. When working to windward, each *leg* or tack is a *board* and, depending on the length of each leg, there may be *long boards* and *short boards.*

If a gust of wind comes along, threatening to capsize the boat, the coxswain must ease the pressure of wind on his sails, so he puts the tiller *down* (away from the wind, toward the *lee* side). He is *luffing* then as the boat's bow swings into the wind and the luffs of the sails shake so that wind is spilled. If he attempts to sail too close to the wind, causing all the sails to shake, and spill wind, the expression is *all in the wind.*

A *reach* is a course that can be made good when sailing off the wind, that is, sailing free, not close-hauled. The wind then is nearly abeam. With the wind forward of the beam, it is a *close reach;* abaft the beam, a *broad reach.*

Running before the wind, sails are sometimes set with booms on opposite sides, *wing and wing.* It is considered the most dangerous point of sailing to have the wind *dead aft* because of the risk, to an inexperienced boatman, of having the boom accidentally swing across the stern to the opposite side. This is a *jibe* (or *gybe*) and at the least can cause considerable damage to spars and rigging. If the maneuver is executed deliberately, with the sail and boom kept under control, there is no danger and this is exactly what happens when *wearing.* Instead of tacking, with the bow passing through the wind, the stern in wearing is brought through the wind.

Another point that must be watched in running before the wind in a tendency to *yaw,* or *veer* suddenly off course. The boat is said to *broach to* if, through bad steering or the force of a heavy sea, she is allowed to slew around with a possibility, as she swings into the wind, of being caught broadside *in the trough.*

To *bring to* is to stop a boat by throwing her head into the wind, (or to come to an anchorage). To *heave to* is to lay the boat with helm to leeward and sails trimmed so that the boat alternately *comes to* and *falls off,* keeping out of the trough. Vessels often heave to in heavy weather. Motor boats heave to when the boat's head is brought into the wind or sea and held there by means of her engines. Larger ships sometimes are allowed to drift in whatever position they will assume relative to wind and sea, with wind on the quarter or even with the ship lying in the trough. That may be their method of heaving to, depending on how the ship will be most comfortable under stress of weather.

A SAILBOAT *lies to* when, without anchoring, she is held in one position with no way on. The bow *pays off* when it swings away (falls off) from the wind. She is kept a *rap full* when sails are filled, not quite close-hauled, and is *pinched* when sailed so close to the wind that the sails shiver. If a boat is *carrying* a heavy *press* of canvas, the helmsman may *ease her* by luffing a little. Lines are eased off when slacked.

Sails are *bent* to spars; lines belayed to cleats or bitts when made fast or secured. Lines *reeve* through blocks or *fairleads* (which guide them in the desired direction). Sails *draw* when they fill with wind and drive a boat; *bag,* when they set too full, with *taut* (tight) leaches and canvas slack. *Slack* is the opposite of taut. One *looses sail* when *unfurling* it. To *furl* sail is to roll it up and secure it to a yard or boom, and unfurl conveys the opposite idea when the sail is made ready for use.

A boat is under *easy* sail if she is not laboring or straining, but when the wind *freshens* it may be necessary to *shorten sail* (reduce the amount of canvas carried). *Douse* and *strike* are synonymous terms used when sail is shortened.

Reefing (spoken of elsewhere in connection with the parts of a sail) consists of reducing the area of a sail by lowering it part way, gathering the foot of the sail along the boom, and securing it with the *reef points.* There are usually several bands of reef points; to *close reef* means to shorten down to the last band, rather than just a *single* or *double reef.* When no sail is set, as happens on occasion when a vessel *scuds* (drives) before a gale, she is under *bare poles.*

MOST confusing are some of the terms having to do with directions relative to the wind. As previously indicated, *windward*

(pronounced windard) means toward the wind, the direction from which the wind blows. A boat goes to windward, but in speaking of the side of a vessel and the parts on that side on which the wind is blowing, it is better to refer to the *weather* side.

Opposed to windward is *leeward* (pronounced looard), the direction away from the wind, toward which it is blowing. The *lee side,* therefore, is away from the wind, and a boat makes *leeway* when blown sideways off her course. A *lee shore* is a good one to *give a wide berth* (keep well clear of it). Many use this term in a mistaken sense, thinking that there is protection from the wind under a lee shore. But since it is one on which the wind is blowing, it is dangerous. When a vessel is caught on a lee shore and has to work her way clear, she is *clawing off.*

As a boat *heels* (*not* keels) to the wind in sailing, the weather side is *up,* the leeward side *down.* Hence the expression, putting the helm or tiller up or down. A boat *carries weather helm* if the tiller must be kept to windward in order to hold her course; *lee helm* if it must be kept to leeward. In a good breeze it is well for a sailboat to carry a little weather helm. Then if the tiller is let go the boat will tend to come up into the wind instead of falling off. The *trim* of the boat, determined by the distribution of the weight of crew and ballast, has much to do with what helm the boat will carry.

Other Terms

FEW will require to have the distinction between *cabin* and *cockpit* pointed out in their application to small boats. Many small rowing and sailing craft are entirely open or partly decked. On small decked boats a cabin is the enclosed space, the cockpit open. In sailing vessels the cockpit is usually a small well aft where the steering wheel is located.

A lot of misunderstanding revolves about the use of the term *sheets.* When speaking of the parts of a boat—not sails—the *foresheets* indicate that space forward of the foremast thwart. The *sternsheets* is the space abaft the after thwart.

When small boats are fitted with sails, the keel is usually not deep enough to provide good sailing qualities so they are fitted with either *centerboards* or *daggerboards.* Their function is the same, but the construction differs. The centerboard lies in a vertical well, its long dimension fore and aft. It can be hoisted or lowered as required, being pivoted at the forward end. The well or box which houses the centerboard in its raised position is watertight and is called a *trunk.* The trunk has *head ledges* (vertical members) at each end and a *cap* on top. Dagger-boards fulfill the same function as a centerboard by increasing the keel area, but are raised and lowered vertically in the trunk, not pivoted.

A *PAINTER* is a line at the bow of the boat, used for towing or *making* the boat *fast.* (One does not "tie a boat up.") A painter at the stern is called a *stern fast.* A *sea painter* is used in life boats when launching them at sea. This is a long line attached to a thwart by means of a *toggle* so that it can be cast off easily, the line being led well forward on the ship, outside all stanchions, etc.

Chocks are metal fittings through which mooring or anchor lines are passed so as to lead them in the proper direction toward a dock, other vessel, etc. *Cleats,* of metal or wood, are fittings with two arms or horns on which lines can be made fast, or *belayed.*

When boats are to be lifted from the water on *davits* or hoists, metal fittings must be attached to the hull, usually the keel, to provide an eye into which hoisting gear can be hooked. These are *hoisting pads,* though on small pleasure boats it is often the practice to use *lifting rings* on deck, with rods passing down to the keel. Cleat and lifting ring may be designed as a combined fitting. *Hoisting shackles* are bolted to *hoisting rods* or pads; into these shackles the lower block of the *boat falls* is hooked.

Boat falls are the blocks and tackle used to hoist and lower boats on davits. A *block* consists of a wood or metal frame or shell containing one or more *sheaves* (pronounced shivs) or rollers in the *sheave hole* (space) between the *cheeks* of the block. Power to pull or hoist anything is greatly multiplied when a line is passed continuously around the several sheaves of a pair of blocks. The blocks with the line constitute a *tackle* (pronounced by seamen taykle). Boats, like fishermen's dories, are *nested* when thwarts are removed and the boats stowed one inside the other. Half a dozen boats, or more, may be so nested.

Cleats and Bitts

While cleats are satisfactory for making lines fast, wooden or metal *bitts* are often preferred where heavy strains are to be carried. These are vertical posts, sometimes single, sometimes double. They may take the form of a fitting bolted securely to the deck but often, as in the case of the wooden *samson post,* pass through the deck and are securely *stepped* at the keel or otherwise strongly fastened.

Towing bitts are also called *towing posts.* Where feasible, towing bitts on a towboat are located as near amidships as possible to permit the stern of the towing boat to swing for better maneuvering. Sometimes round metal pins are fitted through the head of a post or bitt to aid in belaying the line. Such a pin is a *norman pin.* They are also used to secure rudder heads.

Slings of wire rope or chain are used when handling boats on *booms* or *cranes.* Booms are also rigged out from a ship's side for small boats to ride to when alongside. When a boat handled on davits aboard a ship is to be secured at the *davit heads,* it is held in position by *gripes* against *strongbacks,* which are spars lashed between davits. Gripes may be of canvas or tarred hemp with a wood mat backed with canvas. If the boat is secured in a *cradle* or *chocks* on deck the gripe may be of chain or metal, tightened down by means of *turnbuckles.* These are threaded metal devices having left- and right-hand threads so that the eyebolts, hooks or shackles at either end may be drawn together as the turnbuckle is screwed up. Turnbuckles are commonly spliced into rigging on sailing craft so *shrouds* and *stays* can be *set up.* When rigging is set up, the slack is taken out.

Boat hooks, mentioned elsewhere, hardly need definition. They are simply poles with metal hook fittings on the end used when a boat comes into a dock to *fend off* (prevent hitting) or to pick up a mooring. *Fenders,* of various kinds, have already been defined.

Docks, Piers and Harbors

Speaking of docks and related subjects, a distinction must often be drawn between terminology technically right when applied to ships and commercial craft and that which is more appropriate for small pleasure craft. For example, *marina* and *yacht basin* come to mind when the average yachtsman thinks of a protected basin offering facilities for the berthing (tie-up) of pleasure craft. A shipmaster might think of a *dock* as an artificial basin, protected perhaps by jetties and breakwaters, with facilities for loading and unloading his vessel. A boatman, on the other hand, usually thinks of a dock as the structure he builds at the edge of the bank or shore in protected waters for his boat to lie to, as distinguished from the situation where a boat lies to a permanent *mooring* in an *anchorage,* away from the shore.

Piles, that is, substantial stakes, are often driven into the bottom at marinas to form individual *slips* in which boats can be berthed. When piles are used to support structures such as bridges, they are referred to as *piers.* A *wharf* is a structure built on the shore of a harbor extending into deep water so that vessels may lie alongside to load or unload cargo or passengers. In the United States, a wharf running at an angle to the shore line may also be referred to as a *pier.* One makes fast *to* a pile, but *alongside* a wharf. Whether he makes fast to or alongside a pier depends on what kind of pier he has in mind. Fishermen in small boats often make fast under a bridge *to* the piers supporting it, but if it is the wharf-like pier that is under discussion then the vessel makes fast *alongside.*

Boats are *hauled out* of the water on inclined planes at the water's edge called *ways* (marine way or marine railway), the framework which supports her as she is hauled out being called a *cradle.*

Jetties are dikes or embankments connected to the land; when these are used to protect a harbor, and have no connection with the land, they are generally referred to as *breakwaters.* *Groins* are jetty-like dikes built out at roughly a 90-degree angle from the shore to prevent erosion of the shore line.

A *harbor* is an anchorage which affords reasonably good protection for a vessel, with shelter from wind and sea. Strictly speaking, it applies to the water area with whatever breakwaters, jetties, etc., are needed for its protection. *Port* is a more comprehensive term,

including not only the harbor but, collectively, all the facilities for freight and passengers as well, such as docks, wharves, piers, warehouses and similar structures.

Miscellaneous Terms

Here are a few miscellaneous terms you may use more or less frequently. *Bilge keels* are narrow keels sometimes applied at the turn of a vessel's bilge to help reduce her rolling. *Ground plates* are sheets of anti-corrosive metal secured to the bottom below the water line, to which electrical ground wires are attached. *Teredos* are a type of shipworm which may bore into a boat's bottom if unprotected by copper paint. A *stuffing box* is a metal fitting (usually bronze) which fits around the propeller shaft to prevent water from entering the hull. The *shaft,* of course, connects the engine and propeller.

Secure, in nautical terms, does not mean obtain, but rather to make fast, or safe. One *secures for sea* when he puts extra lashings on movable objects to prevent their shifting. *Scope* is the length of anchor line paid out from hawse pipe, or bow chock, to anchor, often expressed as a ratio to the depth of water. A *round turn* is taken when a line is passed completely around a spar, bitt, rope or other object. *Two-blocks* is the term used when a tackle has been hauled up so that the blocks meet. *Signal halyards* are light lines used for hoisting flags and signals to spreaders, yard arms, etc.

Galley smoke pipes are sometimes called *Charley Nobles.* Closets, aboard a boat, are called *lockers* and a *hanging locker* is one deep enough for full-length garments. When something is put away in its proper place aboard ship, it is *stowed; lazarettes* are compartments in the stern of a vessel used for stowage. *Overhead* is a nautical term for ceiling or roof. Properly, you have no roof on a boat, and *ceiling,* in nautical use, is the sheathing or planking inside the frames, as distinguished from the outer planking. When the stem or stern of a boat *rakes* (is not perpendicular), the term *overhang* describes the projection of the upper part of bow or stern beyond a perpendicular from the waterline. A *jumper* is a preventer rope, wire or chain used to prevent a spar from giving way in an upward direction. A job is done *smartly* when done quickly, in a neat, efficient, shipshape manner.

Some Terms Relating to Courses, Bearings, etc.

A *great circle* is a circle on the surface of a sphere made by intersection of a plane through the sphere's center. A *meridian* is a great circle of the earth, passing through its poles. *Magnetic meridians* are irregular lines on the earth's surface, passing through the magnetic poles. They indicate the direction of the earth's magnetic field.

A *course* is the direction of movement prescribed for a vessel from one place to another. A *true course* is one taken from the chart with reference to true north. (The angle between a vessel's keel and the geographic meridian, when the vessel is on course.) The *magnetic course* is the angle between a vessel's keel and the magnetic meridian passing through her position. A *compass course* is the course as indicated by a vessel's compass. (The angle between a vessel's keel and the direction indicated by the north point of the compass card when the vessel is on course.) The *course steered* is the direction in which a vessel is steered, and may be given a true, magnetic or compass value. The *heading* is the direction a vessel's bow points at any given time. This may not coincide with her course. A *track* is the *course made good,* that is, the actual path of the vessel over the bottom. (Usually given a true value.) A *bearing* is the direction of a terrestrial object from an observer, and may be given a true, magnetic or compass value. A *relative bearing* is the direction of a terrestrial object from an observer, relative to the vessel's heading, best measured in degrees from 000 to 360.

Variation is the angle between true north and the direction of north as indicated by a magnetic compass unaffected by deviation. (It is easterly if the north point of such a compass points to the east of true north, westerly if it points west of true north.) *Deviation* is an error in a magnetic compass caused by magnetic influences on the vessel. (Easterly if the north point of the compass points east of magnetic north, westerly if it points west of magnetic north.) *Compass error* is the algebraic sum of variation and deviation.

CHAPTER VI

THE ART OF
Anchoring

design rather than on mere mass.

The result is that old-fashioned conceptions of good ground tackle must now be revised, especially in the matter of required weights, when the newer types of equipment are carried. To say that you carry a 30-pounder aboard your boat doesn't mean much till you specify whether it is a Herreshoff type, a Navy anchor, a Northill, a Danforth, or some other, and know the type of bottom it will be buried in.

The war proved to be a great laboratory for the testing of ground tackle as was demonstrated when scores of thousands of landing craft

GROUND TACKLE

IN anchoring, as in every other art, there are good and bad practices. No one technique may be claimed as the only right and successful method, but out of the experience of boatmen over the years have been distilled certain principles which, if observed, will help the amateur to "stay put" when he lets his anchor go.

In the last analysis, power to hold is the real criterion of effective anchoring. If you hold—and know you'll hold—with a 3:1 scope and light anchor, while your neighbor drags with double the weight and 7:1 scope as recommended by the book, then no one can deny you've practised your art better than he.

There are so many variables entering into the picture —the size, type and weight of the boat, whether she is light or shallow draft, the area she presents to the wind in freeboard and superstructure, the weight and design of anchor, the nature of the bottom, the amount of sea running, to mention a few—that any attempt to reduce the subject to hard and fast rules would be futile.

Not only that, but practices vary in different parts of the country. On some rocky coasts they swear by the old-fashioned heavy kedge with chain. In other localities where hard sand bottoms prevail, the light spidery sand anchor is popular, with manila for the rode. And, in every locality, you'll find most of the popular types of ground tackle represented in any given fleet of boats, regardless of the preponderance of one particular make.

For many years, the yachtsman's choice in anchors was narrowed down to a relatively few types—notably the sand anchor, the old triangular-fluked kedge with a dull bill, or a Navy (patent) anchor. Then improved variations of each began to put in an appearance, and radically new designs as well, based scientifically on good

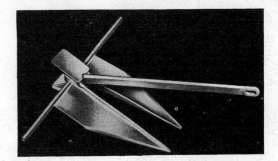

Danforth's newest anchor is the Hi-Tensile, which has demonstrated tremendous holding power for its weight. At upper left, one of the older patterns of the kedge

relied on their Danforths to haul them off invasion beaches, and light weight Northills saved precious tons of carrying capacity for fleets of seaplanes.

While no one will deny the necessity of selecting anchors heavy enough to hold under any conditions you may ever meet, there is little point in carrying a hundred pounds of weight when a 30-pounder of better design might give you equal, or greater, holding power.

To those unfamiliar with the types of anchor in common use on boats today, the popular conceptions of anchors are usually of the Navy type often seen housed in the hawse pipes of large Naval and commercial vessels or, at best, the older pattern of kedge, illustrated in one of the photographs. Too often anchors are bought for small craft on the basis of this limited knowledge, on the false assumption that the best patterns must have been chosen for the larger ships.

Reference to the labeled sketch at this point is suggested, to gain familiarity with the correct names of the anchor's various parts.

The Kedge

For purposes of broad classification, anchors are of either the stock or stockless design. The kedge is of the stock pattern, while the Navy anchor is stockless, so that the shank can be hauled into a hawse pipe. The older types of kedge are best identified by their roughly triangular flukes and relatively dull bill. This latter feature is a handicap to the fluke's getting a good bite into a hard bottom, and if it doesn't penetrate to bury the fluke deep, holding power is poor. It is a fact, however, that in soft muddy bottoms such an anchor will sink down because of its weight and the broad flukes may hold where a narrow fluked anchor of the sand type would slice through and never hold.

Again, the old kedge is often spoken of highly by those who habitually anchor on rocky bottoms. They prefer a large heavy hook and use a buoyed trip line to free it if it fouls under a rock. This latter trick will be discussed more fully elsewhere.

Right: The thimble, shackle and eye splice are commonly used to secure manila line to the anchor ring. The key and its lashing are also shown

Left: Wilcox Crittenden's Yachtsman type of anchor, labeled to indicate names of the various parts

Left: Modern light weight Danforth anchors chocked on deck. Note the windlass and bow chocks

A weakness of the conventional kedge is the triangular shape of fluke, presenting a shoulder square with the arm around which a turn of the anchor line may foul as a boat swings with changing current or shifts of wind. Once the line (sometimes referred to as the cable or rode) has fouled the arm projecting above the bottom, its holding power is nil, because that's the very principle you'd use in freeing a fouled anchor—to draw the projecting arm up and out, instead of hauling on the ring.

Several anchor manufacturers have taken the good qualities of the kedge and have redesigned it to overcome the objectionable features. Characteristic of these improved models are the Herreshoff and the Yachtsman's type (illustrated in the labeled photograph), in both of which the bill is sharper for better penetration of hard bottoms, and the fluke is diamond-shaped to eliminate the shoulder and so permit the line to slip past it.

Sand Anchors

The trawl or sand anchor resembles the kedge except that the fluke is small and the bill sharp to enable the anchor to bite in hard bottoms, and bury to the shank. Sand anchors vary in the proportioning of their parts and particularly in the shape of the arms, so that there may be considerable difference in the holding power of different patterns of equal weight.

One of the best sand anchors is the Bedell type. In hard bottoms it bites in smartly and, once it has a chance to bury to the shank, it develops tremendous holding power even on a relatively short scope. So hard does it hold that it is sometimes necessary to use power to break it out, snubbing the shortened anchor line on the bitt.

Folding Types

Stock-type anchors may be made with a fast stock or with a loose stock. In the latter type, a key is required to pin the stock in its open position when set up ready for use. When the key is withdrawn from its slot, the stock can be folded back alongside the shank for better stowage. In the Bedell pattern, the T-shaped key is an integral part of the stock. A T-shaped slot is cut in the shank to correspond. When setting it up, the stock passes through in one position only. It is then given a 180-degree turn and is ready for use, with no loose keys to pin in place.

Some of the folding types are also arranged to permit folding of the arms but, in the case of the kedge, much of the holding power is lost because the arms must be straight to fold compactly. Some of the light weight anchors, to be discussed later, are much better in this respect, as the folding feature is not achieved at the expense of holding power.

The Stockless Anchor

Coming now to consideration of the stockless types, the old Navy anchor is probably the one most often reviled on small craft because, on the one hand, if it is heavy enough to hold, it is a back-breaker to handle due to its high ratio of weight to holding power—and, on the other hand, if the weight is kept within reason, it cannot be trusted to hold. Large ships have plenty of mechanical power to handle heavy Navy anchors which stow compactly in the hawse pipes but on a small pleasure craft the problem is entirely different.

In addition to compactness, Navy anchors do have these virtues, that there is no fluke projecting above the bottom to foul the line, and they lie flat on deck without need for folding a stock. Because of these features, there have been a number of variations of the Navy pattern, some of which are highly regarded.

anchor, the Danforth has a round rod through the crown which prevents the anchor from rolling, yet does not stop it from penetrating or interfere with its stowage in a hawsepipe. Since the flukes fold as in the Navy type, the Danforth lies flat on deck, and is easy to handle and stow.

Holding power of the Danforth has been rated at anywhere from triple to ten or twenty times that of some of the older types. The Navy has replaced many of its old patent anchors with Danforths of half the weight, or less. During the war 328-foot LST's carried 3,000-pound Danforths on the stern which were let go well offshore before the landing craft hit the beach. When ready to retract from the beach, powerful winches would sweat up on the anchor cable and pull the LST off stern-first against the power of the ship's engines running ahead.

Of more direct interest to small boat owners, perhaps, are reports by boatmen of practical experiences in weathering bad blows when lying to comparatively light anchors. One 40-footer, for example, rode out a 100-mile hurricane to a 30-pound Danforth (Mark II) without dragging. By older standards, a kedge of 120 pounds might have been indicated for this boat on the basis of recommendations of 3 pounds of heavy anchor per foot of boat length.

A new Danforth, the Hi-Tensile, is now in production, in sizes up to 3000 pounds, with flukes fabricated from rolled alloy steel sections, drop forged alloy steel shanks, and seamless steel stocks.

Left: A Bedell sand anchor (at extreme left) and a Herreshoff type. Note the difference in area of the flukes. Below: A pair of Yachtsman's type anchors chocked on deck and lashed down. Note balancing bands on the anchor shanks, placed at the center of gravity. Hook on the davit tackle is hooked into this ring to swing the anchor aboard

The Danforth
(Light weight type)

Undoubtedly one of the best developments along this line is the Danforth, which has the unique feature of being equally adaptable to large vessels and small boats. Tens of thousands of Danforths were used on scores of different types of war boats, from small miscellaneous harbor craft up to large ocean-going ships.

In the Danforth anchor, flukes are long and sharp, designed so that heavy strains will bury the anchor completely. Tests have shown that the anchor will tend to work down through soft bottoms to firmer holding ground below, burying part of the cable as well. In place of a stock through the head of the

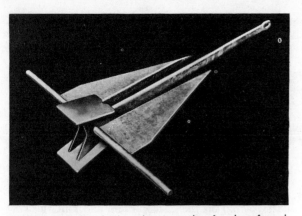

The Danforth Standard anchor is made of a drop-forged alloy steel shank, fabricated alloy steel flukes and drawn seamless tubing stock welded to the flukes. It holds 30 to 200 times its own weight, depending on conditions

Danforth also makes a Standard model in which the flukes are fabricated from alloy plate instead of cast steel. Holding power of the Hi-Tensile model is said to be about equal to Danforth Standard anchors of about twice the weight. A 5-pound Danforth has held a 40-foot cruising sloop in all bottoms, including soft mud six feet deep, in 25-mile winds. A special Danforth is made for small craft such as row boats, in 2½ and 4½-pound Standard models.

The CQR Plow

Another innovation, of the stockless type, is the Laughlin CQR plow anchor. Of English origin, the plow is now made in this country as well, has been given numerous severe tests and has been highly recommended by users. This anchor takes its name from the unusual design of its flukes, which resemble a plow. When let go, the anchor lies on its side on the bottom. As soon as a pull is put on the cable, it rights itself driving the point of the flukes in, and then buries the flukes completely.

Though difficulty has been experienced at times in getting the anchor to bite in kelp-covered or rocky bottoms, this would be a hard test for most anchors. In normal bottoms of sand, mud or clay, tests showed that it outheld older stocked anchors by about 4 to 1, and held 11 times better than the old stockless.

The Northill

Proof of the claim that weight is of less significance than scientific design to achieve holding power is evidenced in results obtained with lightweight anchors like the Northill. The Northill is made in a utility model of hot-dipped galvanized Ductilon. For compact stowage, the stock of the Northill utility anchor is arranged to fold up against the shank.

Light weight anchors have proved a boon both on seaplanes like the big clippers, where no excess weight can be tolerated, and on boats, where the weight of necessary ground tackle often governs the size of boat a man can conveniently handle single-handed.

The Northill has a stock at the crown instead of at the ring end, adding to the anchor's holding power when the flukes are buried. Arms are at right angles to the shank, and the broad reinforced flukes are set at a carefully computed angle to assure a quick bite and deep penetration. A relatively sharp-pointed bill aids in causing the anchor to bite in smartly as soon as a pull is exerted on the cable, and narrow fluke arms allow the anchor to dig deep.

Figuring holding power as a ratio to anchor weight which, in the final analysis, is the best and most significant means of making a comparison, the Northill has demonstrated holding power as high as 60 to 1, against 3 or 4 to 1 for Navy anchors or 7 or 8 to 1 for some of the kedges. In tests, a 12-pound Northill has outheld a 300-pound Navy stockless.

Northill also makes a small boat anchor for craft like rowboats, outboards and small sailboats. The weight is less than 3 pounds and it is fabricated from heavy gauge steel, hot-dip galvanized. The small boat anchor is only 12 inches long but has the same patented design as the larger models.

The Northill utility is now made in 6, 13, 27, 47, 75 and 105-pound sizes. For an average cruiser about 35 feet in length, Northill recommends a regular anchor of 13 pounds weight, with a spare emergency Northill of 27-pound size.

Grapnels and Mushrooms

Grapnels are another of the stockless type of anchor, having four or five curved claw-like arms. These are thin and spidery with little holding power in soft bottoms. Some types with arms reinforced to prevent bending under heavy strain, are used on bottoms of rock or coral, with the deliberate intent of hooking under a rock or into a crevice. A buoyed trip line under such conditions is generally made fast to a ring in the crown so it can be retrieved.

Mushroom anchors, stockless, having a cast-iron bowl at the end of a shank, are the popular choice for permanent moorings, where they have tremendous holding power when down long enough to be imbedded deep in the bottom. A refinement of this type incorporates in its design a heavy bulb cast into the shank near the ring to increase the holding power. Much greater reliance can be placed on standard types of mushroom anchor than on the concrete blocks or iron car wheels sometimes used as substitutes.

The Manila Rode

The line or cable used with an anchor is often called the rode. On small boats it is commonly of manila or galvanized chain—in some cases, flexible stainless steel wire.

A majority of small pleasure craft use manila, because it is light and easy to handle without a winch. As a boat surges in a seaway at anchor, manila is elastic enough to stretch and cushion the shock, which eases the load on the anchor and mooring bitt.

Sisal, a substitute, with its projecting ends of fiber, is not as nice to handle as manila, and is only 80 percent as strong. If sisal must be used, it should be a size larger than manila.

Some yachtsmen prefer bolt rope to the regular manila. Because of its greater strength, it can be used in one diameter smaller than the standard manila—or, in equal diameters, it provides an extra factor of safety. A special refinement is whale line—strong, soft, free from kinking, and easy to handle.

Chain

Manila, in diameters up to 1 inch, 1¼, or even 1½ inches, is satisfactory on boats up to about 50 or 60 feet in length—even larger, under normal conditions. Manila more than 1½ inches in diameter is hard to handle so chain is indicated for larger craft. BBB grade is recommended, and the boat should be equipped with a winch having a wildcat on one end to fit the chain.

From this it should not be inferred that chain is not also in use on smaller craft. On boats that cruise extensively and have occasion to anchor on rock or coral, chain is often preferred—in fact, regarded as indispensable, as it stands chafing where manila won't.

A combination often recommended, especially for light weight anchors, is the use of four or five fathoms of chain shackled between the anchor and the manila rode. This is intended to take chafing of the bottom and as a protection against sharp fluke edges. At the same time it tends to lower the angle of pull and help give the anchor a bite. Some cruising men who have had extensive experience in anchoring on rough coral bottoms claim this to be inadequate, and prefer chain throughout.

Chain, especially in the larger diameters, has considerable weight and produces a sag in the anchor line that acts like the "spring" in manila to ease shocks from surging. However, when the sag is out, it is generally agreed that the shock on both boat and anchor is greater than with manila. Too much emphasis should not be placed on the cushioning effect of a chain's sag, in small sizes.

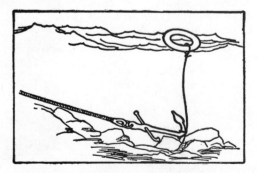

A buoyed trip line to the crown will permit the anchor to be hauled up fluke first if fouled under a rock

When a boat swings about her anchor with wind or current and fouls a turn of line around an arm, holding power is destroyed.

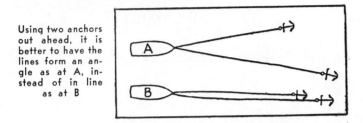

Using two anchors out ahead, it is better to have the lines form an angle as at A, instead of in line as at B

One test, made in a moderate wind with a generous scope of 10 to 1, revealed not a single link of chain resting on the bottom.

On the other hand, in larger sizes, exhaustive tests on a 104-footer with ½-inch and ⅝-inch chain showed the weight of chain to be beneficial, reducing the maximum load on the anchor to as little as 5 percent of that recorded in a similar test with a wire rope rode. Under similar conditions, manila rope reduced the maximum load about 50 percent, as compared with wire cable. Conclusions drawn from the tests were that heavier anchors, cable and deck gear were required when using wire rope because of the heavier surge load on the anchor.

Chain is easy to stow in lockers and doesn't soak up moisture like manila, which requires drying on deck before stowage. Sand doesn't stick to chain and mud can be washed off, but sand penetrating the strands of manila is bad for the rope, chafing fibers like an abrasive and reducing its strength.

The weight of chain in the bow of some small boats may be an objection, but this can be overcome by dividing a long chain cable into two or three shorter lengths, stowed where convenient, and shackled together as necessary.

Nylon Rope

Though it costs considerably more than manila, nylon rope has become very popular for anchor, mooring and tow lines. Extremely elastic (stretching a third or more with safety) it absorbs sudden strains that snap other ropes. Nearly double the strength of manila, ⅜" nylon is as strong as ½" manila; ¾" nylon equals 1" manila. It is light in weight per pound of strength, and also resists rot, decay and mildew.

Nylon should be unreeled from the coil like wire, not up through the coil like manila. Neither should it be towed when new to take out the kinks. When splicing, tape and then fuse the ends with a hot knife. Strands should be kept twisted, and an extra tuck taken, the ends to be left a little longer, when trimming, until the splice is well set under strain. Splice thimbles in tightly to prevent them from dropping out when the nylon stretches. Seizings should be made tightly so they cannot slip.

If necessary, nylon can be stowed wet, but it is best to keep it away from continued moisture, heat and chemicals. In use, it is recommended that it be covered or shaded from the sun, especially when new, as ultraviolet light may damage surface fibers. Like manila, it should be protected by chafing gear at chocks and other points of wear. A length of chain between nylon rode and anchor is especially desirable on rough bottoms, to reduce chafe.

Wire Rope Rode

Reference has been made to wire rope as an alternate to the use of the more conventional manila or chain for the rode. In recent years, flexible stainless steel wire rope has proved its outstanding merit for pennants on permanent moorings because of its strength and resistance to chafe and abrasion.

In addition, many fine yachts have also been equipped with wire for the regular anchor cable in preference to manila or chain. One 70-footer, for example, saved 1,500 pounds of weight by using 75 fathoms of ⅝-inch stainless steel instead of the heavier chain.

Wire rope is spooled evenly on the drum of a special winch designed for its use, permitting a long length to be carried compactly in small space on deck. Kinks are disastrous, but spooling on the drum takes care of that.

Due regard, of course, should be paid to the necessity of providing anchors of sufficient holding power, in the light of findings reported on comparative anchor loads with wire, manila and chain.

Securing the Rode to the Ring

Various methods are used in securing the rode to the anchor ring. With manila, the preferred practice is to work an eye splice around a thimble and use a galvanized shackle to join the thimble and ring. With this kind of rig, it is a good idea to put a bit of graphite grease on threads of the shackle pin and wire it to prevent its working out.

Incidentally, the key which locks the stock of a folding anchor should also be wired or lashed to hold it in its keyway.

With a thimble and shackle, a ready means is provided of backing up your manila with a length of chain, if desired, shackling the chain in turn to the anchor ring. Shackles should be large enough so as not to bind the manila against the ring and cause chafing.

ANCHOR BEND

ANCHOR BOWLINE

Some boatmen would rather bend their manila directly to the ring, using an anchor bend and seizing the free end to the rode. In the Chesapeake, and elsewhere, they use a bowline with an extra round turn around the ring, pointing out that this makes it easy to turn the line end for end occasionally, which is good practice, or to remove the line from the anchor for easy handling when stowing, etc.

Another convenient rig on small craft is merely to work a big eye splice in the end of manila, passing it through the ring, over the anchor while the stock (on stock types) is folded along the shank, and then tighten the eye by hauling it up on itself at the ring.

Shackles, of course, are the accepted method of securing chain cables to the anchor, stout swivels being an added refinement.

The bitter end of an anchor cable (the inboard end) should preferably be made fast to some part of the boat to guard against loss in case the anchor goes by the board accidentally. Sometimes this is accomplished by leading the line below, perhaps through a deck pipe, and securing to a samson post or other strong timber. On sail boats, it may be secured to a mast. On small boats where the entire length of rode is carried on deck, it is feasible to have an eye splice in the bitter end to fit the post, run this down close to the deck and use a clove hitch above the eye splice to adjust the scope.

Pitch of the fluke on the Northill anchor causes it to penetrate and dig in instantly. Here the anchor is already turning to its ultimate horizontal position. In the Northill the stock is at the crown end, rather than the ring end, as in kedges

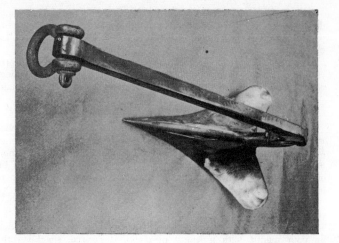

Stowage of Ground Tackle

ONE or two—sometimes three—anchors are generally carried on the forward deck ready for use. If rodes are stowed below at the anchorage, at least one should be made ready and secured to its anchor before getting under way from the dock or mooring. The obvious reason, of course, is that the "hook" should be ready to let go at all times on an instant's notice in case of engine failure —unlikely, but a possibility.

To prevent deck anchors from coming adrift when the boat rolls and pitches in a seaway, it is imperative that they be carried in chocks and lashed down against jumping out of the chocks. One way to do this is to fit hardwood blocks to the deck, notched to receive the fluke edges and ring end of the anchor, bedding the blocks in white lead or marine glue before fastening them down.

Standard types of cast bronze chocks are also available from marine supply dealers to take most anchors. In either case, eye bolts or rings should be provided so that the shank (and folded stock, if any) can be lashed down securely with light line.

Commonly a spare anchor for emergencies or extreme conditions of weather is carried below. This, too, requires careful chocking as a heavy anchor, gone adrift, could easily loosen a bottom plank with its pounding. Weight of this should be carried on floors or frames, not planking.

In any case, stow the spare so that it can be made ready on short notice, as its sole value may some day depend on your being able to get it over *quickly* without first digging it out from under an accumulation of gear.

Rope and Chain Lockers

Except for small craft which carry their line coiled

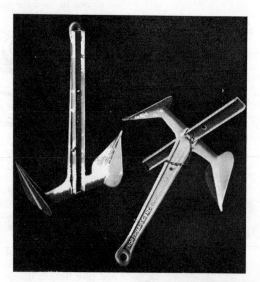

At top: The non-fouling plow type of anchor made by Maxim Silencer Company. Above: Northill's Utility type, made of galvanized Ductilon, showing stock in folded and open positions. Right: View on the forward deck of a yacht carrying stainless steel rope neatly spooled on the drum of a special winch

forward on deck or in an open cockpit, the usual practice is to provide rope and chain lockers in the forepeak. Chain dries quickly as it comes from the water and can be fed down into the locker through a deck pipe as it comes off the winch.

Not so with manila, which should be thoroughly dried on deck before stowing below, where it should be carefully coiled for immediate use. Gratings on deck are an aid in drying before stowage, and the lockers below should be well ventilated and also provided

with gratings or any other arrangement that will permit a good air circulation at all times. Dark wet lockers are a favorite point of origin for destructive dry rot. A hatch over the rope locker that can be thrown open to sun and air is a fine feature.

Deck pipes for manila are available through which the line can be fed below and certain types of bitts are made hollow with an opening in the aft side through which a rode can be passed.

Lines are sometimes flemished down on deck by starting with a free end and winding the line spirally in a clockwise direction to form a flat mat. This looks shipshape but, if allowed to remain long in one spot, will stain the deck. Loose coils permit the line to dry better.

Care of Anchors and Chain

Galvanized anchors are usually coated by the hot-dip process which leaves a tough protective finish, normally requiring no care except ordinary washing off of mud that may be picked up in use. Occasionally, they are freshened up in appearance by a coat of aluminum bronze during spring fitting-out.

Stainless steel, used in Northill anchors, retains its bright luster for years. Slight surface discolorations may be removed by brushing with a 25 percent solution of nitric acid (1 part nitric acid to 3 parts water) and rinsing with fresh water.

On muddy bottoms chain will often come up pretty well fouled with the sticky black stuff because its weight has caused it to lie on the bottom, where even a light strain would keep all but a few feet of manila from touching bottom. Obviously, the chain needs thorough cleaning and on some of the larger craft a hose is provided on deck for the purpose. At best, it's a messy job.

Care and Inspection of Manila

Manila definitely requires good care if it is to give good service, being subject to chafe, and deterioration from a number of causes. The care of manila has been dealt with elsewhere at length so the best we can do here is to hit the high spots.

In the first place, good practice dictates the holding in reserve at all times of one long spare cable in good condition, of a diameter proportioned to the heaviest of your anchors. Splices or bends are never as strong as one single continuous length, yet some boatmen like the idea of dividing long lengths of line into two or three sections for added convenience in handling, shackling lengths together only when necessary.

Lengths of line in regular use may be turned end for end periodically, as most of the chafe and wear comes on the anchor end. On small boats it is often feasible to standardize on one size of line for all rodes. A new one

can be laid by in the spring as a spare and the old spare is then put into regular service.

In any case, a cardinal principle requires that manila line be kept clean to keep grit out of the fibers, and well dried on deck before stowing. An occasional washing with a low-pressure hose, using fresh water, is helpful. High pressure is bad because it tends to drive sand deeper instead of washing it out.

Throwing a strain on a kinked line is fatal to manila. To a lesser degree, short bends are likewise injurious. For this reason the best deck hardware is designed to allow an easy bend at chocks, bitts and cleats. Chafing gear at points of contact can be rigged of strips of canvas wrapped about the line and sewed or lashed with marlin, depending on whether it is to be permanent or temporary. Rubber hose is also used, slitting it spirally so it can be clapped on without sliding down the length of the line.

Periodic inspection of manila pays big dividends. Things to look for are abrasion, broken or frayed fibers or yarns, variation in the size and shape of strands, rot, and acid stains. Rope that has lost its elasticity needs replacement. The same is true if outer fibers are half worn. Inside fibers, when the rope is twisted to expose the interior, should be clean and bright, as they appear in new rope.

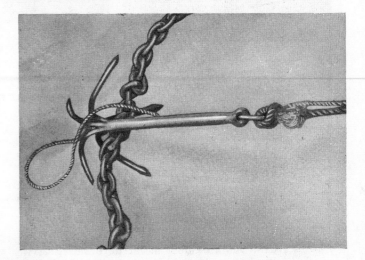

Above: The grapnel is sometimes used for recovering objects lost on the bottom. With a buoyed trip line to the surface, it is also used for anchoring on rocky bottoms. At left, note the windlass with niggerhead for manila and wildcat for chain. Note grating for ventilation of the rope locker. Falls of the davit tackle can be hooked into ring on balance band secured to the anchor shank

Excessive bending or overloading are revealed by white powdered fiber inside, and broken yarns.

Number of Anchors to Carry

The number of anchors to be carried aboard will be conditioned upon several things—the size of boat, whether she is used only in sheltered waters or cruises extensively offshore, and, to some extent, the type of anchor.

Though some small boats are occasionally found with only a single anchor, this can by no stretch of the imagination be considered adequate. Even discounting the possibility of fouling one anchor so badly that it cannot be retrieved, there are many occasions when it is desirable to lay to two. Again, one anchor heavy enough for extreme conditions would be a nuisance in ordinary weather.

Many boats carry two anchors, proportioning the weight in the ratio of about 40 percent in one, 60 percent in the other. Three are undoubtedly better. This allows for two to be carried on deck—a light one for brief stops while some

Above: Kedge and Navy anchors carried on deck. Manila line is belayed on the windlass and deck pipes permit leading line below for stowage. Ventilation to the locker is provided. At left: Diagram showing how the Laughlin COR plow anchor rights itself and buries

one is aboard, and a medium anchor for ordinary service including anchorages at night in harbor. The third might well be a big spare, carried below, selected with an eye to its holding no matter what else lets go, under extreme conditions of wind and weather.

Some experienced yachtsmen carry four, though they probably are in the minority.

How Heavy?

An old rule-of-thumb proportioned the weight of anchors to boat length, granting of course that length is not the sole criterion and assuming a necessary digression from the rule in exceptional cases. One such rule, based on kedges of better design, indicated a small anchor of ½ pound per foot of length, a medium anchor of 1 pound per foot, and a large anchor of 2 pounds per foot.

Very roughly speaking, that probably would serve well enough as a point of departure for a great majority of the average types of boat, though that meant a total of 140 pounds of kedge on a 40-footer.

Certain naval architects, realizing the necessity of even greater weight for safety aboard offshore cruising craft, adopted a formula, using two anchors, of 1½ to 1¾ pounds per foot overall for one anchor, 2¼ to 3 pounds per foot for the other. That would figure a total weight of 150 to 190 pounds in two anchors.

Such formulas were accepted for boats up to about 70 feet in length, two figures being provided as a range to allow for variation in displacement, windage, etc.

Next heavier in the scale of recommended anchor weights was a formula which provided (for two anchors with weights distributed 40 : 60) a total of 3½ to 4 pounds per waterline foot for 25-30-footers, and increasingly heavier weights up to a total of about 8 pounds per foot for 70-footers. Upwards of 35 feet, a third anchor of 1¼ to 1¾ pounds per foot was added.

Another formula takes into account the fact that gross tonnage might often be a better measure of required anchor weights than length. While tonnage is not convertible into feet, analysis of the figures shows that in the case of ordinary cruisers of 40-50 feet, where tonnages may vary from about 17 or 18 up to 25 or 26 tons, the weight of a single anchor runs about 1½ pounds per foot; in motor yachts of about 80 to 100 feet, it figures about 2¼ to 3¼ pounds per foot; in sailing yachts, 2½ pounds for a 40-footer, 3 pounds for a 60-footer, 4 pounds for a 100-footer.

All these figures serve to show how widely recommendations may vary and from them the yachtsman may make his selection if he is kedge-equipped.

Boiling all these facts down, and bearing in mind that they represent a consensus of the best available recommendations for kedge type anchors (not the newer anchors like Danforth and Northill) we get an overall picture something like this:

WEIGHT OF KEDGES (IMPROVED DESIGN)
Per Foot of Boat Length

	Small Kedge	Service Anchor	Heavy Spare
Motor Boats	½ pound	1-1½ pounds	2-3 pounds
Sail Boats	1-1½ pounds	1½-3 pounds	2½-4 pounds

Holding Power of Modern Anchors

With the development of new type anchors which have conclusively demonstrated, both by test and practical experience in use, a vastly greater ratio of holding power to weight, it becomes evident that the old figures are obsolete, when choosing a newer type of anchor, unless due consideration be given to the relative holding power of the new one as compared with the kedge.

Thus, if the old figures show that a 50-pound kedge

is indicated for your boat for normal service, any manufacturer can readily give you the weight in his design which has outheld that anchor.

It is not within the scope of this article to set forth all the comparative data amassed by various manufacturers in their tests. Some facts are, however, interesting and pertinent.

It has been found, for example, that the normal strain on an anchor due to wind and current in average weather, is relatively small. Furthermore, current is a relatively small factor as compared with the pressure exerted by the wind on exposed surfaces. The surge resulting when a boat pitches at anchor in a seaway throws a tremendous strain on the boat and all her ground tackle. And the weight of the boat is another significant factor.

The principal dimensions that determine the holding power required are: overall length, beam, hull depth and draft, displacement and height of superstructure.

The Northill Company has evolved a simple formula for determining the holding power (in pounds) required for average conditions of wind and weather, based on the boat's gross weight, or displacement, as follows:—

HOLDING POWER REQUIRED (AVERAGE CONDITIONS)

Type of Boat	Percentage of Gross Weight
Centerboard Sailboats	5%
Small Motor Boats	6%
Larger Cruisers (Motor)	7%
Keel Type Sailboats	10%

When It Starts to Blow

Where two anchors will be carried, the table above can be used to determine the holding power required of the smaller of the two. However, wind pressure varies as the square of its velocity, so Northill uses another formula to take into account extreme conditions where a boat, surging hard on her ground tackle in open water, is anchored in a gale.

For sailboats, where heavier displacement and windage in masts and rigging must be considered:

$$\text{Pull in pounds} = \frac{AV^2}{186}$$

For motor boats the formula is slightly modified:

$$\text{Pull in pounds} = \frac{AV^2}{220}$$

In the above, V is the velocity of the wind in miles per hour. A is a factor derived by multiplying height (from water line to deckhouse top) by the overall beam.

The result obtained from this formula should be regarded as a minimum holding power, adding roughly a third as a safety factor to allow for those elements that cannot be exactly calculated, such as yawing which changes the area exposed to the wind, and surging (an important factor) which varies with the sea that is running.

Northill Weights

Figures on recommended weights of Northill Utility anchors show that for the lighter of two anchors a 13-pounder is suggested for boats up to 40 feet over all, a 25-pounder for boats 45-55 feet. A 25-pounder is suggested as the larger anchor for 25-30-footers, a 45-pounder for 35-55-footers.

Even lighter weights can be used in the Northill folding type, according to the figures, which recommend: one 6- and one 12-pounder on 25-30-footers; one 12- and one 20-pounder on 35-40-footers; one 12- and one 30-pounder on 45-footers; one 20- and one 30-pounder on 50-55-footers; and one 30- and one 50-pounder on boats 60 feet over all.

The Load on an Anchor

In a paper read by R. S. Danforth before the Society of Naval Architects and Marine Engineers summarizing results obtained in a series of anchoring tests, it was revealed that the load on an anchor is made up of four components:—

(1) Wind pressure, equal to .0043 AV^2 (in which A is the cross-sectional projected area above water, in square feet; and V is wind velocity in knots.)

(2) Load due to current, equal to resistance of the vessel and propeller traveling through water at the speed of the current.

(3) Load due to surge. The formula states that this load amounts to nearly 100 times the displacement in long tons, times the speed in knots squared, divided by the distance in which the vessel is stopped.

(4) A somewhat similar shock load due to the vessel's rising vertically on a sea—particularly on short scope—trying to lift the anchor. Long scope (10:1) tends to reduce this load. Short scopes (3 or 4:1) make it severe.

Referring to the surge load—(3), above—and noting how great it may be, and the factors involved, it is easy to see why the elasticity of good manila is of such consequence in reducing the overall load on an anchor, and how effective the weight of chain may be, as the load is gradually absorbed in lifting it.

Holding Power in Various Bottoms

The manufacturer, in recommending a weight of anchor, will take into consideration variations in his own particular design's holding power in different types of bottom.

Danforth has published a scale of anchor weights for boats 12 to 200 feet in length, which allows for varying conditions of weather and holding ground. It must be remembered that anchor weights given are for the Danforth anchor and would be grossly inadequate in old-fashioned anchors.

The Danforth table is intended only as a general guide; the correct size for your boat may be smaller or larger, depending on the bottom, scope possible, exposure, and such factors.

ANCHOR RODES — AVERAGE LENGTH AND DIAMETER, MANILA AND CHAIN

TABLE 1
MOTOR BOATS, CRUISERS, LIGHT SAILBOATS

W.L. Length Boat (Feet)	Service Anchor Length Rode (Fathoms)	Service Anchor Dia. Manila (Inches)	Heavy Anchor Length Rode (Fathoms)	Heavy Anchor Dia. Manila (Inches)	Heavy Anchor Dia. BBB Chain (Inches)
20	16	7/16	20	1/2	*1/4
25	19	1/2	26	5/8	*1/4
30	23	5/8	32	3/4	*5/16
35	26	5/8	38	7/8	*3/8
40	30	3/4	44	1	*3/8
45	33	7/8	50	1⅛	7/16
50	36	1	56	1¼	1/2
55	40	1⅛	62	1⅜	9/16
60	43	1⅛	68	1⅜	5/8
65	46	1¼	74	1½	11/16
70	50	1¼	80	1½	3/4

TABLE 2
CRUISING AUXILIARIES, OR HEAVY MOTOR CRUISERS WITH LARGE SUPERSTRUCTURE

W.L. Length Boat (Feet)	Service Anchor Length Rode (Fathoms)	Service Anchor Dia. Manila (Inches)	Service Anchor Dia. BBB Chain (Inches)	Heavy Anchor Length Rode (Fathoms)	Heavy Anchor Dia. Manila (Inches)	Heavy Anchor Dia. BBB Chain (Inches)
20	17	1/2	*3/16	25	1/2	*1/4
25	22	5/8	*1/4	33	5/8	*5/16
30	26	3/4	*5/16	40	3/4	*3/8
35	31	7/8	*3/8	48	1	7/16
40	36	1	3/8	55	1⅛	1/2
45	41	1⅛	7/16	63	1¼	1/2
50	46	1⅛	7/16	70	1⅜	9/16
55	50	1¼	1/2	78	1½	3/8
60	55	1¼	1/2	85	1½	11/16
65	60	1⅜	5/8	93	1⅝	3/4
70	65	1⅜	5/8	100	1⅝	3/4

*Manila often preferred to chain.

—From Northill Anchoring Handbook

SUGGESTED DANFORTH ANCHOR SIZES

Maximum Length of Boat (Ft.)	STANDARD Working Anchor	STANDARD Storm Anchor	HI-TENSILE Lunch Hook	HI-TENSILE Working Anchor	HI-TENSILE Storm Anchor
12	2½	4	..	..	..
16	4	8	..	..	5
20	8	13	4 (Std.)	5	12
30	13	22	5	12	18
40	40	65	12	18	28
60	40	65	18	28	60
80	85	180	28	60	90
100	180	200	60	90	..
125	200	300	90	..	..
150	300	500	..	..	..
200	500	750	..	..	..

It is to be noted that in this table, as in all other tables and formulas, figures are not supposed to be absolute. They do, however, provide an excellent guide.

In the table below are given the average results of hundreds of tests made by various authorities to determine anchor holding power.

RESULTS OF ANCHOR HOLDING TESTS

(Anchor weight and holding power in pounds)

Weight of Anchor Tested	Stockless	Kedge	Danforth Standard	Danforth Hi-Tensile
IN HARD SAND				
2½-3	..	..	760	..
4-6	..	70	1,470	2,600
8-12	30	125	..	11,600
13-18	..	180	7,500	..
22-31	..	230	9,600	..
IN MUD				
2½-3	..	..	165	..
4-6	..	40	200	210
8-12	15	100	..	2,600
13-18	..	170	1,200	..
22-31	..	90	2,000	..
IN VERY SOFT MUD				
2½-3	..	..	105	..
4-6	..	30	150	280
8-12	10	60	..	950
13-18	..	105	285	..
22-31	..	..	1,250	..

Testing Holding Power

A simple test that any boat owner can make has been suggested by the owner of a 40-foot auxiliary sloop. He states that a well powered boat can use her engine to throw a load on an anchor greater than she will normally register when riding to her anchor.

The pull of an engine can be approximated by multiplying the horsepower by 20, a value that works out about right for a fairly heavy-duty propeller. With a high-speed propeller of small diameter, the pull is reduced somewhat.

The anchor to be tested is let go astern and scope of 7 or 8:1 paid out before making fast. Then the engine is speeded up till the anchor drags. Sufficient speed is maintained to drag the anchor at one or two knots, meanwhile noting the engine r.p.m. Testing other anchors the same way provides a basis for comparison in the varying rates of r.p.m. required to move each.

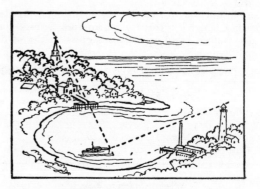

When anchoring, always try to select a pair of ranges to determine the exact position. It's best if they're visible at night

Actual test readings of the load can be made by using spring scales in the line, rigged if necessary to permit a small scale to register heavy loads. If a lever-operated winch is available, the scale can be attached at the end of the lever. The scale's reading is then multiplied by the ratio of the radius of the lever arm to the radius of the drum on which the chain or rope is carried.

The originator of this idea determined that his 40-footer, powered with a 52 h.p. engine driving a 20 by 12 propeller through 2:1 reduction, under full power pulled about 1,000 pounds. Under normal conditions of anchoring, he found that the boat would rarely surge to a higher value than 400 pounds, especially if generous scope were paid out.

When making a comparison of holding powers it is interesting to note that holding power is proportional to the area of buried fluke multiplied by the distance it is buried in the bottom. Consequently, for given areas of fluke, the design which permits deepest penetration is the most effective.

WEIGHT AND STRENGTH — MANILA, NYLON, CHAIN AND WIRE ROPE

	APPROX. WEIGHT OF 100' IN AIR				ROPE—Breaking Strength		CHAIN—Proof Test		WIRE ROPE—Breaking Strength			
Diameter	Nylon Rope	Manila Rope	BBB Galv. Chain	6 x 19 Fiber Core Wire Rope	Nylon Yacht Rope	Manila Yacht Rope	BBB Gal. Coil Chain	High Strength Alloy Chain	Iron Wire Rope 6 x 19	Gal. Plow Steel Wire Rope 6 x 19 Fiber Core	Gal. Improved Plow Steel Wire 6 x 19 Fiber Core	Stainless Steel Wire Rope 6 x 19 IWRC
1/4	1.6	1.9	76	100	1,300	650	2,700	6,500	2,200	4,300	5,000	*6,400
5/16	2.6	3.2	115	160	2,000	1,150	3,700	.....	3,200	6,700	7,700	*9,000
3/8	3.8	4.0	170	230	2,900	1,550	4,600	13,000	5,000	9,600	11,000	*12,000
7/16	5.2	5.1	225	310	3,900	1,900	6,200	.....	6,400	13,000	15,000	16,300
1/2	6.9	6.5	295	400	5,000	2,900	8,200	22,000	8,400	17,000	19,000	22,800
9/16	8.8	8.5	350	510	6,200	3,800	10,200	.....	10,600	21,000	24,000	28,500
5/8	10.8	11.2	430	630	7,500	4,800	12,500	33,000	12,800	26,000	30,000	35,000
3/4	15.8	13.8	600	900	10,700	5,900	17,700	46,000	18,200	37,000	43,000	49,600
7/8	21.8	20.8	810	1230	14,200	8,400	24,000	.....	21,400	50,000	58,000	66,500
1	28.5	25.2	1050	1600	18,500	9,900	31,000	.....	28,000	66,000	75,000	85,400

* 7 x 19.

Figures above are taken from the booklet "Anchors and Anchoring" published by Danforth Anchors. They point out that the values given are approximate, varying with different brands and manufacturers. To provide a reasonable safety factor, they advocate limiting working loads to 1/5 the rated breaking strength of rope and wire rope, or ½ the proof test value to which chain is pre-stressed during manufacture

The Technique of Anchoring; Scope; Increasing Holding Power; Recommendations for Permanent Yacht Moorings

THUS far we have discussed only equipment, our ground tackle. Let's consider now the technique—the art of anchoring. As a matter of fact, good equipment is more than half the battle; anyone can easily learn to use his gear correctly.

On the other hand, if your anchors are of doubtful holding power, and your lines too short, then you can never escape the uneasy feeling associated with wondering whether, some day, you'll find yourself dragging on a lee shore. No part of your boat's equipment is more important, so don't stint here.

Before you can think about how to anchor, you must decide where you'll anchor, and here, as in all other phases of seamanship, a little foresight pays off handsomely.

Selecting an Anchorage

There will be times, of course, when you will stop briefly in open water, coming to anchor for lunch, a swim, to fish, or perhaps to watch a regatta—but, in the main, the problem of finding an anchorage comes down to choice of some spot where there's good holding bottom, protection from the wind, and water of a suitable depth. Such an anchorage is the kind you'd look for in which to spend the night, free from anxiety about the weather.

The chart is the best guide in selecting such a spot. Sometimes you will be able to find a harbor protected on all sides, regardless of wind shifts. If not, the next best choice would be a cove, offering protection at least from the direction of the wind, or the quarter from which it is expected. As a last resort, anchorage may be found under a windward bank or shore—that is, where the wind blows from the bank toward the boat. In this case, watch for wind shifts, which could leave you in a dangerous berth on a lee shore.

Anchorages are sometimes designated on charts by means of an anchor symbol—two flukes to signify a deep-water anchorage for large craft; one fluke, for small boats. Areas delineated on the chart by solid magenta lines, marked perhaps by white buoys, are established anchorage areas, though the spots sought by small boats are seldom so marked. Never anchor in cable areas or channels, both indicated by broken parallel lines.

Characteristics of the Bottom

Character of the bottom is of prime importance. While the type and design of anchor fluke has a direct bearing on its ability to penetrate, as we have already noted, it can be stated broadly that mixtures of mud and clay, or sandy mud, make excellent holding bottom for most anchors; firm sand is good if your anchor will bite deep into it; loose sand is bad. Soft mud should be avoided if possible; rocks prevent an anchor from getting a bite except when a fluke is lodged in a crevice; and grassy bottoms, while they provide good holding for the anchor that can get through to firm bottom, often prevent a fluke from taking hold.

Characteristics of the bottom are always shown on charts. By making a few casts with the hand lead, a check can be had on the depth, and if the lead is armed with a bit of hard grease or tallow, samples of the bottom will be brought up as a further check.

Relatively shallow

Right: An improved type of mooring buoy, made by Winner Mfg. Co., of balsa wood, in which the chain runs through the buoy. Below: A grating is provided on deck here on which to dry manila line. Note the Herreshoff anchor (left) and hand-operated davit hoist

depths are preferred for an anchorage, because a given amount of scope (the length of line paid out) will then provide better holding and reduce the diameter of the circle through which the boat will swing. However, due consideration must be given to the range of tide, so that a falling level does not leave you aground, impaled on the exposed fluke of your own anchor, or bottled up behind a shoal with not enough water to get out at low tide.

Approaching the Anchorage

Having selected a suitable spot, try to run in on some range ashore, selected from marks identified on the chart, crossing ranges or referring your position to visible buoys and landmarks to aid you in locating the spot. Later these aids will also be helpful in determining whether you are holding or dragging, especially if the marks are visible at night and it comes on to blow after dark.

If there are rocks, shoals, reefs or other boats to consider, give them all as wide a berth as possible, keeping in mind a possible swing of 360 degrees about the anchor with wind shifts or current changes.

Remember, too, that large yachts nearby may swing to a much longer scope than you allow—and, conversely, that you may swing much further than a smaller boat nearby lying on short scope. Such conditions bring about an overlapping of the swinging circles.

The risk of fouling a neighboring craft is aggravated when, in a current, the deep draft vessel holds her position in a current, while a light draft boat swings to a shift of wind not strong enough to influence the other.

The boat that has already established her location in an anchorage has a prior claim to the spot and can't be expected to move if you later find yourself in an embarrassing position. Consequently, allow room enough so that you can pay out more scope if necessary in case of a blow, without being forced to change your anchorage, perhaps after dark.

The way other boats lie, together with the set of nearby buoys, will help to determine how you should round up to the chosen spot. Estimate the relative effects of wind and current on your own boat and come up, slowly, against the stronger of these forces—in other

words, heading as you expect to lie after dropping back on the anchor. Running through the anchorage, take care that your way is reduced to a point where your wake cannot disturb other boats.

Letting the Anchor Go

These preliminaries disposed of, you are ready to let the anchor go. One man—unless you are forced to work single-handed—should be stationed on the forward deck. Enough line should be hauled out of the locker and coiled down so as to run freely without kinking or fouling. If previously detached, the line must be shackled to the ring, stock set up (if of the stock type) and keyed.

Despite the fact that in certain localities some experienced boatmen have adopted the practice of letting go while the craft has headway, depending on way to snub the anchor and give it a bite, the amateur motor boatman would do well to make it a standing rule never to let go while the craft has headway.

In a motor boat, the bow can be brought slowly up to the spot where the anchor is to lie, and headway checked with the reverse gear if necessary. Then, just before the boat begins to gather sternway slowly in reverse, the anchor can be lowered easily over the side till it hits the bottom, crown first.

Never stand in the coils of line on deck and don't attempt to "heave" the anchor as far as you can by casting it as far as possible from the side of the boat. Occasionally, with judgment, a light anchor in a small boat can be carefully thrown a short distance—taking care that it lands in its holding position—but the best all-around rule is to lower it as described above. That way, the possibility of fouling the anchor is minimized.

With the anchor on the bottom and the boat reversing slowly, line can be paid out as the boat takes it, preferably with a turn of line around the bitt. When a scope of about 7 or 8 times the depth has been paid out, snub the line by holding and the anchor will get a quick sure bite into the bottom, after which the line can be shortened if the anchorage is so crowded that such a scope would be excessive. Snubbing too soon will usually result in causing the anchor to drag. Sometimes the anchor may be shod with a clod of mud adhering to flukes, in which case it is best to lift it, wash it off and try again. (On a very soft bottom light weight anchors can often be set better at shorter scope by "feeling them in" by hand.) When you must work single-handed, you can get your ground tackle ready to let go, long before you arrive at the anchorage, bring the boat up to the chosen spot, and then lower the anchor as the boat settles back with wind and current, paying out line as she takes it.

Making Fast

After the anchor has gotten a good bite, and the proper scope pa'd out, the line can be made fast and the motor shut off.

On small boats equipped with a Samson post, the best and easiest way to secure is with a clove hitch,

Left: Complete permanent mooring equipment, including mushroom anchor, chain, buoy, swivel, and pennant. Pennant is led from the chain but may be attached at top of buoy if a strong rod passes through the buoy. Below: Two types of mooring swivel, and a device used to hook a rope bridle to chain when anchoring at night. Ball bearing swivels are also available

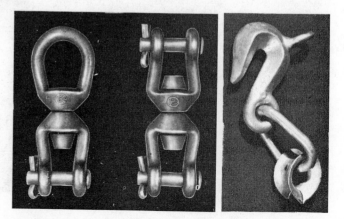

down first and have a man tend the line carefully as you manuever the bow off to one side before letting the other go. Then you can settle back on both lines, adjusting scope as necessary. Fouling the wheel in slack line under the boat in maneuvers like this is disastrous.

With good handling, it is possible to get two anchors down single-handed. The easiest way is to settle back on one anchor, making fast when the proper scope has been paid out. Then go ahead easily with the propeller, rudder over enough to hold the line out taut so you can keep an eye on it at all times. When the line stands out abeam, stop your headway, go forward and let the other anchor go, drop back and adjust the lines to equal scope.

Two anchors are sometimes laid for increased holding power in a blow. The important thing to remember in this connection is that it is far better to have your weight concentrated in one anchor, than divided into two. Behind this principle is a law that states that, for equal holding power, the square of the weight of a single anchor will equal the sum of the squares of the weight of two smaller anchors. In other words, one 50-pounder ($50^2 = 2500$) will hold as much as a 30-pounder ($30^2 = 900$) and a 40-pounder ($40^2 = 1600$) combined.

Stern Anchors

In crowded anchorages, boats sometimes lie to anchors bow and stern. The easiest way to get these down is to let the bow anchor go first, and then drop back with wind or current on an extra long scope, drop the stern anchor, and then adjust the scope on both as necessary, taking in line forward. This arrangement is all right if current is

similar to that usually thrown when making fast to a spile. The principal objection to the clove hitch on a small post is that it will sometimes jam pretty tight, especially when wet, if the strain is very heavy. On winches, three or four round turns can be taken on the niggerhead, belaying the end on a cleat or belaying pin. Where a stout cleat is used to make fast, take a round turn around the base of the cleat, one turn over each horn crossing diagonally over the center of the cleat, and finish with another round turn about the base.

The fundamental idea in making fast is to secure in such a manner that the line can neither slip nor jam. If the strain comes on top of a series of turns on a cleat, then it will be practically impossible to free if you want to change the scope, without first taking the strain off it by using the power.

If it becomes necessary to shorten scope, clear the bitt first of old turns or hitches. Don't throw new ones over the old.

A trick worth using when the sea is so rough that it is difficult to go forward on deck—especially if you are single-handed—is to set up the anchor in the aft cockpit, lead the line forward on deck through a closed chock, and back aft to the cockpit. When you're ready to let go it can be dropped on the weather side from the cockpit, and the line secured on a bitt or cleat aft.

Using Two Anchors

Deep draft sailboats lie well head to the wind but motorboats often "tack" back and forth at anchor. Skiffs, with high freeboard and little draft forward, are among the worst offenders in this respect.

You can stop this yawing by laying two anchors, lines leading out from either bow, making an angle of about 45 degrees between them. To do this, get one anchor

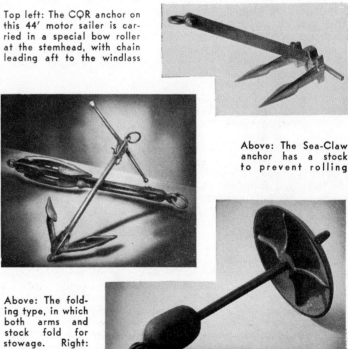

Top left: The CQR anchor on this 44' motor sailer is carried in a special bow roller at the stemhead, with chain leading aft to the windlass

Above: The Sea-Claw anchor has a stock to prevent rolling

Above: The folding type, in which both arms and stock fold for stowage. Right: Mushroom mooring anchor with bulb cast in shank

the principal factor, but in a hard blow, with wind abeam, a great strain would be thrown on the ground tackle.

Sometimes a stern anchor will be useful if you seek shelter under a windward bank. The stern anchor can be let go aft, estimating the distance off carefully as it is dropped, and scope paid out as the boat is run up toward the bank. A second anchor can then be bedded securely in the bank, or a line taken to a dock or tree.

The stern anchor will keep the stern off and prevent the boat from ranging ahead. But, again, watch that stern line, while the propeller is turning!

A berth on the weather side of a dock is a bad one as considerable damage can be done to a boat pounding heavily against spiles, even with fenders out. Anchors can help to ease the situation in a case where such a berth is unavoidable. Keeping well up to windward, angling into the wind as much as is practicable, have a man let one anchor go on a long scope off the quarter (the port quarter, if you'll lie starboard side to the dock). As he pays out scope, run ahead and get another off the port bow, judging positions of both so you can drop down to leeward toward the dock on equal scope, with lines tending off at a 45-degree angle. Properly executed, this maneuver will prevent you from hitting the dock, and the lines you then carry ashore will be needed only to prevent the boat from moving ahead or astern.

Occasionally, on a hot day, you may be able to get a little more shade from the canopy and a little more breeze in the cockpit if the boat is anchored with only a stern anchor. If it blows up, the anchor is more readily gotten up from the bow. To accomplish this, the line can be made fast to the stern bitt when anchoring and then led forward along the deck outside all stanchions and made fast forward, allowing only a little slack. Then when you are ready to get under way you can cast off the line aft and the boat will swing around.

Fishermen have a trick of holding a boat from yawing, using only a single anchor. A bridle is made fast to the anchor line, and led to an after bitt. Then, as more scope is paid out on the bow line, the bow pays off to one side and the wind or current holds it there. A little adjustment on the lines forward and aft will locate a position where the boat will usually lie quite steady.

Increasing Holding Power

If you have reason to doubt that your main anchor is going to hold in a heavy blow, you can increase its holding power by sending a kellet or sentinel down the anchor line about half way to the anchor. This can take the form of a weight, such as a pig of ballast, or a light anchor. Using a light anchor, a snap hook can be seized to its ring and the snap clipped over the anchor line. With a line made fast to the ring, the small anchor can be sent down and checked at the proper distance. Any device of this kind serves to lower the angle of pull on the anchor and puts a sag in the line which eases shocks, as it has to be straightened out before the load is thrown on the anchor.

How effective this can be is evidenced by one test made aboard a 104-footer in which a 30-pound weight, suspended from the ⅝-inch wire cable, reduced the maximum anchor load nearly 50 per cent.

A better arrangement would be to carry a good length of chain, even if you are normally equipped with manila line, and cast a 25- or 50-pound pig of lead with a ring bolt in it. These can be stowed away somewhere as ballast—and probably never used. Then, in a pinch, you can break out your biggest anchor, shackle on the chain, and the weight at its end, and then your best and longest length of manila. Such a rig would be hard to beat.

Scope

As yet we have touched only briefly on the matter of scope, indicating that a scope of about 7 or 8:1 is about right right for ordinary conditions. This means that the length of line from bow chock to anchor will be 7 or 8 times the distance from the bow chock to the bottom. There is risk in considering water depth as the important item in this ratio if we overlook two factors—the height of freeboard at the bow, and the range of tide. If we anchor in 10 feet of water at low tide with 60 feet of line, we have a scope, theoretically, of 6:1. But if the bow chock is 5 feet above the water level, and the tide rises another 5 feet, we'd find that the actual ratio has been reduced to 3:1.

Government tests have indicated that proper scope ratios, depending on conditions, will range from 5:1 to 10:1. Even in a hard blow, in an exposed anchorage, the chances are that you will never need a scope of more than 15 to 1 with an anchor of suitable holding power.

Short scope reduces an anchor's holding power as the line, leading up to the surface at a sharp angle, is tending to break the anchor out. As the pull is brought down more nearly parallel with the bottom, the fluke digs in deeper with increased strain on the line. Surging of a boat as she pitches in a sea throws a great load on an anchor, particularly on a short scope. With long scope, the angle of pull is not only better, but the elasticity of a long line cushions the heaviest shocks materially.

Anchor line can be marked with short pieces of twine at convenient intervals as a measure of scope, links of chain painted white. Without such definite markings, the amount of scope is too much a matter of guesswork.

Getting Under Way

When you are ready to get under way, run up to the anchor slowly under power, so that the line can be taken in easily without hauling the boat up to it. Ordinarily the anchor will break out readily when the line stands vertically.

As the line comes in, it can be whipped up and down to free it of any grass or weed it may have picked up. This gets rid of it before it comes on deck. If the anchor is not too heavy mud can be washed off by swinging it back and forth near the surface as it leaves the water. With care, the line can be snubbed around a bitt and the anchor allowed to wash off as the boat gathers headway. Two things must be watched: don't allow the flukes to hit the topsides, and be careful that the water flowing past the anchor doesn't get too good a hold and take it out of your hands.

Line should be coiled loosely on deck and allowed to dry thoroughly before stowing below. When the anchor is on deck, the stock (if there is one) can be folded and the anchor lashed down securely in its chocks.

On larger craft, equipped with a davit, the anchor can be brought up with the winch to a point where a light tackle can be hooked into a ring in the balancing band on the anchor's shank. With the anchor suspended over the side, mud can be washed off with a hose.

In all this anchor handling, try to avoid letting the anchor hit the hull at any time as planking is soft and will get badly gouged and dented. Guests often are eager to "help" by getting the anchor up, but unless they have had some experience, it's better to handle this part of the job yourself.

If an anchor refuses to break out when you haul vertically on the line, snub it around the bitt and go ahead with the engine a few feet. If it doesn't respond to this treatment, it's an indication that the anchor may have fouled under some obstruction. To clear it, try making fast to the bitt and running slowly in a wide circle on a taut line. Changing the angle of pull may free it, or a turn of line may foul the exposed fluke and draw it out.

Sometimes a length of chain can be run down the anchor line, rigged so that another boat can use her power to haul in a direction opposite to that in which the anchor line tends, thus changing the angle of pull 180 degrees.

If the anchor is not fouled in something immovable, it may be broken out by making the line fast at low water and allowing a rising tide to exert a steady strain. Or, if there is a considerable ground swell, the line may be snubbed when the bow pitches low in a trough. There's some risk of parting the line this way, in case the fluke is fouled worse than you think.

Things to Guard Against

A potent source of trouble is carelessness in not stowing lines on deck so they can't get adrift. If a bight or end of line slips over the side while the boat is under way, it is almost certain to run back under the bottom and get hopelessly fouled in the propeller.

Guard against dragging. By crossing two ranges on shore, as mentioned earlier, you can locate an exact spot and tell whether or not you have dragged. Even a single range, abeam, will serve if the wind doesn't shift.

If ranges are not lighted so that they can be picked out at night, you can rig a drift lead (the lead line will do). Simply lower it to the bottom, leaving slack to allow for the boat's swinging, and make fast. If it comes taut, you've dragged. Don't forget to pick it up before getting under way.

Chafing is another source of trouble. Wherever the line comes in contact with chocks or rails, and has a chance to rub back and forth under a continuous strain, look out for chafe which wears the outer fibers and may seriously weaken the line. Mooring pennants are particularly susceptible to this. Laying at anchor, you can "freshen the nip" by paying out a little more scope from time to time, or parcel the line at the point of chafe with strips of canvas wrapped around it. Permanent chafing gear is used sometimes, the first at 7 or 8 fathoms, and others at intervals of about 5 fathoms. This serves also as a check on the scope paid out.

Another thing to keep an eye on is fouling of the anchor. If you've handled your ground tackle carefully when letting go, you're all right until the boat swings around the anchor with wind shifts or change of current. If a turn of the line catches the fluke, the anchor is sure to break out. Anchors that bury completely and have no fluke to project above the bottom are free from this problem.

In Rocky Bottoms

Fouling in a rocky bottom is something that can be guarded against before letting go. A buoyed trip line is the answer. Some anchors have a ring at the crown but in any case a light line can be made fast at the crown, long enough to reach the surface, where it is buoyed with a block of wood, ring buoy or some similar small float. If the anchor doesn't trip at the first pull on the anchor line, haul in the trip line, and the anchor will be withdrawn, crown first.

An alternate scheme is to "scow" the anchor by bending the anchor line to the crown, leading it back along the shank, and stopping it to the ring with a light lashing of twine. With sufficient scope, the strain is on the crown and not on the lashing. When hove up short, the strain is on the lashing and when this parts, the anchor comes up crown first.

Kedging, and Anchoring at Night

The term "kedging" is sometimes applied to the use of a light anchor carried out to deep water in a dinghy to haul a boat off a bar. If you ever have to resort to this, coil the line down carefully in the dinghy, so that it pays out freely from the stern of the dinghy as you row. The dink might well become unmanageable in a wind or strong current if an attempt is made to pay the line out from the deck of the stranded boat.

Anchoring at night, you must display a white 32-point light, visible at least a mile, rigged forward at a height of not more than 20 feet above the hull. Vessels over 150 feet in length show a white light forward 20 to 40 feet above the hull, and another aft at least 15 feet lower than the forward light. Vessels over 300 gross tons at anchor display a black ball as a day mark. In certain areas specially designated by the Secretary of War as anchorage areas, no lights need be displayed at night on vessels less than 65 feet in length.

Permanent Moorings

As a result of several hurricanes since September 1938, much attention has been given to the question of just what constitutes adequate mooring equipment for various sizes of motor and sailing craft, moored in a fleet at a yacht club anchorage.

The Coast Guard has ruled that boats in the metropolitan New

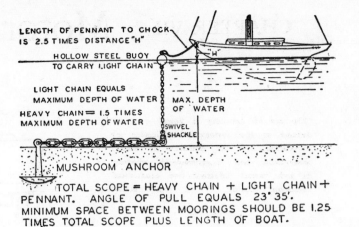

LENGTH OF PENNANT TO CHOCK IS 2.5 TIMES DISTANCE "H"

HOLLOW STEEL BUOY TO CARRY LIGHT CHAIN

LIGHT CHAIN EQUALS MAXIMUM DEPTH OF WATER
HEAVY CHAIN = 1.5 TIMES MAXIMUM DEPTH OF WATER

MAX. DEPTH OF WATER

SWIVEL SHACKLE

MUSHROOM ANCHOR

TOTAL SCOPE = HEAVY CHAIN + LIGHT CHAIN + PENNANT. ANGLE OF PULL EQUALS 23°35'. MINIMUM SPACE BETWEEN MOORINGS SHOULD BE 1.25 TIMES TOTAL SCOPE PLUS LENGTH OF BOAT.

Diagram of good mooring practice recommended by the Lake Michigan Yachting Association and approved by the U. S. Coast Guard. A weight added at the shackle between lengths of chain would increase the holding power

York area must have mooring permits obtained from the Captain of the Port. Yacht clubs, cooperating with the Coast Guard, have required members to provide proper ground tackle.

The problem of the Manhasset Bay Yacht Club at Port Washington, L. I., is typical of that existing in numerous anchorages. Here about 200 boats are moored in a limited space. If it were possible to permit each boat to use a length of chain equal to from 5 to 7 times the depth of water (maximum 30 feet), safety would be assured, but this would require a swinging radius of several hundred feet for each boat, which is not possible.

The plan finally adopted by this club involves the use of a mushroom anchor of ample weight, a good length of heavy chain, a shorter length of light chain, and a manila, stainless steel or compound rope for a pennant. Their recommendations are given in the table below.

Inasmuch as hurricanes and many of the season's worst storms are likely to occur toward the end of the summer boating season, boat-owners—and especially those who leave their craft in the water during the fall months—are advised to make a careful mid-season inspection of all their mooring gear. Some of our worst blows have occurred in September and, to weather them, anchors, chain, manila, and every other part of the mooring equipment must be in better condition than might be considered adequate for mid-summer weather.

SUGGESTIONS FOR PERMANENT YACHT MOORINGS
For Wind Velocities Up to 75 M.P.H.

Boat Length Overall	Mushroom Anchor (Min. Wt.)	Heavy Chain		Light Chain		Pennant			Total Scope (Chocks to Mushroom)
		Length	Diameter	Length	Diameter	Length (Minim.)	Diameter (If Manila)	Diameter (If Stainless Steel)	
—FOR MOTOR BOATS—									
25	225	30	$\frac{7}{8}$	20	$\frac{3}{8}$	20	1	$\frac{9}{32}$	70
35	300	35	1	20	$\frac{7}{16}$	20	$1\frac{1}{4}$	$\frac{11}{32}$	75
45	400	40	1	20	$\frac{1}{2}$	20	$1\frac{1}{2}$	$\frac{3}{8}$	80
55	500	50	1	20	$\frac{9}{16}$	20	2	$\frac{7}{16}$	90
—FOR RACING TYPE SAILBOATS—									
25	125	30	$\frac{5}{8}$	20	$\frac{5}{16}$	20	1	$\frac{9}{32}$	70
35	200	30	$\frac{3}{4}$	20	$\frac{3}{8}$	20	$1\frac{1}{4}$	$\frac{11}{32}$	70
45	325	35	1	20	$\frac{7}{16}$	20	$1\frac{1}{2}$	$\frac{3}{8}$	75
55	450	45	1	20	$\frac{9}{16}$	20	2	$\frac{7}{16}$	85
—FOR CRUISING TYPE SAILBOATS—									
25	175	30	$\frac{3}{4}$	20	$\frac{5}{16}$	20	1	$\frac{9}{32}$	70
35	250	30	1	20	$\frac{3}{8}$	20	$1\frac{1}{4}$	$\frac{11}{32}$	70
45	400	40	1	20	$\frac{7}{16}$	20	$1\frac{1}{2}$	$\frac{3}{8}$	80
55	550	55	1	20	$\frac{9}{16}$	20	2	$\frac{7}{16}$	95

NOTE:—Heavy chain to be shackled to mushroom anchor, light chain shackled to end of heavy chain. With stainless steel pennants, use special bow chocks and mooring bitts to eliminate sharp bends.

CHAPTER VII

Motor Boat Handling

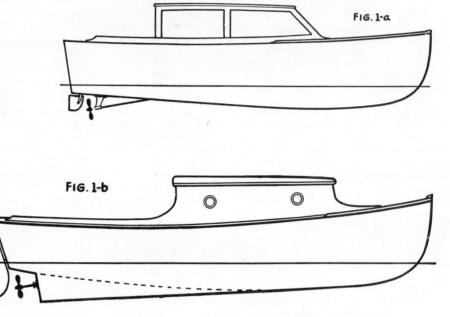

FIG. 1-a

FIG. 1-b

How disposition of draft, free-board and superstructure varies. Fig. 1-a shows a type in which draft is greater forward than aft. At b, this condition is reversed

WITHOUT a doubt some of the finest exhibitions of skill in the art of handling motor boats are often given by men who may never have read a printed page on the subject of seamanship. Their facility at the helm of a motor boat is their sheepskin from the sea's school of experience—in which the curriculum, admittedly, may be tough.

Witness, for example, the consummate skill some commercial fisherman might display in maneuvering his skiff into a tight berth under adverse weather conditions, finally to bring her up against the wharf in a landing that wouldn't crack an egg. Such proficiency, developed over long years of meeting every conceivable kind of situation, eventually manifests almost as an instinct, prompting the boatman to react right whether he has time to think the problem out in advance or not.

Sometimes the old-timer's methods might appear, to a novice, to verge on carelessness, but that's probably because the old salt in a practical way understands exactly what the minimum requirements are for the safety of his craft and therefore doesn't waste any time on non-essentials. Consequently if he uses three lines where the text book says six, don't jump to the conclusion that he wouldn't know how to use more if they were needed.

So, in approaching a study of the principles of boat handling, it's helpful to keep in mind that the goal is not so much to be able to repeat verbatim definitions or the prescribed answers to a set of questions for the sake of passing a quiz as it is to understand the "why" of some of the curious capers your boat may cut when you're out there handling her. If she stubbornly refuses to make a turn under a given set of conditions, or persistently backs one way when you want her to go the other, you will be less likely to make the same mistake twice when you understand the reasons behind her behavior.

All of which leads up to this very fundamental thought. Learn all you possibly can about the principles according to which average boats respond under normal conditions; supplement this with all the experience you can get aboard your own boat and other types as well, and then learn to act so that controlling elements aid you rather than oppose you.

Some of the ideas to be developed later may seem applicable only to larger vessels, but remember that some day you may be at the wheel of a strange 70-footer instead of your own familiar 30-footer. Then the significance of these points will be more apparent.

No two boats will behave in identical manner in every situation, so great is their individuality. This applies even to "standardized" craft which to outward appearances may be alike as two peas in a pod. Exactly how the boat will perform depends on many things—among them the design; the form and shape of the hull's underbody; the construction; the shape, position and area of the rudder; the trim; speed; the weight; load; strength and direction of wind and current; and the nature of the sea, if any.

Effect of Wind and Current

Wind and current are particularly important factors in analyzing a boat's behavior as they may cause her to respond precisely opposite to what you would expect without these factors to reckon with. As a case in point, many motor boats have a tendency to back into the wind despite anything that can be done with the helm.

Given two boats of roughly the same size (see Figure 1), one of which (A) has considerable draft forward but little aft, and another (B), with relatively greater draft aft but more superstructure forward—you will find radical differences in their handling qualities. What governs is the relative area presented above water to the wind as compared with the areas exposed to the water, both fore and aft.

The former (A), with wind abeam, might hold her course reasonably well when the bow of the latter (B) would persistently pay off, requiring considerable rudder angle to hold her up. On the other hand, with wind and sea aft, B might go along about her business with little attention to the helm while A insisted on "rooting" at the bow and yawing off her course despite the best efforts of the helmsman.

As a general rule, the boat with low freeboard and superstructure but relatively deep draft (C, Fig. 2), tending toward the sailboat type, will be less affected by wind and more by current than the light draft motor boat (D, Fig. 2) with high freeboard and deckhouses. The latter floats relatively high in the water and has little below the waterline to hold her against wind pressures acting on areas exposed above water to drive her to leeward.

Now, turning to Figure 3, we find what might be termed an average type of motor boat. Her greatest draft is aft where the freeboard is low and her greatest exposure to windage is presented by the relatively higher bow and cabin forward. Obviously her bow will be affected by wind pressures more than the stern. With wind abeam, the tendency would be for her bow to be driven to leeward more than the stern. To offset that, she would need a certain amount of rudder angle to hold her on her course and compensate for leeway.

Figure 2—Proportion of draft to height above water has a great bearing on how the boat handles. At 2-c, the deep-draft sailboat type; at 2-d, a motorboat with high superstructure and shallow draft

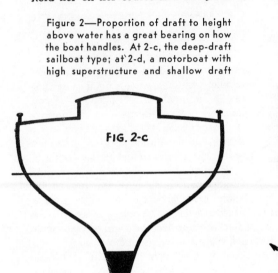

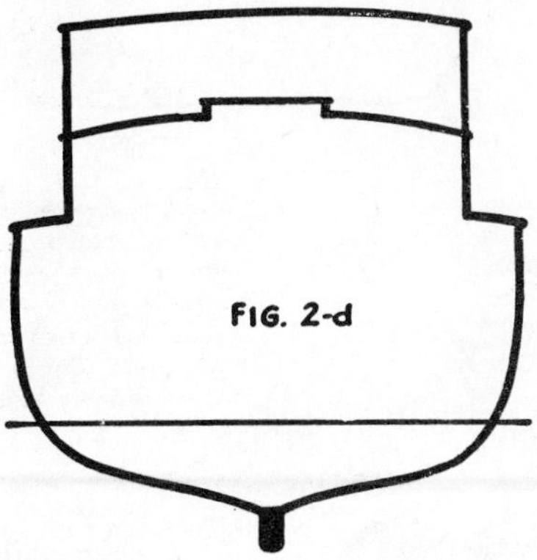

Figure 4—The port side is always the port side, and the starboard side starboard, regardless of whether the boat is making headway or sternway. The boat illustrated has left rudder; don't say starboard helm

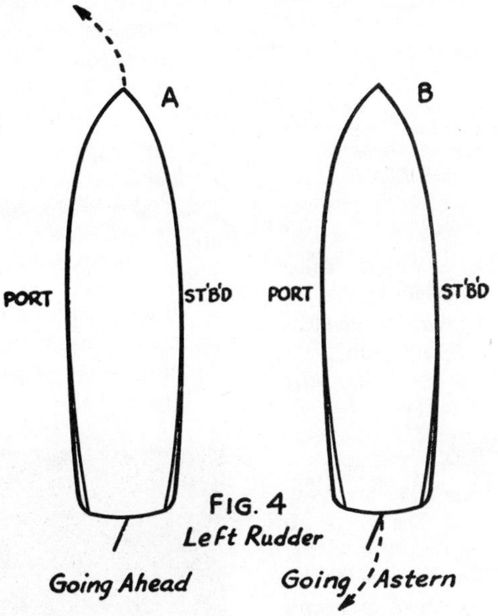

For the same reason if she is drifting in a smooth sea with engine stopped, wind pressure on her bow will make the bow pay off so that the wind finally is brought abaft the beam. The action might almost be compared to that of a sailboat in which a flattened jib, but no other canvas, is set.

But, just as an illustration to show how boat behavior may vary, suppose it is raining and the canvas side curtains are buttoned down on that same

Figure 3—Sketch of what might be termed an average cruiser, in its relative proportions of draft, freeboard, superstructure, etc. If allowed to drift without control from propeller and rudder she would probably bring the wind abaft the beam

cruiser. Here a new factor is introduced and the windage aft is increased to such an extent that it may more than offset the effect of the windage forward. Under such conditions she might be very hard to handle in close quarters because of the great amount of total windage compared to her draft.

Some boats require humoring under certain conditions. For example, because of a combination of excessive superstructure forward and little draft at the bow, it may be practically impossible to turn a boat in close quarters by the conventional technique.

Helmsman Must Develop Judgment

From these and many other variations in boat behavior it begins to be evident that the boatman must develop judgment, based on understanding of the individual boat he is handling and the forces acting upon her. Combinations of conditions are infinite, so he must be able to appraise the situation and act promptly, with decision.

A good helmsman will be prudent and try to foresee possibilities, having a solution in mind for the problem before it presents itself. On that basis, it's likely that he'll never meet an "emergency." To cite a simple example, if you're running down a narrow channel with a strong wind abeam, and you have a choice as to which side to take, the windward side is the better bet. If the engine should stop, you'll probably then have a chance to get an anchor down before going aground on the leeward side.

By the same token, you wouldn't skirt the windward side of a shoal too closely. To leeward, in case of engine failure, you would drift clear, but to windward you'd be driven down on the shoal. A strong current might have the same effect, and would have to be taken into account.

As another example of how the helmsman should try always to be prepared for possibilities, suppose you are approaching a bridge having a narrow draw opening with a strong wind or current setting you down rapidly on it. If you were to approach the opening at an angle, and power or steering gear failed, you'd be in a jam. On the other hand, if you straighten out

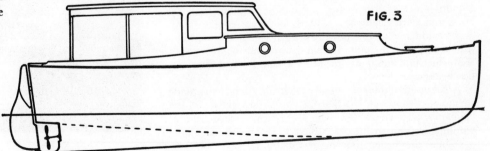

your course while still some distance off so you will be shooting down the center of the opening in alignment with it, the chances of doing any damage are practically nil because her straight course will tend to carry her through in the clear in any case.

In developing your boat sense, draw from as many sources as possible. Observe the way experienced yachtsmen, fishermen and Coast Guardsmen handle their boats, making due allowance for differences in your own boat when you try similar maneuvers.

Terminology of Boat Handling

Before getting too deep into discussion of actual problems of maneuvering it is necessary in advance to get some of the correct terminology fixed in mind.

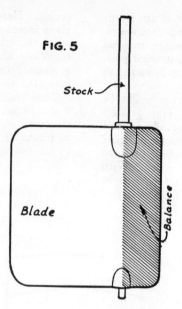

FIG. 5

Stock

Blade

Balance

Figure 5—A balanced rudder, in which part of the blade area (the shaded section) projects ahead of the rudder stock

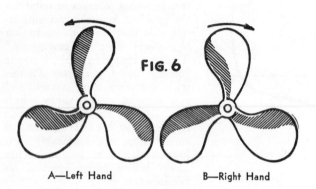

FIG. 6

A—Left Hand   B—Right Hand

Figure 6—Left-hand and right-hand propellers. This is how they turn when you stand astern of them, looking forward at the aft side of the blades

Of course everyone knows that the port side of a boat is the left side facing forward, while the starboard is the right side. This is easy to visualize while the boat has headway but when the boat is reversing the operator may face aft and get all mixed up when the terms right, left, starboard and port are used.

Therefore, bear in mind that the port side is the port side no matter which way the boat is going. When we speak of the boat's going to port it means that her bow turns to port when she has headway and her stern to port when she has sternway. Figure 4 makes this clear. At A the boat has headway and her bow is turning to port. At B she is going astern and her stern is going to port.

The old terms of port helm and starboard helm have now given way to new terms which prevent misunderstanding. In Figure 4 the boat has left rudder in both cases and with headway, as at A, her bow goes to port. Right rudder, which is not illustrated, is just the opposite. The rudder is then on the starboard side of the boat's centerline and her bow goes to starboard when the boat has headway.

A balanced rudder is one in which the area of the blade surface is distributed so that part of it lies ahead of the rudder stock. See Figure 5. An unbalanced rudder would have the stock attached at the edge of the blade.

While the proportion of this balanced area may be only 20 per cent of the total rudder area, it exerts considerable effect in taking strain off the steering gear and

making steering easier, though it may slow the boat on a turn more than the unbalanced type.

Right and Left Hand Propellers

Propellers are right-handed or left-handed, depending on the direction of their rotation. It is vital that the difference be understood because this has a great bearing on how a boat maneuvers, especially when reversing. To determine the hand, stand outside the boat, astern of the propeller, and look forward at the driving face of the blades. If the top of the propeller turns clockwise when driving the boat ahead, it is right-handed; if counterclockwise, left-handed. This is illustrated in Figure 6. A is left-handed; B, right-handed.

Most propellers on marine engines in single-screw installations are right-handed although some (notably on converted engines) are left-handed. In any maneuvering problems which follow, the assumption is that the propeller on the boat under discussion is right-handed unless specifically noted to the contrary.

In twin-screw installations the ideal arrangement is to have the tops of the blades turn outward for better maneuvering qualities. Figure 6 might be taken as an illustration of this, in which the port engine swings a left-hand wheel, the starboard engine a right-hand wheel.

Don't be confused by the term right- and left-hand as applied to the engines that are driving the propellers. If you stand inside the boat, facing aft toward the engine, and the flywheel turns counter-clockwise (as in most marine engines) it is a *left-handed engine* and requires a *right-hand propeller*. See Figure 7. A right-hand engine takes a left-hand wheel.

How the Propeller Acts

Motor boats are driven through the water by the action of their propellers which act almost like a pump, drawing in a stream of water from forward (when

Figure 7—Direction of rotation is marked on this marine engine flywheel housing. This is a left-hand engine, as shown by the counterclockwise direction of the arrow. It takes a right-hand propeller

going ahead) and throwing it out astern. This stream moving astern reacts on the water around it to provide the power for propulsion. Sometimes an analogy is drawn between propeller action and a screw thread working in a nut, but this fails to give a correct picture of what really is happening at the propeller.

Actually all of the water drawn into the propeller does not flow from directly ahead like a thin column of water but for

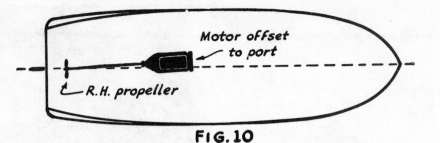

FIG. 10

Figure 10—Ordinarily engines are installed on the center line, but unequal blade thrust tends to make stern go to starboard, bow to port (assuming a right-hand propeller). Sometimes shaft is splayed to one side of the center line as illustrated to offset that tendency

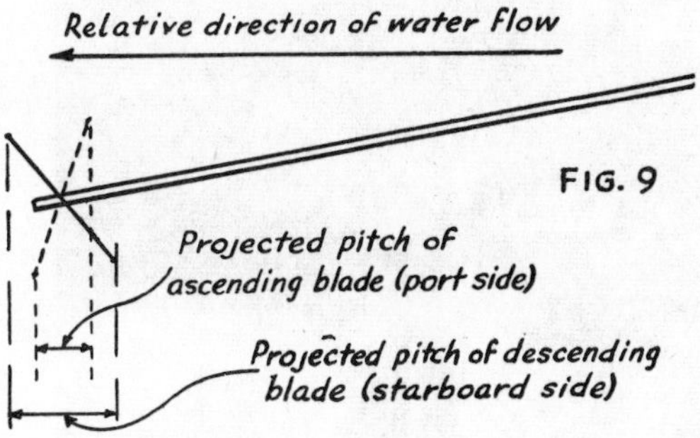

Figure 9—With rudder amidships, bow of boat with right hand propeller may swing to port. Angularity of the propeller shaft has the effect of increasing the pitch of the descending blade relative to that of the ascending blade, so greater thrust is exerted on starboard side

FIG. 9

Relative direction of water Flow

Projected pitch of ascending blade (port side)

Projected pitch of descending blade (starboard side)

Figure 8—The screw current which drives a boat through the water. Here the boat has headway. Suction current is shown leading into the propeller, the discharge current driven out astern

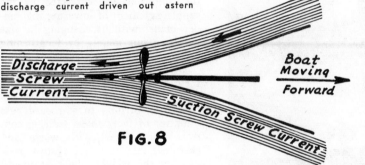

FIG. 8

Discharge Screw Current

Boat Moving Forward

Suction Screw Current

Unequal Blade Thrust

Finally, there is another factor of some moment that needs to be understood in analyzing a boat's reaction to propeller rotation. While this has been sometimes referred to as sidewise blade pressure, it is more properly an unequal thrust exerted by the ascending and descending blades of the propeller. See Figure 9.

Here we are looking at the starboard side of a propeller shaft, inclined, as most shafts are, at a considerable angle to the water's surface and to the flow of water past the propeller blades. The actual pitch of the blades as manufactured, of course, is the same, but the water flows diagonally across the plane in which the blades revolve.

Figure 9 shows clearly how the effect of this is to increase the pitch of the descending starboard blade as compared with the ascending port blade, when considered relative to the direction of water flow past the propeller.

The importance of this factor is reduced as the shaft angle is decreased, and naval architects, taking cognizance of this, sometimes take pains to have the engine installed as low as possible to keep the propeller shaft nearly parallel to the water's surface and the flow of water past the blades. This naturally contributes to propeller efficiency, and is a worth-while factor to be considered wherever consistent with other requirements of the design. Limitations in some designs, however, make it necessary for the engine and shaft to be installed at a considerable angle.

Effect of Unequal Blade Thrust

The relatively greater pitch of the blade on the starboard side has the effect of creating a stronger thrust on this side with the result that the bow of the boat tends to turn to port. Putting it another way, insofar as this single factor is concerned, there is a natural tendency for the stern of a single screw boat with right-hand propeller to go to starboard when the propeller is going ahead, and for the stern to go to port when it is reversing.

Again, when such a boat has headway the bow apparently wants to turn to port if the rudder is held amidships, so a certain amount of right rudder may be necessary to maintain a straight course. To correct it, shafts are sometimes splayed to port, as in Figure 10, or a small trimming tab attached at the after edge of the rudder blade, on the side toward which the boat tends to pull.

The effect is a great variable, so small in some cases as to be negligible; quite pronounced in others.

our purposes here it can be considered as coming in generally parallel to the propeller shaft. The propeller ejects it and as it does so imparts a twist or spiral motion to the water, its direction of rotation dependent on the way the propeller turns. This flow of water set up by the propeller is called screw current.

Suction and Discharge Screw Currents

Regardless of whether the propeller is going ahead or reversing that part of the current which flows into the propeller is called the suction screw current. The part ejected from the propeller is the discharge current. See Figure 8. The latter is not only spiral in motion but is also a more compact stream than the suction current and exerts a greater pressure than the suction current.

By locating the rudder behind the propeller in this discharge current a greater steering effect is possible than if it were to be placed elsewhere, to be acted upon only by water moving naturally past the hull. For that reason a twin-screw cruiser is likely to have twin rudders, one behind each propeller, thus keeping their blades at all times more directly in the propeller's discharge current. Exactly what the effect of each part of the screw current on the boat's behavior will be depends upon what part of the boat it is acting upon.

There is also a wake current. This is a body of water carried along by a vessel with her as she moves through the water due to friction on her hull. This has its maximum effect near the surface, is practically of no consequence at the keel.

for that pivoting point to move aft.

Different boats require varying degrees of rudder angle to compensate for any tendency to fall off from a straight course. Depending on differences in construction, arrangement of rudder blade, and the hand of the propeller, the bow may tend to fall off to port or starboard. These are all factors that the helmsman should understand before attempting maneuvers with a boat.

Using a concrete example to make the significance of the last point more clear, a certain group of boats of almost identical design were found to have a strong tendency to pull off course to port. In some of these, the condition was corrected by the simple expedient of lowering the rudder blade, without changing its size or shape but merely by lengthening the stock an inch or two.

Before correcting that condition, these boats would make a quick and easy turn to port but would be obstinate in turning to starboard. As a matter of fact, unless steering controls were rigged with worm and gear to hold the wheel against pressure on the rudder, the boat would immediately swing into a short circle to port the instant the wheel was left unattended. While this is an exaggerated condition, far from normal, it does illustrate the handling characteristics the helmsman must pay attention to, especially in an unfamiliar boat.

Then again, the state of the sea will have an effect on a boat's performance. A heavy, deep draft boat or one which is heavily loaded will carry her way through the water longer than a light one when the propeller is disengaged by throwing the reverse gear lever into neutral. This is likely to be even more marked in a seaway, the light displacement boat losing her way against the sea much sooner than a heavier craft would.

How the Rudder Acts

Although there are some boats, like fast hydroplanes, which have bow rudders, the conventional arrangement for steering on most boats is by means of a vertical rudder blade at the stern pivoted in hangers or on its stock so that movement of the steering wheel or tiller throws it to port or starboard of the boat's centerline.

In a sailboat, having no propeller, when the boat has

WE have seen how the helmsman has many things to consider when handling boats, due partly to individual characteristics which cause them to respond differently under identical conditions of wind, weather and current.

We have dealt too with the effect which draft and freeboard have on a boat's behavior, showing how high freeboard creates windage which acts to drive a boat to leeward whereas deep draft gives her a grip on the water with which to oppose that tendency.

The general principle is easily observed in the case of a deep keel sailboat, where deep draft acts to hold her on her course, and minimum freeboard is designed into her to reduce the windage factor.

Not only the draft, but the trim, has a bearing on a boat's handling qualities. Later we will see how the effect of rudder action in steering is to cause a boat to pivot about a point near the bow. But if she trims by the stern, that is, deeper than normal aft, the tendency is

Figure 11. With right rudder, as boat moves from A to B to C, stern is driven against the piles, with risk of damage. Rudder should be amidships till boat is clear

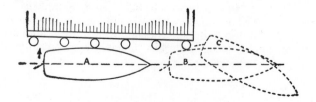

headway water flows past the hull and if the rudder is moved to one side of the keel a resistance on that side is created together with a current at an angle to the keel. The combined effect is to throw the stern to port with right rudder, to starboard with left rudder.

But note that any control from the rudder is dependent on the boat's motion through the water. Even if she is drifting, with motion relative to the bottom, but none so far as the surrounding water is concerned, her rudder has no effect. Only when the water flows past the rudder and strikes it at an angle does the boat respond. The faster she is moving, the stronger the rudder effect. It makes no difference how her headway has been produced—she may even be in tow—there is control as long as there is motion relative to the water.

Propeller Current's Action On Rudder

In a motor boat the situation is different than that encountered in a sailboat. Here the rudder blade is almost invariably directly in the discharge current of the propeller which is pumping a strong stream of water astern. Moving the rudder to one side of the keel deflects the stream to that side. The reaction which pushes the stern in the opposite direction is much stronger than it would be in the absence of that powerful jet.

PROPELLER AND RUDDER ACTION UNDER THE

CONDITIONS ENCOUNTERED IN MANEUVERING

Above: A fine harbor, but a difficult berth for the boatman to maneuver into. Left: A boat with no way on has no control from her rudder. Yet she can be turned here almost in her own length by proper use of rudder and power

At very slow propeller speeds the boat's headway may not be sufficient to give good control over the boat if other forces are acting upon her at the time. For example, with a strong wind on the port beam, even with rudder hard over to port, it may not be possible to make a turn into the wind until the propeller is speeded up enough to exert a more powerful thrust against the offset rudder blade.

Here is a fundamental principle to remember in handling motor boats. In close quarters a motor boat can often be turned in a couple of boat lengths by judicious use of the power. If, for example, the rudder is set hard to starboard (that is, right rudder) while the boat has no headway and the throttle is suddenly opened, the stern can be kicked around to port before the boat has a chance to gather headway. The exact technique of turning in limited space will be described in detail further along.

Keep Stern Free to Maneuver

As soon as the boatman understands the underlying difference between the steering of a boat and a car, he will always be conscious of the need to keep the stern free to maneuver in close quarters. Furthermore, when he lies alongside a dock, a float or another boat, and wants to pull away, he will never, automobile-fashion, throw the wheel over until the stern is clear.

To set the rudder to starboard, for example, while

lying port side to a dock and then attempt to pull away by going ahead would only throw the port quarter against the dock piles and pin it there, to slam successively into one pile after the other as the boat moves ahead, with the likelihood of doing plenty of damage. See Figure 11.

Steering gears on motor boats are almost invariably rigged today so that they turn with the rudder, that is, turning the top of the wheel to port throws the rudder to port. Consequently, with the usual rig, the boat having headway, putting the wheel over to port gives her left rudder which kicks the stern to starboard so that the bow, in effect, moves to port. Conversely, turning the wheel to starboard gives her right rudder, throwing the stern to port so that the boat turns to starboard.

Turning Circles

When the boat has headway and the rudder is put over to make a turn (to starboard, let us say), the stern is first kicked to port and the boat then tends to slide off obliquely, "crab-wise." Due to its momentum through the water it will carry some distance along the original course before settling into a turn, in which the bow describes a smaller circle than the stern. The pivoting point about which she turns may be between one-fourth and one-third of the boat's length from the bow, varying with different boats and changing for any given boat with the trim. See Fig. 13.

While there is always a loss of speed in making a turn, the size of a boat's turning circle will vary but little with changes in speed, assuming a given rudder angle. Whether she makes it at slow speed or at wide open throttle, the actual diameter of the turn is about the same.

Stops are invariably put on a rudder to limit its maximum angle. Beyond that point an increase of rudder angle would result, not in a smaller turning circle, but a larger one. That's why Naval vessels usually have a maximum rudder angle of 35 degrees.

When the boat has sternway (reversing) the rudder normally would be turned to port (left rudder) to turn the stern of the boat to port, while right rudder should normally tend to turn the stern to starboard in backing. However, the subject cannot be dismissed as easily as that and we shall see later how, under certain circumstances, the effect of the reversing propeller may more than offset the steering effect of the rudder.

Just as the speed of a boat is cut down in shallow water, so the depth has an effect on a boat's steering. Even though the keel may not actually be touching the bottom, it will be noticed that the boat's response to

rudder action in shallow water is almost always sluggish.

Let us consider now a number of typical situations to see how the average motor boat will respond to propeller and rudder action (assuming a single screw boat with right-hand propeller).

No Way On, Propeller Turns Ahead

Picture her first without any way on, engine idling and rudder amidships. Being dead in the water there is no wake current to act on the propeller blades. Now the clutch is engaged and the propeller starts to turn ahead. Until she gathers headway, the unequal blade thrust (refer back to Figure 9) tends to throw her stern to starboard. As she gets headway, wake current enters the picture, increasing pressure against the upper blades (remember wake current is strongest at the surface, has little effect at the bottom of the keel) and this tends to offset the effect of unequal blade thrust.

What happens under identical conditions, except that the rudder is hard over at the time the propeller is engaged? In this case the propeller's discharge current strikes the rudder and exerts its normal effect of kicking the stern to port with right rudder, or stern to starboard with left rudder. With right rudder the kick to port would be much stronger than the effect of unequal blade thrust.

With Headway, Propeller Going Ahead

After the boat has gathered normal headway, with

The helmsman should have an unobstructed view, especially in the danger zone from dead ahead to two points abaft the starboard beam. This dinghy creates a blind spot dead ahead

rudder amidships, the average boat tends to hold her course in a straight line fairly well. From a purely theoretical standpoint, the unequal blade thrust, with a right-hand wheel, should tend to move the stern to starboard, and bow to port. However, in most cases, this is a relatively unimportant consideration.

by the reversing propeller instead of away from it.

Going back now to the case where the boat has headway and the propeller is reversed—this time with rudder over to port, let us say. Here the situation is more complicated. As before, we have the unequal blade thrust and propeller discharge current both driving the stern to port.

In addition there are two opposing factors. If the boat has much way on (ahead) her left rudder tends to throw the stern to starboard. However, her propeller suction current is being drawn in from astern in such a manner that it strikes the back of the rudder blade, tending to drive the stern to port.

Which combination of factors will be strongest depends on the amount of headway the boat has. If she has been travelling at some speed, the steering effect of the left rudder will probably be the dominant factor and her stern would be thrown to starboard at first.

Below: A 17' runabout executing a hard-over turn at full throttle, banking inward automatically. Note how right rudder kicks the stern to port, with the stern describing a wider circle than the bow in turning

Above: Boats under sail have no propeller discharge current to increase the rudder's effect in steering. Their maneuverability is limited, and there are many tight places into which a motor boat could be worked where the sailboat would not dare venture

It is only in a comparatively few cases that the unequal thrust of the propeller blades has a very pronounced effect.

Now, the boat having headway, assume the rudder is put to starboard. The water flowing past the hull hits the rudder on its starboard side, forcing the stern to port. The propeller's discharge current intensifies this effect by acting on the same side and the boat's bow turns to starboard, the same side on which the rudder is set. With rudder to port the action would naturally be just the opposite.

With Headway, Propeller Reversing

A boat has no brakes as does a car, so she depends on reversing the propeller to bring her to a stop. Assuming that the boat has headway, rudder amidships, and the propeller is reversed, the effect is to throw the stern to port as the boat loses its headway. The rudder has no steering effect in this case, and unequal blade thrust of the propeller (which, remember, is reversing) tends to throw the stern to port. At the same time the propeller blades on the starboard side are throwing their discharge current in a powerful column forward against the starboard side of the keel and bottom of the boat, with nothing on the port side to offset this pressure. The stern, of necessity, is thrown to port.

This principle explains why a boatman will bring his boat up to a landing port side to the dock, if he has a choice. The stern then is thrown in toward the dock

As this steering effect weakens with reduced headway, the propeller slowing her down, then the effect of the suction current is added to help the tendency of the stern to port until eventually, with all her headway l ed, even the steering tendency to starboard is lost and all factors combine to throw the stern to port.

No Way On, Propeller Reverses

Now if the boat is lying dead in the water with no headway, rudder amidships, and the propeller is reversed, we again have that strong tendency of the stern to port as the discharge current strikes the starboard side of the hull. You see, in each of the cases where the discharge current of the reversing propeller is a factor, the strong current on the starboard side is directed generally toward the boat's bow but upward and inward in a spiral movement. The descending blade on the port side, on the other hand, tends to throw its stream downward at such an angle that its force is largely spent below the keel. Therefore, the two forces are never of equal effect.

Until the boat gathers sternway from her backing propeller it would not matter if the rudder were over to port or starboard. The discharge current against the starboard side is still the strong controlling factor and the stern is thrown to port. (Come back to this later when we discuss the matter of turning in a limited space.)

With Sternway, Propeller Reversing

Now visualize the boat gathering sternway as the propeller continues to reverse. Here arises one of the seemingly mystifying conditions that baffle many a helmsman during his first trick at the wheel. The novice assumes that if he wants to back in a straight line his rudder must be amidships, just as it must be when he goes ahead on a straight course. Under certain conditions his boat may even respond to *right* rudder as he reverses by going to *port,* which is exactly what he doesn't expect, and if he is learning by trial and error he comes to the conclusion that it depends on the boat's fancy, while rudder position has nothing to do with control.

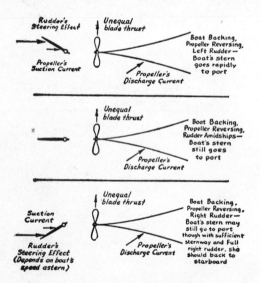

Fig. 12. Three different situations where a boat is backing, her propeller reversing, with rudder set in various positions. Some boats back to port no matter how the rudder is set, but usually with right rudder and good sternway, they can be turned to starboard, though the turn to port is much better

However, let's analyze the situation to see if he's right and whether there is anything that can be done about it. Fortunately, there is.

At the outset we can rule out any effect of wake current as that force now is spent at the bow. Considering first the most obvious case, let's assume we have left rudder. Here there are four factors all working together to throw the stern to port. Unequal blade thrust is pushing the stern to port; the discharge current of the propeller is adding its powerful effect; and now we add the steering effect of the rudder acting on the aft side of the rudder blade, against which the suction current of the propeller is also working.

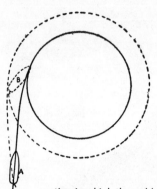

The distance a vessel moves in the direction of her original course, after the helm has been put over, is called the advance

Fig. 13. When a boat's rudder is put over to make a turn, her stern is kicked away from the direction in which the rudder moves. Then, after sliding obliquely along the course (as shown from A to B) she settles into a turning circle in which the bow describes a smaller circle (solid line) than the stern (dotted line)

Boat Tends to Back to Port

Remember this condition well for it is the answer to why *every single screw vessel with right-hand propeller naturally backs to port* easily when she may be very obstinate about going to starboard when reversing.

Now, while backing to port, let's bring the rudder amidships and see what happens. Here we have eliminated the effects of suction current and steering from the rudder, leaving unequal blade thrust and the discharge current to continue forcing the stern to port.

Assuming further that we have not yet gathered much sternway, let's put the rudder to starboard and see if we can't possibly make the boat back to starboard as you might expect she should with right rudder. The forces of sidewise blade pressure and discharge current still tend to drive her stern to port, but the suction current of the propeller wants to offset this. The effect of the discharge current is stronger than the suction so the tendency is still to port. Now, with sternway, the steering effect of right rudder is to starboard, but as yet we haven't way enough to make this offset the stronger factors.

Steering While Backing

Just about the time we are about to give it up on the assumption that she can't be made to back to starboard, we try opening the throttle to gain more sternway. This finally has the desired effect and with full right rudder we find that the steering effect at considerable backing speed is enough (probably) to turn her stern to starboard against all the opposing forces. How well she will back to starboard—in fact, whether she will or not—depends on the design.

All of this means that if the boat will back to starboard with full right rudder, she may also be made to go in a straight line—but not with rudder amidships. There's no use trying. She will need a certain amount of right rudder depending both on her design and the speed. Some boats, while their backing to port is always much better than to starboard, can be controlled with a reasonable degree of precision by one who understands the particular boat he is handling.

In cases, boats may even be steered backwards out of crooked slips or channels—not, however, without a lot of backing and filling if there is much wind to complicate the situation. Generally the trick is to keep the boat under control, making the turns no greater than necessary so as to prevent the boat from swinging too much as a result of momentum and making it correspondingly difficult to get her straightened out again.

In maneuvers of this kind it is best to set the rudder first and then get added maneuvering power by speeding up the propeller in the desired direction, instead of trying to swing the rudder after the propeller is turning fast either ahead or astern.

With Sternway, Propeller Turning Ahead

There is one other situation to be considered, where we wish to kill our sternway by engaging the propeller to turn ahead. Regardless of rudder position, unequal blade thrust with the propeller going ahead now tends to throw the stern to starboard while the suction current is of no consequence. Unequal blade thrust may or may not be offset by the steering effect and the discharge current.

With rudder amidships, there is no steering effect and the discharge current does not enter our calculations. Therefore the stern will go to starboard. Now if you throw the rudder to port the discharge current of the propeller hits the rudder and drives the stern to starboard —even though the normal steering effect of left rudder would be to send the stern to port, with sternway. The powerful discharge current from the propeller going ahead is the determining factor.

If the rudder is put to starboard, the steering effect works with the unequal blade thrust tending to move the stern to starboard but the discharge current strikes the starboard side of the rudder and acts to kick the stern to port. Application of enough power so that the force of the discharge current outweighs the other factors will result in the stern going to port.

Propeller Action Governs

From this analysis it will be seen that in a single screw boat one must constantly keep in mind what the propeller is doing in order to know how to use the rudder to best advantage. What the propeller is doing is even more important than whether the boat at the time may have headway or sternway.

To cite an example to make this clear, let's suppose you are backing in a direction that brings your port quarter up toward a dock. The tendency if you were to try to steer away from it would be to use right rudder. But the efficacy of that would be doubtful, because of the boat's inclination to back to port.

Therefore, we plan to kick the stern away by going ahead with the propeller so we set the rudder to port (left rudder, *toward* the dock), throw the reverse gear lever into the forward position and go ahead strong with the engine. The discharge current checks the sternway and, striking the rudder, throws the stern to starboard, clear of the dock.

It takes a lot of experience with any given boat to learn all her whims and traits—to know her strong points and use them wisely to overcome the weak ones. But boats, like individuals, do respond to understanding treatment.

Kiekhaefer Aeromarine Motors photograph

A group of outboard boats racing in a choppy sea. A high degree of skill and experience is required of their pilots to prevent capsizes. The outboard differs from the inboard in that the propeller, instead of a rudder, turns to provide steering

TECHNIQUE OF HANDLING THE BOAT

WHEN MANEUVERING IN CLOSE QUAR-

TERS. BACKING TO PORT AND TO

STARBOARD. THE PROBLEM OF LEAV-

ING AND PICKING UP MOORINGS

Approaching a dock, station someone at both bow and stern to
handle lines

PROFICIENCY in motor boat handling is a matter of 10 percent principles, 90 percent application of these principles in practice. Therefore, the sooner we get afloat and start experimenting, the better. We've absorbed enough of the theory to have a broad idea of what to expect in practice; the next step is to get at the helm of a boat and actually learn by doing.

Here are a few basic ideas to keep in mind, summarized from what has gone before. Remember that the boat is always under better control with headway than when she has sternway, because of the effect of the propeller's discharge current on the rudder when steering.

Until the boat has gathered headway the stern has a tendency to swing (to starboard, with right-hand propeller) even with rudder amidships, as the propeller starts to turn ahead. With good headway, rudder angle is the principal factor affecting control.

Backing, there is a strong tendency to go to port regardless of rudder angle, except (ordinarily) with full right rudder and considerable sternway. To back in a straight line you need a certain amount of right rudder varying, probably, with the speed.

With no way on there is no rudder control, yet the stern can be kicked rapidly to port or starboard by putting the rudder over and applying plenty of power before the boat has a chance to gather way.

With left-hand propeller, the boat's reaction will be contrary to that outlined for the right-hand propeller.

The first step in applying these principles will be to take the boat out in open water—preferably on a day when there is little wind and no current. These factors should be ruled out at first and studied separately later, after the boat's normal reactions are fully understood.

With unlimited room to maneuver and no traffic to worry about, try putting the boat through all the maneuvers already discussed. Practice with every combination of conditions—with headway, sternway, and no way on; with right-rudder, left rudder and rudder amidships; with propeller turning in the direction of the boat's way, and also those cases where the propeller is turning opposite to the direction of the boat's way.

In each of these maneuvers note whether the rudder or propeller has the greater effect; note, too, how changing the speed alters the boat's response. Put the rudder hard over each way and see what happens when considerable power is applied before the boat has any way on.

Practice turns to determine the size of the boat's turning circle and the space required to bring the boat to a full stop with varying amounts of way, up to full speed.

Later, when these fundamentals are mastered, go out again and observe how wind and current and sea alter the situation. Note how she tends to back into the wind until good steerageway is reached. How, if she is lying in the trough in a seaway, she tends to stay there with rudder amidships, because wave action is stronger than her natural tendency in smooth water to back to port.

Watch too how her stern starts to settle, and the bow comes up, when you get into shoal water. If there's just enough water to permit her to run without grounding, a wave will pile up on her quarter, steepest on the shallower side, as the natural formation of the wake is disturbed.

You should, of course, pick your maneuvering grounds from the chart to avoid danger of grounding, but if you see the first wave of your wake stretching away on the quarter in a sharp inverted V, tending to break at the top, beware of shoal water on that side.

Getting Under Way

Whenever you are about to get under way, assuming that you are starting a cold motor, don't spend too much time at the dock or mooring "warming up". There are a few things to check before getting under way and by the time these have been taken care of you will be ready to cast off and let the warming up of the motor be accomplished under load, at about half speed. Long periods of idling are bad for the clutch and the motor will warm up better and quicker with the propeller engaged.

Before casting off, check the oil pressure and see that the cooling water is circulating. In most all marine installations sea water is circulated through the engine water jackets. Leaving the jackets, part or all of this water goes into the exhaust to be discharged overboard. Until this water flows from the exhaust pipe it is unsafe to get under way.

If the water doesn't circulate, investigate at once as overheating can cause much damage, especially if the cold water is suddenly picked up and pumped into the hot cylinder block. Cracking of the casting might result.

Never race the motor as it idles, especially when cold. If the propeller is the right size and the throttle stop properly set, the motor should be able to take the propeller when the clutch is engaged at idling speeds. Boats don't require transmissions with a change of speeds as in cars, because the propeller slip automatically takes care of picking up the load gradually as the clutch is engaged.

After the clutch is in, the throttle (which almost invariably is hand-operated) can be opened gradually. Roughly speaking, normal cruising should be done at about two-thirds or three-quarters throttle. The extra few hundred revolutions available at wide open throttle seldom yield an increase in speed proportionate to the extra power required and the corresponding increase in fuel consumption.

One caution to observe when first learning to maneuver the boat is to avoid operating at too high a speed. Later, after you have become more familiar with the boat and its response to wheel and throttle, you will be able to use more power in certain situations—to accomplish a quick turn, for example—without getting into a jam.

Checking Headway

Before attempting the maneuver of picking up a mooring you will want to experiment with the technique of checking the boat's headway while she is out in open water. Having no brakes, you must reverse the propeller to bring the boat to a stop. In by-gone days when many boats had no reverse gears the engine itself had to be stopped, permitting the

boat to coast up to a landing, and it was often quite a trick to estimate exactly when the ignition should be cut. Reverse gears make the problem relatively simple. Some diesel engines today, especially in the larger sizes, have no reverse gear, but depend on stopping the engine and starting them up in reverse in order to check the boat's way.

Your experiments will show how effective the propeller is in killing the boat's headway. Generally speaking the larger diameter propellers, acting on a large volume of water, will exert the greatest effect. Small propellers, poorly matched to heavy hulls, may churn up considerable water before they are able to overcome the boat's momentum.

One popular type of standardized cruiser was formerly equipped with a powerful slow-turning engine and a foot-operated clutch. This would have to be thrown out, as in a car, before engaging the reverse gear lever by hand. When the clutch was re-engaged by easing up on the foot pedal the big propeller, reversing, would stop the boat almost like a car equipped with four-wheel brakes.

Right: Initiation in boat handling. Dozens of new owners acquiring rapidly the rudiments of maneuvering a boat on a cruise through the New York State Barge Canal. Below: No room for miscalculation here, when turning

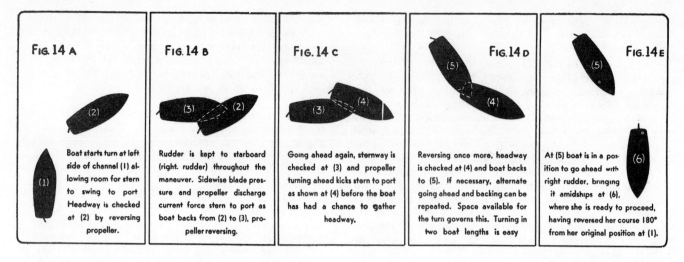

FIG. 14 A Boat starts turn at left side of channel (1) allowing room for stern to swing to port. Headway is checked at (2) by reversing propeller.

FIG. 14 B Rudder is kept to starboard (right rudder) throughout the maneuver. Sidewise blade pressure and propeller discharge current force stern to port as boat backs from (2) to (3), propeller reversing.

FIG. 14 C Going ahead again, sternway is checked at (3) and propeller turning ahead kicks stern to port as shown at (4) before the boat has had a chance to gather headway.

FIG. 14 D Reversing once more, headway is checked at (4) and boat backs to (5). If necessary, alternate going ahead and backing can be repeated. Space available for the turn governs this. Turning in two boat lengths is easy.

FIG. 14 E At (5) boat is in a position to go ahead with right rudder, bringing it amidships at (6), where she is ready to proceed, having reversed her course 180° from her original position at (1).

Many fast boats, like our modern PT's, can be stopped in an incredibly short distance. When their throttles are closed, the boat changes her trim suddenly and headway is quickly lost, even before the propellers are reversed.

Whenever it is necessary to go from forward into reverse or vice versa, close the throttle to slow the engine down while going through neutral. If you make a practice of cracking the reverse gear from full ahead to full astern, look out for trouble. This is hard on the gear even if it doesn't fail—which it might do just when you're counting on it most.

Turning in Close Quarters

Turning a boat in a waterway not much wider than the boat's length often seems a bugbear to the novice but, once he has mastered the technique, it's no more difficult than turning a car on a narrow road.

Take a look at figure 14. The situation sketched might apply in many cases. Perhaps you've run to the head of a dead-end canal and must turn around. Or possibly the waterway is a narrow channel, flanked by shoals. In the former case you must allow room so the swinging stern doesn't hit the canal bulkhead; in the latter, a similar allowance must be made to avoid throwing the stern up on shoal water.

Referring to Figure 14-a, we start at (1), on the left side of the channel, running at slow speed. Putting the rudder hard over to starboard, the boat swings toward position (2), her headway being checked by reversing. *Always* execute this maneuver by going ahead to starboard, backing to port, to take advantage of the boat's natural tendency, as explained before.

Now (see 14-b) *leave the wheel hard over to starboard* (right rudder). Normally you would expect to use left rudder in backing from (2) to (3), but this is unnecessary as the boat has no chance to gather sternway. As the reversing propeller stops the boat at (2), open the throttle for an instant and the stern will be kicked around to port to position (3).

Any attempt to shift from right rudder while going ahead to left rudder while going astern only results in extra gymnastics at the wheel at a time when you want your hands free for the throttle and reverse gear lever.

Throttling while we engage the clutch to go ahead, the sternway is checked at (3). Opening the throttle again, just for an instant, keeps the stern swinging to port toward position (4)—see Figure 14-c. Now the operation described in 14-b is repeated, backing from position (4) to (5) as shown in 14-d.

If this happens to be a bulkheaded slip you are maneuvering in, allow plenty of room so that the port quarter is not thrown against the head of the slip as you go ahead again at (5)—see 14-e. The stern will continue to swing to port as the boat straightens away toward (6). At this point the rudder can be brought amidships, the boat having executed a 180-degree turn.

Figure 15 illustrates the successive steps required to work out another practical problem in boat handling. Suppose (see 15-a) you are in a narrow slip or canal at

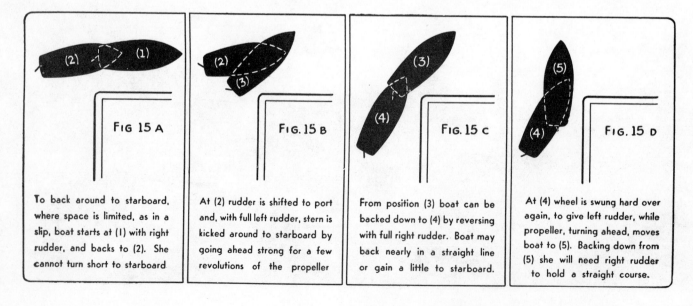

FIG 15 A To back around to starboard, where space is limited, as in a slip, boat starts at (1) with right rudder, and backs to (2). She cannot turn short to starboard.

FIG. 15 B At (2) rudder is shifted to port and, with full left rudder, stern is kicked around to starboard by going ahead strong for a few revolutions of the propeller.

FIG. 15 C From position (3) boat can be backed down to (4) by reversing with full right rudder. Boat may back nearly in a straight line or gain a little to starboard.

FIG. 15 D At (4) wheel is swung hard over again, to give left rudder, while propeller, turning ahead, moves boat to (5). Backing down from (5) she will need right rudder to hold a straight course.

position (1) and want to back around a sharp turn, to starboard. Reversing with full right rudder, you will not be able to turn short enough to steer around the 90-degree angle. Most likely you will back to a position about as indicated at (2), gaining a little to starboard. Now (see 15-b) by going ahead with left rudder the stern is kicked over to starboard, placing the boat at (3).

Reversing once more, with full right rudder, the boat backs to (4), necessitating our going ahead once more with left rudder. This puts the boat at (5) (15-d) in a position to back down on the new course.

Note that if she is expected to back down in a straight line from (5) she will need right rudder, though not necessarily hard over.

Backing to Port

Figure 16 illustrates a variation of the maneuver just described. Suppose the boat is lying in a slip, at A, and wishes to back out into the channel, space being limited. Figure 15 showed how it would be necessary to work her around if the turn were to starboard. In Figure 16 her problem would be exactly the same if she had to back around in the direction of C.

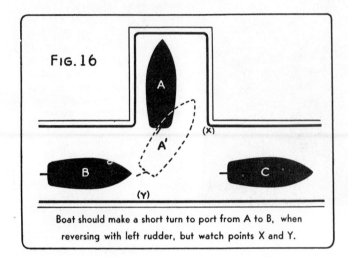

FIG. 16

Boat should make a short turn to port from A to B, when reversing with left rudder, but watch points X and Y.

However, if there is a choice, and she can back out to port, the probability is that with left rudder she will work around from A to B without any special maneuvering. To do it, her initial position in the slip must be about as shown at A with some clearance on her port side, but considerably more on the starboard side.

Clearance on the port side is needed because in reversing her stern immediately starts to move to port. More clearance on the starboard side is necessary because the bow will swing over toward point (x) as she backs.

In fact, points (x) and (y) are the ones to watch in executing this maneuver. If the boat shouldn't turn as short as expected, and doesn't swing directly from A to B, but takes a position as shown by the dotted lines at A', the starboard bow is in danger of touching at (x) and the starboard quarter at (y). This could be corrected at A' by going ahead with the propeller a few revolutions, using right rudder, to kick the stern over to port. This must be done carefully as there is no latitude here for much headway.

Having straightened her up, you could then back with left rudder to B and finally square away with rudder amidships to proceed toward C.

Leaving a Mooring

For permanent berths, boats lie either at docks or moorings. Most yacht clubs have anchorages for members' boats, using mushroom anchors and mooring buoys to which the boat is secured by a pennant or mooring line over the forward bitt.

Getting away from the mooring when you are about to start a cruise is among the simplest of maneuvers, yet there is a right and a wrong way to go about it. The principal hazard in doing it wrong is the possibility of getting either the mooring line or dinghy painter fouled in the propeller. Handling of the boat is dictated by whatever is necessary to accomplish this with a minimum of fuss.

As soon as the motor is running, shorten up the dinghy painter so that the reversing propeller cannot pull any slack down into it, to be hopelessly fouled around the shaft and wheel. See that any boarding ladders, fenders or boat booms are aboard and send a man forward to let the mooring line go. The pennant usually has a small block of wood or metal buoy to float the end, making it easy to pick up again on return to the mooring.

In a river or stream where there is a current, the boat will lie head to that current (unless the wind is stronger). But in a bay on a calm day there may be neither wind nor current to move the boat even when the mooring line is let go. To go ahead under such conditions would almost certainly result in fouling the propeller.

To avoid this, back away a few boat lengths, far enough so you can keep the buoy in sight and allow sufficient room to clear it when you go ahead, with particular regard for any swinging of the stern. Whether you back away straight or turn as you reverse depends largely on the position of neighboring boats in the anchorage.

Until you are clear of the anchorage, run well throttled so as not to create a nuisance with your wake. Then, as you open up to cruising speed, the dinghy can be dropped back near the crest of the second wave astern. If she is astern of that crest, she will tow too hard, running "uphill" with bow too high. Shorten the painter from this point until the pull on it lessens as she flattens out to a better trim, but don't have her run "down-hill" either, if there is any tendency for her to yaw off the course.

When There Is Wind or Current

When your mooring is in a stream or if a tidal current flows past it, the boat will be set back when the mooring line has been let go. This usually simplifies the problem of getting away; reversing may not be necessary.

In a wind (assuming the current is not stronger) the boat will be lying head to the wind. As she drops back from the mooring, whether or not the reverse gear is used, the bow will pay off to one side and shape the boat up to get away without additional maneuvering.

All boats with considerable freeboard have a strong tendency to "tack" back and forth as they lie at anchor in a wind, and the same is true to an extent at permanent moorings unless the gear is so heavy as to retard this action.

If the bow is "tacking" this way and you want to shape the boat up to leave the buoy on one side or the other, wait till the boat reaches the limit of her swing in the right direction and then let the pennant go. The bow will pay off rapidly as she catches the wind on that side.

Sometimes, if the boat isn't too big or the wind too strong, you can help to cast the bow in the right direction by holding the pennant to one side so that the wind will catch that side and cause her to pay off toward the other.

Picking Up the Mooring

Returning to the anchorage when the cruise is finished, approach your mooring at slow speed, noting carefully how other boats are lying at their buoys. They are heading into the wind or current (whichever is stronger) and your course in approaching the buoy should be roughly parallel to the way they line—up-wind or against the current. Shorten the dinghy painter as necessary.

Now slip the clutch into neutral when you estimate that you have just way enough to carry you up to the buoy. A man should be stationed on the bow with a boathook to pick up the pennant float when it comes within reach. If you see that you are about to overshoot the mark, reverse enough to check the headway as the bow comes up to the buoy. If you fall short, a few extra kicks ahead with the propeller should suffice.

Don't expect the man forward to do the work that the engine should accomplish in holding the boat in position until the signal is given that the pennant eye has been secured on the bitt. Watch especially that the boat doesn't tend to drop astern while the man forward tries to hang on with the boathook. Also try to avoid having the buoy chafe unnecessarily against the hull.

When running through an anchorage keep an eye peeled for other moorings so as not to foul or cut them. If yours is the only mooring in the anchorage, you will have to gauge the effect of wind and current on your own boat as best you can so as to approach up-wind or against the current or directly against any combination of these factors. Don't try to execute this maneuver with wind abeam or astern. When the pennant is secure forward, and only then, the motor can be stopped.

LANDING AT DOCKS UNDER VARIOUS CONDITIONS OF WIND AND CURRENT,

TO WINDWARD AND LEEWARD. MOORING WITH ANCHORS AT A DOCK

THE knowledge you have already acquired in turning a boat where space for maneuvering is limited will stand you in good stead when you tackle the next problem of bringing her in neatly to a dock or float.

The factors involved here are, in part, the same as in coming to a mooring, with certain modifications. For example, when you pick up a mooring you have wind and current to consider, generally determining the angle of your approach. Wind and current must also be reckoned with at docks, but there are many occasions when the angle of approach to a dock is not a matter of choice.

With no wind or current to complicate the situation, landing, with a right-handed propeller, can be accomplished most effectively by bringing the boat in port side to the dock. Our previous analysis of propeller action when reversing makes the reason for this clear.

Don't come in with a grand flourish at high speed but throttle down gradually to keep the boat under control. When you see that you have way enough to reach the dock, slip the clutch into neutral and use the reverse gear as and when necessary to check headway as the boat goes into her berth.

If your speed has been properly estimated you will be several boat lengths from the dock when the clutch is thrown into neutral. Coming in at too high a speed

you will be forced to go into neutral a long way from the dock (losing maneuverability with the propeller disengaged) or face the alternative of trusting the reverse gear to check excessive headway.

This is a good time to exercise judgment, keeping the way necessary for good maneuverability, yet using no more than required. Remember that just because a destroyer does her maneuvering at 15 knots it doesn't follow that it would be good seamanship to do the same with a little cruiser where 15 knots represents her maximum speed, or better.

As the reversing propeller throws its discharge current against the starboard side aft, the stern is carried to port. For this reason it is customary to approach, not exactly parallel with the dock, but at a slight angle— say 10 to 20 degrees. Then as she comes up to the dock her stern will be brought alongside (see figure 17) with the boat parallel to the dock, properly berthed.

In docking, lines should be kept ready to run fore and aft and fenders placed if necessary to keep the boat from chafing against unprotected piles.

Wind or Current Parallel to Dock

When the dock happens to be on the shore of a river or bank of a tidal stream so that the current flows parallel to it, it is best to govern the direction of approach by the current flow, even though this puts the starboard side toward the dock. Heading into the current will enable you to keep the propeller turning over slowly— right up to the moment of reaching the dock, if the current is strong enough.

The same is true if wind is the force you are opposing. If your course puts the wind over the stern you will have to make a wide swing, starting far enough from the dock to permit you to round up to leeward of it, coming in against the wind. To miscalculate here by not allowing room enough for the turn would be embarrassing, as you head for the bank with wind or current sweeping you downstream. Hence the importance of preliminary practice in open water, noting the size of turning circles under various conditions, before attempting the actual docking maneuvers.

In starting a turn like this, even at some distance from the dock, it will be necessary to throttle down long

before the dock comes abeam. Otherwise the wash the boat throws may carry along and leave you wallowing in your own wake just when you're trying to come alongside.

In coming up against wind or current, you use that force to check your headway, instead of the reverse. Therefore, allowance usually need not be made for the effect of a reversing propeller.

Landings Down-Wind or With the Current

Avoid, if you can, the landing in which wind or current is setting you down towards the dock in the direction of your course. In cases of this kind you are dependent on your reverse gear and even though they are practically 100 percent dependable, an error in judgment or minor motor ailment would put you on the spot.

However, you will meet such situations, where space does not permit a turn before docking. For example, suppose you are coming in to a canal lock with a strong wind astern. Hold the speed down to a minimum consistent with adequate control and by all means take the port side of the lock, unless there is no choice.

Plan to get a line out from the stern or port quarter as soon as headway is checked. If necessary, the boat would lie well enough temporarily to this line alone, whereas to get a bow line fast first and then miss making the stern line fast would be to risk being turned end for end by the wind. This has happened repeatedly to inexperienced boatmen on their first cruise through canals, to the embarrassment of other boats already berthed along the lock walls.

If you have a couple of hands aboard, assign one to the bow and one to the stern to handle lines, with instructions not to make fast until headway is checked. The seriousness of checking the boat's way by means of a snubbed bow line instead of reversing the propeller is only too obvious. If single-handed, you will have to work smartly, with a stern line fast to the after bitt coiled ready to carry ashore, and a bow line, preferably run in advance along the deck back to the cockpit. Such

lines of course would have to be led outboard of all stanchions, to be clear when taken ashore.

The problem is no different if you are making your landing with a fair current. In either case you must be ready with the reverse on the approach, using it as strongly as necessary to hold the boat against its momentum and the push of wind or current. The propeller ordinarily should be turning over slowly in reverse for the last boat length or two of headway, the throttle being opened gradually and as needed to kill all headway at the right instant.

When Boats Lie Ahead and Astern

Let's vary the problem by assuming that boats are already lying at the dock, leaving you little more than a boat length to squeeze into your berth. The technique is decidedly not the one you are accustomed to in parking a car at a curb.

Referring to Fig. 18, boats A and B are already in their berths astern and ahead, respectively, of the berth we, in boat C, want to slip into. The position of boat A necessitates our going in at a greater angle than if the dock were clear, and there is no room to go either ahead or astern once we have nosed up to position C-2.

Consequently a man is stationed forward to take a line (in this case technically called an after bow spring) leading aft from the forward bitt to a pile or bollard on the dock. He takes a turn around the pile and holds fast while we go ahead with the propeller, setting the rudder to starboard. The spring prevents the boat from going ahead and the stern is thrown in toward the dock until she assumes her final position against the dock, as at C-3.

As the boat swings in, the spring must be slacked off a little and often a fender or two will be necessary at the point of contact.

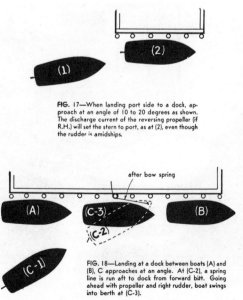

FIG. 17—When landing port side to a dock, approach at an angle of 10 to 20 degrees as shown. The discharge current of the reversing propeller (if R.H.) will set the stern to port, as at (2), even though the rudder is amidships.

FIG. 18—Landing at a dock between boats (A) and (B), C approaches at an angle. At (C-2), a spring line is run aft to dock from forward bitt. Going ahead with propeller and right rudder, boat swings into berth at (C-3).

Using Wind or Current

In a case such as that covered by Fig. 18, with conditions the same except for a wind from the south (assume boats A and B are headed east) we could have used the wind to advantage in bringing the boat in.

Under such conditions the boat could be brought up parallel to her final position at C-3, allowing the wind to set her in to her berth at the dock. The bow, probably, would come in faster than the stern, but this would not matter.

During this maneuver, the engine would be idling and, if there were any tendency for the boat to go ahead or astern, it could be offset by a turn or two of the propeller as needed, to maintain her position midway between A and B.

A variation of this problem is sketched in Fig. 19, where a current is flowing east. Here the boat is brought up to a position C-1 parallel to her berth at C-2. The propeller will have to be turning over very slowly in reverse (perhaps at the engine's idling speed) to hold her at C-1 against the current.

Now if the rudder is turned slightly to port the boat will tend to move bodily in toward the dock, though the stern is likely to come in first. An after quarter spring should be run first, to hold the boat against the current as the propeller stops turning.

Only enough rudder and power should be used to work the boat slowly sidewise. Too much power will put her out of control and too much rudder may cause her stern to go to port too fast, permitting the current to act on the boat's starboard side.

Under identical conditions, except for a current setting west instead of east, the propeller would be allowed to turn slowly ahead, just enough to hold the boat against the current. Then, with rudder slightly to port, the boat would edge off sidewise to port, the bow coming

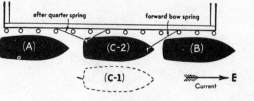

FIG. 19—The boat can be worked sidewise into her berth, using the current, by setting the rudder to port and using just enough power to offset the drift of the current. In this case, propeller must be reversed to hold her against the current.

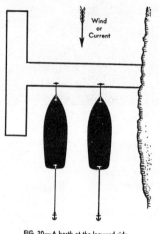

FIG. 20—A berth at the leeward side of a dock, using a stern anchor

in slightly ahead of the stern. The forward bow spring would be the first of the mooring lines to make fast in this case.

Landing on the Leeward Side

Sometimes you will run into situations where a pier or wharf juts out into the water, with wind blowing at right angles to it, giving you a choice of sides on which to land. If there is much wind and sea, the windward side can be very uncomfortable as the boat will pound against the piles.

The rougher it is, the more important it becomes to take the leeward side. The wind will then hold her clear, at the length of her mooring lines. If there is much wind you will have to work smartly when bringing the boat up to such a berth and it will help to have men ready at both bow and stern to run the mooring lines.

The bow line of course must be run first and made fast. The stern line may present more of a problem since the boat has had to approach at an angle to allow for the wind's tendency to blow the bow off. The stern line can be heaved ashore by the man aft to the other on the dock, after the latter has made his bow line fast. The bow line, if necessary, can be used as a spring to bring the stern in by going ahead with rudder to starboard, on the principle sketched in Fig. 18.

This maneuver, single-handed, would be difficult. It could be accomplished by getting a bow line off to use as a spring, working the stern up to the dock with the power, and lashing the wheel, (unless you have a worm-and-gear steerer) to keep the rudder to starboard while you get a stern line fast.

Often it is a question of just how smartly the boatman works as to how much maneuvering he must go through. If he knows his boat and his crew know their job, he probably will get his lines ashore fast enough so that the spring line may not be needed to get the stern in.

Stern Anchor to Leeward

Fig. 20 illustrates a method by which boats often line up at a dock beam to beam. Each has a secure berth on the leeward side of the dock and a maximum number of boats are accommodated for a given amount of dock space. The principal objection is the difficulty of stepping ashore from the bow.

A good example of how a group of yachts can lie to a relatively small dock by using anchors to keep them off, and bow or stern lines, as the case may be, to the dock

The arrangement shown makes a very snug berth even in a hard blow but a shift of wind might necessitate a shift of berth if the wind came abeam, throwing a heavy strain on the stern line and anchor.

The principle of getting into a berth like this is obvious from the sketch. Simply run up against the wind or current, propeller turning over just fast enough to give steerageway, and have a man let the anchor go over the stern, paying out line until the bow is close enough to get a line on the dock. The stern line is available as a check though the helmsman should make it his business to bring the bow up as required without over-shooting his mark and hitting the dock.

After passengers have been discharged the bow line can be slacked and the stern anchor line shortened, though this means that one person must be aboard. If all are to go ashore, adjust the stern line so that it just checks the boat from touching the dock. Then if there is room, carry the bow line off at an angle to another pile. This increases the clearance at the bow, and the wind or current acting on one side will help to hold her clear.

The sketch is not to scale. Often the scope of the anchor line astern will need to be much greater than that indicated to provide holding power in a given depth. Seven times the depth of water is a rough and ready rule to determine the scope of anchor lines though this is qualified by dozens of factors.

Using Anchors to Windward

If you see that a berth on the windward side of a dock is inevitable and there is reason to believe that the hull will suffer even with fenders strategically placed, plan in advance to get anchors out to windward. This trick is not used nearly as often as it should be, especially if the boat is to occupy such a berth for a considerable time.

You will need a man on the bow and another on the stern to handle anchor lines, though in a pinch the helmsman can handle the stern line if he takes every precaution to keep slack lines from fouling the propeller. Referring to Fig. 21, the stern anchor is let go from the quarter when the boat is at A, moving slowly ahead, to be checked at B, when the man forward lets his anchor go. If someone is tending the line aft, the helmsman can back a little as necessary to place the boat as the wind carries her down to her berth at C.

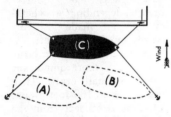

FIG. 21—Laying anchors to windward from the bow and quarter to keep a boat from pounding on the windward side of a dock.

On the other hand, if the helmsman must leave his wheel and tend the stern line, then the boat can be jockeyed into position merely by adjusting the length of the various lines. This probably will necessitate hauling in some of the stern line while the bow line is slacked away. Throughout, the lines should be carefully tended. Dock lines can be run from the port bow and quarter.

Note that at A and B the boat is not parallel to the dock, but has been headed up somewhat into the wind. As she drifts in, after the engine is put in neutral at B, the bow will come in faster than the stern.

This plan should be used with a full understanding of the great strain the anchor lines are carrying with the wind hitting the boat abeam, especially if there is some sea running as well. The stronger the wind and the rougher the sea, the longer the scope required if the anchors are to hold without dragging.

If you plan to land on the windward side of the dock without using anchors to hold her off, make due allowance for leeway on the approach and keep the bow somewhat up to windward if possible, checking headway while abreast of the berth you will occupy. Then have fenders handy as she drifts in.

When Current Sets Toward the Dock

Let's suppose now a situation in which the boat must find a berth off a dock in such a position that the current will be flowing from the boat toward the dock. See Fig. 22.

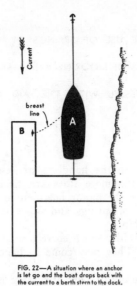

FIG. 22—A situation where an anchor is let go and the boat drops back with the current to a berth stern to the dock.

In this hypothetical case it may be assumed that the outside of the dock, which ordinarily would be the natural choice for landing, must be kept clear for ferries, perhaps, or other boats, while the lower side of the dock is also restricted for some reason. The only remaining berth is above it, at A in the illustration.

This situation should be sized up to determine exactly where the anchor is to be let go, with certainty that you will have sufficient scope. If your anchor drags here, you will be in a bad spot as the current will set the boat down on the dock. Therefore make sure that the anchor really gets a bite.

The spot where the anchor is to be let go may be approached from any direction as long as the boat is rounded up into the current. The procedure, if we wish to land bow to the dock with a stern anchor out, has already been outlined in Fig. 20. This, however, is not feasible above the dock because of the difficulty of backing away into the current when leaving.

After the anchor has been let go, the boat can be dropped back toward her berth at A, simply by paying out more scope on the anchor line. The current will do the work though the engine could be used to help control the boat's position if wind tended to throw her out of line.

Just before the stern reaches the dock, a stern line can be made fast to a pile, after which the boat's position can be adjusted by the lines as desired. If the anchor is holding securely (and the berth should be left if it isn't) the stern can be brought close enough to the dock for passengers to step comfortably ashore.

The boat should not be left unattended in this position as she may safely be if berthed as in Fig. 20. In Fig. 22, where a convenient wing of the dock is available alongside the boat, a breast line could be run as shown. Then, before leaving the boat, the anchor line could be shortened to give ample clearance at the stern. Slacking the stern line would permit stepping ashore at B, after which the stern line could be adjusted from the dock.

The breast line is left slack but is available to haul the boat back in to B when boarding again after slacking the stern line. If the breast line is made fast too far aft it would be difficult to haul the stern in because of the "tacking" action of the boat in the current Made fast forward of amidships, the boat will come in readily.

Landing Starboard Side to Dock

Though a dock on the port side is preferable, as already explained, a good landing at a dock on the starboard side can be made, if care is exercised.

Referring to Figure 22-a, the boat is approaching the dock at (A), nearly parallel to it, engine idling or turning over just enough to insure control.

Just before it is necessary to reverse to check the headway, the rudder is shifted to full left (at B) to swing the stern in toward the dock. If she does not respond, give the propeller a kick ahead while the rudder is full left. This definitely kicks the stern in and, as she swings, the reverse can be used to kill the headway.

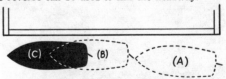

FIG. 22a—Making a landing with the starboard side of the boat toward the dock. Approaching slowly at (A), nearly parallel with the dock, rudder is shifted to full left at (B), swinging stern to starboard. At this point, give the boat a kick ahead with the propeller (if necessary) to swing the stern Then reverse to check headway.

PRINCIPLES UNDERLYING THE USE OF SPRINGS IN HANDLING

BOATS AT A DOCK. METHODS OF MOORING AND MAKING FAST.

TURNING (WINDING) A VESSEL WITH THE AID OF LINES

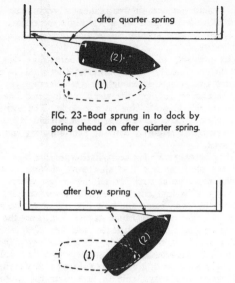

FIG. 23–Boat sprung in to dock by going ahead on after quarter spring.

LINES play an important part in the handling of vessels at a dock. Obviously, the larger the craft the more lines are likely to be called into play. It would be absurd for the motor boatmen to burden his 30-footer with a spider-web of breasts, springs and other lines that would be appropriate only on a large ship.

Nevertheless, it is well to be familiar with correct terms and the functions of lines that may be used. They may come in handy some time—though not necessarily all at once.

Motor boatmen often speak loosely of bow and stern lines—and little else—depending on whether the line is made fast forward or aft and regardless of the direction in which it leads or the purpose it serves. To be strictly correct, according to nautical terminology, there is only one bow line. This is made fast to the forward bitt and run along the dock as far as practicable to prevent the boat from moving astern.

FIG. 24–Bow swung sharply in toward dock by going ahead on an after bow spring.

Conversely, a stern line, properly, leads from the after bitt to a distant pile or bollard on the dock astern of the boat, to check her from going ahead. The special virtue of such lines as applied to small boats is the fact that, with but little slack, they still allow for considerable rise and fall of the tide.

Breast lines, on the other hand, lead athwart-

ships nearly at right angles to the vessel and to the dock, to keep her from moving sidewise away from her berth. Large craft may use bow, waist or quarter breasts, depending on whether they are made fast forward, amidships or aft.

Naturally breasts on large vessels are more important than on small craft. If a vessel has a 100-foot beam, her bow is 50 feet from the dock and the bow breast must be somewhat longer than that. On a small boat with 10-foot beam, the bow is only 5 feet from the dock, and other lines may serve to keep her from moving away from the dock.

Another point to remember is the fact that a majority of small pleasure boats have only two bitts or cleats—one forward and one aft—to make fast to and no other cleats amidships or elsewhere, to which waist lines can be made fast.

As we shall see later, a small boat might be adequately moored with springs

Large cruisers are ordinarily berthed at floats only for brief periods while taking on and discharging guests and supplies. A couple of fenders and lines at bow and stern suffice. No allowance need be made at a float for tide

MacGramlich

128

alone, using no breasts. Sometimes boatmen attempt to make fast to a dock with bow and stern breasts only and get into trouble because slack must be left in the line to allow for tide. If adjusted right for low water, they may be entirely too slack at high water and the boat gets a chance to catch in some stringer or projection of the dock when her bow or stern swings in.

The Use of Springs

Springs are not as long as bow and stern lines, but they lead forward and aft to check motion astern and ahead, respectively. There may be four springs—the forward bow spring, the after bow spring, the forward quarter spring, and the after quarter spring. Bow springs are made fast to the vessel at the bow, quarter springs at the quarter.

Forward springs lead forward from the ship to the dock, so the forward bow and quarter springs check motion astern. After springs lead aft from the vessel to the dock. Thus the after bow and quarter springs check motion ahead.

To keep this clear in mind, remember that the terms forward and after applied to such lines relate to the *direction* in which the line runs *from* the vessel, not to where it is made fast, the latter being indicated by the terms bow, waist and quarter.

We have already seen (Figure 18, Part Four) how, by means of an after bow spring, the stern can be brought in to a dock by going ahead with rudder set away from the dock. In this case the boat lay obliquely to the face of the dock, with bow against it.

Now if the boat lay parallel to the dock but some distance off, she could be breasted in bodily by hauling in on bow and stern breasts, but with a vessel of any size this might require considerable effort.

Ideal permanent berthing facilities for scores of boats are supplied here in this yacht basin, with individual slips for each boat

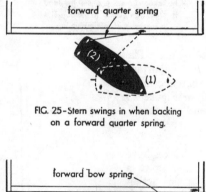

FIG. 25–Stern swings in when backing on a forward quarter spring.

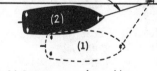

FIG. 26–Reversing on a forward bow spring, the boat comes in nearly parallel to the dock.

Effect of After Springs

If it were possible to secure an after spring at the boat's center of gravity, she could be sprung in bodily to the dock and her parallel alignment (or any other position) could be held by means of the rudder as the propeller goes ahead, because the stern would be free to swing as the discharge current acts on the rudder.

Actually this is not feasible as we probably have only the bow and stern (or quarter) bits to make fast to, while the center of gravity may be nearly amidships. Now if we rig an after quarter spring, and go ahead with rudder amidships, the combination of forces is such that the boat will be sprung in nearly parallel to the dock. Her stern will come in till the quarter touches the dock, while the bow may stand off somewhat. (See Figure 23).

If the rudder were put to port at position (1) in Figure 23, in the expectation that the bow would thus be thrown to port, it would be seen that the effect is negligible, as the stern is prevented from being kicked to starboard by the taut spring. Putting the rudder to starboard would throw the stern in to port fast, however.

Now, turning to Figure 24, let's rig the after spring from the bow instead of the quarter and see what happens.

With rudder amidships, going ahead on this bow spring will cause the bow to be swung abruptly in toward the dock, as the bit describes an arc of a circle, the length of the spring its radius. With left rudder, the bow turns in even faster as the stern is thrown to starboard further away from the dock. With right rudder some of the bow's sharp turn inward to port toward the dock is offset but probably not enough to bring the boat in parallel

FIG. 27-Usual method of mooring a small vessel to a dock with springs. Lines required are (1) bow line, (2) stern line, (3) after bow spring, and (4) forward quarter spring.

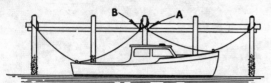

FIG. 28-Use of mooring lines at a dock. Note eye splice of after bow spring (A) run up through the eye (B) of the forward quarter spring. Either can be cleared without removing the other

—unless the spring is made fast further aft.

Reversing on a Spring

The action is just the opposite if we reverse on a spring. Turning to Figure 25, note how the stern is swung sharply in toward the dock by the action of the forward quarter spring when reversing. Compare this action with that illustrated in Figure 24, picturing the boat turned end for end.

Now note what happens, as in Figure 26, when backing on a forward bow spring. The turning effect of the spring on the boat is not important here, and she springs in nearly parallel to the dock in an action which might be compared with that in Figure 23 —once again considering the boat turned end for end.

Making Fast at a Dock

Boatmen located on fresh water streams and lakes have no tidal problem confronting them when securing to a dock with mooring lines, but failure to take this action into account in tidal waters can part lines, and even sink the boat.

Springs provide an effective method of leaving a boat free to rise and fall, while preventing her from going ahead or astern or twisting in such a way as to get caught on dock projections.

The longer a mooring line can be, the more of a rise and fall of tide it can take care of with a minimum of slack. Yet every line must be allowed slack enough so that all do not come taut together at either extreme stage of the tide.

As a general rule, where space permits, a bow line should be run well ahead of the boat to the dock, and a stern line well aft. If these two lines are run off at an angle of about 45 degrees to the centerline of the boat, they will often prove sufficient for small pleasure boats, breasts being entirely unnecessary and the springs (one or two) resorted to only if the necessary slack of bow and stern lines allows the boat to move about too much at her berth.

Mooring a 100-Footer

What might be considered a typical satisfactory arrangement of mooring lines on the average cruiser or yacht—even up to 100-footers—is illustrated in Figure 27. Only three cleats, piles or bollards are required on the dock to make fast to, the middle one of which comes about amidships. Both the after bow spring and the forward quarter spring can be run to this, while bow and stern lines run forward and aft, respectively, to the two other points on the dock.

Breast lines here would be superfluous, serving no useful purpose, and therefore should be omitted. In the service, 110-foot sub-chasers find this arrangement adequate and there is no point in burdening smaller craft with more, except under unusual conditions. Some yachtsmen prefer to run the stern line to the outboard bitt.

If two lines are used anywhere with the idea of getting double the strength of one, they must be of equal length when strain is put upon them. Otherwise one carries the load first and parts, and then the other follows suit.

A boat moored as shown in Figure 27 will lie comfortably at her berth, regardless of changes in tide level, shifts of wind or current, or the wash of passing boats. This last factor can be a serious matter if lines are laid in such a manner that the boat is free to surge fore and aft because of too much slack.

Two Lines on One Bollard

The most convenient way of using mooring lines is to have an eye splice of suitable size in the end which goes ashore, to be dropped over the pile or bollard. Figure 27 shows both the after

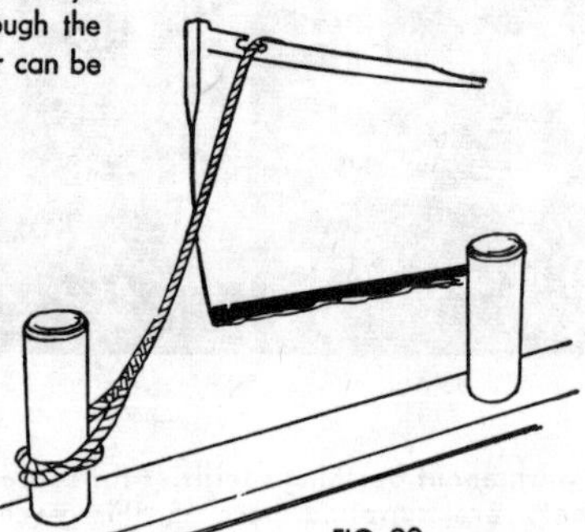

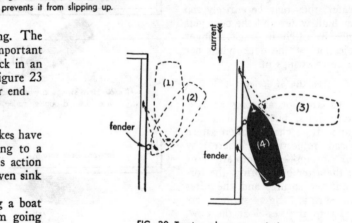

FIG. 29
An extra round turn in the eye splice of a mooring line should be taken around a pile if the lead is high from dock to deck. This prevents it from slipping up.

FIG. 30-Turning a boat at a dock, using the current and springs.

bow spring and the forward quarter spring secured to a single bollard about amidships. If these are dropped one over the other, the upper one must first be cleared in order to get the lower one free.

Inasmuch as one or the other of these springs may be needed to get clear of the dock, depending on wind and current conditions at the time, it is well to rig these so that either can be freed without disturbing the other.

Assuming that the eye splice of the forward quarter spring has been placed on the pile first, take the splice of the after bow spring and run it up from below through the eye of the quarter spring and then drop it down over the pile. (See Figure 28).

This way either line can be cleared without disturbing the other, though it may be necessary to use a little power to ease the strain on one if its eye happens to nip the other line between itself and the pile.

If a boat has considerable freeboard, the tide is high, and dock piles are relatively short, so that a mooring line leads down at a fairly sharp angle from deck to dock, there may be some risk of its slipping up over the top of the pile. An extra round turn of the eye splice taken over the pile will prevent this. (See Figure 29.)

Heaving Lines

Part of the essence of good seamanship lies in knowing when a certain method of procedure is applicable to the size of vessel one is handling. Use of big ship technique on small motor boats is amusing to a boatman. Application of motor boat principles aboard a big vessel may be distressing to a ship captain.

So it is with heaving lines. When a small motor boat is brought up smartly to a dock, there is rarely any need for springs or heaving lines, though a spring is often helpful in getting clear when leaving.

On small boats the mooring lines are properly kept neatly coiled until needed and then broken out of the locker for use in docking just before required. Manila lines of even 50 and 60-foot yachts are relatively light—say between 1-inch and 1½-inch diameter—and can be handled easily as the boat is brought alongside. Sending out any unnecessary springs or sending lines out too soon is not in order.

The lines of a big vessel are heavy hawsers, hard to handle, and impossible to heave. Therefore they make use of heaving lines, which are light lines weighted at the end by a "monkey's fist" (an intricate woven knot which encloses the weight.) This heaving line is bent to the hawser near the eye splice—not in the loop where it might be jammed when a strain is thrown on the hawser—and the line is sent from ship to dock or dock to ship as soon as possible as a messenger.

On small boats this is more of a principle to remember for possible use than a precept to practice in ordinary run-of-the-mill docking maneuvers. Generally your crew can step ashore with necessary lines and there is no need for getting lines out at some distance from the dock, as in ship-docking procedure.

Even if necessary to heave your regular mooring lines on a small boat, they will carry some distance if properly coiled, half held loosely in the left hand and the remaining half heaved by the right, all uncoiling naturally in the air, without fouling up into a knot and falling short. If necessary, a weight can be added at times to carry a line but this is seldom used.

If, in passing a line for towing purposes, for example, you had to send a heavier line a long distance, then break out the heaving line principle and use it to good advantage.

Turning a Boat at a Dock

Turning a boat at a dock—called winding ship in the case of a large vessel—is easy if wind or current is used as an aid, or if the engine is used in the absence of these factors.

Figure 30 illustrates a boat lying, at position (1), with her stern toward the current and the problem is to turn her to head into the current. The first step is to let all lines go except the after bow spring.

Normally the effect of the current will then be sufficient to throw her bow in toward the dock and her stern out into the stream toward the position sketched at (2). If any factor, such as a beam wind, tends to keep her stern pinned against the dock, the stern can be kicked out by going ahead easily with right rudder. A fender should be kept handy as a protection to the starboard bow.

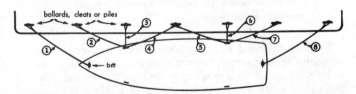

FIG. 31—When a vessel is large enough to justify the use of breasts in addition to springs, her mooring lines may be used as shown—(1) bow line, (2) forward bow spring (3) forward (bow) breast (4) after bow spring (5) forward quarter spring (6) after (quarter) breast (7) after quarter spring (8) stern line. Don't burden a small boat with them all. Aboard ships, mooring lines are numbered from the bow aft, depending on where they are secured aboard ship.

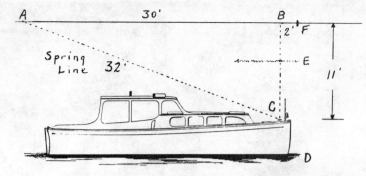

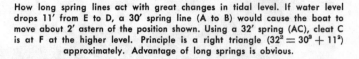

How long spring lines act with great changes in tidal level. If water level drops 11' from E to D, a 30' spring line (A to B) would cause the boat to move about 2' astern of the position shown. Using a 32' spring (AC), cleat C is at F at the higher level. Principle is a right triangle ($32^2 = 30^2 + 11^2$) approximately. Advantage of long springs is obvious.

Some steps should be taken to prevent the bow from catching on the dock as she swings, thus exerting a great leverage on the spring. A small boat may roll the fender a little and the boat can be eased off by hand, but in larger craft it is customary to reverse the engine just enough to keep the bow clear, as shown at (3).

As she swings in with the current, the fender should be made ready near the port bow as shown at (4). At this point she may tend to lie in this position, depending on just how much strain there is on the bow spring. If she does not come alongside readily, perhaps helping her by going ahead a little with right rudder, a forward quarter spring can be rigged. Then, by taking a strain on the quarter spring, and easing the bow spring, she will set in to her new berth.

Larger vessels executing this maneuver would get a forward bow spring out on the port bow when the ship reaches position (3), rigging it not from the extreme bow but a point further aft. Going ahead easily with right rudder on this spring alone (the first one having been cast off), the ship could be kept under control and eased in nicely.

In turning a boat this way it is always easier and better to make the turn with the bow to the dock rather than the stern. The procedure would be the same as outlined in a case where wind is blowing in the direction in which the current sets in the illustration.

Turning at a Dock with Power

Considering a problem similar to that sketched in Figure 30, except that we assume there is neither wind nor current to assist in turning, the power of the engine can be used to swing her.

Going ahead on an after bow spring with right rudder (starboard side being toward the dock as in the figure) would throw the stern out away from the dock, a fender being used as in the previous illustration to protect the bow. In this case the stem is allowed to nose up against the dock, using another fender if necessary to cushion it.

As the boat swings toward a position at right angles to the dock, the spring will have to be eased. With the bow against the dock, engine going ahead slowly, and rudder amidships, the boat can be held in this position while the bow spring is cast off from the dock and re-rigged as an after bow spring on the port side. With right rudder again, the stern will continue to swing all the way around, fenders being shifted once more to protect the port bow.

This is a principle that has many applications and will be found useful in dozens of situations when the theory is understood. In a berth only inches wider than the overall length of the boat, without room to go ahead and astern, she can be turned end for end with no line-hauling or manual effort of any kind.

If there happens to be wind or current holding her against the dock, the first half of this maneuver can be used to get the stern out into the stream, preliminary to backing away when ready to get clear of the dock.

This cutter has a chock in her rail at the waist, through which her springs are rigged here to check motion fore and aft. If much strain is to be carried, the length of the doubled stern lines should be equalized. A spring rigged from the waist can be of great value in handling a boat at a dock, as the stern is free to swing

vent her from backing further and this causes her to pivot as the stern is pulled around to starboard, as at (C). As she continues to back toward (D), the boat assumes a position parallel to the outer face of the dock.

At (D), the spring can be cast off the bollard and carried further up the dock to be made fast elsewhere as a stern line, if the boat is to remain in this new berth. The bow line in turn can be used to control the bow and prevent the boat's swinging too far; then made fast as necessary, perhaps to the bollard formerly used to secure the spring.

This method is especially useful when there is a breeze off the dock that would tend to blow her away if maneuvering without lines. No manpower is required and it can be accomplished leisurely in a seamanlike manner.

In the event that the maneuver is used preparatory to getting under way, the bow line is not required. When the boat has pivoted far enough, with starboard quarter near the corner of the dock, the engine can be idled while the spring is cast off the bollard and brought aboard. Getting under way from such a position, the rudder must be set amidships till the quarter clears the dock, then full left rudder turns her bow out into the stream.

THE USE OF SPRINGS IN WORKING A

BOAT AROUND THE END OF A DOCK.

GETTING CLEAR OF DOCKS UNDER

VARIOUS CONDITIONS OF WIND AND

CURRENT. FENDERS AND SIDEBOARDS.

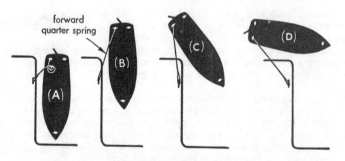

FIG. 32-Use of a forward quarter spring when backing a boat out around the end of a dock. When spring is taut, boat reverses with full right rudder.

ELSEWHERE we have discussed the technique of backing a boat out of her slip, turning either to port or starboard, preparatory to getting under way. A variation of this is illustrated in Figure 32, where the boat is pictured lying in a slip at right angles to the outer side of a dock.

The problem may be to back her around so as to have her lying along the outside of the dock, or the principle might be used as a method of backing clear of the slip, preliminary to getting under way, especially if there is little room for maneuvering. The idea in this case is to use a forward quarter spring.

At (A) in the illustration, the boat is shown lying starboard side to the dock. The first step is to make the spring ready from a point near the corner of the dock to the after bitt, either amidships if there is only one, or the bitt on the starboard quarter, if there are two.

With the spring ready, but left slack and tended, the bow line is cast off, or slacked away and tended by a man on the dock and the boat is backed easily with full right rudder. At (B), a strain is taken on the spring to pre-

Spring lines used this way should have a loop of convenient size in the end, formed either by an eye splice or a bowline so as to slip quickly and easily off the pile, bollard or cleat, yet stand the strain of holding the boat against application of power, without slipping. The eye splice is best; the bowline is quickly turned into the end of a line having no splice.

In this or any other maneuver involving the application of engine power against the spring, it is obvious that the strain must be taken up slowly and easily. A sudden surge of power puts a load on deck fittings that they were never designed to carry—may even tear cleats right out by the roots, so to speak. If the fastenings hold, the line

may part—perhaps with a dangerous snap, as the parted ends lash out.

Once the strain has been taken up easily, proper deck fittings and good line of adequate size will stand the application of plenty of power, in those cases where the power is really needed. Bear this principle in mind when you are preparing to tow or in passing a line to a stranded boat with a view toward hauling her off.

Holding the Boat with One Spring

While we are talking of springs there is another trick worth remembering that deserves to be used more often. See Figure 33.

In the illustration we assume that you have run up along the leeward side of a dock, to remain there for just a short time while you pick up guests or perhaps put some one ashore. Instead of getting lines out to make fast fore and aft as you would for a longer stop, or expect the crew to hold the boat against the wind's pressure, try using one line as an after bow spring, as illustrated.

After coming alongside, rig the line and go ahead easily till it takes a strain; then go ahead, with left rudder, with power enough to hold the stern up against the dock. This is a maneuver that you can accomplish single-handed without too much difficulty, by having your spring fast to the forward bitt as you come in, with the end ready to pass ashore for someone on the dock to drop over a pile.

Single-handed, you might prefer to use the spring double, with the bight of line around the pile and both ends of the line fast to your bitt. Then, when your guests are all aboard, you can slip the engine into neutral, cast off one end and haul the spring back aboard without leaving the deck. This would be helpful if the wind were of some force, the bollard well back from the dock edge, and no one ashore to assist. This way there would be no risk of the boat's

Docking instructions are given to an approaching boat from the marine control tower of one of the world's largest marinas. In canals, restricted waters, anchorages, and in the vicinity of other boats, speed should be moderate to prevent damage from the wake

being blown off as you step ashore to cast off the line.

In any case, when the line has been cast off forward, the wind will cause the boat to drift clear of the dock, the bow ordinarily paying off faster than the stern. Whether you go ahead or reverse to get under way will be dependent on the proximity of other docks and boats, etc., and whether your course is to be up or down-stream. The same maneuver would be applicable if current were setting in the direction that the wind is blowing in the illustration.

Using Springs to Get Clear of a Dock

When either wind or current tends to set the boat off the dock as shown in Figure 33 there is little difficulty in getting clear when you are ready to get under way. In Figure 34, however, we have assumed a situation in which the wind (or current) tends to hold the boat in her berth against the windward side of the dock. This is a bad berth if there is wind enough to raise much of a sea.

If the principle of the spring is not used in a case like this there may be a great deal of effort expended with boat hooks and manpower doing a lubberly job, with the possibility, even, of damage to the boat. Correct use of an after bow spring is the seamanlike solution.

Referring to Figure 34 (A), all mooring lines have been cast off except the after bow spring. If the boat has been lying to bow and stern lines only, the stern line can be cast off and the bow line transferred to a position on the dock as shown to convert it into a spring.

Going ahead easily on the spring with right rudder tends to nose the bow in and throw the stern up into the wind away from the dock. If it does not respond with the rudder hard over, open the throttle to provide the kick necessary to work the stern around against wind pressure. Depending on the nature of the dock

FIG. 33-Making a brief stop on the leeward side of a dock, boat can be held in position by going ahead on an after bow spring with rudder hard over (in this case, to port).

and type of boat, you may need a fender or two at the critical spots between dock and boat.

At (B), it is evident that the continued turning of the stern would throw a great strain on the spring. Therefore, it is generally necessary to ease the spring, yet keep the stem from slipping along the dock. One of the best ways to accomplish this is to have the spring made fast on the bitt by means of several round turns and a half hitch. With the half hitch cast off, the turns can be allowed to slip a little to ease the spring as necessary.

At (C), the boat has turned far enough so that the stem is not likely to slip, though the boat could be allowed to turn further till her stern was squarely into the wind. At this point the spring and fender can be gotten aboard and the boat backed away with rudder amidships.

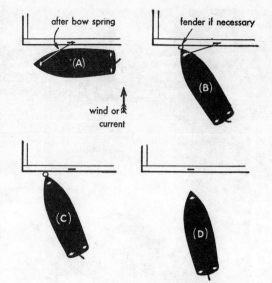

FIG. 34–How an after bow spring is used to leave the windward side of a dock. Boat goes ahead on the spring with rudder set toward dock, then backs away into the wind.

board, because of the effect of sidewise blade pressure (with a right-handed wheel). This usually is of little consequence as it takes but a moment to get forward and cast off.

With a worm-and-gear type steerer, which holds its position against pressure on the rudder, or any other type of control that will maintain rudder angle without a hand on the wheel, it can be set in a case like this for just enough right rudder to compensate for the effect of sidewise blade pressure.

Leaving Dock with Wind or Current Astern

The procedure just outlined can be used in getting away from a dock if the wind or current comes from astern—which is along the lines of the technique described in connection

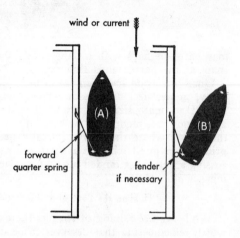

FIG. 35–When wind or current is ahead, backing on a forward quarter spring turns the stern in and bow out, shaping the boat up to get clear by going ahead.

When Single-Handed

This is another of those maneuvers that can be accomplished single-handed with little effort if done in a seamanlike manner. If single-handed, the rudder must be set amidships when the stern has worked up into the wind, giving the helmsman a chance to go forward and cast off the spring. Furthermore, it will not be easy for him to go forward and ease his spring, but this can sometimes be done by momentarily going into neutral, which allows the spring to pull the stem toward the bollard. This, however, may not be expedient with much wind, requiring the help of a man forward to handle it properly.

When the boat lies with head to the dock and rudder amidships, there may be a natural tendency for her to work her stern around to star-

with Figure 30 for turning a boat at a dock.

Instead of merely casting off all lines and going ahead in such a situation, it is better to get the maneuverable stern out away from the dock, shaping the boat up to go astern first, before going ahead on the course. The reason, obviously, is that this technique gets the boat away from the dock where there is no risk of scraping her topsides as you pull away—especially if the rudder is not exactly amidships.

Fenders are generally required to protect the hull when lying alongside docks, even in quiet water. In rough water, or when there is passing traffic, good fenders become increasingly important

134

Turning again to Figure 34, but assuming the wind is east or that the current sets westward (top of diagram being north) the after bow spring allows her stern to go out into the stream, to be kicked out if necessary by power, going ahead with right rudder. Often in such a case the stern swings out without aid from the power.

When the boat has swung anywhere from 45 to 90 degrees, depending on circumstances of the particular case, the spring is cast off and the boat reverses far enough to clear the dock nicely when you go ahead with left rudder.

Leaving Dock with Wind or Current Ahead

Now, referring to Figure 35, let's consider the boat as lying with her bow toward the north. There is a wind from the north or a current which sets south so that its effect is in a line parallel to the dock and opposite to the direction in which the boat is heading.

If, in attempting to get clear of this berth, all lines were cast off immediately, the boat might drift bodily back along the dock or, if power were applied ahead, the helmsman would have to exercise care that the boat was kept exactly parallel in order to pull away without damage.

Again, it is more seamanlike to use a spring (unless the boat is so small that a person stepping aboard at the bow can merely push her bow out enough.) This time we need a forward quarter spring on the port side. It is likely that this is already in use as one of the dock mooring lines, so all other lines can be cast off.

If the bow does not swing out at once with the effect of wind or current, backing easily on the spring will pull the stern in toward the dock, probably necessitating use of a fender on the port quarter to protect the hull.

In maneuvers where the bow swings in toward the dock, the fender is not always important if the bow has a good metal rub strip and the topsides are well flared. On the other hand, in cases like the one under discussion, the stern comes in against the dock and a fender is usually in order, especially if the topsides tumble home. Good stout metal-shod rubrails are a fine thing on any boat that has occasion to maneuver much around docks.

In Figure 35, when the bow has swung out as sketched at (B), the boat has been shaped up to pull directly away by casting off the spring and going ahead with rudder amidships.

Fenders

We have noted from time to time in the foregoing illustrations the necessity of protecting the hull with fenders in maneuvering around rough dock piles, or in lying alongside other craft. Articles on equipment have repeatedly pointed out the desirability of carrying plenty of good fenders, but often the equipment actually provided falls far short of being adequate.

The standard types of yacht fenders are satisfactory if large enough and provided in sufficient number. When a boat lies at a dock with no motion, except the rise and fall of tide and the flow of current, even the lightest of guardrails may be alright. But you can't count on these ideal conditions to prevail at all times.

The combination of topsides that are heavily flared forward, tumble home aft, high superstructure that reaches out practically to the deck edge, and comparatively light guard moldings, possibly of wood not even metal-shod with half-oval, all make for potential damage when the boat starts to roll and pound against piles, either as a result of the swell created by passing craft or wave action from the wind or a ground swell.

The ordinary fenders (not "bumpers") for pleasure boats are of several types of construction—canvas covers filled with ground cork for small craft; woven manila or cotton covers, also cork-filled; and all manila rope, braided so that no central core or filler is required. Newer types include those of rubber construction containing minute gas-filled cells; others have canvas covers enclosing sponge rubber, shredded rubber or cork and rubber. Kapok is also used as a filling.

The smallest of these fenders sometimes have a grommet, eye or rope ring at one end only, to take the pennant by which it is suspended from fender hooks on the boat. Better practice is to have an eye at each end so that the fender can be rigged horizontally as well as vertically, sometimes by hanging it over the pile, instead of from the boat where it moves as the boat moves.

Half a dozen substantial fenders are not too many to carry and if the boat is equipped with few, or no, hooks, go over it with a critical eye to see that stout fender hooks are placed where needed.

In the Navy and Coast Guard, fenders for what they call small craft, like subchasers and patrol boats, often consist of a 25-pound ball of woven rattan surrounded by a finishing external layer of manila rope. Still larger craft use cylindrical fenders, of all-rattan construction, which are pliable, springy, resilient, and drain quickly, thus drying out rapidly after a thorough soaking.

Boats that have been taken over by the Government for Coast Guard duty have been subjected to far more vigorous service than they ever saw in the days when their operations were restricted simply to pleasure cruises. Cruisers have had to tie against rough sea walls, piers intended for the use of liners, and go alongside freighters and every other type of vessel—perhaps while under way, and worse, in a seaway.

These problems have been successfully solved by the Coast Guardsmen, Reservists, and Auxiliarists who man them; a page from their experiences, as reported in an Auxiliary publication, might well be borrowed by those yachtsmen who wish to be ready to cope with any contingency.

Sideboards or Fenderboards

The solution to many of these problems of protecting the hull has been found in the use of sideboards or fenderboards, carried aboard in addition to a full complement of good heavy fenders. Yachtsmen have carried such boards in some cases but, due to lack of stowage space or other considerations, they have not always been of suitable size.

If fenders are hung vertically from the boat's side, they give protection in cases where there is a horizontal string piece to bear against as the boat moves fore and aft. If there are vertical piles to lie against, vertical fenders cannot be expected to stay exactly in place. Movement of the boat fore and aft shifts them between the piles and their value is destroyed. Hanging the fender horizontally by both ends is only a slight improvement, and then only if hung on the pile where it is independent of the boat's movement fore and aft. As a matter of fact, even this doesn't provide well for rise and fall of the tide.

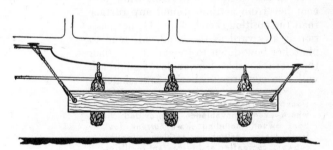

FIG. 36—A side board or plank to be used in conjunction with ordinary fenders proves invaluable in cases where adequate protection to the hull cannot be provided by fenders alone.

The publication mentioned describes the fenders and sideboards used to protect a 66-footer from battering against sea-walls, piers, and large vessels during the course of strenuous duty, both summer and winter. Her fenders were a foot in diameter, 40 inches long, of ¾-inch woven manila. Her sideboards were of 2¾ by 10-inch oak, 8 to 10 feet long. A foot from each end, holes were bored transverse to take ¾-inch manila pennants, eye spliced through the holes.

This combination worked with complete success whereas three previous boards fashioned of 1½ by 12-inch yellow pine had been snapped by battering against the pier.

On boats with a heavy flare forward, they cant the sideboard so that the forward end projects above the deck line to prevent the flared overhang from catching on the top of the pile. Wind, tide, and suction often have a tendency to hold a small craft alongside a larger vessel under way and it was found that an extra cylindrical fender held between the sideboard and the larger vessel's sides permitted the patrol boat to get away easily, as the fender rolled.

The applicability of sideboards and fenders to boats lying side by side is easily seen. If each craft suspends several fenders over the side with a horizontal sideboard to bear directly against the board of the other, each is as comfortable as though moored to a dock and there is no possibility of damage even to high rolling superstructures because the hulls are held well apart.

The method of rigging sideboards is illustrated in Figure 36.

Some berths provide for piles to tie to, lying off a dock so that boats lie beam to beam, each occupying its own individual slip. In one variation of this, catwalks are provided between the various boats to allow more convenient access to each.

Figure 37 illustrates a problem where a boat must be backed into such a berth in a basin. Complicating the situation is a bulkhead along the east (leeward) and south sides, which prevents approach from any direction except west, down-wind.

If the space between piles and the south bulkhead is sufficient to allow the boat to make a turn, going ahead with right rudder, as in 2-3-4-5, she may round up this way, until, as in (5), she has headed partly into the wind.

If space, turning power, or wind prevent her from getting around any further than the position sketched at (4), her position is awkward as the wind will tend to blow her bow down to leeward faster than the stern so that her angle of approach will not conform with the path sketched

Docking arrangements in a large marina, where every convenience is provided the boat owner, including shore current, fuel, fresh water, telephone service, supplies, showers, recreation and restaurant facilities, etc. Some craft lie bow into the dock, others stern to. In such places, boat owners soon become adept at berthing their craft

at 6-7-8. In that case, she would have to work out another technique.

Assuming that she can round up under power to position (5) with right rudder, she has been placed so that she can back along the line 6-7-8 without shifting her rudder. Remembering that the stern normally tends to port, and that with full right rudder she might back practically in a straight line, it can be seen how her position at (5) allows for the wind to blow the bow down to leeward.

At (7) her bow should still be somewhat up into the wind, and her starboard quarter close to the pile (F). Having her head up into the wind more than is shown at (7) is alright as a kick ahead with left rudder will straighten her out to exactly the right angle. If that kick throws her stern too close to the pile (F), idling a moment allows the wind to carry her down into position.

As she passes pile (F), a line should be passed to it—or picked up if one is attached to the pile—and made fast forward when a man at the stern has been able to

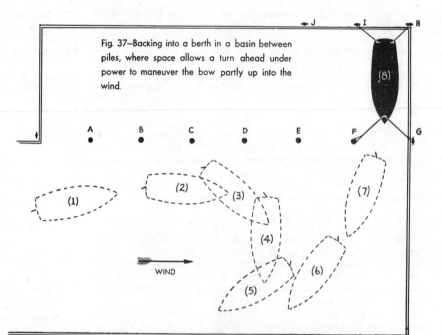

Fig. 37—Backing into a berth in a basin between piles, where space allows a turn ahead under power to maneuver the bow partly up into the wind.

WIND

get another line on cleat I. Lines to cleats (G) and (H) can be run at leisure.

Before the line to (G) is fast, backing easily draws the stern close enough for a man to step ashore from the stern. Adjusting and securing the line at (G) after all are ashore prevents the boat from going too far astern.

When Maneuvering Room Is Limited

With a good breeze, it might be impossible to get the bow around as shown at (5). In that case there is an alternative, using springs. You might approach close to the line of piles A B C D with the intent of bringing her up

M. Rosenfeld

Left: Bollards are set in recesses of lock walls to take lines when passing through locks. This boat has locked down, cast off lines, and is ready to proceed on the lower level. Above: Boats moored in a basin between piles, stern to a dock

alongside piles (C) and (D), heading east, as at position (1), Figure 38. Now run an after bow spring, doubled, from the bitt around pile (D) and back to the bitt. Going ahead easily with left rudder will cause the stern to swing around to the south as at (2). Engine idling, she will swing completely around and if the spring is slacked a little she will lie starboard side against piles (E) and (F), as at (3). It may be necessary to back a little between positions (2) and (3).

Now rig a forward quarter spring on the starboard side to pile (F) and cast off the bow line to (D). The reason why this was doubled is now evident, as you can get the line back aboard by casting off the second hitch.

Reversing on the quarter spring throws her bow to the south and her stern in toward her berth as at (4). This spring can be carried forward by a crewman walking along the starboard side to the bow, where it becomes the forward bow spring to (F) when secured to the forward bitt.

Approaching Up-wind

In Figures 37 and 38, if this were not a closed basin, so that approach could be made against the wind, heading west, it would be comparatively easy to swing up into a position approximately as shown at (7) in Figure 37, heading perhaps more closely into the wind—say a 45-degree angle from the line of piles—with starboard quarter close to pile (F). This would have been accomplished by turning with left rudder as the berth came abeam.

Figure 39 illustrates such a case. At (2) left rudder, while the boat is still moving ahead, throws the stern in toward the slip and pile (F) as at (3). Backing with right rudder brings her down to position (4), the bow sagging off to leeward somewhat, while the rudder is set to port and the propeller given a strong kick ahead. This throws the stern up to windward as at (5), shaping the boat up to back in with right rudder.

Between positions (4) and (6) it may be necessary to go ahead and back several times but in any case the combination of the engine kicking the stern to windward while the wind blows the bow to leeward can be used effectively to work her in neatly.

Another alternative, at (3), would be to pass a line around the pile (F) and hold on while the wind blew the bow to leeward just enough to shape the boat up, as at (5), to back in. A little reversing between positions (3) and (5) might be indicated. At (5), of course, the line from the starboard quarter is cast off and carried forward to become the forward bow spring on the starboard side, secured to pile (F) for mooring.

Getting Clear of a Pile

In your maneuvering around piles, as outlined in foregoing illustrations, there is a possibility that you may sometimes be caught in a position where the wind or current or both will act to pin the boat against the pile and

take advantage of the greater width for turning, then come back upstream against the wind to dock.

Preferably, if there is room, the helmsman should wait till he is beyond the dock before he starts his turn as this would allow more room for straightening out at the dock. Referring to the illustration, he has slowed down, the boat is under control and he gauges his distance from the east bank so that there is just sufficient room for the stern to swing to port with right rudder at (B) without hitting the bank.

From experience in this maneuver he knows that in the absence of wind he can round up nicely through track A-B-C-D-E-F with full right rudder at low speed. Now if he tries the same thing at low engine speed with the northerly wind, instead of moving from (C) to (D), the wind catches him abeam and tends to hold the bow down to leeward as at (D').

At (D') he would be in a bad way, forced to reverse to avoid hitting the west bank and fortunate if he could

hold her there so that she is temporarily unmaneuverable.

The solution to this predicament is to rig a forward spring from the pile to a bitt aft, preferably on the side of the boat away from the pile, as shown in Figure 40. Then, by reversing with left rudder, the boat can be wound around the pile and her bow brought into the wind or against the current as in position (2), properly shaped up to draw clear by going ahead with the power as the spring is cast off the pile.

In getting clear from this point, it may be necessary to use a little left rudder to keep the stern clear of the pile, but not enough to throw her stern so far over that the starboard quarter is in danger of hitting the other pile.

As a matter of fact, at position (2) the wind may catch the bow on the port side, easing the boat away from the pile, so that you will be in a position to pull directly away with rudder amidships—always alert, however, to throw the stern one way or the other if needed by proper use of the rudder.

Speed and the Boat's Turning Circle

Earlier in this series when we were discussing the general principles of a boat's response to rudder action, we observed that speed has very little effect on the size of the turning circle. The general rule is that the rudder angle will control the diameter of the turning circle; the faster the speed, the shorter the time in which the turn is completed.

While this is theoretically true, there are situations where a burst of speed for a short period may help the boat to turn within the limits of a channel or stream where she couldn't turn at very low engine speeds.

Consider the following case in point. In Figure 41, we have a boat bound south in a narrow canal or stream with a strong northerly wind, her dock being on the west side. The south end of the illustration may represent the dead end of a canal or the stream may continue further. This is irrelevant except that if the stream widens further on it would be wise to go on down-stream and

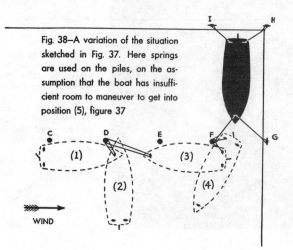

Fig. 38—A variation of the situation sketched in Fig. 37. Here springs are used on the piles, on the assumption that the boat has insufficient room to maneuver to get into position (5), figure 37

Fig. 39—In this case, arrangement of the bulkheads in the basin permits approach against the wind, varying the technique employed to back into the slip.

back out quickly enough to prevent his bow from being driven down by the wind on the south bank, if this is a dead end.

Therefore at (B), if the boat is moving slowly, a sudden burst of power at the propeller acting on the full right rudder will bring her around quickly. At (D) the helmsman must be ready to close his throttle in order to prevent the boat from gathering so much way that landing at the dock is difficult.

This is not a maneuver to be guessed at, but if you have occasion to make the same one repeatedly in bringing her in to her usual berth, you will soon get to know whether the strength of the wind will allow you to use these tactics or whether you must resort to some other procedure such as landing down-wind and allowing her to turn at the dock on a spring.

Plan Maneuvers in Advance

In previous pages we have outlined most of the basic ideas or principles by means of which the average single-screw motor boat

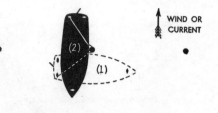

Fig. 40—How to get clear of a pile when pinned against it by wind or current.

can be handled when maneuvering around docks and moorings. Obviously the number of possible situations, considering the differences in boats, and the strength, direction, and effect of wind and current is almost infinite. Usually, however, the application of one of the principles we have mentioned, modified perhaps to suit conditions, will permit a seamanlike handling of the problem.

Understanding these principles as a background, you will be less likely to work in opposition to the forces of the elements and will use the control you have over the boat with propeller, rudder, and lines to best advantage. The seamanlike solution usually requires the least manpower and is accomplished with a minimum of confusion, fuss, shouting of orders, and other unnecessary hindrances to an orderly accomplishment of the task.

Even though you know the principles you are to use in executing a maneuver, you will find that it pays to think out in advance the steps you will take, and their succession. With a plan of action clearly worked out, you can take each step slowly and easily, and have time to keep the boat under perfect control. This does not conflict in any way with the truth that there will be occasions that call for bold, swift, and decisive action. Rather, under such circumstances, the need for calm ordered judgment is accentuated.

The lubberly handling of a situation may eventually achieve the end that is sought, but often at the expense of strained lines, fittings, and equipment, not to mention the nerves, muscles, and temper of both skipper and crew.

Common Sense in Executing the Plan

If your planned line of action requires amendment or even complete abandonment because of unforeseen conditions, don't hesitate to act accordingly. If, for example, your plan for a clean approach to a dock has been upset by a freak current you couldn't calculate, back off and square away for another attempt. That in itself is good seamanship and good judgment regardless of how others may judge your apparent "miss" on the first try.

Common sense, if you act with deliberation, will enable you to work out a solution for any combination of conditions. Sometimes, understanding the idiosyncrasies of your own boat, you may put it through evolutions never mentioned in the books but if it achieves your end better than conventional practice, it's still good seamanship.

When you are at the helm and you have men on deck handling lines, issue the necessary orders to each so that all action is coordinated and under your control, instead of having two or three acting independently to cross purposes. This is especially imperative when your crew is not familiar with boats or your method of handling one.

Orders to the Crew

On larger vessels here are some of the orders used in connection with the handling of lines at a dock. You can be the judge as to whether you consider them appropriate on your own boat, having due regard for its size and the number of men in the crew. The

giving of such orders presupposes that crewmen will understand what they mean.

When docking, the order *"Stand by to dock"* puts the crew in readiness, each standing by his respective line, seeing that it is properly coiled ready to heave. If no men are available on the dock to receive lines, others aboard stand ready to step ashore to receive the lines.

At the command *"Heave——(bow line, stern, line, or whatever line is named)"* deck men heave the line named to the dock.

"Take in slack on——" requires deckmen to take a turn on the cleat or bitt and pull in slack.

"Take a strain on——" means that deckmen are to pull lines named up tight, taking an extra turn if necessary on the cleat or bitt, but allowing it to slip.

"Ease off on——" means that the line should be allowed to slip off more freely.

"Hold (or snub)——" means to check the line temporarily.

"Secure lines" means to make fast permanently, adjusting to proper length and rigging chafing gear if necessary.

In each case the blanks above imply that a line or lines will be named to complete the order.

On leaving a dock, the order *"Stand by the lines"* prepares men on the dock to stand by bollards ready to cast off lines and men on deck to take them in when ready. This is followed by the order,

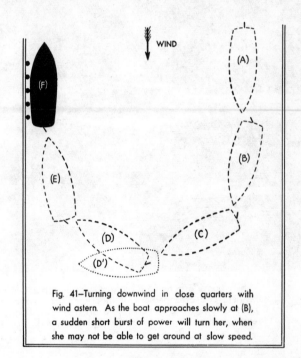

Fig. 41—Turning downwind in close quarters with wind astern. As the boat approaches slowly at (B), a sudden short burst of power will turn her, when she may not be able to get around at slow speed.

"Cast off the lines" at which dock men clear the lines from the bollards and toss them to deck men, keeping them clear of the water, if possible.

As previously explained, the procedure is so simplified on a small boat that docking may involve only the stepping ashore of one man each at bow and stern with their respective lines, others to be passed as and if required after these are secured.

One mistake that crewmen often make in helping to handle lines on a small boat is that, in their eagerness to assist, they insist on snubbing them immediately when as a matter of fact the skipper wants them merely to be tended and left slack so that his boat is free to be maneuvered further with the power. A case in point is where the boat is coming in to a landing at a dock and the bow man snubs his line instead of allowing the boat to ease up and draw alongside as the skipper intended.

One caution that cannot be emphasized too strongly is that, in handling lines, whether they are mooring lines, anchor lines, or any other kind, they must not be allowed to get over the side in such a way that they will be sucked down into the propeller and wrapped around the shaft and wheel.

Resumé of Factors Affecting Control of Single-Screw Boat

To sum up all the effects which the skipper of a single-screw (R. H.) boat must have in mind as he maneuvers his craft, the following will provide a condensed summary.

I—ENGINE
(1) *Going ahead*—No effect (or slight tendency of bow to port).
(2) *Going astern*—Stern goes to port, bow to starboard.

II—RUDDER
(1) *With headway*
(a) Left rudder turns stern to starboard, bow to port.
(b) Right rudder turns stern to port, bow to starboard.
(2) *With sternway*
(a) Left rudder turns stern rapidly to port, bow to starboard.
(b) Right rudder usually turns stern to starboard, bow to port, if sternway is sufficient. With little sternway, boat may back in a straight line, or stern may even go to port.

III—CURRENT
(1) Sets boat bodily in direction of its flow.
(2) Other factors interacting (boat held, for example, by waist breast), current normally acts with greater effect on the stern because of deeper draft here.

IV—WIND
(1) Usually affects bow more than stern, throwing it to leeward.
(2) Engine backing, boat backs into wind.

V—TWO OR MORE FACTORS COMBINED
(1) Helmsman must determine relative effects of each on basis of his experience with the boat.

When boats are tied up alongside each other beam to beam, careful attention should be paid to the placing of fenders and arrangement of mooring lines so that no damage will result from the wash of passing boats. If a boat is lying to an anchor and another ties alongside, the added pull may cause the anchor to drag. A little extra scope of line may be all that is needed.

IT is important to note that everything that has been said thus far in regard to the handling of a boat has presupposed a single-screw craft with right-hand propeller, a category which includes the vast majority of pleasure boats.

Twin screws, however, are becoming more and more popular, partly because of their superior maneuverability. In the twin-screw boat, the propellers are usually arranged so that the tops of the blades turn outward, so that the starboard wheel is right-hand, the port wheel is left-hand. The effect of this is to give a maximum of maneuverability.

Going ahead with the starboard wheel for a turn to port, the offset of the propeller from the center line is adding its effect by throwing the stern to starboard. Similarly, offset of the port wheel going ahead helps the steering effect when the port propeller is turning ahead for a turn to starboard.

When reversing, the starboard wheel throws its discharge current against the starboard side of the hull to help the turn of the stern to port. Likewise, the port propeller reversing throws its stream against the port side of the hull to help the swing of the stern to starboard. See figure 44.

The important factors in turning and steering are thus combined by the outward turning wheels. The steering effect is exerted in the same direction as the turning moment caused by the off-center location of the propellers.

One or Two Rudders

While some boats are rigged with a single rudder between the propellers in the midships line, this arrangement is more common in larger vessels. The trend today in pleasure boats is to use twin rudders, one each directly behind the propellers in the discharge currents. This, too, improves maneuverability by rudder.

It is readily seen that the location of two propellers, one each on the port and starboard sides at some distance from the center line of the keel, gives the operator of such a boat the means of throwing one side or the other ahead or astern, independent of rudder control. In fact, much of the boat's maneuvering at low speed is done without touching the steering wheel, as the two throttles are the principal key to flexibility of control.

If there is only one rudder, a little thought will show that its chief influence in slow-speed maneuvering is felt only when it is placed astern of a propeller going ahead. Its effect behind a propeller reversing is negligible.

Visualize, for example, such a boat making a short turn bow to starboard, by going ahead on the port propeller, and astern on the starboard wheel. If the single rudder is put to starboard (right rudder) nothing is accomplished due to lack of headway. See (A), Figure 42. The rudder is set obliquely behind the reversing starboard wheel and there is no blade behind the port wheel to increase its turning effect. The port engine going ahead is trying to turn the bow to starboard yet it can act on the rudder blade only when the rudder is set for a turn to port, as in (B), Figure 42.

Putting it another way, with a single rudder (neglecting for a moment the action of the starboard propeller) if the port propeller is turned ahead to swing the bow to starboard, turning the rudder to starboard throws it away from and out of the port propeller's discharge current. If the rudder is set to port to get into that current, its steering effect would be to kick the stern to starboard and thus offset the tendency of the port propeller to swing the bow to starboard.

Twin rudders are generally used on twin-screw boats, permitting blades to be located directly in the propellers' discharge currents. Independent controls for each of the engines are symmetrically located at the wheel. Note the radar antenna

At reasonable speeds, the twin-screw boat can be handled by, and is responsive to, its rudder whether the blade area is all in a single midships rudder or divided between two. Maneuvering in tight corners, the rudder can be set amidships and forgotten while the reverse gear controls are handled to throw the propellers ahead or astern and the throttles are used to control the relative amount of power applied on each.

Turning in a Boat Length

To make a tight turn, a single-screw boat must make a little headway and sternway as the stern is kicked around. Furthermore, it involves going ahead and astern with the propeller, even though the rudder is set to star-

Twin-screw boats have a great advantage over single-screw craft in maneuvering. If the boat in the center of the illustration above is twin-screw, she backs the starboard engine to get clear of the berth, goes ahead with the port engine to turn, and finally squares away with both engines ahead, after which she steers by rudder

board (right rudder) throughout. The throttle, too, must be tended to apply sudden bursts of power without allowing the boat to gather way.

In contrast to this, the twin-screw boat can be made to turn in a circle the diameter of which is only a little greater than her length. The turn to port is accomplished as readily as a turn to starboard since such effects as sidewise blade pressure on two propellers rotating in opposite directions offset each other.

Turning bow to starboard, the rudder can be set amidships, while the port engine goes ahead and the starboard engine reverses. See Figure 43. The engines will probably be turning at nearly, not exactly, the same speed. The boat drives forward more easily than it goes astern and the propeller at a given r.p.m. has more propelling power ahead than astern. Therefore the r.p.m. on the reversing starboard wheel may be somewhat higher than that on the port propeller, to prevent her from making some headway as she pivots.

By setting the throttle for the reversing starboard engine this can be left alone and the port throttle is adjusted till the size of the turning circle is established. A rate of r.p.m. can be found where she is actually turning in her own length. If the port engine is then speeded up a little, the circle is larger and she makes some headway. If the port engine is slowed down, the circle is also larger but she makes some sternway as the reversing starboard wheel pulls her around, stern to port.

One Propeller Going Ahead or Back

Again, there is the alternative of casting the stern one way or the other by going ahead or backing on one pro-

Fig. 42–Why twin-screw boat with one rudder is maneuvered at low speed with propellers, rudder being kept amidships.

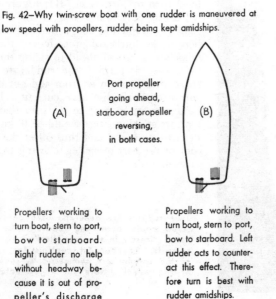

Port propeller going ahead, starboard propeller reversing, in both cases.

(A) Propellers working to turn boat, stern to port, bow to starboard. Right rudder no help without headway because it is out of propeller's discharge current.

(B) Propellers working to turn boat, stern to port, bow to starboard. Left rudder acts to counteract this effect. Therefore turn is best with rudder amidships.

peller only without turning the other propeller at all. Some headway or sternway in these cases accompanies the turn.

Referring to (A), Figure 44, a kick ahead on the port propeller throws the stern to port, bow to starboard, as in a single-screw boat with right rudder. If there are twin rudders, right rudder helps this kick. A kick ahead with the starboard wheel throws the stern to starboard, bow to port, as shown at (B). Reversing the port wheel only, pulls the stern around to starboard and vice versa. See sketches (C) and (D).

When reversing with one propeller, the other being stopped, sidewise blade pressure, discharge screw current and the offset of the working propeller from the center line all combine to throw the stern in a direction away from the reversing propeller.

Using Springs With Twin Screws

When a twin-screw vessel is lying at a dock and a spring is used to throw the bow or stern out as an aid to getting clear, one engine may be used. For example, with an after bow spring, going ahead on the outside engine only, throws the stern out away from the dock. Or propellers can be turned in opposite directions.

Sometimes a twin-screw vessel is gotten clear of a dock by rigging a forward bow spring and reversing the propeller on the dock side to throw the propeller discharge current on that side forward between the boat and dock as a "cushion." Naturally this is most effective if the dock under water is solidly bulkheaded rather than built on open piling. The discharge current from the inside wheel forces the boat away from the dock and the line is then cast off. Further reversing on the propeller nearest the dock while the other propeller turns ahead,

Fig. 43—Turning twin-screw boat, bow to starboard, stern to port, in her own length. Rudder amidships, port propeller going ahead, starboard propeller reversing (probably at somewhat higher r.p.m. than port propeller). Changing r.p.m. can give her headway or sternway as she turns.

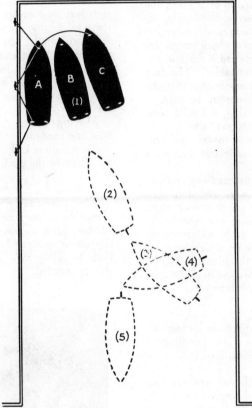

Fig. 45—Twin screw 110-footer leaving berth between two others in a slip. At (1) stern has been sprung out by going ahead on a bow spring to (A), starboard engine going ahead, port engine reversing. At (2) spring having been cast off, she has backed clear with both engines reversing. At (3) sternway is checked and stern kicked around to (4) by going ahead on the starboard engine. At (5) she is straightened out and, after headway is gained, responds to her rudder which has been left amidships during the maneuver

as necessary, shapes the boat up to get the stern clear. The speed of the two motors will vary with conditions of wind and current and the rudder is left amidships till the boat is clear and ready to pull away.

Docking a Twin-Screw Vessel

Landing at a dock, a twin-screw vessel will approach at slow speed at an angle of 10 to 20 degrees, as is the case with a single-screw boat. When she has just way enough to carry her in nicely, the rudder is swung over to the side away from the dock to bring the stern in as the engines are thrown into neutral. To check headway as she comes up parallel to the dock, the outboard engine is reversed.

Landing either port or starboard side to the dock is accomplished with equal ease because of the starboard propeller turning counter-clockwise as it reverses in a port-side landing, or the port propeller turning clockwise in reverse on a landing starboard side to the dock.

Steering With the Throttles

In maintaining a straight course with a twin-screw vessel, the speed of the motors can be adjusted so that the leeward engine compensates for the effect of leeway. That is, the leeward engine can be turned a little faster to hold the bow up into the wind.

If she happens to sustain some damage to her steering gear, whether it be the rudder(s) or any part of the gear inboard, she can still make port by steering with the throttles. One motor can be allowed to turn at a constant speed—the starboard one, let us say. Then opening the throttle of the port motor will speed up the port propeller and cause a turn to starboard. Closing the throttle of the port motor slows down the port propeller and allows the starboard wheel to push ahead, causing a turn to port. And we have also shown that she is at no great disadvantage when she finally maneuvers into her berth after getting into port as the throttle and reverse gears are adequate for complete control here too.

Response to Rudder While Backing

A twin-screw vessel starting from a position dead in the water, with both propellers backing at the same speed, is at a great advantage over the single-screw vessel as she can be made to take any desired course by steering with her rudder whereas the single-screw vessel, it will be remembered, is obstinate about backing her stern to starboard. In the twin-screw vessel opposite rotation of the propellers means that the forces which normally throw the single-screw vessel off course are balanced out.

In addition to use of the rudder, the twin-screw vessel offers the possibility of using her throttles to speed up one motor or the other as an aid to steering while maintaining her sternway or she can even stop one propeller or go ahead on it for maximum control in reverse.

While the twin-screw vessel backs as readily to starboard as to port, she is still subject to the effect of wind, waves, and current though the helmsman is in a better position to exercise control over them as we have seen in the case of leeway, offset by different engine speeds instead of holding the rudder offset from the midships line.

Other Twin-Screw Maneuvers

If one propeller is stopped while the boat has headway, the bow necessarily turns in the direction of the propeller that is dead. Consequently, if one engine of a twin-screw power plant fails, and the boat is brought in on the other, a certain amount of rudder angle on the side of the operating propeller is necessary in order to maintain a straight course, or some kind of drag must be towed on the side of the working propeller.

A basic principle in the maneuvering of a twin-screw vessel is to use the rudder primarily in relation to the direction of the vessel's movement through the water (that is, whether she had headway or sternway). Elsewhere, it will be recalled, the principle as given for the single-screw vessel was that the rudder should be considered in relation to the direction in which the propeller happens to be turning, regardless of whether the vessel has headway or sternway.

When a twin-screw vessel has headway, both propellers turning ahead, and a quick turn to starboard is desired, the starboard engine is reversed with right rudder. The fact that the vessel has headway in this instance means that the right rudder adds its steering effect to shorten the turn.

With sternway, both propellers reversing, if a quick turn to port is wanted, the port engine is thrown ahead, with left rudder. Again, due to the vessel's sternway, the rudder's effect is added to that of the propellers in causing a short turn to port.

If a twin-screw vessel has considerable headway and her engines are reversed with rudder hard over, the stern will normally swing away from the rudder (to port with right rudder and vice versa) until the headway is overcome by the reversing engines. After she has gathered sternway, her stern tends to work toward the side on which her rudder is set. Then the vessel's stern in the illustration just cited would eventually move to starboard with right rudder, after her headway had changed to sternway.

Handling a 110-Footer

Data used by the Coast Guard Auxiliary in its instruction courses includes an actual example of the handling of a 110-foot sub-chaser, which is so excellent that it is given here practically verbatim.

In Figure 45 the chaser is the middle one of three tied abreast lying port side to a dock headed toward the beach. Let's call the boats A, B, and C. Our boat is B, the middle one; A is at the dock; C is the outside boat.

The engines are warmed up preliminary to getting under way and when they are ready lines are cleared as follows: First, C's bow breast is cast off from B's bow and run to A, forward of B's stem, with some slack to allow B to maneuver a little.

C now casts off all lines except the bow breast which has been transferred to A and gets a heaving line ready for use after B has pulled out.

B then casts off all lines securing her to A except an after bow spring which is slacked a little to allow B, going ahead, to get the bulge of her bow past that of A's bow and thus permit B to pivot better.

B now goes ahead 1/3 on the outside (starboard) engine and back 1/3 on the inside (port) engine. Two men are standing by with fenders. As B moves slowly ahead a few feet, the spring line takes the strain and the stern works out, to starboard.

Backing Clear

C is being swung along with B but no lines secure the two vessels and there is nothing to prevent B from drawing clear as she backs both engines 1/3 after having swung her stern far enough around to starboard.

With B clear, C heaves to A the line she has already prepared. At this point she can either run a stern breast to A

and heave in on it or else rig an after bow spring to draw alongside A by using power. In the latter case, she will go ahead on the inside (port) engine and reverse the outside (starboard) engine. If the bow breast to A tends to check the swing of C's bow, it must be slacked. Back alongside A, C rigs all mooring lines to A as she was formally secured to B.

B, in the meantime, has backed out into the slip and backs the port engine 2/3 while the starboard engine continues to back at 1/3. The effect of this will be to give her better clearance from the dock and swing her while backing.

Checking Sternway and Turning

The boat draws well clear of the dock under this maneuver but presently gathers too much sternway so that starboard engine is thrown ahead 2/3 which checks the sternway and causes her to turn more rapidly, throwing the bow around to port.

When finally straightened out in the slip, both engines are run at 1/3 ahead to gather steerage-way. Then both are stopped (idled in neutral in the case of boat with reverse gears) while steering with the rudder and a long blast is blown on the whistle as a warning prior to leaving the slip.

Moving out of the slip, the current catches the port bow and tends to set the vessel back toward the dock so she is given a short kick ahead on the starboard engine to offset it. Clear of the dock, she goes ahead 2/3 on both engines.

Returning to Her Berth

The same chaser is now ready to return to her berth alongside another vessel. Keeping well out in the stream till the slip is almost abeam, she turns and passes into the slip about midway between the piers, favoring one side a little to allow for current. No abrupt changes of course will be needed.

Here's a typical installation of twin engines under the deck of a modern cruiser. Sometimes, symmetrical pairs are installed, opposite rotation, tops of propellers turning outward for best maneuverability. Controls are carried up to the helm. Dual controls are often used on flying bridges.

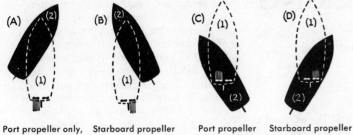

Fig. 44—What happens in a twin-screw boat when one propeller is thrown ahead or astern.

(A) Port propeller only, going ahead

(B) Starboard propeller only, going ahead

(C) Port propeller only, reversing

(D) Starboard propeller only, reversing

Engines are stopped (or idling in neutral) passing the pier heads while the vessel is steered to a point just ahead of the other vessel's pilot house. The angle of approach to the other vessel should be small. If it appears that the angle is too wide the helm should be used decisively to place her in position in plenty of time to straighten out.

With reduced speed, the quartermaster handles the wheel smartly, using considerably more helm to achieve a given response than he would need if the vessel had good headway. What he does is to get the bow to swing, then shifts the rudder smartly for a moment, then shifts back to the midships position.

Engines are kept stopped (or idling) as she comes in at a moderate angle, her bow about six feet from that of the other vessel. A bow spring is passed, slack taken up and secured. Now the outside (starboard in this case) engine is backed 1/3 while the inside (port) engine goes ahead 1/3. This is just a momentary kick to be repeated if necessary.

The effect of the reversing outside engine is to kill the headway and swing the stern to port toward the other vessel, assisted by the kick ahead on the inside engine. The last of the headway, acting on the spring, also contributes to the same effect. No heaving lines have been used during this maneuver and, under ideal conditions, only the outside engine will be called on for a short kick astern while the inside engine may not be needed at all.

THE FINE ART OF DOCKING

A few words on handling the small boat

EVERY day, in hundreds of ports the world over, vessels are brought to dock, undocked, and moored. All manner of vessels, from 25,000-ton supertankers to tiny harbor tugs, are handled expertly — even casually — by men to whom the sea is a profession. From all this, and often from bitter experience and mishap, comes a wealth of knowledge on ship handling which could well be used by the skipper of a small boat.

The purpose of this article is to bring out several of these ship-handling "kinks" which are particularly adaptable to small-boat maneuvering. Kinks which will ease the day-to-day docking of these craft—but, more important, aid during those times when foul weather and adverse seas make docking, more than ever, a matter of precise judgment and practical skill.

These are by no means *the* ways to dock a boat. But perhaps among them you will find one or two methods which will treat you well, or will be of particular use to your type of boat or waters.

To handle a boat, or a ship, you must first *know* it. Know what it will do, how fast it will do it, and in what space. No article or text can give you this knowledge—it can come only from actual experience and practice. But attention can be drawn to certain basics which will enable you to get much more from experience. Some of the more important of these. . . .

A. THE PROPELLER CONTROLS THE DIRECTION OF A BOAT WHEN DOCKING, ALMOST AS MUCH AS THE RUDDER.

A vessel with a propeller that turns in a clockwise direction when viewed from astern with the engine turning ahead (called a right-handed vessel) is the most common. This vessel's bow will usually swing to port slowly when going ahead, even with the rudder amidships, *but* the stern will swing rather sharply to port when the vessel is going astern, often regardless of where the rudder is. For left-handed vessels the effects are reversed.

B. THIS "TURNING EFFECT" OF THE PROPELLER IS MUCH MORE PRONOUNCED WHEN GOING ASTERN.

Since much of a rudder's effect comes from the wash of the propeller rushing past it, if the engine is reversed this wash will be directed in a direction *away* from the rudder and much of the effect of the helm is lost. The propeller takes over in a pronounced fashion.

C. BRIEF SPURTS OF FULL ENGINE POWER MAY BE USED TO TURN THE BOW OR STERN OF THE VESSEL AS DESIRED, WITHOUT GETTING THE BOAT UNDER WAY.

With the rudder to starboard, a brief spurt of the engine at full-ahead power will swing the bow to starboard *but*, if the engine is cut off before the vessel gathers way, most of the power of the engine will have gone into turning the vessel rather than getting it moving through the water. The heavier the boat, the more this is so. Don't be afraid to gun your engine full-ahead momentarily to gain maneuverability. A boat's a pretty heavy thing and it won't shoot ahead the moment power is applied.

D. THE WIND, TIDE, AND CURRENT CAN OFTEN BE AS MUCH HELP IN DOCKING AS THE ENGINES AND HELM.

Nature will often dock your boat for you, if given half a chance. Why waste gas and temper fighting her. A good policy many times is "Ride with the current."

Now to the actual processes of docking. These will be presented in outline form so as to make it easier to grasp the details without wading through a lot of text. The word "wind" will be used to cover whichever factor has the most effect on the vessel at the moment, whether it is actually the wind, or whether it may be tide or current. In conditions of calm or still water almost any of the methods outlined will work equally well. Boats are shown port side to the docks; for the reverse condition, simply reverse the rudder orders, but maintain the same engine speeds and directions.

LEAVING A DOCK

ALONGSIDE DOCK; WIND AHEAD (Fig. 1)

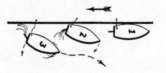

1. Single up to one stern line No power, no rudder.
2. Let the wind swing the bow out,

perhaps helping with boathook or with brief *spurts* of full ahead against a rudder hard right. (But watch port quarter.)

3. When the bow has swung out 15 or 20 degrees, hard left rudder and spurts of full ahead to swing stern out clear of the dock. (This is rarely done by smallboat handlers, consequently the stern scrapes along the dock as they pull away. There is no reason for this when a few guns of the engine and a bit of rudder will get you away without a scratch.)

4. Let go the line when the boat is a few feet off the dock and go ahead slow steering her *gradually* away from the dock with slight rudder. (Too much rudder will swing the stern right back against the dock and you'll end up no better off than if you had left it there to begin with.)

WIND OFF THE DOCK (Fig. 2)

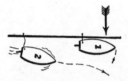

1. Single up to one stern line and let the wind swing the bow out. Ease off on the stern line and the stern will go out as well. You're now clear of the dock, both bow and stern, without a scratch or a touch of the throttle.
2. Let go the line. Slow ahead and steer her away *easily*.

WIND ASTERN (Fig. 3)

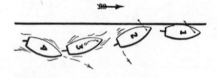

1. Single up to a bow line.
2. Let the wind swing the stern out from the dock or use the engine in spurts of full ahead against a hard left rudder.
3. Engine astern to back off slowly— cast off line and use rudder to back her off properly.
4. When well clear of dock, ahead engine and easy right rudder to steer her away.

WIND ON THE DOCK (Fig. 4)

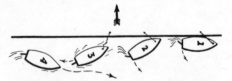

1. Single up to one bow line led well aft onto the dock. Spurts of full ahead against a rudder hard left to swing the stern out.
2. Medium to full astern (depending on wind) to back her away from the dock. The stern will swing slowly to port

of its own accord. Help it to do so with rudder if desired. When boat is roughly parallel to the dock let go line. . . .

3. Slight right rudder and full ahead. Or (Fig. 5).

1. Single up to one stern line led well up onto dock.

2. Medium to full astern to swing bow out. *No* rudder.

3. Rudder half left and engine slow ahead to swing stern out. When away a bit, let go line and steer her off carefully. Power used here will depend, again, on the force of the wind.

LEAVING A SLIP (Fig. 6)

This method will work on both a walled slip or with a boat moored bow or stern to a dock between two stakes or pilings.

1. Single-up to one stern line of a length sufficient to reach from the stern chock forward about ⅔ the length of the vessel. Make the outboard end of this fast to the outer end of the slip.

2. Slow astern till the line is taut, then hard left rudder and the boat will swing her stern to port easily and under *full control*. The line acts as a pivot. This method is especially useful in restricted waters where there is little room to "pull out" from the slip. I know of no method that will get a boat out of a slip in less space or with better control.

3. Cast off when out far enough and slow ahead giving a *slight* kick of left rudder to swing the stern out clear of the end of the slip or the dock.

This maneuver will do equally well for almost all conditions of wind and sea. More or less power or rudder may be needed but the steps are exactly the same.

This "controlled backing" method keeps you, the slip and your neighbor free from scrapes and gouges, fits of temper . . . and repair bills.

DOCKING

ALONGSIDE; WIND AHEAD, OR OFF THE DOCK (Fig. 7)

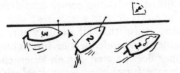

1. Approach slowly at an angle of about 30 to 40 degrees to the dock.

2. Engine astern to stop her about 1

foot off the dock—bow line ashore.

3. Right rudder and spurts of full ahead to bring the stern in or allow the wind to drift her in.

4. Tie up.

WIND ASTERN (Fig. 8)

1. Approach *closely* to dock, about 10 to 15 degrees.

2. When near to dock, one or two feet, right rudder and spurts of full ahead to *start* stern swinging in. As soon as the stern begins to swing in (Boat about parallel to dock). . . .

3. Full astern to stop her. This action will keep the stern swinging in toward the dock. (Only practice will tell just where to shift from ahead to astern.)

4. Bow should now point about 5 to 10 degrees *outward* from the dock. Stern line onto dock. Let her bow now drift into the dock after stopping engine or help it in with spurts of full ahead against hard left rudder.

5. Tie up.

WIND ONTO THE DOCK (Fig. 9)

1. Approach the dock at a *steep* angle (60 to 80 degrees) to allow you to use the engine as a brake on the boat's headway. This is vital in any heavy wind.

2. Full astern to stop bow about a foot or two off the dock. Ease her with a boathook if possible. Bow line ashore.

3. Let the wind swing the stern in— braking its speed with the rudder hard right and the engine astern. (This will also help to keep the bow from being forced into the dock.

4. Tie up.

I've had this method succeed where winds were of sufficient force to send other boats crashing into docks in a shower of paint chips and splinters.

ENTERING A SLIP
WIND ANYWHERE BUT ASTERN (Fig. 10)

1. Approach slowly and roughly parallel to end of slip till you are able to pass a line to the cleat or piling nearest your approach.

2. Astern to slow the approach and *stop* her just *short of* the far piling, with the line taut.

3. Rudder hard left and gun ahead on engines to swing her into the slip using the line and the piling as a pivot.

5. Ease her into the slip and tie up.

WIND ASTERN (Fig. 11)

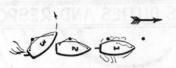

1. Approach as previously described but use enough astern power to stop her positively. Pass a stern line and

2. a bow line, hauling both as taut as possible.

3. Using both engines, wind and rudder, ease her around and into the slip.

4. Tie up.

This is one of the best methods to use in any reasonably fresh wind as the control you have over the boat is positive and there is very little chance that she can get out of control.

A FEW TIPS TO SUM UP . . .

1. Try to visualize just what conditions will be at the dock *before* you get there.

2. Use fenders generously and pad your slip or dock well.

3. Keep your engine in good shape and your control cables taut.

4. Keep your mooring lines healthy and use chafing gear whenever possible.

5. Favor a bight of line around a piling as the last line to let go, (as it is an easy matter to let go the end on the vessel to cast off).

6. Watch lines to see that they don't foul your propeller.

7. Remember that a boat will pivot about a point about ⅓ of its length aft from the bow and will not "follow the front wheels" as does a car. When the bow goes to starboard *the stern will also swing out to port* so that when turning, a boat cuts a considerably wider path than its beam. It goes around a turn in a sort of "crab-fashion."

Now try the outlined maneuvers (in easy weather first though) and see how they treat you. I believe you'll find them kind to your boat, safe under most conditions, and easy to learn and use.

A boat handled properly is a joy to see and a joy to sail. A boat barreling in towards a dock with a bone in her teeth then shuddering as the clutch squeals into astern, or one creeping toward a dock cautiously, like a shy miss to a dance floor, is painful to watch for a sailor and awkward for the skipper.

If a skipper knows his boat, uses common sense, and the proper maneuvers, and isn't afraid to use his engines and the winds to help him, he will find his reputation as a ship-handler on the increase to say nothing of his enjoyment.

The Skipper
HIS DUTIES AND RESPONSIBILITIES

THE yachtsman is properly interested in the pleasure and comradeship that he obtains with his boat; the rigorous routine of a battleship has little, if any, place on the bridge of a 40-foot cruiser. However, we amateurs can learn from Navy practices. As many of these practices have as their sole purpose insurance of the safety of the ship and her personnel, it is especially appropriate for us to know something of them and apply to our own cruising those that will contribute to our own safety. The first responsibility of a skipper is the safety of his ship and his people.

Leadership and Discipline

SUPPOSE we think first about leadership and discipline. These are subjects that are rarely considered by the yachtsman but in them we find much that can be of value in that sudden emergency for which all of us who cruise must always be prepared.

Discipline; shades of a hickory stick. But, discipline is not subservience; discipline is self-control. It means prompt and cheerful obedience to necessary laws and regulations, laws and regulations designed for the sole purpose of our safety. It also means a square deal to our shipmates; the skipper who expects discipline of his crew must likewise discipline himself. A well-disciplined boat is a secure and safe boat.

Discipline does not mean a long string of commands with a crew constantly scurrying about the deck. Gold braid is not necessary to discipline. Discipline does not mean that all the joy is gone out of the job. There can be discipline on board the smallest yacht without there being any apparent show of it. Real discipline is a function of leadership and leadership can be exercised in dungarees on board a 20-foot sailboat; it is a characteristic that all of us should cultivate and practice.

Leadership is based on three things: (1) each man must know himself, his abilities and his limitations; (2) he must know his job, know it so well that he doesn't have to think about the details of doing it; (3) he must know his men and his boat and what he can reasonably expect of them in an emergency.

Authority and Obligations

FROM the lowest third class Petty Officer to the Admiral of the Fleet, every man of the Navy charged with authority has two functions to perform: (1) his function as a military leader; (2) his function as a specialist in some technical phase of his profession. It is relatively easy for any of us to become technically skilled in shaping a course, making a mooring, even swabbing a deck. All of these have to do with our technical ability and are equally applicable in the Navy and in amateur cruising.

But there usually comes a time, and it is always an emergency when seconds count, when there are too many jobs for even the most skillful of us to handle them all. This is the time when our capacity for leadership will bring us to port or put us aground. In one way, leadership on a motor cruiser is even more important than it is on an aircraft carrier; our friends on board may not be skilled in the operation of a boat. We have to make up for their lack of technical ability.

Let's look at it another way. There is an old saying that you get more out of a job when you have to work at it; the average guest on board should more quickly feel at home and should have pleasanter memories of his cruise if he has some of the boat's work to perform, if he must coordinate his efforts with those of his shipmates. As skippers, we all welcome the guest who is eager to turn to and do his share.

E. Levick

The skipper's first obligation is the safety of his boat and crew

The Good Skipper

A GOOD SKIPPER will privately catalog in his own mind the abilities of his guests and think ahead to the tasks that he will request them to do should an emergency arise. He may and should go one step further; without making it obvious, he should see to it that all on board are given various jobs to do not only so that he can find the best spot for each but also so that they are able to do more than one thing. Our first obligation is the safety of our boat and her people.

One good U. S. Power Squadron skipper makes it a practice to have "informal formal" watches, which amount to Navy watch, quarter, and station bills. From the stories told of cruises in his schooner, everyone on board has a bang-up good time, as well as a safe cruise. This man is a real leader and he doesn't hesitate to work at it.

Let's not try to define leadership; there have been as many definitions of this word as there have been writers. Any intelligent man thoroughly understands the meaning and significance of the term. Taking honesty and integrity for granted, it is the first characteristic that a man should develop. Out of leadership comes confidence, pride, emulation on the part of our associates; out of it will come the pleasant cruise that all of us want.

Next to leadership comes forehandedness or foresightedness. A first class skipper doesn't wait for an emergency to arise; he has long before formulated several solutions to any emergency with which he may be faced. Commander Frost, one of the foremost destroyer captains in the Navy, put it something like this: "The most expert captain is the first to admit how often he has been fooled

George Rupprecht

where, through a failure to exercise common sense, we did things as silly as that suggested above. The old adage "use your head" applies equally well on shipboard.

One more quotation from Commander Frost. He has defined the art of handling a ship: "Systematic application of knowledge and skill, acquired by study, observation and experience, in effecting the safe, smart, effective and economical operation of your ship." Think it over.

Courtesy

THERE IS a courtesy extended by large ships that is worthy of attention: dipping the ensign when passing a ship of the Navy. Pleasure craft frequently do not do this but it is a mark of respect that it is highly desirable for all to show. As your bridge draws abeam the bridge of the Naval vessel, dip the ensign and immediately hoist it two-blocks. All persons on board except the helmsman should face the warship and stand at attention. Any in uniform should salute.

Duties and Responsibilities

WE COME now to the duties and responsibilities of a skipper, of those activities with which you must be familiar while on the bridge.

Approximately in the order of their importance, the responsibilities of the skipper or of the man having the watch are as follows:

Safe navigation of his boat.

Safe and efficient handling of the boat in company with or in the the presence of other boats.

Safety of personnel and materiél on board.

Rendering assistance to all in danger or distress.

Smart handling and smart appearance of the boat.

Comfort and contentment on board.

A good log.

These are some of the instructions that the U. S. Navy gives to watch officers, men who are charged with the responsibility for the ship. They form a pattern that all of us, whatever the size of our craft, can follow with benefit. They presuppose that a man know himself, his job, his crew, and his ship. Let's see what they mean in terms of actual practice.

Before a boat can be gotten under way, it is important that a check-up be made to determine if she is ready to sail. Not alone should the equipment required by law be on board and in proper condition for use but all navigational and other equipment should be at hand. Water and gasoline tanks should be sounded, the ground tackle inspected, stores checked, and all those other little odd jobs that can be done at the mooring, but not at sea in an emergency, completed. These things sound elementary and worthy of little consideration but all of us can recall results that might have been different had the

by some trick of wind or current. Dangerous situations develop with startling suddenness so even when things look easiest, watch out. Have an answer to every threat and a trick to take you out of every danger." An officer must always look ahead, a minute, an hour or a day as the circumstances of his situation dictate. And, whether we like it or not, a yacht skipper is an officer, good or bad.

Vigilance

NEXT in importance to forehandedness is vigilance. In no position more than that of the skipper is "eternal vigilance the price of safety." He must see intelligently all that comes within his vision, outside and inside the ship. And his vigilance must extend beyond this to the faculty of foreseeing situations as well as seeing them. The rule of the airlines that a pilot must be able to get into alternate fields as well as the airport of his destination holds meaning for the boat skipper too.

One more check point; it is common sense. The successful skipper has a sense of proportion and of the fitness of things; let us adjust ourselves to our situation. For example, it is obviously ridiculous to dress in white flannels and blue coat when kedging off, although we might do so when the ladies are on board of a quiet Sunday afternoon. Yet we all probably can recall cases

proper attention been given in advance to such minor details.

The Navy provides each ship with a check list that the officer must use before he takes charge or gets the ship under way. The yachtsman could profitably make up his own check list and either actually or mentally go over it as he steps from the dock to the deck. The whole subject of safety is so important that every yachtsman should consider himself disqualified until he so thoroughly knows the requirements that he executes them as second nature.

Physical Condition of the Skipper

Another point in the safe navigation of a ship has to do with the physical condition of the skipper. The constant vigil which is necessary requires the complete possession of all faculties as well as a sense of physical well-being. No man should expose his boat or his people to danger, except in an extreme emergency, unless he is in good physical and mental condition.

The good skipper will not permit any of his personnel to take needless risks. If a dangerous job that may result in a man being swept overboard has to be done, he will insist that that man wear a life jacket. This may not be customary in yachting circles but that omission does not justify contempt for danger. In this connection, the state of the weather should be carefully observed and every effort made before getting under way to ascertain what the weather will be for the period of the cruise. A little foresight in this regard may save a ship or a life.

The Lookout

A small cruiser cannot readily utilize the lookout routine of the large vessel but the implication of vigilance and caution of that routine should be acknowledged. We should make it a matter of pride that we, as skippers, will observe any danger before any other person on board sights it; this is definitely our responsibility.

Important Things to Do

Here is a short check list of things to do:

1. Frequently check and plot the boat's position when in sight of land or aids to navigation; be certain of the identification of the objects used to fix position.

2. Take soundings and heed their warning.

3. Note the effect on the boat of wind and current, especially in close waters or when maneuvering with other boats.

4. Do not follow other boats blindly; steer a safe course and do not assume that the other fellow is on a safe course.

5. When in doubt as to position, slow down promptly; do not wait until the last minute.

6. Remember that the other fellow may not see us and always be alert immediately to take such steps as will prevent a collision.

In conclusion, for those of us who wish to cruise tomorrow as well as today, let us think first of the things that spell safety; then the fun will take care of itself.

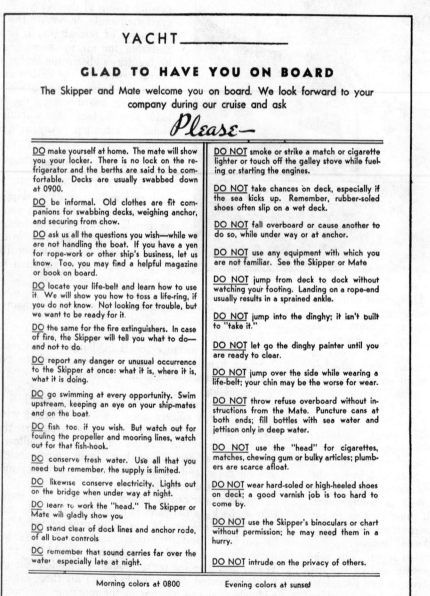

Regarding Refuse

The admonition (see note at left) against throwing refuse overboard is more than a matter of etiquette alone—it is based on law. Complaints received by both the Coast Guard and Army Engineers concerning refuse in coastal waters have fostered an official appeal by both agencies to the public. While asking each citizen to do his part voluntarily the appeal pointed out that "throwing, discharging, or depositing either from or out of any floating craft or from the shore refuse matter of any kind into any navigable waters of the U. S. or into any tributary of any navigable waters from which the same shall float or be carried into such navigable water is a violation of federal law (33 USC 407)." And for any who might take the warning lightly the appeal adds that such violation is punishable by a fine not exceeding $2500, not less than $500 or by imprisonment for not more than one year nor less than 30 days, or by both fine and imprisonment.

Elon Jessup

BOAT MAINTENANCE

THERE is nothing more pitiful than a boat that has been neglected. It seems to cry out to you that this condition is not its fault but the shabbiness is the crime of an owner that didn't deserve the privilege of owning a vessel of any sort. Yet maybe more criminal is that boat which at a distance looks fine with a new coat of paint but underneath is a rotting hull.

Boats are like human beings; it doesn't take them long to go to seed. A gentleman would no more think of going without shaving, washing, or keeping himself well groomed than flying without an airplane. Then why should he let his boat get in a decrepit state? Therefore there is only one answer and that is to always keep your boat shipshape and Bristol Fashion. This means a place for everything and everything in its place; and everything in good order.

Let us first discuss equipment and supplies. There is nothing that we depend upon so much as lines. We use them to anchor, to tie up, to go aloft, to go overside, and in fact almost everything we do depends upon the use of them. It is not only our duty but also for the sake of our safety that these be kept in good condition. We must be sure that our lines are dry before stowing; if not, they will rot. And, we must be sure that they are stowed in a well ventilated compartment, for if it is not well ventilated we might just as well have not dried them. The same reasoning goes for sails, oilskins, and any other materials of the same sort.

The use of clean, dry, and well-ventilated compartments is not only for the saving of the lines, sails, etc. but for the safety of the hull itself. If these compartments as well as all other parts of the boat are not well ventilated the result will be the rotting of the hull and this means extensive repairs and a big bill. Again, in

KEEP YOUR BOAT SHIPSHAPE FROM
STEM TO STERN, KEEL TO TRUCK

one Bermuda race a few years ago, spontaneous combustion in an unventilated oilskin locker was the cause of a fire aboard one of the schooners.

All equipment should be well marked and kept in specific places. Any article with labels should have the contents painted on the bottle or can proper; it is a good idea even to remove the paper labels, as they soak off and foul up the lazaret. Some people use adhesive tape on the articles and print the contents on the tape; others merely place a letter on each different item (A means potatoes, B means beans, C means sunburn ointment) and keep a key list on board. The only trouble with the latter method is if you lose the key list you're sunk.

If all equipment is clearly marked and always in a certain place it eases the Skipper's mind, to say nothing of adding to his safety. Not only is he sure of having everything but doesn't worry for the first day trying to remember what he has forgotten. In order to carry this thought out successfully it is necessary and good seamanship to have and use a sailing check list. A sailing check list is a list of all items that a competent skipper will investigate and provide for, relating to the boat, her equipment, supplies, stores, condition and to her operation, prior to shoving off from the mooring. If this list is kept aboard, and if the skipper checks off each item before he shoves off there will never be any need to worry about being without the necessary equipment.

The hull is, to say the least, a very important part of a

boat. No matter how good your superstructure is, if your hull is rotten you just have no boat. In order to preserve this hull we must at all times keep it well painted. Every year the old coat of paint should be sanded down before new is applied and, every so often, depending on how thick the old coats of paint are, all paint should be burned off, the hull sanded, seams and scars white leaded before a new coat of paint is applied.

Special care is to be paid to the bottom. This is of course a most important item. The bottom must be kept covered with anti-fouling paint. This type of paint, usually a copper paint, has properties that tend to keep worms out of the bottom as well as to discourage marine growth that attaches itself to the bottom.

There are two theories about applying bottom paint. Some say that the boat should be put into the water as soon as the paint has been applied, that is, while it is wet, while others state that the paint should be dry be-

Above: The engine should be kept in the best of shape at all times. Left: Guard against electrolytic action by using zinc slabs on underwater fittings. Note how the propeller has been totally destroyed by this action which takes place between dissimilar metals under water

fore launching. Follow the manufacturer's directions on the can.

Bright work, such as spars, natural wood finishes of any sort receive special care. All of these need a good sanding at least yearly and must be kept well covered with spar varnish. Those parts of the bright work that receive a lot of wear or spray need to be given more than one coat of varnish a season. Unless bright work is kept well covered the weather will get into the wood and the result is that it will turn dark and in extreme cases black.

To keep bright work looking well is a lot of work. No matter how much care is taken it will turn a little darker each year. This means that every so often it will be necessary to remove all of the varnish with varnish remover, sand the bare wood, and start with a fresh coat. In recent years more and more boats have appeared with almost no bright work at all. The cabins and spars are painted and in fact the only part left natural is the trim around the ports and hatches. This turn toward little or no bright work has even invaded the interiors which a few years ago would have been looked upon as sacrilege. No matter how much old-timers view this trend with alarm it does have this advantage—it does not reduce the protective qualities which are the main reasons for keeping surfaces covered and it does make less work.

Canvas decks present a special problem. They must be kept covered with a good deck paint for protection but the less paint you put on the better. If you get too much paint on the decks, not only will it crack but they will become smooth. This is not so good especially on a small boat, as a smooth deck makes for precarious footing in wet weather. This has been overcome in some sections by sprinkling sand on the decks while the paint is still wet. Also, some paint manufacturers are putting out a special paint with a non-skid surface. In the past few years the use of white deck paint has become increasingly popular. The reasoning behind this is that white reflects heat and as a result the cabin is much cooler.

Betwixt wind and water, that part of the vessel at or near the waterline, is the most difficult part of the hull to keep protected. This is because it is always getting wet and drying off and also that the water causes a lot of friction at this part. Here is used a special quick-drying paint called boot-topping, the principal ingredients of which are varnish and dryer.

If there is any metal to be painted, be sure to use a priming coat of anti-corrosive paint against the metal first. The two most popular types of this paint in use are red lead and aluminum. Many feel that red lead is an all around best as it has practically no injurious effect on the metal, as well as having excellent adhesion, wearing, and covering qualities. Its disadvantage is that it is a heavy paint. The advantage in the use of aluminum paint is that it is light. It is specially important if your boat has a metal bottom that anti-corrosive paint be used before the anti-fouling paint, the reason being that the ingredients of bottom paint are oxides of mercury and copper and if they come in contact with steel, corrosion will result. Also, the anti-fouling paints offer no protection to the hull against sea-water corrosion.

The question of painting the bilges is another moot one. Some owners always keep them painted while others merely use linseed oil. Those using the oil state that paint will cause the bilge to rot and of course the other school say just the opposite. Of course some sort of preservative is helpful and it is felt that what you use is not important. I know many good seamen from both schools; some use paint and others use oil and neither have had cause to be sorry.

Rules for Painting

There are a few simple rules that if carried out will cause no worry through painting. These are:
1) Never paint over a wet, dirty, or greasy surface.
2) Never paint during wet weather.
3) Never paint before cleaning and sanding.
4) Do not continuously apply new over old coats.
5) Never apply paint heavily.
6) Paint with reasonable frequency.
7) Putty after the priming coat.
8) Never use a blow torch immediately after applying paint remover.
9) Never scrape or sand near fresh paint.

There is a generally preferred order for painting the various parts of a boat as follows:
1) All interiors, including bilge (if painted) and engines.
2) Spars.
3) Cabin exterior and decks.
4) All deck gear, cockpits, ventilators, hatches, etc.
5) Hull topsides.
6) Bottom.
7) Boot-topping.

Inspections Necessary

Besides keeping all surfaces well covered there are many other parts that must be inspected regularly. For example, on some boats you must be constantly on the lookout for electrolysis. This chemical reaction is caused when different metals such as brass or bronze and iron come together or in close proximity to each other. This is often noticeable on boats between an iron rudder and a bronze propeller. Cases have been known where the rudder is just eaten up. This can be checked by placing a zinc plate nearby and the zinc will be affected instead of the iron. However, if this is done, care must be taken to watch the zinc plate and replace it whenever necessary.

Regular checks of shaft logs, stuffing boxes, bearings, under water connections, and the propeller are essential. Be sure to avoid sharp bends in wire rigging or stays as this impairs the efficiency of wire rope. Your steering system and cables should be gone over often. If your steering system goes wrong in a tight place you will not only damage your own vessel but may also injure some person or another boat. It is a *must* to have an auxiliary steering gear. This is easily rigged up with a tiller to fit over the rudder post. This gear should be readily accessible and easily rigged.

All equipment as well as the hull itself must be kept clean at all times. This also includes the bilges. There is nothing that gets dirty easier than a boat. Not only is it uncomfortable to try to live on but it is injurious to the hull and the equipment. Regular cleaning makes for little work to keep your boat spic and span but if you let it go it is a hard job to clean up.

Care of the Engine

In a motor boat the engine is the only means of propulsion and in an auxiliary it is the means of getting in and out of tight places. Therefore the engine is something that should be in the best of shape at all times and should always start at once. All of us are not good mechanics but all of us should be able to (1) Read and follow the manufacturer's instruction book; (2) Know

enough not to fool with something we are not sure of but get a good engine man on the job; and (3) Take the U.S.P.S. Mechanical Instruction Course or some other equally good engine course.

However, here are some things which we all can do not only in order to keep running but also to keep down expenses.
1) Constantly check oil level; change oil regularly.
2) Keep batteries filled and fully charged.
3) Keep grease cups filled; turn down and clean regularly.
4) Oil starter, generator, and distributor regularly.
5) Check all studs, bolts, screws, wires, etc. for tightness.
6) Check engine and propeller shaft alignment.
7) Keep engines clean, especially all filters.
8) Check cooling system, including intake, regularly.
9) Keep fuel lines tight; check for vibration.
10) Check all electric wiring regularly.
11) Do not run with a slipping clutch.
12) Do not race a cold motor.
13) Cool down engine before stopping it.
14) Engage clutch only at moderate speeds.
15) Do not depend on reverse gear to stop suddenly.
16) Carry spare parts and know how to install them.
17) Carry proper tools.

Before, we spoke of a sailing check list that all competent skippers checked before each run. In order to assist the skipper in preventing breakdowns, every boat should have an inspection check list on board and in use. An inspection check list is a list of all items the skipper will regularly inspect, and the scheduled periods for such inspections with a place for the skipper to write in the date of each inspection, in order to keep his boat well found.

The Winter Lay-up

Perhaps the greatest damage done to a boat is during the long winter months when she is laid up. In the north boats are usually pulled out during the winter while in the south they are usually left overboard. Of course these call for a slightly different technique.

In general these are the things to do when laying up for the winter:
1) Thoroughly clean the bottom, decks, cockpit, bilge, all compartments, and lockers.
2) Apply a coat of good anti-fouling paint to the bottom and sand down and prime all marred surfaces.
3) Drain the fuel system, tanks (when gas is not rationed), lines, pumps and the carburetor.
4) Thoroughly clean the engine, sand down and apply a coat of primer to all marred places.
5) Drain and flush out all water systems and tanks; drain the toilets.
6) Thoroughly overhaul the motor and all mechanical gear; flush and drain the engine cooling system; flush and refill the crankcase with fresh winter grade oil, cleaning and refilling all grease cups at the same time; coat the cylinder walls with oil.
7) Grease all brightwork.
8) Remove the batteries and place on charge.
9) Leave all floorboards up, doors ajar, ports and skylights open, hatches partly open, drawers and lockers open.
10) Carefully fit a well-made winter cover, provided with ventilating ports if boat is to be stored outdoors.

Once a boat is Shipshape and Bristol Fashion it doesn't take much work to keep her so. It is only when she is allowed to become run down that the work is heavy.

CHAPTER VIII

SEAMANSHIP

(See also page 439a)

WHEN the term seamanship is used, it commonly suggests the thought of handling a boat offshore in open water, perhaps under stress of weather. At least, that is where this quality meets the acid test. The size of the boat has little bearing on its seaworthiness. This is conditioned more upon its design and construction. The average cruiser is seaworthy enough for all the conditions she is likely to encounter in the use for which she is intended.

Every boat, obviously, has its limitations and ordinary judgment dictates that the one designed for lake and river use should not be expected to be suitable in all weather offshore. It is a fact that just what a boat will do is governed to a great extent by the skill of the man at the helm. Thus a good seaman will bring a poor craft through a blow that a novice might not be able to weather with a larger, more seaworthy vessel.

Rough weather is purely a relative term and what seems a terrible storm to the fair-weather man may be nothing more than a good breeze to the man who has known the sea in all its tantrums. When the going begins to get heavy, various types of boats will behave differently depending on their size and design, the way they are trimmed or loaded, and the nature of the sea.

Large shallow bodies of water, such as Lake Erie, kick up an uncomfortable sea in a hard blow, because the depth is not great enough to permit the waves to assume their natural form. The result is a short steep wind sea with breaking crests. Miles off shore in the open ocean with the same amount of wind, there might be a moderate sea running but the greater depth permits the wave to assume a smoother form, without broken crests.

Head Seas

Little difficulty will be experienced by the average well-designed cruiser when running with the seas head on. Some spray may be thrown or, if the sections are full forward, there may be a tendency to pound somewhat with the impact of the bow against the seas. However, she is likely to handle well enough while the seas are met head on or nearly so. If the seas are steep-sided and the speed too great, it will be necessary to slow down. This will give the bow a chance to rise in meeting each sea instead of being driven deep into it.

In the worst seas, it may help to run slightly off the course, taking the seas a few points off the bow. This will give the boat an easier motion. The more headway is reduced in meeting heavy seas the less will be the strain on the hull.

In the Trough

If the course to be made good is such that it will force the boat to run in the trough of a heavy sea with wind abeam and the seas striking the hull broadside on, it may be well to resort to what might be called a series of tacks, except that the wind is brought first broad on the bow, then broad on the quarter.

This results in a zig-zag course that makes good the desired objective, while the boat is in the trough only for brief intervals while turning. With the wind broad on the bow, the behavior should be satisfactory; on the quarter, the motion will be less comfortable but at least it will be better than running in the trough.

Running Before a Sea

Running dead before a sea is well enough if the stern can be kept up to the waves without being thrown around off the course. This is known as yawing. But when the sea gets too heavy, the boat tends to rush down a slope from crest to trough and, stern high, the propeller comes

Seamanship of the highest order is required of the skippers and crews of boats participating in ocean races, where they often are driven hard to win

M. Rosenfeld

out of water and races while the rudder, also partly out, loses its grip on the water and the sea takes charge of the stern. At this stage she may yaw so badly as to broach to, that is to say, be thrown broadside into the trough. This must be avoided at all costs.

Checking the headway to let the seas pass usually has the desired effect. While seldom necessary it is often recommended that towing a long heavy line astern will also help to check the boat's speed and keep her running straight. Obviously the line must be carefully handled and not allowed to foul the propeller. Cutting down the engine speed will reduce the strain imposed on the motor by alternate laboring with stern deep down before an overtaking sea and racing as the head goes down and the propeller comes out at the crest.

The ordinary swell off shore is seldom troublesome on this point of running but the steep wind sea of the lakes and shallow bays makes steering difficult and reduced speed imperative. Excessive speed down a steep slope may cause a boat to pitchpole, that is, drive her head under in the trough, tripping the bow, while the succeeding crest catches the stern and throws her end over end. When the going is bad enough to allow risk of this, it helps to keep the stern down and the head light and buoyant, by shifting weight if necessary.

Taking a Boat Through Inlets

When the offshore swells run into the shallower water along the beach, they build up a steeper ground swell because of the resistance created by the bottom. Natural inlets on sandy beaches, unprotected by breakwaters, usually build up a bar across the mouth. When the ground swell reaches the bar, its form changes rapidly and a short steep-sided wave is produced which may break where the water is shallowest.

This fact should be taken into consideration when approaching from offshore. A few miles off, the sea may be relatively smooth while the inlet from seaward may not look as bad as it actually is. The breakers may extend clear across the mouth, even in a buoyed channel.

The shoals shift so fast with the moving sand that it is not always feasible to keep the buoys in the best water. Local boatmen often leave the buoyed channel and are guided by the appearance of the sea, picking the best depth by the smoothest surface and the absence of breakers. A stranger is handicapped in such a situation because he may not have knowledge of uncharted obstructions and so does not care to risk leaving the buoyed channel. In a case of this kind he should have a local pilot if possible. Otherwise it will sometimes pay well to anchor off, if necessary, an hour or two and follow a local boat in.

If it becomes necessary to pick a way through without local help, there are several suggestions which may help to make things more comfortable. Don't run directly in but wait outside the bar until you have had a chance to watch the action of the waves as they pile up at the most critical spot in the channel, which will be the shallowest. Usually they will come along in groups of three, sometimes more, but always three at least. The last sea will be bigger than the rest and by careful observation it can be picked out of the successive groups.

When you are ready to enter, stand off until a big one has broken or spent its force on the bar and then run through behind it. Ebb tide seems to build up a worse sea on the bars than the flood, probably due to the rush

This big yacht is practically hidden in the trough of a heavy ground swell

of water out against and under the incoming ground swell. If the sea looks too bad on the ebb, it may be better to keep off a few hours until the flood has had a chance to make.

Heaving To

When conditions get so bad offshore that the boat cannot make headway and begins to take too much punishment, the usual sailboat practice is to heave to, that is, to carry just enough canvas, principally aft, to keep the vessel's head to the sea or a few points off where she can ride comfortably without making progress ahead. Ships sometimes are hove to by allowing them to drift in any position relative to the sea they will naturally assume.

Neither of these practices is feasible with a motor boat as her comparatively high bow and lack of canvas permits her to fall off broadside to the sea, in the trough, and she is not big enough to be left to her own devices as the liner might be. On the other hand motor boats are seldom caught out where they must weather prolonged blows.

For short periods, when the fuel supply permits, the average motor boat will be most comfortable when the propeller is allowed to turn over slowly, giving steerage way enough to keep her head to the seas or a few points off, depending on the period of the waves and the motion of the boat.

The Sea Anchor

In extreme cases, a sea anchor is occasionally used. This consists of a canvas cone-shaped bag having an iron hoop to keep it open at the mouth. To this hoop a heavy line is attached which is paid out from the bow and made fast to the forward bitt. A trip line is attached to a ring at the end of the cone. This is used to spill the bag and make it easier to haul the anchor back aboard. In use, the theory of the anchor is not to go to the bottom and hold, but merely to present a drag or resistance which will keep the boat's head up within a few points of the wind as she drifts off to leeward. Such anchors are sometimes equipped with an oil can which permits oil to ooze out slowly and form a slick on the surface, thus preventing the seas from breaking.

A motor yacht in mid-Atlantic running before a heavy winter sea. Note the dory securely lashed down on deck

In the absence of a regular sea anchor, any form of drag rigged from spars, planks and canvas or other material at hand that will float just below the surface and effectively keep the boat from lying in the trough, would be worth trying. The oil might be distributed from a bag punctured with a few holes and stuffed with oakum or waste saturated with oil. If it could be launched successfully and swamped, with a stout line securely attached, a dinghy could be tried in lieu of the sea anchor, but such procedure is easier to talk about than to accomplish, when conditions are bad enough to justify the attempt.

Use of Oil in Rough Water

Many experiences of late years have shown that the utility of oil for the purpose of modifying the effect of breaking waves is undoubted and the application simple.

The following may serve for the guidance of seamen, whose attention is called to the fact that a very small quantity of oil skillfully applied may prevent much damage both to ships (especially of the smaller classes) and to boats by modifying the action of breaking seas.

The principal facts as to the use of oil are as follows:

1. On free waves, *i.e.,* waves in deep water, the effect is greatest.

2. In a surf, or waves breaking on a bar, where a mass of liquid is in actual motion in shallow water, the effect of the oil is uncertain, as nothing can prevent the larger waves from breaking under such circumstances, but even here it is of some service.

3. The heaviest and thickest oils are most effectual. Refined kerosene is of little use; crude petroleum is serviceable when nothing else is obtainable; but all animal and

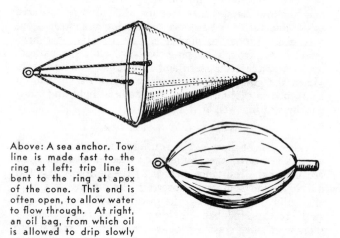

Above: A sea anchor. Tow line is made fast to the ring at left; trip line is bent to the ring at apex of the cone. This end is often open, to allow water to flow through. At right, an oil bag, from which oil is allowed to drip slowly

vegetable oils, such as waste oil from the engines, have great effect.

4. A small quantity of oil suffices, if applied in such a manner as to spread to windward.

5. It is useful in a ship or boat, either when running or lying-to, or in wearing.

6. No experiences are related of its use when hoisting a boat at sea or in a seaway, but it is highly probable that much time would be saved and injury to the boat avoided by its use on such occasions.

7. In cold water the oil, being thickened by the lower temperature and not being able to spread freely, will have its effect much reduced. This will vary with the description of oil used.

8. For a ship at sea the best method of application appears to be to hang over the side, in such a manner as to be in the water, small canvas bags, capable of holding from 1 to 2 gallons of oil, the bags being pricked with a sail needle to facilitate leakage of the oil. The oil is also

Although this fast cruiser is throwing a lot of spray, there's not much of a sea running, just a chop created by the wind

frequently distributed from canvas bags or oakum inserted in the closet bowls.

The position of these bags should vary with the circumstances. Running before the wind, they should be hung on either bow—e.g., from the cathead—and allowed to tow in the water.

With the wind on the quarter the effect seems to be less than in any other position, as the oil goes astern while the waves come up on the quarter.

Lying-to, the weather bow, and another position farther aft, seem the best places from which to hang the bags, using sufficient line to permit them to draw to windward while the ship drifts.

9. Crossing a bar with a flood tide, to pour oil overboard and allow it to float in ahead of the boat, which would follow with a bag towing astern, would appear to be the best plan. As before remarked, under these circumstances the effect can not be so much trusted.

On a bar, with the ebb tide running, it would seem to be useless to try oil for the purpose of entering.

10. For boarding a wreck, it is recommended to pour oil overboard to windward of her before going alongside. The effect in this case must greatly depend upon the set of the current and the circumstances of the depth of water.

11. For a boat riding in bad weather from a sea anchor, it is recommended to fasten the bag to an endless line rove through a block on the sea anchor, by which means the oil can be diffused well ahead of the boat and the bag readily hauled on board for refilling, if necessary.

The Dinghy in Rough Water

In rough water a dinghy becomes somewhat of a nuisance. In moderate weather it will prove tractable enough if properly designed. And if the boat is large enough to secure the tender properly aboard, there will be no difficulty in bad weather. But when it becomes necessary to tow it in a heavy following sea, it alternately lags astern on the back of a wave and then surges ahead on the forward side of another in an attempt to run the towing boat down. A long strong line is necessary and another line towed from the ring in the dinghy's transom will form a drag and prevent it from yawing so badly.

Towing Small Boats

One of the cardinal principles of seamanship requires that you be ready on any and all occasions to render assistance to other craft in need of aid. This may necessitate your taking another boat in tow. A long strong line will be needed, especially in rough water. When conditions will permit towing a small boat close up, it will be noticed that the length of line has considerable effect on the amount of resistance offered by the tow. If the stern of the tow is deep in the trough of a stern wave, she will tow much harder than if she is hauled in a few feet to get her up on the crest. When riding on the forward slope of one of the waves, a small boat may tow so easily at times as to take most of the strain off the tow line, but in this position she will yaw at the slightest provocation.

When a boat has two bitts aft instead of a single one amidships, a bridle is often rigged to tow from both, instead of throwing the whole load on one side. A heavy tow with the line made fast to a bitt aft will handicap a towing boat in maneuvering as her stern is prevented from swinging freely. If it is possible to make the line fast further forward, maneuvering will be much easier.

Seamanship is a fascinating study—and an endless one. The deeper a boatman goes into it, the more he learns. The more he learns, the more he realizes that there is yet to learn. Volumes have been written on the subject and their aid is invaluable in getting a grasp of the principles, but in the final analysis seamanship is a faculty to be developed and used, and not a mere set of principles to be understood or talked about.

Lifeboats aboard a liner mounted on gravity davits. Cradles roll down by gravity and swing out. A searchlight is provided on the rail for illumination

Lifeboat Seamanship

HANDLING BOATS UNDER OARS ALONGSIDE A

VESSEL. LAUNCHING AND GETTING THEM

BACK ABOARD. REQUIRED LIFEBOAT EQUIPMENT

WHILE yachtsmen in the normal course of events do not require a specific knowledge of lifeboats, there is much that can be learned from a study of this type of craft and its handling. Ordinarily the handling of lifeboats at sea in effecting a rescue calls for that consummate brand of seamanship which is the ultimate test of a seaman's ability to handle a boat in rough water.

Furthermore, under existing conditions today, yachtsmen do find themselves in situations where this kind of knowledge is invaluable; later they can apply it in the handling of their own dories and dinghies, and cruisers and yachts as well.

Because of the stories associated with the seaworthiness of lifeboats, of their survival in storms that get liners into difficulties in mid-ocean, amateur boatbuilders often get the notion that the ideal pleasure boat would be a lifeboat—on which they propose to build a cabin, and then install an engine. Nine times out of ten this is a mistake, as there are dozens of complications that arise in the conversion and dozens of reasons too why the lifeboat does not permit the working out of accommodations, etc., that the average yachtsman expects in a pleasure boat.

Many different types of boat classify as lifeboats and not all do represent the ultimate in seagoing design—strange as that may seem. The double-ended whaleboat is admittedly one of the finest small boats ever designed to weather a blow in the open ocean. Men who have spent a lifetime at sea have expressed an opinion that they would sooner entrust themselves to a whaleboat than any other floating craft of its inches. Coming down from the true whaleboat used on the seven seas from pole to pole, modern whaleboats embody most of the essential characteristics of design that have accounted for the well-justified fame of the original type.

On the other hand there are lifeboats, notably of metal construction, which have little in common with the wooden whaleboat. Their lines are certainly not those which would appeal to one who appreciates the graceful sweeping curves of a fine yacht. Their chief claim to seaworthiness is based rather on strong watertight construction, and the design is such that they will carry a maximum number of passengers which, in the final analysis, is the real function of a lifeboat.

Though some lifeboats do have a transom (square) stern, most are double-enders because of certain inherent advantages, principally in following seas or in a surf, where they are less likely to ship water, broach to, or get out of control than their broadsterned brothers.

Both wood and metal are used in construction, depending on the type. The original whaleboat was entirely of wood and relatively light, considering the kind of service it was expected to stand up to. Planking, for example, might not exceed ½-inch in thickness.

Lifeboats are driven by oars or sails, and many of the larger ones today are driven by inboard marine engines of the same type which powers our pleasure boats. The super-liner America, when she was launched in 1939, was equipped with fourteen lifeboats of which ten were engine-driven. They had a capacity of 135 persons each and were, at that time, the largest ever built in this country.

There is another type of propelling device used on lifeboats in which hand-operated vertical levers are placed near the thwarts and connected by suitable shafting and gears to a propeller. All the difficulties encountered in handling oars in a crowded boat—especially with inexpert oarsmen—are overcome with this propelling gear. On ocean-going and coastwise ships, lifeboats with a capacity of less than 60 persons may be fitted with this gear. If the capacity is more than 60, those which are not motor-driven are also equipped with the hand-operated gear.

An essential part of a lifeboat's construction is a series of air tanks, designed to keep her afloat if capsized and filled with water. Hanging in bights from the gunwales on each side are lifelines. These bights are not more than 3 feet long and in each there is a seine float that hangs within a foot of the waterline.

To drain water from lifeboats, they are fitted with drain holes in the bottom, often with automatic plugs, though wooden boats may be supplied with two plugs for each hole, secured by chain. Obviously one of the most important things to watch before a lifeboat is launched is to see that drain holes are properly plugged.

Plates attached to lifeboat hulls by the builder give the cubical contents of the boat and the number of persons it is designed to carry. The same information is lettered on the bow and the number of persons the boat may carry also appears on the topsides of at least two of the thwarts. Name of the ship to which the boat belongs is also lettered on the bow, with the boat's number.

A lifeboat's number is not like the registration number of the motor boat, but rather indicates its place aboard the vessel. If there are boats on both sides of the ship, odd-numbered boats are on the starboard side, even numbers on the port side. Number 1 is forward (starboard side), followed by number 3, 5, 7, etc., going aft. Number 2 is forward (on the port side), followed by 4, 6, etc., going aft. If nested, the boat under number 1 is 1-A; under number 2, 2-A, etc.

Rigid inspections and drills are prescribed in order to keep all lifeboats in good condition and crews skilled in their handling. At least once every year boats must be thoroughly overhauled and painted. Except in an emergency, no repairs or alterations can be made without the consent of local inspectors. The falls must be in readiness for immediate use at any time, and protected from ice. Propelling gear, whether motor- or hand-operated, must be operated ahead and astern five minutes or more once a week. Obstructions on deck which would interfere with the launching of boats are definitely prohibited.

On passenger vessels a ladder is provided for each set of davits so passengers can descend to the boats. The larger ships have searchlights to supply illumination for launching and when the boat lies alongside.

The equipment with which every lifeboat must be provided is prescribed by law and varies with the service in which the ship is engaged. There are separate provisions for ocean-going and coastwise vessels; inspected seagoing barges navigating oceans or in coastwise trade; vessels on the Great Lakes; and vessels on bays, sounds, and lakes other than the Great Lakes. (See tabulation of equipment required on the lifeboats on vessels navigating oceans or coastwise, also illustrations of lifeboat equipment.)

All equipment must be in good condition and aboard the boat before the vessel leaves port, remaining there throughout the voyage. Loose articles of equipment must be securely attached to the boat and nothing which does not properly belong to the boat's equipment may be stowed in it at any time.

There are three kinds of davits used in launching and hoisting lifeboats—gravity, radial or round bar, and quadrantal. In the gravity type there are two parallel tracks,

Photographs by M. Rosenfeld

About to go to the assistance of a vessel at sea, a big Coast Guard cutter launches one of her boats. Note the quadrantal type davits, sea painter ready, and iron ring around the falls instead of frapping lines, to keep the boat from swinging

arranged athwartships, on which cradles carrying the boat travel. The upper part of the track is at a 30-degree angle from the horizontal; the lower outboard part is vertical.

In launching, with the gravity type, the gripes which secure the boat are released and a brake lever is raised, permitting the cradles to go out and down. These cradles are designed so that the boat is automatically swung out clear of the ship's side as they approach the vertical part of the track. When the boat reaches the embarkation deck, tricing lines swing the boat in toward the ship's side and frapping lines are passed around the falls above the lower block to keep the boat from swinging. Then the tricing lines are cast off and the brake lever is lifted again to lower the boat to the water.

Radial or round bar davits are the type one commonly sees aboard yachts, consisting of a pair of curved arms which carry the tackle required for handling the boat. The boat rests on deck in chocks. In launching, round bar davits are swung aft far enough to permit the bow of the boat to clear the forward davit. Then the forward davit is swung outboard, taking the bow of the boat with it, followed by the after davit which swings the boat's stern out. Frapping lines are passed to hold it, and the boat is lowered to the water by means of the falls.

Quadrantal davits have a pair of perpendicular arms, one each at bow and stern, with curved arms reaching over the boat's hoisting hooks. At the foot, the arms are pivoted so that they can be swung outboard in an arc by cranking the handle of a worm-and-gear mechanism. Frapping lines and falls are used the same as described for the round bar type of davit. The boat normally is carried on deck in chocks.

In many boats, releasing gear is provided in the form of a hook at each end of the boat, connected by a chain, the purpose of which is to permit both falls to be released simultaneously as the boat hits the water. The chain leads along the side of the boat through fair leaders, with an operating grip near the stern. When this is pulled, the hooks are upset on their pivots and the boat is free. Other types of releasing gear accomplish the same purpose by means of lever-operated shafting along the bottom of the boat; still other devices permit the hooks to be released independently by hand.

On the voyages of ocean-going and intercoastal craft, each lifeboat (and life raft) must be in charge of a

During a boat drill covers and strongbacks (the spars between davits against which boats are griped) are removed. Plugs are then put in the drain holes, painters let out and tended and ladders secured in place. All boats are swung out in readiness for lowering and frapping lines are passed around the falls to keep the boats from swinging. Where one set of davits handles more than one boat, the outboard boat is swung out. When possible, boats are actually lowered to the water and the crew drilled in handling oars, sails, or whatever power is provided for the boat.

The man in charge of each boat sees to it that every member of his crew is familiar with his respective duties. On passenger vessels every member of the crew must participate, at least once every three months, in a drill in which he is required to pull an oar.

The Manual for Lifeboatmen and Able Seamen, now published by the United States Coast Guard, contains about forty questions and answers for lifeboatmen which give, in condensed form, the essence of the information one should have in connection with the equipment, use and handling of lifeboats. Yachtsmen would do well to make this part of their basic knowledge of seamanship. The questions and answers are given here as they appear in the Manual:

Q. How do you know how many persons a lifeboat is allowed to carry? A. The number of persons allowed is stated on the builder's plate attached to the boat, is painted on the bow of the boat, and also on at least two of the thwarts.

Q. How are lifeboats num-

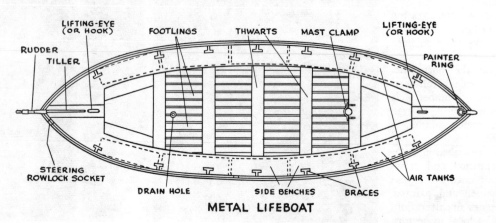

LIFTING-EYE (OR HOOK) · FOOTLINGS · THWARTS · MAST CLAMP · LIFTING-EYE (OR HOOK) · RUDDER · TILLER · PAINTER RING · STEERING ROWLOCK SOCKET · DRAIN HOLE · SIDE BENCHES · BRACES · AIR TANKS

METAL LIFEBOAT

Left: Names of parts of a metal lifeboat. Below: One of the metal lifeboats of the super-liner America, equipped with manually operated propelling gear. Levers at the thwarts are connected by shafting through gears to a propeller

licensed deck officer or a certificated lifeboatman. On coastwise, Great Lakes, bay and sound vessels, they must be in charge of a licensed officer, or certificated able seaman. One man is designated as second in command and it is the responsibility of the person in charge to see that he has a list of the crew (of his own boat or raft) and also that the crew know their duties.

Lifeboat and fire drills are held at least once each week, and also before leaving port when a passenger vessel's voyage will require more than a week. Signals for the boat drill are sounded on the vessel's whistle—seven short blasts and one long blast—and the same on the general alarm bell. Whistle signals may also be used to give the commands required when handling the boats, in which case one short blast means "Lower the boats"; two short blasts, "Stop lowering"; three short blasts, "Crew dismissed from boat stations."

bered on board a vessel? A. The boats are numbered from forward toward the stern, odd-numbered boats being on the starboard side (1, 3, 5, 7, etc., in order), and even-numbered boats being on the port side (2, 4, 6, 8, etc., in order). If the boats are nested, number 1A is carried under number 1, number 2A under number 2, etc.

Q. In what part of a lifeboat are the hatchets kept? A. One is kept at the bow and one at the stern of the boat.

Q. What is a sea painter? A. A sea painter is a long line led well forward on a vessel, outside of everything. It is to be secured to the second thwart in the lifeboat with a toggle or in such a manner that it may be cast off easily.

Q. Describe a sea anchor. A. A sea anchor is a cone-shaped canvas bag. The open end is fastened to an iron

Note—2 boathooks, 8 feet long and 1½ inches diameter also required. See also additional equipment listed at end of this article.

EQUIPMENT REQUIRED ON LIFEBOATS
(Ocean or Coastwise Vessels)

1 *bailer* with lanyard attached
1 *bucket* with lanyard attached
1 liquid *compass*
12 red self-igniting *distress lights* in a watertight metal case
1 canvas *ditty-bag* containing sailmaker's palm, needles, sail twine, marline and marline-spike
2 enamelled *drinking cups*
1 *flashlight* with one extra lamp in a portable watertight metal case
2 *hatchets*, attached by lanyards, one at each end of the boat
1 gallon of *illuminating oil* in a metal container
1 *lantern*
1 *lifeline* (around the boat)
2 *life preservers*
1 *locker* or box for storage and preservation of small articles and equipment
1 *mast*, or more, with at least one good sail and proper gear for each, the sail and gear protected by a suitable canvas cover. (North of latitude 35 degrees North a vessel equipped with radio is required to have only one lifeboat on each side of the vessel so equipped.) Motor lifeboats are exempt from this requirement.
1 box of friction *matches* in a watertight container
A single-banked complement of *oars*, with 2 spare oars and a steering oar. Motor lifeboats and those equipped with hand-operated propelling gear must be equipped with four oars and one steering oar.
1 *painter*
Plugs, or automatic plugs, for drain holes. Decked lifeboats having no plug hole must be provided with at least two *bilge pumps* .
1 airtight receptacle containing two pounds of *emergency provisions* for each person. Condensed milk must be included on all passenger vessels on international voyages.
1 set and a half of thole pins or *rowlocks*, attached by separate chains
1 *rudder* having either tiller or yoke and yoke lines
1 *sea anchor*
1 *signal pistol* with lanyard attached, and 12 red lights
1 gallon of *storm oil* in a container
Wooden *water breakers* or suitable tanks filled, with spigots, and containing 1 quart of fresh water for each person
MOTOR LIFEBOATS, in addition to the above, must carry 2 carbon tetrachloride *fire extinguishers*, one or two *bilge pumps* (depending on the size of the boat), *searchlight* with 2 spare bulbs, and *radio*.

---

ring which keeps the bag spread out. A bridle is attached to the ring, and secured to the other end of the bridle is a smaller ring or grommet to which the drag line is made fast. A tripping line of smaller size, but 2 fathoms longer than the drag line, is attached to the small closed end of the sea anchor and led through a fair lead attached to the iron hoop at the open end.

Q. How is a sea anchor used? A. A sea anchor is used as a drag to keep the boat's head to the wind and sea and to prevent rapid drifting. When held by the drag line, with trip line slack, it is wide open and drags through the water with considerable resistance. A container of storm oil, having a small opening for the continuous discharge of the oil, may be secured to the sea anchor.

Q. How is a sea anchor hauled in? A. A sea anchor is hauled in by its tripping line which upsets it so that it is brought in small end first with greatly reduced resistance to its passage through the water.

Q. What may be used in lieu of a sea anchor? A. A tarpaulin or anything similar may be attached to some oars lashed together, one edge being weighted down by attaching to it any heavy object, and after bridling the whole so that it will drag as nearly upright in the water as possible, it may be used very effectively in lieu of a sea anchor.

Q. What oil is used as storm oil? A. Animal or vegetable oil is used whenever available, although fuel oil will be effective if the water temperature is fairly high. The effect of any oil is less at lower temperatures of the water.

Q. What is the effect of storm oil? A. Storm oil does not lessen the size of seas, but does tend to prevent them from combing or breaking. It will usually be of aid in any sea in which a lifeboat can live.

Q. What are the parts of an anchor? A. The parts of an anchor are stock, shank, fluke, crown, arm, and shackle or ring.

Q. What are the parts of an oar? A. The parts of an oar are the handle or gripe, leather, loom, blade, and tip.

Q. Of what woods are oars usually made? A. Ash, but any wood of equal length of grain and equal strength may be used, such as beech, birch, etc. Racing oars are usually made of spruce.

Boat Falls

Q. What is the usual size of boat falls? A. The manila line used is usually from 2 to 4 inches in circumference, depending on the size and weight of the boat. With a threefold purchase, the standing part is rove over the center sheave. On all ocean, coastwise, Great Lakes, and on new bay and sound passenger vessels, wire falls and mechanical means for lowering boats are required if the height of the boat deck exceeds 20 feet from the lightest seagoing draft.

Q. Why are lifeboats usually "double-enders"? A. "Double-end" boats are more seaworthy. They are less likely to ship water in a following sea, and less likely to broach to. They are easier to steer in a following sea, easier to handle alongside a vessel, and much easier to handle in a surf.

Q. What is a frapping line? A. A frapping line is any piece of line passed around a boat fall above the lower block, one end being made fast on deck and the other being hauled taut and belayed to prevent the boat from swinging.

Q. Which oar is the stroke oar in a lifeboat? A. The oar nearest the stern in a single-banked boat. In a double-banked boat, the port and the starboard oars nearest the stern are both stroke oars.

Launching and Getting Away from the Ship

Q. If you were in charge of a lifeboat, how would you proceed to get the boat launched and away from the ship under oars? A. Muster the crew; see that they all have on life preservers properly adjusted; remove the boat cover and strongback; hang the ladder over the side; have one bow and one stroke oarsman lie in the boat and see that the plug is in or that the automatic bailer is free, and that the life lines are clear; have the painter led well forward outside of the davits and tended; let go all gripes and the boat chocks; remove the reel covers; tend the falls; slack davit guys and swing the boat out; set davit guys taut and belay; have stroke oarsman place steering oar in readiness; place all crew in boat, station two men at each fall, one to see that falls are kept clear and one to lower; lower away on both falls evenly; have bow and stroke oarsmen ready with boathooks to fend off from vessel's side; trip releasing gear as soon as boat is water-borne; take passengers aboard, either at embarkation deck or after boat is in water, seeing that they all have on properly adjusted life preservers; shove boat's bow off and have crew commence rowing, giving them the following orders: "Let go the painter"; "Stand by your oars"; "Up oars"; "Let fall"; "Give way together." If the boat is under radial davits, guy the boat out as described above; if under quadrantal davits, crank the boat out; if under gravity davits, place one hand on brake lever, raising it slowly, keeping the boat well under control, and permit the boat to roll down the runway, controlling it by frapping lines.

Launching in a Seaway

Q. How would you launch a boat in a heavy seaway? A. The vessel should first be hove to on a heading that will reduce the roll, and which will offer as good a lee as possible for the boat to be launched. Some vessels are better in the trough, some with the sea on the bow, and some with a quartering sea. A boat may be launched with care by a well-drilled crew under adverse conditions. If the boat is not fitted with skates, mattresses should be slung up and down the side. Prior to lowering, oil should be used over the vessel's side so that the oil will keep spreading. If the vessel is rolling, the boat itself should be kept from swinging as much as possible by frapping lines until ready to lower. If the vessel is pitching, the boat should be kept from swaying by keeping the painter taut and by using a stern fast in the same manner. When ready, the frapping lines should be tended, the boat should be lowered away smartly, the releasing gear should be tripped as soon as the boat is water-borne, and the boat should be sheered off immediately from the vessel's side by using the steering oar and sea painter.

Q. If you were in charge of a lifeboat, how would you prevent it from swinging as the vessel rolled when the boat is at the embarkation deck? A. By the use of frapping lines passed around the falls above the lower block.

Q. What are the most important things to be done before a boat is lowered? A. Make sure that the drain plug is in place, and that the painter is carried forward and tended.

Q. In a lifeboat which is not equipped with simultaneous releasing gear, which fall should be unhooked first? A. If the vessel is stationary or has headway, the after fall should be unhooked first. If the vessel has sternway, the forward fall should be unhooked first.

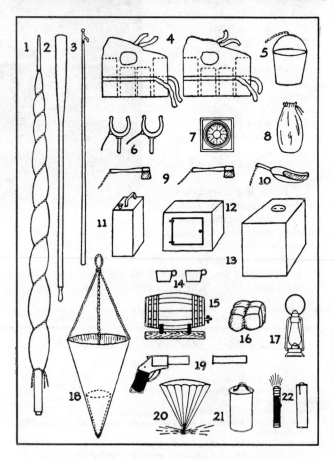

Lifeboat equipment: (1) mast and sail, (2) oars, (3) boat hook, (4) life preservers, (5) bucket, (6) rowlocks, (7) compass, (8) ditty bag, (9) hatchets, (10) bailer, (11) 1 gallon oil, (12) container, (13) bread-box, (14) drinking cups, (15) water breaker, (16) matches, (17) lantern, (18) sea anchor, (19) pistol and cartridge, (20) flare, (21) distress signals, and (22) flashlight and container

Coming Alongside a Vessel

Q. If you were in charge of a lifeboat, how would you proceed to come alongside a gangway under ordinary conditions, and what orders would you give? A. Come up to the vessel from astern so that the boat is parallel to the vessel when about 100 yards from the gangway, and then give the order "In bows," whereupon the two bow oarsmen boat their oars and stand by with boathooks; when the boat is about two boat lengths from the gangway, give the order "Oars," followed by "Boat your oars," whereupon all of the oars are boated; next sheer the bow in toward the gangway, and when it nearly touches, shift the helm and sheer the bow out, bringing the stern in. Due regard, of course, must be had for wind, tide, and sea. It is customary to have a painter ready at hand at the gangway, and led well forward on the vessel, for use in moderate weather.

Getting the Boat Back Aboard

Q. If you were in charge of a lifeboat, how would you proceed to put it aboard under ordinary conditions? A. Bring the boat alongside the vessel under the davits; get the painter and make it fast; send all of crew except one bow and one stroke oarsman on board by the ladder; have bow oarsman hook on forward fall, then have stroke oarsman hook on after fall; immediately thereafter commence hoisting; if both falls are not led to the same winch, see that boat comes up evenly; as soon as boat is clear of water, have stroke oarsman pull drain plug; when block-and-block, pass stoppers and belay falls; then proceed to take boat in on deck according to type of davit used, the process being the opposite of what is used in launching.

Q. What boats are always kept ready for immediate launching?

A. The emergency boats. These boats are of suitable size, built for use under all conditions of wind and sea in an emergency, such as rescue of man overboard, rescue of persons from a wreck, carrying out lines, etc. Generally they are of whaleboat type with finer lines than the ordinary lifeboat.

Q. How would you place passengers in a lifeboat? A. So that the boat is on an even keel and the weight equally distributed fore and aft, and so that the handling of the oars is not interfered with; and with the women and children in the center of the boat, so as to protect them as much as possible from spray.

Q. What is the meaning of the order "Back water?" A. To do with the oar the opposite of what is done in rowing, or, in other words, to row backwards.

Q. What is the meaning of the order "Stern all?" A. To take the way off a boat which has headway. To carry out the order, the blades of the oars are dipped very slightly in the water on the backstroke only for a few strokes, and the depth to which the oars are dipped is increased gradually as way is lost, until finally the blade is submerged to the same depth as in rowing ahead. When way is off the boat, a well-drilled crew will commence without further orders to "Back water."

Lifeboat Seamanship

Q. If you were hove to by the sea anchor and the dragline carried away, how would you keep the boat's head up to the wind and sea? A. By using the oars.

Q. When steering a boat by compass, where should the compass be placed? A. Aft where it is convenient for the man steering the boat to see, and secured so that the lubber's line is as close to the center line of the keel as possible.

Q. If you were heading for a particular place or point of land, and fog shut in, what would you do? A. As soon as signs of fog appeared, take a compass bearing of the place or point, and then steer by compass.

Q. What lights should you display on a lifeboat at sea at night? A. From sunset to sunrise, the boat's lantern hoisted as high as possible on the mast or on a spare oar.

Q. What would you do in a lifeboat at sea at night if you saw the lights of a vessel and you desired assistance? A. Use a distress light until an answer is received. If the vessel is a considerable distance off, use the signal pistol until an answer is received.

Q. What is the Coast Guard signal meaning "Do not attempt to land in your own boats"? A. By day a red flag and a white flag waved together; by night a red lantern and a white lantern waved together.

Q. What is the Coast Guard signal meaning "This is the best place to land?" A. By day, a man beckoning on the beach; by night, two torches burning together on the beach.

Landing a Lifeboat Through Surf

Q. How would you land a lifeboat on the beach with a strong wind on shore, a high sea, and heavy surf? A. If it is possible for the lifeboat to live in the sea, it is probably better to wait outside the breakers until the sea moderates. There are many cases where lives have been lost in attempting to go through surf at a time when the boat was perfectly safe outside the breakers. Watch carefully when approaching and find a place where the surf is least heavy; head directly for the beach, towing the sea anchor over the stern spreading oil, and having the oarsmen pull an easy stroke to keep a strain on the dragline so as to prevent the stern from being thrown around by the sea and the boat capsized. If necessary, use additional oil to prevent the seas from combing and breaking. When on the last sea and making the beach, have the oarsmen pull vigorously so that the boat will go up on the beach as far as possible and will not capsize.

Handling Motor Lifeboats

Q. In a motor lifeboat, how does the torque of the propeller affect the boat when the ordinary right-handed marine engine is used? A. With the helm amidships and the engine running ahead, the boat's head gradually goes to port. With the helm amidships and engine going astern, the boat's stern goes to port rapidly. A small amount of right rudder is necessary to counteract this tendency when going ahead. As the effect of the torque is greater when going astern, advantage may be taken of this tendency when maneuvering in close quarters, by turning the boat to the right. By going ahead with right rudder, and astern with left rudder, and repeating the process, the stern is sheered rapidly to port and the boat is quickly turned. In handling lifeboats, it is best to use the engines at a moderate speed, both ahead and astern, while maneuvering in order to get the maximum benefit in steering of the action of the propeller stream against the rudder.

Q. Is the action of the rudder on a motor lifeboat more pronounced than on a large vessel? A. It is, because of comparative rudder areas. A motor lifeboat can be steered when going astern much better than a vessel can.

Manually Operated Propellers

Q. Describe a manually operated propeller as used in a lifeboat. A. The manually operated propeller eliminates the use of oars. The usual clutch, shafting, stuffing box, and propeller found in a motor lifeboat are used. Bars run the length of the boat and are connected to the propeller shaft by a system of gears. Motive power is furnished by the movement of the bars in a fore-and-aft direction by the occupants of the boat (either passengers or crew), causing the propeller to rotate. The whole device is so constructed that no previous instruction is necessary for its operation. The direction of rotation of the propeller, and hence the direction of motion of the boat, may be reversed by means of the clutch.

Additional Lifeboat Equipment

In its Navigation and Inspection Circular No. 11-52, dated October 20, 1952, the U. S. Coast Guard specified the following additional lifeboat equipment as required for vessels in ocean or coastwise service:

- 1 bilge pump.
- 2 buckets instead of 1.
- 1 first aid kit.
- 2 buoyant heaving lines.
- 1 jackknife.
- 1 lifeboat gunwale ladder (lifeboats for 60 or more persons only).
- 2 painters instead of 1.
- 2 buoyant smoke signals (hand-held smoke signals may be retained until 3 years from date of manufacture, but all replacements shall be of the buoyant type).
- 3 quarts of water per person instead of 1.
- 1 pound of condensed milk per person when not on an additional voyage.
- 3 grab lines.

Surf Seamanship

METHODS OF HANDLING BOATS IN THE SURF.
HELMSMANSHIP. EFFECT OF WIND, SEA AND
SHALLOW WATER ON STEERING. HEAVING TO

OF all phases of seamanship, taking a small boat through the surf probably calls for the greatest skill. There are some types of small boats of such excellent design that they will live through fairly heavy seas, even when mismanaged to a certain extent—provided they are in deep water. But when the ground swell rolls in on a beach or bar, and the natural formation of waves is broken up, curling breakers are produced that carry power enough to capsize any but the expertly handled and well designed boat.

The difficulties lie in the steepness of the curling breaker's shoreward side and the speed at which it is driving on the beach. The boat with buoyancy enough to live in a surf is so light that it can be picked up by a breaker and carried like a surfboard at astonishing speed. If caught even slightly off the end-on heading that allows breakers to pass, she may broach to and capsize despite the best efforts of her crew. Or she may be carried end-on at increasing speed on the shoreward side of a roller,

stern rising and bow lowering, until the bow is buried in a trough and the stern is thrown somersault fashion over the bow, pitchpoling.

When approaching a line of breakers along the beach from the seaward side it is hard to form an accurate idea of just how rough the surf is, the character of the seas that the boat will be running through, and just where the surf may be a little less heavy, or offer some kind of opening for the landing. From seaward the surf will always appear smoother than when viewed from the beach. Therefore a primary rule to be laid down is that extreme caution must be exercised before entering the surf.

It is generally possible, however, to wait just outside the breakers for a time, studying the succession of seas as they roll in. It will be noted that the outer line of breakers is ordinarily the heaviest so that a boat taken safely through them usually has a good chance of getting all the way to the beach—if handled properly. Somewhere along the beach, because of the configuration of outer bars, the trend of the shoreline, or rock formations, there may be one spot where the surf is a little easier to run.

For example, an inlet from seaward might appear so prohibitive because of high surf breaking on an outer bar, even in the buoyed channel, that one would hesitate to enter unless there were no alternative. Yet with a little study it may be found that this bar, curving around the inlet mouth, has left passes between its extremities and

Fishermen land a loaded dory on a flat sand beach through the surf, the shore crew standing by with block and tackle to haul the boat clear of the breakers

H. Armstrong Roberts

the beach proper. Running down to the leeward end of the bar, it is possible that the shoal itself acts almost as a breakwater behind which it would be possible to pass in smooth water, without actually entering the breakers at any point.

Conditions are not always as ideal as that but it illustrates the point that every advantage should be taken of whatever natural conditions may exist that would help to provide some sort of clear channel or smooth out the breakers. Even off-lying rocks, skirted to leeward, may help, though rocky beaches must be approached with extra caution because of the increased hazard of submerged rocks added to that of the breakers.

Current must be considered, in its effect in setting a boat off her intended course to a certain spot on the beach. Currents often set diagonally on the beach or run parallel to it. Leeway caused by a cross wind may also complicate the problem.

After a spot has been chosen for the proposed landing, it is wise to lay off that spot a while outside the outermost breakers, watching the seas as they come in. It is not uncommon to find that there will be a succession of heavy swells followed by a period when the seas are relatively smoother and less dangerous. Study of this sequence may help to allow a series of bad seas to break, taking advantage of the comparative lull that follows to make the run for the beach.

Knowing the two fundamental hazards that make surf dangerous to a small boat will help one to take steps to avoid conditions creating the hazard. The risk of broaching to will be avoided if the boat, by oars, a drag, or any means available, is kept end-on to the breakers. The risk of pitchpoling after being driven down and carried forward at breakneck speed on the shoreward side of the breaker will be eliminated if, by the power of oars, or a drag, the shoreward progress can be stopped as a breaking wave approaches. In this way the wave passes the boat without carrying her shoreward.

Before entering the surf, the boat should be trimmed so that the ends are relatively light, that is, no heavy weight in either extreme end. In the distribution of weight, it is best to keep the shoreward end of the boat lighter than the seaward end. So trimmed, she will be less likely to broach.

Landing Stern First

Boats may be landed either bow or stern to the beach. It is generally agreed that the latter method is safest for an inexperienced crew. Just before getting into the breakers, the boat is turned to head seaward and the crew backs water to send the boat toward the beach stern first. The great advantage of this method is that, at the approach of a breaker coming in from seaward, the crew can pull a few strokes to meet it and then resume their backing when the sea has passed. If the boat is very small and the sea heavy, this is conceded to be good practice.

An alternative to this method is to drop an anchor just outside the surf, with sufficient line in the bow to reach the beach and then back in with the oars, paying out line as you go. In a practical way the surge of the sea may be sufficient to drive the boat in without oars. The anchor line is always ready to keep the bow up to the seas, as a strain is kept on it at all times. If there is no one on shore to assist in beaching or launching this is a good method as the line is then available for use in hauling the boat out through the surf again when launching.

The Surf Line

Boats are also backed in to the beach with the aid of a surf line made fast to the stern of a motor boat just outside the breakers. The motor boat may anchor or just keep way enough on to hold her position against the current, while line is veered out from the bow of the boat in the surf as necessary. The surf line, buoyed perhaps with floats or life jackets to keep it near the surface and prevent its fouling the bottom, aids the oarsmen in keeping the bow head on to the approaching seas.

Once the boat has gotten ashore it is possible, with the surf line, to send it back and forth through the surf—as

163

for example to land several loads of supplies or to bring fresh water out to a vessel from shore—by securing a hauling line to the stern (shoreward end) of the landing boat. The hauling line is veered out from the beach as the crew of the motor boat hauls in the surf line. Then on the next trip to the beach the hauling line is hauled ashore while the surf line is veered out from the anchored boat. The boat can be handled this way whether or not there are any occupants in the boat to assist with the oars.

M. Rosenfeld

Richard H. Anthony

Above: This type of motor lifeboat, even if rolled over in a breaking sea, would right and bail herself out automatically. Left: A Coast Guard crew returns to the station after surfboat drill. Skilled crews can take such a boat through an amazingly heavy surf. Note the long steering sweep

Landing Bow to the Beach

If the boat is not a double-ender, the chances of getting through to the beach are probably best if one of the methods described above is adopted, in which the bow is kept to seaward. In any case, regardless of the type of boat or the method of landing, every effort should be made to watch the seas closely so as to avoid if possible their breaking around the boat. By a little skillfull maneuvering it is often possible to place the boat so that seas break either ahead or astern.

If conditions are such that it would be safe to head for the beach bow-on instead of stern first, a sweep or steering oar should be used on the stern instead of a rudder. When a breaker is seen building up astern, all oarsmen should back water hard to hold the stern up against the wave to allow it to pass. As soon as it has passed the oarsmen row hard for the beach, coming in on the back of the wave while the breaker spends itself ahead of the

boat, shoreward. As is the practice of the Coast Guard, the two oars furthest aft can be used to help the coxswain at the steering oar to keep the boat under full control.

Oarsmen on the after thwarts are sometimes placed so that they face shoreward. Then when a breaker rolls in they are in a position to exert all their power, rowing against the breaker rather than having to back water. In this case, more oarsmen should face forward than aft, as it takes plenty of pulling power to hold the boat up to the oncoming seas and prevent broaching.

What has been said elsewhere of the value of a drogue or sea anchor when running before a following sea applies as well to running the surf. Any kind of weight or drag towed astern (if landing bow-on) will help to keep the stern up to the sea. A pig of ballast, a bucket or a basket or any kind of improvised drag will be better than nothing. A regular sea anchor is recommended as the tripping line permits it to be upset at will so as to cut down the drag when not needed. The sea anchor can be towed from 10 to 20 fathoms of line and, if desired, an oil bag can be used on the sea anchor to help in smoothing the crested seas. If the landing is being made with the aid of a motor boat outside the surf, oil can sometimes be distributed to advantage from the off-lying boat.

Under Sail or Motor

When a boat that is to be landed on the beach approaches the surf under sail, her mast and sails should be taken down outside the breakers and the boat taken through under oars. The only exception to this is the case where just a moderate sea may be breaking on a steep beach, when the boat may be sailed right onto the beach under a small amount of headsail.

As a matter of fact, in all the other cases discussed above we have assumed that the problem is one of landing on a relatively flat beach where successive lines of breakers extend some distance seaward.

Whether under sail or oars, the problem is different on a steep beach because the only breakers of consequence then will be directly on the beach. In such a case the practice is to keep the speed of the boat up right onto the beach, swinging her broadside as she lands so as to haul her bodily up out of reach of the next sea as quickly as possible.

Motor surf boats should enter the surf at a moderate speed, steered by a steering oar in place of the rudder, which should be unshipped. An oar on each quarter will help in steering. Instead of attempting to run right on the beach under power, it is better to cut the motor and ship oars to land. A sea anchor or drogue will probably be needed from the stern to check the boat's headway, and one man should stand ready with a knife or hatchet to cut either the tow line or tripping line if necessary.

In rowing to seaward through a surf, the same caution about dodging the breakers applies, as in landing. If the surf is heavy and there is a head wind to buck,

it will be necessary to get up just as much speed as possible when meeting a breaker that can't be avoided. However the oarsmen may be powerful enough to drive the boat harder than is necessary merely to prevent her from being carried astern by an approaching wave. In such a case checking the way somewhat will enable her to pass over the sea easier than if driven through so hard that the bow falls abruptly as the wave passes by.

Helmsmanship

One of the attributes of a good seaman is the ability to steer well—another of those faculties that is developed not by study, but by practice. Not all of the principles laid down for the proper steering of a ship will apply to small pleasure boats. Nevertheless if one is posted on the fundamentals applicable to large vessels, the chances are he'll do a better job at the wheel of small craft. And, by the same token, the experience pleasure boatmen have acquired in handling small boats is today serving them well aboard cutters, patrol craft and other good sized vessels.

Right: One of the attributes of a good seaman is the ability to steer well. Steering by compass in rough weather is something of an art

M. Rosenfeld

Left: Close-hauled, with her lee rail awash, this yawl is being driven hard in an ocean race. Wind pressure on sails keeps her from rolling as a motor boat would in a beam sea. For that reason, small steadying sails are carried on some motor boats used regularly off shore in heavy weather

There are certain commands given to a helmsman which need explanation. The old expressions of "port helm" and "starboard helm" have given way to *right rudder* and *left rudder,* respectively, because the latter admit no possibility of confusion in interpretation.

The terms right and left are used with standard orders, preceding the command itself, so that the helmsman can start immediately to apply the rudder, while he awaits the rest of the command which tells him how much rudder is required. For example, the command may be *right full rudder, right standard rudder,* or *right standard half rudder.*

If the maximum available rudder arc is 35 degrees, full rudder is likely to be only 30 degrees, the remaining 5 degrees being used only in emergencies. Standard rudder and standard half rudder are relative terms, differing on various ships. When a group of vessels is operating as a unit, a command of (right or left) standard rudder turns them all in the same radius, though the actual rudder angle varies on each.

Rudder amidships, obviously, requires the helmsman to align the rudder in the fore and aft centerline of the ship. If the rudder is to be turned a specified number of degrees,—10 degrees to port, let's say—the command is *left 10 degrees rudder.* If the rudder angle is to be increased, the command is *give her more rudder;* decreased, *ease the rudder.* With the rudder at 15 degrees, *ease to 10* would indicate to the helmsman exactly how much the rudder is to be eased.

Coast Guardsmen prepare to launch a surf boat

Handsomely is a nautical expression that means exactly the opposite of what a landsman might expect. It means gradually, moderately or carefully. Consequently if the command is *right, handsomely,* it calls for only a slight change of course—to the right, in this case.

To check the swing of a ship, without stopping it entirely, is to *meet her. Steady* or *steady as you go* or *steady so* means to hold her on the course you are steering at the time. If the command is given while the ship is still swinging, the helmsman notes the course when the command is given, and steadies on that course.

When the course to be made good is a little to one side of the set course, the command may be *nothing to the right,* or *nothing to the left.* If the latter, the helmsman knows he must not let the ship go to the left of the ordered course.

In maneuvering, an officer may order *shift the rudder.* The ship, for example, might have been turning to starboard with right rudder. As headway is checked, the rudder is changed from right to left at the command and the vessel would continue to turn in the same direction as she gathers sternway.

Mind your rudder means to stand by for an order or perhaps to pay better attention to the steering. However, if the ship is getting off her course too much—to the right, let us say—the command is *mind your left rudder* (that is, use more left rudder to counteract the tendency the ship has toward the right of her course).

Commands from an officer of the deck are repeated by the helmsman. Then, when the command has been executed, he reports—as, for example, "Steady on course 189, Sir." The officer's acknowledgment may be "Very well" if the report is correct or acceptable, or the reply may be "Keep her so" if the helmsman is to continue to steer the course reported.

Steering by Compass

AT sea, most steering is naturally done by compass, requiring the helmsman to keep the lubberline of the compass (representing the ship's head) on that mark of the compass card which indicates the course to be steered. If the course is 100 degrees and the lubberline is at 95 degrees, the helmsman must swing the ship's head, with right rudder, 5 degrees to the right, so that the lubberline is brought around to 100. Remember, the card stands still while the lubberline swings around it. Any attempt to bring the desired course on the card up to the lubberline will produce exactly the wrong result.

As a vessel swings with a change in course, there is a tendency for the inexperienced helmsman to allow her to swing too far, due to the momentum of the turn and the lag between the turning of the wheel and the ship's response to rudder action. That's why it is necessary to meet her (as explained above) so that the ship comes up to, and steadies on, the new course without over-swinging.

A crooked course, yawing from side to side, brands the inexperienced helmsman. A straight course is the goal to shoot at; this can be achieved, after the ship has steadied, by only slight movements of the wheel. It calls for anticipation of the ship's swing and correction with a little rudder instead of letting her get well off the course before the rudder is applied. A zig-zag course is an inefficient course. The mileage is longer and any offset of the rudder from the centerline tends to retard the ship's progress.

A good helmsman will not only use small amounts of rudder, but he'll also turn the wheel slowly. His eyes will be on the compass, not on the ship ahead, unless he has specific orders to the contrary. There are times, for example, when he may be ordered to steer for a certain landmark or other object.

In piloting small craft, it is often better to pick out a distant landmark, or a star at night, to steer by. This helps to maintain a straight course as the compass is smaller and less steady than aboard a larger vessel. The helmsman can then drop his eye periodically to the compass to check his course.

Effect of Wind and Sea

A BEAM wind will exercise considerable effect on the steering as the bow, with its relatively greater proportion of freeboard to draft, tends to be driven off more than the stern, and the rudder angle must be sufficient to compensate for this. In a heavy sea, the direction from which the seas are coming will have a bearing on the steering. A head sea will be less troublesome than a following sea.

Driving into a head sea, the ship will probably be slowed down to prevent unnecessary pounding, and the swing of the bow will have to be corrected with slight rudder changes. In a following sea, the tendency for the stern to be thrown around by overtaking waves (yawing) must be anticipated and checked as much as possible. When the stern is tossed high before an overtaking sea, if it tends to be thrown to starboard, the helmsman must meet her by applying right rudder.

Broaching should be avoided at all costs. Ordinarily if the seas are not too bad, it is possible in handling a small boat to watch astern for the big seas that cause the boat to yaw too much. Then by speeding up the engine, with rudder set against the direction of the yaw, the corrective effect of the rudder will be enough to straighten her out and keep the stern up to the sea. As the wave passes the bow, the throttle can be closed again to its previous setting.

Shallow Water

SMALL craft in heavy following seas such as are built up on inlet bars and in big shallow lakes sometimes tend to broach to despite anything that can be done by the helmsman. Rudder hard over one way, the boat may run in the opposite direction. When conditions are as serious as that, a drag astern, consisting of a small sea anchor or length of heavy line has been recommended as an aid in keeping the stern up to the sea. The great risk in speeding up too much when the boat has acquired considerable momentum down the descending side of a wave is that of pitchpoling. If she is allowed to trip by running the bow under in the trough between steep seas, the sea astern may throw her end over end.

Shallow water, besides tending to create a more bothersome steep-sided sea when the wind blows hard, also has a decided effect on the speed and steering of a vessel. A suction is created, the stern settles, and speed is decreased because of the change in the vessel's trim. Propeller and rudder action are both sluggish, so that response to the wheel is not as good as it will be in deep water.

In a small motor boat with exhaust at the stern near the waterline, warning of shallow water is often had before actual grounding, as the exhaust starts to bury under water and a difference in its sound is detected. This happens without any change in the throttle setting.

Beam Seas

ALL vessels have what is known as a period of oscillation, or rolling period, which is the time required by a vessel to roll from one side to the other. If this period happens to coincide with the period of the waves in which she is running, as in a beam sea, the synchronism should be broken by a change of course (and speed, if necessary), to avoid excessive rolling. It is seldom necessary, in such a case, to meet the seas squarely bow-on. Slight changes of course often damp the rolling enough to make the vessel comfortable. If the ship is disabled, with power not available, then the only way to prevent heavy rolling is to get out a sea anchor or drogue to hold the bow up to the sea, used perhaps in conjunction with storm oil if the waves are breaking.

Occasions may arise, as in preparing to heave to, when a vessel that has been running before a following sea must be brought around head to sea. This calls for skill and judgment and a knowledge of the steering qualities of the particular vessel involved. By watching carefully the procession of waves as they pass, taking into consideration their height and the distance between them and space required for the turn, it will usually be possible to avoid having her caught beam on to a dangerous oncoming sea.

Invariably a boat is under better control when her engine is going ahead rather than in reverse. The propeller, in the first instance, is throwing a stream of water past the rudder blade. In general, if left to her own devices, with engines stopped, the bow of the average boat (and most larger vessels) will fall off until the wind comes abaft the beam, because of the relative height of bow and superstructure forward as compared with that aft where the draft, too, is normally greater.

Methods of Heaving To

WHEN the going gets so bad at sea that it would be dangerous for a vessel to pursue her course it is time to heave to, a maneuver that varies in its execution with the type of vessel under consideration. Motor vessels, both single and twin screw, will usually be most comfortable if brought around head to sea, using just enough power to maintain bare steerageway, without making any considerable progress through the water. In fact, the vessel is likely to be making leeway, even though kept bow on to the sea. Sailing craft, heaving to, shorten sail and trim it so that the vessel alternately comes up to the wind and falls off, but not enough to get into the trough of the sea. Large steamers often heave to as a small motor vessel might, turning over their engines enough to maintain steerageway only, head to sea. This is not invariably the case, however, with large steamers.

The object always is to lay the vessel in such a position that she will take the seas most comfortably. That might mean allowing her to drift naturally, perhaps with the sea on the quarter, and sometimes using oil to create a slick on the surface which prevents waves from breaking. Some ships even lie in the trough when hove to, showing how much the practice varies with the size and type of vessel under consideration.

How Large Vessels Use Oil

THE use of oil in rough water has already been discussed in connection with the handling of lifeboats and small craft in heavy weather. Large vessels also use oil at times. It is interesting to note that only two gallons per hour is regarded as sufficient.

Vessels lying to a sea anchor use oil by bending the oil bags to the sea anchor or its cable. If scudding before a gale, the oil bags can be hung over the bow, or if lying to in a heavy cross sea the oil can be spread from bags hung over both sides. The general principle involved is to get the oil slick to spread to windward if possible and around the vessel in such a way that she stays in the slick. If the oil goes off to leeward or astern it is of no use.

Sea anchors can be used only if there is sufficient sea room as there is naturally a steady drift to leeward. When a vessel is driven down onto a lee shore and is forced to use her regular ground tackle to ride out a gale, it is imperative that a constant watch be maintained to guard against dragging. Merely having a heavy anchor down doesn't guarantee her safety. If ranges are taken as landmarks ashore dragging can be detected. Engines may have to be used to ease the strain on the anchor during the worst of the blow and a long scope of cable will give the anchor its best chance to hold.

The cruiser below is running in a ground swell offshore, taking the seas abeam. If, on this particular heading, she rolled too heavily, a slight change of course would probably reduce the rolling. Every boat has what is called a period of oscillation.

Other Fine Points in Motor Boat Seamanship

M. Rosenfeld

HANDLING MOTOR BOATS ALONGSIDE VESSELS; RENDERING ASSISTANCE TO VESSELS IN DISTRESS; USE OF BOAT AND BREAST LINES; TOWING

•

This Coast Guard cutter has maneuvered into position to put a line aboard a vessel to take her in tow. Two seamen are using shoulder guns to shoot a light line across to the other craft

IN peace time, little emphasis is likely to be placed on the technique of handling motor boats alongside large vessels—probably for the reason that the situation seldom presents itself. In the Navy, Coast Guard and Merchant Marine it's different, where the bringing of motor-driven launches, lifeboats, and landing boats of all kinds alongside gangways is part of the regular routine. Often these small "boats" are as big as our pleasure cruisers and the manner of their handling would be similar, if not identical. A parallel, though not exact, could also be drawn in the handling of motor dinghies alongside yachts.

From the standpoint of boat handling, the principal differences lie in the fact that in the service the coxswain of a boat may be dealing with a heavily built craft loaded with men or cargo. The reactions of his heavily loaded boat to helm and power are necessarily different. He cannot depend on manpower to hold or fend off a heavy boat in a seaway as a yachtsman might hold a dinghy with a boathook. Skillful seamanship is brought into play so that mechanical power and appliances do a neat job with little effort where the untrained man might make a lubberly landing.

Just because boats used aboard large vessels are often more stoutly built than pleasure craft is no excuse for giving them unnecessarily rough treatment. Neither can the yachtsman's comparatively frail dinghy be expected to do some of the things that are entirely feasible when boats are built to stand a lot of hard punishment. But underlying both problems are certain broad principles which apply generally to all cases. The good seaman will vary his technique by sizing up the prevailing conditions at the time and be governed by the qualities and characteristics of the boat he is handling. It might be definitely *unseamanlike* to handle a 16-foot dinghy like a steel invasion barge.

To get down to cases, let's consider a situation in which a 30- or 40-foot motor-driven boat is to be brought alongside the gangway of a ship. We will assume it is on the starboard side and that the ship is at anchor, heading into the current. The problem is somewhat the same as when a boat is to be landed at a dock or float, port side to the dock.

Remember that the propeller (if right-handed, as it is likely to be), when reversed to check the boat's headway, will have a tendency to throw the stern to port. For this reason we approach, not exactly parallel to the outboard side of the gangway, but at a slight angle, toward the ship's bow.

If our original course had been downstream with the current, it would have been necessary to swing in a wide arc to make the approach at the desired angle, speed reduced so as not to have our own wake rolling in to complicate matters just as we come alongside.

The approach would be the same if the ship were making headway, as the boat would have to be brought alongside in the direction the ship is heading. If the ship were making sternway, it would be best not to come alongside at all, unless there were no alternative. Then the boat would have to approach from the opposite direction, heading in the direction toward which the ship is making sternway. Water churning along the vessel's side, thrown by her backing propeller, might make the maneuver difficult, if not impractical, so the further (toward the ship's bow) the boat can keep away from this disturbance, the better, in such a case.

However, to get back to the original illustration, we are approaching the gangway, speed reduced to a point where the boat is under perfect control—and not too much dependence placed on the reverse gear. While rare, there is always a possibility of failure somewhere between the throwing of a lever for the back-up and the desired response from the propeller.

If we had come barging in at cruising speed, depending on a spectacular four-wheel-brake stop, engine churning hard in reverse, the probability of failure would be proportionately increased, due to the strain imposed on the reverse gear. Actually just good steerageway only is needed, to offset the current or sea against which the boat is heading.

When the boat has reached a point where the reduced headway is just sufficient to carry her by her own momentum to the gangway, we go into neutral and ease up alongside using the rudder to bring the boat within reach of the gangway, but clear of it by a foot or two to avoid possible damage by contact if the boat rolls or pitches. Then the reverse can be used to check any slight excess of headway.

Men at bow and stern should be posted to fend off with boathooks but, especially with heavily loaded boats, they should not be expected to hold the boat in position by this means alone. A heavy boat drifting naturally astern without power would simply drag them overboard.

The heavier the boat the more momentum she will carry when taken out of gear; a light boat will lose her way quicker. This element enters into a determination of just when to take the engine out of gear on the approach.

If there is to be any error in judgment, it had better be on the side of falling short, in which case an extra kick or two ahead with the propeller brings her up. The risk of overshooting the mark is this: if the outboard bow happens to be caught by wind or current, it will set the bow to port toward the ship's side and then the boat will be set obliquely down on or under the gangway. This could be very serious in a seaway and plenty of damage might be done; the boat would be out of control and manpower alone probably would not be sufficient to fend her off. The stronger the current or the heavier the wind and sea, the larger will this factor loom.

At the risk of repetition, we emphasize again the importance of having the boat under complete control at all times, the control being provided by the rudder and propeller and not by manpower. A seaman will handle his boat at all times—not only in a maneuver like this—in

such a way that failure of any part of his equipment, whether it be a stalled engine, failure of his reverse or steering gear, or any other unforeseen contingency, will not leave him in a precarious situation.

When opportunity presents, experience should be gained through practice in this type of maneuver, first in smooth water in moderate current. Then when the emergency arises requiring allowance for added factors like a confused sea or cross wind, the coxswain will have more confidence in his ability to cope with the situation.

Under extreme conditions a vessel might lighten the task of the small boat by providing a lee. This could be done by casting the ship's bow to starboard with the rudder or, if steaming slowly, by holding a course that will allow the boat to work under the vessel's lee. Oil from the steamer's bow might help in cases. If the boat is rising and falling in heavy swells, it is imperative that she be kept clear.

M. Rosenfeld

The cutter here is lowering a boat to be sent over to the schooner. Note the knotted life lines hanging down into the boat from the span between davits, giving crew something to hang on to

Using a Boat Line

Whenever a sea is running or the current is strong, a bow line should be passed to the ship to aid in handling the boat. A boat line, so called, is a long bow line rigged in a special way and used much the same as a sea painter.

If the boat is to lie alongside the gangway for a period of time, some effective means of holding her in position must be devised, without making fast to the gangway. To accomplish this, a boat line is led from a substantial cleat or bitt, not on or near the stem head, but out on the port bow (starboard bow, in case the boat is lying to the ship's port side), to a point well forward on the ship.

A short line or a line from the boat's stem head will not produce the desired result. A long boat line back from the stem and off the boat's centerline permits the current to catch the boat on that side and sheer her away from the ship. With the boat line on the port bow, the rudder is set to starboard and the boat stands away from the ship clear of the gangway, at any desired distance.

To study a similar type of action and understand the principle, try towing a dinghy some time at slow speed with the painter made fast, not to the stem, but to a ring on the port bow. She tends to sheer off to starboard of the boat's wake and could be held there with rudder set to starboard.

When the boat line has been rigged, a man at the tiller can set the boat in toward the gangway or away from it, merely by changing the rudder angle. The engine ordinarily will not be needed at all because the action of the current on the rudder blade gives the necessary control. In fact, the engine should be used only against a heavy sea or strong tideway, and then only with a great deal of care, as the power applied must not be enough to allow the boat to gather any headway.

A very fine degree of control can be exercised with a boat line. The line, not manpower or engine power, does the holding against wind and current, and the rudder holds her off just the right distance. A coxswain might hold his boat well off for some time and then ease in with a slight change in rudder angle just long enough to allow a person to step aboard, then sheer off again—the boat never actually coming in contact with the gangway.

One who understands this principle can easily rig sea painters and boat lines and use the general idea in dozens of ways in handling boats.

The Breast Line

A breast line can be used in conjunction with the boat line to good advantage. Properly rigged, the boat can be left unattended.

From the same cleat on the inboard bow (the ship side), or another cleat near it, a second line is rigged in a thwartship direction as a breast line to control the distance the boat will stand away from the gangway. With half rudder the boat tends to sheer well off; the breast line can then be trimmed so that the boat's position is limited at a certain distance. Then the boat will hold that position, setting obliquely to the current as the current pushes the stern in toward the ship.

Note that this result has been achieved with only two lines, and no stern line. Experiment some time when conditions of wind, sea and current are right, in laying a boat alongside a dock this way so that she stands clear, instead of pounding against the dock. Of course it's necessary to watch for any shift of wind or change in current direction as either might alter the whole set-up. One thing that stands in the way of a more general application of this principle is the fact that comparatively few cruisers have bitts, cleats or rings placed right for the boat line. They have to be substantially fastened, particularly if they are to be used in a heavy seaway. Many utility boats could be so rigged to advantage.

John Madigan

A breeches buoy is used to remove the crew of a vessel grounded along the coast. Here a Coast Guardsman aims the line-throwing gun so that the projectile and shot line will fall across the vessel's deck

Rendering Assistance to Vessels

It is an unwritten law of the sea that one should never pass up an opportunity to render assistance to any vessel in need of aid. Of course this is one of the primary functions of the Coast Guard, but there are plenty of occasions when a little timely help on the part of a fellow boatman may save hours of labor later after the tide has fallen or wind and sea have had a chance to make up.

As often as not, assistance is likely to take the form of a tow line passed to another to get him out of a position of temporary embarrassment or perhaps to get him to a Coast Guard station or back to port in case of failure of any of his gear.

While the actual occurrences are not frequent, the possible combinations of conditions are so varied that they could not be enumerated. For the sake of illustration,

Breeches buoy drill, in which the "wreck pole" on the beach in the background is used for practice instead of a grounded vessel. A hawser is sent out to the wreck after the shot line and on this hawser the breeches buoy (below) travels, one person at a time being hauled ashore by means of an endless whip line

however, consider a case where a boat has gone aground on a sand bar. The bar we'll assume is exposed to a long sweep of wind which, together with the current, is tending to drive her harder aground. A rising wind is building up a heavier sea which pounds against her hull and unless she is hauled off promptly she may be left in an uncomfortable spot over the succeeding tide.

The average motor boat draws considerably more water aft than she does forward and, unless the bar is steep where the boat has struck, she is likely to have hit first with the aft end of the keel while the bow is driven around part way at least, further up on the bar—in a position, perhaps, almost as though she had hit head on or nearly so.

Unless the motor boatman has confidence in his ability to render effective assistance and not pile up alongside the other fellow, he had better hunt up the nearest Coast Guard crew or some other pleasure craft equal to the job. However, the task is easy now if she is gotten off without delay.

The grounded boat is in effect on a lee shore, a bad place for another vessel to be working. In all her maneuvering she must consider the possibility of getting out of control herself, and avoid it at all costs. Loss of control might be due to engine failure or to being caught too close to shoal water broadside to the sea, unable to swing out into deeper water, or to loss of maneuvering power when the tow line is made fast.

Probably the most effective way to proceed in a situation of this kind would be to determine, from the relative direction of wind and current, how an anchored boat would lie and then drop an anchor well off in deep water using a long scope of line. If you can get close enough to the stranded vessel to heave a line, you will probably want your boat to lie dead to windward. If the current sets at some angle to the wind and you cannot reach her with a heaving line, you may be able to anchor so that a light line can be floated down with the current, buoyed by a life preserver. After a light line has been sent over, the heavier tow line can be bent on and hauled across. Use a long husky line for the towing and, if it is new, see that there are no kinks in it when the strain is put upon the line.

If neither heaving nor floating the line down is feasible, a man may be dropped back in a dinghy on a long painter, using the oars to guide the boat rather than to provide all the pulling power.

With a long scope of anchor line the boat can be worked to port or starboard as necessary to guide a floated line down into position to reach the stranded boat. This probably can be done with the rudder, setting it to port or starboard as necessary, perhaps using the engine power judiciously to carry the boat further than she normally would "tack" at anchor.

When the tow line has been sent across by any of these methods, it is made fast to the after bitt or cleat on the towing boat and to the bow or stern of the stranded boat, depending on conditions. Sometimes, when the tide has fallen, leaving the boat partly out of water, a line is passed completely around her, so that the strain is transferred to the hull instead of a bitt or cleat, which might be torn out of the deck. If her keel is fast for its full length on a shelving bar, it may be necessary to tow her off stern first. If wind and current permit and the bow is free to swing, it may be better to make the tow line fast to the bow of the stranded boat. These conditions and the exact positions of the boats will determine which is feasible.

With the tow line fast, the towing boat goes ahead easily with her engine, taking slack out of the line, while the anchor line is tended by a man forward. If it is necessary to open up the throttle to get power enough to start her, be alert to close it once the boat has been freed, for the reason that the anchor is still down. Note that in all this maneuvering the anchor line has held the bow up into wind and sea in the right position for towing and has enabled the boat safely to drop back into relatively shoal water without getting fast herself.

Even with the most skillful handling, without the anchor to windward, the towing boat would be in a bad way if her rudder failed to hold her up to wind and sea, the stern being bound by the tow line while the bow fell off with wind and current.

The anchor can be gotten back aboard as the towing boat comes slowly up to it. By this time the stranded boat will be well clear of the bar. When there is plenty of sea room to maneuver, the tow line can be transferred from stern to bow on the towed boat, if she has been hauled off stern first.

Through all of this maneuvering, it is imperative to see that all lines are kept clear so as not to foul the propeller and that no sudden surge is put on a slack line.

Maneuvering to Take a Vessel in Tow

SOMEWHERE in the course of your boating experience you are likely to run up against a situation where you wish to take another vessel in tow. In good weather with no sea running the problem is comparatively easy, involving little more than the maneuvering of your boat into position in line with, and ahead of, the other boat and the passing of a tow line.

There are, however, some fine points of seamanship to be taken into consideration if you are faced with a similar problem in heavy weather. In the first place, the disabled craft is likely to be lying with the wind abaft the beam, a position she would probably assume if left to her own devices with no control from engine and rudder. Visualize a practical situation: a vessel lying on a general northerly heading with wind and sea sweeping in on her port quarter, from the southwesterly quadrant.

Approaching from astern (that is, on a northerly heading) you will place your boat on a heading parallel to that of the other vessel. Before ranging ahead to get into position for towing you must determine on what side you will work. All other factors being equal, you will normally choose the starboard side, thus working up under the starboard bow (assuming that your boat has a right-handed propeller, as it probably does.)

The reason for choosing the starboard side is this: with your own boat under the other's starboard bow, if you back up to maneuver, your stern is thrown to port by the backing propeller. If you get too close you can easily kick ahead and get clear. If you are under her port bow you might put yourself in a position where you cannot maneuver in either direction, as your stern is thrown to port away from the ship and your own starboard side is drawn up toward her port bow.

Despite this general consideration, the situation must be studied broadly to size up the relative rate of drift of the two vessels during the time you are engaged in passing the tow line. If

the distressed vessel is deep in the water due to flooding, she .s likely to drift slower than the rescuing vessel which is lighter and more buoyant and thus more exposed to the wind. Otherwise because of height of superstructure, draft, etc., the disabled vessel may very well drift faster than the one coming to her assistance.

While coming up from astern you can probably determine the relative drift. Then if you are drifting faster than the other vessel, go to windward of her. If you are drifting slower than the other vessel go to leeward of her. In either case the boats will gradually draw closer together as you work, so that you will not be blown too far apart. If the boats get too close, you have the maneuvering power to get clear when necessary.

Furthermore, if the maneuver is handled in this manner, then as you draw ahead of the other vessel you will be setting naturally up into a position dead ahead of the other craft, in the right position for towing instead of being set off at an angle broad on her bow. In any case be sure to allow yourself sufficient maneuvering space and don't be caught in a spot where you cannot get clear.

Getting a Line Aboard

UNDER most ordinary circumstances, in good weather, or in cases where both boats are relatively small, it is feasible to heave a light line across to the disabled craft. A light line with a "monkey's fist" in the end can be sent a considerable distance if the line is held so that it uncoils naturally like a spring and doesn't foul up in a snarled tangle in midair. If you can be to windward when the heave is made, so much the better.

With larger craft, especially in the open sea in bad weather, when it may be dangerous to stand in too close, a line-throwing gun fired from the shoulder is a handy device. This is used by the Coast Guard and one of the accompanying illustrations shows the gun in use. A light line is carried by a projectile which can be aimed with considerable accuracy so as to fall across the other vessel's deck. Sometimes a line can be gotten over by buoying it and floating it across.

Regardless of the method used, it is usually handiest to send a light line across first and then bend the heavier towing hawser to it. Under certain circumstances a small boat is used to carry the line over, but the difficulty here is that if the weather is fine you can safely maneuver the big boat close and therefore don't need the small boat; if the weather is bad then the difficulties of handling the small boat make this method equally impractical.

If it is decided that it would be of value to create a slick between drifting vessels in which a boat can work, then the oil is spread by the leeward vessel, on the theory that the boats will drift faster than the oil slick and the windward vessel will drift down into it.

When a small boat is used to run a line, most of the coil should be carried in the boat and paid out over the stern as necessary. Trying to make a line fast to the boat and pulling away as the line is paid out from the larger boat, with a big bight of line dragging in the water, is almost always impractical. If the shoulder gun is used, work up to windward if possible.

Whatever tactics are employed to get the towing line or hawser ready, try to maneuver in such a way that, by the time the tow line is ready on both boats, your own craft will be nearly in correct position to start towing instead of somewhere off abeam or elsewhere, with a long bight of heavy line in the water to straighten out.

Generally speaking, it is best for the towing boat to pass her tow line to the other craft. In the case of small boats that may have a painter shackled to the bow this is very important as the line cannot be cast off quickly at the shackle in an emergency. In any case someone should tend the tow line and be ready to cut with knife or hatchet if necessary.

Towing

TOW LINES should never be made fast in any manner that would prevent their being cast off or cut on an instant's notice. On large craft this is sometimes accomplished by having a shackle somewhere in the tow line near the stern attached with a pelican hook or slip hook. This type of hook is hinged in such a manner that a link holds it in the closed position. In an emergency the link could be knocked off and the hook would upset, releasing the tow line at the shackle.

When the tow line has been secured, go ahead slowly to take up the slack, never with a sudden surge. If the size of the boat permits, a man can stand aft and pay line out gradually, though keeping

Handling a heavy towing hawser aboard a Coast Guard cutter

a strain on it at all times so that the load is taken up easily.

The general theory in towing is to make the tow line fast on the towing boat, not near the stern but at some point further forward, ahead of the rudder. In a practical way there may be no alternative. The only bitt or cleat substantial enough to tow from may be one on the aft deck. If this is the case it will be noted that, with a heavy tow, the response of the boat to its rudder will be sluggish as the stern has to drag the tow with it when moving to port or starboard.

On this theory a tug which does a lot of towing and which must be highly maneuverable has her towing bitt well forward of the stern so that the stern is free to swing in response to rudder action around the towing bitt as a pivot. This is a rather crude way to express it, but it illustrates the principle. As the stern swings, the tow line sweeps across it from quarter to quarter and no deck fixtures are put in the way to foul the hawser.

If there is a chock in the stern amidships and this is used as a lead for the towline, expect the maneuvering action to be sluggish just as though the line were made fast to a bitt at that point. If the line tends to chafe at the chock, it may be parcelled (wrapped) with canvas to take the chafing and protect the line.

Aboard larger vessels, a length of chain is sometimes shackled to the wire rope or manila hawser, the chain passing through the chock with the shackle outboard. This not only takes the chafe but helps in case the tow sheers far off on the tow boat's quarter, as the abrupt bend under heavy strain would be bad for wire or manila, whereas the chain can take it. Chafing gear for chain can be made by wrapping sheet copper ($\frac{1}{8}$ to $\frac{1}{4}$-inch thick) around the chain in the form of a sleeve.

Easing the Strain on Towlines

MANILA makes a good tow line because of the spring in it, or stretch. Anything that tends to produce such a spring to ease heavy shocks when towing in heavy weather is helpful. It is on this principle that long heavy tow lines are used for easy towing. The sag in the tow line is desirable and can be increased if necessary by bending a kedge anchor to the middle of the line. This will relieve excessive strains on the towing hawser. In rough weather a long tow line should be used, even if the tow is light.

One exception to the general rule of towing at the end of a long line in bad weather is a case where a small boat is towing astern of a larger vessel. Here it may be wise to reverse the procedure by using a relatively short line to keep her close up under the larger vessel's counter. In this way she can be trimmed with bow out of water and will have the benefit of comparatively smooth going in the vessel's wake as the craft ahead smoothes out heavy seas before her.

When towing, boats should be kept "in step", as it were, by adjusting the length of tow line so that the boat and her tow are both on the crest or in the trough of seas at the same time. Under certain conditions, with a confused sea, this may be largely a theoretical consideration, but the general principle is to prevent, if possible, a situation where the tow is shouldering up against the back of one sea, presenting a maximum of resistance while the towing boat is trying to run down the forward slope of another sea. Then when this condition is reversed, the tow alternately runs ahead and surges back on the tow line with a heavy strain. If there is any degree of uniformity to the waves, the strain on the hawser will be minimized by adjusting it to the proper length.

Boats in Tandem

WHEN several boats are to be taken in tow in a string, unless they are all light and the water is smooth, it's bad practice to tow by separate lines from bow to stern of each of the boats in the string (as barges might be towed in tandem). This imposes too heavy a strain on the bow and stern of boats near the head of the string. To get around this, run a substantial tow line, heavy enough to take the strain of towing all boats, back to the bow of the last boat in the string. Intermediate boats can then make fast to the main tow line with slip lines as necessary.

For maximum towing power, whenever the trim of the towing boat can be materially altered by shifting weights, it is well to keep the stern well down by moving heavy weights aft. The propeller, deep in the water, will get a better grip. Too near the surface it will tend to cavitate and send a frothy wake astern without accomplishing any real work, especially if the tow is heavy.

A small boat in tow should preferably be trimmed a little by the stern because trimming by the head causes her to yaw. In a seaway the condition is aggravated and it becomes increasingly important to keep the bow relatively light.

In smooth water motor boats may at times borrow an idea from tugs which often, in harbor or sheltered waters, take their tow alongside for better maneuverability. If the tow is a big one the tug will make fast on the quarter.

173

How the Coast Guard Aids Stranded Vessels

(From the U. S. Coast Pilot)

COAST GUARD (lifesaving) stations and houses of refuge are located upon the Atlantic and Pacific seaboards of the United States, the Gulf of Mexico, and the Lake coasts.

The stations are manned throughout the year by crews of experienced surfmen.

All lifesaving stations, except inactive stations, are fully supplied with boats, wreck guns, beach apparatus, and restoratives.

The lifesaving stations are provided with the International Code of Signals, and other means of visual signaling, and vessels can, by opening communications, be reported; or obtain the latitude or longitude of the station, where determined; or information as to the weather probabilities in most cases; or, where facilities for the transmission of messages by telephone or telegraph are available, request for a tug or Coast Guard cutter will be received and promptly forwarded.

The station crews patrol the beach from two to four miles each side of their stations between sunset and sunrise, and if the weather is foggy the patrol is continued through the day. A continuous lookout is also maintained at every station night and day.

Each patrolman carries warning signals. Upon discovering a vessel standing into danger he ignites one of these, which emits a brilliant red flame of about 2 minutes' duration, to warn her off, or, should the vessel be ashore, to let her crew know that they are discovered and assistance is at hand.

If the vessel is not discovered by the patrol immediately after striking, rockets, flare-up lights, or other recognized signals of distress should be used. If the weather be foggy, some recognized sound signal should be made to attract attention, as the patrolman may be some distance away at the other end of his beat.

Masters are particularly cautioned, if they should be driven ashore anywhere in the neighborhood of the stations, to remain on board until assistance arrives and under no circumstances should they attempt to land through the surf in their own boats until the last hope of assistance from the shore has vanished. Often when comparatively smooth at sea a dangerous surf is running which is not perceptible 400 yards offshore, and the surf when viewed from a vessel never appears as dangerous as it is. Many lives have been lost unnecessarily by the crews of stranded vessels being thus deceived and attempting to land in the ship's boats.

The difficulties of rescue by operations from the shore are greatly increased in cases where the anchors are let go *after entering the breakers,* as is frequently done, and the chances of saving life correspondingly lessened.

Rescue with the Lifeboat or Surfboat

THE patrolman after discovering your vessel ashore and burning a warning signal, hastens to his station or the telephone for assistance. If the use of a boat is practicable, either the large lifeboat is launched from its ways in the station and proceeds to the wreck by water, or the lighter surfboat is hauled overland to a point opposite the wreck and launched, as circumstances may require.

Upon the boat reaching your vessel the directions and orders of the officer in charge (who always commands and steers the boat) should be implicitly obeyed. Any headlong rushing and crowding should be prevented, and the captain of the vessel should remain on board, to preserve order, until every other person has left.

Women, children, helpless persons, and passengers should be passed into the boat first.

Goods or baggage will positively not be taken into the boat until all are landed. If any be passed in against the remonstrance of the officer in charge, he is fully authorized to throw the same overboard.

Rescue with the Breeches Buoy or Life Car

SHOULD it be inexpedient to use either the lifeboat or surfboat, recourse will be had to the wreck gun and beach apparatus for rescue by the breeches buoy or the life car.

A shot with a small line attached will be fired across your vessel. Get hold of the line as soon as possible and haul on board until you get a tailblock with a whip or endless line rove through it. The tailblock should be hauled on board as quickly as possible to prevent the whip drifting off with the set or fouling with wreckage, etc. Therefore if you have been driven into the rigging, where but one or two men can work to advantage, cut the shot line, and run it

through some available block, such as the throat or peak halyards block, or any block which will afford a clear lead, or even between the ratlines, that as many as possible may assist in hauling.

Attached to the tailblock will be a tally board with the following directions in English on one side and French on the other:

"Make the tail of the block fast to the lower mast, well up. If the masts are gone, then to the best place you can find. *Cast off shot line, see that the rope in the block runs free,* and show signal to the shore."

As soon as your signal is seen, a 3-inch hawser will be bent onto the whip and hauled off to your ship by the lifesaving crew.

If circumstances permit, you can assist the lifesaving crew by manning that part of the whip to which the hawser is bent and hauling with them.

Making the Hawser Fast

WHEN the end of the hawser is got on board, a tally board will be found attached, bearing the following directions in English on one side and French on the other:

"Make this hawser fast about 2 feet above the tailblock, see all clear and that the rope in the block runs free and show signal to the shore."

Take particular care that there are no turns of the whip line around the hawser. To prevent this, take the end of the hawser up between the parts of the whip before making it fast.

When the hawser is made fast, the whip cast off from the hawser, and your signal seen by the lifesaving crew, they will haul the hawser taut and by means of the whip will haul off to your vessel a breeches buoy suspended from a traveler block, or a life car, from rings running on the hawser.

If the breeches buoy be sent, let one man immediately get into it, thrusting his legs through the breeches. If the life car, remove the hatch, place as many persons therein as it will hold (four to six) and secure the hatch on the outside by the hatch bar and hook, signal as before, and the buoy or car will be hauled ashore. This will be repeated until all are landed. On the last trip of the life car the hatch must be secured by the inside hatch bar.

Signals from the Wreck

IN signaling as directed in the foregoing instructions, if in the daytime, let one man separate himself from the rest and swing his hat, a handkerchief, or his hand; if at night, the showing of a light and concealing it once or twice will be understood; and like signals will be made from shore. (See also Wreck Signals, p. 177.)

Circumstances may arise, owing to the strength of the current or set, or the danger of the wreck breaking up immediately, when it would be impossible to send off the hawser. In such a case a breeches buoy or life car will be hauled off instead by the whip or sent off to you by the shot line, and you will be hauled ashore through the surf. If your vessel is stranded during the night and discovered by the patrolman—which you will know by his burning a brilliant red light—keep a sharp lookout for signs of the arrival of the lifesaving crew abreast of your vessel.

Some time may intervene between the burning of the light and their arrival, as the patrolman may have to return to his station, perhaps 3 or 4 miles distant, and the lifesaving crew draw the apparatus or surfboat through the sand or over bad roads to where your vessel is stranded.

Lights on the beach will indicate their arrival, and the sound of cannon firing from the shore may be taken as evidence that a line has been fired across your vessel. Therefore, upon hearing the cannon, make strict search aloft, fore, and aft for the shot line, for it is almost certain to be there. Though the movement of the lifesaving crew may not be perceptible to you, owing to the darkness, your vessel will be a good mark for the men experienced in the use of the wreck gun, and the first shot seldom fails.

Remain by the wreck until assistance arrives from the shore, or as long as possible. If driven aloft, the inshore mast s the safest.

If not discovered immediately by the patrol, burn rockets, flare-up, or other lights, or if the weather be foggy, fire guns or make other sound signals.

Make the shot line fast on deck or to the rigging to prevent its being washed into the sea and possibly fouling the gear.

Take particular care that there are no turns of the whip line around the hawser before making the hawser fast.

Send the women, children, helpless persons, and passengers ashore first.

Stranding, Assisting
And Towing

As applied to the small boat

IF you do a normal amount of boating, and poke your bow into a normal number of strange places, the chances are that someday you may go aground. It is equally possible that some day a balky motor may force you to ask a tow from a passing boat, or you may be on the passing boat from which a tow is requested.

In either case, you should know what to do, and why.

Simple stranding is more often an inconvenience than a danger and, with a little 'know how' and some fast work, the period of stranding may be but a matter of minutes.

If it should happen in that before-mentioned strange harbor, the very fact that it is strange presupposes that you have been feeling your way along and so, probably, have just touched bottom lightly, in which case you should be off again with a minimum of difficulty, *provided* that your immediate actions do not all tend to put you hard aground.

One's first instinctive act on going aground is to throw his engines into reverse and gun them to the limit in an effort to pull off, which may be the one thing that you should *not* do.

If in tidal waters, the first thing to consider is, of course, the stage of the tide.

If the tide is making, and the sea quiet enough so that the hull is not pounding, time is working for you, and whatever you do to assist yourself and the boat will be much more effective after a little time has passed. If, on the other hand, you grounded on a falling tide you will have to work quickly and do exactly the right things or you will be fast for several hours.

About the only thing you know offhand is the shape of the hull, its point of greatest draft, and consequently the part most apt to be touching, but bottom contours may be such that the premise will be true. However, if the hull shows any tendency to swing, due to the action of wind or waves, the point about which it pivots is most apt to be the part grounded.

The type of bottom requires immediate consideration. If it is sandy, and you reverse hard, you will be apt to wash a quantity of sand from astern and throw it directly under the keel, with the obvious result of bedding the boat more firmly to the bottom. Always exercise discretion in reversing while aground due to the risk of pumping sand or mud into the engine. If the bottom is rocky and you insist on trying to reverse off, you may drag the hull and do more damage than with the original grounding. Too, if grounded forward, the

well known tendency of the stern to swing to port, when reversing with a right-hand wheel, may swing the hull broadside onto exposed pinnacles or to a greater contact with a soft bottom.

How to Use a Kedge

The one *right* thing to do immediately after grounding is to take out a kedge and get it set hard.

Unless the boat has really been driven on, the service anchor should be heavy enough. Put the anchor *and* the line in the dinghy, make the bitter end fast to the stern bitts or to something solid and row out as far as possible, letting the line run from the stern of the dinghy as it uncoils. Taken out this way, the oarsman's task will be much easier than if he tries to drag the line from the large boat through the water.

When setting out the kedge, consider again the sideways turning effect of a reversing single screw and, unless the boat has twin screws, set the kedge at a compensating angle from the stern. If the propeller is right hand (as with a standard marine motor) set the anchor slightly to starboard of the stern. This will give two desirable effects. When pulling together with kedge line and reverse the boat will have practically a straight pull on it, and when used alternately, first pulling on the line and then giving a short surge with the reverse, the action may give a sort of wiggling action to the stern and the keel, which will be a real help in starting the boat moving.

A Tackle Helps

If you can possibly find a couple of double-sheave pulleys and a length of suitable line on board, make up a handy-billy or fall and fasten it to the kedge line. Then you can really pull! Such a handy-billy should be a part of the boat's regular equipment, anyhow.

Whatever else you may do, during the entire period of grounding, persist in keeping that kedge-line as taut as the combined strength of those on board can make it. You may be agreeably surprised by having the boat yield suddenly to

Placing anchors (Fig. 1) to free a grounded boat, and (Fig. 2) how to make a tow line fast to allow for wind or current and improve maneuverability

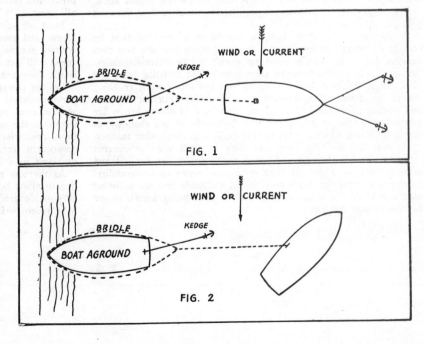

that continued pull, especially if a passing boat throws a wake to help lift the keel off the bottom.

If the bottom is sandy, that same pull, with the propeller going *ahead* may result in washing some sand *away* from under the keel, with the desired result. If the kedge line is kept taut you may try it with a clear mind. At least you will not do any harm.

Run your crew, if you have one, from side to side to roll the boat and make the keel work in the bottom. If you have spars, swing the booms outboard and put men on them to heave the boat down, thus raising the keel line. Shift ballast or heavy objects from over the portion grounded to lighten that section and if you have to, remove some internal weight by loading it into the dinghy or by taking it ashore if that is possible.

Take soundings all around the position where the boat lies.

It is possible that a swing of the stern to port or starboard may do more for you than any amount of straight backward pulling, and the soundings will reveal any additional depth that may exist on either side to help you out.

Two kedges set out at an acute angle from either side of the stern and pulled upon alternately may give that desired stern wiggle that will help you to work clear.

All of the above is written with the assumption that the boat is grounded, but not holed or strained open. If either of these last has happened, you may be far better off where she lies than you would be if she were in deep water again. If she is badly stove, you may want to take an anchor ashore, to hold her or to pull her further in until temporary repairs can be made. Perhaps, as the tide falls, the damaged portion may be exposed far enough to allow some outside patching; always presupposing that you had foresight enough to have something aboard to patch with! A piece of copper sheathing, some tacks and a can of pitch or roofing compound will do wonders in such a situation.

Even though the hull is unharmed, and you are finally left with a falling tide to sit it out for a few hours, you may as well be philosophical and get over the side and make good use of those hours. Undoubtedly you would prefer to do it under happier circumstances, but this may be your chance to get at that outside stuffing box, or get a good check on the condition of the bottom, or do any one of a number of little jobs that you could not do otherwise, short of a haulout.

If she is going to be left fairly high and dry, keep your eyes on her layover condition. If there is anything to get a line to, even another kedge, you can make her lay over on whichever side you choose, as she loses buoyancy. If she is deep and narrow she may need some assistance in standing up again, particularly if she lays over in soft mud. Both the suction of the mud and her own dead-weight will work against her in that case.

Assisting the Stranded Boat

PERHAPS, in spite of all you could do, she would not come off without assistance. Whether you are on board the stranded boat or the assisting one there are several things you should know.

It is of primary importance to see that the assisting boat does not join the other in its trouble!

It may seem easiest to bring a line in to a stranded boat by coming in under engine power, bow on, passing the line and then backing out again, but the maneuver should not be attempted unless one is sure that there is water enough under the assisting boat, and also, unless the boat backs well, without too much stern crabbing due to the action of the reversed screw. Wind and current direction will greatly affect the success of this maneuver. If all conditions are adverse and tend to swing the boat broadside to the shallows as she backs it will be best to try to pass the line in some other manner.

Perhaps the assisting boat may back in, with wind or current compensating for the reversed screw, thus keeping her straight and leaving the bow headed out with consequent better maneuverability. In any case, after the line is once passed and made fast, the assisting boat should do the actual pulling with engines going ahead, to get full power into the pull.

If conditions are such that a close approach is unwise, it will be far better for the second boat to drop anchor, or even two anchors, well off the stranded boat and then send the line over in a dinghy, or else buoy the line and attempt to float it in to the grounded boat. If wind or current or both are broadside to the direction of pull, the assisting boat would best stay anchored even while pulling, for as soon as she takes the strain, particularly if the line is fast to her stern, she will have lost her own maneuverability, and will gradually make leeway, which could eventually put her aground broadside. (See Fig. 1).

If the pulling must be done with the assisting boat under way, the line should be made fast well forward of the stern so that while hauling, she can angle into the wind and current and still hold her own position. (See Fig. 2).

Tremendous strains can be set up, particularly on the stranded boat, by this sort of action, even to the point of carrying away whatever the tow-line is made fast to. It is far better to run a bridle around the whole hull and pull against this bridle rather than to risk starting some part of the stern by such straining. The assisting boat should also be bridled if there is any doubt of her ability to withstand such concentrated strains.

Towing Techniques

AT last the stranded boat is free and ready to move off under her own power, or to be towed to her home mooring. From here on these remarks apply to any tow.

When approaching a boat, dead in the water, with the intention of passing a line, if there is any kind of sea running, do not be dramatic and try to run in too close. Just buoy a long line with several life preservers, tow it astern and take a turn about the stern of the disabled one, but don't foul their propeller in so doing. The occupants will be able to pick it up with a boathook from the cockpit with far less fuss than by any heave-and-catch method.

The forward bitts are usually rugged and so the towed one may make fast the line at that point; then, with someone at the wheel to assist by steering, there is little more to do other than to have an anchor ready to run if, for any reason, the tow-line is cast loose.

The tow boat, however, requires some real handling!

The worst possible place to make fast the tow-line is to the stern of the lead boat, since the pull of the tow prevents the stern from swinging properly in response to the rudder and thus interferes with the boat's maneuvering ability. The tow-line should be made fast as near amidships as possible, as in tug and tow boat practice. If no suitable place is provided, it is best to make a bridle from the forward bitts, running around the superstructure to a point in the forward part of the cockpit. Such a bridle will have to be wrapped with chafing gear wherever it bears on the superstructure or any corners, and even then, some chafing of the finish is almost bound to occur. The tow-line should be made fast so that it can be cast loose if necessary or, failing that, have a knife or hatchet ready to cut it. That line too, is a potential danger to anyone near if it should break and come whipping forward, so keep a wary eye upon it at all times.

Start off easy! Don't try to dig up the whole ocean with your screw, and merely end up with a lot of cavitation and vibration without getting anywhere in particular. A steady pull at a reasonable speed will get you there just as fast and with far less strain on boats, lines and crews.

Let out plenty of scope so that the line will make a long catenary curve to act as a spring, thus reducing sudden jerks. If there is any sea running, adjust the line so that both boats are climbing the slopes of the waves and sliding down the back-slopes at the same time, otherwise the line will be alternately taut and slack, with consequent terrific jolts that will either strain things unnecessarily or result in a broken line.

As the tow gets into protected, quiet waters, shorten up on the line to allow better handling in close quarters. Also swing as wide as possible around buoys, channel turns, etc., so that the tow will have room to follow.

CHAPTER IX

Fog Signals; Day Marks;
Signals for a Pilot;
Life-Saving and Distress Signals

(See Chapter IV, pages 61-77)

·A Coast Guardsman, signaling at night from the beach to a vessel in distress, indicates the best place to land by vertical motion of a white light or flare

International Life Saving Signals

Signals to be used by lifesaving stations when communicating with ships in distress and by ships in distress when communicating with lifesaving stations are as follows:

(1) Replies from shore station to distress signals made by a ship:

(a) *Signal:* By day: white smoke signal. By night: white star rocket. *Signification:* You are seen. Assistance will be given as soon as possible.

(2) Landing signals for the guidance of small boats bringing away the crew of a wrecked ship:

(a) *Signal:* By day: vertical motion of a white flag or the arms. By night: vertical motion of a white light or flare. A range (indication of direction) may be given by placing a steady white light or flare lower and in line with the observer. *Signification:* This is the best place to land.

(b) *Signal:* By day: horizontal motion of a white flag or arms extended horizontally. By night: horizontal motion of a white light or flare. *Signification:* Landing here highly dangerous.

(c) *Signal:* By day: horizontal motion of a white flag, followed by the placing of the white flag in the ground and carrying of another white flag in the direction to be indicated. By night: horizontal motion of a white light or flare, followed by the placing of the white light or flare on the ground and the carrying of another white light or flare in the direction to be indicated. *Signification:* Landing here highly dangerous. A more favorable location to land is in the direction indicated.

(3) Signals to be employed in connection with the use of shore lifesaving apparatus:

(a) *Signal:* By day: vertical motion of a white flag or the arms. By night: vertical motion of a white light or flare. *Signification:* In general "Affirmative." Specifically: "Rocket line is held." "Tail block is made fast." "Hawser is made fast." "Man is in the breeches buoy." "Haul away."

(b) *Signal:* By day: horizontal motion of a white flag or arms extended horizontally. By night: horizontal motion of a white light or flare. *Signification:* In general "Negative." Specifically: "Slack away." "Avast hauling."

Distress Signals—Inland Rules

BY DAY:—(1.) A continuous sounding with any fog signal apparatus, or firing a gun.

BY NIGHT:—(1.) Flames on the vessel, as from a burning tar or oil barrel, etc. (2.) Continuous sounding with any fog signal apparatus, or firing a gun.

Distress Signals—International Rules

(1) A gun or other explosive signal at intervals of about 1 minute.

(2) Continuous sounding of any fog signal apparatus.

(3) Rockets or shells, throwing red stars fired one at a time at short intervals.

(4) Signal by radiotelegraphy, or other method, consisting of the group ...———... in the Morse Code.

(5) Signal by radiotelephony consisting of spoken word "Mayday."

(6) The International Code signal NC.

(7) A signal consisting of a square flag and above or below it a ball, or something resembling a ball.

(8) Flames on the vessel (as from a burning oil or tar barrel).

(9) A rocket parachute flare showing a red light.

NOTE:—Radio signal (12 dashes sent in one minute—each dash 4 seconds, each interval 1 second) has been provided to actuate auto-alarms of other vessels.

Submarine Distress Signals

A submarine of the United States Navy which may be in need of assistance releases a red smoke bomb.

A submarine which may be compelled to surface in the vicinity of surface craft releases a yellow smoke bomb. Surface vessels should keep clear of the yellow smoke bombs.

A yellow marker buoy, telephone-equipped, may be released by a submarine in distress on the bottom.

Any person sighting a red smoke bomb rising from the surface of the water or a yellow distress marker buoy (about 3 feet in diameter) should report the time and location immediately to the nearest Naval authority or Coast Guard unit.

Aircraft Distress Signals

When an aircraft desires to call upon a surface craft to render assistance to survivors or planes in distress, the aircraft will: (1.) Circle the vessel at least once, (2.) Fly across the bow of the vessel at a low altitude, opening and closing the throttle, or changing propeller pitch, when possible, (3.) Head in the direction of the rescue scene. This is repeated until the vessel acknowledges by following. An Aldis lamp, radio or dropped message is used, if possible, to explain the situation.

The surface craft should follow the aircraft or indicate that it is unable to comply by hoisting the international flag NEGAT, or by other visual or radio means.

Radar Search

A wooden boat that may be the object of a search by Coast Guard patrol or rescue craft should hoist a large metallic object aloft to aid in detection by radar, which is effective by night and in periods of low visibility as well as by day. Metallic objects below decks are likely to be shielded by hull or bulwarks.

Manual Distress Signal

The Coast Guard has approved a manual type of distress signal now officially recognized under Inland, Great Lakes and Western River rules. With this method no special equipment is required.

To make it: (1) Start by raising arms outstretched at shoulder level. (2) Drop them *slowly* to the sides. (3) Repeat as often as necessary. A handkerchief, towel, shirt or rag in each hand will increase the range of visibility.

FOG SIGNALS

(See Figures 53–62)

(To be given, whether by day or night, in fog or thick weather, such as mist, falling snow, or heavy rain storms)

A COMPARISON OF INTERNATIONAL, INLAND, GREAT LAKES AND WESTERN RIVER RULES

NOTE: A prolonged blast means a blast of 4 to 6 seconds' duration.

	International Rules	Inland Rules	Great Lakes Rules	Western River Rules
How signals are given when *under way*	Steam vessels:—Whistle or siren Sailing vessels and Vessels towed:—Fog horn	Same as International	Steam vessel:—Whistle Sailing vessel (not in tow):—Fog horn (See special cases below)	Steam vessel:—Whistle or siren Sailing vessel:—Fog horn
Fog signal equipment required (For MOTOR BOATS, see special regulations below)	Power-driven vessels:—Whistle or siren, sounded by steam, or substitute for steam; fog horn (mechanical); bell Sailing vessels (20 gross tons or over):—Fog horn and bell	Same as International	Steam vessels:—Whistle, sounded by steam or substitute for steam, audible 2 miles; bell Sailing vessels:—Fog horn and bell	Steam vessels:—Whistle or siren Sailing vessels:—Fog horn (Sailing vessels over 20 gross tons also carry a bell)
Steam (power-driven) vessel under way (See Fig. 53)	1 prolonged blast at intervals of not more than 2 minutes	1 prolonged blast at intervals of not more than 1 minute	3 blasts at intervals of not more than 1 minute (except when towing raft)	3 blasts at intervals of not more than 1 minute (2 of equal length. last one longer)
Steam (power-driven) vessel under way but stopped and having no way on (See Fig. 55)	2 prolonged blasts (1 second between) at intervals of not more than 2 minutes	Not mentioned	Not mentioned	Not mentioned
Sailing vessels under way (See Figures 60, 61, 62)	Starboard tack, 1 blast Port tack, 2 blasts in succession Wind abaft the beam, 3 blasts in succession Intervals in each case not more than 1 minute	Same as International	If not in tow, same as International	Same as steam vessel, but uses fog horn
Vessels at anchor or not under way (See Figures 56, 58)	Ring bell rapidly for 5 seconds at intervals of not more than 1 minute* Vessel aground, in addition to anchor signal, gives 3 strokes on bell, before and after	Same as International	At anchor or aground, ring bell rapidly 3 to 5 seconds at 2-minute intervals. In addition, every 3 minutes, sound signal on whistle or horn—1 short, 2 long, 1 short blasts in quick succession.	Same as International
Vessels at anchor or not under way (over 350 ft.)	In addition to bell in forepart of vessel, sound gong in after part, at intervals of not more than 1 minute*	Not mentioned	Not mentioned	Not mentioned
Vessels towing or towed (See Figures 57, 59)	Vessels when towing, laying or picking up a submarine cable or navigation mark, or under way but not under command or unable to maneuver:— 1 prolonged blast (on whistle) followed by 2 short blasts, at intervals of not more than 1 minute Vessel towed gives 1 prolonged blast, followed by 3 short, on whistle or fog horn	1 prolonged blast (on whistle) followed by 2 short blasts, at intervals of not more than 1 minute. Vessel towed may give same signal (on fog horn)	Steamer towing raft:—Sounds at intervals of not more than 1 minute, a screeching or Modoc whistle for 3 to 5 seconds Vessel towed:—At intervals of 1 minute strikes bell four times (twice in quick succession, followed by a little longer interval, then twice in quick succession again)	Vessel towing sounds 3 distinct blasts of equal length at intervals of not more than 1 minute
Small craft or craft not otherwise provided for	Vessels of less than 20 tons, rowboats, and seaplanes on the water, if they do not give regular signals prescribed above, make some other efficient sound signal at intervals of not more than 1 minute (On small seagoing vessels, gong may be used instead of bell)	Rafts and other watercraft not provided for above navigating by hand power, horse power, or river current, sound 1 blast of fog horn or equivalent signal at intervals of not more than 1 minute	Vessels under 10 registered tons, if they do not give regular signals prescribed above, make some other efficient sound signal at intervals of not more than 1 minute. Produce boats, fishing boats, rafts, or other watercraft navigating by hand power or river current, or anchored or moored in or near channel or fairway, not in port, sound fog horn or equivalent signal at intervals of not more than 1 minute	Not mentioned
Drift net vessels attached to nets, and vessels engaged in trawling, dredging, dragging, or linefishing with lines out (over 20 gross tons) (See Figure 54)	1 blast at 1 minute intervals (whistle or siren if power-driven; fog horn if sail) each blast followed by ringing bell. May substitute blast of several notes of higher and lower pitch Under 20 tons, need not make this signal but, if they do not, must make some other efficient signal at 1 minute intervals	Not mentioned	Not mentioned	Not mentioned
Speed in fog or thick weather	Moderate speed, with regard to circumstances and conditions. Power-driven vessel hearing, forward of beam, fog signal of vessel, position of which is not ascertained, must stop and then navigate with caution until danger of collision is past	Same as International	Moderate speed. Steam vessel hearing, from direction not more than 4 points from right ahead, fog signal of another vessel, must reduce speed to bare steerageway, then navigate with caution until vessels have passed.	Moderate speed. Steam vessel hearing, forward of beam, fog signal of another vessel, must reduce speed to bare steerageway, then navigate with caution till vessels have passed

FOG SIGNAL EQUIPMENT FOR MOTOR BOATS

WHISTLE	Motor boats, under way, give their fog signals on the whistle, not on a fog horn. Boats of Class 1, 16'–26'; Class 2, 26'–40'; and Class 3, 40'–65' carry an "efficient" whistle or other sound-producing mechanical appliance. With respect to motor boats, a blast of at least 2 seconds is considered a prolonged blast. A mouth whistle capable of producing a 2-second blast that can be heard at least ½ mile, has been held to be in compliance with the law, on Class 1 only. However, an efficient electric or air horn is preferable, especially on boats with deckhouses. On Classes 2 and 3, whistle must be audible 1 mile. On Class 3, it must be power-operated; on Class 2, hand or power; on Class 1, hand, mouth or power.	BELL	Class 2 and Class 3 carry an efficient bell.
		FOG HORN	NOT required on MOTOR boats.
		EXEMPTIONS	OUTBOARD MOTOR BOATS competing in a race previously arranged and announced or tuning up for such a race are exempt from carrying the above equipment. All boats of Class A, under 16', are also exempt.

* International Rules now authorize, in addition to bell signals at anchor, a warning signal of three blasts (1 short, 1 prolonged, 1 short)

FOG SIGNALS

GIVEN, DAY OR NIGHT, IN FOG OR

THICK WEATHER, SUCH AS MIST,

FALLING SNOW, OR RAIN STORMS

Fig. 53
Right: In a fog, a steam or motor vessel (this includes motor boats) under way on inland waters sounds a prolonged blast (4 to 6 seconds) on the whistle at intervals of not more than 1 minute. On the high seas, under International Rules, the signal is also 1 prolonged blast, but at intervals of not more than 2 minutes. On the Great Lakes, she sounds 3 blasts in rapid succession every minute (except when towing a raft)

Fig. 54
Left: Under International Rules, fishing craft such as drift net vessels attached to nets, and vessels engaged in trolling, dredging, dragging or line-fishing with lines out (if over 20 gross tons) must sound 1 blast at 1 minute intervals, each blast followed by the ringing of a bell. Power-driven vessels use their whistle or siren for the blast; sailboats their fog horn. Optionally, they may sound a blast consisting of a series of alternate notes of higher and lower pitch. Fishing vessels under 20 tons may give some other efficient signal at 1 minute intervals. Inland Rules and Great Lakes Rules do not make special provisions for such craft

Fig. 55
Right: The International Rules (only) also provide for the power-driven vessel under way, but stopped and having no way on. She gives two prolonged blasts on the whistle at intervals of not more than 2 minutes (1 second between blasts). Such a signal is given when a vessel is navigating in a fog and headway is stopped so that the navigating officers can more readily listen for the fog signal on some aid to navigation. It is also used when two vessels approach each other, giving the usual fog signals for vessels under way, and have come so close that it is necessary for safety for one or both to stop headway. Two blasts then indicate headway has been stopped; 1 blast that she still has way on

Fig. 56
Left: Vessels at anchor or not under way (when in a fairway) ring a bell rapidly for 5 seconds at intervals of not more than 1 minute, under both Inland and International Rules. On the Great Lakes, they would ring the bell rapidly for 3 to 5 seconds at intervals of not more than 2 minutes, followed by four blasts in quick succession, every 3 minutes on whistle or horn—1 short, 2 long, 1 short. The same signal is prescribed for a vessel aground in or near a channel or fairway on the Great Lakes. On the high seas, a vessel over 350 feet in length at anchor or not under way, in addition to the bell which she sounds forward, strikes a gong aft at 1 minute intervals

Fig. 57

Left: On the high seas a vessel laying or picking up telegraph cable or a navigation mark, or a vessel which is under way but not under command or unable to maneuver, sounds 1 prolonged blast on the whistle followed by 2 short blasts. This signal is given at 1-minute intervals

Fig. 58

Right: Courts have held that, even though vessels aground and vessels at anchor are, under Inland Rules, in the same category as far as lights are concerned, it would be proper for a vessel aground in a fog to give a distress signal (continuous sounding of the whistle) as a fog signal to distinguish her from a vessel at anchor, which rings a bell at 1-minute intervals. (See Fig. 56.) A vessel aground, under International Rules, gives the signal for a vessel at anchor, and three strokes on the bell before and after it. Great Lakes rules prescribe that vessels aground *must* give the same signal as a vessel at anchor (ringing bell for 3 to 5 seconds at 2-minute intervals, followed by 1 short, 2 long, 1 short blasts in quick succession, every 3 minutes, on whistle or horn)

Fig. 59

Left: A vessel towing, on inland waters or the high seas, gives a prolonged blast on the whistle followed by 2 short blasts, at intervals of not more than 1 minute. Under Inland Rules, the vessel towed may give the same signal as the vessel which is towing, except on a fog horn. On the high seas, the vessel towed sounds 1 prolonged blast followed by 3 short blasts, on the whistle or fog horn. On the Great Lakes a vessel being towed strikes a bell 4 times (twice in quick succession, then twice in quick succession again) at 1 minute intervals. The vessel towing gives the usual Great Lakes signal for a vessel under way of 3 blasts on the whistle in rapid succession every minute, except that steamers towing a raft sound every minute a screeching or Modoc whistle for 3 to 5 seconds

Fig. 61

Below: A sailing vessel on the starboard tack sounds a fog signal of 1 blast on the fog horn at intervals of not more than 1 minute

Fig. 60

Below, right: A sailing vessel on the port tack sounds 2 blasts in succession on the fog horn every minute. Fog signals for sailboats are the same under Inland and International Rules, and on the Great Lakes also (unless being towed)

Fig. 62

Above: When the wind is abaft the beam the fog signal for a sailing vessel is 3 blasts on the fog horn in succession, at 1 minute intervals

BLACK

BLACK

Fig. 63 (Left)—A vessel not under control on the high seas shows a day mark consisting of two black balls vertically arranged placed in a position where they ccn best be seen. On other waters, the same day signal is displayed by self propelled suction dredges underway with their suctions on bottom.

BL. & WH.

RED

Fig. 64 (Left)— On waters other than the high seas, vessels which are moored or anchored and engaged in laying pipe or operating on submarine construction display in the day time two balls in a vertical line, the upper ball being painted with alternate black and white vertical stripes and the lower ball bright red.

BLACK

Fig. 65 (Left)— Vessels over 65 feet (on inland waters) anchored in a channel display one black ball. On the high seas, it is used by anchored vessels regardless of length.

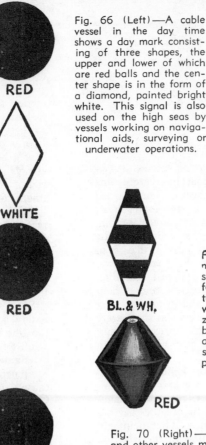

RED

WHITE

RED

Fig. 66 (Left)—A cable vessel in the day time shows a day mark consisting of three shapes, the upper and lower of which are red balls and the center shape is in the form of a diamond, painted bright white. This signal is also used on the high seas by vessels working on navigational aids, surveying or underwater operations.

RED

RED

Fig. 67 (Left)— Dredges held in a stationary position show two red balls in the day time, vertically arranged and placed in a position where they can best be seen.

BL. & WH.

RED

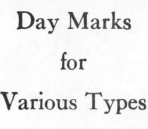

Day Marks
for
Various Types
of
Vessels

(See also pages 69 and 78)

Fig. 69 (Left)—A vessel towing a submerged object in the day time shows two shapes, one above the other, in the form of a double frustum of a cone base to base, the upper shape being painted with alternate horizontal stripes of black and white and the lower shape being painted bright red.

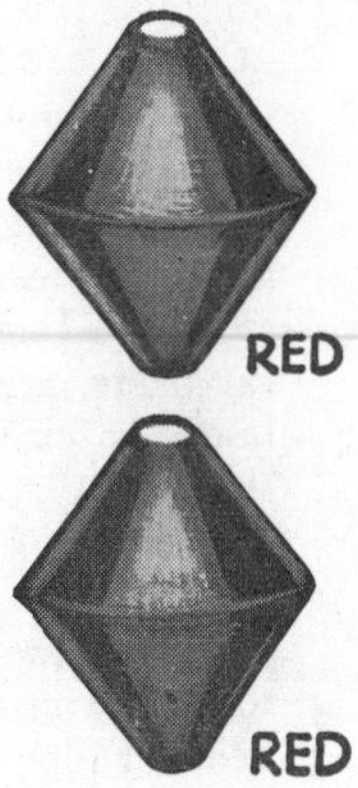

RED

RED

Fig. 70 (Right)—Steamers, lighters and other vessels made fast alongside a wreck or moored over a wreck, display two double frustums of a cone base to base, both of which are painted bright red.

Fig. 71—A fishing vessel in the day time may display a basket in the rigging.

Special Signals for Minesweepers

The maneuverability of a minesweeper is hampered by its sweeping operations. To indicate the nature of their work they display special signals, and all vessels are cautioned to keep out of their way.

By day, all vessels towing sweeps show a day signal consisting of a black ball at the fore masthead and a black ball at each yardarm. At night, 32-point green lights are used in place of the black balls, exhibited in the same positions. The lights are shown only to warn friendly ships.

Special Signals for Survey Vessels

By day, surveying vessels of the Coast and Geodetic Survey, under way and engaged in surveying, may carry in vertical line, not less than 6 feet apart, where best seen, three shapes not less than 2 feet in diameter. The highest and lowest are green and globular; the middle one white and diamond-shaped.

These signals do not relieve them from complying with rules regarding right of way; and, at night, when surveying under way, they carry the regular lights prescribed by the rules.

An anchor in a fairway, when surveying, they show by day two black balls in vertical line 6 feet apart; at night, two red lights in the same manner. A flare-up is shown if necessary.

When necessary, small survey boats also carry these special signals but the distance between the balls or lights may be reduced to 3 feet.

Special Signal—Coast Guard Buoy Tenders

On waters other than the high seas, United States Coast Guard buoy tenders, engaged in repair work on aids to navigation, display two orange and white vertically striped balls in vertical line. To prevent damage from their wash, passing vessels should slow down to not more than 5 m.p.h. On the high seas, vessels working on aids to navigation would display, vertically, a white diamond between two red balls.

Pilot Signals

A pilot may be obtained by displaying: By day—(1) International Code Signal G, (2) International Code Signal P. T. (3) the Pilot Jack hoisted at the fore. Either G or P. T. means "I require a pilot," (see Volume I, H. O. 87). By night—(1) The pyrotechnic light (blue light) every 15 minutes, (2) a bright white light, flashed or shown at short or frequent intervals just above the bulwarks for about a minute at a time, (3) the International Code Signal P. T. by flashing light.

Signals for Drawbridges

Signals for the opening of drawbridges vary in different localities. A common signal is three blasts of the whistle, as on the Harlem River, New York. If the draw is ready to be opened, the bridge answers with three blasts; if not, two blasts. Always consult the Coast Pilot for specific regulations.

Safety at Sea

CHAPTER X

IT may be said with little fear of successful contradiction that the motor boat has become the safest modern form of travel. The hazard which attaches to the use of a well-found boat, properly handled by an intelligent, careful person, is negligible. Analysis shows that most accidents are avoidable. Experience has proved that even minor misfortunes rarely visit the boatman who knows that his boat is sound, equipped according to the dictates of law and experience, and is handled with reasonable judgment and prudence. Examining this a little further, it is evident that safety at sea is conditioned, not upon the caprice of chance or the elements, but upon the boat and the man who is responsible for her.

This being the case, what is the logical procedure to guarantee that safety which we know is attainable? Modern boats, built by reputable manufacturers, are essentially seaworthy because they are honestly built to proved designs. That points in the first place to the proper course in the selection of a good sound boat. There is no necessity of trying some freak of questionable worth. If you have no experience on this subject, it is easy enough to avail yourself of the services of one who is qualified. Proper servicing each season will keep your boat in condition.

It is up to the owner to see that the equipment required by law is aboard and ready for use, supplemented by other items used even more than the legal accessories. It is also up to the owner to decide whether or not he is satisfied to navigate his craft in hit-or-miss fashion or prefers to understand the simple principles of elementary piloting and utilize them in enjoying safer and more scientific cruises. The law does not demand it, but you, the owner, are privileged to spend an hour or two occasionally absorbing the contents of the Pilot Rules so that you may know your legal rights and duties. Plenty of literature is available on the subject of how a boat should be operated; other boatmen are always glad to lend a hand in getting you started right. Your experience can be gathered in easy stages, without effort and without risk; a cruise on the Sound or other inland body of water is a more reasonable initiation than a passage to Bermuda. Add this all up and what do you get? It puts the question of safety squarely up to the individual. Whatever you do toward making your own boat safe and handling it more safely profits the other fellow as well.

Specifically, then, what can we do about it? Safety afloat begins ashore. Probably the first thought that comes to mind is that of safeguarding against fire. Fire is usually traceable to the galley or engine room, where faulty installation, improper equipment or carelessness in operation are the direct cause. All of these things are under our control. Gasoline fumes, mixed with air, form an explosive mixture. These fumes, being heavier than air, find their way to the bottom of the bilge. The obvious answer is prevention—make it impossible for gasoline, in either liquid or gaseous form, to get into the bilge in the first place. Then keep the bilge clean and ventilate the engine compartment thoroughly and there will be nothing that can be ignited. Leakage of liquid gasoline into the bilge can be prevented by proper installation, using strongly built gasoline tanks, copper tubing for fuel lines, leak-proof connections, tight fittings and lengths of flexible metallic fuel hose to take care of vibration. Gasoline vapors created when the tanks are filled must be prevented from finding their way down through open hatches and companionways. Finally, avoidable sparks and flames should not be permitted in the engine room.

One of the most essential requirements in proper installation of the fuel system is that there be a tight connection between the gasoline tanks and the filling plates on deck. If the filler is located outside of the coaming, spillage will go overboard while the pipe from deck plate to tank will prevent

M. Rosenfeld

Safety features aboard a modern sea-going cruiser. Note the radio direction finder, radiotelephone, depth sounder, manual control for the built-in fire extinguishing system, portable fire extinguisher, modern engine controls and instrument panels for twin engines, spherical compass, windshield wiper, and searchlight control. This particular boat is also equipped with Photo-Electric Pilot to hold her automatically on course. The direction finder gives accurate bearings and positions, even in fog

leakage or spillage below deck. The filler pipe should run to the bottom of the tank and suitable vent pipes for the tanks should lead outside the hull. A fuel indicator if used should be of the most approved type. If the fuel supply of auxiliary lighting plants and generating sets is not drawn from the main tank, the separate tanks should be installed with fillers and vents similar to those of the main tank.

There are several precautions that may be taken in the engine room. Carburetors should be equipped with flame arresters for protection against backfire, and pans

M. Rosenfeld

covered with fine mesh brass screen should be attached under the carburetor to collect drip. Leakage will be sucked back into the engine if a copper tube is run from the bottom of the pan to the intake manifold. When possible, switches and fuses should be installed outside the engine compartment. If this is not feasible they should be enclosed and placed as high above the floor as convenient, preferably not less than four feet. Shut-off valves should be placed close to each tank and also at the carburetor, and no petcock or other provision for drawing gas in the engine room should be allowed. A type of diaphragm packless valve for fuel, gas and oil lines is now available which is pressure-tight in any position. Tested by Underwriters Laboratories under high pressure in open, half open, and closed positions, it safeguards against leakage at the valves.

Every possible precaution should be taken to insure that not even a single drop of fuel leakage can find its way into the bilge.

Gas tanks are sometimes located above self-bailing cockpit floors, and if a valve is placed between the tank and decking, the engine can be stopped by shutting off the valve and no gas will be left below decks. The ignition and lighting systems should be checked occasionally to see that wires are in good condition and all connections tight. Devices are now available which will disclose, at the throw of a

Ventilation of bilges in motor and fuel compartments is one of the most important considerations in motor boat safety. Air ducts, as shown at left, should draw from the lowest point in the bilge, where vapors settle. Below: Cutaway view showing how a built-in fire extinguishing system can be installed, with manual and/or automatic control, to flood engine compartments with carbon dioxide in case of fire

switch, whether inflammable vapors are present in the boat. These are doubly valuable because they warn of leakage not only of gasoline but also of bottled gas such as might be used for cooking. Lining the engine compartment and under side of cockpit floors with fireproof or fire-resistant insulation is a worth-while feature, and serves as a sound dampener as well.

To ventilate the engine compartment, large pipes should be run down into the bilge at each corner of the engine room. It is better to leave these entirely open, with no provision for closing them, than to run the risk of having them accidently closed. The amount of water they will ship in a seaway is of no great consequence. Two of the ducts should be equipped with electric blowers. If the suction type of fan is used to draw the air out, their motors must be explosion-proof, shielded against sparking. Otherwise they must be located outside of the exhaust duct. Running the fans for ten minutes before and after starting the engine will clear the bilge of fumes and vapors. This provides a positive system that can be relied upon. A common tendency is to depend on the opening of hatches and ports to air out an engine compartment before starting but the fact remains that the heavy fumes, if present, are down low in the bilge and the only sure way to get them out is to drive them out with blowers. In cases where a boat is so small as to make the installation of blowers impractical, at least the pipes, of generous size, can be installed with ventilating scoops facing forward on two inlet pipes and two more reversed, facing aft, to draw the fumes out the outlet passages. In cases where the ventilating ducts cannot be laid out to advantage, openings can be cut in the fore and aft bulkheads of the engine compartment, as low as possible. Leaving ventilators open fore and aft in a boat, the draft produced will tend to carry out the fumes, instead of keeping them confined at the most vulnerable spot.

Gassing Up

WITH an installation that provides the safety features outlined above, an important first step has been taken. Further precautions should be observed every time gasoline is taken aboard. Before the tank fillers are opened or hoses or cans brought aboard, the engine and any other motors or fans that could possibly produce a spark should be stopped. Fires in the galley or any other open flame aboard should be extinguished. Smoking at the time should be rigidly prohibited. A precaution that is frequently neglected is to close all doors, hatches, ports and windows. The obvious purpose of this is to prevent fumes from traveling down through such openings into the cabin, engine room or bilge. After these points have been checked, exercise care in the handling of the fuel so that all of it goes into the tank and not one drop below decks. While fueling have the metallic end of the filling hose in contact with the metal pipe leading to the tank. After the fueling, any spillage on deck should be wiped up. Then before any motors are started or flames of any kind lighted, throw all ports and other windows wide open and wait at least five minutes for all compartments to air out.

All this may sound like complicated, unnecessary procedure, but if it means only a few dollars extra in installation cost and requires but a few minutes more to handle fuel in a safe and sane way, isn't it worth it?

The law requires you to carry a fire extinguisher, stating that it must be of a type capable of promptly and effectually extinguishing burning gasoline. This includes carbon dioxide, carbon tetrachloride, and foam types. Soda and acid, sand, or salt and sand are not approved. It is also required that they be full and in working condition. As a result of the phraseology of the regulations, a single one-quart extinguisher might pass the law, but on the average small cruiser, for your own protection, at least two are desirable. One of these should be in the galley, the other mounted outside the cabin near the wheel. Preferably this latter extinguisher should be of larger size, depending on the requirements of the boat. The ideal arrangement is to suppplement these hand extinguishers with a built-in system in which carbon dioxide is carried in cylinders under pressure and piped to compartments to be protected. These can be arranged to operate automatically and

may also be supplied with remote manual control. When discharged, the compartment is filled with a non-inflammable gas which smothers the fire.

Extinguishers should be examined at least once a year, certainly before the boat goes into commission. The foam type should be discharged, cleaned, and recharged. If it is of the tetrachloride type, some of the liquid should be discharged, throwing the stream both up and down to make certain that piston and valves are working properly. Then it should be refilled and it is recommended that it be swung by the handle seven or eight times before being replaced in its bracket. In the carbon dioxide type it is necessary to weigh the cylinder containing the gas to see that it is exactly the same as the full weight stamped on the valve, cylinder, or tag as the case may be. This will reveal whether or not it is fully charged. If not, it should be recharged While the cylinder is disconnected, the pull cord of the control can be tested by removing the cover of the handle box. The cord should work easily. When the cylinder is replaced, it must stand with valve and lever in the same relative position, with no slack in the cord.

Water is of no use in extinguishing a gasoline fire. The burning gasoline floats on the surface and the use of water serves only to spread it. However, there are occasions when it might be used. It will extinguish a blaze made by burning alcohol and is also all right in other places where gasoline is not present. Consequently a bucket is a desirable thing to add to your equipment, along with an axe. Larger craft should be supplied with a fire pump and hose.

Government Equipment

ANOTHER thing required on motor boats over 16 feet is a whistle or other sound-producing device. This is used to give passing whistle signals and it is necessary to have a clear understanding of the Pilot Rules in order to make these signals correctly. Thus you will be able to understand the other fellow's intentions and to signal him your own. Collisions can't occur when there is this mutual understanding of intended action and compliance with the specific rights and obligations of each vessel, as outlined in the rules. The effectiveness of your whistle depends on its being heard. The law requires that the sound-producing device be "efficient." Make sure that yours is powerful enough so that it cannot be drowned out by other noises.

Motor boats 26 feet in length or over were once required to carry a fog horn, but this requirement was lifted by the Motor Boat Act of 1940. Fog signals are made on the whistle. They do not consist of making a noise whenever it might seem necessary but rather of sounding long blasts on the whistle at prescribed intervals, according to the Pilot Rules. In fog the range of visibility is reduced, so due caution must be exercised. A lookout should be posted and the speed reduced in order to have the boat under complete control at all times. While courts have held that moderate speed would be such as to permit a boat to stop within the range of visibility it is conceivable that even this might not be slow enough. Half the range of visibility would be safer under some circumstances. Fog may be regarded by some as a hazard from the navigational standpoint, but it holds no terror for the man who pilots scientifically. Knowing your position and your course at all times, even in strange waters, inspires a confidence that is ample reward for the slight effort involved in learning the simple principles of piloting. A fog bell is also required on motor boats of more than 26 feet in length. This is used only while at anchor or aground.

It should be obvious that your life preserver equipment must be in strict compliance with the law, with regard to type, condition, number, etc. On boats not carrying passengers for hire, ring buoys are approved as life preservers. At least one of these is a desirable item of equipment on every boat, for use in case a person happens to go overboard. When a ring buoy is wanted there is no time to bother with lashings that have to be untied or cut. Hooks are made upon which they can be hung, close to the helmsman's position. These hold the ring securely in a clip but release without effort. If necessary to use lashings, they should be light enough to be broken when needed. A good idea is to provide at least one such ring of the type that automatically lights when it hits the water. Some cushions pass as life preservers but be sure they are fitted with two loops and have a tag attached showing they have been approved.

The best seaman is the one who is prepared for any contingency, before the need arises to meet it. At the call of "man overboard," seconds count and a well planned line of action will enable you to act quickly and effectively without confusion. The ring buoy should be heaved immediately, even if the person is a skillful swimmer. The engine should be thrown into neutral for an instant till it is seen that the person is clear of the propeller, and then re-engaged while the rudder is put hard over and the engine opened up for a quick turn, going ahead. Whether or not you turn to port or starboard had best be decided by experiment in advance. Ordinarily a boat with a right-handed propeller should turn quickest to port but practical experience shows that some boats behave otherwise. By this maneuver you should be able to get back to the buoy, with boat under perfect control, in less than a minute. You might find that reversing and backing will be more effective for your boat, but the odds are against it. At any rate make a few tests. Throw a paper or cardboard box overboard and experiment in recovering it until you know precisely what to do if the need should ever arise. Circumstances will dictate best procedure as to how to approach the man in the water. Although the boat can best be kept under control by approaching from leeward, maneuvering into a position to windward of him will provide a lee as the boat drifts toward him.

If you run at night, you are required to carry lights. The law specifies that screens must be provided for the colored side lights of boats over 26 feet so they will not shine across the bow. All white lights must be visible 2 miles, colored lights 1 mile. Remember that the only reason the law was drafted was for the sake of the safety of your own boat and that of others you may meet. So be sure your lights are always in good working order and that they are strong enough to throw a good clear beam far enough to serve the purpose intended. They must not be obstructed by superstructure or other parts of the boat. Some lights are equipped with electric light bulbs for regular use but are rigged to burn kerosene in emergency. This is a wise provision. A powerful searchlight will often be useful but it should be used with consideration. If you have ever had one played into your deckhouse when you were trying to spot channel buoys, you know the consequences of their misuse.

Other Essential Equipment

MOST of the equipment mentioned thus far is legal equipment and we have no alternative but to carry it. The cause of safety afloat, however, can be greatly furthered by some advance thought on the matter of being prepared to handle any situation that may arise. When you select your ground tackle, you can't prepare only for the mid-summer afternoon in ten feet of water in a quiet bay with not even a gentle breeze stirring. Your heaviest anchor (which should be but one of three) should be husky enough and your spare anchor line should be long and strong enough to hold you no matter how hard it blows in whatever waters you may find it necessary to anchor in.

A well-built boat won't leak—much. But you ought to be prepared to handle a leak if it should develop, suddenly, for any cause. That doesn't mean the installation of a toy pump that will squirt a few gallons a minute, but a good sized one that will throw fifteen or twenty gallons every sixty seconds without too much effort on the part of the pumper. An additional engine-driven or separate electric pump is even better.

Every boat should be equipped with the means to rectify minor engine ailments, at least. This means a good kit of tools, and spare engine parts such as spark plugs, coil, condenser, distributor points, gaskets, etc. Eventually you will accumulate a considerable store of reserve supplies. You may have a few carpenter's tools, extra lines of all sizes, marlin, an assortment of nails, screws, washers, and bolts, wire, tape, caulking cotton, paint, etc. If you have sails you will carry a repair kit, containing twine, wax, needles, palm, fid, and similar articles. All of this extra gear should be kept stowed away in shipshape manner where it can be found when wanted, and not thrown loosely into lockers all over the boat.

A medicine cabinet or first-aid kit should be aboard. Another thought would be to provide some sort of emergency rations to be kept aboard at all times, such as canned foods, hard tack or pilot biscuits, and plenty of fresh water. Then if you ever find it necessary to spend a day or two away from any source of supplies it need not be a hardship. This of course will be in addition to any regular food supplies put aboard for a cruise and should never be drawn upon except in such an emergency.

If you plan to do much cruising outside or go in for deep-sea fishing, twin engines will meet your requirements better than a single one. They should be complete separate units, each with its own fuel system, propeller and rudder—neither dependent upon the other. On a single engine, dual ignition is a valuable feature, operating either on battery, coil and distributor, or magneto with impulse coupling. In a battery system a spare storage battery, wired to be charged by the engine and available for immediate use when required, is also good practice.

For regular offshore work, a moderate amount of canvas on a motor boat will steady her in a seaway and even provide a certain amount of steerage way if necessary, even though she may not be able to go to windward. Steering gear should be inspected often enough to see that it is thoroughly dependable. Some form of emergency steering in case the regular gear should fail should be planned and provided in advance. This may consist of nothing more elaborate than a strong spare tiller. By allowing the squared head of the rudder stock to extend above the quadrant or regular tiller to a point perhaps above the cockpit floor or other convenient height, the emergency tiller can be rigged in a matter of seconds.

Your navigating equipment ought to be complete and you should know how to use it. The minimum would include a good compass, properly installed, with deviation card; parallel rules or protractor; dividers; pelorus or bearing finder; a patent log or engine tachometer and watch; lead line; up-to-date charts; corrected Light Lists; Tide Tables; Current Tables and Coast Pilot.

If You Require Assistance

REMEMBER that the principal function of the Coast Guard is to render assistance to mariners. They stand ready at all times, and their aid is just as available to the owner of a yacht as it is to the master of an ocean liner. Try to equip your boat and handle it in such a manner that you will not require outside assistance but if you should, don't hesitate to call them. You can signal for aid by hoisting the ensign upside-down; firing a gun or any other explosive signal at intervals of about a minute; by continuously sounding a fog horn, whistle or bell; displaying the international code signal NC; or a distance signal consisting of a square flag with a ball, or something resembling a ball, above or below it; even by simply raising and lowering your outstretched arms, slowly and repeatedly.

For night use a water-tight outfit containing flares or rockets should be aboard. One type of signalling equipment provides a pistol and cartridges which throw a brilliant flare several hundred feet in the air where it is suspended for more than half a minute, burning with an intense light visible about twenty-five miles. These are also useful in flood-lighting a considerable area at night when entering a strange harbor or inlet, locating a buoy, launching a dinghy, or recovering one that has come adrift, or locating something that has gone overboard at night.

More and more small craft are being equipped with the devices which contribute so greatly to safety aboard the larger vessels. Even the common radio set is helpful today in getting the daily weather broadcasts. One need not set out on a long run if he has fore-knowledge of an approaching storm. The radio direction finder is thoroughly practical aboard the comparatively small yacht, occupying but little space and giving accurate positions and courses regardless of conditions of visibility. The radio telephone is also opening up new possibilities in the way of continuous intercommunication between ship and shore. Small radio outfits which combine receiving and transmitting ability in a single unit are now in use. On larger yachts the fathometer gives a continuous visual indication of depth, with all that that implies of more precise, scientific navigation, confidence and safety at sea.

Boats can be made safe and kept safe. There is no excuse for not providing that safety when its accomplishment is so easy. It may never be possible in any form of travel or transportation to eliminate completely every little mishap and inconvenience in connection with its use, but in boating we certainly can provide against such occurrences so as to practically remove any element of hazard. For safer navigation, remember the seaman's three L's—log, lead and lookout. To promote general safety afloat, uphold the unwritten law of the sea—stand by and lend a hand whenever you are able to render assistance.

FIRST AID FOR PLEASURE CRAFT

THE size of the boat, the number of people, the length of the cruise, the geographical area for which the cruise is planned and the hazards likely to be encountered determine the variety and quantity of first-aid materials needed. First-aid materials should be an integral part of every boat's equipment, irrespective of the size of the boat or the purpose for which it is used. It should be noted here that the first-aid kit must be kept in an accessible location and that each person aboard should be made aware of its availability and location.

Basic First-Aid Materials

There are certain basic first-aid materials which should be carried aboard all classes of boats. Bandages should be carried that are ready for instant use; each dressing should be individual and a complete dressing in itself. Each bandage should be sterilized and designed to provide protection against infection and contamination.

Antiseptics should be packaged so that the solution stays at its original strength from the time it is packaged until it is used. This type of packaging is available in a swab that contains a hermetically sealed ampoule contained in a sleeve of multi-layered cardboard so that when the ampoule is broken, there is no chance for the user to be cut from the glass. A close-packed cotton tip saturates instantly and then is applied to the wound area. The advantage of this type of packaging is that there is no wastage, spillage or deterioration of the product due to the one-application hermetically sealed ampoule.

The basic first-aid materials should also include burn treatments to take care of sunburn or burns caused by other hazards. Scissors should be included also as they have multiple uses aboard a boat. Blunt-end forceps are a necessity to remove splinters. They should always be of the blunt-end variety so as to preclude the possibility of doing further injury by probing which is not a first-aid measure.

There are several types of ready-made first-aid kits which are specially designed, tested and generally approved for marine use.

The Coast Guard Kit

1. Coast Guard Kit: This is a kit which is required aboard Merchant Vessels, Life Rafts and Life Boats; U.S.C.G. Reg. 94.20-15 (I) and 75.20-15(1). U.S.C.G. Approval number 160.041-3-0. This kit is of 20-gauge steel, waterproof and painted to prevent rusting and contains twenty-four (24) units of the following basic first-aid materials:

5 units	4" Bandage Compress, 1 per
2 units	2" Bandage Compress, 4 per
2 units	1" Adhesive Bandages, 16 per
3 units	Triangular Bandages, 1 per
1 unit	Eye Dressing Packet, 3 per
1 unit	2" x 6 yd. Gauze Bandage, 2 per
1 unit	Tourniquet, Forceps & Scissors, 1 ea (dbl. unit)
1 unit	Wire Splint
1 unit	Ammonia Inhalants, 10 per
1 unit	Antiseptic Swabs, 10 per
1 unit	Aspirin Compound Tablets, 6½ gr., 5 vials of 20 per (dbl. unit)
3 units	Petrolatum Gauze, 3" x 18", 4 per

It is well designed for the purpose for which it is intended, but it is too bulky and heavy for pleasure craft under 65'.

Cylindrical Yachtsman's Kit

2. Cylindrical Yachtsman's Kit. This is specifically designed for boats under 65'. It consists of a light-weight aluminum cylinder, treated to resist salt corrosion and rust. Because of its unique mounting brackets it can be mounted on the bulkhead, in the main cabin or cockpit, or under the seat in smaller boats. The canister houses a vinyl roll-up which contains items of the prepackaged type which are always ready for instant use. Another important feature is that the vinyl roll-up, containing the first aid items, can be removed from the canister and taken to the scene of any accident either aboard the boat or ashore. With this type of first-aid kit there is no chance of deterioration or corrosion from salt water. A list of the items contained in the cylindrical kit are as follows:

2 units	1" Plastic Adhesive Bandages, 16 per
1 unit	Burn Compound, ¾ oz., 2 per
1 unit	Ammonia Inhalants, 10 per
1 unit	2" Bandage Compress, 4 per
1 unit	4" Bandage Compress, 1 per
2 units	Merthiolate Swabs, 10 per
1 each	Scissors and Forceps

The Life Raft Kit

3. Another type of first-aid kit is one which is used by commercial airliners traveling over water for use in the aircraft life rafts. The C.A.A. Life Raft Kit, specifications CAA 42.24, contain these items:

2 units	1" Adhesive Bandages, 16 per
1 unit	Burn Compound, ⅛ oz., 6 per
1 unit	Ammonia Inhalants, 10 per
2 units	Antiseptic Swabs, 10 per
1 unit	Eye Dressing Packet, 3 per
2 units	2" Bandage Compress, 4 per
2 units	4" Bandage Compress, 1 per
2 units	Aromatic Spirits of Ammonia, 4 per
1 unit	Triangular Bandage
1 unit	Tourniquet, Forceps & Scissors (dbl. unit)

This kit contains basic unit first-aid materials and is in a heat-sealed waterproof vinyl container. This is more adaptable to life boats and life rafts and dinghies for emergency only rather than for everyday use because, once the plastic container is opened, it cannot be readily closed again to protect the contents. It should be considered as a piece of emergency equipment and should not be cannibalized for use of minor wounds.

All three of the above types of kits are manufactured by the Medical Supply Company of Rockford, Illinois. The kits and the replacement units as needed may generally be secured through Marine Supply Dealers.

Unit Packaging

The advantages of kits of this type are: All first-aid materials are packaged in a standard unit-size package (4" x 2⅛" x ⅝") as set forth by the Division of Simplified Practices, U.S. Bureau of Standards Code R178-41. Due to the relative infrequency of use of various items in first aid, units should be designed to cope with only one injury. The antiseptics, ointments and such should be packaged to treat the smallest injury on the theory that more than one may be used to take care of the less-frequent larger injuries. This safeguards against contamination, leakage, evaporation and changes in pharmaceutical and therapeutic values over long periods of storage. It also eliminates the remnants of partially used surgical dressings which become soiled and unsterile after once having been opened.

Each package outlines proper first-aid instructions for use. Recognize, too, that first aid is usually rendered by a layman whose primary occupation is not medical work. Irrespective of the skill or amount of training he has, his practice of first aid is at best a by-product of his principal work. Thus, the materials chosen for the 'first-aider' must be designed to be as foolproof and easily used as it is possible to make them. This is why this type of packaging is used by the American Red Cross, U.S. Coast Guard, U.S. Bureau of Mines, telephone and utility companies as well as the Army and Navy as being the most practical for first-aid emergency use.

Medicine Cabinets: Most cruisers over 26' have medicine cabinets in the head where additional first-aid supplies may be stored. A word of caution should be sounded here—this cabinet should supplement rather than replace the first-aid kits as outlined above since the contents are not portable to the scene of the emergency. It should contain the items which normally are stocked in the medicine cabinet at home such as aspirin, upset stomach remedies, etc.

How to Administer First Aid

RULE ONE. *Always take the first aid to the victim, not the victim to the first aid.* It would be highly impractical to attempt the instruction of first aid in this small space. It is the skipper's responsibility for his passengers and crew to acquaint himself with the proper first-aid procedures. This can be done through classes given by each Chapter of the American Red Cross in a standard first-aid course without charge. It should be remembered that when you are aboard your boat and at sea, you are out of immediate touch with professional medical attention and, therefore, preparedness is necessary.

RULE TWO. *When you are giving first aid, take your time.* Usually there is more damage done by the well-meaning amateur than was ever caused by the actual injury. Remember, there are only three instances when speed in giving first aid is required: 1—When the victim has stopped breathing; 2—When there is arterial bleeding; and 3—When the victim has been bitten by a poisonous snake. The measures required in these instances are taught in the standard first-aid course, and you may acquire the American Red Cross Manual from the local chapter of your Red Cross. The Snake Bite Manual is published by the National Safety Council, 425 N. Michigan Avenue in Chicago, Illinois. These two manuals will cover all contingencies which would normally arise under these conditions.

It should be noted that we have eliminated splints from the first-aid kits for the following reasons: The average first-aider is not qualified to set a broken limb; it is much safer to place the limb in pillows or blankets, tying them securely around the fractured members so that no further damage will be done. And always remember that first aid should stop at first aid . . . which is administering aid and comfort to avert further complications until professional medical attention can be obtained. When transporting a victim, take your time . . . prepare him carefully for the journey . . . and don't complicate the situation with speed.

Artificial Respiration

Every boatman should have a working knowledge of the rudiments of artificial respiration. Minutes count, so be prepared to act quickly if the occasion arises. New mouth-to-mouth method widely approved by first-aid organizations.

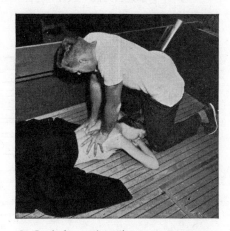

3. Rock forward until your arms are approximately vertical. Let the weight of the upper part of your body exert even pressure downward. Keep your elbows straight. Important: Take great care to avoid excessive pressure, which might damage subject's ribs

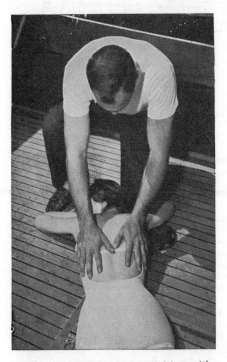

1. Place subejct in prone position with face turned to one side and resting on hands, placed one on the other with fingers barely overlapping. Remove foam and debris from mouth, draw tongue forward. Waste no time. Everything is secondary to getting air into the lungs

The Holger-Nielsen Method
(See figures 1-5)

Prompt, efficient application of artificial respiration has been responsible for saving the lives of thousands ot persons over the years and knowledge of this important branch of first aid is essential to all those who operate small craft. One technique extensively used in Scandinavia and the United States is the Holger-Nielsen method, illustrated in the accompanying photographs from Texaco-Waterways Services' well known handbook *Cruising With Safety.* Just as in the case of older methods, it is extremely important to take these three steps once the victim has resumed natural brathing; treat for shock by keeping him warm; keep him quiet; and call a physician.

Mouth-to-mouth Respiration

More recently the American Red Cross has approved mouth-to-mouth artificial respiration as best for adults as well as children. Older manual methods are still considered acceptable for rescuers who cannot or will not use the new system.

Instructions given by the Red Cross for use of the mouth-to-mouth method are as follows:

1. If there is foreign matter visible in the victim's mouth, wipe it out quickly with your fingers or a cloth wrapped around your fingers.

2. Tilt the victim's head back so the chin is pointing upward. Pull or push the jaw into a jutting-out position. These maneuvers should relieve obstruction of the airway by moving the base of the tongue away from the back of the throat.

3. Open your mouth wide and place it tightly over the victim's mouth. At the same time pinch the victim's nostrils shut or close the nostrils with your cheek. As an alternative, close the victim's mouth and place your mouth over the nose. Blow into the victim's mouth or nose. The first blowing efforts should determine whether or not obstruction exists.

4. Remove your mouth, turn your head to the side, and listen for the return rush of air that indicates air exchange. Repeat the blowing effort. For an adult, blow vigorously at the rate of about twelve breaths a minute. For a child, take relatively shallow breaths appropriate for the child's size, at the rate of about twenty a minute.

5. If you are not getting air exchange, recheck the head and jaw position. If you still do not get air exchange, quickly turn the victim on his side and administer several sharp blows between the shoulder blades in the hope of dislodging foreign matter.

Tubes have been developed and are now generally available at drugstores to facilitate use of the new method.

4. Release the pressure without jerking and rock slowly backward, sliding hands along arms until the little fingers touch subject's elbows. If help is available, have subject covered with a blanket or coat to reduce shock. Loosen tight clothes

2. Kneel on either knee or on both if that's more comfortable. Place hands on subject's back so that their heels are just below an imaginary line running between the armpits. Fingers should be extended to distribute pressure over the full width of back

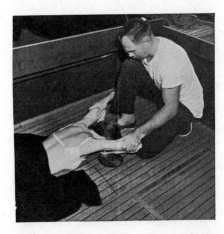

5. Draw arms upward and toward you with just enough lift to feel resistance and tension. As you rock backward, the arms of the subject will be drawn toward you. Then, complete the cycle by dropping subject's arms. Repeat the cycle 12 times per minute

Suggestions for Safety in Construction, Fueling and Operation

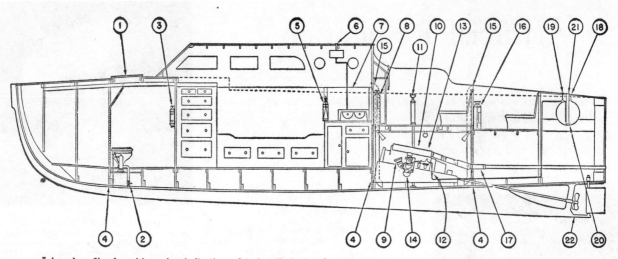

Inboard profile of a cabin cruiser indicating safety installations and construction recommended to minimize the hazards most commonly found on powerboats.

1. Escape hatch big enough for adult to pass through in case of emergency.

2. Accessible seacock on toilet discharge which can be closed when cruiser is unattended.

3. Portable one quart carbon tetrachloride fire extinguisher.

4. Watertight bulkheads.

5. Portable 4-lb. carbon dioxide fire extinguisher.

6. Alcohol stove fuel tank arranged to fill through house deck.

7. Woodwork close to stove insulated and protected with sheet metal.

8. Manually operated fire-extinguishing system using carbon dioxide, serving the engine compartment.

9. Flame Arrestor on air intake of engine carburetor to baffle any possible backfire.

10. Storage battery in ventilated lead-lined box, protected by cover to prevent tool or metal object falling on terminals and causing flash. (Located on stbd. side of motor.)

11. Fixed Navy-type bilge pump with strainer on suction pipe.

12. Shut-off valve on gasoline fuel line near carburetor.

13. Accessible seacock on intake for circulating water for cooling the engine.

14. Drip pan (closed) with drain connection to engine intake manifold.

15. Ventilating pipes running down all the way to bilge in all four corners of engine room, connected with cowl-type ventilators on deck.

16. Portable 2½-gallon foam type extinguisher.

17. Exhaust pipe insulated with asbestos where it passes through bulkhead.

18. Vent pipe leading outboard from gasoline tank, so gasoline vapors will discharge outside hull.

19. Shut-off valve on gasoline fuel line near tank with extension to deck for accessible operation.

20. Gasoline fuel tank with baffle plate and with filling pipe extending nearly to bottom of tank.

21. Deck fill connected to top of gasoline tank so any overflow will drain overboard.

22. Metal skeg shoe protecting propeller from striking obstructions.

TYPES OF INSTALLATIONS

1. *Best Installation:* Fill pipe firmly attached to tight deck plate. Fill pipe extends to bottom of tank with well to form liquid seal. Vent pipe discharges to open air, away from all hull openings, hatches, doors, windows, ports, etc. Outboard end of vent screened.

2. *Fairly Good Installation:* Fill pipes firmly attached to tight deck plates, but not extended to bottom of tank with liquid seal well. Tank can be exploded from ignited fill pipe. Vent led to open air with screened outboard end. Location of the vent outlet should be kept clear of all hull openings.

3. *Dangerous Installation:* Fill pipes firmly attached to deck plates, but vent pipes discharge all vapors to inside of boat. Fumes may be ignited by a backfire, a lit match, by electrical apparatus of any kind, or by a fire in the galley stove. Unless vent pipe is led to open air, a tight deck fill pipe is *no* protection.

4. *Very Dangerous Installation:* Both fill pipe and vent pipe end inside of hull. All vapors escape to interior of boat. Tank will overflow in filling and spill liquid fuel to bilge. Possible static spark from fill connections or funnel may ignite gasoline.

Note: *Do not* place fill pipes inside of deckhouses or cockpits. *Do not* use small diameter tubing for vents. They will cause bubbling and spilling at the fill pipes.

FILLING INSTRUCTIONS

1. Fuel tanks should be properly installed and vented.

2. Fueling should be completed before dark except in emergencies.

3. Whenever boat is moored at service station for fueling:
A. Do not smoke, strike matches, or throw switches.
B. Stop all engines, motors, fans, and devices liable to produce sparks.
C. Put out all lights and galley fires.

4. Before starting to fuel:
A. See that boat is moored securely.
B. Close all ports, windows, doors and hatches.
C. Ascertain definitely how much additional fuel the tanks will hold.

5. During fueling:
A. Keep nozzle of hose, or can, in contact with fill opening to guard against possible static spark.
B. See that no fuel spills get into hull or bilges.

6. After fueling is completed:
A. Close fill openings.
B. Wipe up *all* spilled fuel.
C. Open all ports, windows, doors and hatches.
D. Permit boat to ventilate for at least 5 minutes.
E. See that there is no odor of gasoline in the engine room or below decks before starting machinery or lighting fire.
F. Be prepared to cast off moorings as soon as engine starts.

SAFETY PRECAUTIONS

1. Do not overload the boat.

2. Do not take chances with fire and explosion.

3. Do not tolerate an installation which lacks modern safeguards.

4. Do not allow gas or oil in the bilge.

5. Do not operate near swimmers in the water.

6. Do not allow rubbish to accumulate.

7. Do not make temporary repairs except in emergencies.

8. Do not use gasoline stoves.

9. Do not use kapok-filled life preservers to sit upon, as such action compresses the filler and destroys its efficiency.

10. Do not fail to provide life belts for children.

11. Do not be afraid of a boat—respect it.

12. Do not forget your wake can damage others.

13. Do not fail to reduce speed through anchorages.

14. Do not fail to take precautions against fouling other boats when anchoring.

15. Do not lie at anchor with short cable; allow sufficient scope.

16. Do not fail to exercise sober judgment at all times.

(Data on this page from U. S. Coast Guard and National Fire Protection Association publications.)

SAFETY PRACTICES Afloat

KNOWLEDGE of the right technique in maneuvering a motor boat should be supplemented by an understanding of related principles that contribute toward safety in operation. The two go hand-in-hand—both are needed to round out the qualifications of an able boatman.

Safety practices in boat handling were formerly a primary concern of the Bureau of Marine Inspection and Navigation, functions of which have been transferred to the U. S. Coast Guard and the Bureau of Customs. They have prescribed regulations pertaining to safety devices required on motor boats by law and in this connection publish detailed regulations governing lights, whistles, bells, life preservers, fire extinguishers, flame arrestors, ventilating equipment, etc. These regulations have been discussed elsewhere at great length.

The inspectors, however, go one step farther. In addition to the prescribed regulations, they have also compiled a vast amount of information on safety practices which they suggest and recommend. As all this is of vital interest to the motor boat operator, a digest of it is given herewith.

Placing emphasis first on the means of making the boat safe with respect to gasoline in the bilge, it is pointed out that all petroleum vapors are heavier than air. Settling to the lowest point in the bilge, they may lie dormant in the engine compartment for some time, but remain a potential hazard if exposed to an open flame, lighted cigarette, or electric spark.

Therefore, accumulation of such vapors must be prevented by keeping gasoline out of the bilge and by adequate ventilation. Sources of ignition of these vapors must also be eliminated, as well as pockets in the hull where they might be trapped.

For seaworthiness and safety, reliable equipment, suitable materials for boatbuilding and equipment, and high-grade construction are essentials. Use of fire-retardant materials wherever practicable is suggested.

Water-tight bulkheads (or as tight as practicable) are recommended to isolate bilges of fuel and machinery spaces from those of living quarters. Bulkheads may be double diagonal wood, steel plate or equivalent. Waterproof plywood is often used in the bulkheads of pleasure boats. Again, where practicable, two means of exit should be provided from compartments where persons may congregate or sleep. Thus, in a small craft having only one cabin and cockpit, a hatch forward in addition to the regular companionway aft is a desirable feature.

The mistaken notion that a boat can carry weight anywhere as long as she appears to trim right in the water should be corrected. Addition of heavy superstructure is particularly bad, as is the shifting of heavy weights such as motors, ballast, tanks, machinery, etc. Where stability is concerned, no shifts of major weights or changes in design should be considered without the advice of a qualified naval architect. Amateur boatbuilders sometimes ruin boats by deviating from architect's plans in which the proportioning of weights has been given the most painstaking attention.

The entire electrical installation should comply rigidly with the best and most modern safety practices, taking due consideration of the

Navigating equipment should be in keeping with the type of cruising the boat is used for. Note the clock, barometer, sextant, barograph, binoculars, radio direction finder, and radiobeacon chart included in the equipment on this offshore auxiliary

Note, in illustration below, the heavy insulation around the exhaust pipe in this installation.

fact that the requirements of marine installation are, if anything, more exacting than other applications where salt- and moisture-laden atmospheres are not prevalent. Wiring and other electrical equipment should be installed correctly in the beginning and kept safe by frequent inspection.

Every boat owner or person who contemplates the operation of a motor boat should make it his responsibility to know the regulations and customs pertaining to operation and navigation, especially of the type of craft he handles. This assumes double significance where long cruises are planned, coastal or offshore. A few of the subjects which his knowledge should embrace include ability to read the barometer, right of way, whistle signals, running lights, aids to navigation, and a thorough understanding of charts. There are many others.

On every cruise (including even those in familiar waters) carry appropriate navigating equipment—charts, dividers, compass, and parallel rules or protractor are only the bare minimum. Have your compass adjusted or prepare your own deviation card, first checking to see that the instrument is correctly installed. It is suggested that compasses on wooden vessels be checked every two or three years; on steel vessels, every year.

Shifting of any major items of metallic equipment such

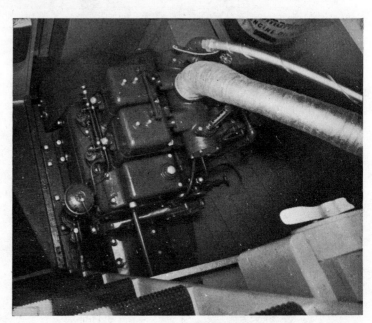

as engines, tanks, machinery, anchors, etc., always necessitates a check for possible changes of deviation.

A first-aid kit together with suitable instructions should be aboard every motor boat no matter how remote the possibility of its ever being needed or however short the cruise.

One of the most modern aids to safe navigation today is radar, which is now applicable to yachts. It penetrates fog and darkness, showing landmarks, buoys and other craft as pips of light on an indicator or scope. Pleasure boats should carry a folding radar reflector to be hoisted in thick weather. They make a wooden boat as conspicuous as a steel vessel in radar scopes and are especially valuable if the boat becomes the object of a radar search. By means of RATAN, a new navigational aid, shore installations in selected areas (Sandy Hook, for example) can transmit an excellent radio image of the area they cover, on a VHF television channel. To receive it, all the boatman needs is a television receiver tunable to VHF. Small sets which can be operated on 12 volts are becoming available. Within the limits of areas covered, TV receivers for RATAN would provide safety at a fraction of the cost of radar.

Periodically the hull should get a thorough inspection inside and out. This is usually taken care of in the spring fitting-out season. Seams of a wooden hull that require attention should be caulked by one who understands the art, as permanent injury may be done to planks and fastenings by improper caulking of a hull while dry. All exposed fastenings should be examined. The same applies to ports and other openings in the hull which rely upon gaskets for water tightness.

A clean hull is a safe hull. Bilges should be cleaned in the Spring with strong solutions of washing soda or some commercial preparation and flushed with water. Some of these solvents are intended to be thrown into the bilge periodically and pumped out with the bilge water after they have had time to accomplish their cleansing action.

Underwater fittings should have an annual inspection. This includes such parts as shafts, propellers, rudders, struts, stuffing boxes, and metal skegs. Stuffing boxes should be repacked as often as necessary (usually annually) to keep them from leaking, shafting checked for alignment and excessive wear and propellers examined to see if they require truing up.

Fittings which pass through the hull near or below the water line should have sea cocks installed close to the planking to permit positive closing. Inspection in the Spring before the boat is launched should be made to see that such fittings and their fastenings have not been damaged, or attacked by electrolytic action. Where hose is used over pipe nipples for connections, hose clamps should be used.

Engines should be suited to the hulls they power. Extremes of underpowering and overpowering are equally bad. Original installations and subsequent changes require the advice of a naval architect or one thoroughly familiar with this phase of boat design.

Conversions of automobile engines for marine duty by amateur mechanics are invariably a source of trouble because of basic differences between the two types in characteristics. Lubrication and cooling are the chief problems. Selection of accepted types of marine engines is advised.

All but the smallest craft should carry at least two anchors of ample holding power with sufficient cable to hold under adverse conditions of wind and weather. Roughly eight times the depth of water is the scope needed for holding although more might be required if the bottom is poor holding ground. A spare cable should be carried for the extra anchor.

All should be stowed so as to be readily accessible in emergency such as engine failure on a lee shore, or in heavy traffic. Boatmen who cruise offshore should provide a sea anchor and be familiar with its use.

Permanent moorings should be arranged according to the best accepted practice.

In addition to mushroom anchors of ample weight and sufficient scope of chain from anchor to buoy, a strong manila (or stainless steel wire rope) pennant should be used from buoy to boat, properly protected from chafing. Frequent inspection of the pennant will reveal whether it should be renewed. Renewal is especially desirable before the hard blows likely to occur late in the season.

All life-saving equipment needs a certain amount of care. Buoyant cushions should not be handled roughly in using them as cushions; their efficiency as life-saving devices depends on their being in good condition. Cushions usually get plenty of air but the regular cork or kapok jackets are often relegated to some dark unventilated locker where they are forgotten. This is bad practice. They should be clean and dry at all times, stowed in well ventilated racks or other suitable compartments where they will be quickly accessible.

In addition to any power bilge-pumping equipment which may be provided, it is well to install a good substantial hand pump capable of handling considerable quantities of water easily.

Pans are recommended under the engine to catch any oil leakage so that it can be removed promptly before it gets into the bilge. However, it should not be allowed to accumulate and remain in the pan.

Exhaust Lines

Exhaust pipes should be installed so that they cannot scorch or ignite woodwork. Where necessary, gratings can be used to prevent gear from touching the pipe. Any leaks must be rectified at once to prevent the escape of exhaust gases into various compartments.

Exhaust manifolds should be water-jacketed (standard marine engine practice) and engine cooling water discharged through the exhaust pipe, entering as near the manifold as practicable.

Where the nature of the installation prevents the discharge of all cooling water through the exhaust pipe, it is recommended that a length of not less than 12 diameters of pipe be water-jacketed like the manifold, the remainder supported by non-combustible hangers and kept clear of the woodwork by at least 1½ inches.

If the first 12 diameters are not jacketed, or cooled by water, woodwork within 6 inches should be protected by ⅛-inch asbestos board covered with sheet metal, allowing a dead air space of at least ¼ inch between wood and asbestos and clearance of not less than ½ pipe diameter between pipe and the surface of such protection. Non-combustible packings should be installed where exhaust pipes pass through water-tight bulkheads.

There should be no traps in the exhaust line and only a minimum number of bends or elbows. Ninety-degree elbows or bends of less than 5 diameters radius are not recommended. Suitable materials for pipe are cast or wrought iron, or copper tubing of sufficiently heavy gauge, jacketed or carrying all of the cooling water discharged from the engine. Gauges suggested for copper tubing are #14 B.W.G. for 2-inch O.D.; #12 B.W.G. for 4-inch O.D.; and #10 B.W.G. for 6-inch O.D. In runabouts, #16 B.W.G. for tubing up to 3 inches O.D is acceptable.

Flexible Exhaust Connections

When steam hose or other non-metallic material is used for flexibility, it should conform to the following requirements: 1. A substantial length of water-cooled metal exhaust pipe and a water-cooled silencer should be installed between the flexible section and the exhaust manifold. 2. All cooling water from the motor should pass through the flexible section. 3. Material of the flexible sections should be specially adapted to resist the action of oil and heat. 4. The flexible section should be suitably reinforced to prevent crushing or panting by extra thickness of wall or built-in wire winding. 5. As installed it should not be bent sufficiently to unduly stress or crimp the inner or outer linings or to permit local impingement of exhaust gases.

Unless of down-draft type, carburetors should have a closed drip collector. Air intakes are to be directed so that backfires cannot blow into the bilges and should be fitted with flame arrestors according to regulations.

Fuel Tank Construction and Installation

Fuel tanks should be installed so as to be secure against moving in a heavy seaway. It is best if gas tanks can be located in separate water-tight compartments higher than the water line, with water-tight pans below them suitably fitted with overboard drains. Considerations of design may make this impossible.

Preferably tanks should be installed to permit removal for periodic inspection and cleaning. Locating them in remote sections of the hull necessitates excessive length of piping. Use of portable tanks below deck is not good practice.

Number 18 gauge (U. S. Std.) is specified for tanks of non-corrosive metals or alloys—14 gauge for iron or steel, except that 18 gauge is acceptable in runabout tanks of iron or steel up to 35 gallons capacity, and 16 gauge up to 70 gallons. Hot dipped galvanizing inside and out is recommended for iron and steel.

Seams of copper tanks should be rolled, riveted, and

The radio direction finder is independent of night and weather conditions, permitting bearings to be taken to provide lines of position regardless of visibility. Intersections of two or more lines give a fix. This yacht is also equipped with radiotelephone and radar

The carburetor of every gasoline engine installed after April 25, 1940, must be equipped with a flame arrester. However, they are not required on outboard motors

Shut-off valves are desirable both at the tank and carburetor. In the best installations they will be arranged so that they can be operated from outside the compartments in which tanks are located. Also recommended is a heat-actuated device to shut off the fuel supply, automatically in case of fire. Valves should be of non-ferrous metal with ground seats installed to close against the flow. Types which depend on packing to prevent leakage at the stem should not be used.

Fuel lines should be of seamless drawn annealed copper tubing or copper pipe, run so as to be in sight for easy inspection, protected from damage and secured against vibration by soft non-ferrous clips with rounded edges. Ferrules of non-abrasive material may be used to conduct piping through steel decks or bulkheads. In rubber-mounted engine installations, a short length of flexible tubing with suitable fittings should be used near the carburetor to prevent leakage or breakage as a result of vibration. Such a flexible section or copper loop is desirable in all installations.

soldered, or rolled and brazed—on ferrous metal, welded, or riveted and welded. All outside rivet points and heads should be welded. If the tanks are not cylindrical or have flat heads they should be fitted with strong baffle plates. Cylindrical tanks are recommended for pressure.

The safety factor for tank construction should be not less than four. Test for a gravity tank is a static head of 10 feet of water above the tank top, while pressure tanks should withstand twice the working pressure or the test for gravity tanks, whichever is greater.

Outlets or drains for drawing off gas are not recommended. Taps for drains must be tightly plugged. Outlet for the fuel piping is preferably taken from the top of the tank.

Fill and Vent Pipes

Filling pipes and sounding holes should be fitted with gas-tight connections to the deck outside the coaming so spillage and vapors will go overboard. The fill pipe should extend nearly to the bottom of the tank with a strainer in the throat of the fill. Separate sounding holes should not be larger than ½ inch I.P.S. and kept closed except when sounding.

Vent pipes leading outboard should be at least ⅜-inch I.P.S. on tanks up to 100 gallons—½-inch, 100 to 150 gallons—¾-inch, 150 to 300 gallons—1-inch, 300 to 500 gallons. In boats that heel, such as auxiliaries, the port tank vent should be led to the starboard side and vice versa.

The fill and vent fittings may be combined in a single anti-explosion unit. Where vents terminate on the hull, the outlet should be fitted with a flame trap inside the hull to protect against flare backs from outside sources of ignition. Vents should never terminate in closed spaces such as engine compartments or under deck.

Gauge glasses and try cocks are not recommended though other methods of indicating fuel level may be used if they do not expose liquid or vapor inside the boat or permit it to get below. Auxiliary tanks should be filled and vented the same as the main tanks.

Depth recorders take over, electronically, the job of "heaving the lead." They give a continuous record of depths, which may be recorded on a graph

Tube fittings should be of non-ferrous drawn or forged metal of the flared type and tubing properly flared by tools designed for the purpose, preferably annealing the tube end before flaring. Pipe fittings should be of non-ferrous metal with standard pipe threads, the joint being soldered after being made up. Cast fittings should be tinned.

A strainer should be installed in the fuel line inside the engine compartment, properly supported so that its weight is not carried by the piping, and a shut-off provided on both sides of the strainer for cleaning purposes.

When the boat is laid up for any considerable length of time, the entire fuel system should be drained.

NINE RULES FOR THE SAFE OPERATION OF

MOTOR BOATS. SAFETY SUGGESTIONS FOR

DIESEL-POWERED BOATS. INSTALLATION

AND CARE OF FIRE-EXTINGUISHERS, STOVES,

HEATERS AND ELECTRICAL EQUIPMENT

Safety in Operation

THE practices listed below are nine good rules which boatmen should observe as a matter of habit in the operation of their boats. These have to do mainly with the safe and proper handling of gasoline. In this connection, it is pointed out that explosive vapors may be of such proportions as to be practically odorless, and may also travel some distance from the point of leakage. They do not escape from the bilge by natural means but must be drawn or forced out.

Here are the rules as given:

1. All gasoline connections should be tight.

2. Care should be taken not to expose gasoline in closed spaces through spilling, drawing off, storage, or use in any kind of cleaning, no matter how small the quantity.

3. Ventilation as adequate as possible should be insured by attention to all arrangements therefore, both before starting and while running.

4. Naked lights, however small, should not be carried into compartments where gasoline vapor may be present.

5. The entire boat, especially the engine compartment, should be kept clean and free from flammable rubbish, loose oil and grease, and dirty waste or rags. Clean waste and rags should be kept in metal-lined lockers or containers. Similar receptacles should be provided for waste and rags coated with oil or paint; but such accumulation must be kept to a minimum by frequent disposal ashore.

6. In fueling, before tank fills are opened or gasoline brought on board, all engines, motors, and fans should be shut down, galley fires put out, and all doors, ports, windows, and hatches closed. On completion, after hose or cans have been removed, any spillage should be wiped up and the boat opened. If practicable, it should remain open for at least five minutes before starting any engine or motor or lighting a fire. No smoking should be permitted during the fueling operation.

7. In order to guard against a possible spark while fueling, the nozzle of the hose or can should be put in contact with the fill pipe or funnel *before* starting to run

Cleanliness is a great aid to safety in galleys, engine rooms and elsewhere. Insulation of bulkhead above the stove and provision for ventilation are good features

in gasoline and this contact should be kept until after the flow has stopped. When main and auxiliary machinery is mounted on rubber, a suitable ground connection should be provided to a metal portion of the hull or hull fittings to prevent the accumulation of a static charge.

8. Lockers in which oiled clothing is carried should be cool and well ventilated on account of the danger of spontaneous combustion.

9. Paint and varnish removers are generally highly flammable and particular caution should be exercised during their use to see that there is ample ventilation and no open lights, fires, or smoking.

Ventilation

Included in the recommendations for safety practices afloat are a set of requirements having to do with the proper ventilation of all enclosed compartments aboard motor boats.

The general rule is that any compartment in which a motor is located, particularly the lower portion and the bilges, should be provided with means of ventilation which can be depended upon to remove effectively any possible accumulation of flammable or explosive vapor. Where considerations of hull design and construction permit, compartments in which tanks are located should be ventilated in a similar manner.

Where such compartments are closed, permanently open inlet and outlet ducts extending to the bilges should be installed. Of these, two inlets should lead to the wings at one end of the compartment and two outlets from the wings at the opposite end. Where the compartments are not closed, good practice dictates installation of at least one duct in the forward part of the boat and one in the after part.

Whenever practicable, the outlet ducts should be fitted with wind-actuated self-trimming or rotary exhauster heads, or power-operated exhausters. If the latter are used, the motor should be installed outside of the ducts as high as possible above the flooring. The size of the vents should be proportioned to the beam of the boat, allowing at least two square inches of vent area per foot of beam.

Installation, wiring and all electrical apparatus used in electric exhaust fan installations should meet detailed requirements outlined by the Bureau. No electrical devices which may create a source of ignition through spark-

ing should be allowed in spaces where vapors may be present. Exhaust fans should be operated for at least five minutes before starting and after stopping the engine.

While the carburetor does undoubtedly aid in removing vapors while the engine is running, its effectiveness is more or less an unknown quantity and cannot take the place of other prescribed means of ventilation. Furthermore, such vapors cannot be consumed by the engine until after it is in operation.

On boats having no exhaust fan, all means of natural ventilation should be made effective. This includes the opening of all doors and ports and the trimming of ventilator cowls to the wind before the motor is started. Under no circumstances permit the lighting of matches, smoking or the presence of any other possible sources of vapor ignition until you are sure the boat is thoroughly aired out.

Fire Extinguishing Equipment

All fire extinguishing equipment aboard, both of the hand type and also permanently installed systems, should be of approved type. A fixed carbon dioxide smothering system is recommended by the Bureau for motor and tank compartments, bilges, and galleys. Tables are available showing the quantity of gas required for given spaces.

Both manually and automatically operated smothering systems are available. The spaces to be protected by such systems should be enclosed and contain only the usual number of openings such as ports, companionways and doors.

The Bureau's code of safe practices includes recommendations for the proper handling of fuels used for cabin heating, cooking, refrigeration, etc., and the equipment used for these purposes.

Batteries should be secure against shifting in any kind of seaway, no matter how heavy. Note clean-cut wiring, use of clips, and insulated hatch cover. Decks of auxiliary (below) are kept clear, with anchors stowed in chocks on cabin trunk. Life lines are an additional safety feature

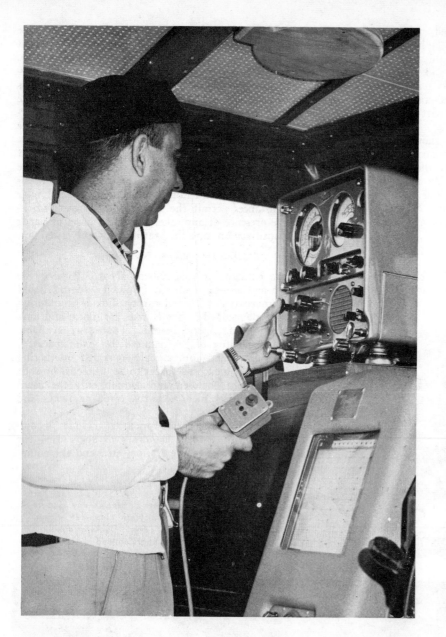

When the stove is of a type using liquid fuel, the oven should not be under the open burners because of the possibility of overflow of fuel in case the burners happen to be extinguished.

Clearance of not less than 3 inches is desirable between the bottom of a coal, charcoal, or wood stove and the deck on which it rests. Stove pipes must be of good construction, well insulated and secured.

With solidified alcohol as fuel, the containers should also be secured against movement. Using liquid fuel, a catch pan ¾-inch deep should be provided beneath the stove as a safeguard, wherever wet priming is the means of lighting the burners. Gasoline should never be used for priming.

Where the tank is of large capacity, it should be separate from the stove, either mounted outside, or with an outside fill pipe and vent if the tank must be inside. Tanks integral with the stove, as is the case with many small outfits, should be properly baffled from the burners.

Both gravity and pressure are acceptable in alcohol stoves but valves should be used at the tank of gravity or siphon systems. With outside tank, an additional valve should be fitted at the stove.

Suggestions regarding liquid alcohol stoves are generally applicable to fuel oil and kerosene types. Any system which may be affected by roll or listing is not recommended. Burners should be kept clean and never primed while hot.

Requirements for the tanks containing fuel for such equipment are substantially the same as those previously outlined for the main fuel tanks. Types of fuel are electricity, coal, coke, wood, canned heat (solidified alcohol), liquid alcohol, kerosene, liquified and compressed gas, and gasoline. Of these, electricity is said to be the safest, while gasoline does not receive the official approval of the inspectors.

In best practice, cooking or heating stoves are not placed in the same compartment with machinery or gasoline tanks. Limits of space in small craft often prevent the adoption of this ideal arrangement; in such cases it is suggested that the stove be located as far as possible from carburetor and tank connections.

Stoves generate enough heat to necessitate the protection of surrounding woodwork within 12 inches of the bottom and sides or 24 inches above the stove top. Protection should consist of ⅛-inch asbestos board covered with sheet metal, allowing ¼-inch air space between the asbestos and woodwork.

Portable stoves are not recommended; the fixed type should be secured so rigidly that shifting with the roll or pitch of the boat is impossible, even under extreme conditions. If a portable stove must be used, it should be secured temporarily, clear of woodwork, while in use.

Fairly comprehensive instructions are given in the complete text of the recommended practices with respect to stoves using liquified or compressed gas. These should be studied in full by users of such systems. For marine use, such equipment should be listed by the Underwriters' Laboratories.

Vapors from petroleum gas are heavier than air so that they would behave like gasoline vapors in settling to the bilge if allowed to escape. Mixed with air, they are explosive and should have odorants mixed with the fuel as a warning in case of leakage.

Installation should be in accordance with recommendations furnished with the system; brief printed instructions and labeled diagrams for operation and maintenance should be posted in a convenient place aboard for reference.

Heaters and Hot Water Boilers

For cabin heaters and hot water boilers, gasoline is not advocated as a fuel, nor bubble-feed furners of any type. Portable kerosene heaters are not advised, either. Recommendations for galley stoves in respect to installation and operation apply generally to heating equipment. Gas-burning heaters should be equipped with an automatic device to shut off the supply if the flame is extinguished. Pilot lights should not be used.

Flame-operated ice machines are not recommended; motors of electric types should be located as high as possible above the bilge.

Electric lanterns and flashlights are considered preferable to oil lamps and lanterns which produce a naked flame, or any type of gasoline lamp. Portable electric lights today make a very satisfactory source of emergency lighting in case of failure of the main lighting system, and there are many kinds of dry-battery-operated lamps and lanterns from which to choose.

Electrical Equipment

Wiring and electrical equipment should be inspected annually by someone competent to determine its actual condition in accordance with the following principles.

Installations of 32 volts and over should comply with the code of recommended practices for shipboard installations published by the American Institute of Electrical Engineers.

For installations of 32 volts or less, the following practice should always be used as a guide.

Generators and motors should be located in dry, accessible, ventilated places. Independent generators and motors should be mounted as high above the floor as feasible to keep them away from any possible splash of bilge water or contact with low-lying vapors. If they must be installed low or in pockets of the hull, they should be of explosion-proof type. Generators and motors of the main engine should be fused at the generators.

Switchboards must also be kept dry, accessible and ventilated, located preferably outside the engine compartment. Backs should be metal-incased, with provision for access. Uninsulated current-carrying parts should be mounted on non-absorbent non-combustible high dielectric composition.

A master switch should be installed on the main panel and an additional switch used if the starting motor is on an independent circuit. Switches not mounted on the switchboard should be enclosed. Each circuit should be fused.

Gases are generated when batteries are charging so installation of these units should be such that the gas will be dissipated either by natural or induced ventilation. Acid batteries should be set in lead pans and alkaline batteries insulated from metal contact. Batteries should be installed so they cannot possibly shift even in a heavy seaway and must be readily accessible for inspection. If it is impracticable to keep the batteries out of the engine or fuel tank compartments, they should be screened so as to prevent possibility of a spark through dropping a metal object across the terminals. Terminals should be of the soldered lug type.

Manufacturers of standard types of marine engines equip their engines with ignition wiring of a type in conformity with the code of recommended practice. They also supply ordinarily a wiring diagram to be used as a guide in installations of necessary wiring to instrument panels, batteries, lights, etc. Where a reputable manufacturer's wiring diagram is not available, detailed information may be taken from the complete text of the code including such factors as the proper size and type of wire to be used, taking into consideration given voltage drops and the amount of current to be carried. Formulas and tables are given in the code.

Hatches are desirable not only for the ventilation they provide below decks but also to provide access to decks in an emergency. Note, too, the generous sized ventilators.

As a general precaution all wiring should be of stranded type instead of single wire as an added safeguard against breakage by vibration. No conductors smaller than #12 A.W.G. should be used.

Outside conductors should be protected by metal kick pipes or tubes and terminate in water-tight receptacles. All wiring should be run as high as practicable above the flooring. The extended use of conduits and metal tubing is not recommended because of the liability of moisture to accumulate inside. Surface wiring should be protected in accordance with the National Electric Code. Concealed wiring may be unprotected but should be held in place by non-ferrous clips with rounded edges not over 14 inches apart.

Lead-sheathed unarmored conductors and conductors armored with spiral wound flat metal stripping are not recommended though suitable types armored with metallic basket weave or helical wire, with or without inside lead sheathing, may be used.

Joints and splices should be secure. If not made by solderless wire connector listed by the Underwriters, splices should be soldered. Ends of stranded conductors clamped under terminal screws should be formed and soldered unless fitted with solderless lugs listed by the Underwriters.

Splices, unless provided with insulated wire connectors, should be taped with rubber and friction tape to provide insulation equal to that of the conductor. Switches, fuses, sockets, and similar accessories should be standard National Electric Code types for the load to be carried and listed by the Underwriters.

Lighting and power switches and light fixtures in the engine room, forepeak, lazarette and galley (if gas is used for the range) should be explosion-proof. Under-deck explosion-proof switches are recommended throughout. Junction boxes instead of junction blocks, and Edison base lamps and sockets instead of bayonet lock type, are recommended. Magnetic starting switches approved by the Underwriters mounted close to the starting motors and explosion-proof starting motors and generators are also recommended.

The prudent skipper tunes in latest weather bulletins before plotting his day's course, especially when considering a long run offshore.

On wooden vessels protection against damage by lightning may be provided by grounding vertical projections in general compliance with land practice as recommended by the National Fire Protection Association code.

Safety Suggestions for Diesel-Powered Boats

Operators of diesel powered boats can contribute to the safety of this excellent type of installation by observation of the following suggestions. The relatively safe characteristics of the fuel, as compared with gasoline, are no justification for negligence in the application of principles calculated to assure the highest possible degree of safety afloat.

It is recommended that, in diesel-powered boats, the same precautions be taken as for gasoline against the leakage of fuel oil into closed or partially closed compartments. Likewise the caution requiring the entire boat to be clean and free from flammable material applies with equal force. Also the same care should be exercised in fueling. Adequate ventilation of the engine compartment should be provided and the use of naked lights in the bilge or poorly ventilated parts of machinery or tank compartments should be prohibited.

Where diesel fuel tanks are filled under pressure the area of the vent should at least equal the area of the filling pipe.

The feed pipe from tank to engine should be of seamless steel or annealed seamless brass or copper tubing, tested to at least 1½ times maximum working pressure. Connections should be made up with ground joints or on continuous metallic gaskets in counterbores.

Where water is the heating medium in service tanks, coils should be easily removable. The coils should be kept tight to insure against leakage of oil into the muffler water-heater.

Where fuel requiring heating above its flash point is used in centrifugal purifiers, the purifiers and all connections must be gas-tight. The purifier is best located in a compartment separate from the engine room. When electric motor-driven, the motors should be of explosion-proof type with controller outside the compartment in which the purifier is located.

General provisions with respect to piping of the exhaust line as given for gasoline installations apply in diesel installations except that copper pipe should never be used for diesel exhausts. Where water jacketing is not used around the exhaust pipe or muffler, woodwork within 9 inches should be protected by ¼-inch asbestos board covered with sheet metal, leaving a dead air space of ¼-inch between asbestos and wood, and clearance of not less than ⅓ pipe diameter between the pipe and surface of such protection. Some efficient type of spark-arresting device should be installed in funnel exhausts.

The provisions regarding electrical equipment, ventilation and fire extinguishing equipment are substantially the same as those given for gasoline installations.

Where gasoline auxilaries must be used in a diesel-powered vessel, the suggestions applicable to gasoline engines should be followed. Gasoline feed tanks for auxiliaries should preferably be mounted on deck, but if necessary to install them below deck then the requirements as previously given for gasoline tank installation should be observed.

Fire Protection Standards

The National Fire Protection Association, 60 Batterymarch Street, Boston 10, Massachusetts, has made exhaustive studies in the field of motor boat safety, with the purpose of drafting a comprehensive set of fire protection standards for motor boats. Their publication, Fire Protection Standards for Motor Craft, is highly recommended for detailed study by every motor boat owner and operator. The standards they have adopted are not compulsory regulations in the sense that they are required by the Coast Guard on all motor boats, but they do indicate what is currently considered good practice toward making inboard-powered motor craft as free from the fire hazard as practicable. They may safely be followed as a guide toward achievement of the highest possible level of safety practically attainable.

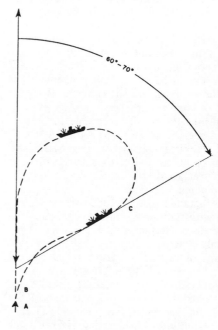

The Williamson Turn, used on large Naval vessels, particularly in rough weather and periods of low visibility, to pick up a man overboard. Alarm is sounded at A, rudder put hard over at B to right (side from which man fell) to throw propeller away from him. Speed is maintained until (C) heading 60° from original course. Rudder then put hard over in opposite direction (left, in this case) and held till ship returns to original course (at D). Engines are stopped and vessel drifts down to man in the water.

CHAPTER XI

Marlinespike
Seamanship

The Care of Rope;
Knots, Bends,
Hitches, Splices;
Blocks and Tackles

The size of rope should be matched to the block it reeves through. Chafe at blocks can cause serious damage

A PUBLICATION of the National Lead Company contains excellent advice to painters on the care of rope used in rigging scaffolding and for similar jobs. In it they make ten salient points which boatmen may observe with profit.

The anchor and mooring lines, standing and running rigging, and similar manila gear that constitute one of the most important parts of a yachtsman's equipment may be used with intelligent care—to which it will respond with years of useful service—or it may be abused by ignorance and neglect, ruining it in short order.

This question, important as it is in normal times, assumed increasing significance during the war as boatmen used up their manila. Sources of supply for manila fiber in the Philippines were temporarily cut off, so that the Government had to divert all existing stocks of manila fiber and cordage to war use.

Manufacturers met the emergency by producing rope of sisal for civilian use. While this was satisfactory as a war-time manila substitute, its strength is about 80 percent that of genuine manila, which is much better for boat use. This calls for a proportionate increase in diameter to provide equivalent strength, and when a line must reeve through a block, the size of the sheave and clearance in the hole, or swallow, must be watched. Too small a sheave and too little clearance are equally bad.

These ten commandments for the care of rope may not be all inclusive, but it is safe to say that if they are observed a boatman may very well, in many cases, be able to double the useful life of his rope. Here they are:

I. Look Out for Kinks

One sure way to destroy the value of a piece of line is to allow it to get a kink in it and then put it under strain. For example, you decide to play the Good Samari-

tan and break out your new spare line to haul a stranded boat off a bar. The new line is unruly and doesn't handle like the well-used anchor line, so there are a dozen kinks between your quarter bitt and his samson post when you ease the clutch in and open the throttle. In thirty seconds, you'll take more out of that line than you would in thirty weeks of normal service—*if* you don't shake those kinks out first.

What happens is this: The fibers are overstressed at the sharp bend, weakening fibers inside the strands. Rapid wear follows and later the line may part at that spot, right at a critical time—through no fault of its own.

The time to start watching for kinks is in the very beginning when the rope is first taken from the coil. There are right and wrong ways of doing this. The right way is to lay the coil on deck with the *inside* end *down* according to direction on the tag attached to the coil. Now reach down into the coil and pull this inner end up through the center, unwinding counter-clockwise. If it uncoils in the wrong direction, turn the coil over and pull the end out from the other side.

Inasmuch as kinks are most troublesome in wet weather, yachtsmen have more to watch than those who use their rope ashore. Wet rope shrinks as the fibers swell and the lay shortens.

Knots have the same effect as a sharp kink. Some knots may take 40 to 50 per cent out of a rope's efficiency. A good splice, on the other hand, will allow a rope to retain 85 to 95 per cent of its original strength. Therefore, if a splice is indicated, *don't* use a knot.

TO LENGTHEN THE LIFE OF YOUR ROPE

OBSERVE THESE TEN SIMPLE RULES

Running rigging on a windjammer. Sails are power on wind-ships; their rigging is as important as the engines of motor boats

2. Keep Your Rope Clean

Simple cleanliness in taking care of rope pays big dividends. In the course of use it is bound to pick up mud and sand. When this occurs, the rope should be draped in loose loops over a rail and hosed down gently, with fresh water if available. Don't use a high pressure stream with the intent of doing a more thorough job, as this will only force dirt and grit deeper into the rope. After washing, allow it to dry and then rap or shake it thoroughly to get out any remaining particles of dirt.

3. Stow Carefully

Careful stowage is a *must*. Rope should always be stowed in a dry place where it will not be exposed to excessive heat or moisture. Free air should be allowed to circulate through loops and coils; therefore, good ventilation must be provided in rope lockers.

Never toss anchor or other lines carelessly into a locker after wetting, nor throw tarpaulins or any other equipment over them to hinder air circulation. Rot fungus and mildew will grow on a wet line stowed in a locker and destroy its life in short order. The same applies to a dry line stowed in a damp unventilated locker.

Always dry lines thoroughly on deck *before* stowing below. Then hang up light lines on pegs and coil heavy ones down loosely on gratings that will allow free ventilation from below as well as above.

Strange as it may seem, alternate wetting and drying result in quicker deterioration than occurs in a rope that is always wet. Nevertheless, the way anchor and dock lines are used aboard a boat there is no alternative except to dry them carefully and stow them between periods of use.

While it is essential that the rope be dried, don't expose it to intense heat, near a hot stove, exhaust pipe, etc. Such treatment, through rapid evaporation, will make the rope brittle by drawing out the natural oils of the fiber as well as the cordage solution which the manufacturer puts into the rope. This solution is applied to the rope when it is made as a treatment to check evaporation of the natural fiber moisture, to make the rope water-resistant, and to serve as a lubricant to reduce the wear normally caused by friction.

4. Guard Against Chafe and Abrasion

Chafe and abrasion are among rope's worst enemies. Heavy coils are sometimes dragged along the ground instead of being carried on the shoulder. Dragging over a rough surface causes the outside fibers to be cut or rubbed off while grit works inside the strands and is equally destructive in cutting inside fibers.

Rope should never be allowed to rub on sharp edges, or one rope chafe against another. Surface wear is accelerated and fraying often starts as a result of it. If it is necessary to have a rope pass over a sharp edge like a rail on the deck edge or a badly designed chock, rig a canvas pad to prevent excessive tension from damaging the fibers.

When riding to an anchor for considerable periods, it is always well to "freshen the nip" by paying out a little line to bring the chafe of chocks in another place.

Chafing gear of canvas will protect the line from this source of trouble; it is particularly desirable on mooring lines where chafing always comes in one spot. Some boatmen carry a split length of rubber hose which can be readily clapped on the line where required.

Another trick to lengthen the life of a line like an anchor line or halyard, where most of the wear comes on one end, is to turn the line end for end occasionally. Any rope ends that do not terminate in a splice should be whipped to prevent fraying.

When making fast at a dock, select smooth round spiles of good diameter to make fast to, and shun square or rectangular timbers with sharp corners. If there is no alternative, pad the sharp edges.

5. Prevent Slipping

WHEN using rope on the drums of winches or hoists it is bad practice to let the rope slip on the drum as it revolves. This not only increases wear on the rope, but the sudden jerks as the rope is snubbed strain the fibers badly.

Similarly the rope should not be allowed to lie against the revolving drum of a hoist or winch. In addition to objectionable chafe, there is the element of heat from friction to be considered; this may be enough to burn the fibers.

6. Avoid Small Blocks

THERE are two sources of trouble when rope is expected to run over too small a block. On the one hand there is excessive internal friction. Wear from such friction is always present when rope runs over the sheaves of blocks and the smaller the sheave diameter, the greater the friction. On the other hand, there is the external wear as the rope chafes against the inside of sheave holes providing insufficient clearance. Faulty alignment of blocks which causes the rope to rub against the sides, or cheeks, of the blocks is also bad. A combination of this internal friction and external chafe breaks down fibers much faster than would be expected in normal use.

One place where trouble of this kind shows up quickly if installation is faulty is in the use of small sheaves in the steering lines or cables. These get a great deal of hard usage and their life can be extended by the use of sheaves of generous diameter.

In tackles, when matching blocks to rope, use a block with a shell length of at least 3 inches for 3/8-inch (diameter) rope; 4 inches for 1/2; 5 inches for 5/8; 6 inches for 3/4; 7 inches for 7/8; 9 inches for 1 inch; and 12 inches for 1 1/4-inch rope.

Care should be exercised to see that sheaves are never allowed to become rough or rusty. See to it that they are well lubricated to reduce friction and to prevent their seizing. A sheave frozen by rust or corrosion on its pin would work havoc on a piece of rope.

7. Don't Lubricate

AS mentioned above, the manufacturer has already treated the rope with an oil or solution which preserves it and lubricates internal fibers. This may account for roughly 10 per cent of the rope's weight. Users are cautioned not to attempt to improve upon the manufacturer's work by using additional lubricant of any kind upon it. The treatment given the rope originally when manufactured prolongs its life and retains its strength.

8. Beware of Chemicals

BOTH acids and alkalis attack rope. Consequently it should never be stowed any place where it might be brought into accidental contact with chemicals or even be subject to exposure to the fumes. In testing storage batteries with a hydrometer, for example, acid dropped on a rope will burn it badly. Even paint and drying oils, like linseed, should not be allowed to get in contact with it.

Alkalis and acids burn the fibers and kill the life of rope by rendering the fibers brittle. Wet rope is more susceptible to chemical fumes than if it were dry. Rust, too, is bad for rope. If a line must be used around chemicals, it is essential to check it frequently. Spots of discoloration are a danger sign showing when fibers have broken down.

9. Never Overload

AN old saw has it that you should never send a boy to do a man's job. So it is with rope. If all available statistics show that you should have a 3/4-inch anchor line, don't try to get away with 1/2-inch. Better be safe than sorry.

Many tables have already been published giving suitable sizes of anchor and mooring lines for motor and sailing craft of all sizes. However, note again that substitution of sisal for manila calls for increased diameter.

The table which accompanies this article will serve as a guide in this respect. It shows the minimum strain carried by one standard brand of both manila and sisal in commercially available sizes, together with safe working strains for each.

The factor of safety to be allowed in determining the load on a rope is commonly taken as 5. That is, if a rope must lift 500 pounds, a rope of sufficient tensile strength to handle 2,500 pounds should be selected. If the load ever exceeds 75 per cent of the rope's breaking strength the chances are good that it will be permanently injured. In that case, it may fail unexpectedly, without warning.

TABLE OF COMPARATIVE STRENGTHS—MANILA AND SISAL					
		Manila		Sisal	
Dia.	Circ.	Min. Strain Carried	Safe Working Strain	Min. Strain Carried	Safe Working Strain
1/4	3/4	600	120	480	96
3/8	1 1/8	1350	270	1080	216
1/2	1 1/2	2650	530	2120	424
5/8	2	4400	880	3520	704
3/4	2 1/4	5400	1080	4320	864
7/8	2 3/4	7700	1540	6160	1232
1	3	9000	1800	7200	1440
1 1/8	3 1/2	12,000	2400	9600	1920
1 1/4	3 3/4	13,500	2700	10,800	2160
1 1/2	4 1/2	18,500	3700	14,800	2960
2	6	31,000	6200	24,800	4960

10. Don't Use Frozen Rope

WHILE this is a problem seldom encountered by the average yachtsman whose boat is normally laid up in freezing weather, it is still a matter of moment to those, such as charter boat fishermen, etc., whose activities often run right through the winter. Rope that has been allowed to freeze after a wetting is readily broken and therefore cannot be trusted. The only practical solution if this happens is to thaw it out and dry it thoroughly before putting it back into service.

How to Inspect Your Rope

CAREFUL periodic inspection should, in a practical way, enable you to renew lines long before they have deteriorated to a point where they might be considered unsafe, even though theoretically a scientific breaking test might be insisted upon for some services. Here are things to look out for:

In an external examination of the rope, watch out for abrasion and broken fibers, variations in size and shape of the strands, and rot. Excessive wear on the outside is revealed when fibers appear to be about half worn through. Then it is time to renew the rope. Acid stains, frayed strands and broken yarns should be all revealed in such an examination, which should include the entire length of the rope.

The fibers should have a certain luster, and evidences of dryness or brittleness should be viewed with suspicion. A good rope will have a certain feel that distinguishes it from another out of which the life has gone. The sound rope will have a certain pliability, stretch and flexibility that is never present in a limp, dead worn-out rope. A good rope will be free from splinters of fiber—just another earmark of quality in good rope.

Now twist the strands so as to open the rope up, revealing the condition of interior fibers. Evidence of white powdered fiber is a danger signal warning of excessive internal bending, tension and wear. Repeat this test in several places. If yarns (the twisted fibers) appear inside to be clean, bright and free from spots of discoloration the chances are that the rope is still in good condition—assuming the exterior is also O.K.

Signs of damage due to overloading are also found in the interior yarns. A rope in which these inner yarns have been broken or partly broken by excessive loading can never be trusted.

A rough and ready breaking test that the owner can apply is to unlay about a foot of one yarn and break it with the hands. If this single yarn breaks easily, the rope undoubtedly has lost its strength. Again scientists may demand more scientific tests. When black or brown discoloration spots reveal the action of acid or chemical fumes, use this breakage test frequently.

The simple overhand knot used to keep the end of a rope from unlaying. This knot jams and may become almost impossible to untie. A better knot for the purpose is shown in:

The figure eight knot. This does not jam.

Overhand   **Figure Eight**

The square or reef knot, perhaps the most useful knot known. The rope manipulated by the right hand (this is the rope leading from the left side of the sketch and terminating in the arrow in A) is turned over the other rope in tying both the first and second half of the knot. Learn to always turn this rope over the other and the knot can be tied with certainty in the dark. If the rope manipulated by the right hand is first turned over and then under the other rope the treacherous granny knot will result.

Square or Reef Knot

Do not use the square knot to tie together lines of different sizes, as it will slip. The reef or square knot is used for tying light lines together (not for tying heavy hawsers), for tying awning stops, reef points, cord on packages, and in fact is put to such numerous uses by sailors that many landsmen call it the sailor's knot. The knot has one serious fault. It jams and is difficult to untie after being heavily stressed.

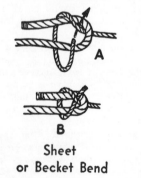

Sheet
or Becket Bend

The sheet or becket bend, known to landsmen as the weaver's knot, is used for tying two lines together. It will not slip even if there is great difference in the sizes of the lines. To make the knot secure for connecting hawsers for towing, the free ends of the lines should be stopped down with twine in the manner illustrated in the figure of the reeving line bend.

Knots, Bends,

THE real problem in advising the boatman as to the knots he should learn to tie and use is to select the few that are of real utility on the average cruiser and exclude the numerous knots which, although serving a special purpose excellently, are of little practical use to the average boatman.

The short list of knots described below and illustrated in the accompanying sketches will meet all ordinary situations. Better know these knots—practice until they can be tied with certainty in the dark or blindfolded—than to have a superficial knowledge of a greater number of knots, including many that are of little practical value.

A knot or splice is never as strong as the rope itself. It is stated that the average efficiency of knots varies from about 50 to 60 per cent of the rope itself, but a well-made splice has about 85 to 95 per cent of the rope's strength. Splices, therefore, are preferred for heavy loads.

✦

The bowline, a knot second in usefulness only to the square knot. The bowline will not slip, does not pinch or kink the rope as much as some other knots, and does not jam and become difficult to untie. By tying a bowline with a small loop and pass-

Bowline

ing the line through the loop the running bowline is obtained. This is an excellent form of running noose.

Bowlines are used wherever a secure loop or noose is needed in the end of a line, such as a line which is to be secured to a bollard in making a boat fast to a pier or wharf. They may also be used in securing lines to anchors where there is no time to make a splice. Hawsers are sometimes connected by two bowlines, the loop of one knot being passed through the loop of the other.

Clove Hitch

The clove hitch is used for making a line fast temporarily to a pile or bollard.

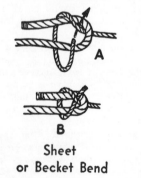

Two Half Hitches

Two half hitches are used for making a line fast to a bollard, pile, timber, or stanchion. Note that the knot consists of a turn around the fixed object and a clove hitch around the standing part of the line.

Correct method of making fast to a cleat. The half hitch which completes the fastening is taken with the free part of the line. The line can then be freed without taking up slack in the standing part.

Correct Method
of Making Fast to a Cleat

Incorrect Method
of Making Fast to a Cleat

Common incorrect method of making fast to a cleat. The half hitch is taken with the standing part of the line and the line consequently can not be freed without taking up slack in the standing part. Accidents have been caused by the use of this type of fastening on lines which must be freed quickly.

The reeving line bend, so called because it is used to connect lines which must pass through a small opening, such as a hawse pipe.

Reeving Line Bend
Free ends must be
stopped down with twine

Hitches & Splices

It may be of some interest to recall that the strength of a rope is derived largely from the friction that exists between the individual fibres, yarn and strands, of which the rope is made. The twisting of these fibres into yarn, then into strands, hawsers and finally cables is always carried out in such a manner as to increase the amount and effectiveness of the friction between the rope elements. In the tying of knots this principle of making use of friction is also applicable, for in this manner, much more can be accomplished by the use of a simple knot, so tied that the strain on the rope adds to the knot's holding power, than will ever develop from a conglomeration of hitches, many of which serve no useful purpose, and which, moreover, make it more practicable in the end to cut the rope than to untie the knots. From the examples which follow it will be evident that wherever possible the most effective use is made of friction between two or more portions of a knot in order to increase its holding power.

✢

Fisherman's Bend

The fisherman's bend, also called the anchor bend, is handy for making fast to a buoy or spar or the ring of an anchor. In some localities it is preferred to the thimble and eye splice for attaching the anchor line to the ring. As is evident from the illustration, it is made by taking two round turns around the ring, then passing the end under both turns to form a half hitch around the standing part of the line. For further security, a second half hitch is taken around the standing part only, or in place of the last half hitch, the end may be stopped down or seized back to the line with twine.

Two Methods
of Whipping a Rope End

All butt-ended ropes should of course be whipped to prevent raveling of the strands. Two common methods for doing this are shown in the sketch. While these figures are not strictly to scale this has been done purposely in order that there should be no difficulty in following the several steps involved in either of the two methods.

✢

When two ropes are to be permanently joined, provided they do not have to pass over a sheave or through a block, a short splice is better than a knot because of its strength. For pulley work, the long splice is better because the short splice almost doubles the size of the rope.

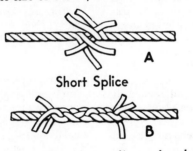

Short Splice

To make a short splice, unlay the strands of both rope ends for a short distance, preferably seizing the ends of strands to prevent them from untwisting. Now join the ends together so that the strands of one rope lie alternately between the strands of the other, as in sketch A. If desired, one set of strands can be temporarily tied down. Strands of the opposite set are then tucked over and under the strands of the rope, against the twist or lay of the rope. Pass each tuck over one strand, under the second, and out between the second and third. This tucking of the strands would be done the same way in an eye splice.

After one set of strands has been tucked, repeat the operation by working the other set of strands into the opposite rope. The splice is finished by taking two more tucks with each of the six strands. See sketch B. For a good finish, the splice can be rolled under foot on deck. Never trim the projecting ends of strands off too close.

For a neater finish, the splice can be tapered by cutting out a third of the yarns before taking the next to the last tuck, and half of the remaining yarns of each strand before the final tuck.

Long Splice

When the ropes are to be permanently joined without increasing the diameter, so that it will render freely through a block, the long splice is useful. In this case, unlay the strands of both rope ends about four times as far as required for a short splice.

Now join them, with strands alternating, as though beginning a short splice. Next unlay one strand of one rope and in its place lay the opposite strand from the other rope. The process is repeated for two other strands, but in the opposite direction.

This accounts for four strands. The remaining two are allowed to remain in the position they took when the rope ends were first placed together, the result at this stage appearing as in the sketch. However, instead of tucking the ends against the lay as in a short splice, each tuck in a long splice is made with the lay of the rope so that it follows continuously around the same strand. Tapering, as previously described, can be done by cutting out part of the yarns.

A Few Tips

Practice these knots with a couple of short lengths of line and put them to practical use. Always keep lines dry and clean. Keep ends of lines neatly served or whipped with twine to prevent unlaying. Serving or whipping is preferable to the crown knots or splices sometimes used to prevent unlaying as these knots and splices prevent reeving the line through the openings of a block which would otherwise take the line nicely.

The knots, hitches, bends and splices just described are sufficient for all practical purposes aboard the average pleasure boat. To make them with facility in a seamanlike manner, have some experienced yachtsman, sailor or fisherman show you how he'd do it, especially the bowline, clove hitch and splice.

Those who may wish to go into this subject intensively are referred to the Encyclopedia of Knots and Fancy Rope Work which contains 3100 examples of knots, ties, splices, etc.

Marlinespike Seamanship

THE ART OF HANDLING AND

USING LINES ABOARD BOATS.

COILING, FAKING, FLEMISH-

ING; WORMING, PARCEL-

LING AND SERVING. IMPOR-

TANT KNOTS AND SPLICES

THERE is nothing that distinguishes a seaman from a lubber as much as his proficiency in marlinespike seamanship. There is nothing more pitiful than seeing someone make fast with a multitude of turns around a pile finished off with many fancy loops only to see a puff of wind cause the boat to tug and the entire conglomeration fall apart and the boat begin to drift. Again, it is impossible to keep a boat shipshape and Bristol fashion, if the ends of your lines have "cow's tails" (frayed or untidy ends of rope).

First let us all make sure that we understand certain terms. Marlinespike seamanship deals with rope and the methods of working it. *Rope* is cordage of all types and sizes; fiber, wire, small cordage. *Small stuff* is small cordage, usually made of tarred hemp, such as spun-yarn, marlin, ratline, houseline, roundline, frequently used as seizing, for whipping, worming and serving line. *Line* is a general term applied on board ship to a piece of rope in use.

There are very few ropes on shipboard. Here is a good question to ask boating friends or to send to a quiz program, "How many ropes are there aboard ship and name them"? There are but nine ropes on board ship. These are bell ropes, man ropes, top ropes, foot ropes, bolt ropes, back rope, yard rope, bucket rope, and tiller rope. There may be one or two more but we don't want to start a fight like the one a few years ago on naming the masts in proper order on a seven-masted schooner. The main thing to remember is that you don't tie up with a *rope* but you use a *line* and you don't haul in a sail with a *rope* or a *sheet-rope* but with a *sheet*.

There are various types of fiber rope, mainly Manila, Hemp, Cotton, and Flax. Manila rope is used for general purposes on shipboard. It is made from the fibre of the Abaca plant which is principally found in the Philippine Islands. The fibre from these plants is spun into twisted yarn and the yarn twisted into strands. Then

Anchor line neatly coiled, clockwise, on deck. Note the grating below it to aid in drying

these strands are twisted together, using a laying machine to make rope. Usually the rope is made from three strands but sometimes four-strand rope is made. A cable is made by twisting three ropes together. To keep rope from unlaying easily, each successive step is twisted in the opposite direction. This is done as follows: yarn—right-handed; strands—left-handed; rope—right-handed; and cable—left-handed. However it is possible to get left-handed rope and in this case the procedure is reversed.

Hemp rope is made in the same manner as manila but the fibres come from the hemp plant. This plant is cultivated extensively in the United States and also in Italy and Russia. Hemp is usually used for small stuff but is also used on shipboard as standing rigging when wire rope is not used, and as standing rigging it is usually tarred. This preserves it from deterioration from dampness, but reduces its strength and flexibility.

Cotton is used for lead lines and taffrail log lines. It is also in great usage as running rigging on small sail boats. Signal halliards are made of unfinished flax twine.

The size of rope is measured in different ways. Fibre rope is measured by its circumference, although most yachtsmen have always designated it by its diameter. On the other hand wire rope is designated by its diameter. Therefore, two-inch wire rope is much thicker than two-inch fibre rope. Of course, the length of both wire and fibre rope is measured in fathoms. Small stuff is usually designated by the number of threads it contains. The largest of small stuff is ratline stuff, which is usually 3-stranded, right-handed and may have 8 threads to the strand, in which case it would be 24-thread. The length of small stuff is measured either by the fathom or by the pound. On shipboard small stuff is generally used for seizing, whipping, etc.

Fibre rope will last a long time if proper care is taken of it. Special care must be taken from the first, as it is most important that a new coil of rope be uncoiled properly. If this is not done the new rope will be full of kinks and there is nothing so injurious to rope as kinks. Although it has been written, read, and told many times the proper method of uncoiling a new coil of rope is so important that it bears repeating.

To do this, place the coil so that the front is up, with both fag ends visible on this face. Pull the inside fag end (the fag end at the inside of the coil) from the front. This will take out the turn in the rope, caused in coiling, and should avoid kinking. If necessary, pull the inside fag end from the back to the front of the coil before uncoiling. Never use the outside fag end to uncoil and never uncoil from the back.

Fibre rope will shrink when wet, and because of this fact it is necessary to loosen all standing fibre rigging whenever wet. If this is not done the shrinking will cause an injurious strain on the

Right: Main sheet tackle rigged with a double block (movable) on the boom and single block (fixed) on deck. The extra single block (foreground) does not increase power but serves as a fairlead. Note eye splice around thimble

Left: Line is flemished down for neatness by laying it down in close concentric coils, one against the other, in the form of a flat mat, free end at the center. If left long in one spot it may discolor the deck. It does not dry as well as a loose coil

rope. The rigging should be kept slack until dry. Rope will deteriorate rapidly from continued dampness and therefore should always be dry before stowed. To dry, it is best to coil down loosely and place where the sun can get at the rope and the air can pass freely all about it. Of course, rope should never be stowed in a locker that is not well ventilated and dry; for if not, there is not much use in drying the rope as it will rot the locker.

No attempt should ever be made to put a maximum strain on fibre rope as that will just about ruin a piece of line, even if it is brand new. We well remember a number of years ago we had a house moved and the mover had brand new manila. We said that it was a fine piece of line and would like it afterward. He replied it would be all right; but after they had pulled and hauled on it there was nothing left but a shell. The rope was no more good. Sharp bends are another thing to guard against. It must always be remembered that the safety of the rope decreases after each time it is used and, if care is not taken, all fibre rope will deteriorate rapidly.

Wire rope is generally used on board cruising boats as

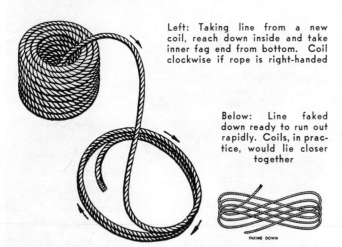

Left: Taking line from a new coil, reach down inside and take inner fag end from bottom. Coil clockwise if rope is right-handed

Below: Line faked down ready to run out rapidly. Coils, in practice, would lie closer together

Wire anchor rope spooled on the drum of a windlass to keep it from kinking

standing rigging; however, on a number of sail boats it is also used as running rigging. Steel is almost exclusively used in making wire rope. It is sometimes galvanized and can be had in stainless steel, which is fine but expensive, in order to preserve it from corrosion. Some wire rope has a hemp core. This greatly increases the flexibility and also acts as a cushion against sudden stress or heavy pull.

Great care must also be taken of wire rope. It should always be kept on a reel when not in use and must be reeled off and not slipped off over the ends of the reel. If kept in a coil it should be rolled off at all times. If a kink ever gets into a wire rope it is a disaster, as this practically ruins it. As with fibre rope, sharp bends will cause an excessive strain and greatly impair the efficiency.

It is important to note that whenever you see broken wires or when the diameter of the outside wires is worn to one-half the original diameter, it is time to condemn the rope as it is no longer safe.

When line is left on deck, or put in a locker, it is not thrown down in a heap. Not only would this give a lubberly appearance, but if you needed to use the line, especially in a hurry, it might kink or tangle. For safety and good seamanship we always either coil, fake, or flemish down a line.

A line is generally coiled down, always with the lay, when it must be kept ready for emergency use, clear for running. To make a straight coil, a circular bight of the secured end is laid and successive bights are placed on top. When all the line has been used, the entire coil is capsized to leave it clear for running.

When the entire length of a line must be run out rapidly it is usually faked down. To do this a short length of the free end is laid out in a straight line and then turned back to form a flat coil. Successive flat coils are then formed, laying the end of each coil on top of the preceding coils.

When great neatness is desired a line is flemished down. Successive circles of the line are wrapped about each other with the free end at the center. When it is finished it looks like a mat and with an old piece of line can be used as one.

A disadvantage of coiling down is that you must watch out for kinks. With a flemished down line care must be taken to prevent coils from falling back and fouling the preceding coil. If a line is flemished down and left on a deck for some time it will mark the deck as well as remain wet on the under side, and therefore deteriorate. On small boats lines are usually either coiled down or flemished down.

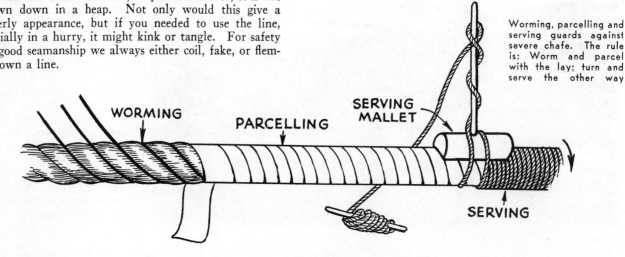

WORMING   PARCELLING   SERVING MALLET

SERVING

Worming, parcelling and serving guards against severe chafe. The rule is: Worm and parcel with the lay; turn and serve the other way

Before a person dares to take a boat out he should be able to make a bowline, two half hitches, clove hitch, and square knot. This is not all he should know, but they are the absolute minimum. The following are those that every competent seaman should know:

A—Knots in the end of a rope:
1. Overhand
2. Bowline
3. Running bowline
4. Bowline on a bight
5. French bowline
6. Sheepshank
7. Blackwall hitch
8. Figure 8
9. Cat's-paw

B—Knots for bending two ropes, or two ends of the same rope together:
1. Square or reef
2. Two bowlines
3. Single and double sheet or becket bend
4. Single and double carrick bend
5. Reeving line bend

C—Knots for securing a line to ring or spar:
1. Fisherman's bend
2. Timber hitch
3. Timber and half hitch
4. Two half hitches
5. Round turn and two half hitches
6. Rolling hitch
7. Clove hitch
8. Studding sail tack bend
9. Studding sail halyard bend

D—Knots worked in the end of a rope:
1. Wall knot
2. Wall and crown
3. Single Matthew Walker
4. Lanyard knot

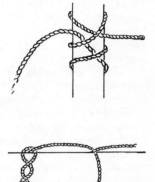

The sheepshank (above), used to shorten a line. Lay the bight in three parts and take a half hitch around each doubled part. The cat's paw (left), used to secure a line to a hook. Make a double loop by twisting two bights of the line as shown

The rolling hitch (right) used to bend a line to a spar or rope. Close turns up tight and take the strain on the arrow-tipped end. The timber hitch (lower right) temporarily secures a line to a spar or timber, as in towing. The half hitch shown is sometimes omitted. If used, it should be taken first. In both hitches, strain should be kept on the line to make it hold

A splice it nothing more than weaving a piece of line back into itself or into another piece. Not only do splices look shipshape: they show good seamanship as they decrease a rope's efficiency very little. A knot impairs the efficiency of rope about 45 per cent, whereas a good splice will take out only from 5 to 15 per cent. There are four main splices:

EYE SPLICE—Where a permanent eye is desired in the end of a line.

SHORT SPLICE: To join quickly and permanently two lines where full strength is not necessary and when an enlarged section is not objectionable.

LONG SPLICE: To join permanently two lines where full strength is not necessary and minimum increase in cross-section is desired.

BACK SPLICE: To put an enlarged, finished end on a line.

Besides the four general classes of knots and the splices, there are other types of work that all seamen should be able to do.

STOPPER ON A ROPE: A length of rope secured at one end used in securing or checking a running line.

STRAP ON A ROPE: Turns taken around a standing part with the tackle hooked through the bights.

MOUSE A HOOK: A method of closing the open part of a hook with small stuff to assist in preventing the object to which it is hooked jumping out.

GROMMET STRAP: A grommet or continuous loop of rope, used to attach permanently a hook to a block.

SEIZING: The lashing together of two ends of rope by continuous turns of small stuff.

As said before there is nothing more unseamanlike than cow's tails on the end of a line. There are many ways to prevent this such as a back splice, wall knot, etc., but perhaps the best method is by whipping. This is done by continuously wrapping small stuff around the end of the line you wish to keep from unlaying. There are two basic methods of whipping—plain, done by hand, and sewed. Sewed whipping is preferred as it is easier to get taut and much harder to pull off. The advantage of whipping over the other methods of eliminating cow's tails is that it does not increase the size of the rope. This can work as a disadvantage; for example, a sheet can run through all the blocks, making it necessary to re-reeve. Another type, such as a wall and crown, will not allow the end to run through a block.

There is nothing that wears rope so fast as chafing. In order to prevent this, it is necessary to rig chafing gear. When the chafe is of only temporary nature the rope can be protected by wrapping a piece of canvas around it. However, when the chafe will be more or less permanent or severe the line should be wormed, parceled, and served.

WORMING: consists of following the lay of the rope, between the strands, with small stuff, tarred, to keep the moisture out and for filling out the round of the rope.

PARCELING: consists of wrapping the rope spirally with long strips of canvas, following the lay of the rope and overlapping.

SERVING: consists of wrapping small stuff over the parceling opposite to the lay of the rope, to form a taut, protective cover.

All seamen should be able to work with canvas and a needle. You should provide yourself with a sewing kit consisting of a small canvas kit bag, two or three short and long needles, some beeswax, and some small stuff. The long needle, usually triangular, straight, or curved, is generally used for sewing canvas, while the short needle, usually broad, straight or curved, is generally used for rope work.

There are four main types of stitches used in sewing canvas. Flat is used for seams in sails, tarpaulins, etc.; round is for making duffel bags; baseball, where a snug edge-to-edge fit in canvas is desired; and herringbone is for very stiff or painted canvas.

NOTES ON
BLOCKS AND TACKLES

THE use of blocks and tackle, (pronounced tay-kle) or, to use a higher sounding name, mechanical appliances, on board a small cruising type boat is very limited. However the competent seaman should have a basic knowledge of them, as their use enables one man to do the work of many.

Blocks and tackle on small boats are almost entirely confined to sail boats where the hoisting of heavy sails, as well as setting them, requires some means for one or two men to match the strength of many. No matter how small the sail boat, the sheets usually run through one or more blocks, which means we have a mechanical appliance. To see how this aids, go for a sail in a 20-foot boat, in a moderate breeze, and bend a line to the boom. While underway attempt to trim in the sail with your improvised sheet. It will come in but it will be a struggle, so try it with the regular system of blocks and tackle and you will

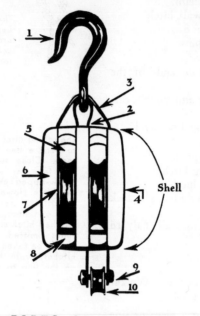

PARTS OF A BLOCK

1. Hook
2. Inner Strap
3. Outer Strap
4. Pin
5. Swallows
6. Cheeks
7. Sheaves — either plain, roller, or self-lubricating
8. Breech
9. Becket
10. Thimble

which is fitted one or more sheaves (pulleys—the word is pronounced shiv), and is designated according to the number of sheaves it contains, such as single, double, or triple. The size of the block to be used is, of course, determined by the size of the rope to be reeved. If a fibre rope is being used, usually manila, the size of the block should be three times the circumference of the rope and the diameter twice the circumference. Therefore, if 2-inch manila is being used the block would be 6 inches (three times the circumference) and the sheave 4 inches (twice the circumference). Wire rope is also used but usually only as halliards on sail boats.

The term tackle is used for an assemblage of falls (ropes) and blocks. When you pass ropes through the blocks you reeve them and the part of the fall made fast to one of the blocks or the weight, as the case may be, is known as the standing part, while the end upon which the force is to be applied is called the hauling part. To overhaul the falls is to separate the blocks; to round in is to bring them together; and chock-a-block or two blocks means they are tight together.

Tackles are named according to the number of sheaves in the blocks that are used (single, two-fold, three-fold purchases), according to the purpose for which the tackle is used (yard-tackles, stay-tackles, etc.), or from names handed down from the past (luff-tackles, watch tackles, gun-tackles, Spanish-burtons, etc.). The tackles that may be found aboard cruising boats, and should be known are:

SINGLE WHIP: A single fixed block with the standing part attached to the weight. (Fig. 1)

GUN TACKLE PURCHASE: Two single blocks with the standing part attached to the fixed block and the weight attached to the moveable block. The falls are reeved from the fixed block where the standing part is made fast, through the moveable block and then the hauling part is reeved through the fixed block. (Fig. 2)

LUFF TACKLE: A single and a double block, with the double block fixed and the weight attached to the single moveable block. The standing part is made fast to the moveable block from which the falls are reeved through one of the sheaves in the double fixed block, then through the single moveable block, and then the hauling part is reeved through the remaining sheave of the fixed block. (Sometimes called a watch tackle). (Fig. 3)

TWO-FOLD PURCHASE: Two double blocks with the weight fixed to the moveable block. The standing part is made fast to the fixed block and the falls are reeved from there through one of the sheaves in the moveable block, to one of the sheaves in the fixed block,

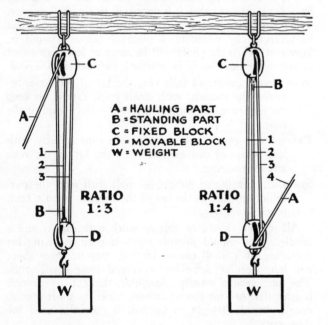

A = HAULING PART
B = STANDING PART
C = FIXED BLOCK
D = MOVABLE BLOCK
W = WEIGHT

RATIO 1:3

RATIO 1:4

The number of falls leading to and from the moveable block determines the ratio of force to weight necessary for lifting

see with what ease the sail comes in. About the most common use on a motor boat is in hoisting your dinghy.

A block consists of a frame of wood or steel inside of

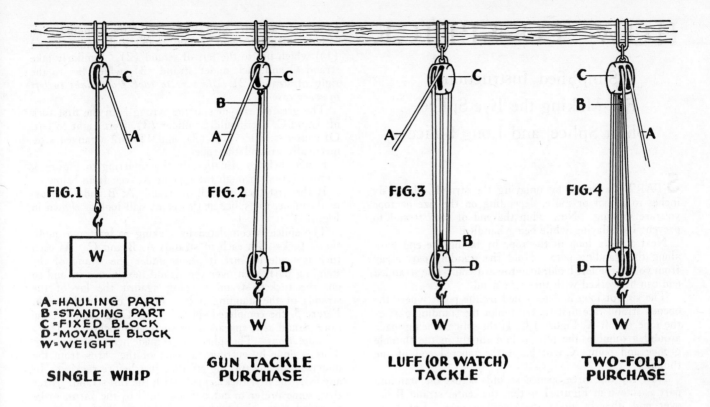

A=HAULING PART
B=STANDING PART
C=FIXED BLOCK
D=MOVABLE BLOCK
W=WEIGHT

FIG.1 — **SINGLE WHIP**

FIG.2 — **GUN TACKLE PURCHASE**

FIG.3 — **LUFF (OR WATCH) TACKLE**

FIG.4 — **TWO-FOLD PURCHASE**

Some of the common tackles that are found aboard cruising boats

then again through the moveable block (other sheave), and then the hauling part is reeved through the remaining sheave of the fixed block. (Fig. 4)

There are, of course, a number of other purchases, the heaviest commonly used aboard ship being a three-fold purchase, which consists of two triple blocks. It must be remembered the hauling part reeved through a triple block should be led through the center sheave; if not, the block will cant causing it to bind, and, in extreme cases, to break the block. This is especially true with a three-fold purchase.

To Obtain the Greatest Efficiency

To get the greatest mechanical efficiency the hauling part should lead from the block with the most sheaves, and if both blocks have the same number it is best for the hauling part to lead from the moveable block. It is also best to have the block with the greatest number of sheaves the moveable block, as the number of falls leading to and from the moveable block determines the ratio of force to weight necessary for lifting.

As diagrammed, there are three falls leading from the moveable block and the ratio of force to weight would be 1:3. Now change the blocks—the single block fixed and the double block made moveable with the weight attached and the hauling part leading from it. Notice that, counting the hauling, there are four falls leading to or from the now moveable block, and the ratio becomes 1:4 which is quite an increase. See illustration. The stated

BY MEANS OF A BLOCK OR TWO

CONTAINING ONE OR MORE SHEAVES

POWER FOR HAULING OR HOISTING

CAN BE MULTIPLIED AS REQUIRED

rule of force to weight does not take friction into consideration, and the more sheaves the falls pass the more friction.

In using blocks and tackle the utmost care must be taken in having the proper size blocks for the rope used.

BLOCK AND ROPE SIZES

Size of Block (Length of Shell)	Diameter of Rope	Size of Block (Length of Shell)	Diameter of Rope
3	⅜″	9	1″
4	½″	10	1⅛″
5	9/16″-⅝″	12	1¼″
6	¾″	14	1⅜″
7	13/16″-⅞″	15	1½″
8	⅞″-1″	16	1⅝″

If the rope is too big it will jam and if too small it will slip out of the sheave and jam between the cheeks (sides of a block) and the sheave which will cause untold damage. Also be careful that the proper size of rope and type of tackle is used in reference to the weight to be lifted. There are many tables to give you this. Also your blocks must be lubricated, clean, well painted or varnished (if wooden), and they must be so placed when in use that they will not be crushed or beaten against a spar or other gear.

The entire study of mechanical appliances is a lengthy and technical one, but also immensely interesting. There has been no effort to cover the subject, but only to give a few notes in order that an introduction be made. As said before it allows one man to do many men's work, or it is a "boy doing a man's job."

HOW TO SPLICE

Simplified Instructions
For Making the Eye Splice,
Short Splice, and Long Splice

START the splice by unlaying the strands, about six inches to a foot or more, depending on the size of rope you are splicing. Now whip the end of each strand to prevent its unlaying while being handled.

Next form a loop in the rope by laying the end back along the standing part. Hold the standing part away from you in the left hand, loop toward you. The stranded end can be worked with the right hand.

The size of loop is determined by the point where the opened strands are first tucked under the standing part of the rope (point X, Figure 1). If the splice is being made around a thimble, the rope is laid snugly in the thimble groove and point X will be at the tapered end of the thimble.

Now lay the three opened strands across the standing part as shown in Figure 1 so that the center strand B lies over and directly along the standing part. Left-hand strand A leads off to the left; right-hand strand C to the right of the standing part.

Tucking of strand ends A, B and C under the strands of the standing part is the next step. Get this right and the rest is easy. See Figure 2.

Start with the center strand B. Select the topmost strand (2) of the standing part near point X and tuck B under it. Haul it up snug but not so tight as to distort the natural lay of all strands. Note that the tuck is made from right to left, against the lay of the standing part.

Now take left-hand strand A and tuck under strand (1), which lies to the left of strand (2). Similarly take strand C and tuck under strand (3), which lies to the right of strand (2). *Be sure to tuck from right to left in every case.*

The greatest risk of starting wrong is in the first tuck of strand C. It should go under (3), from right to left. Of course, strands (1), (2), and (3) are arranged symmetrically around the rope.

It may help to visualize this by referring to Figure 3, a cross-section through the rope at X, seen from below.

If the first tuck of each of strands A, B and C is correctly made, the splice at this point will look as shown in Figure 4.

The splice is completed by making at least two additional tucks with each of strands A, B and C. As each tuck is made be sure it passes under one strand of the standing part, then over the strand next above it, and so on, the tucked strand running against the lay of the strands of the standing part. This is clearly shown in Figure 5, the completed splice. Note C, C¹ and C², the same strand as it appears after successive tucks.

Suggestions—The splice can be made neater by tapering. This is done by cutting out part of the yarns from the underside of the tucking strands, just before tucking. In any case, the first tuck is made with the full strand. After that, some prefer to cut out one-third of the yarns, make a second tuck; then cut out another third of the yarns, and make the third tuck. This produces an even taper. Others prefer to make two tucks with the full strands, and two more with strands halved. Fishermen often take two or three full tucks without tapering at all.

After the splice is finished, roll it on deck under foot to smooth it up. Then put a strain on it and finally cut off the projecting ends of the strands.

If the rope is heavy or new and cannot be easily opened by twisting in order to make the tucks, use a fid to open

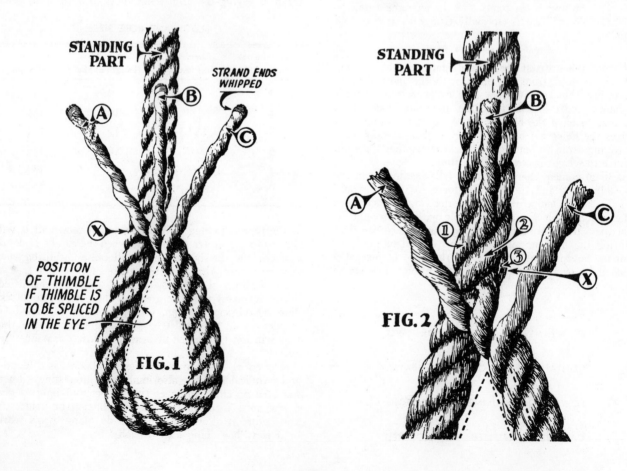

STANDING PART

STRAND ENDS WHIPPED

POSITION OF THIMBLE IF THIMBLE IS TO BE SPLICED IN THE EYE

FIG. 1

STANDING PART

FIG. 2

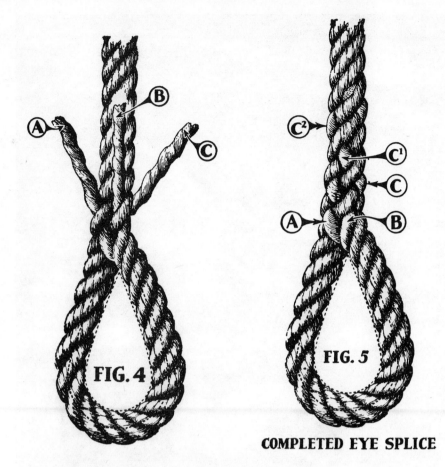

FIG. 4

FIG. 5

COMPLETED EYE SPLICE

Figure 5, at the left, indicates how the eye splice should look when completed. A thimble, if spliced in, would fit as shown by the dotted lines. A short splice is illustrated in Figures 6 and 7, below

How to Make a Short Splice

A short splice is used where two ropes are to be permanently joined, provided they do not have to pass through the sheave hole of a block. The splice will be much stronger than any knot.

The short splice enlarges the rope's diameter at the splice, so in cases where the spliced rope must pass through a sheave hole, a long splice should be used.

To start the short splice, unlay the strands of both rope ends for a short distance as described for the eye splice. Whip the six strand ends to prevent unlaying. A seizing should also be made around each of the ropes to prevent strands from unlaying too far. These seizings can be cut after the splice is completed.

Next "marry" the ends so that the strands of each rope lie alternately between strands of the other as shown in Figure 6. Now tie all three strands of one rope temporarily to the other. (Some omit this step; it is not absolutely essential.)

Working with the three free strands, splice them into the other rope by tucking strands exactly as described for the eye splice, working over and under successive strands from right to left against the lay of the rope.

Next cut the temporary seizing of the other strands and repeat, splicing these three remaining strands into the opposite rope.

Just as in the eye splice, the short splice can be tapered as desired by cutting out yarns from the strands after the first full tuck is made. Figure 7 shows how the short splice would appear if not tapered, before finally trimming off the ends of strands. Never cut strand ends off too close. Otherwise when a heavy strain is put on the rope, the last tuck tends to work out.

the strands. This is a smooth tapered tool of hard wood about 1½ or 2 inches at the butt, tapered to a point in a length of a foot or more.

When unlaid strands tend to untwist, give them a little extra twist as the tucks are made so that the strands keep their strand-like quality and do not appear as a bunch of loose yarns in the finished splice. Watch this specially after cutting out yarns.

When setting the tucked strands up taut, haul them successively back, *toward the loop,* not in the direction of tucking. See that each set of tucks leaves all strands neatly in place, not distorted by excessive strain on some strands, too little on others.

In splicing heavy lines, a temporary whipping is sometimes put around the rope itself to prevent strands from unlaying too far.

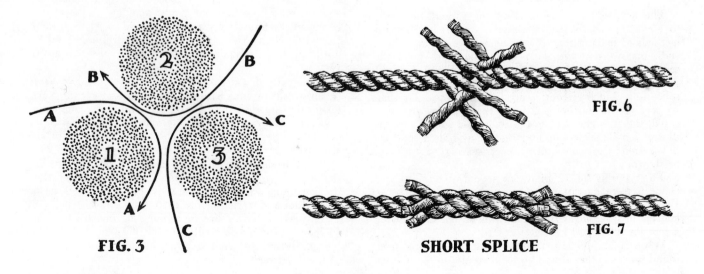

FIG. 3

FIG. 6

FIG. 7

SHORT SPLICE

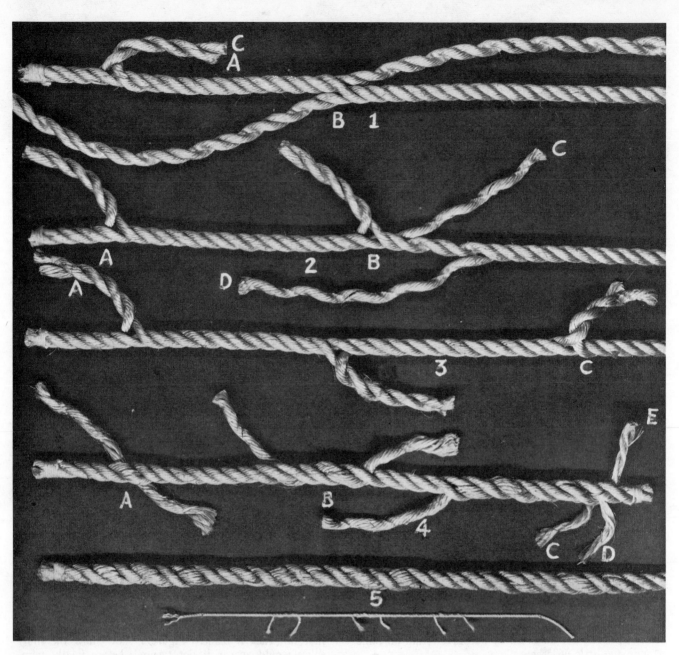

While the short splice is excellent from the standpoint of strength and neatness, as compared to a knot, there are times when the spliced line must reeve through a block. In such cases, the long splice should be used. Illustrated above are the successive steps in the making of a long splice

How to Make a Long Splice

The long splice is used where the spliced ropes are to reeve through blocks or sheaves. There are several methods of making this splice. Some splicers unlay both ends, marry as in the short splice and work from the center both ways. But by starting as in Fig. 1 (above) you do not lose any of the lay of strands. For a long splice in a 3-inch circumference line allow not less than six feet, as the farther apart the three splices are staggered, the stronger will be the completed splice. In the illustration 2-inch circumference rope was used, but the illustration does not allow proper spacing of tucks to be shown.

To start this splice, unlay one strand of one rope for about 6 feet and cut off, leaving about one foot as in Fig. 1, strand C. Then unlay strand from other rope and lay in space formerly occupied by strand C, allowing a foot for splicing as in Fig. 1 at A.

When laying the first strand A (Fig. 1), plan the spacing of splices so that B will be about central in the finished

long splice. Next unlay a strand from right hand rope and a strand from left hand rope and lay the left hand strand in the respective space formerly filled by the strand from right hand rope as in Fig. 2. Continue strand C until all three strands are about equal distance as in Fig. 3.

Then with all pairs of strands (for example Fig. 4A) tie an overhand knot with all yarns flat and even. Next take spike and tuck strands over one and under one as in Fig. 4B, unlaying strands sufficient to allow yarns to lay flat when tucked. Make another full tuck with all strands.

You now have an overhand knot and two full tucks. Halve each strand and tuck as in Fig. 4C, again halve the remaining yarns and tuck as in Fig. 4E. Roll tucks under foot and stretch before cutting off ends. Fig. 5.

To make a long splice in fishing line, make the same as above, using a sail needle to tuck the strands. In the bottom illustration, ends were not cut off, showing proper distance between splices.

210

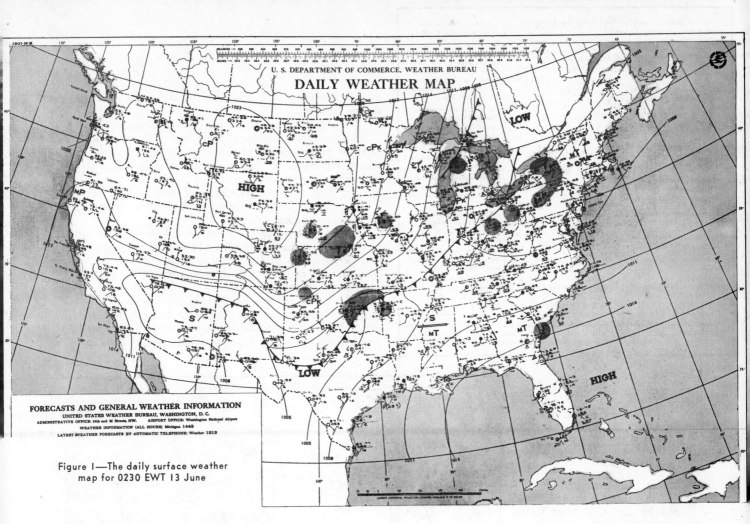

U. S. DEPARTMENT OF COMMERCE, WEATHER BUREAU

DAILY WEATHER MAP

FORECASTS AND GENERAL WEATHER INFORMATION
UNITED STATES WEATHER BUREAU, WASHINGTON, D. C.
ADMINISTRATIVE OFFICE: 24th and M Streets, NW.   AIRPORT OFFICE: Washington National Airport
WEATHER INFORMATION (ALL HOURS) Michigan 1449
LATEST WEATHER FORECASTS BY AUTOMATIC TELEPHONE: Weather 1212

Figure 1—The daily surface weather
map for 0230 EWT 13 June

Weather....AND THE YACHTSMAN

CHAPTER XII

ONE thing about these last few years—we won't say whether it is good or bad—has been the veritable deluge of writings on navigation, on meteorology, on a host of subjects in which we yachtsmen have an interest, real or fancied. For much of this storm of words we can look to our national need for quickly and effectively equipping thousands of men with a working knowledge of these matters. The aura of mysticism has been dissipated; the equations and long words so dear to the heart of the physicist or mathematician have been eliminated. We ordinary mortals have been given a better chance to learn, to learn without impairment of understanding of the fundamental concepts on which our knowledge of that subject matter must rest. We have had forcibly impressed upon us the necessity for using what we know, as well as the wisdom of adding to our storehouse of knowledge.

Perhaps in no other subject of interest to yachtsmen is this development so true as it is of Weather. We can recall the club member whom we once approached in awe, with reverence. If he deigned to speak at all, he would solemnly mention barometric tendency or frontogenesis or some equally occult term, then carefully scan the morning sky and pronounce his verdict: "The Star boats will have a fair wind this afternoon, if it doesn't rain." And he would be right, more often than not. Today we can be just as good as he was, and without nearly

so much effort as he had to expend in obtaining his understanding. The U. S. Weather Bureau, the Bureau of Aeronautics of the U. S. Navy, have attended to that. Before we get into the whys and wherefores of the weather, however, let's understand clearly that all the knowledge in the world isn't much good to us unless we use it. Thereon hangs a story (and can't we all see ourselves in Commodore Stanford's shoes!)

Alfred Stanford, twice Commodore of the Cruising Club of America, in his pungent little book "The Pleasure of Sailing" (Published by Simon and Schuster, New York City, 1943) tells this story on himself. He is writing of the Simple Virtues—foresightedness, industry, cheerfulness—and their practical value in yachting.

"I am thinking of a little cruising sloop at anchor in Block Island Harbor of a quiet evening. It is in the soft and mellow month of June. The glass is rising, but the wind is backing. The air is light and variable as we turn in at about ten.

"A few puffs come in from the north. The sky has clouded over. But it is early in the sailing season. My weather instinct is dulled—I didn't observe the mackerel sky of two days ago, or take in the cloud bank that hung over Fisher's Island and the New London shore as we

211

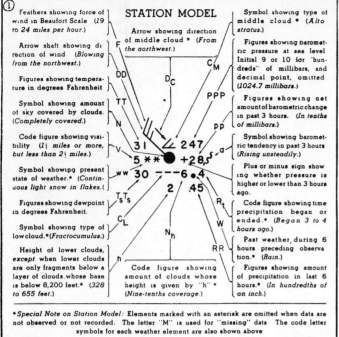

distant Placentia Bay. So pants, sneakers and socks get thoroughly wet.

"I can dry them out at our trusty Shipmate stove.

"But someone discovers there are only two small sacks of briquettes and not much kindling. We can go ashore for more, of course. Champlin's dock is just a few cable lengths away.

"But how can we get the stuff back aboard, dry? That small problem is deferred in the interest of getting on some dry clothes.

"Just as I have finished the second dressing of the morning, a sudden rolling of the little ship makes it clear that her bow has paid off. She is lying broadside to the chop that has built up with the rising wind.

"We are dragging.

"All of us now rush on deck to get the second hook down without considering how much wiser it would be not to have two anchors down, but one with a cherub weight and twice the scope of anchor rode. But again

Figure 3, above, shows a daily surface weather map station model. Figure 4, at the right, the daily surface weather map for 1930 EST 17 April 1940

sailed by in the afternoon.

"Even my weather knowledge is dulled by disuse. I have forgotten the initial overlapping, compressive effect of a downward-moving cold-air mass in conjunction with an advancing low-pressure area. Of course the barometer would rise; it has to.

"As I sleep peacefully, four days of cold, driving rain are on the way. And plenty of wind with the disturbance.

"In Salt Pond Harbor at Block Island; the narrow entrance channel runs right out to the north northeast. This means every bit of the weather will drive right in on us.

"Along about four in the morning a slight hum of wind in the rigging penetrates my dreams. I lie in a snug, dry cabin, too lazy and too comfortable to move. By dawn there are rain squalls. It is cold.

"The awning was not rigged, I recall at breakfast. The trickle of water that comes down through the skylight is duplicated over the bunks in several places. By the time I get into action, the bunk is damp and the blankets have been wet—much more than I imagine, for no surface pool stays long on the absorbent material of bedding.

"In setting the awning, I go up on deck with only an oilskin coat on. No need for oily pants or boots! This is just a bit of June rain in near-by Block Island, not

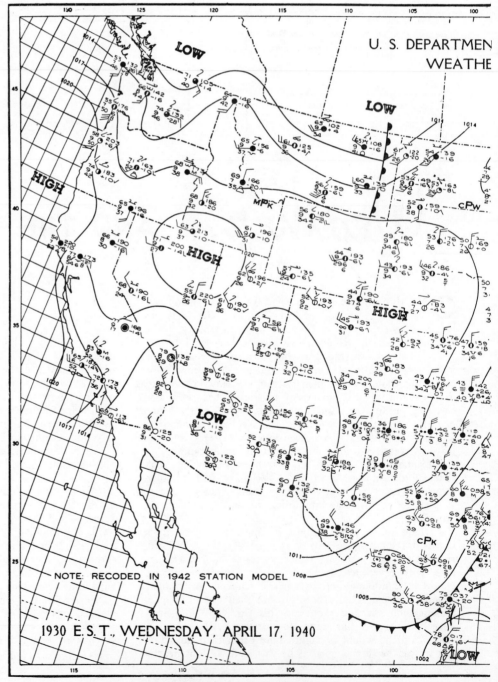

U. S. DEPARTMEN
WEATHE

NOTE: RECODED IN 1942 STATION MODEL

1930 E.S.T., WEDNESDAY, APRIL 17, 1940

we are all wet and cold by now and must hurry to get the chore done. We want to be below, out of the piercing wind. It is more like March on deck now than June.

"It seems impossible to believe that only yesterday we were stripped to the waist, basking in the sun and thinking how fine summer was.

"Clearly we are in for a three- to four-day northeaster as we see the storm-warning flags flying straight out from the Coast Guard signal mast. Why didn't we notice them before?

"Grumbling and wet, we stumble below. Why didn't someone bother to get a weather report yesterday on the radio?

"Let's try now. I get the little portable set out from the end of the starboard bunk where I tossed it to make room for the breakfast dishes. It happened to be under a drip and is wet. Hopefully I turn it on. It is dead.

"We get out of our soaked clothes and rummage for some time to dig out the last dry clothing we have aboard.

FORECASTING REDUCED TO SIMPLE TERMS

"It is unnecessary to go on, isn't it?

"Do I need to record that this ship's company found it too rough to make the trip ashore in the dinghy for wood, coal and provisions by the time they got around to it after lunch? Do I need to describe in painful detail how the two anchors fouled each other later that night?

"Or can we see the misery of those next few days fairly clearly now, the logic of one mistake leading to the next? Anyone who has sailed even a little bit knows the rest of the story."

All the signs were there, all the tools we need: the weather map, radio reports, local observations, understanding of cause and effect. They asked only to be read and used. Suppose, in this little series of articles, we take them apart, see what they are and how we may apply them in our cruising.

We don't know the precise dates of Commodore Stanford's experience but here is a daily surface weather map, the Weather Bureau having kindly given us permission to reproduce it. It records the weather conditions existing at 0230 Eastern War Time on Saturday, 13 June, a few years ago. (Figure 1.) Many of us ashore, in peacetime, would see this map in our morning paper; some of us would receive a copy by subscription direct from the Weather Bureau.

Out over Lake Erie is a heavy, black line, with sharp barbs on its easterly side. To the northwest there is another similar but shorter line. These are cold fronts. To the eastward of each are dotted gray, shaded areas; rain is falling in these localities. Over east central New York State appear the letters mT; a mass of moist (maritime), warm (tropical) air lies ahead of the cold front. Behind the front is a mass of cold polar continental air (the symbol cPK). The colder, drier air is moving eastward, thrusting a wedge under the warmer, moist air, lifting it and pushing it toward Block Island. Something is bound to happen.

A cold front does not always bring a storm or even invariably bring rain. But it is like a polar bear; never to be trusted. When the weather map shows a cold front, it is time for us to the

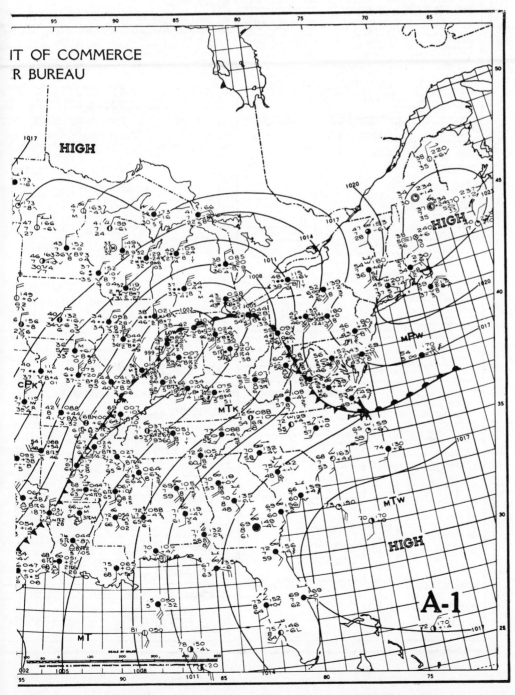

Analysis of the Weather Map—Explanation of Symbols

eastward of it to be on guard. A cold front can bring a sharp drop in temperature, a heavy rain, poor visibility, squalls, a wind shift of as much as 180 degrees with a doubling in velocity, all within a few hours. A cold front is a bad weather factory that often works overtime. So, if we would go cruising that week-end, it will pay us to watch for the signs that tell us when it is close aboard: the fluctuating barometer, in summer a warm, moist wind from the south, the thickening clouds on the westerly and northwesterly horizon.

It will pay us, too, to keep our radio tuned for weather broadcasts. There are many stations, located throughout the United States, that, in peacetime, broadcast weather reports at specified times in plain language (voice, not code) on frequencies that can be received on many commercial radio sets. Again by courtesy of the Weather Bureau, here are summaries of the essential information that would have been broadcast for those of us cruising near Block Island.

Saturday morning, 13 June: Scattered thunderstorms this afternoon, continued warm and humid today. Southerly winds. Thunderstorms and slightly cooler tonight.

Sunday morning, 14 June: Scattered showers today and tonight; much cooler tonight, with winds backing to northerly.

Sunday afternoon, special: Fresh northerly winds tonight; small craft warnings hoisted Block Island to Portland.

Monday morning, 15 June: Continued cool with fresh winds. Small craft warnings remain hoisted Block Island to Portland.

Tuesday morning, 16 June: Little change in temperature. Winds slackening. Rain continues today and tonight.

ALL we need in order to know to what station, on what frequency, at what time we should listen is a copy of "Radio Weather Aids to Navigation" (HO 118), published by the Navy Hydrographic Office and available from the Government Printing Office. When cruising midwestern waters, a copy of the companion volume "Radio Weather Aids to Navigation—Great Lakes" may be obtained from any Great Lakes Branch Hydrographic Office. For our Block Island example, on page 3 of HO 118, we find station NMF at Winthrop, Massachusetts broadcasting (voice) on 2,662 kilocycles at noon and midnight, EWT, with special warnings broadcast immediately on receipt from the Weather Bureau. That's all the mystery there is to this important phase of our subject. What about the other phases — reading the weather

map, making and interpreting local observations, understanding something about weather causes and effects—that we need if we are to become proficient in determining what the weather is likely to be, right where we are cruising?

On first glance, the weather map appears to be a staggering array of symbols, small and large. There are those heavy lines represent-

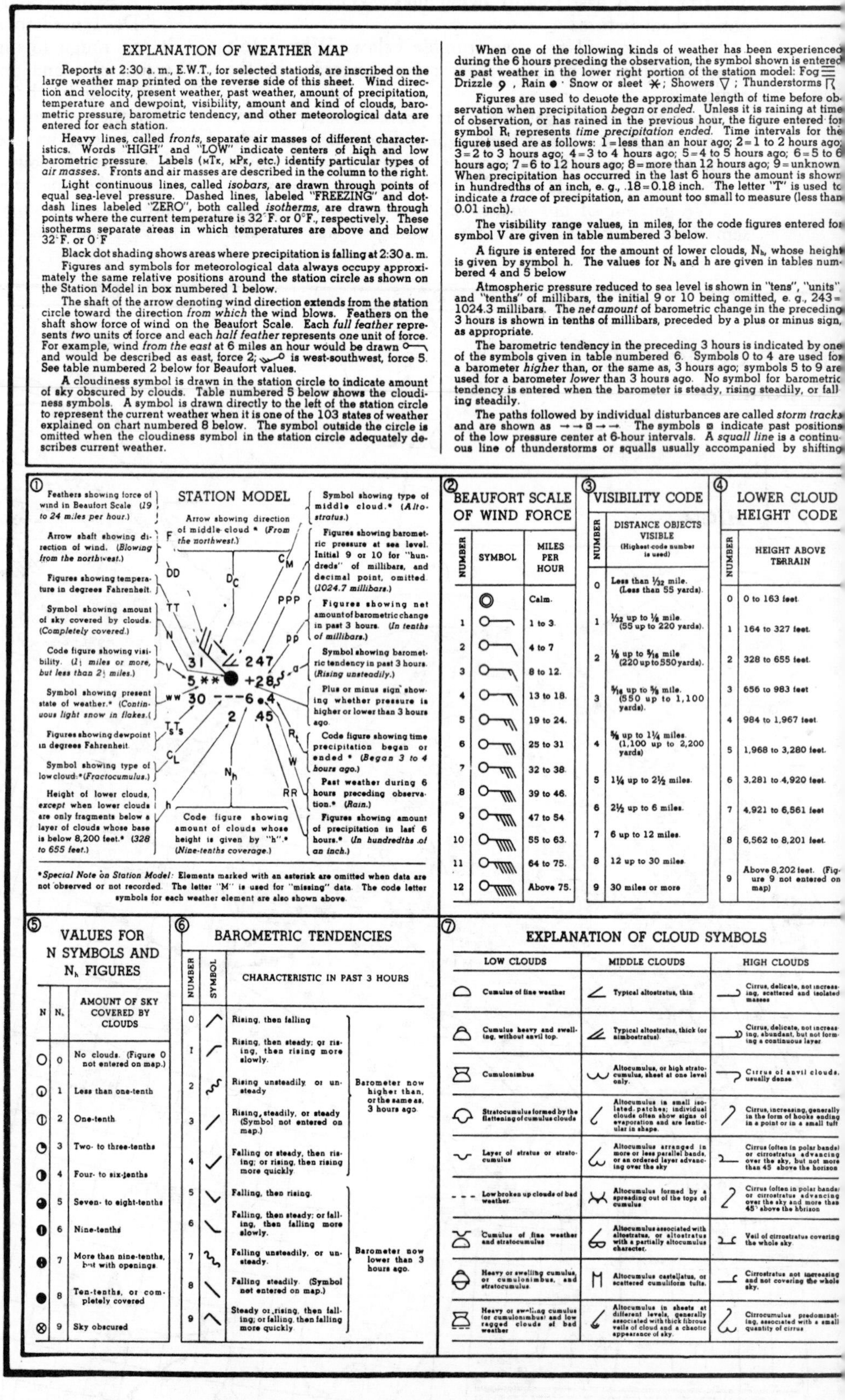

EXPLANATION OF WEATHER MAP

Reports at 2:30 a. m., E.W.T., for selected stations, are inscribed on the large weather map printed on the reverse side of this sheet. Wind direction and velocity, present weather, past weather, amount of precipitation, temperature and dewpoint, visibility, amount and kind of clouds, barometric pressure, barometric tendency, and other meteorological data are entered for each station.

Heavy lines, called *fronts*, separate air masses of different characteristics. Words "HIGH" and "LOW" indicate centers of high and low barometric pressure. Labels (мTк, мРк, etc.) identify particular types of *air masses*. Fronts and air masses are described in the column to the right.

Light continuous lines, called *isobars*, are drawn through points of equal sea-level pressure. Dashed lines, labeled "FREEZING" and dot-dash lines labeled "ZERO", both called *isotherms*, are drawn through points where the current temperature is 32° F. or 0° F., respectively. These isotherms separate areas in which temperatures are above and below 32° F. or 0° F.

Black dot shading shows areas where precipitation is falling at 2:30 a. m.

Figures and symbols for meteorological data always occupy approximately the same relative positions around the station circle as shown on the Station Model in box numbered 1 below.

The shaft of the arrow denoting wind direction extends from the station circle toward the direction *from which* the wind blows. Feathers on the shaft show force of wind on the Beaufort Scale. Each *full feather* represents *two* units of force and each *half feather* represents *one* unit of force. For example, wind *from the east* at 6 miles an hour would be drawn ⊙— and would be described as east, force 2; ⟋ is west-southwest, force 5. See table numbered 2 below for Beaufort values.

A cloudiness symbol is drawn in the station circle to indicate amount of sky obscured by clouds. Table numbered 5 below shows the cloudiness symbols. A symbol is drawn directly to the left of the station circle to represent the current weather when it is one of the 103 states of weather explained on chart numbered 8 below. The symbol outside the circle is omitted when the cloudiness symbol in the station circle adequately describes current weather.

When one of the following kinds of weather has been experienced during the 6 hours preceding the observation, the symbol shown is entered as past weather in the lower right portion of the station model: Fog ≡; Drizzle 9, Rain ●; Snow or sleet ✳; Showers ▽; Thunderstorms ℞

Figures are used to denote the approximate length of time before observation when precipitation *began* or *ended*. Unless it is raining at the time of observation, or has rained in the previous hour, the figure entered for symbol R₁ represents *time precipitation ended*. Time intervals for the figures used are as follows: 1 = less than an hour ago; 2 = 1 to 2 hours ago; 3 = 2 to 3 hours ago; 4 = 3 to 4 hours ago; 5 = 4 to 5 hours ago; 6 = 5 to 6 hours ago; 7 = 6 to 12 hours ago; 8 = more than 12 hours ago; 9 = unknown When precipitation has occurred in the last 6 hours the amount is shown in hundredths of an inch, e. g., .18 = 0.18 inch. The letter "T" is used to indicate a *trace* of precipitation, an amount too small to measure (less than 0.01 inch).

The visibility range values, in miles, for the code figures entered for symbol V are given in table numbered 3 below.

A figure is entered for the amount of lower clouds, Nₕ, whose height is given by symbol h. The values for Nₕ and h are given in tables numbered 4 and 5 below

Atmospheric pressure reduced to sea level is shown in "tens", "units" and "tenths" of millibars, the initial 9 or 10 being omitted, e. g., 243 = 1024.3 millibars. The *net amount* of barometric change in the preceding 3 hours is shown in tenths of millibars, preceded by a plus or minus sign, as appropriate.

The barometric tendency in the preceding 3 hours is indicated by one of the symbols given in table numbered 6. Symbols 0 to 4 are used for a barometer *higher* than, or the same as, 3 hours ago; symbols 5 to 9 are used for a barometer *lower* than 3 hours ago. No symbol for barometric tendency is entered when the barometer is steady, rising steadily, or falling steadily.

The paths followed by individual disturbances are called *storm tracks* and are shown as → ⊠ → ⊠ →. The symbols ⊠ indicate past positions of the low pressure center at 6-hour intervals. A *squall line* is a continuous line of thunderstorms or squalls usually accompanied by shifting

① STATION MODEL

Feathers showing force of wind in Beaufort Scale (19 to 24 miles per hour.)

Arrow shaft showing direction of wind. (Blowing from the northwest.)

Figures showing temperature in degrees Fahrenheit.

Symbol showing amount of sky covered by clouds. (Completely covered.)

Code figure showing visibility. (1½ miles or more, but less than 2½ miles.)

Symbol showing present state of weather.* (Continuous light snow in flakes.)

Figures showing dewpoint in degrees Fahrenheit.

Symbol showing type of low cloud.* (Fractocumulus.)

Height of lower clouds, except when lower clouds are only fragments below a layer of clouds whose base is below 8,200 feet.* (328 to 655 feet.)

Symbol showing type of middle cloud.* (Altostratus.)

Arrow showing direction of middle cloud. (From the northwest.)

Figures showing barometric pressure at sea level. Initial 9 or 10 for "hundreds" of millibars and decimal point, omitted. (1024.7 millibars.)

Figures showing net amount of barometric change in past 3 hours. (In tenths of millibars.)

Symbol showing barometric tendency in past 3 hours. (Rising unsteadily.)

Plus or minus sign showing whether pressure is higher or lower than 3 hours ago.

Code figure showing time precipitation began or ended * (Began 3 to 4 hours ago.)

Past weather during 6 hours preceding observation.* (Rain.)

Figures showing amount of precipitation in last 6 hours.* (In hundredths of an inch.)

Code figure showing amount of clouds whose height is given by "h".* (Nine-tenths coverage.)

*Special Note on Station Model: Elements marked with an asterisk are omitted when data are not observed or not recorded. The letter "M" is used for "missing" data. The code letter symbols for each weather element are also shown above.

② BEAUFORT SCALE OF WIND FORCE

NUMBER	SYMBOL	MILES PER HOUR
0	◎	Calm.
1	◯—	1 to 3.
2	◯⟍	4 to 7
3	◯⟍	8 to 12.
4	◯⟍	13 to 18.
5	◯⟍	19 to 24.
6	◯⟍⟍	25 to 31
7	◯⟍⟍	32 to 38.
8	◯⟍⟍	39 to 46.
9	◯⟍⟍	47 to 54
10	◯⟍⟍⟍	55 to 63.
11	◯⟍⟍⟍	64 to 75.
12	◯⟍⟍⟍	Above 75.

③ VISIBILITY CODE

NUMBER	DISTANCE OBJECTS VISIBLE (Highest code number is used)
0	Less than 1/32 mile. (Less than 55 yards.)
1	1/32 up to 1/8 mile. (55 up to 220 yards.)
2	1/8 up to 5/16 mile. (220 up to 550 yards.)
3	5/16 up to 5/8 mile. (550 up to 1,100 yards.)
4	5/8 up to 1¼ miles. (1,100 up to 2,200 yards.)
5	1¼ up to 2½ miles.
6	2½ up to 6 miles.
7	6 up to 12 miles.
8	12 up to 30 miles.
9	30 miles or more

④ LOWER CLOUD HEIGHT CODE

NUMBER	HEIGHT ABOVE TERRAIN
0	0 to 163 feet.
1	164 to 327 feet.
2	328 to 655 feet.
3	656 to 983 feet.
4	984 to 1,967 feet.
5	1,968 to 3,280 feet.
6	3,281 to 4,920 feet.
7	4,921 to 6,561 feet.
8	6,562 to 8,201 feet.
9	Above 8,202 feet. (Figure 9 not entered on map)

⑤ VALUES FOR N SYMBOLS AND Nₕ FIGURES

N	Nₕ	AMOUNT OF SKY COVERED BY CLOUDS
◯	0	No clouds. (Figure 0 not entered on map.)
◑	1	Less than one-tenth
◑	2	One-tenth
◑	3	Two- to three-tenths
◑	4	Four- to six-tenths
◑	5	Seven- to eight-tenths
◑	6	Nine-tenths
◕	7	More than nine-tenths, but with openings.
●	8	Ten-tenths, or completely covered
⊗	9	Sky obscured

⑥ BAROMETRIC TENDENCIES

NUMBER	SYMBOL	CHARACTERISTIC IN PAST 3 HOURS	
0	⟋	Rising, then falling	
1	⟋	Rising, then steady; or rising, then rising more slowly.	
2	⟋	Rising unsteadily or unsteady	Barometer now higher than, or the same as, 3 hours ago.
3	⟋	Rising, steadily, or steady (Symbol not entered on map.)	
4	✓	Falling or steady, then rising; or rising, then falling more quickly	
5	⟍	Falling, then rising	
6	⟍	Falling, then steady; or falling, then falling more slowly.	
7	⟍	Falling unsteadily, or unsteady.	Barometer now lower than 3 hours ago.
8	⟍	Falling steadily. (Symbol not entered on map.)	
9	⟍	Steady or rising, then falling; or falling, then falling more slowly	

⑦ EXPLANATION OF CLOUD SYMBOLS

LOW CLOUDS	MIDDLE CLOUDS	HIGH CLOUDS
Cumulus of fine weather	Typical altostratus, thin	Cirrus, delicate, not increasing, scattered and isolated masses
Cumulus heavy and swelling, without anvil top.	Typical altostratus, thick (or nimbostratus)	Cirrus, delicate, not increasing, abundant, but not forming a continuous layer
Cumulonimbus	Altocumulus, or high stratocumulus, sheet at one level only.	Cirrus of anvil clouds, usually dense.
Stratocumulus formed by the flattening of cumulus clouds	Altocumulus in small isolated patches; individual clouds often show signs of evaporation and are lenticular in shape.	Cirrus, increasing, generally in the form of hooks ending in a point or in a small tuft
Layer of stratus or stratocumulus	Altocumulus arranged in more or less parallel bands, or an ordered layer advancing over the sky	Cirrus (often in polar bands) or cirrostratus advancing over the sky, but not more than 45° above the horizon
Low broken up clouds of bad weather	Altocumulus formed by a spreading out of the tops of cumulus	Cirrus (often in polar bands) or cirrostratus advancing over the sky and more than 45° above the horizon
Cumulus of fine weather and stratocumulus	Altocumulus associated with altostratus, or altostratus with a partially altocumulus character.	Veil of cirrostratus covering the whole sky
Heavy or swelling cumulus, or cumulonimbus, and stratocumulus	Altocumulus castellatus, or scattered cumuliform tufts.	Cirrostratus not increasing and not covering the whole sky.
Heavy or swelling cumulus (or cumulonimbus) and low ragged clouds of bad weather	Altocumulus in sheets at different levels, generally associated with thick fibrous veils of cloud and a chaotic appearance of sky.	Cirrocumulus predominant, associated with a small quantity of cirrus

Figure 2. Daily surface weather map — explanation of symbols

ing fronts, the letter combinations defining the air masses, light solid lines (called isobars) connecting points of equal barometric pressure, perhaps light dashed lines (called isotherms) connecting points of equal temperature, words such as HIGH (H) and LOW (L), a multitude of little symbols marking many cities that are called station models, shaded areas. These are merely the weatherman's shorthand and he helps us out by printing a complete explanation on the back of every map (Figure 2); it is not necessary for us to memorize them although it is surprising how soon and easily individual ones are learned.

At frequent, regular intervals throughout the day and night, hundreds of Weather Bureau observers situated all over the United States, simultaneously note the weather conditions prevailing at their stations and telegraph their observations to various forecast centers. There the skilled meteorologists of the Bureau plot these data on maps and prepare their forecasts. The map for 0230 EWT is published daily; additional maps prepared at other times are used by the Bureau, the airlines, and other specialized persons.

We don't have to be able to draw a weather map in order to be able to read one but we can review to advantage the method of analysis used by the meteorologist.

First, he plots the station models for all localities on which he has reports. Figure 3 is an illustration of this model. It gives a wealth of particulars on the weather at that station at the time of observation plus information on certain phases of the past weather. Both instrumental and visual observations are recorded. It's a pretty complete picture.

Second, he locates any fronts, using yesterday's maps as a guide. Let's take an actual case, as analyzed by Dr. B. C. Haynes, Senior Meteorologist of the U. S. Weather Bureau and published by the Bureau in its booklet "Analysis of a Series of Surface Weather Maps." Figure 4 is the finished map for 1930 EST Wednesday, 17 April 1940. Given the station models, how was it completed?

Fronts are weather factories; they develop when two different masses of air, each of which wants to retain its individuality, meet. Fronts are marked by a difference in the temperatures of the two air masses, a difference in dewpoints (the temperature at which the air is saturated with moisture), differences in barometric pressure and pressure tendency, differences in wind direction and velocity. To make a start, we examine the station models and find that the lowest barometric pressure (998.0 millibars for this map) is at a station in western Indiana. Note that the general wind pattern over Kentucky, Tennessee and the southwestern states is from south to southwest. Over Illinois, Missouri, Kansas and the central plains states the general wind pattern is northwest to north. Different air masses must be over each of these regions and these air masses must be separated by a front. Beginning at our station in western Indiana we will draw this front.

To confirm our finding that a front exists, we look at the next station due west of our starting point; it is located in central Illinois. Here are the salient data of the two station models:

	Western Indiana	Central Illinois
Air temperature...	65°	37°
Dewpoint	60°	36°
Pressure	998.0 mb	1,004.4 mb
Pressure Tendency	—2.2 mb	+2.4 mb
Wind direction....	SW	N
Wind velocity (force)	4	5

The differences are sharp; we are on the right track.

We continue southwestward across Illinois, southeastern Missouri, central Arkansas, the northwestern tip of Louisiana, eastern Texas, into Mexico, all the time comparing the station models and placing the front between those showing the critical

---

inds and heavy showers, and is indicated as ←—SQUALL LINE—→ when occurs.

FRONTS AND AIR MASSES

The boundary between two different air masses is called a *front*. Im-rtant changes in weather often occur with the passage of a front. Half rcle and/or triangular symbols are placed on the lines representing fronts indicate the classification of the front. The side on which the symbols e placed indicates the direction of movement. The boundary of rela-vely cold air of polar origin advancing into an area occupied by warmer ;, usually of tropical origin, is called a *cold front*. The boundary of rela-vely warm air advancing into an area occupied by colder air is called a *arm front*. The line along which a cold front has overtaken a warm front called an *occluded front*. A boundary between two air masses, which ows little tendency at the time of observation to advance into either the arm or the cold areas, is called a *stationary front*. Air mass boundaries e known as *surface fronts* when they intersect the ground, and as *upper r fronts* when they do not. Surface fronts are drawn in solid black, fronts oft are drawn in outline only.

Front symbols, with arrows to show their direction of movement, are ven below:

◖◗◗	Warm front (surface)	◠◠◠	Warm front (aloft)
▲▲▲	Cold front (surface)	△△△	Cold front (aloft)
◗▲◗	Occluded front (surface)	▼◗▼◗	Stationary front (surface)

A front which is disappearing or decreasing in intensity is labeled RONTOLYSIS".

A front which is forming or increasing in intensity is labeled "FRONTO-ENESIS"

Masses of air are classified to indicate their origin and basic charac-ristics. For example, the letter P *(Polar)* denotes relatively dry and cold r from northerly regions. The letter T *(Tropical)* denotes relatively moist d warm air from southerly regions. Letters placed *before* the letters T d P indicate *maritime* (m) or *continental* (c) classification. Letters placed *after* T and P show that the air mass is *colder* (k) or *warmer* (w) than the surface over which it is moving. Mixtures of air masses are denoted by plus signs (+), and transitional changes of air masses from one type to another are indicated by arrows (⇒). One air mass above another is indicated by placing the label for the higher air mass above the other, with a separating line. Air mass symbols composed of the following letters are used:

m = Maritime; c = Continental; A = Arctic; P = Polar; T = Tropical; E = Equatorial; S = Superior (very dry); k = colder and w = warmer than the surface over which it is moving.

PRECIPITATION MAP

The precipitation map contains the same United States stations as the large weather map. When precipitation has occurred at any of these stations in the 24-hour period ending at 2:30 a. m., E. W. T., figures denoting the total amounts, in hundredths of an inch, are entered at the station circle. When the figures for total precipitation have been compiled from incomplete data the figure on the map will be underlined.

The geographical area in which precipitation has fallen in the last 24 hours, ending at 2:30 a. m., E. W. T., is covered by black dot shading.

TEMPERATURE MAP

The temperature map contains the same United States stations as the large weather map. The figures entered above the station circles denote *maximum* temperatures reported from these stations during the last 24 hours, ending at 2:30 a. m., E. W. T. The figures entered below the station circles denote *minimum* temperatures for 24 hours, ending at 2:30 p. m., E. W. T., of the previous day.

Light gray shading, labeled "COLDER" or "WARMER", indicates the area in which current temperatures recorded at 2:30 a. m., E. W. T., are 10° to 19°F. higher or lower than 24 hours ago.

Dark gray shading, labeled "MUCH COLDER" or "MUCH WARMER", indicates the area in which current temperatures recorded at 2:30 a. m., E. W. T., are 20°F., or more, higher or lower than 24 hours ago.

Inquiries regarding this map should be addressed to Chief, U. S. Weather Bureau, Washington 25, D. C.

EXPLANATION OF PRESENT WEATHER SYMBOLS

Symbol	Meaning
≡	Low fog, whether on ground or at sea.
∞	Haze, but visibility 5/8 miles (1,100 yards) or more.
§	Dust devils seen.
<	Distant lightning.
=	Light fog (visibility 5/8 miles (1,100 yards) or more).
≡)	Fog at a distance, but not at station.
•)	Rain within sight.
*)	Snow within sight.
ϟ)	Thunder, without precipitation at station.
S)	Duststorm within sight, but not at station.
∇	Ugly, threatening sky.
∧	Squally weather.
⩓	Heavy squalls in last three hours.
)(	Waterspouts seen in last three hours.
⊃	Visibility reduced by smoke.
S	Blowing dust, but visibility 5/8 miles (1,100 yards) or more.
9	Signs of tropical storm (hurricane).
•]	Rain in last hour, but not at time of observation.
*]	Snow in last hour, but not at time of observation.
,]	Drizzle in last hour, but not at time of observation
•]	Continuous or intermittent rain in last hour, but not at time of observation.
*]	Continuous or intermittent snow in last hour, but not at time of observation.
⁑]	Continuous or intermittent rain and snow, mixed, in last hour, but not at time of observation.
∇]	Rain showers in last hour, but not at time of observation.
∇]	Snow showers in last hour, but not at time of observation
△]	Hail (or rain and hail) showers in last hour, but not at time of observation.
ϟ]	Light or moderate thunderstorm, with precipitation in last hour, but no precipitation at time of observation.
ϟ]	Heavy thunderstorm, with precipitation in last hour, but no precipitation at time of observation.
S)	Duststorm or sandstorm
|S	Duststorm or sandstorm, has decreased.
S	Duststorm or sandstorm, no appreciable change
S	Duststorm or sandstorm, has increased.
S	Line of duststorms.
⇒	Storm of drifting snow.
+	Light or moderate storm of drifting snow, generally low.
⇸	Heavy storm of drifting snow, generally low.
+	Light or moderate storm of drifting snow, generally high.
⇸	Heavy storm of drifting snow, generally high.
⊜	Fog (visibility less than 5/8 miles (1,100 yards)).
≡]	Moderate fog in last hour, but not at time of observation.
■]	Heavy fog in last hour, but not at time of observation.
≡|	Fog, sky discernible, has become thinner during last hour.
≡|	Fog, sky not discernible, has become thinner during last hour.
≡	Fog, sky discernible, no appreciable change during last hour.
≡	Fog, sky not discernible, no appreciable change during last hour.
|≡	Fog, sky discernible, has begun or become thicker during last hour.
|≡	Fog, sky not discernible, has begun or become thicker during last hour.
≡	Fog in patches.
⊙	Drizzle (precipitation consisting of numerous small drops.)
,	Intermittent light drizzle.
, ,	Continuous light drizzle.
⁏	Intermittent moderate drizzle.
⁏	Continuous moderate drizzle
⁏	Intermittent heavy drizzle.
⁏	Continuous heavy drizzle.
⌶	Drizzle and fog.
⁏	Light or moderate drizzle and rain.
⁏	Heavy drizzle and light rain.
⊙	Rain.
•	Intermittent light rain.
• •	Continuous light rain.
⁚	Intermittent moderate rain.
∴	Continuous moderate rain.
⁝	Intermittent heavy rain.
⁘	Continuous heavy rain.
≡	Rain and fog.
⁑	Light or moderate rain and snow, mixed.
⁑	Heavy rain and snow, mixed.
⊛	Snow.
*	Intermittent light snow in flakes.
* *	Continuous light snow in flakes.
⁑	Intermittent moderate snow in flakes.
⁂	Continuous moderate snow in flakes.
⁑	Intermittent heavy snow in flakes.
⁂	Continuous heavy snow in flakes.
≡	Snow and fog.
△	Snow grains.
△	Sleet.
—	Ice crystals.
ⓥ	Showers of rain.
ⓥ	Showers of snow.
∇	Showers of light or moderate rain.
∇	Showers of heavy rain.
∇	Showers of light or moderate snow.
∇	Showers of heavy snow.
∇	Showers of light or moderate rain and snow.
∇	Showers of heavy rain and snow.
∇	Showers of snow pellets.
◊	Showers of light or moderate hail, or rain and hail.
◊	Showers of heavy hail, or rain and hail.
ϟ	Thunderstorm, with precipitation falling at time of observation.
ϟ]	Rain and thunder in last hour, but only rain at time of observation.
ϟ]	Precipitation and thunder during last hour, but only snow (or rain and snow mixed) at time of observation.
ϟ	Light thunderstorm, without hail, but with rain at time of observation.
ϟ	Light thunderstorm, without hail, but with snow at time of observation.
ϟ	Light thunderstorm, with small hail, at time of observation.
ϟ	Moderate thunderstorm, without hail, but with rain at time of observation.
ϟ	Moderate thunderstorm, without hail, but with snow at time of observation.
ϟ	Moderate thunderstorm, with small hail, at time of observation.
ϟ	Heavy thunderstorm, without hail, but with rain at time of observation.
ϟ	Heavy thunderstorm, without hail, but with snow at time of observation.
ϟ	Thunderstorm, combined with duststorm, at time of observation.
ϟ	Heavy thunderstorm, with hail, at time of observation.

differences. We have drawn a front on our map, but what kind of front is it?

To the west and northwest of this front, the station models show relatively colder air moving from the north or northwest; to the east and southeast they show relatively warmer air moving from the south. The colder air is moving toward the front. As it is colder and heavier, it pushes the warmer, lighter air eastward before it, at the same time driving under this warmer air and lifting it off the ground. Cold air is displacing warm; we have a cold front.

Are there any more fronts to be found? The United States is a pretty large piece of land. Starting again at our station in western Indiana, suppose we work eastward this time. Through southern Michigan and northern Ohio we again find differences in wind direction and velocity, in air temperature and dewpoint. These differences remain quite sharp all the way to western Pennsylvania. We have located another front, a warm front this time as the somewhat colder air north of our line is retreating to the northeast and warmer air south of line is following and replacing the colder.

As we continue eastward from western Pennsylvania, the front becomes more obscure; the differences between the air masses become less pronounced. On the other hand, reports of rain, overcast skies and fog continue. The winds are lighter. We draw in a stationary front (neither air mass moving appreciably against the other) all the way across West Virginia, Virginia, and North Carolina to the sea.

Warm fronts and cold fronts are active weather factories; a stationary front is a potential weather factory. The latter may gradually dissipate or it may resolve itself into an active front.

Taking a final glance at the map and station models, we notice another wind shift and temperature difference in eastern Montana. Applying the same technique, we locate another, a short, warm front in this region. We now have our frontal analysis complete.

The third step is to analyze our map for pressure indications; we need to know the pattern of the isobars, where high and low pressure centers exist, the nature of the pressure field. Water flows from high pressure to low. The rotation of the earth upsets that analogy appreciably for air. Because of this rotation, the wind blows, not directly from high to low pressure, but nearly parallel to the isobars and only slightly across them toward the low pressure. The more closely spaced the isobars, the stronger the winds in that area. The closely spaced isobars mean that a greater pressure difference exists, hence the winds are stronger, but the earth's rotation still makes them blow almost along the isobars. Observe the wind direction arrows on the station models, then note the direction of adjacent isobars. Compare the force of the wind, as indicated by the number of feathers on the arrow, with the spacing of the isobars.

Drawing in the isobars, which are always shown on the weather maps we obtain, is a job for the professional meteorologist. We need to note them carefully, as they tell us much about the winds and the winds bring us much of our weather. Incidentally, the fact that barometric pressures are reported in millibars need not disturb those of us used to reading a barometer graduated in inches of mercury; the Weather Bureau prints a conversion scale on every map.

LATER on in this series, we will delve into the wind-barometer table for, afloat, it is the changes in the wind and the changes in the pressure that tell us much about what weather to expect. Let's get back to our map.

We have a low pressure center in western Indiana. We find a high pressure center in northeastern Nevada and another off the coast of Maine. There is a high over the central plains states, another over central Canada, and others off the South Atlantic and Pacific coasts. In addition to our western Indiana low, there are lows in the southwest, off the east coast of Texas, over western Canada.

As we approach our long cold front, the isobars become more closely spaced; the pressure differences are greater and the winds are stronger. It is not too promising a time for a comfortable cruise along the east coast, the Gulf, Mississippi or Great Lakes. Perhaps we had better figure on overhauling the engine during the next day or two.

The fourth step is to determine the kinds of air masses on either side of each front. A given air mass (as we will observe in a subsequent article) has its own individual properties; these properties tell us much about the kind of weather we can expect. Having located our fronts and completed the pressure analysis, we can label these air masses. Look at Figure 4 again.

In the southeastern United States, the wind and pressure gradient indicate that an air mass is moving from over the warm waters of the Gulf northward across the southeastern states. The high temperatures and high dewpoints (see the station models) tell us that this air is warm and moist. As this is a late afternoon (1930 EST) map, the air has been further heated for many hours by re-radiation of the sun's heat by the earth. The land then is probably hotter than the air, which means that the air can be heated still more as night approaches. This air is unstable. The thunderstorms and showers, cumulus and towering cumulonimbus clouds reported at various stations confirm this diagnosis. We label this air with the symbol mTk, meaning that it is unstable, tropical moist air, air that can result in foul weather.

LOOKING north of the front along the Atlantic Coast, we note that the winds and pressure gradient indicate an onshore movement of air from over the Atlantic Ocean. Temperatures and dewpoints are fairly low, fog and low clouds are shown at many stations. These are signs of moist, stable polar air so we label it mPw, the w indicating that it is relatively warmer than the land over which it is moving and hence not given to heating from below. It will lose heat to the earth; more low clouds, fog and light rains are probable.

To the west of our main cold front, we observe northerly winds, low temperatures and low dewpoints. Many stations report stratocumulus clouds and a few report cumulus clouds. The temperatures recorded tell us that this air mass is being warmed as it moves southward. We again have unstable air. However, as it came from the northward over Canada and not from over an ocean, it is unstable, continental, polar air. We label it cPk.

Studying our map still more, we find stable continental polar air over the Dakotas (cPw) and unstable moist (maritime) polar air (mPk) over the northwestern states.

We place the symbol mTk over Kentucky or southern Ohio, the symbol mPw north of the main frontal system in the Atlantic Ocean at latitude 39°N, the symbol cPk over Missouri, cPw over North Dakota, and mPk over Idaho.

The meteorologist is now ready to prepare his forecast and we are ready for a yachtsman's reading of the daily surface weather map.

How the Yachtsman
Reads the Daily
Surface Weather Map

C. F. Brooks

W. J. Humphreys

Figure 7 (top). Altocumulus clouds. This is the active form of this middle-altitude cloud, denoting a thunderstorm is probable. As it grows into cumulus, the warning is confirmed; soon cumulonimbus clouds will form and the storm will break. Lower, Figure 8 shows stratocumulus clouds. Especially in summer, when these clouds grow denser or close up on blue sky, rain is probable. Photographs courtesy U. S. Weather Bureau

IF we should visit the friendly Washington office of the U. S. Weather Bureau and ask for a copy of the current weather map, we would be greeted with a pleasant smile and the question: "What weather map? We have weather maps and weather maps!" Yes, the Bureau prepares many types of weather map; what we want is the daily surface weather map. Figure 1, page 220, is a reproduction of the new form of this map as adopted on 1 July 1944; on the reverse side is the explanation of terms, reproduced as figure 2, pages 214-215.

In peace-time, the daily surface map is issued simultaneously by many branch offices of the Weather Bureau, each office inserting the forecasts for its region in the block at the left side. It is available daily by subscription to all citizens of the United States. (Requests for subscriptions to the Daily Surface Weather Map should be sent to the Superintendent of Documents, Government Printing Office, Washington (25), D. C., and not to the Weather Bureau.) It is also available, in modified form, in our newspapers. We will use figure 1 quite a little.

Another excellent version of surface weather conditions is the Special Weather Map published by the Bureau for limited distribution under the wartime meteorological training program of the Civil Aeronautics Authority. There are two maps for each day. One is for data reported at 0230 EWT and is the same, with one exception, as the regular daily surface weather map. The other is for observations made at 1430 EWT. Thus, we have national weather information at 12-hour intervals. The value of this feature is illustrated by figures 3, 4, 5 and 6 where figures 3 and 5 record the usual 0230 observations and figures 4 and 6 give the intervening weather at 1430 EWT.

Figures 3 through 6 forcibly demonstrate the fact that weather moves and may move rapidly. Suppose we had been cruising off Cleveland in Lake Erie that Saturday and Sunday in April. (We should not have been, had we seen the maps of Friday or Saturday morning!) Here is a portion of the weather sequence reported on the Cleveland station model:

	Saturday		Sunday	
Item	0230	1430	0230	1430
Wind direction	NE	SW	N	N
Wind force	4	4	3	3
Air temperature	43°	60°	38°	36°
Dewpoint	37°	48°	36°	33°
Barometer (millibars)	1004.7	995.6	999.0	1007.1
Barometer tendency	—2.4	—2.4	+2.4	+1.6
Sky overcast?	Yes	Yes	Obscured	Yes
Fog?	No	No	Thick	Light
Rain?	No	Yes	No	No
Thunderstorms?	No	Yes	No	No

The wind shift Saturday afternoon was substantial,

the drop in temperature from Saturday to Sunday afternoon was large. Saturday brought thunderstorms; Sunday brought fog. Look closely at figure 6. Beginning just south of Chicago and running east northeast over Cleveland all the way to the low pressure center is a line of small arrows. These arrows depict the track of the storm; it passed right across Cleveland, traveling the 350 miles from its starting point between early Saturday morning and the middle of Saturday afternoon. Old Man Weather simply won't let us take too many liberties.

This Special Map has another valuable feature not included on the Daily Map. Across its base is a vertical cross-section of the atmosphere showing certain weather conditions from the surface of the earth far up into the atmosphere. Fronts, the freezing level, precipitation

H. T. Floreen

Figure 9. Cumulus clouds. These are the cumulus of fair weather. Should they grow in size, darken and thicken across the sky as a warm summer day progresses, a thunderstorm is likely. They are signs of unstable air, of air upset by vertical currents

(vertical dashed lines), the highly significant cloud formations (the dotted areas labeled with letters) are all there for us to see. Our chances of making a sound local forecast are greatly enhanced, as we will see subsequently when we put similar cross-sections to work.

Some of us have already written to the Chief of the Weather Bureau and told him we might be interested in subscribing to the Special Map. If enough of us write him perhaps he will be able to arrange for its general issuance.

Return now to our daily surface weather map, figure 1. What are its features and limitations (from our point of view) ; what associated services are normally available from the U. S. Weather Bureau to help us utilize this map in our cruising?

This map shows by symbol the weather conditions existing at specified localities for the date and at the time stated on the map. These instantaneously-occurring conditions are "frozen" on the map but they by no means are frozen in fact. It always must be remembered that

the recorded observations necessarily truly portray weather conditions only for the time given.

Based on these observations, the meteorologist prepares his forecasts. The one printed on the map is for geographical regions of appreciable size and indicates the weather to be expected in the next 36 hours from time of observation. If only because of the extent of territory and period of time involved, the forecast is couched in general terms. There is as yet no infallible method, mathematical or otherwise, that will permit the meteorologist to guarantee that the weather will develop, in a given locality or over a number of days, precisely according to a predetermined pattern. That is why there is a continuous flow of weather news over the teletype circuits and radio stations of the airways; it is often a matter of life or death for them to be accurately informed of weather conditions at particular places.

We yachtsmen are brothers with the aviators in this case. We want to know what conditions to expect in the waters we plan to cruise, for the duration of our cruise. Unlike the aviator, we have no teletype sequence reports and we have no organization for frequently obtaining up-to-the-minute weather maps. Once we leave a major city and certainly while afloat we generally are denied the latest map.

We cannot expect, to say nothing of obtain, detailed long-term forecasts from the Weather Bureau; we cannot receive the current weather map. What purpose is served, then, by subscribing to and carefully reading a map that, in its details, is out-of-date when we receive it?

Many of us can receive, and after the war most of us probably will be able to receive, radio (voice) reports on the weather. Some of us are now able, and all of us who want to can learn how, to observe and evaluate the weather as it develops in our own localities. Later on in these articles we will return to these matters. If we are to do a really good job of interpreting these radio reports and local observations, we need, in addition to knowledge of weather causes and effects, a sound basic picture against which to judge them. This is where the weather map comes in. It gives us the necessary background information; it makes us alert as to developments that can take place; it tells us for what warning signs in particular we should look and approximately where and when we should look for them.

To help us out (and for other reasons!) the U. S. Weather Bureau normally, but not during the war, has

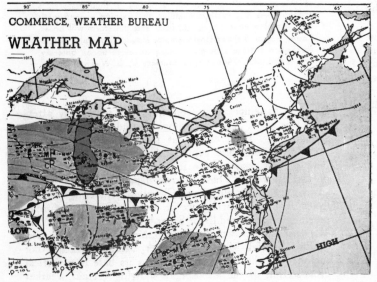

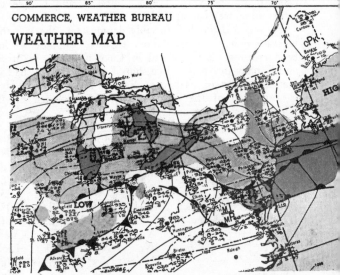

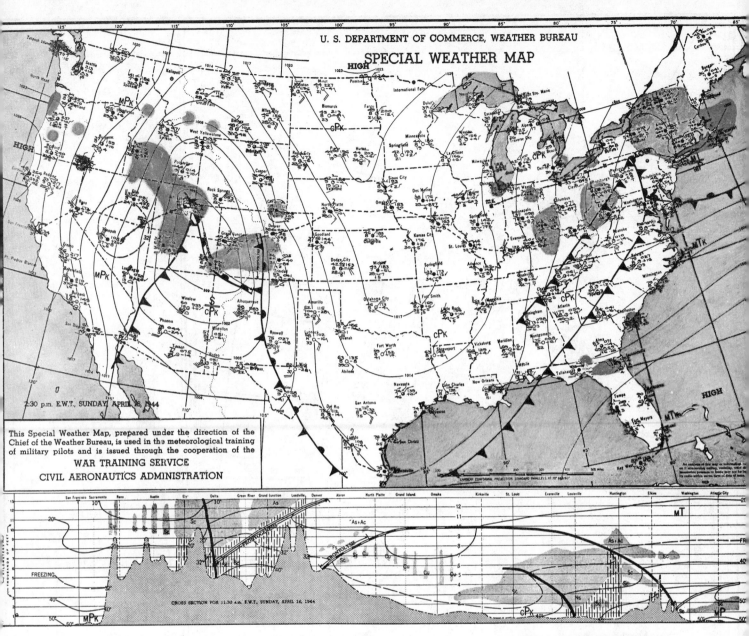

U. S. DEPARTMENT OF COMMERCE, WEATHER BUREAU

SPECIAL WEATHER MAP

2:30 p.m. E.W.T., SUNDAY APRIL 16, 1944

This Special Weather Map, prepared under the direction of the Chief of the Weather Bureau, is used in the meteorological training of military pilots and is issued through the cooperation of the

WAR TRAINING SERVICE
CIVIL AERONAUTICS ADMINISTRATION

CROSS SECTION FOR 11:30 a.m. E.W.T., SUNDAY, APRIL 16, 1944

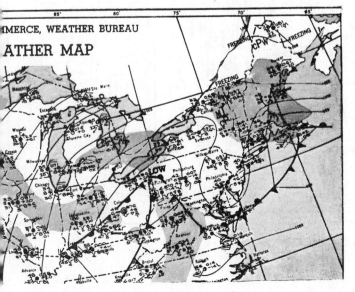

MERCE, WEATHER BUREAU

ATHER MAP

---

provided the following additional services. First, at noon on Tuesdays and Thursdays special five-day weather outlook reports are issued. These give us a very good, but general, picture of the weather we may expect. They are available from field offices of the Bureau, in the daily press, over the radio. Second, some 75 field offices

Figures 3, 4 and 5 (opposite page and at left) showing the northeast quadrant only of the Special Weather Map for, successively, 0230 EWT 15 April 1944; 1430 EWT 15 April; and 0230 EWT 16 April. Figure 6 (above) is the Special Weather Map for 1430 EWT 16 April, 1944. For explanation of symbols, see Fig. 2, Page 214.

EXPLANATION OF CROSS SECTION

The adjacent upper air cross section may be thought of as a thin vertical slice cut through the atmosphere from the Pacific to the Atlantic, and extending from the ground to a height of 14,000 feet above sea level The points on the ground on which this vertical cross section rests are shown on the adjacent weather map by the dashed blue line connecting San Francisco and Atlantic City

Pilot balloon and radiosonde data used in drawing the cross section are taken from reports of observations made approximately 3 hours earlier than the surface observations. As a result of this time interval, conditions shown on the cross section may not coincide with conditions shown on the weather map

The sloping surfaces which separate air masses of different characteristics are called fronts, and are indicated as follows.

    warm front;
    cold front;
    stationary front.

Isotherms of actual temperature in degrees Fahrenheit are drawn as light continuous lines. The 32° F. isotherm is labeled "freezing" and is drawn as a light broken line.

Vertical black dashed lines denote precipitation currently falling.

The symbols used to designate air mass types, precipitation forms and thunderstorms are the same as used on the surface map. Self-explanatory notations are also used to indicate special conditions

Vertical black dashed lines are used to indicate falling precipitation.

The approximate vertical and horizontal extent of clouds are indicated by light dot shading. It should be understood, of course, that it is not possible to show individual clouds, and that the cloud forms shown are merely symbolic of the existing clouds, which in nature are more numerous than represented on the cross section

Cloud type abbreviations used: High clouds; Ci = Cirrus, Cc = Cirrocumulus, Cs = Cirrostratus Middle clouds; Ac = Altocumulus, As = Altostratus, Acc = Altocumulus castellatus. Low clouds; Sc = Stratocumulus, St = Stratus Ns = Nimbostratus Fc = Fractocumulus, Fs = Fractostratus. Clouds of vertical development; Cu = Cumulus Cb = Cumulonimbus, Cm = Cumulus mammatus

issue amplified 36-hour local forecasts each morning; these, too, are disseminated via our newspapers and broadcasting stations. Third, airways weather forecasts are available at all airport weather offices and over the airways communications network (voice) at six-hour intervals every day. In addition, special regional and terminal forecasts, giving many intimate details of the weather, are being broadcast nearly constantly. Finally, special warnings of storms and other major weather developments are published widely and promptly; the hurricane warnings dropped by aircraft in the Caribbean furnish one example, small craft

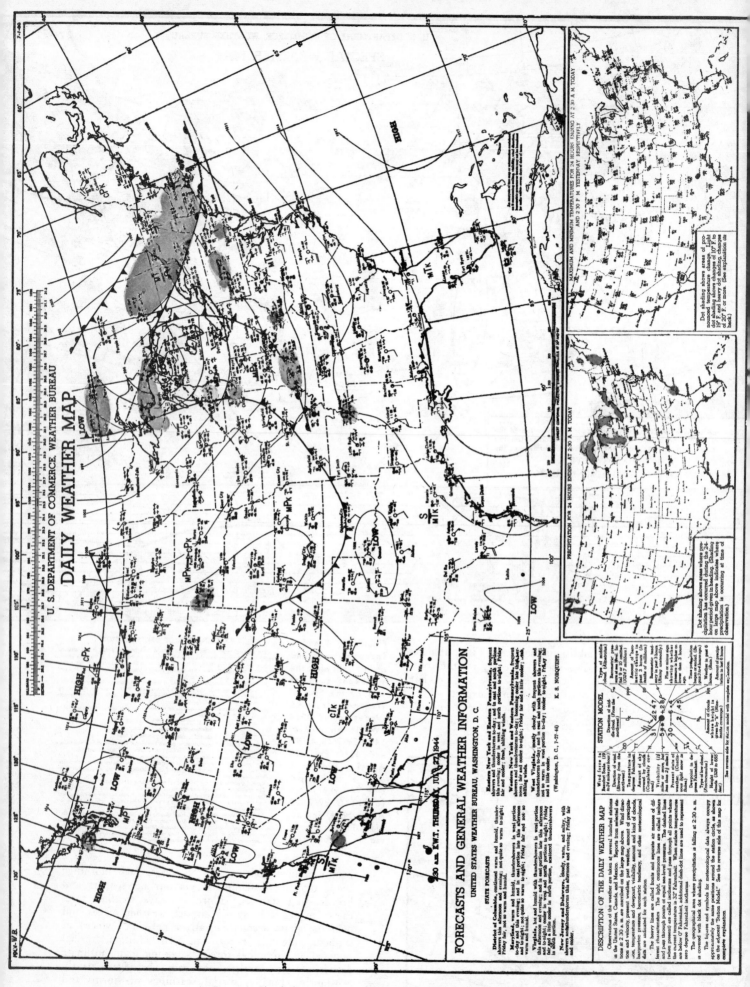

Figure I. The daily surface weather map for 0230 EWT 27 July 1944

220

and storm signals flying from Coast Guard Stations another.

It is a pretty helpful thing to be able to read the daily surface weather map, more helpful to read it each day and every day. There are four things necessary to the preparation of our own estimate of the weather, based on the map.

FIRST, we must acquire a complete mental picture of the weather conditions shown on the latest map available to us. We note particularly the conditions obtaining in our cruising locality and note generally the weather prevailing elsewhere.

Suppose we are planning a run down the Potomac from Washington on 27 July. That morning we receive our copy of the 0230 EWT surface weather map (Figure 1). The Washington station model tells us that at that time the sky was slightly (0.2 to 0.3) overcast with altocumulus clouds (Figure 7), the wind was nearly south, force 4, the pressure was 1006.4 millibars falling slightly, then steady, the air temperature was 80°, the dewpoint 70° and the visibility seven miles. The official forecasts for the District, for Maryland and eastern Virginia indicate nothing worse than a hot, humid day with thundershowers in the afternoon and evening. Not a bad day to try to escape from Washington, especially as we notice that it is mighty hot and sultry as we read the map. Looking southwest along our course down the Potomac, we note that the station models at Snow Hill, Richmond and Norfolk show clear skies and higher, rising, then falling, barometers. Knowing, however, that the weather moves generally from west to east in the United States, we are more interested in the lower, denser cloud formations, for example, the stratocumulus clouds (Figure 8) reported at Elkins and Pittsburgh, and the more sharply falling barometers of nearby stations to the west and northwest. We also observe the the mass of mTk over our locality. We know that this is unstable moist tropical air, air that can bring foul weather. We have a pretty good local picture, plus some warnings, as we look over the balance of the map.

To the westward, we observe two cold fronts, the more easterly one being part of a storm system with its low pressure area over northern Michigan and its warm front crossing New York state. (We will return to this storm later on; right now we need only to note its presence.) Moist, unstable polar air is behind these fronts, moving eastward toward us. Those altocumulus clouds reported at Washington at 0230 are a sign in themselves; these clouds generally precede a cold front by about 300 miles.

THE second step in reading the map is to project these weather conditions ahead in time and space; knowing what they were at 0230 we want to estimate what they will be later in the day. Looking at the map of 26 July and knowing that these fronts are probably moving eastward or northeastward at perhaps 20 knots, we decide that this weather may pass over us that evening. We know, too, conditions being what they are, that thunderstorms are likely to occur as the front passes over us. We conclude that the forecaster knows his job (!) and that it will be a good idea to watch for warning signs in the sky, to tune in Station NMN at Norfolk at 1150 EWT for the latest weather forecast, at 1350. 1550 and 1750 for any special warnings (HO 118).

We get under way from the club about 0930 on a fair course. Our crew having the boat well in hand, we decide to estimate how the weather will change as the day progresses. Then we can judge the probable sequence of warning signs. This is the third thing we do in "reading" our map.

The air is hot and humid and we know it to be unstable. As the sun continues to heat the earth and the earth continues to radiate this heat to the air, we realize that this instability will increase. We are on the water, so we know that the air can pick up more and more moisture. As this unstable, moist air is lifted higher and higher above the surface of the earth, we know that more and more of its moisture content is going to condense to form larger and larger clouds. As these clouds grow the chances of rain become greater. We decide to watch for cumulus clouds (Figure 9) growing and turning gray at the base as the afternoon wears on.

Knowing something of the habits of cold fronts, we will also watch for increasing cloudiness to the west and northwest, for an unsteady barometer, for an increase and backing of the wind.

We have the situation well in hand; there is no need now to wonder or worry, so we relax and enjoy our cruise. For we have already benefitted from the fourth, last and most important thing in our map reading; knowing the causes of weather developments and applying this knowledge in interpreting the map.

A MINOR emergency with the dink, which is towing astern, causes us to miss the 1150 radio weather report. But we are not much concerned; we know what to look for and can tune in later for any storm warnings. We check the barometer and notice that it has fallen slightly since our last reading at 1000. Lunch is welcomed by all hands and we continue pleasantly on our course downstream. As the afternoon wears on, the barometer is more and more unsteady, the wind backs and rises a bit and the clouds thicken and deepen across the sky. The 1550 radio report warns us

Photo by U.S. Navy

Figure 10. Cumulonimbus cloud, the thunderstorm cloud, a mark of highly unstable air with violent vertical air currents. It is a weather factory complete in itself. Heavy rain can be observed falling from the base of the cloud; hail and strong winds are also among its products.

that severe thunderstorms threaten early in the evening. The 1750 broadcast confirms this warning and estimates that the storm will arrive about 2000.

About 1800 we make our anchorage. Being weather-wise, we set the hook with special care, pay out plenty of rode and make sure we have clearance for swinging, as well as such protection as the shore provides. Following a hearty dinner, all gear topsides and below is secured. As dark, menacing cumulonimbus clouds (Figure 10) grow to westward with lightning and thunder increasing and the wind begins to sing in the rigging, we take a final look around and add a lashing or two here and there. We are ready and we know we are in a stout ship.

About 2015 the storm breaks. Rain and hail pelt down; the wind screams. We start the engine and keep it idling just in case we should drag or otherwise need full control. After a strenuous hour or so, the wind and rain slacken, the wind is steady from the northwest, the barometer rises and the temperature falls. Gradually the clouds break up and the stars are with us. The next morning, after a fine sleep, we continue on course to learn from the radio that 1.85 inches of rain had fallen during the storm and that some damage had been done. The day is clear, cooler and less humid, with a west wind force 2. The official forecast is for fair skies and moderate temperature tonight and Saturday. Our long week-end is off to a safe start.

SUPPOSE we summarize the principal features of the weather map that we should observe. In the next part we can begin to discuss characteristics and to analyze weather causes and effects.

The first thing we should read on the latest daily surface weather map available to us is the official forecast for our state or region. We might just as well have this background. These courteous chaps down at the Weather Bureau are right far more often than they are wrong; their batting average is about 0.850. Not bad, especially against a pitcher as tough and wily as Weather.

Next, we want to study carefully the data of the station models for those cities nearest our location. If we are in or near a station model city, we should compare specific weather conditions, such as clouds. air temperature, dewpoint, barometer, wind direction and velocity, for our time with those for the map time (0230 EWT). We should then judge the significance of any differences in light of our knowledge of weather fundamentals. We also need to pay particular attention to the data of stations west of us.

Third, we identify the air mass in which we are situated. We need to know if it is relatively warmer than the earth and hence possibly productive of low clouds and fog or whether it is relatively colder and therefore a good breeding area for massive clouds and thunderstorms. We need to know if it is dry (continental) or moist (maritime) air; clouds, fog and rain cannot form without sufficient moisture in the air. We need to know if it is cold (polar) air, which is relatively dense and heavy, or warm (tropical) air and consequently lighter, exerting a lesser pressure on the surface of the earth. All of these items are quickly revealed by the air mass symbol printed on the map.

It is a pretty good idea, at this stage, to get out yesterday's map and make comparisons of the station model data and the local air mass. We'll be making similar comparisons from here on. Weather in the United States moves in a general pattern from west to east; as it moves it changes but there is always a reason for any change. Substantial differences between the weather reports of two successive days tell us that powerful causes have been at work; minor differences suggest sluggish weather. We must estimate how the weather will change as it moves.

FIFTH, we go afield over the map, looking for highs and lows and comparing their extent and locations with those shown on yesterday's map. Highs generally, but not invariably by any means, indicate fair weather to come; lows are likely to produce storms. We should note particularly the location, east or west, of these highs and lows in comparison to the waters we plan to cruise. We should note whether they are moving toward or away from us. While we are looking for the high and lows, we might as well check up on the spacing of (distance between) isobars, those solid lines connecting points of equal barometric pressure. If they are close together, the pressure gradient is strong; the weather will move more rapidly and change more violently. If they are widely spaced, the pressure gradient is weak; the weather will move slowly and change gradually.

The pressure tendency data—whether the barometer is rising or falling and, if so, at what rate—will help us in evaluating the strength of any weather changes. If we can remember it, it is helpful to know that highs tend to move toward localities having a rising pressure tendency while lows tend to move toward places having a falling tendency; like pressures attract each other. By comparing successive maps, we can estimate the speed and direction of movements of our pressure centers and judge whether any will pass over or near our waters.

The principal source of rain, winds and generally foul weather in the United States are two types of storm: the extra-tropical cyclone, the thunderstorm. The latter is frequently associated with the former type, especially in summer, but often occurs separately. Our other major weather enemy is fog. Fog, like a thunderstorm, occurs locally due to the characteristics of the air mass present; we cover these possibilities when we check the map for air masses, especially mTk and mTw, as we saw previously and will note in more detail another time. Fog and thunderstorms also occur with the passage of fronts; the extra-tropical cyclone is a frontal system.

OUR seventh observation of the weather map is for fronts, those weather factories that can cause most any weather develop-

ments. We have already discussed cold fronts; look for them first. They usually bring sharp changes in the weather, with thunderstorms and perhaps a heavy rain of relatively short duration. Locate them on the map, judge their speed and direction of movement and be prepared for a concentrated dose of foul weather. Warm fronts are somewhat gentler but they take so long to get out of the way. The rain and fog hold on and on and on. We must decide if a warm front is likely to pay us a visit during our cruise.

Then there is the stationary front, the front that cannot make up its mind as to what it wants to do. But it will do something eventually, if only to dissipate, so we spot it in relation to ourselves. The fourth type is the occluded front, a front formed by a cold front that has overtaken and swallowed a warm front. A fully occluded front is weather indigestion in its last stages; in the early stages, it is the extra-tropical cyclone.

Let's take another look at Figure 1. Over the New England states, just ahead of the warm front, is a dotted gray shaded area indicative of rain; it is quite extensive. All of the station models in this area report fully overcast or obscured skies; some of them report fog. Over the Great Lakes at the western extremity of this warm front is a low pressure center, labeled LOW on the map. More rain, thunderstorms, and overcast skies mark the hapless city of Sault Ste. Marie. A cold front curves south and then southwest from this low. This system of a warm front ahead of a cold front, with the two fronts joined in a low pressure center is called an extra-tropical cyclone. Its direction of movement is indicated by the isobars in the V joining the warm to the cold front; this is known as the warm sector. Washington is in the warm sector and the cold front portion will probably pass over it. Extra-tropical cyclones bring us all the bad weather of low pressure centers, of warm fronts, of cold fronts, plus a few variations of their own. It behooves us always to look carefully for them on the weather map. To make themselves even more interesting, these storms are likely to appear in families of 2, 3, or 4; having found one, perhaps the biggest one, look for others.

To judge whether they will affect our cruise, we must estimate their maturity and extent as well as direction of movement and time of arrival at our station. Maturity is easily determined; the greater the proportion of the cold and warm fronts shown in the occluded front symbol, beginning at the low pressure center, the older the storm and the less violence it has left to expend on us. The lengths of the cold and warm fronts and the dimensions of the warm sector (the V) reveal the extent of the storm. Comparison with yesterday's map assists us in estimating its speed and direction of movement. The worst spot is the low pressure center itself; judge its movement carefully. Note on Figure 1 that there is a line of small arrows leading to the low from a point near Des Moines; the Weather Bureau thus tells us the track of the storm. The little boxes along this line of arrows indicate the position of the center at six-hour intervals.

Finally, we look over the map, especially those sections ahead of cold fronts, for the squall line symbol. None shows on Figure 1 (unless our eyes are worse than we thought); they are the exception rather than the rule. But they mean strong winds and violent wind shifts, heavy rain and hail; a squall line is a continuous line of thunderstorms. As such, it deserves our utmost respect; we simply do not knowingly cruise into a squall line.

These, then, are the weather map features we need to observe. Their interpretation must await future discussion.

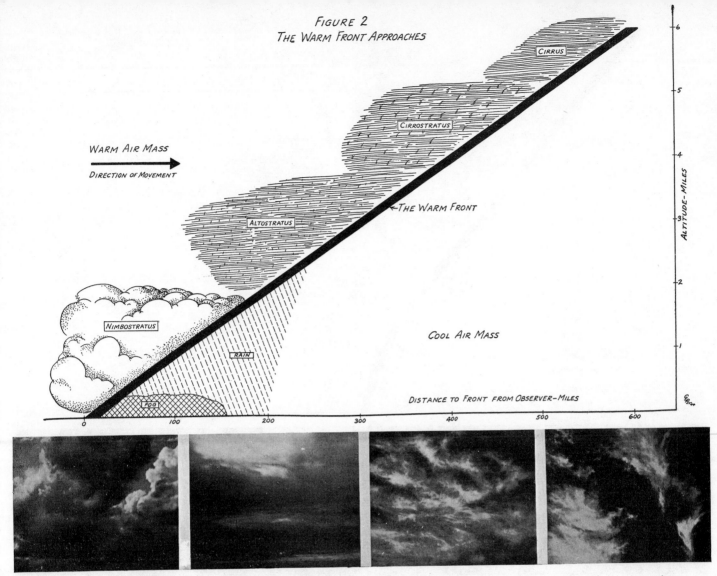

Figure 2
The Warm Front Approaches

Warm Air Mass

Direction of Movement

Cirrus

Cirrostratus

Altostratus

← The Warm Front

Cool Air Mass

Nimbostratus

Rain

Fog

Distance to Front from Observer—Miles

0   100   200   300   400   500   600

Altitude—Miles

Swelling cumulus above nimbostratus   Thick altostratus   Fibrous cirrostratus   Tufted cirrus increasing

Characteristics

Of the Various

Types of Storms;

Extra-tropical

Cyclones,

Thunderstorms,

Hurricanes

And Tornadoes

P REVIOUSLY we remarked that the principal sources of rain, winds and generally foul weather in the United States are two types of storm: the extra-tropical cyclone, the thunderstorm. There are other storms—the hurricane, the tornado—that are usually more destructive but it is a fact that these two types bring us most of our weather troubles. Fog is another enemy not to be taken lightly, as we shall see, but let's concentrate on storms right now. If we would take proper and timely precautions for them, we should know something of their characteristics.

A definition of an extra-tropical cyclone, useful in the United States, is: A traveling system of winds rotating counterclockwise around a center of low barometric pressure and containing at birth a warm front and a cold front. It is just as nasty as this string of words suggests and is the chief immediate cause of the day-to-day changes in our weather.

We saw what one looked like on the daily weather map. Figure 1 is a diagram (plan view) of the birth, development and death of an extra-tropical cyclone. Our thanks are due Captain Charles G. Halpine, USN, for permission to reproduce this diagram from his book "A Pilot's Meteorology," published by D. van Nostrand Company. Incidentally, this is one of the best and most readable books available, for yachtsmen as well as aviators.

In part (a) of Figure 1, we have a warm air mass, probably moist tropical air, flowing northeastward and a cold air mass, probably polar continental, flowing southwestward. They are separated by a heavy line representing the boundary or front between them. Having different properties, these two air masses start fighting, as in part (b). The cold air from behind pushes under the warm air; the warm air rises up over the cold air ahead of it. A cold front is born on the left, a warm front on the right. Where they are connected together, the barometric pressure is lowered and the air starts circulating counterclockwise around this low. At the rear of the cold front, a high pressure area develops. At the same time, the whole system keeps moving in a general easterly direction. The crosshatched area represents rain. When

223

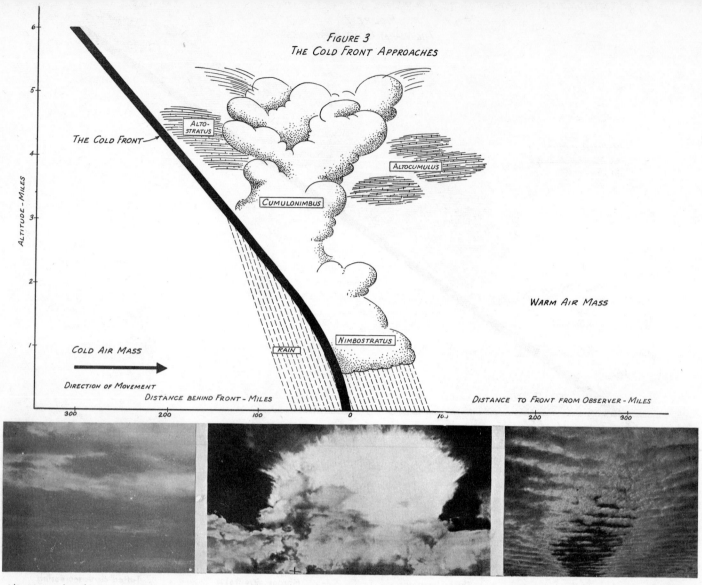

FIGURE 3
THE COLD FRONT APPROACHES

THE COLD FRONT

ALTO-STRATUS

ALTOCUMULUS

CUMULONIMBUS

WARM AIR MASS

NIMBOSTRATUS

RAIN

COLD AIR MASS

DIRECTION OF MOVEMENT

DISTANCE BEHIND FRONT - MILES

DISTANCE TO FRONT FROM OBSERVER - MILES

ALTITUDE - MILES

Altostratus, breaking up in rear of storm

Cumulonimbus

Banded altocumulus, advancing ahead of storm

Below: Figure I. Diagram of development of extra-tropical cyclone. (Reproduced by courtesy of Captain C. G. Halpine, U.S.N., and D. van Nostrand Co., Inc.)

(A)

(B)

(C)

(D)

(E)

(F)

warm, moist air is lifted, as it is when a cold air mass pushes under it or when it rises up over cold air ahead, its temperature falls. When its dewpoint is reached, any excess water vapor condenses to form first clouds and then rain.

In parts (c) and (d) of Figure 1, the storm matures, the low pressure deepening more and more, the clouds and rain increasing and the winds becoming stronger. In part (e), the cold front begins to catch up with the warm front and swallow it; an occluded front is formed. The storm is now at its height. It will do about one-half of its mischief while in occlusion. In part (f), it is well along to dissipation; after a while longer, the weather should clear, as the high pressure area reaches us. Unless there is another member of the family tagging along behind! Extra-tropical cyclones often occur in families of two, three or four storms. It takes about one day (24 hours) for this disturbance to reach maturity with three or possibly four days more required for complete dissipation. Not a pleasant prospect if we are caught afloat the Saturday before Labor Day. In winter, these storms occur on the average of twice a week in the USA; in summer they occur somewhat less frequently and are less severe. Their movement is eastward to north of east at a velocity in winter of about 700 miles per day and in summer of perhaps 500 miles per day. Finally, this storm usually covers a large area geographically; it does not blow up and away but can affect a given locality for days.

The component parts of an extra-tropical cyclone are:

1. A warm front, with its two conflicting air masses and its weather.
2. A cold front, with its two conflicting air masses, one of which (the warmer) is common with the warm front, and its weather.
3. A center of low barometric pressure with its wind system, at the junction of the fronts.
4. A high pressure area behind the cold front.

224

In early May a few years ago some of us were cruising down the Mississippi. We noticed on the weather map that there was an extra-tropical cyclone far to the southwest, its center moving ENE along a path that would leave us SSE of it. The warm front, the warm sector between the fronts, and the cold front would pass over us if we continued our cruise. Being stubborn, we kept on but watched carefully for the approaching trouble.

The first day the weather was fine with gentle winds and light fluffy cumulus clouds. The next morning we observed cirrus (Ci) clouds (figure 2) to the westward and noted that the barometer was falling. As these slowly thickened, we knew that the warm front was perhaps 500 miles, about one day, away. As the day wore on, the barometer fell more rapidly, the wind blew increasingly strong from the southeast, and the clouds thickened to the cirrostratus (Cs) of figure 2. A halo appeared around the sun. Altostratus (As) clouds (figure 2) next were seen approaching from westward. Knowing that these clouds precede a warm front by about 200 to 300 miles and that rain can be expected about 200 miles ahead of the front, it required no magician to tell us that we had better begin securing ship and breaking out the oilskins. We observed that the spread between the air temperature and dewpoint temperature was growing less and less; it looked as though we could also expect fog. We decided to anchor until the warm front had passed over.

Next came the low nimbostratus (Ns) rain clouds (figure 2), the barometer continuing to fall and the temperature slowly to rise. The visibility grew worse and worse. The ship's bell began its clamor and we spent a not too comfortable night. By morning, it was raining steadily and the air was warm. The wind had veered to SSW. Finally, the clouds began to break, the barometer stopped falling, the rain gradually ceased. Knowing that it might be anything from a few hours to a day or more before the cold front struck us, we got underway, keeping our eyes peeled for altocumulus (Ac) clouds to the westward. The watch below was set to airing the cabins and our duffle as we ran through the remainder of the warm sector.

About 1000 the next morning, the lookout spotted the altocumulus clouds (figure 3); the cold front was perhaps 150 miles away. As the day was hot and quite humid, we figured that thunderstorms were probable and that they might be severe. We decided to anchor early, about 1500, and prepare for the worst. The barometer was jumpy, the wind was south and increasing. Nimbostratus (Ns) clouds with cumulonimbus (Cb) (figure 3) towering out of them appeared to the west. Rain set in and the wind rose sharply. As in our trip on the Potomac, we had a busy few hours—and were mighty glad that we had known enough to recognize and time the warning signs. By morning the storm was over and we continued our cruise with a blue sky and fair winds.

Thus, we passed through an extra-tropical cyclone. Figure 4 is a picture of it, again with acknowledgement to Captain Halpine. The central portion is a plan view of the storm; the lower portion is a vertical cross-section along the line CD, our "Course" through the storm. The cloud sequences and the rain are clearly shown (Cb symbol omitted). Had we passed north, instead of south, of the center, the upper diagram would represent the clouds and weather. If we don't know where the center is? That's easy. Face the wind. The center will bear approximately 110° from our heading. Then we know whether to expect something bad or something worse.

As we experienced in the foregoing case, thunderstorms can occur along with cold fronts. If the air is sufficiently unstable, as in the summer, they may occur in warm

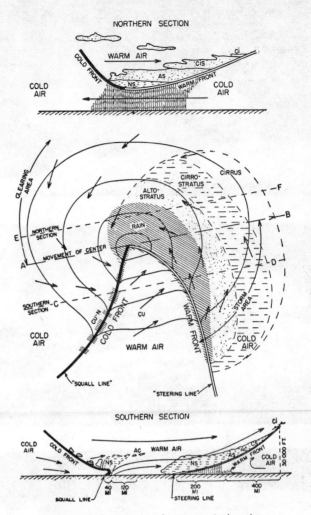

Figure 4. Cross-sections of extra-tropical cyclone. (Reproduced by courtesy of Captain C. G. Halpine, U.S.N., and D. van Nostrand Co., Inc.)

fronts, just ahead of the frontal passage. They also develop on their own in a single air mass without a frontal passage. These are the local thunderstorms so prevalent in the late afternoon and early evening of a hot, sultry day.

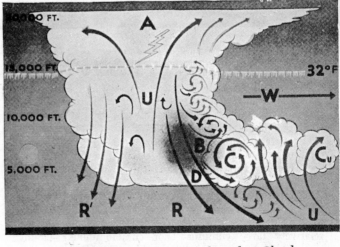

Key to Diagram of Cumulonimbus Cloud

A —Anvil Top
B —Dark Area
C —Roll Cloud
Cᵤ—Advance Cumulus Clouds
D —Down Drafts

U —Up Drafts
R —Primary Rain Area
R' —Secondary Area
W —Wind Direction

Figure 5. Diagram of thunderstorm cloud. (Courtesy of Aviation Training Division, U. S. Navy)

Figure 6. Growth of the anvil of thunderstorm cloud. The upper photograph was taken at 1200, the middle at 1220, the lower at 1230 from the same position as the storm developed. (Courtesy, U. S. Weather Bureau)

We know a thunderstorm as a storm of limited duration, arising only in a cumulonimbus cloud, attended by thunder and lightning, and marked by abrupt variations in temperature, pressure and wind. A line squall is a lengthy row of thunderstorms stretching across the country. In either form, a thunderstorm is a very undesirable shipmate.

Incidentally, a shower is a smaller brother, though the rainfall and wind in it may be of considerable intensity. It characteristically is the product of isolated relatively large cumulus (not cumulonimbus) clouds separated from one another by blue sky. It is not accompanied by thunder and lightning.

In all cases, the prime danger signal is a cumulus cloud growing larger. Every thunderstorm (cumulonimbus) cloud has four distinctive features, although we may not always be able to see all four as other clouds may intervene in our line of sight. Figure 5 shows these four features; the anvil top is better illustrated in figure 6. These three photographs of an anvil were taken from the

same position over a period of one-half hour!

Figure 5 is a drawing, by courtesy of the Navy Bureau of Aeronautics from their booklet "Thunderstorms" (Aerology Series Two), of a cumulonimbus cloud; it shows these four features diagrammatically. Starting at the top, we notice the layer of cirrus clouds, shaped like an anvil and consequently called "anvil top," leaning in the direction of the upper wind. This tells us the direction in which the storm is moving. The next feature is the main body of the cloud; it is a large cumulus of great height with cauliflower sides. It must be of great height, as it must extend above the freezing level if the cirrus anvil top is to form. Cirrus clouds are composed of ice crystals, not water droplets. The third feature is the roll cloud formed by violent air currents along the leading edge of the base of the cumulus cloud. The fourth and final feature is the dark area within the storm and extending from the base of the cloud to the earth; at the center this is rain, at the edges hail and rain.

Now a thunderstorm has no respect for anyone, least of all a group of yachtsmen pleasure bent. Let's let Harold tell the story in his own words; he got mixed up in a line squall on Chesapeake Bay late in July.

"About twenty boats from the Yacht Club went up the Rappahannock River last week-end, the occasion being a Southern Chesapeake Bay all-sail regatta. It was as good as anything I have seen for several years, and we had an enjoyable time except that we took an awful trimming coming back.

"Mrs. B. and I were asked to go with another couple in a 30-foot cruiser. The trip is quite long, it being about seventy miles from our home port on the Lower Bay to Urbanna on the Rappahannock, where the regatta was held. As you know, the Chesapeake is quite wide and kicks up considerably with southerly winds.

"Going up on Friday it was a perfectly glorious day on the Bay; Saturday and Sunday during the sail races the weather was also fine. On Monday, about three o'clock in the afternoon, when we were nearly two-thirds of the way home and about five miles east of York Spit Light, we experienced one of the worst storms that I have ever been through on the Bay. The storm did a lot of damage on shore and it was one time on a small boat that I was really scared.

"Many other boats were traveling down, some ahead and some behind us, and the whole fleet was completely scattered. In fact, two of the large sailboats couldn't be located for about thirty-six hours, but everyone was finally checked in. The thing that upset us most was the fact that our engine went out due to gasoline in the tanks sloshing around violently, causing sediment to settle in the lines and to clog the filters. Between getting out a sea anchor, clearing the gas lines, and looking after a sailing dinghy which we were towing astern on a long bridle, we had our hands full. For one and one-half hours we slogged into it with the engine turning over just enough to give us headway.

"We took an awful slamming about, wrecked most of the china and glassware and soaked down everything in the interior of the boat. The seas were coming clean over the bow and aboard. Finally, the weather cleared and we made port but I think that's all the sailing I want this season."

HAROLD is an old hand, a waterman. Subsequent correspondence developed that he had tried to get hold of a weather map, just to check on things, but had been unable to locate one. The cruiser was not equipped with a radio. A series of hot, humid summer days on the Chesapeake not infrequently brings violent thunderstorms. Had he been able to get the 0230 EWT map of that July Monday, or to get radio weather reports, he undoubtedly would have timed his departure to arrive home much earlier in the day. That map revealed a squall line of thunderstorms extending from North Carolina to New York City, right across the Bay. The air mass involved was mTk: thunderstorm air. As the day progressed and the air near the Bay was heated and its moisture content further increased, a severe storm was certain. A good thing for us to remember is that a telephone call to any U. S. Weather Bureau office, during peace or war, will immediately provide us with any necessary warning.

Obviously, it behooves us to be able to recognize an approaching thunderstorm, to know the conditions that will produce one. Once it appears, we must judge whether it will pass over us, estimate its intensity, and figure how much time we have to batten down hatches.

There are three requirements for the formation of a thunderstorm. One, there must be strong upward air currents, such as are caused by a cold front under-running warm air or by heat radiated from the surface of the earth on a hot summer day. Warm, moist air being forced up a mountain slope can also produce a thunderstorm. Two, the parcels of air forming the storm must be unstable, that is, relatively lighter than their neighbors outside the storm, and willing therefore to keep on being pushed higher and higher until they pass the freezing level. Tropical air colder than the surface over which it is moving makes a good candidate. Third, the air must be moist. That's why thunderstorms like rivers and lakes, like the sea. Without moisture, there can be no clouds and no rain. The most promising thunderstorm air is mTk (tropical maritime colder than the earth); whenever it appears in our cruising area, alone or ahead of a cold front, we need to be very suspicious.

THUNDERSTORMS occur most frequently and with the greatest intensity in the Summer, in the USA; they are rare in Winter. While they may strike at any hour over the land, over rivers and inland lakes they vastly prefer the late afternoon or early evening. The earth has been a good "stove" for many hours, heating the air to produce strong upward currents. Over the ocean, thunderstorms more commonly occur just before sunrise. Water gains and loses heat far less rapidly than does land; it takes these additional hours to do the job at sea. Finally, thunderstorms are most frequent and most violent in tropical latitudes; they thin out and lose intensity as the higher latitudes are reached. The southeastern states often experience as many as four thunderstorms (and they are often potent ones) a week in Summer.

As we have remarked previously, a thunderstorm is an individual weather factory. Ahead of the storm, there are variable shifting surface winds; the first steady wind usually will be felt about five miles ahead of the roll cloud. As the roll cloud passes over us, violently turbulent winds may be expected, followed by strong downdrafts as the main cloud reaches us. Heavy rain and often hail begin to fall just abaft the roll cloud. The rain continues but the hail lessens as the core of the storm approaches. Interestingly

enough, the hail is generally thickest in the clearer air surrounding the core. There may be winds as high as sixty miles an hour near the storm center. At the rear of the storm, downdrafts again will be experienced but the fall of rain will be noticeably lighter. The weather quickly clears with passage of the storm; it even has been known to bring cooler, refreshing temperatures and lower humidities.

If the cumulonimbus cloud is fully developed and towers to normal thunderstorm altitudes, 35,000 feet or more in Summer, the storm will be severe. The winds and wind shifts will be violent; there will be heavy rain and hail; hailstones as large as baseballs have been observed in more than one thunderstorm. If the anvil top is low, say only 15,000 feet or so, as it usually is in Spring and Fall, the storm will be less severe but it will still be a storm. If the cumulonimbus cloud is not fully developed, particularly if it lacks the anvil top and roll cloud, a heavy shower will be experienced. Watch for winds shifts, however; they can take the sticks out of her. Another intensity indicator is the lighting; the greater the proportion of vertical to horizontal lightning, the more intense the storm will be.

If the cumulonimbus cloud is due north or due south of us, the chances are that we will miss most or all of the storm; the normal course of the storm is ENE. If it is due east of us, and there is no indication, from other clouds for example, that the upper air winds are from the east, we are safe. If the cloud is west of us, lash down all gear.

WE can time the approach of the storm, once the cloud is visible, by a series of bearings. If we wish, we can estimate its distance off another way. The lightning and thunder occur practically simultaneously but we see the lightning much sooner than we hear the thunder. Consequently, time this interval, in seconds. Multiply the number of seconds by 0.2; the result will be the distance off in miles. Thunderstorms travel at about 25 miles per hour. Thunder can be heard up to about 10 miles; lightning can be seen at a still greater distance.

So much for thunderstorms; a few other storms deserve brief attention. First, we must not forget that a cold front, or a warm front, or a low pressure center, each independently can bring us foul weather. We previously have had enough examples so that none is necessary here. Secondly, while they are of concern principally only to those of us cruising the Gulf of Mexico and off the southeast Atlantic coast in Summer and early fall, a hurricane is not a toy. The winds and rain are bad enough; the tidal conditions associated with this type of storm are frequently equal or greater mischief-makers. The third type of storm we should mention is the tornado; while they cut a narrow swath, they do cut a deep one. Tornadoes have wrecked boats on the Mississippi and elsewhere in the southern tier of states, especially in the Spring. Hurricanes are usually well-reported and their course forecasted by the Weather Bureau; this is not true of tornadoes. The latter are local in character, springing up quickly and having relatively short lives. Hurricanes are very extensive storms, with long tracks and a life cycle ordinarily of some days duration. In waters and at seasons when they are likely, we want to keep our radios tuned for any possible warning. Once we receive that warning, there is only one place for the yachtsman: ashore. A small boat, no matter how skillfully handled, cannot live in these storms. Unless the owner possesses more than his share of Guardian Angels.

Storms are enemies; we may founder or we may experience only discomfort. Our chances of the latter instead of the former are enhanced if we are forwarned of their approach and promptly take all possible precautions.

The Causes of Fog—
How, Why, Where and When
It Forms—Radiation,
Advection and Frontal Types

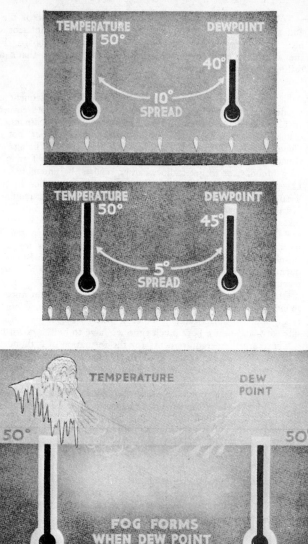

THE essential part is not always to know things; it is to know how to reason about them. This truism applies to fog. There are at least six types of fog; to attempt to remember the intimate details of each would take all the joy out of our cruise. The basic causes of fog are few in number and easy for us to recall. What we want is a working knowledge of these causes; then we can judge if and when fog is likely to upset our plans.

Fog is merely a cloud, whose base rests upon the earth, be the latter land or water. It consists of water droplets, suspended in the air, each droplet so small that it cannot be distinguished individually yet present in such tremendous numbers that objects close at hand are obscured. That's about all we need to remember in order to reason things out about fog; it is the key to the lock. Let's prove it.

If we are to have innumerable water droplets suspended in the air, there must be plenty of water vapor originally in that air. If droplets are to form from that vapor, the air must be cooled by some means so that this moisture vapor will condense. If the droplets are to condense in the air next to the earth, the cooling must extend to the

Fig. 1—Why fog forms. (Reproduced by courtesy of Aviation Training Division, U. S. Navy.) Figure 2—A graph of a series of air and dewpoint temperatures

earth; the droplets are suspended, so they can't fall. If the fog is to have any depth, successively higher layers of air must be cooled sufficiently to cause condensation in them. Fog forms from the ground up. Thus, the land or water must be colder than the air next to it, the lower layers of air progressively must be colder than the layers above them.

If water vapor is to condense out of the air, then the temperature of the air must be lowered to or below the dewpoint temperature, that is, the temperature at which the air is saturated with water vapor and below which condensation of water vapor will occur. We can lower the air temperature, by cooling, as above, until it falls to the dewpoint. Or, we can increase the dewpoint, by adding more water vapor to the air, until it equals the air temperature. Air, as it passes over rivers and lakes, over the oceans, over wet ground is likely to pick up water vapor and have its dewpoint raised. Rain

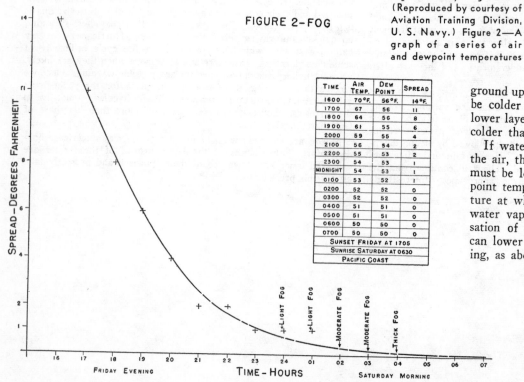

FIGURE 2-FOG

TIME	AIR TEMP.	DEW POINT	SPREAD
1600	70°F.	56°F.	14°F.
1700	67	56	11
1800	64	56	8
1900	61	55	6
2000	59	55	4
2100	56	54	2
2200	55	53	2
2300	54	53	1
MIDNIGHT	54	53	1
0100	53	52	1
0200	52	52	0
0300	52	52	0
0400	51	51	0
0500	51	51	0
0600	50	50	0
0700	50	50	0
SUNSET FRIDAY AT 1705			
SUNRISE SATURDAY AT 0630			
PACIFIC COAST			

falling from higher clouds can increase the amount of water vapor in the air near the earth.

So, all we need to do to judge the likelihood of fog formation is periodically to measure the air temperature and dewpoint temperature and see if the spread (difference) between them is getting smaller and smaller. The Navy, in its Aviation Training booklet "Fog" (Aerology Series 3) has provided us with a pretty good diagram of the change in spread; it is reproduced here as Figure 1.

Figure 2 is a graph of a series of air and dewpoint temperatures. By recording these temperatures and plotting their spread over a period of several hours, as is indicated by that part of the curve drawn as a solid line, we have a basis for forecasting the time at which we are likely to be fog-bound. The dot-dash portion of the curve represents actual data but it could just as easily have been drawn by extending the solid portion. If an error were made in this extrapolation, it would probably indicate that the fog would form at an earlier hour. Which is on the safe side; we would be secure in our anchorage some

time before the fifty-ninth minute of the eleventh hour!

Note that the curve is not a straight line. While the average decrease in spread is about one and one-half degrees (Fahrenheit) per hour, the decrease is at a much greater rate in the earlier hours. So long as we do not make unreasonable allowances for a slowing up in the rate of change of the spread, this also will help to keep us on the safe side.

Visibility in light fog may vary from 5/8 to six miles; in moderate fog it may be as much as one-half mile. Dense fog, with the visibility less than 5/16 mile, is just no fun at all, especially when we are off the rock-bound coast of Maine.

How do we determine the dewpoint? There is a simple-to-operate, inexpensive little gadget known by the horrible name of sling psychrometer. The Taylor Instrument Companies have very kindly provided us with an illustration: figure 3. A sling psychrometer is merely two thermometers, mounted in a single holder with a handle that permits it to be whirled overhead. One thermometer, known as the dry-bulb, has its bulb of mercury exposed directly to the air. The other thermometer, known as the wet-bulb, has its bulb covered with a piece of gauze. We soak this gauze in water, so that the bulb is moistened. Whirling it in the air, water is evaporated from the wet-bulb thermometer, thereby cooling it, as evaporation is a cooling process. This thermometer, then, indicates what the temperature of the air will be when it is saturated with water vapor. This is called the wet-bulb temperature. The dry-bulb thermometer, of course, shows the actual temperature of the air. From the wet-bulb temperature and dry-bulb temperature, the dewpoint may be determined by referring to a suitable table. However, as we are far more interested in knowing the spread, or difference, between the air temperature and dewpoint, we will save ourselves some work by using another table (Table 1), its use being explained in the next two paragraphs.

If the air is already actually saturated with water vapor, then none can evaporate from the gauze and both thermometers must show the same value. The dewpoint then has this same numerical value and so the spread between air temperature and dewpoint must be zero. If the air is not already saturated with water vapor, the wet-bulb thermometer, due to the cooling effect, will give a lower reading than the dry-bulb thermometer. We subtract the wet-bulb temperature from the dry-bulb

TABLE 1

AIR TEMPERATURE — DEWPOINT SPREAD

(All figures are in degrees Fahrenheit at 30" pressure)

Difference Dry-Bulb Minus Wet-Bulb	Air Temperature Shown By Dry-Bulb Thermometer												
	35	40	45	50	55	60	65	70	75	80	85	90	95
1	2	2	2	2	2	2	2	1	1	1	1	1	1
2	5	5	4	4	4	3	3	3	3	3	3	3	2
3	7	7	7	6	5	5	5	4	4	4	4	4	4
4	10	10	9	8	7	7	6	6	6	6	5	5	5
5	14	12	11	10	10	9	8	8	7	7	7	7	6
6	18	15	14	13	12	11	10	9	9	8	8	8	8
7	22	19	17	16	14	13	12	11	11	10	10	9	9
8	28	22	20	18	17	15	14	13	12	12	11	11	10
9	35	27	23	21	19	17	16	15	14	13	13	12	12
10	-	33	27	24	22	20	18	17	16	15	14	14	13
11	-	40	32	28	25	22	20	19	18	17	16	15	15
12	-	-	38	32	28	25	23	21	20	18	17	17	16
13	-	-	45	37	31	28	25	23	21	20	19	18	17
14	-	-	-	42	35	31	28	26	24	22	21	20	19
15	-	-	-	50	40	35	31	28	26	24	23	21	21

Opposite   Difference Dry-Bulb Minus Wet-Bulb and
Under   Air Temperature Shown By Dry-Bulb Thermometer
Read   Value of Spread: Air Temperature minus Dewpoint Temperature

Based on U.S. Weather Bureau Psychrometric Tables

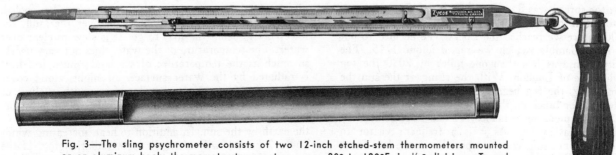

Fig. 3—The sling psychrometer consists of two 12-inch etched-stem thermometers mounted on an aluminum back; thermometer temperature range 20° to 120°F. in ½° divisions. Turned wood handle, with swivel. Furnished with case to protect thermometers when not in use. (Reproduced by courtesy of Taylor Instrument Companies)

Fig. 4A—Advection fog is common along many coasts
(Courtesy of Aviation Training Division, U. S. Navy)

cover cuts it off. The earth radiates most of this heat to warm the air above it. After sunset, the earth continues to lose heat, cooling itself at a more rapid rate. If the air is nearly still, moist and warmer than the earth, the layers of air next to the earth will be cooled. The air temperature will fall, approaching the value of the dewpoint temperature. When these are sub-

temperature. With this difference and the dry-bulb (the air) temperature, we consult Table 1 and find directly the corresponding spread between the air temperature and the dewpoint temperature. This is the figure we want. Simple enough; practically all of us did it back in our high school physics class.

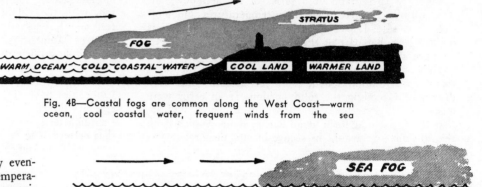

Fig. 4B—Coastal fogs are common along the West Coast—warm ocean, cool coastal water, frequent winds from the sea

Fig. 5—The most persistent sea fog is an advection fog that forms when air blows from warm sea to cold sea

If, in the late afternoon or early evening, the spread between the air temperature and dewpoint is less than approximately 10°F, and the air temperature is falling, fog or greatly restricted visibility will probably be experienced in a few hours. These critical values are emphasized by the heavy line above which they lie in Table 1. Incidentally, should we ever want to know the dewpoint temperature itself, all we need do is to subtract the spread figure given in the table from the temperature shown by the dry-bulb thermometer. Thus, when the dry-bulb thermometer indicates an air temperature of 70°F and the difference between the dry-bulb and wet-bulb temperatures is 11°F, the spread is 19°F and the dewpoint is 51°F.

Several years ago, having saved our vacation for a last long October cruise, we sailed north from Seattle through the Sound and Deception Pass to the Islands. After loafing contentedly among them for some days, we shaped a course for Victoria. The weather had been kind to us; the winds were light but we were in no hurry. Our plans, such as they were, called for departure from Victoria on the 19th. During the night of the 18th, a continuous light drizzle set in, clearing as the sun rose the next morning. We checked the weather maps and reports, to learn that a mass of stable, maritime polar air was stagnant over most of the Northwest. Winds were light and the pressure gradient weak, with the barometer reading close to 1020 millibars (about 30.13 inches).

As so often happened at Victoria in bygone years, our departure was delayed beyond the intended hour. Stagnant, stable, moist air in October in those waters usually spells fog. Crossing the Straits, we checked the Almanac to learn that sunset would occur about 1710. At 1530, with Port Townsend abeam, we began to take dewpoints; the spread was 8°. By 1600, it was 7°. Fog was sure to form before midnight; at 10 knots it would be 2000 before we reached the Locks. We decided to put in at Port Gamble, which we raised about 1745. The visibility then was less than one mile; by 2030 the fog reminded one of London. With the rising of the sun the next morning, the fog began to thin, though it was not until long after lunch on the 20th that we got under way again for our mooring at home. We had been delayed by a typical radiation fog. As it is a frequent visitor to United States cruising waters, especially in the late Summer and Fall, let's take a good look at it.

The sun heats the earth all day long, unless cloud

stantially equal, fog will form. There are five requirements for radiation fog (some of us call it ground fog) formation.

First, the air must be stable, that is, the air at the earth must be colder than the air aloft with the water or land still colder than the air adjacent to it. Second, the air must be moist; there can be no fog without moisture. Third, the sky must be clear with little or no cloud cover, so that the earth readily can lose its heat. Fourth, the winds must be light. If there is a dead calm, the lower layers of air will not mix with the ones above. As air is a poor conductor of heat, the fog will form only in these lower layers to a height of perhaps two to four feet; it will not be deep. A mild turbulence, say winds of three to five knots, will deepen the fog but will not dissipate it. Fifth, it helps a lot if the character of the terrain is such as to permit the fog to accumulate; depressions, valleys, coastal bays off rugged shores are good candidates.

Radiation fog is most prevalent in the middle and high latitudes. It is a local affair, occurring most frequently in low lands and valleys, especially near lakes and rivers, where we may cruise. The cool air drains down into and stagnates in these terrain depressions; the lake or river aids the process by contributing moisture to raise the dewpoint. Radiation fog also raises hob in coastal waters; ask any "Downeaster."

This fog, which may be patchy or dense, forms at night or in the evening, after the land or water has cooled. When the sun rises, it will burn off over the land, the lower layers being the first to go. It is slow to clear over water. The temperature of the water does not vary nearly so much as the temperature of the land; much less heat is radiated by the water surface. At night, cloud cover hinders fog formation, as it interferes with cooling of the earth. By the same token, cloud cover during the day hinders fog dissipation, as it interferes with heating of the earth by the sun. In addition to heat, increasing winds (over 7 knots) will often dissipate radiation fog. If the fog should drift out over warm water or warm land (sand for example), it will clear quickly.

When it forms in the early morning, say around 0300, it will develop its maximum density about 0700, and should dissipate by about 1000. If it forms shortly after sunset, it will be very slow to clear.

If it is suspected that radiation fog is likely to form, we need only to use our sling psychrometer and Table 1. If about 1600, the spread between air and dewpoint temperatures is less than 10°, fog before midnight, slow to clear the next day, is probable. The less the spread, the earlier the fog will form and the later it will dissipate. If the spread at 1600 is between 10° and 20°, fog will probably form between midnight and 0600 the next morning, and should clear between 1000 and 1200. If the

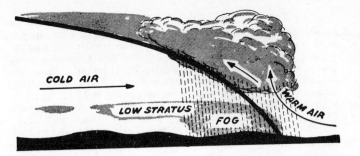

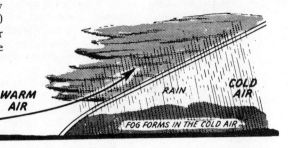

Figures 7 and 8 courtesy Aviation Training Division, U. S. Navy

Fig. 7 (left)—Warm front fog and Fig. 8 (above)—Cold front fog

figure 5 its formation at sea. Advection fog may form day or night, winter or summer, over land or sea.

For us, the most bothersome type probably is coastal advection fog (figure 4). When steady winds displace a mass of relatively warm, moist air over colder water or land, fog may blanket a great length of coastline and, especially at night, may extend for hundreds of miles inland up river valleys and over the countryside. The otherwise friendly sea breeze may also bring us this type of fog, though in this case it is generally of limited extent and is rare in Summer.

Off-shore winds carrying warm, moist air out over colder water can also result in formation of advection fog; in this case, it forms over the water and may extend many miles out to sea.

For an example, let's go to the Pacific coast, where the water nearer the land often is colder than the water to westward. The prevailing winds are onshore and the air frequently contains large quantities of water vapor. Figure 4B illustrates the result, especially at those seasons of the year when the land temperature is still lower than the temperature of the coastal waters. But, to make our Western friends feel better, the same thing can happen when onshore winds carry air across the Gulf Stream and then on westward across the colder Atlantic coastal waters.

This type of fog also forms when air is blown across the Gulf Stream and then over the Labrador Current off the Grand Banks; a similar effect is found in the Pacific.

Advection fog also may form over the larger inland lakes, as warm air is carried over their colder surface. Along the Mississippi and Ohio rivers, a special type of this fog, known as steam fog, is a particular hazard to late evening cruising in the Fall. In this case, cold air that is nearly saturated with water vapor is blown by light winds over the much warmer water of these rivers. The resulting fog is often patchy, though it may be dense, and sunshine the next morning will dissipate it. Steam fog also is often seen early in a frosty morning over a mountain lake.

Advection fog is generally much harder to dissipate than is radiation fog; a wind shift or substantial increase in wind velocity is required, as the sun has little effect. Of course, the passage of a cold front through it will change the visibility in a hurry! Advection fog is generally long-lasting fog, carried by the winds. Cloud cover hinders its breakup and sunshine has no effect on it over the water though it may thin it a bit over the land. It can cause days and days of misery.

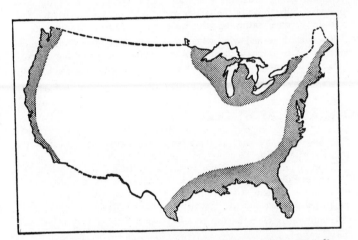

Fig. 6—Land areas in the United States most often affected by advection fog. (Courtesy Aviation Training Division, U. S. Navy, and McGraw Hill Book Company, Inc.)

spread is 20° to 30°, fog may form just before sunrise and clear soon thereafter. If the spread is greater than 30°, radiation fog is unlikely.

Radiation fog annoys us in the late Summer and Fall; advection fog can annoy us at any season. (Advection means transfer by horizontal motion.) Winds blowing warm, moist air over a colder surface cause advection fog. The air is cooled and fog forms; it may be carried for hundreds of miles by the wind. Advection fogs forming along the Gulf Coast have been carried all the way to Lake Michigan, right up the Mississippi Valley, as some of our friends found out one week-end. At sea, this fog may extend from the low to high latitudes.

There are several types of advection fog, but all have the same basic requirements for formation. First, there must be a wind to carry the air mass and the resulting fog. Second, the air must be moist or must pick up sufficient moisture as it moves. Third, the air must be warmer than the surface over which it is moving, with the air at the higher levels still warmer than the air below. Fourth, the surface—land or water—temperature must be progressively colder in the direction in which the air mass and fog are moving. Figure 4, again by courtesy of the U. S. Navy from its "Flying the Weather," illustrates the formation of advection fog along the coast and

WEATHER map air mass indications (for example, tropical maritime air warmer than the surface beneath it, mTw) give us some warning of its possible approach. The relative air, land and water temperatures, plus the wind direction and knowledge of the area from which the air mass is moving afford checks on these indications. Finally, periodic measurement of the air and dewpoint temperature spread again will stand us in good stead.

In the United States, the principal land areas most frequently affected by advection fog include the Pacific Coast, from Puget Sound to Lower California, the Atlantic Coast, from Maine to Florida, the entire Gulf Coast and the Great Lakes region. Figure 6, from the Navy's "Aerology for Pilots", published by McGraw-Hill Book Company, shows these areas; most of us have probably been caught more than once.

The U. S. Weather Bureau tells us the favorite resorts of sea fog. Suppose we take the figures for the Summer months of June, July and August. On the Pacific Coast, we'll take our observations of the weather every day about 0400. Along the Gulf Coast, we'll take them about 0600 and along the Atlantic Coast about 0700. Which may seem unfair to San Franciscans, but the data available are all for Greenwich Noon. We'll give the results in terms of the number of times fog was reported, expressed as a percentage of the total number of all weather observations.

Coastal Region	*Fog Reported*
Maine	For more than 20% of the observations
Middle Atlantic...	For more than 5% and less than 20% of the observations
Pacific Coast.....	For more than 5% and less than 20% of the observations
South Atlantic....	For less than 5% of the observations
Gulf	For less than 5% of the observations

Which should make the Golden Gate feel better.

THE third principal classification of fog is frontal or precipitation type. Warm fronts and cold fronts are not satisfied to bring us rain and wind, oftentimes they must add fog to our troubles. Warm rain falling through colder air near the surface of the earth is the cause. Fortunately, this type is more prevalent in winter than in summer.

The warm front type is the more common, more extensive, and consequently more annoying, especially along the Atlantic Coast. Figure 7, taken from the Navy's "Flying the Weather" illustrates its formation. The warm, moist air riding up over the colder air ahead produces a continuous, warm rainfall. As these warm water droplets fall through the cold air ahead of the front, this cold air becomes saturated with water vapor. If the wind is strong, low stratus clouds and perhaps light fog will form in the cold air. If the wind is light, moderate to thick fog will form in advance of the front and will extend through most of the region over which the rain is falling. A warm front moves slowly; consequently such fog thickens gradually but is frequently very extensive. It clears abruptly when the front passes over us.

In the cold front type, the rain area is narrower and the front moves faster; it is more restricted in width and duration, developing and dissipating quite quickly. It is more prevalent along the Pacific Coast. Figure 8 indicates the manner in which it forms. The rain falling from the warm air that is being lifted by the cold air mass, falls through the colder air at and behind the front. The cold air becomes saturated with water vapor and fog results.

Knowing how and why, where and when fogs form, it isn't difficult for us to forecast them with an accuracy of gratifying proportions. All we need is this knowledge, Table 1 and our gadget. Lady Luck is helpful, too.

GREAT LAKES WEATHER FORECAST (LAFOT) CODE

The Weather Bureau of the U. S. Department of Commerce publishes a series of storm warning facilities charts designed especially for boatmen and pleasure craft operators. They cover, by sections, coastal waters, the Gulf of Mexico and the Great Lakes. These provide the latest available data as to where and when weather forecasts can be obtained for navigational purposes.

In addition to the schedules they publish of Weather Bureau forecasts, and weather broadcasts from commercial radio and TV stations, they include, for Great Lakes areas, the schedule of coded weather forecasts on the Lakes known as LAFOTS. These are issued in code and broadcast by U. S. and Canadian radiotelephone stations (marine wave lengths) on schedules as published on the charts.

The LAFOT code consists of groups of five figures represented by the letter symbols "DDffW," supplemented by plain language words. The first two digits, "DD," indicate the wind direction according to Table I. When the two figures for "DD" are the same, the wind is expected to hold steady from that direction during the forecast period indicated in the LAFOT. If the figures for "DD" are different, the winds will vary between the two directions indicated.

Figures for the third and fourth digits, "ff," give the wind velocity expected in knots (nautical mph). Variations from the forecast wind velocity may be expected. For winds below 16 mph, variations from the forecast velocity will usually run as high as 40% and occasionally 70%; for velocities 16 mph and above, variations will run as high as 20% and occasionally 30%. The figure for the last digit "W," gives the average weather expected according to Table II.

Table I: Symbol D-Wind Direction

CODE FIGURE	DIRECTION
0	Calm
1	Northeast
2	East
3	Southeast
4	South
5	Southwest
6	West
7	Northwest
8	North
9	Variable

Table II: Symbol W-Weather

CODE FIGURE	WEATHER
0	Fine (mostly clear)
1	Cloudy (or overcast)
2	Thundersqualls
3	Showers
4	Rain
5	Fog (visibility ½ mile or less)
6	Lake steam (visibility ½ mile or less)
7	Light to moderate snow
8	Freezing rain
9	Heavy snow (visibility ½ mile or less)

LAFOTS cover 24 hours divided into two 12-hour periods; the periods in LAFOTS being identified by the words "FIRST" and "SECOND." In LAFOTS transmitted by U. S. radiotelephone stations commencing shortly after midnight, the "FIRST" period begins at 1 am, and the "SECOND" 12 hours later at 1 pm, EST. For LAFOTS broadcast a few minutes after 6 am, 12 noon and 6 pm, EST, the "FIRST" period starts at 7 am, 1 pm, and 7 pm, EST, respectively. In LAFOTS issued by the Dominion Public Weather Office, at Toronto, for broadcast by Canadian radiotelephone stations, the "FIRST" period commences at the time of broadcast and the "SECOND" 12 hours later.

Examples of U. S. LAFOTS issued for broadcast shortly after midnight EST:

SUPERIOR: First 18347 west half 11189 east half. Second 87240 west half 88277 east half. Much colder with temperature falling to 15 by late evening.

MICHIGAN: First 99113 becoming 11193 middle period and 18301 end period. Second 87310.

Examples of above LAFOTS as translated: Lake forecasts for two 12-hour periods, the first commencing at 1 am and the second starting 12 hours later or at 1 pm, EST.

Lake Superior: First period, northeast to north winds, 34 mph with light to moderate snow west half of Lake and northeast 18 mph with heavy snow east half of Lake. Second period, north to northwest winds 24 mph, fine weather west half and north 27 mph with light to moderate snow east half of Lake. Much colder with temperature falling to 15 degrees by late evening.

Lake Michigan: First period, variable winds, 11 mph with showers becoming northeast 19 mph with showers middle of period and northeast to north winds, 30 mph and cloudy end of period. Second period, north to northwest winds, 31 mph with fine weather.

Synopsis: Each LAFOT Bulletin also contains a brief weather summary giving position of Lows, Highs, Fronts and other features on the weather map within a radius of 600 miles of the Lake Region.

Note: When Small Craft, Gale or Whole Gale warnings have been issued for any Lake, the appropriate U. S. LAFOTS will also contain a statement indicating the type of display and the area along the Lakes where warning displays are in effect.

Great Lakes Weather Bulletins (LAWEB) are issued by the U. S. Weather Bureau for broadcast every six hours during the navigation season. LAWEB broadcast schedules are published on the charts.

LAWEB Bulletins are issued in two parts. Part I contains plain language reports of wind direction and velocity and/or barometer reading data from land stations in the Lake Region.

Part II comprises reports from ships underway on the Lakes when more than 4 miles off shore. Positions of ships are given in distance in miles and direction from well-known landmarks; wind direction to 16 points of the compass and velocities in miles an hour. Ice data, in season, are added when reported by ships.

Visibility and weather are included in both land and ship station reports when visibility is less than ⅝ mile. Observations are taken one hour and 30 minutes prior to the time of each broadcast.

Left: Figure I. A modern aneroid barometer, calibrated in both millibars (outer scale) and inches (inner scale) of mercury. Second hand indicates pressure tendency. The usually misleading words "Rain—Change—Fair" do not appear. (Courtesy Taylor Instrument Co.)

Weather Signs

The Barometer

We have already discussed fog and how we can use a sling psychrometer to help us in forecasting its occurrence. There are a few other weather instruments, useful afloat, with which we should be familiar.

The aneroid barometer (figure 1) is an old shipmate. The one illustrated was developed by the Taylor Instrument Companies and is similar to the standard used by the U. S. Navy. It has several interesting features.

First, notice that the words "Fair—Change—Rain" do not appear. Such indications, unfortunately found on many aneroid barometers, are usually meaningless. It is not the actual barometric pressure that is so important in forecasting; it is the direction and rate of change of pressure. Plus, as we shall see in a few minutes, the direction and character of the wind. So these likely-to-be-misleading words are not printed on the dial face of this barometer.

Second, there are two pressure scales. Not a few of us are accustomed to thinking of barometric pressure in terms of inches of mercury, so the inner scale is graduated in these units. Weather maps are now printed with the pressures shown in millibars and many radio weather reports specify this value. Consequently, the outer scale is graduated in millibars. We don't have to worry about conversions between units as the barometer face has both calibrations.

Third, it is a rugged instrument, a feature not to be despised on board a 40-footer. It has a high order of accuracy. (No, I do not get a commission on their sale! What we are interested in here is cataloging the features for which we should look when we are about to select a barometer.

Fourth, it has the usual second, or reference, indicator hand so we can keep track of changes in pressure.

Now, a good barometer is a very helpful gadget, provided a few things. Provided we read it at regular intervals and make a record of the readings. Provided we recognize that there is much more to weather than just barometric pressure. Remember our definition of a cyclonic storm? It was, in part: A traveling system of winds rotating counterclockwise around a center of low barometric pressure.

An individual reading of the barometer tells us only the pressure being exerted by the atmosphere

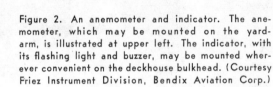

Figure 2. An anemometer and indicator. The anemometer, which may be mounted on the yardarm, is illustrated at upper left. The indicator, with its flashing light and buzzer, may be mounted wherever convenient on the deckhouse bulkhead. (Courtesy Friez Instrument Division, Bendix Aviation Corp.)

TABLE I

WIND-BAROMETER TABLE

WIND DIRECTION	BAROMETER REDUCED TO SEA LEVEL	CHARACTER OF WEATHER
SW to NW	30.10 to 30.20 and steady	Fair, with slight temperature changes for one or two days.
SW to NW	30.10 to 30.20 and rising rapidly	Fair followed within two days by rain.
SW to NW	30.20 and above and stationary	Continued fair with no decided temperature change.
SW to NW	30.20 and above and falling slowly	Slowly rising temperature and fair for two days.
S to SE	30.10 to 30.20 and falling slowly	Rain within twenty-four hours.
S to SE	30.10 to 30.20 and falling rapidly	Wind increasing in force, with rain within 12 to 24 hours.
SE to NE	30.10 to 30.20 and falling slowly	Rain in 12 to 18 hours.
SE to NE	30.10 to 30.20 and falling rapidly	Increasing wind and rain within 12 hours.
E to NE	30.10 and above and falling slowly	In summer with light winds rain may not fall for several days. In winter rain in 24 hours.
E to NE	30.10 and above and falling fast	In summer, rain probably in 12 hours. In winter, rain or snow, with increasing winds will often set in when the barometer begins to fall and the wind set in NE.
SE to NE	30.00 or below and falling slowly	Rain will continue 1 or 2 days.
SE to NE	30.00 or below and falling rapidly	Rain with high wind, followed within 36 hours by clearing and in winter colder.
S to SW	30.00 or below and rising slowly	Clearing in a few hours and fair for several days.
S to E	29.80 or below and falling rapidly	Severe storm imminent, followed in 24 hours by clearing and in winter colder.
E to N	29.80 or below and falling rapidly	Severe NE gale and heavy rain, winter heavy snow and cold wave.
Going to W	29.80 or below and rising rapidly	Clearing and colder.

Reproduced by Courtesy of U.S. Weather Bureau

on the earth's surface at the particular instant of observation. We can't do much forecasting with that one reading. But suppose we have logged the pressure at fairly regular intervals, as follows:

Time	Pressure	Change
0700	30.02 inches	—
0800	30.00	–0.02
0900	29.97	–0.03
1000	29.93	–0.04
1100	29.88	–0.05
1200	29.82	–0.06

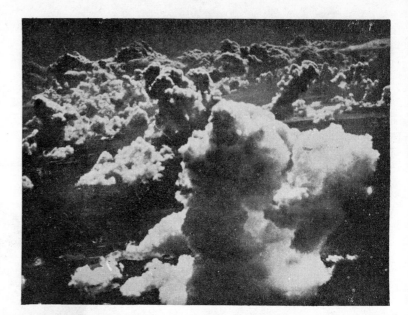

We wouldn't need the Delphic Oracle to tell us that trouble was brewing. The pressure is falling, at an increasing rate. A fall of 0.02 inch per hour is a low rate of fall; consequently, this figure would not be particularly disturbing. But a fall of 0.05 inch per hour is a pretty high rate.

Figure 3 (left): Forecast—Changeable Weather; Rain. To the right are cirrus clouds, to the upper left are cirrocumulus. In the center are cirrostratus, at the bottom stratocumulus. Rain is likely to fall soon. Figure 4 (above): Weather —Warm and Sultry. Forecast—Thunderstorms. The heavy, towering cumulus cloud in the foreground, backed up by castellated altocumulus and cumulus clouds, foretells a thunderstorm and summer squall. (Courtesy U. S. Weather Bureau)

Next, there is a normal daily change in pressure. The pressure is usually at its maximum value about 1000 and 2200 each day, at its minimum value about 0400 and 1600. The variation between minimum and maximum may be as much as 0.05 inch change in these six hour intervals (about 0.01 inch change per hour). Thus, when the pressure normally would increase about 0.03 inch (0700 to 1000) our pressure fell 0.09 inch.

Suppose, now, that we also observed, around 1200, that the wind was backing, east to north, and that the barometer continued to fall at a high rate. A rocky lee shore close aboard would not be pleasant to contemplate as a severe northeast gale with heavy rain is on its way. On the other hand, given the same barometer reading of about 29.80, rising rapidly with the wind going to west, we could expect clearing and cooler weather. Quite a difference.

The late Professor E. B. Garriott when he was Chief Forecaster in the U. S. Weather Bureau prepared a famous table—The Wind-Barometer Table—and we reproduce it as table 1. It is a good thing to post on board near our barometer. The foregoing example is taken from this table.

Then there are a few general rules that are often helpful. First, foul weather is usually forecast by a falling barometer with winds from the east quadrants, clearing and fair weather is usually forecast by winds shifting to west quadrants with a rising barometer. Second, there are the rules formerly printed on every Weather Bureau daily surface weather map:

"When the wind sets in from points between south and southeast and the barometer falls steadily, a storm is approaching from the west or northwest, and its center will pass near or north of the observer within 12 to 24 hours, with the wind shifting to northwest by way of south and southwest.

"When the wind sets in from points between east and northeast and the barometer falls steadily, a storm is approaching from the south or southwest, and its center will pass near or to the south of the observer within 12 to 24 hours, with the wind shifting to northwest by way of north.

"The rapidity of the storm's approach and its intensity will be indicated by the rate and amount of the fall in the barometer."

There are some other generally useful barometer rules. With our sling psychrometer we can determine the air temperature, so: a falling barometer and a rising thermometer often forecast rain; barometer and thermometer rising together often forecast fine weather. A steady, slow rise in the barometer forecasts settled weather, a steady, slow fall unsettled or wet weather. A rapid rise in the barometer forecasts clearing with high winds, a rapid fall a storm. Finally, the barometer forecasts changes in

the weather some hours ahead of their occurrence; it is not a last-minute warning agent.

In using barometer indications for local forecasting, it is vitally important that we remember that all weather changes result from unequal heating of the atmosphere and these changes are modified by the characteristics of the earth in our locality. All rules must be checked against our experience in our own cruising waters before we can place full confidence in their validity.

How do we measure the characteristics of the wind? Every sailor is familiar with the wind direction indicators that may be mounted at the masthead. Because a boat, at anchor or under way, can head in any direction all around the

Figure 5. Forecast—Severe Storm. The squall line clouds mark an advancing cold front; the storm will be severe, with a sharp, violent shift in the wind, rain and probably hail. (Courtesy U.S. Weather Bureau)

compass, a few mental gymnastics are necessary before we can use this indicator or an owner's flag or club burgee to determine the true direction of the wind. At anchor, the fly will give us the bearing of the wind relative to the boat's head; this must be converted to true bearing of the wind itself. We can use our compass to obtain these values, provided we know its deviation on our heading and know the variation for our anchorage. Then we need to remember that wind direction is always stated as the true direction from which, not toward which, the wind is blowing. There's nothing difficult about these gymnastics, but there is a tremendous difference in the significance of a NE and SW wind.

Underway, estimating direction, and

Table 3. Beaufort Scale. (Courtesy Aviation Training Div., U. S. Navy)

Beaufort number	Map symbol	Seaman's description of wind	Terms used by U.S. Weather Bureau	Velocity m.p.h.	Velocity, knots	Estimating velocities on land	Estimating velocities on sea	Probable mean height of waves in feet	Description of sea
0		Calm	Calm	Less than 1	Less than 1	Smoke rises vertically	Sea like a mirror		Calm (glassy).
1		Light air	Light	1-3	1-3	Smoke drifts; wind vanes unmoved.	Ripples with the appearance of scales are formed but without foam crests.	½	Rippled.
2		Light breeze		4-7	4-6	Wind felt on face; leaves rustle; ordinary vane moved by wind.	Small wavelets, still short but more pronounced; crests have a glassy appearance and do not break.	1	Smooth.
3		Gentle breeze	Gentle	8-12	7-10	Leaves and small twigs in constant motion; wind extends light flag.	Large wavelets. Crests begin to break. Foam of glassy appearance. Perhaps scattered white caps.	2½	
4		Moderate breeze	Moderate	13-18	11-16	Raises dust and loose paper; small branches are moved.	Small waves, becoming longer; fairly frequent white caps.	5	Slight.
5		Fresh breeze	Fresh	19-24	17-21	Small trees in leaf begin to sway; crested wavelets form on inland water.	Moderate waves, taking a more pronounced long form; many white caps are formed. (Chance of some spray.)	10	Moderate.
6		Strong breeze	Strong	25-31	22-27	Large branches in motion; whistling heard in telegraph wires; umbrellas used with difficulty.	Large waves begin to form; the white foam crests are more extensive everywhere. (Probably some spray.)	15	Rough.
7		Moderate gale		32-38	28-33	Whole trees in motion; inconvenience felt in walking against the wind.	Sea heaps up and white foam from breaking waves begins to be blown in streaks along the direction of the wind.	20	Very rough.
8		Fresh gale	Gale	39-46	34-40	Breaks twigs off trees; generally impedes progress.	Moderately high waves of greater length; edges of crests break into spindrift. The foam is blown in well-marked streaks along the direction of the wind.	25	High.
9		Strong gale		47-54	41-47	Slight structural damage occurs.	High waves. Dense streaks of foam along the direction of the wind. Sea begins to roll. Spray may affect visibility.	30	
10		Whole gale	Whole gale	55-63	48-55	Trees uprooted; considerable structural damage occurs.	Very high waves with long, overhanging crests. The resulting foam, in great patches, is blown in dense white streaks along the direction of the wind. On the whole, the surface of the sea takes a white appearance. The rolling of the sea becomes heavy and shocklike. Visibility is affected.	35	Very high.
11		Storm		64-75	56-65		Exceptionally high waves. (Small and medium-sized ships might for a long time be lost to view behind the waves.) The sea is completely covered with long white patches of foam lying along the direction of the wind. Everywhere edges of the wave crests are blown into froth. Visibility affected.	40	
12		Hurricane	Hurricane	Above 75	Above 65		The air is filled with foam and spray. Sea completely white with driving spray; visibility very seriously affected.	45 or more.	Phenomenal.

*To record the velocity in knots of HURRICANES of greater intensity than Force 12, the new scale is: 13, 72-80 kts.; 14, 81-89 kts.; 15, 90-99 kts.; 16, 100-109 kts.; 17, 110-118 kts.

Figure 6. Forecast—Fair today. The rising sun is dimly seen through stratocumulus clouds. The storm has passed; fair but colder weather may be expected. (Courtesy U. S. Weather Bureau)

velocity too, of the wind is more difficult. Someone else, to wit, the Hydrographic Office of the Navy, having worked it out, we might as well use their results. Table 2 is based on the wind tables of "American Practical Navigator" (Bowditch—HO 9), 1936 edition. Using our true course and speed, we can determine from this table the (approximate) true wind direction and velocity, provided we have the apparent direction and velocity. Our wind indicator or owner's flag will give us the apparent direction; for apparent velocity we need something else.

One thing else is an anemometer; the Friez Instrument Division of Bendix Aviation Corporation has kindly supplied us with an illustration, figure 2. The anemometer proper is designed for mounting at the masthead or on the yardarm; the indicator with its buzzer and flashing light may be mounted in the cabin. The unit is so designed that the number of buzzes or flashes per minute directly equals wind velocity, in statute miles per hour or knots as the case may be. Thus, all we need to do is to throw the switch and count the buzzes or flashes occurring in one minute. If we are at anchor, this is the actual or true surface wind velocity; if we are underway, we need Captain Bowditch's table, as the velocity given by the anemometer will be the apparent, not true, velocity. Sounds very complicated and horribly expensive; in practice, it is neither. The caption beneath the table tells us how to use it.

Another method is to use Admiral Beaufort's table and our seaman's eye. Table 3 is the Navy's—Aviation Training Division—latest modification; notice the several means for estimating wind velocity. For convenience, we record it in units of Force, i.e., Beaufort number. All wind velocities on weather maps are given in this

Weather
and the
Yachtsman

Part Five

unit. Wind direction can be judged by observing the direction in which any wave-crests are breaking or the direction in which any clouds are moving. The former tells us the direction of any surface winds, the latter the direction of winds aloft. In weather forecasting, winds aloft are the more important.

We don't need to determine wind direction and velocity with great precision but reasonable estimates are mighty helpful in preparing our own local forecasts. Estimating direction to two or four points is sufficient; within one Beaufort number is enough for velocity. By observing these factors regularly and making a record of them, we are warned of potential weather developments as the wind shifts direction and changes its velocity. Even a steady wind, however, has its meaning. Along the Pacific Coast, local west winds often bring rain, as they pick up moisture in their travel over the ocean and are strengthened by the prevailing westerlies. On the other hand, local east winds, blowing off the coastal mountain ranges, oppose the prevailing westerlies and are not so likely to bring rain. Along the Atlantic Coast, local west winds usually bring fair weather, local easterlies foul weather.

These, then, are the only strictly weather instruments we really need on board: a sling psychrometer, an aneroid barometer, an anemometer. Costing, in total, considerably less than a dinghy, they are better preventive medicine against storms than the dink is curative.

In addition to our instrumental weather observations, there are many visual weather signs that we can note, without interfering with our primary purpose: an enjoyable cruise. Let's take a quick look at some of them.

Weather is always on the move, though at times it may move haltingly. In the USA, it moves because the winds aloft are prevailing winds, the prevailing westerlies. Consequently, it moves generally from west to east. The ebb and flow of the different air masses give us our fronts and their weather effects. Because of these surges back and forth in the air, weather moves in an irregular path, at a variable speed. As the weather moves, it changes, although over a relatively short time interval it tends to continue its existing state. It behooves us, then, to observe the present and immediate past (last six hours) state of the weather, sky and sea. This is our point of departure for using visual observations in local forecasting.

Visual Weather Signs

First, we want to check for visibility. Haze, dust and smoke are nearly as important as fog itself. The particles of solid matter suspended in the air and reducing the visibility are nuclei on which water vapor can condense. Unless the water vapor present in the air does condense, we can have no fog, no clouds, no rain. If haze progressively restricts our vision, we have a warning sign that worse may be in store for us.

Second, we should note the clouds. How much of the sky is covered; what form or forms of cloud are present; in what direction are they moving; are they increasing or decreasing in amount, rapidly or slowly; are they lowering or lifting; what is the sequence of cloud forms across the sky? The clouds constitute a whole weather study in themselves. We saw in our previous story on Storms how clouds can be used to time the approach of foul weather. We have space here only for the briefest additional mention of their significance. (Two excellent publications are: "Clouds, Fog and Aviation," by Dr. W. J. Humphreys, published by Williams & Wilkins Co., Baltimore, in 1943 and "Codes for Cloud Forms and States of the Sky," Circular S, U.S. Weather Bureau No. 1249, published in 1938, available from Superintendent of Documents, Government Printing Office, Washington (25), D.C.

The greater the proportion of the sky covered by clouds, the greater the likelihood of wet weather. If the clouds thicken gradually, then the chances are that they will break up slowly; foul weather may continue for some time. If the clouds are moving toward us, the storm will probably affect us. If they are moving east to west, instead of the customary west to east, foul weather is near at hand. If the clouds are moving rapidly, the storm will arrive very soon. The high-flying ice-crystal cirrus clouds, being the ones

---

TABLE 2

TRUE FORCE AND DIRECTION OF THE WIND

from its

APPARENT FORCE AND DIRECTION ON A BOAT UNDERWAY

APPARENT WIND VELOCITY Knots	SPEED OF BOAT							
	5 Knots TRUE WIND		10 Knots TRUE WIND		15 Knots TRUE WIND		20 Knots TRUE WIND	
	Points off Bow	Velocity Knots	Points off Bow	Velocity Knots	Points off Bow	Velocity Knots	Points off Bow	Velocity Knots
I. APPARENT WIND DIRECTION IS DEAD AHEAD								
Calm	D. As.	5 K.	D. As.	10 K.	D. As.	15 K.	D. As.	20 K.
4 K.	"	1	"	6	"	11	"	16
8	D. Ah.	3	"	2	"	7	"	12
12	"	7	D. Ah.	2	"	3	"	8
16	"	11	"	6	D. Ah.	1	"	4
22	"	17	"	12	"	7	D. Ah.	2
30	"	25	"	20	"	15	"	10
42	"	37	"	32	"	27	"	22
60	"	55	"	50	"	45	"	40
II. APPARENT WIND DIRECTION IS 4 POINTS (BROAD) OFF THE BOW								
4 K.	11 pts.	4 K.	14 pts.	8 K.	15 pts.	12 K.	15 pts.	17 K.
8	7	6	11	7	13	11	14	15
12	6	9	9	9	11	11	13	14
16	5	13	7	11	10	12	11	14
22	5	19	6	16	8	15	9	16
30	5	27	6	24	7	22	8	21
42	4	39	5	36	6	33	6	31
60	4	57	5	53	5	51	6	48
III. APPARENT WIND DIRECTION IS 8 POINTS OFF THE BOW (ABEAM)								
4 K.	13 pts.	6 K.	14 pts.	11 K.	15 pts.	16 K.	15 pts.	20 K.
8	11	9	13	13	14	17	14	22
12	10	13	12	16	13	19	13	23
16	10	17	11	19	12	22	13	26
22	9	23	10	24	11	27	12	30
30	9	30	10	32	10	34	11	36
42	9	42	9	43	10	45	10	47
60	8	60	9	61	9	62	10	63
IV. APPARENT WIND DIRECTION IS 12 POINTS OFF THE [(BROAD ON THE QUARTER)								
4 K.	14 pts.	8 K.	15 pts.	13 K.	15 pts.	18 K.	15 pts.	23 K.
8	14	12	14	17	15	21	15	26
12	13	16	14	20	14	25	15	30
16	13	20	14	24	14	29	14	33
22	13	26	13	30	14	34	14	39
30	13	34	13	38	13	42	14	46
42	12	46	13	50	13	54	13	58
60	12	64	13	67	13	71	13	75

CONVERSION OF POINTS OFF BOW TO TRUE DIRECTION OF WIND

POINTS OFF BOW	BOAT'S HEADING -- TRUE							
	000°	045°	090°	135°	180°	225°	270°	315°
I. WHEN WIND DIRECTION OBTAINED FROM TABLE ABOVE IS OFF STARBOARD BOW								
Dead Ahead	N	NE	E	SE	S	SW	W	NW
4 points	NE	E	SE	S	SW	W	NW	N
8	E	SE	S	SW	W	NW	N	NE
12	SE	S	SW	W	NW	N	NE	E
Dead Astern	S	SW	W	NW	N	NE	E	SE
II. WHEN WIND DIRECTION OBTAINED FROM TABLE ABOVE IS OFF PORT BOW								
Dead Ahead	N	NE	E	SE	S	SW	W	NW
4 points	NW	N	NE	E	SE	S	SW	W
8	W	NW	N	NE	E	SE	S	SW
12	SW	W	NW	N	NE	E	SE	S
Dead Astern	S	SW	W	NW	N	NE	E	SE

Abbreviations: D.As.=Dead Astern. D.Ah.=Dead Ahead. K.=Knots. **pts.**=Points off bow

TO USE THIS TABLE

1. With Wind Direction Indicator: Determine Apparent Wind Direction off the Bow

2. With Anemometer: Determine Apparent Wind Velocity, in Knots

3. Enter Upper Part of Table: Use portion for nearest Apparent Wind Direction Opposite Apparent Wind Velocity and under nearest Speed of Boat, read Wind Direction in Points off Bow and True Wind Velocity in Knots. Note whether True Wind Direction is off Starboard or Port Bow.

4. Enter Lower Part of Table: Use portion for proper Bow: Starboard or Port. Opposite Points off Bow and under nearest Boat's True Heading, read True Wind Direction.

5. Log: Record True Wind Direction as obtained from Lower Part of Table and True Wind Velocity as obtained from Upper Part of Table in Boat's Weather Log.

Based on Table 32 AMERICAN PRACTICAL NAVIGATOR - BOWDITCH - HO 9   1936 Edition
by permission of Hydrographer, U. S. Navy.

most greatly influenced by the prevailing westerly winds, normally move at roughly 45 to 50 knots. Middle altitude clouds, altostratus and altocumulus, move at about 35 and 25 knots, respectively. Cumulus and cumulonimbus clouds usually have velocities of about 15 to 20 knots. Stratus (sheet) type clouds normally move more rapidly than do the cumulus type; the latter are influenced by the great vertical air currents creating them as well as by the prevailing horizontal winds. A timid series of relative bearings will help us judge the speed of movement.

We have had photographs of many cloud forms in our previous pages. It must suffice here that we summarize their more important indications, with figures 3 through 6 to illustrate how some clouds forecast the weather.

Cirrus clouds are often the advance agents of a storm; they precede warm fronts and extra-tropical cyclones. As they thicken to cirrocumulus or cirrostratus, they forecast the probability of rain within 24 hours. If they appear to converge in bands near the horizon and especially if they extend more than 45° above the horizon, they indicate foul weather to come.

The middle altitude clouds are perhaps the most important forecasters. Whether thin or thick, altostratus mark the central part of a typical storm. Altocumulus occurs in seven recognized varieties, some of which are welcome harbingers of fair weather. If seen in small isolated patches, not increasing in extent nor growing denser, or tending to form a single flat sheet at one level in sky, slowly evaporating to uncover more and more blue sky, this cloud form indicates fair weather to come. But, should altocumulus clouds appear in castellated or domed form and in several sheets at different altitudes in a confused sky, a thunderstorm is probable.

The low level clouds—stratus, stratocumulus, nimbostratus or fractostratus and fractocumulus—frequently are rain producers. When these appear and grow denser, the storm is upon us.

Finally, we have the clouds of vertical development, those cottony cumulus puff-balls so characteristic of a warm summer day and the massive cumulonimbus thunderstorm cloud to which we have already paid our humble respects.

Learning to recognize clouds is like learning to identify the stars. Long hours of pleasant cruising and watchful eyes are the necessary preludes. During the summer day, particularly, the clouds tend to the cumulus—piled up—variety. Near sunset, as the earth and air cool, these begin to flatten out and the sratus—sheet—

variety may form as the night wears on. From these stratus night clouds we often get a drizzling rain early in the morning when the air is at its lowest temperature and therefore able to hold only the minimum amount of water as vapor. After sunrise, the stratus clouds burn off as the water droplets evaporate in the warming air and so the weather clears.

Clouds, and the sequence of cloud forms across the sky, are timely weather signs. There are a few other visual observations we can make to our advantage.

Some of us got a quiet chuckle out of one newspaper reporter's account of the Normandy invasion; he had more poetry than science in his head. The weather on D-Day was not of the best. This reporter was writing his observations as his ship headed east toward

TABLE 7 B

LOCAL WEATHER OBSERVATIONS

Time -- ZT. Navy Style
Latitude - degrees, minutes
Longitude - " "
Course - degrees psc
- " true
Speed - Knots
Barometer - in. or mb.
- tendency
Clouds - form
- moving from
- amount
- changing to
Sea - condition
- swells
- moving from
Temperatures - air, dry bulb
- dewpoint
- water
Visibility
Wind - direction, true
- shifting to
- velocity, true
- force (Beaufort)
Weather - present

Figure 7B, Local Weather Observations

the rising sun. This is what he wrote: "The weather had been bad all night long and we wondered what was in store for us when we hit the beaches in the morning. Then, as we were standing in, the sun broke through the clouds and the most beautiful rainbow I have ever seen formed in the sky. One end appeared to rest in the north country and the other to touch the soil of France, a perfect symbol to our French brothers that their day of liberation was at hand." Noble sentiments and a true forecast for France. But pure hokum as far as the rainbow was concerned. A rainbow can be seen only when our back is to the sun. In the morning, a rainbow is seen when looking westward, not eastward. Why? Rainbows result from sunlight striking a sheet of water droplets and being reflected toward the observer. A morning rainbow suggests rain for us later in the day, as the moisture-laden air moves eastward toward us. An evening rainbow suggests a clear night and sunny day tomorrow; the excess moisture is being carried farther away from us.

All of us know that a bright blue sky means fine weather. There is good scientific reason for that, but we won't go into it here! Likewise for sound cause, a vivid red sky at sunset means fair weather tomorrow but a vivid red sky at sunrise means foul weather today. If at sunset, the sun appears diffuse and glaringly white or if the sun should set behind dark clouds, with a falling barometer, foul weather may be expected later that night or in the morning.

TABLE 7 A

BOAT WEATHER LOG

Yacht_____ At/Passage_____ to_____
Day___ Date_____ Time Zone_____ Skipper_____

1. Latest Weather Map: Date___ Time_____ Summary of forecast and of principal regional weather features:_____

2. Radio Weather Reports Received (state source and time):_____

3. Local Weather Observations (see over for record)

4. Remarks and Local Forecast for Next___ Hours (state time forecast effective):_____

Figure 7A, Boat Weather Log

Finally, the sea itself may telegraph storm warnings ahead. Long, high swells rolling in tell us that powerful winds have been at work some distance away. The longer the swells are, the heavier the storm that produced them. If the storm is approaching us, the swells will increase, often before the sky reveals any warning sign. Should the swells rise greatly or become very confused, it would be good seamanship to seek shelter immediately. Should the swells fall away or any confusion of the sea die out, before the sky clouds over, we would go merrily on our way. These are signs that all experienced boatmen recognize.

It is much more important for us to observe the weather as it develops than it is for us to keep a fancy record of our observations. Most of us get enough "pencil-pushing" during the week without taking along a thick pad of forms and an extra box of leads on the week-end cruise. But sometimes it is handy to know how the record might be kept: what items we should write down at what times. So figure 7 has been included; it is similar to the Weather Log used in the Weather Course of the United States Power Squadrons.

Figure 7-A is the face sheet, figure 7-B the reverse side. The first weather items recorded are the results of our weather map reading and of radio reports received. These are basic to all intelligent forecasting. Then we use the reverse side to note our local observations. Sufficient columns are available to permit recording these data six times during one 24-hour day, or at four-hour intervals. That's not a bad interval. Entries can be made using the U. S. Weather Bureau code symbols (it makes us better map readers) or any other way we want, provided we use the same scheme consistently.

From these records we prepare our forecast, being not too anxious to make it cover a long period of time. Forecasting much more than 12 hours ahead is likely to reduce our batting average.

In the concluding pages of this weather yarn we will discuss the preparation of local forecasts.

Barometer Readings

Barometer readings in weather reports are given in terms of sea level pressure. This means that the barometer reading at a weather station on the Great Lakes is first corrected for the height of the barometer above the lake, then corrected for the height of the lake above sea level and the resultant is announced as the barometer reading whether the term "sea level reading" is stated or not.

To obtain the "above water" correction add 0.01 inch for every 10 feet of exposure above the water line. Following are the corrections for each of the Great Lakes to obtain sea level readings:

Lake Superior	0.64
Lakes Michigan, Huron, St. Clair	0.62
Lake Erie	0.61
Lake Ontario	0.26

An example of the manner in which this information may be utilized is as follows: A vessel in the Detroit River takes a barometer reading of 29.72 at 7:00 P.M. The barometer is located 30 feet above the water line. On the WJR broadcast at 11:15 P.M. the Detroit barometer for 7:00 P.M. is announced at 30.42. The correct reading for the ship's barometer at 7:00 P.M. should have been 29.77, computed as follows:

Announced 7:00 P.M. barometer reading	30.42 (Sea level)
Correction for lake level	(—) .62
Height above water correction	(—) .03
Correct ship barometer	29.77
Actual reading	29.72
Error	(—) 0.05

The barometer should be re-set by increasing the reading 0.05 or by applying this correction to each reading.

Conversion Table for Inches and Millibars

Inches	Millibars	Inches	Millibars
28.44	963	29.77	1008
28.53	966	29.86	1011
28.62	969	29.94	1014
28.70	972	30.03	1017
28.79	975	30.12	1020
28.88	978	30.21	1023
28.97	981	30.30	1026
29.06	984	30.39	1029
29.15	987	30.48	1032
29.24	990	30.56	1035
29.32	993	30.65	1038
29.41	996	30.74	1041
29.50	999	30.83	1044
29.59	1002	30.92	1047
29.68	1005	31.01	1050

Preparation of
Local Forecasts

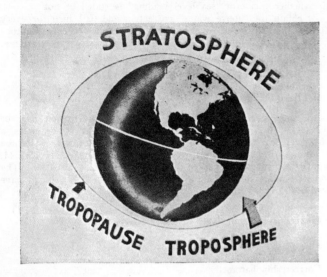

Figure 5. The atmosphere surrounding the earth is made up of two main parts: the lower portion, next to the earth's surface, known as the Troposphere; the upper portion, known as the Stratosphere. These parts are separated by a narrow band known as the Tropopause. All of our weather developments occur in the Troposphere, which varies in depth from about 25,000 feet over the polar regions to 36,000 feet in the middle latitudes to some 60,000 feet over the equator. All the energy received on the surface of the earth is radiated from the sun. As this energy is re-radiated from the earth, the air above the earth is heated. Much more energy is received, and re-radiated, over the equator than is received and re-radiated over the polar regions. As a result, the air over the equator tends to rise and the colder air over the poles tends to sink. (Reproduced by Courtesy of Aviation Training Division, U. S. Navy)

A YACHTING friend once remarked, without malice aforethought: "Why bother with weather maps and radios and a ton of instruments? They just clutter up my cabin and my mind. I stick my head out of the companionway and look to westward. That tells me all I need to know about the weather." Not a bad idea. Except that too many of us have an excessively large bump of curiosity. We not only want to know that the weather will be bad, but we also want to know how bad the weather is going to be, how soon it is going to be bad, and how quickly it will be fair again. If our interest were merely whether the weather is to be good, bad, or indifferent, an intelligent, quick look to westward often would suffice. When we start to refine our information or when we haven't had thirty-odd years of experience in sticking our head out of the companionway, then we need to do something more than that.

Local weather signs—the ones we can see out the companionway—help us a great deal in forecasting the probable weather, for short periods of time. Weather is always on the move; the weather 100 miles to westward—which we cannot see too well even when on deck—will be with us in about four hours. Again, some visual weather signs indulge in "double-talk." The cloud sequence preceding a relatively innocuous warm front is likely to be the same as the cloud sequence preceding a violent extra-tropical cyclone. The former may bring us several days of miserable rain; the latter may dismast us. If any

question of the safety of our boat and her people is involved, we must assume that the more severe weather disturbance is approaching.

Consequently, several things are necessary if we are to prepare intelligent local forecasts, forecasts that should make our cruising safer and more enjoyable. First, we need all the official background information we can get: the latest available weather map, the latest radio weather reports. They give us information on what to expect and when to expect it, information that we cannot always get by local observation.

The features for which we look on the daily surface weather map are:

1. The official forecast for our state and region, plus any storm or small craft warnings.
2. Data of the station models for cities in our cruising area, to westward and to windward.
3. The air mass in which we are situated and others approaching and likely to affect us; the stability or instability of the air.
4. Highs and lows, spacing of the isobars, and pressure tendencies.
5. Isotherms; when shown. The air temperature and dewpoint patterns.
6. Wind pattern and cloud conditions.
7. Storms: extra-tropical cyclones, squall lines, thunderstorms.
8. Fog. Signs of air-mass fogs and of fogs accompanying fronts.
9. Fronts: cold, warm, stationary, occluded.
10. Precipitation areas.

In noting these features, we judge the direction and movement of the weather and decide whether it is likely to change (if so, how) before it reaches us. We then estimate the character of the weather that may affect our cruise. The use of the weather maps of the immediately preceding several days together with local observation of

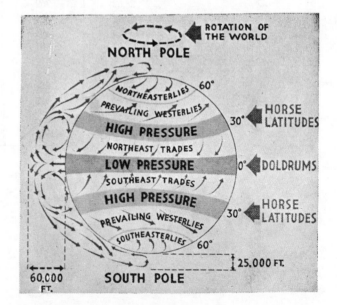

Figure 6. General Air Circulation. The rising air over the equator results in a low barometric pressure at that part of the earth's surface. The sinking air over the polar regions results in a high barometric pressure there. As air flows from highs to lows, there is a tendency for the air, at the earth's surface, to flow from the poles toward the equator. Up near the Tropopause, or roof, the air flow is from the equator to the poles. However, some of this air sinks to form a high pressure belt at about 30° North and South Latitudes. This interchanges of air between equator and poles is influenced by the earth's rotation from West to East, which deflects the winds and gives us our prevailing westerlies and northeasterlies. (Reproduced by Courtesy of Aviation Training Division, U. S. Navy)

240

the actual weather existing at the time of our map-reading, will help us immensely in estimating the future weather.

By referring to HO 118 (Radio Weather Aids to Navigation) or its Great Lakes counterpart, we can make a list of the broadcasts to which we can listen while afloat: stations, frequency, time, nature of information. With our weather map as background, we have the best obtainable official picture of the weather; we have a sound basis for our forecasts.

The second thing we must do to prepare intelligent local forecasts is to recognize the limitations of local observations. Our "double-talk" example is one such limitation. Further, local signs of general storms often precede the disturbance by not more than twelve hours, sometimes by a much shorter interval. Storms developing locally are even worse offenders; they may give us only one hour of warning. We should observe and record the weather, as it develops locally, continuously at regular intervals and we should prepare forecasts only for a few hours in advance.

Third, we need to have a good idea of how the weather usually develops in our cruising area. Significant weather signs of the Pacific Coast may indicate nothing on the Great Lakes or Ohio River. We need experience in observing and interpreting weather in our waters; a good practice is to compare our forecasts with the actual weather as it develops.

Finally, it helps a lot when we know the primary causes of weather disturbances and can judge whether these causes are likely to exist in our locality. We can't control the weather; we can control our boat.

Probably the most important of all local observations is the combination of wind direction and velocity with barometric pressure and pressure tendency. It is a fairly long-time warning; it suggests the degree of severity of any storm. Previously we took a good look at the instruments—aneroid barometer, thermometer, anemometer—we can use to measure these weather developments. We discussed the wind-barometer table that helps us judge the coming weather. We need to use these instruments and this table, or their equivalents, regularly and we need to know how to interpret their readings. For our purpose here, let's assume we are experts in these observations.

Just to be on the safe side, however, suppose we refer to the wind-barometer table (p. 233) and summarize some of the more important general rules.

1. A falling barometer and winds from east quadrants, forecast foul weather approaching from westward.
2. Winds veering to west quadrants indicate clear weather to come, but a backing wind following passage of a storm suggests more foul weather.
3. The barometer changes usually occur before there is a shift in the wind.
4. A low pressure area tends to deepen and the wind to increase in velocity as the low approaches a body of water.
5. A veering (clockwise) wind and a rising barometer usually mark clearing or fair weather.
6. A backing (counterclockwise) wind and a falling barometer forecast foul weather.
7. There is a normal diurnal (daily) fluctuation in the barometer. In the interval from 0400 to 1000, it rises about 0.05 inch, then decreases by the same amount to 1600, then rises 0.05 inch by 2200, then decreases again until 0400 the next morning. The average, hourly diurnal change is thus slightly less than plus or minus 0.01 inch.

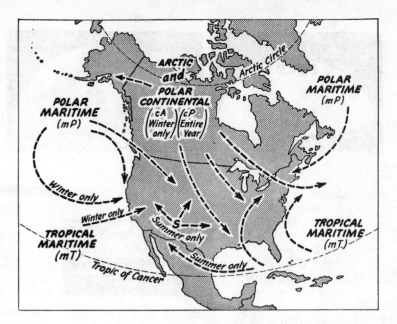

Figure 7. North American Air Masses. The source regions and directions of movement of the air masses influencing North American weather are shown on this map. Air remaining in contact with the earth's surface gradually acquires properties characteristic of the surface beneath it. Then, as this air mass subsequently moves over the earth, its properties, and its conflicts with other air masses that it may encounter en route, cause changes in the weather of the area invaded. (Reproduced by Courtesy of Aviation Training Division, U. S. Navy)

8. After allowing for the diurnal variation, a change of 0.02 inch per hour in the barometer is a small change, but a variation of 0.05 inch per hour, especially when the glass is falling, is a change not to be ignored.

As we haven't as yet paid too much attention to temperature indications, maybe it would be still better if we also summarized some temperature indications before we accepted the mantle of expert. If the temperature of the air is at its normal value for the season, or just slightly colder, fair weather is probable. If the evening air temperature is much above normal, the weather is likely to be unsettled. A rising air temperature, when accompanied by a rising barometer, forecasts fine weather. Clearing weather is often forecast by a falling thermometer and a steady barometer. If the air temperature rises and the barometer falls, a storm is possible.

We also had a good look at the sling psychrometer. As the spread between the air temperature and dewpoint temperature lessens, fog is likely. As it increases, fair weather is in prospect. If of a warm, sunny morning, the dewpoint is 70°F or higher and the wind is from the south, a thunderstorm is probable later in the day.

Next, we need to be able to read all visual signs—the clouds, state of the sky and sea—that may appear. Forecasting from a long list of disjointed rules may be dangerous: in our efforts to remember them all, we are likely to get hopelessly confused. But, we can stifle our pride and post the more useful ones on the deckhouse bulkhead, so let's summarize some of them, limiting ourselves to those having a scientific basis and eliminating all the merry but sometimes misleading jingles..

A. The Sky

1. Bright blue sky: fair weather
2. Vivid red sky—(a) at sunset: fair tomorrow
   (b) at sunrise: probably foul today
3. Gray sky at sunset: foul tomorrow
4. Cloudless sky at sunset: fair tomorrow and cooler

2. Cc-Cirrocumulus—
    (a) weak disturbance approaching
    (b) growing denser: rain in 24 hours
3. Cs-Cirrostratus—
    (a) thickening: rain in 6 to 24 hours
    (b) veil over entire sky: warm front or cyclone

5. Rainbow—
    (a) in morning: rain later today
    (b) in afternoon: fair tonight and tomorrow
6. Halo or corona around sun or moon: storm approaching
7. Moon rises clear with W wind: fair tonight and tomorrow

The cold air is heavier than the warm air . . . therefore it slides underneath

The intersection of this surface with the earth is the line shown on the weather map

These fronts often extend from several hundred miles to well over a thousand or two

Figure 8. How Fronts Form. As air piles up in the polar regions, the pressure increases until it becomes so strong that the northeasterly current from the pole breaks into the area of the prevailing westerly wind. The middle latitudes, lying between the cold and warm areas of the earth, become a battleground, where cold air from the north and warm air from the south clash. Cold air and warm air, on meeting, do not mix readily. The cold air, being heavier, slides beneath the warm air. A sloping boundary surface, a front, separating the two air masses is formed. (Reproduced by Courtesy of Aviation Training Division, U. S. Navy)

B. The Sun

1. Sun appears weak and washed out: rain probable
2. Sun disappears in cirrostratus clouds: rain
3. Sun at sunset diffuse and white: storm
4. Sun sets in dark clouds, barometer falling: foul tonight
5. Sun sets like ball of fire: fair and warmer tomorrow
6. Sun rises out of gray horizon into clear: fair today

C. General Cloudiness

1. Decreasing or breaking up: clearing weather
2. Increasing: foul weather approaching
3. Moving east to west, in USA: storm near
4. Moving rapidly: storm near
5. Two or more layers moving in different directions: unsettled
6. Clouds in E to S quadrants: rain in 24 hours
7. Middle or low clouds, N to W: fair for a day or so
8. Cloudy day clears at sunset: fair tomorrow
9. Night clouds burn off after sunrise: fair today
10. General cloudiness with E wind: storm to south
11. General cloudiness with W wind: storm to north
12. Maximum cloudiness normally occurs about noon, minimum in late evening

D. Fog

1. Lifting reluctantly in morning: more fog and rain to come
2. Clearing early in morning: fair today
3. Forming locally early in the evening: slow to clear tomorrow
4. Forming locally late at night: early to clear tomorrow
5. Riding a steady S or SW wind: slow to clear

E. Individual Clouds

1. Ci-Cirrus—
    (a) increasing to W: warm front or cyclone, 12 to 24 hours
    (b) moving E to W: rain in 24 hours
    (c) moving rapidly, especially from SW: foul
    (d) converging in bands near horizon: foul
    (e) thickening, especially with S wind: rain
    (f) backed by overcast or gray sky: foul
    (g) of anvil: thunderstorm near
    (h) not increasing, drifting or standing still: fair
    (i) dissolving as sun rises: fair

4. Ac-Altocumulus—
    (a) in small, isolated patches: fair
    (b) evaporating: fair
    (c) domed: thunderstorm possible
    (d) with altostratus: rain probable
5. As-Altostratus, thickening: warm front or cyclone
6. St. Stratus: light, steady rain
7. Sc-Stratocumulus—
    (a) growing denser: rain
    (b) after showers have passed: clearing
8. Ns-Nimbostratus: rain
9. Cu-Cumulus—
    (a) massing to windward: storm
    (b) growing as summer day passes: thunderstorm
    (c) small, isolated patches: fair
10. Cb-Cumulonimbus: thunderstorm
11. Cumulus type clouds: produce showers and thunderstorms, unstable air
12. Stratus type clouds: produce steady, long-continued rain, stable air

F. Cloud Sequences

1. Ci to Cc or Cs: rain in 24 hours
2. Ci to Cs to As to Ns: steady rain, fog, warmer
3. Ci to Cs or Cc to Ac to Cb: warm front, with thunderstorms
4. As to Ac to Ns or Cb: cold front, squalls, thunderstorms, wind shifts
5. Cc to Ac: thunderstorm approaching
6. Ac, turreted, to Cu, large: thunderstorm approaching
7. Cs or Cc to As, thick, to St: heavy, rain, colder
8. Daytime; Cu growing to turreted Cu, to Cb: thunderstorm, air mass type
9. Evening; Cu to Ac or Sc to St: steady rain tomorrow
10. Ns or As to Ac, Ac then diminishing: clearing

Weather Causes and Effects

Finally, it may also be helpful if we summarize the general summer weather pattern usually associated with each major weather cause.

1. Polar (P) air is usually relatively cold and dry; it flows south over the United States. A polar air mass brings mostly clear skies over the land, but cloudy—cumulus type—skies over relatively warm water. Visibility is good. Winds are light to moderate northerlies. The weather is likely to be fair. This air mass generally follows the passage of a cold front.

2. Tropical (T) air is usually relatively warm and moist; it flows north over the United States. A tropical air mass will bring warmer weather; may produce showers or continued rain. Visibility is likely to be restricted. Over relatively cool water, low stratus clouds and fog are prevalent. Over relatively warm water, thunderstorms are likely.

3. A cold front is usually accompanied by strong, shifting surface winds, squalls, and thunderstorms. Clouds will often be of the cumulus variety. Cold front weather is often severe but the storm quickly passes.

4. A warm front is usually marked by great sheets of low clouds, by fog and poor visibility, by steady rain. The winds are not likely to be violent but the foul weather will probably continue for some time.

5. An extra-tropical cyclone means that we will experience some combination of the weather associated with a warm front and a cold front.

When translating the meaning of weather map indications into the precautions we should take afloat, it is well to remember that weather disturbances vary in intensity. Not all extra-tropical cyclones produce a violent storm, not all warm fronts produce only cloudy skies. Necessarily as good seamen, we will prepare for the worst and then we can be only agreeably surprised.

Local Forecasting

Now, with all our expert ratings and our knowledge of the weather, the weather map and radio reports, we should be ready to do some local forecasting, more especially, some local forecasting for specific weather hazards.

Like most everything else connected with boats and boating, there is a gadget we can use. It's a pretty good one, too. It is the Guest Weathercaster and with it we need a barometer and wind vane plus two observations of the pressure, wind direction and general state of the weather, these observations to be made about six hours apart. The Weathercaster is put up in book form, the cover being equipped with four concentric, lettered dials. One dial is for barometric pressure, another for pressure tendency, the third for wind direction and the fourth for current state of the weather. Each dial may be moved independently; when all four are properly oriented, a code number is revealed. This number is translated into a weather forecast by referring to the tables which, with a very complete set of instructions, form the balance of the book. Simple to use, it forecasts conditions for a period of 12 to 24 hours.

Cold Fronts

But, suppose we want to do our own guessing. First, cold fronts, with their usually attendant squall lines, deserve our respect. Here are the steps we might take in determining whether one is likely to catch us afloat this week-end:

1. Before sailing, check over the latest available weather map and make an "estimate of the situation." Does the map show a cold front? More than one? Where are they located? Are they likely to affect us during our cruise? When? Where? Mildly or severely?

2. After getting underway, listen regularly to the radio weather reports. We know what stations, at what times, we can tune in, so that's easy.

3. While underway, at the first opportunity, or, better still, before casting off, prepare a check-list of the warning signs that we can observe as we cruise, in the order of their occurrence at our probable stations, thus:
   a. Direction in which clouds should first appear, probably to W or NW.
   b. First cloud form we should see, probably altostratus, and distance it is ahead of the cold front, about 300 miles.
   c. Cloud sequences: probably altostratus, then altocumulus, then nimbostratus or cumulonimbus.
   d. Barometer activity; for a cold front, it will first be erratic, falling and rising, falling and rising. Then it will fall, as the front nears, rising sharply after the front passes.
   e. Wind; first from the south, increasing in velocity, with a shift to north as the cold front passes.
   f. Temperature; down, after the front approaches and passes us.

It is a mighty good idea to time the approach of the front so we can take adequate precautions for the safety and comfort of our crew. To refresh our memory, let's refer to the cold front diagram (page 224). The cloud sequence isn't quite the same as that described above; the weather isn't always uniform, so there is more than one sequence: another kind of "double-talk."

Warm Fronts

If it is a warm front, with its usually less severe but long-lasting miserable weather, our procedure is:

1. Before sailing, check the latest available weather map and make an estimate of the situation, as for a cold front.

2. After getting underway, listen regularly to the radio weather reports.

3. Prepare our check-list of warning signs:
   a. Clouds should first appear to SW.
   b. First cloud form will probably be cirrus, about 600 miles ahead of the front.
   c. Cloud sequence: Cirrus to cirrostratus to altostratus to nimbostratus, if the air is stable, which means that the front will be relatively mild but foggy and the rain long-lived; if the sequence is cirrus to cirrocumulus to altocumulus to cumulonimbus, as it is when the air is unstable, expect strong winds and heavy rain, a thunderstorm.
   d. Barometer, falling, often at an increasing rate.
   e. Wind from SE or SSE and increasing; it will shift to SSW or SW as the front passes.
   f. Temperature, gradually rising.

We should time the approach of the front and again we refresh our memory by reference to the warm front diagram, page 223. Only one cloud sequence is shown on it.

Extra-tropical Cyclones

For an extra-tropical cyclone, remembering that it is a combination of a warm front, a cold front, a low pressure area, and a wind system, our procedure would be:

1. Before sailing, check the latest available weather map and make an estimate of the situation: always this fundamental step.

2. After getting underway, listen regularly to the radio weather reports.

3. Prepare our check-list of warning signs:
   a. Determine our probable position with respect to the low pressure center at the time of its passage by applying the law of storms. Facing the wind, center will bear approximately 110° from our heading.
   b. Depending on our probable position relative to the low, at its time of passage, make up lists similar to those for warm fronts and cold fronts. Figure 4 (page 225) will help us do this.

4. Time the approach of the storm and govern ourselves accordingly!

Clouds

CLOUDS differ from fogs only in their location. Both appear when air is cooled below the point at which dew begins to form. The principal distinction lies in the fact that clouds usually result from the cooling caused by upward drafts of air, so that clouds generally are separated from the earth, except on mountain tops. Fog, on the contrary, is found when air at or near the earth's surface is cooled. Fog has been called a cloud on earth—cloud, a fog in the sky.

Clouds assume an infinite variety of forms but are grouped into the following general classifications. Abbreviations are given in parentheses.

CIRRUS (Ci)—Detached clouds of delicate and fibrous appearance, without shading, generally white in color, often of a silky appearance. Cirrus appears in the most varied forms, such as isolated tufts, lines drawn across a blue sky, branching feather-like plumes, curved lines ending in tufts, etc.; they are often arranged in bands which cross the sky like meridian lines, and which, owing to the effect of perspective, converge to a point on the horizon, or to two opposite points (cirrostratus and cirrocumulus often take part in the formation of these bands).

CIRROCUMULUS (Cc)—A cirriform layer or patch composed of small white flakes or of very small globular masses, usually without shadows, which are arranged in groups or lines, or more often in ripples resembling those of the sand on the seashore.

CIRROSTRATUS (Cs)—A thin whitish veil which does not blur the outlines of the sun or moon, but usually gives rise to halos. Sometimes it is quite diffuse and merely gives the sky a milky look; sometimes it more or less distinctly shows a fibrous structure with disordered filaments.

ALTOCUMULUS (Ac)—A layer (or patches) composed of laminae or rather flattened globular masses, the smallest elements of the regularly arranged layer being fairly small and thin, with or without shading. These elements are arranged in groups, in lines, or waves, following one or two directions, and are sometimes so close together that their edges join. The thin and translucent edges of the elements often show irisations which are rather characteristic of this class of cloud.

ALTOSTRATUS (As)—Striated or fibrous veil, more or less gray, or bluish in color. This cloud is like thick cirrostratus but without halo phenomena; the sun or moon shows vaguely, with a faint gleam, as though through ground glass. Sometimes the sheet is thin, with forms intermediate with cirrostratus. Sometimes it is very thick and dark, sometimes even completely hiding the sun or moon. In this case differences of thickness may cause relatively light patches between very dark parts; but the surface never shows real relief, and the striated or fibrous structure is always seen in places in the body of the cloud.

Every form is observed between high altostratus and cirrostratus on the one hand, and low altostratus and nimbostratus on the other.

Rain or snow may fall from altostratus, but when the rain is heavy the cloud layer will have grown thicker and lower, becoming nimbostratus; but heavy snow may fall from a layer that is definitely altostratus.

STRATOCUMULUS (Sc)—A layer (or patches) composed of laminae, globular masses or rolls; the smallest of the regularly arranged elements are fairly large; they are soft and gray, with darker parts. These elements are arranged in groups, in lines, or in waves, alined in one or in two directions. Very often the rolls are so close that their edges join; when they cover the whole sky they have a wavy appearance.

STRATUS (St)—A low uniform layer of cloud, resembling fog, but not resting on the ground.

NIMBOSTRATUS (Ns)—A low, amorphous, and rainy layer, of a dark gray color, usually nearly uniform; feebly illuminated seemingly from inside. When it gives precipitation it is in the form of continuous rain or snow. But precipitation alone is not a sufficient criterion to distinguish the cloud which should be called nimbostratus even when no rain or snow falls from it.

There is often precipitation which does not reach the ground; in this case the base of the cloud is usually diffuse and looks wet on account of the general trailing precipitation, virga, so that it is not possible to determine the limit of its lower surface.

CUMULUS (Cu)—Dense clouds with vertical development; the upper surface is dome shaped and exhibits rounded protuberances, while the base is nearly horizontal. When the cloud is opposite the sun the surfaces normal to the observer are brighter than the edges of the protuberances. When the light comes from the side, the clouds exhibit strong contrasts of light and shade; against the sun, on the other hand, they look dark with a bright edge.

CUMULONIMBUS (Cb)—Heavy masses of cloud, with great vertical development, whose cumuliform summits rise in the form of mountains or towers, the upper parts having a fibrous texture and often spreading out in the shape of an anvil. The base resembles nimbostratus, and one generally notices virga. This base has often a layer of very low ragged clouds below it (fractostratus, fractocumulus). Cumulonimbus clouds generally produce showers of rain or snow and sometimes of hail, and often thunderstorms as well. If the whole of the cloud cannot be seen the fall of a real shower is enough to characterize the cloud as a cumulonimbus.

Predicting Thunderstorms and Fog

WHEN it comes to thunderstorms, we have two types to consider. First, the thunderstorm that accompanies a cold or warm front, known as the frontal type. Second, the thunderstorm that blows up locally (but to us not surprisingly!) in the late afternoon of a warm summer day, known as the air mass type. Our procedure, in each case, would be:

A. Frontal Type

1. Before sailing, check the latest available weather map. A well-developed low headed NE, a tropical maritime cold air mass, mTk, or a squall line en route to our position, each affords us a potent warning.
2. After getting underway, listen regularly to the radio weather reports.
3. Prepare our check-list of warning signs:
   a. A cirrostratus cloud sheet may mount from NW against a S wind.
   b. Domed or turreted cumulus clouds will probably appear, dark and low on the horizon.
   c. The barometer will begin to fall, slowly at first.
   d. A gusty wind will set in and increase, blowing toward the storm.
   e. A dark rain curtain and perhaps lightning will be visible under the cloud-bank and approaching us.
   f. If the storm cloud is due north or due south of us, we will probably avoid the foul weather.

B. Air Mass Type

1. Before sailing, check the latest available weather map. If an mTk air mass is approaching, we should be particularly observant.
2. In the morning, determine the dewpoint temperature of the air, especially if the day is hot and humid, with light southerly winds.
   a. If the dewpoint is 70°F or more, a thunderstorm that afternoon is likely.
   b. If the dewpoint is 60°F or less, a thunderstorm that day is not probable.

3. Observe the clouds closely as the day progresses
   a. Cumulus clouds swelling and darkening as the day wears on indicate that a thunderstorm is probable.
   b. The barometer will fall and an increasing gusty wind will set in, blowing toward the storm.
   c. When the underside of the darkening cumulus turns slate-blue, the storm is near.
   d. Note development of the anvil top and roll cloud.
4. Judging probable severity.
   a. The hotter and more humid the day, the greater the intensity.
   b. The greater the proportion of vertical to horizontal lightning, the more violent the storm and the nearer it is.
   c. If the cumulonimbus cloud is fully developed and towers to a great height, the storm will be very severe.
   d. If the cloud lacks the anvil top or roll cloud, or both, or if the top is relatively low—only 15,000 or 18,000 feet high—the storm will be less violent.

Timing the impact of a thunderstorm is important, as this storm can do us great damage yet gives us little warning. We must get our boat secured and take all measures possible for the safety of our crew. Thunder can be heard up to ten miles or so, lightning seen from a somewhat greater distance. As sound travels in air about one mile in five seconds, timing the interval between lightning and thunder will tell us the distance off. Thunderstorms move at a speed of about 18 knots.

In both cases—frontal and air mass thunderstorms—it behooves us to judge whether the necessary conditions for their occurrence exist. These conditions are:
1. High humidity, that is, plenty of moisture vapor in the air.
2. Warm air.

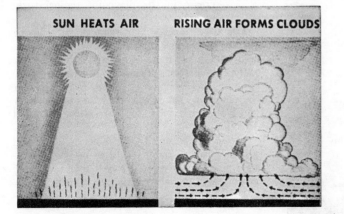

Figure 1. Air Mass Thunderstorm. Re-radiation of energy received by the earth from the sun heats the air. As the air rises, it cools and clouds will form as moisture vapor in the air condenses. If the vertical air currents are strong enough, if the air contains sufficient moisture vapor, an air mass thunderstorm results. (Reproduced by Courtesy of Aviation Training Division, U. S. Navy)

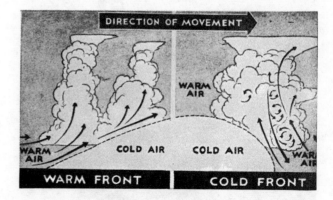

Figure 2. Frontal Thunderstorms. The frontal surface forces the warm air aloft. As the warm air rises, it cools and moisture vapor condenses to form clouds. If the action continues long enough, thunderstorms result, being concentrated in a zone about 15 to 50 miles wide and extending for perhaps hundreds of miles along the front. The cold front type is usually the more violent; the front is steeper and the warm air is lifted suddenly. An older name for a cold front is Squall Line. (Reproduced by Courtesy of Aviation Training Division, U. S. Navy)

3. Nearly calm, heavy air, especially for the air mass type.
4. Unstable air; the presence of cumulus clouds tells us that the necessary vertical air currents are at work.

When the storm arrives over us, the wind will shift, blowing away from the storm; the barometer will rise. Gradually the heavy rain will slacken though strong winds may continue for some time. It is sound seamanship always to assume that any thunderstorm will be severe.

Forecasting Fog

Forecasting the occurrence of fog is likely to be a bit more interesting for those of us who are mechanically minded. Out comes the sling psychrometer, our table of air temperature—dewpoint spread (Table 1, page 229), and a sheet of graph paper.

1. Before sailing, check the latest available weather map, noting particularly any mTw air masses or fog producing fronts moving toward our cruising waters. The station models of the cities over which any suspicious air mass has passed should be examined for fog symbols.
2. While underway, regularly check the air temperature, water temperature and dewpoint spread, emphasizing the last-named from about 1600 on.
   a. If the air is warmer than the water, fog is possible.
   b. If the dewpoint spread begins to narrow, fog is possible:
      0-10° spread, fog before midnight, slow to clear.
      10-20° spread, fog between 0000-0600, clearing 1000-1200.
      20-20° spread, fog just before sunrise, clearing early.

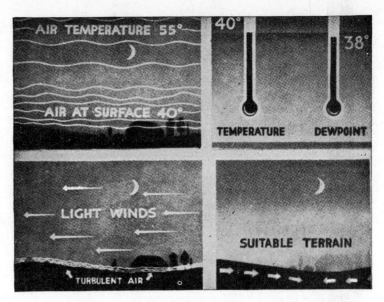

Figure 3. Requirements for Radiation Fog. (1) The air must be warmer just above than it is at the surface of the earth and the sky must be cloudless or nearly so. (2) There must be enough moisture in the air; the dewpoint must be nearly the same as the air temperature. (3) The winds must be light but there must not be a dead calm. (4) The terrain, as a valley, must allow the fog to accumulate. (Reproduced by Courtesy of Aviation Training Division, U. S. Navy)

30° or more spread, fog unlikely.
   c. Our graph of dewpoint spread versus time will help us judge the fateful hour of formation.

Fogs, particularly advection fog, may last for days. Knowledge of the causes of fog is a great help in forecasting their occurrence and dissipation.

For thunderstorms, the air must be unstable, that is, colder than the water or land over which it is moving. For fog, the air must be stable, that is, warmer than the water or land. Also, the air must be moist and this moisture must condense if fog is to form. The requirements for radiation fog are:
1. Stable, moist air.
2. Little or no cloud cover.
3. Light winds, but not a dead calm.
4. Terrain, such as valleys, into which the air and fog may drain.
5. A drop in the air temperature, an increase in the dewpoint temperature, or both.

For advection fog, the requirements can be quickly summarized: winds blowing a warm, moist, stable air mass over progressively colder surfaces. Correct forecasting is stimulated by knowing the air masses likely to reach us, their characteristics and the land or water over which they may pass and by knowing the wind direction.

Steam fog is found with moist, cold air and warm water in some localities, as the Mississippi and Ohio Rivers. Frontal fogs form only when warm or cold fronts pass over us.

Forecasting on a Race to Gloucester

Now that we are experts in forecasting, let's take an actual experience of a weather-wise skipper. In June of 1940, the Cruising Club, due to the war, substituted for its New York to Bermuda race, a race from Block Island to Gloucester, Massachusetts, around

Knowing the causes of fog helps in forecasting it

Cape Cod. Among the entrants was Pierre S. du Pont, 3rd, owner and captain of the 64-foot schooner Barlovento. Pete is Chairman of the Weather Course Committee of the United States Power Squadrons and a blue-water sailor who knows and respects the weather. It is with his kind permission that this race log of Barlovento is partially reproduced here.

Table 2 is a tabulation of the data essential to our purpose. Remarks from the log are given below; read them in conjunction with Table 2.

Monday, June 24

All hands called at 0630 to prepare for getting underway. Underway at 0830. Drizzling. At 0900 stood out of harbor and set all working sails except jib. Genoa jib and fisherman set up in stops. Wind gradually diminishing. Across line for start of race at 1000, on starboard tack. Genoa set, fisherman still in stops. Shifted to port tack, setting fisherman, at 1030. Tacked at 1115. No wind. Finally, a gentle draft from NW, shifting to E. At 1400, SE wind which gradually increased during afternoon. Genoa taken in at 1600, fisherman at 1900. Under working sails only, continued on port tack until 2015. Sea rough. Foresail taken in after tacking. Wind blowing hard during whole watch.

Tuesday, June 25

Wind continued to blow hard. Came about on port tack at 0215. Log reading 104 miles. Wind velocity increased during 4 to 8 watch, with sea getting rougher. About 0800, wind moderated and sea appeared more regular. Fog set in about 1000. Foresail set at 1130 as wind died and sea calmed. Fisherman set at 1310. Tacked ship at 1400. No steerageway, sails idly flapping until about 1600. Wind started to blow from W and gradually freshened. Jibed, set genoa and balloon staysail at 1800. Wind from WNW and increasing. At 1850 heard fog horn on Nantucket Lightship; abeam 1947. Sea very smooth, ship making good speed. After 2000, wind began to moderate slowly, still blowing from WNW. Heard bellows type fog horn astern during this watch but could see nothing.

Wednesday, June 26

Sea gradually getting smoother but there was still a heavy swell from the E. As wind moderated, it got very puffy, blowing strongly in the gusts. At 0500, wind shifted more to N; trimmed all sails. Wind continued to shift. Forced to take in balloon staysail; set foresail and fisherman staysail. Held this rig until 0800, when shifted to starboard tack. At 0925, lowered genoa and set jib; wind and sea had increased. At 1020, wind was so strong it was necessary to relieve the ship by taking in the fisherman. Wind kept increasing all morning; lowered foresail at noon. Received noon radio weather report, predicting strong northerly (head) winds. At 1300, decided to abandon race. Came about on port tack, took off mainsail and jib, reset foresail. Engine started. Shaped course for Pollock Rip Channel. Took in foresail,

reset main and jib at 1530. Pollock Rip at 1700. Dropped anchor in Nantucket Harbor 2130.

Data for the Forecasts

Pete read the signs correctly. Let's take a look at the information he had.

The latest weather map available before the start of the race on 24 June was the 0730 surface map of 23 June. In those days, air masses were not labeled and fronts were not shown on this map. But the data for Block Island were: Pressure—29.94″. Temperature—59°, increasing. Wind velocity—10 mph, from west. Precipitation—none in last 24 hours. The marine forecast for Sandy Hook to Eastport predicted moderate E winds in south portion with cloudy weather for 24 June. The general forecast for the southern New England States predicted cloudy weather with showers for the 24th. To westward, there was a moderate low—29.59″—centered

			WIND		BOAT SPEED Knots	STATE OF WEATHER
DATE	E.S. TIME	BARO-METER "Hg.	Direc-tion	Knots	Force		

"BARLOVENTO"
SALT POND HARBOR to NANTUCKET HARBOR
June 24 to 26, 1940.

DATE	E.S. TIME	BAROMETER "Hg.	Direction	Knots	Force	BOAT SPEED Knots	STATE OF WEATHER
24 June	0900	29.62	-	-	-	-	Overcast, drizzle
	1000	29.62	S	11	4	-	Overcast, drizzle
	1100	29.62	Calm	0	0	-	Rain
	1200	29.62	E	0	0	1.0	Rain
	1300	-	-	-	-	-	Rain
	1400	29.59	ESE	16	4	4.0	Rain
	1500	29.59	ExS	16	4	6.0	Rain
	1600	29.59	ESE	19	5	6.8	Rain
	1700	29.59	ESE	23	6	6.5	Overcast
	1800	29.59	ExS	24	6	6.5	Overcast
	1900	29.59	ESE	25	6	5.0	Overcast
	2000	29.55	SxE	26	6	4.5	Rain
	2100	-	SxE	30	7	7.0	Overcast
	2200	29.55	SxE	26	6	7.0	Rain
	2300	29.54	SE	29	7	7.5	Overcast
	2400	29.54	SE	29	7	6.0	Rain
25 June	0100	29.54	SxE	23	6	5.5	Rain
	0200	29.54	ESE	23	6	5.5	Rain
	0300	29.55	ENE	25	6	5.0	Overcast
	0400	29.55	E	24	6	5.0	Overcast
	0500	29.54	E	29	7	5.0	Overcast
	0600	29.55	E	30	7	5.0	Overcast
	0700	29.55	E	29	7	6.0	Overcast
	0800	29.55	ExS	26	6	5.5	Overcast
	0900	29.55	E	26	6	6.0	Overcast
	1000	29.50	E	24	6	6.0	Overcast
	1100	29.50	E	23	6	6.0	Fog
	1200	29.50	ESE	13	4	4.0	Fog, drizzle
	1300	29.50	ENE	10	3	1.0	Fog
	1400	29.48	Variable	0	0	0	Fog
	1500	29.50	Variable	0	0	0	Fog
	1600	29.51	Variable	0	0	0	Fog
	1700	29.54	WSW	13	4	3.0	Fog
	1800	29.56	W	12	4	5.0	Heavy overcast
	1900	29.56	WNW	16	4	8.0	Heavy overcast
	2000	-	-	-	-	-	Fog
	2100	29.56	WNW	13	4	6.0	Fog
	2200	29.55	WNW	12	4	6.0	Fog
	2300	29.54	WNW	10	3	5.3	Fog
	2400	29.59	NW	11	4	5.5	Fog
26 June	0100	29.58	WNW	16	4	7.0	Overcast
	0200	29.60	WNW	9	3	5.0	Overcast
	0300	29.55	WNW	10	3	5.5	Overcast
	0400	29.55	WNW	14	4	6.5	Overcast
	0500	29.51	NNW	16	4	6.7	Overcast
	0600	29.50	NxW	12	4	5.5	Overcast
	0700	-	NxW	10	3	4.0	Rain
	0800	29.47	ENE	12	4	4.0	Rain
	0900	29.40	NxE	18	5	7.0	Rain
	1000	29.35	NE	22	6	6.0	Rain
	1100	29.35	N	23	6	6.5	Rain
	1200	29.35	N	30	7	5.5	Rain
	1300	29.35	N	30	7	7.0	Cloudy
	1400	29.40	NxW	33	7	7.0	Cloudy
	1500	29.40	NxW	33	7	6.0	Cloudy

TABLE 2

over Iowa, with general rainfall and thunderstorms west and east of the low all across the nothern tier of states.

By 1000 on Monday the 24th (Table 2), the barometer was down to 29.62", a drop of slightly more than 0.01 inch per hour since 0730 Sunday. Not too good, but not desperate, either; it could mean merely fairly steady rain for a day or so. But, as the log shows, the glass continued to drop, steadily though slowly. At 0300 Wednesday, it took a nose-dive reaching a low of 29.35" that afternoon.

Until Tuesday noon, the wind continued to blow steadily from the SE or E at force 6 to 7. Then it shifted abruptly to the W and fog set in. The wind continued to back and the barometer to fall. The noon radio report on Wednesday merely served to confirm the Captain's forecast of more bad weather to come. It kept right on raining and blowing most of the time through Sunday.

Through the courtesy of Conrad P. Mook, of the Special Scientific Services Division of the U. S. Weather Bureau, we saw the original manuscript weather maps, four per day, of that week in June. On Monday, an extra-tropical cyclone was approaching the waters of the Sound. A secondary center of this cyclone passed just south of Barlovento during Tuesday afternoon. Look at the log; observe the wind shift and change in the weather. At the same time, an upper air cold front formed in the secondary center swept overhead. On Wednesday, the occluded portion of the old cyclone died out and there were now low pressure areas NE and SE of the ship. The wind increased and shifted to NW, as the log shows.

Early Thursday morning, a second cold front, which was a part of the same great cyclonic system to which the first cold front belonged, swinging counter-clockwise, passed over Nantucket and the weather began to clear. Friday was much improved, until late that evening. Another extra-tropical cyclone, centered NW of Nantucket, then began its tricks. About 0130 Saturday morning the warm front of this cyclone, with storm warnings flying from the Coast Guard flagstaff, passed Nantucket, followed by the cold front around midnight of the same day. It certainly was a marvelous week for a sailing race! The backing wind and steadily falling barometer didn't lie to us this time.

Pete abandoned the race but he was snug in Nantucket harbor. Not a shroud nor stay nor sail required the slightest repair, nor did he lose his ship. We said at the beginning that he is weather-wise.

U. S. Storm Warnings

After much preparatory work and consultation with marine groups, yacht clubs, shipping agencies and other coastal interests, a new and simplified system of Coastal Warning Displays was put into effect January 1, 1958 by the Weather Bureau, Department of Commerce.

Under the new method, only four separate signals are used during the day, instead of the seven separate flag signals formerly employed in the Weather Bureau's Storm Warning Display System. During the night, only four comparable lantern signals are used for Small Craft, Gale, Whole Gale, and Hurricane warnings.

The Weather Bureau emphasizes that these visual storm warnings displayed along the coast are supplementary to—and not a replacement for—the written advisories and warnings given prompt and wide distribution by press, radio and television. In most cases, important details of the forecasts and warnings in regard to the time, intensity, duration, and direction of storms, cannot be given satisfactorily through visual signals alone.

Following is a detailed explanation of the new signals:

Small Craft Warning: One red pennant displayed by day and a red light above a white light at night to indicate winds up to 38 mph (33 knots) and/or sea conditions dangerous to small craft operations are forecast for the area.

Gale Warning: Two red pennants displayed by day and a white light above a red light at night to indicate winds ranging from 39 to 54 mph (34 to 48 knots) are forecast for the area.

Whole Gale Warnings: A single square red flag with a black center displayed during daytime and at night to indicate winds ranging from 55 to 73 mph (48 to 63 knots) are forecast for the area.

Hurricane Warning: Two square red flags with black centers displayed by day and a white light between two red lights at night to indicate that winds 74 mph (64 knots) and above are forecast for the area.

By radio.—Storm warnings and storm advisories issued by the United States Weather Bureau are broadcast, after clearance through military authorities, by designated United States Naval and Coast Guard radio stations. A large number of commercial radio stations also broadcast storm warnings under the same clearance requirements although at somewhat irregular intervals.

Radio schedules of storm warnings and weather information broadcast from United States and foreign stations are contained in Hydrographic Office Publication 206 entitled, "Radio Weather Aids to Navigation."

Coast Guard vessels now display storm warning signals. Headquarters of the Coast Guard are supplied with weather information by the Weather Bureau and Coast Guard vessels receive instructions to fly the proper signals when storms are approaching. The shore stations where storm warning signals are displayed are listed in the various Coast Pilots. The Pilots also contain general information as to the prevailing weather in areas covered by each book.

In 1945, display of storm warning signals from lightships was authorized. These signals consist of the standard Weather Bureau flag hoists, displayed by day. No night signals are displayed. The storm warning signals are flown only while the lightships are on station, not while proceeding to and from station.

Yachtsmen will find much interesting weather information on the various pilot charts of the North Atlantic and North Pacific Oceans issued by the Hydrographic Office of the Navy Department. These amount practically to monthly weather maps of the oceans and in addition give a vast amount of valuable data on subjects closely allied to weather and weather forecasting.

Storm Warning Facilities Charts, prepared by the Weather Bureau, are available from the Superintendent of Documents, Washington 25, D. C., at 5 cents each. Eleven charts cover the coastal waters of the United States and the Great Lakes. In addition to locating points where storm warning signals are displayed, the charts list commercial broadcasting stations, Telephone Company and Coast Guard stations which broadcast weather reports, and times of broadcasts.

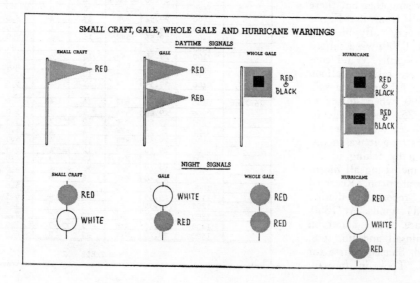

SMALL CRAFT, GALE, WHOLE GALE AND HURRICANE WARNINGS

CHAPTER XIII

The Compass

Learning to Box the Compass—Points and Degrees—The Meaning of True and Magnetic Courses — Placing the Compass on Board

THE subject of this Lesson is the Compass. This is one of the most important subjects in the whole Course. This Lesson will be closely allied to subjects discussed in Chapter XIV. Therefore, to have a complete knowledge of the subject it will be necessary to consider the two chapters together.

No one should be afraid or discouraged in his study of the compass. It is true that the manner in which the subject is usually presented is so complex and complicated that it gives one the idea that the compass is a very mysterious and generally misunderstood device. But such is far from the real truth. As a matter of fact, a study of the compass is not necessarily complex but can be made simple and readily understood. As the compass is the mariner's greatest friend it is hoped that everyone will carefully study these pages and follow the course as enthusiastically as they have the previous chapters.

Fig. 131, above. The compass should always be conveniently located in the helmsman's line of sight so that his eye can drop down to it readily without diverting his attention from the course ahead. A modern spherical compass is illustrated. Fig. 131a, left. An excellent mounting of the binnacle, permitting bearings to be taken over the compass. The binnacle light should be of low intensity, and arranged so that there can be no disturbing glare

Fig. 132. In the diagram at the right some liberties are taken, for the sake of simplification, in illustrating the behavior of the magnetic compass. Its needle tends to align itself, not with the geographical (true) meridians converging at the north pole, but rather with magnetic lines of force surrounding the earth, terminating at the magnetic north pole in the general area indicated at MN. These lines of force are neither straight nor constant, varying according to the locality and the particular year. Aligning itself with a magnetic meridian, the compass (disregarding deviation) determines magnetic directions, courses, bearings and headings, as distinguished from the true directions established by reference to the true geographical meridians. The angular difference between a true meridian and a magnetic meridian is the variation at that particular locality. At A, true north lies on the boat's course, while her compass (disregarding deviation) points, roughly, to MN. Similarly, at B, C, and D, the compass tends to align itself with the magnetic meridian of the locality. At A and B, variation is westerly; at D it is easterly; at points near C it approaches zero. There is a slight yearly change in variation at any particular place (as indicated on the chart). This annual change is small and can be considered nearly constant although it does vary slightly at times

Therefore, determine to conquer the subject of the compass and you will never regret it.

Trust Your Compass

As an introductory remark we should like to advise everyone to believe in his compass. Many more disasters have occurred on account of one's disbelief in his compass than to the contrary. It is true that the compass has errors but these errors are easily determined and after they have been determined make the compass as accurate as a watch. Therefore, believe what your compass tells you and it will always guide you to safety.

The Magnetic Poles

When reference is made in this text to a magnetic north pole, it must be understood that this is not a precise point toward which the compass needle points exactly. It does point to it, approximately, because the needle tends to align itself with lines of force surounding the earth, terminating at the North and South Magnetic Poles, the locations of which do not coincide with the geographic (true) poles. Since these lines of force are not straight, the compass may point slightly east or west of the magnetic north pole at any given point. The magnetic north pole is located in an area somewhat north of Hudson Bay; the geographic (true) north pole is at the extremity of the earth's axis of rotation.

What the Compass Is

The compass is nothing more than a magnet suspended so as to be allowed to swing freely in a horizontal plane. In theory, an ordinary knitting needle magnetized by drawing a toy magnet along its length a few times, and suspended from the center by means of a thread so that it can swing in a horizontal plane, is as much of a compass as the ones we use on our boats to-day. If such a needle is magnetized and suspended it will immediately assume a north and south position.

But the compass, as we know it, consists of a number of magnetized needles bound together, and suspended or pivoted from beneath. On this bundle of magnetized needles we have a card mounted to give us a better sense of direction, and allow us to determine directions other than north and south, which would be the only two indicated by the magnetized needles if we had no card mounted thereon.

There has been little or no change in the mariner's compass for centuries. In theory and construction, it is practically the same as it was more than one hundred years ago. The only changes which have been made are refinement in its construction, and the markings on the compass card.

The Dry Compass

The older compasses were known as dry compasses; that is, simply magnetic needles and a card pivoted at the center. Naturally such an arrangement was very sensitive and responded to the motion of the ship very freely. With the coming of the steam engine, and later, the internal combustion motor, it was found that the vibrations set up by the machinery were such as to keep the compass card in constant motion, which naturally made it unreliable as a navigating instrument. The development of the liquid compass followed, and this type overcomes to a large extent the difficulty and trouble experienced with the dry compass.

The Liquid Compass

The liquid, or wet compass, is practically no different from the dry compass, with the exception that a liquid generally consisting of a mixture of 55 per cent. water, and 45 per cent. alcohol is introduced into the bowl of the compass, and then the latter is sealed up. The liquid not only prevents the compass needle and card from responding to small vibrations due to power plants and the sea, but also tends to buoy up or float the needle and card, and . thus make it rest more lightly on its pivot. This allows the card to turn more freely as the ship is turned, or rather to hold its position more steadily as the ship's bow is turned away from the compass.

The smaller and less expensive compasses use kerosene as the filling liquid, and some of the newer makes use oil instead of alcohol and water. On account of the nature of the various kinds of fluids used, the compass as we know it is practically non-freezable in ordinary latitudes.

One of the great advances in the construction of modern compasses is the development of the spherical compass. This has a hemi-spherical shaped glass top which magnifies the card. Furthermore, with this type of construction, the card is much steadier.

Gyro-compasses are mechanical compasses that depend for their directive force on the principles of the gyroscope. They seek the true meridian rather than the magnetic meridian. As they give true courses, bearings, etc., it is unnecessary to apply variation and deviation. Due to their size, cost and more complicated mechanism, they are used primarily by relatively large vessels.

Dialing his course, this skipper sets his magnetic compass pilot for automatic steering. Besides steering the course accurately and automatically at all speeds, the boat can also be handled at any time by a remote control. The craft can be steered from the bow, anywhere on deck, or even from a crow's nest, when necessary, to con the boat in strange waters

The Lubberline

Compasses are fitted with a gimbal ring to keep the bowl and card level under every circumstance of a ship's motion in a seaway, the ring being connected with a binnacle or compass box by means of journals or knife edges.

On the inside of every compass bowl is drawn a vertical black line called the lubberline, and it is imperative that the compass be placed in the binnacle or on the boat so that a line joining the pivot and the lubberline shall be parallel to the keel of the boat. Thus, the lubberline always indicates the compass direction on which the boat is heading.

The Card

While a compass card may be graduated in either points or degrees only, most of those used today on

Fig. 134 (right). The new compass card, graduated in both degrees, 0 to 360, and in quarter points. An older type of card had degree markings running from 0 at North and 0 at South to 90 degrees at East and West. The only difference between the two cards is in the method of naming various directions by degrees. In both cards North is 0 degrees. However, on the old card South is also 0 degrees while East and West are each 90 degrees. Northeast, Southeast, Southwest, and Northwest in the old card are designated at 45 degrees. In other words we work from 0 degrees at North and South towards 90 degrees at East and West. In the new compass cards the designations run from 0 degrees to 360 degrees around the card in a clockwise direction. In this card Northeast is 45 degrees, East 90 degrees, Southeast 135 degrees, South 180 degrees, Southwest 225 degrees, West 270 degrees, Northwest 315 degrees, etc. (See also Fig. 148.)

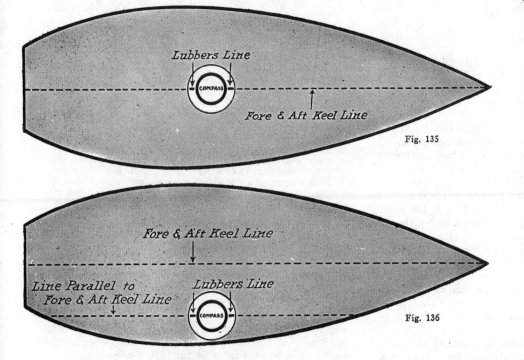

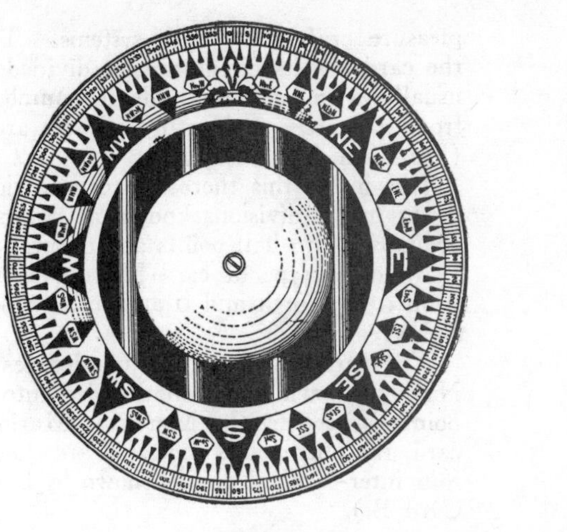

Fig. 135

Figs. 135 and 136. (At the left.) The correct placing of one's compass aboard his boat is very important. If possible place the compass over the keel line. Be sure that an imaginary line drawn through two of the lubberlines and the center of the compass is directly over the keel line and not at an angle with the keel line. If a lubberline does not correctly indicate the boat's bow then the compass will be worse than useless. When the compass can not be placed in the center of a boat over the fore and aft keel line and must be located to one side, then an imaginary line drawn through the lubberlines and the center of the compass must be exactly parallel to the fore and aft keel line as indicated in Fig. 136.

Fig. 136

Fig. 137. This figure is intended to indicate one of the two ways of naming the quarter points of the compass. The arrows indicate the numerical order of naming the quarter points, viz.: . ¼, ½ and ¾, or ¾, ½ and ¼, depending upon the direction of the arrow. In this method of naming the quarter points (which is known as the older method) we work from each cardinal and inter-cardinal point toward the 22½-degree points as indicated by the arrows, thus, N ¼ E, N ½ E, N ¾ E, N x E, N x E ¼ E, N x E ½ E, N x E ¾ E, NNE. Now note how the fractional points change, thus: NE x N ¾ N, NE x N ½ N, NE x N ¼ N, NE x N, etc.

Fig. 138. This figure indicates the other or newer or Navy method of designating quarter points. As in Fig. 137 the arrows indicate the numerical sequence of the fractional points thus: N ¼ E, N ½ E, N ¾ E, N x E, N x E ¼ E, N x E ½ E, N x E ¾ E, N NE ¼ E, N NE ½ E, N NE ¾ E, NE x N. Now a change to this: NE ¾ N, NE ½ N, NE ¼ N, NE, NE ¼ E, NE ½ E, NE ¾ E, NE x E, NE x E ¼ E, NE x E ½ E, NE x E ¾ E, E NE, E NE ¼ E, E NE ½ E, E NE ¾ E, E x N, E ¾ N, E ½ N, E ¼ N

pleasure craft show both systems. The outer edge of the card has its circumference divided into 360 degrees, usually with each tenth degree numbered. This reads from 0 degrees at North clockwise around to 360 (0). (See Card A at the right.)

Just inside this there is a concentric circle graduated in 32 major divisions known as points, each subdivided ordinarily into half-points and quarter-points.

An older type of card had degree markings running from 0 at North and 0 at South to 90 degrees at East and West.

The card divided into 360 degrees is known as the Navy type, while the one divided into both degrees and points is used by the Merchant Marine. On the Navy card, the only points indicated are the four cardinal and four inter-cardinal points, shown by heavy markers. (See Card B.)

Points

Division of the compass card according to points is a most interesting one. While the use of the card divided into degrees from 0 to 360 is becoming more popular, many boatmen prefer the point system. It is well to be familiar with both.

As mentioned above, the card is divided into 32 major divisions known as points, each one of these points having a particular name. The four principal or cardinal points are known as North, South, East and West.

The inter-cardinal points are the ones midway between the cardinals, and these are given a name which is a combination of the points which they bisect; that is, the point midway between North and East is known as Northeast, etc. This gives us eight divisions.

We now subdivide these eight divisions in half, and once again we give these eight new points names which are combinations of the two points which they are midway between. For example, the point midway between North and Northeast is North Northeast. That point midway between South and Southwest is South Southwest.

To get the additional 16 points it is simply necessary to divide points which we have already determined in a similar way as before. Here again the new points will have names corresponding to the points to which they are adjacent. The word "by" will be used in all of these 16 new points. For instance, the point between North and North Northeast is known as North by East, because it is adjacent to North, and in an easterly direction from North. The point between Southeast and South Southeast is known as Southeast by South, because it is adjacent to the inter-cardinal point Southeast, and in a southerly direction from it.

Quarter Points

For the purpose of steering more accurate courses than would be possible by following only 32 points, we must subdivide the points into halves and quarters. The naming of these quarter points is most interesting, and must be thoroughly mastered by the motor boatman.

Naturally it will be seen that every quarter point might have two names; that is, it might refer to the point either to the right or to the left of it. For example, the quarter point just to the right of North could logically be called North ¼ East, or it might be called North by East ¾ North. Either of these designations would probably convey to the man at the wheel the course which it was desired that he should follow. However, and perhaps unfortunately, there is a certain method of calling these quarter points, and again we are confronted with two methods instead of one.

The illustration above shows four types of cards available today. Card A has its outer edge divided into 360 degrees, quarter-points concentrically arranged on the inner circle. Card B is Navy style, divided into 360 degrees, clockwise from 0 at North to 360, every 10th degree numbered. Cardinals and intercardinals are the only point divisions indicated on this type of card. At C, the quarter-points show at the outer edge while the 360-degree divisions are superimposed upon the quarter-points. At D, the card is divided into quarter-points only. Many prefer cards C and D for sailing vessels because of their plainness

The older method appears to many to be the most logical one, although both are correct. (See Figs. 137, 138, 143 and 148.)

Fig. 148 gives a complete comparison of the point and degree methods of naming compass directions. It is not assumed that this table will be memorized but its existence should be kept in mind for future reference.

Mounting the Compass in the Boat
(See Figs. 135 and 136)

A compass may be of the most expensive type and, in itself, highly accurate yet useless in running courses if it is incorrectly installed in the boat. The lubberline, as has been pointed out, represents the boat's head but only if the compass itself is so placed with respect to the keel or boat's center line that it too will lie in a line parallel with the keel.

When possible, it is well to have the compass in the boat's center line, over the keel. It should be located ahead of the wheel at a height where it will be easy to read and in such a manner that the helmsman's eye can drop down to it easily without actually having his attention diverted from the course ahead.

If the center of the compass cannot be placed amidships directly over the fore and aft keel line, then a line should be struck parallel to the keel line and the lubberline should lie in this line.

Preferably the wheel and compass, if they must be on one side, should be on the starboard side, giving a clear view of the danger zone from dead ahead to two points abaft the starboard beam.

Electrical wires near a compass may affect it. When two wires are contained in a single cable, the effect of each is neutralized. In the case of single conductor wires, it is well to twist pairs together for the same reason.

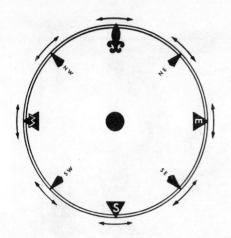

Fig. 139 (left). To learn to box the compass, first memorize the four cardinal points, North, South, East and West. Intercardinals, Northeast, Southeast, Northwest and Southwest derive their names by combination of the cardinal points on each side of the inter-cardinal. Fig. 140 (right). To obtain the next 8 points, call the desired point by a name which is a combination of the nearest cardinal and inter-cardinal. Thus we have North Northeast between North and Northeast, West Southwest between West and Southwest, etc.

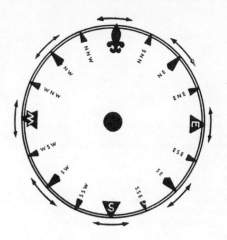

Fig. 142. (Below.) In order to steer more directions or more closely than would be possible by the use of the 32 points alone it becomes necessary to subdivide the points into quarter-points, half-points and three-quarter points. Each of these ¼-points has a particular name depending upon its position relative to the points on each side of it. See Figs. 137, 138, 143 and 148

Fig. 141. (At the left.) To obtain the remaining 16 points we again bisect the space between the sixteen we have already learned and give the new points a name which is a combination of the cardinal or inter-cardinal point to which they are adjacent and the word "by" according to the direction in which the new point is from its cardinal or inter-cardinal point. For example, the new point adjacent to North toward East will be known as N x E. When it is adjacent to North but to the westward of it it is known as N x W. The point adjacent to Northeast and to the eastward of it is NE x E, etc.

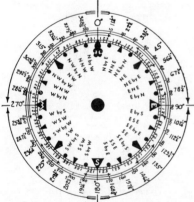

Fig. 143. (At the right.) The compass card with the names of the 32 points and the 96 quarter-points. (See also Figs. 137, 138 and 148.) The motor boatman should become thoroughly conversant with the names of all the points and quarter-points. He should be able to box the compass by quarter-points, forward and backward completely around the compass card or through any quadrant

Fig. 144. A good form of binnacle and steering wheel when these must be placed on one side of the boat due to the fact that the companionway is in the center. It is preferable to have the compass and helmsman's position on the starboard side rather than on the port side as such a location will give the helmsman an unobstructed view of the so-called danger zone which extends from dead ahead to two points abaft the starboard beam. It will be remembered that when other boats are in this danger zone approaching your course they will have the right of way over you and it will be necessary for you to give way. It will therefore be seen why it is essential that the helmsman should have a clear and unobstructed view of this danger zone. If the helmsman's position and compass were on the port side it then might be that his view of the danger zone would be obstructed by equipment on deck, bow, dinghy, passengers, etc.

Fig. 146 (below). An excellent arrangement for the compass and binnacle. In this case the compass is located in the center line of the ship directly over the keel line

Fig. 145. The compass rose shows both magnetic and true directions. On every chart there are several of these roses; the one nearest the locality in question should be used. Roses on the newest charts have three circles. The outer circle is calibrated in degrees from 0° to 360° with zero at true north. These divisions indicate true directions. The two inner circles give magnetic directions in both points and degrees, with the arrow indicating magnetic north. The inner circle is divided into 32 major parts, which are the 32 points of the compass. Each major division is subdivided into four parts which represent the quarter points of the compass. The middle circle shows magnetic directions in degrees. When referring to magnetic directions or magnetic courses, one of the inner circles must be used, depending on whether you are working in points or degrees. On older charts magnetic directions are given in points only, not in degrees. In the center of the rose, variation for the locality is given, together with the amount of annual change. In this illustration, there is no change

254

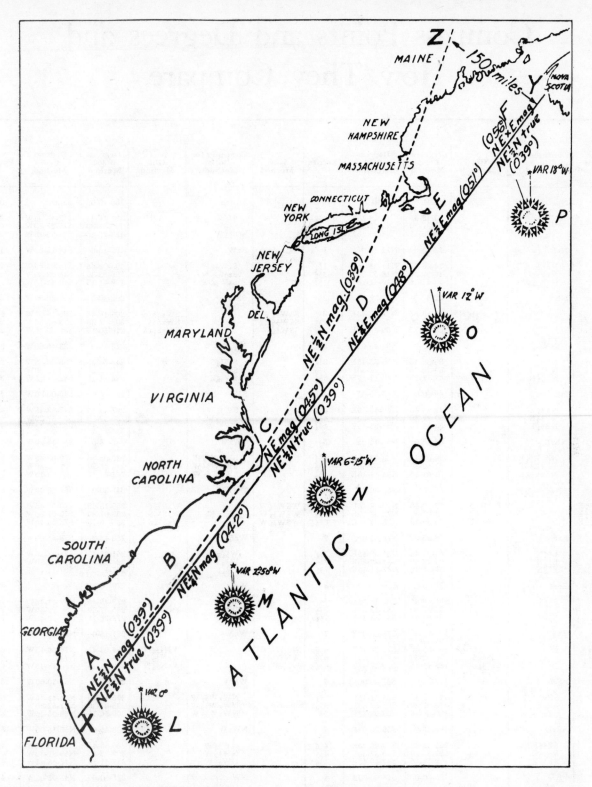

Fig. 147. This figure is intended to indicate the difference between true and magnetic courses and how magnetic directions differ depending upon the particular locality on the earth's surface where the mariner is. For example, one intends to lay a course along the Atlantic Seaboard from Florida to Nova Scotia, say from point X to point Y. If he drew a straight line between these two points as indicated in the figure above and determined the magnetic direction of this line at point A he would find the magnetic course to be NE ½ N (039°). If he steered this magnetic course of NE ½ N (039°) expecting that it would take him up the Coast to Nova Scotia along the straight line X Y he would soon come to grief. Not only would he fail to clear Cape Hatteras but this course would take him well inside of Cape Cod and theoretically would land him in the forests of Maine at point Z which is 150 miles from the point in Nova Scotia which he desired to reach when he set out from Florida. Of course, the reason for this is because a magnetic course of NE ½ N (039°) at point A is not in the same direction as a NE ½ N (039°) magnetic course is at points B, C, D, E, or F

On the other hand motorboatmen will see that everywhere along the straight line XY the true courses are identical. In other words, the true course at X is NE ½ N (039°) which is the same at B, C, D, E, and F. To steer the proper course along the straight line XY it will be necessary for the motorboatman from time to time to change his compass course, i.e., at B his magnetic course would be NE ¼ N (042°); at C, NE (045°); at D, NE ¼ E (048°); at E, NE ½ E (051°) and at F, NE x E (056°)

The compass roses are indicated at L, M, N, O, and P. These roses indicate magnetic directions and the differences or variation in the direction of North is very evident. The star over each rose indicates true North

Compass Points and Degrees and How They Compare

New Method	Common for Both Methods	Old Method	Degrees 0-360 Method	Degrees 0-90 Method	Points	New Method	Common for Both Methods	Old Method	Degrees 0-360 Method	Degrees 0-90 Method	Points
	North		North	North			South		180- 0-0	South	0
	N¼E		2-48-45	N2-48-45E	¼		S¼W		182-48-45	S 2-48-45W	¼
	N½E		5-37-30	N5-37-30E	½		S½W		185-37-30	S 5-37-30W	½
	N¾E		8-26-15	N8-26-15E	¾		S¾W		188-26-15	S 8-26-15W	¾
	NxE		11-15-0	N11-15-0E	1		SxW		191-15-0	S11-15-00W	1
	NxE¼E		14-03-45	N14-03-45E	1¼		SxW¼W		194-03-45	S14-03-45W	1¼
	NxE½E		16-52-30	N16-52-30E	1½		SxW½W		196-52-30	S16-52-30W	1½
	NxE¾E		19-41-15	N19-41-15E	1¾		SxW¾W		199-41-15	S19-41-15W	1¾
	NNE		22-30-0	N22-30-0E	2		SSW		202-30-0	S22-30-00W	2
NNE¼E		NExN¾N	25-18-45	N25-18-45E	2¼	SSW¼W		SWxS¾S	205-18-45	S25-18-45W	2¼
NNE½E		NExN½N	28-07-30	N28-07-30E	2½	SSW½W		SWxS½S	208- 7-30	S28-07-30W	2½
NNE¾E		NExN¼N	30-56-15	N30-56-15E	2¾	SSW¾W		SWxS¼S	210-56-15	S30-56-15W	2¾
	NExN		33-45-0	N33-45-0E	3		SWxS		213-45-0	S33-45-00W	3
	NE¾N		36-33-45	N36-33-45E	3¼		SW¾S		216-33-45	S36-33-45W	3¼
	NE½N		39-22-30	N39-22-30E	3½		SW½S		219-22-30	S39-22-30W	3½
	NE¼N		42-11-15	N42-11-15E	3¾		SW¼S		222-11-15	S42-11-15W	3¾
	NE		45- 0-0	N45- 0-0E	4		SW		225- 0-0	S45-00-00W	4
	NE¼E		47-48-45	N47-48-45E	4¼		SW¼W		227-48-45	S47-48-45W	4¼
	NE½E		50-37-30	N50-37-30E	4½		SW½W		230-37-30	S50-37-30W	4½
	NE¾E		53-26-15	N53-26-15E	4¾		SW¾W		233-26-15	S53-26-15W	4¾
	NExE		56-15-0	N56-15-0E	5		SWxW		236-15-0	S56-15-00W	5
	NExE¼E		59-03-45	N59-03-45E	5¼		SWxW¼W		239-03-45	S59-03-45W	5¼
	NExE½E		61-52-30	N61-52-30E	5½		SWxW½W		241-52-30	S61-52-30W	5½
	NExE¾E		64-41-15	N64-41-15E	5¾		SWxW¾W		244-41-15	S64-41-15W	5¾
	ENE		67-30-0	N67-30-0E	6		WSW		247-30-0	S67-30-00W	6
ENE¼E		ExN¾N	70-18-45	N70-18-45E	6¼	WSW¼W		WxS¾S	250-18-45	S70-18-45W	6¼
ENE½E		ExN½N	73-07-30	N73-07-30E	6½	WSW½W		WxS½S	253-07-30	S73-07-30W	6½
ENE¾E		ExN¼N	75-56-15	N75-56-15E	6¾	WSW¾W		WxS¼S	255-56-15	S75-56-15W	6¾
	ExN		78-45-0	N78-45-0E	7		WxS		258-45-0	S78-45-00W	7
	E¾N		81-33-45	N81-33-45E	7¼		W¾S		261-33-45	S81-33-45W	7¼
	E½N		84-22-30	N84-22-30E	7½		W½S		264-22-30	S84-22-30W	7½
	E¼N		87-11-15	N87-11-15E	7¾		W¼S		267-11-15	S87-11-15W	7¾
	East		90- 0-0	East	8		West		270- 0-0	West	8
	E¼S		92-48-45	S87-11-15E	7¾		W¼N		272-48-45	N87-11-15W	7¾
	E½S		95-37-30	S84-22-30E	7½		W½N		275-37-30	N84-22-30W	7½
	E¾S		98-26-15	S81-33-45E	7¼		W¾N		278-26-15	N81-33-45W	7¼
	ExS		101-15-0	S78-45-00E	7		WxN		281-15-0	N78-45-00W	7
ESE¾E		ExS¼S	104-03-45	S75-56-15E	6¾	WNW¾W		WxN¼N	284-03-45	N75-56-15W	6¾
ESE½E		ExS½S	106-52-30	S73-07-30E	6½	WNW½W		WxN½N	286-52-30	N73-07-30W	6½
ESE¼E		ExS¾S	109-41-15	S70-18-45E	6¼	WNW¼W		WxN¾N	289-41-15	N70-18-45W	6¼
	ESE		112-30-0	S67-30-00E	6		WNW		292-30-0	N67-30-00W	6
	SExE¾E		115-18-45	S64-41-15E	5¾		NWxW¾W		295-18-45	N64-41-15W	5¾
	SExE½E		118-07-30	S61-52-30E	5½		NWxW½W		298-07-30	N61-52-30W	5½
	SExE¼E		120-56-15	S59-03-45E	5¼		NWxW¼W		300-56-15	N59-03-45W	5¼
	SExE		123-45-0	S56-15-00E	5		NWxW		303-45-0	N56-15-00W	5
	SE¾E		126-33-45	S53-26-15E	4¾		NW¾W		306-33-45	N53-26-15W	4¾
	SE½E		129-22-30	S50-37-30E	4½		NW½W		309-22-30	N50-37-30W	4½
	SE¼E		132-11-15	S47-48-45E	4¼		NW¼W		312-11-15	N47-48-45W	4¼
	SE		135- 0-0	S45-00-00E	4		NW		315- 0-0	N45-00-00W	4
	SE¼S		137-48-45	S42-11-15E	3¾		NW¼N		317-48-45	N42-11-15W	3¾
	SE½S		140-37-30	S39-22-30E	3½		NW½N		320-37-30	N39-22-30W	3½
	SE¾S		143-26-15	S36-33-45E	3¼		NW¾N		323-26-15	N36-33-45W	3¼
	SExS		146-15-0	S33-45-0E	3		NWxN		326-15-0	N33-45-00W	3
SSE¾E		SExS¼S	149- 3-45	S30-56-15E	2¾	NNW¾W		NWxN¼N	329-03-45	N30-56-15W	2¾
SSE½E		SExS½S	151-52-30	S28-07-30E	2½	NNW½W		NWxN½N	331-52-30	N28-07-30W	2½
SSE¼E		SExS¾S	154-41-15	S25-18-45E	2¼	NNW¼W		NWxN¾N	334-41-15	N25-18-45W	2¼
	SSE		157-30-0	S22-30-00E	2		NNW		337-30-0	N22-30-00W	2
	SxE¾E		160-18-45	S19-41-15E	1¾		NxW¾W		340-18-45	N19-41-15W	1¾
	SxE½E		163-07-30	S16-52-30E	1½		NxW½W		343-07-30	N16-52-30W	1½
	SxE¼E		165-56-15	S14-03-45E	1¼		NxW¼W		345-56-15	N14-03-45W	1¼
	SxE		168-45-0	S11-15-00E	1		NxW		348-45-0	N11-15-00W	1
	S¾E		171-33-45	S 8-26-15E	¾		N¾W		351-33-45	N 8-26-15W	¾
	S½E		174-22-30	S 5-37-30E	½		N½W		354-22-30	N 5-37-30W	½
	S¼E		177-11-15	S 2-48-45E	¼		N¼W		357-11-15	N 2-48-45W	¼

Fig. 148. Table showing the names of all points and quarter points of the compass by all methods as well as two methods of using degrees

CHAPTER XIV

Compass Errors

Variation, Deviation, True and Magnetic Courses, Allowing for
Compass Errors. Various Methods of Determining Deviation

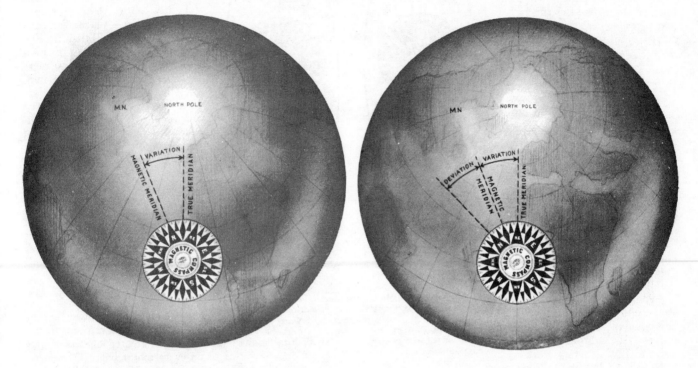

Fig. 149. Variation is the angle between two lines drawn from the ship's position. One is a magnetic meridian passing through the magnetic north pole MN, the other a line passing through the geographic (true) north pole. If the north point of the compass card is drawn to the west or left of geographic north (as shown), variation is westerly. If it is drawn to the east or right of geographic north, variation is easterly. (See also Fig. 132, previous chapter.) When changing from magnetic to true courses, or vice versa, allow for variation only. When changing from true to compass courses, or vice versa, allow for both variation and deviation

Fig. 150. In addition to variation, there may be another error of the compass, caused by various magnetic substances on the boat itself attracting or repelling certain points of the compass. This error is known as deviation. When the north pole of the compass is turned to the left, or to the west from its normal position, as illustrated above, the deviation is said to be westerly. If the north pole is pulled toward the east, or to the right, the deviation is said to be easterly. Obviously, the deviation is different for each particular boat, and furthermore, is different for each particular heading of the boat

CHAPTER 13 was devoted to the preliminary study of the compass and the learning of the various names for the thirty-two points of the compass and all of the quarter points. There is also some reference to variation and deviation and to the meaning of true and magnetic courses. We now come to a further consideration of the compass, and principally to its errors and the application of variation and deviation as they apply to small boat practice.

While the compass is subject to certain errors to be explained in this chapter, these errors may be readily determined and allowed for. Therefore, every motor boatman should study his compass, learn to believe in it and make use of it on every possible occasion.

Variation

(See Fig. 132)

If you were on your boat at the position marked *A*, and your boat was heading as indicated by the dotted line, she would be heading true North, but the compass would be pointing in a decidedly different direction, indicated by the dotted line from *A* to a point marked *MN*. In other words, your boat would be headed true North, but the

magnetic heading would be quite different. This angular difference between the true North and the magnetic North is known as the variation of the compass, shown in Fig. 132 by the angle between North Pole, *A*, and *MN*.

This variation is not constant; it is different with every change in geographical location. If your position is at *B*, your boat is still heading true North, and your compass towards *MN*. The angle between true North and magnetic North at *B* is different and smaller than when at *A*. In other words, the variation at *B* is less than at *A*. In both cases magnetic North has been to the West, or to the left, of true North, which makes the variation westerly.

Now consider your position at *C*. In this case your boat is heading toward true North, and also toward magnetic North. If the magnetic meridian coincides exactly with the true direction of geographic north, there is no variation. (The magnetic meridians are never perfectly straight lines.)

At *D* we again have a variation, but in this case magnetic North is to the East, or to the right of, true North, and we have an easterly variation. At *E*, the boat is heading toward true North, but going away from magnetic North. In such a case, while the boat is heading North, the compass is pointing South, and we have 180 degrees variation.

Change in Location

Variation is different for every geographical location. Near New York City variation is about 12 degrees westerly; around Portland, Me., it is about 17½ degrees westerly. As we go West variation becomes less and less until in the vicinity of Lake Superior we have zero variation. Farther West than this the variation becomes easterly, and increases in magnitude.

Determining Variation

(See Figs. 158 and 159)

The amount of variation in a given locality is shown on the Government chart of that area. Fig. 159 shows a compass rose. Several are printed on each chart. The note in the center of this rose, "Variation 23 degrees 00 minutes East, 1947" gives the variation at the particular location where this rose is printed. From the statement directly below, "Annual decrease 3 minutes," it will be seen that variation is not a constant quantity, but is increasing or diminishing almost all the time. To calculate what the variation would be in 1950, we subtract 9' and get 22° 51' E.

Now turn to Fig. 158, showing the newest type of compass rose. Note that there are three circles. The outer circle has its zero at true North and in-

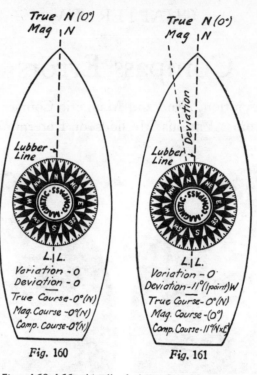

Fig. 160   **Fig. 161**

Figs. 160-166. In all of these figures the boat shown is assumed to be heading true north, but with various amounts and combinations of variation and deviation. The compass card shown on the diagrams indicates the exact position which the card would take depending upon the particular amount of deviation which is specified. For example, in figure 160, as there is neither variation nor deviation the boat will be heading toward magnetic north, as well as true north (0°) and the lubber line of the compass will also be opposite the north pole of the card. In figure 161, which has a deviation of 11° (1 point), the north pole of the compass will be pulled around 11° (1 point) toward the left and the lubber line will be opposite the 11° (N x E) point of the compass. Consequently in figure 161 the compass course to be steered in order to make good a magnetic course of North with 11° (1 point) westerly deviation will be 11° (N x E).

dicates true directions. The inner circles have the zero or North point oriented so as to point to Magnetic North in the locality for which the rose is given. In this particular illustration the magnetic North point of the compass is pulled or displaced 12 degrees to the left or west of true North. Thus the variation is 12 degrees (slightly more than 1 point) West. In Fig. 159, the variation is East. Note too that in Fig. 158, no annual change is indicated, whereas in Fig. 159 there is an annual decrease of 3 minutes in the amount of variation. With the new type of compass rose, one may take magnetic directions from the inmost circle in points and quarter points, or from the new intermediate circle in degrees.

Deviation

One error entering into both magnetic and true courses is caused by magnetic substances such as iron and steel on our boats. The error caused by the effect which this magnetic substance has on our compass, moving the needle one way or the other, is called deviation. It exists to a greater or less degree on every motor boat. Moreover, deviation is not constant; it is different in amount for every different heading of a boat.

Fig. 151 shows why this difference in the amount of deviation

(NOTE—In these illustrations, courses are given in degrees, and equivalents to the nearest quarter-point.)

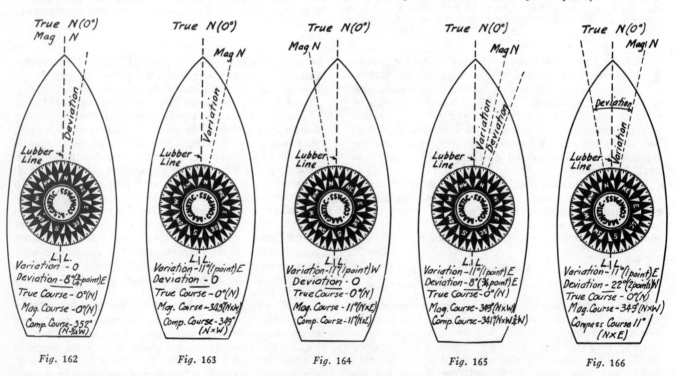

Fig. 162   **Fig. 163**   **Fig. 164**   **Fig. 165**   **Fig. 166**

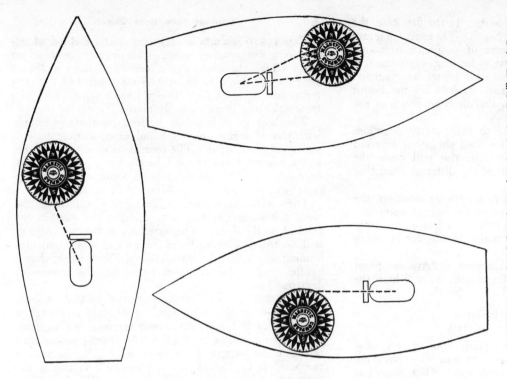

Fig. 151 (left). These diagrams illustrate why deviation on any particular boat is different for each heading of the boat. The diagram of the engine is assumed to be the center of magnetic substances on the boat which have an effect upon the compass and cause deviation. In the case of the boat at the extreme left, which is heading in a northerly direction, this magnetic influence is nearest the south and southwest poles of the compass and is deviating the compass to right or left, depending on whether the magnetic influence is positive or negative. In the case of the boat heading in the easterly direction this influence is nearest the west and southwest poles of the compass. In the case of the boat heading westerly it will be seen that the magnetic influences are nearest the north and northeast poles of the compass and consequently affect the compass in an entirely different way on this heading

Fig. 152 (below). This table shows the various methods of applying variation or deviation when changing from true courses to magnetic courses, magnetic courses to compass courses and compass courses to true courses, or vice versa. The known or given courses are shown in column A, and courses to be found in column B and the direction of variation or deviation in column C. Column D shows whether the variation or deviation (Column C) should be applied to the right or to the left of the known course (Column A) to determine the unknown course (Column B). For example, suppose the true course were southwest and it was desired to find what the magnetic course would be in a locality having one point westerly variation. By referring to Figure 152 one will see that to change from a true to a magnetic course with a westerly variation comes on line number 1. Under column D it states to apply the variation to the right. Therefore, the point to the right of southwest would be southwest by west, which is the magnetic course sought. Again if the true course were southwest and we desired to find the compass course with the variation of one point west and the deviation of one-half point east, we will find the correct method of doing this given on line 3. The net error in this case, that is, one point westerly variation and one-half point easterly deviation, amounts to a net westerly error of one-half point, which, according to the table, should be applied to the right. Therefore, the compass course would be southwest one-half west

	(A) Known or given course	(B) Course to be found	(C) Variation or Deviation Separately or the sum of the two	(D) To Find the Course (B) apply variation or deviation (C) to the right or left of known course (A) as follows:	
				by points	by degrees 0° to 360
1	True	Magnetic	West	Apply Var. to Right	Add
2	True	Magnetic	East	" Var. to Left	Subtract
3	True	Compass	West	" Var ± Dev. to R.	Add
4	True	Compass	East	" Var ± Dev. to L.	Subtract
5	Magnetic	True	West	" Var. to Left	Subtract
6	Magnetic	True	East	" Var. to Right	Add
7	Magnetic	Compass	West	" Dev. to Right	Add
8	Magnetic	Compass	East	" Dev. to Left	Subtract
9	Compass	True	West	" Var ± Dev. to L.	Subtract
10	Compass	True	East	" Var ± Dev. to R	Add
11	Compass	Magnetic	West	" Dev. to Left	Subtract
12	Compass	Magnetic	East	" Dev. to Right	Add

Note: If courses are given in degrees (old method) with 0° at south and 90° at west above application does not hold good.

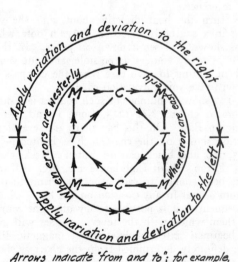

Arrows indicate "from and to"; for example, to find a compass course (C) from a true course (T) apply errors to the right when error is westerly, and to the left when error is easterly, or to go from a magnetic course (M) to a true course (T) apply error to the right when error is easterly and apply error to the left when error is westerly

Fig. 153 (at the right). This figure shows diagrammatically the same points which are brought out in the table above, namely, methods of applying compass errors to the right or left when changing from one kind of a course to another. It should be remembered that when changing from a magnetic to a true course, or vice versa, allow for variation only. When changing from magnetic to compass courses, or vice versa, allow for deviation only. When changing from true to compass courses allow for both variation and deviation, that is, the algebraic sum of both occurs. Here we have three boats. In the first case, the boat is heading approximately North. The engine diagram is used to represent the center of magnetic attraction on the boat. When the boat is heading approximately North, as shown, the pull of this center of magnetic attraction will be exerted most strongly on the South point of the compass, and in the direction which is approximately Southeast.

As the boat swings around to the easterly direction, it is apparent that the attraction is on altogether different points of the compass. Naturally, this will cause the compass to have a deviation decidedly different from that of the first case.

As the boat swings around to a westerly direction, the pull of the magnetic substance on the boat is again different, and causes an entirely different effect on the compass. In other words, the deviation is different on every different heading.

It cannot be assumed that because we have one point westerly deviation when heading North we will have the same amount when heading East or South.

Determining Deviation
(See Figs. 155, 156, 157)

The question now arises not only how to determine the deviation of one's compass, but how to correct the compass so that no deviation will exist. The former is simple, the latter, more difficult. It is much simpler to determine the deviation, know how much it is, and let it exist, than to attempt to correct and compensate for this error on small motor boats. However, one method of compensating the compass is given at the conclusion of this chapter. For practical purposes, most of the deviation can be eliminated by this method.

To determine the amount of deviation, it is simply necessary to choose a number of courses the direction of which can be determined from one's chart, and then put one's boat over these courses, and note the direction shown by the compass.

For example, choose two points on the chart which are directly North and South of each other; that is, two lighthouses, buoys, headlands, or other points which can be readily distinguished. Put the boat over this course, and note the course which the compass shows. Perhaps it will be North by East. Make a note of this for future reference.

Now turn the boat directly about, and she will be heading in a southerly direction. Again note what the compass shows, and set it down on paper. In this way pick out as many courses as possible, and put your boat over them, noting in each case what the compass shows, which will give you a deviation card.

Fig. 157 shows a number of such courses laid out from Government chart (No. 1213, Long Island Sound) of Huntington Bay. On this bay there are several aids to navigation shown on the chart such as lighted bell buoy No. 15, red and black can off Eaton's Neck, can buoy No. 13, Eaton's Point Lighthouse, etc., etc. All of these aids are near enough to each other to permit their being seen from a boat in any position on the bay.

Consequently, it is possible to lay off eight courses between them which with the reverse courses will give the motor boatman sixteen courses whose magnetic direction may be definitely determined from the chart as shown in Fig. 157. By putting the boat over each of these sixteen courses, and observing the direction as shown by compass on the boat, and then comparing these compass headings with the actual magnetic courses shown by the chart (Fig. 157) one can readily determine his compass deviation on the various headings.

Bearings on a Near Object

Fig. 155 represents a very convenient method of determining deviation by means of bearings on an object on shore. Fig. 156 illustrates a method of using a distant object which could be located on the chart, but Fig. 155 represents an object (A) close at hand on shore, such as a tree, stake or a mark specially placed.

The boat is anchored in a fixed position, preferably with several anchors out bow and stern, so that she will swing only as desired. The compass is then taken ashore, and a bearing taken from A to the boat. As there will be no deviation to the compass on shore, a correct magnetic bearing can be obtained from A to the boat.

Then with the compass in its correct position on the boat, a bearing is taken with it from the boat to the mark A on the shore. The difference in the two bearings will be the deviation of the compass on that particular heading which the boat is then on. (That heading shown by the compass lubberline corrected for the amount of deviation just determined.)

For example, if the bearing from the mark A on shore to the boat (as indicated with the compass on shore) is 292° (W N W), then the correct magnetic bearing from the boat to A will be 112° (E S E). If the compass bearing from the boat to A (as indicated by the compass on the boat) is 124° (S E x E), then the deviation is 12° (about 1 point) westerly. As the lubberline is indicating 11° (N x E) (I, Fig. 155) this, corrected for 12° (1 point) westerly deviation, shows the boat to be heading 359° (almost due North) magnetic.

The boat is then swung around a little (II, Fig. 155) and another compass bearing taken on A. Perhaps this bearing will be 118° (S E x E ½ E) and as the magnetic bearing 112° (E S E) has not changed then on this heading 315° (N W) the compass will have a deviation of 6° (½ point) west. Swing the boat to another position (III, Fig. 155) and take a bearing on A. Perhaps this bearing will be 112° (E S E), which is the same as the magnetic bearing. Therefore on this heading 236° (S W x W) the compass shows zero deviation. Proceed in the same way until the boat has been swung all around (360°) obtaining as many bearings on A as is convenient.

Reciprocal Bearings

Another method of determining compass deviation is by taking what are known as reciprocal bearings. This method calls for work of a more exacting nature than any of the foregoing methods, and while it is extremely serviceable for obtaining compass deviations on large boats and vessels, it is not altogether suitable for obtaining compass deviations 1or small boat use where it is impossible to obtain a compass bearing of an object on shore quickly, with accuracy. This method calls for placing an observer on shore with a compass, and another observer on board the boat at the boat's compass.

A system of prearranged signals must be worked out, so that at the instant a signal is given from the boat or by the observer on shore, such as the waving of a handkerchief or the dropping of a flag, a bearing will be taken from the boat to the observer's position on shore, and at the same instant a bearing will be taken by the observer on shore of the boat's position. The bearing by the shore compass, reversed, is the magnetic bearing of the shore station from the boat. The difference between this bearing and the bearing by the boat's compass represents the deviation.

A number of such observations should be taken from the boat to the shore, and the shore to the boat, with the boat on different headings.

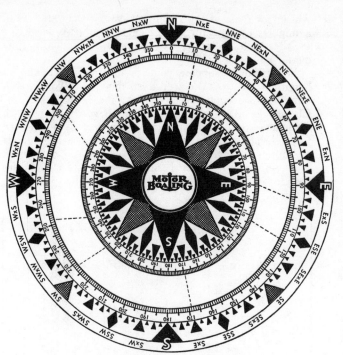

Fig. 154 (left). This is a convenient form of deviation card to indicate the amount of deviation on various headings. The card consists of an inner compass and on outer one. The outer compass indicates magnetic directions and the inner compass the directions as shown by your own compass. The directions which would be shown by your own compass corresponding to the correct magnetic directions are indicated by connecting the corresponding points by dotted lines. For example, if one's compass showed zero deviation on a course of 11° (N x E) then the 11° marks on the two compasses would be connected by a dotted line. If when sailing a 37° (NE ¾ N) course one's compass indicated 34° (NE x N) then these two marks would be connected by a dotted line as shown. If on a heading of 96° (E ½ S) magnetic one's compass showed 90° (E) then these two marks would be connected as shown. The same method is followed entirely around the compass card. The method of using such a deviation card is easy. For example, supposing it was desired to steer a magnetic course of 228° (SW ¼ W). Then by referring to the deviation card and following the dotted line opposite 228° on the outer compass one would see that it led to the mark 225° (SW) on the inner compass. This would be the direction to steer

Fig. 155 (below, left) represents a method of determining deviation by means of bearings of an object on shore. The boat is anchored bow and stern so that it may be swung at any desired heading. The compass is taken ashore, placed at any point "A" and a bearing taken from "A" to the boat. As there will be no deviation on shore a correct magnetic bearing can be obtained from "A" to the boat. The reverse bearing is found to be 112° (ESE), for example. Then the compass is returned to the boat and the bearing taken from the boat to point "A" with the boat heading in a northerly direction. It might be found this bearing is 124° (SE x E), whereas the correct magnetic bearing as indicated by the compass on shore was 112° (ESE); therefore, it will be readily seen that the compass is showing a deviation of 12° (about 1 point) west when the boat is heading north. Next swing the boat so that she will head 315° (NW) and take another bearing by the compass on the boat to point "A." This may be 118° (SE x E ½ E) for example, which will indicate a deviation of 6° (½ point) west on a heading of 315° (NW). The boat is then swung to another heading, 236° (SW x W) for example, and a bearing taken from the boat to point "A." In this case the bearing might be 112° (ESE) which is the correct magnetic bearing also; therefore the compass has zero deviation on its 236° (SW x W) heading. The boat should be swung through as many headings as possible and results noted on a deviation card

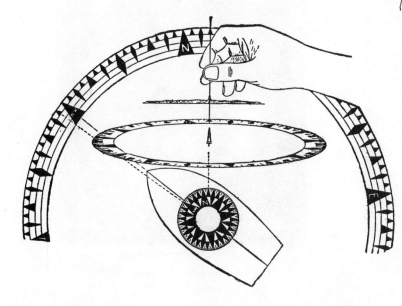

Correct magnetic bearing, Boat to A 112°(ESE)

Compass bearing (Boat heading 0°(N)
Boat to A, 124°(SE x E) ∴ Deviation = 12°(I pt) W

Compass bearing, Boat heading 315°(NW)
Boat to A, 118°(SE x E ½ E) ∴ Deviation = 6°(½ pt) W

Compass bearing, Boat heading 236°(SW x W)
Boat to A, 112°(ESE) ∴ Deviation = 0

Note: Compass shown above represents the position it would assume only when boat is heading north. Position when boat is heading 315°(NW) & 236°(SW x W) are not shown

0°(N)

315° (NW)

236° (SW x W)

112°(ESE) Magnetic Bearing
124°(SE x E) Compass Bearing when boat is heading North

Shore Line

A

Fig. 156 (left) indicates a method of determining deviation by means of a bearing on a distant object. The outside semi-circle is included in the diagram merely for illustrative purposes as an indication that the lighthouse (shown with a strip of shore line immediately below the hand) bears 8° (N ¾ E) magnetic from the ship's position. This magnetic direction is really determined from the chart. With a boat heading in any direction, say 315° (NW), by taking a bearing of the distant object with one's own compass it will be observed that the object bears say 11° (N x E). As the correct magnetic bearing is 8° (N ¾ E) and the compass bearing 11° (N x E) when the boat is heading 315° (NW), it immediately shows that the compass has 3° (¼ point) westerly deviation at this heading

261

Easterly and Westerly Deviation

When the north pole of your compass is swung to the right, or toward the East by the magnetic substance on the boat, the deviation is said to be easterly. When the north pole is swung to the left or to the West, we have a westerly deviation. Deviation refers to the north point of the compass, and to no other point.

Local Attraction

There is another error to which the compass is subject, but fortunately it occurs very infrequently—local attraction. This deflection of the compass needle is caused by magnetic influences not on the ship itself, excluding of course the magnetic poles, which account for variation. The effects of local attraction are sometimes felt when a ship is in port, in close proximity to docks, other vessels, machinery and masses of iron and steel. In port, this error is seldom troublesome but it may also be experienced at sea where it could be a source of danger unless taken into account.

There are few places where local attraction exists naturally, the principal examples being found in certain parts of Lake Superior and several spots off the coast of Australia. Information regarding this compass error is always given on the charts affected and in the Coast Pilots and other Government publications.

Kinds of Courses

The three methods by which bearings or courses may be expressed are:

(a) *True,* when they refer to the North geographical pole.

(b) *Magnetic,* when they refer to the magnetic meridian. To change magnetic courses to true courses, the former must be corrected for variation.

(c) *Compass,* when they refer to the particular boat's compass on each particular heading and must be corrected for the deviation on that heading for conversion to the magnetic course and for both deviation and variation for conversion to true bearings or true courses.

The Sun Compass

Another method of determining deviation involves the use of a sun compass or shadow pelorus. With it any amateur can determine deviation within a quarter-point.

The sun compass is essentially a reversed compass card, so mounted in a box that it can be rotated about its center. At the center a hole is drilled, and a straight wire three or four inches long projects vertically upward. On the box a line A, corresponding to the lubber line of the magnetic compass, is cut, and the sun compass is so placed on the boat that the mark A will represent the bow of the boat either by being in line with the bow if the sun compass is in line with the keel of the boat, or else so that an imaginary line drawn through A and the center of the compass will be parallel to the keel of the boat.

The sun causes a shadow to fall from the upright wire, and this shadow cuts a point indicating the heading of the vessel. By comparing this heading with the heading as indicated by the boat's compass, the deviation can be read off directly. Tables show at what figure on the sun compass the line at A must be set for any time of day.

To find the true course by means of the sun compass, first determine the *local* time of day. This is done by adding or subtracting a certain amount from the standard time as shown by your watch, if it is correct. The amount to add or subtract is determined by whether your position is east or west of the standard time meridian

which, for most of the Atlantic Coast, is the 75th. Add 4 minutes of time for every degree your position is east of the 75th meridian (or your own standard time meridian).

For example, suppose you are in Vineyard Sound in longitude 70° 30′ West; add 18 minutes to your watch time. If you happened to be near the western shore of Chesapeake Bay in longitude 77° (west of the 75th meridian) you would subtract 8 minutes from watch time to get local time. (Latitude and longitude of thousands of stations are given in the Tide Tables.)

Having found the local time, we next add or subtract a correction found in Table III. These values vary with the date.

TABLE III—Correction in Minutes					
(April 1 to October 1)					
Date	Corr.	June 5-10	(+1)	Aug 26-29	(—1)
		11-15	(0)	Aug 30-Sept 2	(0)
April 1-5	(—3)	16-20	(—1)	Sept 3-6	(+1)
6-9	(—2)	21-24	(—2)	7-9	(+2)
10-11	(—1)	25-30	(—3)	10-11	(+3)
12-16	(0)	July 1-4	(—4)	12-13	(+4)
17-20	(+1)	5-10	(—5)	14-16	(+5)
21-26	(+2)	11-31	(—6)	17-19	(+6)
Apr 27-May 3	(+3)	Aug 1-Aug 12	(—5)	20-22	(+7)
May 4-15	(+4)	13-17	(—4)	23-25	(+8)
16-27	(+3)	18-22	(—3)	26-28	(+9)
May 28-June 4	(+2)	23-25	(—2)	29-31	(+10)

With the corrected time, we enter Tables I and II, interpolating for our latitude. For example, Table I gives true bearings of the sun at latitude 41°, Table II at latitude 45°. If your latitude is 43°, the approximate bearing would be half way between those given for 41° and 45°. Approximate bearings can be found for any latitude between 35° and 50° and all longitudes, remembering that standard times in this country are figured from the 75th, 90th, 105th and 120th meridians.

If the bearing is before noon, the card of the sun compass is revolved clockwise from zero (keeping A toward the bow of the boat) until the bearing of the sun in degrees as obtained from Tables I and II is opposite mark A. Where the shadow cuts the inner calibration of the sun compass card will then be found the true course on which the boat is heading. In the afternoon, the card would be turned counter-clockwise, starting from zero at A. *(See tables, page 264.)*

The sun compass or shadow pelorus

Fig. 157 (right) shows a good method of determining compass deviation by putting the boat over a number of courses, the magnetic directions of which can be determined from the chart. Note, for example, the section of Huntington Bay shown here. An examination of the chart shows a number of fixed aids to navigation, buoys, headlands, etc. There is a lighted bell buoy, No. 15, off Lloyd Point, lighted bell buoy No. 11 B and a red-and-black can off Eatons Neck, can buoy No. 13 off Eatons Point, Eatons Point Lighthouse, Lloyd Harbor Lighthouse, a lighted buoy off the entrance to Northport Bay, etc. Magnetic directions between each two of these can be taken easily from the chart. For example, the red-and-black can bears 87° (E ¼ N) from bell buoy No. 15. Therefore, if the boat is sailed over this course and the compass indicates any other heading than 87° (E ¼ N), a certain amount of deviation is present on this heading. Turning about and sailing the reverse course from the red-and-black can toward bell buoy No. 15, we find the magnetic course is 267° (W ¼ S) and the compass heading should agree with it. If it does not, then there is deviation on this particular heading, and the amount is easily determined. The same principle can be applied on all the other headings, and deviations on many headings determined

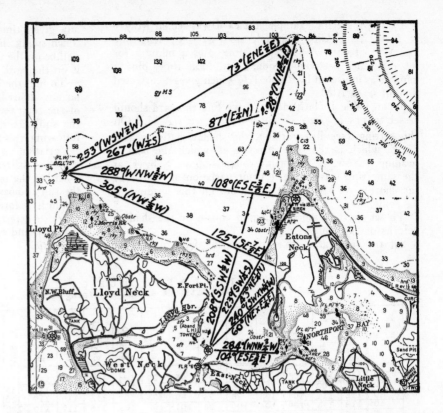

Fig. 158 (left) shows the new type of compass rose. The variation in this instance (near New York) is 12°00' westerly, equivalent to a little more than one point. Westerly variation means that the magnetic north is to the left or westward of true north. In this new style compass rose, it will be noted that true directions are given in the outside circle in degrees. The two inner circles both give magnetic directions, the inmost circle being divided into points and quarter points, the middle circle in degrees. When determining true courses, one uses the outer circle. When finding magnetic courses in points, the inner circle must be used. For magnetic courses in degrees the new intermediate circle may be used

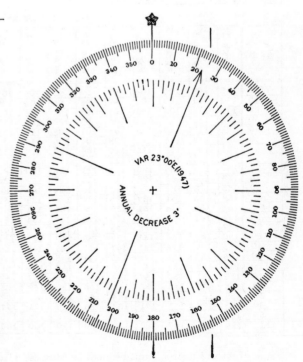

Fig. 159 (right) shows the older type of compass rose in which the inner magnetic circle is calibrated only in points and quarter points. Note that in this case, the variation (near Seattle) is easterly. Observe too that the amount of annual change in variation is given—a decrease of 3° per year in this locality. In other areas it is increasing, while Fig. 158, above, shows that in New York waters there is no annual change. In Figure 159, the variation at Seattle is shown to have been 23°00' east in 1947, indicating that the compass needle is deflected more than two full points to the right or east of true geographic north. Off the coast of Georgia near Savannah in 1946, there was no variation and no annual change

Taking a specific example, the card was set on May 1 at New York City (latitude 40° 42′ N., longitude 74° W.) at 9:15 A.M. watch time, plus 4 minutes for the difference between standard and local time, plus 3 minutes as indicated by Table III, which gives a corrected time of 9:22 A.M.

From Table I (latitude 41°) we find the card should be set to 115 at 9:20, or about 116 at 9:22 A.M. On this setting (see illustration), the shadow falls at SSE ⅜ E, which is the true direction in which the boat is heading. Now, if the boat's compass shows S by E at the same time (assuming 1 point variation as shown by the chart), we know that deviation, on this heading, is ⅜ point.

To set the boat on any desired course by the shadow pelorus or sun compass:

Set the sun's azimuth (true bearing from north) at any given time, at the boat's head as explained above. Then swing the boat's bow to starboard or port and she will be on the desired course when the shadow falls across it on the card.

To find the boat's *magnetic* course, or to steer the boat on any desired magnetic course, allow for the *variation* of the compass for the *locality* of the boat *before* setting the sun's azimuth at the boat's head, according to the following rule:

Variation *easterly,* allow to the *left* of the *true* azimuth; variation *westerly* allow to the *right* of the true azimuth.

Either the *true* or the *magnetic* course can be found by the sun compass. If the *variation* is applied to the true azimuth before setting the sun compass, the *magnetic* course is determined. If it is *not* applied, the *true* course is found, and *variation must be allowed for to convert to magnetic.*

TRUE BEARINGS OF THE SUN
For Latitude 41 and adjoining Parallels.

A.M.	March 16	April 3	April 16	May 1	May 16	June 15	Aug 2	Aug 16	Aug 30	Sept 18	Sept 23	Oct 1	Oct 14	Nov 3	Nov.15	Dec. 15	Feby 2	Feby 15	March 3	P.M.
VIII	112	107	103	98	94	90	95	99	104	109	111	113	117	121	123	126	123	120	116	IV
10	114	109	105	100	96	92	97	101	105	111	113	115	119	123	125	128	125	122	118	50
20	116	111	107	102	98	94	99	103	107	113	115	117	120	125	127	130	127	124	118	40
30	118	113	109	104	100	96	101	105	109	115	117	119	122	127	129	132	129	126	122	30
40	120	115	111	106	102	98	103	107	112	117	119	121	125	129	131	132	129	126	122	20
50	122	117	113	108	104	99	105	109	114	119	121	123	127	131	133	134	131	128	124	10
IX	125	119	115	110	106	101	107	111	116	122	123	125	129	133	135	138	135	132	128	III
10	127	122	117	113	108	104	109	114	118	124	126	128	131	135	138	140	137	134	130	50
20	129	124	120	115	111	106	112	116	121	127	128	130	135	138	139	142	139	136	130	40
30	132	127	123	118	113	108	114	115	123	129	131	133	136	140	142	144	142	139	133	30
40	134	129	125	120	116	111	117	121	126	132	133	135	138	142	144	146	144	141	135	20
50	137	132	128	123	119	113	120	124	129	134	136	138	141	145	146	148	146	144	139	10
X	140	135	131	126	122	116	123	127	132	137	139	141	143	147	148	151	148	146	143	II
10	143	138	134	129	125	120	126	130	135	140	142	143	146	149	151	153	151	149	146	50
20	146	141	138	133	129	123	130	134	138	143	145	146	149	152	153	155	153	151	148	40
30	149	144	141	137	132	127	133	137	142	147	148	149	152	155	156	158	156	154	151	30
40	152	148	145	140	136	132	137	141	145	150	151	152	155	157	158	160	158	157	154	20
50	155	151	149	145	141	135	142	145	149	153	154	156	158	160	161	162	161	159	157	10
XI	159	155	153	149	145	140	146	150	153	157	158	159	161	162	164	165	164	162	160	I
10	162	159	157	154	150	146	151	154	157	161	161	162	164	166	166	167	166	165	164	50
20	166	163	161	159	156	152	157	159	162	164	165	166	167	168	169	170	169	168	167	40
30	169	167	166	164	162	158	162	164	166	168	169	169	170	171	172	172	172	171	170	30
40	172	172	170	169	168	165	168	169	171	172	172	173	173	174	174	174	174	174	173	20
50	176	176	175	174	174	173	174	175	175	176	176	177	177	177	177	177	177	177	177	10
XII	180	180	180	180	180	180	180	180	180	180	180	180	180	180	180	180	180	180	180	XII

For Latitude 45 and adjoining Parallels.

A.M.	March 15	April 1	April 15	May 1	May 15	June 15	Aug. 1	Aug. 15	Aug. 30	Sept. 15	Sept. 21	Oct. 1	Oct. 15	Nov. 1	Nov. 15	Dec. 15	Feby. 1	Feby. 15	March 3	P.M.
VIII	112	109	105	102	97	94	97	102	105	109	112	114	118	121	124	127	124	121	117	IV
10	114	111	107	104	99	95	99	104	107	111	114	116	120	123	126	129	126	123	119	50
20	116	113	109	106	101	97	101	106	109	113	116	118	122	125	128	131	128	125	121	40
30	118	115	111	108	103	99	103	108	111	115	118	121	124	127	130	133	130	127	123	30
40	121	117	113	110	105	101	105	110	113	117	121	123	126	129	132	135	132	129	125	30
50	123	119	116	112	108	104	108	112	116	119	123	125	128	132	134	137	134	132	127	20
IX	125	122	118	115	110	106	110	115	118	122	125	127	130	134	136	139	136	134	130	III
10	128	124	120	117	112	109	112	117	120	124	128	130	133	136	139	141	138	136	132	50
20	130	127	123	120	115	111	115	120	123	127	130	132	135	138	141	143	140	138	134	40
30	133	129	126	122	117	113	117	122	126	129	133	134	137	140	142	145	142	140	137	30
40	135	132	128	125	119	116	119	125	128	132	135	137	140	143	145	147	145	143	139	20
50	138	135	132	128	123	119	123	128	131	135	138	140	142	145	147	149	147	145	142	10
X	141	138	134	131	126	122	126	131	134	138	141	142	145	147	149	151	149	148	144	II
10	144	141	137	134	130	125	130	134	137	141	144	145	148	150	152	154	152	150	147	50
20	147	144	141	138	133	129	133	138	141	144	147	148	150	153	154	156	154	153	150	40
30	150	147	144	141	137	133	137	141	144	147	150	151	153	156	158	156	156	155	153	30
40	153	150	148	145	141	137	141	145	148	150	153	154	156	158	159	160	159	158	156	20
50	156	154	151	149	145	141	145	149	151	154	156	157	159	161	162	163	162	161	158	10
XI	159	157	155	153	150	146	150	153	155	159	159	160	162	163	164	165	164	163	161	I
10	163	161	159	157	154	151	154	157	159	161	163	163	165	166	167	168	167	166	164	50
20	166	165	163	162	159	156	159	162	163	165	166	166	168	169	169	170	169	169	167	40
30	169	168	167	166	164	162	164	166	168	169	169	171	172	172	173	172	172	172	171	30
40	173	172	171	171	169	168	169	171	171	172	173	173	174	174	175	175	175	174	174	20
50	176	176	176	175	175	174	175	175	176	176	176	177	177	177	177	177	177	177	177	10
XII	180	180	180	180	180	180	180	180	180	180	180	180	180	180	180	180	180	180	180	XII

Tables of the sun's true bearings for latitudes 41 and 45 degrees for use in conjunction with the sun compass

DETERMINING DEVIATION

By BEARING OF SUN
At SUNRISE AND SUNSET

An easy method of determining the deviation of one's compass is to take a magnetic bearing of the sun as it rises or sets. From the data on this page of true bearings at sunrise and sunset, the error of the compass can be readily determined.

For example, the sun's true bearing as it rises (Latitude 41°N) on July 29 is 64°; at sunset 296°. To obtain the correct magnetic bearing, add to the true bearing of sunrise or sunset (Fig. 1) a westerly variation (or subtract an easterly variation) obtained from the compass rose on the chart at the particular location where you are. The difference between the corrected magnetic bearing and the compass bearing will be the deviation—thus:

July 29 sunset, true bearing:	296°
add 12° westerly var.	12
correct mag. bearing:	308°
Bearing by compass:	290°
*Easterly Deviation:	18°

*On the heading on which bearing is taken.

Due mainly to the effects of refraction the center of the sun is in the true horizon when its lower limb is still elevated about 20 minutes of angle above the visible horizon or, for estimation by eye, 2/3 of the sun's diameter.

To find the true bearing of the sun at sunrise and sunset, graphically, requires knowledge of the latitude and the sun's declination only. The latitude may be taken from the chart and the declination from the nautical almanac or, close enough for this purpose, from the accompanying table (Fig. 2).

The diagram (Fig. 3) provides a graphic method of reducing this information to true bearings. From the point on the diagram where the straight declination line intersects the curved latitude line lay a straight edge to the center of the compass rose. The straight edge will pass through the true bearing on the rose.

If the diagram is to be preserved, cement it to cardboard and provide a string through the center of the rose instead of the straight edge.

Fig. 4 illustrates graphically the dates on which various bearings of sunrise and sunset occur for approximately 10-degree changes, sunrise and sunset having the most northerly bearings (about 58° in latitudes 41°—43°N) from June 6 through July 8 and most southerly from December 7 through January 6.

The diagram is not restricted to the sun only but may be used for any celestial object whose declination is within the limits of the diagram. The fixed stars and planets whose declination may be taken from the nautical almanac are convenient if the horizon is clear. These objects are in the true horizon when they are elevated about the diameter of the sun or moon above the visible horizon. The moon can be used if it is quite clear; the time of setting is taken just as it disappears and since its declination changes rapidly this factor must be taken from the nautical almanac for the Greenwich time at the time of observation.

SUN'S TRUE BEARING AT RISING AND SETTING
For Latitudes 41°, 42°, 43° North

	Date	Rise	Set		Date	Rise	Set
	1– 6	122°	238°	JUNE	1– 5	60°	300°
	7–12	120	240		6–30	58	302
JANUARY	13–18	119	241		1– 8	58	302
	19–23	117	243		9–15	60	300
	24–27	116	244	JULY	16–21	61	299
	28–31	115	245		22–26	63	297
					27–30	64	296
	1– 3	113	247		31	65	295
	4– 6	112	248		1– 3	65	295
	7– 9	110	250		4– 7	67	293
	10–12	109	251		8–10	68	292
FEBRUARY	13–16	108	252		11–14	69	291
	17–18	106	254	AUGUST	15–17	71	289
	19–21	105	255		18–20	72	288
	22–24	104	256		21–23	74	286
	25–27	102	258		24–26	75	285
	28	101	259		27–29	76	284
					30–31	78	282
	1	100	260		1– 3	79	281
	2– 4	99	261		4– 6	81	279
	5– 6	98	262		7– 9	82	278
	7– 9	97	263		10–11	83	277
	10–12	95	265		12–14	85	275
	13–14	94	266	SEPTEMBER	15–16	86	274
MARCH	15–17	93	267		17–19	87	273
	18–19	91	269		20–21	89	271
	20–22	90	270		22–24	90	270
	23–24	89	271		25–27	91	269
	25–27	87	273		28–29	93	267
	28–29	86	274		30	94	266
	30–31	85	275		1– 2	94	266
					3– 4	95	265
	1	85	275		5– 7	97	263
	2– 4	83	277		8–10	98	262
	5– 7	82	278		11–12	99	261
	8– 9	81	279	OCTOBER	13–15	101	259
	10–11	79	281		16–18	102	258
APRIL	12–14	78	282		19–20	104	256
	15–17	76	284		21–23	105	255
	18–20	75	285		24–26	106	254
	21–23	74	286		27–29	108	252
	24–26	72	288		30–31	109	251
	27–29	71	289		1	109	251
	30	69	291		2– 4	110	250
					5– 8	112	248
	1– 2	69	291	NOVEMBER	9–12	113	247
	3– 6	68	292		13–15	115	245
	7– 9	67	293		16–19	116	244
MAY	10–13	65	295		20–24	117	243
	14–18	64	296		25–29	119	241
	19–23	63	297		30	120	240
	24–29	61	299	DECEMBER	1– 6	120	240
	30–31	60	300		7–31	122	238

Fig. 1. To the bearings given above, add the westerly variation (or subtract the easterly variation) to obtain the correct magnetic bearing at sunrise or sunset. (For figures 2, 3 and 4, see next page.)

APPROXIMATE TRUE BEARINGS

AT SUNRISE AND SUNSET

FOR LATITUDES 41°–43° N

Fig. 4 (above). In this latitude, the farthest north bearing of the sun at sunrise is 58°, which bearing is practically constant from June 6 through July 8. This corresponds to the most southerly bearing of 122° from Dec. 8 through Jan. 6

SUN'S APPROXIMATE DECLINATION

DAY	JAN	FEB	MAR	APR	MAY	JUN	JUL	AUG	SEP	OCT	NOV	DEC	DAY
1	23 S	17½ S	7¾ S	4¼ N	15 N	22 N	23¼ S	18¼ N	8½ N	3 S	14½ S	21¾ S	1
2	23 S	17 S	7½ S	4¼ N	15½ N	22 N	23 N	18 N	8¼ N	3½ S	14½ S	21¾ S	2
3	23 S	16½ S	7 S	5 N	15½ N	22¼ N	23 N	17¾ N	7¾ N	3½ S	14¾ S	22 S	3
4	22¾ S	16½ S	6¾ S	5½ N	15¾ N	22¼ N	23 N	17½ N	7½ N	4 S	15¼ S	22¼ S	4
5	22½ S	16¼ S	6¼ S	5¾ N	16 N	22½ N	22¾ N	17¼ N	7 N	4½ S	15½ S	22¼ S	5
6	22½ S	16 S	6 S	6¼ N	16¼ N	22½ N	22¾ N	17 N	6¾ N	4¾ S	15¾ S	22¼ S	6
7	22¼ S	15½ S	5½ S	6½ N	16½ N	22½ N	22¾ N	16½ N	6 N	5½ S	16 S	22¼ S	7
8	22¼ S	15¼ S	5 S	7 N	17 N	22½ N	22½ N	16¼ N	6 N	5¾ S	16½ S	22½ S	8
9	22¼ S	15 S	4¾ S	7½ N	17¼ N	23 N	22½ N	16 N	5½ N	6 S	16¾ S	22½ S	9
10	22 S	14½ S	4½ S	7¾ N	17½ N	23 N	22¼ N	15¾ N	5¼ N	6½ S	17 S	22½ S	10
11	22 S	14½ S	4 S	8 N	17¾ N	23 N	22¼ N	15½ N	4¾ N	6¾ S	17¼ S	23 S	11
12	21¾ S	14 S	3½ S	8½ N	18 N	23 N	22 N	15¼ N	4½ N	7½ S	17½ S	23 S	12
13	21½ S	13½ S	3 S	8¾ N	18¼ N	23¼ N	22 N	15 N	4 N	7½ S	17¾ S	23 S	13
14	21½ S	13¼ S	2¾ S	9¼ N	18½ N	23¼ N	21¾ N	14½ N	3¾ N	8 S	18 S	23¼ S	14
15	21¼ S	13 S	2½ S	9½ N	18¾ N	23¼ N	21¾ N	14¼ N	3¼ N	8½ S	18¼ S	23¼ S	15
16	21 S	12½ S	2 S	10 N	19 N	23¼ N	21½ N	14 N	3 N	8¾ S	18½ S	23¼ S	16
17	20¾ S	12¼ S	1½ S	10¼ N	19¼ N	23¼ N	21¼ N	13¾ N	2½ N	9 S	18¾ S	23¼ S	17
18	20½ S	12 S	1¼ S	10½ N	19½ N	23½ N	21 N	13½ N	2 N	9½ S	19 S	23½ S	18
19	20¼ S	11½ S	¾ S	½ N	19¾ N	23½ N	21 N	13 N	1¾ N	9¾ S	19¼ S	23½ S	19
20	20¼ S	11¼ S	½ S	½ N	20 N	23½ N	20¾ N	12¾ N	1½ N	10 S	19½ S	23½ S	20
21	20 S	10¾ S	0	11¼ N	20 N	23½ N	20½ N	12½ N	1¼ N	10½ S	19¾ S	23½ S	21
22	19¾ S	10½ S	¼ N	12 N	20¼ N	23½ N	20½ N	12 N	1 N	10½ S	20 S	23½ S	22
23	19½ S	10 S	¾ N	12¼ N	20½ N	23½ N	20¼ N	11¾ N	¾ N	11¼ S	20¼ S	23½ S	23
24	19¼ S	9¾ S	1¼ N	12½ N	20¾ N	23½ N	20 N	11¼ N	½ S	11½ S	20½ S	23½ S	24
25	19 S	9½ S	1½ N	13 N	20¾ N	23½ N	19¾ N	11 N	½ S	11½ S	20½ S	23¼ S	25
26	18¾ S	9 S	2 N	13¼ N	21 N	23¼ N	19½ N	10½ N	1 S	12¼ S	20¾ S	23¼ S	26
27	18½ S	8½ S	2¼ N	13¾ N	21¼ N	23¼ N	19¼ N	10¼ N	1¼ S	12½ S	21 S	23¼ S	27
28	18¼ S	8¼ S	2½ N	14 N	21¼ N	23¼ N	19 N	10 N	1¾ S	13 S	21¼ S	23¼ S	28
29	18 S	8 S	3¼ N	14¼ N	21½ N	23¼ N	19 N	9½ N	2¼ S	13¾ S	21½ S	23¼ S	29
30	17½ S		3½ N	14½ N	21¾ N	23¼ N	18½ N	9¼ N	2½ S	13½ S	21½ S	23¼ S	30
31	17½ S		4 N		21¾ N		18½ N	9 N		14 S		23½ S	31

TRUE BEARING AT RISING AND SETTING

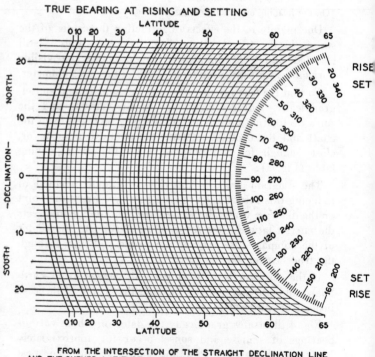

FROM THE INTERSECTION OF THE STRAIGHT DECLINATION LINE AND THE CURVED LATITUDE LINE DRAW A LINE TO THE CENTER OF THE AZIMUTH CIRCLE. THE LINE DRAWN WILL INTERSECT THE CIRCLE AT THE TRUE BEARING AT RISING OR SETTING

Fig. 2 (at left). Figures for sun's declination to be used in Fig. 3, (above) to determine graphically the true bearing of the sun at sunrise and sunset for any day in the year

COMPASS DEVIATION CARD

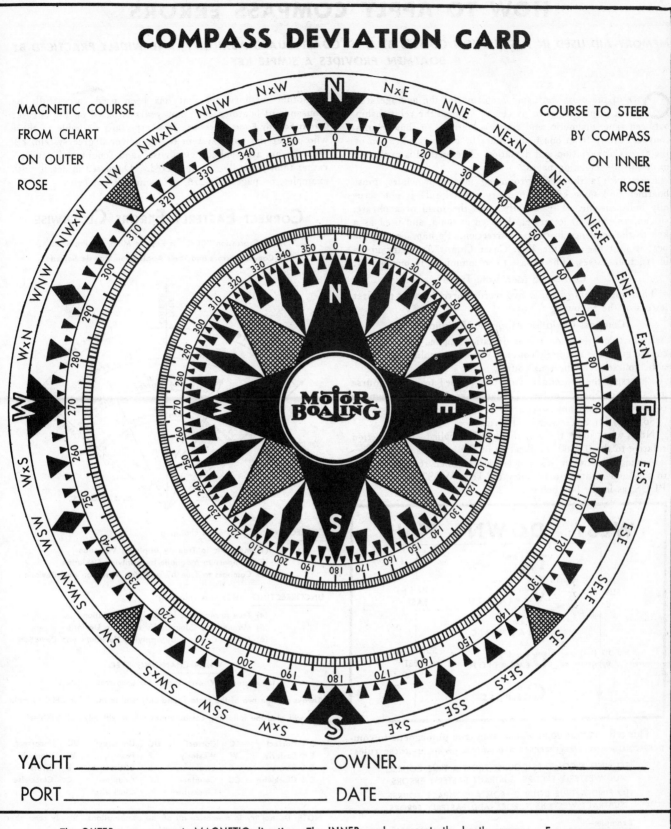

MAGNETIC COURSE
FROM CHART
ON OUTER
ROSE

COURSE TO STEER
BY COMPASS
ON INNER
ROSE

YACHT_____ OWNER_____

PORT_____ DATE_____

The OUTER rose represents MAGNETIC directions. The INNER card represents the boat's compass. For every compass heading for which the deviation is known, draw a line from that compass point or degree to the magnetic course (on the outer rose) when on that heading.

TO FIND THE COMPASS COURSE: Start at the outer rose with the magnetic course (as plotted on the chart) and follow the lines to the inner card, from which the compass course is read.

TO CORRECT COMPASS COURSE TO MAGNETIC: Start with the compass course on the inner card and follow the lines to the outer rose from which the magnetic course (to be plotted on the chart) is read.

DO NOT USE THIS METHOD WHEN CORRECTING OBSERVED BEARINGS. In such cases, first find the deviation for the boat's heading when the bearing is taken. Then apply that deviation to the bearing, East or West, as required.

Any CHANGE in the location o' iron or untwisted electric wires within six feet of the compass will change its deviation. A new card must then be constructed.

HOW TO APPLY COMPASS ERRORS

MEMORY AID USED IN INSTRUCTION CLASSES BY U. S. COAST GUARD AUXILIARY, AND WIDELY PRACTICED BY BOATMEN, PROVIDES A SIMPLE KEY

ONE of the most confusing problems for the average student of piloting is to fix clearly in mind the relationship between true, magnetic, and compass courses, so that he may convert readily from one to the other by proper application of the errors of variation and deviation. The method is explained in detail in succeeding pages.

Even with a thorough grounding in the principles, most boatmen find some kind of memory aid helpful—if not actually indispensable. This usually takes the form of a phrase, slogan, or group of letters easily fixed in mind, and used as a key to the sequence in course correction. Perhaps one of the best is that used by the U.S. Coast Guard Auxiliary in its instruction classes. The phrase to be committed to memory is:

Can Dead Men Vote Twice?

The first letters of these five words correspond to the first letters of the following terms:

Compass-Deviation-Magnetic-Variation-True

From this it is evident that deviation applied to a compass course gives the magnetic course. Variation applied to a magnetic course gives the true course.

Reversing the procedure, variation applied to a true course gives the magnetic course. Deviation applied to a magnetic course gives the compass course.

So much for the *sequence* of terms.

Now, what about the way the error is applied—the *direction* relative to the 0°-360° calibration of the compass card?

Arrange the five terms in a vertical column, reading bottom to top, and commit to memory the key: WEST—DOWN—PLUS, as in the box below.

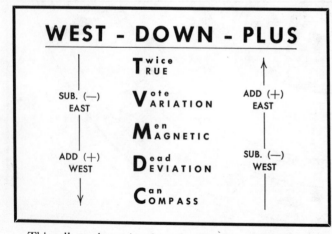

This tells us that going *down* from true to magnetic to compass courses, *westerly errors* are *added,* giving us these rules:

TO FIND A COMPASS COURSE FROM A TRUE COURSE, ADD WESTERLY ERRORS, SUBTRACT EASTERLY ERRORS

TO FIND A TRUE COURSE FROM A COMPASS COURSE, SUBTRACT WESTERLY ERRORS, ADD EASTERLY ERRORS

Example:—

True course as plotted on the chart	180°
Variation for the locality (shown on the chart)	12° W
Deviation (for our boat on this heading)	4° E

What is the compass course to steer?

Following the rule:

TRUE COURSE	180°
VARIATION (WEST) ADD	12°
MAGNETIC COURSE	192°
DEVIATION (EAST) SUBTRACT	4°
COMPASS COURSE	188°

Another memory aid that has been used successfully by thousands of boatmen for many years is based on the phrase: **Correct Easterly Errors Clockwise.** It is especially valuable to those who prefer the point system to the newer degree system, because errors are applied "clockwise" and "counter-clockwise," rather than "added" or "subtracted." Discussed in detail, with examples, on pages 271-273, it is summarized below.

CORRECT EASTERLY ERRORS CLOCKWISE

If the Expression "CEEC" is Kept in Mind, All Problems of Compass Errors and Their Application May Be Solved

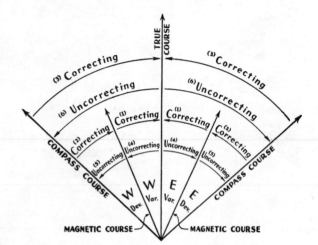

CORRECTING (C) is changing

(1) Magnetic to True by applying Variation
(2) Compass to Magnetic by applying Deviation
(3) Compass to True by applying Variation and Deviation

UNCORRECTING (UC) is changing

(4) True to Magnetic by applying Variation
(5) Magnetic to Compass by applying Deviation
(6) True to Compass by applying Variation and Deviation

WHEN CHANGING CEEC

for westerly (W) errors, and for uncorrecting (UC):-

Always change two of the factors (and only two) in the basic **CEEC** formula.

This will give the following combinations which will solve all problems:-

C	Correct	C	Correct	UC	Uncorrect	UC	Uncorrect
E	Easterly	W	Westerly	E	Easterly	W	Westerly
E	Errors	E	Errors	E	Errors	E	Errors
C	Clockwise	CC	Counter-Clockwise	CC	Counter-Clockwise	C	Clockwise

NOTE: Do not try to memorize all of the combinations. Simply remember **CEEC,** and that in order to obtain all other combinations you must always change two of the factors in **CEEC** and only two.

Can't remember CEEC? Try Cannibals Eat Every Captive

STILL ANOTHER MEMORY AID—A reader, rejecting both the CDMVT and CEEC suggestions for jogging his memory, uses the word HAWSER. Dropping the first and last letters, he has **AWSE,** which he interprets to mean **Add Westerly—Subtract Easterly** errors in converting to compass courses (uncorrecting). When correcting (compass-to-magnetic-to-true), he naturally reverses the first and third letters.

IN order to clearly understand the mariner's compass it is well to have some knowledge of the physical laws which govern its behavior. A piece of iron or steel which attracts other iron or steel is called a magnet. Some ores have this property and are known as natural magnets. A piece of iron or steel may, by specific treatment, be made a magnet. Such a magnet will have its attractive force concentrated in two places, which are known as its poles, but its attractive force or magnetic flux will make itself apparent in varying degree throughout the entire area surrounding the magnet. This area is known as the field of the magnet. The magnetic flux makes itself felt through the field in a definite manner following certain paths or directions. These paths are termed lines of force.

Most of us are familiar with the manner in which iron filings will arrange themselves if scattered about the field of an ordinary bar magnet. The filings show very clearly the lines of force through the field and their concentration at the poles. It can be demonstrated experimentally that each filing actually becomes a small temporary magnet and arranges itself in a very definite position with regard to the bar or relatively large magnet.

While it is not strictly true, for the purposes of this discussion the earth may be considered as a huge spherical magnet having its poles located in the north and south polar regions. As such a magnet it will have a magnetic field. Throughout its field will be an infinite number of lines of force. The mariner is concerned with those lines of force which are present upon the surface of the earth and which may be considered as running from the north to the south magnetic poles. At any point on such a magnetic line of force the direction along the line towards the earth's north magnetic pole is termed magnetic north and the direction toward the south magnetic pole is termed south magnetic. It is to be noted that

VARIATION AS A FACTOR IN COMPASS ERROR—PRACTICAL PROBLEMS IN THE APPLICATION OF COMPASS ERRORS

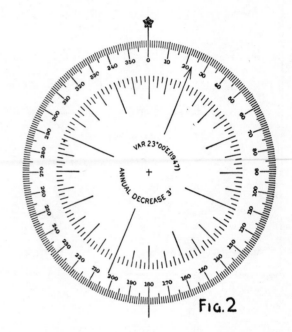

VAR 23°00'E (1947)

ANNUAL DECREASE 3'

FIG. 2

the north or the south magnetic direction from any point is not the true bearing of the north or south magnetic pole from the point, but the direction along the line of force passing through the point. The direction of the line of force passing through any point on the earth is termed the magnetic meridian of the point.

A magnet of bar or needle form, suspended in the earth's magnetic field, so as to be free to swing, will, like the iron filing in the field of a small magnet assume a very definite position. In general it will come to rest along one of the earth's lines of force, pointing north and south magnetic. Its poles are named for those poles of the earth toward which they point. That is, the pole pointing in the general direction of the earth's north magnetic pole is termed the north pole of the magnet and that pointing in

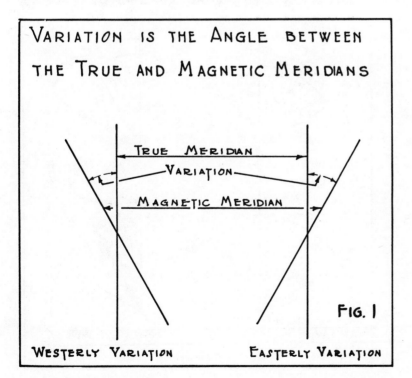

VARIATION IS THE ANGLE BETWEEN THE TRUE AND MAGNETIC MERIDIANS

TRUE MERIDIAN

VARIATION

MAGNETIC MERIDIAN

WESTERLY VARIATION   EASTERLY VARIATION

FIG. 1

A CLEAR EXPLANATION OF

THE COMPASS, ITS ERRORS

AND THEIR APPLICATION

eral direction of the north magnetic pole. This gives rise to an error of the compass known as variation.

The line passing through a point on the earth and the north and south geographic poles is known as the true meridian of the place. It has already been stated that direction of the magnetic line of force at such a point, which is the direction assumed by a compass needle unaffected by anything but the earth's magnetic flux, is the magnetic meridian of the point. Hence the variation of the compass at any place may be defined as the angle between the true and magnetic meridians at that place.

Variation is termed easterly if the upper half of the magnetic meridian is to the east of the true meridian and west if the upper half or branch of the magnetic meridian is to the west of the true meridian.

The earth's lines of force do not run as great circles passing over the earth and through the magnetic poles but change their direction over the globe, making many different angles with the true meridians. Hence variation differs with locality and on a long course the mariner must take into account the change in variation as he proceeds upon the voyage. On the Great Circle course from New York to Liverpool the variation changes over ten degrees in six hundred miles. Off the coast of Florida the variation is zero, while in the vicinity of Cape Sable, Nova Scotia it is 18° W. An aviator departing from Florida for Nova Scotia, would, if he failed to take the change

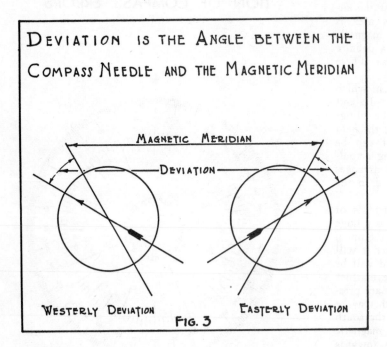

DEVIATION IS THE ANGLE BETWEEN THE COMPASS NEEDLE AND THE MAGNETIC MERIDIAN

MAGNETIC MERIDIAN

DEVIATION

WESTERLY DEVIATION   EASTERLY DEVIATION

FIG. 3

the general direction of the earth's south magnetic pole is termed the south pole of the magnet.

The mariner's compass is a refinement of such a freely suspended needle, upon which has been placed a graduated card and the whole suitably placed in a liquid for damping purposes so that its apparent motion will not be too violent. The mariner does not see the north or south poles of the magnet of his compass, but sees the direction of these poles depicted on the compass card, so that in actuality the compass card may be considered to behave as does the freely suspended needle.

The earth's magnetic and geographic poles do not coincide. The north magnetic pole is at present located in approximately latitude 71° north and longitude 96° west. The south magnetic pole is not diametrically opposed to it but is in approximately latitude 73° south and longitude 156° east. Hence the north point of the compass does not point to the geographic pole but along a magnetic meridian or line of force in the gen-

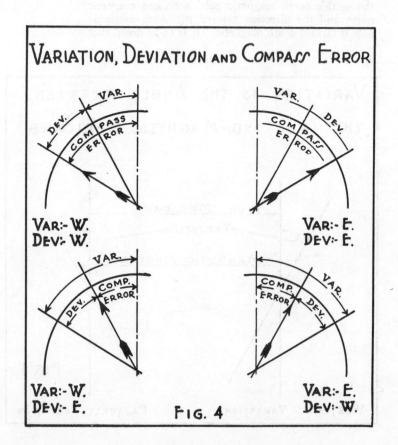

VARIATION, DEVIATION AND COMPASS ERROR

VAR.   VAR.
DEV.   DEV.
COMPASS ERROR   COMPASS ERROR

VAR:- W.   VAR:- E.
DEV:- W.   DEV:- E.

VAR.   VAR.
DEV.   DEV.
COMP. ERROR   COMP. ERROR

VAR:- W.   VAR:- E.
DEV:- E.   DEV:- W.

FIG. 4

DEVIATION TABLE.
FIG. 5

SHIP'S HEAD P.S.C.	DEV.	SHIP'S HEAD P.S.C.	DEV.	SHIP'S HEAD P.S.C.	DEV.
0°	14° W.	120°	15° E.	240°	4° E.
15°	10° W	135°	16° E.	255°	1° W.
30°	5° W.	150°	12° E.	270°	7° W.
45°	1° W.	165°	13° E.	285°	12° W.
60°	2° E.	180°	14° E.	300°	15° W.
75°	5° E.	195°	14° E.	315°	19° W.
90°	7° E.	210°	12° E	330°	19° W.
105°	9° E.	225°	9° E.	345°	17° W.
				360°	14° W.

in variation into consideration, find himself not in Nova Scotia but lost over the woods of Maine. A quick picture of the changes in variation over the earth's surface may be obtained by consulting the Hydrographic Office chart number 1706. Lines are drawn on this chart through all places having the same variation.

Variation not only changes with locality but generally changes its value slowly in any given place. In piloting and small boat sailing which involves the use of Coast and Geodetic Survey charts the mariner finds upon the chart not only the value of the variation, but the rate, amount, and direction of the annual change given upon the compass rose. See Figure 2. This rose is a double one. The outer circle is graduated in degrees from 0° to 360° and is placed so that its zero or north point and 180° or south point lie on a geographic or true meridian. The inner circle is graduated in points and while having the same center as the outer rose is turned so that its north-south axis lies along the magnetic meridian. The angle and direction of the variation for a given year is stated on this rose, together with the annual rate of change and its direction. Compass roses on the newest charts give magnetic directions in degrees as well as points.

A piece of iron brought near a mariner's compass will cause the card to move and indicate a direction other than that of the magnetic meridian. A steel ship, having a magnetic field of her own, will exert a similar force upon her compasses and introduce an error, beyond variation, which the navigator must take into account. Though not so great, all vessels have their own magnetic fields and the action

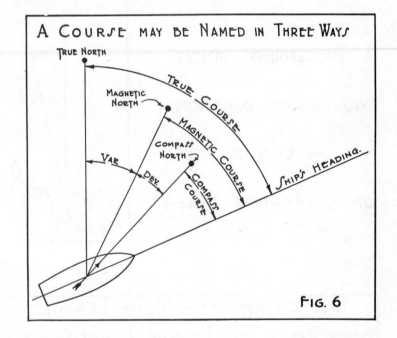

A COURSE MAY BE NAMED IN THREE WAYS

FIG. 6

of these fields is to cause the compass needle to take a position at some angle to the magnetic meridian instead of along it. This angle is termed deviation. There was once a vessel named Carnegie built at great expense of wood, bronze and other non-magnetic material which had practically no magnetic field and hence no deviation on her compasses. Such a vessel is of course, beyond the means of the average yachtsman and he must make the best of his situation and make allowances for deviation.

Deviation is the angle between the compass needle and the magnetic meridian. If the compass needle or compass north is to the east of the upper or northerly branch of the magnetic meridian the deviation is termed east; if the compass north is to the west of the upper or northerly branch of the magnetic meridian it is termed west. It will be readily seen that it is possible to have various combinations of deviation and variation. The navigator may be faced with westerly variation and have either easterly or westerly deviation upon his compass; he may likewise have easterly variation and either deviation on his compass. In any event the angle between the direction of the compass north and the true meridian is known as the compass error (sometimes referred to as total error) and is similarly denoted east or west as the compass north lies to the east or west of the upper branch of the true meridian.

Deviation is not constant on a vessel, but varies with the heading of the boat, and in the case of steel ships, with their position on the earth. The wise motor boatman equips himself with a table of deviations applying to his own boat.

A course may be defined as the angle which the ship's keel makes with some line of reference. There are three of these lines of reference in common usage, the true meridian, the magnetic meridian and the direction of compass north. Hence one course may be named in three ways, *true*,

A SUCCEEDING ARTICLE

WILL DESCRIBE DEVIATION

AND THE CONSTRUCTION

OF A DEVIATION TABLE

magnetic, or *compass.* The true course is the angle between the ship's heading and the true meridian. The magnetic course is the angle between the ship's heading and the magnetic meridian. The compass course is the angle between the ship's heading and the compass needle. It is important to observe that *no matter how the course be defined it is sailed over one track only.*

A vessel is steered by compass. The course angle is given to the helmsman as a compass course. The navigator or pilot, on the other hand, determines from his chart the true or the magnetic course, very simply, but not the compass course. Such a magnetic course must be converted to a compass course before it may be used by the helmsman, that is, a course stated with reference to the magnetic meridian must be

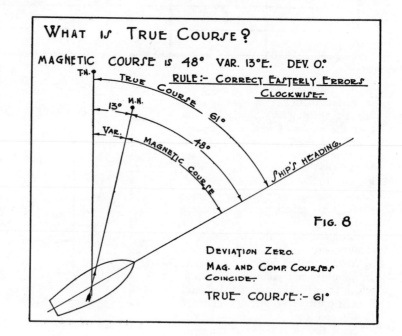

Fig. 8

restated with reference to the compass needle. Similarly it is necessary for other purposes at times, to express a magnetic course as a true course, or vice versa, or a compass course as a magnetic course. Since bearings are angles expressed with regard to the same three lines of reference, as are courses, it is frequently necessary to convert from one system to another. Bear in mind that *a course or a bearing exists only as one direction* and that its expression as compass, magnetic or true does not change its direction, but merely expresses this direction *as an angle with respect to a line of reference.* The conversion of a course from one system to another may be done by the application of one simple rule,

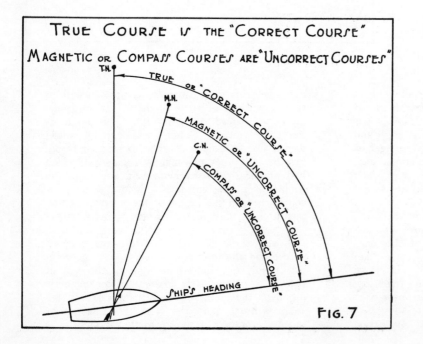

Fig. 7

270

the derivation of which will be found to be quite logical.

If it is assumed that the ideal manner of stating a course is that which is absolute and involves no variable factor, it must be conceded that this is the case when a course is given as true, that is. stated with reference to the true meridian. A less ideal manner of expression is that involving one variable, variation. This is the case when courses are expressed as magnetic. The least ideal manner of expression is that involving both variable factors, variation and deviation. which is the case when a course is stated as compass. For purposes of euphony let the word *correct* be used instead of ideal. Then the true may be termed the correct course and magnetic or compass courses termed less correct or for want of a better term *uncorrect* courses. Conversion of courses from compass to magnetic and from magnetic to true is then termed CORRECTING and the conversion from true to magnetic and from magnetic to compass is termed UNCORRECTING.

The rule for all course conversion may now be stated: when correcting apply easterly errors clockwise; for convenience abbreviated to CORRECT EASTERLY ERRORS CLOCKWISE.

In applying this rule it is obvious that it must be changed to suit specific cases. The conversion may be correcting or uncorrecting; the error may be easterly or westerly; and the direction of its application, clockwise or counterclockwise. The rule has three changeable words and confusion may be avoided by remembering that in any change from the basic statement, CORRECT EASTERLY ERRORS CLOCKWISE, ALWAYS TWO and ONLY TWO of the four words are changed at one time. Though it is not advisable to remember the variations of the rule, they are stated here to illustrate their applications.

1. CORRECT EASTERLY ERRORS CLOCKWISE. Used when correcting with an easterly error.

2. CORRECT WESTERLY ERRORS COUNTER-CLOCKWISE. Used when correcting with a westerly error.

3. UNCORRECT EASTERLY ERRORS COUNTER-CLOCKWISE. Used when uncorrecting with an easterly error.

4. UNCORRECT WESTERLY ERRORS CLOCKWISE. Used when uncorrecting with a westerly error.

The terms clockwise and counterclockwise are used to denote the angular direction in which the error is applied. A compass is graduated from 0° to 360° in a clockwise direction. An error of 10° applied clockwise to a course of 45° gives a resultant course of 55°. An error of 15° applied counterclockwise to a course of 255° gives a resultant course of 240°. A number of examples are given and illustrated.

MAGNETIC TO TRUE. VARIATION EASTERLY.
RULE: CORRECT EASTERLY ERRORS CLOCKWISE.

From figure 8 it is readily seen that the magnetic course of 48° now expressed as the course with reference to the magnetic meridian, will, if expressed with reference to the true meridian or corrected, be increased by 13°, the amount of the easterly variation; i.e., the error of 13° East is applied to the magnetic course of 48° in a clockwise direction to obtain the true course of 61°.

MAGNETIC TO TRUE. VARIATION WESTERLY.
BASIC RULE: CORRECT EASTERLY ERRORS CLOCKWISE.

Figure 9, the basic rule is not directly applicable here. The error is not easterly but westerly. The conversion remains a correction, so that the only other word which can be changed in the rule is clockwise, and the rule becomes CORRECT WESTERLY ERRORS COUNTERCLOCKWISE, in accordance with the statement made that always two and only two of the words in the rule are changed for any application.

The magnetic course of 68° now expressed with reference to the magnetic meridian will, if expressed with reference to the

true meridian, or corrected, be diminished by 14°, i.e., the error of 14° W is applied in a counterclockwise direction to obtain the true course of 54°.

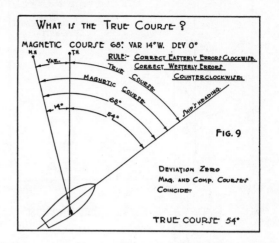

TRUE TO MAGNETIC. VARIATION EASTERLY.

BASIC RULE: CORRECT EASTERLY ERRORS CLOCKWISE.

Figure 10, the basic rule is not directly applicable here. The error is easterly, but the conversion is uncorrecting. Always two and only two words of the basic rule may be changed, so that for this application the rule becomes UNCORRECT EASTERLY ERRORS COUNTERCLOCKWISE.

The true course of 72° now given with reference to the true meridian, if stated with reference to the magnetic meridian, or uncorrected will be diminished by 11°, i.e., the easterly error of 11° is applied to the true course of 72° in a counterclockwise direction giving a magnetic course of 61°.

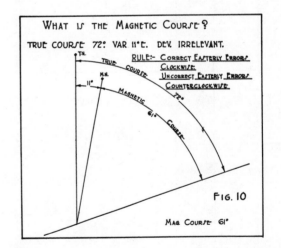

TRUE TO MAGNETIC. VARIATION WESTERLY.

BASIC RULE: CORRECT EASTERLY ERRORS CLOCKWISE.

Figure 11, the basic rule is not directly applicable here. The error is westerly and the conversion uncorrecting. Always two and only two of the words of the rule may be changed and for this case it becomes UNCORRECT WESTERLY ERRORS CLOCKWISE. The true course of 84° stated with reference to the true meridian, if stated with reference to the magnetic meridian, or uncorrected, will be increased by 10°, i.e., the error of 10° W is applied to the true course in a clockwise direction, giving a magnetic course of 94°.

271

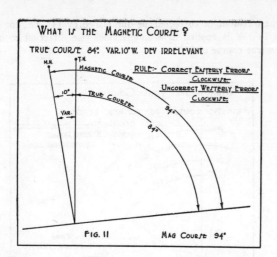

WHAT IS THE MAGNETIC COURSE?

TRUE COURSE 84°. VAR.10°W. DEV IRRELEVANT.

RULE:- CORRECT EASTERLY ERRORS
Clockwise
Uncorrect Westerly Errors
Clockwise

FIG. 11   MAG COURSE 94°

COMPASS TO MAGNETIC. DEVIATION EASTERLY.

BASIC RULE: CORRECT EASTERLY ERRORS CLOCKWISE.

Figure 12, this conversion is performed exactly as in figure 8.

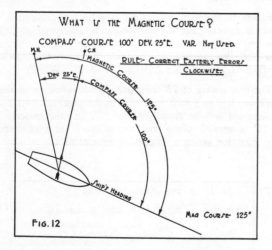

WHAT IS THE MAGNETIC COURSE?

COMPASS COURSE 100° DEV. 25°E. VAR. Not used.

RULE:- CORRECT EASTERLY ERRORS
CLOCKWISE

FIG. 12   MAG COURSE 125°

COMPASS TO MAGNETIC. DEVIATION WESTERLY.

RULE: CORRECT WESTERLY ERRORS COUNTERCLOCKWISE.

Figure 13, proceed as in figure 9.

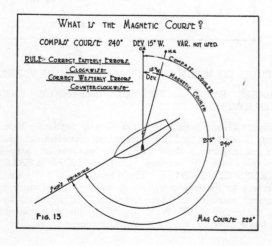

WHAT IS THE MAGNETIC COURSE?

COMPASS COURSE 240° DEV. 15°W. VAR. Not used.

RULE:- Correct Easterly Errors
Clockwise
Correct Westerly Errors
Counterclockwise

FIG. 13   MAG COURSE 225°

MAGNETIC TO COMPASS. DEVIATION EASTERLY.

RULE: UNCORRECT EASTERLY ERRORS COUNTERCLOCKWISE.

Figure 14, proceed as in figure 10.

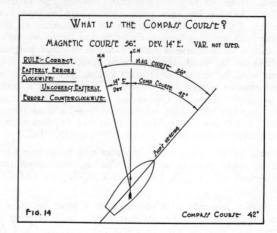

WHAT IS THE COMPASS COURSE?

MAGNETIC COURSE 56°. DEV. 14°E. VAR. not used.

RULE:- Correct
Easterly Errors
Clockwise
Uncorrect Easterly
Errors Counterclockwise

FIG. 14   COMPASS COURSE 42°

MAGNETIC TO COMPASS. DEVIATION WESTERLY.

RULE: UNCORRECT WESTERLY ERRORS CLOCKWISE.

Figure 15, proceed as in figure 11.

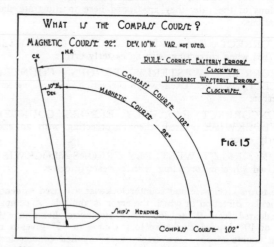

WHAT IS THE COMPASS COURSE?

MAGNETIC COURSE 92°. DEV. 10°W. VAR. not used.

RULE- Correct Easterly Errors
Clockwise
Uncorrect Westerly Errors
Clockwise

FIG. 15   COMPASS COURSE 102°

COMPASS TO TRUE. VARIATION EAST DEVIATION EAST.

RULE: CORRECT EASTERLY ERRORS CLOCKWISE.

Figure 16, the total or compass error, the combined variation and deviation is 19° E. Method of procedure is the same as in figure 8.

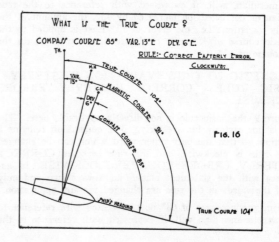

WHAT IS THE TRUE COURSE?

COMPASS COURSE 85° VAR. 13°E. DEV. 6°E.

RULE:- Correct Easterly Error
Clockwise

FIG. 16   TRUE COURSE 104°

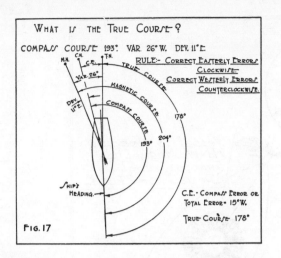

FIG. 17

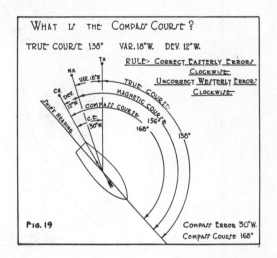

FIG. 19

TRUE TO COMPASS. VARIATION EAST DEVIATION WEST.

RULE: UNCORRECT.

Figure 18, the total error obtained by combining 25° easterly variation and 11° westerly deviation is 14° E.

Proceed as in figure 10.

COMPASS TO TRUE. VARIATION WEST DEVIATION EAST.

RULE:

Figure 17, the total error, obtained by combining 26° westerly variation and 11° easterly deviation is 15° W.

Proceed as in figure 9.

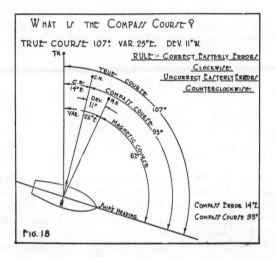

FIG. 18

TRUE TO COMPASS. VARIATION WEST DEVIATION WEST.

RULE: UNCORRECT WESTERLY ERRORS CLOCKWISE.

The compass or total error is 30° W.

Proceed as in figure 11.

Careful study of these examples will enable one to become familiar with the methods of course conversion. The same methods are followed where courses are expressed in the point system, the use of the term clockwise and counterclockwise assuring the novice against inadvertently applying the errors in the wrong direction.

For any vessel a navigator must have a deviation table. In a succeeding article the method of constructing such a table for a small boat will be explained.

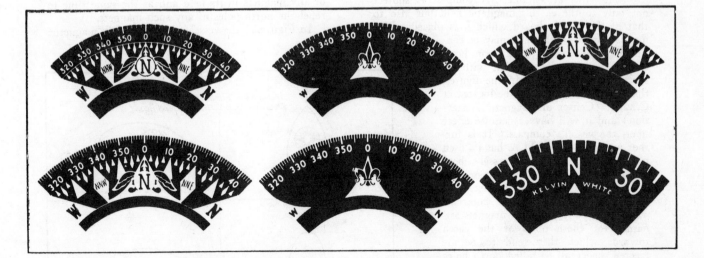

Some of the most modern compasses are equipped with a reverse type of card, in which the background is black with degree or point markings (or both) in white. This is easily read and not tiring on the eyes, either day or night.

Courtesy Wilfrid O. White and Sons, Inc.

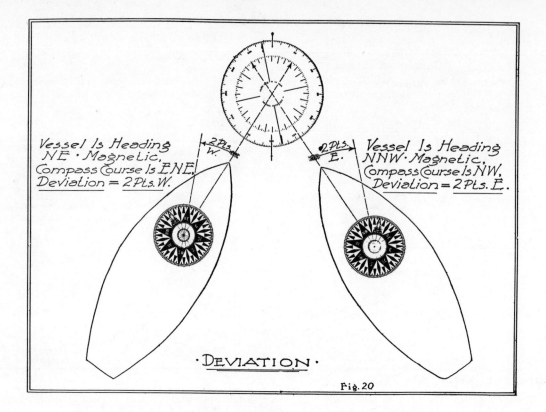

Vessel Is Heading NE · Magnetic, Compass Course Is ENE, Deviation = 2 Pts. W.

2 Pts. W.

2 Pts. E.

Vessel Is Heading NNW · Magnetic, Compass Course Is NW, Deviation = 2 Pts. E.

·DEVIATION·

Fig. 20

DEVIATION—HOW TO FIND IT
AND HOW TO
ALLOW FOR IT

D EVIATION is not constant on a vessel but varies with the boat's heading. The reasons for this are simple. A compass is subject not only to the earth's magnetic field but also to that of the vessel aboard which it is placed. The magnetic field of the boat may be considered as concentrated in one large magnet in a specific position with respect to the compass. In the figures, this magnet is assumed to be located at C.M.A. (Center of Magnetic Attraction) and it will have a definite effect upon the vessel's compass. It is further assumed that C.M.A. has its own north pole towards the vessel's bow and its south pole towards her stern.

It is characteristic of magnets that like poles repel and unlike poles attract each other. Poles of magnets are names for those poles of the earth towards which they tend to be attracted, hence all so-called north poles of magnets are possessed of a magnetism unlike that of the earth's north pole and like that of its south pole, while all so-called south poles of magnets are possessed of a magnetism like

that of the earth's north magnetic pole and unlike that of its south. If two magnets are brought in proximity they will attract each other only if their unlike poles are brought together; if their like poles are brought together they will repel each other. In the figures the magnet C.M.A. is fixed on the boat; therefore its field is fixed. Its forward end or north pole will tend to attract the south poles of any magnets in its field and at the same time to repel the north poles of any such magnets.

In Figure 21 the vessel is heading north magnetic.

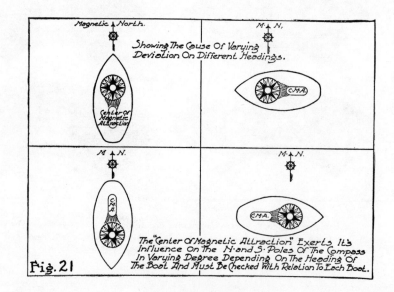

Magnetic North.

M. N.

Showing The Cause Of Varying Deviation On Different Headings.

Center Of Magnetic Attraction

C.M.A.

M. N.

M. N.

C.M.A.

C.M.A.

The "Center Of Magnetic Attraction" Exerts Its Influence On The N· and S· Poles Of The Compass In Varying Degree Depending On The Heading Of The Boat And Must Be Checked With Relation To Each Boat.

Fig. 21

The north point of the compass (possessed of a magnetism unlike that of the earth's north magnetic pole) is attracted by the earth's north magnetic pole, being at the same time repelled by the north of the magnet C.M.A. At the same time the south-seeking, or south pole of the compass is attracted not only by the earth's south pole but by the closely proximate north pole of the magnet C.M.A. Thus when the vessel is on this heading the forces of the earth's field and that of the vessel coincide and there is no deviation of the compass.

If C.M.A. were non-existent no change in the position of the compass needle would be apparent for any heading of the boat. The boat could be headed in any direction, the compass needle would remain absolutely stationary and the lubber line of the compass move around the stationary card to indicate the actual magnetic heading of the boat. But as the position of the magnet C.M.A. relative to that of the compass needle is changed with each change in the vessel's heading, its effect on the compass needle is likewise changed and the needle or card instead of remaining still, deviates from its original position and takes up a new one. When the boat heads west, magnetic, as in Figure 21, the compass needle is subject to the same forces as before, but that of

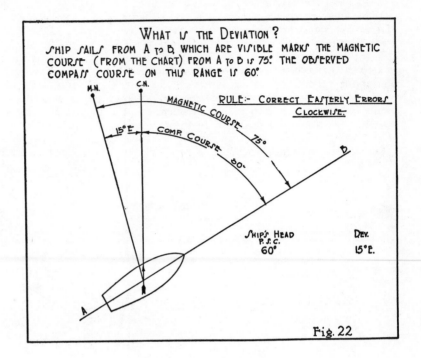

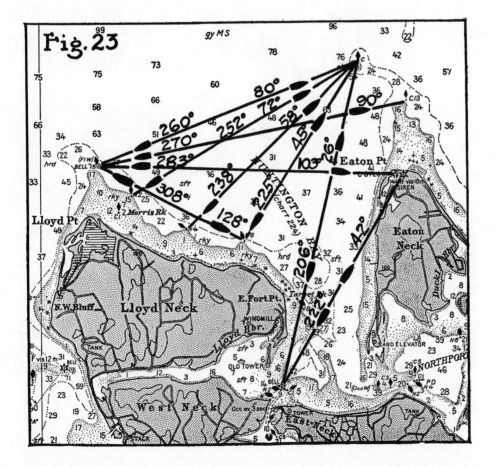

Figure 23. A series of easily located courses which can be sailed to determine compass deviation on these headings

275

C.M.A. is applied from a different direction. The north pole of the magnet C.M.A. attracts the south of the compass and repels the compass north, tending as before to force the compass to take up a position such that its axis is in line with the fore-and-aft line of the ship, while the earth's magnetism tends to keep the compass in line with the magnetic meridian, which in this heading is athwartship. As a result of these two forces the compass needle takes up an intermediate position as shown and the compass has a westerly deviation on this heading.

When the vessel heads east magnetic as in Figure 21 the same forces are again acting on the compass needle but that of C.M.A. is applied from a still different direction. The force of C.M.A. still tends to keep the north point of the compass in the direction of the vessel's bow, which is now to the eastward. Again the combination of the two forces results in the compass card taking an intermediate position, this time with its north to the eastward of magnetic north, resulting in an easterly deviation.

On the heading south magnetic (Figure 21) the magnet C.M.A. still tends to keep the north point of the compass card toward the boat's bow. The earth's force directs the compass north towards the stern of the vessel and the compass card once more takes up an intermediate position, this time with a westerly deviation.

Thus it is seen that in the case of this vessel, deviation is zero when the vessel heads north, magnetic; it is easterly when she heads east magnetic, and westerly when she heads west or south magnetic. If the magnet flux of the boat could actually be resolved into the equivalent of the one magnet C.M.A., it could be neutralized by placing a magnet of like strength in the position of C.M.A. with its poles in the opposite direction to those of C.M.A. It is not practical to do this, but since the magnetic flux or power of a magnet varies inversely as the square of its distance from the point of affectation, small magnets placed close to the compass will neutralize the effect of very much larger ones which are more remote. Small compensating magnets of this type are generally all that is necessary to reduce the deviation on small yacht compasses to a very small factor. Properly placed by one skilled in this practice, these compensating magnets will reduce the deviation to zero in three quadrants and leave not over three or four degrees in the fourth.

Without going into a technical discussion as to the reasons therefor, it may be stated that since motor boats are principally constructed of wood the deviations of the compass do not change in value for changes in the latitude of the vessel, and hence whether or not the compass is compensated it is not a difficult matter for the small boat operator to determine the deviation of the compass for different headings, tabulate them, and provided he makes no changes in the magnetic

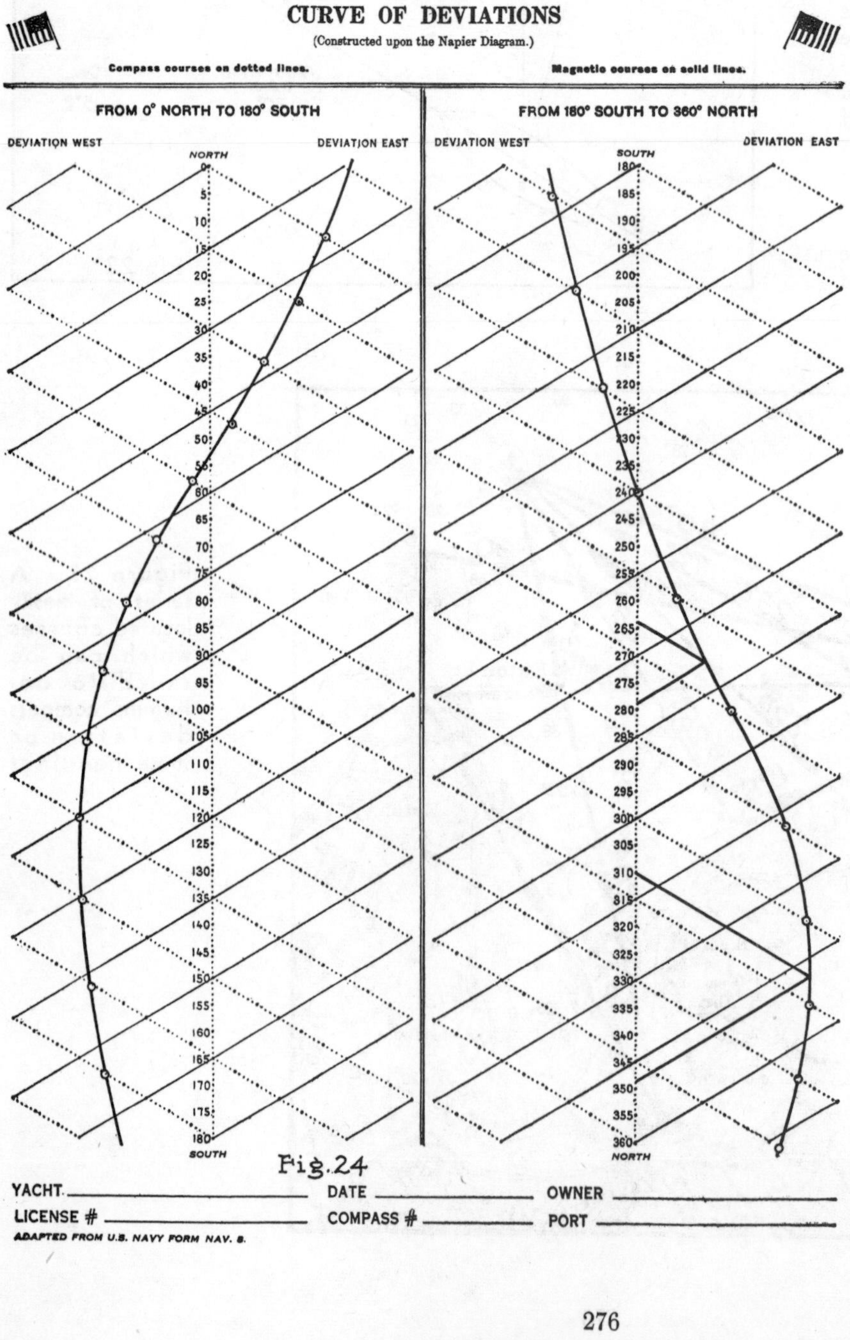

CURVE OF DEVIATIONS
(Constructed upon the Napier Diagram.)

Compass courses on dotted lines.   Magnetic courses on solid lines.

FROM 0° NORTH TO 180° SOUTH   FROM 180° SOUTH TO 360° NORTH

DEVIATION WEST   DEVIATION EAST   DEVIATION WEST   DEVIATION EAST

Fig. 24

YACHT_____ DATE _____ OWNER _____
LICENSE # _____ COMPASS # _____ PORT _____
ADAPTED FROM U.S. NAVY FORM NAV. 8.

Figure 24. The Napier diagram affords a quick and convenient means of reading the deviation on any heading

Figure 25. Another form of deviation card showing in the outer rose the magnetic directions connected to the corresponding compass directions on the inner rose

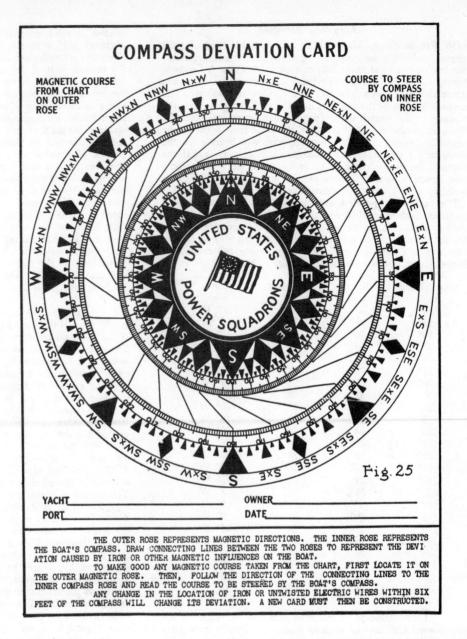

COMPASS DEVIATION CARD

MAGNETIC COURSE
FROM CHART
ON OUTER
ROSE

COURSE TO STEER
BY COMPASS
ON INNER
ROSE

UNITED STATES POWER SQUADRONS

Fig. 25

YACHT_____   OWNER_____
PORT_____   DATE_____

THE OUTER ROSE REPRESENTS MAGNETIC DIRECTIONS. THE INNER ROSE REPRESENTS THE BOAT'S COMPASS. DRAW CONNECTING LINES BETWEEN THE TWO ROSES TO REPRESENT THE DEVIATION CAUSED BY IRON OR OTHER MAGNETIC INFLUENCES ON THE BOAT.

TO MAKE GOOD ANY MAGNETIC COURSE TAKEN FROM THE CHART, FIRST LOCATE IT ON THE OUTER MAGNETIC ROSE. THEN, FOLLOW THE DIRECTION OF THE CONNECTING LINES TO THE INNER COMPASS ROSE AND READ THE COURSE TO BE STEERED BY THE BOAT'S COMPASS.

ANY CHANGE IN THE LOCATION OF IRON OR UNTWISTED ELECTRIC WIRES WITHIN SIX FEET OF THE COMPASS WILL CHANGE ITS DEVIATION. A NEW CARD MUST THEN BE CONSTRUCTED.

structure of the vessel and her fittings, have a permanent deviation table suitable for use anywhere. Deviation is the angle between the magnetic meridian and the compass needle. Determination of deviation merely requires the observation of the position of the compass magnet or card at a time when the direction of the magnetic meridian is known.

This may be done in many ways, but probably the simplest from the standpoint of the average motor boat man are those of running ranges or crossing a range on different headings. Both these methods involve the selection of visible objects, whose positions are clearly marked on a chart, from which the magnetic direction of the range may be determined. Figure 22 illustrates the determination of deviation by sailing such a range. A and B are two visible objects. From the chart the range AB or the magnetic course from A to B is found to be 75°. The vessel starts from a point near A and heads for B, keeping AB on the boat's fore and aft line, being directed on this course not by compass but by steering directly for B. While on this course, the course indicated by the compass is found to be 60°. The difference between the compass course (60°) and the magnetic course (75°) is 15°. Conversion from a compass to a magnetic course is *correcting,* the error of 15° must be applied to the compass course of 60° in a

clockwise direction in order to give a magnetic course of 75° and therefore by application of the rule—*correct easterly errors clockwise*—the error is 15° easterly.

Figure 23 illustrates a number of such ranges on a chart. If a boat be directed over these courses by visible observation of the marks, and her compass headings be observed on the respective courses, the deviation for each such heading may be readily determined and tabulated. The table so derived may not of necessity be of a series of stations evenly spaced from 0° around the card to 360°. It is desirable to tabulate the deviation for every 15°. This may be better accomplished by sailing across a known magnetic range and observing the compass bearing of the range each time it is crossed. The difference between the observed compass bearing of the range at each crossing and its known magnetic bearing, is the deviation of the compass for that heading of the vessel per standard compass. Our coasts abound with such ranges. It is not difficult to find such a range. Observation of the compass bearing will be rendered easier if the compass has an azimuth circle for taking bearings.

DO NOT RELY ON THE COMPASS

UNLESS YOU HAVE PREPARED AN

ACCURATE TABLE OF DEVIATIONS

Recording Deviation

Off Provincetown, Mass., there is a veritable host of such ranges. Selecting the range of the white can off Shank Painter Bar and its two land range marks, (see U. S. Coast & Geodetic Survey Chart No. 341), which bears 58° magnetic, a boat sails across this range on a calm day on a number of headings. The compass bearing of the range is noted at each crossing, as is the heading of the vessel p.s.c. (per standard compass) and the whole is tabulated. In each case the difference between the magnetic bearing and the observed compass bearing is the deviation for the particular heading. The error is east if the magnetic bearing is obtained by applying the error in a clockwise direction to the compass bearing and west if obtained by applying it in a counterclockwise direction.

The figures in the first and last columns now constitute a deviation table for this compass, for headings p.s.c. It is obvious that this particular compass has deviations much greater than would be met with in general, but this will serve very well to illustrate the importance of taking full cognizance of the change of deviation due to change of heading.

Ship's Head p.s.c.	Bearing p.s.c.	Bearing mag.	Deviation
0°	32°	58°	26° E
15°	39°	58°	19° E
30°	46°	58°	12° E
45°	53°	58°	5° E
60°	62°	58°	4° W
75°	70°	58°	12° W
90°	77°	58°	19° W
105°	82°	58°	24° W
120°	86°	58°	28° W
135°	88°	58°	30° W
150°	88°	58°	30° W
165°	86°	58°	28° W
180°	82°	58°	24° W
195°	77°	58°	19° W
210°	71°	58°	13° W
225°	65°	58°	7° W
240°	58°	58°	0°
255°	49°	58°	9° E
270°	37°	58°	21° E
285°	25°	58°	33° E
300°	20°	58°	38° E
315°	19°	58°	39° E
330°	22°	58°	36° E
345°	25°	58°	33° E

THIS table is of value in applying deviation to observed compass bearings such as might be taken in the course of general piloting, but it does not give the pilot a ready table of deviations to apply to magnetic courses to determine the courses to steer. Its use for this purpose entails a considerable amount of interpolation by trial and error methods. Suppose we wish to find the course to steer in order to make good 30° magnetic. The deviation for 30° compass cannot be applied, for this deviation (12° E, from the table) results in a compass course of 18°. This is not correct, for the deviation from the table for 18° compass is about 18° E, which applied to the compass course of 18° shows that not the required 30° but 36° magnetic is being made good. The deviation selected is too small and it becomes necessary to try various values for the deviation until one is found that may be proved correct by trial and error. It will be found ultimately that a deviation of 22° E will be the proper one to use. Then 22° E applied to 30° mag. gives a compass course of 8°. From the deviation table the deviation for 8° which is approximately midway between the stations 0° and 15° is 22° E and therefore proved the proper one to apply.

The Napier Diagram
(See Fig. 24, Page 276)

THIS tedious trial and error method may be eliminated by the construction of either a steering card or a table of deviations for magnetic headings. These may be derived easily by means of a conversion curve. The simplest of conversion curves is that constructed upon the Napier diagram. A Napier diagram is a series of equilateral triangles constructed upon both sides of a base line. The form shown is adapted from that in use by the U. S. Navy. For convenience all the sides of the triangles making a positive angle of 60° with the base line are printed as solid lines, while all those sides making a positive angle of 120° with the base line are printed as dotted lines. Since the triangles are equilateral the scale of the base line is the same as that of the sides. If the base line be laid off to a scale to represent degrees, this same scale may be applied to the inclined lines to represent a specific angle, so that a base line graduated from 0° to 360°, that is from North through East, South, West and back to North may conveniently represent the graduations of a compass card, while the deviations of the compass may be plotted for any heading, to the same scale, on one of the two lines passing through the base line at the point marked for that particular heading. Once more for convenience, the inclined lines or triangle sides are drawn through the base line every fifteen degrees of its length. In the old days when points were in common use, the base line was graduated in points and the inclined lines drawn through every point designation on the base line. In constructing the curve from a series of deviations for headings p.s.c. one is concerned only with the dotted lines. All such deviations are plotted on the dotted lines of the diagram. Easterly deviations are laid off to the right of the base line and westerly deviations to the left of the base line.

THE deviation from the table for the heading 0° p.s.c. is 26° E. On the dotted line passing through the point marked 0° on the diagram measure off a length to the right of the base line equal to 26° of the base line. Mark this point. It will be noted that for further convenience, the dotted lines are dotted every degree of their length, to the same scale as the base line, and that every fifth degree is marked a trifle more heavily than the others, so that it is very easy to locate the twenty-sixth dot from the base line on the line in question. The deviation (taken from the table) for 15° p.s.c. is 19° E. Mark the nineteenth dot on the dotted line running to the right through the scale point denoted as 15°. Proceed in a similar manner with the 30° and 45° headings. The 60° heading has a deviation of 4° W. This is laid off as before with the exception that being a westerly deviation it is measured to the left of the base line. The deviation is marked in this manner for each of the headings for which it is known, care being taken to use only the dotted lines and to mark easterly to the right and westerly to the left of the base line. A fair curve is then drawn through all these points. This is the conversion curve. It is possible that this curve will not pass immediately through every one of the points, but it will be sufficiently close to render any error in its position negligible. The curve is of great value.

Just as the length of the dotted line intercepted between the curve and the base line on a specific heading represents, to the scale of the base line, the deviation for that heading p.s.c., so does the length of any solid line intercepted between the curve and the base line on a specific heading, represent, to the same scale, the deviation for that heading magnetic. It becomes immediately obvious that the deviation for the magnetic heading 30° if measured with dividers, is 22° and its direction is East.

Using the Napier Diagram

FROM the Napier diagram the exact deviation for any heading, compass or magnetic, may be secured by measuring the length of the dotted or solid line passing through the point on the scale representing the heading, and the curve. Furthermore the compass course corresponding to a given magnetic course, may be readily obtained. A line is drawn from the point on the base line corresponding to the magnetic course, to the curve, parallel to the solid line. From this intersection a second line is drawn back to the base line, parallel to the dotted line. The point of intersection between the second line and the base line, indicates the compass course.

To find a magnetic course corresponding to a given compass course, a line is drawn from the point on the base line corresponding to the compass course, to the curve and parallel to the dotted line. From this intersection a second line is drawn back to the base line parallel to the solid line, intersecting the base line at the point which indicates the required magnetic course.

To make good a magnetic course of 279° the ship must steer 264°. This is secured by drawing through the point marked 279° a line parallel to the solid or magnetic course lines. From the point where this line intersects the curve another line is drawn parallel to the dotted or compass course lines. This line, it will be observed, cuts the base line at the course to steer, which is 264°.

A lighthouse is observed dead ahead bearing 310° p.s.c. Its magnetic bearing (349°) is easily found from the diagram in the following manner. The compass bearing (310°) is first located on the base line. A line is then drawn from this point to the curve parallel to the dotted line. From this intersection a line is drawn back to the base line, parallel to the solid line. The second plotted line meets the base line at 349°, the required magnetic bearing.

The Deviation Card

Now it will not be found convenient to be constantly referring to a Napier diagram and its graphic method of solution, but the deviations for magnetic headings may be taken off the diagram in the manner just illustrated, from the solid lines and a table made such as the one which follows:

Ship's Head Magnetic	Devi- ation	Steer p.s.c.
0°	37° E	323°
15°	32° E	343°
30°	22° E	8°
45°	9.5° E	35.5°
60°	9° W	69°
75°	21° W	96°
90°	27° W	117°
105°	30° W	135°
120°	30° W	150°
135°	29° W	164°
150°	25° W	175°
165°	22° W	187°
180°	17.5° W	197.5°
195°	14° W	209°
210°	10° W	220°

Ship's Head Magnetic	Devi- ation	Steer p.s.c.
225°	5° W	230°
240°	0°	240°
255°	5° E	250°
270°	11° E	259°
285°	18° E	267°
300°	25° E	275°
315°	32° E	283°
330°	36° E	294°
345°	39° E	306°

The column headed "Steer, p.s.c." gives the compass course to steer to make good the corresponding desired magnetic course. Once the deviations for magnetic headings have been secured a deviation diagram such as has already appeared in these columns may be constructed. (See Introduction to Navigation, W. M. Angas) or a card of the type illustrated may be used. The outer rose represents magnetic courses and the inner rose the corresponding compass courses to steer. Lines are drawn connecting corresponding courses, having been derived from the original table and the second table of deviation for magnetic headings. Any desired course may be secured at a glance, the interpolation between stations involving very little chance of error, whether the card or the two deviation tables are used.

It is obvious that the compass used in this little discussion is woefully uncompensated, and that one might search diligently for a long time to find a boat whose compass had such gross deviational errors, but this was intentionally selected with a view to emphasizing the ease with which deviation may be determined and the general simplicity of the methods of procedure.

NOTE.—In the deviation table given on the preceding page, it will be noted that the magnetic bearing of the range is given as 58°. If an average of all bearings p.s.c. be taken by dividing their sum (1,359°) by the number of observations (24), it will be found that the average bearing p.s.c. is 56.63° or, taking it to the nearest degree, 57°. If it were possible in a practical way to make all observations with absolute precision, this average would probably agree exactly with the magnetic bearing. In other words, from a purely theoretical angle, the sum of the bearings p.s.c. and the sum of the magnetic bearings would be equal.

COMPENSATING COMPASSES ON YACHTS

A YACHT that has been compensated for deviation gives its owner an added sense of security whenever he is compelled to use the compass at night or in a fog. It relieves the pilot of considerable mathematical gymnastics and he does not have to worry as to whether or not he has applied his deviation in the wrong direction. There are less than a dozen men in the country who are recognized as expert ship compass adjusters. Their charges are usually approximately $50.00 and it is $50.00 well spent by the yachtsman.

There are many times, however, when the yachtsman is a long way from a port where a competent compass adjuster might be found. The yachtsman is then compelled to either adjust his own compass or to swing the ship and construct a deviation table or a Napier diagram.

The time when a yachtsman needs his compass is usually during a fog or on a night run when he certainly has enough mental hazards to confront him without the worry of applying deviation, and deviation applied in the wrong direction is worse than no correction at all.

For the past twenty years, the writer has used a system of adjusting yacht compasses that can do the trick in far less time than it would take to compute a deviation table. It requires no pelorus or instrument of any kind. It requires no mental gymnastics, no calculation or computations. In fact, this system is so simple that it seems ridiculous that it has not come into widespread use among small boat owners.

This system of compensating compasses was originally devised by Major William E. Hoke, of the Maryland Yacht Club, over a quarter of a century ago. There are only one or two fundamental rules to follow and accuracy is guaranteed. The error is read directly on the compass card. The reading is corrected and the final work is easily checked so that there could be no chance of an unknown error.

We will assume that we are going to adjust the compass on a standard 35-foot stock model cruiser of the conventional type. Our first step is to purchase from some marine supply house, compass or nautical instrument establishment two compensating magnets. These consist of several small magnetized steel rods within a brass tube. Some are marked N for the north end; others are colored red for the north end and blue for the south end. Marine hardware stores usually charge about $1.00 apiece. Compass adjusters who make them up to order usually charge about $3.00 each.

Only two magnets will be required for our cruiser and, sometimes, only one will be necessary. The next thing we will need is a stack of old newspapers consisting of about a dozen or more of the average daily newspapers, a ball of twine, and a handful of old washers, bolts or discarded spark plugs. Half a dozen copper tacks or copper staples for attaching the magnets to the boat will complete the list of things that we need before shoving off from the dock. To use this method, it is not even necessary to have a chart on board.

We cruise out into the harbor until we find a buoy with a clear path and sufficient water so that we could make a run from the buoy either to the north or to the south and another run either to the east or to the west. If possible, this buoy should be away from busy harbor traffic so that other boats may not interfere with our maneuvers. While we are en route to the buoy, we will take one of the daily papers and wad it up into a roll about as large as a basket ball. We will tie a string around this large ball of loosely wadded newspapers and leave about three feet of cord, to the end of which we will attach one of the discarded washers, bolts or spark plugs. We will be careful to see that everything is in its place that would be on an ordinary cruise. Of course, we will see that the magnets that we intend to use are far enough away from the compass so as not to affect the compass card

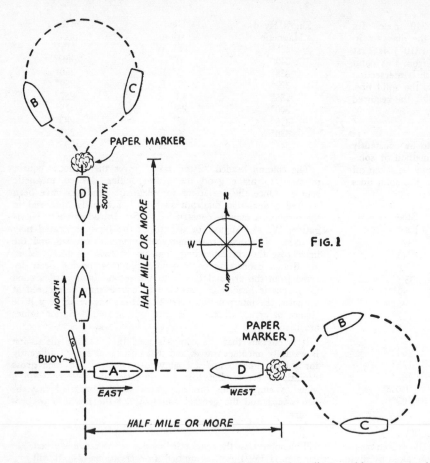

PAPER MARKER

HALF MILE OR MORE

FIG. 1

PAPER MARKER

HALF MILE OR MORE

during our first maneuvers. Naturally, we will also see that all hammers, tools, and junk are not close to the compass.

Arriving at the buoy, if we intend to use a course north of the buoy, approach the buoy from the south. We will pass the buoy as close as we dare without taking any paint off the side of our little ship. Having cleared the buoy, we will steer north, by the uncorrected compass. The helmsman will be instructed to keep his eyes glued to the binnacle and hold the boat on this north compass course. We will continue on this north compass course for possibly three-quarters of a mile or more. In fact, we will hold the course just as long as we can clearly see the buoy which we originally passed. When we decide that we have run far enough, we will toss over the stern and clear of the wake, one of our newspaper balls with its string and sinker attached.

As soon as this is done, the helmsman will immediately turn quickly to the left as in position B, figure 1. Then, he will throw the helm hard over and make a complete right-hand turn, coming around to position C in figure 1. As soon as he spots the floating paper ball, he will head directly for it, run it down and pass over it. The ball, being made of paper, will not hurt the propeller. The sinker, while not heavy enough to drag the paper ball under, is heavy enough to keep the wind from moving the paper during the short space of time that it takes our cruiser to make its complete turn.

Having crossed the paper ball and in position D, the helmsman will immediately steer directly for the buoy that he originally left. When he is headed directly for this buoy, the compass should read 180 degrees, or due South, provided there was no deviation on board our cruiser to affect the compass.

We will assume that instead of reading 180 degrees as the compass should, that the compass card showed a reading of 200 degrees at the lubber line. In that case, in order to adjust our compass, we must remove 10 degrees of this 20-degree error. With the helmsman still heading directly for the buoy and paying no attention to the compass on the return trip, an assistant will take one of the magnets and place it in position A, as shown in figure 2. If the magnet increases the error and causes the compass card to swing toward 210, then the adjuster should immediately turn the magnet end for end which will swing the compass card back to the left of the 200-degree point.

Placing the magnet closer to the compass as in C, figure 2, will swing the compass card further to the left of 200. In position D, it will swing the card back towards 200. We will place the magnet at A, C, or D at the point where the compass card will show 190 degrees at the lubber line. At this point, we will lightly tack the copper tacks or staples to hold the magnet in place.

Returning to the buoy where we started, we will pass the buoy, swing around and repeat the operation, using a second paper ball. This time, when we cross the paper ball and have headed back to the buoy, if we did our work correctly during the first maneuver, the compass card should read due South or 180 degrees.

We will assume, however, that we were a little careless on the first maneuver or the helmsman was a little nervous and as a result, on this second maneuver, instead of the compass reading due South or 180 degrees, that the compass read instead 178 degrees. In this case, we have reduced the deviation on a north and south run from ten degrees to one degree. By moving our magnet a hair's breadth away from the compass, we will be able to take out this remaining one degree and a third trip over this north and south run will undoubtedly show that there is no error whatsoever remaining.

There are only two rules we must remember in this operation and they are: when correcting the compass error on a north and south run, the magnet *must* be placed in position A or if there is not sufficient room at position A then at position A', on the opposite side of the compass. Placing the magnet at B will have no effect on the compass on a north and south run. Another thing to remember is that the middle of the magnet *must* be on the fore-and-aft line passing through the middle of the compass. This fore-and-aft line of the middle of the compass is, of course, parallel to the keel. The magnet must not be placed off center as shown in position E, figure 2.

It is a very good idea before starting the maneuvers to mark this fore-and-aft line and athwartship line in chalk. If you will always remember that the magnets must be at right angles to the fore-and-aft line for north and south runs and must be at right angles to the athwartship line on west or east runs, and that the center of the magnets must be on their respective lines, then you will have no trouble in compensating a compass by this method.

Having removed the compass error from the north and south runs, we will approach the buoy from the west and repeat the entire procedure by running to the eastward, dropping our paper ball marker and returning to the buoy. If, on the return run, there is no error in our compass on an east and west run, then the compass should read 270 degrees. If, however, it should read

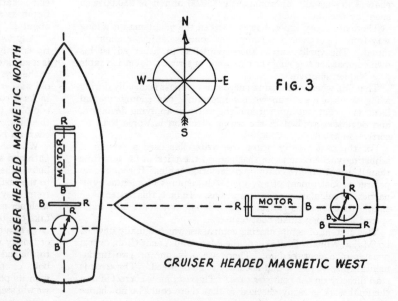

FIG. 3

CRUISER HEADED MAGNETIC NORTH

CRUISER HEADED MAGNETIC WEST

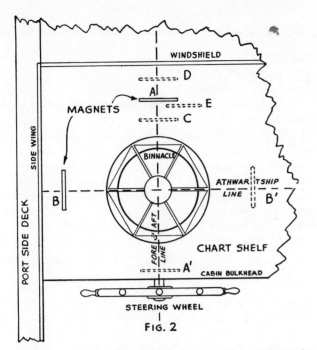

In the illustration above, note that A and A' are athwartship magnets (placed in the fore and aft line). Magnets B and B' are fore and aft magnets (placed in the athwartship line)

FIG. 2

THIS same principle of compass correction has been used by large steamships where the nature of the cargo has upset the arrangement of the compensating magnets. For example: we will assume that we are on a large steamship off the Jersey Coast and that we have determined that Barnegat Light Ship is 230 degrees magnetic, distance 45 miles. We will also assume there was no light ship or buoy or object in the vicinity. We determined our position by celestial observation and we know that our compass is considerably out of adjustment because of our cargo.

In this case, we would put our ship temporarily on the reverse course of 230 degrees or 50 degrees and would throw over the taffrail an empty barrel or vegetable crate. After running on the reverse course of 50 degrees for a short distance, we would throw overboard another crate or barrel, make a complete turn, pass over the last crate or barrel thrown overboard and head directly for the first one. If there was no deviation in the ship, the compass would show the correct course of 230 degrees.

We will assume that instead our ship's compass shows a compass reading of 250 degrees. Then half-way between 250 degrees and 230 degrees or 240 degrees would be the correct magnetic course that we want, and after passing over the original buoy or crate, we would continue and instruct the helmsman to steer a course of 240 degrees per ship's compass which would be equivalent to a magnetic course of 230 degrees. If our speed was ten knots, we would expect to hit Barnegat Light Ship right on the nose four and a half hours later.

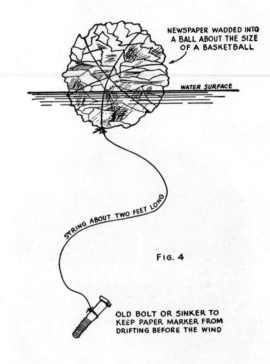

FIG. 4

276 degrees, then we will so arrange our magnet that it will read 273 degrees and we will check our work as explained in the north and south maneuvers.

If there is not sufficient water for us to run north from the buoy, we can, of course, run south from the buoy and the same applies on the east and west runs. The entire operation may require anywhere from thirty minutes to two hours. With a helmsman who can hold a steady compass course, one can usually take out all of the error on either return trip on the first return trip, and often half a mile is a sufficient distance to run. At other times, in a stubborn case, it may take three or four runs before all of the error has been removed.

On the modern stock cruiser of today, most of the error is found on the east and west runs and very little error is found on the north and south runs. Figure 3 shows the relative position of the motors, the magnets and the compass on both north and west runs. The letter R indicates the north end, or red end of the compass or magnet, and B indicates the south or blue end of the compass or magnet. Remember that opposites attract; that the blue end of the magnet will attract the red end of the compass and repel the blue end. When the magnet is first placed in position, if the error as shown on the compass card is increased instead of corrected, it is only necessary to reverse the ends of the magnet.

Compass Adjustment on Large Vessels

The compensation of a compass on a large vessel is a complex matter, to be undertaken only by an expert skilled in this specialized field. It involves correction of such errors as semi-circular deviation, heeling error, etc. The latter, as the name implies, is caused when a vessel heels. To offset the effect of vertical iron in a vessel, causing semi-circular deviation, a compass adjuster uses flinders bars of soft iron, placing them vertically near the compass. Quadrantal spheres are the hollow balls of soft iron placed to port and starboard of the compass to correct for quadrantal deviation. Those wishing a detailed discussion of the subject are referred to Dutton's *Navigation and Nautical Astronomy*.

Adjust Your Compass

*You can count on your compass
if it is accurate; if it isn't,
here's what to do*

By ROBERT C. BEARD
(Former Professional Compass Adjuster)

Two hundred degrees!
Mr. Dumhed was fuming. His compass should have read due south.

Mrs. Dumhed came over to see what the shouting was about. "Look, Martha!" I just paid a compass adjuster forty-five bucks to guarantee me one degree accuracy on this blasted compass, and look, there it is, almost twenty degr—."

He stopped short, his eyes wide like dinner plates. The compass was reading due south. He took a swig from the beer can in his hand and looked again. Still south. He gulped the rest of his beer and slammed the can down where it had been a few moments before—alongside the compass. "This damn thing is making a fool of me!"

And it was. Even as he stared at the compass, it began to swing west again, silently, defiantly, until it came to rest at two hundred degrees. Dumhed blinked, and opened another beer.

This little incident might actually have happened, as have many more like it. Beer cans are often steel, and many yachtsmen drive their craft with the wheel in one hand and a beer can in the other. May I recommend the old-fashioned bottle? Glass is non-magnetic.

Right now, before you begin a new season, take a long look at your compass. Consider what it means to you. Out in the blue, you won't find white lines to mark your road, and often the next buoy won't be visible. You may follow charted courses from buoy to buoy, and a little uncalculated compass deviation will be of minor consequence as long as the water is deep and the weather fair. If you miss a marker, you can find it with the glasses and get back on course. But how about night runs? And what if a fog purrs in? Will you be able to spot your buoy then? Suppose you are running a narrow channel in shallow water. A small amount of deviation may put you aground. For example, a four-degree error will set you about 370 feet off course for every mile traveled.

Nor need you be on a cruise to depend on an accurate compass. Suppose you are anchored just half a mile from shore, catching the kind of fish you won't have to lie about. Suddenly, in rolls one of those pea-soup fogs. You can wait for it to pass, staying put, perhaps, past nightfall when the fog may vanish in a strong wind. If you have a poor compass, or none at all, you're in trouble. And the smaller your boat, the bigger your trouble. Obviously the safety of your boat depends heavily upon the accuracy of your compass.

Magnetic compass theory basically is simple. The "north-seeking" pole of the magnetized compass needle is constantly attracted toward the North magnetic pole of the earth. The case in which the needle is freely mounted can be turned in any direction and the needle will continue to point North. So you mount the whole thing in a boat and think you have a reliable direction indicator. And you have, but with complications.

The practical application of the compass is more complex than the basic theory on which it operates. The actual amount of magnetic force present to keep the compass needle pointed north is extremely small. Anything magnetic, or made of some magnetic material (iron or steel) that is placed in the vicinity of the compass will (Continued on next page) influence the compass needle so that it will no longer point to the magnetic north pole. The engine, steering gear and tachometer cables are often bad offenders, but let me point out some other common culprits that are seldom considered.

Recently a doctor-boatman asked me to compensate his compass. Now the doctor, a sort of do-it-himselfer, had installed in his cabin a remote speaker from his bridge-mounted radiotelephone. The speaker was mounted directly under the wheelhouse. There was no use trying to correct the compass with the speaker in that position, because every loudspeaker contains a powerful magnet.

With the speaker relocated in the cabin, I set about correcting the compass, only to find it "locked" to the boat. Whichever way we turned the boat, the compass needle followed instead of pointing north. Tests with a small magnet showed that the tachometer cable, steering wheel and steering column were highly magnetized inside the wheelhouse. They had received from the loudspeaker an induced magnetic field, retained even after the speaker was removed. I demagnetized these parts and was then able to correct the compass.

In another case I was asked to recheck a compass that had been adjusted by someone else six months before. The owner said it had been "acting funny lately." When we turned the boat the compass locked in and followed for almost 180 degrees; then it popped loose and swung back about 100 degrees. When we turned in the opposite direction, the compass again locked in at one point and repeated the performance. After a couple of hours with no success in cancelling or even locating the offending magnetic field, I overheard the owner mentioning that he had recently remodeled the head. It was located directly beneath the compass area. A few questions elicited the fact that he had replaced his old plastic medicine cabinet with an enameled steel one. It required only the removal of four screws to get the new cabinet out of the head, whereupon the compass returned to normal.

A Mr. Bentleg (the names are fictitious, the facts are not) called one day to announce that he would not pay my compass compensation bill until I removed eight degrees of error which he and a Navy-Commander friend had observed during a weekend cruise. I had guaranteed less than one degree of deviation. When I boarded his boat for a recheck I promptly moved a radio direction finder that was near the compass a few feet away. It had not been there when I did the compensation. This restored Mr. Bentleg's compass to one degree accuracy. Remember the doctor's remote speaker? Well, RDF's as well as all radios contain loudspeakers which have powerful magnets. *(Keep all radio equipment well away from your compass—at least 3 feet.)*

Mr. Zilch complained that I did a poor job on his compass. His had been a tough one, but, when finished, it was within my one degree standard. I rechecked and found that a six-degree error did indeed appear on two headings. The appearance of a new deviation such as this invariably indicates that a new magnetic influence has been introduced or else someone has tampered with the compass adjustments. I began searching for changes. This led me to the galley, located in this boat directly below the compass station. On a bulkhead was a magnetic knife holder. I removed it, rechecked the compass and found it working properly.

You can compensate your own compass by any of several methods, and achieve reasonably good results. It's easier, of course, to have a professional compensator do it, but one is not always available. And then, too, it's cheaper to do it yourself. Fees vary from $30 to $60 for 60-foot and smaller boats (if the charge is higher I consider it excessive; if it is less, check out the person's competence). Let's take a step-by-step look at correcting a compass.

First, consider the lubberline. No amount of compass correction will put you on course if the lubberline (the vertical line on the forward inner side of the compass bowl) is not parallel to the keel of your boat. To check it, find the beam center of your boat on a line across the compass. Then measure the distance from the center of the compass to the beam center. Now find the beam center across the stern rail or transom and mark the spot that is the same distance from beam center as is the compass. Stretch a string between this spot and the lubberline. This string is parallel to the keel. With one eye, sight along the string toward the compass so that the lubberline is hidden from your sight behind the string. Now observe the center-pin on the compass card. It should also be under the string. If it appears to one side of the string the compass must be turned slightly until both lubberline and center-pin are in line with the string. When this is accomplished tighten the compass securely.

Now look around the compass. Is all equipment in its proper place? Stow any tools, hardware and so on that is around the compass. See that there are no magnetic knife holders or loudspeakers within several feet of the compass in any direction, including straight down! And turn off all electrical equipment which is *not always used when cruising.*

The simplest compass check you can make is to run charted ranges. But the odds are you will have no one location with enough ranges to check all compass points. Since your compass can be accurate on some headings and off on others, we will not be satisfied with range running. Let's proceed to method two, a clever technique devised years ago by Major W. E. Hoke of the Maryland Y. C. (See also pp. 279-281.) Get two compensating magnets. These are slender magnets about two inches long encased in a chrome-plated tube with a mounting hole at each end. You will need some tiny brass wood screws for the mounting. Then gather some newspapers, a ball of string and a few light weights like bolts, washers or discarded spark plugs. Cruise to a buoy having deep enough water for your boat for at least a half mile in all directions. The right spot should have little or no current flow, and the day should be windless and calm to minimize drift error. Using the newspapers, make several loosely formed paper wads about the size of a beach ball. Tie each one so it will hold its shape, and let about three feet of string dangle from it. To the end of each string attach a weight.

Approach the buoy from the south, passing it closely with your compass pointing exactly north. Hold that course for about a half mile. At this point ask your assistant to drop one of the floats over the stern and clear of the wake. Immediately turn your boat 180 degrees as to run down the float, passing directly over it with your bow headed for the buoy. If your compass is correct, it will read exactly 180 degrees, or south. Let's assume it is reading 200 degrees instead. Since reversing your course doubles the magnetic error, your actual compass error is one half that indicated, or 10 degrees. While continuing your course for the buoy, ask your assistant to place one of the magnets athwartships about one foot forward of the compass and exactly on the compass centerline. He should then gradually move the magnet closer until the compass needle reads 190 degrees. If the needle swings the wrong way, he must swing the magnet ends around. When the proper location has been reached, secure the magnet to the surface with a strip of adhesive tape. When you reach the buoy, come about and repeat the run north. If you were careful the first time, your compass will read exactly south on the return leg to the buoy. If it is still a few degrees off, move the magnet slightly forward or aft as needed to remove *half* the indicated error while the boat's course is held dead on the buoy. If a third check shows that you have corrected the north-south run, screw the magnet into place, being careful not to move it. The smallest shift will re-introduce a change into the compass reading.

Now do the same for east and west headings. Run east from the buoy for about half a mile, drop a float, turn and cruise over the float while heading for the buoy. If on the return run the needle does not point exactly west, remove half the error by placing the other magnet on either side of the compass, on its centerline, and parallel to the lubberline. As before, start from about a foot from the compass, and slowly decrease the distance until the correction is gotten. Do not screw the magnet into place until by rechecking you know that all error is gone.

Although you cannot correct errors that may exist on inter-cardinal headings yourself, it is well to know if there are any. To do so, make the same buoy-and-float checks for NE-SW runs and for NW-SE runs. Record any errors on a card that will be kept near the compass, remembering again that the actual error is *half* the error indicated on the return run. Use this deviation card when cruising courses on or near the inter-cardinal headings. For courses between the inter-cardinal and cardinal points, simply prorate the error. If you have no error on east and ten degrees of error on NE, for example, you will have five degrees of error on ENE. (Be sure to note whether the deviation is plus or minus.) Most wooden boats have negligible inter-cardinal deviation once the compass has been compensated. Steel hulls, however, pose a different and much more complex problem. If your boat is steel-hulled, and you have considerable inter-cardinal deviation, it may be necessary to install iron balls on each side of your compass. This is a job for the professional compensator.

The Darrach method of compass correction is method three on your list. It uses the course reversal basis also, but instead of a buoy and paper float it employs a sun-shadow instrument to show exact course reversal. This gimballed device has a vertical center-pin whose shadow falls onto a horizontal disc, the outer edge of which is calibrated in degrees. On a sunny day you simply head your boat north (you do not need a buoy for a starting point) by compass and set the instrument so the pin-shadow falls on zero degrees. Then turn the boat south according to the shadow reading, and note your compass heading. If it shows 180 degrees, your compass is okay. If it shows, say, 190 degrees, you have a five degree error. As with Hoke's method, the Darrach instrument indicates twice the actual error. One major advantage of the sun-shadow method is that neither wind nor current affect your readings.

After the four cardinal points have been corrected, put your boat on a north heading with the instrument shadow on zero degrees. Now slowly turn the boat through a full 360 degree circle. Your assistant will watch the sun instrument and call all the compass points as the shadow crosses them. You as a third person watch the compass and, if there is any deviation, this cross-check will point it up immediately, revealing what course to steer for any given magnetic heading.

If your compass has such large errors that the small magnets will not make the needed correction, or if the compass needle is magnetically locked to the boat even though you have taken all the precautions I have described, this means that a strong magnetic field exists nearby. The first suspects are the steering mechanism and tachometer cables. To test these and other objects for magnetism, I use a .001″ machinists thickness gauge. This is a paper-thin strip of steel about six inches long, one-half inch wide and a mere one one-thousandth of an inch thick. I touch one end of it to the suspected part, then gently pull away. If there is any magnetism present the end of the thin steel will stick to the magnetic part. Open the wheel housing to test all metal parts there.

When the offending part has been located, you can demagnetize it by borrowing from an electronics service shop either his color TV degaussing coil or his magnetic tape bulk erasing coil. Before doing any demagnetizing, *remove the compass from the boat* to prevent accidentally demagnetizing the compass needle. Connect the demagnetizing coil to the shore line. Holding it about one foot from the part to be demagnetized, turn it on and keep it on! Do not let it turn off for any reason, until this procedure is finished. Move the coil slowly toward the part until it is in contact with it. Then, still slowly, move it all over the part and around it. Finally, very slowly draw the coil away from the part for about five feet before turning it off. If your finger slipped and allowed the coil to turn off momentarily during the process, you will have 'o repeat the whole process to be sure of complete demagnetization. Replace the compass, recheck the lubberline and proceed with compensation as before.

Now that your compass is squared away, let's see what happens when you run your windshield wipers, depth sounder, running lights or any electrical device you sometimes use. Head the boat north and pick a landmark. While your helper holds a steady course by landmark, turn on the windshield wipers for about five seconds while watching the compass closely. Repeat this test several times to detect even the slightest swing of the compass that may be caused by the wipers. If there is no reaction, don't rejoice yet. Any piece of electrical gear that affects the compass will cause a maximum deviation on two (diametrically opposed) headings. Half way between these two headings there will be no deviation at all. If your compass shows no deviation on a north heading with the wipers running, it may be that the wipers are not affecting it at all. Or, it may be that north is one of their points of no effect. To test, turn your boat 90 degrees and repeat the test on east or west headings. If the operating wipers still cause no deviation, they are not affecting the compass.

If you do observe deviation on either of these trials, the next step is to slowly turn your boat and test with the wipers every 10 degrees until you find a heading on which no deviation occurs. (Seldom does this null point coincide with the cardinal headings; the odds are against it.) When you find a null, make a note of it. Then swing the boat exactly 90 degrees from the null point. Here your test will indicate maximum deviation. For example, let's say the compass swings plus 10 degrees from this point when you run the wipers. If you now turn your boat 180 degrees and repeat the test, you will observe another maximum deviation, except that it will be 10 degrees minus. Note these headings for use in plotting a deviation card by which to steer compass courses when cruising with the wipers on.

Here's a simple way to prepare a deviation card from your notes. Divide your card into two columns, with thirty-six lines and spaces in each column. Entitle column one, COMPASS COURSE DESIRED and column two, COMPASS COURSE—WIPER RUNNING. In column one on line 1 write 0 degrees; on line 2, 10 degrees; on line 3, 20 degrees, and so on until you reach 350 degrees on the bottom line. Assume that in your tests with the wiper running the null point was 40 degrees by compass. Since there was no deviation on this heading, write 40 degrees under column two on the same line which has 40 degrees written under column one. Your second null is opposite 40 degrees on the compass, 220 degrees, so write 220 degrees under column two on the same line which has 220 degrees in column one. Your points of maximum deviation were 90 degrees each way from the null points, or at 130 degrees and 310 degrees. Assuming your error was plus 10 degrees at 130, you now write 140 degrees under column two on the same line which has 130 written in column one. At 310 degrees your error was minus 10 so you now write 300 degrees in column two on the line

which has 310 degrees in column one. From this data you can prorate the errors for all other headings and complete column two.

Using the same example, you will notice that you develop 10 degrees of error as you turn from 40 degrees (no error) to 130 degrees (maximum error). Since this is a 90-degree turn, you are increasing your error by approximately 1 and 1/10 degrees for every 10 degrees you swing the boat. On line five in column two you have entered 40 degrees. On line six you can now write 51.1 degrees, on line seven, 62.2 degrees, etc. When you pass 130 degrees, the error decreases at the same rate until it is zero at 220 degrees. Opposite 140 degrees, column two will show 148.7 degrees; opposite 150 degrees, 157.8 degrees. From there to 310 degrees, the error increases again at the same rate, except that it is now "minus" and must be subtracted from the values given in column one. Column two (opposite 230 degrees) will read 228.9 degrees; (opposite 240 degrees), 237.8 degrees; etc. At 310 degrees you have your maximum deviation, 300.1 degrees. Just ignore that .1 degree computational difference; you can't steer that closely anyway. Beyond 310 degrees the error decreases again until you are back to 40 degrees. With all the calculation done, you can read directly from column two the course to be steered, with the windshield wipers running, to achieve the course shown in column one.

It is necessary to repeat all the foregoing procedures for each piece of equipment near the compass. Fortunately not many of them will throw a compass as do wipers; you may find you will have no more deviation cards to prepare. But don't take it for granted. I have seen a 12° error caused by lighting the instrument panel.

281d

COMPASS COMFORTS

A Review of the High Spots of Chapters XIII and XIV

The compass is the mariner's greatest friend. Trust it and it will be the surest means of getting you where you desire to go.

+

Don't be afraid or discouraged in your study of the compass. It can be made very simple and easily understood.

+

True, the compass has errors. These can be readily determined and will make your compass as accurate as a watch.

+

The compass is a magnet, so suspended that it will swing freely in a horizontal plane.

+

In the mariner's compass, the card with directions marked thereon (points and degrees) is attached to the magnetic needle.

+

The compass needle tends to align itself with lines of magnetic force surrounding the earth, which terminate at the North and South magnetic poles.

+

The lines of magnetic force are not straight, so the compass may point slightly east or west of the magnetic pole, depending upon your location on the earth's surface.

+

The magnetic poles are *not* coincident with the geographic poles which are located at the extreme top and bottom of the earth's sphere.

+

The magnetic north pole is located in an area somewhat north of Hudson Bay. The location of the magnetic south pole is also known.

+

A gyro-compass is mechanical. In the gyro-compass the directive forces seek the true meridians instead of the magnetic meridians as is the case of the magnetic (mariner's) compass.

+

The mariner's compass is a "wet" compass. The bowl contains a liquid, generally of water and alcohol or other special fluid. This liquids tends to "buoy-up" the card as well as dampen its movement from the effect of power plant vibration and the sea. It allows the card to turn freely as the ship is turned.

On the inside bowl is drawn a vertical black line known as the lubber line.

+

The compass must be so placed in the binnacle or on the boat that a line drawn from the center (pivot) of the compass to the lubber line, is parallel to the keel of the boat.

+

With the compass correctly placed on the boat, the lubber line will always represent the bow of the boat and will indicate the compass direction on which the boat is heading.

+

The compass card may show degrees only or points only or a combination of the two.

+

The cards on most compasses used for small boats almost always show both degrees and points.

+

The North point on the card is always marked 0° and/or North.

+

Cards are now uniformly marked clockwise from 0° at North around through 360° thus: East 90°, South 180°, West 270°, etc.

+

An older type of card was marked 0° at both North and South and 90° at both East and West.

+

While the degree method of using the compass is now pretty universal, the older point method is still used by some "old time" skippers.

+

With the point method, the compass card is divided into 32 points. The four *cardinal* points are named, North, East, South and West. All of the other points are named by using a combination of these names.

+

As the angular distance between points is large (11¼°) to make for more accurate steering, the points are further divided into quarter points.

+

Under most favorable conditions, one is a good helmsman who can keep his boat on her course within ¼ point (about

3°). Even this small error would throw you about ½ mile off your course in a 10-mile run.

+

Electric wires near a compass may affect it. If the wires are twisted the magnetic effect is reduced.

+

Your compass does not indicate "true" directions except in localities where the variation is zero (and there is no deviation).

+

Your compass does not indicate magnetic directions except in cases where the deviation is zero.

+

Deviation may be taken out of one's compass mechanically by compensation. But compensation must be done for each particular boat and with the boat on a number of headings.

+

Variation can not be removed mechanically. It is always with us. Each compass rose on the chart indicates the amount and direction of variation at that particular spot. (It will vary slightly at other localities.)

+

The two principal compass errors which must be accounted for are variation and deviation. (There are a few others but they do not amount to much.)

+

Variation results from the fact that the magnetic poles are not located at the same places on the earth as the geographical poles. As the compass tends to point to the former and as the charts and other navigation data refer to the latter, this difference or error must be accounted for.

+

The other compass error, deviation, results (mostly) from magnetic substances and electric currents on one's own boat.

+

Courses or directions referred to the geographic north are known as true courses or true directions—those referred to the magnetic poles, are magnetic courses or magnetic directions. The angular difference between these two is called variation. (Don't consider this as the correct technical definition). The amount of this variation for any particular locality is shown in the center of the compass rose on the chart.

+

Variation is not constant but changes slightly from one year to the next and from one locality to another. The chart shows the amount of the changes.

It is important to keep in mind when considering the three kinds of courses—true, magnetic and compass—that the "true" course is always the CORRECT course.

+

When working from compass and/or magnetic courses to/toward true courses, one is always CORRECTING.

+

When working from true courses to/toward magnetic and/or compass courses, and from a magnetic to a compass course one is always UNCORRECTING.

+

So, when changing from one kind of course to another, first consider whether you should CORRECT OR UNCORRECT. The rest is easy.

+

Many slogans have been suggested to help one remember the operations when Correcting and Uncorrecting. Ours is "CORRECT EASTERLY ERRORS CLOCKWISE" — "CEEC" —"Crews Eat Everything Chewable" — "Captain Eats Eggs Constantly"—"Cruisers Enjoy Ebb Current" and many more.

+

The CEEC—Correct Easterly Errors Clockwise—can be changed into the formula for meeting *every* condition of correcting and uncorrecting, with easterly or westerly errors, of variation and deviation, by *always* changing *two* and only *two* of the factors, thus—

CWECC: Correct Westerly Errors
        Counter Clockwise
UCWEC: Uncorrect Westerly Errors
        Clockwise
UCEECC: Uncorrect Easterly Errors
        Counter Clockwise

+

If you are working from a compass course to a true one, you are CORRECTING. Your E (error) in CEEC is the algebraic sum of the deviation and variation.

+

If you are working from a magnetic course to a true one, you are CORRECTING. Your E in CEEC is the amount of the variation.

+

If you are working from a compass course to a magnetic one, you are CORRECTING. Your E in CEEC is the amount of the deviation.

+

If you are working from a true course to a compass course, you are UNCORRECTING. Your E (error) is the algebraic sum of your variation and deviation.

If you are working from a true course to a magnetic course, you are UNCORRECTING. Your E is the variation.

+

And the only other possible case is: working from a magnetic course to a compass course, you are UNCORRECTING and E (error) will be the amount of the deviation in your compass on the particular heading of the boat.

+

The latter case (above) is perhaps the most common one for you on your boat, in order to determine the course you should steer with your compass to make good a magnetic course taken from the chart. The formulae will be—

UCEECC: Uncorrect Easterly Errors
        Counter Clockwise
UCWEC: Uncorrect Westerly Errors
        Clockwise

+

The USPS, in the remarks on one of its compass lessons has the following to say (copyrighted):

"For rather obvious reasons, the geographic north pole is a standard reference point, but since this is neither a visible object, nor generally accessible, some other secondary reference is needed. Surveys have been made of the earth's magnetic field, and the magnetic meridians delineated. However, additional magnetic and electro-magnetic fields arising on our boat may alter the direction of the compass needle and thus give rise to a third reference system, the compass north. Thus any given direction may be expressed by the clockwise angular measurement from the zero or north point of one of these reference lines. It is essential that the student recognize that the true, magnetic and compass values all refer to the same direction and do not represent three different lines."

+

Magnetic Compass: This may be the dry type, with fixed card and moving needle; their general instability makes them unsuited for boat work. The wet, or mariner's, compass, has the needles attached to the card.

+

Installation: This is of course individualized for each boat, but basically must provide a usable position, with a line through the pivot and lubber line, parallel to the keel. It should be as far as possible from magnetic materials such as motors, stove, refrigerator, tools, chain, etc. Twisted wires should be used for any circuits in the binnacle.

+

Compass Errors: Variation, deviation, heeling, local attraction, lightning and magnetic storms may cause the compass to point to other than true north.

Variation: The earth, behaving as a huge magnet, with a major pole at about 73°N, 100°W, causes magnetic materials to be aligned with the magnetic field. This latter is asymmetrically related to geographic meridians—any angular difference in direction is the variation.

+

According as the magnetic meridian is inclined east or west of the geographic meridian, the variation is labeled east or west. Imaginary lines through points of zero variation are *agonic* lines, and those through places with the same variation, are *isogonic* lines.

+

Deviation: The additional magnetic and/or electro-magnetic forces arising from boat structure or equipment also exert a directing influence on the compass, often to deflect the zero from the magnetic meridian; this angular displacement is deviation. Ferrous material, whether already magnetized or not, is the causative agent. Brass, bronze, aluminum and most stainless steels are without effect.

It is most convenient to assume that all the boat forces are concentrated at one point, and the vector for this magnetic center can be combined with the earth's field to show the resultant force.

According as the north end of the compass needle is deflected east or west of the magnetic meridian, deviation is labeled east or west, similar to variation. Likewise, in order that a single rule may be used for converting, the same pattern is followed, as for variation.

+

Compass Error: As a collective item this term represents the algebraic sum of variation and deviation; this will save time in a number of problems.

+

Determination of Deviation: Since deviation is unique for each compass installation, it is necessary to check each compass for such error. Any procedure, whereby comparison can be made with a series of actual compass values and the known magnetic directions will serve to determine deviation. Ranges, reciprocal bearings, bearings on distant objects and sun azimuths may be used. Local conditions will determine which method is best suited, but the distant object method can nearly always be adapted.

+

Lightning and Magnetic Storms: If a ship is struck by lightning, any ferrous material may acquire new magnetic properties, and the deviation should be checked. Magnetic storms, although infrequent in low latitudes, may cause marked and erratic behavior of the compass.

Kay Lawrence

Above: The lighthouse is one of the pilot's principal assurances of safe navigation. Right: The lens of Kilauea Point Light

CHAPTER XV

Lighthouses, Lightships, Buoys and Other Aids to Navigation

Aids to Navigation Maintained by the United States Coast Guard. The Significance of the Coloring of Navigational Aids and of Their Light and Sound Signals. The Characteristics of Lights. The Use of Radiobeacon Signals, Range Lights, and Unlighted Aids. Intracoastal Waterway Aids.

(See color plate, page 42)

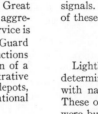

Jurisdiction

THE maintenance of aids to marine navigation is a function of the United States Coast Guard, having been placed under that organization on July 1, 1939, and consists of the maintenance of lighthouses, lightships, radiobeacons, fog signals, buoys, and beacons upon all navigable waters of the United States and its possessions; including Atlantic and Pacific Coasts of continental United States, the Great Lakes, the Mississippi River and its tributaries, Puerto Rico, the approaches to the Panama Canal, the Hawaiian Islands, and Alaska.

The chief administrative officer is the Commandant of the Coast Guard, with headquarters at Washington, D. C. Under his direction the functions of establishment, construction, maintenance, and operation of aids to navigation are carried on through administrative and engineering divisions in Washington, and by the various district offices. Because of the wide geographic distribution of aids to navigation on the seacoasts, the Great Lakes, and navigable rivers of the United States, with an aggregate coast line of over 40,000 miles, the field work of the service is carried on by district organizations. There are 11 Coast Guard districts, carrying on lighthouse work, as well as other functions of the Coast Guard. Each district is under the supervision of a commander, assisted by a suitable engineering and administrative force, and equipped with the necessary supply and buoy depots, and with suitable vessels for the maintenance of the navigational aids.

Early History

The maintenance of aids to marine navigation is one of the oldest Federal functions, the work of erecting and maintaining lighthouses being provided for at the first session of Congress by Act of August 7, 1789 (the 9th law enacted by Congress). Twelve lighthouses which had previously been built by the Colonies were ceded to the new Federal Government, and became the nucleus of a system of navigational aids which over a period of 150 years has been increased to a present total of over 29,000.

Federal maintenance of navigational aids was first carried on under the direct supervision of the Secretary of the Treasury. Somewhat later, when the duties of the Secretary of the Treasury

had greatly increased, administration of the navigational aids was delegated to the commissioner of the revenue. In 1820, the superintendence of the lighthouse establishment was assigned to the fifth auditor of the Treasury, and in 1845 again transferred, this time to the Revenue Marine Bureau, an organization which later became the Coast Guard. The collectors of customs through all this period served as local superintendents of lighthouses.

A Lighthouse Board was created in 1852, to administer the constantly expanding service, being composed of officers of the Army and Navy, and of civilian scientists. In 1903 the Lighthouse establishment was transferred from the Treasury Department to the newly created Department of Commerce, and in 1910, the Lighthouse Board was superseded by the Bureau of Lighthouses in that Department. On July 1, 1939, the Lighthouse Service was consolidated with the United States Coast Guard.

The United States Coast Guard today maintains over 29,000 aids to marine navigation. The greater number of these are lighthouses, automatic lights, and buoys. There are also about 145 radiobeacons, 31 lightship stations, and about 1,500 fog signals. The appropriations and allotments for the maintenance of these aids total about $11,000,000 annually.

Lighthouses, Their Significance to the Mariner

Lighthouses are the signal stations by means of which mariners determine their exact position. Mariners had once to be satisfied with natural landmarks, from which to obtain their bearings. These often being lacking at points where most needed, towers were built, and eventually lights were placed in many of them. The modern lighthouse represents the scientific development of this same idea, the signalling equipment being the culmination of many years of striving to overcome the limitations of visibility and audibility.

Coloring of structures. Color is applied to lighthouses and automatic light structures for the purpose of making them readily distinguishable from the background against which they are seen, and to distinguish one structure from others in the same general vicinity. Solid colors, bands of color, and various patterns are applied solely for these purposes. Minor light structures are sometimes painted black or red, to indicate the sides of the channel which they mark, following the same system used in the coloring of buoys. When so painted, red structures mark the

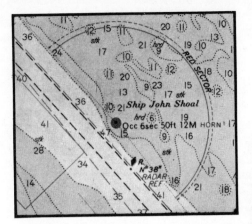

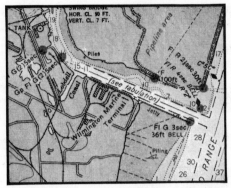

Fig. 77 (left). The light on Ship John Shoal, as it appears on the chart. According to the abbreviated description, this is a white light, occulting **every** 6 seconds, 50 feet high, visible 13 miles. A red sector covers the shoals, and the fog signal is a horn. This is one of the principal lighted aids for the ship channel in the upper part of Delaware Bay.

Fig. 78 (below, left). Twin range lights, used here to keep the mariner in the dredged channel of a river. A new type of range light uses only one lantern. When the vessel is in mid-channel, the light shows white; on the right side of the channel entering from seaward the light shows red; on the left side, green. Another type shows a fixed light in mid-channel, changing to occulting or flashing at the sides.

Fig. 79 (below). Numerous lights and other aids to navigation in the vicinity of Cape Henlopen. Lights are placed at the ends of the breakwaters to guide vessels into the Harbor of Refuge and the inner harbor. Different colors and characteristics enable the pilot to distinguish and identify them

right side of the channel, and black structures the left side of the channel, entering from seaward.

Light colors and characteristics. The colors of the lights shown from lighthouses, and their characteristics or manner in which they flash, are for the purpose of distinguishing one light from others in the general vicinity and avoiding confusion with lights used for other purposes. The length of the flashes and the intervals between may be accurately timed, and positive identification made by consulting the Light Lists. The colors of minor lights, when red or green, may also have the further significance of indicating the side of the channel which the light marks, red being on the right, and green on the left side entering from seaward.

Fog signal characteristics. Fog signals, both at lighthouses and on lightships, sound distinctive blasts. This is for the purpose of distinguishing one station from another. The characteristic of every fog signal is given in the Light Lists, and many of them are also given on the charts. All signals sound on a definite schedule, and positive identification may be made, even when the sending station is not visible, by timing the length of the blasts and the intervals between. With practice, mariners may also differentiate between the signals produced by the different types of apparatus.

Daybeacons

There are many aids to navigation which are not lighted. Structures (not buoys) of this type are called daybeacons. They vary greatly in design and construction, depending upon their location, and the distance to which they must be seen. A daybeacon may consist of a single pile with a daymark at the top, a spar with a cask at the top, a slatted tower, or a structure of masonry.

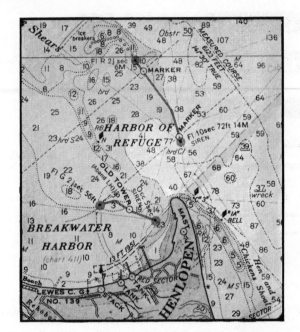

Figs. 72 to 76. Unlighted aids or daybeacons are used for marking obstructions, entrances to harbors, important turning marks in a channel, etc. There are many and various shapes used. Some may be merely a pile or stake occasionally with a pointer indicating the channel. Others are timber structures carrying a target or some characteristic feature. Others are iron or steel spindles with a barrel or cage work at the top. Some types are monuments of stone. Some are strong, braced reinforced concrete tripods. A complete description is found in the Light Lists

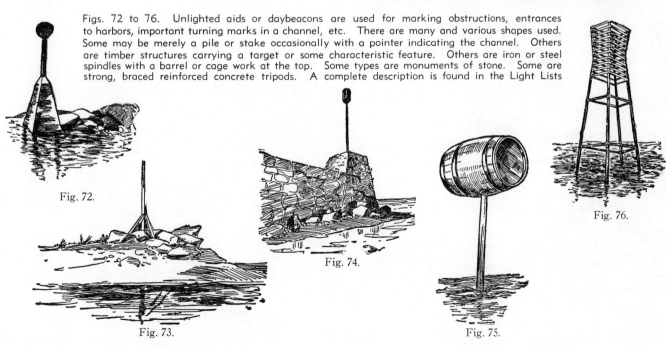

Fig. 72.

Fig. 73.

Fig. 74.

Fig. 75.

Fig. 76.

283

Illustration	Symbols and meaning		
	Lights which do not change color	Lights which show color variations	Phase description
	F. = Fixed	Alt. = Alternating.	A continuous steady light.
	F. Fl. = Fixed and flashing.	Alt. F. Fl. = Alternating fixed and flashing.	A fixed light varied at regular intervals by a flash of greater brilliance.
	F. Gp. Fl. = Fixed and group flashing.	Alt. F. Gp. Fl. = Alternating fixed and group flashing	A fixed light varied at regular intervals by groups of 2 or more flashes of greater brilliance.
	Fl. = Flashing	Alt. Fl. = Alternating flashing.	Showing a single flash at regular intervals, the duration of light always being less than the duration of darkness. Shows not more than 30 flashes per minute.
	Gp. Fl. = Group flashing.	Alt. Gp. Fl. = Alternating group flashing.	Showing at regular intervals groups of 2 or more flashes.
	Qk. Fl. = Quick flashing.	-----------	Shows not less than 60 flashes per minute.
	I. Qk. Fl. = Interrupted quick flashing.	-----------	Shows quick flashes for about 4 seconds, followed by a dark period of about 4 seconds.
	S-L. Fl. = Short-long flashing.	-----------	Shows a short flash of about 0.4 second, followed by a long flash of 4 times that duration.
	Occ. = Occulting.	Alt. Occ. = Alternating occulting.	A light totally eclipsed at regular intervals, the duration of light always equal to or greater than the duration of darkness.
	Gp. Occ. = Group occulting.	-----------	A light with a group of 2 or more eclipses at regular intervals.

Light colors used and abbreviations: W = white, R = red, G = green.

Fig. 80-81. Characteristic light phases which distinguish one light from another and thus aid in identification without confusion. The symbols (abbreviations) and meanings are given for lights which do not change color, as well as those which show color variations. A description of each characteristic phase is included. The time required for a light to pass through a full cycle, or set of changes in its characteristic, is called its period. See also color plate, page 42.

Daybeacons are colored, as are lighthouses, to distinguish them from their surroundings and to provide a means of identification. Daybeacons marking the sides of channels are colored and numbered in the same manner as buoys and minor light structures; red indicating the right side entering, and black the left side entering.

Range Lights

Two lights, located some distance apart, visible usually in one direction only, and used together, are known as range lights. They are so located that the mariner by bringing them into line has placed himself on the axis of a channel, and if he so steers his ship that they remain continuously in line, he will remain within the confines of the channel. Entrance channels are frequently marked by range lights, and the Delaware River on the Atlantic Coast, and the Columbia River on the Pacific Coast are examples of channels marked by ranges.

The lights of ranges may be of any color, and may also be fixed or flashing; the principal requirement being that they stand out distinctly from their surroundings. Most range lights lose brilliancy rapidly as a ship diverges from the range line. Ranges should be used only after a careful examination of the charts, as it is particularly important to determine for what distance the range line can be safely followed, information not obtainable from the lights themselves in all cases.

Lightships

Lightships serve the same essential purpose as lighthouses. They take the form of ships only because they are to occupy stations at which it would be impracticable to build lighthouses. Hulls of lightships in United States waters are almost invariably painted red with the name of the station in white on both sides. Relief lightships are placed on station when regular lightships are being overhauled. All the signals, the masthead light, the fog signal, and the radiobeacon, have distinctive characteristics, so that the lightship may readily be identified under all conditions. A riding-light on the forestay indicates the direction that the ship is heading, and as lightships ride to a single anchor, this also indicates the direction of the current.

Present day lightships are built of steel, with either steam or Diesel engine propulsion. Power for the operation of the signals is obtained from suitable auxiliary machinery. Each lightship has a crew of from 6 to 15 men.

Modern Lighthouses

Electricity is the illuminant now used in most of the larger lighthouses, electric incandescent lamps placed inside the larger sizes of lenses producing beams of as much as 9,000,000 candlepower where such brilliance is required. The flashing characteristics which distinguish many of the lighthouses are produced by revolving the entire lens, a work which was formerly performed by weight-driven clockwork, but which is now efficiently accomplished by means of electric motors. Lenses which are aggregates of highly polished glass prisms are assembled in a variety of types to produce whatever characteristic will best differentiate a particular light from its neighbors.

The larger light stations are also fitted with fog signals, various types of sounding devices such as diaphones, trumpets, oscillators, sirens, and horns being employed.

A typical fog-signal installation consists of gasoline or oil engine driven air compressors, discharging compressed air into a large storage tank. From the air tank or receiver, the air is allowed to flow to the sounding device under the accurate control of a signal timer, which coordinates fog signals, the light in the tower, and the radiobeacon signals. The fog signals at some stations are operated by electricity, particularly where commercial current is available.

At the present time many of the lighthouses which were originally cared for by resident keepers are operated automatically, particularly where such aids have become of less importance through the establishment nearby of more effective modern signals. There are also large numbers of automatic lights on inexpensive structures, cared for through the periodic visits of the lighthouse tenders or of keepers placed in charge of a group of such aids. Most automatic lights are operated on compressed acetylene gas or by means of some form of electric battery. The apparatus used for these purposes has become so highly developed that the small automatic lights have a degree of reliability nearly equalling that of the attended lighthouses.

Significance of Intracoastal Waterway Aids

This waterway, frequently referred to as the Inside Route, is a comparatively shallow channel lying parallel to and extending for nearly the entire length of the Atlantic and Gulf coast lines. Dredging operations which have extended over a period of years have provided an almost continuous inside passage from the North Atlantic states to Florida and the Gulf of Mexico. In the portion of this waterway south from Norfolk, Va., the aids to navigation are colored and numbered from north to south along the Atlantic Coast and from east to west along the Gulf Coast. Black buoys, beacons, and light structures mark the left or port side proceeding south, while aids on the right or starboard side are colored red. In addition to the colors black or red, Intracoastal Waterways aids also have a band, border or other mark painted yellow. This is the special mark of the Intracoastal Waterway. Where the Intracoastal Waterway crosses rivers, harbors, or other bodies of water, which are marked in the usual manner for entering from the sea, the seacoast aids bear, in addition to their regular markings, a yellow square on the left or port hand and a yellow triangle

Figs. 82-84. Lightships are placed at important stations where it is not feasible to build a lighthouse. Distinctive characteristics, such as masthead lights, fog signals, and radiobeacons—all described in the Light Lists—aid in their identification. Station names are painted conspicuously on their sides. Relief lightships, painted red, with word RELIEF on the side, are placed on station while regular lightships are being overhauled. When the Coast Guard's ten-year modernization program is complete, only Oregon's Columbia River and Washington State's Swiftsure lightships, of the original 24, will remain. They will maintain stations off the Pacific Northwest coast in positions where it would be impractical to build offshore stations.

The new and the old in offshore light stations. Lightships have been used since 1820 but in 1961 the Coast Guard built the first of its Texas-tower-type structures on the station at the southern approach to Massachusetts' Cape Cod Canal formerly guarded by Buzzards Bay Lightship. In the photograph (left) the relief lightship temporarily on duty at that time is shown leaving her post after commissioning of the permanent structure (just astern of her). Code flags (PC) indicate she is not in her position on station

Left: Split Rock Lighthouse, standing on a rocky cliff in Minnesota on Lake Superior, is one of the most frequently visited. Its incandescent oil vapor lamp, in a third order lens, produces 370,000 candlepower. The light stands 168 feet above the lake and is visible 22 miles

Left: Fire Island Lighthouse rises 167 feet above the low south shore of Long Island (N. Y.). This is one of the most important navigational aids to ships bound for New York Harbor. First erected in 1827, the present tower of brick was built in 1858

Right: Portland Head Lighthouse, at Cape Elizabeth, Me. The original station went into commission in 1791, construction having been started a year earlier by the Colony of Massachusetts. The present light is 32,000 candlepower

Extreme right: Navesink, the first primary seacoast light to be electrically lighted, overlooks New York Lower Bay from the Highlands of Navesink, N. J. Its 9,000,000 candlepower beam is visible 22 miles

Left: Old and new lighthouses at Cape Henry, Va., marking the entrance to Chesapeake Bay. The original lighthouse (1791) was the first to be built by the Federal Government. The new tower is of cast iron plates. The old tower is not used as a lighthouse

Right: Eastern Point Lighthouse (Mass.) has guided Gloucestermen for more than a century. The present white brick tower, built in 1890, replaces one built in 1832

LIGHTHOUSES

Right: Isolated Cape Spencer Lighthouse, 150 miles from a town, marks the northern entrance from the Pacific into the Inside Passages of Southeastern Alaska. It is a primary light, fog signal and radiobeacon station

Photographs by

U. S. Coast Guard

Above: Ponce de Leon Lighthouse, six miles below Daytona Beach, Fla., guards the long section of coast between the light at St. Augustine and Cape Canaveral

Below: Sullivan's Island Lighthouse, on the north side of Charleston Harbor (S.C.) Entrance, most powerful in Western Hemisphere, has 20 million candlepower, visible 20 miles. One of the world's tallest lights (structure is 140 feet high) built in 1962, it is equipped with an elevator.

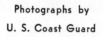

Left: Tillamook Rock Lighthouse, standing a mile offshore at Tillamook Head, Oregon, is one of the most exposed stations on the Pacific Coast. The protecting glass of the light, 133 feet above sea level, has been smashed several times by stones driven by great storm waves. Landing at this station is often difficult, if not impossible

Right: Jupiter Inlet Lighthouse lights the northern approach to the passage around the Florida Reefs. The station is equipped with radiobeacon and a million candlepower light. Construction, in 1860, was beset with many difficulties

Left: The skeleton iron structures of the lighthouses of the Florida Reefs between Miami and Key West are practically hurricane-proof. Six of them, similar in appearance, are located at Fowey Rocks, Carysfort Reef, Alligator Reef, Sombrero Key, American Shoal, and Sand Key. Each is manned by four keepers

Fig. 87 (right). Scotland Lightship, well known to New York and New Jersey yachtsmen and to the masters of all kinds of vessels approaching and leaving New York by way of the harbor entrance off Sandy Hook. Eastward of the Hook, she is stationed at the lower (SE) end of South Channel in 63 feet of water, a few miles to the westward of Ambrose. The hull is red, and she has two masts and a circular gallery at each masthead. She shows an occulting white light, and a fixed white riding light of 250 cp is carried on the forestay. The fog signal is a diaphragm horn sounding a group of 2 blasts every 20 seconds

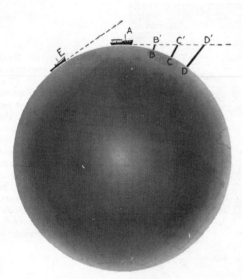

Fig. 88 (left). This illustration shows why it is necessary to have a lighthouse of a particular height in order that the light can be seen for a given distance. If one's boat is at point A, his line of vision is along the horizontal dotted line. The horizon is in that direction from him. A lighthouse at B to be visible from A must have a height equal to BB'. At C, to be visible from A, it must have a height equal to CC'. A lighthouse at D must have a height equal to DD', in order to be seen from the boat at A. The boat at E can see neither the boat A nor the lighthouse at B, C or D as her line of vision is along the dotted line at E. (See also Fig. 29, page 419, for larger scale illustration)

Flashing: Showing single flashes recurring not faster than thirty per minute, the flashes being shorter than the eclipses.

Fixed and flashing: A fixed light varied at regular intervals by one or more flashes of greater brilliance.

Group flashing: Showing at regular intervals groups of flashes.

Quick flashing: Showing not less than 60 short flashes per minute.

Interrupted quick flashing: Showing quick flashes for about four seconds, followed by a dark period of about four seconds.

Short-long flashing: Showing a short flash and then a long flash, this combination recurring about eight times a minute.

Occulting: A steady light totally eclipsed at intervals, the intervals being no longer than the light periods.

Group occulting: A steady light totally eclipsed by a group of two or more eclipses.

Alternating: Lights in which two or more of the colors white, red, and green are used.

on the right or starboard hand, to indicate that they also mark the Intracoastal Waterway. (See chapter on Buoys.)

Visibility and Candlepower of Lights

Under normal atmospheric conditions the visibility of a light depends upon its height and intensity; the distance due to the former being known as the geographic range, and to the latter as the luminous range. As a rule, for the principal lights the luminous range is greater than the geographic, and the distance from which the principal lights are visible is limited by the horizon only, and under some conditions of atmospheric refraction, the glare or loom of the light and occasionally the light itself may be visible far beyond the computed geographic range of the light. On the other hand, and unfortunately more frequently the case, these distances may be greatly lessened by unfavorable weather conditions due to fog, rain, snow, haze or smoke. Weak and colored lights are more easily obscured by such conditions. The distances of visibility are given in nautical miles.

The intensity of lights is indicated in the Light Lists in terms of candlepower. The chief purpose of these figures is to indicate the relative brilliance of various lights, so that the mariner may judge if a light may be expected to be seen at a great distance or only when approached fairly close to.

Light Characteristics

To avoid confusion, lights are given distinct characteristics, the following being employed:

Fixed: A continuous steady light.

Importance of Radio Navigational Aids in Small Boat Handling

The recent production and marketing of inexpensive radio direction finders has greatly increased the importance of the U. S. Coast Guard radiobeacon system to small boat owners and handlers. It is now possible to get a low cost radio direction finder for approximately $200. These are compact, portable units operating on self-contained batteries. Another new development is the automatic direction finder, which continuously indicates the bearing of a station on a dial.

Radiobeacons are radio stations installed at lighthouses, on lightships, or at other points well known to mariners, for sending out radio signals in all directions for the guidance of mariners. Each radiobeacon is located at a definite point shown on the charts, and is readily distinguished from other radiobeacons by the characteristic of its signal, as is a lighthouse by its distinguishing light beams. The radiobeacons operate within the frequency range 285–325 Kc. set aside for this purpose. Hundreds of radiobeacons are operated in the waters of the United States and possessions by the U. S. Coast Guard.

Complete detailed instructions for the installation, calibration, operation, and maintenance of radio direction finders aboard vessels are given in the instruction books accompanying the instruments but a brief description of a radio direction finder and of its operation follows.

A radio direction finder consists essentially of a small loop antenna capable of rotation and equipped with a pointer operating over a dial graduated in degrees, as is a ship's compass, and a

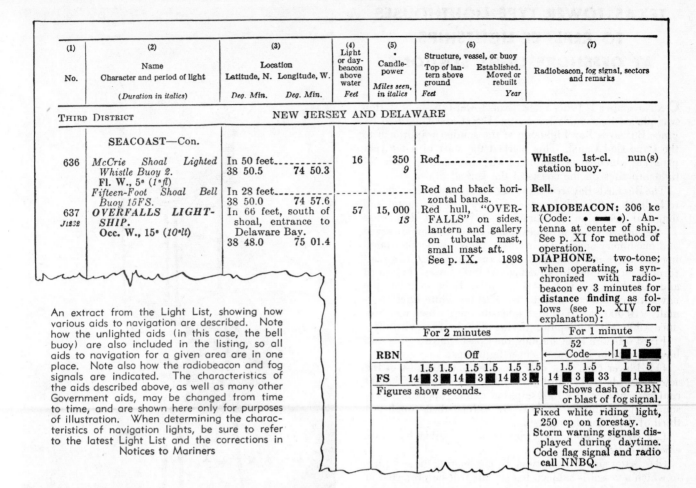

(1) No.	(2) Name Character and period of light (Duration in italics)	(3) Location Latitude, N. Longitude, W. Deg. Min. Deg. Min.	(4) Light or day-beacon above water Feet	(5) Candle-power Miles seen, in italics	(6) Structure, vessel, or buoy — Top of lantern above ground Feet / Established. Moved or rebuilt Year	(7) Radiobeacon, fog signal, sectors and remarks
	THIRD DISTRICT	NEW JERSEY AND DELAWARE				
	SEACOAST—Con.					
636	*McCrie Shoal Lighted Whistle Buoy 2.* Fl. W., 5ˢ (1ˢfl)	In 50 feet_____ 38 50.5 74 50.3	16	350 *9*	Red_____	Whistle. 1st-cl. nun(s) station buoy.
	Fifteen-Foot Shoal Bell Buoy 15FS.	In 28 feet_____ 38 50.0 74 57.6	_____	_____	Red and black horizontal bands.	Bell.
637 J1232	*OVERFALLS LIGHT-SHIP.* Occ. W., 15ˢ (10ˢlt)	In 66 feet, south of shoal, entrance to Delaware Bay. 38 48.0 75 01.4	57	15,000 *13*	Red hull, "OVER-FALLS" on sides, lantern and gallery on tubular mast, small mast aft. See p. IX. 1898	RADIOBEACON: 306 kc (Code: • ▬ •). Antenna at center of ship. See p. XI for method of operation. DIAPHONE, two-tone; when operating, is synchronized with radiobeacon ev 3 minutes for **distance finding** as follows (see p. XIV for explanation):

	For 2 minutes	For 1 minute
RBN	Off	52 ◄—Code—► 1 ■ 1 1 5 ■
FS	1.5 1.5 1.5 1.5 1.5 1.5 14 ■ 3 ■ 14 ■ 3 ■ 14 ■ 3 ■	1.5 1.5 1.5 1 5 14 ■ 3 ■ 33 1 ■ 1
Figures show seconds.		■ Shows dash of RBN or blast of fog signal.

Fixed white riding light, 250 cp on forestay. Storm warning signals displayed during daytime. Code flag signal and radio call NNBQ.

An extract from the Light List, showing how various aids to navigation are described. Note how the unlighted aids (in this case, the bell buoy) are also included in the listing, so all aids to navigation for a given area are in one place. Note also how the radiobeacon and fog signals are indicated. The characteristics of the aids described above, as well as many other Government aids, may be changed from time to time, and are shown here only for purposes of illustration. When determining the characteristics of navigation lights, be sure to refer to the latest Light List and the corrections in Notices to Mariners

radio receiver provided with head phones or loud speaker. The loop antenna may be integral with and mounted directly on the receiver if the superstructure of the boat on which it is used is of wood. If the pilot house is of metal construction, the loop must be mounted above the pilot house and is connected to the dial and rotating handwheel near the receiver by a shaft. The original installation and calibration require approximately the same care as for a magnetic compass, and changes in rigging or erection of additional antennas on a vessel should not be undertaken without carefully recalibrating the radio direction finder afterward.

To get a radio bearing, the navigator tunes his receiver to the frequency of the radiobeacon on which the bearing is desired, having before him a list of the radiobeacon stations with their frequencies and characteristic signals. When a signal is heard and the station identified, he is prepared to take a bearing on it. The loop is rotated, causing the signal to be heard either fainter or louder. A brief manipulation of the loop handwheel, to which the dial pointer is attached, is usually sufficient to discover the point at which the signal is heard faintest, or at which, preferably, no signal is heard. With the handwheel in this position, the bearing is read. A simple procedure is usually provided to determine which of two possible bearings, 180° apart, is the correct one.

If the radio direction finder dial is of the "dumb" card type, indicating degrees from the ship's head, a simultaneous reading of the ship's heading on the steering compass must also be taken. The reading of the "dumb" radio direction finder card added to the reading of the steering compass (and minus 360 if the total is larger than this) is the direction of the radiobeacon from the observing vessel expressed in degrees "per steering compass." By applying the proper correction for deviation, a bearing in degrees magnetic is obtained, and this in turn is converted into degrees true by applying the proper variation.

The methods of navigation by the use of radio bearings are the same as with visual bearings on lighthouses or other known objects. A most important practical difference is that radio bearings may be obtained at great distances, and the outstanding advantages of radiobeacons as navigational aids are their availability at all times regardless of fog, rain, or snow, and the

fact that their range is many times as great as even the most powerful visible signal. In general, radiobeacons are located at all important entrances and at outstanding intermediate points along the coast. Many are also placed in sounds and bays, notably Long Island Sound, Chesapeake Bay, and Puget Sound, as well as on the Great Lakes. Full details regarding the location and operation of radiobeacons are given in the Light List, published annually, and on radiobeacon charts, of which three are now published showing respectively the Atlantic and Gulf, Great Lakes, and Pacific Coast areas. These radiobeacon charts, suitable for posting in pilot houses or elsewhere near radio direction finders, are no longer issued as separate sheets, but are bound into the Light Lists. (See illustration, page 471d.) All changes are announced in the Notices to Mariners.

Significant changes were made in June 1963: the sequencing of six radiobeacons on a single frequency, the elimination of the distinction between fair and foul weather operation, the adjustment of service ranges, and the incorporation of a long dash at the end of the characteristic identifier. In the system of time sharing, the six beacons to be sequenced will each transmit for a period of 1 minute in consecutive rotation. The order of rotation is according to the assigned sequence number as indicated by Roman numerals I through VI. Some radiobeacons continue to operate every minute without interruption.

Many radiobeacons are equipped also to send synchronized radio and air sound fog signals for distance-finding purposes. A vessel provided with a radio receiver covering the band 285-325 Kc. may, by a single observation, determine its distance from the station, when the vessel is within audible range of the sound signal. Any radio receiving set capable of receiving on the proper frequency is sufficient, although if the vessel has a radio direction finder, and takes a radio bearing at the same time, its position is at once determined by both the distance and the bearing. Distance-finding signals are based on the fact that radio signals are transmitted practically instantaneously, and that sound signals in air travel at the rate of 1 mile in about 5 seconds. The approximate distance in miles from the sending station is readily obtained by measuring the time in seconds between the reception of the radio and of the sound signals and dividing by 5.5 for nautical miles (5 for statute miles).

TEXAS TOWER-TYPE LIGHTHOUSES TO REPLACE LIGHTSHIPS AT OFFSHORE LIGHT STATIONS

O n November 1, 1961, a new Texas tower-type light station was placed in commission by the U.S. Coast Guard to replace Buzzards Bay Lightship at the southern approach to the Cape Cod Canal. This marked the start of a ten-year program which when completed will eliminate 22 of the 24 lightship sites off the coasts of the United States.

The Buzzards Bay structure has four main steel legs driven to bedrock 268 feet below the surface, with horizontal and diagonal steel pipe cross-bracing. A 70′-by-70′ deckhouse 71 feet above water provides quarters for a crew of seven and machinery space. The roof serves as a helicopter landing and there is a boat landing at the waterline. The platform is surmounted by an octagonal light tower. Fog horn and radiobeacon tower above the main light complete the navigational aid equipment. The flashing white light (normally 910,000 cp) has a high intensity optic which will produce 9,000,000 candlepower during periods of low visibility.

Fixed offshore light stations, the Coast Guard points out, have five major advantages over lightships:

(1) Lower cost. Not only was the $950,000 cost of the new Buzzards Light substantially less than the $1,500,000 replacement cost of a lightship, but annual operating, personnel and maintenance costs are estimated at roughly a third of those for the lightship.

(2) Greater luminous range, made possible by more efficient optics.

(3) Better signal projection. By eliminating the swinging to which a vessel is subject, fog signals will be projected in the most useful direction under any given circumstances.

(4) More accurate guidance, because the towers do not swing and cannot be blown off station in violent storms.

(5) Long life. Towers are expected to last 75 years, as compared with the average 50-year-span of lightships.

Thirty-seven-year-old Buzzards Bay Lightship, first of 22 to be replaced during the next decade by fixed offshore structures. Off station here, she flies the code flags PC ("I am not in my correct position") at the port spreader. The jack flies forward, national ensign aft, commission pennant and Coast Guard ensign at the starboard spreader, and a four-letter identifying call sign, in code. Black ball signifies she is at anchor.

On four steel stilt-like legs bedded in rock, the new Buzzard's light station will always be "on station," regardless of weather.

An additional factor influencing the Coast Guard's decision was the increasing age of lightships, which has resulted in excessive maintenance and repair costs.

In addition to manned structures like the Buzzards Bay station, the Coast Guard is also building un-manned light towers such as the one which replaces Brenton Reef lightship at the entrance to Narragansett Bay.

The current program of building fixed light installations, though relatively new as a deep-water project, traces back to 1878 when a tower was installed at Fowey Rocks off the Florida Keys.

In the case of nearby lighthouses where offshore towers may not be feasible, scientific advances in optics, acoustics, and electronics today provide the means whereby such navigational aids can be improved to the extent that, when combined with minor floating aids, the combination can provide better service than the lightship.

UNITED STATES COAST GUARD
BUOYAGE OF THE UNITED STATES
Significance of Shapes, Coloring, Numbering, and Light Characteristics
Symbols shown adjacent to Buoys are those used on Charts to indicate such Aids

LATERAL SYSTEM

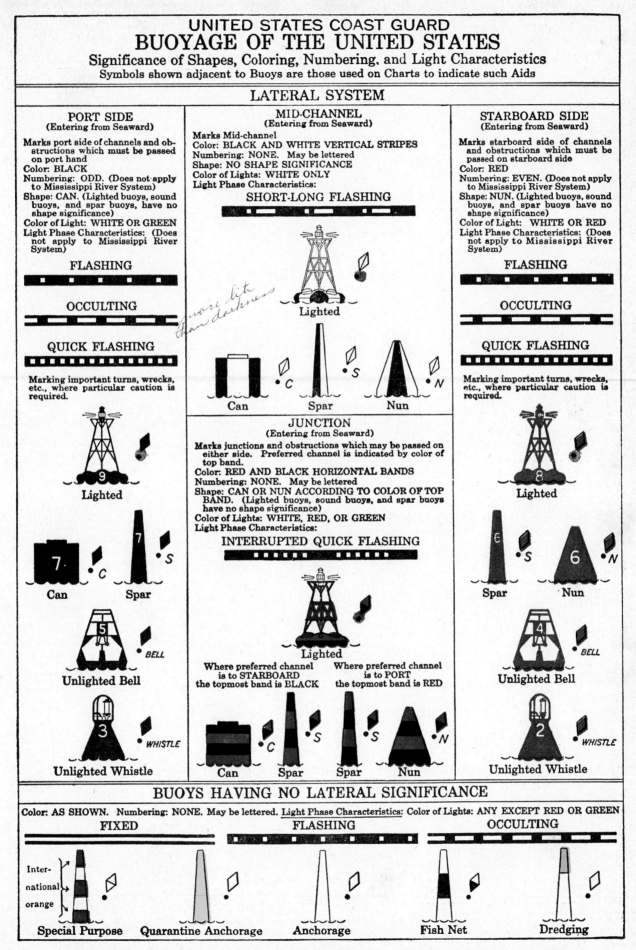

PORT SIDE
(Entering from Seaward)

Marks port side of channels and obstructions which must be passed on port hand
Color: BLACK
Numbering: ODD. (Does not apply to Mississippi River System)
Shape: CAN. (Lighted buoys, sound buoys, and spar buoys, have no shape significance)
Color of Light: WHITE OR GREEN
Light Phase Characteristics: (Does not apply to Mississippi River System)

FLASHING

OCCULTING

QUICK FLASHING

Marking important turns, wrecks, etc., where particular caution is required.

Lighted

9

7

Can   Spar

5   BELL

Unlighted Bell

3   WHISTLE

Unlighted Whistle

MID-CHANNEL
(Entering from Seaward)

Marks Mid-channel
Color: BLACK AND WHITE VERTICAL STRIPES
Numbering: NONE. May be lettered
Shape: NO SHAPE SIGNIFICANCE
Color of Lights: WHITE ONLY
Light Phase Characteristics:

SHORT-LONG FLASHING

Lighted

Can   Spar   Nun

JUNCTION
(Entering from Seaward)

Marks junctions and obstructions which may be passed on either side. Preferred channel is indicated by color of top band.
Color: RED AND BLACK HORIZONTAL BANDS
Numbering: NONE. May be lettered
Shape: CAN OR NUN ACCORDING TO COLOR OF TOP BAND. (Lighted buoys, sound buoys, and spar buoys have no shape significance)
Color of Lights: WHITE, RED, OR GREEN
Light Phase Characteristics:

INTERRUPTED QUICK FLASHING

Lighted

Where preferred channel is to STARBOARD the topmost band is BLACK

Where preferred channel is to PORT the topmost band is RED

Can   Spar   Spar   Nun

STARBOARD SIDE
(Entering from Seaward)

Marks starboard side of channels and obstructions which must be passed on starboard side
Color: RED
Numbering: EVEN. (Does not apply to Mississippi River System)
Shape: NUN. (Lighted buoys, sound buoys, and spar buoys have no shape significance)
Color of Light: WHITE OR RED
Light Phase Characteristics: (Does not apply to Mississippi River System)

FLASHING

OCCULTING

QUICK FLASHING

Marking important turns, wrecks, etc., where particular caution is required.

Lighted

8

6   6

Spar   Nun

4   BELL

Unlighted Bell

2   WHISTLE

Unlighted Whistle

BUOYS HAVING NO LATERAL SIGNIFICANCE

Color: AS SHOWN. Numbering: NONE. May be lettered. Light Phase Characteristics: Color of Lights: ANY EXCEPT RED OR GREEN

FIXED   FLASHING   OCCULTING

International orange

Special Purpose   Quarantine Anchorage   Anchorage   Fish Net   Dredging

The significance of shapes, colors, numbers and light characteristics in the United States buoyage system.

TYPES OF AIDS TO NAVIGATION
INTRACOASTAL WATERWAY

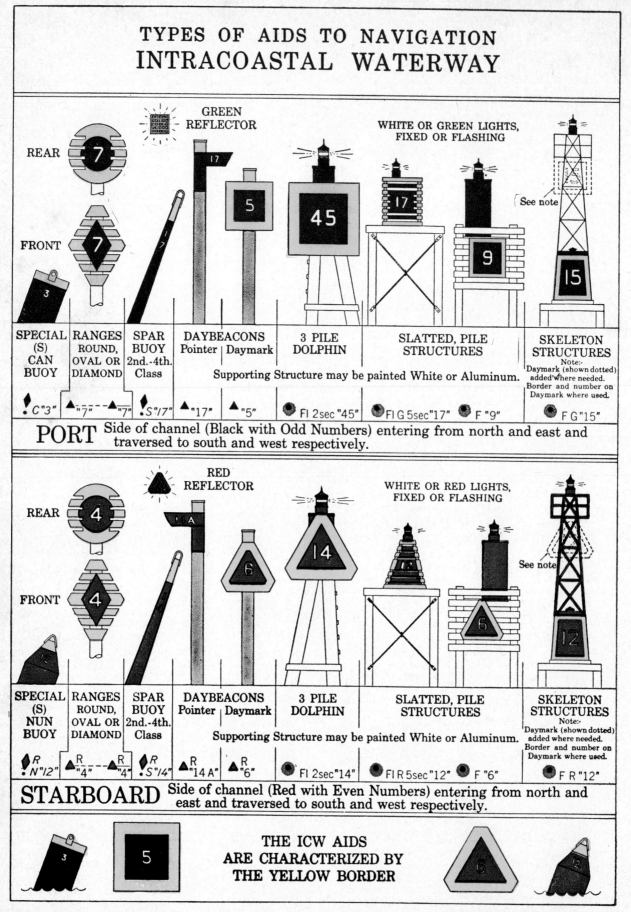

Aids to navigation on the Intracoastal Waterway are distinguished by a special border or other mark painted yellow. Aids on this waterway are colored and numbered from north to south along the Atlantic Coast and from east to west on the Gulf Coast.

Boatmen on non-federal waters will enjoy the safety of uniform aids to navigation, without inter-state confusion.

Uniform markers, supplementing U.S. Coast Guard's lateral system in use on federal waters, when implemented by the respective states, will simplify navigation and promote safety in waters under state control

New Buoyage System
for State Waterways

Piloting from port to port down the Atlantic Seaboard, picture the confusion that would result if, each time you crossed a state line, you encountered a radical change in buoyage. You don't, of course, because the United States Coast Guard has adopted a uniform system to mark the federal "navigable" waterways under its jurisdiction. These include not only coastal waters but lakes and rivers navigable to the sea.

If you know the essentials of the federal system, you can cruise with confidence because, even in strange waters, each distinctive shape, marking, color or number conveys a familiar meaning. In those rare cases, as in cross channels, where some confusion could exist, a glance at the chart will eliminate it.

But on waters wholly within state boundaries (not navigable to the sea) a different condition prevails. Here the state assumes responsibility for its own waters, with respect both to the operation of boats and establishment of any navigational aids or regulatory markers required.

Until recently, no effort had been made to create a nation-wide measure of standardization. With trailer-borne craft traveling freely these days from state to state over the highways, the boatman has been figuratively "at sea" in trying to decipher the significance of what had been intended for him as "aids to navigation."

Now, at long last, a constructive step has been taken. Boating legislators from more than 30 states met re-

cently at San Francisco with U.S. Coast Guard and other representatives of the federal government at a conference called by the Advisory Panel of State Officials to the Merchant Marine Council, in cooperation with the Council of State Governments.

Seeking standards for waterway marking, their buoyage committee drafted a report which was subsequently approved and adopted. The problem was divided into two general parts: (1) the establishment of a system of markers to indicate regulatory areas, speed zones, restricted areas, etc. and (2) the development of navigational aids to supplement the Coast Guard's federal system.

(1) Regulatory Markers

On federal waters, the boatman can turn to his charts, light lists, coast pilots and other publications for information on natural hazards, zoned areas, directions, distances, etc., to supplement the knowledge he gets from buoys, daybeacons, and other aids. On state waters, he will now have a uniform system of water signs or markers that will, in themselves, convey their message without reference to any publication—an obvious advantage, especially to inexperienced boatmen.

Just as Intracoastal Waterway markers are distinguished by a special yellow border or other yellow mark, international orange and white will identify state regulatory markers. On buoys, a 3-inch orange band will be used at top and bottom, and on the white area between bands a geometric shape will appear, also in orange. A diamond shape denotes danger. A diamond with a cross indicates a prohibited area. A circle signifies zoning or control. A square or rectangle will convey other information. On shore structures, the orange bands are optional.

The geometric shape conveys the basic idea of danger, control, etc., so the boatman can tell at a distance whether to keep away or approach closer for more information. To convey a specific meaning, spelled-out words or recognized abbreviations will appear within the shape. The sole exception to this is the cross within a diamond, used to absolutely prohibit boats from an area because of danger to the boat, to swimmers in a protected zone, or for any other reason sufficient to warrant exclusion by law.

Initials, symbols and silhouettes have been avoided to minimize risk of misinterpretation. In some cases, words may be needed outside the geometric shape to give the reason, authority or some clarification of the specific meaning. Shown in an accompanying illustration are the designated shapes with typical qualifying words, the significance of each shape, and a partial list of suggested words suitable for use with this system.

(2) The Uniform Buoyage System

In selecting types of buoys for use in waters not marked by the Coast Guard, the object was to make the state system compatible with the federal. To this end, regulations have been drafted, the substance of which is as follows:

(a) On well-defined channels (including rivers) the federal system of all-black and all-red buoys has been adopted. These will be located in pairs at both ends of a channel, leaving no doubt that boats should pass between the solid black and the solid red.

If necessary to stagger these in a channel, they will be close enough to eliminate possibility of confusion and will be placed in conformity with the coloring of buoys at ends of the channel. Numbers, if any, will be white and may be reflectorized—odd numbers on black, even numbers on red.

(b) Where there is no well-defined channel or the obstruction is such that it might be approached from more than one direction, a cardinal (compass point) system is used. A *white buoy* with *black top* directs boats to pass to the NORTH or EAST of it. A *white buoy* with *red top* directs boats to pass to the SOUTH or WEST of it. Numbers, if used, will be white, may be reflectorized, and placed in the top (colored) area of the buoy. Width of the top colored band is to be about a third of the buoy's height above water. Odd numbers would be used on black-topped buoys, even numbers on red-topped.

(c) To direct boats outside an obstruction, away from shore (around the end of a reef, for example) a red-and-white vertically striped buoy is used, the white stripe twice the width of the red. This warns boats not to pass between the buoy and the nearest shore.

(d) Size, shape and material of buoys are discretionary with the state, and the term "buoy" is taken to refer to fixed as well as floating navigational markers.

(e) Use of reflectorized material is also discretionary. If used on lateral buoys, red reflectors would appear on solid red buoys, green reflectors on solid black buoys. All others would use silver or white reflectors.

(f) Light on buoys are to be of the flashing type: red on all-red buoys, green on all-black buoys, white on all others.

(g) On bridges, fixed red lights will mark limits of the safe channel, a single fixed green light over the center of the channel indicating maximum vertical clearance at that point.

Mooring buoys, in the state system, will be white with a blue horizontal band. Water structures such as ski jumps, diving platforms, etc., are to be painted white.

States are urged to give official recognition to the "diver's flag" (red with white diagonal stripe) adopted by the Underwater Society of America to warn surface craft away from areas where divers are submerged.

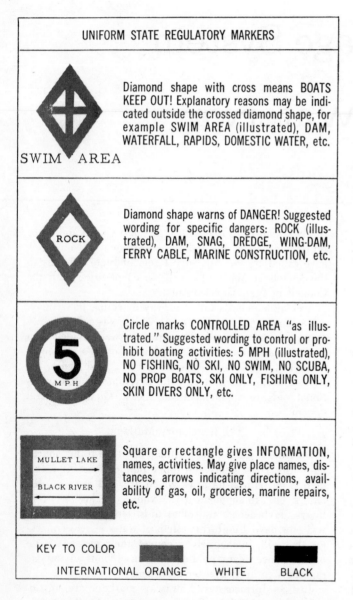

UNIFORM STATE REGULATORY MARKERS

SWIM AREA — Diamond shape with cross means BOATS KEEP OUT! Explanatory reasons may be indicated outside the crossed diamond shape, for example SWIM AREA (illustrated), DAM, WATERFALL, RAPIDS, DOMESTIC WATER, etc.

ROCK — Diamond shape warns of DANGER! Suggested wording for specific dangers: ROCK (illustrated), DAM, SNAG, DREDGE, WING-DAM, FERRY CABLE, MARINE CONSTRUCTION, etc.

5 MPH — Circle marks CONTROLLED AREA "as illustrated." Suggested wording to control or prohibit boating activities: 5 MPH (illustrated), NO FISHING, NO SKI, NO SWIM, NO SCUBA, NO PROP BOATS, SKI ONLY, FISHING ONLY, SKIN DIVERS ONLY, etc.

MULLET LAKE / BLACK RIVER — Square or rectangle gives INFORMATION, names, activities. May give place names, distances, arrows indicating directions, availability of gas, oil, groceries, marine repairs, etc.

KEY TO COLOR — INTERNATIONAL ORANGE — WHITE — BLACK

Uniform state regulatory markers (as indicated above) will convey their meanings to the boatman without need for reference to charts or other publications.

How buoys might be placed in a typical waterway under state jurisdiction

BLACK	**ALL BLACK BUOY** indicates boat should pass between it and its companion all-red buoy. Used with all-red buoy to mark a **well defined channel**. If numbered, has odd number, colored white. Numbers may be reflectorized (green). If lighted, flashing green.	**WHITE RED-STRIPED**	**RED-STRIPED WHITE BUOY** indicates boat should not pass between buoy and nearest shore (cardinal system). Used when reef or obstruction requires boat to go **outside** buoy (away from shore). White stripes to be twice the width of red stripes. Reflector or light, if used, is white; the light flashing.
RED	**ALL RED BUOY** indicates boat should pass between it and its companion all-black buoy. Used with all-black buoy to mark a **well defined channel**. If numbered, has even number, colored white. Numbers may be reflectorized (red). If lighted, flashing red.	**WHITE BLUE BAND**	**WHITE BUOY WITH BLUE BAND** indicates anchorage or mooring. Used in areas where watercraft are permanently anchored or moored.
WHITE BLACK-TOPPED	**BLACK TOPPED WHITE BUOY** indicates boat should pass to NORTH or EAST (cardinal system). Used where there is no well-defined channel. Reflector or light, if used, is white; the light flashing.	**RED WHITE STRIPE**	**SQUARE RED FLAG WITH WHITE DIAGONAL STRIPE** indicates presence of a DIVER. Adopted by Underwater Society of America for use during diving activities. Boatmen are warned to KEEP AWAY from flag area to avoid submerged divers.
WHITE RED-TOPPED	**RED TOPPED WHITE BUOY** indicates boat should pass to SOUTH or WEST (cardinal system). Used where there is no well-defined channel. Reflector or light, if used, is white; the light flashing.	KEY TO COLOR —	

KEY TO COLOR —

BLACK	WHITE	RED	BLUE

Types of buoys proposed for state waters to supplement those in use on coastal waters

Some states have prepared charts for waters under their control. As a further step toward nation-wide uniformity in navigational aids, it has been recommended that they adopt as standard the chart symbols currently in use by the U.S. Coast and Geodetic Survey and the U.S. Corps of Engineers.

Taken in conjunction with the ground gained by establishment of federally guided consistent state numbering laws under the Federal Boating Act of 1958, the new buoyage regulations mark a significant milestone in the trend toward uniformity of laws under which the boatman operates.

The adoption of these regulations by the respective states will be a progressive matter, as might be expected. For example, at the time of going to press it is reported that California is in the process of developing regulations to implement a system based on the proposals outlined. New York and Hawaii are working on similar regulations. Nevada, Missouri, Alabama and South Dakota have authority to implement the proposal without additional legislation. Connecticut and Maryland expect to use at least part of the system. Montana, Florida, Arizona and Colorado may require legislation to implement the proposal. The wider the acceptance of the uniform system by the fifty states, the more value it will have for boatmen in general.

CHAPTER XVI

BUOYS—

WHAT THEY MEAN AND HOW TO USE THEM

Various Types, Colors and Numbers— The Spar, Can, Nun, Bell, Whistle, Lighted, and Combination Buoys

THE primary function of buoys is to warn the mariner of some danger, some obstruction, or change in the contours of the sea bottom, that he may avoid the dangers and continue his course in safe waters. The utmost advantage is obtained from buoys when they are considered as marking definite identified spots, for if a mariner be properly equipped with charts, and knows his precise location at the moment, he can readily plot a safe course on which to proceed. Such features as size, shape, coloring, numbering, and signalling equipment, are but means to these ends of warning, guiding, and orienting.

The buoyage system as found in waters of the United States consists of several different types of buoys, each kind designed to serve under definite conditions. Broadly speaking, buoys serve as day-marks during the daytime, those having lights are also available for navigation by night, and those having sound signals are more readily located in time of fog as well as by night. The following are the principal types:

Spar Buoys

Spar buoys are usually large logs, trimmed, shaped, appropriately painted, and moored with a suitable length of chain and a sinker to anchor them. They vary in length from 20 to 50

The maintenance of aids to navigation is a function of the U. S. Coast Guard. Below is a view of their depot at Staten Island, with a buoy tender lying at the dock. Above, the crew of a tender repairs a lighted buoy.

Left: Undergoing a servicing, a big lighted whistle buoy is tested and painted. Note its size relative to the men at work on it

buoys four gongs of different tones, with one clapper for each gong, take the place of the bell. As the sea rocks the buoy, the clappers strike against the gongs sounding four different notes. A new type of gong buoy has only one gong, so that it sounds one note instead of four.

Whistle Buoys

Whistle buoys provide a sound signal which is useful at night and also during fog or low visibility. Such buoys also serve as day-marks. They are used principally in open and exposed places where a ground swell normally exists, as the whistle is sounded by compressed air produced by the motion of the buoy in the sea. Whistle buoys have a conical shaped top, above which the whistle projects, protected by cage work. These buoys have no shape significance. In combination buoys, having lights as well as whistles, the whistle is located within the lattice-work tower, immediately below the light. A type of sound buoy is now being introduced in which a trumpet is sounded at regular intervals by mechanical means.

feet, depending upon the depth of water in which they are moored. Spar shaped buoys are also constructed of steel plates.

Can and Nun Buoys

Can and nun buoys are built up of steel plates, in various sizes. They are moored with chain affixed to a sinker of appropriate weight.

Bell Buoys

Bell buoys serve with considerable effectiveness both by day and night, and also during fog, and are much used because of their moderate maintenance cost. Most bell buoys are sounded by the motion of the buoy in the sea, four clappers being loosely hung so that they are readily set in motion. Newer types of bell buoys are operated by compressed gas or electric batteries, their strokes sounding at regular intervals, and are particularly useful in sheltered waters.

Gong Buoys

Gong buoys are used to give a distinctive characteristic when there are several bell buoys in one vicinity. In these

Right (above): Coast Guardsmen freeing a lighted buoy from its sheathing of ice. Theirs is the task of keeping buoys in operation and on station

Right: Encrusted with barnacles and in need of an overhaul, a group of nun buoys is brought back to a Coast Guard depot for reconditioning. Much of their length is below water

Station buoys, colored the same as regular aids, are placed alongside lightships and important buoy stations to mark them in case the regular aid is carried away. Lightship station buoys bear the letters LS above the initials of the station. In the illustration, a spar marks the station of the combination light and bell buoy. Cans and nuns are also used as station buoys. Note saw teeth on guards designed to cut the towing hawser of tugs if fouled by a tow, thus preventing damage to buoy

way is marked from the north Atlantic states to the lower coast of Texas, regardless of the compass headings of individual sections.

Coloring of Buoys

All buoys are painted distinctive colors to indicate their purpose or the side of the channel which they mark.

Red buoys mark the right hand side of channels, entering from seaward.

Black buoys mark the left hand side of channels, entering from seaward.

Red-and-black horizontally banded buoys mark obstructions, or a junction of one channel with another, and indicate that there is a channel on either side. If the topmost band is red, the principal channel will be followed by keeping the buoy on the right hand side of the vessel, when entering from seaward. If the topmost band is black, the principal channel will be followed by keeping the buoy on the left hand side of the vessel, when entering from seaward. (NOTE: When proceeding toward the sea, it may not be possible to pass on either side of these buoys, and the chart should always be consulted.) Buoys marking wrecks are generally placed on the seaward or channel side of the wreck, as near to it as practicable. Caution should be used in passing, as the wreck may shift.

Black-and-white vertically striped buoys indicate the middle of a channel, and should be passed close to, but on either side, for safety.

White buoys mark anchorages.

Yellow buoys mark quarantine anchorages. (Boat-shaped radio current buoys, also painted yellow, fitted with antennas and displaying, at night, two quick-flashing red lights in vertical line, have been used in survey work to determine current velocities and direction.)

White buoys with green tops mark areas in which dredging is being carried on, or a survey is being conducted.

Black-and-white horizontally banded buoys mark the limits of areas in which fish nets and traps are permitted.

Red or black (unlighted) buoys with white tops have the same significance as similar buoys without the white top, the white painting being added so that the buoys may be readily picked up at night by a ship's searchlight.

Numbering of Buoys

Most buoys are given numbers, which are painted conspicuously upon them. These numbers serve to indicate which side of the channel the buoys mark, and also facilitate the locating of the buoys upon the charts.

Numbers increase from seaward and are kept in approximate sequence on the two sides of the channel by omitting numbers as required.

Odd numbered buoys mark the left hand sides of channels entering from seaward.

Even numbered buoys mark the right hand sides of channels entering from seaward.

Numbers followed by letters, such as 24A, 24B, 24C, indicate that buoys have been added to a channel and the series not at once renumbered.

Numbers followed by letters, such as 1 DR, are used on important buoys, particularly those marking isolated offshore dangers. The letters are initials of the station name, in this instance Duxbury Reef, and the number has the usual significance.

Letters, without numbers, are applied in some cases to black-and-white vertically striped buoys marking fairways, and to red-and-black horizontally banded buoys marking junctions or bifurcations.

Lighted Buoys

The type of lighted buoy in general use today burns compressed acetylene gas, contained in steel tanks inside the buoy. From the tanks the gas is conveyed by tube to a flasher set in the lantern at the top of the buoy. A valve mechanism operated by the gas pressure permits a definite amount of gas to pass the burner at intervals, to be ignited by a pilot flame which burns continuously. The period and length of the flash may be adjusted to produce a definite characteristic. Flashing lights have a period of light shorter than the period of darkness while occulting lights have a light period equal to or greater than the period of darkness. A few buoys are lighted electrically and the number is increasing.

Combination Buoys

These are lighted buoys which are also fitted with some form of sound signal, such as a bell, gongs, a whistle, or a trumpet.

The Lateral System

The coloring and numbering of buoys are determined by their position with respect to the navigable channel as such channels are entered and followed from seaward toward the head of navigation. This method, known as the lateral system, is uniform in all United States waters and is described in detail herein under the headings Coloring and Numbering. As all channels do not lead from seaward, arbitrary assumptions must be made in order that the system may be consistently applied. In the coloring and numbering of offshore buoys along the coasts and along traffic routes not leading distinctly from seaward or toward headwaters, the following system has been adopted: Proceeding in a southerly direction along the Atlantic coast, in a northerly and westerly direction along the Gulf coast and in northerly direction along the Pacific coast, will be considered as proceeding from seaward, and accordingly coastal buoys which are to be kept on the right hand side are red and have even numbers. On the Great Lakes offshore buoys are colored and numbered from the outlet of each lake toward its upper end. The Intracoastal Water-

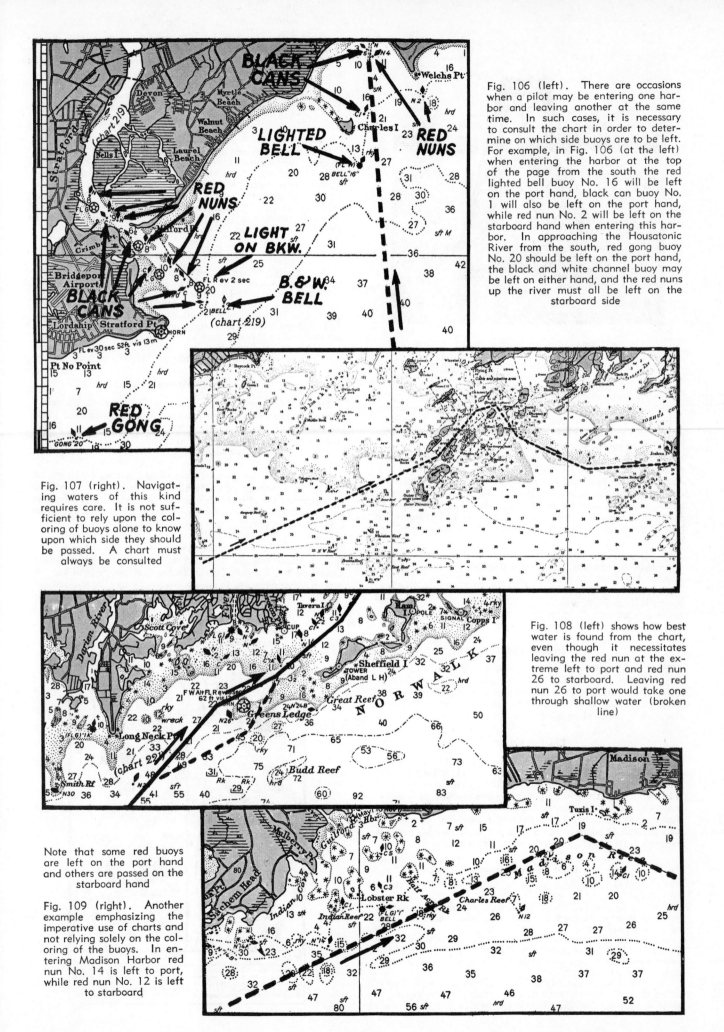

Fig. 106 (left). There are occasions when a pilot may be entering one harbor and leaving another at the same time. In such cases, it is necessary to consult the chart in order to determine on which side buoys are to be left. For example, in Fig. 106 (at the left) when entering the harbor at the top of the page from the south the red lighted bell buoy No. 16 will be left on the port hand, black can buoy No. 1 will also be left on the port hand, while red nun No. 2 will be left on the starboard hand when entering this harbor. In approaching the Housatonic River from the south, red gong buoy No. 20 should be left on the port hand, the black and white channel buoy may be left on either hand, and the red nuns up the river must all be left on the starboard side

Fig. 107 (right). Navigating waters of this kind requires care. It is not sufficient to rely upon the coloring of the buoys alone to know upon which side they should be passed. A chart must always be consulted

Fig. 108 (left) shows how best water is found from the chart, even though it necessitates leaving the red nun at the extreme left to port and red nun 26 to starboard. Leaving red nun 26 to port would take one through shallow water (broken line)

Note that some red buoys are left on the port hand and others are passed on the starboard hand

Fig. 109 (right). Another example emphasizing the imperative use of charts and not relying solely on the coloring of the buoys. In entering Madison Harbor red nun No. 14 is left to port, while red nun No. 12 is left to starboard

A bell buoy, sounded by the motion of the buoy in the sea as clappers strike the bell. Newer types of buoy carry radar reflectors.

Shapes of Buoys

Definite shape characteristics have been given to a large portion of the unlighted buoys used in United States waters, to indicate which sides of the channels they mark. Cylindrical buoys with flat tops are known as can buoys, and if painted black, mark the left hand sides of channels entering from seaward. Conical buoys with pointed tops are known as nun buoys, and if painted red, mark the right hand sides of channels entering from seaward. Cylindrical or can buoys, painted in red-and-black horizontal bands, with the topmast band black, are used to indicate an obstruction or a junction of one channel with another, where the principal channel entering from seaward lies to the right of the buoy.

Can or nun buoys with black-and-white vertical stripes indicate the middle of a channel, and may be passed safely on either side. In these the shape has no significance.

No special significance is to be attached to the shapes of spar buoys, bell buoys, whistle buoys, gong buoys, lighted buoys, or combination buoys, their purpose being indicated by their coloring, numbering, or the characteristic of the light.

Sizes of Buoys

The various types of buoys are made in different sizes to fit them for service in waters of different depths and varying degrees of exposure. These sizes in no way affect the significance of the buoys and need not be taken into consideration by mariners except as a means of judging distances.

Color of Lights

For all buoys having lights, the following system of coloring is used. Green lights are used only on buoys marking the left hand sides of channels entering from seaward. Red lights are used only on buoys marking the right hand sides of channels entering from seaward. White lights may be used on either side of the channel, and such lights are frequently employed in place of colored lights at points where a light of considerable brilliance is required, particularly as leading or turning lights.

Light Characteristics

Fixed lights (lights that do not flash) may be found on either red or black buoys.

Flashing lights (flashing at regular intervals and at the rate of not more than 30 flashes per minute) are placed on either black buoys or on red buoys.

Quick flashing lights (not less than 60 flashes per minute) are placed on black buoys and on red buoys at points where it is desired to indicate that special caution is required, as at sharp turns or sudden constrictions.

Interrupted quick flashing lights (the groups consisting of a series of quick flashes, with dark intervals between groups of about 4 seconds) and placed on buoys painted in red-and-black

horizontal bands, indicating obstructions or a junction of one channel with another.

Short-long flashing lights (groups consisting of a short flash and a long flash, the groups recurring at the rate of about 8 times per minute) are placed on buoys painted in black-and-white vertical stripes, indicating a fairway or the middle of a channel where the buoy should be passed close to. The light is always white.

Reflectors

Reflectors are placed upon many unlighted buoys, and greatly facilitate the locating of the buoys at night by means of a searchlight. Reflectors may be white, red, or green, and have the same significance as lights of these colors. Scotchlite reflective sheeting is also used extensively by the Coast Guard for marking unlighted buoys. This flexible plastic film is easy to attach to a reasonably smooth surface and has angularity features not available in the conventional glass reflector.

Fish Net Buoys

Particularly, though not exclusively, in the Chesapeake Bay area, buoys are used to mark the limits of areas in which fish nets and traps are permitted, such areas and the buoys being indicated also upon the charts. These buoys are chiefly spars, and are painted in black-and-white horizontal bands. Unlike the vertically striped black-and-white buoys, they carry identification numbers. Temporary buoys, orange-and-white horizontally banded and topped by a blue-and-white flag on a mast, have been used in research work by the Fish and Wildlife Service.

Intracoastal Waterway Aids

The aids to navigation marking the Intracoastal Waterway have a characteristic yellow marking in addition to their usual coloring to indicate which side of the channel they mark. Buoys have a yellow band at the top. Single pile beacons have a yellow band at the top. Daymarks on light structures have a yellow border.

In addition to the special Intracoastal Waterway coloring, all aids in this waterway are painted in the usual manner to indicate which side of the channel they mark. All aids in this waterway are colored and numbered from north to south along the Atlantic coast and from east to west on the Gulf Coast.

Where the Intracoastal Waterway follows another waterway, the aids in which are colored and numbered in the opposite direction, a yellow triangle is placed on black buoys, and a yellow square on red buoys. This indicates that buoys with the triangular markings are to be considered as nun buoys, and the square marked buoys as can buoys, insofar as a vessel following the Intracoastal Waterway is concerned.

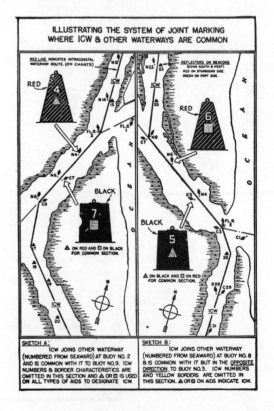

Brief History of Buoyage

Buoyage of navigable waterways in this country was undertaken at least as early as 1767 when, according to available records, buoys were in use in the Delaware River. The earliest types were simply solid wooden spars or were built up of staves, similar to a barrel. This stave construction was employed in small buoys used near Boston about 1808, but these gave way to spar buoys about 1820, supplemented by iron buoys in 1850. A marked improvement was effected in 1900 when tall can and nun buoys were introduced. In 1881 the first lighted buoy, burning oil, was put into service outside New York Harbor. Electricity was employed from 1888 to 1903 in the Gedney Channel in New York lower bay. Current for these buoys was supplied through cables from shore, but this system proved impractical. Buoys lighted by compressed acetylene gas stored in tanks within the buoy itself, the type of lighted buoy in general use today, were introduced in 1910. Bell buoys, in which the bell is struck by clappers actuated by the rolling of the buoy in the sea, have been in service since 1885; and now buoys are also in service in which the bell is struck at regular intervals by a mechanism operated by compressed gas. Whistle buoys, the whistle sounded through motion of the buoy in the sea, have been employed since 1876. Similar buoys are now available in which a trumpet is sounded by electrical means. Tests have also been made of buoys fitted with automatic radiobeacons, and the use of these is expected to be extended. Recently, experiments have been made to develop a buoy which would reflect radar signals better than the standard type of buoy. These test buoys are painted with orange and white vertical stripes.

Notices to Mariners

When vessels are in active operation, the owners or operators should keep themselves fully informed of the proposed changes in the navigational aids in the vicinity in which they intend to cruise. Information regarding changes in aids is made available by the Coast Guard through its weekly Notice to Mariners, and through radio broadcasts. Notices to Mariners are, on application to the Coast Guard, mailed without charge to individuals who have definite use for them, and to yacht clubs and similar organizations having facilities for making their contents available, by posting or otherwise. In addition to these printed notices issued from Washington, each District Commander issues from time to time Local Notices to Mariners with respect to aids to navigation in his district. These local notices cover emergency matters as well as temporary misplacements and outages. They are similarly made available to organizations such as those noted and to newspapers for publication.

Buoys in British Waters

In British waters, more significance is placed on shape than on the color of buoys. For example, buoys found on the starboard hand are painted in any one color, but one may find *either* a red *or* a black buoy on his starboard hand. However, it will be a pointed top buoy, bullet-nosed in shape. Port hand buoys in England are either single-colored or parti-colored, in shape resembling generally the frustum of a cone. Among these are included the red-and-white and black-and-white checkered buoys not found in United States waters.

The U. S. Coast Guard is constantly at work improving its aids to navigation so that they may better serve the boatman and mariner. Above, at the left, the world's first atomic buoy is launched at the Coast Guard Yard in Baltimore, Md. The test buoy is lighted by SNAP-7A (the Atomic Energy Commission's Systems for Nuclear Auxiliary Power), a strontium-90 thermoelectric system. The power system consists basically of a thermoelectric generator, a voltage converter, and small battery. The generator converts heat energy from strontium-90, a waste product of fission used as a fuel source, to electrical energy. There are no moving parts, and the ten-year life of the generator and battery is a great advantage over present systems which must be recharged every year or two. The three other illustrations (center and right) show new types of buoys designed with built-in reflectors to serve as a better target for radar than the older conventional shapes. At left center is the new-type can buoy; at right center, the nun; and at the right an unlighted mid-channel buoy with black and white vertical stripes. The vertical stripes signify that the mid-channel buoy may be passed close-to on either side. (Official U. S. Coast Guard photographs).

CHAPTER XVII

Government Publications

(*See pages 491-493*)

THE pilot is dependent upon accurate charts in navigating unfamiliar waters. However, to supplement this information, he has recourse to a number of other publications issued by the Government. These include Tide Tables, Current Tables, Coast Pilots, Light Lists, Tidal Current Charts and several others. Utilizing all the data available from these sources, he is able to prepare himself with detailed local knowledge on any body of navigable water.

Charts of coastwise waters are prepared by the Coast and ʻGeodetic Survey of the Department of Commerce. This division also issues the Tide Tables, Current Tables, Tidal Current Charts for certain harbors and Coast Pilots. Catalogs issued by them give information on other publications of the Department of Commerce and contain outline maps showing the area covered by each chart together with its respective catalog number. The various Light Lists are published by the United State Coast Guard.

Charts are kept up to date by means of a weekly bulletin called Notice to Mariners, a free publication of the Oceanographic Office, U. S. Navy. Now issued in two parts, Part I covers the Western Hemisphere, Part II the Eastern Hemisphere. In addition to these, there are local Notices issued by the Commanders of Coast Guard Districts. These are usually best suited to the needs of yachtsmen who do not require information on remote or foreign waters.

Tide and Current Tables, Coast Pilots, Light Lists, Tidal Current Charts, Notices to Mariners, and Other Publications of the Government Useful to the Pilot. A Discussion of Tides and How They Are Caused

The Notices give detailed information on the establishment of new aids to navigation, discontinuance of, or changes in existing aids, and data of any kind which will affect the information given on charts or other publications. The numbers of the charts and the pages of the publications affected are given with each note for convenience in making the necessary changes. When the chart numbers are printed in bold-face type, the changes are of a permanent character and the publications affected may be corrected accordingly. Where the information is of a general or temporary nature or is based on unauthenticated reports, the chart numbers are printed in light-face type. This indicates that the information given should be noted simply that the mariner may be in possession of all the facts relating to the area in question, without making permanent corrections.

All boatmen are urged to cooperate with the Federal Government in keeping the buoyage system up to its highest plane of efficiency and helpfulness by reporting any facts they may have concerning damage to buoys, ex-

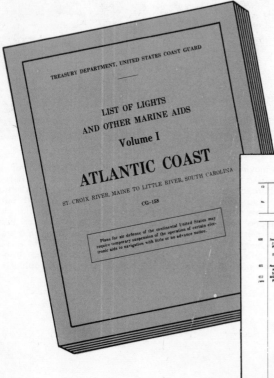

Light Lists are now available in five volumes, covering the coasts, Great Lakes and Mississippi River system. Illustrated is Volume I, listing aids to navigation on the Atlantic Coast from St. Croix River, Maine, to Little River, South Carolina, embracing the First, Third and Fifth Coast Guard Districts. Extract shows descriptions of some of the aids at the eastern end of Long Island.

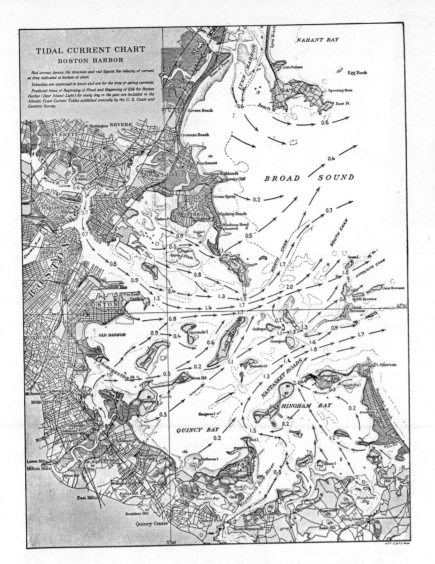

TIDAL CURRENT CHART
BOSTON HARBOR

Red arrows denote the direction and red figures the velocity of current at time indicated at bottom of chart.

Velocities are expressed in knots and are for the time of spring currents.

Predicted times of Beginning of Flood and Beginning of Ebb for Boston Harbor (Deer Island Light) for every day in the year are included in the Atlantic Coast Current Tables published annually by the U. S. Coast and Geodetic Survey.

there are four volumes, one of which covers the East Coast of North and South America, another the West Coast of North and South America. The East Coast Tide Tables alone contain predictions for 47 reference stations and differences for about 2,000 stations in North and South America.

The Tide Tables give the predicted times and heights of high and low water for each day of the year at a number of important points known as reference stations or standard ports. Portland, Boston, Newport, and Sandy Hook are thus among the various points for which detailed tidal information is given in the East Coast Tables. Additional data are tabulated showing the difference in the times and heights between these reference stations and thousands of other subordinate stations. From this table, called Tidal Differences and Constants, the tide at virtually any point along the coast may be easily computed.

It seems advisable at this point to depart long enough from the strictly practical to consider some of the fundamental causes of tides

tinction of lights, shifting of shoals and channels, and all information of like nature. Reports relating to defects of any sort in aids to navigation should be communicated as quickly as possible to the nearest District Commander of the Coast Guard. Data concerning dangers to navigation, changes in shoals and channels and similar information affecting charts or publications of the Coast and Geodetic Survey should be sent to the director of that division at Washington, D. C., or to the nearest Coast and Geodetic Survey Field Station.

Tide Tables are of great value in determining the height of water at any place at a given time. These are calculated in advance and are published annually in several volumes. At present

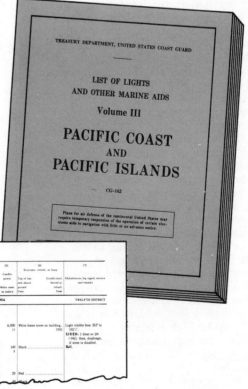

Above: One of the 12 charts in the Tidal Current Chart of Boston Harbor, showing currents 4 hours after high water at Boston. Right: Aids to navigation on the Pacific Coast are described in Volume III of the Light List. An extract from it appears below.

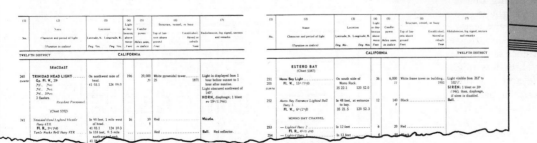

301

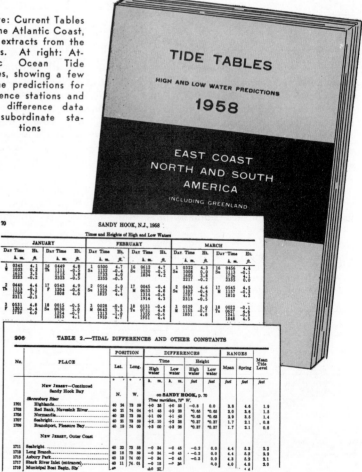

side this layer of water, each point on the earth's surface would then have two high and two low tides each day, following each other in alternate and regular succession. However, the surface of the earth is not surrounded by such a uniform layer but is broken up by land masses of varying contour and the ocean depths likewise vary so that the regularity of these cycles is disturbed more or less depending or the nature of the coast-line.

When the high tide has reached its maximum level, and the low tide its minimum, there are periods of no apparent change, known as the stand. The difference in level between high and low water at a given place is called the range. Note that so far we have been dealing only with a vertical movement of the water.

Now the periodic rising and falling of the water set up tidal currents in the bays and arms of the ocean along the coasts. This horizontal flow toward the coasts is called flood tide; away from the coast, ebb. At the end of both flood and ebb, before the current has turned, there are periods of no apparent flow known as slack water.

It is important to note that the

and currents. A general understanding of these causes will help considerably in an intelligent use of the tables.

All bodies respond to the universal law of gravitation, the intensity of the attraction depending on the size of the bodies and the distance separating them. Thus it is that the moon, being nearest to us of all the heavenly bodies, controls the tides of the earth by tending to draw the water of the oceans toward it. The sun exerts a similar influence but of much less intensity than that of the moon.

If the earth were surrounded by a layer of water of uniform thickness, the tendency of the moon's attraction would be to draw the water out at the points of the earth directly toward and away from the moon. These points would accordingly experience a high tide, or raising of the water level. Between those two points, around the earth, the water would be drawn away, and these places would experience a lowering of the water level, or low tide. The terms high tide and low tide refer, properly, to the upper and lower limits of the water's rise and fall.

As the earth revolves on its axis, once in twenty-four hours, in-

Above: Current Tables for the Atlantic Coast, with extracts from the tables. At right: Atlantic Ocean Tide Tables, showing a few of the predictions for reference stations and tidal difference data for subordinate stations

302

times of no vertical movement (stand) do not necessarily coincide with the times of no horizontal movement (slack). If the coast-line were absolutely regular they probably would, but due to the retardation of the flow as it runs into bays, inlets and other indentations of the coast, the current may be running at strength while the level has reached its highest or lowest point.

Obviously then the Tide Tables cannot be consulted when determining the time of a fair current. Neither is the time of slack water as shown in the Current Tables any guide to the time of high water. The condition just described is commonly seen at our inlets, where the current sometimes continues to run flood into the bays hours after the water has stopped rising. In the same way the ebb current may still be flowing with great velocity while the level has already begun to rise.

Practically everyone has observed the fluctuations in the height of tide and strength of currents at the different phases of the moon. This is caused by the variation in the combined gravitational pull of moon and sun as they assume relatively different positions in space. The sun, though much larger than the moon, is infinitely more remote from the earth, the factors being such that the sun's tide-producing influence is about two-fifths that of the moon. The earth is making a yearly circuit around the sun; the moon a monthly revolution about the earth. At full moon and new moon, the three bodies are most nearly in a direct line (as they are during an eclipse) and the tide-producing forces of sun and moon combine in causing higher high tides and lower low tides. These are called spring tides. At the first quarter and third quarter phases of the moon, the sun and the moon have assumed positions in space at an angle of 90 degrees, as seen from the earth. At these times the tidal influences of the two bodies tend to oppose each other, resulting in lower high tides and higher low tides. These are known as neap tides.

An inspection of the Tide Tables will also reveal a difference between the heights attained by the two high tides of one day at any given place. This is a difficult thing to explain in a few words without illustrations but it may be said that it is due to the fact that they are equal only when the moon is directly over the equator. Otherwise when the earth revolves on its axis 180 degrees, a given point on the earth will be at a greater or lesser distance from the point of the highest high water. This condition gives rise to four different terms—higher high water, lower high water, higher low water, and lower low water.

Tidal height at a given point varies from month to month and from year to

Below—General catalog of charts and U. S. Coast and Geodetic Survey publications, from which one can determine the area covered by each chart, its scale, price, etc. Sales agencies for such publications are also listed. Lower—One section of the Coast Pilot, issued in a series of volumes for coasts of the United States and its possessions. Each includes sailing directions, depths of water, courses, strength of currents, location of repair facilities and supplies and much additional data of value in navigating unfamiliar waters, as indicated in the extract shown

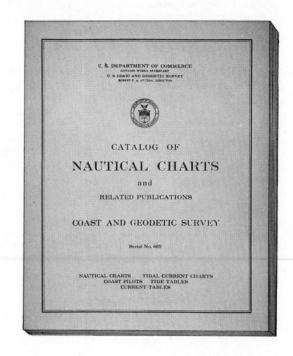

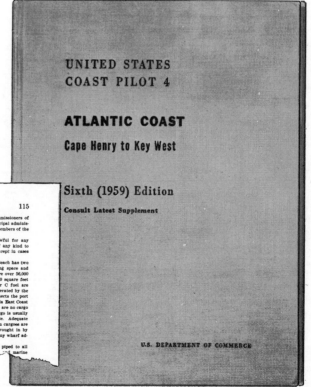

year. The monthly variation is due to the fact that the earth is not at the center of the moon's orbit. When the moon is close to the earth it exerts the greatest influence on the tides and the high tides resulting from this maximum attraction are called perigees. Apogees are the lower tides resulting when the moon is at its greatest distance from the earth. In a similar manner the yearly variation in the tide is caused by the varying attraction of the sun as its distance from the earth becomes greater or less.

Other factors having a pronounced influence on the height of tide are the barometric pressure and wind. The effect of a prolonged gale of wind from a certain quarter is sometimes sufficient to offset all of the other factors.

While there are normally two high and two low tides every twenty-four hours, they are on an average almost an hour later each day. This is due to the fact that the lunar day is about fifty minutes longer than the solar day. That is, reckoning time by the sun, the moon will pass over a given point somewhat less than an hour later each day. Consequently there will be times when a high or low tide may skip a calendar day, as indicated by a blank space in the Tide Tables. If it is a high tide that has skipped it will be noticed that the previous corresponding high occurred late in the foregoing day and the next one is due early the following day.

It will also be noted that at certain times, some stations listed in the Tide Tables appear to have only one high and one low tide each day. This condition arises when the configuration of the land and the periods between successive tides are such that one tide is reflected back from the shore and alters the influence of the succeeding tide.

Sometimes the diurnal inequality (that is, the difference in height of the two high waters or the two low waters of each day) is so increased as to cause only one low water each day. These tides are not unusual in the tropics and consequently are called tropic tides. Equatorial tides occur near the time when the moon is over the equator; the tendency toward producing diurnal inequality is then at a minimum.

The depths given in the Tide Tables must naturally be reckoned from some plane of reference or datum, as it is called. From the previous discussion of the great variations to which the tide is subject, it is evident that there are a number of different planes to which the heights might be referred. Actually the predictions in the tables are based on the same datum as that used in making the charts of any given locality. The plane used for the Atlantic Coast is mean low water, which is the average of all low waters. On the Pacific Coast it is the average of the lower of the two low waters of each day.

All of the factors which can be determined in advance are taken into account in tide predictions, but in the use of the tables it should be borne in mind that certain factors, particularly the wind, cannot be forecast. Ordinary care should therefore be exercised, especially since low waters may go considerably lower than the level shown in the Tide Tables.

Explanation of the Tables

Table I of the Tide Tables, which gives the predicted times and heights of high and low water at the main reference stations, is practically self-explanatory. Where no sign is given before the predicted height, it is to be added to the depths as given on the chart. When the height is preceded by a minus (—) sign, the depths are to be subtracted. Time is given in Navy style—four figures 0000 to 2400.

Table II, Tidal Differences and Constants, gives the information necessary to find the time and height of tide for thousands of subordinate stations by the application of simple corrections to the data given for main reference stations. The name of the reference station in each case is given in bold-face type at the head of the particular section in which the subordinate station is listed. The following information is given in separate columns: latitude and longitude of the place, differences in time of tide and height of high water, mean range of the tide, and mean tide level.

To determine the time of high or low water at any station in Table II, use the column headed Differences, Time. This gives the hours and minutes to be added (+) or subtracted (—) from the time of high or low water at its reference table, shown in bold face type.

The height of tide, referred to datum of charts, is obtained by means of height differences or ratios. A plus (+) sign indicates the difference is to be added to the height at the reference station; a minus (—) sign indicates it should be subtracted.

Where height differences could give unsatisfactory predictions, ratios may be substituted for heights. Ratios are identified by an asterisk. These are given as a decimal fraction to be multiplied by the height at the reference station.

In the column headed Ranges, the mean range is the difference in height between mean high water and mean low water. The spring range is the average semidiurnal range occurring semimonthly when the moon is new or full. It is larger than the mean range where the type of tide is either semi-diurnal or mixed, and is of no practical significance where the type of tide is diurnal. Where the tide is chiefly of the diurnal type the table gives the diurnal range, which is the difference in height between mean higher high water and mean lower low water.

Figures once given for the High Water Interval have been omitted in recent editions of the Tide Tables. They simply represent values from which the time of high tide can be computed when the time of the moon's transit is known (that is, the time at which the moon bears true south). *See pages 351-353.*

A rough workable formula is given in Chapter XXVII, page 412, for determining the height of tide at any given time between high and low water. Those who wish to work with greater precision will find Table III of the Tide Tables of value. By its use close calculations can be made for any given time between high and low water and for any range of tide. Other tables in this publication give astronomical data such as time of moonrise and moonset, sunrise and sunset, etc.

Current Tables

The Current Tables are made up in much the same form as Tide Tables. However, instead of times of high and low water, the Current Tables give times of maximum flood, maximum ebb and the time of the two slack waters. The velocity at strength of the current is given in terms of nautical miles per hour (knots).

In the second part of the tables covering Current Differences and Constants, the latitude,

TABLE FOR FINDING HEIGHT OF TIDE ABOVE LOW WATER AT ANY HOUR OF THE EBB OR FLOOD		
FALLING TIDE Hours after high water	RISING TIDE Hours after low water	CONSTANT Ebb or Flood
0	6	1.0
1/2	5 1/2	0.98
1	5	0.92
1 1/2	4 1/2	0.84
2	4	0.75
2 1/2	3 1/2	0.63
3	3	0.50
3 1/2	2 1/2	0.38
4	2	0.26
4 1/2	1 1/2	0.16
5	1	0.08
5 1/2	1/2	0.025

1. Find rise of tide for given day in Tide Tables (difference between heights of nearest high and low tides)
2. Enter column 1 or 2 on line corresponding to time for which height of tide is to be calculated
3. In column 3, find constant given for that time
4. Multiply constant obtained in (3) by total rise of tide (1)

longitude and time difference columns are used in the same manner as in the Tide Tables. The column headed Velocity Ratio gives a decimal fraction which may be multiplied by the velocity at the reference station to determine the velocity at the subordinate station.

Near the coast and in inland tidal waters the current from slack water increases in velocity for a period of about three hours when the maximum velocity or the strength of the current is reached. The velocity then decreases for another period of about three hours when slack water is again reached and the current begins a similar cycle in the opposite direction. The current that flows toward the coast or up a stream is known as the flood current, while the one that sets from the coast or down a stream is known as the ebb current. In the columns headed Maximum Currents there are given the flood direction, average velocity, ebb direction and average velocity at strength of current. The flood and ebb directions are given in degrees, true, reading clockwise from 0° at north to 359° and are the directions toward which the current flows. The average velocities given represent the mean velocities of all strengths of flood and ebb currents.

Current Tables are published in two volumes—Atlantic Coast, North America; and Pacific Coast, North America, and Philippine islands. A table from which velocity may be computed for any given period of the current flow is included in the Current Tables.

Tidal Current Charts

Tidal Current Charts are available for eight bodies of water —New York Harbor, Boston Harbor, San Francisco Bay, Tampa Bay, Long Island Sound and Block Island Sound, Narragansett Bay to Nantucket Sound, Delaware Bay and River, and Puget Sound (in two parts). These are made up in the form of a series of twelve reproductions of the chart of the locality. Each of the charts indicates the direction and velocity of the tidal currents for a different hour. The currents in the various passages are traced with red arrows and the velocities are noted at numerous points. By following through the sequence of the charts the hourly changes in velocity and direction are easily determined. These charts make it possible to get an excellent picture of just how the tidal currents act in the various passages and channels throughout every part of the entire twelve-hour cycle.

Where the currents sometimes run at great velocities, as they do in Hell Gate, and especially where the tidal currents are complex, flowing often in opposite directions at the same stage of tide, a great advantage may be gained by consulting one of these charts. A few minutes study may well be the means of carrying the strength of a fair current through the entire passage, instead of needlessly bucking an unfavorable flow for a long period. As is the case with all current predictions, it must be remembered that the velocity figures refer to normal or average conditions and consequently a strong wind from certain quarters may have a decided influence, both as to time and strength.

Current Diagrams

As mentioned in a previous paragraph, current diagrams for important bodies of water are included in the Current Tables. They enable the pilot to determine the strength and general direction of the current flow as he takes his boat through the waterway. They also show graphically when a departure should be made from a given point in order to carry a favorable current through the passage. The current diagram for Chesapeake Bay has been reproduced on a larger scale and is issued as a separate publication.

Tide and current surveys have been made in a number of the important harbors and waterways of the United States. The data derived from these surveys are made available through a series of special publications which give in considerable detail the results of all observational data relating to tides and currents available for each waterway covered. These may be purchased at the office of the Coast and Geodetic Survey or from any of its agencies.

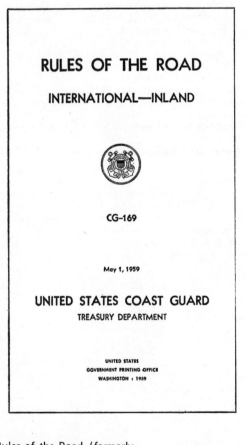

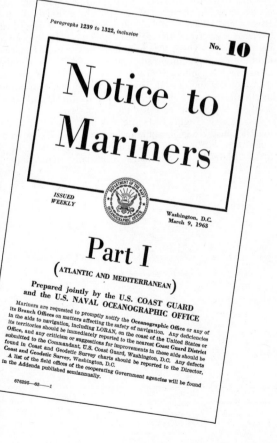

Notice to Mariners, right, a free weekly publication prepared jointly by the U. S. Coast Guard and the U. S. Navy Oceanographic Office by which charts and other Government publications are kept up to date. Part I covers the Western Hemisphere, Part II the Eastern Hemisphere. In addition, local Notices are issued by Coast Guard District Commanders for their respective districts. Shown below is an extract from the Notice illustrated

Rules of the Road (formerly called Pilot Rules), above, published by the Coast Guard, contain the rules relating to the navigation of vessels, including display of lights, fog signals and passing signals, day signals, speed, etc.

I   562

★ (1254) CHESAPEAKE BAY—James River—Controlling depths.—Surveys by the Corps of Engineers show controlling depths at M.L.W. in the improved James River channel as follows: In September–November 1962 a depth of 25 feet for a width of 200 feet from Hopewell (37°19'28'' N., 77°16'40'' W.) to Richmond Deep Water Terminal; thence in March 1957–November 1961 a depth of 17 feet for a width of 200 feet to a point about 150 yards south of the locks; thence shoaling to a minimum depth of 8 feet for a width of 200 feet or 15 feet in the northeast 100 feet to the locks.
    Approximate position: depth note: 37°20'30'' N., 77°17'15'' W.
    Note.—The Corps of Engineers should be consulted for changing conditions

Coast Pilots

Naturally the amount of information which can be given on charts is definitely limited. The volumes which supply detailed instructions for the navigation of coastal waters are called Coast Pilots. They are printed in book form, in eight volumes, some of which cover foreign coasts. The Atlantic Coast is covered by four volumes.

The various volumes of the Coast Pilot contain complete and explicit sailing directions between all ports together with recommended courses and exact distances. Channels, with their controlling depths, and all dangers and obstructions are fully described. Local information on intricate inland channels which cannot be navigated to advantage by chart, is included in great detail. Harbors and anchorages are given, with particular information on those points at which facilities are available for boat supplies and marine repairs. Information regarding canals, docks, bridges, wrecks, etc., which cannot be adequately expressed on the chart, due to limitations of space, is also contained in the Pilots. Supplements to the latest editions are issued with each volume, giving corrections and additions up to the date of issue.

The Coast Pilot data concerning the Intracoastal Waterway from New York to Key West, which was formerly published in a separate volume, is now covered in the regular Atlantic Coast Pilots for the areas concerned.

For the Great Lakes and other waters covered by U. S. Lake Survey charts, the publication corresponding to the Coast Pilot is called the Great Lakes Pilot, formerly known as the U. S. Lake Survey Bulletin. This is an annual publication, kept up to date during the navigation season by seven monthly supplements issued from May to November.

Two comparatively recent publications are of great value to persons navigating the inland routes along the Atlantic and Gulf Coasts. Both are available from the Superintendent of Documents, Washington 25, D. C. Entitled Intracoastal Waterway, it is published in two parts. Part I is the Atlantic Section, covering the Atlantic Coast from Boston to Key West. Part II is the Gulf Section, from Florida to the Rio Grande. Principal features of the waterway are briefly described, with considerable data of interest to the yachtsman.

Light Lists

Light Lists for all coasts of the United States and its island possessions, the Great Lakes, and the Mississippi and Ohio Rivers, are issued by the United States Coast Guard and may be purchased from the Superintendent of Documents, Washington, D. C. These lists describe, for the use of mariners, the lighthouses, lightships, radiobeacons, and buoys maintained in all navigable United States waters by the Coast Guard. This data includes the official name of the aid, the characteristics of its light, sound, and radio signals, its structural appearance, position, and dimensions for taking angles.

In the new Light Lists, lighted and unlighted aids appear together in their geographic order, with amplifying data on the same page. While the new publications may still be referred to as "Light Lists," the name is officially changed to "List of Lights and Other Marine Aids." The book is about the size of the new Coast Pilots. Aids are listed for each district in this order: seacoast, major channel, Intracoastal Waterway, minor channel and miscellaneous.

Light Lists are published in five volumes as follows:

Volume I, Atlantic Coast, St. Croix River (Maine) to Little River (South Carolina)

Volume II, Atlantic and Gulf Coasts, Little River (S.C.) to Rio Grande River (Texas)

Volume III, Pacific Coast and Pacific Islands

Volume IV, Great Lakes, U. S. and Canada

Volume V, Mississippi River System

All Coast Guard light lists are for sale by the Superintendent of Documents, Government Printing Office, Washington 25, D. C., and by sales agencies as listed quarterly in the weekly Notices to Mariners.

Charts, Coast Pilots, Tide Tables, and Current Tables of the coasts covered by Coast Guard Light Lists of the Atlantic and Pacific Coasts, are published by the United States Coast and Geodetic Survey, Department of Commerce, Washington 25, D. C., and are for sale by that agency and by sales agencies as listed quarterly in the weekly Notices to Mariners. Charts and related publications for the Great Lakes covered by the Great Lakes Light List are published by the United States Lake Survey, Corps of Engineers, United States Army, Detroit, Mich. Maps and related publications for the Mississippi River system covered by the Mississippi and Ohio Rivers Light List are published by the various District Engineer offices, Corps of Engineers, United States Army, located in the area.

Other Publications

Besides the foregoing publications, which are those commonly used on cruising boats, a copy of the American Practical Navigator by Bowditch is recommended. This has long been recognized as the accepted authority on questions of piloting and navigation. It is published by the United States Oceanographic Office and will be found very useful.

Other Government publications which contain useful information for the amateur skipper are H.O. 117, Radio Navigational Aids; H.O. 118, Radio Weather Aids to Navigation; H.O. 103, International Code of Signals. Visual; H.O. 104, International Code of Signals, Radio; Daily Weather Reports and the Weather Map; and the Yachtsman's Guide (published by MoToR BoatinG).

Further information on publications will be found on page 491.

Branch Oceanographic Office Service

Branch Offices of the U. S. Oceanographic Office in principal ports render great service to yachtsmen. They have on hand latest hydrographic information and are equipped with charts covering the world, Sailing Directions, Light Lists, Tide and Current Tables, and data on navigation, together with Manuals and Tables. The naval officers in charge of these offices are only too willing to give boatmen the benefit of their knowledge and experience, when planning a short cruise or an ocean voyage.

CHAPTER XVIII
The Chart

Reading and Interpreting the Chart, How Charts Are Made and What to Look for on Them—Meaning of the Symbols and Marks

See also pages 398-404

CHARTS, the subject of the present lesson in MoToR BoatinG's Course in Piloting are among the most essential items of equipment carried on boats. The navigator is dependent at all times upon the correctness and accuracy of the information shown on the charts and it is the duty of various government agencies to see that the information supplied is correct at all times. A chart is a miniature representation on a plane surface of certain portions of the earth's surface plotted according to the definite systems of projection. They generally include an outline of adjacent lands and such artificial features that are useful as aids to navigation. They show the depths of water, the location of obstructions, dangerous areas, the parallels of latitude and longitude and other information according to the special use for which the chart is intended.

There are several ways in which charts are constructed. The method commonly used for navigation charts is Mercator's projection. This system assumes that the earth is a cylinder and in accordance with this assumption the meridians of longitude which in a sphere converge at the poles are opened out and become straight lines. This necessitates a stretching out in the width of everything in the higher latitudes. In order to preserve the geographical relation the lengths are stretched proportionately, with the result that everything in the high latitudes is on a larger scale as compared with places in lower latitudes. An island, for example, in the neighborhood of the equator would appear much smaller than an island of the identical size in the neighborhood of the poles, both being plotted to the same scale. The cylinder on which the projection is made is assumed to be tangent to the earth at the equator. The rectangles formed by the intersection of the meridians of longitude and parallels of latitude will have variable altitudes which increase from the equator according to known laws. The proportionate

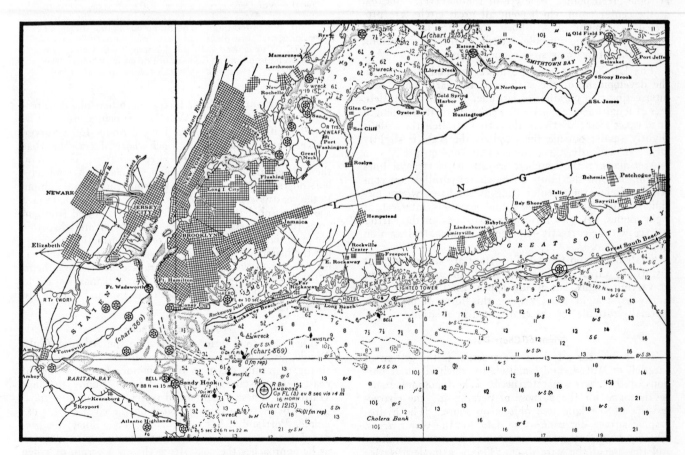

Fig. 168. Small portion of the general coastwise chart number 1108, Approaches to New York. This in the original covers the entire zone lying between Nantucket shoals on the east and Five Fathom Bank light vessel on the south. It is on an exceedingly small scale and only intended to be used for off-shore navigation. Such general features as the principal sea coast lights and light vessels are prominently shown as well as a general outline of the land and location of cities. The principal deepwater buoys which would be observed by a large vessel in approaching a harbor are also indicated. For comparative purposes Figs. 169 and 170 are reproductions of the same locality as shown on larger scale charts reduced in the same proportion. References to these charts numbers 1215 and 369 are printed in red on the originals. Soundings are given in fathoms and on the original, curves of depths running through 10, 20, 40, 50, 100 and 1,000 fathoms are indicated. In the drawing the 10 fathom curve appears and a portion of the 20 fathom line is just visible in the corner

increase is expressed in minutes at the equator as a unit and the length of the meridian as increased between equator and any given latitude constitutes the number of Meridional parts corresponding to that latitude. This information is all tabulated for ready reference.

A straight line between any two points on the Mercator chart is a rhumb line, cutting all meridians at the same angle. This feature makes it especially convenient in plotting courses. However, a great circle (shortest distance between two points on the earth's surface) is a curved line on the Mercator chart so that radio bearings, which follow great circles, cannot be plotted as straight lines on a Mercator chart without correction.

Methods of Projection

Another form of chart construction is the polyconic system of projection. This is used particularly for the plotting of surveys and is also used to some extent in the charts of the United States Coast and Geodetic Survey. This projection is based upon the development of the earth's surface upon a series of cones, a different one being used for each parallel of latitude. The vertex is in the point where a tangent to the earth at that latitude intersects the earth's axis. The distortion of the figure is less than in any other method of projection and the relative sizes are more correctly preserved.

There is still another method called Gnomonic projection. This system assumes a plane tangent to the earth at some given point. The eye of the observer is located at the center from which point all great circles are projected as straight lines. These charts are not used for general navigating purposes except in the polar regions, where the Mercator system cannot be used.

The Lambert projection, a newer method, is based on the development of the surface of the earth on a cone intersecting two parallels of latitude. On these parallels, arcs of longitude are represented either in their true length or to exact scale. Between these two parallels the scale is slightly small; outside the parallels the scale is slightly large. Practically, the error is of no consequence.

Meridians on the Lambert projection are straight lines meeting beyond the limits of the chart; parallels are concentric circles, their center lying at the point where meridians intersect. Meridians and parallels intersect at right angles. Angles formed by two lines on the earth's surface will be correctly represented on a chart drawn on this projection.

Small figures on the earth's surface are shown without distortion. Great circle courses would intersect meridians at varying angles but would appear on the chart practically as straight lines, making this form of projection especially suitable for the charts used in aviation.

Origin of Chart Data

The origin for all chart construction is the system of parallels of latitude and longitude to which all other portions of the chart are referenced. The topographic survey is made for the purpose of determining the characteristics of the land and objects on shore. The hydrographic survey determines the data for the water areas. The depths of bottom are determined by many soundings and the use of the wire drag. This is a modern device by means of which obstructions in the nature of pinnacle rocks can be quickly located. The soundings are plotted on the chart in correct relation to other objects and in the finished chart only such are included which are necessary to give a clear idea of the depths.

Who Issues Charts

Three departments of the Government issue charts, as follows: The Coast and Geodetic Survey of the Department of Commerce publishes from its surveys charts

which are suited to the purposes of navigation, commerce, and public defense. The Oceanographic Office in the Navy Department has charge of the duplication of charts and plans issued by other nations, and the publication of charts by the Navy of coasts not under the jurisdiction of the United States; the Corps of Engineers in the War Department issues charts of the Great Lakes.

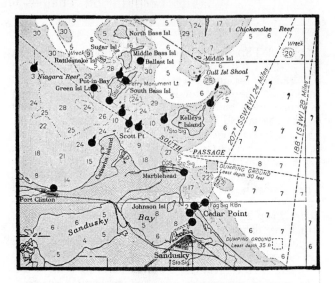

Part of Lake Survey chart No. 3, Lake Erie (published by the War Dept.), scale 1 to 400,000 (polyconic projection). Areas with depths to 30 feet, on this earlier chart, are tinted blue. The numerous lights (black circular spots) are black dots in a magenta circle on the chart. This is used with the diamond-shaped buoy symbol on lighted buoys. Courses are given in degrees (true) and points (magnetic) with distances in statute miles

The charts of the Great Lakes and other inland waterways are published by the War Department Corps of Engineers, with headquarters at United States Lake Survey Office, Detroit, Michigan. Their charts differ somewhat from the Coast and Geodetic Survey charts. They show the courses and distances between various points and harbors on the chart. The buoy system is in general similar to the coastwise charts. Depths of water on new charts are shown on tinted areas up to 24 feet, the 1, 2, 3 and 4-fathom areas tinted successively lighter. Depths greater than this are given on untinted areas. Useful information concerning the heights of water, tabulation of magnetic variation, lists of dry docks, and other data are printed on them. All lighted aids are emphasized by a small magenta circle printed over them which causes them to stand out clearly on the chart.

Four Series of Charts

There are four series of charts on the Atlantic, Gulf, Pacific, and Philippine Island Coasts, the first series consisting of sailing charts, which embrace long stretches of coasts—for instance, from the Bay of Fundy to Cape Hatteras. These are intended to serve for offshore navigation, or between distant points on the coast, as for example, Portland, Me., to Norfolk, Va. They are prepared for the use of the navigator in fixing his position as he approaches the coast from the open ocean, or when sailing between distant coast ports. They show the offshore soundings, the principal lights and outer buoys and landmarks visible at a great distance.

The second series is known as the general charts of the coast. They are on a scale three times as large as those of the first series, and embrace more limited areas, such as the Gulf of Maine, etc. They are intended for coastwise navigation when the vessel's course is mostly within sight of land, and her position can be fixed by landmarks, lights, buoys, and soundings.

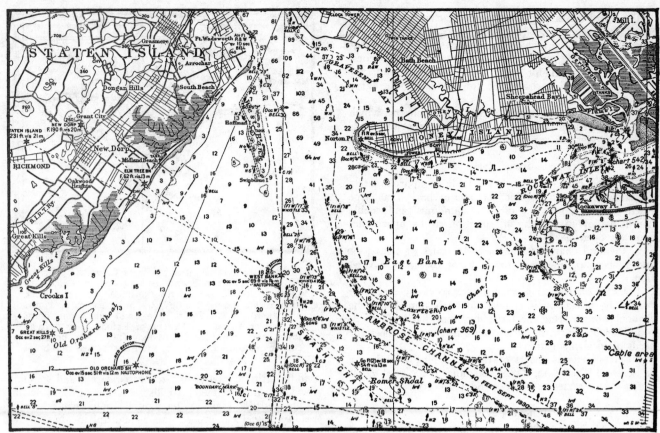

Fig. 169. Portion of chart number 1215. Approach to New York, Fire Island Inlet to Sea Girt Light. Original on a scale of 1 to 80,000. The size of this chart is such that all buoys and other aids to navigation can be readily shown. Note the many lighted buoys along Ambrose Channel. The steering ranges for the channel are Staten Island Light and West Bank Light. The ranges for the Swash channel are the New Dorp and Elm Tree beacons. The visibility of these lights is plainly indicated and these ranges are used continuously. The depth of water can be given in greater detail, the soundings being given in feet

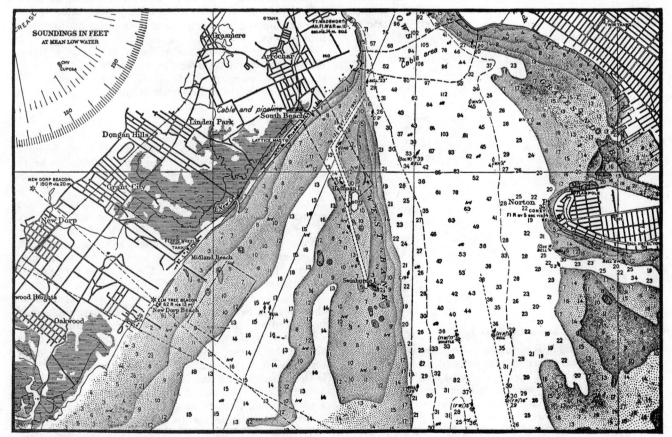

Fig. 170. Portion of chart number 369 New York Harbor. This is a large scale detail chart on a scale of 1 to 40,000 or twice as large as Fig. 169. On this one the soundings are indicated in feet at mean low water. Much greater detail is possible as will be noted by the shoal water indications in the tinted zones, the wharfs, buildings, streets and other features being more plainly indicated. Conspicuous objects which will aid the navigator in locating his position are shown. The vertical and horizontal lines which appear on the charts are the meridians of longitude and parallels of latitude. The figures giving this information appear at the edges of the original chart

The third series comprises the coast charts, which are constructed on a scale five times as large as that of the second series. One inch on these charts represents about one nautical mile, or one and one-seventh statute miles. They are intended for close coastwise navigation, for entering bays and harbors, and for navigating the large inland waterways.

The fourth series embraces the harbor charts, which are constructed on large scales intended to meet the needs of local navigation.

Scales Used

1. Sailing charts, mostly on a scale of approximately 1:1,200,000, which exhibit the approaches to a large extent of coast, give the offshore soundings, and enable the navigator to identify his position as he approaches from the open sea.

2. General charts of the coast, on scales of 1:400,000 and 1:200,000, intended especially for coastwise navigation.

3. Coast charts, on a scale of 1:80,000, by means of which the navigator is enabled to avail himself of the channels for entering the larger bays and harbors.

4. Harbor charts, on large scales, intended to meet the needs of local navigation.

NOTE.—General charts of the Philippine Islands are on scales 1:1,600,000, 1:800,000, and 1:400,000; coast charts are on scales 1:100,000, and 1:200,000.

Distances By Scale

The table below will give the length of a nautical and statute mile on the several scales used in constructing charts, that is, in the scale 1:1,200 the chart is ⅟₁₂₀₀ part of the actual linear dimensions in nature (or 100 feet to the inch), equal to 60.8 inches to a nautical mile, and 52.8 inches to a statute mile, and so on. A nautical mile is a minute of an average great circle of the earth, and its length is 6,080 feet, or 1,853.2 meters. A statute mile is 5,280 feet, or 1,609.3 meters.

Scale	Nautical mile Inches	Statute mile Inches
1:1,200	60.803	52.800
1:2,400	30.401	26.400
1:4,800	15.201	13.200
1:5,000	14.593	12.672
1:10,000	7.296	6.336
1:15,000	4.864	4.224
1:20,000	3.649	3.168
1:30,000	2.432	2.112
1:40,000	1.824	1.584
1:50,000	1.459	1.267
1:60,000	1.216	1.056
1:80,000	.912	.792
1:100,000	.730	.634
1:200,000	.365	.317
1:400,000	.182	.158
1:1,000,000	.073	.063
1:1,200,000	.061	.053

Measuring Distance

If no scale of miles is given, latitude scales on the east and west edges of the chart may be used for measuring distances. If the places are on the same meridian, their distance apart is most readily estimated by finding the difference of latitude in minutes. Distances between points situated on lines that make an angle with the meridians may be measured by taking between the points of the dividers a small number of subdivisions near the

NOTE:—On June 17, 1954, the Department of Defense adopted the international nautical mile of 6,076.10333 feet (1,852 meters) and on August 31, 1954, the Coast Guard adopted the same standard.

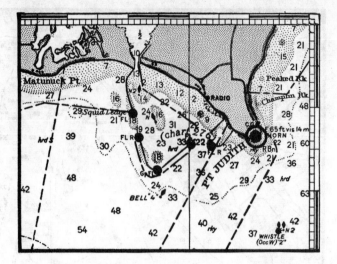

A small section from the corner of C. and G. S. chart 1211, Block Island Sound, showing longitude scale at the top, latitude scale at the right. On the latter, each minute is a nautical mile (2.7 miles shown). Lights are shown on Pt. Judith, the breakwaters and lights thereon enclosing the Harbor of Refuge, also a radio tower, and Coast Guard Station. The dashed lines enclose a cable area; long and short dashes fish trap areas

middle latitude of the line to be measured, and stepping them off on that line. All distances measured by means of the latitude scale are in nautical miles which can be readily converted into statute by multiplying by 1.15.

Notes on Charts

The source of a chart and the authority upon which it is based should be considered. The mariner will naturally feel the greatest confidence in a chart issued by the Government of one of the more important maritime nations which maintain a well equipped office for the especial purpose of acquiring and treating hydrographic information. He should be especially careful that the chart is of recent issue and bears corrections of a recent date—facts that should be clearly shown on the face of the chart. Notes on charts should always be read with care, as they may give important information that can not be graphically represented.

Dates on Charts

Charts bear three dates, which should be understood by persons using them: (1) The date (month and year) of the edition, *printed* on the latest charts below the border in a central position; (2) the date of the latest correction to the chart plates, *printed* in the lower left-hand corner below the border; (3) the *date of issue, stamped* below the border and just to the left of the subtitle. Charts show all necessary corrections as to lights, beacons, buoys, and dangers, which have been received to the *date of issue,* being hand corrected since the latest date printed in the lower self-hand corner. All small but important corrections occurring subsequent to the *date of issue* of the chart are published in Notice to Mariners and should be applied by hand to the chart immediately after the receipt of the notices. The date of the edition of the chart remains unchanged until an extensive correction is made on the plate from which the chart is printed. The date is then changed and the issue is known as a new edition. When a correction, not of sufficient importance to require a new edition, is made to a chart plate, the year, month, and day are noted in the lower left-hand corner. All the notes on a chart should be read carefully, as in some cases they relate to aids or dangers not clearly charted.

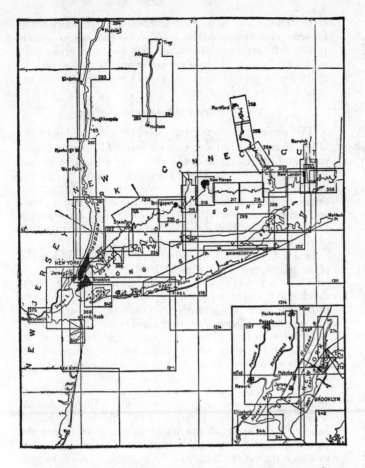

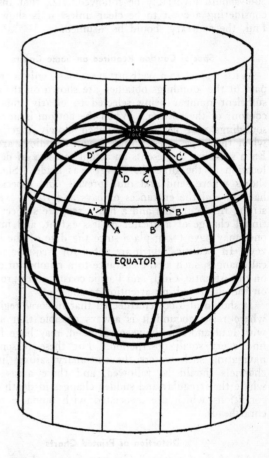

Fig. 171 (left). A reproduction of a typical page taken from the catalogue of charts, coast pilots, and tide tables as published by the United States Coast and Geodetic Survey. It will be noted that the numerous rectangles indicated cover the territory embraced in the various charts published. The relative size of the charts discussed under Figures 169 and 170 can be clearly distinguished. The general coastwise charts for offshore navigation are not shown on this index. On the adjacent page of the catalogue is noted the number, title, state, scale, size in inches and the price of each of these various charts. The chart user can quickly determine which charts are necessary to him and also their cost by referring to the catalogue

Fig. 172 (right). All large scale charts are constructed on what is known as Mercator's projection. This means roughly that the chart is constructed on the theory that the earth is a cylinder. The meridians of longitude, which converge at the poles are opened out and become straight lines. This necessitates a stretching out in width of everything in the higher latitudes. To preserve correct proportions everything in the higher latitudes is on a larger scale than at the equator. The particular advantage of this method is that the track of a vessel can be represented by a straight line instead of a curve as it would be in the case of a sphere. In our diagram the points marked A, B, C, and D on the earth's surface become the points A', B', C', and D' when projected on to the chart according to this method of construction

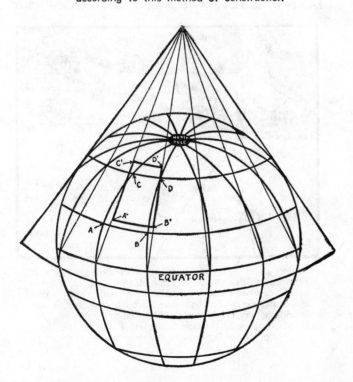

Fig. 173 (left). Another method of plotting charts is the polyconic shown in this sketch. This system while not used for navigation particularly is adapted to the plotting of surveys. It is based on the development of the earth's surface on a series of cones, a different one being taken for each parallel of latitude. The vertex is in a point where a tangent to the earth at that latitude intersects the earth's axis. The distortion is less in this method than in the others and a straight line on this type of chart approaches very closely a great circle. It is only on charts of very large extent that the curvature becomes apparent. The parallels of latitude are curves, this being apparent to the eye upon all except the largest scale of charts

Accuracy of Charts

The value of a chart depends upon the character and accuracy of the survey on which it is based, and the larger the scale of the chart the more important do these become. In these respects the source from which the information has been compiled is a good guide. This applies particularly to the charts of the Alaska Peninsula, Aleutian Islands, Arctic Ocean, and part of Bering Sea, and the Philippine Islands. The early Russian and Spanish surveys were not made with great accuracy, and until they are replaced by later surveys these charts must be used with caution.

With respect to these regions the fullness or scantiness of the soundings is another method of estimating the completeness of a chart. When the soundings are sparse or unevenly distributed, it may be taken for granted that the survey was not in great detail. A wide berth should, therefore, be given to every rocky shore or patch, and this rule should invariably be followed, viz., that instead of considering a coast to be clear unless it is shown to be foul, the contrary should be assumed.

Special Caution Required on Some Coasts

With respect to a well-surveyed coast, only a fractional part of the soundings obtained are shown on the chart, a sufficient number being selected to clearly indicate the contour of the bottom. When the bottom is uneven, the soundings will be found grouped closely together, and when the slopes are gradual fewer soundings are given. Each sounding represents an actual measure of depth and location at the time the survey was made. Shores and shoals where sand and mud prevail, and especially bar harbors and the entrances of bays and rivers exposed to strong tidal currents and a heavy sea, are subject to continual change of a greater or less extent, and important ones may have taken place since the date of the last survey. In localities which are noted for frequent and radical changes, such as the entrance to a number of estuaries on the Atlantic, Gulf, and Pacific coasts, notes are printed on the charts calling attention to the fact.

It should also be remembered that in coral regions and where rocks abound it is always possible that a survey with lead and line, however detailed, may have failed to find every small obstruction. For these reasons when navigating such waters the customary sailing lines and channels should be followed, and those areas avoided where the irregular and sudden changes in depth indicate conditions which are associated with pinnacle rocks or coral heads.

Distortion of Printed Charts

All of the Coast and Geodetic Survey charts are now printed by lithography on dry paper and have little if any distortion. A lithographed chart may be distinguished from a plate printed chart by the feel of the surface, the former being smooth while the latter is rough. Lithographed charts also are usually tinted in colors while the others are in black and white.

Caution in Using Small-Scale Charts

It is obvious that dangers to navigation can not be shown with the same amount of detail on small-scale charts as on those of larger scale; therefore in approaching the land or dangerous banks regard should be had to the scale of the chart, and the largest scale chart available should be used. A small error in laying down a position means only yards on a large-scale chart, whereas on a small scale the same amount of displacement means large fractions of a mile. For the same reason bearings to near objects should be used in preference to objects farther off, although the latter may be more prominent, as a small error in bearing or laying it down on the chart has a greater effect in misplacing the position the longer the line to be drawn.

Planes of Reference

The plane of reference for soundings on Oceanographic Office charts, made from United States Government surveys, and on Coast and Geodetic Survey charts of the Atlantic coast of the United States is mean low water; on the Pacific coast of the United States as far as the Strait of Fuca it is the mean of the lower low waters, and from Puget Sound to Alaska the Survey has adopted the harmonic or Indian tide plane, which is roughly that of the lowest low waters observed.

In Hydrographic Office charts of the Great Lakes the plane of reference is the mean level of the lake in 1847, which is 4.7 feet lower than the high water of 1838, the highest water recorded; a plane sufficiently low to insure the safe navigation of a vessel of less draft than the soundings shown over that locality.

In Lake Survey charts the soundings are referred to a plane of reference which is the mean elevation of the lake above mean tide of New York (adjusted levels of 1903).

Care must be taken to study the notes on the charts and compare them with the monthly bulletins issued, which give the mean elevation of the lake at the time of issue and the state of the water in the lake during the past month and its probable state for the coming month in order that corrections can be properly applied to find the proper depth.

On most British Admiralty charts the plane of reference is the low water of ordinary springs; on French charts the low water of equinoctial springs.

In the case of many charts compiled from old or various sources the plane of reference may be in doubt. In such cases, or whenever not stated on the chart, the assumption that the reference plane is mean low water gives the largest margin of safety.

Whichever plane of reference may be used for a chart, it must be remembered that there are times when the tide falls below it. Low water is lower than mean low water

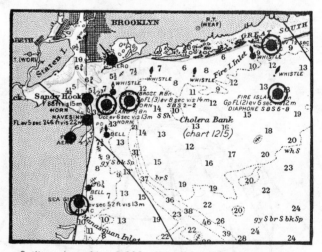

Sailing chart No. 1,000, for offshore navigation only, from Cape Sable, N. S., to Cape Hatteras, N. C., is on a small scale and not much concerned with detail along the coast, except for lightships, outer buoys, wrecks, etc. Soundings are in fathoms. A variation line (11° W) passes diagonally through Sandy Hook. Note the three lightships, lighthouses and numerous wrecks

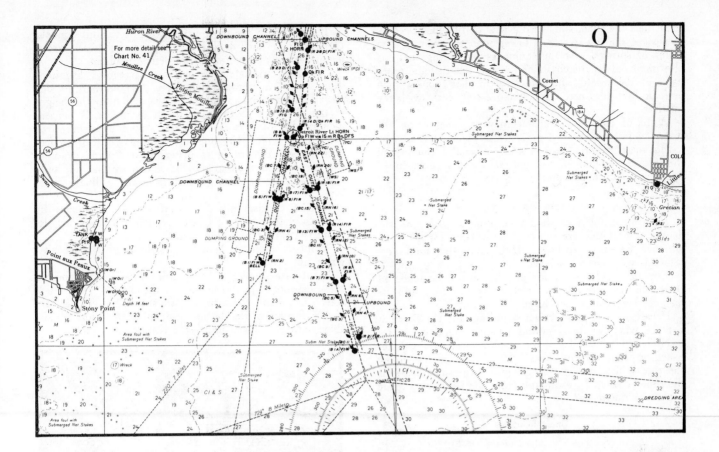

Fig. 175. Above: Portion of coast chart No. 39, west end of Lake Erie. Charts of the Great Lakes and certain other inland waterways are published by the War Department, Corps of Engineers. Principal sales office is the Lake Survey Office, Detroit. U. S. Engineer Offices at Buffalo and Chicago and the U. S. Canal Office, Sault Ste. Marie, Mich., make counter sales only. Lake Survey charts of the Great Lakes, Lake Champlain, New York Canals and Lake of the Woods are on the polyconic projection. They differ somewhat from Coast and Geodetic Survey charts. The courses (in degrees) and distances (statute miles) are an excellent feature. The magenta discs on the original chart (reproduced here in black) make all lights conspicuous. Within the red spot appears a dot in black. The practice of leaving red buoys to starboard and black buoys to port entering harbors from seaward is the same as on salt water. Soundings are in feet. Areas with depths of less than 24 feet are tinted blue, with the depths in feet. The deepest tints are in the shallowest water. The plane of reference is low water datum; there are no tides. Naturally, reproductions of the kind illustrated here are not for use in navigation. For that purpose always get the original charts, corrected to date of use.

Fig. 176. Right: This is a section of Coast and Geodetic Survey chart No. 251 showing a portion of the head of Buzzards Bay (Massachusetts), scale 1 to 20,000, reproduced about half chart size. At lower right is the range for the old Cape Cod Canal entrance channel. The new Hog Island channel, with mooring basin dredged to 32 feet, is clearly shown as well as shoals of varying depth defined by fathom curves. Depths are in feet. A railroad bridge with vertical lift (upper right) spans the canal, also a cable area. The old channel is closed by the dike at Hog Island. Data on the canal is given on a note on the chart

about half the time, and when a new or full moon occurs at perigee the low water is lower than the average low water of springs. At the equinoxes the spring range is also increased on the coasts of Europe, but in some other parts of the world, and especially in the Tropics, such periodic low tides may coincide more frequently with the solstices.

Wind or a high barometer may at times cause the water to fall below even a very low plane of reference.

On coasts where there is much diurnal inequality in the tides the amount of rise and fall can not be depended upon, and additional caution is necessary.

Mean Sea Level

The important fact should be remembered that the depths at half tide are practically the same for all tides, whether neaps or springs. Half tide, therefore, corresponds with mean sea level.

The tide tables give, for all the ports, the plane of reference to which tidal heights are referred and its distance below mean sea level.

If called on to take special soundings for the chart at a place where there is no tidal bench mark, mean sea level should be found and the plane for reductions established at the proper distance below it, as ascertained by the tide tables, or by observations, or in some cases, if the time be short, by estimation, the data used being made a part of the record.

Chart Readings

(See Fig. 179, also pages 324-328)

Chart reading aims to give such explanation concerning the various symbols and standards as will establish easily remembered relations between these graphic representations and the physical features which they represent. Briefly stated, the standards governing charts are the following:

The "shore line" is the boundary between water and land at high water. This boundary is shown by a continuous line wherever data are sufficient to plot the same with any degree of accuracy; otherwise a dashed line is used, indicating "approximate" delineation.

Vertical lettering is used for any feature dry at high water and not affected by the movement of the waters. (See the designation of Towers and Bell in the illustration at the right.)

Leaning lettering is used to describe such features as are parts of the hydrography. (See the manner in which *hrd s* is used to indicate hard sand in the same illustration.)

Very often, on smaller scale charts, a small reef can not be distinguished from a small islet; the proper name for either might be "———— Rock." Following the standard of lettering the feature in doubt is an islet if its name is in vertical letters, but is a reef if lettered in leaning characters.

Topography

The general topography is indicated by hachures, contours, or sketch-contours. Hachures and sketch-contours indicate approximately the relative position of summits and valleys and degree of connecting slopes. Whenever the contours are based upon an accurate survey of altitudes, a note stating their value—contour interval—is found under the title of the chart.

Symbols denoting vegetation have been designed to present pictorially the characteristics of the various kinds of growth. For example: The mangrove symbol consists of irregular ribs connected and studded with leaves.

The nature of the shore is indicated by various symbols, rows of fine dots denoting sandy beach; small circles denote gravel; irregular shapes denote boulders.

Cliffs are indicated by bands of irregular hachures. The symbol is not a "plan view," but rather a "side elevation," and its extent is in proportion to the height of the cliff, not to the plan. For example: A perpendicular cliff of 100 feet will be shown by a hachured band much wider than one representing a cliff of 15 feet with slope. According to principles of "plan" drawing the perpendicular cliff could be shown by one line only and could not be distinguished from the ordinary shore line.

Houses, roads, railroads, trails, etc., are shown by symbols well known, and are frequently lettered by descriptive text or proper *names*.

Numbers upon the land express the height, above high water, in feet.

Lights are shown by heavy solid dots or by 6-pointed stars, depending upon the scale of the chart. Their characters, *i.e.,* distinctive features, are stated in full or abbreviated form; in the latter case an explanation of the abbreviations is given under the title of the chart.

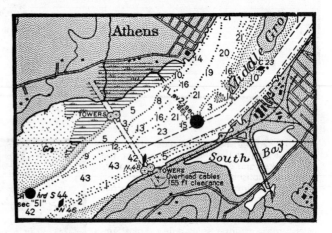

Part of C. and G. S. chart No. 283 (Hudson River), scale 1 to 40,000. Clearance of the overhead cables is indicated, and position of their supporting towers on and near shore. Nun buoys on the chart, of course, are symbolized in red, not black, as in the reproduction

Depths

Depths of water are shown very clearly by numbers which indicate the depth in feet or fathoms as the case may be, below mean low water. It is well to examine the chart to determine whether the soundings are in feet or fathoms, or even a combination of the two. Some charts are made with depths under thirty feet given in feet, while greater depths are given in fathoms. Further, these charts would have the depths in feet on tinted areas so that they can be quickly distinguished. Contour lines which run through all depths of the same dimensions are shown on most charts. A line consisting of a particular characteristic dotted line will run through all depths and can readily be followed.

Fathom Curves a Caution

Except in plans of harbors that have been surveyed in detail, the 5-fathom curve on most charts may be considered as a danger line, or caution against unnecessarily approaching the shore or bank within that line on account of the possible existence of undiscovered inequalities of the bottom, which only an elaborate detailed survey could reveal. In general surveys of coasts or of little-frequented anchorages the necessities of navigation do not demand

(Continued on page 316)

NEW CHARTS FOR SMALL CRAFT

New Series 101 charts of the Potomac

River better adapted to use on small boats.

Other areas to be charted in same style

ONE of the current projects of the U. S. Coast & Geodetic Survey has been the development of a new kind of chart specifically intended to meet the needs of the small boat owner. Several types were proposed and submitted to 24,000 boatmen for opinions and suggestions. Final result was the adoption of Small-Craft Chart Series 101 covering, initially, the Potomac River. This has served as a prototype for the charting of other selected areas as funds become available. The program is expected to be well advanced within the next decade.

The new charts are printed on 14½″ by 32″ paper, folded into four panels. The river is divided into three cruising areas, each sheet carrying insets, photographs, and facility information to amplify basic chart coverage. The scale is 1:80,000, with the Washington area enlarged to 1:40,000. On the reverse side of each sheet are the detailed inset charts, tabulations of depths, tides, facilities and supplies and aerial photographs of important areas, helpful in visualizing what the charted area looks like. This is particularly valuable at harbor entrances, marina approaches, etc.

Charts are printed in five colors: buff overprint for land areas; blue tint extended to the six-foot depth curve; red for restricted, danger, and fish trap areas and for emphasis on such features as aids to navigation, anchorages, pipelines, cable areas, etc. A green tint is used to define the low water line. Place names, projections, and scales are in black.

Many practical suggestions offered by boatmen were incorporated into the final version of the charts. Large compass roses show both true and magnetic bearings, magnetic headings are given on course lines, and distance scales are given in both charts and insets. Useful data are included on tides and currents, the current arrows giving both average direction and velocity. In addition, there's a helpful digest of information on basic rules of the road and whistle signals, radiotelephone weather forecasts, storm warning signals, and principal chart symbols and abbreviations.

Boatmen will welcome the detailed listing of points where they can obtain marina services, hull and engine repairs, fuel, water, ice, restaurant and lodging facilities ashore, and supplies of all kinds.

Charts now available in the Small Craft series, in addition to #101 (Potomac River) include 116-117 (which together cover the entire north shore of Long Island Sound and south shore from Port Jefferson to Throgs Neck and City Island); #141 (Florida Keys from Miami to Marathon, including Florida Bay); #152 (Galveston Bay); #165 (San Francisco Bay); and #184 (Seattle-Bellingham, and the San Juan islands).

Early in 1963 the Coast & Geodetic Survey started to publish the first of another new series of compact charts, in size and utility similar to those mentioned above, to replace the more than 60 charts of the Intracoastal Waterway from Norfolk, Va., to Brownsville, Texas.

Areas covered by the first of the new charts are as follows:—#824 A-B (Sandy Hook to Little Egg Harbor); #826 A-B (Little Egg Harbor to Cape May); #829 A-B (Norfolk to Albemarle Sound, including the Dismal Swamp route; #831 A-B (Albemarle Sound to the Neuse River, N. C.); #841 A-B and #843 A-B (Brunswick, Ga., to Eau Gallie, Fla.); #845 A-B (Eau Gallie to West Palm Beach); #847 A-B (West Palm Beach to Miami); #855 A-B (Cross-Florida Okeechobee Waterway (St. Lucie Inlet to Fort Myers); #856 A-B (Fort Myers to Port Charlotte); and #857 A-B (Port Charlotte to Tampa Bay).

The new Intracoastal charts are accordion-folded, measuring only 7⅜ by 15 inches, convenient to handle even in a small skiff. The plan is to revise and publish them annually, usually to coincide with the boating season in each area. If space permits, additional offshore hydrography will be added to new editions, to provide continuity for vessels plying between the waterway and the open sea.

A new chart (#690, same size as the Intracoastal charts) covers Lake Washington and the Ship Canal.

Several years will be needed to convert all charts to the new compact format, to check out boating facilities through field inspection and to assemble other data planned for this project.

The Coast Survey's objective is to include within the wrap-around covers of the folio, just about everything the small boat pilot needs to know about the area he is cruising.

Below: Of special value to the boatman is the listing of depths, tides, facilities and supplies for areas covered by the chart. Note how the location of the facilities available on the Little Wicomico are spotted on the inset chart at bottom of page

		DEPTHS		TIDES			FACILITIES								SUPPLIES													
NO	PLACE	APPROACH – FT	ALONGSIDE – FT	MEAN RANGE FT	HOURS EARLIER THAN WASHINGTON	BERTHS	GAS ENGINE REPAIR	MARINE RAILWAY	HULL REPAIRS	LAUNCHING RAMP	LIFT - TONS	ELECTRICITY	TOILETS	SHOWERS	MEALS	LODGING	MOTOR - CHARTER	BOAT - RENTAL - ROW	BAIT - TACKLE	GASOLINE	DIESEL OIL	PUMP CAN	WATER	ICE	TRUCK	GROCERIES	HARDWARE	BOTTLED GAS
=4A	LITTLE WICOMICO RIVER		5½	0.8	6	B	S	E			P	E	TS	ML	RM		BT	P	P	WI	G			B
=4B	LITTLE WICOMICO RIVER		5	0.8	6	N										BT	P			G		H	
=4C	LITTLE WICOMICO RIVER	5	6½	0.8	6		HE	90															
=4D	LITTLE WICOMICO RIVER	5	6½	0.8	6		HE	85															
8 A	COAN RIVER	9	4	1.4	7½	N								RM	B	C	T	WI	G				
8 B	COAN RIVER	9		1.4	7½									P									
8 C	COAN RIVER	8	6½	1.4	7½	B	HE	50						C					G		H		
8 D	COAN RIVER	11	9	1.4	7½									C			G					
10 A	SMITH CREEK	10	8	1.5	7½	B	N				E	T		RM	BT	P	P	WI	G	H	B
10 B	SMITH CREEK	10	5	1.5	7½	B	N					TS	M	RCM	BT		I		G		B
10 C	SMITH CREEK	10	10	1.5	7½	B	NS	HE	80	P-10	E	TS		RCM	BT	P	P	WI	G	H	B
10 D	SMITH CREEK	10	6	1.5	7½	B	S	E			E	TS	ML	RC	BT	P		WI	G		B

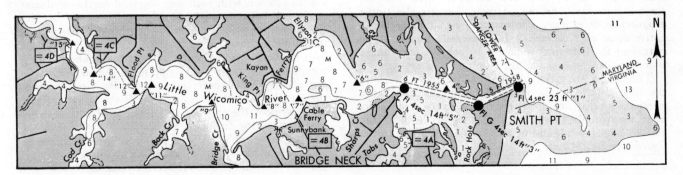

Insets are used liberally to show local cruising areas in greater detail. This inset (-4) for the Little Wicomico River is typical. Depths under six feet are tinted blue. Channel markers (black triangles in this reproduction) are in red and black on the original

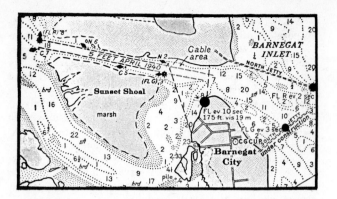

A portion of U. S. C. and G. S. chart No. 825, New Jersey Intracoastal Waterway, which shows the 5-foot dredged channel inside Barnegat Inlet, marked by can, nun and lighted buoys, with jetties protecting the inlet. Marshes are tinted green on the chart, shoal areas of less than three feet blue. A pile and exposed wreck are shown near the bottom

the great expenditure of time required for so detailed a survey. It is not contemplated that ships will approach the shores in such localities without taking special precautions

The 10-fathom curves on rocky shores is another warning, especially for ships of heavy draft.

A useful danger line will be obtained by tracing out with a colored pencil or ink the line of depth next greater than the draft of the ship using the chart. For vessels drawing less than 18 feet the edge of the sanding serves as a well-marked danger line.

Charts on which no fathom curves are marked must especially be regarded with caution, as indicating that soundings were too scanty and the bottom too uneven to enable the lines to be drawn with accuracy.

Isolated soundings, shoaler than surrounding depths, should always be avoided, especially if ringed around, as it is doubtful how closely the spot may have been examined and whether the least depth has been found.

Hydrography

Soundings or depths are not under the rule of lettering; they might be found vertical, leaning, or both upon one chart so as to distinguish the data furnished by different authorities. The U. S. Oceanographic Office shows the soundings by means of vertical block figures, considered the clearest type. The figures denote fathoms or feet, always stated in the title of the chart.

The extent of fairway and water areas restricting navigation to limited draft, is indicated by a system of lines, called "fathom lines." They are lines connecting equal depths, generally showing the limits of area of depth of 1 fathom, 2, 3, 5, 10, and multiples of 10 fathoms.

The 1-, 2-, and 3-fathom lines either have a stippled edge or the areas within the 3-fathom lines are covered with a light-blue tint which readily distinguishes them from deeper waters. On some charts the areas between the 3-fathom lines and the 5-fathom lines are also tinted a lighter shade of blue. On many of the older charts the entire areas of 1, 2, and 3 fathoms are stippled. The nature of the bottom is indicated by abbreviations under sounding, explained under the title of the chart.

The depths are given for the time of low water, and the least depths of all obtained during the survey are selected, so that the hydrography is represented in its most unfavorable condition. Increases of depth at the various stages of tide can be ascertained and added to the figures upon the chart.

Dredged Channels

These are generally shown upon the chart by two broken lines to represent the side limits of the improvement together with the depth and date. The depth is the controlling depth through the channel on the date charted and does not mean that this depth obtains over the full width of the channel, nor that the depth has not subsequently changed due to either shoaling or dredging. Those changes are often of frequent occurrence; therefore, when vessels' drafts approximate the charted depth of a dredged channel local information as to conditions should be obtained before entering.

Ranges

Ranges are shown by lines of dashes and by continuous lines, the latter are only shown as far as a ship may follow the range in safety. The bearings are given as "true" and are expressed, upon later charts, in degrees of a protractor divided into 360, starting at North and following the hands of a clock.

The compasses upon the charts are divided in accord with this new system. The outer rose, divided into degrees, is the "true" compass, the inner rose, divided into quarter points, is the "magnetic," and set upon the variation for the epoch stated in the central legend.

Dangers and Aids to Navigation

Reefs, ledges, sunken rocks, rocks awash, and foul ground are marked by symbols. Discolored water, ripples, current, and weeds are noted by symbol or lettering.

Wire drags are used to sweep areas where pinnacle rocks and other dangers might escape detection by isolated soundings. The wire drag establishes a safe minimum depth in areas known to be free of such hazards. These areas are outlined on new charts by green lines; depths within them will be at least as great as that given on the chart in green numbers.

Aids to navigation are shown by symbols and by abbreviations, or by as much descriptive text as the scale of the chart may admit.

To render these symbols distinct it is necessary to greatly exaggerate these aids in size, as compared with the scale of the chart; therefore certain parts of the symbols have been agreed upon to indicate the exact position of such aids, as follows:

The center of the base line of any symbol presenting a horizontal line, namely, mooring buoys, beacons, light vessels.

How Buoys Are Shown

All buoys, excepting mooring buoys, are shown by compressed diamond-shapes and a small dot, denoting the anchor ring. This dot indicates the proper position. To avoid interference with other features upon the chart it is often found necessary to show the diamond-shape at various bearings to the anchor ring, so that at times the symbol might be upside down. Since the buoys are also shown with such superimposed marks, as drums, cones, and balls attention should be given to the fact that the anchor ring does *not* touch the diamond shape, while the distinguishing marks are *joined* to the top of the buoy-symbol. For example: Numerous soundings close together might compel the buoy to be shown so that the top of the symbol bears in the opposite direction from the actual position; the isolated dot is the "position" part of the symbol, the opposite ring (connected with the buoy by a staff) is the distinctive mark.

The buoy symbol is shown "open"—in outline—for buoys of any color other than black; black buoys are shown by "solid" shape. If the buoy system shown upon the chart consists of the black and one other color only, the explanation under the title will ascribe such color to

Fig. 177. An inset in the pilot chart for the month of July, North Atlantic Ocean. Green lines (on the original chart) show annual change in the variation of the compass, direction of movement of the north end of the needle *being* indicated East or West. Solid blue lines and figures give normal reduced barometric pressure; dotted blue lines show normal temperature for the month. Lines connecting points where variation is the same are called isogonic lines. Those joining points of no variation are agonic lines. *See also page 320*

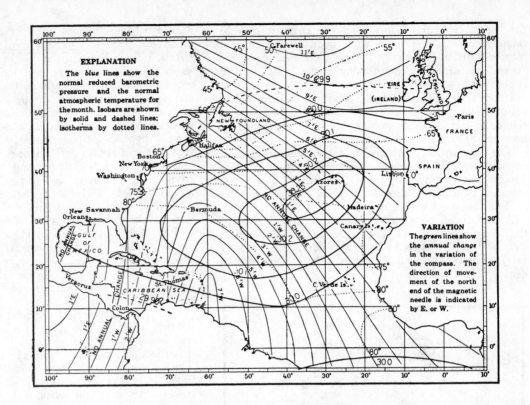

See also page 320

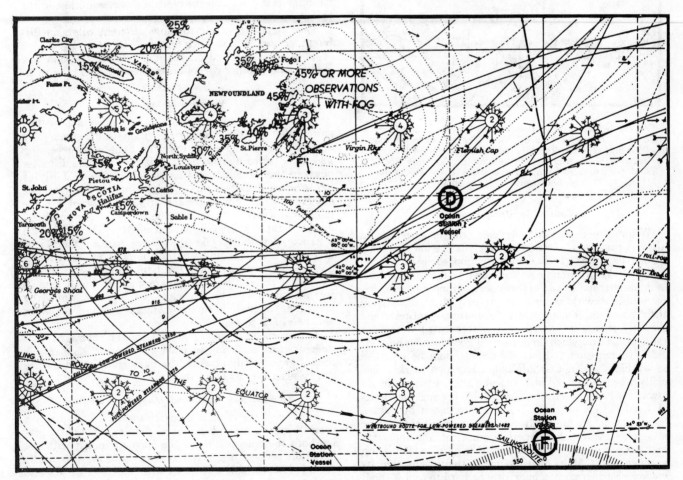

Fig. 178. This is a small portion of the pilot chart of the North Atlantic for the month of July. Dotted lines in blue on the original indicate the percentage of days in which fog can be expected for the month. The highest percentage will be noted as 45. The full lines represent the accepted tracks for full-powered and low-powered steamers. The wind rose (in blue on the original) in each 5-degree square shows the character of prevailing winds. Arrows fly with the wind.

Length of the arrow gives percentage of the total number of observations in which the wind has blown from that point. The number of feathers shows the average force (Beaufort scale). Figures inside the circle give percentage of calms, light airs, and variable winds. Ocean station vessels (lettered red circles) supply meteorological information. The (red) long-short dashed line indicates extreme limit of ice. Small (blue) arrows indicate currents; velocity given in miles per day

317

the "open" symbol. Thus upon one chart it may be found to denote "red buoy" while upon another chart it may be stated as "white" or "green"; the meaning of the "open" symbol *varies,* the meaning of the "solid" symbol is always the same—"black."

Upon any chart containing buoys of various colors besides black the color will be found stated by abbreviation or in full alongside each symbol or in the form of a note on the chart.

The buoy symbol, with anchor dot surrounded by rays, denotes a "lighted" buoy; surmounted by a crescent (points downward) denotes a "whistling" buoy; surmounted by a half disk with dot *above* the same denotes a "bell" buoy. See note below.

A line drawn between the upper and lower points of the diamond-shape (longer axis) denotes "vertical stripes"; a line drawn between the side points (shorter axis) denotes "horizontal stripes"; both lines drawn denote "checkered" buoy.

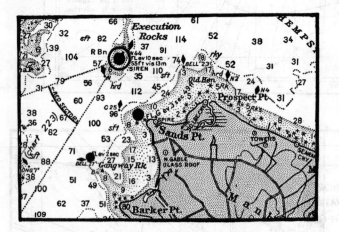

At the western end of Long Island Sound, C. and G. S. chart 1213, scale 1 to 80,000. The red sector of the light on Execution Rocks is delineated by dotted lines, a beacon (black triangle, Bn) stands on Gangway Rock, and numerous rocks along the shore both underwater (+) and awash (*) are shown

Caution in Using Buoys

While buoys are valuable aids, the mariner should always employ a certain amount of caution in being guided by them. It is manifestly impossible to rely on buoys always maintaining their exact position, or, indeed, of finding them at all. Heavy seas, strong currents, ice, or collisions with passing vessels may drag them from their positions or cause them to disappear entirely, and they are especially uncertain in unfrequented waters, or those of nations which do not keep a good lookout on their aids to navigation. Buoys should therefore be regarded as warnings and not as infallible navigation marks, especially when in exposed places; and a ship's position should always, when possible, be checked by bearings or angles of fixed objects on shore. The lights shown by lighted buoys can not be implicitly relied upon; the light may be altogether extinguished, or, if intermittent, the apparatus may get out of order. A buoy may be hard to identify on a rough night, if its light is intermittently obscured by waves. Furthermore, a buoy may be hard to find if small craft are anchored near it, as they often do when fishing. Though prohibited by law, boats sometimes tie up to buoys.

Identification of Lights

Before coming within range of a light the navigator should acquaint himself with its characteristics, so that when the light is sighted it will be recognized. The charts, sailing directions, and light lists give information as to the color, character, and range of visibility of the various lights. Care should be taken to note all of these and compare them when the light is seen. If the light is of the flashing, revolving, or intermittent variety, the duration of its period should be noted to identify it. If a fixed light, a method that may be employed to make sure that it is not a vessel's light is to descend several feet immediately after sighting it and observe if it disappears from view. A navigation light will usually do so while a vessel's light will not. The reason for this is that navigation lights are, as a rule, sufficiently powerful to be seen at the farthest point to which the ray can reach without being interrupted by the earth's curvature; they are therefore seen the moment the ray reaches the observer's eye on deck, but are cut off if the light is lowered. A vessel's light, on the other hand, is of limited intensity and does not carry beyond a point within which it is visible at all heights.

Care must be taken to avoid being deceived on first sighting a light. The glare of a powerful light is often seen beyond the distance of visibility of its direct rays by the reflection downward from particles of mist in the air. The same mist may cause a white light to have a reddish tinge, or it may obscure a light except within short distances. A fixed light when first picked up may appear flashing, as it is seen on the crest of a wave and lost in the hollow.

Some lights are made to show different colors in different sectors within their range. In such lights one color is generally used on bearings whence the approach is clear and another covers areas where dangers are to be found.

Visibility of Lights

When looking for a light, the fact must not be forgotten that aloft the range of vision is increased. By noting a star immediately over the light a good bearing may be obtained by pelorus or compass. All the distances given in the light lists and on the charts for visibility of lights are calculated for a height of 15 feet for the observer's eye. For a greater or less height of eye the table of distances of visibility due to the height published in the light list should be consulted. To obtain the distance of visibility take the square root of the height in feet of the light and multiply it by 1.15, which will give the distance in miles the light can be seen at the sea level; add to this the square root of the height in feet of your own eye above the sea level multiplied by 1.15 and you will have the distance in miles the light will be visible to you.

This intrinsic power of a light should always be considered when expecting to make it in thick weather. A weak light is easily obscured by haze and no dependence can be placed on its being seen.

The Compass Rose, and Magnetic Variation

The top of the chart is generally north. In addition a compass rose is printed in several places on the chart giving both the true north and the magnetic north with the variation between them at the time the chart was made. As this is a variable quantity the annual rate of increase or decrease is noted from which the variation at any time can be quickly found.

Upon charts of small scale and greater territory, coast charts, and ocean charts, "variation lines" are given because the magnetic conditions differ greatly in the various localities represented upon one chart.

NOTE: The most recent sheets summarizing symbols and abbreviations used on charts show the compressed diamond shape and dot as a standard buoy symbol, differentiating several special specific types of buoy by lettering or abbreviations alongside the symbol as follows: bell, BELL; gong, GONG; whistle, WHIS; can, C; nun, N; spherical, SP; spar, S. The newest charts use a heavy black dot for a light, emphasized by a solid magenta spot of color instead of an open circle.

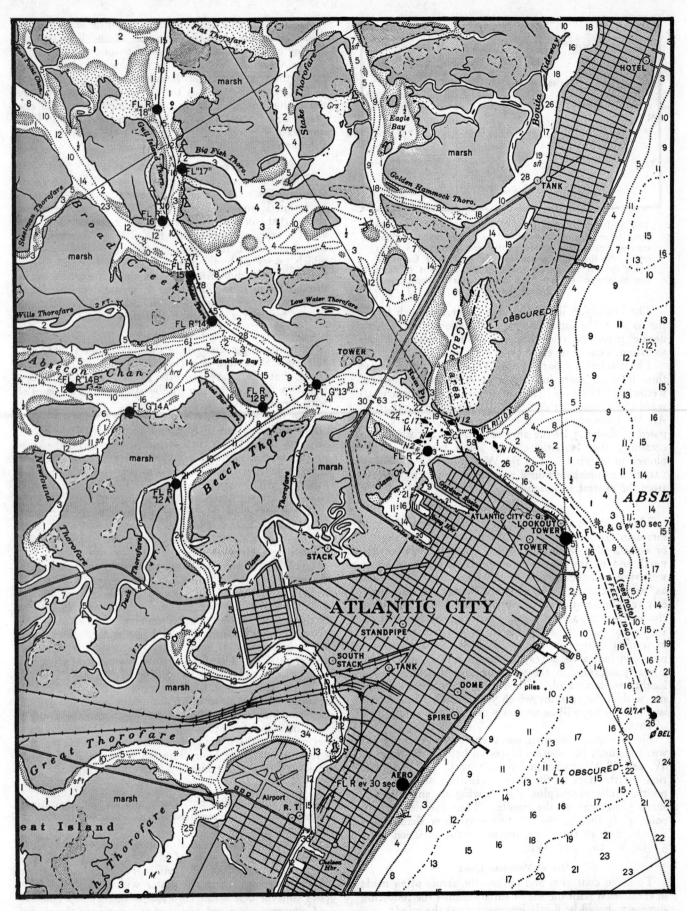

This is a portion of C. and G. S. chart No. 826 of the New Jersey Intracoastal Waterway, scale 1 to 40,000, reproduced to the exact size as it appears on the chart. The black line tracing the inside route is actually red on the chart. Water areas with a depth of less than 6 feet are shaded in a light blue which does not reproduce here. The shading emphasizes the white areas, of greater depth. Note the cable area, two wrecks just below Golden Hammock Thorofare, the dredged inlet channel, dotted lines showing the area inshore of which the light at the inlet is obscured, and the prominent landmarks all clearly identified. Where circular black spots appear in the reproduction, the chart shows a star in a yellow tinted circle, denoting a light. Changes are frequently made in the data shown on charts. For example, the aero light at Atlantic City now flashes at a different rate than that shown on the chart. The channel into Atlantic City often shifts, necessitating the changing of the position of the buoys. All such changes are published in the weekly Notice to Mariners.

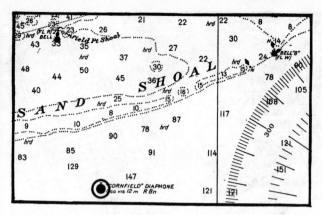

The outlines of Long Sand Shoal, chart 1212, Eastern Long Island Sound, are defined by the 3- and 5-fathom curves, tinted blue where depths are less than 3 fathoms. At the bottom appears the symbol of Cornfield lightship (in yellow on the chart). Portions of both the magnetic (inner) and true (outer) compass rose are at the right

The "variation lines" are lines connecting such localities as show the same amount of variation of a magnetic needle from the true meridian. The amount of this variation is stated on each, or on every fifth line.

The Variation Chart of the World, No. 2406, shows these lines for every full degree of variation; W. denotes westerly variation—i.e., the magnetic needle points westward of the true meridian. E. denotes easterly variation. All W. lines are continuous lines; all E. lines are composed of dashes. In the absence of any other source for obtaining the "variations," the ship's position can be plotted upon this Chart of the World and the amount of variation can be ascertained to sufficiently accurate degree from the nearest variation line.

Annual Change

The magnetic variation of the compass from the true meridian does not remain the same, but changes slightly or considerably in any locality. The movement of the north end of the magnetic needle is to eastward or to westward and the amount of this movement is expressed as "annual change." An eastward change *decreases* westerly variation and *increases* easterly variation; a westward change increases westerly and decreases easterly variation. Figures in parentheses on the chart represent the "rate" or annual change in the variation of the compass, the plus sign indicating a yearly increase and the minus sign a yearly decrease in the value of the variation for the locality so designated. When using the chart at a time not within the year for which year the Variation Chart was compiled it will be necessary to apply the annual rate of change.

For example, a mariner uses a chart two years after it was compiled; his position is spotted halfway between 5° W. and 6° W. variation lines, giving 5° 30′ W. variation for the date of the chart. He then finds that the position falls near (plus 2′), showing an annual westward movement of the needle. Thus the needle will point 4′ farther to the left two years later than shown for the date of the chart, increasing the variation from 5° 30′ W. to 5° 34′ W.

Use of Variation Lines

To avoid confusion and obviate the errors often made in connection with the use of variation lines the following summary should be firmly impressed upon the mind:

The lines or curves simply *connect* equal values; they do not represent by their direction the direction or pointing of the needle. Along a line which runs northwest-

ward upon the chart the variation might be easterly. By coincidence only may the direction of the line and the bearing of the magnetic north be the same.

The value of "variation" is the amount of arc separating the true north and the magnetic north.

The value of "rate" is the amount of arc covered by the change in the pointing of a magnetic needle in one year's time; thus, along a "rate" curve running in a northeasterly direction upon the chart the compass needle may steadily have a westward movement.

Local Magnetic Disturbance

The term "local magnetic disturbance" or "local attraction" has reference only to the effects on the compass of magnetic masses external to the ship. Observation shows that such disturbance of the compass in a ship afloat is experienced only in a few places. Magnetic laws do not permit of the supposition that it is the visible land which causes such disturbances, because the effect of a magnetic force diminishes in such rapid proportion as the distance from it increases that it would require a local center of magnetic force of an amount absolutely unknown to affect a compass half a mile distant.

Tidal Streams

In navigating coasts where the tidal range is considerable especial caution is necessary. It should be remembered that there are indrafts to all bays and bights, although the general run of the stream may be parallel with the shore.

The turn of the tidal stream offshore is seldom coincident with the time of high and low water on the shore. In some channels the tidal stream may overrun the turn of the vertical movement of the tide by three hours, forming what is usually known as tide and half tide, the effect of which is that at high and low water by the shore the stream is running at its greatest velocity.

The effect of the tidal wave in causing currents may be illustrated by two simple cases:

(1) Where there is a small tidal basin connected with the sea by a large opening.

(2) Where there is a large tidal basin connected with the sea by a small opening.

In the first case the velocity of the current in the opening will have its maximum value when the height of the tide within is changing most rapidly, i.e., at a time about midway between high and low water. The water in the basin keeps at approximately the same level as the water outside. The flood stream corresponds with the rising and the ebb with the falling of the tide.

In the second case the velocity of the current in the opening will have its maximum value when it is high water or low water without, for then there is the greatest head of water for producing motion. The flood stream begins about three hours after low water, and the ebb stream about three hours after high water, slack water thus occurring about midway between the tides.

Currents

Along most shores not much affected by bays, tidal rivers, etc., the current usually turns soon after high water and low water.

The swiftest current in straight portions of tidal rivers is usually in the middle of the stream, but in curved portions the most rapid current is toward the outer edge of the curve, and here the water will be deepest. The pilot rule for best water is to follow the ebb-tide reaches.

Countercurrents and eddies may occur near the shores of straits, especially in bights and near points. A knowledge of them is useful in order that they may be taken advantage of or avoided.

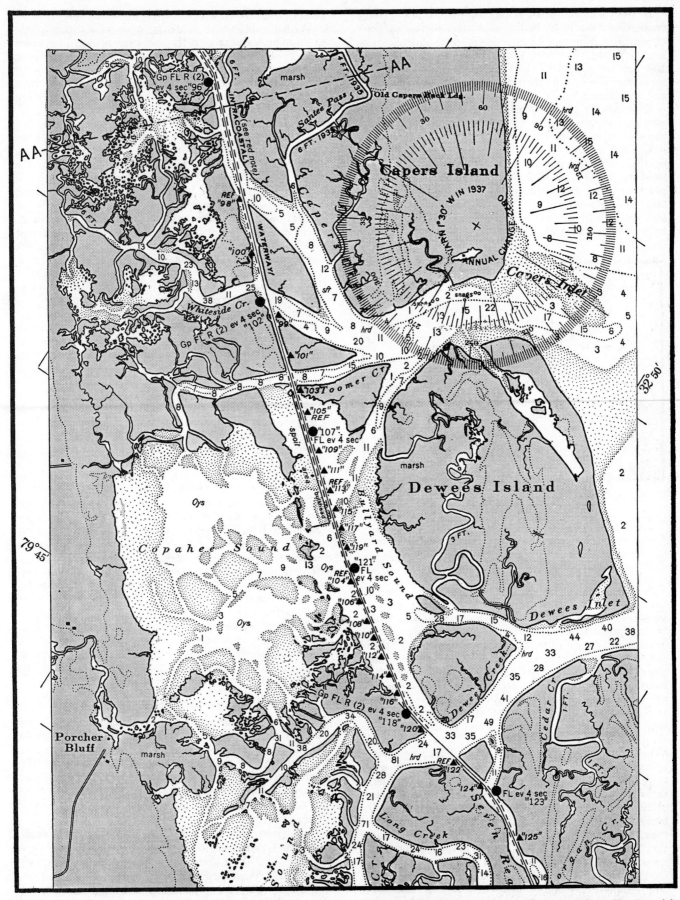

A portion of one of the new C. & G. S. charts (No. 837) of the Intracoastal Waterway from New York to Florida. This is one of the new 800 series, scale 1 to 40,000. The reproduction here is exactly the same as it appears on the chart. The route, threading bays, sounds, rivers, etc., is shown in red on the original chart (a black line in the reproduction). Note particularly the triangular symbols denoting beacons, reflectors (REF), spoil areas and bulkheads along the dredged channel (parallel broken lines) and the obstructions, designated "snags", in the inlet. The line AA —— —— AA shows where this strip of chart joins the next. Because of the strip form of this chart, North is not at the top. The aids to navigation along the Intracoastal Waterway have a characteristic yellow marking in addition to their usual coloring to indicate which side of the channel they mark. This yellow coloring does not show on the charts.

A swift current often occurs in the narrow passage connecting two large bodies of water, owing to their considerable difference of level at the same instant. The several passages between Vineyard Sound and Buzzards Bay are cases in point. In the Woods Hole passage the maximum strength of the tidal streams occurs near high and low water.

Tide rips are generally made by a rapid current setting over an irregular bottom, as at the edges of banks where the change of depth is considerable.

Current arrows on charts show only the most usual or the mean direction of a tidal stream or current; it must not be assumed that the direction of a stream will not vary from that indicated by the arrow. The rate, also, of a stream constantly varies with circumstances, and the rate given on the chart is merely the mean of those found during the survey, possibly from very few observations.

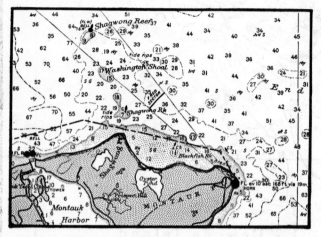

Montauk Point, as it appears on C. and G. S. chart 1212. Note the tide rips near Shagwong Rock, shoals and reefs offshore, covered by a red sector of the light, breakers at the point, and outlying spots with depths of less than 5 fathoms. Inshore of the line indicated by long and short dashes is a fish trap area

Fog Signals

Sound is conveyed in a very capricious way through the atmosphere. Apart from the wind, large areas of silence have been found in different directions and at different distances from the origin of the sound signal, even in clear weather. Therefore too much confidence should not be felt as to hearing a fog signal. The apparatus, moreover, for sounding the signal may require some time before it is in readiness to act. A fog often creeps imperceptibly toward the land and is not observed by those at a lighthouse until it is upon them, whereas a vessel may have been in it for many hours while approaching the land. In such a case no signal may be sounded. When sound travels against the wind it may be thrown upward; in such a case a man aloft might hear it when it is inaudible on deck. The conditions for hearing a signal will vary at the same station within short intervals of time. Mariners must not, therefore, judge their distance from a fog signal by the force of the sound and must not assume that a signal is not sounding because they do not hear it. Taken together, these facts should induce the utmost caution when nearing the land or danger in fog. The lead is generally the only safe guide and should be faithfully used. In regions where the shores are high and rocky the echo of the whistle frequently gives warning of too close an approach to shore. In narrow passages it is often possible to keep in mid-channel by directing course so that the echoes from both

shores are heard at approximately the same time.

With the object of rendering more substantial service to shipping, submarine bells have been installed on many light vessels and buoys in the coastal waters of the most advanced maritime countries and they have been proved to possess an advantage over aerial sound signals, both in regard to the certainty and the range of transmission.

Tides

A knowledge of the tide, or vertical rise and fall of the water, is of great and direct importance whenever the depth at low water approximates to or is less than the draft of the vessel and wherever docks are constructed so as to be entered and left near the time of high water. But under all conditions such knowledge may be of indirect use, as it often enables the mariner to estimate in advance whether at a given time and place the current will be running flood or ebb. In using the tables slack water should not be confounded with high or low tide nor a flood or ebb current with a rising or falling tide. In some localities the tide may be at a high or low water stand while the current is at its maximum velocity.

The Tide Tables published by the Coast and Geodetic Survey give the predicted times and heights of high and low waters for most of the principal ports of the world and tidal differences and constants for obtaining the tides at all important ports. These tables are now issued in four volumes.

The Coast and Geodetic Survey is charged with the survey of the coasts, harbors, and tidal estuaries of the United States and its insular possessions and issues the following publications relating to these waters as guides to navigation: Charts, Coast Pilots, Tide Tables, Current Tables, and a catalogue of these publications.

Coast Pilots

Coast Pilots, relating to surveyed waters of the United States, Puerto Rico, Virgin Islands, Alaska, Hawaiian Islands, and the Philippine Islands, contain full nautical descriptions of the coast, harbors, dangers, and directions for coasting and entering harbors. At intervals of about one year supplements are issued, containing the more important corrections since the publication of the volume. The supplements are printed on one side of the paper only, so that they may be cut and pasted in the appropriate places in the volume. Supplements and other corrections for any volume can be obtained, free of charge, on application to the Coast and Geodetic Survey, Washington, D. C., or any of its field stations, provided the volume itself has not been superseded.

Tide and Current Tables, Current Charts

The Coast and Geodetic Survey Tide Tables are issued annually in advance of the year for which they are made and contain the predicted times and heights of the tide for each day in the year at the principal ports of the world, including the United States and its possessions. Tables of tidal differences are given by means of which the tides at about 6,000 intermediate ports may be obtained.

Tide tables are published in four volumes: (1) Europe and West Coast of Africa, (2) East Coast North and South America, (3) West Coast North and South America, (4) Central and Western Pacific Ocean and Indian Ocean.

Current Tables are published separately as Current Tables, Atlantic Coast, North America; and Current Tables, Pacific Coast, North America, and Philippine Islands. These tables contain the predicted times of slack water and the times and velocities of strength of current in a number of important waterways, together with a table of differences by means of which similar predictions can be obtained for numerous other places.

Tidal Current Charts are published by the Coast and Geodetic Survey for Boston Harbor, New York Harbor, Tampa Bay, San Francisco Bay, Long Island Sound and Block Island Sound, Naragansett Bay to Nantucket Sound, Delaware Bay and River, and Puget Sound (in two parts). These publications show the direction and velocity of the current throughout the waterway for each hour of the tidal cycle.

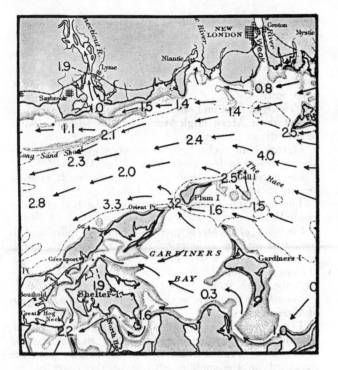

A small portion of the tidal current chart of Long Island Sound and Block Island Sound, showing the direction and velocities (in knots) of the currents in The Race and Plum Gut three hours after "Slack, Flood Begins" at The Race. Note the 4-knot current in The Race at its strength and the differences in the current set depending on land configuration. The arrows are red in the original chart. The complete set of charts consists of twelve, one for each hour of the flood and ebb

Sales Agencies

Agencies for the sale of the charts, Coast Pilots, Tide Tables, and Current Tables of the Coast and Geodetic Survey are established in many ports of the United States and in some foreign ports. They can also be purchased in the office of the Coast and Geodetic Survey, Washington, D. C., or any of the field stations. If ordered by mail, prepayment is obligatory. Remittances should be made by check or money order, payable to the "Coast and Geodetic Survey, Department of Commerce." Postage stamps can not be accepted. The sending of money in an unregistered letter is unsafe. Only catalogue numbers of charts need be mentioned. The catalogue of charts and other publications of the Survey can be obtained free of charge on application at any of the sale agencies or to the Coast and Geodetic Survey, Washington, D. C.

Lists of Lights, including buoys and other daymarks of the United States, its insular possessions, and the Great Lakes are published by the U. S. Coast Guard and may be purchased from its sale agencies or from the Superintendent of Documents, Washington, D. C. Local Notice to Mariners, relating to the same waters, is published by the U. S. Coast Guard; this publication can be obtained free of charge on application to any Coast Guard District Commander.

Navigational Charts Under Red Lights

It has been long recognized that after exposure of the eyes to artificial light at night a considerable length of time is required for the eyes to again become "dark adapted" and for the possessor to be able to see in the dark with any degree of success. This is an important matter for the seaman, especially when vessels are under darkened ship condition much of the time.

The Navy Department has made a study of the effect of lights of different colors, and found that exposure to white and blue light required 10 to 30 minutes for a person to become properly dark adapted, but only a few seconds after exposure to red light. From this standpoint red is the preferred color for lighting whenever needed by persons requiring night vision. This red color effect may be attained by the use of red bulbs, red shields or filters, or by the use of red goggles by the personnel affected.

In connection with these studies, the Oceanographic Office found that the use of red lights seriously affected the legibility of certain nautical charts. The buff color used for the land tint, the orange for indicating navigational lights, and the red color used for various purposes on these charts are all invisible under red lighting. While it is desirable to retain colors on the charts for daylight use, it has become necessary to revise the color scheme in order that they may be serviceable both in daylight and under red lighting conditions.

This situation was met by the Oceanographic Office through the use of a gray tint for land areas, a magenta to replace the orange tint for lights, and substituting a purple color for red. Blue is continued for shallow-water areas. These colors are distinguishable from each other under the red light, each appearing as a different shade, but not as a different color.

Price and Correctness of Publications

The charts and publications of the U. S. Oceanographic Office are sold to purchasers *at cost of printing and paper,* which selling price is printed on each such chart or other publication. Every agent of the Oceanographic Office is strictly forbidden to sell these articles at any price higher than that printed thereon. Any purchaser or would-be purchasers who is asked or required to pay more than the official price for any such chart or publication is requested to report the case in full to the "Oceanographic Office, Navy Department, Washington, D. C.," at once, in order that steps may be taken to protect such purchasers.

Purchasers of charts should consult the weekly Notice to Mariners for corrections subsequent to the date of issue of the charts.

Chart Symbols and Abbreviations

A COMPLETE SUMMARY OF THE SYMBOLS AND ABBREVIATIONS USED ON NAUTICAL CHARTS PUBLISHED
BY THE OCEANOGRAPHIC OFFICE AND THE COAST AND GEODETIC SURVEY, INDICATING WHICH
CONFORM TO THE STANDARD FORM PROPOSED BY THE INTERNATIONAL HYDROGRAPHIC BUREAU

THE nautical chart can convey to its user much or little, depending on the extent of his understanding of the sometimes curious little symbols which indicate, to the trained eye, a rock here, a wreck there, safe deep water perhaps between—all appropriately marked with beacons, buoys and suitable marks to reveal the position of both aids and dangers to navigation.

Symbols have been used for years to designate the many features shown on charts. However, recently, a standard form has been proposed by the International Hydrographic Bureau. Some of the symbols used on nautical charts published by the Coast and Geodetic Survey and the Oceanographic Office conform to this proposed standard, while others do not.

In the accompanying illustrations are shown the symbols and abbreviations which appear on the nautical charts of the Oceanographic Office and the Coast and Geodetic Survey. These have the approval of the Federal Board of Surveys and Maps of the United States of America. Alongside these symbols and abbreviations will be found numbers, in accordance with the standard form of the International Hydrographic Bureau. Vertical figures indicate that the designated symbol or abbreviation is in conformity with the proposed standard of the International Hydrographic Bureau. Slanting figures mean that the symbol or abbreviation shown either differs from that of the International Hydrographic Bureau or else does not appear on their proposed standard. Where the figures are enclosed in parentheses the symbols or abbreviations are in addition to those shown on the proposed standard.

Symbols and abbreviations shown herewith will be used on all charts made by the Coast and Geodetic Survey and the Oceanographic Office in the future. Cases may occur where symbols and abbreviations that have been superseded may still appear on charts that have not been extensively revised subsequent to this standard. The symbols shown here all relate to nautical charts; others not commonly used on nautical charts are shown on a standard symbol sheet issued by the Board of Surveys and Maps.

How Features Are Grouped

In this new classification, the various features are broadly grouped as follows: A, The Coast Line; B, Coast Features; C, The Land; D, Control Points; E, Units; F, Adjectives; G, Harbors; H, Topography; I, Buildings; J, Miscellaneous Stations; K, Lights; L, Buoys and Beacons; M, Radio Stations; N, Fog Signals; O, Dangers; P, Various Limits; Q, Soundings; R, Depth Contours and Tints; S, Quality of the Bottom; T, Tides and Currents; and U, The Compass. In addition, a table is included for convenience in converting meters, fathoms, and feet.

Simple inspection of various symbols and abbreviations reveals their meaning and use better than any description could. However, there are certain general principles which should be kept in mind when analyzing the data to be found on a nautical chart.

General Principles

Soundings, for example, may be expressed in either feet or fathoms. One should refer to the title of the chart to determine which is used. A fathom, of course, is six feet.

Heights of land and other conspicuous objects are given in feet above Mean High Water (unless otherwise noted in the title of the chart.)

Elevations of rocks, lighthouses, contours and hills are also expressed in feet above Mean High Water.

Elevations of mountain peaks, if underlined, refer to heights in feet above Mean Sea Level.

The *coast line* as charted represents the line of Mean High Water.

Visibility of lights is given in nautical miles and is computed on the assumption that the observer's eye is fifteen feet above water level.

Dredged channels are shown by limiting dash lines with the depth, month and year of latest examination.

Longitudes as shown on the chart refer to the Meridian of Greenwich.

The *Mercator projection* is always used for the construction of navigational charts unless another method of projection is noted in the title of the chart. They are computed on the middle latitude of the chart or the middle latitude of a series of charts.

Marginal notes are explained in the Coast Pilot and Sailing Directions, with additional information in chart catalogs. If the abbreviation N.A. 1927 appears in the upper right-hand corner of the chart, it means North American Datum of 1927."

It should be noted, in reading a chart, that the use of *capitals* and the style of *lettering* given herewith is not always rigidly adhered to in the construction of some charts. Furthermore, the use of *colors* is optional.

Temporary Changes

In addition to these general considerations, caution is to be observed with respect to *temporary changes* affecting lights, buoys and day beacons. When an aid to navigation has been destroyed or removed, but is to be re-established (being temporarily replaced by an aid of a different characteristic) its status is indicated in red by means of the following abbreviations:

D	— Destroyed, to be re-established.
T R B	— Temporarily replaced by a red buoy.
T B B	— Temporarily replaced by a black buoy.
T F B	— Temporarily replaced by a fixed white lighted buoy.
T F R B	— Temporarily replaced by a fixed red lighted buoy.
T FL B	— Temporarily replaced by a flashing white lighted buoy.
T FL R B	— Temporarily replaced by a flashing red lighted buoy.
T FL G B	— Temporarily replaced by a flashing green lighted buoy.

A. The Coastline

1 Shoreline unsurveyed

c Stones or gravel

Rocky

Not rocky, high | Not rocky, low

Contours

d Rock, uncovers at datum of soundings

3 Cliffy coastline (Bluffs)

f Sand and gravel

4 Sandhills or dunes

g Coral, uncovers at datum of soundings (See O-10)

5 Stony or shingly shore

6 Sandy shore

7 Mangrove — Symbol used only in small areas

8 Swamp or marsh — Symbol used only in small areas

12 Breakers along a shore

breakers

If extensive

13 Limiting danger line

11 Foreshores

a Mud flats

b Sand

KEY TO COLORS

TAN

BLUE

GREEN

B. Coast Features

	Abbr.	Term
1	G.	Gulf
2	B.	Bay
(2a)	B.	Bayou
3	Fd.	Fiord
4	L.	Loch, Lough, Lake
5	Cr.	Creek
(5a)	C.	Cove
6	In.	Inlet
7	Str.	Strait
8	Sd.	Sound
9	Pass.	Passage, Pass
10	Chan.	Channel
11	Entr.	Entrance
13	Mth.	Mouth
14	Rds.	Roads, Roadsted
15	Anch.	Anchorage
16	Hbr.	Harbor
17	P.	Port
(17a)	P.	Pond
18	I.	Island
19	It.	Islet
20	Arch.	Archipelago
21	Pen.	Peninsula
22	C.	Cape
23	Prom.	Promontory
24	Hd.	Head
25	Pt.	Point
26	Mt.	Mountain
	Mt.	Mount
27	R.	Range
29	Pk.	Peak
30	Vol.	Volcano
32	Bld.	Boulder
(33)	Str.	Stream
(34)	R.	River
(35)	Slu.	Slough
(36)	Lag.	Lagoon
(37)	Thoro.	Thorofare
(38)		
(39)		
(40)		
(41)		

C. The Land

1 Contours

-610-
-606-

1 Contours, approximate

(a) Contours, approximate
-610-

(b) Form lines, no definite interval
-610-
-606-

2 Hachures

3 Glacier
Glacier

O TREE
A conspicuous clump or single tree of any kind useful as a landmark

5 Isolated trees

9 Deciduous woodland
wooded

10 Coniferous woodland
wooded

(11) Elevation of top of trees
2560 T.T.

(12)

D. Control Points

	Symbol	Term
1	△	Triangulation point
2	○	Fixed point
3	256	Summit of height (Peak) (when not a landmark)
(a)	256	Peak, accentuated by contours
(b)	256	Peak, accentuated by hachures
(c)	256	Peak, when elevation has not been determined
(d)	256	Peak, when a landmark
4	⊕ Obs. Spot	Observation spot
5	B.M.	Bench mark
6	See View	View point
(9)	Astr.	Astronomical
(10)	Tri.	Triangulation
(11)	U. S. E.	United States Engineers
(12)		
(13)		

E. Units

	Abbr.	Term
1	hr.	hour
2	min.	minute
3	sec.	second
4		meter
5	km.	kilometer
6	in.	inch
7	ft.	foot
8	yd.	yard
9	fm.	fathom
11	M.	nautical mile
12	kn.	knot
13	lat.	latitude
14	long.	longitude
17	cor.	correction
(18)	alt.	altitude
(19)	ht.	height
(20)		
(21)		

F. Adjectives and other abbreviations

	Abbr.	Term
1	gt.	great
3	lrg.	large
4	sml.	small
7	mid.	middle
9	anc.	ancient
12	conspic.	conspicuous
16	dist.	distant
17	abt.	about
(19)	aband.	abandoned
(20)	extr.	extreme
(21)	concr.	concrete
(22)	bet.	between
(23)	estab.	established
(24)	exper.	experimental
(25)	discontd.	discontinued
(26)	fl.	flood
(27)	mod.	moderate
(28)	maintd.	maintained
(29)	elec.	electric
(30)	priv.	private, privately
(31)	prom.	prominent
(32)	std.	standard
(33)	subm.	submerged
(34)	approx.	approximate
(35)	cor.	corner
(36)	Cl.	clearance
(37)	No.	number
(38)	Ave.	avenue
(39)	Hy.	highway
(40)	explos.	explosive
(41)		

Group A of the new classification shows features of the coastline; B, abbreviations of coast features; C, the land; D, control points; E, abbreviations for units; and F, adjectives

As precision has been made for additions to the symbols from time to time, it is suggested that the reader obtain a copy of Chart No. 1, Nautical Chart Symbols and Abbreviations, an Oceanographic Office publication available from their sales agents in principal ports. The symbols shown on these pages are typical. Chart No. 1 is more comprehensive and has the advantage of being shown in color. It also includes a complete alphabetical list of abbreviations.

G. Harbors

1	Anch.	Anchorage, large vessels (see P-12)
2	Anch.	Anchorage, small vessels
3	Hbr.	Harbor
6	Bkwr.	breakwater
8		jetty (partly below M.H.W.)
(8a)		jetty (small scale)
9	Pier	pier
11		groin (partly below M.H.W.)
12	Anch. prohib.	Anchorage prohibited
13		spoil ground
14	Trap	fish traps (actual shape charted)
(14a)	Fsh. stk.	fishing stakes when dangerous
16	Ldg.	landing place
18	Whf.	wharf
21	Dol.	dolphin
26	Quar.	Quarantine
29	Cus. Ho.	Customhouse
33	B. Hbr.	Boat Harbor
35		dock
36		dry dock (actual shape shown on large scale charts)
37		floating dock (actual shape shown on large scale charts)
39		patent slip (marine railway)
(39a)	Ramp	ramp
40		lock (point upstream)
45		lock
(46)	Obsy.	Observatory
(47)		

H. Topography

1	Roads (Rds.)
2	Track, footpath, or trail
3	Railway (single or double track) Railway (Ry.) Railroad (R.R.) Same grade Ry. above Ry. below
4	Overhead cable (Ovhd. Cab.)
5	Power transmission line
8	River (R.) or Stream (Str.)
9	Intermittent stream
10	Lake (L.)
12	Marsh (See A-8) Canal Lock Sluice Ditch
13	Canal or ditch (point upstream)
14	Bridge (fixed) (Br.)
15	Drawbridge, in general
16	Swing bridge, that can be opened

17	Pontoon bridge, that can be opened
(17a)	Lift bridge
(b)	Bascule bridge, that can be opened (dotted line in Red)
19	Ferry (Fy.)
21	Dam
(25)	Levee
(26)	Lava flow
(27)	Log boom
(28)	Submerged piling, piling, stumps, and snags Submд. pile Pile stumps snags
(29)	Tunnel (railroad or road)
(30)	Viaduct
(31)	
(32)	

I. Buildings

When the buildings are prominent, they may be shown by landmark symbol with descriptive note. (See The landmark symbol is used to indicate positions of objects when accurately determined.

1		City or town (large scale)
(1a)		City or town (small scale)
3	Vil.	Village
4	Cas.	Castle
5	Ho.	House
8	Ch.	Church
10		Temple
12		Mosque
13		Minaret
14	Pag.	Pagoda
16	Mony.	Monastery
18	Cem.	Cemetery
19	Ft.	Fort (actual shape charted)
23		Airplane landing field Airport (large scale)
24		Small scale Airport (military) Airport (civil)
(24a)	(Red)	
(24b)		
26		Street
27	Tel.	Telegra
29	P.O.	Post Office
30	Govt.	Government
32	Hosp.	Hospital
34	Magz.	Magazine

35	MONU.	Monument
36	CUP.	Cupola
37	elev.	elevation elevator elevated
40	RUINS	Ruins
41	TR.	Tower
42		Windmill
44	CH.	Chimney, Stack
46		Oil tank
47	Facty. GAB	Factory
(56)		Gable
(57)	Sch.	School
(58)	H.S.	High School
(59)	Univ.	University
(60)	Inst.	Institute
(61)	Co.	Company
(62)	Corp.	Corporation
(63)	Cap.	Capitol
(64)	C.H.	Courthouse
(65)	Cath.	Cathedral
(66)	Bldg.	Building
(67)	Pav.	Pavilion
(68)	Ltd.	Limited
(69)	Apt.	Apartment
(70)	Tp.	Telephone
(71)		
(72)		

KEY TO COLORS

TAN

BLUE

GREEN

Symbols relating to harbors are included in Group G, those showing various characteristics of topography in Group H. At the right, in Group I, are given the symbols and abbreviations used in designating buildings on a chart. Charts are tinted tan, blue and green to aid in differentiating certain features. See key to colors at the right

J. Miscellaneous Stations

No.	Abbr.	Description
2	Sta.	Station
3	C.G.	Coast Guard (similar to L.S.S.)
(3a)		When the building is a landmark
6	L.S.S.	Lifesaving Station (See No. J-3)
7	Rkt. Sta.	Rocket station
8	Pil. Sta.	Pilot Station
9	Sig. Sta.	Signal Station
10	Sem.	Semaphore
19		Flagstaff
(20)		Weather Bureau Signal Station
(21)		Flagpole
(22)		Flag tower
(23)		Lookout tower
(24)		Standpipe
(25)		On land
(26)		

K. Lights

No.	Abbr.	Description
1	Lt.	Position of light
2		Light
3	L.H.	Lighthouse
4	AERO	Aeronautical light
5		Lighted beacon
6		Lightship
7		Lighted buoy
10	REF.	Reflector
(17)	Priv. maintd.	Private light (maintained by private interests; to be used with caution)
21	F	Fixed
22	Occ	Occulting
23	Fl	Flashing
24	Qk Fl	Quick flashing
(24a)	I Qk	Interrupted quick
26	Alt	Alternating
27	Gp Occ	Group occulting
28	Gp Fl	Group flashing
(28a)	S-L	Short-long
29	F Fl	Fixed flashing
30	F Gp Fl	Fixed group flashing
31	Rot.	Rotating
(39)	min.	minutes
(40)	sec.	seconds
44		visible
(44a)	M.	nautical mile
47	Gp.	group
49	SEC.	sector
61	Vi.	violet
63	Bu.	blue
64	G.	green
65	Or.	orange
66	R.	red
67	W.	white
(67a)	Am.	amber
68	OBSC.	obscured
69	(U)	unwatched
70	Occas.	occasional
71	Irreg.	irregular
73	Temp	temporary
80	Vert.	vertical
81	Hor.	horizontal
(82)	D.	destroyed
(82a)	Exting.	extinguished
(83)	V.B.	vertical beam
(84)	Exper.	experimental
(85)	R.	range
86	AERO	aeronautical
(87)		
(88)		
(89)		

L. Buoys and Beacons

On entering a channel from seaward, buoys on starboard side are red with even numbers, on port side black with odd numbers. Light on buoys on starboard side of channel are red or white, on port side white or green. Mid-channel buoys have black and white vertical stripes. Obstruction buoys are green, or have red and black horizontal bands. This system does not always apply to foreign waters. The dot of the buoy symbol, and the small circle of the light vessel and mooring buoy symbols indicate their positions.

No.	Abbr.	Description
1		Position of buoy
2		Lighted buoy (on magenta disc)
3	BELL	Bell buoy
(3a)	GONG	Gong buoy
4	WHIS	Whistle buoy
5	C	Can buoy
6	N	Nun buoy
7	SP	Spherical buoy
8	S	Spar buoy
(8a)		Checkered buoy
12		Lightship
14		Fairway buoy (B. & W. V.S.) (Mid-Channel)
18	RB	Junction buoy (R. & B. H.B.)
19	RB	Isolated danger buoy (R. & B. H.B.)
20	G	Wreck or obstruction buoy (R. & B. H.B.) or (G.)
22		Mooring buoy
24	Y Quar.	Quarantine buoy
(27)	BW	Fish trap buoy (W. & B. H.B.)
(28)		Anchorage buoy
(29)	Priv. maintd.	Maintained by private interests; to be used with caution
31	H.B.	Horizontal bands
32	V.S.	Vertical stripes
33	Chec.	checkered
41	W.	white
42	B.	black
43	R.	red
44	Y.	yellow
45	G.	green
(46)	Br.	brown
(47)	Gy.	gray
(48)	T.B.	temporary buoy
52	W.Bn. R.Bn. Bn.	Fixed beacons (unlighted daymarks)
(52a)	MARKER	Private aid to navigation
53	Bn.	Beacon (See L-52)
63	Tank	Landmark
(63a)		Landmark, position approx
(64)	REF.	Reflector
(65)		Note: Buoy and beacon symbols with topmarks may be shown on charts of foreign waters

M. Radio Stations

No.	Abbr.	Description
1	R Sta.	Radio station
2	R. Tp.	Radio telephone
3	R. Bn.	Radiobeacon
7	R.D.F.	Radio direction finder station
9	R. Tr.	Radio tower
(9a)	R. Mast	Radio mast
(10)	R. Tr. (WEAF)	Commercial broadcast
(11)	Ra.	Coast radar station
(12)	Racon	Radar responder beacon
(13)	Ra. Ref.	Radar reflector
(14)	Ra.(conspic.)	Radar conspicuous object
(15)	Ra. Mk.	Ramark

N. Fog Signals

No.	Abbr.	Description
1	Fog Sig.	Fog Signal Station
6	SUB-BELL	Submarine fog bell (mechanical)
7	SUB-OSC.	Submarine oscillator
8	NAUTO.	Nautophone
9	DIA.	Diaphone
11	SIREN	Fog siren
12	HORN	Fog trumpet
13	HORN	Fog horn
14	BELL	Fog bell
15	WHIS.	Fog whistle
16	REED	Reed horn
17	GONG	Gong
(18)	D.F.S.	Distance-Finding Sta.
(19)	GUN	Fog gun
(20)		

O. Dangers

No.	Abbr.	Description
1		Rocks which do not cover; with their elevations above M.H.W.
2		Rocks that cover and uncover, with heights in feet above datum of soundings
(3a)		When rock of No. 2 is considered a danger to navigation
(4a)		Sunken rock
(4b)		When rock of No. 4a is considered a danger to navigation
(4c)		Shoal sounding on isolated rock replaces symbol
(6a)		Sunken danger with depth cleared by wire drag (Feet or fathoms)
10		Coral or rocky reef (below datum of soundings) See A-11g
11		Stranded wreck (any portion of hull above datum of soundings)
12		Sunken wreck with only masts visible
14		Dangerous sunken wreck with less than 10 fathoms of water over it. (See No. 6a)
(14a)		A number of sunken wrecks
(14b)		Obstruction of any kind
16		Sunken wreck, not dangerous to navigation or over which the depth exceeds 10 fathoms
17		Foul ground
18		Overfalls or tide rips
19		Eddies
20		Kelp, any kind
(20a)		
(20b)		
21	Bk.	bank
22	Shl.	shoal
23	Rf.	reef
24	Le.	ledge
25		breakers (see A-12)
27	Obstr.	obstruction
28	Wk.	wreck
(28a)	Wks.	wreckage
33	Cov.	covers
34	Uncov.	uncovers
35	Rep.	reported
(35a)	Shoal (rep. 1945)	shoal reported
36	Discol.	discolored
41	P.A.	position approximate
42	P.D.	position doubtful
43	E.D.	existence doubtful
44	Pos.	position
(46)		
(47)		

In Group J are the symbols for miscellaneous stations; Group K, symbols and abbreviations for lights; Group L, buoys and beacons; M, radio stations; N, fog signals; and O, dangers to navigation. With reference to item K7, a distinction should be noted between the different systems which indicate the position of a lighted buoy on Oceanographic Office and British Admiralty charts. On U.S. charts, the position is indicated by the black dot found in the center of the magenta disc. On British Admiralty charts, the position is indicated by a small circle in the middle of the base line. The light star and colored-light dot are at the top of the buoy symbol. The letter designation shown near the base of the buoy symbol on British Admiralty charts refers to the color of the buoy, not the color of the light. Navigators using British Admiralty charts should refer to B. A. Chart #5011. (Signs and Abbreviations on Charts Issued by the Hydrographic Department, Admiralty.)

U. Compass

VAR 12°30' E (1947)
ANNUAL INCREASE 2'
MAGNETIC
ALL IN MAGENTA COLOR

Compass Rose

The outer rose is in degrees with zero at true north. The inner circles are in points and degrees with the arrow indicating magnetic north.

21	brg.	bearing
23	mag.	magnetic
24	var.	variation
(27)	deg.	degrees
(28)	dev.	deviation
(29)		
(30)		
(31)		

1	N.	north
2	E.	east
3	S.	south
4	W.	west
5	NE.	northeast
6	SE.	southeast
7	SW.	southwest
8	NW.	northwest

KEY TO COLORS

TAN BLUE GREEN

T. Tides and Currents

1	H.W.	high water
(1a)	H.H.W.	higher high water
2	L.W.	low water
(2a)	L.L.W.	lower low water
3	M.T.L.	mean tide level
4	M.S.L	mean sea level
6	Np.	neap tide
7	Sp.	spring tide
(8a)	M.H.W.	mean high water
(8b)	M.H.H.W.	mean higher high water
(9a)	M.L.W.	mean low water
(9b)	M.L.L.W.	mean lower low water
10	I.S.L.W.	Indian spring low water
17	Str.	stream
18		current, general
19		flood stream (current)
20		ebb stream (current)
23	vel.	velocity
24	kn.	knots
(25)		Current Diagram, with explanatory note (magenta)
(26)		

S. Quality of the Bottom

1	Grd.	ground
2	S.	sand
3	M.	mud
4	Oz.	ooze
5	Ml.	marl
6	Cl.	clay
7	G.	gravel
8	Sn.	shingle
9	P.	pebbles
10	St.	stones
(10a)	Sp.	specks
11	Rk.	rock
(11a)	Bld. (s)	boulder (s)
12	Ck.	chalk
13	Qz.	quartz
14	Co.	coral
(14a)	Co. Hd.	coral head
15	Md.	madrepore
(16a)	Vol. Ash.	volcanic ash
17	La.	lava
18	Pm.	pumice
19	T.	tufa
20	Sc.	scoriae
21	Cn.	cinders
22	Mn.	manganese
23	Sh.	shells
24	Oys.	oysters
25	Ms.	mussels
26	Spg.	sponge
27	Grs.	grass
28	Wd.	weeds
32	Fr.	foraminifera
33	Gl.	globigerina
34	Di.	diatom
35	Rd.	radiolaria
36	Pt.	pteropod
37	Po.	polyzoa
39	fne.	fine
40	crs.	coarse
41	sft.	soft
42	hrd.	hard
43	stf.	stiff
44	sml.	small
45	lrg.	large
46	stk.	sticky
47	brk.	broken
(47a)	rky.	rocky
50	spk.	speckled
51	grty.	gritty
53	fly.	flinty
54	glac.	glacial
56	wh.	white
57	bk.	black
59	bu.	blue
60	gn.	green
61	yl.	yellow
63	rd.	red
64	br.	brown
66	gy.	gray
67	lt.	light
68	dk.	dark
(69)	Ca.	calcareous
(70)		
(71)		
(72)		
(73)		
(74)		

P. Various Limits

i	Leading line (Range line)
4	Limit of sector (Magenta disc)
5	Channel or course recommended
(5a)	Alternate course
7	Submarine cable (Lines and words in Red)
8	Pipeline
9	Submarine pipe line (Red)
9	Maritime limits in general
10	Limit of fishing zone (fish trap areas bounded by broken lines)
11	Limit of dumping ground (see P-9 & G-13)
12	Anchorage limit (magenta)
13	Limit of airport
16	International boundary (also State boundary)
18	Ice limits
(21)	Bdy. Boundary
(22)	Bdy. Mon. Boundary monument
(23)	Reservation line
(24)	
(25)	

Q. Soundings

2	No bottom sounding
5	Dredged channels (controlling depth may be shown in separate note) 30 FEET (MAY 1939)
9	Swept areas (shown by green tint) (not yet covered by sufficient hydrographic surveys to show adequate soundings)
(9a)	Areas swept by wire drag to depth indicated
(16)	Stream
(17)	See general remarks 13
(18)	

R. Depth Contours & Tints

Feet	Fathoms	
0	0	GREEN
6	1	BLUE
12	2	BLUE
18	3	LIGHT BLUE
24	4	LIGHT BLUE
30	5	
36	6	
60	10	
120	20	
180	30	
240	40	
300	50	
600	100	
1,200	200	
1,800	300	
2,400	400	
3,000	500	
6,000	1,000	
12,000	2,000	
18,000	3,000	
Or 10 fathoms and greater		
Or	BLUE 10 BLUE 100 COLOR	

Conversion Tables

Meters	Feet		Feet	Meters
0.30	1		1	3.28
0.61	2		2	6.56
0.91	3		3	9.84
1.22	4		4	13.12
1.52	5		5	16.40
1.83	6		6	19.68
2.13	7		7	22.97
2.44	8		8	26.25
2.74	9		9	29.53
3.05	10		10	32.81

Meters	Fathoms		Meters	Fathoms
0.46	$\frac{1}{4}$		10.52	$5\frac{3}{4}$
0.91	$\frac{1}{2}$		10.97	6
1.37	$\frac{3}{4}$		11.43	$6\frac{1}{4}$
1.83	1		11.89	$6\frac{1}{2}$
2.29	$1\frac{1}{4}$		12.34	$6\frac{3}{4}$
2.74	$1\frac{1}{2}$		12.80	7
3.20	$1\frac{3}{4}$		13.26	$7\frac{1}{4}$
3.66	2		13.72	$7\frac{1}{2}$
4.11	$2\frac{1}{4}$		14.17	$7\frac{3}{4}$
4.57	$2\frac{1}{2}$		14.63	8
5.03	$2\frac{3}{4}$		15.09	$8\frac{1}{4}$
5.49	3		15.54	$8\frac{1}{2}$
5.94	$3\frac{1}{4}$		16.00	$8\frac{3}{4}$
6.40	$3\frac{1}{2}$		16.46	9
6.86	$3\frac{3}{4}$		16.92	$9\frac{1}{4}$
7.32	4		17.37	$9\frac{1}{2}$
7.77	$4\frac{1}{4}$		17.83	$9\frac{3}{4}$
8.23	$4\frac{1}{2}$		18.29	10
8.69	$4\frac{3}{4}$		18.75	$10\frac{1}{4}$
9.14	5		19.20	$10\frac{1}{2}$
9.60	$5\frac{1}{4}$		19.66	$10\frac{3}{4}$
10.05	$5\frac{1}{2}$		20.12	11

The remaining groups of symbols are as follows: P, various limits; Q, soundings; R, depth contours and tints; S, quality of the bottom; T, tides and currents; and U, the compass. Conversion tables are also included

NOTES ON
CHARTS

A navigational chart is a reproduction of a portion of the spherical earth on a flat sheet of paper. Distortion appears in all methods of projection, so the one chosen is that one with the least distortion for a specific purpose.

+

Mercator projection is most commonly used for nautical charts. The Polyconic projection is used for charts of inland waters. The Gnomonic, Lambert and other forms have limited application to small boat needs.

+

Mercator charts are generally projected from the center of the earth onto a cylinder surrounding it and tangent to the equator. Splitting the cylinder and laying it out flat produces the Mercator chart.

+

On a Mercator chart lines to represent latitude and longitude are straight and intersect at right angles. The meridians are shown as parallel; therefore any line which intersects them at the same angle can represent a course.

+

On Mercator charts a course is a straight line, a feature that makes the Mercator system most useful to the navigator. This line is called a rhumb line or loxodromic curve. It cuts meridians at the same angle and spirals toward the poles in a constant true curve.

+

While shown as parallel lines on a Mercator chart, meridians converge at the poles and, therefore, areas near the poles are expanded laterally to preserve proper ratios. Vertical dimensions are also enlarged.

+

Expansion of the latitude causes a changing scale as used for measurement. A small segment at mid-latitude of a course is selected and used as a unit of measure. An average scale is printed on large scale charts.

+

The difference between one minute of latitude at the north and south borders of a Mercator chart is so small that it will have no measurable effect for practical purposes.

+

Mercator charts can be constructed mathematically using tables found in Bowditch.

+

Mercator projection does not lend itself to polar areas. Tables of Conversion angles appear in Bowditch which are used to apply as corrections to compensate for great circle paths of radio beams.

As areas covered by charts increase various scales must be used to show necessary detail. Harbor, coastal, general, sailing, and special scales are available.

+

Dates of issue are printed in lower right border of charts. Out of date charts should not be used unless they have been continuously checked and corrected with the Notice to Mariners.

+

Much special data appears on charts such as scale, datum level, restricted areas, anchorages, cables, fishing limits. etc.

Charts enable the navigator to visualize courses and bearings and to obtain numerical values for such lines.

+

The direction of lines can be referenced to the geographic or true north as primary references.

+

Until the compass errors have been mastered use only true directions and the true rose. Later, the magnetic rose may be used.

+

Work neatly and accurately. In plotting bearings these obviously are from boat to object. The use of reciprocals is not necessary and may lead to confusion.

+

Draw courses in solid lines, letter C (course) above and S (speed) below. Bearings are also drawn solid, with time and true direction below. Construction lines are faint or dashed.

+

Angles are marked, fixes are shown by a small circle properly labeled with latitude and longitude in small box close by.

+

Polyconic projection, largely used for survey work, is generally most faithful and largely used for charts of inland waters.

+

The central meridian on polyconic charts is straight. The others are curved and converge toward the pole. Parallels are non-concentric circles. The grid may appear rectangular on large-scale charts but the curvature is plainly apparent on large area charts.

+

Since polyconic meridians are not parallel, directions must be taken from the nearest compass rose.

Polyconic charts are provided with a uniform scale reading in statute miles. The latitude scale on the side margins will supply nautical mile scales as with Mercator charts.

+

Polyconic inland charts frequently carry courses and bearings. Directions are given in degrees true, and distances in statute miles.

+

Gnomonic charts are useful in laying down great circle courses, later transferred bit by bit to Mercator charts. Distortion is pronounced on Gnomonic charts as distance from point of tangency increases.

+

Transverse Mercator charts are being used to replace Gnomonic charts for polar areas.

+

Charted visibility of lights is for a 15-foot height of eye; the distance is recorded in nautical miles.

+

When recording latitude and longitude always remember to include north-south and east-west designations.

+

Check alignment of plotting tools frequently against the chart grid or compass rose.

+

Having selected a desirable position in an anchorage on the chart, lay off cross bearings and steam in slowly on one bearing, letting go the anchor when the other object is on its bearing.

+

Clearance heights for a bridge are usually given for the center span and for mean high water.

+

In using a chart on which soundings are few, indicating the lack of a thorough survey, the area should be navigated with caution, following lines of soundings when practicable.

+

In taking the values of magnetic variation lines from a chart, due consideration should be given to the epoch for which they are calculated.

Navigators will sometimes find it convenient when laying off a long course on the chart, and the parallel ruler will not reach from the departure to destination, to fold up the bottom or side of the chart as the case requires, laying the edge between the two points.

+

Note the issuance of new editions of Oceanographic Office charts as announced in the Notice to Mariners, and it will better serve safety and convenience to replace the old corrected copy aboard the ship.

+

The soundings on charts are given for mean low water, mean lower low water, low-water ordinary springs, or low-water extraordinary springs. At the time of spring tides the charts having the datum of mean low water and mean lower low water indicate more water than actually exists; and those soundings reduced to low-water ordinary springs are not low enough to meet the depth conditions of certain astronomical conditions, or the results liable to attend sustained high winds or a very high barometer.

+

Buoys placed by the U. S. Government on offshore stations are colored and numbered from north along the east coast of the United States and from south along the Pacific coast.

+

With the advance of cold weather, buoys may be changed in certain rivers and harbors to such types as better resist the run of ice. This is usually done with no further notice than the note in the light lists.

+

In winter buoys are liable to be dragged from their stations by running ice.

The arc of visibility given to a light which is cut off by intervening land, may vary with the distance of the observer from the light. When the light is cut off by land that slopes to the shore it may be seen over a wider arc by a ship at a distance than by one close at hand.

+

The light of a lighthouse may be distinguished from that of a vessel by reducing the height of the eye. If the light disappears below the horizon it indicates distance beyond the horizon, if it remains visible with low height of eye it indicates the probability of a vessel showing a light of low visibility and considerable altitude.

+

A paste made of lampblack and a light oil smeared over the arc and vernier of a sextant and wiped off, not only cleans the arc but by filling up the graduations makes them more easily read. Care should be taken that the lampblack is without grit.

+

A steamer in a current is borne over the bottom at the same rate and in the same direction as the water about her. Her steaming speed is neither decreased nor accelerated. The mariner has no means of knowing the current drift except by observations, bearings, or less accurately, by soundings. The log only shows distance through the water, hence when the ship's run as established by fixes (which is the distance over the ground) is greater than a distance shown by an accurate log, a favorable current has been experienced, and conversely, less distance, an unfavorable current.

+

When anchoring always allow for the rise and fall of the tide.

+

A pair of colored glasses is very useful to a watch officer when the ship has the sun ahead.

+

It is dangerous for the navigator to depend on his memory.

Figs. 180 and 181. The lead line. Leads for motor boat use may be had from five pounds up. Five pounds is about the lightest practicable, good for depths up to 100 feet. The line should be braided cotton, not less than 30 fathoms, and marked as shown in the text below. These two illustrations show alternate methods of casting the lead. In either case the lead is cast from a position well forward on the starboard side. The boat's headway should be reduced and the lead cast forward so that by the time the lead reaches bottom, the line is perpendicular

A Discussion Dealing

With Those Instruments

With Which Every

Motor Boatman

Should Be Familiar—

The Lead, Log,

Course Protractor,

Pelorus, etc.

CHAPTER XIX

Piloting Instruments

See pages 392-397

THIS chapter deals primarily with the instruments used in piloting. Here we will discuss only briefly the actual use of the instruments as this will be taken up in more detail in the next lesson. However, every student of piloting should become familiar with the few instruments which it is necessary to have aboard for coastwise and inland work so that he will recognize them and know something about them when the time for their actual use arrives.

The Lead and Lead Line
(See Figs. 180 and 181)

Of the instruments necessary for successful piloting, a motor boatman should be familiar with a few of the most common ones. Of these the lead line is probably the most useful. As is well known, the lead line is a device for determining the depth of water, and consists essentially of a suitably marked line having a piece of lead of a certain definite shape, somewhat similar to a window weight. For use on motor boats leads of various weights are used, ranging from five to fourteen pounds. A lead line of twenty-five fathoms is sufficient for all ordinary purposes. The deep sea lead weighs from 30 to 100 pounds, and a line of 100 fathoms or upwards is employed.

Lines are generally marked as follows:

2 fathoms from the lead, with 2 strips of leather.
3 fathoms from the lead, with 3 strips of leather.
5 fathoms from the lead, with a white cotton rag.
7 fathoms from the lead, with a red woolen rag.
10 fathoms from the lead, with leather having a hole in it.
13 fathoms from the lead, same as at 3 fathoms.
15 fathoms from the lead, same as at 5 fathoms.

List of Navigating Instruments for Small Boats

Compass
Celluloid Course Protractor
Dividers (bronze)
Pelorus or Bearing Finder
Patent Log and Log Line
Lead and Lead Line
Good Timepiece
Deviation Card
Log Book

Also Latest Edition of the Following

Charts
Coast Pilot
Lake Survey Bulletin
Tide and Current Tables
Light List

---

17 fathoms from the lead, same as at 7 fathoms.
20 fathoms from the lead, with 2 knots.
25 fathoms from the lead, with 1 knot.
30 fathoms from the lead, with 3 knots.
35 fathoms from the lead, with 1 knot.
40 fathoms from the lead, with 4 knots.
And so on.

Fathoms which correspond with the depths marked are called "marks." The intermediate fathoms are called "deeps." The only fractions of a fathom used are the half and quarter. The length of lead lines should be checked up frequently while wet. The bottom of the lead is hollowed out, and the hole is filled with tallow or a like substance by means of which a sample of the bottom is brought up. The process of filling the lead with tallow is called "arming the lead."

In recent years, new markings have been developed primarily for small-boat use, well adapted to pleasure craft, in which plastic markings replace those discussed above. The depth, in fathoms, is indicated by numbers on the markers. Up to 10 fathoms, each fathom is marked, and half-fathoms are indicated by yellow strips.

(NOTE: The actual method of using the lead and lead line in navigation and piloting will be explained in detail in Chapter XX.)

Modern Sounding Devices

In bygone days, sounding machines were often used instead of the deep-sea lead to record ocean depths. One common type (the Kelvin) used a wire to lower a glass tube to measure pressure corresponding to the depth. In recent years, sonic depth-finders, working on electronic principles, have been developed so highly that the old sounding machines have been rendered obsolete.

The trend in sonic depth-finders has been toward the use of supersonic frequencies operating outside the audible range of sound. A transducer is installed on the hull to transmit a supersonic signal which is reflected from the bottom and picked up again by the transducer. Timing the interval required for the signal to reach bottom and return to its point of origin provides a means of measuring the distance, or depth, just as the time interval between a boat's whistle blast and the audible echo reflected from a cliff is a measure of distance off.

A typical depth finder will require one other unit, in the deckhouse, to send a signal, amplify the echo and record the depth in a visual form. Depths, calibrated in feet or fathoms, may be shown on a dial or may be plotted automatically as a continuous record in graph form.

Echo depth sounders are amazingly accurate even in relatively shallow water, and today are made in such compact units that their installation is practical even on small cruisers. On larger craft where depth observations may be required at more than one position, remote indicators are available.

The sonic depth-finder has become one of the more valuable piloting aids to the pleasure boatman.

The Patent Log
(See Fig. 183)

The log is a device for determining the distance which a boat has run through the water. There are three principal kinds of logs known as the patent log, chip log, and the ground log. Of these three, the patent log is the only one used to any extent today.

The patent log consists of a registering device, tow line, and a rotator. The registering device is generally made fast to some permanent position near the stern of the boat, and the length of tow line used must be sufficient to extend beyond the effect of the boat's wake. The rotator is attached to the outer end of the log line, and is a small spindle with a number of wings or blades extending radially in such a manner as to form a spiral, and when drawn through the water in the direction of its axis rotates about that axis after the manner of a screw propeller. The registering device is so calibrated that instead of registering the number of total turns of the rotator and log line, it will register in nautical miles.

The patent log is by no means perfect, especially when used on small boats. It is subject more or less to error, sometimes as great as 10 per cent. The patent log naturally registers distance which the boat has run in the water, and does not indicate distance relative to some point on land. In other words, to get the net actual distance run, allowance must be made in the reading of the patent log for currents, leeway and such errors. The patent log cannot be depended upon for actual reading at low speeds—that is, speeds of less than five or six miles per hour. Wave motion also has considerable effect upon the operation of the patent log.

The Chip Log
(See Fig. 184)

The chip log is not used to any great extent at the present time. The chip log consists of three principal parts, known as the log-chip, log-line, and the log-glass. The log-chip is a thin piece of wood, weighted at one edge sufficiently to make it float upright in the water. As it is thrown overboard from the boat, it assumes a position at rest relative to the boat. In other words, the log-chip remains in a fixed position, and the boat sails away therefrom. A log-line is made fast to the log-chip in a suitable manner at one end, the other end of which is wound upon a reel kept aboard the boat.

After the log-chip has been thrown overboard, the log-

line will begin to unwind from the reel, which is generally mounted on a spindle, to be held in one's hands. At a distance of 15 to 20 fathoms from the log-chip a permanent mark is placed to allow sufficient length for the log-chip to clear the wake of the boat. The rest of the line is divided into lengths of 47 feet 3 inches, called "knots," by pieces of fish line thrust through the strands. The number of strands of line or knots which leave the reel or pass over the taffrail of the boat in a given time, in the time which it takes the log-glass to empty itself, will be an indication of the speed of the boat.

The log-line is so attached to the chip that when the entire length of the line has been withdrawn from the reel the sharp pull will cause one of the attachments in the log-chip to disconnect, and the log-chip will then float in a position of least resistance, and can be drawn aboard the boat without difficulty.

The Ground Log

The ground log follows in a general way the principles which govern the chip log; except that a lead which sinks to the bottom is used in place of a chip, which floats in a fixed position. The ground log indicates speed relative to the land, and no corrections for current, etc., are necessary.

Modern Logs

New types of logs and speedometers may be purchased today which are usually actuated by water pressure on a fitting installed on the bottom of the boat. It is a great convenience in piloting to have such an instrument permanently installed so that speed or mileage can be read directly from a calibrated arc on or near the engine instrument panel.

The Chronometer

The chronometer, the timepiece used on ships, differs from the clock or other timekeeping instruments in that it is constructed to perform its work with greater precision. Correct time, or regularity of a timepiece on shipboard is absolutely essential.

Chronometers should be handled with the greatest care and should not be subject to jarring, sudden shock or extreme changes in temperature.

As it is beyond the power of human skill to make anything absolutely perfect, it follows that all chronometers have more or less error. After this error has been reduced to a minimum there is no further effort made to adjust the chronometer. However, it is essential that the amount which the chronometer varies each day should be known, and the variation should be constant or nearly so. This error is known as the *rate* of the chronometer and the amount which the chronometer gains or loses each day is called the *daily rate*.

To insure a uniform rate the chronometer should be wound at the same time each day, although it may be capable of running a much longer period than twenty-four hours.

When using the chronometer for the purpose of observations, etc., a correction must be made to its reading for the chronometer's rate. For example, if the chronometer were known to be absolutely correct on June 1, and to have a daily rate of $+ \frac{1}{8}$ second, then when taking an observation on September 1, $11\frac{1}{4}$ seconds would have to be subtracted from the chronometer time to obtain the correct time.

Clock Time and Sun Time

Did you ever realize that the time as shown by our watches and clocks in every day life is not correct? Very few times a year, and then only at certain locations on the earth, are they correct? They are all fast or slow, depending upon several things.

Fig. 182. The pelorus or bearing finder, installed on or near the bridge, to take bearings when locating position. It may also be used when determining deviation by bearings. The bronze disc is marked like a compass card and pivoted so that any point or degree can be set opposite the lubber line. The disc is set to correspond with the ship's compass, corrected for deviation, and bearings of objects may be read by the sighting vanes. For a boat which can be kept on a steady course, this method is suitable. However, in rough water, or on a sailing boat, set the dummy compass card so that 0°-180° is lined up with the lubbers line. Variation may be applied to this setting, offsetting the 0° to the right or left as applicable. Then no certain or steady course is necessary in order to have the dummy compass card oriented correctly, but a relative bearing will be obtained, which *added* to the compass course will give *true* bearing at all times. This is true only if there is no deviation. Should there be deviation it may be applied to the resulting bearing, or if remaining on a steady basic course it may be applied with the variation and set on the dummy compass. On practically all types of boats and ships, it is usually more feasible for the helmsman to continually note the compass course while someone else obtains the bearing, than to steer an exact course, thus orienting the dummy compass correctly

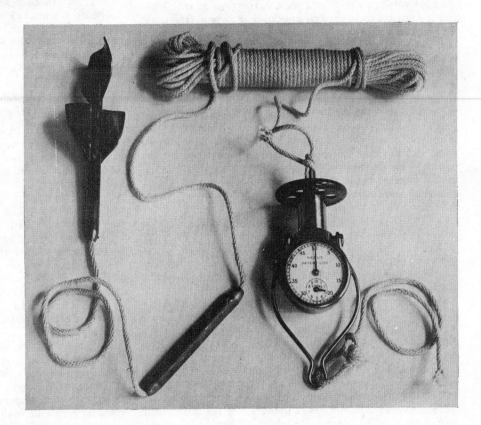

Fig. 183. The patent log, used for determining distance run, and speed. A log line connects the rotator to a registering device which is made fast near the stern of the boat. The log line must be long enough so the rotator is clear of the wake as it is towed astern. In use, the rotator revolves as it is towed through the water, and the log line transmits this rotary motion to the registering device which is calibrated so that the distance run can be read directly on the dial. The one illustrated is calibrated from 0 to 50 miles, fractions, in tenths, being read on the small dial below. To determine speed with the aid of the log, the time required to run a given distance must be taken. Rotators may be had suitable for measuring distance in either statute or nautical miles, but naturally care must be exercised that these are not confused in use. Patent logs are subject to errors, varying with the boat's speed, condition of the sea, distance astern the rotator is towed, etc.

Fig. 184. The old chip log, consisting of the log-chip, log-line and log-glass. The log-chip is a thin piece of wood, weighted so it will float perpendicularly. The chip is thrown from the stern and the log-line is allowed to flow freely over the rail. The line is marked at intervals of 47 feet 3 inches, called "knots", and the number of knots that pass over the rail in the time that it takes for the glass to empty itself is a direct measure of the speed

Of course, time is nothing more or less than our crude way of expressing the position of the sun at any particular moment, as it is the sun which is the master key to our lives, as well as to everything inanimate. At ten in the morning the sun has a certain position in the sky, at eleven o'clock it has another position, at four still another, and so on. But at eleven o'clock yesterday the sun did not have the same position that it had at eleven today, nor was the sun overhead (noon) yesterday exactly twenty-four hours before it was overhead today.

Equation of Time

In other words, there is a small variation in the time it takes the sun to go around the earth every day—that is, it is slightly more or slightly less than twenty-four hours from noon to noon, depending upon the time of the year. This variation from twenty-four hours is called the equation of time, and may amount to as much as sixteen and one-half minutes.

There is another error in the time shown by our watches which is much greater than the error of the equation of time. Everyone knows that noon is the time at which the sun is supposed to be directly overhead or to bear true south (in northern latitudes). As explained above, it does not bear exactly true south every twenty-four hours. Furthermore, if the sun is overhead (bearing true south) at New York when the clock is indicating noon, it is not overhead at Boston, Syracuse, Buffalo, or any other place which is not in the same longitude as New York. At Boston, when it is noon at New York, the sun is bearing west of south, while at Syracuse and Buffalo it is bearing east of south. In other words, it is past noon at Boston, and before noon at Buffalo. But it would not be convenient for the clocks at Boston to be showing 12:12 and those in Buffalo 11:40, while those in New York were at 12 noon. Great inconvenience in the routine of our daily lives would result from such an arrangement.

Longitude and Time

As the earth revolves around its axis every twenty-four hours (or nearly so) and as any circle drawn around the earth is divided into 360 degrees, it is apparent that one hour of time will be equivalent to 15 degrees on the circle drawn around the earth. As east and west distance on such a circle is known as longitude, an hour's time will represent 15 degrees of longitude, and four minutes of time, one degree.

As there is a difference of longitude of over 50 degrees between the Atlantic and Pacific Coasts of the United States, it follows that there will be a difference of time of something over 200 minutes as indicated by the sun. Such a difference is too great to neglect. That is, it would not be feasible to have the clocks in New York and San Francisco indicate the same hour. If such were the case, then when the clocks indicated twelve o'clock noon at San Francisco, the sun would be low down on the horizon and it would have been daylight for only a few hours. It is not practical to have the clock time and real time as indicated by the position of the sun differ by more than one hour.

As mentioned above, one hour's difference in sun time represents 15 degrees difference in longitude. The standard meridians of longitude which have been chosen in this country are the 75th, 90th, 105th, and 120th. Places having these longitudes have clock times which agree with the sun time, except for the slight error caused by the equation of time. Places located to the east of these meridians have clock times which are slower than sun time, and the clocks in localities to the west of the standard meridians are fast.

The Course Protractor
(See Figs. 185 and 186)

The course protractor has generally superseded the ancient parallel rulers for the purpose of transferring the direction of the line drawn on the chart to the compass rose on the chart, in order to determine its direction. In using the course protractor, its center should be placed on the chart exactly over the boat's position. The arm of the protractor is then swung around to the nearest compass rose on the chart, making the hair line down the center of the arm pass directly over the center of the compass rose.

Holding the protractor arm firmly in this position, the compass part of the protractor is then swung around until the hair line cuts the same compass point or degree on the protractor compass as it cuts upon the compass rose. The compass and the rose are now parallel, or, in other words, they have the same variations. Holding the protractor compass firmly against the chart, the protractor arm is moved until its center line cuts the point on the chart where it is desired to lay a course. The compass course either in points or degrees can then be read off directly.

Should the boat's compass have any deviation, the course can be easily corrected to take account of this error by simply turning the protractor compass around, while holding the arm against the chart—clockwise if the error is easterly, and counter-clockwise if the error is westerly.

The Pelorus or Bearing Finder
(See Figs. 187, 188 and 189)

In order to take observations and bearings of distant objects with any degree of accuracy, it will be necessary to have some form of bearing finder or pelorus. The pelorus as it is manufactured and sold today by the dealers in nautical instruments is so very expensive that for the little use which the motor boatman has for such an instrument it would hardly pay him to go to the expense of purchasing one. However, with a little care, a home-made bearing finder may be constructed which under ordinary conditions will be found to give fairly accurate results.

Fig. 187 illustrates such a bearing finder. A circular piece of hard wood is cut out for the base of the instrument, and four series of tacks are placed 90 degrees apart, as shown. These tacks have the same function as the lubber-line on the compass bowl. On the wood base a compass card is mounted; this may be one of those distributed for advertising purposes, or home-made, as the owner prefers. The compass card is mounted at its center to the base, so that it may be freely revolved around its center. Mounted at the same center will be seen a horizontal arm which rests directly on the compass card. This horizontal arm is provided at each end with vertical members, which are about six inches in height, and have small holes near their upper extremity, through which the distant object is sighted.

To use this bearing finder it is simply necessary to mount it in some suitable position on the boat, so that one set of tacks will represent the bow of the boat exactly as the lubberline on the compass does. The compass card of the bearing finder is then turned by hand, so that these tacks will be opposite that point on the compass card which represents the correct heading of the boat at the particular moment the bearing is to be taken. Keeping the pelorus base and its compass card in this position, the movable sighting vanes of the instrument are then turned so that it is possible to obtain a bearing of the desired distant object by sighting through the two holes in the uprights. The bearing of the object will then be indicated on the compass card below through an opening in the horizontal member of the sighting vanes. If possible, sights or bearings on a number of distant objects should be taken, and the bearings plotted on one's chart as a check.

Fig. 185 (left). The course protractor consists of a celluloid disc marked in compass points and degrees, with a movable celluloid arm pivoted at the center of the disc. After the course has been laid on the chart, clear of all dangers and obstructions, the center of the protractor is placed on the ship's position. Then the movable arm is swung around so that its edge passes through the center point of the nearest compass rose on the chart. Noting the compass point or degree which the arm cuts on the chart's compass rose (NE by E ¼ E in the illustration), the protractor disc is next rotated till the arm cuts the same point or degree on both protractor disc and compass rose. Meanwhile the protractor must not be allowed to slip from its position with arm cutting the center of the chart rose and disc centered on the boat's position. Note in Figure 186 how the dashed line cuts the NE by E ¼ E point of both protractor disc and chart compass rose

Fig. 186 (right). Holding the protractor disc firmly on the chart to prevent it from slipping, the next step is to swing the protractor arm around until the edge of the arm lies along the plotted course of the boat. At the point where the arm cuts the protractor disc, the course can then be read. In the illustration at the right, the arm cuts the disc at NE ½ N. This is the course (in this case magnetic). Deviation must be allowed for in arriving at the compass course to be steered by the helmsman. A simple way to do this is to rotate the protractor disc by the amount of the deviation—to the right if deviation is easterly, to the left if it is westerly. If for example, the deviation were one point East, the disc would be rotated one point clockwise and the hairline would show the compass course to be NNE ½ E. On the other hand, if the deviation were ½ point West, then the disc should be rotated ½ point counter-clockwise from its original position and the arm, cutting the disc at NE, would show that the compass course to steer is NE

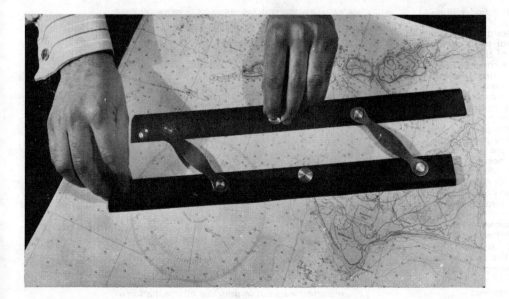

Some prefer to use parallel rulers (left) instead of the course protractor when laying a course on the chart. The two straightedges of the ruler are kept in parallel alignment by connecting links. Thus one arm of the ruler can be laid along the course line drawn on the chart, and the ruler moved, in as many successive steps as necessary, until an edge of the ruler cuts through the center of the chart compass rose. Then the course can be read, either in points or degrees, on the circumference of the compass rose

Fig. 187. This is a form of home-made pelorus or bearing finder. It consists of a circular piece of hard wood as a base with four series of tacks placed at right angles or at 90° apart as shown. These tacks have the same function as a lubber line of the compass. On the wood base a compass card is mounted. This may be of any form desired and if it is not possible to obtain one of those compass cards used for advertising purposes one may be made at home. This compass card is mounted at its center so that it may be freely revolved. Mounted at the same center there is a horizontal arm which rests directly on the compass card. This arm is provided at each end with vertical members which are about six inches in height and have small holes at each upper extremity through which object is sighted

NOTE: Because of the difficulty of holding a course and taking a bearing at the same time, it is helpful to have an assistant when using the pelorus.

Fig. 188. To use the bearing finder illustrated in Fig. 187 (above) it is only necessary to mount it in some suitable position on the boat so that one set of tacks on the base will represent the bow of the boat exactly as the lubber line of the compass does. The compass card of the bearing finder is then turned by hand so that these tacks will be opposite that point on the compass card which represents the correct course of the boat at the particular moment that the bearing is taken. Keeping the pelorus base and this compass card in this position the movable sighting vanes of the instrument are then turned so that it is possible to obtain a sight of the desired distant object through the holes in the two uprights. The bearing of that object will then be indicated on the compass card below, through one of the openings in the horizontal member of the sighting vane. If possible sights or bearings on a number of different objects should be taken as a check. In using this pelorus it is essential that the boat be on on even keel when the bearing is taken. See Fig. 182 for description of the method of taking relative bearings

Fig. 189. The sight vane. This is an instrument which is mounted directly on the top of the glass of the compass. It may be revolved on a pin which fits into a depression in the center of the glass or is sometimes arranged with a frame which fits over the outer edge of the compass top. The one illustrated above can be rotated by means of the two short pins projecting upward at each side of the frame of the sight vane. The bearing is taken by aligning the two vertical sighting vanes or pins with the object, the bearing being read under the horizontal line connecting them. Various forms of sight vanes are mnaufactured by compass manufacturers but in principle all are the same

THE practice of Piloting is a fascinating pastime. It is a pleasing game where the results if satisfactory are a source of enjoyment, but if the deductions and judgment be in error it may lead to disagreeable consequences. Thus a stake is placed for the participator in coastwise piloting to compete for. So many motor boat men run haphazard along the coast depending on the sight of familiar landmarks and good luck for a position that a few words on the subject may be found profitable.

The instruments used in Piloting, besides the compass, are mainly the lead, log and some device for taking bearings. Usually a simple contrivance fitted with two sight vanes that fits on the compass is all that is necessary in small vessels. In larger boats a pelorus may be found. This is a brass plate engraved as a compass, capable of being so turned as to set it on the heading of the boat. There is a set of sight vanes fitted to revolve on the face of the dial, and the whole is supported on a standard. Sometimes instead of a brass plate ground glass is used with the compass painted upon it in black; in such peloruses an electric light is placed beneath the dial to facilitate its use in night work. The sextant is often found to be of use in taking angles.

CHAPTER XX

Piloting

How to Navigate Strange Waters With a Feeling of Safety and Security

Note: This chapter on Piloting deals briefly with only the more elementary phases of the subject. A more complete and advanced treatise will be found in the chapter on Advanced Piloting on pages 392-439

Fig. 210. The Bow and Beam Method. An observation is taken of the object C at 45° or 4 pts. on the bow (boat A). The log is then read or the time noted. Another bearing is taken when the same object C is abeam and log again read or time noted. The distance run from A to B will be the distance off from the object C at the time of the second bearing

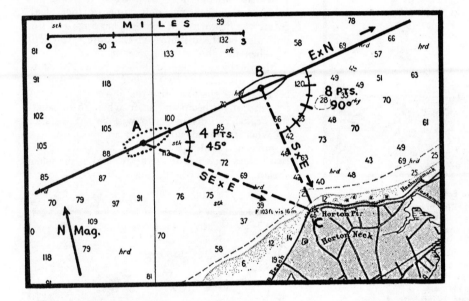

There are many different methods for finding a boat's position, depending upon the number of objects in sight, their bearing relative to the heading of the vessel, and the character of the bottom and depth of water.

Four Point Bearing

The most commonly practiced method is known as the "Four-Point Bearing" (Bow and Beam to some). (See Fig. 210.) It is a standing order on all well navigated vessels that no lighthouse be passed without taking a four-point bearing. The log reading is noted when the lighthouse (or other charted landmark) is four points (45°) on the bow and the same course is held until it bears abeam when the log is again read. The distance run between bearings is the distance off the lighthouse when abeam. Care must be exercised in ascertaining the distance run over the bottom. If a current should be against a vessel the log will show more miles than have been made and, vice versa, if a fair current is experienced more miles will be made over the bottom than the log indicates. It is the distance made over the bottom that shows us our distance off the light. Many vessels have been stranded on

the Florida Reefs through miscalculation or no calculation of the Gulf Stream current when using the four-point bearing.

If your vessel has no log you will have to determine the distance run by other means. If you have calibrated your ship's speed at various revolutions of the motor, a very close approximation of the distance run can be determined by noting the time of taking the first bearing (45°) and the time of taking the second bearing (90°). These will give you the time run between bearings and from your R.P.M.—Speed curve, you can easily calculate the distance run during this period of time.

The diagram (Fig. 210) shows a right triangle with an angle of 45° known, and a side given. It is a mathematical fact that all three angles of a triangle always add up to 180°, and as we have here two angles equal to 135°, it clearly shows that the third angle must be also 45°. It is a well known theorem that the sides of a triangle opposite equal angles are equal. Hence it will be seen that the distance run is the same as the distance off the lighthouse.

It often becomes desirable to get a position, or at least an approximation, when a four-point bearing is not available. A single bearing of an object laid down on the chart shows the mariner that he is somewhere on this line. A sounding taken at the same time will, if the shore is shelving uniformly, give a good approximation of the position.

Two Bearings and a Run

With a single object in sight another method known as two bearings and the run between, for lack of a better name, is sometimes resorted to. (See Fig. 211.) In such

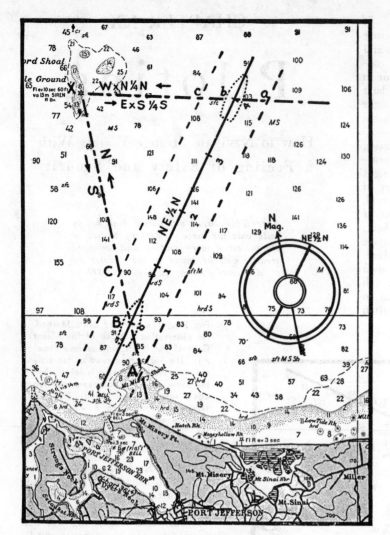

bearing is taken a certain number of degrees off the bow, say 20°, and again when 40°, noting at the same time the run between them. As in a four-point bearing the distance run is the distance off the light or other object at the time of taking the second bearing. This is valuable in that it gives the position before the light is abeam and in case shoals or ledges lie off, it is most desirable to know the position before reaching them.

The 7/10 Rule

This problem furnishes the navigator with further valuable information (provided he uses two points and four points on the bow) (Fig. 212) in that if he takes 7/10 of the distance run it will be the distance the boat will pass the light when abeam. This is called the Seven-tenths Rule.

26½°-45° Bearing

An easy method to determine before you come abeam of the object, how far off the object you will be when you are abeam, is take a bearing of the object when it bears 26½° from your course, note the log or time; then when it bears 45° take another bearing, note time or log. Calculate the distance run between bearings and this will also be the distance off the object you will be when the object comes abeam.

Should by any chance it have been desired to get the distance when too late for a four-point bearing, note the log when the object bears 26½° forward of the beam and again when 26½° abaft the beam; the distance run will be the distance off when it was abeam. Or if an approximation is sufficient read the log when the object bears two points forward of the beam, and again when abeam. Multiply the distance run by 2½ to get

Fig. 211 Above: Two Bearings and a Run Between. Lines are drawn on a chart corresponding to the two bearings and the dividers are set at a distance equal to the run between bearings. Two points on the lines parallel to the course may be located which will be the boat's positions at the time of taking the bearings

Fig. 212 Right: Doubling the Angle. In this method a bearing of the object D is taken from any position A and the log is read. The boat is kept on the same course until the bearing of D is twice as many points on the bow as it was when the first bearing was taken. The log is then read again. The distance off the object at the time the second bearing is taken at B will equal the distance run between bearings

a case take a bearing of the object, read the log, and after an interval, during which the course has not been changed, and the bearing has changed not less than 30°, again read the log and note a second bearing. Lay both bearings on the chart, take the distance run on the dividers, and holding the points always in the direction of the course from each other, carry them in between the bearings until their convergence brings the points of the dividers each on a bearing line. These points will indicate the first and second positions of the boat. Remember it is always the run over the bottom that is used, and if current is against or with the boat the log distance must be respectively decreased or increased.

Doubling the Angle

There is a method known as Doubling the Angle on the Bow (see Fig. 212), where the

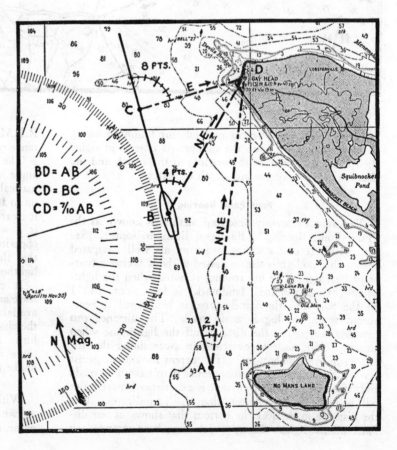

$$BD = AB$$
$$CD = BC$$
$$CD = \frac{7}{10} AB$$

the distance off. By similarly taking a bearing when the light is one point forward of the beam and multiplying the run by 5 a fairly accurate distance off the light is obtained.

Special Bearings

The following sets of bearings bear such a relation to each other that the run shown by log between bearings (corrected for current) will equal the distance off when the object is passed abeam:

20°–30°, 21°–32°, 22°–34°, 23°–37°, 24°–39°, 25°–41°, 26°–43½°, 26½°–45°, 27°–46°, 28°–48½°, 29°–51°, 30°–53½°, 31°–56°, 32°–59°, 33°–61½°, 34°–64½°, 35°–67°, 36°–69½°, 36½°–71°, 37°–72°, 38°–74°, 39°–77°, 40°–79°, 41°–81°, 42°–83½°, 43°–86°, 44°–88°, 45°–90°.

Cross Bearings

All that has been said refers to the problem of locating a boat when one object is visible. Should two objects be available the method of cross bearings (see Fig. 214) is most practical, for the position is given immediately without waiting during a certain run. The objects should be hardly less than 30° apart

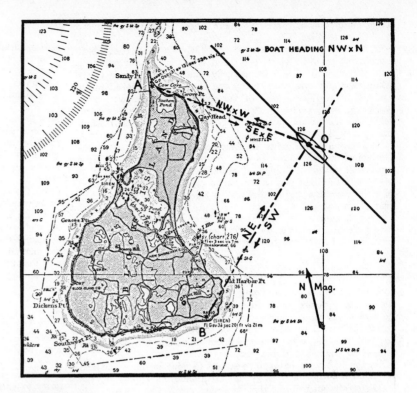

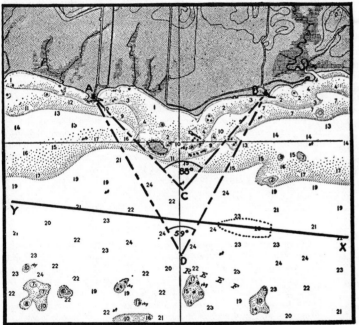

Fig. 214 Above: Cross Bearings. This is used to locate one's position when the two objects A and B are visible and can be located on the chart. A bearing is taken of each at the same time and these bearings lines are drawn on the chart. The boat's position will then be at point O at the intersection of the two lines

Fig. 215 (Left): The Double Danger Angle. From C, clear of inshore dangers, lines AC and BC are drawn, and angle C measured (88°). From D, clear of the offshore reef, angle D is plotted (59°). On course XY, the vessel is safe as long as the observed angle between A and B is more than 59°, but less than 88°

and the nearer 90° the better results. The procedure is to take a bearing of each object as quickly as possible, correct for deviation if the compass rose diagram on the chart is magnetic, and also for variation if it is a true diagram, and lay them down on the chart. The boat is somewhere on each of these lines or bearings and hence must be at their intersection. This is an accurate method, but a mistake might not be detected, so if a third object be in sight, a third bearing passing close to or through the intersection of the other two, makes an absolutely correct position.

The Danger Angle

There is a wrinkle known as a Danger Angle (see Fig. 215) which is a very useful method of insuring safety in passing a dangerous rock. There must be two charted objects in sight and properly located in relation to the

shoal or rock. At a safe distance off the rock make a dot on the chart, and draw a line from it to each object, points A and B in the diagram. An ordinary protractor will measure the danger angle (88°) at the intersection of the lines (at C). If the vessel gets in closer to the rocks than the point of safety the angle will become larger and if further away will become smaller.

Sometimes a Double Danger Angle is used where another rock exists outside the first and it is necessary to navigate between them. In such a case the vessel is protected from the inner rock by a danger angle as shown in Fig. 215. Inside the outer rock at a safe distance a point is set down and by drawing lines to each object another danger angle is established. While the first angle is not allowed to get any larger this second angle is not allowed to get any smaller. Thus both rocks are passed in safety.

The pilot depends very materially upon the buoys, spindles and beacons maintained as aids to navigation, but this trust should not be too implicit, as buoys get adrift and sometimes drag or are dragged from their positions. But along such coasts as ours where the Government is alert to maintain an efficient system, buoys are quickly returned to their proper positions. Unfortunately this is not true everywhere. The same is true of the reliability of lighthouses. There are hundreds of them along more isolated coasts than ours where too much confidence might lead to disaster.

It should be remembered that red starboard hand buoys bear even numbers while black port hand buoys carry odd numbers. And that conical or nun-shaped buoys are starboard hand buoys while cans and cylindrical buoys are black. Spar shaped buoys are common to both sides of the channel. The fairway buoy black and white vertically striped, should be passed close aboard, while the danger or obstruction buoy, black and red horizontal bands, should be given a good berth.

The visibility of lights is computed for a height of fifteen feet above the sea, so a man on a motor boat will not see a light until well within its range of visibility. An occulting light is one where the light period is equal to or greater than the period of eclipse, while a flashing light has a period of light shorter than that of eclipse.

An unknown white light seen at night should be avoided. It may indicate a wide variety of craft or obstructions from a mast-head light of a steamer to a rowboat.

Qualities of a Pilot

A pilot to be successful must be a man of ability. He must possess an intimate knowledge of the whole coast along which he navigates, of its currents at all times, he must be able to handle his vessel as a row boat and know the rules of the road so well that he acts almost without thinking, for he traffics where the commerce is heaviest.

On the Lakes we have pilots second to none in the world and on the coast they are as good. Mentioning the pilots on the Lakes recalls an incident that happened a few years ago and is worth repeating. A long file of steamers were plying as usual through the narrow channels between Lake Huron and Lake Erie when during a squall one of them parted or jammed her wheel ropes and came into collision with another steamer, which was sunk in the channel. There was only time to show a single white lantern from the forward part of the wreck, for coming up astern was a large steamer towing a barge. The captain and the mate of the latter steamer were peering vigilantly ahead in the blackness when they were startled by the unfamiliar light. The captain had but a few seconds to decide what to do, when from the invisible bank close aboard came a woman's voice, "Look out for the wreck, Cap'n." A quick helm and the steamer passed through the narrow opening between the wreck and the bank with only a few feet to spare. The bilge of the barge took the bottom at the edge of the channel, listed and slid along into the deep water in safety.

A Piloting Problem

It might be interesting to work out a problem in piloting applying the various methods which have just been mentioned for locating one's position. Fig. 220 illustrates a problem of piloting on Long Island Sound which is not unlike the conditions met on many other bodies of water which are so popular for motor boating.

In piloting or running courses it is essential that one know the speed of his boat with considerable accuracy. The patent log is perhaps the most convenient method of determining the speed of one's boat. However, this instrument is not an absolute necessity inasmuch as by a little practice and experience one is able to determine the speed of his boat at different revolutions of the motor. This process of determining the speed of one's boat, of course, can be done in several different ways, the simplest of which is by putting the boat over a course of known length. A log should always be kept whenever one cruises in his boat. Enough data will soon be obtained so that the motor boatman will know with a good degree of accuracy the exact speed of his boat under various conditions of weather and sea.

In the piloting problem which follows dealing with Fig. 220, both methods of determining distance covered are included. If a patent log is used the readings of the log should always be checked by taking the time of passing objects, and then by measuring the distance on the chart between these objects it is possible to calculate the speed of the boat from this data. Although both methods are mentioned below, yet one should not get the idea that it is absolutely necessary to employ a patent log to carry on piloting, for this can be done by the other method alone if it has to be.

Laying the Course

It is desired to sail from point A opposite Larchmont to a point at Q when Eaton's Neck bears 176° (See Fig. 220). The first step is to lay the course. The chart should be closely examined for depths and obstructions to navigation. A line or lines should be drawn on the chart to indicate the course which the boat is to take all the way from A to Q. It might be necessary to sail over a number of different courses in order to clear all obstructions. However, if one course can be laid out from starting point to destination so much the better. By examining the chart, Fig. 220, it will be seen that a straight line can be drawn on the chart which will extend from A to Q and will clear all obstructions such as Jackson Shoal, Duryee Middle Ground and the shoal water off Lloyd's Neck. Therefore it can be assumed that one's boat can safely take this course.

The next step is by means of a course protractor or the parallel rules to determine the direction of this course-line AQ by transferring the direction of this line to the compass rose by the method shown in Figs. 217 and 219. If this is done one will find that the magnetic direction to be steered with zero deviation will be 86°.

Bow and Beam Bearings

We will assume that our boat has a speed of 8 knots which will require 7½ minutes to cover one nautical mile. Starting from a position A at 10 A. M., assuming no current, we head our boat 86°. The first chance we have to locate our position in order to check our course and speed and to determine whether we are really following the line AQ will be by taking a bow and beam bearing of the light buoy off Mamaroneck Harbor, lettered B in Fig. 220. Therefore, when buoy B bears 45° (4 points) on our port bow we will be prepared to note the time as well as note the reading of the log if we are using one. As our course is 86° then 45° off this course would be 41°. So when buoy B bears 41° from our boat we can assume that we are somewhere on the line BC. At 10:15 buoy B bears 41° and the log reads 2.00 miles. We continue on this same course until buoy B is abeam or bears 356°. We again note the time, which in this case is 10.21, as well as the log reading which shows 2.8 miles. Therefore, as it has taken us 6 minutes to sail from C to D which, converted into distance, as the speed is 8 knots, we see the distance between C and D is 0.8 mile. Therefore, we know we are the same distance off B in a direction 176°, that is, 0.8 mile. From this, then, we can locate position D at once.

Cross Bearings

Continuing on our course of 86° our next chance to locate our position will be by means of cross bearings on Sands Point and Matinicock Point lights, lettered F and E on the diagram. A bearing is taken on light F and this bearing is found to be 226°. At the same time a bearing is taken on light E which is found to bear 114°. Lines are then drawn on the chart in these directions and intersected at point G which must be our position. The log is found to read 3.3 and the time to be 10:25 A. M.

Two Bearings and Run Between

Matinicock Point light buoy is the next convenient mark for locating and checking our position. The method known as Two Bearings and the Run Between will be found convenient in this instance. The first bearing taken is found to be 131° and we continue our course to some other point and take another bearing which we find to be 221°. A log reading at the taking of the first bearing is 4.3 and the time 10:32. The log when the second bearing was taken read 6.3 and the time was 10:47. Therefore, the time between bearings was 15 minutes, which is equivalent to 2.0 miles. We now draw from point E, lines in the direction 311° and 41° which are the reverse of the two bearings. With our dividers set at a distance equivalent to 2.0 miles and held in 86° direction, corresponding to the course of the boat, we locate points H and J, which are 2.0 miles apart, which gives us the two positions H and J which we sought.

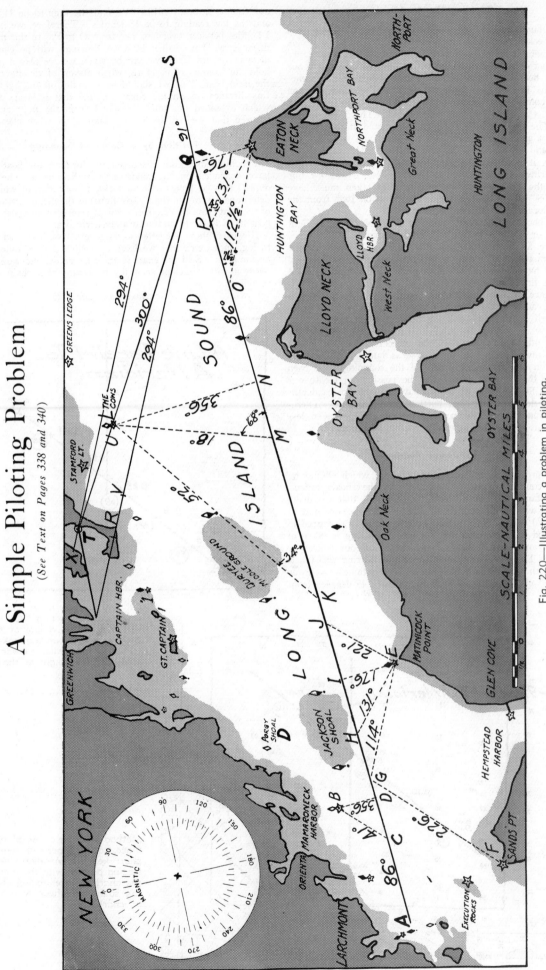

A Simple Piloting Problem

(See Text on Pages 338 and 340)

Fig. 220—Illustrating a problem in piloting.

339

Doubling the Angle

The light buoy on The Cows, point L, gives us another opportunity of checking our position a little farther on. We decide to use the method known as doubling the angle. Therefore, we take a bearing of the light at L when it is 34° (3 points) on our port bow or bears 52° from us. This locates our position somewhere on the line KL but does not give us the exact location of K. We continue on the same course 86° until the same light L bears 68° (6 points) on our bow or 18°. This gives us the line LM. The time and log readings were noted at the moment both the first and second bearings were taken and were 7.0 and 10.5 miles and 10:52:30 A. M. and 11:19 A. M. respectively. Accordingly, it is an easy matter to calculate the distance run between bearings which we find to be 3.5 miles. Therefore, our position at the time the second bearing was taken must have been 3.5 miles off the light L and in the direction 198° from the light. This locates the position M exactly.

Another check will be the location of point N when the light L is abeam or when it bears 356°. As the points D, G, H, J, and M have all been plotted on the chart and a line drawn through them which should be a straight line, if our sailing and observations have been accurate then point N should also be on this straight line continued, and should bear 176° from light L and a distance of 1.25 miles from point M. This distance is determined readily as the time and log reading at point M were noted as well as the time and log reading when light L was abeam.

The buoy off Lloyd's Neck will be another convenient means of checking our position, as our course as laid out passes this buoy close on our starboard hand. If the soundings had been recorded on the chart it would also be possible to locate our position off Lloyd's Neck, as the shaded section indicates depths of 18 feet or less and the clear portion greater depths. Therefore, if a sounding was taken which at any time showed less than 3 fathoms we would know we were off our course.

26½-45 Degree Bearings

Our next problem is to locate the point Q, which should be reached by continuing our 86° course. As the shoals extend for some distance off Eaton Neck it is essential that we make sure that we will be far enough off when we are abeam of it to clear the shoal water. The method known as the 26½ degree-45 degree method will determine this for us. A bearing is taken of Eaton Neck and when it bears 26½ degrees off our course or when it bears 112½°. The time at which this bearing was taken is 11:46 and the log reading 14.2 miles. We continue to sail our course of 86° until the Eaton Neck Light bears 45 degrees from

our course or bears 131°. We find the time to be 11:56 A. M. and the log reading to be 15.3 miles. Therefore, we have sailed 1.1 miles between bearings, i.e., from O to P. In this method the distance we have sailed between bearings will be equal to the distance off the light we will be when we are abeam of it if we hold our course. Therefore, when abeam of the light or when the light bears 176° we should be 1.1 miles off the light. Laying this distance off on the chart we find that it clears the shoals which extended out into the sound from the light and we are assured that we will be a safe distance off when abeam.

Position by a Chain of Soundings

The methods so far discussed for locating the boat's position have depended on the navigator's ability to see one or more objects such as buoys or landmarks, the location of which can be determined from the chart. By figuring the distance and direction of the boat from that known point of reference, the position of the boat itself is easily and accurately arrived at.

However, there are often cases where visibility is so poor, due to fog, snow, etc., that we have no visible charted object to rely on for a fix. Still the chart is the sure guide, and we may get a position with sufficient accuracy by means of a chain or line of soundings.

(Continued on page 342)

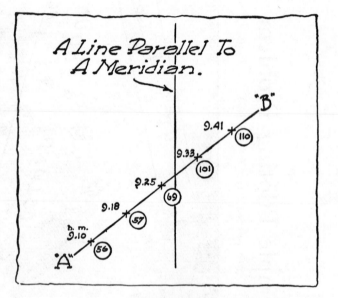

On transparent paper indicote the vessel's course = Line "A" — "B" = with relation to a line of Meridian, with record of soundings taken at intervals of one mile, allowance to be made for the height of the tide.

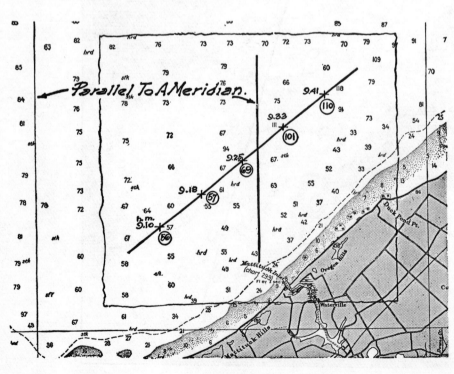

Method of using a line of soundings. Place tracing paper with soundings on chart keeping Meridian line on the tracing parallel with the Meridians on the chart. Move tracing about until the soundings check with soundings on chart.

Fig. 217. A convenient form of course protractor made out of a compass card and a piece of string. A hole is punched at the center of the card and the string drawn through it. To use this protractor place the compass card on the chart, its center coinciding with the boat's position. The string is stretched so it cuts the center of the nearest compass rose on the chart. The point on the compass rose which the string cuts is noted and then the compass card is revolved so that the string will cut the same point on the card as it does on the rose. As shown the string is cutting the point NE½E on the rose and the card of the protractor has been revolved so that the string cuts this same point, NE½E. (See Fig. 219)

Fig. 218. A convenient form of position locator, by means of which the position of one's boat can be accurately located when one object which can be located on the chart is visible. The method of using this diagram is to take a bearing of some object such as a lighthouse, an aid to navigation or some prominent landmark noting the time and log reading and the number of points off the bow which the object bears. The same course is held until the same object is abeam and then the time and log reading is again noted. If a log is used, then the difference between the two log readings will give the distance run between bearings. If no log is used, then by knowing the speed of the boat and the time between bearings, the distance run can be readily calculated. After the miles sailed between two bearings, that is, between the first bearing and the 90-degree bearing have been calculated simply use the figures at the bottom of the diagram and follow along the vertical line opposite this figure until it meets the diagonal line corresponding to the number of points off the bow which the object was at the time of taking the first bearing. Then follow along in a horizontal direction from this intersection to the left hand margin and the figures there will represent the number of miles away which the object is when it is abeam or at the time of the second bearing

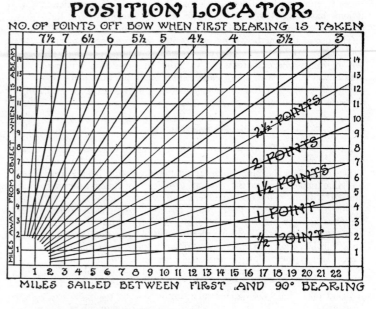

POSITION LOCATOR
NO. OF POINTS OFF BOW WHEN FIRST BEARING IS TAKEN
MILES SAILED BETWEEN FIRST AND 90° BEARING

Fig. 219. After the protractor has been set as indicated in Fig. 217, then to obtain the course which must be steered to reach any given point carry the string to the object which it is desired to reach, keeping the compass card firmly in position with the left hand. The string which extends from the center of the compass card to the point on the chart to which one desires to sail will cut a certain point on the compass card at the left. This will be the magnetic course which must be steered to make good this course. In the illustration at the left the center of the compass rose is at a point off Throggs Neck, at the entrance to Long Island Sound. The string extends to the wharf on Beldens Point, City Island. The course to be steered is NNE ¼ N

One sounding, in itself, is not of much value except to show the nature of the bottom. But by holding a known course and taking additional soundings at regular intervals we get something that can be used to advantage. On a piece of tracing paper, a line is drawn which will correspond with the meridian line on the chart. Then the boat is held on a fixed compass course. This is converted to a true course by applying deviation and variation, and the resulting *true* course is plotted on the tracing paper with reference to the meridian.

The next step is to take a sounding and note the time and depth on one point of the line. The depth naturally must be corrected for the height of the tide as the charted depths refer to low water. Then the course plotted on the tracing paper is run, and the boat's speed *over the bottom* figured, either by engine revolutions or by the log, due allowance being made for the effect of wind and current in aiding or retarding the boat. When the boat has covered a mile over the bottom, another sounding is taken and the time and depth again noted on the course line on the tracing paper, at a point which is equivalent to one mile from the first sounding according to the scale of the chart we are using.

Plotting the Soundings

Then at regular intervals—every six minutes, for example, for a ten-knot speed—a series of half a dozen or more soundings is taken and plotted on the tracing paper. Now the tracing paper is placed on the chart in the approximate position of the boat and moved about, the meridian line being kept parallel at all times to the meridian line on the chart. Presently, if the calculations have been accurate, a point will be found where the soundings on both chart and paper agree and the position is fixed.

The use of this method is not well suited to shore lines that are foul, with outlying rocks and very irregular depths, nor does it tell anything where there is no variation in the depth. There are, however, a great many cases when other piloting methods cannot be used, that the chain of soundings proves an excellent check on position. *See also page 411.*

Radio Position Finding

Radio direction-finder sets on board ship enable bearings to be taken of transmissions by other ships, aircraft, and shore stations. When located in the pilot house or on the navigating bridge, the direction finder enables the navigating officer to obtain bearings himself without reference to others and without delay.

Due to the great value of radio bearings, particularly when visibility is poor and when sights of heavenly bodies cannot be obtained, the radio direction-finder on board ship deserves the same consideration and care as are given to the sextant and compass. It has the following characteristics in common with the two latter navigational instruments: the readings are subject to certain errors; these errors may be reduced by skillful and intelligent operation; the dangers of using erroneous readings may be greatly reduced by the intelligence and good judgment of the mariner. In order to acquire experienced judgment in the operation of the instrument, it is essential that the mariner himself use it as much as practicable.

Troubles from interference and weak signals are greatly reduced by the use of direction finders of proper selectivity.

The bearings given by the set are relative bearings and the true bearings are obtained by applying the ship's heading to the bearings taken. On some ships the set is mounted over the ship's compass so as to permit the bearings to be read directly from the compass card. In either case the bearings must be corrected for radio deviation as shown by the calibration curve of the set.

No exact rules can be given as to the accuracy to be expected in radio bearings taken by a ship, as the accuracy depends to a large extent upon the skill of the ship's operator, the condition of the ship's equipment, and the accuracy of the ship's calibration curve. Mariners are urged to obtain this information for themselves by taking frequent radio bearings when their ship's position is accurately known and by recording the results. United States radio-beacons are operated on hourly schedules regardless of weather conditions, giving mariners opportunity to make such frequent observations, and often to check the results directly with visual bearings.

Skill in the operation of the radio direction-finder can be obtained only by practice and by observing the technical instructions for the set in question. For these reasons the operator should study carefully the instructions issued with the set and should practice taking bearings frequently so that when bearings are needed he can obtain them rapidly and accurately.

Fix by Radio Bearings

Radio bearings may be used in the same manner as other lines of position to obtain a fix if due regard is always given to the fact that, like lines of position obtained from heavenly bodies, radio bearings are subject to possible errors. Some of the uses of radio bearings in obtaining a fix are: cross bearings taken on two or more stations, a single bearing crossed with a line of position of a heavenly body, a bearing and a sounding, a bearing and a synchronized air or submarine signal and two bearings on the same station and the distance run between bearings.

Circular radiobeacons send out waves of approximately uniform strength in all directions so that ships may take radio bearings of them by means of the ship's radio direction-finder sets. This is the most common type of radiobeacon used by surface ships. Due to the many factors which enter into the transmission and reception of radio signals, a ship cannot estimate with any degree of accuracy its distance from a radiobeacon either by the strength of the signals received or by the time at which the signals were first heard. Mariners should give this fact careful consideration in approaching radiobeacons. In using radio bearings in approaching lightships it is important that the courses be set at all times to pass safely clear; the risk of collision can be avoided by ensuring that the radio bearing does not remain constant.

Synchronized Signals for Distance-Finding

At some radiobeacon stations, sound signals, either submarine or air, or both, are synchronized with the radiobeacon signals for distance-finding. The methods in use employ as a rule distinctive signals to indicate the point of synchronization, and make use, for determining distance, of the lag of signals traveling through air or water as compared to the practically instantaneous travel of the radio signals. (Elapsed time in seconds between receipt of a radio signal and a corresponding sound signal divided by 5.5 gives distance in nautical miles.)

Additional information on direction-finder sets on board ship may be found in "Instructions for the Operation and Calibration of Direction-Finder Equipment," published by the U. S. Navy Department, Bureau of Engineering and "Radiobeacons and Radiobeacon Navigation," published by the U. S. Coast Guard. Both of these publications are for sale by the Superintendent of Documents, Washington, D. C. Readers are also referred to Oceanographic Office publication Number 205, which includes details of direction-finder stations, radio beacons, time signals, etc.

Distance by Echo

A rough and ready method of determining distance, in passages or other bodies of water where sheer cliffs will produce an echo, is to sound a short blast of the whistle and time, preferably by stop watch, the interval before the echo is received.

Divide the interval in seconds by 2 (because the sound has to travel to the shore and it takes an equal length of time for the echo to return), and multiply that figure by 1,000, which is a very rough figure for the speed in feet per second of sound in air. (Actually, at 32 degrees F. the speed is 1100 feet per second; at 72 degrees F., 1120 feet; but 1,000 is good enough for a rough estimate.)

For example, you sound a whistle blast and time the interval till the return of the echo at 5 seconds. Half that is 2½; multiply by 1000 and you have 2500 feet or a distance off of approximately ½ mile.

This is sometimes called "dog-bark navigation" and is used to some extent in the inside passage to Alaska on the British Columbia coast. If the echo can be received from both shores, a vessel can be kept in the middle of the passage by holding a course that will cause the echo from both sides to be received simultaneously.

Note:—*Radio bearings are great circles. Therefore a correction is required before plotting a radio bearing on a Mercator chart. A conversion table giving this information is contained in H.O. 205, Radio Navigational Aids.*

NOTE: The following is a brief resume of the relative value of certain methods of piloting and information on soundings, etc., from Coast Pilot and Oceanographic data. For a complete discussion of piloting methods, see also Chapter XXVII

Methods of Fixing Position

A navigator in sight of objects whose positions are shown upon the chart may locate his vessel by any of the following methods: (1) Cross bearings of two known objects; (2) the bearing and distance of a known object; (3) the bearing of a known object and the angle between two known objects; (4) two bearings of a known object separated by an interval of time, with the run during that interval; (5) sextant angles between three known objects. Besides the foregoing there are two methods by which, without obtaining the precise position, the navigator may assure himself that he is clear of any particular danger. These are: (6) the danger angle; (7) the danger bearing.

In discussing these methods it is assumed that (1) is so familiar to all mariners as to require little explanation; (2 and 3) are seldom employed and will be passed over without comment; (4) two bearings of a known object separated by an interval of time, with the run during that interval, is a most useful method, certain cases arising thereunder being particularly easy of application. Such cases are (1) *doubling the angle on the bow*—when the angular distance on the bow at the second bearing is twice as great as it was at the first bearing, the distance of the object from the ship at the second bearing is equal to the run between the two bearings. A case where this holds good is familiar to every navigator as the *bow and beam bearing*, where the first bearing is taken when the object is broad on the bow and the second when it is abeam; in that case the distance at second bearing and the distance abeam are the same and equal to the run between bearings; (2) when the first bearing is 26½° from ahead and the second 45°, the distance at which the object will be passed abeam will equal the run between bearings.

Value of Two Bearings on One Object

The method of obtaining position by two bearings of the same object is one of great value, by reason of the fact that it is frequently necessary to locate the ship when there is but one landmark in sight. Careful navigators seldom, if ever, miss the opportunity for a bow and beam bearing in passing a lighthouse or other well-plotted object. It involves little or no trouble and always gives a feeling of added security, however little the position may be in doubt. If about to pass an object, abreast of which there is a danger, a familiar example of which is when a lighthouse marks a point off which are rocks or shoals, a good assurance of clearness should be obtained before bringing it abeam, either by doubling the angle on the bow or by using the 26½°–45° bearing. The latter has the advantage over the former if the object is sighted in time to permit of its use, as it may be assumed that the 45° (bow) bearing will always be observed in any event, and this gives the distance abeam directly.

It must be remembered that, however convenient, the fix obtained by two bearings of the same object will be in error unless the course and distance are correctly estimated, the course made good and the distance over the ground being required. Difficulty will occur in estimating the exact course when there is bad steering, a cross current, or when a ship is making leeway. Errors in the allowed run will arise when she is being set back or ahead by a current or when the logging is inaccurate.

Fixing Position by Sextant Angles

The most accurate method available to the navigator for fixing a position relative to the shore is by plotting with a protractor, sextant angles between well-defined objects on the chart. This method, based on the "three-point problem" of geometry, should be in general use.

In many narrow waters also where the object may yet be at some distance, as in coral harbors or narrow passages among mudbanks, navigation by sextant and protractor is invaluable, as a true position can in general be obtained only by its means. Positions by bearings are too rough to depend upon, and a small error in either taking or plotting a bearing might under such circumstances put the ship ashore. For its successful employment it is necessary, first, that the objects be well chosen; and second, that the observer be skillful and rapid in his use of the sextant. The latter is only a matter of practice.

Near objects should be used either for bearings or for angles of position in preference to distant ones, although the latter may be more prominent, as a small error in the bearing or angle or in laying it on the chart has a greater effect in misplacing the position the longer the line to be drawn. On the other hand, distant objects should be used for direction because less affected by a small error or change of position. The 3-arm protractor consists of a graduated circle with one fixed and two movable radial arms. The zero of the graduation is at the fixed arm, and by turning the movable arms each one can be set at any desired angle with reference to the fixed arm.

Plotting a Position

To plot a position, the two angles observed between the three selected objects are set on the instrument, which is then moved over the chart until the three beveled edges in case of a metal instrument, or the radial lines in the case of a transparent or celluloid instrument, pass respectively and simultaneously through the three objects. The center of the instrument will then mark the ship's position, which may be pricked on the chart or marked with a pencil point through the center hole. The tracing-paper protractor, consisting of a graduated circle printed on tracing paper, can be used as a substitute for the brass or celluloid instrument. The paper protractor also per-

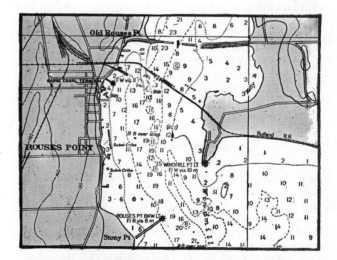

Small section (slightly reduced) of Lake Survey chart No. 171, upper end of Lake Champlain. Water areas up to one fathom depth are dark blue, one to two fathoms white. Note the one- and two-fathom curves. Highway and railroad bridges are shown, also breakwaters, submerged cribs and snags, boulders (Blds), cans (BC), nuns (RN), and wrecks near Barge Canal Terminal

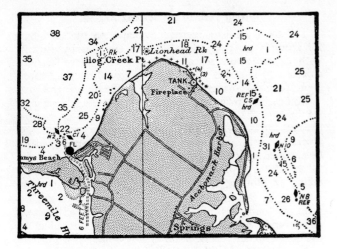

Buoys equipped with reflectors (REF) are shown on this portion of C. and G. S. chart 1212. The channel into Threemile Harbor is shown to be dredged to a depth of 6 feet. Two rocks, never covered, are indicated off the tank on the point, showing *(3)* and *(4)* feet above M. H. W. Three- and 5-fathom curves are outlined, the chart being tinted blue inside the 3-fathom line

mits the laying down for simultaneous trial of a number of angles in cases of fixing important positions. Plain tracing paper may also be used if there are any suitable means of laying off the angles.

Soundings

Soundings taken at random are of little value in fixing or checking position and may at times be misleading. In thick weather, when near or running close to the land, in shoal water, or in the vicinity of dangers, soundings should be taken continuously and at regular intervals, and, with the character of the bottoms, systematically recorded. An exact agreement with the soundings on the chart need not be expected, as there may be some little inaccuracies in reporting the depth on a ship moving with speed through the water, or the tide may cause a discrepancy, or the chart may itself lack perfection, but the soundings should agree in a general way and a marked departure from the characteristic bottom shown on the chart should lead the navigator to verify his position and proceed with caution; especially is this true if the water is more shoal than expected. By laying the soundings on tracing paper, according to the scale of the chart, along a line representing the track of the ship, and then moving the paper over the chart parallel with the course until the observed soundings agree with those on the chart, the ship's position will, in general, be quite well determined.

Use of Sounding Tubes

Although of undoubted value as a navigational instrument the sounding tube is subject to certain defects which, operating singly or in combination, may give results so misleading as to seriously endanger the vessel whose safety is entirely dependent upon an accurate knowledge of the depths. There are various types of tubes in common use which are too well known to require detailed description here. They are all based on the principle that the column of air in the tube will be compressed in proportion to the depth to which the tube is lowered in the water. The principle is sound theoretically, but in practice there are several sources of mechanical errors which affect the result in proportion to the depth of water determined.

Echo Soundings

This method of obtaining soundings is becoming extensively used. Its advantages lie in the fact that rapid and almost instantaneous soundings can be had while the vessel is running at full speed, and the navigator thereby knows at all times the depth of water under his keel. The method of determining the ship's position as described in the preceding sections (Soundings) is eminently applicable when the echo soundings are obtained. Two types of instruments have been brought out. In one type, the returning echo is flashed on a revolving plate and the depth read by an adjacent scale, while with the other type the depths are recorded on a graph.

By means of echo sounding, a vessel can follow the 50 or 100 fathom curve with ease, and in such localities as the Pacific coast and Alaska dangerous points and capes can be rounded in thick weather with utmost safety.

Echo sounding has been developed to such an extent that it is now used by the surveying vessels of the Coast and Geodetic Survey, and has practically replaced the use of the pressure tube.

Radio Direction Finder Bearings

Radio direction finder bearings and positions are especially valuable at night and during fog or thick weather when other observations are not obtainable. For practical navigating purposes radio waves may be regarded as traveling in a straight line from the sending station to the receiving station. Instruments for determining the bearing of this line are now available. The necessary observations may be divided into two general classes: First, where the bearing of the ship's radio call is determined by one, two, or more radio stations on shore and the resulting bearing or position is reported to the vessel; secondly, where the bearing of one or more known radio stations is determined on the vessel itself and plotted as a line of position or as cross bearings. Experiments show that these bearings can be determined with a probable error of less than 2°, and the accuracy of the resulting position is largely dependent on the skill and care of the observer. It must be remembered, however, that these lines are parts of great circles, and if plotted as straight lines on a Mercator chart a considerable error may result when the ship and shore station are a long distance apart. The bearings may be corrected for this distortion.

Radiobeacons

The United States Coast Guard now maintains and operates radiobeacons at a large number of lighthouses and lightships. These radiobeacons send distinctive signals and ships equipped with radio direction finders may readily obtain bearings on these beacons. See page 471d for a chart of the radiobeacon system on the Atlantic and Gulf coasts.

Synchronization of Sound and Radio Signals

At some of the stations the radio and sound signals are synchronized for distance-finding purposes. Reference should be made to the Light List to ascertain which part of the radiobeacon signal and sound signal are coincident. When the sound signal travels through water, the number of seconds intervening between the reception of the radio signal and sound signal multiplied by 0.78 gives the distance of the vessel in miles from the station. Where the sound signal travels through air the distance in miles is obtained by dividing the number of seconds by 5.

KEEP TRACK OF YOUR POSITION

Several methods are available to the navigator to enable him to keep track of his position. From a known point he may advance his position by keeping track of course and speed of the boat. This results in a DR (dead reckoning) position.

+

Alien factors, known or unknown, may cause this to differ from the actual position. Runs out of sight of land should employ celestial observations. Plan the trip with care and adhere to the courses and speeds selected so that frequent DR plots can be made.

+

Should trouble develop, the navigator may get a line of position from a light or radio beacon permitting an approximation of position or a check on the effects of current. He will be able to reach shore, or give an estimated position if help is needed.

+

From experience or guess, the navigator may estimate the effect of wind or current and apply suitable corrections to the DR (dead reckoning) to obtain the EP (estimated position)

+

In dangerous waters the prudent navigator will exaggerate his allowances in order to be on the safe side. While neither DR or EP agree with the actual position, he will have established limits for further operations.

+

When navigational aids are at hand, more complete positioning is possible. A single observation, such as a bearing, provides a line of position which may be straight or circular, depending on the type of observation.

+

The boat must be somewhere on the line of position and while the navigator does not know just where, he does know that he cannot be other than on that line at the time of observation.

+

When position is uncertain, the use of DR coupled with the LOP may supply maximum possible information.

In areas where aids to navigation are infrequent the line of position (LOP) may be all the data to be had. It should not be dismissed lightly as it does supply valuable data.

+

A bearing or a range will supply a straight LOP which passes through the aid and the actual position of the boat. A circular LOP is derived from an observation which provides a distance from an object, such as a vertical sextant angle, a rangefinder, timing from a DFS, or a horizontal angle between two known aids.

+

Convert compass or relative bearings to true before plotting on chart; ranges can be drawn directly, distance off by vertical angle from Bowditch tables.

+

Horizontal angles should be carefully plotted, noting the situation of angles greater and less than 90 degrees. The possible effect of tide upon vertical angle values should be recognized.

A complete position can be secured by two separate LOPs with an interval between. Boat is continued on course and speed. Having been on LOP[1] at first observation this line is advanced by the boat's motion and intersects LOP[2] and is presumed to be at their intersection. This position is labeled a running fix, RF.

+

A running fix, RF, is not reliable if there is any offsetting effect of wind or current. These factors are naturally not always known.

+

A number of bearings may be taken at uniform time intervals. Such bearings should mark off uniform intercepts on the course actually being made good. Trial and error will soon show whether this agrees with the intended course.

Note that a LOP may be regressed as well as advanced. This is not often done in piloting but may be valuable in celestial positioning.

+

Instead of advancing the LOP on the chart, a table of Successive Bearings in Bowditch will facilitate solution of these problems; it does not make them more reliable.

+

The determination of a running fix, RF, may be simplified by noting specific relative bearings and the time between rather than a random selection.

Geometric relations will show that when the relative angle is doubled, the distance off at the second bearing is equal to the distance run between bearings.

+

This doubling the angle is most often used with the 22½-45 degree or the 45-90 degree pairs, although any desired combination can be chosen.

+

With the 22½-45 degree combination it is further possible to predict the distance at which an object will be passed when it is abeam as 7/10 of the distance run between bearings.

+

These special combinations are likewise subject to error, based on the effect of wind and current, and should be used with this knowledge in mind. They may not give the actual position of the boat.

+

When it is possible to make two or more essentially simultaneous observations, the corresponding LOPs when drawn on the chart will intersect and since the boat is on both lines its position will be at the intersection point.

Two circle positions as from two horizontal angles will produce two intersection points, one of these being the position of the boat and the other the central object.

✛

Many combinations of LOPs may be used, such as two bearings, two ranges, a bearing and a range, a bearing and a horizontal angle, etc.

✛

Since there is always the possibility of error, select those combinations which tend to minimize errors. A simple diagram will show that the accuracy of the fix is at a maximum when the LOPs cut each other at an angle of 90 degrees.

✛

An acute or oblique cut will magnify small errors to an indeterminate solution of parallel lines or superimposed circles.

✛

For reasonable accuracy the navigator should try to secure a cut between the angles of 60 and 120 degrees.

✛

Casual observation will frequently indicate whether ranges or bearings will give a good cut. A short run will often improve the relative positions, resulting in a better fix.

✛

It is often difficult to visualize the situation when using horizontal angles. We must avoid producing a revolver and a diagram will best show the proper choice.

✛

A fix obtained by horizontal angles is independent of compass errors. A sextant can easily be read to a half degree. This method lends itself to rough weather use when a pelorus may not be practical.

With a constant heading three bearings may be taken on three objects and the differences between them used as angles just as if taken by a sextant.

✛

Horizontal angles may be plotted by using a three arm protractor or laying the angles on tracing paper and overlaying the chart, with each line passing through the respective aid.

✛

A single LOP, while not defining your position, still tells you where you are not and serves as a limiting line to avoid danger, or a directional guide.

✛

It is often possible to select a limiting line or boundary from the chart and determine its value. The compass value of such a danger bearing is obtained by applying deviation for the heading when the bearing is to be used.

✛

The boat has reached this LOP when the actual observation matches the precomputed bearing.

The circle, which is the locus of all points from which a constant angle will be observed between two points on the circle, can also serve as a limiting boundary, inside or outside of which there is danger or safety.

✛

Inspect the chart and roughly describe a circle which encloses the desired area. From any point on the circle draw lines to the two aids to be used. This precomputed danger angle is recorded and occasional observations with the sextant will show whether the boat is inside or outside the circle.

A vertical angle on an object of known height provides a distance off, and this type of observation may also be used as a pre-computed danger angle.

✛

When rain, fog, darkness, etc., do not permit visual observations, recourse must be had to audible signals, electronic aids, or reference to the bottom.

A sharp lookout should be maintained and speed reduced. It is helpful to stop the engines from time to time in order to listen for bells, horns, breakers or other sounds. A change in the swell may indicate a change in the depth of water.

✛

Fog horns and bells offer possible guidance but imperfect sound reception may make it difficult to hear or locate them. Sea actuated signals, such as bells and whistles, may remain silent on calm days, often the situation during fog.

✛

Echoing whistle signals from high banks may be used with variable success in suitable areas.

✛

Electronic aids serve to best advantage under trying conditions. Refer to the Light List for operation and use of such aids. Note that visibility may be good at the station and the signal may not be in operation.

✛

When in doubt about the depth of water take a sounding. If the bottom is irregular a chain of soundings corrected for tide may be matched with the chart to give an approximation of position. An armed lead will bring up samples of bottom to help in fixing position.

CHAPTER XXI

Tides and Currents

See also pages 417-425

Allowance for Currents and Tides, Leeway, Speed of Boat Through Water and Over Bottom, Short Cuts in Piloting

ONE of the most interesting problems in small piloting is the question of currents, their effect upon speed, and the determination of courses which mu. steered and the time required to make good a given tance or to reach an objective.

Contrary to usual belief, the problem is really compar; tively simple and capable of being solved readily w t. considerable accuracy without the use of higher mathematics.

Kinds of Current Problems

A study of currents resolves itself into three cases, as follows:

1. When the direction of the current is in the same direction as the boat's course or in the opposite direction.

2. When the direction of the current is at right angles to the boat's course; that is, the course of the boat is across the current.

3. When the direction of the current is oblique to the course of the boat; that is, neither at right angles nor directly favorable or adverse. The question as to whether the oblique course of the current favors or retards the progress of the boat must be considered also.

Each of the above cases may be divided into three parts as follows:

a. Determination of the course to be steered to reach a certain object.

b. The time required to reach a certain object or to make good a given distance.

c. The speed of the boat over the bottom.

Current With or Against the Course

Consider first problem 1, that is: When the direction of the current is in the same direction as the boat's course or in the opposite direction. The speed of the boat over the bottom in this instance is simply the algebraic sum of the boat's speed through the water, or in still water, and the speed of the current.

In other words, in the case of an 8 m.p.h. boat working with a 2-mile current the net speed of the boat will be at the rate of $8 + 2$ or 10 miles an hour. In the case of the same boat against an adverse current of 2 miles an hour the resultant speed of the boat over the bottom will be $8 - 2$ or 6 miles an hour.

Speed Through the Water

A boat goes through the water at a speed which is not affected in the slightest by the tide or current. An 8 m.p.h. boat goes through the water at an 8-mile speed no matter whether she has a 5-knot current with or against her.

Wind, weather, waves and other conditions of the sea affect a boat's speed through the water but the current does not.

The compass course to be steered will not be affected by a current which is directly ahead or directly astern. If the course to sail from one point to another is East, the course will be the same whether the current is flowing from East to West or from West to East.

Calculating Time Required

It is often necessary to know the time required for a boat to cover a known distance, assuming the speed of the boat in still water is known or can be calculated. To determine the time, divide the distance in miles and fractions thereof by the speed of the boat over the bottom in miles per hour. The result will be the time required in hours and fractions of the hour.

It is essential that, in making this calculation, the speed of the boat over the bottom be used and not the speed through the water. As explained above, speed over the bottom is the speed in still water, plus or minus the speed of the current, depending upon whether it is astern or ahead.

Figuring the Speed

To calculate speed, divide the distance run by the time in hours required to make the run. This gives speed over the bottom. To this must be added or subtracted the speed of the current to determine the true normal speed of the boat through the water, depending upon whether the boat has had a fair or a head current.

An 8 m.p.h. boat could make no headway against this current in a West Coast passage. At slack water it can be navigated

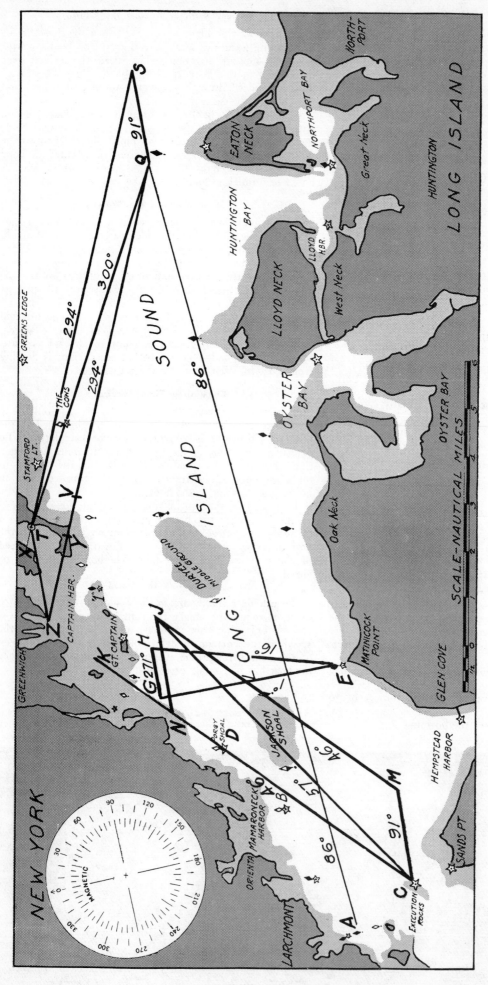

For example: suppose a distance of 12 miles was covered in 1½ hours. Dividing 12 by 1½ the answer would be 8 miles which would be the speed over the bottom.

Now to determine her speed through the water, assuming a 2 m.p.h. favorable current, we subtract 2 from 8 which would give us 6, the true speed of the boat in still water. In this same case, had the boat been held back by a current of 2 m.p.h. in making this run of 12 miles in 1½ hours then to get her true normal speed we add 2 and 8 and the result would be 10 m.p.h.

From the above it will be seen that the motor boatman must have a clear understanding of this difference between a boat's speed through the water and her speed over the bottom. In actual piloting and all problems connected with it, a boat's speed over the bottom must be used instead of her speed through the water.

It is important that the speed of the current be applied in the proper direction. That is, do not subtract from the boat's normal speed when it should be added and vice versa.

Average Speed

It is often assumed that when a boat sails up a river for a certain distance against the current, and then turns and comes down stream for the same distance, her average speed in covering the whole distance will be the same as it would be in slack water. However, such an assumption is incorrect as the average speed of a

Fig. 230. See text for full explanation

boat under such conditions would be decidedly less than the speed she was capable of in still or slack water. For example, a course of eight nautical miles up a river which has a 4-knot current flowing down, and a boat with a normal speed in still water of 8 knots. The time required for the boat to go up stream—that is, eight miles against a 4-knot current—will be two hours, and the time to return down stream with a 4-knot current will be only two-thirds of an hour. Thus, the total time required to go the sixteen miles, one-half of which is with the current, and the other half against the current, will be two and two-thirds hours. Dividing this time into the distance (sixteen nautical miles), gives us a speed of 6 knots as the average for the entire trip. This amount is 2 knots slower than the normal speed of the boat in slack water.

S = Normal speed of boat = 8 knots
C = Speed of current = 4 knots
    Then time required to go 8 (nautical) miles
       up stream   = 2   hours
       And time to go 8 miles down stream = 2/3 hour
       Total time to go 16 miles (½ with and
         ½ against current)   = 2 2/3 hours
A = Average speed = $\dfrac{16}{2.67}$ = 6 knots

Time = $\dfrac{L \times S}{S^2 - C^2}$

Normal speed = $\dfrac{A + \sqrt{A^2 + 4\,C^2}}{2}$

Current at Right Angles to the Course

Situations and conditions of this kind can be more readily solved graphically than by means of mathematics although it is, of course, possible to solve them by the use of trigonometry if it is so desired.

In the case of sailing directly across a current the most important problem generally is to determine the compass course to be steered in order to counteract the current effects. In figure 230, suppose it is desired to sail directly across Long Island Sound from Matinicock Point to Portchester Harbor or from point E to G. The distance between the two points is first determined from the chart and in this instance we find it to be exactly four miles. As our boat has a normal speed of 8 miles an hour it would require ½ hour to sail from E to G in still water.

Next we determine the velocity of the current from our knowledge of local conditions or from some other reliable source. For the purpose of this illustration we will assume that the current is running nearly west (271° magnetic) at a rate of 2 miles an hour. Now as it required ½ hour to cross the Sound from E to G in a northerly direction (our course is 01°) the tide would carry the boat one mile

toward the west by the time the other shore was reached; and therefore instead of reaching point G as desired, the boat would be at a point one mile west of G. Therefore to assure reaching point G we must steer or head our boat on a course somewhat to the eastward of north to counteract for this current which is constantly taking the boat to the westward in her run across the Sound.

To determine the necessary amount to the east of north which we must steer we lay off on the chart a line from G at right angles to EG and determine the point H along this line which in distance from G is equal to the flow of the current during the time it would take the boat to go from E to G under normal conditions which in our instance is ½ hour. This is equivalent to one mile flow of the current. Therefore the length of line GH is one mile.

We now connect points E and H by a line and the direction of this line is the course which must be steered or the direction in which the bow of the boat must be headed to go from E to G with a westerly (271°) current of one mile an hour. It is now an easy matter to determine the direction of this line EH by transferring it to the compass rose on the chart by means of a course protractor. In our example we find this to be 16°.

Time Required to Run from E to G

Under these conditions it is only necessary to measure the length of the line EH and then find out what distance this length represents according to the scale of the chart. In our example we find the distance to be 4.2 miles and as the normal speed of the boat is 8 miles an hour it will therefore require .525 hours which is equivalent to 31½ minutes to make this run.

NOTE: This graphic method which has just been described is subject to a slight error but in cases where the speed of the current is less than 25% of the speed of the boat this error is so small as to be of no consequence.

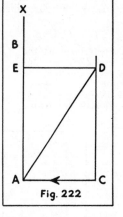

Fig. 222

Figure 222. Current Diagram When Sailing at Right Angles to Current. It is desired to sail from A to X; lay off on the chart, on the line AX, a distance AB equal to one hour's run of the boat in still water; lay off AC which, in direction, is opposite to the direction of the current and make the distance from A to C equal to one hour's flow of the current. From C lay off a line parallel to the course line AB and on this line locate a point D so that AD = AB. The compass direction of AD will be the compass course which must be held to sail from A to B. To calculate the time required to cover the distance from A to X draw a line from D parallel to the current line AC which will meet the line AB at E. The distance AE will then represent the speed of the boat over the bottom in miles per hour and by using this speed in the usual way to sail a distance equal to AX the time required to cover the distance is determined.

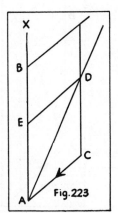

Fig. 223

Figure 223. Current Diagram When Direction Is Forward of Beam.—In this case as in figure 222 it is desired to sail from A to X; a distance AB is laid off on AX equal to an hour's run of the boat in still water. A line is drawn from A in the reverse direction from the current and the point C is located, the distance from A equal to an hour's run of the current; from C we draw a line parallel to AB and locate a point D on it so that AB = AD. Then the compass direction of AD will represent the direction which must be steered under these conditions. To calculate the time to go from A to X or the speed of the boat over the bottom, draw a line DE which will be parallel to AC. BE will then represent the amount which the boat has been retarded by the current, therefore, the time required to go from A to B in hours will be $\dfrac{AB}{AB - BE}$ or in other words the net speed of the boat over the bottom will be equal to AB — BE.

Current Oblique, Forward of the Beam
(See also Fig. 228, page 488)

If the direction of the current is other than dead ahead or astern or at right angles to one's course the case is not quite as simple but the course to be steered and the time required under conditions of a diagonal cross current may be quite readily determined graphically. Take in the case of Figure 230; When it is desired to go from Execution Rocks, lettered C, to Porgy Shoal Light, lettered D; as in the case when the current was at right angles to the boat's course, we again connect the starting point C with the finishing point D by means of a line. We determine the distance between these two points from the scale of the chart and find it to be 5 miles.

Now on CD or CD extended, we find a point K which is equal in distance from starting point C to an hour's run of the boat in still water, or in our case 8 miles. From C we draw a line CM which in direction is opposite to the direction of the flow of the current or in our case, 91°, nearly east. Point M is located on this line at a distance from C equal to one hour's flow of the current or in our case two miles.

We now draw a line from M parallel to CD and locate point J on it so that CJ will be equal to an hour's run of the boat in still water or 8 miles. The direction of CJ will be the course which must be steered and by transferring the direction of this line CJ to the compass rose we find this direction to be 57° which is the course which must be steered to run from Execution Rocks to Porgy Shoal Light.

To calculate the time required to run from C to D under these conditions, we draw a line from J parallel to the current line CM which will meet the line CD extended at N. Now the distance measured by the line NK will represent the amount which the boat has been retarded by the current in one hour's running time in still water. By measuring this distance with a pair of dividers we find it to be equivalent to 1.6 miles. Therefore the speed of our boat over the bottom will be 8 minus 1.6 or 6.4 miles an hour. As the distance from C to D has been found to be 5 miles, therefore the time required will be 5 divided by 6.4 or .78 hour which is equivalent to 47 minutes.

Figure 224. Current Diagram When Current Is Abaft the Beam.—In this case, in figures 222 and 223, it is desired to sail from A to X. This case is very similar to the preceding ones with the exception that the current instead of retarding the boat's progress through the water, more or less aids it. In this case we lay off AB equal to one hour's run of the boat in still water and from A the line AC, which in direction will be opposite to the direction of the current and the distance AC will be equal to one hour's flow of the current. Draw a line from C parallel to AX and locate point D on this line, so that AD = AB. Then the direction of the line AD will be the direction which must be steered to make good a course from A to B with a current AC. To calculate the speed over the bottom, we draw a line from D parallel to AC and meeting AX at E. The distance BE will represent the distance which the boat has been helped along in one hour's time by the current. Therefore, the speed of the boat over the bottom equals AE and the time required to go from A to X = $\frac{AX}{AE}$

(See also Fig. 228, Page 488)

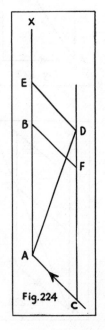

Fig. 224

Figure 225. The Horizontal Danger Angle.—To be sure that he will clear a charted danger such as a submerged shoal, rock or other obstruction is one of the mariner's principal worries. If he is running in sight of land on which there are two or more objects in view which can be definitely located on the chart, then the problem becomes fairly simple and he may apply the method commonly known as the Danger Angle. Fig. A illustrates this method. Points A and A' are on land or are such that they can be definitely spotted on the chart. Point O is the nearest point to the danger it is desired to approach when sailing on course C D. Point O may also be readily located on the chart. Proceed by drawing a circle through the three known points A O A'. This circle must include all portions of the danger. The angle A O A' may be measured with a protractor. Now to be sure that the danger will be safely cleared frequent bearings should be taken while the boat is on her course. If these bearings are taken at such points as P, P2, P3, etc., and the angle subtended by the objects A and A' in each instance (that is angles A P1 A'; A P2 A'; A P3 A', etc.) is less than the angle A O A', then the mariner will know that his course is safe to clear the danger which he is desirous of avoiding. However, if the angle is equal to or greater than A O A', the boat should at once sheer off to avoid the danger.

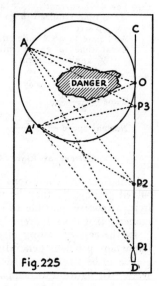

Fig. 225

Current Oblique, Abaft the Beam
(See also Fig. 228, page 488)

Another instance in oblique current sailing is where the current tends to favor the boat's progress through the water rather than to retard it as in the instance just described. But the method of procedure is the same.

For example, if it is desired to sail from point Q to V it is apparent that a westerly current will considerably assist the boat. To determine the course which must be steered we lay off from Q a line 91° magnetic equal in length to an hour's flow of the current, namely two miles. This gives us the line QS. We now draw a line from S which we will call SX parallel to QV but of an indefinite length. We determine a point on this line SX which represents the distance from Q equal to an hour's run of the boat through the water or in our case 8 miles. This gives us point T. A line is drawn from Q to T and its direction is found to be 300° which is the direction which must be steered to make good the course of 294° between Q and V.

To find the time to hold this course in order to reach point V lay off a line from T parallel to the current line QS. This will intersect QV extended at Z. Locate a point Y on QV extended so that the length QY will represent one hour's sailing of the boat under normal conditions in still water, that is, 8 miles. Then YZ will represent the amount which the boat has been aided by the current in one hour. Therefore the speed of the boat over the bottom will be QY plux YZ or 8 plus 1.7 which is equal to 9.7 miles. As point V is 7.3 miles from Q the time required to cover this distance QV will be 7.3 divided by 9.7 or .75 hour or 45 minutes.

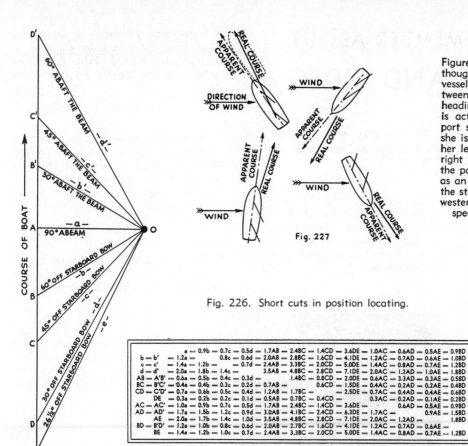

Fig. 226. Short cuts in position locating.

Figure 227. (left) Leeway is generally thought of as the sidewise movement of a vessel, but technically it is the angle between the direction in which the vessel is heading and the direction in which she is actually going. Notice that when the port side of a vessel is the windward side she is then said to be on the port tack and her leeway makes her real course lie to the right of her apparent course. Leeway on the port tack therefore has the same effect as an easterly compass error and leeway on the starboard tack has the same effect as a westerly error. The above rules hold irrespective of the direction of the wind.

In Figure 226, at the left, will be found a handy graphic illustration by means of which many short cuts can be made in locating one's position. The diagram at extreme left shows various bearings relative to the boat's course, while the accompanying table shows the relationship between the distances involved. Knowing certain factors, others can be arrived at by a simple calculation. For example, the run from C to B being known, distance b from B to O can be calculated from the formula BC = 0.4b.

Figure 229 (below). The Victory Leeway Calculator.—This diagram is a graphic reproduction to aid the pilot by showing angularity of one- to four-point courses for distances as far as one is likely to use in the ordinary alongshore navigation. It is intended mainly as a help in quickly calculating the allowance to be made for any force (current, wind or sea), which will tend to set the ship sideways on her course and can be used for ordinary amounts of leeway for distances up to 25 miles or on a "per hour" basis for longer distances. As an illustration suppose you are south and east of Long Beach so that Scotland light vessel bears W. distant 22 miles, and your speed is 9 miles per hour. Also suppose the current is flood, and wind S.W. moderate. Calculate the distance current, sea and wind will set you to the north either by the "current diagram" (Figs. 222-224) or approximate it from information gained by consulting chart, Current Table or Coast Pilot. Suppose current influence be ⅞ mile per hour and adding another ⅛ mile for sea and wind we have a total leeway of 1 mile per hour. With distance of 22 miles and 9 miles per hour speed it will take about 2½ hours for the run and the total "leeway" in that time will be 2½ miles. Now run along bottom row of figures (which indicate distance) to 22; then where that perpendicular crosses between the lines of 2 and 3 in the right margin (indicating leeway) we will find the nearest diagonal from compass card in lower left corner is marked "½ point" which is allowance to be made. As course was west and the flood sets to the north and west a course of West ½ South will bring you out at Scotland if your other calculations were correct. On the same basis of facts, figuring for the "per hour" method, with hourly speed of 9 miles in bottom row of figures and 1 mile in the figures on right margin, the intersection will be very close to the "½ point diagonal." In the above, the word "leeway" is used in a very broad sense as its regular meaning is the error caused by wind and sea only but for purposes of illustration it is made to include also the current error. This diagram could also be used to determine allowance for current and wind when working a traverse table in dead reckoning.

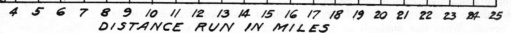

DISTANCE RUN IN MILES

POINTS TO REMEMBER ABOUT
CURRENTS AND TIDES

The term for the horizontal motion of large masses of water is current. It may be further defined as ocean current, wind-driven current, river current and tidal current.

✛

Well defined currents which have been surveyed, exist in the oceans, and are clearly shown on the Pilot Charts.

✛

The frictional effect of wind blowing over water generates a water current.

✛

In the northern hemisphere, this sets about 40 degrees to the right in open water and perhaps 20 degrees to the right in restricted areas. The resulting velocity of the water may be approximately 2 per cent of the wind velocity.

✛

Local conditions have a marked effect on the expected direction, however, and table 5, Rotary Tidal Currents, of the Current Tables should be consulted for specific stations.

✛

River currents are often unpredictable except for direction. Velocity in mid-channel is usually greatest, but mid-channel is not always mid-stream.

✛

Eddies and reverse currents may be found near shore and sub-surface velocities and directions do not always agree with surface data.

✛

Both current and tide result from the gravitational effect of the sun and moon on the earth's water envelope. A great wave of water on the earth follows the moon as it travels around the earth.

✛

The effect of the moon generally predominates because it is closer to earth and the effect is strengthened when sun and moon are in alignment.

✛

For practical purposes it can be assumed that a tidal bulge is created over the oceans. When this impinges on the shores, energy is expended in heaping up the tides.

The changing water gradients thus bring about an increasing horizontal flow.

✛

The occurrence of SLACK and STAND of the tide are usually out of phase except for unbroken coast stations. Local hydrography and coast outline are the controlling factors in most tidal and current situations.

In reasonably cyclical fashion, ocean waters are flung on the shores and enter bays and inlets as a FLOOD CURRENT. This inward flow slows and ceases causing SLACK, then reverses direction causing EBB CURRENT.

✛

During each flow the current reaches a maximum velocity, STRENGTH, which often exceeds 12 knots. (In some localities.)

✛

When a canal or a strait connects two bodies of water with differing tidal stages, a preferential flow of water takes place due principally to the difference in heights.

✛

This form of flow or current is a HYDRAULIC CURRENT and Part B of Table 3, Current Tables, will permit interpolation of values.

✛

Current tables contain complete daily data for the time of slack water, flood and ebb, maxima, and velocities at strength for numerous important stations.

Current characteristics for times other than those listed can be obtained by interpolation through Table 3. Current velocity is not directly proportional to time.

✛

By applying corrections involving time and velocity from Table 2 to appropriate Reference Stations, complete data for practically all places and sub-stations can be arrived at. Interpolation is used for determining intermediate values.

✛

Slack water is not an instantaneous event. Table 4 is provided to supply time and velocity for various current strengths.

✛

Currents offshore are generally weaker and differ from the usual ebb and flood in that they follow a circular pattern which leads to the term ROTARY CURRENTS.

✛

Rotary currents may possibly be the primary motion of water in large masses. It is only when reflected from shores that the ebb-flood sequence is produced.

✛

Current diagrams, available for many areas, provide the most practical method for selecting times at which to carry favorable currents.

Tidal current charts offer the most useful picture of current conditions for a limited number of localities.

✛

Tide and Current Tables are based on Standard time. Weather may upset the predictions and should always be taken into account.

TIDAL MOTION

Casual observation in tidewater areas shows that there is a rhythmic vertical motion of the water. It will rise from LOW WATER to a crest, HIGH WATER, and then fall again to repeat the cycle.

+

When vertical motion ceases the condition of STAND is reached. The difference in height between any adjacent pair of high and low waters is the RANGE.

+

The A.M. and P.M. highs or lows or both may differ appreciably in respective heights. This is called DIURNAL INEQUALITY.

The tides are associated closely with the motion of the moon so that the passage of the moon over your meridian serves as a reference to the time of high water.

+

The time between the passage of the moon and the actual time of high water is termed the LUNITIDAL INTERVAL, usually the HIGH WATER INTERVAL.

+

The moon changes its relative position in the sky rather rapidly and therefore causes correspondingly rapid changes in the tide pattern.

+

When the moon is high or low with respect to the equator, we have TROPIC or EQUATORIAL tides.

+

When the moon is close to the earth at PERIGEE we may expect greater tidal motion than when it is at APOGEE, the opposite condition, furthest from the earth.

+

The sun also contributes to the tide-raising force and the relative positions of the sun and moon must be considered.

+

At new and full moon SPRING tides may be of greater range than normal, and at quarter moons NEAP tides are often of less extent than average.

The moon rises on the average about fifty minutes later each day; the corresponding stage of the tide occurs about fifty minutes later each day. The TIDAL DAY is then 24 h and 50 m. This may be decreased (PRIMING) or increased (LAGGING).

+

In some areas, the lunar effects are subordinated to those of the sun, and only one well defined high and low water are observed for each day. These are DIURNAL tides, as distinct from the more unusual SEMIDIURNAL tides, with two highs and lows per day.

+

The actual cause of tide is still controversial but it is generally conceded that a tidal bulge of water follows the moon in its path about the earth causing the rise and fall and currents when this encounters the land. No matter how generated the effect of this water flow is exaggerated in narrow inlets.

+

Tide and current should not be confused. Tide is the vertical rise and fall of the water level while current is the horizontal flow of water moving from place to place.

+

To measure the rise and fall of the tides a standard base line has been established. As an added safety measure this DATUM LEVEL is chosen to approximate the lower tidal stages.

+

On the Atlantic Coast of North America an average is taken of all low waters and is called MEAN LOW WATER.

+

On the Pacific Coast the diurnal inequality is more pronounced and only the lower of the daily lows is averaged to give MEAN LOWER LOW WATER.

+

In some areas, such as Europe and South America where spring tides are important, MEAN LOW WATER SPRINGS are derived from the lows occurring at spring tides.

Certain arbitrary references are used as the datum used for some ports on large rivers.

+

It should be noted that data from the Tide Tables are corrections to the charted depths and not the actual depths of water.

+

Tide Tables like the Current Tables tabulate the time and height corrections for a selected group of stations for all high and low waters. Time used is STANDARD TIME with a 24-hour clock.

+

Should an intermediate stage of the tide be required, interpolation must be used with Table 3. Practice will produce efficiency in interpolation.

+

To avoid the frequent tendency to use 100 minutes in the hour when adding or subtracting time it might be advisable to write times as 12-34 instead of 1234, until greater facility is obtained by practice.

+

A comprehensive list of secondary stations appears in the Tide Tables as Table 2. This contains corrections to be applied to the data for the reference stations to obtain values at the substation.

The height of tide at any time can be determined by the use of Table 3. Instructions for determining such corrections both mathematically and graphically appear in the Tide Tables. After the correction has been arrived at, do not forget to apply it to the charted depths.

+

Current "set" is expressed in direction, i.e., Northeast or 45°; current "drift" is expressed in velocity, i.e., 3.4 miles per hour or 3.4 knots.

Time and Tide

"There is a tide in the affairs of men

Which, taken at the flood, leads on to Fortune."

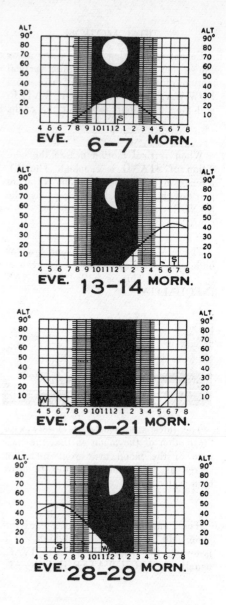

Right: Extracts from the monthly moonlight diagrams (June, 1944) published on the back of Hydrographic Office pilot charts, giving data for days of full moon, third quarter, new moon, and first quarter in 40 degrees north latitude

HAD the Bard of Avon been half the pilot he was a poet, he must have hesitated before penning this immortal philosophic gem. Perhaps he deliberately exercised poetic license, knowing that an exact interpretation of terms would never sanction use of the expression "flood tide." "There is a current..." he could more properly have written, but only at the expense of the rhetorical excellence of his lines.

"Time and tide," runs another well-worn adage, "wait for no man." But man, biding his time for a suitable tide, can utilize this phenomenon of Nature as a tool to lighten his labors, expedite his plans, even achieve victory in certain ventures.

The ship waits for high water, puts to sea with the ebb. Her skipper catches the top of the flood to insure an extra margin of safety under his keel over critical shoals in shallow channels. The boatman carries a tidal current upstream against the river's seaward sweep, or beaches his craft without benefit of ways on some distant strand for repairs.

Certain it is that, among all the factors weighed by Allied strategists in designating D-days for the invasion of hostile shores, the simple elemental consideration of tide must be one of prime importance—if not, in some cases, even paramount.

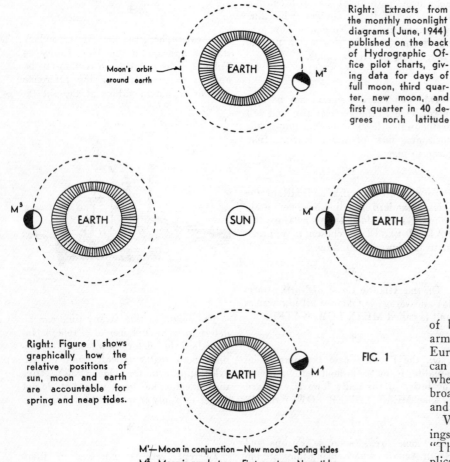

Right: Figure I shows graphically how the relative positions of sun, moon and earth are accountable for spring and neap tides.

M¹—Moon in conjunction—New moon—Spring tides
M²—Moon in quadrature—First quarter—Neap tides
M³—Moon in opposition—Full moon—Spring tides
M⁴—Moon in quadrature—Third quarter—Neap tides

FIG. 1

To carry out his secret mission, the commando times his departure from a British port to hit the beach in France near high water. Tide is on his side when landing craft creep quietly to the very base of the cliff to be scaled. Six hours later, his closest possible approach might leave him a mile from high water mark—a perilous mile to finish afoot, perhaps exposed to enemy fire, with barely a blade of grass for cover.

Whether it be a nocturnal raid by just a handful of men in a couple of boats or the full scale onslaught of an armada needed to deliver telling blows in Europe, the South Pacific or Japan, nowhere can Allied planners reckon without the tide, when modern invasion tactics are based so broadly on utilization of landing boats, large and small.

Winston Churchill, reporting Allied landings on the beaches of Normandy, stated that "This vast plan is undoubtedly the most complicated and difficult that ever has occurred. It involves tides, wind, waves, visibility from both the air and the sea standpoints, and

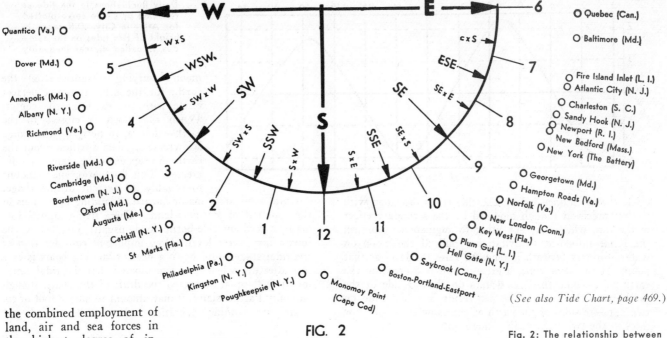

Quantico (Va.) ○
Dover (Md.) ○
Annapolis (Md.) ○
Albany (N. Y.) ○
Richmond (Va.) ○
Riverside (Md.) ○
Cambridge (Md.) ○
Bordentown (N. J.) ○
Oxford (Md.) ○
Augusta (Me.) ○
Catskill (N. Y.) ○
St Marks (Fla.) ○
Philadelphia (Pa.) ○
Kingston (N. Y.) ○
Poughkeepsie (N. Y.) ○
Monomoy Point (Cape Cod) ○
Boston-Portland-Eastport ○
Saybrook (Conn.) ○
Hell Gate (N. Y.) ○
Plum Gut (L. I.) ○
Key West (Fla.) ○
New London (Conn.) ○
Norfolk (Va.) ○
Hampton Roads (Va.) ○
Georgetown (Md.) ○
New York (The Battery) ○
New Bedford (Mass.) ○
Newport (R. I.) ○
Sandy Hook (N. J.) ○
Charleston (S. C.) ○
Atlantic City (N. J.) ○
Fire Island Inlet (L. I.) ○
Baltimore (Md.) ○
Quebec (Can.) ○

6 W   E 6
WxS CxS
5 WSW. ESE. 7
SWxW SW SE SExE
4 8
SWxS SSW SxW S SxE SSE SExS
3 9
2 10
1 12 11

FIG. 2

(See also Tide Chart, page 469.)

the combined employment of land, air and sea forces in the highest degree of intimacy."

For two years before historic D-day, Army Engineers studied every minute detail of the French invasion coast, charting depths and contour lines, obstacles to landing craft, characteristics of the bottom and shore as well, and the most favorable spots for getting on and off the beach. As a result, invasion chiefs were able to calculate conditions at any hour, and beachheads were taken as planned.

At low water, near dawn, engineers and sappers went to work on the mined steel and concrete obstacles the enemy had placed in the hope of wrecking invasion plans. At high water the assault boats went in, most of the casualties to landing craft occuring, according to reports, only after the tide had fallen.

Tide is a great variable. Though it rises and falls in definite and regular cycles, the cycles themselves fluctuate depending on the phase of the moon. And the height it attains at any given point is governed largely by the general configuration of surrounding land masses which tend to alter the regular cyclic movement and modify its action by pocketing water in basins, bays and coastal indentations.

Consequently, in one place we may have a tidal range of only a foot or so, as in certain ports on the Gulf of Mexico—perhaps only a fractional part of a foot, as in Sicily—and in others, the heaving 25- and 30-foot fluctuations that daily visit Liverpool, or the 40- and 50-foot inundations that engulf the tidal flats of Minas Basin in the Bay of Fundy, boiling into streams and estuaries in a bore hurtling landward with the sound of an express train, the speed of a running horse.

Normally, the tidal phenomenon manifests in successive periods of six hours rise and six hours fall, approximately, though in certain localities there will be but one high and one low during the course of a 24-hour day.

Its cause can be traced primarily to the rotation of the earth, the moon appearing to

Fig. 2: The relationship between High Water Interval and the moon's true bearing at high tide. It is high tide at any given station on the outer circle when the moon bears as indicated by the inner circle. For example, it's high tide at the Battery (N. Y.) when the moon bears SE x E true, since the H.W.I. is 8 hrs. 15 min.; at Oxford (Md.), where the H.W.I. is 3 hrs. .01 min., when the moon bears SW. H.W.I. was formerly tabulated in the Tide Tables

Mac Gramlich

Fishermen beached at their wharves in a Down East port by low tide

351

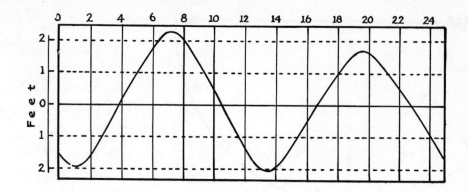

circle the earth once a day. The tide trails the moon with tireless precision though modified by the secondary effect of the sun, which may act either to augment or diminish the lunar influence. Gravitational pull of the moon on waters directly beneath it tends to raise the level at that point. At the same time, a greater pull is exerted on the earth as a whole than on waters on the far side of the earth from the moon. The net result is a high tide on two opposite sides of the earth at the same time, and low tides in the two intermediate quadrants.

Spring Tides and Neap Tides

The sun's influence, because of its distance from the earth, is only two-fifths that of the moon. The relative positions of earth, sun and moon are constantly changing during the lunar month as the moon in its orbit revolves about the earth. So it is evident that the total effect of tide-producing forces varies with the moon's phase. (See Figure 1.)

When the three bodies are in line, as they are at new moon and full moon, tides respond to the combined pull of both moon and sun, and we get higher highs and lower lows. These we call spring tides; this has nothing to do with the season. At first quarter and third quarter, tidal forces oppose each other and result in lower than mean or average highs, and higher than average lows. These are the neap tides.

In studying Figure 1, each of the four cases, M^1, M^2, M^3 and M^4, should be considered by itself as representing a relative arrangement of the earth, sun and moon at one time during the lunar month. Therefore each condition is repeated twelve times during the year as the moon revolves about the earth, giving us all four phases of the moon in one month. Otherwise one might misconstrue the diagram and wrongly believe that the earth had to complete its yearly orbit about the sun to produce the four phases.

Spring tides are good ones to catch when we need big tides for launching, for navigating shoal reaches, or for activities on the beach below the normal low water mark. If you beach a boat on high springs, it may be two weeks before returning springs will float her. Mean highs may only wet her keel and neap tides leave her high and dry even at the hour of high water for that day. So great is the effect of successive conjunctions and oppositions of celestial bodies on the periodic rise and fall of the sea.

Another factor that has a bearing on the degree of rise and fall, or tidal range, is the moon's varying distance from the earth, for the orbit is not a perfect circle with the earth at the center. When the moon is closest to the earth—that is, in perigee—the range is increased; when furthest from the earth—in apogee—the range is decreased. This fluctuation may amount to roughly 20 percent of the range.

Coral reefs are a major hazard to landing operations in the conquest of Pacific islands. There living animal formations feed on tide-borne food, usually just below the lowest low water level. How important consideration of the tidal stage could be to a fleet of landing boats is easy to conjecture when it is remembered that the tidal range might well equal or exceed the draft of the boats, though on many Pacific islands it may amount to only a foot or so.

In one landing operation which was carried out

TABLE 2.—TIDAL DIFFERENCES AND CONSTANTS 273

New York and New Jersey	Latitude	Longitude	Tidal difference Time of tide	Tidal difference Height of high water	Ratio of ranges	High water interval	Mean range of tide	Spring range of tide
	° ' North	° ' West	h. m. Time meridian, 75° W	feet		h. m.	feet	feet
NEW YORK—Continued Long Island, South Side			Reference station, **Sandy Hook**					
Shinnecock Inlet (ocean).	40 50	72 29	−0 50		0.5	6 56	2.3	2.8
Shinnecock Inlet (bay)	40 51	72 29	0 00		0.3	7 41	1 6	1.9
Quogue Bridge, Shinnecock Bay	40 51	72 30			0.2		0.9	1.1
Potunk Point, Moriches Bay	40 48	72 39			0.2		0.8	1.0
Mastic Beach, Moriches Bay	40 45	72 50			0.1		0.5	0.6
Fire Island Breakwater	40 37	73 18	−0 45	−0.5	0.9	7 02	4.1	5.0
Democrat Point, Fire Island Inlet	40 38	73 18	−0 35		0.6	7 02	2.6	3.1
Fire Island Light, Great South Bay	40 38	73 13	+1 05		0.2	8 28	0.7	0.8
Lone Hill, Fire I., Great South Bay	40 40	73 04	+3 25		0.1	10 54	0.6	0.7
Bellport, Bellport Bay.	40 45	72 56	+4 00		0.2	11 26	0.8	1.0
Patchogue, Great South Bay	40 45	73 01	+3 35		0.2	11 05	0.7	0.8
Sayville (Brown Cr.), Great South B	40 44	73 04	+3 40		0.1	11 21	0.6	0.7
Great R., Connetquot R., Gr. South B	40 43	73 09	+3 25		0.1	11 01	0.6	0.7
Bay Shore, Great South Bay	40 43	73 14	+2 35		0.1	10 18	0.6	0.7
Oak Beach, Great South Bay	40 38	73 17	+2 25		0.2	9 55	0.7	0.8
Babylon, Great South Bay.	40 41	73 19	+3 05		0.1	10 34	0.6	0.7
Elder Island, Great South Bay	40 39	73 24	+3 35		0.2	11 02	1.0	1.2
Amityville, Great South Bay	40 39	73 25	+3 20		0.3	10 52	1.2	1.4
Biltmore Shores, South Oyster Bay.	40 40	73 28	+2 35		0.3	9 53	1.4	1.7
Meadow Island, Jones Inlet	40 36	73 34	0 00	−1 2	0.7	7 35	3.4	4.1
Deep Creek Meadow, Hempstead B	40 36	73 32	+0 35		0.6	8 10	2.7	3.3
Green Island, Hempstead Bay.	40 37	73 30	+1 10		0.4	8 45	2.0	2 4

Extracts from an earlier edition of the Tide Tables, Atlantic Ocean, showing (above) tidal differences and constants for subordinate stations on the Long Island coast and (below) data for Sandy Hook, a reference station. The high water interval and ratio of ranges is being omitted from current editions

SANDY HOOK, N. J., 1944   66

	OCTOBER High Time	OCTOBER High Ht.	OCTOBER Low Time	OCTOBER Low Ht.	DAY	NOVEMBER High Time	NOVEMBER High Ht.	NOVEMBER Low Time	NOVEMBER Low Ht.	DAY	DECEMBER High Time	DECEMBER High Ht.	DECEMBER Low Time	DECEMBER Low Ht.
DAY														
	h. m.	ft.	h. m.	ft.		h. m.	ft.	h. m	ft.		h. m.	ft.	h. m	ft.
1 Su	6 41 7 05	5.8 6.1	0 34 12 59	−0.9 −0.8	1 W	7 53 8 18	6.1 5.3	1 46 2 25	−1.1 −1.0	1 F	8 18 8 46	5.7 4.6	2 11 2 55	−0.8 −0.9
2 M	7 27 7 53	6.0 6.0	1 24 1 52	−1.0 −1.0	2 Th	8 39 9 07	6.0 5.0	2 33 3 13	−0.9 −0.9	2 Sa	9 03 9 35	5.4 4.3	2 56 3 41	−0.6 −0.7
3 Tu	8 15 8 40	6.1 5.8	2 13 2 42	−1.1 −1.0	3 F	9 27 9 58	5.7 4.6	3 19 4 01	−0.7 −0.6	3 Su	9 49 10 26	5.0 4.0	3 42 4 28	−0.3 −0.4
4 W	9 02 9 30	6.0 5.4	2 59 3 32	−1.0 −0.8	4 Sa	10 17 10 52	5.3 4.3	4 05 4 49	−0.3 −0.3	4 M	10 38 11 19	4.7 3.8	4 26 5 12	0.0 −0.2
5 Th	9 53 10 23	5.8 5.0	3 44 4 21	−0.7 −0.5	5 Su	11 09 11 48	4.9 4.0	4 52 5 42	0.1 0.1	5 Tu	11 28	4.4	5 14 6 02	0.3 0.1
6 F	10 46 11 17	5.5 4.6	4 30 5 13	−0.3 −0.1	6 M	... 12 02	4.6	5 43 6 40	0.5 0.4	6 W	0 10 12 16	3.7 4.1	6 09 6 56	0.6 0.3
7 Sa	... 11 39	5.1	5 20 6 10	0.1 0.3	7 Tu	0 43 12 55	3.8 4.3	6 40 7 42	0.8 0.5	7 Th	1 06 1 03	3.8 3.9	7 12 7 53	0.8 0.3
8	0 13	4.2	6 16	0.5	8	1 40	3.7	7 55	0.9	8	1 55	3.7	8 15	0.8

successfully, the tide was high enough to clear the reefs for only 50 minutes out of the 24 hours.

Tidal Currents

The periodic tidal rise and fall of the sea is translated into a horizontal flow along coasts and continents as the water runs in and out of bays and sounds and other indentations alongshore. The shoreward motion is called the flood; the receding seaward current the ebb.

High water is often loosely referred to as "flood tide," low water as "ebb tide." This is not only incorrect; it can be misleading. Tide has to do with vertical movement of the surface; current the horizontal motion resulting when high water at a given point moves on to the westward with the moon. Tidal current would be the most explicit term for this flow.

The tidal range at certain points along the invasion coast of France may amount to 20 feet or more. And off that coast are channels where the current velocity may exceed seven knots. That too is a force to be reckoned with. A seven-knot boat wou'd stand still if she tried to buck it, but she'd bowl along at 14 knots running with it.

Speaking broadly, flood current is associated with rising tide levels (in the sense of occurring at approximately the same time), and ebb current with falling levels. But the operator of a landing boat might expose himself to the risk of being left high and dry on the beach—as good as they are at digging their own channels—if he were to assume that the time of the tide's stand (highest or lowest level) always coincided exactly with the time of slack water (no current).

On outer coasts, it is admittedly true that there is generally little difference between the time of high or low water and the beginning of ebb or flood current, but in narrow channels, landlocked harbors, or in tidal rivers, the time of slack may differ by hours from the time of stand.

Coming into a bay or harbor with the flood, the assumption might be that the level is still rising along the beach. As a matter of fact, if it were near the end of the flood, it's a strong probability that the level on the beach has already started to recede. Conversely, if one bucks the tail end of the ebb entering the harbor, he may find depths at piers and docks already increasing.

The Set of Tidal Currents

Another aspect of current conditions along the coast that bears remembering is that the flood current does not necessarily set directly on the beach, and the ebb directly off it. Coastal currents often run diagonally to the beach, perhaps even parallel with it. Of course, this may not be a serious consideration if a high-powered landing boat is charging in full speed to the beach, but in case of a night maneuver, approaching at slow speed to avoid detection, or a commando raid in rubber boats which have to be paddled, this could be a critical factor.

With the point of departure offshore properly chosen with respect to the intended point of landing, boats might drift naturally in with the current to a certain spot on the beach. And, by the same token, it might take considerable muscular effort, or upset plans completely, if crews of paddle-propelled craft had to battle the current before hitting the beach.

Then again, current cuts curious capers when flowing into and out of streams entering the beach. A landing boat might lie off the mouth of a tidal stream, its operator taking note of the strong current surging shoreward in mid-stream. But, taking cover along the banks on

entering, the boatman finds that the current may (probably will) diminish till it reaches almost a dead slack, or even reverse itself in a countercurrent. In cases, a drifting boat would gradually work its way downstream along the bank, when mid-channel currents would sweep it upstream.

Every boatman must have noted this phenomenon, observing how a low-powered boat will travel along for mile after mile close under the bank of a channel or stream in just a moderate current while the big powerful cruiser out in mid-channel bucks her way up against the opposing current, wasting gas, without gaining an inch upon the little fellow inshore.

High Water (Lunitidal) Interval

Tide Tables, available for the waters of the world, formerly showed, in addition to such data as latitude and longitude of the place in question, mean range and spring range of the tide, another interesting figure called the high water interval, expressed in hours and minutes. This interval is also referred to as lunitidal interval or "establishment of the port."

In a dozen words, the high water interval simply means the average interval of time by which time of high tide follows an upper and lower transit of the moon over the meridian of any given locality (that is, when the moon bears due north or south).

Earlier editions of the Tide Tables—in the Tidal Differences and Constants for thousands of subordinate stations based on data given for principal reference stations —would tell us, for example, that at Deep Creek Meadow, Hempstead Bay, Long Island, the high water interval is 8 hours 10 minutes. Seeing the moon due south (at this station, of course) we know it will be high water 8 hours and 10 minutes later.

On the night of full moon, it crosses our meridian (bears due South, true) at midnight so we can expect high water at 8:10 the next morning. At the time of new moon, the moon crosses our meridian at noon so we would expect high water at 8:10 that evening. Therefore the high water interval as given in the tables and the time of high water are approximately the same on the days of new and full moon.

Now the lunar or tidal day is roughly 50 minutes longer than the solar day (due to the moon's revolution about the earth) so that, reckoning time by the sun, the moon will pass our meridian or any given point on earth 50 minutes later each day. Consequently it requires only a simple mental calculation to determine the approximate time of high water for any day before new or full moon—subtracting 50 minutes for each day. Conversely, for any day after the new or full moon, add 50 minutes per day. It's not precise, but it's practical.

"Priming" and "lagging" are terms sometimes used in connection with this interval—the former a shortening of the interval, the latter a lengthening, due to the relative positions of sun and moon.

A quarter of a century ago, the writer sailed the waters of Hempstead Bay (for which the high water interval is given above) in an ancient "one-lunger" with "Uncle Tom" who, with his father and father's father before him, had followed that bay for a livelihood. In anticipation of launching a newly acquired boat of our own, we sat ashore one evening eagerly snatching up nautical nuggets of bay lore he had acquired over several generations. Quizzed about the best time to slide the boat in, Uncle Tom shifted a crusty pipe from port to starboard, squinted an appraising eye at the evening sky.

"Wal," said he, "I should cal'late about 8:00 tomorrow morning, by the looks of that moon. Tide's high when the moon's sou'east."

Mystified, but respecting his instinctive wisdom concerning Nature's phenomena, we made it our business to be on hand with all our gear next morning at 8:00 . . . and caught the high water. We doubt whether Uncle Tom had ever seen a copy of the Tide Tables and we're sure he'd have choked if confronted with any sage observations about "lunitidal intervals."

But that's what he was using, without knowing it.

A little calculation would show that, on the night of full moon, it rises in the east at 6:00 P.M., transits at 12:00 midnight. At 8:10 (the high water interval for this station) the moon is nearing the southeast—by the magnetic bearings which are more familiar to most of us than the true, almost exactly SE. Six hours later, of course, it must be low and the moon will have gone on to the SW.

It makes no difference what the phase of the moon or what the locality on earth, if the high water interval is 8 hours, the tide's high when the moon is in the SE (magnetic) and low when it gets to the SW—half-tide when it's in the south. If you're thinking in terms of true directions, the high water interval should be 9 hours if the moon is to bear SE at high tide.

With a high water interval of 6 hours, the tide will be high when the moon bears true east; low when it bears south. If the interval is 3 hours, the tide is high when the moon's in the SW, low when it's in the SE.

Figure 2 shows the relationship between the value of the high water interval and the moon's bearing at high water for many ports along the Atlantic coast.

We think of high and low water as being roughly 6 hours apart but 6 hours and 13 minutes would be closer because, as mentioned above, the moon is lagging behind about 50 minutes per day and two tidal cycles (two highs and two lows) are completed in 24 hours 50 minutes.

Height of Tide at Any Hour

In the Tide Tables may be found a supplementary table by which the height can be determined for any hour, taking into account the time from the nearest high or low, the duration of rise or fall, and the range. Corrections are calculated to a tenth of a foot. And there are also tables available which give constants so that the tidal height can be computed for half-hour intervals throughout the 6-hour period.

Generally speaking, such precision is better suited to the classroom than to the chart room. There is a one-two-three rule of thumb that will meet practical requirements if you cannot find your tables. According to this rule, the tide rises and falls 1/12 of the range during the first and sixth hours after high and low water slack; 2/12 during the second and fifth hours; 3/12 during the third and fourth hours.

On the back of its Pilot Charts, the Oceanographic Office once published monthly moonlight diagrams for some time, which gave a wealth of information on times of sunrise, sunset, phases of the moon at any time, its altitude, number of hours of moonlight and the times of its crossing the prime vertical and meridian for each day that the bearings occur between 4:00 P.M. and 8:00 A.M. Diagrams were given for every ten degrees of latitude from 0 (the equator) to 60 degrees. To mariners and yachtsmen in general the information was both interesting and useful, especially when we remember how closely the moon's migrations are tied up with the problems of navigation, both by day and night.

CALCULATING SLACK WATER SPEEDS IN A CURRENT

Elsewhere in this chapter will be found a discussion of how slack water speeds may be calculated as a result of two runs, one upstream and one downstream, in a current. It is a fallacy to believe that the distances up and down can be merely totaled and divided by the total time for the run. It would be equally incorrect to divide the total time up and downstream by two as a basis for figuring slack water speed over the distance one way. An average of the *speed* upstream and the *speed* downstream will, however, give a correct figure, exactly the same as if run over a slack water course. The six formulas below are developed from one basic formula and may be used to find speed, distance or current when the time and one other factor are known.

S = Speed through the water, in knots

S_b = Speed over the bottom, in knots.

C = Current in knots.

D = Distance over the bottom in nautical miles.

T_u = Time in minutes, upstream.

T_p = Time in minutes, downstream.

Upstream $S_b = (S-C)$, Downstream $S_b = (S+C)$

Basic formula: $D = \dfrac{T \times S}{60}$

Distance upstream = Distance downstream

$$\underline{\text{③}} \quad S = \frac{60D(T_u + T_p)}{2 T_p T_u}$$

$$\underline{\text{④}} \quad D = \frac{2 T_p T_u S}{60(T_p + T_p)}$$

$$\underline{\text{⑤}} \quad C = \frac{60D(T_u - T_p)}{2 T_p T_u}$$

$$\underline{\text{⑥}} \quad D = \frac{C \times 2 T_p T_u}{60(T_u - T_p)}$$

$$\underline{\text{①}} \; C = S \times \frac{(T_u - T_p)}{(T_u + T_p)} \;,\quad \underline{\text{②}} \; S = C \times \frac{(T_u + T_p)}{(T_u - T_p)}$$

Example 1. Distance and Current not known.
Boat speed 7 knots. What is velocity of the current?
Time up, 10 min., Time down, 3.5 min.
$C = \dfrac{7 \times (10-3.5)}{(10+3.5)} = \dfrac{7 \times 6.5}{13.5} = \dfrac{45.5}{13.5} = 3.37$ knots.

Or if the Distance and Speed not known
What is the speed?
$S = \dfrac{3.37 \times (10+3.5)}{(10-3.5)} = \dfrac{3.37 \times 13.5}{6.5} = 7$ knots.

To Find	When known factors are: Time Upstream, Time Downstream and:	Use formula
Boat Speed	Distance	③
Boat Speed	Current	②
Distance	Current	⑥
Distance	Boat Speed	④
Current	Boat Speed	①
Current	Distance	⑤

354

Fig. 246. Right: Underway or at anchor, a boat having only bow and stern staffs flies the yacht club burgee forward, yacht ensign aft. Formerly a club officer's flag or a private signal was sometimes flown at the bow staff underway, being replaced by the club pennant at anchor. This practice is giving way to use of the club pennant, which should be flown with the ensign. On a boat of the type illustrated, an officer's flag or private signal would be flown from a staff amidships

Fig. 247. Left: In addition to the bow and stern staffs, most cruisers have a signal mast. The club pennant flies forward, ensign aft, and owner's private signal from the masthead. Club burgees are almost universally triangular shaped pennants. The owner's private signal is swallow-tailed, sometimes rectangular. The yacht ensign is rectangular. Better practice would avoid the use of initials on the private signal

CHAPTER XXII

Flag Etiquette

(See Table, page 360, also illustrations in color, pages IX, X, 42 and 383)

Fig. 248. Right: Club burgee at the bow and officer's (commodore's) flag at the truck is correct practice. The ensign aft is not visible here. Officer's flag takes precedence over the private signal and is flown in place of the latter. The officer's flag should be flown only with the burgee of that club of which the yachtsman is an officer. If he flies the burgee of a club of which he is a member, not a flag officer, then the private signal replaces the officer's flag. Burgees of two clubs should never be flown at the same time

Fig. 249. Left: On motor boats with a gaff, when underway only, the ensign may be flown at the gaff instead of the stern staff. Strictly speaking, the yacht ensign should be flown only on licensed yachts, for which it was originally designed as a signal. Though generally used on pleasure boats of all sizes, no law requires a boat under 16 tons to fly it. Despite traditional use it would be better to fly the American ensign, our national flag, at the place of honor in preference to the yacht ensign

Fig. 250. Left: In addition to the club burgee forward, ensign aft and private signal at the masthead, this boat flies a rectangular blue flag at the starboard yardarm. The latter, the owner's absent signal, indicates he is not aboard

Fig. 251. Above: When the owner is not aboard, but guests are, the guest flag is flown. This is a rectangular blue flag with white diagonal stripe, displayed at the starboard yardarm both at anchor and underway. The guest flag is also flown when the owner is not aboard but members of his family are. Club pennant, private signal and ensign are displayed in the usual manner

Fig. 252. Below: Members of the United States Power Squadrons are urged to display the Squadron ensign when aboard their boats—but only when a member of the Squadron is in command. The Squadron ensign is flown from 8:00 A. M. to sundown. It is recommended that it be flown from the stern staff, although it is also flown at the starboard yardarm. Club burgee is shown forward; amidships is the signal designating a flag lieutenant of the United States Power Squadrons

Fig. 253. Above: A member of the United States Power Squadrons may fly the Squadron ensign at the starboard yardarm with the yacht ensign at the stern staff. Club burgee is at the bow, private signal at the masthead. The Squadron ensign is also flown sometimes from the stern staff instead of the yacht ensign and the latter position is recommended, though practice is about equally divided

Fig. 254. Right: Though seldom seen, the American ensign is properly flown at the stern staff, in preference to either the yacht ensign or U. S. P. S. ensign. Here the Squadron ensign flies at the starboard yardarm (or position corresponding to it in this type of boat), a small pennant above it denoting the winner of a Squadron piloting contest. The rectangular flag at the masthead, in place of a private signal, denotes a local Squadron lieutenant. Club pennant is at the bow. Call letters of the boat's radiotelephone appear on the flag at the port yardarm

Fig. 255, Right: Coast Guard Auxiliary vessels, when properly inspected and approved and an Auxiliary member is aboard, may display the Auxiliary flag—on vessels without a mast, at the bow staff; on vessels with one mast, at the truck; on vessels with two or more masts, at the main truck. Here the U.S.P.S. Ensign is also flown at the starboard spreader, yacht ensign aft. Club pennant (not shown) is at the bow staff. The Auxiliary ensign should be hoisted (immediately after the national ensign) at 8:00 a.m. and lowered (immediately before the national ensign) at sunset

Fig. 256. Below: This shows a real jack staff and the only correct way in which the jack should be flown—never from the bow staff of a single-masted motor boat. The definition of jack staff is "a short staff, raised at the bowsprit cap, upon which the union jack is hoisted." The jack is flown only at anchor on Sundays, holidays or other festive occasion. Never haul down the club flag to replace it with a jack

Fig. 257, Above: The pennant of a Coast Guard Auxiliary officer (flotilla commander, in the illustration) may be displayed, night and day, at the starboard spreader, when the officer is aboard an Auxiliary vessel within the District in which he is a member. On vessels without a mast, it may be flown at the bow staff in place of the Auxiliary flag. An efficiency pennant, when awarded, is flown from the same halyard as the Auxiliary flag, and inferior to it. If a Coast Guard officer takes command, he hoists the Coast Guard ensign in place of the Auxiliary flag, and replaces the yacht ensign with the American ensign

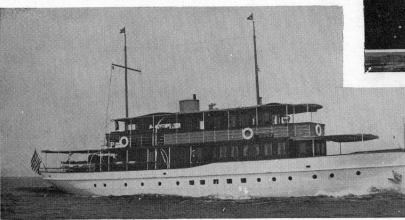

Fig. 258. Left: A motor boat with two pole masts underway flies the club burgee from the fore masthead, not from the jack staff at the bow. Owner's private signal is at the main masthead, ensign aft. At anchor, she flies the same colors except on Sundays or holidays when the jack should be flown from the jack staff forward. No flag is flown from the jack staff underway. Only yachts with at least two masts and jack staff should fly the jack

Fig. 259. Below: Though sometimes seen on commercial vessels underway, the jack should never be flown by a yacht, pleasure boat or Naval vessel when underway. This is a Government quarantine boat and properly flies the American ensign aft, which would also be good practice in a pleasure boat. However, no yacht can properly fly the jack unless it has at least two masts and a jack staff forward—and then only at anchor on Sundays, holidays or special occasions

Fig. 260. Above: Small Coast Guard picket boats fly the Coast Guard ensign from the truck of a short mast as shown. A commission pennant above the ensign is flown to indicate the fact that the boat is in commission, on duty

Fig. 261. Right: This boat properly flies the flags appropriate to her type as a motor boat, even though she has steadying sail. Club burgee is flown forward, owner's private signal at the masthead, ensign aft. The distinction to be made here is that she is strictly a motor boat, whereas a sailboat would observe other practice as prescribed for its type. (See table, page 360.)

Fig. 262. Left: No yacht should ever fly a flag with a name spelled out upon it, whether it be the name of the boat or otherwise. In fact, even the use of initials on yacht flags should be discouraged, although it is widely practiced. The only exception is at regattas or on similar occasions in order to identify boats acting in some special official capacity, as used by judges, police, etc. In a race, flags and colors should be struck, except perhaps a flag showing the racing number

Fig. 263. Right: Even though this pleasure boat is at anchor and assuming also that it is a Sunday or a holiday, nevertheless the jack should never be flown on a boat of this type. Only vessels having two or more masts can have a jack staff, from which no other flag is displayed. The club pennant should have been flown forward

Fig. 264. Left: Flags of the International Code are used on national holidays, at regattas and on other special occasions to dress ship. According to the best practice, they should be flown only when the boat is at anchor, though at regattas many boats so dressed are seen underway

Fig. 265. Left below: Under power, this ketch-rigged motor sailer displays the club burgee at the main truck, private signal from the mizzen truck, yacht ensign at the stern staff. The same practice would be correct at anchor. Under sail, however, the ensign is at the mizzen peak

Fig. 266. Below.: A gaff-rigged schooner under sail, with club burgee at the fore truck, officer's flag at the main truck, ensign at the main peak. The officer's flag always takes precedence over the private signal and flies day and night while the boat is in commission. Other colors are flown only from 8:00 A. M. to sundown; time for "making" them being taken from the senior officer present. The ensign is the first of the colors to be made at 8:00 A.M., last at sunset. Colors are said to be "made", whether hoisting or lowering

Fig. 267. Below: A three-masted schooner, gaff-rigged. Club burgee is flown at the fore truck, private signal at the main truck, ensign at the mizzen peak. At the mizzen truck a wind pennant is properly flown

Fig. 268. Right: Under sail, a ketch-rigged motor sailer with Marconi mizzen flies the yacht ensign from the leech of the after (mizzen) sail, a position corresponding to the peak of a gaff-rigged sail. Club burgee is at the main truck, private signal at the mizzen truck. Yawls fly the same flags

Flag[16]	Description	When flown[14]	Motor boat with bow & stern staffs only[6]	Motor boat with bow & stern staffs and signal mast[6]	Motor boat with two masts	Single-masted sailing yachts	Sailing yachts with two masts	Sailing yachts with more than two masts
U. S. ensign, yacht ensign, or USPS ensign[1]	A	8:00 A.M. to sundown	Aft[2]	Aft[2]	Aft[2]	After peak[11]	Aftermost peak[11]	Aftermost peak[11]
Club burgee[13]	B	8:00 A.M. to sundown	Bow	Bow	Foremast	At the truck[12]	At the foremost truck	At the foremost truck
Private signal	C	8:00 A.M. to sundown	Not flown	Masthead	Mainmast	When under way at the truck[12]	At the aftermost truck	At the main truck
Flag officer's flag[8]	D	Day and night[7]	Not flown	In place of private signal	In place of private signal	Instead of burgee at truck	Instead of private signal	Instead of private signal
Union jack[9]	E	At anchor on Sundays and holidays 8:00 A.M. to sundown	Not flown	Not flown	Bow or jack staff	Not flown	Jack staff	Jack staff
Absent flag	F	During daylight during absence of owner from boat	Not flown	Starboard[10] yardarm	Starboard[10] main yardarm	Starboard[10] spreader	Starboard[10] main spreader	Starboard[10] main spreader
Owner's meal flag	G	During daylight during meal hours of owner when at anchor	Not flown	Starboard[10] yardarm	Starboard[10] main yardarm	Starboard[10] spreader	Starboard[10] main spreader	Starboard[10] main spreader
Guest flag	H	During daylight when owner is absent but guests are on board	Not flown	Starboard[10] yardarm	Starboard[10] main yardarm	Starboard[10] spreader	Starboard[10] main spreader	Starboard[10] main spreader
Crew's meal flag	I	During daylight during meal hours of crew when at anchor	Not flown	Port yardarm	Port forward yardarm	Port spreader	Foremost port spreader	Foremost port spreader

A. The United States National Ensign has been referred to in various ways—for example, as the American ensign, American national flag, etc. It should be understood that in every case this means the familiar flag of the United States (the "Stars and Stripes") which is officially our national flag, our national ensign, and our merchant flag.

B. Club pennant or burgee, generally triangular in shape, sometimes swallow tail.

C. Private signal, generally swallow tail in shape, sometimes rectangular.

D. Flag officer's flag, rectangular in shape, blue (with white design) for senior officer(s), red for next lower in rank, white (with blue design) for lower rank. Other officer's flag (except fleet captain) may be swallow tail or triangular in shape, as provided in the regulations of those yachting organizations making provisions for such flags. (See Note 7.)

E. The American jack is a rectangular blue flag with 50 white stars.

F. The absent flag is plain, rectangular, blue.

G. Owner's meal flag is plain, rectangular, white.

H. The guest flag is a rectangular blue flag, crossed diagonally by a white stripe.

I. Crew's meal flag, a triangular red pennant.

The church pennant—the only flag hoisted on the same staff above the ensign (and only when services are being held, aboard a naval vessel at anchor) —is a triangular white pennant with a blue cross.

1. While the best practice calls for the flying of the yacht ensign yet the US ensign may be substituted except on documented yachts.

The ensign of the United States Power Squadrons may be displayed[4] between morning and evening colors:
(a) In place of the U. S. yacht ensign, or
(b) In addition to the U. S. yacht ensign[5]: at anchor or underway, from the starboard main spreader or yard-arm.

Never salute or answer a salute by dipping the U. S. ensign. Salute by dipping the yacht ensign or USPS ensign when flown at the stern or gaff of motor craft, stern staff of sailing vessels under power or at anchor, or at the aftermost peak or leach of sailing craft under sail. Never salute by dipping a flag flown from the yardarm or spreader.

2. When at anchor,[3] at the stern staff. When under way, in inland waters and when meeting or passing other vessels on the high seas, weather and rig permitting, by motor yachts at the stern staff; by motor yachts with gaff at the gaff.

3. At anchor means when not underway.

4. The ensign of the United States Power Squadrons may be displayed only while the yacht is in command of a member in good standing of the U.S.P.S.

5. Correctly displayed.

6. Mastless motor yachts may display, on a staff erected on the superstructure, the flag designated by this code to be flown from the truck of single-masted yachts.

7. Afloat or ashore, when boat is in commission, whether manned or not, whether or not owner is on board. When an officer of superior rank comes aboard officially, his flag should be flown as provided. When aboard unofficially his flag may be flown from another hoist at option.

Other officers of yachting organizations (except the Fleet Captain) rating other than a rectangular flag shall fly it as provided between 0800 and sunset.

8. The fleet captain displays his flag between morning and evening colors only at the bow staff in small boats while performing the duties of his office.

The constitution or by-laws of some clubs provide that the fleet captain shall be a flag officer. In such a case the fleet captain shall display his flag as a flag officer.

9. The union jack may be displayed only at the jackstaff on sailing yachts and at the jackstaff on motor yachts with more than one mast, between morning and evening colors and only while at anchor on Sundays or when dressing ship.

10. Provided the USPS ensign is not being flown at this hoist, with a USPS member in command.

11. By marconi-rigged sailing yachts at the leach of the aftermost sail, approximately two-thirds the length of the leach above the clew; by sailing yachts under power alone and at anchor at the stern staff.

12. Burgee may be flown underway and at anchor; however, is is permissible to substitute the private signal for the burgee on single masted yachts without bow staff when underway. Single masted yachts with bow staff should fly the club burgee from the bow staff when underway and at anchor.

13. A local Squadron's distinguishing burgee, which has been approved by the District and authorized by the USPS Governing Board, may be flown between morning and evening colors, in the place and instead of the club burgee.

14. On entering or leaving a port before or after the time for making colors, a yacht shall display her flags provided there is sufficient light for them to be recognized. Colors shall be lowered promptly after anchoring or after leaving port.

When making colors short-handed, the ensign shall be hoisted first, followed as rapidly as possible by the USPS ensign, the club burgee and the private signal. Flags are lowered in inverse order. Colors are hoisted smartly but lowered ceremoniously. Flag officer's flags though displayed day and night may be lowered and hoisted at colors.

At Squadron or Club rendezvous, marine parades etc., on order of the Commanding Officer, flags may be flown after sundown but must be lowered at or before midnight as ordered.

15. The burgee, private signal and flag officer's flag shall be approximately a minimum of one-half of one inch on the fly for each foot of the highest truck above the water on sailing yachts and ⅝ of one inch for each foot of overall length on motor yachts. The hoist shall be two-thirds the fly. The ensign when flown at the stern shall be approximately a minimum of one inch on the fly per foot of overall length. The hoist shall be two-thirds the fly.

When the USPS ensign is flown from the starboard yardarm, on motor boats, the length of the fly shall be approximately ⅝ inch per foot of overall length of the boat

The night pennant should approximate three-fourths of an inch on the fly for each foot of height of truck above the water, with a hoist of one-tenth of the fly.

16. When a boat is chartered, the flags of the charterer should be flown.

17. Flags authorized by naval, military or recognized yachting organizations may be displayed at option, provided the procedure for flying such flags specified by those organizations is followed.

18. No other flag shall be displayed, except when making signals with the international code or dressing ship.

19. Such flags as the "cocktail flag" etc., being signals, may be flown from a hoist where best seen.

COLORS:—Though the term "colors" is frequently used to include all the flags flown by a boat, a strict interpretation of the definition would restrict its use to the national flag which distinguishes what nation she belongs to. It is also used to refer to the ceremony of hoisting the colors at 8:00 A.M. and lowering at sunset.

The Flag of Your Country

THE flying of flags and colors on motor craft, sailing and other yachts is governed largely by custom. Few, if any, laws or government regulations have ever been enacted on this subject. Mention has seldom if ever been made by Congress in all of its years, of any requirements for the flying of any flag on numbered, undocumented or unlicensed vessels or yachts. Documented yachts are expected to fly the yacht ensign but the enforcement of even this regulation is questionable.

A review or a brief history of the United States National Flag should permit one to better understand some of the fundamentals on which many of the customs of flags and colors are based, especially their evolution for use on the water.

The origin and early history of the use of national flags is very indefinite. This is especially true of the national ensign of the United States. Early Colonial and American history makes very little mention of our flag or flags. Our Navy seems to have begun the use of the Stars and Stripes immediately after the Continental Congress had passed an Act in June, 1777, establishing the Stars and Stripes as the flag of this country. However, it was not until 1895 or some 30 years after the close of the Civil War, that the United States cavalry was given the right to carry the Stars and Stripes as the national standard. It was in 1841 that the infantry first used the national colors. Not until 1876 did the Marines carry the Stars and Stripes.

As the Navy made use of the national flag from the beginning and the other branches of the U. S. government were slow in adopting it, it emphasizes that the Stars and Stripes as the national ensign is a flag of the sea and its right to be flown from yachts is clearly established.

On the subject of the origin and development of the flag from which the Stars and Stripes has been evolved, accounts are too conflicting to warrant placing much credence in them. Prince Edward, afterwards Edward I of England, about the middle of the last half of the 13th century, adopted the Red Cross of St. George, on a white field, as the national flag of England. After James VI of Scotland ascended the throne of England in 1603, as James I, he was much annoyed by the wrangling between the masters of English and Scotch ships when they met at sea as to which one should dip its colors to the other. Therefore, in 1606, he stopped this annoyance and to help unite the two kingdoms into one country, combined the two crosses into a new flag, which subsequently became known as the Union Jack. This he required all vessels of both countries to carry at their mainmast. A century later when the two countries agreed upon their union, a national agreement required the union of the crosses to be used on flags, banners, standards, and ensigns both at sea and on land.

Near the beginning of the revolution, General Washington assigned to the various officers as a distinction of rank, ribbons varying in color and these were worn by them until something more formal was designed. There were practically no flags or colors although some of the individual companies of the Colonial Army are supposed to have brought with them those which they had previously used. Later General Washington urged the vari-ous Colonels to provide for their regiments colors of such design as might appeal to them. This was frequently done and in many instances, some designs of 13 units were used to represent the 13 colonies.

Some of the colonies adopted flags of their own. Massachusetts adopted the Pine Tree, with the motto An Appeal to Heaven. Rhode Island selected one having an anchor and the word Hope and within the canton a union of 13 white stars on a blue field, said to be the first flag on which the 13 colonies were represented by 13 stars.

South Carolina's flag has an interesting history. In September 1775, the Committee of Safety of Charleston instructed Colonel William Moultrie to take possession of Fort Johnson on James Island, which he did. The uniforms of their troops were blue with a silver increscent in the cap. Soon realizing that a flag was needed, he improvised one having a blue field with a white increscent in the canton. This was the flag which sergeant Jasper so gallantly rescued on June 28, 1776, when the fort of palmetto logs on Sullivans Island was attacked by the British Fleet under Admiral Sir Peter Parker. It was under this flag that the Declaration of Independence was read to the people of Charleston on August 8, 1776. When the state came to officially adopt a flag, it took the one which Colonel Moultrie had designed and in recognition of the good services of the palmetto logs, placed upon it a palmetto tree.

While our first flag act was adopted June 14, 1777, by resolution of the Continental Congress and reading as follows: "Resolved, That the flag of the United States be thirteen stripes, alternate red and white; that the union be thirteen stars, white in a blue field, representing a new constellation" yet there is nothing to show that the Revolutionary Army ever carried any flags furnished by the American Congress. Those which were carried were purely personal, each made by or for some officer, company or regiment, and represented the sentiments of the makers. However, the United States Navy began to use the flag immediately after it was authorized by the Continental Congress.

History records only one Stars and Stripes that was carried by the American Army during the Revolutionary War. It was carried by the North Carolina Militia at the Battle of Guilford Courthouse, March 15, 1781, but the stripes were blue and red and the union had a white field with 13 eight-pointed stars. There is also another flag hanging in the State House at Annapolis, which it is claimed was carried by the Third Maryland Regiment in 1781. It has 13 five pointed stars, one in the center,

John Madigan

Near the beginning of the 20th Century, the different departments of our National Government appointed representatives to confer and see if they could not bring order out of chaos. The proportions of Naval flags and Army colors were quite different, the former being much longer in proportion to its height, the latter being much shorter to avoid interfering with the color or standard bearer. It was decided to leave the Army colors alone but to fly the Naval flag from flagstaffs and from Government buildings. Accordingly, following the recommendations of this committee, on October 29, 1912, President Taft issued an executive order defining minutely the proportions and other details of the Stars and Stripes, at the same time approving a custom which had existed in the Navy of placing on their small boats flags having only 13 stars instead of the full complement. The use of only 13 stars on our small or boat flags, was discontinued by an executive order of President Wilson, dated May 29, 1916, and now all flags, colors, etc., used by the United States Government are required to have their full complement of 49/50 stars. In all of the discussion by the conference it does not appear that there was any mention whatsoever of the yacht ensign or the rights or duties of yachts or any other vessels to fly any particular flag.

From the foregoing it will be seen that the United States has only one flag. The use of the yacht ensign is misleading. England has, by law, created a flag for its navy, another for its merchant service, another for yachts and another for its land forces; each is a national flag and entitled to the position and courtesy due the colors of a nation. But, in the United States, wherever, whenever and for whatever purpose the national colors are flown, there is but one flag to fly.

The place of honor for the national colors on land and sea is as follows: on land on a straight mast, at the head; on a mast with a gaff, at the gaff. At sea and at anchor on a steam or motor vessel, at the flag staff aft; on vessels under sail, at the peak; and on vessels with a gaff, at this gaff when under way.

There has never been passed a law compelling boats to fly the national flag or none at all from the place of honor. It has probably never been contemplated that a loyal citizen would ever do otherwise. Yet, we are free to do as we like and in the use of this freedom there has grown the custom of flying the yacht ensign at the point of honor at shore stations and aboard yachts. There are today ardent yachtsmen in high places who believe this custom aboard yachts should be continued.

The yacht ensign had its beginning on August 7, 1848, when the Congress passed "an act to authorize the Secretary of the Treasury to license yachts and for other purposes" providing for the enrollment and licensing of yachts and exempting them from entering and clearing

and 12 arranged in the form of a circle around it. In both of these cases, the flags were purely personal, not official.

The Stars and Stripes preserved in the State House of Boston is claimed to have flown over Fort Independence during the American Revolution but was not carried by the Army. In 1863 each battery of artillery and each company of cavalry was allowed to carry a small flag consisting of Stars and Stripes but that privilege was revoked at the end of the Civil War. The U. S. Marines did not carry the Stars and Stripes as national colors until 1876, yet those which they carried as such in the Mexican and Civil Wars had an eagle in the union.

In none of the three acts adopting the United States national flag is there any mention as to how the stars should be arranged or how many points they should have. In one of the first flags, the stars were sometimes arranged in a circle or with one star in the center and the remaining 12 either in the form of a circle or hollow square, or three horizontal rows of 4, 5 and 4 stars respectively. In a later flag, they were also arranged in several different orders, three horizontal rows of five each or three vertical rows of five each; sometimes in the quincunx order as was the flag that floated over Fort McHenry when Key wrote the Star Spangled Banner.

Apparently about 1841, when the United States Infantry was first given the right to carry the Stars and Stripes, there was a desire on the part of some to preserve their old national colors in the union of the new flag. One of these had an eagle with a bunch of arrows in one claw and the Indian pipe of peace in the other with 13 stars above and a like number below. During the Mexican War, the Fourth Indiana Volunteers carried a flag having in the union an eagle standing on a segment of the globe with a bunch of arrows in one claw, as though intending to conquer the earth.

The American flag is flying here, properly, from the gaff at a yacht club station. The club burgee is at the masthead

at Custom-houses. The third paragraph of the act provided "that all such licensed yachts shall *use a signal* of the form, size and colors prescribed by the Secretary of the Navy." (This paragraph has been subsequently re-enacted as Sec. 4215 Revised Statutes of the United States.) The Secretary of the Navy acted promptly, and on August 26, 1848, he requested the New York Yacht Club to submit a design for this signal. The design they submitted on January 9, 1849, was the then adopted American ensign, which carried thirteen stars in a circle in the blue field and the thirteen red and white stripes (the Betsy Ross flag), in which they placed a fouled anchor in the center of the circle of stars. The Secretary of the Navy accepted the suggestion of the New York Yacht Club and authorized the adoption of the design.

It is the design of the yacht "signal" that has resulted in the present confusion because its similarity in appearance to the national ensign promptly led yachtsmen to fly the "signal" now known as the yacht ensign in place of the national ensign and the custom has grown until at present nearly all pleasure craft, from outboard speedsters up, are flying the "signal" as an ensign. The yacht ensign was created only as a signal for yachts enrolled and licensed (documented) and exempted them from entering and clearing at Custom-houses. Presumably it was to be flown in addition to the national ensign on documented yachts. To fly it from a club mast ashore signifies nothing.

Another interesting fact is that in law the ensign of a vessel does not reveal her nationality, as the Supreme Court of the United States has rendered a decision that only the documents and papers of a vessel, duly complied with, reveal her nationality so the ensign reveals nothing and protects nobody.

As no laws of our land specify what flags are to be flown or not flown or where, then we must look elsewhere to discover the basis of our present practices. Lacking laws or "official" regulations, perhaps the natural conclusion would be to allow custom to dictate the proper procedure. This would be proper if the existing customs were at all uniform or consistent. However, it does not need to be mentioned that the prevailing customs of the flying of flags on small motor craft are anything but uniform and consistent as we find them today. With the boats of the type which the Long Island sailing skippers affectionately refer to as the "Bronx Navy" so far outnumbering the craft which attempt to follow an orderly procedure in the proper display of colors, then "custom" is no longer a worth while factor.

Most Yacht Clubs and yachting organizations have flag regulations as part of their by-laws thus making these regulations official as far as the particular club is concerned. It becomes the duty of the members of such a club to follow this stated routine. Undoubtedly the first

M. Rosenfeld

club to adopt flag routine was the New York Yacht Club. Probably 99 per cent of all clubs have lifted the New York Yacht Club regulations from their year book without change for their own.

Dressing Ship

On national holidays, at regattas and on other special occasions, yachts often dress ship with signal flags of the International Code. Flag officers' flags, club burgees and national flags are not used. The ship is dressed at 8:00 A.M. and remains so dressed from morning to evening colors.

In dressing ship, the yacht ensign is hoisted at the peak or staff aft, and the jack at the jackstaff. Then a rainbow of flags of the International Code is arranged, reaching from the waterline forward to the waterline aft, by way of the bowsprit end to the foretop masthead, then across to the main topmast, and down to the main boom end, allowing several flags to touch the water line from both the bowsprit end and the main boom end. To keep the flags in position, a weight should be attached to the end of each line. Where there is no bowsprit, flags will start at the stemhead.

Flags and pennants should be bent on alternately rather than in any indiscriminate manner. Since there are twice as many letter flags as numeral pennants, it is good practice, as in the Navy, to follow a sequence of two flags, one pennant, etc., etc., throughout. In order to effect a degree of uniformity in yacht procedure, the following arrangement has been proposed:

Starting from forward, AB2, UJ1, KE3, GH6, IV5, FL4, DM7, PO Third Repeater, RN First Repeater, STo (zero), CX9, WQ8, ZY Second Repeater.

The arrangement here proposed is designed to effect a harmonious color pattern throughout.

U.S.P.S. AND YACHT CLUB CODE FOR FLYING FLAGS AND COLORS *

(See also color plate, pages ix-a and ix-b, U.S.P.S. flags and insignia)

YACHTING ETIQUETTE and customs are very exacting in regard to the proper flying of flags and colors. A yacht is known by the colors she flies. If these are incorrectly flown, then the yacht and her owner create a poor impression in yachting circles. It is, therefore, of foremost importance that the correct procedure be followed at all times.

The yacht ensign, by usage and custom, may be considered our national flag for yachts.[1] The USPS ensign is flown by special authority and custom by members in good standing in this organization, in accordance with their rules.

When a yacht is in commission and manned, the following routine and etiquette shall be observed.

Colors shall be made at 0800 and sunset.

Time shall be taken from the senior officer present.

1. Ensign

The United States yacht ensign may be displayed between morning and evening colors:
(a) When at anchor,[2] at the stern staff.
(b) When under way, in inland waters and when meeting or passing other vessels on the high seas, weather and rig permitting, by motor yachts at the stern; by motor yachts with gaff at the gaff; by gaff-rigged sailing yachts at the after peak; by marconi-rigged sailing yachts at the leach of the aftermost sail, approximately two-thirds the length of the leach above the clew; by sailing yachts under power alone, at the stern staff.

2. USPS Ensign

The ensign of the United States Power Squadrons may be displayed [3] between morning and evening colors:
(a) In place of the U. S. yacht ensign as provided in Sec. 1, or
(b) In addition to the U. S. yacht ensign,[4] at anchor or underway, from the starboard main spreader or yard-arm.

3. Burgee

The yacht club burgee may be displayed whenever [5] the ensign is hoisted, between morning and evening colors, at anchor or under way, by
(a) Mastless yachts or single-masted yachts with bow staff, at the bow staff,
(b) Single-masted yachts without bow staff, at the truck,
(c) Yachts with two or more masts at the foremost truck.

4. Squadron Distinguishing Signals

A local Squadron's distinguishing signal, which has been approved by the District and authorized by the USPS Governing Board, may be flown between morning and evening colors, in the place and instead of the club burgee.

5. Private Signal

The private signal may be displayed, between morning and evening colors, by
(a) Mastless yachts when under way, at the bow staff, in place of the burgee,
(b) Single-masted yachts with bow staff, at anchor, or under way, at the truck,
(c) Single-masted yachts, without bow staff, when under way, at the truck in place of the burgee,
(d) Yachts with two masts, at the aftermost truck.
(e) Yachts with more than two masts, at the main truck.

6. Flag Officer's Flag

A flag officer [6] shall display his flag day and night, in place of and instead of his private signal, or in the case of a single masted yacht instead of the burgee, except when racing or displaying the burgee of another club or the race committee flag.

7. Fleet Captain's Flag

The fleet captain displays his flag [7] between morning and evening colors only at the bow staff in small boats while performing the duties of his office.

8. Race Committee's Flag

On a yacht acting as committee boat, the race committee's flag shall be displayed at the main truck in place of the flag otherwise there displayed, at all times while acting as such.

9. Union Jack

The union jack may be displayed between morning and evening colors on motor yachts with two or more masts only, and on sailing yachts at anchor, on Sundays or holidays or when dressing ship, at the jackstaff (not bow staff).

10. Absent Flag

The absent flag, a rectangular blue flag, may be displayed at the starboard main spreader or yard-arm [8] at anchor, or under way, between sunrise and sunset, when the owner is not on board.

11. Guest Flag

A rectangular blue flag with a white diagonal stripe, from top of hoist to bottom of fly, may be displayed at anchor or under way, between sunrise and sunset, at the starboard main spreader or yard-arm,[8] when guests are aboard during the absence of the owner.

12. Owner's Meal Flag

A rectangular white flag may be displayed when at anchor, from sunrise to sunset, during the owner's meal hours, at the starboard main spreader or yard-arm.[8]

13. Crew's Meal Pennant

A red pennant may be displayed when at anchor, between sunrise and sunset, during the crew's meal hours, at the foremost port spreader or yard-arm.

14. Night Pennant

A blue pennant may be displayed at the main truck from evening to morning colors and at all times when no other flags are flown.

15. Other Flags

Flags authorized by naval, military or recognized yachting organizations may be displayed at option, provided the procedure for flying such flags as specified by those organizations is followed.
No other flag shall be displayed, except when making signals with the international code or dressing ship.

16. Racing

While racing, yachts shall comply with pertinent sections of the Racing Rules and any specific instructions of race committees where these conflict with any provisions of Yacht Routine.

17. Size of Flags

The burgee, private signal and flag officer's flag shall be approximately a minimum of one-half of one inch on the fly for each foot of the highest truck above the water on sailing yachts and 5/8 of one inch for each foot of overall length on motor yachts. The hoist shall be two-thirds the fly. The ensign when flown at the stern shall be approximately a minimum of one inch on the fly per foot of overall length. The hoist shall be two-thirds the fly.
When the USPS ensign is flown from the starboard yard arm, on motor boats, the length of the fly shall be approximately 5/8 of one inch per foot of over all length of the boat.
The night pennant should approximate three-fourths of an inch on the fly for each foot of height of truck above the water, with a hoist of one-tenth of the fly.

18. Order of Colors

When making colors short-handed, the ensign shall be hoisted first, followed as rapidly as possible by the USPS ensign, the club burgee and the private signal. Flags are lowered in inverse order. Colors are hoisted smartly but lowered ceremoniously. Flag officer's flags though displayed day and night may be lowered and hoisted at colors.

19. Entering Port Before or After Colors

On entering or leaving a port before or after the time for making colors, a yacht shall display her flags provided there is sufficient light for them to be recognized. Colors shall be lowered promptly after anchoring or after leaving port.

General Note:—Mastless motor yachts may display, on a staff erected on the superstructure, the flag designated by this code to be flown from the truck of single-masted yachts.

Note *:—The constitution or by-laws or printed regulations of some clubs provide a code for flying flags and colors. In such a case a member of that club when flying the burgee of that club should follow the code of his club.
Note 1:—While the best practice calls for the flying of the yacht ensign yet the US ensign may be substituted therefor except on documented yachts.
Note 2:—Yachts moored or made fast to the shore, wharves, etc. and when aground should fly the flags specified by this code to be flown at anchor.

Note 3:—The ensign of the United States Power Squadrons may be displayed only while the yacht is in command of a member in good standing of the United States Power Squadrons.
Note 4:—Correctly displayed.
Note 5:—Except as otherwise herein provided.
Note 6:—Other officers of yachting organizations (except the Fleet Captain) rating a flag shall fly it as herein specified for a Flag Officer's flag.
Note 7:—The constitution or by-laws of some clubs provide that the fleet captain shall be a flag officer. In such a case the fleet captain shall display his flag as a flag officer.
Note 8:—Provided the USPS ensign is not being flown at this hoist.

FLAG CEREMONIES AND ETIQUETTE
AT YACHT CLUB AND SQUADRON MEETINGS
(When desired, the following is suggested)

FLAG CEREMONIES AT SQUADRON MEETINGS

It is better to place the flags with ceremony than to consider them merely a part of the decorations and equipment.

The route of march in advancing the colors will depend upon the size and layout of the meeting place, width of aisles, etc. In the following it is assumed that the flag of the United States and the USPS flag are to be used, mounted on staffs, and with stands properly located in advance.

In small or congested rooms the following is recommended.

The bearer of the flag of the United States stands at the right side of the room, as viewed by the audience, with the bearer of the USPS flag on the opposite side of the room, in the open space between the first rows of chairs and the speaker's platform. (See Note A below.)

The Commander raps his gavel for order, and as soon as obtained announces "We will now have the presentation of the colors. All please rise and stand at attention."

As soon as this is accomplished the Commander orders, "Color Guard—Present the colors." The Color Guard, on the order, march in opposite directions across the room in front of the speaker's platform. At the center point and just before passing, each comes to a distinct stop facing each other. The bearer of the USPS flag dips his flag slightly and as soon as his flag is back up in carrying position both bearers continue their march and place the flags in their respective stands.

As soon as each flag is placed both bearers step back and come to the position of breast salute, facing the flag of the United States.

Referring back in the above, as soon as the bearers start their march across the room, the Commander orders all present "Breast Salute."

As soon as the bearers have come to the position of breast salute as above, the Commander orders "Two." (Second count of the salute routine.) On this order all present return to the position of attention and the color bearers retire.

The Commander then raps his gavel and orders all present "Be seated" or calls for the Invocation, after which he seats the audience.

If a larger hall is used or more formal ceremonies are desired, the flags may be marched up the center aisle or right aisle. If in single file, with the United States flag in the lead, if abreast with the U. S. flag on the right of marchers.

If marching up the center aisle, at the point where the cleared space between the front seats and the table is reached, the bearer of the USPS flag stops momentarily and allows the bearer of the U. S. flag to cross in front of him. The flag dip is used only when the flags meet from opposite directions as in the first method above.

The Commander follows the same sequence of orders as for the first method above.

COLOR RETIRING CEREMONIES

Color retiring ceremonies may properly and easily be followed at all formal business meetings, where there is a definite moment of official closing. It is not recommended at social gatherings.

Color retiring ceremonies are as follows:

Just before declaring the meeting adjourned the Commander gives the order "Color Guard, stand by to retire the colors." On receiving this order, the Color Guard advances and stands directly in front of their respective colors. When both are in position the Commander orders "Attention" and all present rise and stand at attention. When this is accomplished the Commander orders "Color Guard, secure the colors."

Each color bearer at this command removes his flag from the stand and together do an about-face to face the audience, and then hoist the flags to carrying position.

As soon as this is accomplished the Commander orders "Breast salute" and all present except the color bearers comply. As soon as the position of breast salute is accomplished, the color bearers step off together to retrace their presentation march. If the first method described for presenting colors is used, the dipping ceremony is repeated just before they cross in the center of the room. In this method, as soon as the colors reach the side of the room, or if the aisle method is used, as soon as the colors pass from sight or reach the back of the room, the Commander orders "Two" and all present return to the position of attention.

The Commander may now order the meeting adjourned, or may seat the audience first if there are to be informal activities following.

DISPLAY OF FLAGS AT YACHT CLUB AND SQUADRON MEETINGS

1. The flag of the United States should be displayed either from a staff, or flat against the wall above and behind the speaker's table.

2. The flag of the United States should never be draped or laid over anything except a casket, at which time special rules apply.

3. When displayed flat against a wall it should be fastened along the upper edge only, with the union to the flag's right, to the left as viewed by the audience. This applies whether the flag is hung with stripes vertical or horizontal. The horizontal position of the stripes is preferable.

* 4. When displayed on a staff indoors, in an enclosure where there is no platform at the head of the room, the U. S. ensign is stood at the right of the audience; but if there is a platform, the U. S. ensign is displayed on a staff at the left of the audience, namely, at the right of the speaker. The USPS ensign, if also displayed, is stood at the left of the audience where there is no platform, and at the right of the audience (left of the speaker) if there is a platform. If the Canadian ensign is also to be so displayed, it should be at the right of the audience where there is no platform, and at the right of the speaker where there is a platform but just inboard of the U. S. ensign.

5. If the flag of the United States, and another, are displayed with crossed staffs, as at the head of a room, the flag of the United States should be at the flag's right, to left as viewed by the audience, and with its staff in front of the other.

6. If the flag of the United States is displayed with other flags in a group, from staffs, it should be in the center and slightly higher or in front of the other flags.

7. If the USPS flag is to be displayed flat against a wall, it is hung as prescribed for the Flag of the United States, as in paragraph 3 above, but on the opposite wall.

---

* See USPS Officers Manual.

NOTE A—If there is no raised platform for the head table or speaker, the bearers of the U. S. and USPS flags take positions opposite from the positions indicated (see paragraph 4 Display of Flags at Squadron Meetings).

Motor Boats *

MASTLESS VESSELS (with bow and stern staffs)
Foreign national flag at bow staff.
Own ensign at stern staff.

ONE-MAST MOTOR VESSELS (with yard-arm)
Foreign national flag at bow staff.
Own ensign at stern staff.
Club flag at starboard yard-arm.
Private signal or flag officer's flag at masthead.

TWO-MAST MOTOR VESSELS
Underway:—
Club pennant at bow staff.
Foreign national flag at fore-truck.
Private or flag officer's flag at main-truck.
Own ensign at stern staff.
At anchor or dock:—
The practice outlined above for two-mast motor vessels under way is also correct when at anchor, or at a dock.

All Vessels

Hoist your own ensign first and lower last if you are short-handed.

Show your own colors if entering or leaving port before 8:00 A.M. or after sunset, but do not pay honors except from 8:00 A.M. to sunset.

Sailing Vessels

SLOOPS AND CUTTERS
Own ensign at peak when under sail and at stern staff when at anchor or under power.
Club signal at masthead when at anchor.
Private signal at masthead when underway.
Flag officer's flag in place of club flag or private signal.
Foreign flag on forestay at anchor, and forestay or forward starboard shroud one-third mast height when underway.

YAWLS AND KETCHES
Own ensign at mizzen peak when under sail and at stern staff when at anchor or under power.
Club pennant at main-truck.
Private signal at mizzen-truck.
Flag officer's flag in place of private signal.
Foreign flag on forestay at anchor, and forestay or forward starboard shroud one-third mast height when underway.

SCHOONERS OF TWO OR MORE MASTS
Own ensign at after peak when under sail and at stern staff when at anchor or under power.
Club signal at fore-truck at anchor.
Private signal at main-truck.
Flag officer's flag at main-truck in place of private signal.
Foreign flag at bow staff or forestay at anchor, and fore-truck or forward starboard shroud while underway.

* NOTE: *Motor boats with a gaff should fly their own ensign at gaff while underway, but at stern staff while at anchor or tied to a dock.*

NAVAL RESERVE PENNANTS

There are two types of Naval Reserve pennant. (See illustrations, page ix.) The *Naval Reserve Yacht Pennant* is displayed at the fore truck by yachts and vessels commanded or owned by Naval Reserve Officers, designated by the Secretary of the Navy as suitable for service as naval auxiliaries in time of war. The *Naval Reserve Yacht Owners Distinguishing Pennant* is a personal flag flown, preferably at the fore truck, on yachts owned by, or under the command of, individuals who donated yachts or other craft for use by the Navy during World War II. Those awarded this pennant are not necessarily members of the U. S. Naval Reserve.

FLAGS TO FLY ASHORE AT YACHT CLUBS

I. No USPS Activity Ashore or at Yacht Club Anchorage.
　1. Yacht Club Burgee
　2. U. S. Flag**
　3. Senior Y. C. Officer Present
　4. U. S. Jack may be flown on Sundays and Holidays (optional)

II. With USPS Activity Ashore or in Yacht Club Anchorage.
　1. Yacht Club Burgee
　2. U. S. Flag
　3. USPS Ensign*
　4. Senior USPS Officer Present*

** A few clubs fly the yacht ensign but the U. S. flag is preferred.
* Permission to fly should be requested of Yacht Club.

NOTES: If only a Yacht Club single mast with no yard or gaff, only the U. S. Flag should be flown, at the truck.

If a mast with yardarm only, the U. S. Flag should be flown at truck, Club burgee at starboard yard arm, USPS Ensign or other organizational flag may be flown at port yard arm during activities ashore of such organization. Flag sizes should be in keeping with the height of mast. An appropriate length for the U. S. flag (when flown from the masthead) would be ¼ the height of mast—a 6' by 10' flag, for example, on a 40' mast. When flown from the gaff, its length should be ¼ the height at which it is flown. Burgees may be ⅔ the length of the U. S. flag; officers' flags ½ the length of the U. S. flag.

On national holidays and on days of special yachting significance, it is permissible to fly the flags of the International Code.

The code for "flying flags ashore at Yacht Clubs" may be followed for flags flown ashore at the homes of yachtsmen.

Signal flags, such as storm and weather flags etc. should be flown from a conspicuous hoist.

Flags of yachting organizations should not be flown from commercial establishments, except by special permission.

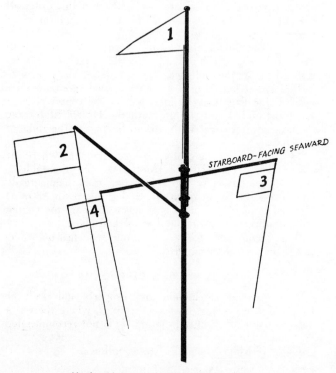

Yacht Club Mast with Yard and Gaff

Honoring An Allied Ensign

JUST as a certain code of etiquette has been adopted to govern the display of flags by American yachts on the waterways of our own nation, so too there is a certain accepted procedure to which pleasure boats should properly adhere when they cross international boundaries into the waters of another nation.

There are only a limited number of positions from which flags may be properly displayed on motor boats and consequently when a foreign flag is to be flown, it must displace one of the flags commonly flown in home waters.

The United States Power Squadrons has adopted a code of flag etiquette which might well be followed by all American pleasure craft cruising in foreign waters.

Motor Boats

For the purposes of this flag code, motor boats may be divided into three general groups: (1) mastless vessels, having bow and stern staffs only; (2) single-masted motor vessels, with yardarm; and (3) vessels with two masts.

For vessels with gaff Ensign is flown at gaff

Mastless vessels. A motor boat having only bow and stern staffs, if in home waters, would fly the yacht club burgee forward and her own ensign aft. In foreign waters, she must obviously keep her own ensign at the place of honor aft. Therefore she has no alternative but to display the national flag of the foreign country which she is visiting at the bow staff in place of her own club burgee. Under no circumstances should she try to fly both flags from one staff at the same time. That principle holds consistently true throughout all flag etiquette.

Motor vessels with one mast. Considering next the motor vessel with one mast and yardarm—possibly the most common of all arrangements aboard cruising motor boats—her own ensign remains at the stern staff and her private signal or officer's flag at the masthead. Her club flag, flown at the bow staff in home waters, is now displayed at the starboard yardarm, giving way to the foreign national flag, which is properly displayed at the bow staff.

Motor vessels with two masts. Some of the larger motor craft have two masts. Assuming that the mainmast has no gaff, then the practise is as follows. Her own ensign is at the stern staff as usual, and her private signal or officer's flag stays at the main truck. The club pennant goes to the bow staff, making way for the foreign national flag at the fore truck. This is correct practice whether the vessel is under way or lying at anchor, or at a dock.

The only variation of this procedure for two-masted vessels is found when the mainmast is equipped with a gaff. In such cases, the gaff takes precedence over the stern staff as the position of honor when the vessel is under way. Therefore the vessel's own ensign flies at the gaff instead of the stern staff when under way. However, when she comes to anchor or ties up to a dock, then the ensign should appear at the stern staff just as it would in vessels without a gaff both at anchor and under way.

Sailing Vessels

Sailing vessels can also be divided into general classifications, insofar as the display of flags is concerned. This classification is based on the arrangement of their masts, and is as follows: (1) sloops and cutters; (2) yawls and ketches; and (3) schooners, whether they have two masts or more.

Sloops and cutters have only one mast, the basic distinction being that the cutter's mast is further aft. Sailing vessels of this type show their own ensign at the peak when under sail, but at the stern staff when at anchor or under power. Most sailboats today have the jib-headed (Marconi) rig. Since such a rig has no gaff, the ensign is flown from the leech of the sail in a position which would correspond with the peak if there were a gaff.

Sloops and cutters fly the club signal when at anchor only, from the masthead. When under way, the private signal takes the place of the club pennant at the masthead. In the event that the owner is a club officer, then his officer's flag is flown instead of the club flag at anchor or the private signal when under way. All

NOTE:—National flags should never be flown at a yard arm for any reason. Correct method of flying a foreign flag (illustrated in this article) applies only when waters of that nation are entered. The foreign national flag should never be flown aboard a yacht to honor a foreign guest. (The U. S. Navy does it only in rare instances.) Ashore, it is common practice among U. S. yacht clubs on the border to fly the Canadian flag at the masthead, with the U. S. flag at the gaff, when they have Canadian entries in races or Canadian flag officers officially in the club house.

SLOOPS AND CUTTERS

UNDER WAY

AT ANCHOR

YAWLS AND KETCHES

AT ANCHOR

UNDER WAY

THREE-MASTED SCHOONERS

UNDER WAY

AT ANCHOR

of this practice is identical whether the vessel is in home waters or abroad.

There is no need to displace any of these flags when going abroad. In foreign waters, the sloop or cutter flies the foreign ensign from her forestay when at anchor, and from the forestay or from the forward starboard shroud (one-third mast height) when under way.

Yawls and ketches have two masts, the larger of which is forward. Their ensign flies at the mizzen peak when under sail, at the stern staff when at anchor or running under power without sails. The club pennant is at the main truck, private signal at the mizzen truck. If the owner is a flag officer of a club, the officer's flag flies at the mizzen truck in place of the private signal. Again, this part of flag practice is identical for home or foreign waters.

To take care of the foreign flag, yawls and ketches, like sloops and cutters, fly it on the forestay when at anchor, and on the forestay or forward starboard shroud (one-third mast height) when under way.

Schooners. The third category of sailing vessels embraces schooners, having two masts or more. Perhaps the best way to show the distinction between the practice in home and foreign waters for them is to outline first the procedure in home waters and then point out the differences in practice when abroad.

At home, the schooner has her own ensign at the after peak when under sail, but at the stern staff when at anchor or under power, without sails set. The club signal is at the fore truck, private signal at the main truck. The flag officer's flag would be flown in place of the private signal at the main truck.

Now, when the schooner is in foreign waters, the practice is the same except that the club signal is flown at the fore truck when at anchor only, (not when under way.) Also, when at anchor, the foreign flag is flown at the bow staff or forestay, but when under way the foreign flag should be at the fore truck or the forward starboard shroud.

CHAPTER XXIII

Yachting Customs and Etiquette

At regattas, moving vessels should proceed slowly and with caution so as not to inconvenience competing boats or anchored craft of spectators

IF etiquette were regarded as no more than blind adherence to certain prescribed conventionalities and amenities of social life, there might be some sound reason why one might question the need for, or desirability of, conforming to the principles of good conduct.

But just as soon as one realizes that these principles are not mere arbitrary laws demanding conformity on the part of all individuals—that they are basically the natural expression of those who instinctively conduct themselves in a sincerely considerate manner toward all, regardless of rank or race—it becomes quite obvious why anyone should voluntarily seek to acquire the traits that distinguish the true gentleman.

In the varied relationships of people in many walks of life, a natural body of customs and accepted procedure inevitably springs up to govern such relationships. Nowhere is this better exemplified than in the various branches of our Governmental service. In the depart-

367

ments that are concerned with diplomacy and statesmanship, observance of correct form is inextricably woven with the act itself. And in military branches of the service it is safe to say that efficient functioning could not possibly be achieved without a similar body of recognized customs.

The bearing and conduct of officers in our national service, who inspire respect from their subordinates by the respect they themselves show even to the lowest in rank, might well be taken as a criterion in civilian life. Discipline that is inspired is a genuine tribute to the one who evokes it, a quality of immeasurable value to the one who learns and practices it. The discipline that is forced by fear or compulsion can never be more than destructive to anyone whom it touches.

The etiquette and customs of the service are of particular interest today due to the increasing activities of our various agencies of national defense. Young men entering the several branches of the service as officers are confronted with numerous problems and questions which may either be obstacles and barriers to their development, or stepping stones to positions of higher responsibility and broader capacity for service, depending largely on whether or not they are gifted with an innate sense of right action, or can acquire it by observing and profiting from the experience of those who have gone before.

A recognition of this fact has prompted the publication of a highly informative and valuable booklet entitled Service Etiquette and Courtesy, by the United States Coast Guard Academy, at New London, Connecticut. Its function is to serve as a guide in questions of procedure to cadets of the Academy. Many of the principles, however, are equally applicable to the problems faced by yachtsmen, especially in the light of the close tie-up today between the activities of amateur yachtsmen and the U. S. Coast Guard through the medium of the Coast Guard Reserve, Coast Guard Auxiliary, and also the widespread organization of the United States Power Squadrons.

Space prohibits more than briefest reference to the highlights only of this manual, but time devoted to an intensive study of it by anyone, in or out of the service, would be well repaid. No better approach to the subject could be found than in the following extract quoted verbatim from the foreword of this handbook:

"A knowledge of rules and customs gives the possessor poise and enables him to meet various situations with ease and confidence. However, the true gentleman reveals more innate qualities; underlying his knowledge of etiquette, customs and usage, there must be sincerity, friendliness, tact, consideration of others, and some imagination. As we embody these qualities in our own characters, our personalities manifest something more than empty courtesy or mere adherence to forms; gentlemanly behavior in the truest sense automatically follows."

Leadership and Discipline

The first part of this Coast Guard pamphlet concerns itself with leadership and discipline. Leadership is said to be largely a matter of intelligent and just administration of authority. Young officers are cautioned against

Frank P. Beauchamp

The correct observance of etiquette and customs plays an important part in the social and formal side of yachting. Members of the United States Power Squadrons are shown above at attention during flag-raising ceremonies at a district rendezvous

assuming, immediately upon being vested with some authority at the time of graduation from an academy, that they automatically have become qualified leaders.

Knowledge along technical and practical lines does not imply a capacity for leadership, which involves a study and cultivation of such qualities as self-control, courage, judgment, simplicity, earnestness, sympathy, faith and loyalty—just a few of many attributes. One of the best methods of acquiring these attributes is to take stock of one's own shortcomings with a view toward eliminating deficiencies and developing in one's self the desirable qualities, rather than to demand of subordinates a perfection one has not himself attained.

In developing a proper attitude toward one's authority in a given position aboard ship, the cadet is told to remember that every man on the ship knows that, except for some accident or his own neglect, he might have stood in his superior's shoes. The knowledge of this fact on the part of every man places upon the officer the burden of showing and proving that he has acquired more than authority—that he has cultivated those qualities of leadership that entitle him to command, and enable him to carry the responsibility which always goes hand-in-hand with authority.

Discipline is to be taught and regarded as the true spirit of an orderly democracy. The right approach recognizes the fact that it should not be a hardship, but rather a natural habit which develops self-control and results in a well regulated life. Expressing the idea of equal privileges and equal rights, discipline of the right kind should not act to reduce men to automatons but rather should inspire all with the power that makes each a potential leader. In the final analysis, its true value will depend largely on whether it is forced, or voluntary.

Another interesting comment that goes far toward shedding a true light on what discipline should mean was contained in an address to students at Columbia University, in which the speaker remarked that discipline too often connoted "an unpleasant and unnecessary use of authority." His belief was that it should rather be taken to mean "scientific cooperation."

Leadership and discipline are logically considered in conjunction. They are inseparable. Given a group of individuals in which all have the qualities of leadership developed to a greater or lesser extent, discipline will give each man an appreciation of the authority vested in their chosen or appointed leader. Consequently they will each lean a shoulder against the wheel in mutual cooperation, and not waste time or mental capacities in envy of their superior's success. The leader, in turn, will have the ability to inspire each to self-development and the voluntary acceptance of higher responsibilities. It is an error for any leader to believe that he can grow no more. With the proper spirit, the leader grows as well as the men he leads.

Comment on the application of this principle to activities in the boating world seems hardly necessary. The yacht club or association that reflects an understanding of these ideas, flourishes. The racing organization that cultivates it, is well-knit. And, of all places, there is none where the demand for capable leadership and the discipline of cooperation is more vital than aboard a vessel—be it ship or yacht or small pleasure boat. The skipper has, must have, final authority. He must be equal to that responsibility. If he is worthy of his trust as a "leader," he will get the cooperation of his crew by "leading," not driving.

(As a guide and reference work, the book Naval Leadership, published by the Naval Institute, has been recommended to young commissioned officers.)

Official Courtesy

PART two of the pamphlet deals with official courtesy, and the first thing that comes to mind in this connection is the matter of saluting.

It seems that the practice had its origin at least as far back as the days of the Romans, when the raising of one's hand, palm forward, was a gesture to show that no dagger was concealed in it. Today, happily, we have other motives in showing respect to superiors. Uncovering the head also dates back to ancient days. Certain types of headgear, however, were not easily removed, so the present day salute evolved as a gesture in which the hand moved to the visor of the hat as if it were going to be removed.

This point, today, is stressed—that deference to superiors does not imply an admission of inferiority, no more than one could logically be accused of cowardice when displaying a wholesome respect for law. Those who might take the attitude that a salute is undemocratic or un-American might well consider this point of view, that courtesy in military affairs is simply an extension of the courtesies, voluntarily rendered, which originate in everyday life. The salute, thus understood, becomes an opportunity to respect the authority an officer represents; any idea of personal inferiority is at once dismissed.

Personal salutes and any other marks of respect usually accorded such individuals are properly given to officers of the Navy, Coast Guard, Army, Marine Corps, Public Health Service, Naval Militia, National Guard and to foreign officers. Certainly no sense of inferiority should attach to the individual who is showing his respect for any of these officers and their attendant authority.

ETIQUETTE prescribes that an enlisted person or officer junior in rank should salute first. Afloat, enlisted men and officers salute a flag officer and all officers senior in rank to themselves. When several officers are in company, those who are entitled to the salute return it. Aboard cutters or at the units to which they are attached officers and enlisted men salute their commanding officer when meeting, passing, or when addressed by him. Senior officers are saluted at the first daily meeting or passing, and whenever addressed. Senior officers or an Executive Officer are also saluted when making an inspection. At other times, it is correct to stand at attention until the officer has passed.

Salutes should begin when the officer is at least six paces away. Head and eyes should always be turned toward the officer and kept so while the hand is raised. The salute itself should be executed with snap, life, never in an indifferent manner and never with coat unbuttoned or with the hand in the pocket, or with cigar, cigarette or pipe in the mouth.

Where a civilian would raise his hat as a mark of respect to a lady, a military man properly uses the military salute.

When the National Anthem is played, or To the Colors sounded, officers and men stand at attention and salute, facing the music. At Escort of the Color, or at Retreat, they face the color or flag. Moving vehicles should be stopped; occupants, excepting the driver, step out and salute; the driver sits at attention.

On official occasions the same respect is paid when the National Anthem of another country is played. Persons in uniform face the flag and use the military salute. Those in civilian clothes stand facing the flag. If a hat is being worn, it is removed and held over the left breast. Women rise and face the flag.

Salutes are not exchanged in public assemblies or conveyances such as theatres, trains, etc. Nor does an enlisted man ever salute when driving a car or truck.

AT mess, when a person calls Attention to indicate entrance of an officer, all present stop eating but remain seated, at attention until the officer leaves or otherwise directs. When addressed, a person rises and stands at attention.

The position on the right is always reserved for a senior in rank. A senior walks to the right of his junior; similarly in a car he sits on the right. When entering cars or small boats, seniors are the last to enter, first to leave. Juniors address their commanding officer as Sir at all times, and pay similar respect to visiting officers of the same rank. When delivering messages, using the form "Captain Blank presents his compliments to Lieutenant Blank and says ....," the junior in rank never presents his compliments to the senior.

When an officer reports at headquarters for duty to a district commander or commanding officer, he also makes a courtesy visit to the home of the commandant, district commander, or commanding officer within 48 hours after reporting.

When calls are made on officers of one's ship or station, procedure varies. A single (unmarried) officer calls on other officers and their families shortly after reporting. If he is married, other officers call upon him first. The exception to this is the case of the commanding officer, upon whom other officers call first. All calls should be returned on the earliest possible occasion.

When officers of ships are exchanging calls, commanding officers exchange visits first. Then wardroom officers of a ship arriving in port call upon the commanding officer and wardroom officers of a ship, or ships, already in port.

Vessels of war are boarded from the starboard side by commissioned officers and visitors accompanying them. Other officers use the port side. This, however, is not invariable if the ship's commanding officer decides circumstances alter the particular case.

Landings across other boats are avoided, never made unless permission is first obtained. Aboard transports and vessels of war, the officer of the deck meets a visiting officer at the gangway.

OFFICERS and men salute the National Ensign upon reaching the quarterdeck whether they approach from a boat, gangway, the shore, or another part of the ship. This salute is made, facing the colors, while standing at the top of the gangway or upon arriving at the quarterdeck. Following this, they salute the officer of the deck. When leaving the quarterdeck, the officer of the deck is saluted first, and then the colors. The deck officer returns both salutes in each case.

When a boat is sent to bring invited guests from a ship at anchor, an officer should accompany the boat; he lends assistance to ladies entering or leaving the boat. When guests of the commanding officer come aboard a ship, the officer of the deck assists ladies or elderly gentlemen at the accommodation ladder.

In cases where an International Salute is rendered, the Ensign of the country so honored is hoisted at the mainmast, flags being broken out at the first gun and hauled down when the last gun is fired (when they are required to be hauled down after the salute).

When ships of the Navy, Coast Guard, foreign men of war, or school ships pass each other at sea within 600 yards (or 400 yards in the case of boats flying flag or pennant), etiquette prescribes that honors be rendered. The officer of the deck has Attention sounded as the jack staffs of the respective vessels pass each other. The junior ship sounds Attention before the senior and waits to give the Carry On signal until the senior ship has done so. All hands on deck or in view of the passing ship are brought to attention. In foreign ports, or wherever full honors are indicated, officers and men are lined up on deck facing the passing vessel and the hand salute is given as the other ship's colors come abreast.

Service Customs

SOMETIMES, unless the accepted form is understood, there is doubt as to how officers should be addressed since the manner of address varies with the rank. In the Navy and Coast Guard, commanders and other officers of higher rank are addressed by their titles, both in official and social life. Lieutenant-commanders and officers junior to them are addressed as Mister, except that the title is used in an introduction or in official or written communications. Cadets are also addressed as Mister so-and-so, socially and in conversation—but as Cadet in written or official communications. Warrant officers are addressed as Mister and enlisted men are addressed by officers by their surnames. Junior officers are often addressed by their seniors by the surname and the same is true between officers of equal rank, unless there is a big difference in age or date of commission.

Etiquette at mess is very exact. Officers must be properly dressed and should ask to be excused before leaving the table. The senior officer at the table is the president of the mess. He is the first to be seated and other officers should not leave the table or ask to be excused until he has left—unless he says that everyone is at liberty to go. A courteous apology is due the president if one arrives at the table late and permission should be requested before being seated. When a commanding officer enters, those at the table rise as a mark of respect. Visitors, accorded the same courtesy and hospitality as callers in the home, are greeted by officers who rise at their entrance. Orders of the commanding officer are taboo as a topic of conversation at the table.

AT social functions such as dances and receptions, guests should be introduced to all members of the unit and everything possible done to put them entirely at ease. If someone has been overlooked, etiquette requires one to introduce himself to the guest, who is then made acquainted with other members. Officers, regardless of grade, properly dance or converse with wives of senior officers, and attention is due the wife of the commanding officer, as well as her guests. Official subjects are not proper subjects of conversation at such social gatherings.

When making introductions at a dance, a gentleman, or lady, may be introduced by mentioning names only. Ladies are not escorted about a room to be introduced in turn to every stranger; gentlemen are taken to the lady to be presented. Young men are presented to their elders; bachelors to married men, unless the bachelor is older. Ordinary citizens are presented to those of official distinction.

Calling hours are between 4:00 and 6:00 or from 8:00 to 9:00 P.M., the latter corresponding to those observed in the Army. In civil life, calls are made in the afternoon. Official calls on district and commanding officers are repeated at their residences within 24 hours after reporting. If the wife of the visited officer is present, then it is proper for the one paying the call to be accompanied by his wife. These calls are brief.

Officers commonly call upon a newly arrived officer as soon as he is situated. Calls are returned within a week or ten days. An officer leaving his station for an extended period, or permanently, calls upon his commanding officer before leaving.

Calling cards are used in the service, the same as in civilian life.

Social Customs

THE question of the correct observance of social customs is so broad in scope that it can be touched upon only lightly here. Under any circumstances, the individual distinguished by natural gentlemanly conduct will stand out regardless of his surroundings as one who has a proper attitude toward the respect and consideration due all with whom he comes in contact.

Association between ladies and gentlemen calls for an attitude of mutual respect, with especial consideration due elderly women. Gentlemen always rise in the presence of a woman who is standing. In churches, homes, clubs, private offices, the reception rooms of apartment houses, etc., the hat is always removed. Out-of-doors, a gentleman who stops to converse with a lady invariably removes his hat, keeping it off while they are together.

When men and women meet in public, the gentleman should never be the first to speak, always awaiting recognition from the lady. Officers at the Coast Guard Academy, however, are permitted to salute ladies who are known to be resident there.

Conditions determine whether or not it is appropriate for a gentleman to offer a lady his arm. When it is, he offers his right arm, never the left. Correct etiquette allows a gentleman to offer his arm to an invalid or elderly lady any time there is reason to believe that the courtesy will be appreciated. Otherwise, in the daytime, the arm is offered to a lady only to assist her in traffic or where walking may be difficult. At night, when it is difficult for a lady to watch her footing, the gentleman always offers his arm. At dinners and balls the lady is escorted to the dining room on her partner's arm. Familiarity toward women is frowned upon in good society, though a gentleman may always offer assistance to a woman when it appears to be needed.

REGARDLESS of the occasion, a man's dress, to be correct, conforms in degree of formality with that of the woman he escorts. This would avoid such incongruous situations as might be presented by a woman in evening dress escorted by a gentleman in a sports or business suit.

When a bow is indicated, the gentleman inclines his body forward from the waist. Hands hanging naturally at the side, heels together, toes outward, one faces directly the person for whom the bow is intended. A hand-shake should be neither a display of physical strength nor a lifeless demonstration, but rather a natural, firm clasp of hands. A slight bow usually accompanies the hand-shake.

Upon entering a drawing room, one first pays his respects to the hostess, then to other ladies present, usually in order of rank. Then the host is greeted and finally other men present. When leaving, one rises and goes directly to the hostess and bids goodbye briefly (naturally, however, not with abruptness), and departs. When a man and woman leave in company, the gentleman waits for the lady to make the first move. After dinner parties, guests usually remain till guests of honor have left.

At teas, dances, balls, receptions and the like, the guests present themselves immediately upon arrival to the hostess, who receives them near the entrance to the room. A lady precedes her escort at the receiving line. The gentleman bows as he shakes hands with the hostess; this is repeated with each of the hostess' attendants. Unless the names of guests are mentioned upon entering, the guests themselves pronounce their names distinctly when presenting themselves to the hostess. If one of a couple or group is acquainted with the hostess, that one presents himself first, introducing the others. Procedure when receiving at formal military dances varies somewhat from this.

When departing from social functions such as the above, the hostess is again at the entrance, and her guests in turn go to her to say goodbye, accompanying this with a bow and hand-shake.

IN general, a gentleman should acknowledge in appropriate manner every courtesy extended him. The form which the acknowledgment takes will vary with the nature of the occasion. A sincere sense of appreciation will prompt him to recognize and acknowledge every generous act performed for his benefit.

In dress and personal appearance, neatness and cleanliness are prime requirements. This includes both scrupulous cleanliness of person and meticulous attention to the details of dress. Officers are required to provide themselves with the uniforms of their rank and maintain them in neat, serviceable condition. For occasions off-duty, they may have civilian clothing. The latter may be worn when on duty at Coast Guard Headquarters, or when employed on shore duty, except at the Coast Guard Academy, Coast Guard Depot, and at Coast Guard stations.

Correct dignified speech, with a capacity for intelligent conversation, are also indicated as distinguishing marks of a gentleman. Good speech implies both correct pronunciation and distinct enunciation. Slang and profanity have no place in the vocabulary of an officer or a gentleman.

THE table manners prescribed for men of the service are precisely those which might be expected of any gentleman in civilian life. Gentlemen assist the ladies in finding places at the table and seating them. Where there are couples, each gentleman assists his own partner (at his right).

Napkins are laid upon the lap, not tucked in the belt, collar or vest, and used only as necessary for the purpose for which they are intended, that is, the removal of particles of food or drink from fingers and lips. When rising at the end of a meal, the napkin is laid, unfolded, beside one's place.

At small dinner parties, one waits before starting to eat till all guests are served or until the hostess starts to eat. On occasions when there are many at dinner, the meal may be started when those in the immediate group have all been served.

When there is any question as to the proper selection of implements from among a great array with which the table is set, one is advised to do as the hostess does. Commonly, they are laid in the order in which they will be used, from the outside in. The knife should never be used in the left hand, nor employed as the fork should be, to convey food to the mouth. After use, the knife, and fork also, is placed across the upper half of the plate with the handle to the right, not upon the table or resting upon both table and plate.

When used with the knife, the fork is held in the left hand; otherwise in the right hand. Thus it is transferred to the right hand before conveying food to the mouth, unless the knife is retained in the right hand. The edge of a fork, not the knife, is used for cutting salad. After eating, both the knife and fork are laid on the plate, ends at the center, handles to the right.

A spoon should be dipped in a direction away from the diner, and used so that the edge of its bowl is at the lips, not in the mouth. It should never be left in cup or glass, but placed in the saucer. Unnecessary noise, in using a spoon to stir, or at any other time during the meal, is obviously not in good taste.

Bread, rolls, etc., should be broken, not cut. Then the small pieces may be buttered and eaten individually. Buttering a whole slice of bread is always regarded as bad etiquette.

The finger bowl is used for cleaning lips and finger-tips; only the finger-tips should be placed in the bowl, one hand at a time. At the conclusion of the meal, guests rise when the hostess does.

YACHT ROUTINE

THE following regulations, particularly applicable to a discussion of yacht etiquette, are taken from that portion of the New York Yacht Club code which deals with Yacht Routine. These deal with salutes, boats, and correct procedure. Other sections, not given here, relate primarily to the display of flags, signals and lights.

Salutes

(See also page 383)

Whistles shall never be used in saluting.

Upon joining the Squadron during the Annual Cruise, the Commodore shall be saluted by all yachts present with one gun.

When the Squadron is disbanded after the Annual Cruise, the Commodore shall be saluted by all yachts present with one gun.

All salutes shall be answered in kind.

Yachts not carrying guns shall salute by dipping the ensign once.

Guns may be used to call attention to signals, but their use otherwise shall be avoided as much as possible.

No guns shall be fired on Sunday.

All salutes herein provided shall be made by dipping the ensign once.

Vessels of the United States and foreign navies shall be saluted.

When a Flag Officer comes to anchor, he shall be saluted by all yachts present, except in cases where there is a senior Flag Officer present.

When the Commodore joins the Squadron during the Annual Cruise, a gun salute is provided in the preceding paragraph, in which case the ensign salute shall not be made, except by yachts which do not carry guns.

When a yacht comes to anchor where a Flag Officer is present, such Flag Officer shall be saluted.

A junior Flag Officer anchoring in the presence of a senior shall salute.

Yachts passing shall salute, the junior saluting first.

Yachts salute on arriving at the home anchorage of another club.

All salutes shall be answered in kind.

A yacht acting as Race Committee boat should neither salute nor be saluted while displaying the Committee Flag.

When coming on board or leaving a yacht, the quarterdeck shall be saluted by touching the cap.

Boats

THE order of entering and leaving boats is—juniors enter first and leave last.

When in boats, Flag Officers, the Fleet Captain, and Race Committee shall display their distinctive flags, Captains their private signals, and Members the Burgee. The flag of the Senior Officer embarked has precedence. When two boats are approaching the same gangway or landing stage, Flag Officers have the right of way.

Boat crews should be dressed alike and in the prescribed uniform. Neck handkerchiefs should always be worn, knotted in front, and cap ribbons should not be tucked under.

Whenever possible, boat booms should be rigged in at night. Otherwise a white light shall be shown at the end.

All boats made fast to the stern of a yacht at anchor shall show a white light.

Procedure

WHEN a Flag Officer makes an official visit, his flag, if senior to that of the yachts visited, shall be displayed in place of the Burgee, while he is on board.

A yacht may display the personal flag of a National, State, or Municipal officer, when such an official is on board, or the National Ensign of a distinguished foreign visitor. This flag should be displayed at the main for the President of the United States, and at the fore for all other officials and visitors.

On the Fourth of July, and when ordered on other occasions, a yacht in commission shall, when at anchor and the weather permits, dress ship at 8:00 A.M. from morning to evening colors. When these days occur on Sundays, the ceremony should be postponed until the following day. In dressing ship rectangular flags should alternate with pennants. Flag Officers' flags and the Burgee shall not be used in dressing ship. The ensign of a foreign nation shall not be displayed except when dressing ship in compliment to such nation, in which case the ensign shall be displayed at the fore truck. When a yacht is dressed, the ensign is displayed in lowered boats.

After joining the Squadron during the Annual Cruise, a yacht shall request permission before leaving. When meeting Squadrons of other clubs, salutes shall be exchanged by the Senior Officer alone. When meeting a single yacht, the salute shall be answered only by the Flagship.

A Flag Officer embarked in a boat, not displaying his distinctive flag, should be considered as present in an unofficial capacity.

PROCEDURE FOR SALUTES BETWEEN VESSELS

Dipping the Ensign in Salute

FEDERAL law prohibits dipping the Flag of the United States (49/50 stars) flag to any person or thing, and only Government vessels are permitted to dip "the Flag" in reply to a dip.

The law does permit organizational or institutional flags to be dipped. The U. S. Power Squadrons Flag, when flown from stern or gaff, may be dipped, or dipped in reply to a dip, since it is an organizational flag.

The status of the Yacht Signal, popularly known as the U. S. Yacht Ensign, (13 stars around an anchor, in the field) is not clear, but since the law covers only the Flag of the United States, the assumption is made that it may be dipped.

In a U. S. Power Squadron Fleet Review the USPS Ensign should be flown from the stern or gaff. Since auxiliary sailing vessels in a Squadron Review will be proceeding under auxiliary power alone such vessels should also fly the USPS Ensign from the stern or gaff.

All vessels in a Review, flying either the USPS Ensign or the Yacht Signal at the stern staff or gaff, should dip this flag when their bow comes abreast the stern of the Flagship and return to full height when their stern passes the bow of the Flagship.

An added mark of respect, and a tight ship, is for all persons visible on deck to stand at attention facing the Flagship, with hand salute held while the flag is in the dipped position.

On this occasion the Flag of the United States should not be flown, but if it is *do not dip it,* and use the hand salute, as described above, only. Do not dip any flag except the flag being flown at the stern staff or gaff.

Hand Salutes

When a vessel is officially reviewing a parade of other vessels, with the senior officer present standing on his reviewing vessel with his staff in formation behind him, only the senior officer gives the hand salute. On a vessel being reviewed, if the skipper has his guests in formation with him, only the skipper gives the hand salute, but if the guests are standing at attention at the rail facing the reviewing yacht as they pass the reviewing point, they all give the hand salute, as the ensign is dipped. The criterion is whether or not the other people aboard are in formation: if in formation, only the skipper salutes, but if not in formation, all salute.

Gun Salutes

Guns should not be used in salutes between yachts unless ordered by a national authority or by the senior officer present.

COMMODORE   VICE COMMODORE   REAR COMMODORE

Clothing for Yachtsmen

CHAPTER
XXIV

(For U.S.P.S. cap and coat insignia, see pages ix-a and ix-b. For U.S.C.G. Auxiliary insignia, see page x.)

BREAKERS ahead, on the shoals of controversy, lie square athwart the course of anyone who would presume to discuss such a question as what constitutes proper garb for the boatman or yachtsman.

When it comes to clothing, most yachtsmen have pretty strong convictions as to whether or not they should, or must, abide by any arbitrary set of regulations. The spokesman of one faction argues that he goes afloat for pleasure and relaxation, and proposes to dress as he pleases—for comfort and practicability. Another group insists on strict adherence to all the proprieties, frowning upon those who cannot be made to conform to the dictates of etiquette, whether it be in dress, the display of flags or anything else.

Who is right? Well, frankly, we cannot believe that it is necessary for all to see eye-to-eye, on any subject. Nor can we find any logical reason why each should not be entitled to his own opinion.

The absence of braid and buttons should not detract any from the merit in a creditable feat of seamanship. And, by the same token, it is conceivable that the fisher-man or boatman in shorts or bathing suit may appreciate the point of view of the yachtsman who finds real satisfaction in knowing, and correctly observing, every detail that the seagoing equivalent of an Emily Post might prescribe. In fact, we would far rather see more of this mutual understanding than to have all conform precisely to one group or another.

Few, we think, deliberately violate the principles of good taste in regard to dress aboard their craft. In some cases it is a matter of not realizing that such principles exist. Errors are often made in the use of various devices and symbols worn on uniforms, and in the choice of the uniforms themselves. Generally those practices would be corrected if the wearer knew he was in error.

One thing is certain. The clothing that might be appropriate and acceptable in one case may be decidedly in bad taste in another. It would be hard to say who would be the more uncomfortable—the outboard mechanic in overalls at a yacht club dinner party, or the commodore in spotless white tinkering with a recalcitrant bit of greasy machinery under a torrid sun.

Let us then leave the choice of clothing to the individual, content to offer a few suggestions as to what has been found to be either satisfactory or accepted in general usage.

The thought most likely to come first to mind at mention of yachting clothes is the conventional uniform worn by boatmen for years. To what extent that uniform will be worn depends, in large measure, on the size of the boat, what one's normal activities are aboard that boat, where it will take him, and the nature of the occasion for which he is dressing.

At regattas, for example, the uniform is almost universally worn, and when visiting a yacht club. Aboard, when there are guests, or during evenings and afternoons at anchor, its use is appropriate. Frequently, on a cruise the uniform will be dispensed with, except on the social occasions requiring its use. On larger craft where there are paid hands to take care of the work of handling and navigating the yacht, a

Cap insignia. Those at left and below used by paid officers only. The one with wreaths (for deck and engineer officers, and stewards) may show owner's flag only. Below, insignia of deck officers, engineers, and radio operators. Paid captains might wear circled anchors, below, or wreath type, left.

Photographs courtesy Commodore Uniform Co., Inc.

SECRETARY

TREASURER

MEASURER

FLEET CAPTAIN

uniform for the owner would seem to be in far better taste than on the small boat where the captain-owner must break out his own anchor, swab his own deck, pump the bilge, bail out the dinghy and attend to numerous other jobs on the side.

On one point, at least, there can be little argument. For the occasions where the uniform is appropriate, it should certainly follow the style prescribed by yacht clubs as correct. For authority, one can do no better on this point than to refer to the code which the New York Yacht Club has adhered to for years. While there may be minor deviations in the practises of other clubs, N.Y.Y.C. regulations are the basic form on which others are patterned.

The service dress prescribed for yachtsmen is a double-breasted sack coat of navy blue or white cloth or serge, with serge or flannel trousers of the same material or of white drill. The cap is of navy blue cloth and has a patent leather visor, chin strap, and buttons. The white cap is the same as the blue with a stationary or removable drill cover. White shirts with black or dark ties are appropriate, and white or black shoes. Sneakers are not worn with a unifom, though they definitely have a place aboard for informal wear. White shoes, white cap and white trousers obviously go together, while the black shoes are worn with the blue trousers and blue cap.

There are a variety of styles of correct yachting cap offered by the manufacturers of uniforms. In every case an emblem or device will be found on the front of the band over the visor. This identifies the club to which the yachtsman belongs and indicates his status in that club. The central part of this device will be an enameled metal or silk embroidered disc showing the distinctive device of the club. This is placed at the intersection of two crossed fouled anchors in gold. If the member happens to hold the office of commodore, he is entitled to three gold stars, one at the top, and one at each side of the anchors.

A vice-commodore, next lower in rank, has the same cap device except that he rates two stars, omitting the one at the top. The rear-commodore has the same device with only one star, placed above the emblem. The N.Y.Y.C. code prescribes that captains (that is, boat owners) and ex-flag officers rate only the two gold fouled anchors and club device, but not the gold stars of incumbent officers. In rare cases, caps are seen with silver stars. In such cases the club has authorized ex-flag officers to use them, though it is not sanctioned in N.Y.Y.C. procedure.

A member of a club, who is not a boat owner, has for a cap device the club emblem with a single fouled anchor placed vertically (according to N.Y.Y.C. regulations). Some clubs sanction, for non-boat-owning members, use of the crossed fouled anchors with the club insignia, reserved for owners only in more formal organizations.

While yacht clubs obviously have no need to prescribe the form of cap device which might be worn by a boat owner who is not a club member, those whose business it is to supply correct uniforms provide for an ornament consisting of the two gold fouled anchors, naturally without the club insignia.

While this practise is sometimes questioned because of the possibility of one's being mistaken for a paid hand, the official cap ornament of a paid deck officer has crossed clear (not fouled)

FLEET SURGEON

RACE COMMITTEE

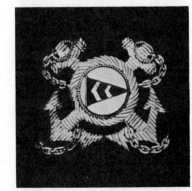

OWNER (Not a club officer)

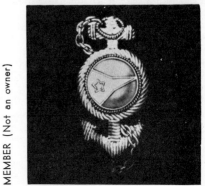

MEMBER (Not an owner)

U. S. P. S. MEMBER

Photographs courtesy Appel Uniform Co., Inc.

373

anchors, encircled by a rope of gold bullion. As the illustrations show, paid hands may also wear the type of insignia which shows crossed club and owner's flags within a wreath. This was quite common in the days of the larger yachts with a big crew. In some cases, the club flag would be omitted, and only the owner's flag displayed in the wreath. The owner decides which device he wishes the paid hands to wear. The skipper of a charter boat is likely to use the crossed clear (not fouled) anchors within the encircling rope of gold bullion.

Other officers of a club are distinguished by certain symbols placed above the regular cap device in gold. A fleet captain, for example, rates a horizontally placed anchor, half an inch long. The secretary is entitled to a maple leaf, the treasurer an acorn, the measurer a gold bar (sometimes an M), a member of the race committee a half-inch anchor placed vertically in distinction to the horizontal anchor of the fleet captain. In at least one club, the letters RC distinguish a race commiteeman. A fleet surgeon is identified by a red cross.

Rank is also designated by the stripes on the sleeve. On blue uniforms, the stripes are black; on white, the stripes are white. A commodore wears five stripes of mohair braid, the upper one finishing in what is known as a trefoil. This might be described as a triple loop, one part vertical, two horizontal. In each loop of the trefoil the commodore wears a gilt star. Regulations, of course, prescribe how wide the stripes are to be ($\frac{3}{8}$-inch), how far from the cuff they are placed, how far apart, the size of stars, etc.

The vice-commodore, next in rank, wears four stripes with trefoil in the upper one, and two gilt stars, one in each of the lower loops. The rear-commodore has three stripes with one star in the upper loop of the trefoil.

Captains (owners), secretaries, treasurers, measurers, fleet surgeons, fleet captains and race committeemen are entitled to two stripes with the trefoil, but no stars. A member only, holding no office, wears a single stripe, with the trefoil.

Ex-flag officers wear the stripes designating their former rank on the sleeve, but omit the stars to which they were entitled when holding office.

Note particularly that in all of the uniform regulations there is no mention of gold braid for the yachtsman, member, owner or club officer. The only gold permissible is the gold fouled anchors of the cap device, the special cap insignia of the secretary, treasurer, etc., and the stars on cap and sleeve.

For the ultra-formal full dress occasion, mess jackets are prescribed. These might be compared to the tuxedo or dinner jacket, and are used in the best nautical circles for evening wear and all formal yacht club functions. The mess jacket is single-breasted, of blue undress worsted, with rolling collar, pointed lapels, trimmed with black silk braid and appropriate collar and sleeve ornament.

U. S. P. S. Uniforms

(See color plate, pages ix-a and ix-b)

UNIFORMS worn by members of the United States Power Squadrons are patterned generally after the regulation yachting uniform prescribed, which they follow in regard to material, color and design. The double-breasted blue coat may be worn with trousers to match or with white trousers in season. Members of southern Squadrons may wear a white uniform of similar style. White shoes are worn with white trousers, black shoes with blue trousers, as in standard yachting practice.

For comfort in warm weather, some of the Squadrons have adopted a type of white sanforized shrunk oxford cloth shirt which may be worn without the coat. The shirt is given somewhat the appearance of a uniform coat by providing it with two pockets with flaps, and shoulder straps. U. S. P. S. buttons are worn in the pocket flaps and epaulet straps. To be worn in conjunction with the shirts, white trousers of sanforized material are available in gabardine, duck or twill.

Regulation caps in either blue or white are in order in the Squadron and may be worn by any member. The official cap device provides for a gold embroidered ship's wheel, eight-spoked, placed so that two upper spokes are at an equal angle with an imaginary vertical center-line. An enamelled disc in the center of the wheel shows the U. S. P. S. ensign with its distinctive blue and white vertical stripes and red field containing thirteen white stars in a circle surrounding a white fouled anchor. The ensign is shown in colors against a white background. Buttons used on U. S. P. S. uniforms are either black or gilt, the design showing a ship's wheel with eight spokes (one spoke

uppermost), the letters U. S. P. S. surrounding a fouled anchor in the center of the wheel. U. S. P. S. bylaws prescribe that black buttons be used on the blue coat, gilt buttons on the white only.

Since the insignia and devices provided for yacht clubs differ from those prescribed for the U. S. P. S., it is evident that certain breaches of etiquette are possible by wearing, at one time, articles associated with two different organizations. This might be compared to wearing two socks which were not mates, or one brown left shoe with a black right one, or displaying at the masthead of one's boat an officer's flag, though the burgee at the bow identifies a club of which the boat owner is a member, but not an officer.

For example, fouled anchors belong on the yachting cap of an amateur yachtsman, the member of a yacht club. But in the center of these anchors belong, not the U. S. P. S. insignia, but that of the yacht club of which the individual is a member.

Again, the sleeve braid with trefoil identifies the amateur yachtsman-member of a club. U. S. P. S. merit marks on the same sleeve are definitely improper.

The key to correct practice, of course, is to wear the insignia of only one organization at a time. And, naturally, avoid the display of any insignia to which you are not entitled.

Paid Hands

We are not concerned here directly with the clothing and insignia worn by paid officers and crew. Suffice it to say that proper uniforms are prescribed for dress, service and work. There are essential differences which distinguish the officer or paid member of the crew from the captain-owner. No trefoils appear on the sleeve of a paid hand. Nor should amateur yachtsmen ever have the name of their craft spelled out upon jerseys or other articles of clothing. Such names may or may not appear on the jerseys of paid seamen. Paid hands such as deck officers, engineers, radio operators and doctors have cap devices with various emblems surrounded by rope or circle of gold bullion. The deck officer, for example, has a pair of crossed anchors (not fouled) within the circle, the engineer a propeller, etc.

The dress uniform of a paid deck or engineer officer includes a double-breasted sack coat of dark navy blue cloth or serge with gilt buttons and trousers and waistcoat of the same material. White dress uniforms are of bleached duck or drill, same pattern as the black suit, but no waistcoat. Black ties are worn by all officers. Double-breasted blue bridge coats worn by deck officers are the same as those worn in the Navy. The blue cap is of dark navy blue cloth with band of mohair braid, black patent leather visor and chin strap. The white cap is the same as the blue, with removable top.

Proper uniforms are prescribed for the steward's department and for seamen, and cap and sleeve ornaments are covered by regulations.

Having read all of the above, one might gather the impression that most boatmen own a wardrobe full of uniforms and never relax in anything less formal. That, however, is not at all true. While the formal occasions mentioned contribute in large measure to the general good fellowship and enjoyment found in yachting circles, if the sport were ever to lose as its basic idea a freedom from the restraint of shore-going conventions, it would very rapidly lose some of its chief virtues, along with many of its adherents.

Informal Clothing

FOR informal use white ducks, gray or tan flannel trousers, and slacks in a variety of colors have all found widespread popularity. Even the shorts and bathing suits, condemned by polite society, have their place where the privacy of free and easy life afloat warrant their use. Slacks and flannels permit a reasonable latitude in choice of clothing appropriate for the season and temperature of the day. Suitable sport shirts are available in a variety of materials. When the cooler days of Fall come along, flannel shirts and warm woolen sweaters are in order.

Blue denim trousers, slacks style and suitably tailored, are available at some of the better outfitters. They make available also a blue denim jacket which completes the outfit. The material is soft and of medium weight and entirely appropriate for all-around informal hard wear afloat.

The yachtsman who is particular to wear the correct style of yachting cap on formal occasions may often go hatless in the Summer time. However, the sun is strong on the water and protection of some kind for head and eyes is often necessary, which probably gives rise to the fairly prevalent custom of wearing the yachting cap when other necessary adjuncts of the properly complete uniform are left in the locker.

Especially among the sailing fraternity a white cloth hat with wide brim all around, often green underneath or with green transparent visor, is popular. Sport fishermen have adopted an idea that originated down east among the lobstermen and sword fishermen. They use a lightweight cloth cap with disproportionately long visor that is an excellent sunshade, protecting the eyes from direct sun glare. If you wear it, you run the risk of having someone accuse you of trying to affect a salty appearance—but then, you will never be able to satisfy everybody, anyway.

Sun glasses are widely used afloat to prevent eye strain from sun glare. Of these, Polaroid glasses are among the best as they are scientifically designed for just this purpose.

Shoes, till recently, presented quite a problem. In the first place, a shoe that cannot be relied upon to give you a sure skidproof footing on a wet or slippery varnished deck, is a total loss on a boat. Coupled with that is the necessity of finding some type of sole and heel that will not scratch fine decks. Rubber and composition soles have been used on shoes for formal wear, but they should have a non-skid tread. Oxfords for formal use are available in black leather, patent leather, white canvas and white buckskin.

For all-around use afloat the best informal footwear available today is a sneaker with some kind of special sole that can be depended upon to give a grip on a wet, heeling deck. Sperry Topsiders, Kleets and Randy Boatshus might be mentioned among those types specially developed to provide better footing afloat. (While not in the realm of clothing, it may be appropriate to mention here that deck paints with non-skid features have also been developed.) Other footwear, such as moccasins, boots, rubbers, etc., are also available with non-skid tread.

Rope soles and sneakers with suction cup tread are often used for a better deck grip. Their value is enhanced if the tread is such that they cannot pick up grit and cinders when worn ashore, to be tracked back on the decks when returning to the boat. Ordinary sneakers are all right afloat, but never with a smooth sole. On a wet deck they are treacherous, to say the least. Crepe-soled footgear, though comfortable, is in the same category.

Wet weather clothing is essential afloat. You may have a closed-in deckhouse for protection while under way, but there are occasions when you must go on deck, nevertheless, to pick up a mooring, make fast to a dock or handle an anchor. Oilskin slickers and sou'westers are the traditional heavy weather garments, but they have a shortcoming in that sooner or later they become hopelessly gummed up, due to the nature of the waterproofing used.

Slickers of rubber, black or white, do not have that propensity to get gummed up. Then, too, in recent years a great variety of lightweight waterproof garments have been developed for yachtsmen and sportsmen. Generally these are a light waterproofed fabric like balloon cloth or cotton. Garments of this kind are available in coat form, either long or short. Some have hoods attached, others are in the form of a waterproof coverall shirt, excellent for fishing.

Special parka-style coats with hood attached are made for yachtsmen, where warmth and light weight, with wind- and water-resistant qualities, are prime requisites. These are made of soft waterproof canvas, backed up with a blanket-like pure wool lining, and will not gum up.

Summing up, then, in response to this question of what to wear afloat, it would seem reasonable that, if the occasion requires the use of a uniform, then the uniform should be correct in detail, according to tradition and the regulations established by better clubs to govern its use. If, on the other hand, the clothing is being chosen for informal wear, comfort and utility will be major considerations. However, if you happen to see some yachtsman wearing gray flannels with his blue uniform coat, there is no use getting too excited about it—you'll see plenty more. A surprising number of them are mighty good yachtsmen—even if the trousers don't match the coat.

YACHT CLUB COMMISSIONING CEREMONIES

The proper procedure for the Annual Going into Commission Ceremony of a yacht club is an important one not always correctly followed by many yacht clubs. The Fleet Captain of the Manhasset Bay Yacht Club, in charge of the Going into Commission Ceremony of that club, worked out a procedure which was both proper and dignified. It is listed below:

Note for M.B.Y.C. Officers and Trustees: Uniform for the Day will be blue yachting jacket and either (1) blue trousers with black shoes and black tie, or (2) white trousers with white shoes and black tie. Caps will not be worn during the ceremony.

1. Color Guard should arrive at 4:30 p.m. (E.D.S.T.) Saturday, May 15, 1954 at Manhasset Bay Yacht Club, Main Street, Port Washington, N. Y. Officer-in-charge should contact the Club's Fleet Captain on arrival.

2. The Color Guard will take a position as shown in the accompanying chart at 4:55 p.m.

3. At 4:55 p.m. the Bugler will sound "first call" in succession at: (1) Club entrance facing parking lot, (2) Inside Club House half way up stairway, and (3) Club terrace in formation position.

4. At 4:55 p.m. the Officers, Trustees and Visiting Flag Officers will form in positions as shown on accompanying chart.

5. Bugler will sound "fall in" and all will come to attention.

6. Color Guard will march to flag mast. Cadet-in-charge will take Ensign halyard with Ensign ready to hoist. Other cadets will take burgee, Union Jack and Commodore's flag ready to hoist. The flags and halyards will be laid out previously by the Dock Captain.

7. The Dock Captain will have men ready to hoist the code flag dress halyards. He will man the signal gun.

8. The Fleet Chaplain will bless the fleet.

9. At conclusion of the Blessing, the Cadet-in-charge of the Color Guard will signal the Dock Captain to fire the gun.

10. The orchestra will play the National Anthem, during which the four flags will be hoisted to their respective raised positions, followed by the hoisting of the code-flags.

11. When the National Anthem is finished and all flags are raised, the Color Guard will march to its formation position.

12. The Cadet-in-charge will report to the Fleet Captain that the Manhasset Bay Yacht Club is now in commission.

13. Color Guard dismissed by Cadet-in-charge and formation disbands.

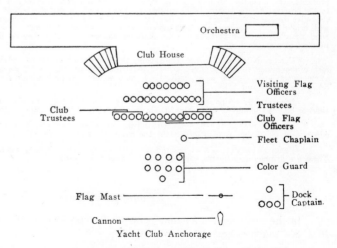

Formation for Commissioning Manhasset Bay Yacht Club

THE log book is the official record of your boat's cruise. The data therein forms an important accessory to piloting as well, not only on the particular cruise in question but for all other trips over the same or approximately the same routes. The data recorded in the log book also may be a contribution to the general fund of knowledge concerning waters used for motor-boat cruising; therefore, the facts and figures entered in the log book should be accurate and conclusive. In the case of large sea-going vessels the entries in the log are frequently referred to as evidence in legal actions.

While there are numerous forms of log books available, most of these are not well suited for motorboat use; rather, they are designed to meet the needs of larger vessels. The log sheet shown with this chapter has been designed especially to meet the needs of both small and large cruising boats whose owners are interested in coastwise cruising and proper piloting. The column headings are self-explanatory and may be kept as completely as desired.

In Column B the names of the important marks, buoys, aids to navigation, etc., which are passed on one's cruise are entered and the time of passing same is listed opposite each in Column A with the distance off in Column E.

The next three columns are used for listing the courses to the next object which is to be passed. If one is dealing in "true" compass courses this data is listed in Column H. If magnetic courses are preferred these should be entered in

CHAPTER XXV

Keep a Log

Column G with the courses corrected for the variation and deviation of the boat's own compass in Column F and the distance to the next objective in Column I. A deviation table for the boat's compass should be available so that it will be possible to determine the compass course from the magnetic course.

The data for columns J and M should be worked out from the chart and listed in advance of starting the cruise or at least before starting on the particular leg of the run in question.

The actual rpm of the motor should be listed in Column J. If the rpms are changed, the time of so changing should be recorded by using a new line on the log sheet.

Column K is for the estimated speed that the boat is making over the bottom which is a far different thing than her speed through the water. This is where the Skipper's real ability and knowledge of his own boat begin to come in. It considers such data as rpm of the motor, direction and force of the wind, set and drift of the current, and condition of the sea, and of course the load which the boat is carrying, condition of her underbody, etc., etc. Experience only can teach one how to apply these varying factors as they affect each boat differently, but constant observation of them will make a Skipper very adept in a short time.

Naturally before one starts on a cruise he has determined his boat's speed at different rpms of the motor. He has become familiar with the tide and current tables published by the government and can determine the effect of a tidal current on a boat's course. The amount which the wind and waves help or retard a boat on her course is something which must also be determined by experience. But this is valuable information and the cruising man should take time to gather all possible data on this subject.

From the Column I and Column K data it will be easy to compute the time which the boat should be abeam of the next object, Column M. Calculate the data for Column M with greatest accuracy and care. It is important especially in the fog or should fog shut down on you after you have made your departure from the last object. The safety of your boat and crew may depend upon how carefully you have worked this out.

The actual time on the course, Column N, is simply the difference between the clock time when you are actually

TABLE I

CLOUD FORMATIONS AND SYMBOLS

CIRRUS, (Ci.)—Detached clouds, delicate and fibrous looking, taking the form of feathers, generally of a white color, sometimes arranged in belts which cross a portion of the sky in great circles, and, by an effect of perspective, converging toward one or two opposite points of the horizon.

CIRRO-STRATUS, (Ci.-S.)—A thin, whitish sheet, sometimes completely covering the sky and only giving it a whitish appearance, or at others presenting, more or less distinctly, a formation like a tangled web. This sheet often produces halos around the sun and moon.

CIRRO-CUMULUS, (Ci.-Cu.)—Small globular masses or white flakes, having no shadows, or only very slight shadows, arranged in groups and often in lines.

ALTO-CUMULUS, (A.-Cu.)—Rather large globular masses, white or grayish, partially shaded, arranged in groups or lines, and often so closely packed that their edges appear confused. The detached masses are generally larger and more compact at the center of the group; at the margin they form into finer flakes. They often spread themselves out in lines in one or two directions.

ALTO-STRATUS, (A.-S.)—A thick sheet of a gray or bluish color, showing a brilliant patch in the neighborhood of the sun or moon, and which, without causing halos, may give rise to coronœ. This form goes through all the changes like the Cirro-Stratus, but its altitude is only half so great.

STRATO-CUMULUS, (S.-Cu.)—Large globular masses or rolls of dark cloud, frequently covering the whole sky, especially in winter, and occasionally giving it a wavy appearance. The layer of Strato-Cumulus is not, as a rule, very thick, and patches of blue sky are often visible through the intervening spaces. All sorts of transitions between this form and the Alto-Cumulus are noticeable. It may be distinguished from Nimbus by its globular or rolled appearance and also because it does not bring rain.

NIMBUS, (N.)—Rain clouds; a thick layer of dark clouds, without shape and with ragged edges, from which continued rain or snow generally falls. Through the openings of these clouds an upper layer of Cirro-Stratus or Alto-Stratus may almost invariably be seen. If the layer of Nimbus separates into shreds or if small loose clouds are visible floating at a low level underneath a large Nimbus, they may be described as Fracto-Nimbus (Fr.-N.), the "scud" of sailors.

CUMULUS, (Cu.)—Woolpack clouds; thick clouds of which the upper surface is domeshaped and exhibits protuberances, while the base is horizontal. When these clouds are opposite the sun the surfaces usually presented to the observer have a greater brilliance than the margins of the protuberances. When the light falls aslant, they give deep shadows; when, on the contrary, the clouds are on the same side as the sun, they appear dark, with bright edges. The true Cumulus has clear superior and inferior limits. It is often broken up by strong winds, and the detached portions undergo continual changes. These may be distinguished by the name of Fracto-Cumulus (Fr.-Cu.).

CUMULO-NIMBUS, (Cu.-N.)—The thunder-cloud or shower-cloud; heavy masses of clouds rising in the form of mountains, turrets, or anvils, generally having a sheet or screen of fibrous appearance above, and a mass of clouds similar to Nimbus underneath. From the base there usually fall local showers of rain or of snow (occasionally hail or soft hail).

STRATUS, (S.)—A horizontal sheet of lifted fog; when this sheet is broken up into irregular shreds by the wind or by the summits of mountains, it may be distinguished by the name of Fracto-Stratus (Fr.-S.).

FRACTO-STRATUS, (Fr.-S.)—A horizontal sheet of lifted fog broken into irregular shreds by wind or the summits of mountains, is distinguished by the name of Fracto-Stratus (Fr.-S.).

FRACTO-CUMULUS, (Fr.-Cu.)—Cumulus, when broken up by strong winds, undergo continual changes. These are distinguished by the name of Fracto-Cumulus (Fr.-Cu.).

Amount of Clouds

In the scale for the amount of clouds 0 represents a sky which is cloudless and 10 a sky which is completely overcast.

Table I, which describes various cloud formations. Amount of clouds is recorded by figures from 0 to 10

TABLE II — MODIFIED BEAUFORT WIND SCALE

Code Figure	Beaufort's Scale	Effect on Sea	Velocity (Knots)	Terms Used in U. S. Weather Bureau Forecasts
0	CALM	Sea like a mirror	Less than 1	Calm
1	LIGHT AIR	Ripples—no foam crests	1–3	Light
2	LIGHT BREEZE	Small wavelets, crests have a glassy appearance and do not break	4–6	Do.
3	GENTLE BREEZE	Large wavelets, crests begin to break. Scattered whitecaps	7–10	Gentle
4	MODERATE BREEZE	Small waves becoming longer. Frequent whitecaps	11–16	Moderate
5	FRESH BREEZE	Moderate waves, taking a more pronounced long form; many white-caps, some spray	17–21	Fresh
6	STRONG BREEZE	Large waves begin to form; extensive whitecaps everywhere, some spray	22–27	Strong
7	MODERATE GALE	Sea heaps up and white foam from breaking waves begins to be blown in streaks along the direction of the wind	28–33	Do.
8	FRESH GALE	Moderately high waves of greater length; edges of crests break into spindrift. The foam is blown in well-marked streaks along the direction of the wind	34–40	Do.
9	STRONG GALE	High waves. Dense streaks of foam along the direction of the wind. Spray may affect visibility. Sea begins to roll	41–47	Gale
10	WHOLE GALE	Very high waves. The surface of the sea takes on a white appearance. The rolling of the sea becomes heavy and shocklike. Visibility is affected	48–55	Do.
11	STORM	Exceptionally high waves. Small and medium sized ships are lost to view for long periods	56–63	Whole Gale
12	HURRICANE	The air is filled with foam and spray. Sea completely white with driving spray; visibility very seriously affected	64–71	Hurricane
13	HURRICANE		72–80	Do.
14	HURRICANE		81–89	Do.
15	HURRICANE		90–99	Do.
16	HURRICANE		100–109	Do.
17	HURRICANE		110–118	Do.

abeam of the object and the entry in Column A. The actual speed, Column O, is also easily computed from Columns I and N, after reaching the object. By comparing the entries in Columns K and O, or Columns L and N, the Skipper will know how good he has been in estimating the effect of the many varying factors on the speed of his boat. In estimating the time he should be at the next object, Column M, he can make due allowance for the amount which his estimate was in error.

The data to be entered at the bottom are physical observations which are worth recording from time to time. Tables I, II, IV and V give a convenient code for listing such data. Data on the estimated set and drift of the current can be obtained from the government current tables.

As an illustration of the proper keeping of the log we will consider a cruise made on Long Island Sound, July 4, from Manhasset Bay, N. Y., to New London, Connecticut, a distance of about 100 miles. Data on the speed of the boat is shown in Table VII and the deviation on easterly and northerly courses in Table VI.

We elect to run our motor at 1400 rpm which gives us a boat speed of exactly 10 miles per hour through the water. We take our departure from Gangway bell buoy number 27 off the entrance to Manhasset Bay at exactly noon, Eastern Standard Time. Our tide table shows us that it will be high water at nearby Willets Pt. at 1242. There is a fresh westerly wind blowing which we estimate to be about 15 miles per hour. This wind is nearly directly astern of us and it kicks up quite a chop. The sky overhead is cloudless, the barometer reads 30.22 and the thermometer 80 degrees.

We elect to run down the Sound, keeping close to the north shore of Long Island until we reach Orient Shoal and then cruise diagonally across the Sound to the entrance of the Thames River. This route will be a little longer than if we should go down the center of the Sound, yet we will be in sight of land at all times with many aids to navigation available as a check on our position should fog shut down on us.

Previous to the start of our cruise we have drawn the courses we are to follow on Coast and Geodetic Survey charts numbers

Table II, which supplies data concerning the force of wind and described in various commonly used forms

1211, 1212 and 1213. We have made these courses pass close to a number of fixed aids to navigation so that the greatest distance between marks is less than 15 miles. We have scaled the distance between the various marks and have entered this data in Columns B and I, with the distance off when abeam in Column E. In scaling from these charts, we do it in nautical miles as there is no statute mile scale on the charts. We convert statute miles by multiplying the distances in nautical miles by 1.15.

In advance, we have also calculated the various magnetic courses between marks and have listed these in Column G, and have applied the deviation of our compass, Table VI, to get our compass courses which we have listed in Column F.

From the known speeds of our boat, Table VII, it should now be an easy matter to determine in advance the time we should be abeam of each of the marks listed in Column B, except for two major conditions which we can not forecast in advance. While we do know that we are going to take our departure from Gangway bell at 1200 on July fourth, yet we have no way of determining in advance what the direction of the wind or condition of the sea will be on that day. Both of these elements might help or retard our progress.

They should always be taken into account, insofar as possible.

The other condition which might develop to change any pre-arranged time schedule is fog. While we have decided to run our motor at 1400 rpm, which gives us a boat speed of 10 miles per hour, should fog shut in on us, the law requires, and safety makes it essential, that we slow down. So if fog comes, our motor will be run at 1000 rpm which is equivalent to a boat speed of 8 miles per hour.

A bad blow might also make it necessary to cut down our engine speed but at this season of the year this is unlikely. On the other hand should head winds be met, the engine might be speeded up slightly to keep our boat speed at 10 miles an hour.

Yet in spite of these unknowns of wind, sea and fog it would

TRIP NO. 14 ...... CRUISE FROM Manhasset Bay...... to ...New London...... DATE ..July 4..

NAMES, ADDRESS, AND TITLES OF GUESTS ABOARD: Mate: W.H.Koelbel, Deckhand: Dan Schroder, George Rupprecht.

Guests: W.F.Bailey, Marybelle Johnson, Ruth B.Smith,

CLOCK TIME (A)	PLACE ABEAM BUOY, LANDMARK OR VESSEL PASSED (B)	TO PORT OR STARBOARD (C)	COMPASS BEARING TO PLACE ABEAM (D)	DISTANCE OFF MILES (E)	COURSE STEERED (F)	MAGNETIC (G)	TRUE (H)	DISTANCE MILES	MOTOR R.P.M. (J)	ESTIMATED SPEED M.P.H. (K)	ESTIMATED TIME TO NEXT OBJECTIVE (L)	SHOULD BE ABEAM NEXT OBJECTIVE AT (M)	ACTUAL TIME BETWEEN OBJECTIVES (N)	ACTUAL SPEED BETWEEN OBJECTIVES (O)	SOUNDING DEPTH (P)	SOUNDING BOTTOM (Q)	REMARKS (R)
12 00	Gangway Bell #27	S	0		051	045		1.3	1400	9.68	8	12 08	8	9.68			
12 08	Execution Light	P			079	079		5.75	"	9.72	35	12 43	34	10.12			
12 42	Matinicock Bell #21	S	0		079	079		8.6	"	10.16	51	13 34	51	10.10			
13 33	Lloyds Bell #15	S	0		084	090		4.6	"	10.4	28	14 02	28	10.28			
14 01	Eatons Point Can #13	S	.25		092	098		14.4	"	10.16	1:25	15 27	1:25	10.18			
15 26	Old Field Point, Gong 11a	S	.3N		092	098		8.05	"	10.25	47	16 14	48	10.05			
16 14	Black Can #9	S	0		092	098		7.3	"	10.50	42	16 56	44	9.96			
16 58	Herod Point Shoal Can #7	S	.3N		092	098		6.3	"	10.50	36	17 32	37	10.20			Dirt in fuel
17 35	Roanoke Shoal Can #5	S	0		079	079		14.6	"	10.65	1:22	18 54	1:22	10.68			Rain
18 57	Hortons Point Light	S	.7N		071	063		7.3	"	10.0	42	19 36	54	9.94			
19 41	Orient Point Shoal Can #3	S	.6N		071	068		12.8	"	9.0	1:25	21 01	28	8.72	65	sft	Mist
21 09	Bartletts Reef Whistle #2A	P	0		071	068		3.35	1000	8.65	23	21 24	38	5.29	45	sft	Mist to fog
21 47	Sarah Ledge Gong	P	0		019	011		3.05	1000	10.00	18	21 42	29	6.32			Fog
22 16	New London, Burr's Dock	P							1400								

FUEL: In Tanks at Start 100 galls. ... Took Aboard ...... At Finish 20 galls Used 80

FRESH WATER: In Tanks at Start 50 galls. ... Took Aboard ...... In Tanks at Finish 42 galls.

RUNNING LIGHTS: Lit at 19 40 ... Extinguished at 22 20 ... Time 12 20. Wind. Force 4. Direction W.

HIGH WATER (time) 12 42 at (place) Willetts Point. ... DAY'S RUN 97.60 +3.5 miles ... Current: Set S.W. Drift (+ or -) m.p.h. 0.32 State of Sea 6

LOW WATER (time) 17 30 at (place) New London. ... TOTAL CRUISE RUN ...... miles ... Weather b. Clouds 0. Visibility ...... miles

OWNER F.W.Horenburger. ... Barometer 30.22 Temperature 80°

378

be well to work out in advance the expected time of arrival at the various points and enter this data in Column M. Then as we proceed down the Sound slight adjustments in these times may be made to correct for any of these conditions unknown at the present moment. Such necessary changes should be small under normal conditions.

But before we can pre-determine these times of passing the various points there is just one more variable which must be taken into consideration—the tides and currents. The current may have a great effect on our speed. But fortunately the Government supplies us with sufficient data on currents to permit us to pretty accurately estimate their effect on our speed. It's a fascinating subject so we will now figure in advance what the effect of the tidal current all the way down the Sound should be on our boat and then later, while we are underway, we'll see how good our estimates have been.

Since we are operating on Eastern Standard Time we can use the times in the Current Tables directly. We find that the Current Diagrams of Long Island Sound refer to the conditions existing in The Race, Long Island Sound, and the two periods of the current cycle listed in tabular form are headed "Slack Flood Begins," and "Slack Ebb Begins."

The tidal current charts are lithographed reproductions showing by means of lines, arrows, and figures, the story of the current for every hour of a complete twelve-hour cycle. A separate chart is printed for each hour and these are referenced to the stage of the cycle called Slack Flood Begins and Slack Ebb Begins, which are tabulated.

Slack Flood Begins as per current diagrams is at 0722 on July 4 and since we plan to start at noon we can use as our first chart the one headed "Five Hours After Slack Flood Begins at The Race." While this is actually 22 minutes later than our schedule we can, for all practical purposes, ignore that one-third hour difference. As a matter of actual fact there would be a barely perceptible difference in the vicinity of Execution Light, although nearer The Race where currents are much stronger than at Gangway Bell. Since we are not concerned with the conditions existing there at the moment we will not worry about it now.

Our first course to Execution Light is 045 degrees and the drift is found to be 0.4 knot and the set practically 225 degrees, or directly opposing our progress. On the inside cover of our Tidal Current Charts appears a correction table which gives a factor by which current velocities are to be multiplied to suit the conditions on any one cycle of the tide. Our maximum predicted flood velocity is 2.9 knots, and the maximum ebb 3.3 knots. The table indicates that for 2.9 knots flood we apply a correction factor which, in this case, happens to be 0.7. Therefore, every current figure which we shall use throughout must be multiplied by 0.7 to give its correct value for the day and time and then by 1.15 to convert to statute miles.

Similarly, on July fourth the time 1314 is given as the Slack Ebb Begins. We can reference all of the rest of our problems to that figure. We find also that the maximum ebb is at 1623 and the predicted velocity on that particular flow is 3.3 knots.

Now, going back to the 0.4 knot found in our first course, we apply 0.7 and se-

cure 0.28 knot and since we are doing all of our problems in statute miles, this turns out to be 0.32 mile against us. Our unit speed of 10 miles will accordingly be reduced to 9.68 miles. In order to learn how long a period of time will be required to cover a distance of 1.30 miles we can apply a formula involving time, speed, and distance in various ways so that any one factor can be found when the other two are known.

Elapsed time = Seconds in an hour multiplied by distance and divided by speed

$$\text{or} \quad \frac{3{,}600 \times 1.3}{9.68} = 8 \text{ minutes } 03 \text{ seconds}$$

therefore, the time required to reach Execution Rock will be 8 minutes. We can discard the seconds as being ultra precise which, after all, is not required. To solve for the other factors in the formula it may be rewritten as follows:

Speed = seconds in an hour multiplied by distance, and divided by the elapsed time in seconds

or: Distance = Elapsed time in seconds multiplied by speed (mph) and divided by seconds in hour.

With these three formulas the problem can be solved in any of its variations. It may also be applied by using minutes instead of seconds, but this has the disadvantage of giving results in minutes and decimals of a minute, which is a less convenient unit. While these formulas have been introduced to indicate the method of solving the time and speed problems, it is very much simpler to locate a table which gives the speed in miles per hour for any reasonable combination of minutes and seconds for a mile. A simple multiplication will then give the time for greater distances. Further times and speeds in this problem will, therefore, be taken from such a table.

We can continue the same current diagram for about one hour. For the second course, to Matinicock bell buoy number 21, our distance by chart is 5.75 miles and we find that on this run two current figures apply, one of 0.4 knot and one of 0.3 knot. Using a mean of 0.35 and multiplying by the correction factor of 0.7 and by 1.15 to reduce to statute miles we get 0.28 mile opposed. Our net speed, therefore, will be 9.72 mph. From

TABLE III

STANDARD ABBREVIATIONS USED ON CHARTS

Relating to Lights

Lt. Light, L.H. Lighthouse, REF. Reflector, F Fixed, Occ Occulting, Fl Flashing, QK Fl Quick Flashing, I Qk Interrupted Quick, Alt Alternating, Gp Occ Group Occulting, Gp Fl Group Flashing, S-L Short-long, F Fl Fixed and flashing, F Gp Fl Fixed and group flashing, Rot. rotating, min. minutes, sec. seconds, M. nautical mile, Gp. group, SEC. sector, Vi. violet, Bu. Blue, G. green, Or. orange, R. red, W. white, Am. amber, OBSC. obscured, (U) unwatched, Occas. occasional, Irreg. irregular, Temp. temporary, Vert. vertical, Hor. horizontal, D destroyed, Exting. extinguished, V.B. vertical beam, Exper. experimental, R. range, AERO aeronautical.

Relating to Buoys and Beacons

C Can, N Nun, Sp Spherical, S Spar, Quar. Quarantine, Priv. maintd. Maintained by private interests, H.B. Horizontal bands, V.S. Vertical stripes, Chec. checkered, W. white, B. black, R. red, Y. yellow, G. green, Br. brown, Gy. gray, T.B. temporary buoy, Bn. beacon, REF. Reflector.

Relating to Fog Signals

Fog Sig. Fog signal station, SUB-BELL Submarine fog bell, SUB-OSC. Submarine oscillator, NAUTO. Nautophone, DIA. Diaphone, SIREN

Fog siren, HORN Fog trumpet or fog horn, BELL Fog bell, WHIS. Fog whistle, REED Reed horn, D.F.S. Distance finding station, GUN Fog gun.

Relating to Bottoms

Grd. ground, S. sand, M. mud, Oz. ooze, Ml. marl, Cl. Clay, G. gravel, Sh. shingle, P. pebbles, St. stones, Sp. specks, Rk. rock, Bld. boulder, Ck. chalk, Qz quartz, Co. coral, Co. Hd. coral head, Md. madrepore, Vol. Ash. volcanic ash, La, lava, Pm. pumice, T. tufa, Sc. scorice, Cn. cinders, Mn. manganese, Sh. shells, Oys. oysters, Ms. mussels, Spg. sponge, Grs. grass, Wd. weeds, Fr. foraminifera, Gl. globigerina, Di. diatom, Rd. radiolaria, Pt. pteropod, Po. polyzoa, fne. fine, crs. coarse, sft. soft, hrd. hard, stf. stiff, sml. small, lrg. large, stk. sticky, brk. broken, rky. rocky, spk. speckled, gry. gritty, fly. flinty, glac. glacial, wh. white, bk. black, bu. blue, gn. green, yl. yellow, rd. red, br. brown, gy. gray, lt. light, dk. dark, Ca. calcareous.

Relating to Dangers

Bk. bank, Shl. Shoal, Rf. reef, Le. ledge, Obstr. obstruction, Wk. wreck, Wks. wreckage, cov. covers, uncov. uncovers, Rep. reported, Discol, discolored, P.A. position approximate, P.D. position doubtful, E.D. existence doubtful, Pos. position. .

When examining a chart we find symbols used which abbreviate features of the lights, buoys, fog signals and nature of bottom

our table we find this is equivalent to 370 seconds per mile. For 5.75 miles. therefore, 2127 seconds or 35 minutes 27 seconds to cover the 5.75 miles, giving the predicted time of 1243.

<table>
<tr><td colspan="2" align="center">TABLE IV
STATE OF SEA SYMBOLS</td></tr>
</table>

TABLE IV
STATE OF SEA SYMBOLS

State of Sea—The state of the sea is expressed by the following system of symbols:

B. — Broken or irregular sea.	M. — Moderate sea or swell.
C. — Choppy, short, or cross sea.	R. — Rough sea.
G. — Ground swell.	S. — Smooth sea.
H. — Heavy sea.	T. — Tide-rips *
L. — Long rolling sea.	

* Tide-rips—Agitation of the surface water caused by the tide passing swiftly over a shoal.

We have still not run out of our first chart of current diagrams which we have been using so continue our computations in the same manner. The current strength is falling so that our speed will not be retarded as strongly for we are approaching the slack water condition and soon will find the current helping us. On the run to Lloyds of 8.6 miles, which will consume more than 50 minutes, we pass out of the first hour and must use the next current diagram sheet headed "Slack Ebb Begins at The Race." Here we find that somewhere between the two charts we have passed through the slack period of the tide. At the start of the leg a current of minus 0.3 gradually stops and runs the other way with greater strength of plus 0.5. We assume, therefore, that a mean of these helped us throughout and our speed has picked up to 10.16 miles, after applying correction factors. This is equivalent to 354 seconds per mile, for 8.6 miles or a total of 3044 seconds, equal to 50 minutes 44 seconds. We are due at Lloyds bell, therefore, at 1334.

The next course carries us to the can buoy off Eaton's Point, a distance of 4.8 miles. Our first estimate of speed indicates about 29 minutes so the Slack Ebb Begins diagram still applies. Our course has changed to 090 degrees and the current set inshore is approximately 090 degrees also. Notice that near shore the current runs counter to the main axis of the Sound. The figure 0.5 knot can reasonably be assumed to apply throughout and this becomes when translated to miles and corrected 0.4 mile. Our speed, therefore, will be 10.4 miles. This requires 346 seconds per mile or for 4.8 miles, a total of 1661 seconds or 27 minutes 41 seconds, say 28 minutes. We are due at Eaton's at 1402.

The next run is a long one, 14.40 miles to the black gong buoy off Old Field Point. The currents on this run are favorable but weak. No definite figures appear, so that we must estimate the probable strength. Further out in the Sound it seems to be about 0.4 knot or slightly more. On our second course we can perhaps estimate a strength of 0.2 knot, which we shall do. This corrected current equals only 0.16 mile, so our speed is computed at 10.16 mph. This is equivalent to 354 seconds per mile or 5098 seconds total equal to 1 hour and 25 minutes. We have progressed thus far in our journey to beyond Old Field Point and by now the time has advanced so that we can use the chart for "Two Hours After Slack Ebb Begins at The Race." Our next course, 098 degrees, carries us to black can number 9 near Rocky Point. A weak current which may be estimated at perhaps 0.3 knot or 0.25 mile helps us and for the next forty odd minutes we will be in it. For our speed 10.25 miles, we require 351 seconds per mile or 2826 seconds or 47 minutes for this leg of 8.05 miles. This brings us to 1614 and we must, therefore, use the "Three Hours After Slack Ebb Begins" diagram for the next hour.

The distance to Herod Point Shoal, can number 7, is 7.30 miles. The current strength along the course selected is about 0.6 knot equivalent when corrected to 0.48 mile, let's say 0.5 mile favorable. Our speed then is 10.5 miles or 343 seconds per mile. It will require 2504 seconds or 41 minutes 44 seconds for the leg, so we set our time down as 42 minutes more, which brings us to Herod Point at 1656. A short run of 6.30 miles

to Roanoke Shoal, can number 5, can be figured at the same current strength and the data for this run works out to be 36 minutes required, due at 1732. At this buoy our courses are changed to a more northerly direction to keep more or less parallel to the shore to Horton's Point. While the light itself is on the shore, our course is laid to a point 0.7 mile offshore. We advance to the next current chart, the one called "Four Hours After Slack Ebb Begins" and while current strengths inshore are only about half of what they are further out in the stream our preference of course keeps us closer to shore. No figures are given along the projected line of our course. The figure 0.6 appears off Roanoke Point, but the figures offshore are greater, running to 1–2 knots. The great volume of water in the Sound is flowing out through the narrower channels of The Race where the current really flows fast. It is safe to assume, therefore, that the strength here will be somewhat greater than 0.6 so let us assume 0.8 knot which in miles is 0.65 mile. Our speed, therefore, is 10.65 miles and will require 338 seconds per mile or a total of 4935 seconds, one hour and 22 minutes, so that we will be abeam of Horton's Point at 1854.

Our next leg takes us to can number 3 off Orient Shoal. We notice that we have now passed out of the scope of the tidal diagram we have been using and since our current tables give us the fact that Slack Flood Begins is at 1922, we accordingly turn to the first chart in the booklet and regard that as being the conditions existing at 1922. We have laid out our cruise only as far as Horton's Point and during the run to Orient Point will be in the conditions indicated. We notice now that the current is no longer favorable but opposed to our progress. And since we are at the edge of the current strength and also some few minutes ahead of the current time of the chart, we can assume slack water for this course and figure our speed at 10 miles without allowances of any kind. The distance of 7.05 miles is accordingly covered in 42 minutes 18 seconds at the rate of 360 seconds per mile, which brings us to Orient Point at 1936.

TABLE V
WEATHER SYMBOLS

Weather—To designate the weather a series of symbols devised by the late Admiral Beaufort is employed. The system is as follows:

b. — Clear blue sky.	r. — Rainy weather, or continuous rain.
d. — Drizzling, or light rain.	
f. — Fog, or foggy weather.	s. — Snow, snowy or snow falling.
g. — Gloomy, or stormy-looking.	
h. — Hail.	t. — Thunder.
l. — Lightning.	
m. — Misty weather.	u. — Ugly appearances or threatening weather.
p. — Passing showers of rain.	w. — Wet, or heavy dew.
q. — Squally weather.	z. — Hazy.

To indicate great intensity of any feature its symbol may be underlined; thus, r., heavy rain.

The same diagram will serve further for the course to Bartlett's Reef bell. This is 12.8 miles distant and will take us about an hour and a quarter. By examining the next chart, "One Hour After Slack Flood Begins," we see that during the later part of this leg we will be opposed by stronger currents and for at least a part of the time by as much as 2.1 knots. The early parts of the run will be opposed by currents of 0.4 and 1.0 knot and, further, our course now will be somewhat diagonally through the current flow and no longer head on to it. We find 0.3, 1.0, 2.1 and 1.6; an average of these is 1.25, and in miles and corrected it is equal to 1.0 mile. Our course is 067 degrees and the set of the current is 270 degrees. We find that while there is a difference of about 22½ degrees in the directions there is not sufficient difference to alter the effect of the current and estimate that our speed throughout the run will be 9 miles—or 400 seconds per mile. For 12.80 miles we will require 5120 seconds or 1 hour 25 minutes and 20 seconds. We are due at Bartlett's Reef bell at 2101.

From Bartlett's to Sarah Ledge gong is 3.35 miles, and conditions on chart "Two Hours After Slack Flood Begins" apply. Current strength is given as 1.7 knots equivalent to 1.35 miles so that our speed will be reduced to 8.65 miles or 416 seconds per mile. For 3.35 miles this equals 1394 seconds or 23 minutes and 14 seconds. Our schedule will then show us due at Sarah Ledge at 2124 almost within sight of our destination. Our last leg will be a run of 3.05 miles up the Thames River to Burr's Landing in New London. Since the current in the river is weak, we again estimate our full 10-mile speed and find at 360 seconds per mile, we will consume 1098 seconds or 18 minutes 18 seconds to complete our journey. We should finish our trip at 2142 if everything goes as per schedule and there are no untoward events to delay or upset the schedule. Our time table is completed and our estimates all entered in the log. Remember that all of these studies have been made prior to our actual cruise of July 4. Wind, weather and uncertainty will now get in their good work and upset our calculations during the course of the cruise.

TABLE VI
DEVIATION OF COMPASS
(From Deviation Card)

Magnetic (Degrees)	Deviation (Degrees)
011	8W
045	6W
068	3W
079	0
090	6E
098	6E

Now let us carry out the keeping of the log during the course of our actual run and see how closely correct our estimates were. Our departure from Gangway bell is made at exactly 1200 as planned. We adjust our speed to 1400 revolutions and prepare to enjoy an exhilarating trip. A moderate westerly breeze and a slight chop lend zest to the action of the boat. Our revolutions are watched carefully and the mate is at the wheel while the skipper prepares to keep the log. The short run to Execution is made exactly on time. At the light we square away from the course down the Sound and find the wind more on the stern. The sun shines brightly so the cook and guests go up on the forward deck to catch some sun tan. The mate steers a careful course; due to the following sea this work requires close attention. Soon the bell off Matinicock appears and is sighted by the guests forward. At the time when it is abeam we find ourselves a minute ahead of schedule, having passed the buoy at 1242. This increase in speed is due to the effect of the following wind and sea. We notice the strength of wind is less and also that the sea is smoother. It is less difficult to steer and the motion of the boat is quieter. Lloyd's Bell appears and is passed at 1333, indicating that we are running closely to schedule, but are ahead by the minute gained in the first leg. The sea becomes quieter and the wind drops still more until soon it is gone and the water is calm. Before long Eaton's Point can appears which is passed at 1401 still one minute ahead of schedule. The mate has been steering for two hours and is now relieved by the skipper who takes over the wheel while the mate keeps the log.

A long run to Old Field Point, almost 14½ miles, is made without incident; the weather gets warmer as the temperature has gone up from 80 to 85 degrees. Before long the gong buoy off Old Field Point comes abeam and is left astern at 1526, still ahead of time. The wind is now coming in a bit more from the south and is so recorded. The course is still 098 degrees and for 8.05 miles to can number 9 near Rocky Point the cruise continues; we arrive there at 1614 and note we have lost the minute and are back on schedule. Apparently the allowance for current was too generous. Here the mate and skipper relieve each other again after a two hour trick at the wheel. We continue

toward can number 7 at Herod Point, course still the same, wind becoming noticeably stronger from the south and we notice a little sea making up. Since we are under the lee of the land it is not uncomfortable. We pass Herod Point can at 1658 and find we have lost still another minute. Wind has increased and we roll pretty heavily in the beam sea and notice that the engine no longer runs steadily. There are interruptions in its rhythm and soon it pops a couple of times and hesitates. The trouble is quickly diagnosed as foreign matter in the fuel and since the boat is equipped with dual gasoline strainers, the skipper goes below and switches the flow to the clean strainer and removes the sediment and dirt from the other. All is well again and we roll along, reaching Roanoke Shoal can 5 at 1735. We find we have lost further time due to the trouble with the fuel and further due to lack of attention to the steering while the engine was cutting up. The weather also has been clouding over and by now we have large masses of heavy cumulo-nimbus clouds. It has become hazy and squally so the oilskins have been brought out in anticipation of showers. The watch is changed again at 1800. While it has clouded over visibility has not been impaired and we make our Horton Point Light on shore. We are abeam of it at 1857, three minutes behind schedule, no doubt due to a lesser current strength than anticipated. It now starts to rain so oilers are put on. There is a moderate sea with a reduced wind, but still misty. Sunset at 1940 and running lights go on. Orient Shoal can 3 is difficult to find as it is getting dark, we are behind schedule by several minutes and it is still misty with reduced visibility. We finally find it at 1941 and are now 5 minutes behind our schedule.

TABLE VII
SPEED OF BOAT

R.P.M.	M.P.H.
1000	8.0
1100	8.5
1200	9.1
1300	9.6
1400	10.0
1500	10.9

The next run will take us diagonally across the Sound to Bartlett's Bell some 12.8 miles and almost an hour and a half further. The misty condition continues, although it is not yet sufficiently thick to require a reduction in speed. We are running more slowly due to the stronger current opposed to us and after relief at the wheel at 8 o'clock we find the cook has the evening meal ready. The course is held carefully and a watch is kept for the light on the buoy. We find a flashing white considerably to starboard of our course and change to examine it more closely. It turns out to be the steamer lane buoy which was on our plotted course but the current has headed us off to the westward more than we anticipated; we make a little greater allowance and at 2109 we are abeam of Bartlett's Reef flashing red whistle. We have lost still more time on our schedule and are now eight minutes behind. The mist is getting thicker and shortly becomes a genuine fog. We reduce our speed to 1000 revolutions and go ahead at 8 miles. Wind has eased off to easterly and very light so that the sea is calm and everything would be perfect except for the fog. We hold our course, but are uncertain as to the effect of the current which is setting us to the westward towards the reef. We decide to check our position and stop the engine so that we may take a sounding. Skipper takes the wheel while the mate makes a cast and reports almost eleven fathoms, 65 feet. We locate the point on our chart which agrees with this depth and once more resume our journey. (If a definite course or similar line of position is not available, a chain of soundings might be required.) Before long we find the gong buoy at Sarah's Ledge. We hear it and pick our way toward it by the sound of its several gongs which make it so easy to recognize. Slowing down and with time lost for sounding we are quite far behind schedule as it is now 2147.

Changing our course up the Thames River we soon lose sight of Sarah Ledge and still find ourselves in a dense fog. While holding our course at 1000 revolutions we are fairly certain of our position, but after some minutes 'on this course feel that it is advisable to obtain a check by another sounding. Once again the engine is stopped and a cast of the lead is made, this time showing only 45 feet, 7½ fathoms. We locate this spot on the chart and find that it checks with our course. We continue with more confidence and as we get up the river we find a slight lifting of the fog which permits us to locate Burr's dock, our destination. We arrive here at 2216 some 34 minutes behind our original schedule, tired and weary from the long journey and the difficulties of coming through the fog. Guests are rowed ashore and delivered to the taxi driver while the crew returns aboard to get a good night's rest. We observe that the schedule, as prepared in advance, was followed fairly closely until the fog shut in and delayed us. Currents were not always up to the strength anticipated and did not help as much as expected. It indicates, however, that close schedules are entirely practical and can be adhered to very closely in all normal weather conditions. Keeping a log forms one of the most interesting and educational features of cruising.

Table VIII (right), boat speed over a measured 1-mile course can be picked out by inspection. For example, if it takes 4 minutes and 19 seconds to run a statute mile (5280-foot) course, the boat's speed is 13.9 statute miles per hour. If the course were a nautical mile (6080 feet), the speed is 13.9 knots (nautical miles per hour). (The international nautical mile, recently adopted by the Coast Guard, is taken to be 6076.1 feet.)

TABLE I—SPEED OVER A MEASURED MILE

Sec.	1 min.	2 min.	3 min.	4 min.	5 min.	6 min.	7 min.	8 min.	9 mid.	10 min.	11 min.	12 min.
0	60.000	30.000	20.000	15.000	12.000	10.000	8.571	7.500	6.667	6.000	5.455	5.000
1	59.016	29.752	19.890	14.938	11.960	9.972	8.551	7.484	6.654	5.990	5.446	4.993
2	58.064	29.508	19.780	14.876	11.921	9.945	8.531	7.469	6.642	5.980	5.438	4.986
3	57.143	29.268	19.672	14.815	11.881	9.917	8.511	7.453	6.630	5.970	5.430	4.979
4	56.250	29.032	19.565	14.754	11.842	9.890	8.491	7.438	6.618	5.960	5.422	4.972
5	55.384	28.800	19.459	14.694	11.803	9.863	8.471	7.423	6.606	5.950	5.414	4.965
6	54.545	28.571	19.355	14.634	11.765	9.836	8.451	7.407	6.593	5.941	5.405	4.959
7	53.731	28.346	19.251	14.575	11.726	9.809	8.431	7.392	6.581	5.931	5.397	4.952
8	52.941	28.125	19.149	14.516	11.688	9.783	8.411	7.377	6.569	5.921	5.389	4.945
9	52.174	27.907	19.048	14.458	11.650	9.756	8.392	7.362	6.557	5.911	5.381	4.938
10	51.428	27.692	18.947	14.400	11.613	9.730	8.372	7.347	6.545	5.902	5.373	4.931
11	50.704	27.481	18.848	14.343	11.576	9.704	8.363	7.332	6.534	5.892	5.365	4.925
12	50.000	27.273	18.750	14.286	11.538	9.677	8.333	7.317	6.522	5.882	5.357	4.918
13	49.315	27.068	18.653	14.229	11.502	9.651	8.314	7.302	6.510	5.873	5.349	4.911
14	48.648	26.866	18.557	14.173	11.465	9.626	8.295	7.287	6.498	5.863	5.341	4.905
15	48.000	26.667	18.461	14.118	11.429	9.600	8.276	7.273	6.486	5.854	5.333	4.898
16	47.368	26.471	18.367	14.062	11.392	9.574	8.257	7.258	6.475	5.844	5.325	4.891
17	46.753	26.277	18.274	14.008	11.356	9.549	8.238	7.243	6.463	5.835	5.318	4.885
18	46.154	26.087	18.182	13.953	11.321	9.524	8.219	7.229	6.452	5.825	5.310	4.878
19	45.570	25.899	18.090	13.900	11.285	9.499	8.200	7.214	6.440	5.816	5.302	4.871
20	45.000	25.714	18.000	13.846	11.250	9.474	8.182	7.200	6.429	5.806	5.294	4.865
21	44.444	25.532	17.910	13.793	11.215	9.449	8.163	7.186	6.417	5.797	5.286	4.858
22	43.902	25.352	17.822	13.740	11.180	9.424	8.145	7.171	6.406	5.788	5.278	4.852
23	43.373	25.175	17.734	13.688	11.146	9.399	8.126	7.157	6.394	5.778	5.270	4.845
24	42.857	25.000	17.647	13.636	11.111	9.375	8.108	7.143	6.383	5.769	5.263	4.839
25	42.353	24.828	17.561	13.585	11.077	9.351	8.090	7.129	6.372	5.760	5.255	4.832
26	41.860	24.658	17.476	13.534	11.043	9.326	8.072	7.115	6.360	5.751	5.248	4.826
27	41.379	24.490	17.391	13.483	11.009	9.302	8.054	7.101	6.349	5.742	5.240	4.819
28	40.909	24.324	17.308	13.433	10.976	9.278	8.036	7.087	6.338	5.732	5.233	4.813
29	40.450	24.161	17.225	13.383	10.942	9.254	8.018	7.073	6.327	5.723	5.225	4.806
30	40.000	24.000	17.143	13.333	10.909	9.231	8.000	7.059	6.316	5.714	5.217	4.800
31	39.561	23.841	17.062	13.284	10.876	9.207	7.982	7.045	6.305	5.705	5.210	4.794
32	39.130	23.684	16.981	13.235	10.843	9.184	7.965	7.031	6.294	5.696	5.202	4.787
33	38.710	23.529	16.901	13.187	10.811	9.160	7.947	7.018	6.283	5.687	5.195	4.781
34	38.298	23.377	16.822	13.139	10.778	9.137	7.930	7.004	6.272	5.678	5.187	4.774
35	37.895	23.226	16.744	13.091	10.746	9.114	7.912	6.990	6.261	5.669	5.180	4.768
36	37.500	23.077	16.667	13.043	10.714	9.091	7.895	6.977	6.250	5.660	5.172	4.762
37	37.113	22.930	16.590	12.996	10.682	9.068	7.877	6.963	6.239	5.651	5.165	4.756
38	36.735	22.785	16.514	12.950	10.651	9.045	7.860	6.950	6.228	5.643	5.158	4.749
39	36.364	22.642	16.438	12.903	10.619	9.023	7.843	6.936	6.218	5.634	5.150	4.743
40	36.000	22.500	16.364	12.857	10.588	9.000	7.826	6.923	6.207	5.625	5.143	4.737
41	35.644	22.360	16.290	12.811	10.557	8.978	7.809	6.910	6.196	5.616	5.136	4.731
42	35.294	22.222	16.216	12.766	10.526	8.955	7.792	6.897	6.186	5.607	5.128	4.724
43	34.951	22.086	16.143	12.721	10.496	8.933	7.775	6.883	6.175	5.599	5.121	4.718
44	34.615	21.951	16.071	12.676	10.465	8.911	7.759	6.870	6.164	5.590	5.114	4.712
45	34.286	21.818	16.000	12.632	10.435	8.889	7.742	6.857	6.154	5.581	5.106	4.706
46	33.962	21.687	15.929	12.587	10.405	8.867	7.725	6.844	6.143	5.573	5.099	4.700
47	33.644	21.557	15.859	12.544	10.375	8.845	7.709	6.831	6.133	5.564	5.092	4.693
48	33.333	21.429	15.789	12.500	10.345	8.824	7.692	6.818	6.122	5.556	5.085	4.687
49	33.028	21.302	15.721	12.457	10.315	8.802	7.676	6.805	6.112	5.547	5.078	4.681
50	32.727	21.176	15.652	12.414	10.286	8.780	7.660	6.792	6.102	5.538	5.070	4.675
51	32.432	21.053	15.584	12.371	10.256	8.759	7.643	6.780	6.091	5.530	5.063	4.669
52	32.143	20.930	15.517	12.329	10.227	8.738	7.627	6.767	6.081	5.531	5.056	4.663
53	31.858	20.809	15.451	12.287	10.198	8.717	7.611	6.754	6.071	5.513	5.049	4.657
54	31.579	20.690	15.385	12.245	10.169	8.696	7.595	6.742	6.061	5.505	5.042	4.651
55	31.304	20.571	15.319	12.203	10.141	8.675	7.579	6.729	6.050	5.496	5.035	4.645
56	31.034	20.455	15.254	12.162	10.112	8.654	7.563	6.716	6.040	5.488	5.028	4.639
57	30.769	20.339	16.190	12.121	10.084	8.633	7.547	6.704	6.030	5.479	5.021	4.633
58	30.508	20.225	15.126	12.081	10.056	8.612	7.531	6.691	6.020	5.471	5.014	4.627
59	30.202	20.112	15.063	12.040	10.028	8.592	7.516	6.679	6.010	5.463	5.007	4.621

TABLE IX
SCALE OF VISIBILITY
(Record number in log)

Scale Number	Prominent Objects Not Visible At
0	50 yards
1	200 yards
2	500 yards
3	½ mile
4	1 mile
5	2 miles
6	4 miles
7	7 miles
8	20 miles
9	More than 20 miles

Table IX (left) gives a scale for visibility of objects at sea, using numbers which can be recorded in the log.

Table X (right) indicates how the state of the sea can be recorded by numbers.

(See also page 468b)

TABLE X
STATE OF THE SEA
(Using Numerals instead of letters. See Table B)

Scale Number	Description Of Sea	Height Of Wave
0	Calm	0 or less than 1 foot
1	Smooth	1 to 2 feet
2	Slight	2 to 3 feet
3	Moderate	3 to 5 feet
4	Rough	5 to 8 feet
5	Very rough	8 to 12 feet
6	High	12 to 20 feet
7	Very high	20 to 40 feet
8	Precipitous	40 feet or more
9	Confused	Record chief direction

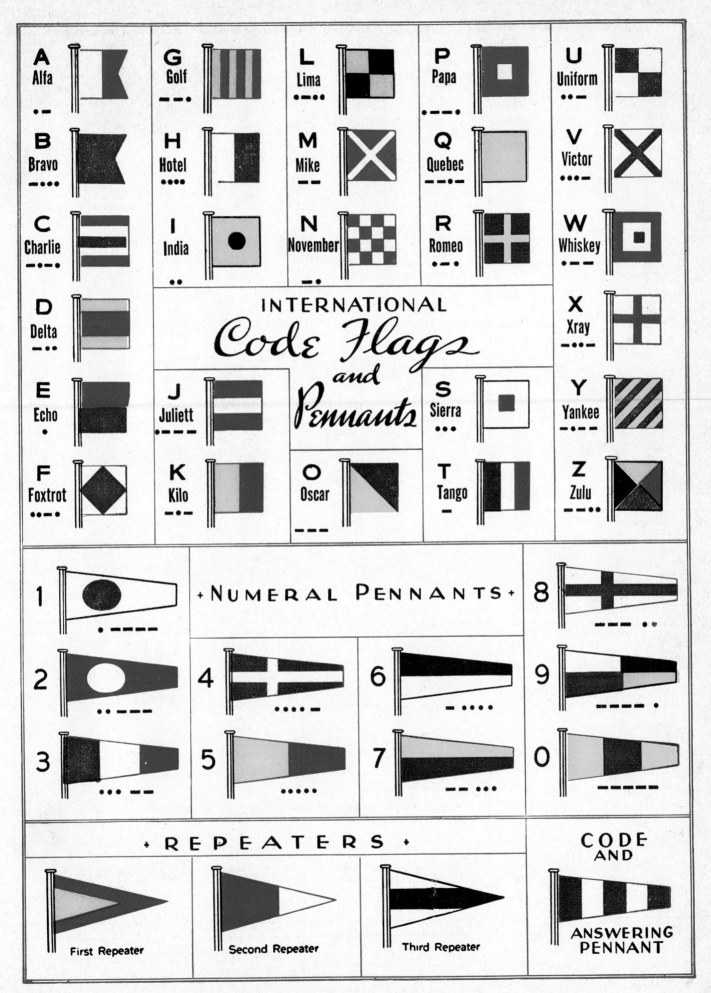

INTERNATIONAL
Code Flags
and
Pennants

A Alfa · —	**G** Golf — — ·	**L** Lima · — · ·
B Bravo — · · ·	**H** Hotel · · · ·	**M** Mike — —
C Charlie — · — ·	**I** India · ·	**N** November — ·
D Delta — · ·		
E Echo ·	**J** Juliett · — — —	
F Foxtrot · · — ·	**K** Kilo — · —	**O** Oscar — — —

P Papa · — — ·	**U** Uniform · · —
Q Quebec — — · —	**V** Victor · · · —
R Romeo · — ·	**W** Whiskey · — —
	X Xray — · · —
S Sierra · · ·	**Y** Yankee — · — —
T Tango —	**Z** Zulu — — · ·

⋆ NUMERAL PENNANTS ⋆

1 · — — — —	**8** — — — · ·
2 · · — — —	**9** — — — — ·
3 · · · — —	**0** — — — — —
4 · · · · —	
5 · · · · ·	
6 — · · · ·	
7 — — · · ·	

⋆ REPEATERS ⋆

First Repeater

Second Repeater

Third Repeater

CODE AND

ANSWERING PENNANT

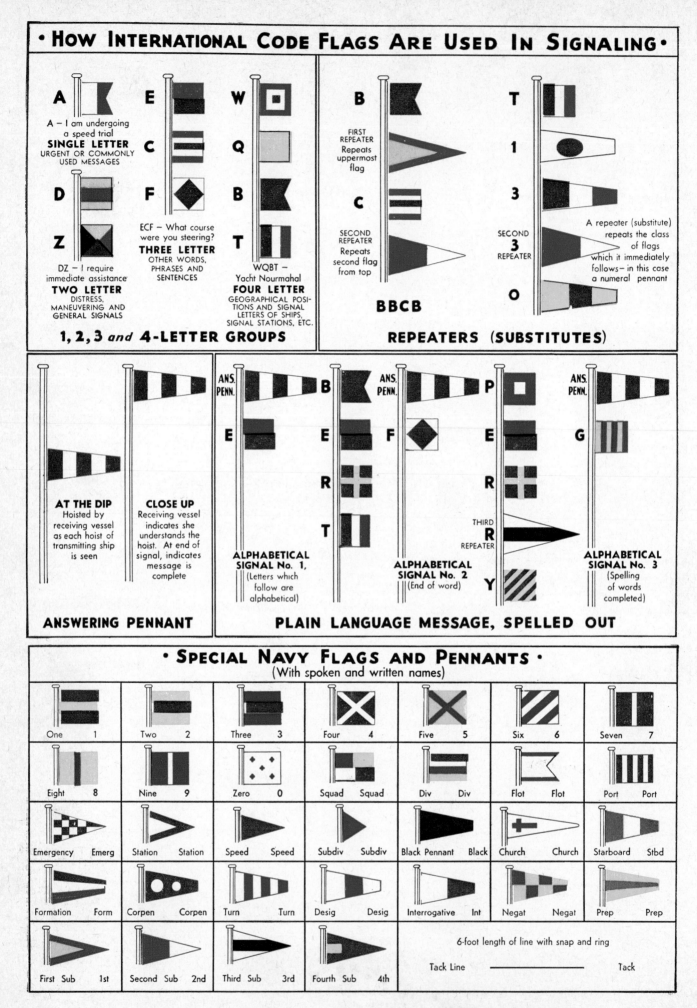

See also page 383

CHAPTER XXVI

SIGNALING

METHODS OF COMMUNICATING BY
MEANS OF INTERNATIONAL CODE
FLAGS, SEMAPHORE, AND FLASHING
LIGHT OR SOUND SIGNALS USING
THE INTERNATIONAL MORSE CODE

VARIOUS forms of signal codes have been used by mariners for many years, but these have not always been international in scope. The need for such a universal system by which ships of all nations could communicate with each other without misunderstanding was brought into sharp focus during the World War of 1914-1918. At that time the International Code of Signals proved inadequate. Revisions were therefor made and a new code drafted, which has now been in general use the world over for a number of years.

In the field of pleasure boating, flags of the International Code are most commonly seen as a decoration for yachts when they dress ship at regattas, on holidays, and so on—much less frequently in the use for which they were basically intended, that of conveying messages from one ship to another. Yet if boatmen were more generally aware of how valuable the ability to signal to other craft might be at times, it is likely that they would regard a knowledge of the fundamentals, at least, an indispensable part of their education in seamanship.

How important a more general knowledge of correct signaling technique among vessels of all kinds really is, is evidenced by the fact that ships of the Navy and Merchant Marine regularly communicate at sea with the express idea of gaining familiarity in the use of the code. Much could be accomplished if yachtsmen as a group would also seize every opportunity to familiarize themselves with its correct use.

As a matter of fact, the former Bureau of Marine Inspection and Navigation once reported that, due to cooperation of the Navy, the Maritime Commission, and the Coast Guard with the Bureau, there had been a definite improvement in signaling efficiency on the part of Merchant Marine personnel.

The international code flags prescribed for flag signaling consist of 26 letter flags, 10 numeral pennants, 3 substitutes or repeaters and a code and answering pennant

For a time the Bureau in its monthly bulletin carried a list of the contacts made between merchant ships and vessels of the Navy and Coast Guard, but within a year they reached such volume that it was no longer practicable to publish it.

For a full, complete explanation of the fundamentals to be outlined in this article, yachtsmen are referred to H. O. No. 87, a publication of the Oceanographic Office of the Navy Department—entitled International Code of Signals (Volume I, Visual and Sound). It may be obtained from the Oceanographic Office at Washington, D. C., or any of its agencies in principal cities. A separate volume deals with radio communication. A copy of H. O. No. 87 and a good set of signal flags should be part of the equipment, not only of every seagoing yacht, but all pleasure boats from fair sized cruisers up. On yachts of the Coast Guard Reserve they would be particularly desirable.

There are four common methods of communicating by means of visual signals. These include: (1) flag signal-

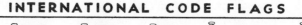

INTERNATIONAL CODE FLAGS

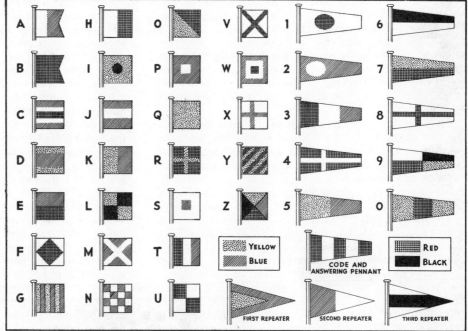

(See also page 383, showing International Code Flags and Pennants in color.)

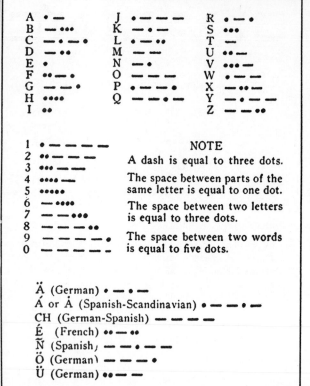

A • —	J • — — —	R • — •
B — • • •	K — • —	S • • •
C — • — •	L • — • •	T —
D — • •	M — —	U • • —
E •	N — •	V • • • —
F • • — •	O — — —	W • — —
G — — •	P • — — •	X — • • —
H • • • •	Q — — • —	Y — • — —
I • •		Z — — • •

1 • — — — —	
2 • • — — —	
3 • • • — —	
4 • • • • —	
5 • • • • •	
6 — • • • •	
7 — — • • •	
8 — — — • •	
9 — — — — •	
0 — — — — —	

NOTE

A dash is equal to three dots.

The space between parts of the same letter is equal to one dot.

The space between two letters is equal to three dots.

The space between two words is equal to five dots.

Ä (German) • — • —
Á or Å (Spanish-Scandinavian) • — — • —
CH (German-Spanish) — — — —
É (French) • • — • •
Ñ (Spanish) — — • — —
Ö (German) — — — •
Ü (German) • • — —

Period • — • — • —	
Semicolon — • — • — •	
Comma — — • • — —	
Colon — — — • • •	
Interrogation • • — — • • (IMI)	
Exclamation Point — — • • — —	
Apostrophe • — — — — •	
Hyphen — • • • • —	
Bar indicating fraction — • • — • (NR)	
Parenthesis — • — — • —	
Inverted Commas • — • • — •	
Underline • • — — • —	
Double Dash — • • • — (BT)	
Distress Call • • • — — — • • • (SOS)	
Attention call, to precede every transmission — • — • — (CT)	

General inquiry call and general call to all stations — • — • — — • — (CQ)

From — • • • (de)
Invitation to transmit (go ahead) — • — (K)
Warning—high power — — • • — —
Question (please repeat after ......) interrupting long messages • • — — • • (IMI)
Wait • — • • •
Break (Bk) (double dash) — • • • — (BT)
Understand • • • — •
Error • • • • • • • • (EEEE etc.)
Received (OK) • — • (R)
Position Report (to precede all position messages) — • — • (TR)
End of each message (cross) • — • — • (AR)
Transmission finished (end of work) (conclusion of correspondence) • • • — • — (VA)

Signals in the Morse code consist of groups of dots and dashes which can be made as a visual signal by flashing light or as a sound signal

ing, with the use of International flags and pennants; (2) flashing light signals; (3) sound signals and (4) the use of semaphore signals. For the second and third methods, the International Morse Code is used.

Flags of the International Code include 26 letter flags, 10 pennants for numerals, 3 substitute or repeater flags, and a code or answering pennant.

In the second and third methods, using flashing light or sound signals, combinations of dots and dashes constituting the International Morse Code express the various letters, numerals and signals. In determining the duration of dot and dash signals, the dot is taken as a unit, a dash equals three units, and the time between any two elements of a symbol is equal to one unit. Between two complete signals, the interval is three units; between two words or groups, five units. This spacing of the letters, words, etc., is an important element of successful signaling.

Flashing light signals are commonly made by exposing and obscuring a light. Sound signals can be made on a siren, whistle, fog horn or any other sound apparatus. Eight words per minute is taken as standard for flashing light signals.

Semaphore signals are made by a signalman holding a pair of hand flags in various positions to designate letters of the alphabet, etc. This is not to be confused with the wig-wag system of flag signaling. As in flashing light signaling, standard practice requires signaling by semaphore at the rate of eight words per minute.

If every message transmitted by means of visual signals had to be spelled out letter for letter, it is apparent that the procedure would become tedious; wasting much time and effort. For this reason, by the use of the code given in H. O. No. 87, words, phrases and even sentences are reduced to a few simple letters. Obviously then one of the first essentials in gaining proficiency in signalling is to be thoroughly conversant with the code book. With such knowledge one will naturally frame his messages so as to utilize phrasing for which code letters have been provided.

In the exchange of messages it is always assumed that the communication is between the masters of the two vessels, unless expressly stated to the contrary.

Signals letters assigned to ships consist of four letters, of which the first letter or two indicate nationality. These agree with their radio call signs. The same principle applies to aircraft except that the signal letters and radio call signs consist of a five-letter group. It should be noted that these letters are used in two ways. Where a ship, aircraft or signal station is spoken *to* or is called, the signal letters precede the communication or signal. But when a signalman wants to speak *of* a ship, that is to say, indicate or refer to a certain ship in his message, he uses her signal letters at the end of his signal.

Not all messages are sent in code; they may be expressed in plain language, spelling out words in full. When ships are referred to in a coded message, their signal letters are used, but when the message is in plain language, then the ship's name is spelled out.

Sometimes, in plain language messages, numbers are written out in full as words in order to eliminate any possibility of error—for example, "one two three" in place of "123." Another safeguard against error, in plain language messages, is to repeat the number, indicating the fact by the word "repetition" directly preceding such

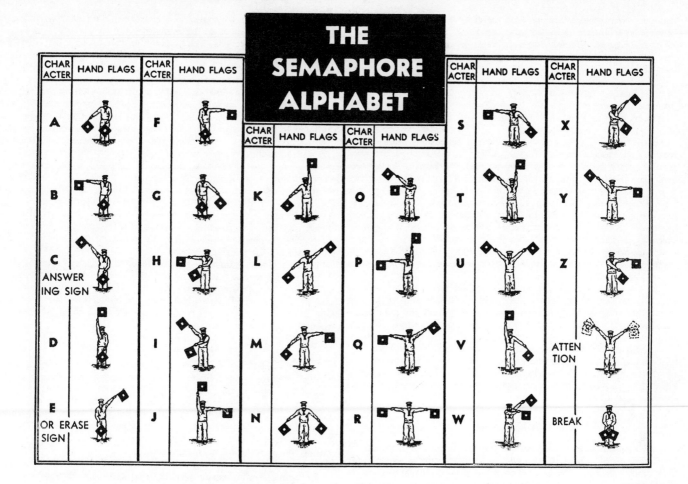

THE SEMAPHORE ALPHABET

CHARACTER	HAND FLAGS	CHARACTER	HAND FLAGS
A		F	
B		G	
C — ANSWERING SIGN		H	
D		I	
E — OR ERASE SIGN		J	

CHARACTER	HAND FLAGS	CHARACTER	HAND FLAGS
K		O	
L		P	
M		Q	
N		R	

CHARACTER	HAND FLAGS	CHARACTER	HAND FLAGS
S		X	
T		Y	
U		Z	
V		ATTENTION	
W		BREAK	

When signaling by semaphore, the signalman uses a pair of hand flags and spells out a plain-language message according to the alphabet illustrated above

repetition—for example, "one two three repetition one two three."

The manner of signaling numbers varies with the method used. In flag signaling, numeral pennants are provided, the shape of which distinguishes the numbers from the letters. In Morse signaling (flashing light or sound), numerals are provided for with distinctive signals, though they may be spelled out. In semaphore, numbers are spelled out. If a decimal point occurs between numerals in a flag signal, the answering pennant is inserted to express it. In Morse, the decimal point sign is the same as a period (. — . — . —). In semaphore it would be spelled out "decimal."

In some cases numbers must be added to a code group to complete its signification. Except when signaling time, bearings or positions, the numbers in such cases are sent as a separate group.

In navigation, time is expressed in terms of hours up to 24, rather than 12 for A.M. and 12 more for P.M. In signaling the same principle applies, so that any time can be expressed in four figures. For example, 2:10 A.M. becomes 0210; 3:12 P.M. would be 1512. In signaling a coded message, the letter T would be joined with these four numerals to form a single group and indicate that the numerals express time—for example, T0210 or T1512. The T always precedes the numerals. In plain language messages (as differentiated from code) the context makes it clear when the message relates to time.

Sometimes the time is signaled from one vessel to another as a check on the chronometer time, in which case the exact instant becomes very important. This is handled by having the time relate to the instant when the signal is hauled down and, if this is done smartly, the time can be checked to a split second. If the message happened to be in Morse, the exact instant would be indicated by sending a long (5-second) dash after the time signal, the end of it synchronized with the exact time which the four-numeral signal expresses.

Courses and bearings are signaled by three figures, interpreted as true, unless expressly designated as magnetic. For example, a course of 45 degrees true would be simply 045; if it is to express a magnetic course of 45 degrees, then the signal would be 045 magnetic. When a course is signaled in code, a suitable code group to express the desired idea would be followed by the three numerals. In the case of a bearing, the letter X is joined to the numerals to form a single group, the X preceding the numerals. X045 would therefore signify "bearing 45 (true)."

Inasmuch as wind and current are often referred to in terms of points of the compass, three-letter code groups have been provided for each of the 32 points. The more or less long-winded Southwest By South is thus cut down, in code, to NTT; Northwest By West to JUV.

To signal a position by giving the latitude and longitude, each would be expressed as a group of four figures, the first group indicating the latitude, the second the longitude. In each case the first two figures indicate degrees; the last two, minutes. When making a signal, each of the two groups of figures would be joined and preceded by the letter P. P4027, P7400 would thus indicate a position in latitude 40 degrees 27 minutes, longitude 74 degrees 00 minutes.

Commonly, it is unnecessary to indicate whether the latitude is north or south and the longitude east or west, since in most cases both are obvious. If required to avoid confusion or misunderstanding, then the N or S can be added directly after the latitude numerals and the E or W directly after the longitude figures. This is often desirable in cases where the position is in a latitude close to the equator or the longitude close to 0 or 180 degrees.

When the longitude runs into three figures, it is usually expedient to drop the first figure since a ship invariably knows her position to the nearest hundred degrees. By doing this, any longitude can be expressed by a four-figure group, though five may be used if necessary to prevent misunderstanding.

Another method of expressing position is by bearing and distance from a given point. In signaling a position by this method, a certain sequence must be observed as follows: first, the bearing from; second, the distance from; third, the point. Thus X021—15—Point Blank would be interpreted as a position 15 miles 21 degrees true from Point Blank. The letter X and three figures will be recalled as expressing the bearing; the 15 group is taken to mean miles unless otherwise stated. The geographical position of the point might be given as a four-letter group from the code book. If, instead of a geographical point, the point of reference happened to be a ship, its position being known, the final group would be the signal letters of the ship referred to.

The time of origin of a message is considered to be the time at which a message is ordered to be made. When it is necessary to insert this time in a signaled message, it is put at the conclusion. The time is expressed in four figures, to the nearest minute. Certain local codes are in use which do not conform to the International Code. Misunderstanding might arise if such local codes were used without explanation. Consequently provision is made for such signals by displaying first the International NMM. This will make it clear that the signals following are not to be interpreted from the International Code book.

CODE FLAGS

WHEN signaling by means of the flags and pennants of the International Code, it is advisable to show only a single hoist at a time. A hoist means one or more groups displayed from a single halyard. The signal is read from top to bottom. (However, in certain organizations, where secrecy is desired, the signal is read from the bottom up. This may explain some strange signal not found in the code book, if read top to bottom.) Each group of letters and/or numerals constitute a separate signal and when several groups are used on one hoist, they naturally must be separated to convey the right meaning. A tackline, consisting of a piece of halyard about 6 feet long, is used to separate such groups.

Signals should be kept flying until answered. There are occasions when more than one hoist may be displayed simultaneously and then an order of sequence must be followed in order to interpret the message correctly. In such cases the hoists are read in the following order: (1) masthead, (2) triatic stay, (3) starboard yardarm and (4) port yardarm. (The triatic stay runs from the main to the foremast head.)

In cases where more hoists than one are flown from a yardarm, the outboard hoist is read first; where more than one are displayed at the triatic stay, the one furthest forward is read first.

The terms superior and inferior are often used in relation to signals. A signal is superior to another if hoisted before the latter, either in point of time or hoist. If hoisted after, it is inferior.

Obviously a visual signal is going to fail of its purpose if it is not clearly visible. For that reason signals should always be flown where they can best be seen by the receiving vessel. This means that each flag must stand out clearly, not enveloped in smoke or fouled by sails, rigging, etc.

How To Call

WHEN calling a particular vessel, her signal letters are hoisted superior to the message which is to follow; otherwise, in the absence of such signal letters, the message would be understood to be addressed to all vessels in sight of the signal. If the other vessel's signal letters are not known, she can be directed or requested to hoist them by displaying the code letter group VH and hoisting the transmitting ship's own signal letters at the same time. As a final alternative, display of the code group NMJ would convey the

message: "I wish to signal to the vessel(s) on bearing indicated from me" and, of course, the bearing would be given to distinguish between several vessels which might be within signaling distance.

In order to understand the procedure followed in answering a signal there are several terms which should be defined. A signal is *at the dip* when hoisted only about half the extent of the halyard; it is said to be *close up* when hoisted to the full extent of the halyard.

In answering a signal then every vessel addressed should hoist the answering pennant at the dip as each hoist is seen, closing up to indicate that the signal is understood. Then when the transmitting ship hauls her hoist down, the answering pennant on the receiving ship is immediately lowered to the dip again so as to be ready to acknowledge the next hoist, in similar manner, when understood. This continues until the message is completed. (It is suggested that the triatic stay should not be used for the answering pennant because of the difficulty in distinguishing whether it is at the dip or close up.) When the transmitting ship has lowered the last hoist, she indicates that the message is complete by hoisting the answering pennant alone, which the receiving ship answers just the same as all previous hoists.

When a signal cannot be clearly distinguished, the receiving ship keeps the answering pennant at the dip and hoists a signal which will convey the reason for the difficulty. If, on the other hand, she can distinguish the signal but does not understand its meaning, she flies the code signal VB indicating: "Signal is not understood though flags are distinguished."

Repeaters or Substitutes

WITH every set of code flags are included three pennant-shaped repeaters or substitutes. These permit the signalman to repeat the same signal flag in a group without carrying extra sets of flags. These substitutes repeat the same *class* of flag that precedes them; that is, following alphabetical flags they repeat them —but if used with numeral pennants they repeat such pennants.

Considering then only the class of flags directly preceding the substitute, the first substitute repeats the top flag; the second substitute, the second flag from the top; and the third substitute the third flag from the top. An answering pennant used as a decimal point is disregarded and a substitute is never used more than once in the same group. If, for example, the signal to be made is ABBA, the hoist reading from top to bottom would be: A, B, second substitute, first substitute. If the signal were 5222, the hoist would be 5, 2, second substitute, third substitute. Note that the second substitute has been used in place of the third numerical and cannot be used again. However, it represents the 2 of the third numeral, therefore the third substitute is used to repeat 2 in the last numeral. T1550 would be signaled T, 1, 5, second substitute, 0, since the substitute in this mixed group of a letter and numerals follows a numeral and therefore repeats the second numeral, which is 5.

When names occur in the text of a message they are spelled out, and alphabetical signals are provided having certain significations. The answering pennant over E (alphabetical signal number 1) indicates that until alphabetical signal number 3 is made, the letters which follow do not represent code signals but alphabetical letters spelling a word. Answering pennant over F (alphabetical signal number 2) signifies the end of a word being spelled or a dot between initials. Answering pennant over G (alphabetical signal number 3) means that the spelling is complete and the signals which follow should be interpreted from the code book.

When naval vessels communicate with merchant ships, they hoist the code pennant and keep it flying while the signal is made. When signal exercises are engaged in between such vessels, or between merchantmen, the code group NMI is used to express: "I wish to exercise signals with you." NML indicates that the "signal exercise is finished."

MORSE CODE

AT this point it would be well to refer to the illustration of the Morse symbols used for both visual and sound signaling. Included in this illustration are some of the more important procedure signals. These procedure signals and signs are in the nature of abbreviated messages, that is, they enable ships to exchange short, concise messages used frequently in connection with signaling.

Procedure Signals

Some of the important procedure signals are as follows:

The letter C (—.—.) means "You are correct."

De (—.. .) in the identity means "From ———." For example, De GXDE means "From ship whose signal letters are GXDE."

G (——.) means "Repeat back." This may be used as a separate signal at the beginning of a plain language message and then signifies that everything which follows should be repeated back, word by word, as received.

R (.—.) means "Message received."

T (—) signifies the receipt of each word in the text of a plain language message.

W (.——) means "I am unable to read your message owing to light not being properly trained or light burning badly." The receiving ship may make this W signal at any time, in which case the transmitting ship should show a steady light until the receiving ship indicates that she is satisfied with the light by stopping the W signal.

AA AA, etc. (.—.— .—.— etc.) is the call for an unknown ship and general call, used to attract attention before signaling a ship the name of which is unknown. It is discontinued when the ship called answers.

T̄TTTT, etc. (————— etc.) is the signal used to answer the above call, discontinued when the transmitting ship stops calling.

NOTE: A bar over letters composing a sign means the letters are to be made as one symbol.

U̅D̅ (.. — — ..) is the repeat sign, used to request repetition of all or part of a message. When it is made singly it means "Repeat the last message." In sound signaling the repeat sign made singly means "I missed the last word (or group); please go back a few words (or groups) and continue the message."

Using The Repeat Sign

THE repeat sign U̅D̅ may be used in conjunction with the signs AA, AB, WA, or WB and an identifying word or group, the last two separated by the space sign. The space sign is II (.. ..) and is used not only in conjunction with the repeat sign but also to separate whole numbers from fractions.

The letters AA, AB, WA, and WB have the following significance:
AA (.— .—) all after.
AB (.— —...) all before.
WA (.—— .—) word or group after.
WB (.—— —...) word or group before.

Thus,

U̅D̅ (alone) means "Repeat the last message."

U̅D̅ AA II VESSEL means "Repeat all after the word VESSEL."

U̅D̅ AB II JEM means "Repeat all before the group JEM."

U̅D̅ WA II KIC means "Repeat the group after KIC."

U̅D̅ WB II FLAGS means "Repeat the word before FLAGS."

Repeat signs are not to be used when a message is not understood or when a message as decoded is unintelligible. In such cases, suitable signals taken from the code should be made.

Other Signs

THE break sign BT (—...—) is used to precede text. It is repeated back but its repetition by the receiving ship is not acknowledged with C by the transmitting ship. (This is amplified under Flashing Light Signaling.)

EEEEE, etc. (..... etc.) is the erase sign, signifying that the last word or group was signaled incorrectly. It is answered with the erase sign. When answered, the transmitting ship repeats the last word or group correctly signaled and then goes ahead with the rest of the message. In the event that the error is not discovered till the message is complete, then the entire message must be signaled over again correctly.

A̅R̅ (.—.—.) is the ending sign used to end all messages. If a whole message is to be cancelled while it is in process of transmission, the correct procedure is to make the erase sign and follow it with the ending sign, thus: E̅E̅E̅E̅E̅ A̅R̅.

PRB is the international code group indicator, used in messages transmitted by Morse code as the first group of coded text and signifies that the message which follows consists of code groups, not plain language.

FLASHING LIGHT

WHEN signaling by flashing light, messages are divided into five component parts: (1) call (2) identity (3) break sign (4) text, and (5) ending. However, it does not follow that all these components will be found in every message.

The call, which begins a message, consists either of the general call (AA AA etc.) or the signal letters of the ship being called. When the receiving ship is ready to take the message, she answers by making the answering sign.

When it is necessary for the two ships to establish their identity, it is done as follows: After the call is answered the transmitting ship makes "de (from)" followed by her signal letters. This is repeated back. Then the receiving ship makes her own signal letters and the transmitting ship repeats back. In the event that either does not repeat back, or does so incorrectly, then the other makes her signal letters again until they are correctly repeated back.

The break sign, as previously indicated, is B̅T̅ and is signaled next, preceding the text which follows. It is repeated back, but the transmitting ship does not acknowledge its repetition by the receiving ship by making the C signal (You are correct) because this is not part of the text of the message. Should the receiving ship fail to repeat back the B̅T̅ (break) signal, the transmitting ship must make it again, until properly acknowledged. When the message requests a repetition, the break sign is not used before the text.

The fourth component is the text. This may be in plain language words or in groups of code, each word or group being signaled separately. As each plain language word is received, the receiving ship acknowledges it by making T. In the case of code groups, numbers (in figures, not spelled out), procedure signals, and signs (except C and punctuation signs) she repeats back as each is made and if such repetition is correct, the transmitting ship makes C. If the repetition is incorrect, then the transmitting ship must make the group again. Similarly, if the receiving ship does not acknowledge receipt of the signal or repeat back, then the transmitting ship must make the last word or group again.

As mentioned in the summary of procedure signals and signs, the ending sign is A̅R̅. This is the fifth and last component of the message, made at the end of the text and answered by the receiving ship by R (Message received).

NATURALLY when ships are exchanging a series of messages, there would be nothing gained by including the call and identity (the first two components) each time. Consequently they would be used at the beginning of the first message but omitted from subsequent messages.

The International Code Book gives many examples of how various types of messages would be exchanged by flashing light, for example: plain language, a coded message, a message with identity omitted, a message with both call and identity omitted, a repetition of a whole message, repetition of "all after" a certain group, repetition of "all before" a certain word, repetition of the "group after" a certain group, and repetition of the "word before" a certain group. The signals made by both transmitting and receiving ships are given, in the proper sequence. The following are given as examples of (1) a simple plain language message and (2) a coded message:

(1) The master of S. S. Malolo (signal letters WMCE) wishes to transmit the message "What weather have you had?" to the master of a passing ship, which is S. S. Accra (signal letters GMQN). The signaling is conducted as follows:

Component	S.S. Malolo Makes—	S.S. Accra Makes—	References and Remarks
Call	AA AA AA, etc.	T̅TTTTTT, etc.	See articles 97, 98 and 111.
Identity	{ De WMCE } GMQN←	De WMCE GMQN	See articles 92 and 112.
Break sign..	B̅T̅	B̅T̅	See articles 100 and 113.
Text	What weather have you had	T T T T T	See articles 95 and 114.
Ending	A̅R̅	R	See articles 108, 94 and 115.

(2) The Italian warship Solferino (signal letters IASJ) wishes to transmit the message. "Have you sighted S. S. Fausto?" to the American merchant vessel Michigan (signal letters KFLN). The message is coded and the signaling is conducted as follows:

Component	S.S. Solferino Makes—	S.S. Michigan Makes—	References and Remarks
Call	AA AA AA, etc.	TTTTTTT, etc.	
Identity	De IASJ De IASJ KFLN	De IASW De IASJ KFLN	Michigan having repeated back incorrectly, Solferino makes the group again. See article 112, last sentence.
Break sign..	BT̄	BT̄	
Text	PRB C NKM C	PRB NKM	See article 109. See articles 91 and 114. Group from signal code signifying "Have you sighted (vessel or object indicated)?"
	OMJZ C	OMJZ	Signal letters of Fausto. See article 43.
Ending	ĀR	R	

Note: The references in the last column of these tabulations relate to article numbers in H. O. No. 87.

SOUND SIGNALING

SOUND signaling should be used only with the greatest of caution, due to the confusion it might create with passing or fog signals. A good rule for yachtsmen would be to become thoroughly familiar with its principles and procedure but never to use it except in emergencies or in cases where there is certainty that no misunderstandings could possibly arise as a result of its use.

A sound signal should be as brief as possible and, except in emergency, communications should be limited to the single-letter signals. In fog or in inland waters where traffic is heavy, sound signals must be kept to an absolute minimum.

When necessary to signal by sound—on whistle, siren, fog horn, or other appliance—the call is made the same as by flashing light (AA AA AA, etc.). However, no call or answer is used with single-letter signals.

The receiving ship answers a call with the answering sign TTTTT, etc., after which the transmitting ship signals her complete message, with no acknowledgement, repetition or interruption from the receiving ship unless the latter happens to miss a word or group. In that case the receiving ship may break in immediately with the repeat sign (ŪD), whereupon the transmitting ship would make the last few words or groups over again and continue. When the transmitting ship has completed the message she makes the ending sign (ĀR), acknowledged by the receiving ship with the final R (Message received).

The code book gives the following example of a communication carried out in Morse signaling by sound. Although the general call is used, the ships do not exchange identities.

S. S. Beechwood, hearing the sound of another steamer's siren, wishes to transmit the message: "Have just passed floating mines." The other ship is S. S. Sirius.

Component	S.S. Beechwood Makes—	S.S. Sirius Makes—
Call	AA AA AA, etc.	TTTTTTT, etc.
Break Sign	BT̄	
Text	Have just passed floating mines	No answer unless a word is missed, in which case makes repeat sign ŪD. See article 121.
Ending	ĀR	R

SEMAPHORE

WHEN a ship wishes to communicate by semaphore (hand flags) she hoists the International Code flag J, a single-letter signal, which means: "I am going to send a message by semaphore." This may be hoisted singly or inferior to a group of signal letters. When the ship addressed sees this, she first hoists the answering pennant at the dip, then close up when ready to take the message.

To designate which one of several vessels is to answer the signal, the semaphore flag is hoisted with a tackline inferior to the signal letters of that ship. A naval vessel wishing to signal by semaphore to a merchantman would hoist the code pennant where it could best be seen, and the merchant ship's signal letters with a tackline superior to the semaphore (J) flag. The semaphore flag flies until the message is completed.

To signal by semaphore, a signalman takes two square hand flags and, using the semaphore alphabet, spells out a plain language message, numbers as well as words being spelled out in full.

First the sender makes the attention sign (waving both flags at arm's length), whereupon the receiving ship should hoist the answering pennant close up. If necessary, the sender then makes the name of the receiving ship, followed by "de (from)" and the name of the transmitting ship. Frequently vessels communicating by semaphore are relatively close to each other. Then, instead of hoisting the semaphore (J) flag and answering pennant, the attention sign and the answering sign (C) may be used.

IN SIGNALING, the signalman faces the ship addressed and as each word is completed drops his arms to the position designated for the break sign. The break sign is also used in spelling double letters; the first letter is made, arms dropped to the break position, and then immediately moved to the second letter. Each word is acknowledged aboard the receiving ship by making C (the answering sign), and if not so acknowledged the word is repeated. When an error is made, the sender makes a succession of E's (EEEEEEE, etc.) then signals the last word that was made correctly and continues his message. The message is completed with the ending sign ĀR.

The code book gives the following example of a message sent by semaphore:

The master of S. S. Lurline (signal letters KIEK) wishes to transmit by semaphore the message: "Can you loan me a kedge anchor?" to the master of S. S. Stora (signal letters GDVR).

Component	S.S. Lurline Makes—	S.S. Stora Makes—	References and Remarks
Call	GDVR tackline } or J	Atten- tion sign	Hoists answering pennant at the dip and close up when ready to read; or makes answering sign C.	See article 129, last sentence.
Identity	Stora de Lurline	C	See articles 129 and 132.
Text	Can you loan me a kedge anchor	C C C C C C C	
Ending	ĀR		

NAMING THE CODE FLAGS

THE 26 letter flags of the International Code (used in flag signaling) are not referred to by letter alone, but are given names. If the flags D T E were seen in a hoist and the signalman reported D T E to the radioman, there would be risk of his being misunderstood, because of the "E" sound in these and other letters. But when the signalman reports Delta Tango Echo (the names given to these flags) it is virtually impossible to misunderstand which flags are referred to.

These flag names, used in flag signaling (given in H.O. #87, Vol. I, Visual, International Code of Signals) are as follows: A—Alfa, B—Bravo, C—Charlie, D—Delta, E—Echo, F—Foxtrot, G—Golf, H—Hotel, I—India, J—Juliett, K—Kilo, L—Lima, M—Mike, N—November, O—Oscar, P—Papa, Q—Quebec, R—Romeo, S—Sierra, T—Tango, U—Uniform, V—Victor, W—Whiskey, X—Xray, Y—Yankee, Z—Zulu.

Formerly a distinction was drawn between certain flag names and the phonetic alphabet equivalent, used in communication to denote letters of the alphabet. For example, the letter A at one time was Able (in communications), but the A flag was named Afirm (in flag signaling). As a result of recent changes, however, the phonetic alphabet and flag names (as given in the previous paragraph) are identical. The latest revision, embodying the new names given in the paragraph above, took effect March 1, 1956.

SIGNAL CODE

M UCH of Volume H. O. No. 87 is necessarily devoted to a listing of the various code letters and groups, with their significance. All signals consist of single, two, three or four letters. Single-letter signals are urgent messages or those in common use. Two-letter signals are next in importance, including distress and maneuvering signals and some general signals in common use. Three-letter signals are used for other words, phrases and sentences. Four-letter signals beginning with the letter A relate to geographical positions. Other four-letter signals are the signal letters of ships, signal stations, etc.

Call letters of ships may be identified from three publications: Signal Letters of the U. S. Merchant Marine, the Berne List, and Lloyd's Register of Shipping. The first of these is available from the Superintendent of Documents, Washington, D. C. (15c). The Berne List is primarily for radio and Lloyd's Register is a large volume generally found in shipping offices but not on shipboard.

The problem of compiling a code from which expressions in any one of seven foreign languages might be taken was a difficult one and certain principles must be followed in its use. These are outlined in the instructions which accompany the code and should be carefully read before attempting to use the code itself. Otherwise, because of the form used, erroneous interpretations might be placed on a message sent in code. Numerous examples help to make the practice of coding clear.

Typical Code Signals from H. O. 87

A	I am undergoing a speed trial.
B	I am taking in or discharging explosives.
C	Yes (Affirmative).
D	Keep clear of me—I am maneuvering with difficulty.
E	I am directing my course to starboard.
F	I am disabled. Communicate with me.
G	I require a pilot.
H	I have a pilot on board.
I	I am directing my course to port.
J	I am going to send a message by semaphore.
K	You should stop your vessel instantly.
L	You should stop. I have something important to communicate.
M	I have a doctor on board.
N	No (Negative).
O	Man overboard.
P	In Harbor (Blue Peter)—All persons are to repair on board as the vessel is about to proceed to sea. (Note: To be hoisted at the foremast head.) At Sea—Your lights are out, or burning badly.
Q	My vessel is healthy and I request free pratique.
R	The way is off my ship; you may feel your way past me.
S	My engines are going full speed astern.
T	Do not pass ahead of me.
U	You are standing into danger.
V	I require assistance.
W	I require medical assistance.
X	Stop carrying out your intentions and watch for my signals.
Y	I am carrying mails.
Z	To be used to address or call shore stations.

Note: Only the single-letter signals F, K, L, O, P, R, U, V, W and Z should be used by flashing. P, T and X, if followed by a numeral group, have other meanings.

AM	Accident has occurred. I require a doctor.
AP	I am aground.
CU	Anchorage is dangerous.
DO	I am drifting and require assistance.
DQ	I am on fire and require immediate assistance.
DV	I have sprung a leak and require immediate assistance.
DZ	I require immediate assistance.
EU	Bar is dangerous.
FV	It is impossible to land.
JT	You should follow me, or vessel indicated.
JZ	I have damaged my rudder. I can not steer.
LJ	I am disabled. Will you tow me in or into place indicated?
LO	My engines are disabled.
LP	My steering gear is disabled.
LT	I am dragging. Can veer no more cable and have no more anchors to let go.
LV	I am in distress for want of fuel.
NC	I am in distress and require immediate assistance.
PT	I require a pilot.
QW	I have on board mail for you, or vessel indicated.
RG	I have telegram(s) for you.
RH	Message has been received.
RJ	Have you any message for me?
RS	Is all well with you?
RV	Where are you bound?
RW	Where are you from?
SD	I am short of lubricating oil. Can you supply?
SE	I am short of petrol. Can you supply?
TH	I have lost my propeller.
TK	I require provisions urgently.
UW	I can not distinguish your flags.
VB	Signal is not understood though flags are distinguished.
WU	What course should I steer to make nearest land?
XY	Can you take me in tow?
YJ	I require water immediately.

Yacht Club Signal Codes

Y ACHT clubs have adopted signal codes of their own, which are not in conformity with signals prescribed by the International Code Book. Furthermore, since the practice among the clubs may vary to a certain extent, the interpretation of such club signals depends largely on a knowledge of the local code as prescribed in the club's year book.

The purpose of the signals prescribed in club codes is principally to provide a means of communication between vessels of the squadron. While the codes do vary, there is a tendency toward standardization of both the meanings of the signals and also the signaling procedure.

In general, signals in the club code will consist of Special, racing and emergency signals (one or two flags, from A to Z, and A to AZ); general signals (two flags, BA and GZ); designation (two flags, HA to HZ); days of the week (two flags, IQ to IZ); hours of the day (two flags, JA to KY); names of places (two flags, NA to WZ); and compass signals (three flags, AQD to AST).

Most clubs provide that yachts using their own club code should hoist the club burgee over the club code flags; otherwise, absence of the burgee would indicate that the International Code is used.

Special Flags

Some flag makers are now supplying flags having special meanings, such as cocktail flag, fishing flag, ball and chain, etc., etc. While such flags are not specifically mentioned in any yacht club code, yet as they would fall into the category of "Signal Flags," they should be displayed on a conspicuous hoist, preferably when not under way.

SIGNALING NAVAL AND COAST GUARD VESSELS

T HERE may be occasions, particularly in time of war, when it is necessary for a pleasure craft to approach a Naval or Coast Guard vessel for the purpose of transmitting vital information. Obviously, no vessel of these services should be bothered with messages unless they are of consequence—dealing, for example, with national defense, or the safety of persons, property, or vessels.

When such a vessel is under way, she should be approached with signal flags flying—the International Code answering pennant at one yardarm, and the three-letter group JGI (urgent message) at the other. By the display of the International Code answering pennant, the naval vessel will understand that the signal is International Code, not Navy Code.

When the naval vessel is ready to receive the message it will hoist the (International Code) answering pennant, after which the message should be completed promptly with International Code Flag hoists.

On craft where signaling equipment is not available, attention may be attracted by waving a flag or any form of pantomime that will convey the idea of a desire to communicate a message. However, if warned by the naval vessel to stand off, the approaching craft should obey instructions regardless of the nature of the message, as naval craft are on serious business, and they may have their own reasons why no craft are to come near.

At night, all lights should be lit, the ensign displayed with flashlight or searchlight played upon it to make it conspicuous and easily identified, and approach should be slow and deliberate, always mindful of the possibility of being warned to stand off. Approach at all times should be toward the starboard side, about where the gangway is located.

If allowed to come alongside, the person in command of the small craft should establish his identity at once, state his business briefly (communicating only to proper officials), follow any instructions exactly, and depart only after permission is secured. Messages should be given only to the Commanding Officer or, in the case of large vessels, the Officer of the Deck.

Advanced Piloting

CHAPTER
XXVII

See also pages
329-334

A modern liquid box compass with 4-inch card, graduated in both quarter-points and degrees

FUNDAMENTALLY, there are three general methods in use among boatmen for taking a vessel from one port to another. The first, employed by a great many owners and operators of small boats, consists simply of sailing by local knowledge alone, depending on acquaintance with home waters to get from point to point. This involves a general knowledge of channels, depths, obstructions and directions, and depends also on the state of the weather. In case of fog or low visibility when the objective cannot be sighted, and landmarks are obscured, the follower of this method of navigation is so seriously handicapped that he is usually compelled to abandon his trip, temporarily at least. At the same time his cruising range is limited to the extent of his knowledge of surrounding waters. We do not mean to disparage the value of local knowledge in boating, as it is indispensable in some localities where a maze of inland channels must be threaded. What we do mean to say is that this particular sort of piloting is of little value when running in fog or in strange waters.

The second method of navigating is far more scientific. It relies upon definite data for locating the boat's position at any time and for plotting a course with confidence and certainty to some new objective which may never before have been visited. This is termed piloting. By the application of simple piloting principles it is possible to take a vessel up or down the coast, fixing the boat's position periodically by reference to landmarks, buoys, lightships and other objects, the positions of which are accurately known from Government charts.

The third system of navigation concerns itself with the location of a ship's position at sea by means of astronomical observations. This is termed celestial navigation and substitutes for the fixed visible landmarks of piloting, the sun, moon, stars and other heavenly bodies. These bodies serve, in deep-sea navigation, as the reference points of known position, from which the ship's position is determined. When weather conditions prevent the navigator from taking observations at sea, he has recourse to the principles of dead reckoning, by which he calculates his position from the distance and direction run from the last known point of departure.

The foregoing, in brief, are the general methods of navigation. We may dismiss the first as being of relatively little value and not strictly a division of scientific navigation. Neither are we particularly interested here in the problems of celestial navigation, inasmuch as the cruises of practically all small boats are confined to inland waters or coastwise trips within sight of land. So it will be our purpose in these articles to discuss only the simple problems of piloting. An understanding of them will enable one to leave his familiar home waters and proceed with confidence to seek new cruising grounds up and down the coast. In this he will find a source of deep and genuine satisfaction and will discover possibilities for enjoyment of his boat surpassing any he has ever before realized.

It will be helpful to approach the study of piloting with a realization of the fact that the principles involved are all extremely simple, and the solution of the problems equally easy when these few principles are clearly understood and applied. In actual practice, piloting generally resolves itself down into the intelligent study of a chart, the laying of a series of courses upon it to delineate the track we wish to follow from point to point, and the sailing of these courses by the use of the compass. In every case, ordinary good judgment is 75 percent of the requirements, knowledge of principles the other 25.

Two general problems are involved in piloting—first, that of finding an exact position at any given time; and second, the determination of a course to steer which will take us to a certain destination. The chart tells us what

Here the compass is shown fitted with an azimuth circle or sight vane. Bearings are taken by sighting over the vertical pins

An excellent type of pelorus, mounted in gimbals to keep the card horizontal while taking a bearing. The vertical sighting arms can be laid flat

Equipment illustrated through courtesy of Kelvin and Wilfrid O. White waters may be safely navigated; the compass enables us to follow these safe tracks.

The instruments which the pilot uses in solving these problems are the compass, chart, course protractor or parallel rules, dividers, the lead line, pelorus and a watch or log for determining the distance run. He has, in addition, certain Government publications such as Tide and Current Tables, Light Lists covering the area he is cruising, and Coast Pilots. These publications are discussed elsewhere.

We shall assume that the reader has a clear understanding of the compass and its errors, variation and deviation, and that he knows how to apply these errors in converting compass courses to magnetic or true, and vice versa. An excellent discussion of this subject will be found in the chapters on the compass, pages 249-281. A correct solution of piloting problems is conditioned upon the correct application of the compass errors to the courses which are plotted on the chart.

The following illustration will show the importance of understanding the compass error and applying it correctly. We might, for example, find from the chart that the magnetic course we wish to make good is NE. If we steer NE by compass, it is almost certain that we will not actually travel over the track we have laid upon the chart, because deviation has probably deflected the compass card so that magnetic NE and compass NE do not coincide. Only in the event that there is no deviation on a compass heading of NE will we travel over the magnetic track we have plotted.

The important thing in connection with the installation of a compass in a boat is that it must be aligned over, or parallel to, the fore-and-aft center line of the boat, that is, the keel. The lubber line is a short vertical black line near the edge of the compass card, painted on the inside surface of the compass bowl. When a line passing through this lubber line and the pivotal point in the center of the card, is parallel to the keel of the boat, the compass is properly installed.

The yacht log, used for measuring distance run. The rotator is towed astern. Spinning as it is drawn through the water, it twists the line and records revolutions on the register in terms of miles

Then, with reference to the position of the card, the lubber line indicates the bow of the boat. We steer a course by holding this lubber line (indicating the boat's head) on the *compass point* or degree *which corresponds to the magnetic or true course* which we have plotted on the chart. Thus, if the *true* course laid on the chart is 45° and the variation 12° west, the *magnetic* course becomes 57°. Then, if we find from our deviation table or Napier diagram that there is also a deviation of 6° west on this heading the *compass* course becomes 63°. Steering 63° by compass, we make good a direction on the chart which can be read as 45° true or 57° magnetic. There is a growing tendency to substitute for the old method of designating courses by points and fractions of points, the newer Navy system which divides the card into 360 degrees, measured clockwise from north as zero.

Another important piloting

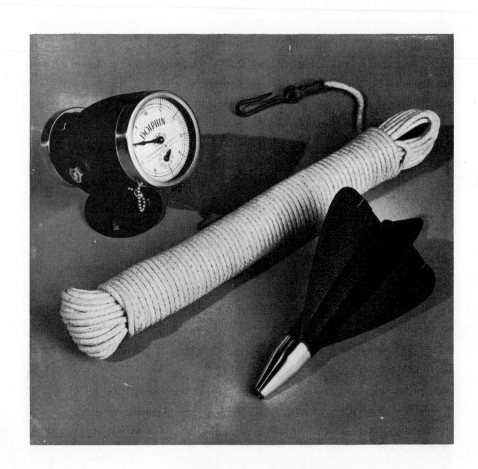

THE ESSENTIALS OF PILOTING ARE EASILY MASTERED.

Photographs by
M. Rosenfeld

TAKE IT STEP BY STEP.

THE INSTRUMENTS USED IN PILOTING—FIRST OF A SERIES OF ARTICLES DEALING WITH PRACTICAL PILOTING PROBLEMS

instrument is the pelorus. This, in principle, is simply a device which enables us to sight over a compass card to determine the bearing of a buoy or landmark. Bearing is the nautical term used to indicate the direction of a line drawn from the boat's position through a given object.

The principle of the pelorus may best be understood by constructing a simple one. A compass card is first secured, similar to the one in the compass. This may be drawn by hand on cardboard or it may be cut out of a printed card frequently used for recording deviation. This is mounted on a circular wooden base, slightly larger than the card. The card is pivoted at the center in such a way that it may be revolved freely and clamped in any desired position. Around the circumference of the wooden base and on its upper surface, four brass tacks are placed, 90° apart.

Next a flat arm is pivoted across the card at the same central point about which the card revolves. If the arm is made of flat strip brass, about six inches of each end may be bent up vertically at right angles to the horizontal position of the arm on the card. Hinging these vertical ends will permit them to be laid flat upon the arm but they must of course be kept vertical when taking a bearing.

A small hole is then bored in the center line of one vertical arm near its top to serve as a peep-sight for the eye. A larger opening at the top of the other vertical arm is then cut and a fine wire attached so that it bisects the opening vertically. A third opening in the horizontal arm on the side of the pivot opposite the eye peep-sight permits us to read the compass card under the arm. A longitudinal wire in the center of this will help in making an exact reading. The center of the small hole, the pivot of the card, and the wires of both openings must all lie in the same vertical plane.

With the pelorus assembled, the wooden base is fixed on some convenient part of the boat where an unobstructed view may be had in all directions. The base is then aligned by the brass tacks just as the compass was lined up by means of the lubber line. A line through two tacks 180° apart must be parallel with the fore-and-aft center line or keel. Now, if we are on a compass course of NE, the lubber line shows at NE on the card in the

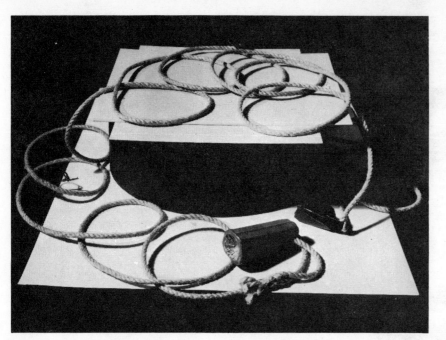

A small lead and line for sounding. This one weighs but three pounds and has only the first three fathoms marked. Some new lead lines have numbered plastic markers at each fathom, and yellow strips at each half-fathom

compass. By revolving the pelorus card so that its NE point is at the forward brass tack on the pelorus base, we are able to bring the two cards into agreement. If we should be passing a lighthouse on this NE course, we could obtain its compass bearing by sighting through the openings in the vertical arms of the pelorus and reading its bearing on the card directly under the opening in the horizontal arm.

With a simple pelorus of this sort, the boat should be on an even keel when taking a bearing. Regular peloruses are mounted in gimbals in the same manner as a compass in order to keep the card level when the boat rolls or pitches. In those rare cases where the boat's compass is in such a position that an unobstructed sight may be taken over the compass itself, the pelorus may be dispensed with by substituting an azimuth circle or sight vane. This is simply a circular frame that fits directly on the compass glass over the card. Vertical pins are provided for sighting the object and the bearing is read under a wire joining the two pins. Two short posts are set in the frame by which the circle may be swung to any desired bearing.

While not recommended as a scientific method of getting a precise bearing, it is possible to make an approximation by sighting the object over the center of the compass with some sort of straight stick, such as an ordinary yard stick. This fact is introduced only to indicate the simplicity of the principle, the several parts of a regular pelorus or sight vane merely being provided to allow greater accuracy and easier use.

There is also a very handy device called the bearing board, made by one manufacturer of nautical instruments. It consists essentially of a flat board on which a dial rotates about a semicircle, graduated in points and degrees from zero at the center to 90 degrees on each side. As the dial, at zero, is aligned parallel with the sides of the board and at right angles to the other edges, the board may be held against any part of the boat which is either parallel with the keel or at right angles to it. A window in the pilot house is generally convenient for the purpose. Then the angle between the boat's course and the bearing of an object may readily be determined by sighting over short posts provided on the dial. The angle, in either points or degrees, is found at the dial point and may be applied to the course.

Now the pilot requires some means of determining how far he has run on a given course from his starting point, or point of departure. In an automobile this is simple enough. If we measure the circumference of a tire and find it to be eight feet, then it will naturally have to make 660 revolutions to

progress a mile. Therefore, we need only connect our speedometer with suitable gearing to a wheel, or some other part of the car that rotates at a proportionate speed, so that a mile is registered every 660 revolutions of the wheel.

However, in measuring distances on the water, we have no solid medium from which to start. Speed- and distance-measuring devices must depend upon the pressure of the water for their operation and indicate only the measure relative to the water. Knowing the speed or distance through the water, allowance may be made for the effect of winds and currents in helping or retarding the boat, and the actual distance made good over the bottom calculated with sufficient accuracy.

Modern instruments, known as logs, are built for permanent installation in a boat, which register mileage through the water by scooping up a stream of water through a fitting on the bottom of the boat and converting this pressure into a measure which can be read upon a calibrated arc. This is a handy instrument and the mileage reading need only be corrected for the effect of wind (leeway) and current (drift).

Speedometers for boats are operated on a similar principle. The pressure of water entering the intake fitting on the boat's hull is transferred by tubing to a calibrated instrument face where it actuates a dial. Knowing the speed of the boat, it is easy to calculate distance from the period of running time, which can be taken with an ordinary watch. Other speedometers utilize the same fundamental principle but are actuated by pressure of the water on a small metallic arm which projects through the bottom of the boat.

Patent Logs

There are other types of logs less frequently used on small craft. The patent log consists of a register, a length of braided line, and a rotator. When the rotator is towed from the stern at the end of the line, the rotator is given a spinning motion which is transferred to the instrument on the stern of the ship where a reading may be taken in nautical miles. The rotator must be kept well clear of the boat's propeller stream and caution must be observed to see that it is neither fouled by weed nor damaged by hitting drift.

The chip-log, seldom used on small boats, consists of a quadrant-shaped piece of wood called the log-chip, a length of line, and a timing device called the log-glass. The line is marked at intervals of 47 feet 3 inches. The chip, weighted to keep it upright in the water, is thrown from the stern and the line is allowed to run out without dragging the chip. The number of 47-foot 3-inch divisions of line passing over the rail in 28 seconds, as measured by the glass, is equal to the number of knots (nautical miles per hour) the ship is making.

Some boats have neither log nor speedometer but are equipped with a tachometer which shows the number of revolutions per minute the engine is turning. This can be used to advantage in computing distances in the following manner. The boat is put over a measured mile course at all of the engine speeds which are likely to be used in cruising. These are tabulated on a card for reference, with the boat speed listed against each engine speed. Then in running a course where the distance must be calculated, the engine is held at one of the tachometer speeds for which we have a tabulated boat speed. The distance can then be figured on the basis of the time run at that particular speed.

Statute and Nautical Miles

In this connection it should be remembered that most measured mile courses are 5,280 feet, the statute or land mile. This is the mile in which the speed of small boats is generally reckoned. However, the scale of miles appearing on Government charts is based on the nautical mile of 6,080 feet, which is the equivalent of one minute of latitude on the earth's surface. Therefore, whenever a distance in nautical miles is taken from the chart, it is important to work with a boat speed in nautical miles. For purposes of conversion from one to the other, statute miles divided by 1.15 will give nautical miles. Nautical miles multiplied by 1.15 equal statute miles. [NOTE:—In 1954, the Department of Defense and the U. S. Coast Guard adopted the International nautical mile of 1,852 meters (6,076.10333 feet) as standard.]

If none of the above instruments is available for figuring speed or distance, then the only method left is to approximate it by running over a mile course with the throttle set at definite points. The difficulty with this is the fact that the throttle setting may be changed in working on the engine or, due to imperfect operation, the engine may not always turn up to its maximum at a given throttle setting.

The Lead—and How to Use It

Another instrument required in piloting is the lead line, used for sounding in determining the depth of water. This consists of a braided cotton line up to 25 or 30 fathoms in length, to one end of which is attached a lead weighing upwards of three pounds. This minimum weight is good for depths of about four or five fathoms. Larger leads up to approximately fourteen pounds are used on small boats for greater depths. The bottom of the lead is hollowed, providing a place in which tallow or grease may be packed. This is called arming the lead. When the lead strikes bottom, particles of mud, sand, shells, or other matter characteristic of the bottom, are caught in the sticky substance with which the lead is armed. These particles may be compared with data on the chart which show the nature of the bottom. An excellent check on the boat's position is often secured in this way.

In taking a sounding, the lead is cast well forward so that it will strike bottom at a point directly below the leadsman as the boat moves slowly through the water. For convenience in reading the depths, lead lines are ordinarily marked as follows: 2 fathoms from the lead—2 strips of leather; 3 fathoms—3 strips of leather; 5 fathoms—white rag; 7 fathoms—red rag; 10 fathoms—leather with a hole in it; 13 fathoms—same as 3 fathoms; 15 fathoms—same as 5; 17 fathoms—same as 7; 20 fathoms—2 knots; 25 fathoms—1 knot; 30 fathoms—3 knots; 35 fathoms—1 knot; 40 fathoms—4 knots, and so on. Lead lines should occasionally be checked when wet to see that the markings are correct. In sounding, allowance should be made for the fact that the leadsman's hand is some distance above the water.

Reporting the Soundings

The fathoms or points on the lead line which are marked are called "marks." Others, which are not marked, are known as "deeps." For example, three fathoms is marked by three strips of leather, and is a "mark." Five fathoms, marked by a white cotton rag, is also a "mark." The four-fathom depth on the line is not marked; this is one of the "deeps."

It is important for the leadsman to understand, and use, these terms when sounding and reporting to the helmsman (or bridge on a larger vessel). The following are given as typical reports, with the respective depths to which they correspond:

DEPTH		REPORT
5	fathoms	*"By the mark five!"*
5¼	fathoms	*"And a quarter five!"*
5½	fathoms	*"And a half five!"*
5¾	fathoms	*"A quarter less six!"*
6	fathoms	*"By the deep six!"*
6¼	fathoms	*"And a quarter six!"*
6½	fathoms	*"And a half six!"*
6¾	fathoms	*"A quarter less seven!"*
7	fathoms	*"By the mark seven!"*

In reporting or calling the soundings the leadsman should always make the number of fathoms the last part of the call. This is seamanlike and is an advantage to the officer on watch as he will generally get the number of fathoms even though through wind or other causes the first two or three words are not clearly understood.

In learning to heave the lead the marks and deeps should be memorized. No difficulty will then be experienced in reporting the cast.

Many owners of small boats find it convenient to carry a sounding pole for working in narrow, crooked channels, or entering strange harbors where the water is relatively shallow. Notches cut in the pole at every foot from the bottom are easily read and accurate soundings may be taken with great rapidity.

Course Protractors and Parallel Rules

The next article of this series will be devoted to a study of the chart and the use of the course protractor or parallel rules in laying courses. We shall therefore pass over these instruments here with a brief reference to their construction so that their use may be better understood in the discussion which follows:

The parallel rules, as the name implies, consist of a pair of straight-edged rulers connected to each other at each end by metal strips. These strips permit one rule to be moved away from the other a distance depending upon the length of the strips. They are so connected that the edges of the rules always retain their parallel relationship. By their use a line can be passed through the center of a compass rose on the chart parallel to any course which may be plotted.

The course protractor is an instrument which can be used instead of the parallel rules in reading the angle of plotted courses. It is composed of only two parts. One of these is a celluloid disc marked like a compass rose in both points and degrees. The other part is a celluloid arm, pivoted at one end in the center of the disc. The arm permits the orientation of the protractor rose so that its north and south points lie in a line parallel to another drawn through the same points of the compass rose on the chart. Then the course can be read directly from the protractor at the point where the course line cuts the rose. Marks along the edge of the arm give distances in nautical miles according to one of the scales in general use on charts.

The U. S. Power Squadrons has a course plotter designed to measure courses and bearings on charts and plotting sheets with a minimum of lost time and motion. Made of plastic, 4" by 14¾", it is similar to Air Force, Navy and Weems-type plotters. The plastic is ruled with parallel lines, with a 180-degree protractor inscribed midway in the length of the instrument. When used to measure courses or bearings, the instrument is placed on the chart with either long edge or any parallel line, alined along the course or bearing. By sliding the plotter along this line until the center or bull's eye of the protractor is over a meridian, the course or bearing can be read at the point of intersection. The instrument is versatile and may be put to several allied uses.

In one type of course protractor (the True-to-Mag protractor made by Frank H. Parks, Portland, Oregon), an extra arm is provided. This can be clamped to the rotating protractor arm in such a way that it indicates the amount of variation, so true and magnetic courses can be read at a glance, without calculation. It is a convenience not only in laying true courses, but also in plotting positions with the radio direction finder.

One simple type of protractor does not require reference to a compass rose on the chart. Made by J. A. Bowers, Montclair, N. J., it consists merely of a rectangular piece of clear plastic with a half-protractor (180°) imprinted on the left side, a rule along the bottom, and instructions on the right side. To determine a course, the protractor is slid along the chart with either long edge aligned with the course. When the center of the dial intersects a parallel or meridian, the true course can be read directly from the instrument. For magnetic courses, variation is applied to the reading.

Dividers are necessary for picking up exact measurements between points on the chart so that they may be transferred to the scale, where distances can be read.

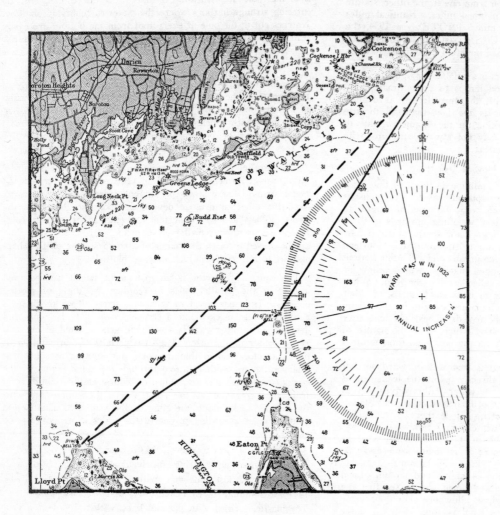

See also

pages 307-328

Figure I. As a general rule it is better practice to lay two short courses between buoys than one long one. This is especially true in thick weather

CHARTS might properly be classified as most important of all the instruments and accessories used in piloting. It would take a skilful boatman indeed to cruise any distance into strange waters without the necessary charts, even if he were equipped with all the other needed devices. On the other hand, practically anyone after a short inspection of the proper charts to determine the more important features could find his way from point to point in good weather simply from information that would be obvious with a few minutes' study. The precision of his piloting might not be of a high order, and he might sail half again as far as would be necessary, but he could nevertheless accomplish his trip safely.

Charts are prepared by various departments of the Government to furnish the pilot or navigator with absolutely accurate representations, to a definite scale, of navigable bodies of water, showing the contour of the land, important landmarks and other useful aids to navigation. They differ from the road map in the great amount of detailed information they give and in the precision with which they are constructed. The need for this accuracy is readily apparent when it is realized that errors of only a small amount in plotting the positions of submerged obstructions would constitute a serious menace to navigation.

It will be seen that complications arise when a spherical surface, such as that of the earth, is to be pictured on a flat or plane surface. A

CHARTS—WHAT THEY SHOW,

HOW THEY ARE USED, AND THE

METHOD OF PLOTTING COURSES

Photographs by

M. Rosenfeld

Figure 2. In laying a course, the protractor rose is first oriented to indicate the same directions as the chart rose. Figure 3 (below). The arm is then swung so that the course can be read where the arm cuts the protractor rose

certain amount of distortion cannot be avoided. However, in the charts we commonly use in piloting, the clever system of projection employed permits us to designate our courses as straight lines, without appreciable error.

There are three methods of projection used in the making of charts—Mercator, polyconic and gnomonic. The latter two we shall pass over briefly as it is the Mercator chart we ordinarily use. In the polyconic it is assumed that a cone is placed over the earth's surface, touching the earth at a parallel of latitude. The apex of the cone is above the earth's pole, at such a distance that the cone is tangent to the earth at the latitude parallel in question. Each point on the earth's surface is then projected outward to the cone. There is little distortion in this type of chart but it is not well adapted to navigational purposes.

The gnomonic projection is developed on the assumption that a plane surface is placed tangent to the earth at a given point. Points on the earth's surface are projected to the plane by lines passing

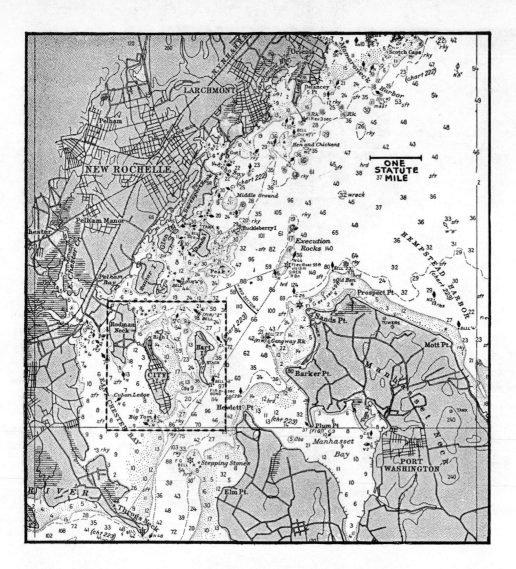

Figure 4. A portion of coast chart number 1213, Western Long Island Sound, scale 1 to 80,000. Note the size of the area enclosed by the dotted lines, as compared with the same area in figure 7. Figure 5 (below) shows some of the standard symbols used on charts

through those points and the earth's center. This is the type of chart used in polar regions where the use of the Mercator projection is not practicable.

In the Mercator chart it is assumed that a cylinder has been placed about the earth, tangent at the equator. The meridians of longitude passing through the north and south poles are then cut and the sections between them opened on the inside of the cylinder in much the same way as sections of an orange peel could be laid back after being cut. In doing this, the meridians of longitude are drawn out east and west so that they appear as parallel straight lines on the cylinder. Near the equator, naturally, the meridians need only be drawn apart a small amount, but in the higher latitudes, where the meridians normally converge, they must be opened out considerably more. Therefore, in order to avoid excessive distortion, the parallels of latitude are also spread apart to a proportionate degree.

This preserves approximately the right shape of objects in high latitudes but their size is relatively greater than that of similar objects in a lower latitude. An island, for example, in 60° latitude would appear considerably larger than a similar island 20° above the equator. Its shape, however, would still be true to its actual proportions The great virtue of the Mercator chart lies in the fact that we can draw upon it a straight line between two points and actually sail that course by determining the compass direction between them. Exactly how this is done we shall see later.

These Mercator charts of the coast which we use in piloting are prepared by the Coast & Geodetic Survey of the Department of Commerce. They may be secured either direct from the main office in Washington, D. C., or at any of the field stations in important cities or from the numerous sales agencies which have been established. A free catalog is issued, showing the area covered by the respective charts.

Rock under water	+
Rock awash (at any stage of the tide)	*
Breakers along shore	
Fishing stakes	
Limiting danger line	
Wreck (any portion of the hull or superstructure above low water)	
Sunken wreck (dangerous to surface navigation)	
Sunken wreck (not dangerous to surface navigation or those over which the depth exceeds 10 fathoms)	
Submarine cable	
Current, not tidal, velocity 2 knots	
Current, not tidal (special usage)	
Tidal currents — Flood, 1½ knots	
Ebb, 1 knot	
Flood, 2d hour	
Ebb, 3d hour	
No bottom at 50 fathoms	
Life-saving station (in general)	L.S.S.
Life-saving station (Coast Guard)	C.G. 161
Lighthouse	
Lighthouse, on small-scale chart	
NOTE.—Light sectors shown by dotted lines	
Light vessels, showing number of mast lights	
Radio station	R.S.
Radio direction finder station (Radio-compass station)	R.f.
Radio tower	R.T.
Radio beacon	R.Bn.

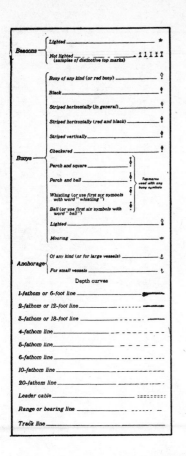

This contains a complete list of the agencies where the charts may be obtained. The cost of the charts is very little as it covers only the expense of printing and distribution.

Charts of the Great Lakes (polyconic projection) are issued by the Lake Survey Office, Federal Building, Detroit (War Department, U. S. Engineers). They differ from coast charts in that they have courses and distances between important points plotted upon them. On lake charts depths under 21 feet are shown in feet in tinted areas and depths beyond the 21-foot limit are shown in fathoms on untinted areas. Foreign charts not published originally in the United States are duplicated by the Oceanographic Office of the Navy Department.

Four different scales are used in the construction of coast charts, showing areas of varying extent. The smaller the area pictured, the greater detail possible. Sailing charts are made to the smallest scale. They cover long stretches of coastline and accordingly can show only the offshore dangers and aids to navigation, together with the more important buoys and landmarks. They are used principally for long runs well off-shore or in fixing position as a ship is approaching shore from seaward.

General coast charts are next in point of area covered, the scale being three times as large as that of the sailing chart. These are used in working along the coast where the boat's position can be frequently fixed by landmarks.

The coast chart generally used on small boats is the third type. These are made on a scale of 1 to 80,000 indicating that each distance on the chart is exactly 1/80,000 part of what it actually is on the earth's surface. This scale figures out so that a nautical mile measures approximately an inch on the chart. An idea of its proportion may be gained from the fact that half of Long Island Sound is shown on one chart. These are the charts used ordinarily for working along the shore and entering harbors.

Figure 6 (above) shows how buoys and fathom lines are symbolized. While these symbols will be found on many charts in current use, reference should also be made to the symbols and abbreviations (pages 324-328) which are being used to create a standard system on all future charts as new plates become necessary

At the right (figure 7) is shown a portion of harbor chart number 223, scale 1 to 20,000. A comparison with figure 4 shows the greater detail possible on large scale charts

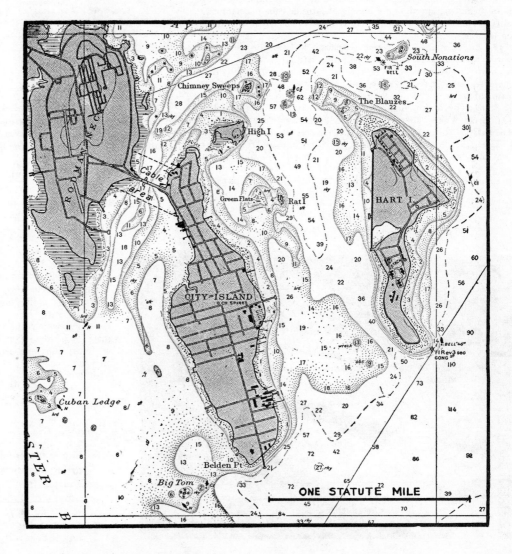

401

Space does not permit the greatest detail on the coast chart, so the fourth series is devoted to harbor charts, drawn on the largest scale. Their size is such that every aid to navigation can be clearly shown without omission of any small details. These are used strictly for local navigation.

Let us take one of the coast charts of the 1200 series and examine it to see what information it supplies. Number 1213 covers the western part of Long Island Sound and is typical of this series. This is in general use by many yachtsmen who have their boats in New York waters.

Parallel lines will be found running north and south. These are the longitude meridians which have been opened out on the Mercator projection to appear parallel on the flat surface. At the top and bottom edges of the chart these lines terminate in a scale from which the longitude west of Greenwich can be read. This scale cannot be used directly as a measure of distance since a degree of longitude represents a greater number of miles at the equator than it does nearer the pole. Meridians may be defined as great circles of the earth passing through the poles. The Greenwich meridian, from which longitude is reckoned, is called the prime meridian.

The horizontal lines are the parallels of latitude. These are further apart than the meridians of longitude because they are separated more and more in the Mercator projection as we go away from the equator in order to preserve the proportion, as explained earlier in the article. In a chart of a region on the equator, the latitude parallels will be the same distance apart as the longitude meridians.

Since a degree of latitude measures 60 miles regardless of its relative position on the earth, the latitude scales at the side of the chart can be used in measuring distance. On a small scale chart it is impossible to give a separate distance scale which will apply to all latitudes shown on the chart. In such cases the latitude scale can be used by taking that portion of it which is opposite the middle latitude of the course or distance being measured. One minute of latitude equals a nautical mile or 6,080 feet. A degree is the equivalent of 60 minutes, or 60 miles.

On charts of the 1200 series a separate scale is given in both yards and nautical miles, though the latitude scale is more accurate. Distances can be picked off the chart with the dividers, transferred to the scale and read directly there in nautical miles. This can be converted to statute or land miles, if desired, by multiplying the number of nautical miles by 1.15. On Great Lakes charts (polyconic projection) distances are taken from scales given in feet, meters, and statute miles.

The next objects of prominence are the compass roses, several of which appear on each chart to simplify the plotting of courses. They appear as concentric circles. The outer one is graduated from zero at north clockwise through 360 degrees.

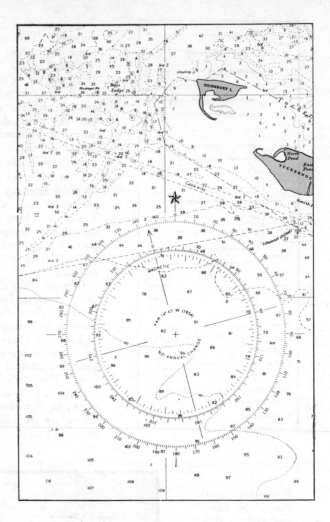

A line through 0 and 180 is parallel with the longitude meridians which pass through the geographic north and south poles. Therefore any direction stated in terms of this outer rose is related to true north and is a true direction or course.

The arrow on the inner rose points to the magnetic north pole. In the case of chart 1213 this is 11¾° west of true north, or approximately one point. This difference between true and magnetic north is the variation, explained in the articles on the compass. At the center of the rose the variation is stated for the year the chart was issued as well as the amount, in minutes, which it is increasing yearly. This annual change is caused by a shifting of the earth's magnetic center of attraction or magnetic north pole.

For ordinary runs, we rarely work with true courses. It is far simpler and easier to use the magnetic rose, since the magnetic directions are the ones which the compass indicates, provided there is no deviation. It is only in cases where we must run long courses, so that the variation changes materially, that it is necessary to work with true courses.

Figure 8 (left). The parallel rules offer an alternate means of taking courses from the chart. Note the excellent chart table provided in this auxiliary. Figure 9 (above), shows a section of chart, illustrating the new type of compass rose

On old charts the magnetic course was always found in points, necessitating a conversion to degrees if the boat's compass card was graduated only in degrees. The newer charts, however, give magnetic directions in both points and degrees. This is a great improvement, as many compasses have cards in which the graduations in points are omitted.

FURTHER examination of the chart shows the shore line, very accurately delineated. This presents an exact picture of the configuration of the land and water areas at high tide. Figures will be found all over the area occupied by water. These are the soundings or depths of water on the exact spots at which the figures are given. On most of our Atlantic Coast piloting charts these depths are given in feet at mean low water, which is the average of all low waters. However, some charts state the depths in fathoms or a combination of feet and fathoms, so it is always best to check the method used by information which appears on the chart.

In those cases where both feet and fathoms are used, the depths of less than 21 feet are shown in feet on tinted areas, greater depths being stated in fathoms untinted. Since the depths given are computed for average low water, there will be times when it is possible that the depths will be slightly less than those indicated. Ordinarily, the tide will be somewhere between low and high so that a certain amount will have to be added to the charted depths. A later article will go into this in greater detail. The figures appearing on the land areas indicate the height of the land in feet above high water.

Dotted lines appear on the chart near shore connecting points of equal depth. These are known as fathom curves or depth curves. They serve as caution lines within which care must be exercised in navigating. If we find from the chart that the curve farthest from shore connects points of five fathoms depth, then all the white area outside of it contains depths of more than 30 feet. Where there are shoals or other obstructions of less depth in this white area, they will be surrounded by a fathom curve, with the correct depths given within it. Whenever the proposed course passes through any of these areas inside a fathom curve it is wise to examine the depths carefully at that point to be certain that there is plenty of water for the draft of the boat.

Interspersed through the soundings there are abbreviations which tell the nature of the bottom. M indicates mud, S sand, gy gray, hrd hard, sft soft, rky rocky, stk sticky, and so on. Any such abbreviations used on a chart are explained in a note on the side of that chart. A comparison of the sample of bottom brought up by the lead in taking a sounding, with the markings on the chart, serves as an excellent check on position.

*LOOKING further on the chart we find numerous little diamond shapes, colored red, black, red and black, or having simply a black outline. These are the buoys. The scheme of coloring and placing them was fully described in a previous chapter on buoyage, and it is a simple matter to identify them on the chart. Their exact position is located by a small black dot placed at one end of the diamond. Black buoys are shown solid black on the chart, while the red ones show red within a black outline. The red and black obstruction buoys are shown with half of the diamond symbol black, half red. White and black mid-channel buoys are shown in black outline with a line drawn through the long axis. A line through the short axis would indicate horizontal striping; through both axes, a checkered buoy. In addition to the color designation a bell buoy will carry the word bell alongside the symbol. Lighted buoys are distinguished by short lines which radiate from the black dot on the symbol. Whistle buoys have a small crescent shape placed at the end of the diamond, and generally carry the word whistle as well. Beacons are represented by a black triangle with the letters Bn.

Letters and numbers placed alongside the buoy symbol aid in identification. Can buoys are indicated by the letter C, nun buoys N, and spars S. W signifies white. Together with the letter will appear the number which the buoy actually carries. When it is lighted, its characteristic is shown in abbreviated form, such as Fl R ev 3 sec (flashing red every 3 seconds.) A few minutes devoted to reading the explanatory matter on the side of the chart will show exactly what all symbols mean and yield a great deal of other valuable information.

Lights are shown by heavy solid dots or stars. These are sometimes more clearly defined by yellow circles. As in the case of buoys, the characteristic of the light is shown in abbreviated form so that it may be positively identified. Sometimes two dotted lines will be found radiating from a light symbol connected by a red arc, labeled red sector. This is frequently used to mark the limits of unsafe waters, the light showing red to anyone within the dangerous sector.

REEFS, rocks, shoals and ledges are all clearly indicated. Small crosses, either alone or surrounded by a dotted circle, denote a rock under water. If the rock is awash at any stage of the tide the cross becomes an asterisk. P D signifies position doubtful; E D, existence doubtful. Submerged wrecks are symbolized by a line crossed with several short lines. Sometimes the word wreck is written in full. If it is not submerged, a different symbol is used, resembling a ship partly sunk, with the bow out of water.

Where larger scale charts are available covering certain harbors, this information is given in red with the chart number. Whenever a larger scale detailed harbor chart can be had, it is always desirable to use it because of the greater amount of information it carries. The data found on a chart are printed in both vertical and leaning type. The vertical lettering denotes that the object is dry at high water; leaning letters would indicate that it was awash, submerged or affected by the water at some stage of the tide.

Where currents are of considerable strength, an arrow is used to show the usual direction. If the current is not tidal, as in some streams and rivers, the arrow carries tail feathers on both sides. Where the current is that created by the flood tide, the feathers appear on one side only. Arrows designating ebb tide are not feathered. The maximum velocity is generally noted near the arrow. Dredged channels are shown by parallel lines of dashes, ranges by lines of dashes and continuous lines.

This covers the more important things which the chart reveals. A half hour devoted to a careful perusal of the chart of home waters will be well repaid by a far better knowledge than can be obtained simply from local knowledge of the water as one sails over the regular courses. In using a chart it is an excellent plan to form the habit of visualizing the landmarks, shore contours, etc., as they will actually appear when sighted. Pick out the most prominent objects and picture how they will bear as the boat sails over the course. A little practice of this sort will help materially in the intelligent use of the chart and in keeping track of the boat's position.

WE come now to the plotting of a course on the chart. Let us suppose we wish to run from Port Jefferson, Long Island, to New Haven, Connecticut. Figure 2 shows a portion of chart number 1212 which covers this area. Coming out of Port Jefferson Harbor we find a bell buoy which serves as a good point of departure. By running close to this we have definitely established a point on the chart from which to lay a course. Glancing at the upper end of the chart, we find that the entrance to New Haven Harbor is protected by breakwaters with lights at each end. Running midway between these, we shall strike the entrance to the buoyed and dredged channel. We note that a straight line from this bell buoy to the breakwater takes us through water of ample depth, free and clear of all obstructions such as rocks and shoals. We therefore draw this line on the chart to indicate the track which we want to make good.

We then place the course protractor (see Figure 2) on the chart with its center over our position at the lower end of the course, that is, at the bell buoy. The next step is to swing the arm of the protractor so that its edge cuts through the center of the compass rose on the chart, as indicated by the dotted line in the figure. (It is unnecessary to draw this dotted line.) This line cuts the magnetic compass rose at a point very nearly NE x E. ¼ E. Knowing this, we are able to rotate the protractor rose until it is also cut at the same point by the protractor arm. Then the relative directions of the same points on both roses are identical. Note that a line through the N and S points of the protractor rose (as indicated by the short arrow in the figure) is parallel to the arrow indicating N on the chart rose. We have simply transferred the chart rose to a convenient position at the starting point of our course so that we can read the course angle directly from the protractor rose.

* NOTE: Changes are gradually being made in charts, as new editions are issued, to bring all symbols into conformity with a standard system adopted by the Coast and Geodetic Survey and Oceanographic Office. See pages 324-328.

Now we hold the protractor rose in position and swing the arm around until it lies along the course. (See figure 3.) It cuts the protractor rose at NE ½ N, (40°) which is the desired *magnetic* course. We cannot steer this course by compass, however, unless there is no deviation on a heading of NE ½ N. So we refer to our deviation table or Napier diagram and according to the rules laid down in the previous discussion of the compass, find the compass course which corresponds to a magnetic course of NE ½ N. Assuming that our deviation has been plotted on the card shown in figure 25 (page 277) we should have to steer a compass course of NNE ¼ E to make good NE ½ N magnetic.

IF parallel rules are used to determine the course angle we arrive at the same result by a slightly different principle. Figure 8 shows a series of courses plotted on chart 1212 to take us safely from the channel north of Shelter Island around through Gardiners Bay and Plum Gut and across Long Island Sound to Duck Island Roads. The second leg of this course lies through Gardiners Bay. To determine its direction by means of the parallel rules, we place the edge of one rule along the course and, holding it firmly in place, we swing the other rule away from the first until it cuts through the center of the compass rose on the chart. The magnetic rose is also cut at NE ½ N, which is the desired *magnetic* course. As noted above, this must be converted to a compass course before we can steer it. Instead of transferring the rose to our course as we did with the protractor, in using parallel rules we transfer the course to the rose. If the connecting links of the rules do not permit reaching the center of the rose in a single step, it may be accomplished in several steps by alternately pushing the separate rules ahead, in each case holding one firmly on the chart to preserve the parallel relationship.

THE following few hints will be found useful in the plotting of courses. Always start and finish the course at definite points which may be easily located. At the beginning, make the successive legs of the course as short as possible, taking full advantage of all buoys and navigational aids, even if this should involve a little longer run. It is remarkable generally how little is added to the total distance run. Thus, in figure 1, on a 10-mile run across the Sound we add only ¼ mile to our distance by laying the course in two steps of five miles each, picking up about half-way an extra buoy which is a full mile off the straight line course. In a later article it will be shown how we could run the single straight course and check our position and distance as the buoy is passed. Take particular care to note the depths of water over which the course line passes and avoid passing too close to unmarked shoals, as the boat may be set off its course by wind and current. How these factors are allowed for will also be developed in a subsequent article. Avoid laying a course across a shoal where the depths are little more than the draft of the boat as shoals sometimes build up and change their depths rapidly.

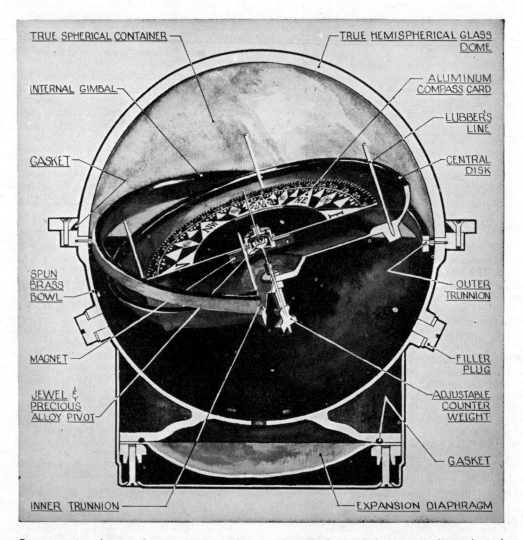

Cut-away view showing the construction and essential parts of one of the most modern spherical compasses, in which the gimbal ring is located inside the hemispherical glass dome. The design is such as to give maximum stability to the card, which is easily read because of the magnifying effect of the spherical glass. The reverse type card has white letters and figures on a black background.
(Courtesy Wilfrid O. White & Sons, Inc.)

HOW THE PILOT FINDS HIMSELF BY TAKING BEARINGS. LINES OF POSITION, AND THE FIX BY CROSS BEARINGS, BOW AND BEAM BEARINGS, DOUBLING THE ANGLE, ETC.

See also pages 335-344

I N piloting, our fundamental problem is to be able to determine the boat's position at any time with reasonable accuracy. This accomplishes two things. It gives us a check by which we may know whether or not the boat is on a predetermined course and, secondly, it gives us a starting point from which to lay a new course in the event that unforeseen conditions make it desirable to run to a different point than that originally decided upon. The method we use in fixing a boat's position is to compare it with locations of visible objects which can be identified and found on the chart.

Let us suppose that we are out in an open bay and wish to run to a certain harbor that is not in sight. As there are no buoys nearby we are not sure of our position. However, on shore in the distance we can see a lighthouse that is familiar. If we can sight that lighthouse over a compass by means of a sight vane or with the aid of a pelorus and find that it bears due north of us, we know then that we are somewhere on a line running south from that object. Such a line is called a line of position.

That in itself, however, does not give us a precise position unless we have some means of knowing just where we are on that line. If we knew how far away the light was we could step that distance off on the chart and find our position. Or we might have some other prominent object in view which appears on the chart. Suppose there is a tower off to the eastward. Then we must also be on a line running west from the tower. Crossing these two lines of position by drawing them on the chart, one south from the lighthouse, one westward from the tower, we know we must be on both lines and therefore can be at only one point, that is, at their intersection. A definite point such as this, establishing the boat's position, is called a fix.

Bearings are in reality lines of position for they give us an idea of our position without determining the exact spot. Two or three such bearings crossed give us a fix. Previously we discussed the construction of the sight vane and the pelorus. In

Figure 10. Getting a fix by bearings on three objects. The boat's position is indicated by the small circle

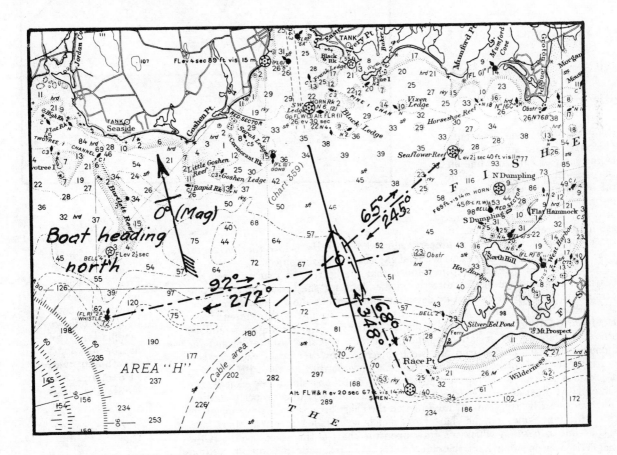

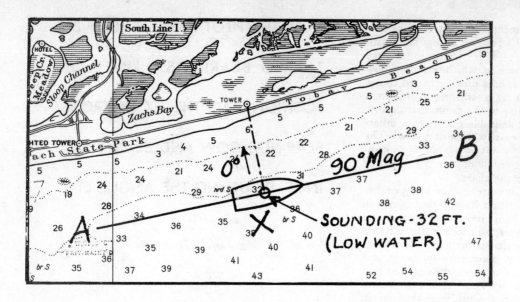

Figure 11. A fix obtained by a single bearing, the distance from the observed object being determined from a sounding

EASY METHODS OF

FIXING POSITION

BY BEARINGS ON

VISIBLE OBJECTS

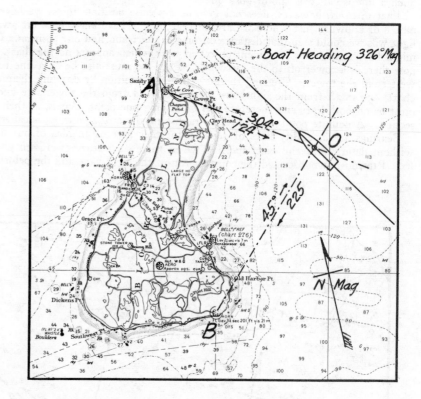

using the sight vane, it is only necessary to sight across the top of the compass card and line up the vertical sighting pins with the object on which we are taking a bearing. The short posts provided on the circular frame are used to rotate the frame to the point where the object is properly aligned. Directly below the horizontal wire connecting the vertical pins we read the bearing of the object.

The important point to keep in mind is that the bearing so read is a *compass* bearing and cannot be plotted directly on the chart for the reason that the compass has probably been affected by deviation and does not show a *magnetic* direction. Ten bearings on the same object from the same point with different boats would probably give ten different compass bearings. Each compass would be affected differently by deviation depending on the particular installation and the amount and proximity of iron and steel objects. However, after each *compass* bearing had been corrected for its own deviation according to the rules given in a previous article, the ten resulting *magnetic* directions should be exactly the same, if the observations have been accurate and the deviations properly applied. That *magnetic* bearing can be laid down on the chart because we have a magnetic rose (the inner one) on the chart from which we can get magnetic directions.

The line of position which we draw upon the chart is the exact reverse of the magnetic bearing; that is, if the object bears 315° magnetic the line of position plotted on the chart is drawn 135° from the object. Where the chart shows only

Figure 12. Locating the boat's position by cross bearings on two landmarks. The nearer 90° apart the objects bear, the more accurate the fix is likely to be

406

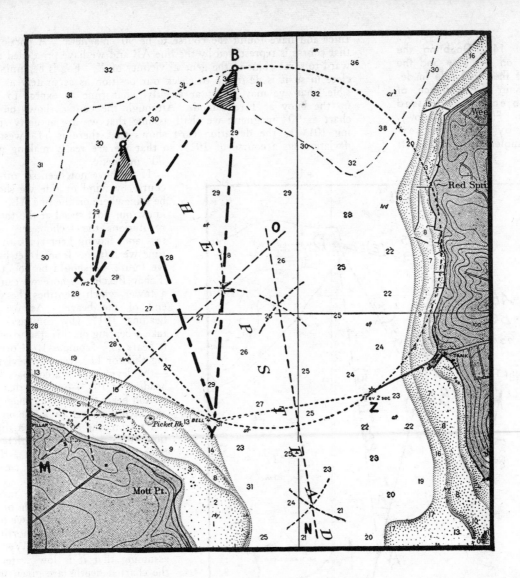

Figure 13. This illustrates the danger of a revolver in getting a fix by horizontal sextant angles on three objects. When the boat is on a circle passing through these objects a fix is impossible

a true compass rose, the observed compass bearing must be corrected for variation as well as deviation. The corrected compass bearing then becomes a true bearing and can be plotted on the chart by reference to the true compass rose, reversing the bearing by adding or subtracting 180°. If the object bears 20° true, then the line of position must be drawn from the object in a direction 200° true.

Now, in taking out the deviation from the deviation table or Napier diagram to apply to a given bearing, it is important to select that deviation which is given for the *heading* of the *boat* at the time the bearing was taken, not the one for the bearing of the object. The reason for this is obvious as it is the direction of the boat's head which determines the amount the compass card is deflected.

Where the pelorus is used for taking the bearing instead of a sight vane, the pelorus card is first rotated so that it indicates the same *compass* heading as the steering compass. The card is then clamped in this position and the boat held exactly on the same compass course. The resulting compass bearing taken by pelorus will be the same as though it were taken directly from the steering compass. Accordingly it must be corrected as in the previous illustration for deviation if we are using the magnetic chart rose, or for both deviation and variation if we are working with a true chart rose. Likewise the plotted magnetic or true line of position is the exact reverse of the bearing, differing from the bearing by 16 points or 180°.

It is possible to apply the deviation to the boat's compass heading before setting the pelorus card. We are then in effect fixing the pelorus card on the boat's magnetic heading. Bearings taken under these circumstances will be magnetic and can be plotted as such upon the chart. Or both the deviation and variation could be applied before setting the pelorus card and the resulting bearings would be true. As a rule, however, the pelorus is brought into agreement with the steering compass and the compass bearings corrected as may be necessary.

With this background of theory, let us take up some actual problems in getting a fix. Figure 11 shows a portion of chart number 1215, approaches to New York. Let us assume that we have laid a course from the bell buoy off Jones Inlet to the bell buoy off Fire Island

Figure 14. Doubling the angle on the bow and the use of the 7/10 rule in determining the distance of an object when passed abeam. Figure 15 (below). A fix by horizontal sextant angles on three objects

Inlet and have found the course to be 90° magnetic. A portion of that course is represented by the line AB and we have proceeded eastward to some point in the general vicinity of X. Fog is beginning to close in so it is desirable to check our position as accurately as possible, that we may know at exactly what time to expect to pick up the buoy at Fire Island. Although the course shows on the chart as 90° magnetic we shall assume that we are actually steering 101° as the deviation card shows that there is 11° westerly deviation on a course of 101°, so that we are really making good 90° magnetic.

If we have not been set off our course by wind or tide we should be somewhere on the line AB. We know our boat speed at the rate of revolutions the tachometer registers and, having kept track of the time we left the Jones Inlet buoy, we figure we should be about off Tobay Beach. Ashore we can see a tower which identifies the west end of the beach. As we are heading 101° (by compass) we take a bearing on this station when it bears 11° (compass). Correcting this for 11° westerly deviation —the deviation for a compass *boat* heading of 101°—we find that the station bears 0° (North) magnetic and accordingly draw a line on the chart from the station in a direction 180° magnetic (South), intersecting our course line AB at X, which should be our correct position.

As a further check we take a sounding and get a depth of 32 feet, which assures us that we have not been set very much north or south of our course. (We are assuming that it is low water as the charted depths are given with reference to low water. Later we shall see how corrections to sound-

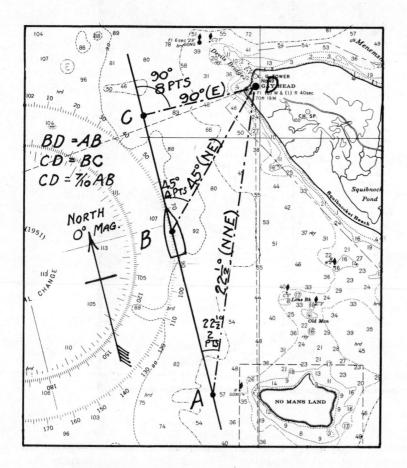

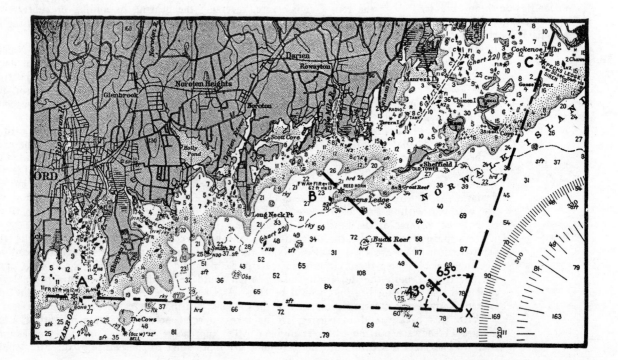

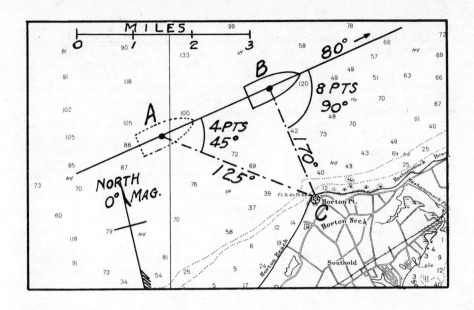

Figure 16. Getting a position by bow and beam bearings. The distance run from A to B equals the distance from B to C

ings may be made for a given stage of tide.) In this case the sounding gives us an excellent idea of our distance from shore as the bottom shelves off gradually and uniformly. Had we gotten a depth of 26 feet we would know immediately that we were not on our course but had been set in toward the beach, either by current, wind or poor steering inside the five-fathom line, necessitating a decided change in course. Otherwise we might finish up on the beach instead of at the Fire Island buoy. We note the time of our bearing and sounding on the chart carefully and since we have the time of our departure from Jones Inlet, we can calculate with considerable exactness just when we should pick up the Fire Island Inlet buoy.

Now in the foregoing illustration we have arbitrarily assumed that only a single landmark is visible. Very frequently there will be two or more objects visible at the same time. Figure 12 illustrates such a case. We are coming in toward the bell buoy at the north end of Block Island from a general southeasterly direction. The boat is on a compass course of 326° and, for the sake of clarity and simplicity, we shall assume at first that there is no deviation on a compass heading of 326°. Both ends of Block Island are clearly visible although the buoy we are heading for is not.

LOOKING ashore for prominent marks we note a lighthouse at the north end of the island and another at the south end. So, without knowing our position as yet, we can take bearings on both objects and find where we are relative to them. The first bearing on the light at Sandy Point (A) shows that it bears 304° from us, so we can lay down one line of position 124° from A on the chart. (We can use the compass bearing as a magnetic direction since we have assumed no deviation.)

Now as rapidly as possible we take the second bearing on the light at B, in order that the boat will not change her position materially between bearings. This bearing tells us that B bears 225° from the boat. Consequently we must be on a line 45° from B and we accordingly draw such a line on the chart. These two lines of position intersect at O, which gives us a fix and determines our position.

In the event that thick weather were closing in on us at this point, it would be a simple matter to lay a new course from O to the bell off Block Island Harbor and from that point a second course in to the breakwater entrance.

This case illustrates the method of getting a fix by cross bearings on two objects. It is the simplest of all methods and is frequently used. At the same time it is very precise if the work is done accurately and the deviation known and correctly applied. Always select objects bearing as near 90° apart as

possible, as this will involve the smallest error in plotting. Never choose objects less than 30° apart nor more than 150°. In these cases the lines intersect in an acute or obtuse angle and a slight error in plotting either line throws the point of intersection too far from its correct position. Near objects are preferable to distant ones from the standpoint of accuracy in plotting but keep in mind that if the boat is under way, very close objects will change their bearing rapidly.

When bearings are taken on three objects for the purpose of getting a fix, it is quite likely that the lines of position will not intersect in a single point. This is due to inaccuracies in observation and plotting. Generally the lines of position will cross in such a manner that a small triangle is formed by the three points of intersection and the boat's position may safely be taken as the central point within the triangle.

Figure 10 illustrates such a problem. Coming from the eastward through The Race, we have rounded Race Point and are crossing the western end of Fishers Island Sound, bound into New London Harbor. Let us assume that there is 6° westerly deviation so that we are steering 6° (by compass) and are actually making good 0° (North) magnetic.

Three bearings are taken in rapid succession. The first shows that Seaflower Reef light bears 71° by compass. Applying to this the westerly deviation of 6° (for a magnetic *boat* heading of 0°, or North) we find that the magnetic bearing is 65° giving us a line of position on the chart 245° magnetic from this light.

The second observation shows that lighted whistle buoy "2A" bears 278° by compass. We again apply the 6° westerly deviation and get a magnetic bearing of 272°. Reversing this, we get a line of position 92° magnetic from the buoy.

The third bearing tells us that Race Point light bears by compass 174°. Applying the westerly deviation, we get a magnetic bearing of 168° and a line of position 348° magnetic from the light.

Plotting these three lines of position we get a fix as shown in figure 10, taking the boat's position to be at the point indicated by the small circle within the triangle.

NO mention was made of the sextant in the earlier article on piloting instruments as this is ordinarily found only on larger craft making extended voyages to sea. However, where a sextant is available it may often be used to advantage in getting a fix by piloting methods. In principle, a sextant is simply a device which enables an observer to measure the angle in degrees, minutes and seconds between two objects. One object is seen directly through a clear glass and the instrument is adjusted by the observer so that the second object is seen reflected by mirrors, directly over the first. The angle between the objects is then read from a calibrated arc.

The last problem showed how a fix was obtained by compass bearings on three objects. Figure 15 illustrates how sextant angles may be used to get a position. A, B and C are three prominent charted objects. The angle between A and B as measured by sextant from the boat's position in the vicinity of X is 43°. The angle between B and C is 65°. These two angles are plotted on a sheet of transparent paper, using a protractor to accurately establish the angles AXB and BXC so that they correspond exactly with the measured sextant angles. When the paper is moved about over the chart, it will be found that there can be only one position for X when the lines AX, BX and CX pass through the three objects observed. This system of getting a fix is easy and accurate and does not require the use of a compass or a knowledge of the amount of compass deviation. This is called the three-point problem.

HOWEVER, in using this method, there is one important caution to be observed. The three objects should be on a straight line, or nearly so. If they are not, the middle object should be nearer the boat than the other two. The reason for this is clearly shown in figure 13. If an observer on a boat in the general area about A or B were to use the buoys X and Y and the light Z to obtain a fix by horizontal sextant angles, he might be somewhere on the circle indicated by the dotted line passing through X, Y, and Z. The dotted construction lines in the figure show how a circle can be described geometrically through any three given points. OM is a straight line perpendicular to a line connecting points X and Y and bisecting the line XY. Similarly ON bisects and is perpendicular to YZ. The intersection of OM and ON at O is the center of the circle BAXYZ.

Now it can be proved geometrically that if the angle between X and Y be measured from various points on the circumference of the circle, it will be exactly the same in all cases. Thus angle XAY equals angle XBY. Therefore an observer would measure the same sextant angle at A as he would at B and in attempting to plot his position on the chart, he would find that his tracing paper could be moved about so that there would be an infinite number of points where his plotted lines would pass through X, Y and Z. He would also find that the curve connecting all those possible positions of his boat would describe the arc XABZ. This condition, where the boat happens to be on a circle passing through the three observed points, is known as a revolver and must be avoided, as a fix under these circumstances is impossible. A compass bearing on any one of the objects would overcome the difficulty as this would definitely establish the direction of one line of position.

BOW and beam bearings are another simple and valuable system of getting a fix. The principle of this method may be briefly stated in the following way: if an object is observed when it bears four points (45°) on the bow and again when it comes abeam then the distance run between observations is the distance the object is being passed abeam. It is unnecessary here to go into the geometrical proof of this case but it may be stated that it depends on a very simple theorem.

To illustrate this problem let us consider figure 16. We shall assume that we are running a course of 80° (magnetic) along the north shore of Long Island and are about to pass the light on Horton Point. If there is no deviation we are steering 80°. Therefore when the light bears 125°, it will be four points off the starboard bow or 45° from dead ahead. The light will bear 125° when we arrive at the point A and at this instant we note the reading of the log (if we have one) or else take the exact time by watch. Holding the course carefully we proceed until the light comes abeam, that is, 8 points or 90° from the bow. In this case it will bear 170°. At this point we again take the reading of the log or watch. If we are using a log the difference in mileage readings will give the distance from A to B directly. With the watch it will be necessary to compute the distance from the elapsed time and speed. Then, if the tachometer shows that the engine is turning 1,000 r.p.m. and we know that the boat makes 8 m.p.h. at that engine speed, a 15-minute run from A to B would mean that we had run two miles between observations, neglecting wind and current. Then we know that we are passing two miles off the light and must be at the point B.

ONCE again, we have a caution to observe. BC will equal AB only when we compute correctly the distance we make good over the bottom. A two-mile-per-hour current against us between A and B would hold us back 15/60 or ¼ of

2 miles. That half-mile deducted from our estimated two-mile run at 8 m.p.h. would mean only 1½ miles made good over the bottom and BC accordingly would be 1½ miles instead of 2. In like manner we must always estimate and allow for the assisting or retarding influence of both wind and current. For the present it will be all right to estimate this. Later in a discussion of current diagrams we shall learn how to make accurate computations where current is involved.

If we are concerned only with determining the *distance* at which we are passing the object abeam, we may disregard deviation, since the principle will hold good regardless of the direction of the course line. The important factor is that the bearings be taken at 4 points (45°) and 8 points (90°). However, if we wish a precise *position*, then deviation must be applied (for the particular heading of the boat) in order to properly chart the magnetic bearings.

IT will be noted that in the previous example of a bow and beam bearing we were, in effect, doubling the angle of the bearing on the bow, that is, 4 points (45°) and 8 points (90°). The same principle may be used in other combinations of angles. For example in figure 14, we are on a course 0° (North) magnetic from No Man's Land to Canapitsit Channel past Gay Head. If a bearing is taken on Gay Head Light when it bears 2 points (22½°) on the bow (A) and again when it bears 4 points (45°) on the bow (B) then BD will equal AB. This is called doubling the angle on the bow and is valuable because it gives a fix before the object is brought abeam. Furthermore, when the 2-point (22½°) and 4-point (45°) combination is used we can determine the distance at which we will pass the object when it comes abeam. The rule is that 7/10 of the distance run between the 2-point (22½°) and 4-point (45°) bearings will be the distance off the object when it is brought abeam. So, we know at B, if we have run 3 miles from A, we are 3 miles from D and will be a little over 2 miles from D when we have brought it abeam at C. As a further check, reverting to our bow and beam problem, the distance run from B to C will also equal CD.

In this illustration, if the boat is on a 0° (North) magnetic course and there is no deviation, at A the 2-point (22½°) bearing, Gay Head will bear 22½° (NNE). At B, the 4-point bearing, it will bear 45° (NE), and at C, with the lighthouse abeam, D will bear due E (90°).

If there were 8° easterly deviation on a boat heading of N magnetic we would be steering 352° by compass to make good 0° magnetic and our bearings would be 14½° at A; 37° at B; and 82° at C. After the corrections have been made to the bearings for deviation, the results would be identical with those plotted in figure 14.

THERE are many combinations of bearings which can be used to determine distance off an object but it is unnecessary to consider any but the more important ones. They are the easiest of application, can readily be remembered and consequently will be used in preference to others that require reference to a book. The only other combination of bearings that it is well to memorize, is 26½°—45°. If the first bearing is taken when the object bears 26½° off the bow and the second taken at 45°, then the distance run between bearings will be the distance off the object when it is passed abeam.

Bowditch's American Practical Navigator is recommended to those who may be interested in the many combinations of bearings possible, both for the determination of the distance of an object at the second of two bearings, and also at the time it will be passed abeam. Another short table in the chapter on Piloting lists the combinations of bearings which will give the distance abeam directly from the distance run.

Summing up the work in the foregoing problems, then, the vital points to fix in mind when applying these principles are the following. The deviation to be applied to a bearing is the one which applies to the *heading* of the *boat* when the bearing is taken. In working with distances, the actual distance made good *over the bottom* must be calculated, not the distance through the water. When working a 3-point problem using horizontal sextant angles, *avoid a revolver* by selecting objects nearly in line.

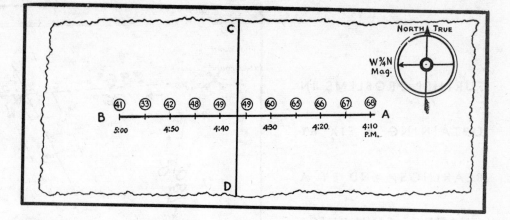

Figure 17. Position by a chain of soundings. The soundings are taken at regular intervals and plotted on transparent paper as shown

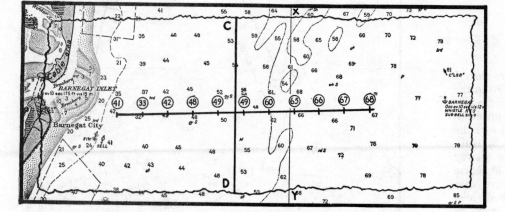

Figure 18. The paper is then moved about on the chart until the sounded depths correspond with the charted depths

See also pages 335-344

FINDING A POSITION BY TWO BEARINGS ON ONE OBJECT, A LINE OF SOUNDINGS, AND BY VERTICAL SEXTANT ANGLE. RANGES, DANGER BEARINGS AND DANGER ANGLES

SEVERAL methods have already been considered by which a fix may be obtained from compass bearings on one object. There is another method which could be used to accomplish the same result, that is, by two bearings and a run between.

Referring to figure 19, let us suppose that we are on a magnetic course of 39° and wish to determine our position, using only the lighthouse at X. As yet we know only the direction of the course we are running. Naturally, as in all previous problems, proper allowance must be made for deviation, if any exists, on a 39° magnetic heading. This will be applied to all courses and lines of position before the magnetic directions are plotted on the chart.

We take our first bearing when the boat is in the general vicinity of B and find that X bears 0° (due North). This gives us a line of position which we plot immediately upon the chart. At the instant of taking the bearing we also record either the reading of the log, or the time by watch. Then we hold the course carefully until the second bearing is taken. Let us assume that the tachometer is registering 1400 r.p.m. and we know from trial runs that this produces a boat speed of 12 m.p.h. On that basis, in a period of 20 minutes we should cover 4 miles. When this time has elapsed we take the second bearing and get a line of position 106° from X. This is also plotted on the chart. Had we used a log, the difference between readings at the two bearings should also give us a distance run of 4 miles.

Now, with two lines of position plotted, we go to the chart compass rose and find our course of 39°. The parallel rules are then set on this 39° magnetic course and the rules are stepped across the chart to a point where the lines of position intercept a distance on the course line of exactly 4 miles as measured by the dividers from the mile scale. The line Bb indicates the position that the rule finally takes, giving us a fix at b. It will be noted that

FURTHER PROBLEMS IN

OBTAINING A FIX BY

BEARINGS, AND BY A

CHAIN OF SOUNDINGS

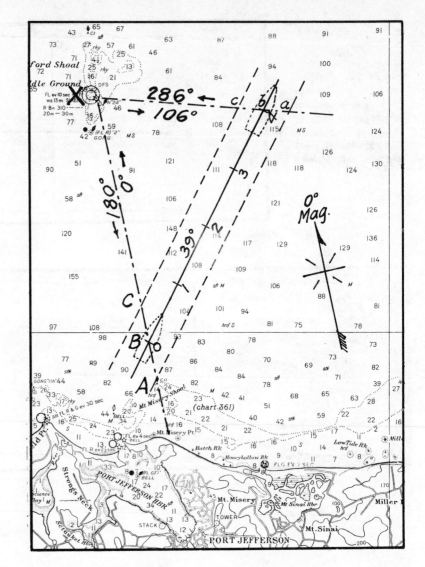

Aa is a greater distance than 4 miles, and Cc is less. As in the former problems where the element of distance is involved, the distance made good over the bottom must be used, by making due allowance for leeway and drift. The above of course is simply an illustrative case and any combination of distances and bearings may be used, but an angle between lines of position of approximately 90° yields the most accurate fix.

The working of the problems thus far considered has been based on the supposition that at least one charted object is visible. A condition might arise, however, where fog or some other cause of low visibility would shut in at a time when no landmark or aid to navigation is in sight, and when the boat's position is only roughly known. In cases of this kind the lead is likely to be invaluable and simply as a matter of prudent judgment, it is wise to keep it going at frequent and regular intervals. A comparison of soundings with the charted depths, along with the information regarding the nature of the bottom as revealed by the chart and the particles brought up by the arming of the lead, is generally sufficient to give a fair idea of the boat's position. At any rate, ample warning will probably be given before the boat gets into foul ground.

The scientific method of using the lead involves the running of a chain of soundings at fixed intervals at a known speed. There are many places where the nature of the bottom is such that this procedure will result in a very accurate fix. Of course, in a case where depths are reasonably constant, it is of little value, but along a coast such as is shown in figure 18, the lead is a sure guide.

Figure 18 reproduces a portion of chart 1216 of the Jersey coast. Let us suppose that we have laid a course from Barnegat lightship for the inlet. Fog closes in and we wish to keep track of our position as closely as possible at all times. Throttling the motor down, we let it turn at a speed that we know from past performance gives us a boat speed of 6 m.p.h. At this rate we cover half a mile every 5 minutes. Then, holding the course of 278° (W ¾ N) magnetic as steadily as possible, we take a sounding at regular 5-minute intervals and carefully record the depths, making allowance for any increase in depth in case it is not low water.

A reasonably accurate table to work from in correcting soundings to charted depths would be as follows: at high water, deduct the entire range of the tide; first hour after high, deduct ⅞ of the range; second hour after high, deduct ¾ of the range; third hour, ½; fourth hour, ¼; fifth hour, ⅛.

Between the first and eleventh soundings, we should have covered five miles

Figure 19. A fix by two bearings and a run between. The distance run, on a given course, will check in at only one point between the plotted lines of position

See also table, page 304

412

which, on the basis of time run from the lightship, should bring us within hearing of the bell buoy. However, it is not visible and cannot be heard, so we stop until a check can be made with the chart.

On a piece of transparent paper (see figure 17) we draw a vertical line CD, which we arbitrarily use to represent a meridian on the chart running north and south *true*. Then with reference to this true meridian we plot a second line, AB, 278° (W ¾ N) *magnetic* to represent the course we have run. Referring to the scale of miles we lay off on the course line from A to B eleven points at intervals of half a mile each to correspond with the intervals at which the soundings were taken. The sounded depths are then recorded at these points in the order in which they were taken.

In the next step (figure 18), the transparent paper is placed upon the chart in the general vicinity of our probable position. Then, with the plotted meridian line CD always parallel to the actual chart meridian XY, the paper is moved about until a point is found where the soundings agree approximately with the charted depths. Our sounding of 60 feet is sure to come very close to the 10-fathom curve, so the paper is moved north and south with this sounding following the curve fairly closely. Another characteristic of the bottom that helps materially is the hole that is found at the last sounding. Note that the depths have consistently decreased until the last sounding, where it suddenly increases about 8 feet. Now if AB is moved north, our 41-foot sounding will not check with the 35-foot depth. If we move AB south, the 33-foot sounding will not check with the 40-foot depth. Therefore, our position is fairly well established at the point indicated by the 41-foot sounding as it is located in the figure. This tells us that in order to pick up the bell buoy, we will have to run about half a mile to the southwest.

Figure 20. The danger bearing. As long as Nash Island light bears 349°, or to the eastward of 349°, there is no danger of striking the ledge at Black Rock

Under certain conditions a sextant can be used for obtaining a fix from a single landmark. If the object is not too far distant and is of considerable height, the angle it subtends at the boat can be measured by sextant. This in conjunction with a bearing will give a fix.

For example, we might be off the Fire Island beach

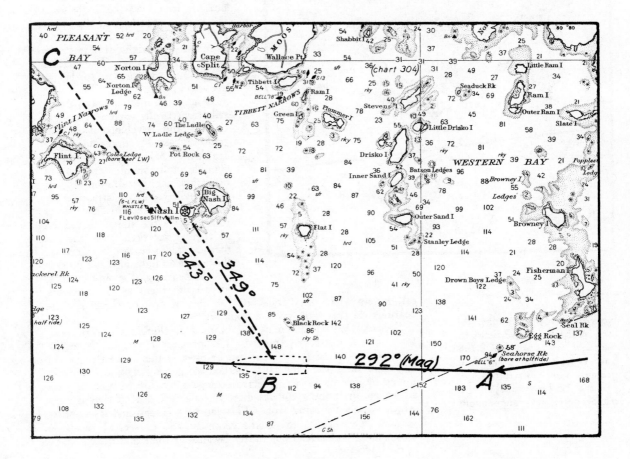

and find that Fire Island lighthouse bears due north magnetic. That gives us a line of position south from the light. The chart tells us that the light is 167 feet above high water. If we measure the angle between the light and water level and get 1°14′ we can turn to table 9 in Bowditch and find our distance from the light in nautical miles. In the column for a heighth of 170 feet we run down to the angle 1°14′ and find opposite this figure in the distance column 1.3 nautical miles. The actual height of the lighthouse is 167 feet instead of 170 so our distance is just a trifle less than the tabulated 1.3.

This method of getting a fix is resorted to only in cases where no other is available as the results secured are not too accurate. A sounding taken in conjunction with the sextant angle would be a valuable check in many cases. A number of other points should also be kept in mind when using this method. The higher and nearer

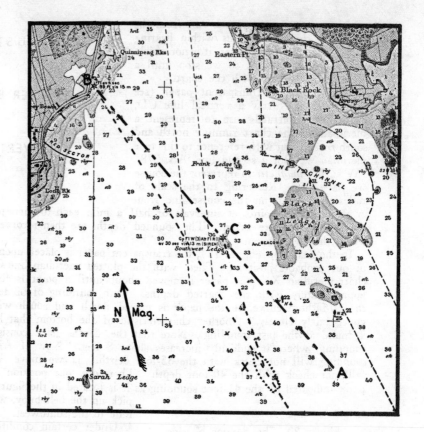

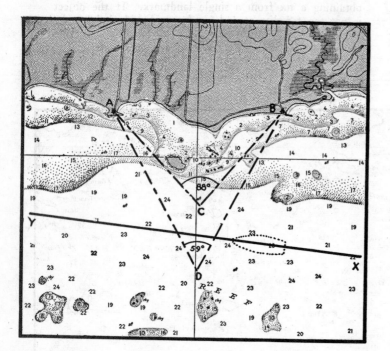

Figure 21 (top). Ranges. As long as the light at C bears to the right or eastward of B, the boat is well clear of all foul ground near Black Ledge. Figure 22 (bottom). The double horizontal danger angle

the object observed, the greater the measured angle will be and the more reliable will be the distance. The observer should be careful to get as near the water as possible in taking the angle since the angle at the base of the object should be 90°. A correction might be made for height of tide if the range is appreciable. The charted heights are given in feet for height above high water.

One of the most important contributions to the science of navigation is the development of the radiocompass direction finder. Sets are now being built, compact enough and simple enough in operation for installation aboard the small yacht or cruiser. By their use operators of small boats can tune in the signals broadcast at regular intervals from the numerous radio-beacon stations on shore and on lightships and quickly get the bearings of several stations, identifying them by characteristic call letters which they transmit. A plot of two or three of these bearings on the chart gives a good fix.

Broadcasting stations may also be used for bearings if their positions on the chart are known. The greatest virtue of the radiocompass lies in the fact that it can be used in the thickest fog or at any other time when the usual methods of getting a fix are rendered useless by low visibility. The radiocompass can also be used to great advantage in running courses directly to a radiobeacon station from which signals are being sent. This can be accomplished if necessary without reference to the boat's compass. Small sets of this type have gained widespread popularity because of their inestimable value in thick weather.

THERE are three general ways in which the pilot can be sure he is clear of hidden dangers without getting a fix. These involve the use of ranges, danger bearings, and danger angles. Figure 21 illustrates one good type of range. A boat is shown at X approaching New London harbor from a general southerly direction. Two prominent lights are located on the chart at B and C and it is found that a line drawn through them passes well clear of all foul ground around Black Ledge. All the water to the south and west of this range is clear of obstructions. As long as B bears to the left or westward of C, the boat is sure to be southwestward of the line AC and consequently in no danger of going aground on the ledge.

Ranges are frequently built at the ends of dredged channels. By keeping them exactly in line, with one structure directly behind the other, or with one light directly over the other, a boat can be held on a straight line down a narrow channel.

There are innumerable cases where charted objects such as headlands, islands, chimneys, towers, etc., can be used as natural ranges in exactly the same way as the lighthouses in the case covered by figure 21. In many localities where channels and obstructions are poorly marked by aids to navigation, fishermen and local pilots navigate safely and surely by means of ranges of this kind.

THE danger bearing functions the same as the range in keeping a boat clear of dangerous ground, except that a single object is used. In figure 20 we have assumed that a boat is bound westward along the Maine Coast and is about to enter Pleasant Bay. Rounding Seahorse Rock bell buoy, a course is laid 292° magnetic in order to carry the boat well clear to the southward of Black Rock. While the boat is on that course there is no danger but the problem is to have a definite check which will prevent turning northward too soon, without going miles out of the way. This is accomplished by taking a danger bearing on Nash Island Light.

A point is selected, at B, which is the logical place to change the course since the new course can be laid straight through from B to C and at the same time it gives Black Rock a sufficiently wide berth. From B a line is drawn through Nash Island Light and it is found that the bearing of the light is 349° magnetic from that point. Therefore, a course of 292° magnetic is held from A until Nash Island Light bears 349° magnetic. The course is then changed to 343°. As long as the light bears 349° or to the eastward of 349°, there is no danger of striking Black Rock, regardless of the exact position of the boat.

SOMETIMES there will be outlying shoals or unmarked reefs along a coast and the problem is to be certain that these dangerous areas are given a sufficiently wide berth. If there should be prominent objects of any kind on shore which can be found on the chart, the obstruction can be safely cleared by the application of the horizontal danger angle.

In figure 22, we are running along a shore unmarked by buoys and spotted with outlying reefs. We wish to take the boat through from X to Y, between the rocks and shoals lying inside of C and the reef indicated outside of D. A point is selected at C on the chart which is well clear of all obstructions along the shore. Lines are plotted from this point through the objects A and B and the angle ACB is measured by means of the protractor. This is found to be 88°.

Similarly, a point D is selected a safe distance inside of the outer reef. The angle ADB, measured in the same way, is found to be 59°. Running through this passage, the angle between A and B is observed by sextant and the course is so shaped that the angle measured from a point between the obstructions is about 75°. That takes the boat through on approximately a middle course between C and D. In no case must the angle ACB be allowed to exceed 88° nor must ADB be smaller than 59°.

The case described above is called the double horizontal danger angle, involving both a minimum and maximum angle. Naturally the same theory may be applied where there is only an inner or outer danger, in which case a single angle is sufficient.

For example, in the same illustration let us suppose there are no outlying reefs anywhere south of the line XY. Inshore of that line we shall assume the water is shoal with a rocky bottom. The point D is selected at a safe distance outside of all dangerous ground and the angle ADB is found to be 59°. If the observed sextant angle between A and B is kept smaller than 59°, the boat will be well clear of all danger.

THE vertical danger angle works on the same general theory but the angle is measured on the height of a single vertical object rather than between two horizontal objects. Figure 23 illustrates the application of this principle. Assuming that there is a tower, chimney or lighthouse of known height on a point of land with an outlying ledge to be cleared, the boat can be taken around it on a generally circular course or past it on a straight course in the following manner:

A point is located on the chart at a safe distance outside the obstruction. The distance between this point and the object to be observed is then measured from the chart scale. The height of the object is also taken from the chart. The angle that the object will subtend at that distance can then be found in table 9 of Bowditch as explained in the case where a vertical sextant angle was used in getting a fix. By holding a given course and checking occasionally to be sure that the observed sextant angle does not exceed the calculated angle the course will be kept clear of the danger. In the case of a long projecting point, if the course is so shaped that the angle remains constant, the boat will make good a circular course around the point at a uniform distance.

Figure 23. The vertical danger angle. By maintaining a certain maximum sextant angle, a boat can be kept well clear of an uncharted outlying obstruction

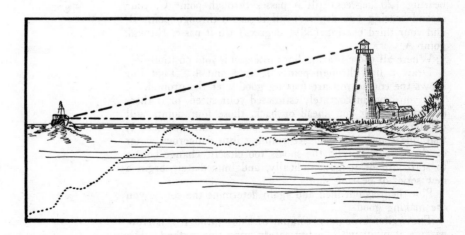

AN ingenious wrinkle in piloting has been worked out and given to us by Capt. J. F. Hellweg, Supt., U. S. Naval Observatory.

Frequently yachts and cruisers get into restricted waters where there are no definite navigational aids. In such cases, if the navigator can see some well defined object on the beach— a tree, a prominent tower, a church steeple, or even a plainly defined mark on a hillside (provided that object is indicated on his chart)—he can navigate with safety by using this method, and without the necessity of hunting some other object to take cross bearings.

Assume that you are standing on a course North true (0 degrees) through a channel between a small island and some unmarked off-lying shoals. Next, assume that there is a church steeple or a water tower on the small island that is marked on the chart.

Through the church steeple or water tower on the chart, draw a line North true (0 degrees), the course you assume you are making good. Estimate your speed over the ground from your log or revolutions, using your propeller revolutions, the condition of your bottom, known tide or assumed tide, etc.

Your first bearing taken shows the church steeple bears 20 degrees true. Plot that first bearing on the chart through the church steeple. You are somewhere on that line, but how distant is not yet known.

Next assume how far you wish to run between sights. Assume this is to be one mile. Then on the line projected North true (0 degrees) from the church steeple, measure off increments of one mile and mark each position A, B, C and D, respectively.

After running North true (0 degrees) for one mile, take your second bearing on the church steeple. It is 26 degrees.

Plot that bearing on the chart showing the steeple bearing 26 degrees. You are some place on that line.

Using a pair of parallel rulers, bring up your first bearing line (20 degrees) till it passes through point A. Point A is a fictitious church steeple exactly one mile North of the real steeple.

Where the first bearing line cuts the second bearing line indicates your position at position (2).

Stand on your course North true (0 degrees) for another mile. Then take your third bearing of the church steeple. It is 38½ degrees.

Plot that bearing on the chart showing the church steeple bearing 38½ degrees true. You are now on that line.

Again using your parallel rulers, bring up your first bearing line (20 degrees) till it passes through point B, and your second bearing line (26 degrees) till it passes through point A. Where those three bearings intersect is your position (3). Stand on your course North true (0 degrees) for another mile. Then take your fourth bearing of the church steeple. It is 65½ degrees.

Plot that bearing 65½ degrees on chart through the church steeple. You are on that line some place.

Again using your parallel rulers, bring up your first bearing (20 degrees) till it passes through point C, your second bearing (26 degrees) till it passes through point B, and your third bearing (38½ degrees) till it passes through point A.

Where all those bearing lines intersect is your position (4).

Draw a line through points 1, 2, 3 and 4. That line shows the course you are making good over the ground.

If you have inaccurately estimated your speed, or if there is a tide setting you ahead or back, those four points will develop a line to starboard or to port of your course. If that line shows that you are running into dangerous water or that you will skirt the shoals too closely, change course to starboard or to port radically, and immediately begin a new series of bearing sights.

Plot them as outlined and again determine the course you are making good.

The writer brought a column of ships through a narrow passage at night with perfect safety using this method. His plots showed he had a strong current from the Eastward setting the vessels on the shoals so they had to change course.

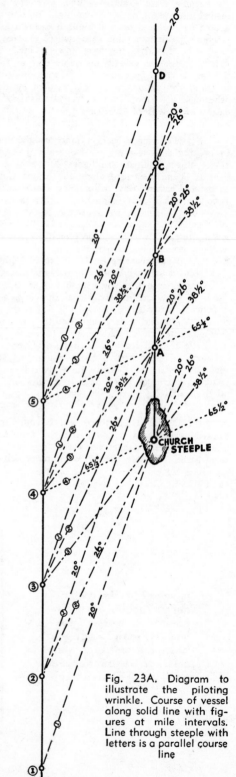

Fig. 23A. Diagram to illustrate the piloting wrinkle. Course of vessel along solid line with figures at mile intervals. Line through steeple with letters is a parallel course line

CURRENT DIAGRAMS—HOW THEY ARE CONSTRUCTED
AND USED WHEN SETTING A COURSE

See also pages 345-349

EVERY boatman, through practical experience, soon becomes acquainted with the fact that the direction of the boat's head on a given course, is not always the same as the track made good over the bottom. Likewise, it often takes a 10-mile boat more or less than an even hour to run a distance of 10 miles. These differences between normal slack water speeds and directions and those actually found in practice, are due to the influence of current and wind, and the action of waves and rough water. The effect of wind and waves varies considerably with the type of boat and prevailing conditions, and accordingly these factors must be handled individually for each particular case. Experience is the only guide in estimating them.

Current, however, (the horizontal flow of the tide or stream) works in a very definite way and with uniform effect on all boats. Therefore it can be calculated with a fair degree of accuracy and allowed for in setting courses. As current is frequently the chief factor to be taken into account and is often of considerable strength, it is helpful to be able to make this calculation scientifically rather than to depend upon a rough approximation.

The principle on which the working of current problems depends is this, that for each hour that a boat is running in a current, it will be set in the direction of the current flow a distance equal to the strength of the current, in terms of miles per hour. It makes no difference whether the course is directly with or against the flow, or quartering obliquely. The effect is the same in each case.

The simplest condition, and the easiest one to understand, would be that of a boat running directly with the set (direction of flow) of the current. Assuming a normal slack water boat speed of 10 m.p.h. and a current of 2 miles, by the end of the hour in which the boat had run off her 10 miles through the water, the current would have carried her down another 2, so that her resulting speed would be 12 miles over the bottom.

On the return trip against the current, she would be retarded

Figure 24. A current diagram in which the current is setting at right angles to the course made good

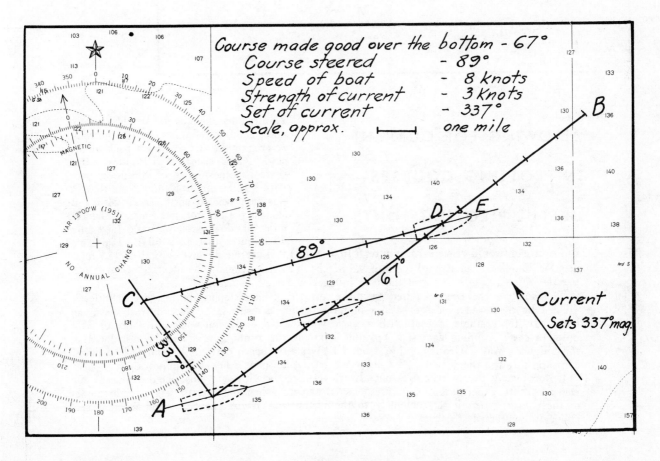

417

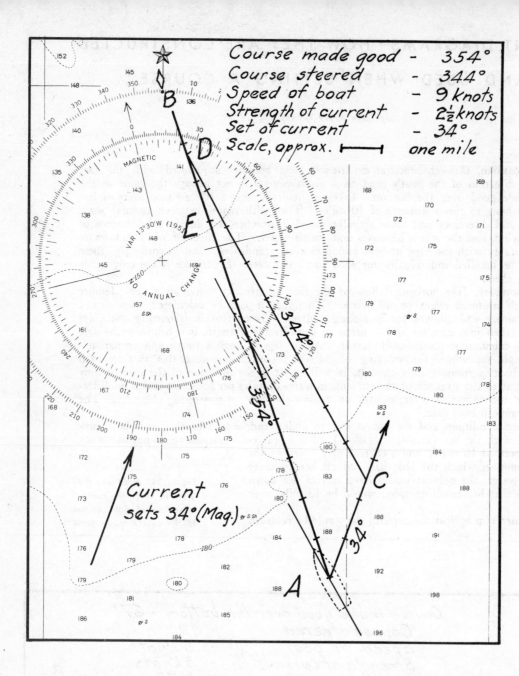

Course made good — 354°
Course steered — 344°
Speed of boat — 9 knots
Strength of current — 2½ knots
Set of current — 34°
Scale, approx. ⊢——⊣ one mile

Current sets 34°(Mag.)

ALLOWING FOR CURRENT

IN PLOTTING COURSES—

USEFUL PILOTING HINTS

2 miles and consequently would actually make good only 8 miles over the bottom. Averaging 12 and 8, we get back to the slack water speed of 10 miles. But there is a possibility of confusion here with a different problem. Note that in this case we averaged *speeds* with and against the current, not *times*. The 10-mile run down-stream would take only 50 minutes (10/12 x 60). The same run upstream would require 75 minutes (10/8 x 60). That would give a total of 125 minutes for 20 miles or an average speed of 9.6 m.p.h. This is obviously the incorrect way to figure the normal or true speed of the boat in slack water.

To calculate the time required to make good a given distance, the distance in miles is divided by the speed over the bottom in miles, giving a result in hours and fractions of an hour. If, for example, a boat with a slack water speed of 12 miles has a distance of 25.2 miles to cover, running against a 1½-mile current, the running time can be calculated in the following way. Deducting 1½ from 12 gives a net speed over the bottom of 10.5 miles. Dividing this into the distance, 25.2 miles, we get 2.4 hours or 2 hours 24 minutes.

Unfortunately the current does not always set directly with or against the direction of our course. Three other general cases are possible, namely, when the current sets at right angles to the course; when it sets obliquely to the course and favors the boat; and when it sets obliquely but retards the boat.

Figure 24 covers the first of these cases. A 12-mile course has been laid 67° from A to B. We have an 8-mile boat and 3-mile current setting 337°, at right angles to our course. Ordinarily, the strength of the current would not be as much as 3 miles, but we have assumed this figure to render the diagram more clear and to make the principle more apparent. The strength and direction of the current may be estimated from local knowledge, taken from the chart when given, or may be secured from the Current Tables issued by the Coast and Geodetic Survey.

After the course AB has been laid, representing the track we wish to actually make good, a second line is drawn from A, the starting point, in the direction toward which the current sets, in this case, 337°. Going to the mile scale on the chart, we set the dividers to 3 miles, which represents the value of one hour's flow of the current. Laying this off on the current line, we get the distance AC. The dividers are then set to 8 miles, representing one hour's run of the boat in slack water. The line CD, completing the triangle, is then drawn, locating D at such a point on the line AB that CD equals 8 miles.

The line CD then represents the direction of the course to steer and we find from the chart that it is 89°. Pointing the bow into

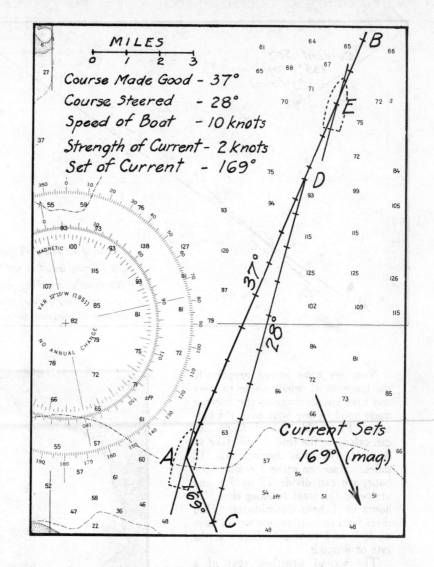

Course Made Good - 37°
Course Steered - 28°
Speed of Boat - 10 knots
Strength of Current - 2 knots
Set of Current - 169°

Current Sets 169° (mag.)

Figure 26. The third type of current problem. Here the current is again setting at an angle to the course, but is retarding the boat's speed

the current at our starting point A, the boat takes a position as indicated by the dotted outline, parallel to the plotted line CD. As she progresses in the easterly direction, the current sets her off to port, so that she actually travels over the track AB, although the boat's head is always pointed 89°, as shown by the several dotted outlines.

The line AD now represents the distance made good over the bottom in one hour's run, approximately 7½ miles. AE, a distance of 8 miles, is the ground we would have covered had there been no current. While it might be supposed that there would be no current against us when it sets at right angles to the course, still the fact that we have to head somewhat off the plotted course into the current, retards us (in this case to the extent of half a mile, in the distance made good). Had we steered 67°, we should have been set off the course 3 miles in an hour's run.

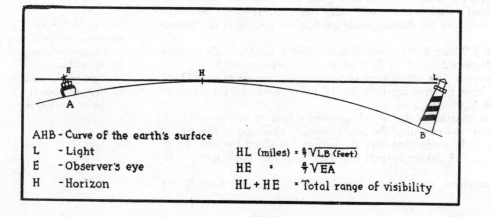

AHB - Curve of the earth's surface
L - Light
E - Observer's eye
H - Horizon

HL (miles) = $\frac{8}{7}\sqrt{LB\text{ (feet)}}$
HE = $\frac{8}{7}\sqrt{EA}$
HL + HE = Total range of visibility

Figure 29. An easy method of figuring the distance at which a light is visible, when the heights of the light and observer's eye are known

419

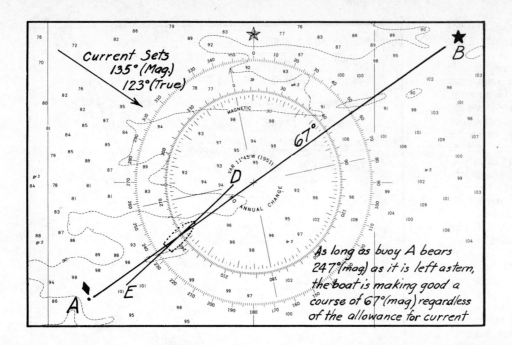

Current Sets
135° (Mag.)
123° (True)

67°

As long as buoy A bears
247°(mag) as it is left astern,
the boat is making good a
course of 67°(mag) regardless
of the allowance for current

Figure 27. A simple but valuable method of checking to determine whether or not the boat is actually making good the desired course in a current

Now we have solved graphically the question of what course to steer and have also determined the distance made good in one hour over the bottom. From this second factor we can calculate the time it will take us to cover the total distance AB, 12 miles. Since we make 7½ miles per hour, we can divide 12 by 7.5 and arrive at the total running time, 1.6 hours or 1 hour 36 minutes. Had there been no current, we would have made it in 1 hour 30 minutes at the rate of 8 m.p.h.

The second situation, that of a current setting obliquely to the course and favoring the boat, is illustrated in figure 25. Let us suppose that we have gotten a fix by cross bearings that locates our position at A, and we wish to lay a course for the buoy at B. The Current Tables show a 2½-knot current setting 34° and our slack water speed is 9 knots.

The first step is to lay the course we wish to make good from A to B. This figures out 354°. AC is then laid off from A in a 34° direction to correspond with the set of the current. The distance AC is 2½ miles as measured from the chart scale and is the equivalent of one hour's flow of the current. CD is then laid off toward B, intersecting AB at a point that makes CD equal to 9 miles, the boat's slack water speed. CD then represents the course to steer, 344°, while AD indicates the distance made good in one hour over the bottom along the line AB.

In slack water, with a 9-knot boat, it would have taken 1 hour and 20 minutes to cover the 12-mile distance from A to B. AE would represent one hour's run. With the quartering current, we actually make good a distance equal to AD, or 10.8 m.p.h. On that basis the running time for 12 miles would be cut down to 1.1 hours or 1 hour 6 minutes.

The third problem to consider is that which involves a current setting obliquely to the course of the boat and retarding the boat's speed. This case is covered by figure 26. The course to be made good over the bottom lies along the line AB in a direction 37° magnetic. A 2-knot current sets 169° and the boat's speed is 10 knots.

As in the previous problems, the first step is to lay off the line AC from A, the

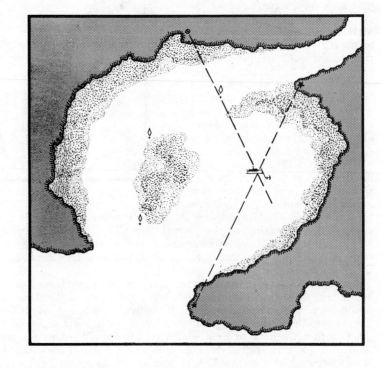

Figure 28. Ranges are one of the pilot's most important aids. This illustration shows how they can be used to find an anchorage on an exact spot

starting point, in the direction of the current flow and of a length equal, in 1-mile units taken from the chart scale, to the strength of the current. CD is then constructed, using as its length 10 units, or 10 miles, to represent the value of the boat's slack water speed. CD is then the course to be steered, 28°, and AD represents the distance made good in one hour's run, approximately 8½ miles.

At a speed, then of 8½ m.p.h. over the bottom, it will take 1 hour and 32 minutes to make good the 13 miles from A to B (13 divided by 8.5). Without current, the boat would normally make good AE instead of AD each hour and the total 13-mile run would require 1 hour 18 minutes.

In all of these problems, the difference between the statute and nautical mile must be kept clearly in mind, and one unit must be used consistently in each case. If the boat's speed is known in statute miles and the current velocity is given in knots, then one must be converted to the other measure, and both laid off in the diagram from the proper scale on the chart. Remember that a speed stated in knots means nautical miles per hour. Since the scale of mile units is usually given on charts in nautical miles and the velocity of currents in the same way, it is ordinarily convenient to convert the boat's statute mile speed to knots and work with nautical miles throughout. If inconvenient, it is unnecessary to work with 1-mile units. A half-mile or any other unit could be taken as well, if it is used consistently throughout. Also bear in mind that when it is said that the current sets east or any other direction, that is the direction toward which it flows.

Note, too, that in these illustrations the set of the current has been plotted in degrees, magnetic, since magnetic courses were used. Current set is given in the Current Tables in degrees, *true,* and allowance for variation must be made in plotting magnetic. If the true set is plotted as taken from the Tables, then courses must also be converted to true if the plotting is to be consistent and accurate.

After drawing a current diagram and figuring an allowance for current, it is a good plan to check this calculation wherever possible in the following way. Referring to figure 27, let us suppose that we have laid a course 67° (magnetic) from the buoy at A to the light at B. There is a current setting 135°, and we have figured from a current diagram that an allowance of 7° is about right for drift. Consequently we are steering 60° as indicated by the line DE.

When the boat has progressed some distance along her course, but before the buoy at A is out of sight, a bearing is taken on it. Naturally it will not bear dead astern down the center line of the boat. If it bears exactly 247°, then we must be on the course from A to B since, if it were in sight from B, it would still be bearing 247°. If it bears to the northward of 247° we have not allowed enough for current and have been set to the south of the course. Conversely, if it bears to the southward of 247°, we have overestimated the strength of the current and are getting too far to the north of the track we wish to make good over the bottom.

This same principle can be applied in making allowance for leeway. The correction to be made to the course for wind depends on so many variable factors that no formula can be given which will be applicable in all cases. However, a little experience with a boat generally gives a fair idea of how it behaves in winds from various quarters. While there may be occasions when an estimate of leeway may be made from the angle which the boat's wake makes with the direction of a line dead astern, it is much more positive to check the actual course being made good by a bearing on a buoy left astern whenever possible.

We have covered now all of the more important problems in laying courses, fixing position and the use of current diagrams. Remember that this is all the theory of practical, useful means of navigating more surely and safely. But the knowledge of these principles is of little value unless it is put into regular practice. Make it a point to apply it at every opportunity, even in fine weather. Then when the time comes on a foggy or squally day, when you must be sure of your navigation, you will have confidence in your ability to plot and hold a safe course and you will feel amply repaid for the effort you have put into study.

The following general suggestions are offered as practical hints which will prove their value many times if observed and put into practice. First, be sure your chart is up-to-date, and then use it. Changes are being made in buoyage to suit shifting channels and shoals, and improvements are constantly under way. Characteristics of lights are often changed to better serve the needs of navigation. The cost of a new chart is small and the slight expenditure might save a great deal of trouble and real expense.

Before laying a course or a series of courses, spend some time in a careful study of the chart. In that way you will be able to familiarize yourself with possible alternate routes, the prominent marks you can utilize in piloting, and you will have a good idea of the lay of the land and how it will appear as you sail your plotted courses. Then, don't be afraid to mark the chart up. Plot the courses clearly and definitely in pencil and note down all directions and distances. Don't trust the memory for any of these details but record them so that there can be no mistake.

Follow the plotted courses implicitly. After coming within sight of your objective, do not abandon the course but follow it to the end and see how closely you would have come out with your calculations of speed, distance and direction. Check your position at every possible opportunity and try to be able to state it exactly at any time. Note on the chart the time of starting every new course and each time some convenient object comes abeam, note the time it is passed. From a few of these observations you will be able to determine the speed you are actually making and you will have a further check on the calculations made at the time of laying the course. If no landmarks are visible, check off your position on the chart each hour on the basis of an estimated speed and note the time alongside of the position. Use cross bearings, bow and beam bearings, danger bearings and ranges as a constant check.

Always steer by compass even if the runs are comparatively short. In this way it will become second nature and your accuracy in steering will be greatly improved when you are surrounded by a blanket of fog with nothing but the compass to guide you. In rough weather, especially with following seas on the quarter, it is sometimes difficult to hold a compass course very closely but it is well worth the effort to run the plotted courses as exactly as possible.

In this connection it is interesting to note that automatic steering has been developed to a point where it is now practicable for small boats. The mechanism required is neither cumbersome nor complicated, consisting of only two units—an automatic compass fitted with a device which registers change in course, and a special quadrant steerer on the rudder post.

On a boat equipped with automatic steering, the navigator can set the course and then leave the wheel, to devote his attention to the problems of navigation, the work of the boat, or even rest and relaxation. The slightest tendency of the boat to deviate from the set course is detected by the automatic compass mechanism, which in turn acts to move the rudder and bring the boat back on a straight course. Accuracy in holding a course to within a degree, or even half a degree, is possible with automatic steering, an impossible feat for even an experienced helmsman.

In steering by compass, check up frequently to see that the needle has not been deflected by iron or steel objects, accidentally left near the compass, to an extent which varies from that shown on the deviation card. An occasional check on ranges or landmarks or over definite courses will serve to warn of any change in the deviation.

It is always good practice to run at definite engine speeds with a view to knowing boat speed just as accurately as possible. Speed through the water is exceedingly difficult to estimate off-hand, especially when one is reluctant to admit that his 15-mile cruiser is actually doing only 10 over a measured course. By constantly checking and keeping track of actual performance a record is soon built up which is invaluable in piloting work. Many owners even go so far as to plot a speed curve for their boats so that they may know at a glance the exact boat speed for any given rate of engine revolutions.

Take full advantage of any possible danger bearings wherever they exist, even if the course plotted seems relatively safe and easy to run. In this way a habit will be formed that may sometimes warn of danger when some unusual current condition is encountered.

In selecting objects for bearings and ranges always choose

natural landmarks in preference to buoys or other objects which may shift their location. Great care is used in placing all aids to navigation and in keeping them in their charted positions, but there is always the possibility of shifting due to collision, storm or similar accident. In fog, keep the lead going at frequent and regular intervals, bearing in mind that a single sounding is of no great value in getting a fix but it does help materially in warning of shoal water. In the absence of other means, a line of soundings at fixed intervals is of great value in getting an idea of position.

DEPTH curves are plotted on charts for a definite purpose and may be put to good use in keeping out of dangerous areas. When entering a strange harbor, use ranges and bearings frequently, even if the chart indicates that it is easy to enter. Use the lead in finding a suitable anchorage, making due allowance for the stage of the tide. Select suitable ranges if possible on shore which will serve to check the exact spot where the anchor is let go. (See figure 28.) The same ranges will also be of value in determining whether or not the boat has dragged anchor.

In setting courses, do not neglect the influence of current and wind. An advantage can often be gained in bucking the current of tidal rivers, especially the ebb, by favoring the bank. Current ordinarily flows the fastest in midstream due to resistance created by the bottom and the banks, and counter-currents are often set up near shore behind points which will actually be favoring when the main flow of the current in midstream is contrary. The best water in a river or other natural channel is generally found in midstream on the straight reaches and on the outside of bends, where the normal tendency of the water is to flow in a wide curve, cutting away the outside bank and building up shoals on the points. As a general rule, the swiftest current will be found along the line of the deepest water.

There are a few points which should be remembered in using lighted aids to navigation at night. Just as buoys may occasionally get adrift, lighted buoys may be temporarily extinguished if the lighting apparatus gets out of order. Before a light comes into range, the chart or Light List should be consulted to determine its characteristic, so that it may be identified on sight. If it is flashing or occulting, the period of light serves as a check on its identity and its color should be noted as well. In the case of a fixed light, it may be distinguished from the light on a vessel when it first comes into range, by lowering the eye a few feet. A navigation light on the horizon would disappear, while the light of the vessel would remain in view.

WHEN the height of a light is known, its range of visibility may be figured approximately from the formula, $R = 8/7\sqrt{H}$, in which R is the range in miles and H the height in feet. (See figure 29.) On this basis, a light 196 feet above sea level would be visible 16 miles ($8/7\sqrt{196}$), provided the observer's eye was at water level. Actually, the eye is elevated somewhat so a second computation must be made in the same manner as above, and the result added to the first. Assuming a height of eye of 16 feet in the above case, an additional 4½ miles ($8/7\sqrt{16}$) must be added to the 16 first computed, making a total visibility range of 20½ miles. Ranges of visibility as given in Light Lists and on charts are figured for a height of eye of 15 feet.

Due to refraction, or bending of light rays in the earth's atmosphere, lights are sometimes seen at much greater ranges than the normal distance of visibility. The glare of a powerful light may also be seen at times before the direct rays become visible. Mist will sometimes have the effect of giving a white light a reddish tinge, or obscure it except at distances much less than the usual range.

Great care should be used when approaching fog signals in thick weather as sound acts in a very unreliable way at such times. Areas of dead spots have been observed in which a fog signal would be inaudible when other areas nearby would be distinctly within the range of audibility. This peculiar effect is not always due to the influence of wind currents, although sound signals traveling against the wind may at times be deflected upward so that a signal could be detected by a man aloft when the same signal would be inaudible on deck.

HOW TO DETERMINE THE TOTAL LENGTH OF RUN
WHEN ROUNDING A HEADLAND

CAPTAIN J. F. HELLWEG, U. S. N. (Ret.), Superintendent of the U. S. Naval Observatory, has applied an old surveying trick to the problem of quickly determining the total length of a run in rounding an irregular headland with many changes of course.

In the illustration below, the ship is at A. You want to know the total run to F on the other side of the headland.

In the illustration, lines are drawn from point to point but after you have become familiar with the method, you merely swing the legs of your dividers from point to point so as to insure that the invisible line determined by the positions of the points of the two divider legs shall be parallel to the coast line and far enough off shore to be in safe water.

The ship is at A. Use dividers and measure distance A to B. Keep dividers' leg point B on point B and swing other dividers' leg A to the right until it touches the dotted line extended backwards from C to B, at point A¹. Hold dividers' A¹ point fast, and extend the B point along line B C till it reaches C.

Now hold C point fast and swing A¹ point to the right until it touches dotted line extended backwards from D to C at point A². Hold the A² point fast and extend the C point along line C D till it reaches D.

Hold D point fast and swing A² point to right till it touches the dotted line extending backwards from E to D at point A³. Hold point A³ fast and extend D point along line D E till it reaches point E.

Next hold E point fast and swing A³ point to the right till it touches the dotted line extending backwards from F to E at point A⁴. Hold A⁴ fast and extend E point along line E F till it reaches point F.

The length of line F A⁴ measures the total distance between the points of the widely separated legs of the dividers and represents graphically the summation of the separate legs A to B, B to C, C to D, D to E and E to F.

This is an old surveying trick that saves much time and is far more accurate than the old standard practice of measuring each leg and then adding the various distances together to get the total distance.

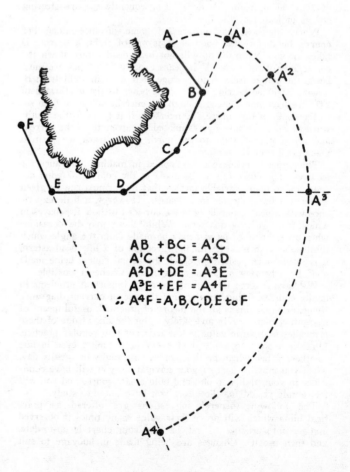

$$AB + BC = A'C$$
$$A'C + CD = A^2D$$
$$A^2D + DE = A^3E$$
$$A^3E + EF = A^4F$$
$$\therefore A^4F = A, B, C, D, E \text{ to } F$$

LEEWAY

What It Is—What It Does

MOST texts and glossaries agree that leeway is a lateral or sidewise movement of a vessel from her course. Some say that wind (or wind and sea, the latter resulting from action of wind) is the sole cause. Others claim

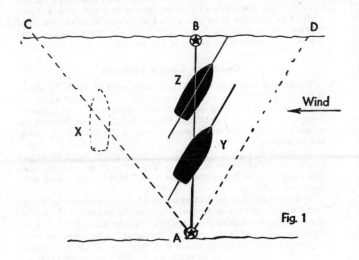

Fig. 1

that lateral movement caused by current is also properly classified as leeway.

An opinion given by the Branch Oceanographic Office in New York adheres to the latter theory—that leeway is leeway, whether caused by wind or current.

The reason why it's important to clarify the cause of leeway is this. Leeway caused by current acts on all vessels with equal effect, regardless of size, trim, load, tonnage, design, or any other factor. On the other hand, leeway caused by wind is a variable conditioned by all of these factors, and more.

Leeway due to current acting on any vessel in a given body of water can usually be estimated pretty closely from data on the set (direction) and drift (velocity) available in Current Tables, Tidal Current Charts, Pilot Charts, Sailing Directions, and other published material based on surveys of current conditions.

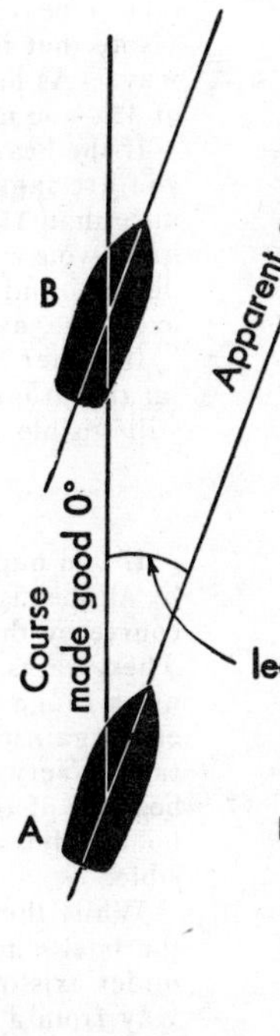

Having the strength of current at the time, its set, the normal slack water speed of the boat, and the course to be made good, it is a simple matter to lay out these factors graphically directly on the chart and determine the course to be steered and the speed the boat actually makes good over the bottom.

This subject of current diagrams has been treated so fully elsewhere that we will dismiss it here simply by

stating that the current factor is properly considered a part of leeway, even when calculated and allowed for separately.

Leeway due to wind is something else again—at least insofar as estimating its effect is concerned. Let's look at Figure 1. We wish to run from A to B. There is a strong easterly wind. If we disregard the wind's effect and steer for B, the wind blowing on our starboard side drives us to leeward. Even though our boat's heading remains parallel (as at X) to the course AB, we are losing ground and will wind up at C, far to leeward of our objective.

The leeway in this case may be expressed either as the distance BC or the angle BAC. The wind is coming from the starboard side and a sailing vessel would be said to be on the starboard tack in this case.

If, in the same illustration, we want to fetch B along the course AB, we shall have to head our vessel somewhat into the wind so that our apparent course (vessel's heading) is along the line AD. At Y and at Z, our heading is still parallel to our original course AD but we are actually making good the track AB toward our objective because of the leeway.

Having arrived at B, our leeway has equalled the distance BD and the angle expressing its value is BAD.

We have intentionally shown the angle BAC as greater than BAD for this reason. If we assume the wind's velocity to be the same in both cases, the leeway will be greater when it strikes the vessel broadside as at X than when it strikes obliquely as at Y and Z.

Let's suppose the run AB represents a couple of hundred miles down one of the Great Lakes. One of the big ore carriers is down-bound with her cargo holds full. Loaded to the Plimsoll mark, she is drawing nearly 20 feet of water with but little of her topsides left exposed to the wind. Like a sail boat with a deep keel, or a centerboarder with board down, she has a relatively great vertical surface below water to provide lateral resistance against leeway. Her leeway is comparatively small even though it blows fairly hard.

Now the same carrier discharges her cargo and returns in ballast over the same course under the same conditions. This time she trims high out of water. Light, she may be drawing only 12 to 15 feet aft and perhaps 6 forward. Her lateral resistance to leeway has been reduced by a very large factor while at the same time her exposure to wind above the water line is proportionately

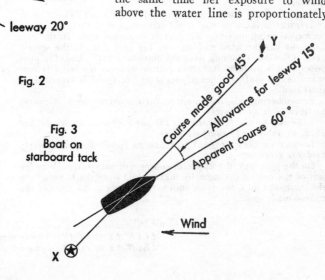

Fig. 2

Fig. 3
Boat on
starboard tack

increased. If she allows no more for leeway on this return trip, she is likely to be driven far off course.

While the loading of pleasure boats is not as important a factor as in the case just cited, you nevertheless have a multitude of types, in which the proportion of draft to exposed topsides and superstructure varies within wide limits. One motor boat will float high *on* the water and leeway will act with maximum effect, as it would on a sailboat with no board to hold her. Opposed to this is the heavily built boat with low freeboard and little superstructure, resting deep *in* the water, with generous draft to hold her against lateral movement. Between these extremes we have every conceivable combination of proportions.

Among sailing vessels you may have on the one hand a comparatively slow craft with high freeboard as against a fast racing type with deep keel and low freeboard. Obviously, the former is going to make more leeway than the latter.

To see just how much leeway can vary, experiment with the board up and down in a centerboard sloop. On the one hand, with board down, she may point fairly high; with board up, she may slide off to leeward and make more leeway than headway.

All of these illustrations are cited to show how many the variables are—the force of the wind, its direction, the amount of sea running across the course, the type of vessel under consideration, her design, speed, load, trim, size, whether driven by sail or motor, etc. Consequently, the effect of leeway resulting from the wind must be a guess. How accurate that guess might be depends to a large extent on one's experience with the craft under consideration.

A vessel in normal trim at sea may steam for days on end without much regard to leeway—yet if she were a type with high freeboard and found herself caught in a severe storm for 24 hours, to neglect the effect of leeway would undoubtedly be a serious navigational error, as she might be driven far off course.

The problem is of even more concern to the motor boatman, because the design of the average motor-driven pleasure boat is such that she feels the wind's effect materially and, in piloting coastal waters, can ill afford to be driven much off her plotted course. Yet this is something that cannot be laid out precisely on paper, as a current diagram might be. Experience must be the guide.

Leeway Does Not Affect the Compass

We shall run afoul of trouble if we think of leeway as having any effect on the compass. Variation and deviation do act on the compass needle and deflect it from a true bearing or course. Leeway doesn't do that. As shown in Figure 1, we are holding a given compass course but we are not making good the course we steer.

Our keel at every instant makes an angle with the track we are actually making good over the bottom. That angle is a measure of the leeway.

Where the compass does enter the picture is in our method of making suitable allowance before running our course so that we can actually make good the desired track over the bottom. Turn now to Figure 2.

Let's suppose we estimate an allowance of 20 degrees for leeway. We wish to run from A to B. After correcting for variation and deviation we find our compass course (without leeway) would be 0 (or 360) degrees. The easterly wind requires us to steer 20 degrees *toward the wind* to overcome the leeway. Consequently we bring the boat's head around to a compass heading of 20 degrees and the force of the wind causes her to slide off to leeward 20 degrees. The course she actually makes good is 0 degrees.

While, strictly speaking, a motor vessel doesn't "tack," it is convenient to think of any vessel concerned with the problem of leeway as being on either the port or starboard tack. In the first case, she has the wind coming over her port side; in the second case, the wind is coming over the starboard rail. And, for purposes of this problem it doesn't matter whether the wind is forward of, or abaft, the beam, except as her speed is retarded or increased.

Remembering this, the rule then for the correction of a course for leeway is as follows:—

* *Leeway on the port tack has the same effect, and can be figured, as an easterly compass error.*

Leeway on the starboard tack can be handled as a westerly compass error.

On the port tack, the apparent course will necessarily be to the left of the course she actually makes good over the bottom. On the starboard tack, the apparent course will lie to the right of the course made good.

Determining the Course to Steer

Going back to Figure 2, we have a course of 0 degrees to be made good, and 20 degrees leeway on the starboard tack. The rule tells us to deal with this as a westerly compass error. According to the basic formula—Correct Easterly Errors Clockwise when going from Compass to Magnetic to True courses—the 20 degrees must be applied clockwise, so the compass course becomes 20 degrees.

It would be equally satisfactory to swing the boat onto the compass heading that would make good the desired course (0 degrees) and then turn her bow *into the wind* as many degrees as required to make the estimated allowance. You get the same result, understand better what you are actually doing and don't have to memorize formulas, which are more or less of a nuisance, anyhow. Visualize this as taking place even if you are working theoretical problems on paper and it will help keep the whole thing clear.

In classroom work the two factors of wind and current are usually treated separately. For example, in traverse sailing, leeway (wind) may be the first correction to the compass course, and the current component the last entry in the column, with both set and drift given, or taken from past observations. In examinations at the Naval Academy, the leeway is given with a stated drift; this is meant to be considered as caused by both wind and current. In practice on board naval vessels the navigator considers both components as cause for leeway.

Checks on Leeway Estimates

While it is true that leeway estimates must be made by guess, there are a few tricks you can use to tell whether your guess has been correct (assuming the necessary conditions are present). Sometimes a glance astern may help some, the angle between the vessel's keel and her wake being a clew to the amount of leeway she is making.

Referring to Figure 3, let's assume you want to run a 45-degree course from lighthouse X to buoy Y. There is an easterly wind and buoy Y is so far distant that it will be picked up only after hours of running.

You estimate that an allowance of 15 degrees should be almost right so you steer a compass course of 60 degrees (15 degrees closer to the wind than the track you want to make good). In the final analysis you're not so much concerned with what the exact compass course is, except to use it in steering. What you must be sure of is that course to be made good—XY. So at intervals you take a bearing on lighthouse X while it is still visible astern. (Note that it will not bear dead astern as it would with no leeway.) As long as that lighthouse bears 225 degrees—the reverse of 45—you must necessarily be making good the desired course.

If the bearing happens to be 215 degrees you would know that you are sagging off to leeward and should make a larger allowance than 15 degrees for leeway. Or if the bearing were 230 degrees you would know then you are making good not 45 but 50 degrees and that your leeway correction of 15 degrees had been excessive, as you are gradually drawing too far to windward.

In either case you can correct your original estimate, get back on the proper bearing, then check again while the lighthouse is still visible astern.

Using a Range

If you happen to be lucky enough to have a range astern, then by all means watch closely and determine your apparent compass course by the boat's heading as you keep steadily on the range. These cases, however, may be few and far between. You can use a range though to advantage in building up a store of experience against the day when an accurate leeway estimate is important. Every time you run a range, note the strength and relative bearing of the wind. Observe its effect on your own particular boat under as many different combinations of conditions as possible.

While the boat is on the range, note its relative bearing from the boat's head. This will be an exact measure of the leeway under existing conditions. If you have occasion to determine leeway from a comparison of the boat's heading with a bearing or range taken from the chart, be sure to take variation and deviation into account, comparing magnetic headings with magnetic bearings or true headings with true bearings.

Otherwise, the leeway you calculate may be even worse than a guess!

* *Putting it another way, in determining the course to be steered*
LEEWAY to STARBOARD shows up as an EASTERLY error.
LEEWAY to PORT shows up as a WESTERLY error.

Piloting In Currents

Time-speed-distance tables for the cruising yachtsman, with a new table of speed factors and course corrections prepared by Cyril G. Veinott, using an electronic computer.

WHEN any boat cruises in a current, the current generally produces two effects: (1) the speed over bottom, or speed of advance, may be more or less than the speed over the surface; and (2) the actual course made good, or course over the bottom, may be different from the heading. The magnitude of these effects can be estimated by a graphical procedure, for any combination of circumstances. They can also be determined, without graphical construction, by the use of a new table, calculated on an Alwac III electronic digital computer. However, an understanding of the graphical procedure will reduce the chances of misinterpreting the table, or of using it incorrectly. For a detailed discussion of the graphic method of constructing current diagrams, the reader is referred to Chapter XXI pages 345-349b, and to pages 417-421.

Where no current is present, and the pilot's problem is a simple matter of determining the time required to run a given distance in slack water, Table A, developed by the author especially for the cruising yachtsman, is a handy reference eliminating the necessity for calculations. The cruising man is usually interested in relatively long runs and thinks in terms of hours and minutes.

It should be self-evident how to use table A, but the following examples will serve to illustrate its use. (*See p. 425a*)

Example 1. At 13 knots, how long does it take to go 36 miles?

Answer. Reading directly from the table, 2 hr. 46 min.

Example 2. At 11 knots, how long does it take to go 43.6 miles?

Answer. Reading from the table

to go 43 miles requires	3 hr. 55 min.
to go .6 miles requires	3 min.
To go 43.6 miles requires	3 hr. 58 min.

Example 3. At 14.3 knots, how long does it take to go 26.4 miles?

Answer. From the table, after the fashion of Ex. 2

to go 26.4 miles at 14 knots requires	1 hr. 53 min.
to go 26.4 miles at 15 knots requires	1 hr. 46 min.
Difference in time for 1 knot	7 min.

Hence, to go 26.4 miles at 14.3 knots requires
1 hr. 53 min. − (0.3 × 7) = 1 hr. 51 min.

It is exactly correct to add times, as in example 2. It is not exactly correct to interpolate between speeds, as done in example 3, because of the reciprocal relationship between time and speed. The error, however, will usually be slight. In the case of example 3, there is no error, as can be found by checking.

For certain purposes, the cruising yachtsman may prefer to use the Calculator described on pages 438a-c.

For most problems, however, involving the calculation or estimation of ETA, the yachtsman may find Table A more convenient and quicker to use, particularly if he will set his engine rpm so as to cruise at a whole number of knots.

CASE I

Finding course and speed of advance from track and speed over water

Any problem involving current can be solved by constructing a triangle to scale, as described on pages 345-349b and 417-421. It is recommended that the yachtsman learn how to lay out such a triangle and solve his problem in this manner. The problem, however, can be solved more simply by use of the accompanying Table B. No graphical construction is needed. (*See p. 425b*)

The following definitions should be kept in mind.

Course. (C) The direction in which the boat is headed.

Speed. (S) The speed the boat is making over the surface, in mph. (Sometimes referred to as RPM speed.)

Drift. (D) The speed of the current, in mph.

Set. The direction towards which the current is moving.

Track. (TR) The direction of an intended track, or the direction of the actual course over the bottom.

Speed of Advance. (SOA) is the actual speed made good over the bottom.

Using Table B to Solve Current Problems

$$Drift,\ in\ per\ cent = \frac{drift,\ in\ mph \times 100}{speed\ over\ water,\ mph}$$

Relative set is the angular distance from the course to be made good (TR) to the set, in whichever direction is the nearer. When measured in a clockwise direction, relative set is positive; when measured in a counter-clockwise direction, relative set is negative. That is,

relative set = set − TR
  if (set − TR) is numerically greater than 180, and positive, subtract 360, obtaining a negative relative set, less than 180.
  if (set − TR) is numerically greater than 180 but negative, add 360, obtaining a positive relative set, less than 180.

Speed of advance (speed over bottom) = speed over surface × SF.

Course to be steered
  = TR − CC when rel. set is positive.
  = TR + CC when rel. set is negative.

In other words, the course correction is towards the current.

(See examples on page 425b)

Table A

TIME REQUIRED TO RUN A KNOWN DISTANCE, AT A KNOWN SPEED

(Time given in hours and minutes)

SPEED — 6 TO 27 — IN MILES PER HOUR

DISTANCE — .1 TO 90 — IN MILES

Dist. miles	6.0	7.0	8.0	9.0	10.0	11.0	12.0	13.0	14.0	15.0	16.0	17.0	18.0	19.0	20.0	21.0	22.0	23.0	24.0	25.0	26.0	27.0
.1	01	01	01	01	01	01	01	00	00	00	00	00	00	00	00	00	00	00	00	00	00	00
.2	02	02	02	01	01	01	01	01	01	01	01	01	01	01	01	01	01	01	01	00	00	00
.3	03	03	02	02	02	02	02	01	01	01	01	01	01	01	01	01	01	01	01	01	01	01
.4	04	03	03	03	02	02	02	02	02	02	02	01	01	01	01	01	01	01	01	01	01	01
.5	05	04	04	03	03	03	03	02	02	02	02	02	02	02	02	01	01	01	01	01	01	01
.6	06	05	05	04	04	03	03	03	03	02	02	02	02	02	02	01	01	01	01	01	01	01
.7	07	06	05	05	04	04	04	03	03	03	03	02	02	02	02	02	02	02	02	01	01	01
.8	08	07	06	05	05	04	04	04	03	03	03	03	03	03	02	02	02	02	02	02	02	02
.9	09	08	07	06	05	05	05	04	04	04	03	03	03	03	03	03	02	02	02	02	02	02
1.0	10	09	08	07	06	05	05	05	04	04	04	04	03	03	03	03	03	03	03	02	02	02
2.0	20	17	15	13	12	11	10	09	09	08	08	07	07	06	06	06	05	05	05	05	05	04
3.0	30	26	23	20	18	16	15	14	13	12	11	11	10	09	09	09	08	08	08	07	07	07
4.0	40	34	30	27	24	22	20	18	17	16	15	14	13	13	12	11	11	10	10	10	09	09
5.0	50	43	38	33	30	27	·25	23	21	20	19	18	17	16	15	14	14	13	13	12	12	11
6.0	1 00	51	45	40	36	33	30	28	26	24	23	21	20	19	18	17	16	16	15	14	14	13
7.0	1 10	1 00	53	47	42	38	35	32	30	28	26	25	23	22	21	20	19	18	18	17	16	16
8.0	1 20	1 09	1 00	53	48	44	40	37	34	32	30	28	27	25	24	23	22	21	20	19	18	18
9.0	1 30	1 17	1 08	1 00	54	49	45	42	39	36	34	32	30	28	27	26	25	23	23	22	21	20
10.0	1 40	1 26	1 15	1 07	1 00	55	50	46	43	40	38	35	33	32	30	29	27	26	25	24	23	22
11.0	1 50	1 34	1 23	1 13	1 06	1 00	55	51	47	44	41	39	37	35	33	31	30	29	28	26	25	24
12.0	2 00	1 43	1 30	1 20	1 12	1 05	1 00	55	51	48	45	42	40	38	36	34	33	31	30	29	28	27
13.0	2 10	1 51	1 38	1 27	1 18	1 11	1 05	1 00	56	52	49	46	43	41	39	37	35	34	33	31	30	29
14.0	2 20	2 00	1 45	1 33	1 24	1 16	1 10	1 05	1 00	56	53	49	47	44	42	40	38	37	35	34	32	31
15.0	2 30	2 09	1 53	1 40	1 30	1 22	1 15	1 09	1 04	1 00	56	53	50	47	45	43	41	39	38	36	35	33
16.0	2 40	2 17	2 00	1 47	1 36	1 27	1 20	1 14	1 09	1 04	1 00	56	53	51	48	46	44	42	40	38	37	36
17.0	2 50	2 26	2 08	1 53	1 42	1 33	1 25	1 18	1 13	1 08	1 04	1 00	57	54	51	49	46	44	43	41	39	38
18.0	3 00	2 34	2 15	2 00	1 48	1 38	1 30	1 23	1 17	1 12	1 08	1 04	1 00	57	54	51	49	47	45	43	42	40
19.0	3 10	2 43	2 23	2 07	1 54	1 44	1 35	1 28	1 21	1 16	1 11	1 07	1 03	1 00	57	54	52	50	48	46	44	42
20.0	3 20	2 51	2 30	2 13	2 00	1 49	1 40	1 32	1 26	1 20	1 15	1 11	1 07	1 03	1 00	57	55	52	50	48	46	44
21.0	3 30	3 00	2 38	2 20	2 06	1 55	1 45	1 37	1 30	1 24	1 19	1 14	1 10	1 06	1 03	1 00	57	55	53	50	48	47
22.0	3 40	3 09	2 45	2 27	2 12	2 00	1 50	1 42	1 34	1 28	1 23	1 18	1 13	1 09	1 06	1 03	1 00	57	55	53	51	49
23.0	3 50	3 17	2 53	2 33	2 18	2 05	1 55	1 46	1 39	1 32	1 26	1 21	1 17	1 13	1 09	1 06	1 03	1 00	58	55	53	51
24.0	4 00	3 26	3 00	2 40	2 24	2 11	2 00	1 51	1 43	1 36	1 30	1 25	1 20	1 16	1 12	1 09	1 05	1 03	1 00	58	55	53
25.0	4 10	3 34	3 08	2 47	2 30	2 16	2 05	1 55	1 47	1 40	1 34	1 28	1 23	1 19	1 15	1 11	1 08	1 05	1 03	1 00	58	56
26.0	4 20	3 43	3 15	2 53	2 36	2 22	2 10	2 00	1 51	1 44	1 38	1 32	1 27	1 22	1 18	1 14	1 11	1 08	1 05	1 02	1 00	58
27.0	4 30	3 51	3 23	3 00	2 42	2 27	2 15	2 05	1 56	1 48	1 41	1 35	1 30	1 25	1 21	1 17	1 14	1 10	1 08	1 05	1 02	1 00
28.0	4 40	4 00	3 30	3 07	2 48	2 33	2 20	2 09	2 00	1 52	1 45	1 39	1 33	1 28	1 24	1 20	1 16	1 13	1 10	1 07	1 05	1 02
29.0	4 50	4 09	3 38	3 13	2 54	2 38	2 25	2 14	2 04	1 56	1 49	1 42	1 37	1 32	1 27	1 23	1 19	1 16	1 13	1 10	1 07	1 04
30.0	5 00	4 17	3 45	3 20	3 00	2 44	2 30	2 18	2 09	2 00	1 53	1 46	1 40	1 35	1 30	1 26	1 22	1 18	1 15	1 12	1 09	1 07
31.0	5 10	4 26	3 53	3 27	3 06	2 49	2 35	2 23	2 13	2 04	1 56	1 49	1 43	1 38	1 33	1 29	1 25	1 21	1 18	1 14	1 12	1 09
32.0	5 20	4 34	4 00	3 33	3 12	2 55	2 40	2 28	2 17	2 08	2 00	1 53	1 47	1 41	1 36	1 31	1 27	1 23	1 20	1 17	1 14	1 11
33.0	5 30	4 43	4 08	3 40	3 18	3 00	2 45	2 32	2 21	2 12	2 04	1 56	1 50	1 44	1 39	1 34	1 30	1 26	1 23	1 19	1 16	1 13
34.0	5 40	4 51	4 15	3 47	3 24	3 05	2 50	2 37	2 26	2 16	2 08	2 00	1 53	1 47	1 42	1 37	1 33	1 29	1 25	1 22	1 18	1 16
35.0	5 50	5 00	4 23	3 53	3 30	3 11	2 55	2 42	2 30	2 20	2 11	2 04	1 57	1 51	1 45	1 40	1 35	1 31	1 28	1 24	1 21	1 18
36.0	6 00	5 09	4 30	4 00	3 36	3 16	3 00	2 46	2 34	2 24	2 15	2 07	2 00	1 54	1 48	1 43	1 38	1 34	1 30	1 26	1 23	1 20
37.0	6 10	5 17	4 38	4 07	3 42	3 22	3 05	2 51	2 39	2 28	2 19	2 11	2 03	1 57	1 51	1 46	1 41	1 37	1 33	1 29	1 25	1 22
38.0	6 20	5 26	4 45	4 13	3 48	3 27	3 10	2 55	2 43	2 32	2 23	2 14	2 07	2 00	1 54	1 49	1 44	1 39	1 35	1 31	1 28	1 24
39.0	6 30	5 34	4 53	4 20	3 54	3 33	3 15	3 00	2 47	2 36	2 26	2 18	2 10	2 03	1 57	1 51	1 46	1 42	1 38	1 34	1 30	1 27
40.0	6 40	5 43	5 00	4 27	4 00	3 38	3 20	3 05	2 51	2 40	2 30	2 21	2 13	2 06	2 00	1 54	1 49	1 44	1 40	1 36	1 32	1 29
41.0	6 50	5 51	5 08	4 33	4 06	3 44	3 25	3 09	2 56	2 44	2 34	2 25	2 17	2 09	2 03	1 57	1 52	1 47	1 43	1 38	1 35	1 31
42.0	7 00	6 00	5 15	4 40	4 12	3 49	3 30	3 14	3 00	2 48	2 38	2 28	2 20	2 13	2 06	2 00	1 55	1 50	1 45	1 41	1 37	1 33
43.0	7 10	6 09	5 23	4 47	4 18	3 55	3 35	3 18	3 04	2 52	2 41	2 32	2 23	2 16	2 09	2 03	1 57	1 52	1 48	1 43	1 39	1 36
44.0	7 20	6 17	5 30	4 53	4 24	4 00	3 40	3 23	3 09	2 56	2 45	2 35	2 27	2 19	2 12	2 06	2 00	1 55	1 50	1 46	1 42	1 38
45.0	7 30	6 26	5 38	5 00	4 30	4 05	3 45	3 28	3 13	3 00	2 49	2 39	2 30	2 22	2 15	2 09	2 03	1 57	1 53	1 48	1 44	1 40
46.0	7 40	6 34	5 45	5 07	4 36	4 11	3 50	3 32	3 17	3 04	2 53	2 42	2 33	2 25	2 18	2 11	2 05	2 00	1 55	1 50	1 46	1 42
47.0	7 50	6 43	5 53	5 13	4 42	4 16	3 55	3 37	3 21	3 08	2 56	2 46	2 37	2 28	2 21	2 14	2 08	2 03	1 58	1 53	1 48	1 44
48.0	8 00	6 51	6 00	5 20	4 48	4 22	4 00	3 42	3 26	3 12	3 00	2 49	2 40	2 32	2 24	2 17	2 11	2 05	2 00	1 55	1 51	1 47
49.0	8 10	7 00	6 08	5 27	4 54	4 27	4 05	3 46	3 30	3 16	3 04	2 53	2 43	2 35	2 27	2 20	2 14	2 08	2 03	1 58	1 53	1 49
50.0	8 20	7 09	6 15	5 33	5 00	4 33	4 10	3 51	3 34	3 20	3 08	2 56	2 47	2 38	2 30	2 23	2 16	2 10	2 05	2 00	1 55	1 51
51.0	8 30	7 17	6 23	5 40	5 06	4 38	4 15	3 55	3 39	3 24	3 11	3 00	2 50	2 41	2 33	2 26	2 19	2 13	2 08	2 02	1 58	1 53
52.0	8 40	7 26	6 30	5 47	5 12	4 44	4 20	4 00	3 43	3 28	3 15	3 04	2 53	2 44	2 36	2 29	2 22	2 16	2 10	2 05	2 00	1 56
53.0	8 50	7 34	6 38	5 53	5 18	4 49	4 25	4 05	3 47	3 32	3 19	3 07	2 57	2 47	2 39	2 31	2 25	2 18	2 13	2 07	2 02	1 58
54.0	9 00	7 43	6 45	6 00	5 24	4 55	4 30	4 09	3 51	3 36	3 23	3 11	3 00	2 51	2 42	2 34	2 27	2 21	2 15	2 10	2 05	2 00
55.0	9 10	7 51	6 53	6 07	5 30	5 00	4 35	4 14	3 56	3 40	3 26	3 14	3 03	2 54	2 45	2 37	2 30	2 23	2 18	2 12	2 07	2 02
56.0	9 20	8 00	7 00	6 13	5 36	5 05	4 40	4 18	4 00	3 44	3 30	3 18	3 07	2 57	2 48	2 40	2 33	2 26	2 20	2 14	2 09	2 04
57.0	9 30	8 09	7 08	6 20	5 42	5 11	4 45	4 23	4 04	3 48	3 34	3 21	3 10	3 00	2 51	2 43	2 35	2 29	2 23	2 17	2 12	2 07
58.0	9 40	8 17	7 15	6 27	5 48	5 16	4 50	4 28	4 09	3 52	3 38	3 25	3 13	3 03	2 54	2 46	2 38	2 31	2 25	2 19	2 14	2 09
59.0	9 50	8 26	7 23	6 33	5 54	5 22	4 55	4 32	4 13	3 56	3 41	3 28	3 17	3 06	2 57	2 49	2 41	2 34	2 28	2 22	2 16	2 11
60.0	10 00	8 34	7 30	6 40	6 00	5 27	5 00	4 37	4 17	4 00	3 45	3 32	3 20	3 09	3 00	2 51	2 44	2 37	2 30	2 24	2 18	2 13
61.0	10 10	8 43	7 38	6 47	6 06	5 33	5 05	4 42	4 21	4 04	3 49	3 35	3 23	3 13	3 03	2 54	2 46	2 39	2 33	2 26	2 21	2 16
62.0	10 20	8 51	7 45	6 53	6 12	5 38	5 10	4 46	4 26	4 08	3 53	3 39	3 27	3 16	3 06	2 57	2 49	2 42	2 35	2 29	2 23	2 18
63.0	10 30	9 00	7 53	7 00	6 18	5 44	5 15	4 51	4 30	4 12	3 56	3 42	3 30	3 19	3 09	3 00	2 52	2 44	2 38	2 31	2 25	2 20
64.0	10 40	9 09	8 00	7 07	6 24	5 49	5 20	4 55	4 34	4 16	4 00	3 46	3 33	3 22	3 12	3 03	2 55	2 47	2 40	2 34	2 28	2 22
65.0	10 50	9 17	8 08	7 13	6 30	5 55	5 25	5 00	4 39	4 20	4 04	3 49	3 37	3 25	3 15	3 06	2 57	2 50	2 43	2 36	2 30	2 24
66.0	11 00	9 26	8 15	7 20	6 36	6 00	5 30	5 05	4 43	4 24	4 08	3 53	3 40	3 28	3 18	3 09	3 00	2 52	2 45	2 38	2 32	2 27
67.0	11 10	9 34	8 23	7 27	6 42	6 05	5 35	5 09	4 47	4 28	4 11	3 56	3 43	3 32	3 21	3 11	3 03	2 55	2 48	2 41	2 35	2 29
68.0	11 20	9 43	8 30	7 33	6 48	6 11	5 40	5 14	4 51	4 32	4 15	4 00	3 47	3 35	3 24	3 14	3 05	2 57	2 50	2 43	2 37	2 31
69.0	11 30	9 51	8 38	7 40	6 54	6 16	5 45	5 18	4 56	4 36	4 19	4 04	3 50	3 38	3 27	3 17	3 08	3 00	2 53	2 46	2 39	2 33
70.0	11 40	10 00	8 45	7 47	7 00	6 22	5 50	5 23	5 00	4 40	4 23	4 07	3 53	3 41	3 30	3 20	3 11	3 03	2 55	2 48	2 42	2 36
71.0	11 50	10 09	8 53	7 53	7 06	6 27	5 55	5 28	5 04	4 44	4 26	4 11	3 57	3 44	3 33	3 23	3 14	3 05	2 58	2 50	2 44	2 38
72.0	12 00	10 17	9 00	8 00	7 12	6 33	6 00	5 32	5 09	4 48	4 30	4 14	4 00	3 47	3 36	3 26	3 16	3 08	3 00	2 53	2 46	2 40
73.0	12 10	10 26	9 08	8 07	7 18	6 38	6 05	5 37	5 13	4 52	4 34	4 18	4 03	3 51	3 39	3 29	3 19	3 10	3 03	2 55	2 48	2 42
74.0	12 20	10 34	9 15	8 13	7 24	6 44	6 10	5 42	5 17	4 56	4 38	4 21	4 07	3 54	3 42	3 31	3 22	3 13	3 05	2 58	2 51	2 44
75.0	12 30	10 43	9 23	8 20	7 30	6 49	6 15	5 46	5 21	5 00	4 41	4 25	4 10	3 57	3 45	3 34	3 25	3 16	3 08	3 00	2 53	2 47
76.0	12 40	10 51	9 30	8 27	7 36	6 55	6 20	5 51	5 26	5 04	4 45	4 28	4 13	4 00	3 48	3 37	3 27	3 18	3 10	3 02	2 55	2 49
77.0	12 50	11 00	9 38	8 33	7 42	7 00	6 25	5 55	5 30	5 08	4 49	4 32	4 17	4 03	3 51	3 40	3 30	3 21	3 13	3 05	2 58	2 51
78.0	13 00	11 09	9 45	8 40	7 48	7 05	6 30	6 00	5 34	5 12	4 53	4 35	4 20	4 06	3 54	3 43	3 33	3 23	3 15	3 07	3 00	2 53
79.0	13 10	11 17	9 53	8 47	7 54	7 11	6 35	6 05	5 39	5 16	4 56	4 39	4 23	4 09	3 57	3 46	3 35	3 26	3 18	3 10	3 02	2 56
80.0	13 20	11 26	10 00	8 53	8 00	7 16	6 40	6 09	5 43	5 20	5 00	4 42	4 27	4 13	4 00	3 49	3 38	3 29	3 20	3 12	3 05	2 58
81.0	13 30	11 34	10 08	9 00	8 06	7 22	6 45	6 14	5 47	5 24	5 04	4 46	4 30	4 16	4 03	3 51	3 41	3 31	3 23	3 14	3 07	3 00
82.0	13 40	11 43	10 15	9 07	8 12	7 27	6 50	6 18	5 51	5 28	5 08	4 49	4 33	4 19	4 06	3 54	3 44	3 34	3 25	3 17	3 09	3 02
83.0	13 50	11 51	10 23	9 13	8 18	7 33	6 55	6 23	5 56	5 32	5 11	4 53	4 37	4 22	4 09	3 57	3 46	3 37	3 28	3 19	3 12	3 04
84.0	14 00	12 00	10 30	9 20	8 24	7 38	7 00	6 28	6 00	5 36	5 15	4 56	4 40	4 25	4 12	4 00	3 49	3 39	3 30	3 22	3 14	3 07
85.0	14 10	12 09	10 38	9 27	8 30	7 44	7 05	6 32	6 04	5 40	5 19	5 00	4 43	4 28	4 15	4 03	3 52	3 42	3 33	3 24	3 16	3 09
86.0	14 20	12 17	10 45	9 33	8 36	7 49	7 10	6 37	6 09	5 44	5 23	5 04	4 47	4 32	4 18	4 06	3 55	3 44	3 35	3 26	3 18	3 11
87.0	14 30	12 26	10 53	9 40	8 42	7 55	7 15	6 42	6 13	5 48	5 26	5 07	4 50	4 35	4 21	4 09	3 57	3 47	3 38	3 29	3 21	3 13
88.0	14 40	12 34	11 00	9 47	8 48	8 00	7 20	6 46	6 17	5 52	5 30	5 11	4 53	4 38	4 24	4 11	4 00	3 50	3 40	3 31	3 23	3 16
89.0	14 50	12 43	11 08	9 53	8 54	8 05	7 25	6 51	6 21	5 56	5 34	5 14	4 57	4 41	4 27	4 14	4 03	3 52	3 43	3 34	3 25	3 18
90.0	15 00	12 51	11 15	10 00	9 00	8 11	7 30	6 55	6 26	6 00	5 38	5 18	5 00	4 44	4 30	4 17	4 05	3 55	3 45	3 36	3 28	3 20

Table B

SPEED FACTORS (SF), AND COURSE CORRECTIONS (CC)
For use in solving current problems

Drift, in per cent of speed over water

Rel. Set	2 SF	CC	4 SF	CC	6 SF	CC	8 SF	CC	10 SF	CC	12 SF	CC	14 SF	CC	16 SF	CC	18 SF	CC	20 SF	CC
000	1.020	00	1.040	00	1.060	00	1.080	00	1.100	00	1.120	00	1.140	00	1.160	00	1.180	00	1.200	00
005	1.020	00	1.040	00	1.060	00	1.080	00	1.100	00	1.119	01	1.139	01	1.159	01	1.179	01	1.199	01
010	1.020	00	1.039	01	1.059	01	1.079	01	1.098	01	1.118	01	1.138	01	1.157	02	1.177	02	1.196	02
015	1.019	00	1.039	01	1.058	01	1.077	01	1.096	01	1.115	02	1.135	02	1.154	02	1.173	03	1.192	03
020	1.019	00	1.037	01	1.056	01	1.075	02	1.093	02	1.112	02	1.130	03	1.149	03	1.167	04	1.186	04
025	1.018	00	1.036	01	1.054	01	1.072	02	1.090	02	1.107	03	1.125	03	1.143	04	1.160	04	1.178	05
030	1.017	01	1.034	01	1.052	02	1.068	02	1.085	03	1.102	03	1.119	04	1.135	05	1.152	05	1.168	06
035	1.016	01	1.033	01	1.049	02	1.064	03	1.080	03	1.096	04	1.111	05	1.127	05	1.142	06	1.157	07
040	1.015	01	1.030	01	1.045	02	1.060	03	1.075	04	1.089	04	1.103	05	1.117	06	1.131	07	1.145	07
045	1.014	01	1.028	02	1.042	02	1.055	03	1.068	04	1.081	04	1.094	06	1.107	06	1.119	07	1.131	08
050	1.013	01	1.025	02	1.038	03	1.050	04	1.061	04	1.073	05	1.084	06	1.095	07	1.106	08	1.117	09
055	1.011	01	1.022	02	1.033	03	1.044	04	1.054	05	1.064	06	1.074	07	1.083	08	1.092	08	1.101	09
060	1.010	01	1.019	02	1.029	03	1.038	04	1.046	05	1.055	06	1.063	07	1.070	08	1.078	09	1.085	10
065	1.008	01	1.016	02	1.024	03	1.031	04	1.038	05	1.045	06	1.051	07	1.057	08	1.063	09	1.068	10
070	1.007	01	1.013	02	1.019	03	1.025	04	1.030	05	1.035	06	1.039	08	1.043	08	1.047	10	1.051	11
075	1.005	01	1.010	02	1.014	03	1.018	04	1.021	06	1.024	07	1.027	08	1.029	08	1.031	10	1.033	11
080	1.003	01	1.006	02	1.009	03	1.011	05	1.013	06	1.014	07	1.015	08	1.015	09	1.015	10	1.015	11
085	1.002	01	1.003	02	1.003	03	1.003	05	1.004	06	1.004	07	1.003	08	1.002	09	1.001	10	.999	11
090	1.000	01	.999	02	.998	03	.997	05	.995	06	.993	07	.990	08	.987	09	.984	10	.980	12
095	.998	01	.996	02	.993	03	.990	05	.986	06	.982	07	.978	08	.973	09	.968	10	.963	11
100	.996	01	.992	02	.988	03	.983	05	.978	06	.972	07	.966	08	.960	09	.953	10	.946	11
105	.995	01	.989	02	.983	03	.976	04	.969	06	.962	07	.955	08	.947	09	.938	10	.929	11
110	.993	01	.986	02	.978	03	.970	04	.961	05	.953	06	.943	08	.934	09	.924	10	.914	11
115	.991	01	.982	02	.973	03	.964	04	.954	05	.943	06	.933	07	.922	08	.911	09	.899	10
120	.990	01	.979	02	.969	03	.958	04	.946	05	.935	06	.923	07	.910	08	.898	09	.885	10
125	.988	01	.977	02	.964	03	.952	04	.939	05	.926	06	.913	07	.900	08	.886	08	.872	09
130	.987	01	.974	02	.960	03	.947	04	.933	04	.919	05	.904	06	.890	07	.875	08	.860	09
135	.986	01	.971	02	.957	02	.942	03	.927	04	.912	05	.896	06	.880	06	.865	07	.849	08
140	.985	01	.969	01	.953	02	.937	03	.921	04	.905	04	.889	05	.872	06	.855	07	.838	07
145	.984	01	.967	01	.950	02	.933	03	.916	03	.899	04	.882	05	.865	05	.847	06	.830	07
150	.983	01	.965	01	.948	02	.930	02	.912	03	.894	03	.876	04	.858	05	.840	05	.822	06
155	.982	01	.964	01	.945	01	.927	02	.908	02	.890	03	.871	03	.853	04	.834	04	.815	05
160	.981	01	.962	01	.943	01	.924	02	.905	02	.886	02	.867	03	.848	03	.829	04	.810	04
165	.981	00	.961	01	.942	01	.923	01	.903	01	.884	02	.864	02	.845	02	.825	03	.805	03
170	.980	00	.961	01	.941	01	.921	01	.901	01	.882	01	.862	01	.842	02	.822	02	.802	02
175	.980	00	.960	00	.940	00	.920	00	.900	00	.880	01	.860	01	.841	01	.821	01	.801	01
180	.980	00	.960	00	.940	00	.920	00	.900	00	.880	00	.860	00	.840	00	.820	00	.800	00

RELATIVE SET — 000 TO 180

Drift, in per cent of speed over water

Rel. Set	22 SF	CC	24 SF	CC	26 SF	CC	28 SF	CC	30 SF	CC	32 SF	CC	34 SF	CC	36 SF	CC	38 SF	CC	40 SF	CC
000	1.220	00	1.240	00	1.260	00	1.280	00	1.300	00	1.320	00	1.340	00	1.360	00	1.380	00	1.400	00
005	1.219	01	1.239	01	1.259	01	1.279	01	1.299	01	1.318	02	1.338	02	1.358	02	1.378	02	1.398	02
010	1.216	02	1.235	02	1.255	03	1.275	03	1.294	03	1.314	03	1.333	03	1.353	04	1.372	04	1.392	04
015	1.211	03	1.230	04	1.249	04	1.268	04	1.287	04	1.306	05	1.325	05	1.343	05	1.362	06	1.381	06
020	1.204	04	1.222	05	1.240	05	1.259	05	1.277	06	1.295	06	1.313	07	1.331	07	1.349	07	1.366	08
025	1.195	05	1.212	06	1.230	06	1.247	07	1.264	07	1.281	08	1.298	08	1.315	09	1.331	09	1.348	10
030	1.184	06	1.201	07	1.217	07	1.233	08	1.248	09	1.264	09	1.280	10	1.295	10	1.311	11	1.326	12
035	1.172	07	1.187	08	1.202	09	1.216	09	1.231	10	1.245	11	1.259	11	1.273	12	1.287	13	1.301	13
040	1.158	08	1.172	09	1.185	10	1.198	10	1.211	11	1.224	12	1.236	13	1.249	13	1.261	14	1.273	15
045	1.143	09	1.155	10	1.167	11	1.178	11	1.189	12	1.200	13	1.211	14	1.222	15	1.232	16	1.242	16
050	1.127	10	1.137	11	1.147	11	1.157	12	1.166	13	1.175	14	1.184	15	1.193	16	1.201	17	1.209	18
055	1.110	10	1.118	11	1.126	12	1.134	13	1.141	14	1.149	15	1.155	16	1.162	17	1.168	18	1.174	19
060	1.092	11	1.098	12	1.104	13	1.110	14	1.116	15	1.121	16	1.126	17	1.130	18	1.134	19	1.138	20
065	1.073	12	1.077	13	1.082	14	1.086	15	1.089	16	1.092	17	1.095	18	1.097	19	1.099	20	1.101	21
070	1.054	12	1.056	13	1.059	14	1.061	15	1.062	16	1.063	17	1.064	19	1.064	20	1.064	21	1.063	22
075	1.034	12	1.035	13	1.035	15	1.035	16	1.035	17	1.034	18	1.033	19	1.031	20	1.029	22	1.026	23
080	1.014	13	1.013	14	1.012	15	1.010	16	1.007	17	1.005	18	1.001	20	.998	21	.993	22	.989	23
085	.995	13	.992	14	.989	15	.985	16	.980	17	.976	19	.971	20	.965	21	.959	22	.952	23
090	.976	13	.971	14	.966	15	.960	16	.954	17	.947	19	.940	20	.933	21	.925	22	.917	24
095	.957	13	.950	14	.943	15	.936	16	.928	17	.920	19	.911	20	.902	21	.892	22	.882	23
100	.938	13	.930	14	.922	15	.913	16	.903	17	.893	18	.883	20	.873	21	.861	22	.850	23
105	.920	12	.911	13	.901	15	.890	16	.879	17	.868	18	.857	19	.844	20	.832	22	.819	23
110	.903	12	.892	13	.881	14	.869	15	.857	16	.844	17	.831	19	.818	20	.804	21	.790	22
115	.887	12	.875	13	.862	14	.849	15	.836	16	.822	17	.808	18	.793	19	.778	20	.763	21
120	.872	11	.858	12	.844	13	.830	14	.816	15	.801	16	.786	17	.770	18	.754	19	.738	20
125	.857	10	.843	11	.828	12	.813	13	.797	14	.781	15	.765	16	.749	17	.732	18	.715	19
130	.844	10	.829	11	.813	11	.797	12	.780	13	.764	14	.747	15	.730	16	.712	17	.695	18
135	.832	09	.816	10	.799	11	.782	11	.765	12	.748	13	.730	14	.712	15	.695	16	.676	16
140	.821	08	.804	09	.787	10	.769	10	.751	11	.733	12	.715	13	.697	13	.679	14	.660	15
145	.812	07	.794	08	.776	09	.758	09	.739	10	.721	11	.702	11	.684	12	.665	13	.646	13
150	.803	06	.785	07	.766	07	.748	08	.729	09	.710	09	.691	10	.672	10	.653	11	.633	12
155	.796	05	.777	06	.758	06	.739	07	.720	07	.701	08	.681	08	.662	09	.643	09	.623	10
160	.790	04	.771	05	.752	05	.732	05	.713	06	.693	06	.674	07	.654	07	.634	07	.615	08
165	.786	03	.766	04	.747	04	.727	04	.707	04	.687	05	.668	05	.648	05	.628	06	.608	06
170	.783	02	.763	02	.743	03	.723	03	.703	03	.683	03	.663	03	.644	04	.624	04	.604	04
175	.781	01	.761	01	.741	01	.721	01	.701	01	.681	02	.661	02	.641	02	.621	02	.601	02
180	.780	00	.760	00	.740	00	.720	00	.700	00	.680	00	.660	00	.640	00	.620	00	.600	00

RELATIVE SET — 000 TO 180

Examples

Page 419, Fig. 26.
Set = 169   Drift = 2   Speed = 10
TR = 37°

Per cent drift $= \dfrac{2 \times 100}{10} = 20\%$

Rel. set = 169 − 37 = +132

From table:
  for 130°; SF = .860 CC = 09
  for 135°; SF = .849 CC = 08
  by interpolation, for 132°; SF = .856 CC = 09

Then: speed of advance = 10 × .856 = 8.56
  course to be steered = 37 − 09 = 28°

Page 418, Fig. 25.
Set = 34   Drift = 2½   Speed = 9
TR = 354

Per cent drift $= \dfrac{2.5 \times 100}{9} = 28\%$

Rel. set = 34 − 354 = −320
                      +360
                      = +40

From table:
  SF = 1.198
  CC = 10°

Then: speed of advance = 9 × 1.198 = 10.782
  course to be steered = 354 − 10 = 344°

Page 417, Fig. 24.
Set = 337   Drift = 3   Speed = 8

Per cent drift $= \dfrac{3 \times 100}{8} = 37.5$, say 38%

Rel. set = 337 − 67 = 270
                     −360
                     = −090

From the table: SF = 0.925
                 CC = 22°

Then: speed of advance = .925 × 8 = 7.4
  course to be steered = 67 + 22 = 89°

TR = 67

Piloting in Currents

CASE II

*Finding track and speed of advance
from course and speed over water*

ON foregoing pages (425-425b) the problem considered was, in non-technical language: I'm going to sail in a known current at a chosen cruising speed (over water) and I know what direction I want to make good over ground; tell me, what course do I steer, and how fast will I actually progress over the ground toward my destination? This can be solved only if the strength (drift) and direction (set) of the current are known.

Another type of current problem which may face the mariner can be stated equally simply: I have been holding a known course (or heading) and cruising at a known speed over water when suddenly I discover I have been sailing in a current, the speed (drift) and direction (set) of which I obtain or estimate; now I wish to determine what direction I am making good over the ground (track) and how fast I am progressing (speed of advance) along this track. This article will enable the mariner to solve this type of problem without graphical construction.

It is recommended that no one attempt to use the tables until he understands how to solve the problem graphically and has actually worked a problem or two by graphical construction. The examples provided in this article can serve this purpose admirably, and the answers given can be used to check the accuracy of the construction. *However, no graphical construction work is needed using the table!*

A graphical method for solving problems of this type is illustrated in Fig. 1. First, line OB is drawn in the direc-

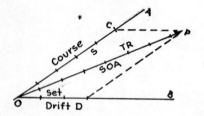

Figure 1.

Effect of a current on the course and speed made good over the bottom.

tion of the set of the current and length OD measured along OB equal (in any convenient scale) to the distance (OD) the current moves in one hour. From D line DP is drawn in the direction of the course being steered, its length (now in the same scale used for OD) equal to the distance the boat would cover over water in one hour. Line OP is then drawn from the starting point to the finishing point; the direction of this line represents the *Track*, TR, or course over ground, and the length of the line indicates the *Speed of Advance*, SOA, or speed over ground.

Another way of explaining the solution to this problem may be helpful. Assume that the engine is stopped (or sails furled) so that the boat has no way; plot the position of the boat at the end of an hour, all the motion being caused by the current. Then pretend that the current stops somehow for an hour while the craft makes way at its own speed for one hour. Plot the course from the

position just found and mark its position along this course line after an hour's run. This new position will represent the actual position of the boat at the end of one hour. The direction from the starting point is the *Track* and the distance from the starting point represents the *Speed of Advance* because it represents the distance made good over ground in an hour.

In Table C, page 425d, drift is expressed relative to the known speed, and set, relative to the course steered. An explanation accompanies the table.

Illustrative examples are taken from pages 417, 418 and 419. See diagrams below and solutions on page 425d.

It might be supposed that the course corrections and speed factors would be the same as discussed in the previous case, but a careful comparison of the tables will reveal that this is not so. To illustrate, suppose that the drift is 20 percent and the relative set 90°. Using Table C for Case II we find that the current sets us off our course by 11°, but we need to alter our course by 12° into the current to compensate for it. Also, when we don't correct our course, the speed factor is 1.02, which means that our speed over ground is two percent greater than our speed over water (but, of course, it isn't getting us where we want to be). If we do "crab" into the current by the required 12°, the speed factor is 0.98, which means that our actual speed of advance is two percent less than our speed over water. Clearly the two cases are not identical.

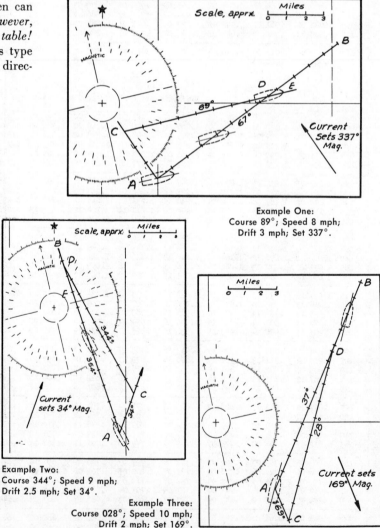

Example One:
Course 89°; Speed 8 mph;
Drift 3 mph; Set 337°.

Example Two:
Course 344°; Speed 9 mph;
Drift 2.5 mph; Set 34°.

Example Three:
Course 028°; Speed 10 mph;
Drift 2 mph; Set 169°.

Table C — Case II

Case II -- To find TRACK and SPEED OF ADVANCE from COURSE and SPEED OVER WATER
SPEED FACTORS (SF) AND COURSE CORRECTIONS (CC)
Drift, in per cent of speed over water

Rel. Set	2 SF	CC	4 SF	CC	6 SF	CC	8 SF	CC	10 SF	CC	12 SF	CC	14 SF	CC	16 SF	CC	18 SF	CC	20 SF	CC
000	1.020	00	1.040	00	1.060	00	1.080	00	1.100	00	1.120	00	1.140	00	1.160	00	1.180	00	1.200	00
005	1.020	00	1.040	00	1.060	00	1.080	00	1.100	00	1.120	01	1.140	01	1.159	01	1.179	01	1.199	01
010	1.020	00	1.039	00	1.059	01	1.079	01	1.099	01	1.118	01	1.138	01	1.158	01	1.178	02	1.197	02
015	1.019	00	1.039	01	1.058	01	1.077	01	1.097	01	1.116	02	1.136	02	1.155	02	1.175	02	1.194	02
020	1.019	00	1.038	01	1.057	01	1.076	01	1.095	02	1.114	02	1.133	02	1.152	03	1.171	03	1.190	03
025	1.018	00	1.036	01	1.055	01	1.073	02	1.091	02	1.110	03	1.128	03	1.147	03	1.166	04	1.184	04
030	1.017	01	1.035	01	1.052	02	1.070	02	1.088	03	1.106	03	1.123	04	1.141	04	1.159	04	1.177	05
035	1.016	01	1.033	01	1.050	02	1.067	02	1.083	03	1.100	04	1.118	04	1.135	05	1.152	05	1.169	06
040	1.015	01	1.031	01	1.047	02	1.063	03	1.079	03	1.095	04	1.111	05	1.127	05	1.144	06	1.160	06
045	1.014	01	1.029	02	1.043	02	1.058	03	1.073	04	1.088	04	1.103	05	1.119	06	1.134	06	1.150	07
050	1.013	01	1.026	02	1.040	03	1.053	03	1.067	04	1.081	05	1.095	06	1.110	06	1.124	07	1.139	08
055	1.012	01	1.023	02	1.036	03	1.048	04	1.061	04	1.073	05	1.086	06	1.100	07	1.113	08	1.127	08
060	1.010	01	1.021	02	1.031	03	1.042	04	1.054	05	1.065	06	1.077	06	1.089	07	1.101	08	1.114	09
065	1.009	01	1.018	02	1.027	03	1.036	05	1.046	05	1.056	06	1.067	07	1.077	08	1.088	09	1.100	09
070	1.007	01	1.014	02	1.022	03	1.030	04	1.038	05	1.047	06	1.056	07	1.065	08	1.075	09	1.085	10
075	1.005	01	1.011	02	1.017	03	1.024	04	1.030	05	1.038	06	1.045	07	1.053	08	1.061	09	1.069	10
080	1.004	01	1.008	02	1.012	03	1.017	04	1.022	06	1.028	07	1.034	08	1.040	09	1.046	10	1.053	11
085	1.002	01	1.004	02	1.007	03	1.010	05	1.014	06	1.018	07	1.022	08	1.026	09	1.031	10	1.037	11
090	1.000	01	1.001	02	1.002	03	1.003	05	1.005	06	1.007	07	1.010	08	1.013	09	1.016	10	1.020	11
095	.998	01	.997	02	.997	03	.996	05	.996	06	.997	07	.998	08	.999	09	1.001	10	1.003	11
100	.997	01	.994	02	.991	03	.989	05	.988	06	.986	07	.985	08	.985	09	.985	10	.985	12
105	.995	01	.990	02	.986	03	.982	05	.979	06	.976	07	.973	08	.971	09	.969	10	.968	12
110	.993	01	.987	02	.981	03	.976	04	.970	06	.966	07	.961	08	.957	09	.954	10	.950	11
115	.992	01	.984	02	.976	03	.969	04	.962	05	.955	07	.949	08	.944	09	.938	10	.933	11
120	.990	01	.981	02	.971	03	.962	04	.954	05	.946	06	.938	07	.930	09	.923	10	.917	11
125	.989	01	.978	02	.967	03	.956	04	.946	05	.936	06	.927	07	.918	08	.909	09	.900	10
130	.987	01	.975	02	.963	03	.951	04	.939	05	.927	06	.916	07	.905	08	.895	09	.885	10
135	.986	01	.972	02	.959	03	.945	03	.932	04	.919	05	.906	06	.894	07	.882	08	.870	09
140	.985	01	.970	02	.955	02	.940	03	.926	04	.911	05	.897	06	.883	07	.870	08	.856	09
145	.984	01	.968	01	.951	02	.936	03	.920	04	.904	05	.889	06	.874	06	.859	07	.844	08
150	.983	01	.966	01	.949	02	.932	02	.915	03	.898	04	.882	05	.865	05	.849	06	.833	07
155	.982	00	.964	01	.946	02	.928	02	.910	03	.893	03	.875	04	.858	05	.840	05	.823	06
160	.981	00	.963	01	.944	01	.925	02	.907	02	.888	03	.870	03	.851	04	.833	04	.815	05
165	.981	00	.961	01	.942	01	.923	01	.904	02	.885	02	.866	02	.846	03	.827	03	.808	04
170	.980	00	.961	00	.941	01	.921	01	.902	01	.882	01	.862	02	.843	02	.823	02	.804	02
175	.980	00	.960	00	.940	00	.920	00	.900	01	.881	01	.861	01	.841	01	.821	01	.801	01
180	.980	00	.960	00	.940	00	.920	00	.900	00	.880	00	.860	00	.840	00	.820	00	.800	00

RELATIVE SET — 000 TO 180

Example Three:

Course=028; Speed=10; Drift=2; Set=169°

Percent drift $= \dfrac{2 \times 100}{10} = 20$

Relative set $= 169 - 28 = 141$

From the table: SF=0.857; CC=9

Then: speed of advance $= 10 \times .857 = 8.6$

Track $= 28 + 9 = 37°$

Case II -- To find TRACK and SPEED OF ADVANCE from COURSE and SPEED OVER WATER
SPEED FACTORS (SF) AND COURSE CORRECTIONS (CC)
Drift, in per cent of speed over water

Rel. Set	22 SF	CC	24 SF	CC	26 SF	CC	28 SF	CC	30 SF	CC	32 SF	CC	34 SF	CC	36 SF	CC	38 SF	CC	40 SF	CC
000	1.220	00	1.240	00	1.260	00	1.280	00	1.300	00	1.320	00	1.340	00	1.360	00	1.380	00	1.400	00
005	1.219	01	1.239	01	1.259	01	1.279	01	1.299	01	1.319	01	1.339	01	1.359	01	1.379	01	1.399	01
010	1.217	02	1.237	02	1.257	02	1.277	02	1.296	02	1.316	02	1.336	03	1.356	03	1.376	03	1.396	03
015	1.214	03	1.233	03	1.253	03	1.273	03	1.292	03	1.312	04	1.331	04	1.351	04	1.371	04	1.390	04
020	1.209	04	1.228	04	1.247	04	1.267	04	1.286	05	1.305	05	1.325	05	1.344	05	1.363	05	1.383	06
025	1.203	04	1.222	05	1.241	05	1.259	05	1.278	06	1.297	06	1.316	06	1.335	07	1.354	07	1.373	07
030	1.196	05	1.214	06	1.232	06	1.250	06	1.269	07	1.287	07	1.306	07	1.324	08	1.343	08	1.361	08
035	1.187	06	1.204	07	1.222	07	1.240	07	1.258	08	1.275	08	1.293	09	1.311	09	1.329	09	1.347	10
040	1.177	07	1.194	07	1.211	08	1.228	08	1.245	09	1.262	09	1.279	10	1.297	10	1.314	11	1.331	11
045	1.166	08	1.182	08	1.198	09	1.214	09	1.231	10	1.247	10	1.263	11	1.280	11	1.297	12	1.314	12
050	1.154	08	1.169	09	1.184	10	1.199	10	1.215	11	1.230	11	1.246	12	1.262	13	1.278	13	1.294	14
055	1.141	09	1.155	10	1.169	11	1.183	11	1.198	12	1.212	12	1.227	13	1.242	14	1.257	14	1.272	15
060	1.126	10	1.139	11	1.152	11	1.166	12	1.179	13	1.193	13	1.206	14	1.220	15	1.235	15	1.249	16
065	1.111	10	1.123	11	1.135	12	1.147	13	1.159	14	1.172	14	1.184	15	1.197	16	1.211	17	1.224	17
070	1.095	11	1.105	12	1.116	13	1.127	14	1.138	14	1.149	15	1.161	16	1.173	17	1.185	18	1.197	18
075	1.078	11	1.087	12	1.096	13	1.106	14	1.116	15	1.126	16	1.136	17	1.147	18	1.158	18	1.169	19
080	1.061	12	1.068	13	1.076	14	1.084	15	1.093	16	1.102	17	1.111	18	1.120	18	1.130	19	1.140	20
085	1.042	12	1.049	13	1.055	14	1.062	15	1.069	16	1.076	17	1.084	18	1.092	19	1.100	20	1.109	21
090	1.024	12	1.028	13	1.033	15	1.038	16	1.044	17	1.050	18	1.056	19	1.063	20	1.070	21	1.077	22
095	1.005	13	1.008	14	1.011	15	1.015	16	1.019	17	1.023	18	1.028	19	1.033	20	1.038	21	1.044	22
100	.986	13	.987	14	.989	15	.991	16	.993	17	.996	18	.999	20	1.002	21	1.006	22	1.010	23
105	.967	13	.966	14	.966	15	.966	16	.967	17	.968	19	.969	20	.971	21	.973	22	.976	23
110	.948	13	.945	14	.943	15	.942	16	.941	17	.940	19	.940	20	.940	21	.940	22	.941	24
115	.929	12	.925	14	.921	15	.917	16	.915	17	.912	19	.910	20	.908	21	.907	22	.907	24
120	.910	12	.904	13	.899	15	.894	16	.889	17	.885	18	.881	20	.877	21	.874	22	.872	23
125	.892	12	.884	13	.877	14	.870	15	.864	16	.858	18	.852	19	.847	20	.842	22	.837	23
130	.875	11	.865	12	.856	13	.848	15	.839	16	.831	17	.824	18	.817	20	.810	21	.804	22
135	.859	10	.847	12	.837	13	.826	14	.816	15	.806	16	.797	18	.788	19	.779	20	.771	22
140	.843	10	.831	11	.818	12	.806	13	.794	14	.782	15	.771	16	.760	18	.750	19	.740	20
145	.829	09	.815	10	.801	11	.787	12	.774	13	.760	14	.747	15	.735	16	.722	18	.710	19
150	.817	08	.801	09	.786	10	.770	10	.755	11	.740	12	.726	14	.711	15	.697	16	.684	17
155	.806	07	.789	07	.772	08	.756	09	.739	10	.723	11	.707	12	.691	13	.675	14	.660	15
160	.797	05	.779	06	.761	07	.743	07	.725	08	.708	09	.690	10	.673	11	.656	11	.639	12
165	.790	04	.771	05	.752	05	.733	06	.714	06	.696	07	.677	07	.659	08	.641	09	.622	10
170	.784	03	.765	03	.745	03	.726	04	.706	04	.687	05	.668	05	.648	06	.629	06	.610	07
175	.781	01	.761	00	.741	02	.721	02	.702	02	.682	02	.662	03	.642	03	.622	03	.603	03
180	.780	00	.760	00	.740	00	.720	00	.700	00	.680	00	.660	00	.640	00	.620	00	.600	00

RELATIVE SET — 000 TO 180

Tables are entered with the drift (in percent of speed over water) at the top, horizontally (2 to 40), and with the relative set of current (000 to 180) in vertical column at left. These yield speed factor (SF) and course correction (CC). See examples below, and compare diagrammatic solutions, page 425c.

Example Two:

Course=344; Speed=9; Drift=2.5; Set=34°

Percent drift $= \dfrac{2.5 \times 100}{9} = 28$

Relative set $= 34 - 344 = \begin{array}{r} -310 \\ +360 \\ \hline +50 \end{array}$

From the table: SF=1.199; CC=10

Then: speed of advance $= 9 \times 1.199 = 10.8$

Track $= 344 + 10 = 354°$

Example One:

Course=089; Speed=8; Drift=3; Set=337°

Percent drift $= \dfrac{3 \times 100}{8} = 38$

Relative set $= \begin{array}{r} 337 - 89 = 248 \\ 248 - 360 = -112 \end{array}$

From the table: SF=0.923; CC=22

Then: speed of advance $= 8 \times 0.923 = 7.4$

Track $= 089 - 22 = 067°$

TWO different types of problems of piloting in currents have been discussed. There is a third type of problem, which I call Case III. In simple terms the problem is: I know the direction I want to go and the *speed over the bottom* I wish to make good; now, what course do I steer and at what *speed over water* (rpm speed) do I need to run? (It is assumed, of course, that the set and drift of the current are known.)

Table D enables the navigator to solve problems of this type, without constructing scale diagrams.

In order to simplify the tables, two new terms are introduced, and illustrated in Fig. 1: Relative Set, the actual angle between *track* and *set*, and Course Correction (CC), the angle by which the *track* must be corrected to obtain the *course*.

In the tables, values of relative set are given up to 180°, as it can always be expressed by an angle of 180° or less, by measuring relative set CW or CCW from the *track*, as needed. The tables give only the magnitude of the *course correction;* the direction in which this correction is to be applied is always against the relative set. That is, you always "crab" into or against the current. It will be noted that, in the table, *drift* is expressed in percent of speed of advance.

For a quick illustration, let us assume we desire to make good a speed of advance of 10 knots, and a 1-knot current is setting directly along the track. In this case, the relative set is 0° and the drift is 10%. Referring to the table, we find that SF = .900 and CC = 00. This means that we need a speed over water of .900 x 10 = 9 knots, and there is no course correction. Of course, we know that the one-knot current is subtracted directly from our speed over water, so we have to make good only 9 knots over water, as the current adds the extra knot to our speed over the bottom.

For such a simple problem, a table is not needed; but if the reader is confused at any time as to how the table was designed to be used, a simple example for which he knows the answer, may be helpful to him in insuring correct use and understanding of the tables. The following examples are taken from pages 417-419.

Piloting in Currents

CASE III

Finding course and speed over water from track and speed of advance

---

Example One

Given: TR 67, Set 337, Drift 3, Speed of Advance 7.4

Calculate:
$$\text{Percent drift} = \frac{3 \times 100}{7.4} = 40.5$$

Rel. set = 337 − 67 = 270 = 90° to port

From the table: SF = 1.077; CC = 22

Then: Speed over water = 7.4 x 1.077 = 7.97 knots
Course to be steered = 67 + 22 = 89°

Example Two

Given: TR 354, Set 34, Drift 2.5, Speed of Advance 10.8

Calculate:
$$\text{Percent drift} = \frac{2.5 \times 100}{10.8} = 23.1$$

Relative set = 34 − 354 = −320 = +40 to starboard

From the table: SF = 0.837; CC = 10.5

Then: Speed over water = 10.8 x .837 = 9.04 knots
Course to be steered = 354 − 10.5 = 343.5°

Example Three

Given: TR 37°, Set 169, Drift 2, Speed of Advance 8.56

Calculate:
$$\text{Percent drift} = \frac{2 \times 100}{8.56} = 23.4$$

Relative set = 169 − 37 = 132° to starboard

From the table: for 130°: SF = 1.164; CC = 8.8
for 135°: SF = 1.176; CC = 8
by interpolation, for 132°: SF = 1.169; CC = 8.3

Then: Speed over water needed = 8.56 x 1.169 = 10.0
Course to be steered = 37 − 8.3 = 28.7°

PILOTING IN CURRENTS: GENERAL RESUME OF THE THREE CASES

		CASE I	CASE II	CASE III
GIVEN		Track	Course	Track
		Speed Over Water	Speed Over Water	Speed of Advance
TO FIND		Speed of Advance	Speed of Advance	Speed Over Water
		Course	Track	Course
Calculate Before Using Table.	% Drift	$\dfrac{\text{Drift X 100}}{\text{Speed Over Water}}$	$\dfrac{\text{Drift X 100}}{\text{Speed Over Water}}$	$\dfrac{\text{Drift X 100}}{\text{Speed of Advance}}$
	Relative Set	SET - TRACK (180° or less to port or starboard)	SET - COURSE (180° or less to port or starboard)	SET - TRACK (180° or less to port or starboard)
Read from table, interpolating, if necessary	SF	Speed factor	Speed factor	Speed factor
	CC	Course Correction	Course Change	Course Correction
ANSWERS		Speed of Advance = (speed over water) X SF	Speed of Advance = (Speed over water) X SF	Speed Over Water = (Speed of Advance) X SF
	If Rel.Set is to Starboard	COURSE = TRACK - CC	TRACK = COURSE + CC	COURSE = TRACK - CC
	If Rel.Set is to Port	COURSE = TRACK + CC	TRACK = COURSE - CC	COURSE = TRACK + CC

Case III -- To find COURSE and SPEED OVER WATER to make good a desired TRACK and SPEED OF ADVANCE
SPEED FACTORS (SF) AND COURSE CORRECTIONS (CC)
Drift, in per cent of speed of advance

Table D — Case III

In use, tables are entered with the drift (in percent of speed of advance) at the top, horizontally (2 to 40), and with the relative set of current (000 to 180) in vertical column at left. These yield speed factor (SF) and course correction (CC). For details of use, see examples in text.

RELATIVE SET — 000 TO 180

Rel. Set	2 SF CC	4 SF CC	6 SF CC	8 SF CC	10 SF CC	12 SF CC	14 SF CC	16 SF CC	18 SF CC	20 SF CC
000	.980 00	.960 00	.940 00	.920 00	.900 00	.880 00	.860 00	.840 00	.820 00	.800 00
005	.980 00	.960 00	.940 00	.920 00	.900 00	.881 01	.861 01	.841 01	.821 01	.801 01
010	.980 00	.961 00	.941 01	.921 01	.902 01	.882 01	.862 02	.843 02	.823 02	.804 02
015	.981 00	.961 01	.942 01	.923 01	.904 02	.885 02	.866 02	.846 03	.827 03	.808 04
020	.981 00	.963 01	.944 01	.925 02	.907 02	.888 03	.870 03	.851 04	.833 04	.815 05
025	.982 00	.964 01	.946 02	.928 02	.910 03	.893 03	.875 04	.858 05	.840 05	.823 06
030	.983 01	.966 01	.949 02	.932 02	.915 03	.898 04	.882 05	.865 05	.849 06	.833 07
035	.984 01	.968 01	.951 02	.936 03	.920 04	.904 04	.889 05	.874 06	.859 07	.844 08
040	.985 01	.970 02	.955 02	.940 03	.926 04	.911 05	.897 06	.883 07	.870 08	.856 09
045	.986 01	.972 02	.959 03	.945 03	.932 04	.919 05	.906 06	.894 07	.882 08	.870 09
050	.987 01	.975 02	.963 03	.951 04	.939 05	.927 06	.916 07	.905 08	.895 09	.885 10
055	.989 01	.978 02	.967 03	.956 04	.946 05	.936 06	.927 07	.918 08	.909 09	.900 10
060	.990 01	.981 02	.971 03	.962 04	.954 05	.946 06	.938 07	.930 09	.923 10	.917 11
065	.992 01	.984 02	.976 03	.969 04	.962 05	.955 07	.949 08	.944 09	.938 10	.933 11
070	.993 01	.987 02	.981 03	.976 04	.970 06	.966 07	.961 08	.957 09	.954 10	.950 11
075	.995 01	.990 02	.986 03	.982 05	.979 06	.976 07	.973 08	.971 09	.969 10	.968 12
080	.997 01	.994 02	.991 03	.989 05	.988 06	.986 07	.985 08	.985 09	.985 10	.985 12
085	.998 01	.997 02	.997 03	.996 05	.996 06	.997 07	.998 08	.999 09	1.001 10	1.003 11
090	1.000 01	1.001 02	1.002 03	1.003 05	1.005 06	1.007 07	1.010 08	1.013 09	1.016 10	1.020 11
095	1.002 01	1.004 02	1.007 03	1.010 05	1.014 06	1.018 07	1.022 08	1.026 09	1.031 10	1.037 11
100	1.004 01	1.008 02	1.012 03	1.017 04	1.022 06	1.028 07	1.034 08	1.040 09	1.046 10	1.053 11
105	1.005 01	1.011 02	1.017 03	1.024 04	1.030 05	1.038 06	1.045 07	1.053 08	1.061 09	1.069 10
110	1.007 01	1.014 02	1.022 03	1.030 04	1.038 05	1.047 06	1.056 07	1.065 08	1.075 09	1.085 10
115	1.009 01	1.018 02	1.027 03	1.036 04	1.046 05	1.056 06	1.067 07	1.077 08	1.088 09	1.100 09
120	1.010 01	1.021 02	1.031 03	1.042 04	1.054 05	1.065 06	1.077 06	1.089 07	1.101 08	1.114 09
125	1.012 01	1.023 02	1.036 03	1.048 04	1.061 04	1.073 05	1.086 06	1.100 07	1.113 08	1.127 08
130	1.013 01	1.026 02	1.040 03	1.053 03	1.067 04	1.081 05	1.095 06	1.110 06	1.124 07	1.139 08
135	1.014 01	1.029 02	1.043 02	1.058 03	1.073 04	1.088 04	1.103 05	1.119 06	1.134 06	1.150 07
140	1.015 01	1.031 01	1.047 02	1.063 03	1.079 03	1.095 04	1.111 05	1.127 05	1.144 06	1.160 06
145	1.016 01	1.033 01	1.050 02	1.067 02	1.083 03	1.100 03	1.118 04	1.135 05	1.152 05	1.169 06
150	1.017 01	1.035 01	1.052 02	1.070 02	1.088 03	1.106 03	1.123 04	1.141 04	1.159 04	1.177 05
155	1.018 00	1.036 01	1.055 01	1.073 02	1.091 02	1.110 03	1.128 03	1.147 03	1.166 04	1.184 04
160	1.019 00	1.038 01	1.057 01	1.076 01	1.095 02	1.114 02	1.133 02	1.152 03	1.171 03	1.190 03
165	1.019 00	1.039 01	1.058 01	1.077 01	1.097 01	1.116 01	1.136 02	1.155 02	1.175 02	1.194 02
170	1.020 00	1.039 00	1.059 01	1.079 01	1.099 01	1.118 01	1.138 01	1.158 01	1.178 02	1.197 02
175	1.020 00	1.040 00	1.060 00	1.080 00	1.100 00	1.120 01	1.140 01	1.159 01	1.179 01	1.199 01
180	1.020 00	1.040 00	1.060 00	1.080 00	1.100 00	1.120 00	1.140 00	1.160 00	1.180 00	1.200 00

Case III -- To find COURSE and SPEED OVER WATER to make good a desired TRACK and SPEED OF ADVANCE
SPEED FACTORS (SF) AND COURSE CORRECTIONS (CC)
Drift, in per cent of speed of advance

RELATIVE SET — 000 TO 180

Rel. Set	22 SF CC	24 SF CC	26 SF CC	28 SF CC	30 SF CC	32 SF CC	34 SF CC	36 SF CC	38 SF CC	40 SF CC
000	.780 00	.760 00	.740 00	.720 00	.700 00	.680 00	.660 00	.640 00	.620 00	.600 00
005	.781 01	.761 02	.741 02	.721 02	.702 02	.682 02	.662 03	.642 03	.622 03	.603 03
010	.784 03	.765 03	.745 03	.726 04	.706 04	.687 05	.668 05	.648 06	.629 06	.610 07
015	.790 04	.771 05	.752 05	.733 06	.714 06	.696 07	.677 07	.659 08	.641 09	.622 10
020	.797 05	.779 06	.761 07	.743 07	.725 08	.708 09	.690 10	.673 11	.656 11	.639 12
025	.806 07	.789 07	.772 08	.756 09	.739 10	.723 11	.707 12	.691 13	.675 14	.660 15
030	.817 08	.801 09	.786 10	.770 11	.755 11	.740 12	.726 14	.711 15	.697 16	.684 17
035	.829 09	.815 10	.801 11	.787 12	.774 13	.760 14	.747 15	.735 16	.722 18	.710 19
040	.843 10	.831 11	.818 12	.806 13	.794 14	.782 15	.771 16	.760 18	.750 19	.740 20
045	.859 10	.847 12	.837 13	.826 14	.816 15	.806 16	.797 18	.788 19	.779 20	.771 22
050	.875 11	.865 12	.856 13	.848 15	.839 16	.831 17	.824 18	.817 20	.810 21	.804 22
055	.892 12	.884 13	.877 14	.870 15	.864 17	.858 18	.852 19	.847 20	.842 22	.837 23
060	.910 12	.904 13	.899 15	.894 16	.889 17	.885 18	.881 20	.877 21	.874 22	.872 23
065	.929 12	.925 14	.921 15	.917 16	.915 17	.912 19	.910 20	.908 21	.907 22	.907 24
070	.948 13	.945 14	.943 15	.942 16	.941 17	.940 19	.940 20	.940 21	.940 22	.941 24
075	.967 13	.966 14	.966 15	.966 16	.967 17	.968 19	.969 20	.971 21	.973 22	.976 23
080	.986 13	.987 14	.989 15	.991 16	.993 17	.996 18	.999 20	1.002 21	1.006 22	1.010 23
085	1.005 13	1.008 14	1.011 15	1.015 16	1.019 17	1.023 18	1.028 19	1.033 20	1.038 21	1.044 22
090	1.024 12	1.028 13	1.033 15	1.038 16	1.044 17	1.050 18	1.056 19	1.063 20	1.070 21	1.077 22
095	1.042 12	1.049 13	1.055 14	1.062 15	1.069 16	1.076 17	1.084 18	1.092 19	1.100 20	1.109 21
100	1.061 12	1.068 13	1.076 14	1.084 15	1.093 16	1.102 17	1.111 18	1.120 18	1.130 19	1.140 20
105	1.078 11	1.087 12	1.096 13	1.106 14	1.116 15	1.126 16	1.136 17	1.147 18	1.158 18	1.169 19
110	1.095 11	1.105 12	1.116 13	1.127 14	1.138 14	1.149 15	1.161 16	1.173 17	1.185 18	1.197 18
115	1.111 10	1.123 11	1.135 12	1.147 13	1.159 14	1.172 14	1.184 15	1.197 16	1.211 17	1.224 17
120	1.126 10	1.139 11	1.152 11	1.166 12	1.179 13	1.193 13	1.206 14	1.220 15	1.235 15	1.249 16
125	1.141 09	1.155 10	1.169 11	1.183 11	1.198 12	1.212 12	1.227 13	1.242 14	1.257 14	1.272 15
130	1.154 08	1.169 09	1.184 10	1.199 10	1.215 11	1.230 11	1.246 12	1.262 13	1.278 13	1.294 14
135	1.166 08	1.182 08	1.198 09	1.214 09	1.231 10	1.247 10	1.263 11	1.280 11	1.297 12	1.314 12
140	1.177 07	1.194 07	1.211 08	1.228 08	1.245 09	1.262 09	1.279 10	1.297 10	1.314 11	1.331 11
145	1.187 06	1.204 07	1.222 07	1.240 07	1.258 08	1.275 08	1.293 09	1.311 09	1.329 09	1.347 10
150	1.196 05	1.214 06	1.232 06	1.250 06	1.269 07	1.287 07	1.306 07	1.324 08	1.343 08	1.361 08
155	1.203 04	1.222 05	1.241 05	1.259 05	1.278 06	1.297 06	1.316 06	1.335 07	1.354 07	1.373 07
160	1.209 04	1.228 04	1.247 04	1.267 04	1.286 05	1.305 05	1.325 05	1.344 05	1.363 05	1.383 05
165	1.214 03	1.233 03	1.253 03	1.273 03	1.292 03	1.312 04	1.331 04	1.351 04	1.371 04	1.390 04
170	1.217 02	1.237 02	1.257 02	1.277 02	1.296 02	1.316 02	1.336 03	1.356 03	1.376 03	1.396 03
175	1.219 01	1.239 01	1.259 01	1.279 01	1.299 01	1.319 01	1.339 01	1.359 01	1.379 01	1.399 01
180	1.220 00	1.240 00	1.260 00	1.280 00	1.300 00	1.320 00	1.340 00	1.360 00	1.380 00	1.400 00

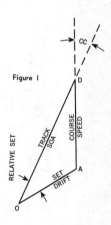

Figure I

Before using these tables to find course and speed over water the author suggests you learn how to solve the problem graphically, thus ensuring an understanding of the principles involved.

'Longshore Piloting

HERE are a number of good piloting wrinkles that might well be stowed away in every boatman's bag of tricks. Their practicability has been thoroughly tested, as many have been used or originated by George W. Rappleyea in numerous day and night delivery runs of new cruisers down the Jersey coast.

One is a trick in making a landfall used, in principle, by Harold Gatty in piloting Wiley Post around the world in eight days. The essence of it is this—to lay your course, *not* for your objective, but decidedly to one side, to allow for possible inaccuracies of leeway estimates.

To illustrate how the principle might be applied by a boatman in piloting let's assume you have been fishing somewhere in the area between Block Island and Martha's Vineyard. See Figure 1. After several hours of trolling, drifting and circling in indeterminate directions, and a possible change in current set, your position is problematical. To make things more interesting, fog closes in, so you decide to run for the nearest harbor, Block Island.

Your best judgment, in the absence of a fix by cross bearings, tells you that you should be somewhere to the eastward of the bell buoy (B, Figure 1) northeast of the harbor, somewhere out in the direction of A. It's a good plan of course to lay the course for an off-lying buoy—as a matter of fact that's what they're for—but even if there were no buoy, there can be merit in laying the course decidedly off to one side of the ultimate objective, Block Island Harbor.

Why? Well, suppose you lay your course for the can buoy directly at the entrance. You're a careful pilot and have estimated your time and speed exactly. On that basis, you expect to pick up the can at 4:00 P. M. Five minutes before the predicted elapsed time has run out, you prudently stop and take a sounding. You get six fathoms. So you hold your westward course, slow down and keep the lead going.

At 4:05, making due allowance for the stage of the tide in correcting the depths you get by sounding, you hit the three-fathom curve. In a limited sense, you have a "line" of position—but *not* a fix. *If* you were on your course, you would have picked up the can along with the three-fathom curve. So now where are we? North or South?

Your first conclusion might be that, because you have run a few minutes over before getting three fathoms, you should be north of the harbor. But what's to say that you weren't actually five minutes' run to the eastward of your estimated point of departure out there at sea? Or that your estimate of actual distance run wasn't in error by that much, because of wind and current?

On the assumption that you are north of the harbor you sound your way south, but no harbor. How far to continue? That can may still be just ahead, obscured by the fog. On the other hand, doubt creeps in. You couldn't be that far off your reckoning—or could you? So there you are, in a fog, literally and figuratively.

If you've missed by a quarter of a mile to the north, you have hit the beach at D; a quarter mile to the south, at E. And there are points both north and south of the harbor where the general trend of the three-fathom line is roughly the same (at F and at E).

Now let's see what would happen if we had laid the course for the bell, well to the north. Our estimate is that we're due to pick it up at 3:40. At 3:35, at 3:40, and at 3:45 we stop and listen —no bell. That's not a sure indication we have missed the buoy by a wide margin because fog plays strange pranks with sound, sometimes causing it to skip one nearby spot and come in clear and strong on the same bearing further away.

So, instead of wasting time in a search for the buoy, we hold our course, and go ahead at reduced speed, keeping the lead going for a rough check on the distance offshore, till we fetch the three-fathom curve. Now, if we've miscalculated by a quarter-mile, we're at G if to the north, at H if to the south. But, we *are* to the *north* of the harbor and so we turn south with confidence along the three-fathom curve.

Had we been on course we would have hit the beach not far from F where the general trend of the curve is north and south. So we steer south but, presently, get greater depths. Conclusion? We're too far north, perhaps at G, or further. So we turn inshore and then follow the curve by sounding. We find the trend is SSW, which is as good as a signpost to tell us we must be at I.

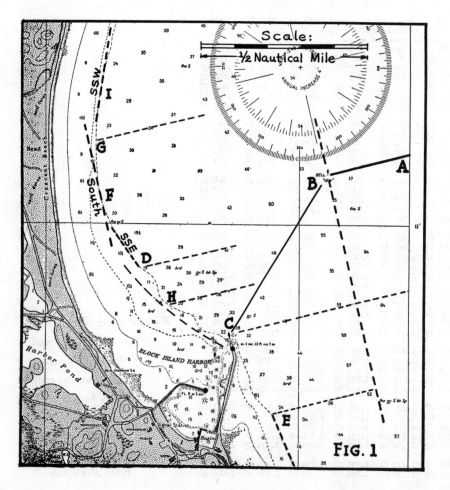

FIG. 1

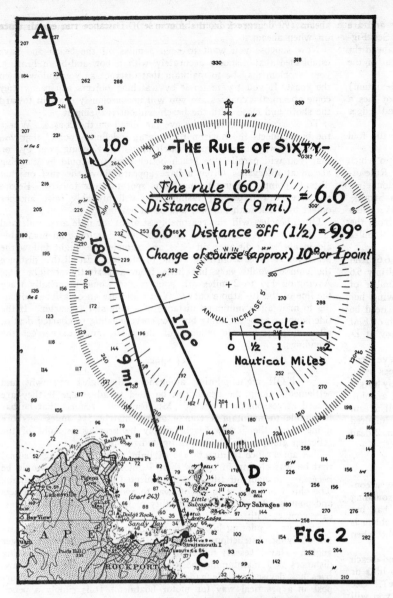

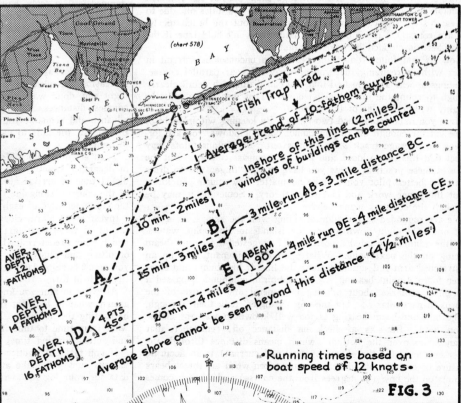

yards, or maybe even the bow staff (if enough time has elapsed for the sharpness of precise details to be dulled a little by memory).

In this particular problem, we laid the course ⅜ mile to the north of the objective. How much allowance is made in any given case varies within limits determined by what you feel would be a maximum possible error under the circumstances. On a long run in from offshore, making a landfall on a beach that trends in a straight line for miles in each direction, with few marks of identification ashore, even if visibility permits using them, you may prefer to make an allowance of a mile or more. It adds little to the total run but eliminates much uncertainty. Familiar objects often look strange in fog, for in clear weather we're seldom as observing as we should be and perspective is lost when a single object is picked up apart from its relationship to usual surroundings.

Some day you may be forty miles offshore, trolling for tuna. If you could have a course recorder aboard, your track after several hours of fishing would resemble the contour of the scrambled parts of a jig-saw puzzle. Remember this wrinkle then, and put it to use. Lay your course a couple of miles up the beach from the inlet you hope to hit. But don't use this blindly, without regard to possible dangers that may line the beach. Study a chart and adapt the principle to the problem at hand.

The Rule-of-Sixty

Here's another useful wrinkle. It's called the Rule-of-Sixty and provides a simple practical way of changing course to clear an off-lying obstruction, without a lot of chart work.

Trending around to the south and later SSE, we know for sure the harbor lies just ahead.

On the other hand, suppose when we had first picked up the three-fathom line, and turned south, our depths decreased. Then we'd know we were south of F. If the trend is roughly SSE, we must be near D and have only to sound our way along another half mile or so, in depths of 2½ fathoms, to lead right in between the entrance can and nun. Touching a two-fathom lump among the 2½-fathom depths, we realize that the abrupt turn, SSW down the entrance channel, is at hand.

By all the perverse laws of nature, this is precisely the time a shift of wind should hustle the fog off to sea, without allowing you the satisfaction of feeling your way right on in behind the breakwater through "pea soup" so thick (as you tell it later) you couldn't see 50

Let's assume you have come out of Portsmouth Harbor and are running a southerly course down the coast to Cape Ann. See Figure 2. Somewhere out off Newburyport you pick up dead ahead the fixed green light on Straitsmouth Island, at the eastern tip of the cape.

Your compass course (magnetic also, assuming no deviation) along the line AC is South (or 180 degrees). A bell buoy lies a mile and a half off the light, offshore of a lot of rocks and ledges you must clear, necessitating a change in course.

You can see the light but you can't see the buoy, nor the foul ground you must avoid off the cape.

Instead of getting out the chart and plotting a position from which a new course can be laid to the buoy, you can apply this Rule-of-Sixty and get your new course by a simple mental calculation.

You know from the chart or Light List that the light on Straitsmouth Island is visible 9 miles, assuming good visibility. (With less than perfect visibility, you'd have to verify your distance from the light by a cross bearing.) But if the night is clear, it's 9 miles distant as it appears on the horizon.

So you divide 60 (the rule) by 9 (the distance) and get 6.6. And you want to clear the light by a mile and a half so you multiply 6.6 by 1½. Result, 10 (9.9 to be precise) and that's the number of degrees you must change your course. Therefore you swing her head around to 170 degrees (180 — 10). Long before you need be concerned about the ledges, you'll pick up the bell buoy north of Flat Ground on the starboard bow and the light on the bell buoy at D, off Dry Salvages, dead ahead.

If you are of the "point" school of helmsmanship, you've been steering South before the change of course at B. Ten degrees being a shade less than 1 full point (11¼ degrees) you're not likely to get out the slide rule to compute the new course. You call it a point, change course to S by E, and find when you bring the bell abeam that you've given it a comfortable berth of a couple of hundred yards, on a course that will put offshore Lighted Whistle No. 2 dead ahead on your course 3 miles further along.

Following the Beach

EARLIER we showed how it was feasible to follow a contour line, which often runs nearly parallel to the beach, by sounding alone. That's well enough as a last resort if visibility is bad but there are a number of helpful hints to remember if your problem is one of following the beach approximately by day or night when objects ashore can be distinguished.

Let's say you wish to parallel the Jersey or Long Island beach (or, for that matter, any average coast where you have no hills or mountains ashore to stand out prominently at long range). See Figure 3. From the deck of the average small boat at sea you will be unable to see the beach if you are more than 4½ miles off, due to the earth's curvature. If you can just make out the beach nicely, you are roughly 4 miles off. This naturally won't hold true if the atmosphere is clouded by haze or rain.

Now as you follow down the beach you unconsciously trend in closer without realizing that you are way off your parallel course. Buildings appear and you find that you can distinguish detail clearly enough to count the individual windows. That means you must be roughly within 2 miles of the beach.

Here you have established two limits. By keeping within sight of shore but far enough off so you cannot count windows, you are following an average track 2 to 4 miles out. Meticulous pilots may object that this is too loose, and insist on compass courses. But the more of these practical stunts you have at your finger tips to draw upon, the better pilot you will be no matter how much you know about the paper work and classroom theory. Sometime it may be so rough the compass won't behave.

We are reminded of the admiral riding with the skipper of a PT boat one wild night down among the islands in Philippine waters. He (the admiral) wanted a position and suggested a bow-and-beam bearing on the next point. Whereupon the lieutenant held up an outstretched arm and squinted along the line of his thumb and forefinger for a 4-point bearing . . . the admiral, confounded, passed a few pithy remarks about piloting in general and the use of the pelorus in particular . . . but the "fix by digits" took them through.

The bow-and-beam bearing is too well known to warrant elaboration here. But as a check on distance off, remember that distance run over the bottom (which means distance through the water corrected for the effects of wind and current) is an accurate measure of distance off, if bearings are taken when an object bears 4 points on the bow (45 degrees from the course) and when it comes abeam (90 degrees from the course.) Distance run equals distance off when abeam.

Now suppose you want to keep 3 miles off the beach and have established that distance accurately with a bow-and-beam bearing, your problem may be to maintain that distance as you follow down the coast. If you try to do it by watching objects ashore as they come abeam, the chances are you will unconsciously draw in toward the shore and close with the beach without realizing it.

To overcome that, keep the eye far ahead on the course. Where the beach meets the horizon there is an indefinite "point" that you can steer for, but never quite catch up with. Keeping your eye on that, you will parallel the beach better than you could by glancing abeam at intervals. Often a haze appears above the surf on that distant "point", helping to mark the spot to steer toward. Before you have drawn too far inshore you will probably raise another object to check with the bow-and-beam bearing.

Often beaches will run reasonably straight for mile after mile and the depth curves will parallel them so closely as to be an invaluable aid in checking distance off. As an example one might follow the beach for 70 miles from Fire Island to Montauk. In all that distance the course would vary but little from a perfectly straight line. Averaging 1½ to 2 miles off, your course would practically trace the line of the 10-fathom curve. You could use an occasional sounding to maintain a minimum distance of a mile and a quarter. If the tide happens to be anything but low, corresponding to charted depths, allow a proportionate amount of the tidal range to correct the soundings.

At Night

FOR night piloting alongshore, the lights of towns and settlements along the beach can be used to advantage if they are spaced at reasonable intervals. Mr. Rappleyea reports that he has been able to maintain a course approximately 5½ miles offshore going down the Jersey beach, simply by keeping in sight of the reflected glow in the sky above lighted towns ashore.

The appearance of direct rays of light would be a danger signal that he was closing in to less than 5 miles, whereupon it would be necessary to haul off till only the reflected glow was visible again. The object of keeping so far off was to avoid the extensive fish nets and pounds offshore, yet the visibility of the glow maintained necessary contact with shore.

Students of piloting know how useful the sextant can be in clearing off-lying obstructions by means of vertical or horizontal danger angles. Naval vessels too have their range finders for measuring distances and maintaining position in formation. Higgins Industries has devised a little gadget which accomplishes the same purpose in a practical way for motor boatmen. It is simply a pencil stamped with a scale, having a 20-inch string attached, with button on the end. By sighting along the string and sliding the finger along the scale the boatman can measure distances with considerable accuracy.

Timetable for Night Piloting

HERE is another ingenious trick which will go far toward increasing the pleasure of night piloting. When you anticipate a night run, don't wait till you are on your way before studying out courses, distances, running time, etc. Go over the entire cruise in advance and acquaint yourself thoroughly with the separate legs of the course, the aids to navigation you will pass, the characteristics of lights, etc.

Then set up a timetable, assuming that you will leave your point of departure exactly at 12:00, and note in orderly fashion the predicted time of arrival abeam of every light and buoy on both sides of the course. Alongside these entries show the compass course and the characteristics of each navigational aid.

Invest in an alarm clock or watch with luminous dial and set it for 12:00 when you start your run from the point of departure on which your predetermined timetable is based. Then as the flashing, occulting and alternating lights successively wink over the horizon you won't have to dash below to puzzle out characteristics and identify each in turn.

At every instant you know where you are, what light you just left astern, what to look for on the course ahead, and when you should be passing the next aid. If need be, the hands can be shifted somewhat from time to time if any great discrepancy between estimated and actual running times should necessitate it.

If you make a practice of keeping timetables of this kind for the various runs you make at night you will soon accumulate a set of data for your log that will prove invaluable on future cruises.

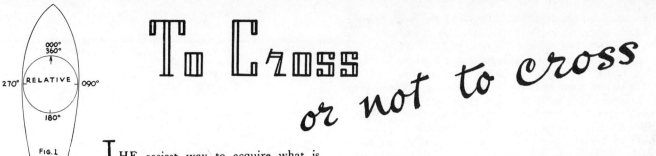

To Cross
or not to cross

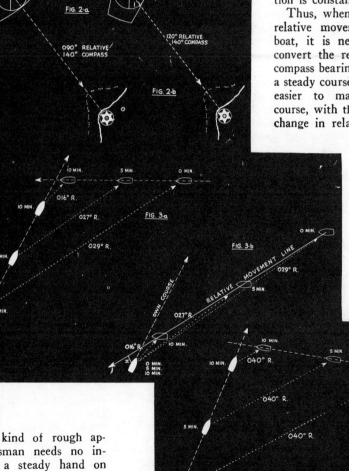

THE easiest way to acquire what is often called a "sailor's eye" is to learn the simple but basic principles of relative movement. The words "relative movement," despite their forbidding sound and the mental picture of relativity, cover a field which is in reality quite easy to master. It is also one of the most useful skills that a sailor can acquire, for it gives quick and accurate answers to problems of moving vessels. For example, you are beating to windward on the port tack, and find a boat coming in on the starboard tack. Will you cross safely ahead, or must you pass astern? Or you find that your motorboat is converging on another boat which has the right of way If you continue on your present course and speed, will you clear her? Or you have laid a course for a buoy, making allowance for wind and current set. Have you made the correct allowance? Relative movement will give you the answers to all such questions.

It should be noted at this point that relative movement applies equally well to all moving objects. Thus the yachtsman can practice his skill ashore, whether he be crossing a street in front of an approaching car, or nearing a cross-roads behind the wheel of his own auto. Whenever there is a possibility of collision, relative movement will solve the problem. Even the hunter shooting at a duck in flight solves a relative movement problem when he determines how much he must lead the target in order to hit it.

In small boat sailing, the same kind of rough application can be made. The yachtsman needs no instruments or diagrams other than a steady hand on the tiller or wheel, a clear eye, and a rough mental diagram. Since the small yacht seldom has a method of taking compass bearings by means of a bearing circle (or pelorus), the bearing of an object is usually taken as a relative bearing.

The relative bearing of any object from your own boat is its angle in degrees measured clockwise from the bow of your own boat. In other words, it is the bearing of the object as seen on a compass rose which is fastened so as to show the fore-and-aft line of your boat as 000° or 360°. Thus an object on the starboard beam will bear 090° Relative, and an object dead astern will bear 180° R. (Fig. 1).

With practice the relative bearing of an object can be estimated within a few degrees. It is obvious, however, that a change in the course of your own boat will change the relative bearings of all objects around her. Thus if you are on a compass course of 050° and an object bears 090° R, the compass bearing of the object will be 140°. (Fig. 2a). Come left to a course of 020° and the same object will bear 120° R, but the compass bearing will remain unchanged at 140°. (This assumes that the compass deviation is constant). (Fig. 2b).

Thus, when determining the relative movement of another boat, it is necessary either to convert the relative bearing to compass bearings or to maintain a steady course. In practice it is easier to maintain a steady course, with the result that any change in relative bearing will be a result of the changing positions of the boats relative to each other, rather than a result of the changing course of your own boat. Since the desired information is the changing positions of the boats relative to each other, this change in relative bearings is all-important.

What we want to know in any crossing or converging situation is: will we cross ahead of or astern of the other boat, or will we hit her? Since the two boats are considered relative to each other, it is convenient to visualize one's own boat as stationary—relative to the other boat. Thus, (1) if the relative bearing of the other boat moves ahead, the other boat will pass ahead; (2) if the relative bearing remains steady, the two boats will collide; (3) if the relative bearing moves aft, the other boat will pass astern.

Fig. 3a shows the first case of a boat passing ahead. The figure represents what happens to the actual positions of the two boats. In Fig. 3b this same case has been reduced to a relative movement diagram, with our own boat represented as stationary. The bearing movement is then clearly seen.

The line connecting the positions of the other boat in Fig. 3b is the line of relative movement, that is, it is the relative course and relative distance travelled by the other boat in relationship to our own boat. It is a straight line (provided both boats maintain their course and speed). This relative movement line when extended passes ahead of our own boat; therefore the other boat, following that line relative to us, will pass ahead. The distance "x" in Fig. 3b is the distance apart that the two boats will be at their closest approach.

In the second case, where the bearing remains the same, the other boat's relative movement line is the reciprocal of the bearing, and the line passes through our boat. The distance "x" is then zero, and the two boats will collide if both maintain course and speed. This is illustrated in Figs. 4a and 4b.

The third case, in which the bearing moves aft, is the opposite of the first case. The relative movement line passes astern of our boat, and the distance "x" is measured from our boat astern to the line, as illustrated in Figs. 5a and 5b.

The foregoing discussion, formulated into rules, would go something like this:

1. Maintain a reasonably steady course and speed.

2. Observe the relative bearing of the approaching boat only when you are as nearly on course as possible, i.e. you must be on the same course each time you observe the other boat.

3. Watch the other boat for changes in course and speed, which obviously will change the relative movement line.

4. (a) If the relative bearing moves ahead, the other boat will pass ahead.

(b) If the relative bearing is steady, the boats will collide.

(c) If the relative bearing moves aft, the other boat will pass astern.

One other useful application of relative movement is in the case of current and/or wind set. In Fig. 6 the boat has set a course which her skipper thinks will put her close aboard the buoy off the shoal. At 0 minutes the buoy bears 340° R; at 5 minutes the buoy bears 350° R. It is clear from this that he is being set down more than he calculated, and that the relative movement line of the buoy will pass ahead of him, i.e. that he will pass on the shoal side of the buoy. If the bearings of the buoy remained steady, he would pass very close to the buoy; and if the bearings shifted gradually away from the bow, he would pass well clear of the shoal and buoy. In Fig. 6a the problem is shown in terms of one's own

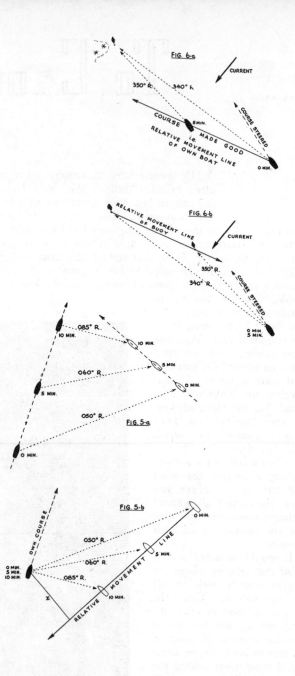

boat moving relative to the buoy. In Fig. 6b, the boat is stationary, and the relative movement line is that of the buoy. Note that the relative movement lines in 6a and 6b are parallel, equal, and opposite.

It should be apparent that in its simple forms the relative movement problem is of real use to the small boat sailor as well as to the naval officer. The yachtsman, lacking radar, can't attempt to plot four targets simultaneously and give their courses and speeds every minute, but he can solve in his head the basic problem of whether it is safe to maintain his course and speed at a time when there's still plenty of room in which to maneuver.

Footnote: In its more refined aspects, the relative movement problem is most accurately solved by a Maneuvering Board Diagram, which is merely a compass rose with circular distance lines inscribed around the center of the rose. These Maneuvering Boards are printed by the Oceanographic Office as H.O. 2665-20 (large) and H.O. 2665-10 (small). A pad of 50 sheets of the small diagrams may be purchased. These diagrams have scales for altering speeds and distances to any desired scale for plotting on the diagram. The only instruments required for using the diagram are parallel rules and a pair of dividers. A scale at the bottom of the board consists of three parallel lines—one for time in minutes, one for distance in yards and miles, and one for speed in knots. If any two of these three factors are known, a straight line through the two will intersect the third line at the correct point. Thus, in a simple example, a line drawn through 10 knots and through 20 (nautical) miles will intersect the time scale at 120 minutes. For a full discussion see pages 430a-d.

The Maneuvering Board

and the Yachtsman

SINCE 1920 the U.S. Navy Hydrographic (now Oceanographic) Office has published a plotting sheet (H.O. 2665) known as the Maneuvering Board which is used by all maritime services for the solution of relative movement problems. The procedure is taught in all navigation and radar courses as a necessary tool in the working of a ship. Complicated movements of a large task force as well as the tracking of a single ship are plotted on maneuvering boards to facilitate the solution of problems of interception and general information such as course and speed of radar contacts.

By using a maneuvering board, parallel ruler and dividers, several problems that confront the yachtsman can be solved. For the privileged owner who has radar aboard the field of use increases ten-fold.

It is the purpose here to present the principles involved, with solutions to a few basic navigation problems which arise when a boat leaves the dock. When a vessel gets under way, the movements of surrounding objects take on a different aspect, sometimes akin to an optical illusion. Some objects, especially moving ones, seem to be doing things that are not actually happening.

To observe the physical appearance of a maneuvering board we look at the accompanying illustration (reduced size). The maneuvering board sheet is about 12 inches square on which is printed, in green, a large circle with bearing lines radiating outward from the center every ten degrees, and ten concentric circles ½ inch apart to indicate speed or distance. On either side of the circle are lines of scale with the numbered marks spaced equal to the distance between the concentric circles. Therefore a speed line drawn out to the fifth circle could indicate 5, 10, 15, 20, or 25 kts depending on your choice of scale.

At the bottom of the sheet are three lines representing a logarithmic scale for use in solving time, speed and distance equations. If two of the quantities are known, the third may be found by drawing a line between them and the answer will be at the intersection of the third line. In Fig. 4 observe the solution to three questions: If you travel 6 miles in 30 minutes, speed equals 12 kts. Traveling at 12 kts, 6 miles will take 30 minutes. If the speed is 12 kts, in 30 minutes you will travel 6 miles. Time, speed, and distance—knowing two, you can solve for the third. This alone makes the maneuvering board valuable. But this is only a small sample of its usefulness.

The first consideration in learning to use the maneuvering board is understanding three basic terms: *actual movement, relative motion*, and *vector diagram*. When a yacht is under way its movement across the water is termed *actual motion*. If it is anchored in some quiet cove the movements of a nearby vessel appear in their actual relationship to the earth's surface. You are observing actual motion. But if you get under way the movement of the other boat appears to be different because you are now observing *relative motion*.

Let us suppose that you are under way and are proceeding north at 5 kts up a channel marked with buoys. You sight a cruiser coming directly toward you, also making 5 kts. The two vessels are converging with a *relative speed* of 10 kts which is simply the sum of your speed and his. Both vessels are passing the stationary channel markers at the same *actual speed* but the distance between them is lessening at the sum of the individual speeds.

As he approaches, you recognize him as a friend from your club and turn around to join him on his southerly course to the fishing hole. As soon as the boats are alongside each other cruising on the same course at the same speed, *relative motion* ceases to exist because he stays in the same place relative to your vessel. Only *actual motion* remains—that of your boats past buoys and over the ground. If your friend's boat develops engine trouble and slows down, again there is relative motion between the two. He will appear to be moving aft because of his reduced speed. This brings out the rule: *relative motion is present only when the actual movements of two or more objects are not the same*.

The *vector diagram* used on maneuvering boards is a series of lines representing actual and relative motion. Each vector, according to its length, represents a statement of fact in the problem. A vector line indicating a course of 045 and speed of 5 kts would be drawn from the center of the plotting sheet outward along the 45° bearing line to a length of 5 units. Always remember, no matter what the problem, your boat remains in the center of the board which is actually moving across the earth with you, and that everything else drawn upon the sheet is *relative* to your course and speed. A vector line indicates graphically the course and speed of the elements in the problem such as your boat, the wind and the current.

Fig. 1 illustrates what is called a true wind problem. Situation: Your sailboat is close hauled on course 080, speed 5 kts. The apparent (or relative) wind is coming over the starboard side from 125° with a speed of 15 kts. You want to sail your boat as close to the wind as possible, say at an angle 45° off the wind.

You wish to know the direction and velocity of the true wind so as to determine whether you can lay the mark on the next tack and the best course you will be able to make to windward.

Solution: Draw your course and speed vector (ER) along bearing line 080 from center out 2½ circles (scale 2:1). From point R draw relative motion line with parallel rulers in the direction toward which the apparent wind is traveling (its course).

With dividers measure the length of 15 kts on the 2:1 scale and lay off on this line from R.

Where this distance ends is point M and a line drawn from the center to M represents *true wind* direction and speed. Since wind direction is never expressed in terms of where it is going we look across the board and see that it is blowing from 142° at a velocity of 12 kts. Now it becomes clear that the movement of the boat through the water caused the apparent wind to shift 17° counter-clockwise from its true direction.

To solve for the new tack we mark the wind's new apparent direction of 169° (add 17° to 142°) and then add the 45° angle on which you wish to sail your boat. This gives the new course of 204°.

One problem common to both sail and motor boats is that of choosing the correct source in traversing an area where current will set the vessel off her intended track if allowances have not been made. In Fig. 2 we have the graphic solution of two questions. What is the current doing? What course do we take to correct for it? To find the answers:

Assume that your cruiser is on course 320° speed 6 kts

and you wish to pass close aboard a light vessel that now at 10:00 is dead ahead, distant 9 miles. As you progress through the water you notice the light vessel is moving to your left; in doing so, it indicates that a current is at work on your port side.

To learn the nature of the current and course needed to correct for it: Plot the original position of the light vessel from you (320° 9 miles).

After fixing your present position, plot the new position of the light vessel from you (310° 7 miles) and label the time 10:29.

Draw in your boat's course and speed vector (ER) of 320° 6 kts (3rd circle using 2:1 scale).

With parallel rulers along the line of relative movement between light vessel plots, move across to point R and in the *same direction* draw a line to some convenient length. Solve the time-speed-distance equation after measuring the distance that the light vessel "traveled" (2.4 miles in 29 min).

This gives 5.2 kts relative speed (from logarithmic scale) which is taken off 2:1 scale and ticked along relative motion line starting at R. This point is labeled M and a line drawn *from M to the center* E represents the direction of the current flow (080°) and its length on 2:1 scale indicates velocity (3 kts).

With this information we can now set a new course. Remembering that our vessel *never* leaves the center of the sheet we must make the light vessel "come to us." A line drawn from the 10:29 position of the light vessel to the center (dotted line) is the line we wish the light vessel to follow on its way to our vessel.

Parallel a line from this, starting at a convenient distance out, but beyond circle No. 3 (6 kts) and draw toward an intersection at point M in the *same direction* as the intended track of the light vessel (line AM).

Fig. 1. How the maneuvering board can be used to determine the velocity and direction of the true wind to aid in setting a new course on the next tack. See the text for details.

Fig. 2. In this problem, the maneuvering board enables the pilot to allow for current setting the boat off her track, and a new course may then be plotted for a given speed.

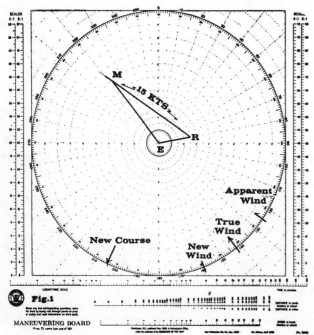

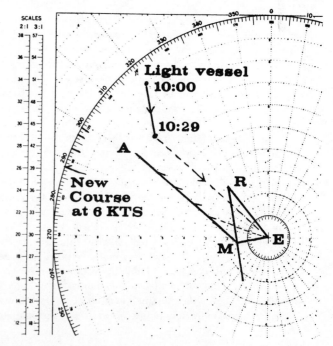

Where this relative movement line crosses the third circle is the course to steer (288°) at 6 kts. It should be noted that there are many possible combinations of courses and speeds available along this line and any increase in speed would then bring a lesser course change and vice versa. For example: looking out along the line we could pick 293° at 8 kts, 297° at 10 kts, or 299° at 12 kts.

The layout of the maneuvering board also lends itself to providing blue-water navigators with an important tool of the trade. It is possible to draw a custom position plotting sheet complete with distance scales and compass rose in a size that can be used anywhere there is a square foot of space to plot. I sometimes use them for plotting lines of position and then transfer only the fix to the large position plotting sheet or navigation chart.

To make such a position plotting sheet we construct a Mercator projection on the maneuvering board as in Fig. 3.

Draw a vertical line (No. 1) and then a horizontal one (No. 2) through the center of the sheet.

Tangent to the sixth circle draw lines (2a) parallel to No. 2.

Pick the latitude that the plot must represent and label line No. 2 (in this case, 35°), then lines No. 2a accordingly 1° lesser and greater (34° and 36°).

From the center draw a line (No. 3) making an angle with the *horizontal* equal to the latitude (35°) represented by line No. 2.

Where this (line No. 3) intersects the sixth circle, draw a line (No. 1a) parallel to longitude line No. 1 and copy on the opposite side. Each circle along the center longitude line will represent 10 minutes of latitude to be used as a mile scale.

Where diagonal line No. 3 crosses each circle drop perpendiculars (dotted lines) to mid-latitude line No. 2 and

it will then be divided in proper length for 10-minute segments of longitude.

As you become more proficient in its use, the maneuvering board becomes a valuable aid in solving problems that would take much longer using other methods. For example the wind problem can be solved in 10 seconds, the current diagram in about a minute. All it takes is a bit of practice and serious use.

In conclusion, a situation worth mentioning, easily understood by plotting on the maneuvering board, is that of collision. If a vessel stays on the same bearing line while the range is closing it becomes immediately clear that she will eventually come in contact with the center. Knowing that your vessel remains forever in this center, you can see that collision will result unless someone changes course to clear the relative movement line plot.

The rule states: *If an approaching vessel remains on a constant bearing while the range closes, collision is inevitable.*

Make a practice of sighting over the compass at surrounding craft and be warned before a situation develops into a scramble for the life jackets. On the floor of the ocean lie too many vessels, even some with radar, whose officers were not alert to the simple fact that "constant bearing—closing range" means collision. (Remember the Andrea Doria!)

In Navy task forces where ships swing left and right in close proximity across each other's bows at high speed, collisions are almost unheard of. This is the result of constant alertness of lookouts and radar operators to the perils of constant bearing.

A pad of 50 maneuvering boards (now numbered 2665-10) may be obtained anywhere that Oceanographic Office charts are sold. At less than a few cents each, this is a small price to pay for safety and easy piloting!

Fig. 3. The offshore navigator can use the maneuvering board to advantage in constructing a position plotting sheet on the Mercator projection for a given latitude, as indicated.

Fig. 4. Extract from a portion of the logarithmic scales given on the maneuvering board, illustrating how they are used to solve time-speed-distance problems as explained in the text.

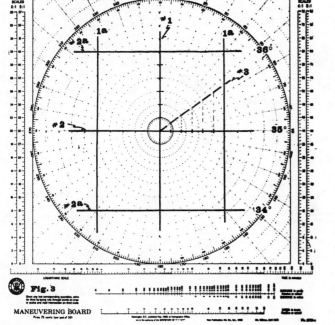

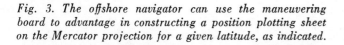

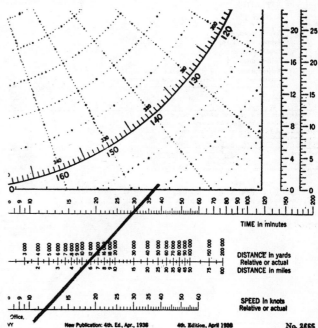

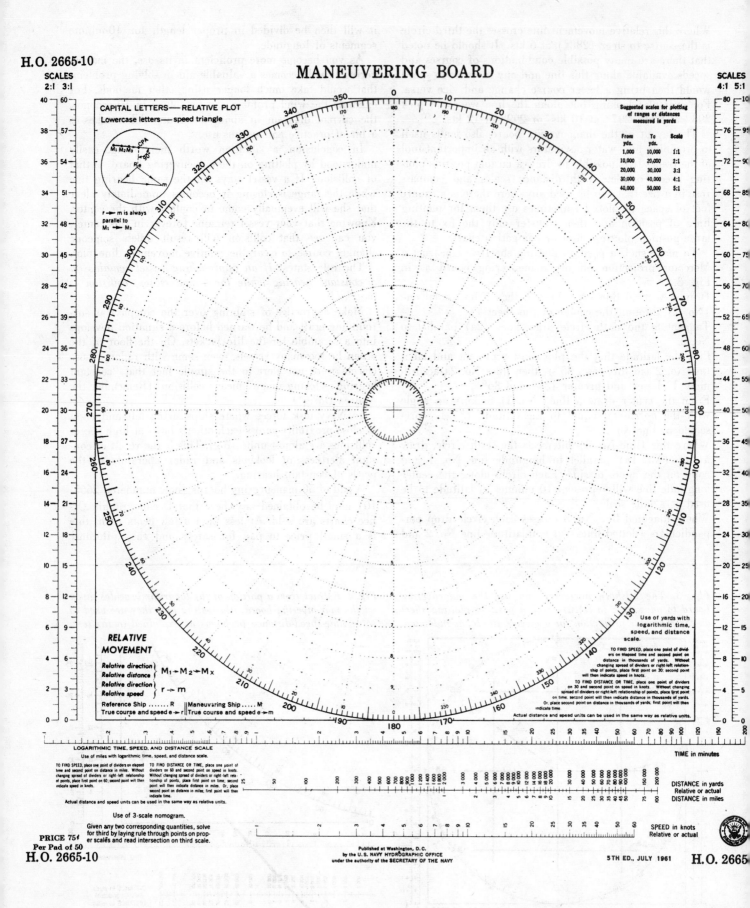

MANEUVERING BOARD

CAPITAL LETTERS— RELATIVE PLOT
Lowercase letters— speed triangle

r → m is always
parallel to
M₁ → M₃

Suggested scales for plotting
of ranges or distances
measured in yards

From yds.	To yds.	Scale
1,000	10,000	1:1
10,000	20,000	2:1
20,000	30,000	3:1
30,000	40,000	4:1
40,000	50,000	5:1

Use of yards with
logarithmic time,
speed, and distance
scale.

TO FIND SPEED, place one point of dividers on elapsed time and second point on distance in thousands of yards. Without changing spread of dividers or right-left relationship of points, place first point on 30; second point will then indicate speed in knots.

TO FIND DISTANCE OR TIME, place one point of dividers on 30 and second point on speed in knots. Without changing spread of dividers or right-left relationship of points, place first point on time; second point will then indicate distance in thousands of yards. Or, place second point on distance in thousands of yards; first point will then indicate time.

Actual distance and speed units can be used in the same way as relative units.

RELATIVE MOVEMENT

Relative direction $M_1 \rightarrow M_2 \rightarrow M_x$
Relative distance
Relative direction $r \rightarrow m$
Relative speed

Reference Ship ...... R   Maneuvering Ship ...... M
True course and speed e→r ‖ True course and speed e→m

LOGARITHMIC TIME, SPEED, AND DISTANCE SCALE
Use of miles with logarithmic time, speed, and distance scale.

TO FIND SPEED, place one point of dividers on elapsed time and second point on distance in miles. Without changing spread of dividers or right-left relationship of points, place first point on 60; second point will then indicate speed in knots.

TO FIND DISTANCE OR TIME, place one point of dividers on 60 and second point on speed in knots. Without changing spread of dividers or right-left relationship of points, place first point on time; second point will then indicate distance in miles. Or, place second point on distance in miles; first point will then indicate time.

Actual distance and speed units can be used in the same way as relative units.

Use of 3-scale nomogram.

Given any two corresponding quantities, solve for third by laying rule through points on proper scales and read intersection on third scale.

TIME in minutes

DISTANCE in yards
Relative or actual

DISTANCE in miles

SPEED in knots
Relative or actual

Published at Washington, D. C.
by the U. S. NAVY HYDROGRAPHIC OFFICE
under the authority of the SECRETARY OF THE NAVY

5TH ED., JULY 1961

PRICE 75¢
Per Pad of 50
H.O. 2665-10

H.O. 2665

430d

Relative Bearings

At A Glance

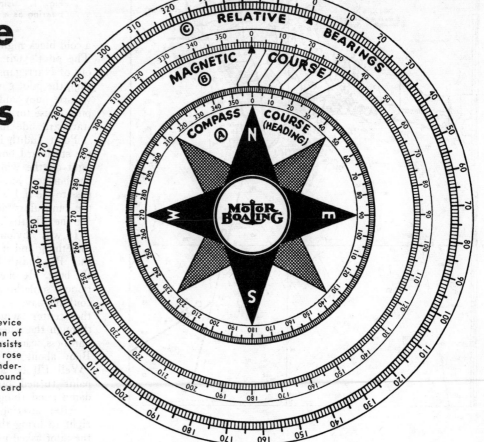

Comdr. Dusinberre's device for the quick conversion of relative bearings consists of an extra compass rose (scale C) placed underneath and pivoting around an ordinary deviation card (scales A-B).

ILLUSTRATED herewith is a simple, but valuable, navigational device worked out by Lt. Comdr. H. W. Dusinberre, U.S.N.R., in the course of practical experience at sea. Briefly, it is a scheme whereby a second compass rose is placed behind, and concentric with, the boat's deviation card, in order to show relative bearings at a glance.

(A relative bearing is one referred to the fore-and-aft line of the vessel from which the bearing is taken. Expressed in degrees relative to the vessel's head, it is independent of such variables as variation and deviation.)

Many boats are equipped (all using a magnetic compass should be) with a compass deviation card, arranged like the A and B scales in the illustration, with both scales on a single card and north and south points of both in alignment. The inner (A) scale represents the compass course or heading of the boat, and next to it, the (B) scale represents the corresponding magnetic course.

As deviation on various courses is determined, by any method, it is recorded on the card by drawing lines between the A and B scales as shown. Thus, to make good a magnetic course of 30 degrees, the vessel must be held on a compass course of 22 degrees. As many of these deviations as possible should be plotted around the 360-degree circle, though only a few are illustrated.

The device utilizes a third scale (C) of relative bearings behind (under) this conventional deviation card, so pinned or pivoted at the center that scale C may be rotated freely around B and set as desired. Setting the 0 point of the relative bearing (C) scale to the boat's magnetic heading permits the navigator to obtain, by inspection, the magnetic bearing corresponding to any relative bearing.

With a dummy pelorus located at any convenient point on the boat, the navigator gets his relative bearings of buoys, beacons, landmarks, etc. At the same time the helmsman calls out the compass heading.

The deviation card (A and B scales) immediately converts the compass heading to magnetic heading. Setting the relative bearing (C) scale to this particular heading (magnetic) then permits immediate conversion of all relative bearings to magnetic bearings which can be plotted on the chart.

For example, two relative bearings are taken—140 degrees and 085 degrees—and the helmsman gives the compass heading of 010 degrees. Compass course 10 degrees (on the A scale) gives magnetic course 17 degrees (on the B scale), by visual interpolation. Now set the 0 degree point of the relative bearing (C) scale to 17 degrees magnetic and 85 degrees relative becomes 102 degrees magnetic, 140 degrees relative becomes 157 degrees magnetic and so on, for any other bearings taken while the vessel is on that particular heading.

For Navy use, there are three discs, as the Navy uses true courses. In this case the inner disc converts compass course to magnetic course, the next disc converts magnetic to true course (set it for the variation in that locality) and the outer disc converts relative bearings to true bearings. Using the third disc, there would be four scales, A, B, C and D. This is easily arranged, where one prefers to work with true courses and bearings.

When bearings are taken with the magnetic compass, using a sight vane directly on the compass (instead of bearings by dummy pelorus), bearings magnetic may be read from this calculator as follows:

Set the C scale in such relation to the B scale that the ship's head per compass on the C scale matches the magnetic heading on B scale. Then every bearing per compass (on C scale) may be converted to bearing magnetic from B scale.

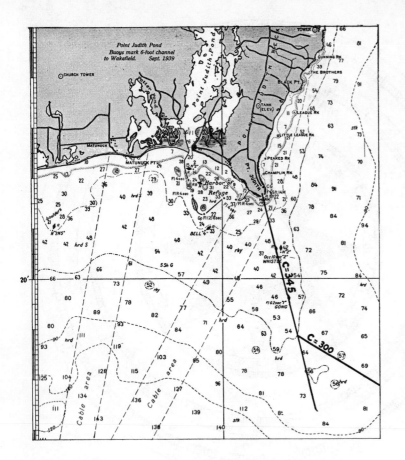

Fig. I. Using a radio direction finder bearing as a course line to pick up a buoy

Piloting In Fog

UPON graduation from high school, with no funds for further education, I turned to the sea for my livelihood. This was only natural in view of the fact that my dad and his four brothers are all sea captains, a tradition which had been passed down for several generations. Conversations at home were practically limited to boats and thus, along with reading many of the texts that lay around our home, I thought I had a good working knowledge of piloting. However, after working as bow watchman, quartermaster, and finally pilot, I soon realized that Dutton, Mixter, Bowditch and others had a great deal to learn about practical piloting—at least, as it is practiced on commercial vessels which operate on a schedule. It is my purpose to point out some of these experiences and show how they can be applied by the yachtsman—also to pass on a few tricks of a highly specialized trade.

I recall one cold January night when I was quartermaster on a sound steamer sailing between Providence and New York when I had an experience which could well happen to a yachtsman. The wind was about northwest and blowing hard. It was

a cold black night and the visibility was excellent. The pilot's wife was aboard and after we got out of Narragansett Bay by Brenton Reef Lightship, the pilot gave me the course to Point Judith whistle buoy and then invited his wife up to the pilot house for a short time. She was seated on the starboard side about four feet from the compass.

Point Judith lighthouse was plainly visible on the starboard bow; however the occulting white light on the whistle buoy had not peeped above the horizon yet. The pilot leaned over the compass to see if I was on the course, then picked up the binoculars and looked into the black night for the whistle buoy.

It was obvious that he was concerned about something and it wasn't long before he remarked that Pt. Judith lighthouse seemed very wide on the bow. He checked the course again and mentioned something to the effect that the wind couldn't have set us over that much. He dropped the center window and the wind whistled through the wheelhouse. Sharp eyes, piercing the darkness, came to focus on Pt. Judith Whistle Buoy about 20 degrees on the starboard bow. "Well I'll be $%&*)(%##æ¢" . . . as the paint turned blue in the wheelhouse. "It's a damn good thing it isn't thick fog out here."

After altering the course 20 degrees to the right to bring the whistler under the jack staff, the pilot asked me if I had a knife in my pocket, to which I replied with an (I-know-better) "NO!" He had me walk around the wheelhouse while he observed the compass. Then he called down through the speaking tube to the freight-deck-watchman to determine if any autos had been stowed forward on the freight deck and received a negative reply.

He stood there at the window gazing into infinity trying to fathom the cause of the compass trouble. Suddenly his face lit up as he turned to his wife and asked if she had her corsets on. Admitting that she did, she was instructed to retire to her room. As Mrs. Pilot vacated the wheelhouse the compass came back to normal and the mystery was solved.

I'll never forget the day that a good-looking blonde walked by the wheel-house and all eyes, including my own, followed her around. When I looked back at the compass, I thought we had gone way off the course.

Fig. 2. A form of log recommended by the author to aid in coastal piloting

AID TO NAVIGATION	TRUE COURSE	VARIATION	MAGNETIC COURSE	DEVIATION	COMPASS COURSE	COURSE REQUIRED	DISTANCE	TIME ABEAM PREDICTED	TIME ABEAM ACTUAL	ELAPSED TIME	SPEED MADE GOOD	REVOLUTIONS	CURRENT	WIND	WEATHER	REMARKS
•LOG• PROWLER DATE July 5 19 48																
Cleveland Ledge	222	15W	237	0	237	237			1305			2000	Fl'd	S.W. light	Clear	Sea Smooth
Bell #5	244	15W	259	0	259	259	9.5	1408	1410	65	8.5	"	"	"	"	"
Hen and Chickens	264	15W	279	0	279	277	9.0	1514	1514	64	8.5	"	"	Mod S.W.	Little chop Cock pick	"
Brenton Reef	007	15W	022	1E	021	021	16.3	1709	1704	110	9.0	"	Ebb	Strong S.W.	Very choppy Castle nasty pick	"
Castle Hill	038	15W	053	2E	051	051	2.2	1719	1719	15	9.0	"	"	"	"	"
Fort Adams		15W					1.8	1731	1732	13	8.3	"	"	"	"	"

However Execution Rocks lighthouse was still dead ahead and the compass was swinging back and forth. I passed the remark that the blonde had made even the compass go haywire. We soon discovered (while looking further at the blonde) that it wasn't her magnetic personality but rather the portable radio she was carrying that had influenced the compass. This is a good point to remember on yachts with blondes aboard.

While employed as a deck hand on a towboat, towing bricks from New York City to West Point up the Hudson, I had another compass experience. It was during the early morning hours enroute to West Point with a load of bricks in tow that I heard the blast of a steamer's whistle ringing through the fog. The second blast indicated that she was getting closer and was about dead ahead. We blew often to enable him to ascertain our position and he returned blast for blast. We eased over to the starboard side of the channel, which is what the good book says to do, and a good choice it was, because as the steamer's bow pierced the fog within the visible range, we were just far enough over to starboard to avoid collision. When the vessel passed us, the bow-watchman could have spit down our smokestack.

This incident was no sooner over when another occurred. We could hear the trains going by on the starboard bank of the river and it was shortly after one of these went by that I reported something dead ahead. The engines were stopped immediately and we were

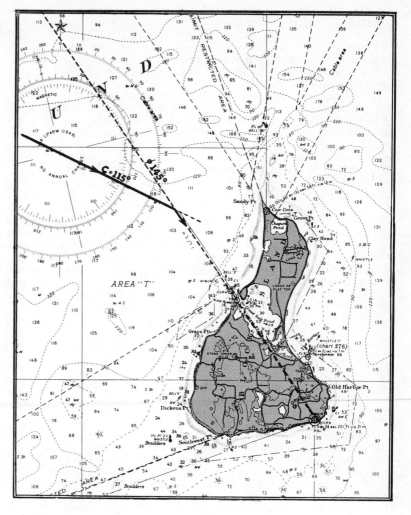

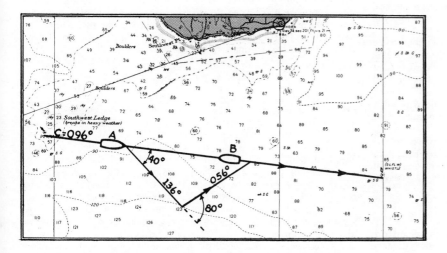

Fig. 3 (above): A course plotted to intercept a radio direction finder bearing that will take the vessel into Block Island. Fig. 4 (left): How to alter course when passing another vessel in a fog

some surprised to find that we were heading straight for the bank of the river at a right angle (90 degrees) to the channel. After a stream of profanity had cleared, the skipper remarked that "anything can happen with these damn trains running so close to the compass."

Fog is one thing we could very well do without, but as long as it insists on sneaking up on us occasionally we might as well prepare for this seagoing smoke. The chances are good that anyone who does any amount of cruising will eventually get caught out in fog so let's get prepared for it. Study your boat thoroughly and know just what she'll do. Then, if you get caught, you won't be so nervous and will use much better judgement.

Let's consider the compass first, as this is the little magic baby we rely so much on when visibility is low. Primarily, the magnetic compass consists of some form of magnetic needle set on a pivot, with a card attached to the needle. If the pivot becomes worn, the compass will be sluggish, that is, when the boat's course is altered, there will be a lag in a noticable change in the lubber's line and it will take some time for the card to settle down after the boat's head has stopped swinging. When this condition exists, it is almost impossible to make a course good, particularly if there is any sea running or if the sea is on the quarter.

When a compass is sluggish, send it back to the manufacturer and let him fix it right. To prevent the compass from becoming sluggish, turn it upside-down when storing for the winter. If your boat tacks back and forth at the mooring, lean the compass on its side by putting a wedge in the gimbals. If your boat is moored near any magnetic disturbances such as electric trolleys or trains, use the same wedging procedure. The pivot will last much longer if proper care is taken.

A compass should set level in the gimbals. If not, there

433

are adjustment screws for this purpose. Air bubbles should not be present in a compass. The lubber's line should conform with the fore and aft line of the boat and the deviation of the compass should be known. Don't ever forget about the things that can attract the compass needle away from magnetic north. Jack-knives, portable radios, *women's corsets,* even the metal ring in a yachting cap can throw the compass off several degrees.

Well! So much for the compass. Now about steering the course that you lay down. Making a course good is an art understood by very few. On a 60-mile run, if you are off one degree, you will finish one mile from the destination. Lay off two courses on a chart with a one-degree difference and note how rapidly they separate. The greatest error made in steering is to try to keep the boat right on the degree and then allow it to go a little the same side of the course. This is particularly true when running with a quartering sea. If the sea is on the starboard quarter, the boat has a tendency to go to the right of the course and, on the other hand, if the sea is on the port quarter, the tendency is to go to the left of the course. It is impossible to keep a boat right on the course all of the time and this is not necessary to be a good helmsman. A good man at the wheel or tiller will ride the course, that is, he allows the boat to go either side of the course the same amount for about the same duration of time.

Making the course good and having an accurate lively compass are of utmost importance while piloting in fog.

Keep a Log

IT WAS MENTIONED before that you must make a study of your boat and the best time to do this is in clear weather. Illustrated (Fig. 2) is a sample log which I would like to suggest for inland and coastwise piloting. In the extreme left-hand column is the station or navigational aid which you expect to pass; next to the right is the true course, variation, and magnetic course as taken from the chart, then the deviation as obtained from the deviation table for the magnetic course. The compass course is the magnetic course after deviation has been applied.

Now comes the guess-work. What course to steer to allow for current, wind, etc.? If your boat is shallow-draft and high-sided, the allowance for wind is going to be more than for the low-free-board deep-draft type of boat. This is guess-work, and experience is the best teacher. Put down a trial course and if this doesn't work, erase it and put down the course you should have steered. By recording the tide and weather conditions on the same line, you will have something to use for future reference.

To study the speed of your boat, record the revolutions, time abeam navigational aids, the distances between them and the elapsed time. With a little experience, you will be able to predict the time you will be at the next mark. The relationship between the speed through water and the revolutions should be a constant for the trip, but may vary somewhat during the season depending on the condition of the bottom. A few barnacles, or a small dent in the propeller, can make a big difference.

The tide conditions are about the same every two weeks and if you run over the same waters every week, and you get caught in fog, look back about two weeks or even four or six weeks and you'll find about the same conditions. If you have kept a log as recommended in this article, things should be simple.

Obey the Pilot Rules

When fog shuts in, there is always a certain amount of anxiety aboard regardless of the confidence you may have in yourself. Start that whistle blowing, and if you hear another vessel ahead, blow often so that he can get a bearing on you. He should reciprocate, so that you can do the same on him. The Inland Rules state that the signal (a prolonged blast of 4 to 6 seconds' duration) should be blown at intervals of not more than one minute. This means you can blow it every 10 seconds if you think it is necessary. Always place someone where the hearing conditions are best and this is usually a point just aft of where the bow wave breaks, but varies with different types of boats.

If it is a dark foggy day, put on your running lights and run at a moderate speed. A moderate speed in fog is that speed at which you can stop your boat in half the limit of visibility. If the visibility is one-quarter mile, you should be able to stop in half that distance If this means that you will have to run too slow to make your courses good, then drop the hook (not in the fairway) and start ringing the bell (for five seconds at one-minute intervals).

Probably the worst conditions encountered in fog are when you have a heavy wet fog that absorbs sound and you are running with a fair wind and tide. Then you are apt to see a vessel ahead before you hear him. However, he will probably hear you, so blow the whistle often under these circumstances.

Altering Your Course

When a boat is located dead ahead by auditory sound bearing, always alter the course to starboard and alter it plenty if sea-room permits. (See Fig. 4.) You probably will ask, what will happen to the course you are trying to make good? The procedure used by most coastwise pilots is as follows: Note the time that you alter the course and when the approaching vessel is clear and you are ready to come back on the original course, alter your course to the left twice the amount you altered it to the right and run the same time, then proceed on your original course.

Referring to the illustration, you hear a vessel ahead and you decide she is approaching fast so you alter the course 40 degrees to the right and note the time. In five minutes the boat is abeam on the port side so you alter your course 80 degrees to the left and run five minutes which should bring you back on the original course line. This is a simple procedure but is not widely known.

In fog, courses should be laid to carry you near sonic aids when possible. After you have come within one minute of running your predicted time out, it is good practice to stop, shut your engines off for a few seconds, and listen. If you don't hear anything, start the engines again and run out that last minute, then stop again. If you don't pick up your mark, try the radio direction finder. Even a single line of position may locate you relative to the mark. Don't forget the sounding lead. A line of position with the R. D. F. and a sounding may give you a good idea of your position.

Sound in fog can be very misleading. Some lighthouses seem to have dead spots or dead areas where the fog signal can't be heard. Execution Rocks in Long Island Sound is a good example of this. Many times I have heard its fog signal miles away while approaching it and then had it fade as if going the wrong way. Finally it would come in again when close aboard and rattle your ears right off.

Remember that your whistle may return in the form of an echo from high land, the side of a ship or even the sails of a large yacht. If you hear an echo from dead ahead . . . *be careful!* I had this experience and heeded the warning when I was pilot on a vessel with 800 passengers aboard. The echo turned out to be a tanker anchored near Brenton Reef Lightship waiting for a pilot. Echos are used by many steamers in close waters.

Using a Radio Direction Finder

A good R. D. F. is a valuable instrument to have aboard, but you must use it often in clear weather for practice and also know its limitations. Sometimes it is possible to use an R. D. F. bearing as a course line to pick up a buoy. (See Fig. 1.) Example: Pt. Judith Whistle Buoy is two miles from Pt. Judith light, which is equipped with a radio beacon. The bearing of the light is 345 degrees from the buoy. On approaching from seaward using an R. D. F. sail east or west whichever the case may be until the radio bearing of Pt. Judith is 345, then sail on that course. If your R. D. F. is dependable, how can you miss the buoy? A sounding lead will also give you a good idea as to your position along the course.

During the summer of 1940, I was pilot on a small excursion steamer running from New London to Block Island. Our passengers had only about two hours' time at the island even when we had clear weather. Therefore, in fog, it was important that we make all our marks right on the button, particularly when we had a competing steamship running the same schedule. The most difficult course to make good was a run from Watch Hill to the New Harbor breakwater. This was a 13-mile run across the tide for a stony breakwater, with nothing but an automobile horn on the end. (The skipper called it worst names than that.) I persuaded the company to install an R. D. F. and with this, we ran a little to the north of the breakwater until Southeast Light radio bearing was 145 degrees. Then we altered our course to this bearing which brought us right up alongside the breakwater. (See Fig. 3.) Using a couple of codfish sinkers on a heavy cod line, we were able to get soundings while going along at a good clip. We had no trouble finding Block Island all summer long.

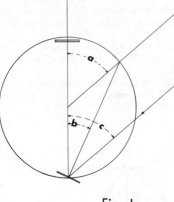

Fig. 1

A NEW
Position
Finder

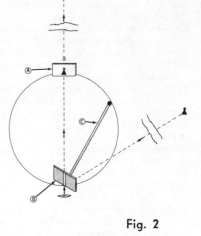

Fig. 2

Fig. 1. Optical principle of Position Finder.

Angle A is angle between two objects on shore being observed.

Angle B is amount index arm, and therefore index mirror, is turned. This is always one-half of angle A.

Angle C is angle of light rays coming from right hand object to index mirror and reflected to horizon mirror. Always the same as angle A.

Fig. 2. The observing portion of the position finder. A, fixed horizon mirror. B, rotatable index mirror. C, index arm. Fig. 3. The instrument positioned on a chart.

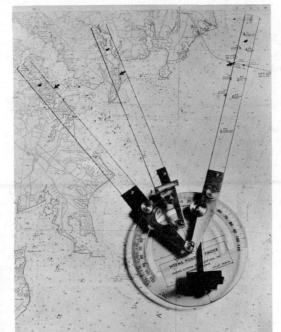

Fig. 3

ONE of the oldest methods of piloting is to measure and plot the angles between three known objects. Although it is a standard method, it has not been widely used in small boats, because a sextant has been required to measure the horizontal angles and a three-armed protractor to plot them. As a sextant is relatively expensive for this use only, those who do not venture on the high seas and use celestial navigation normally do not have one aboard.

The new Position-Finder, handled by Weems System of Navigation, Annapolis, Md., was designed for the yachtsman. It is a combination instrument which can be used both to measure the angles and to plot the position. Not only is there no need for a sextant for making the observations, but also eliminated are the processes of reading angles from the sextant scale and setting those values on a protractor. This results in a saving of time, labor and risk of error. After the observations are taken, the arms are locked in position and the position-finder in effect becomes a three-armed protractor, with the angles already set. The solution is entirely independent of the compass or other instruments. The optical principle employed is shown in Fig. 1.

The observing portion of the instrument (Fig. 2) consists of a fixed horizon mirror (A) in which the reflected image of one object is seen immediately below the true image of the center object, viewed over the top of the mirror. This is called a horizon mirror because it has the same function as the horizon mirror of a marine sextant. The rotatable index mirror (B) is moved by the index arm (C) to reflect the image of the left or right object into the fixed mirror. By viewing through the slot in the center of this mirror, it is possible to use this one mirror for both left and right angles, whereas with a sextant, the index mirror is offset and can be used in one direction only.

The plotting portion of the position-finder consists of three arms, pivoted at one point, at which a pencil mark can be made through a hole onto the chart. The center arm is per-

manently located with an etched center-line 90° to the plane of the horizon mirror. The two movable arms can be locked in position during the observation to avoid any additional setting for plotting. The inside edges of the two movable arms are used for plotting.

How to Use the Position Finder

Choose three objects which can be seen on shore and which can also be easily identified on your chart. The procedure is to measure the angle between the center object and the right-hand object and between the center object and the left-hand one. It is immaterial which angle is measured first.

Move the two plotting arms as far to the rear as they will go. This is to get them out of the way while the angles are being measured. Then, facing toward the center object, look through the slotted index mirror and view the center object on shore above the horizon mirror. Swing the index arm to the right until the right-hand object is seen in the horizon mirror directly under the center object, still seen above the mirror, and lock the index arm in place. Move the right-hand plotting arm against the index arm and lock it in place. You will always see the slot of the index mirror reflected as a line in the horizon mirror when the instrument is properly used.

Unlock the index arm and move it around to the left until the left-hand object is aligned in the mirror under the center object. Lock the index arm in place. Move the left plotting arm against the index arm and lock it in place. Without reading any angles, you have now set the measured angles on the plotting instrument. Place a pencil point on the right-hand object on the chart and place the inside edge of the right plotting arm against the pencil. With the other hand, move the position-finder until the etched line of the center arm and the inside edge of the left arm are over the other two positions on the chart. (Use the removable extension pieces, if necessary.) Mark your position on the chart with a pencil through the center hole of the protractor.

(Fig. 3 shows the position finder positioned on a chart.)

An Old Coasting Stunt

Smalı boat navigators frequently find themselves in spots where the government did *not* erect *any* of the usual aids to navigation, and safe piloting therefore demands extra precautions.

Here's a stunt, suggested by Commodore J. F. Hellweg, U.S.N (Ret.), that will help you lots of times and should reduce the navigator's blood pressure considerably.

You are cruising along an unmarked coast and know little about the tides and also the effect of off-shore and on-shore winds.

You can always pick out some definite object along the shore line. The sharper and more definite it is, the better and the easier your piloting will be. By a sharp object, I mean a well defined object or mark such as a white *vertical* streak on the face of a bluff, or a tall tree clearly seen on the sky line, or a prominent rock. Any of them are better than a mountain or hilltop whose shape may appear to change as you steam past and probably will introduce an error in your work.

As soon as you spot your object (X) on shore, take a bearing of it, and *note the exact time*. Record both in your note book. Then immediately plot the bearing (line XA) and draw a "construction" line representing the course being steered by standard compass and which you hope you are making good.

Next, when the object (X) on shore bears *exactly abeam, note that time,* and plot the bearing (line XB cutting the construction line at point B). Be sure throughout this time to maintain your course accurately (p.s.c.) and your speed by revolutions.

Later, when the object (X) bearing has changed enough to give a good cut, take a third bearing and again *note accurately* the exact time. Plot the third bearing through X (line XC).

As you have recorded the times of each bearing, you can determine the elapsed time between bearings, and can see the ratio between these times.

Take point B where beam bearing cuts the "construction" line as the zero point. Measure off to the right and to the left of point B along the construction line, distances proportionally the same as the two elapsed times *using any scale you want.*

Suppose you ran for 32½ minutes from the first bearing to the beam bearing: and then ran 22½ minutes from the beam bearing to the third bearing. That ratio will then be 32.5/22.5 or 6.5/4.5. Using any scale most convenient (In this problem I used ¼ inch)

spot the two points on the construction line and at those two points *erect perpendiculars* cutting the two bearing lines XA and XC at points A′ and C′. These two perpendiculars of course parallel the beam bearing.

Connect points A′ and C′ and you have your answer. A′C′ *is the course you are making good* and it includes the effect of tides, winds, errors in steering, and errors in speed.

It shows plainly whether you are making good the course you are steering (p.s.c.) or whether you are being set off shore or on shore.

It helps you to determine whether your course "jibes" with the coast line, and therefore is very valuable, particularly along unmarked coasts.

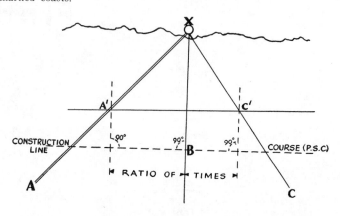

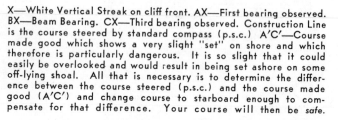

X—White Vertical Streak on cliff front. AX—First bearing observed. BX—Beam Bearing. CX—Third bearing observed. Construction Line is the course steered by standard compass (p.s.c.) A′C′—Course made good which shows a very slight "set" on shore and which therefore is particularly dangerous. It is so slight that it could easily be overlooked and would result in being set ashore on some off-lying shoal. All that is necessary is to determine the difference between the course steered (p.s.c.) and the course made good (A′C′) and change course to starboard enough to compensate for that difference. Your course will then be *safe.*

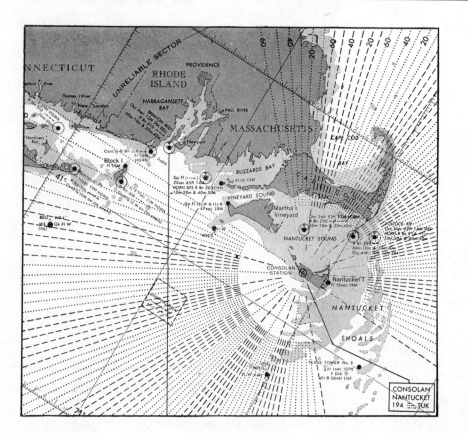

CONSOLAN

Portion of a Consolan chart (HO 16510) published by the Oceanographic Office of the Navy. Consolan, one of the newest radio navigational aids in American waters, has proved of great value to Bermuda racers. A simple radio receiver is required, tunable to the right frequency, and equipped with a beat frequency oscillator. Consolan stations are located at Nantucket (TUK, 194 kc), Miami and San Francisco. The Consolan signal is transmitted as a series of dots and dashes, 60 in all, separated by an "equisignal" or tone. When taking a bearing, the navigator tunes in 194 kc (if he is working Nantucket) and listens for an identifying signal. When transmission is completed he adds up the total of dots and dashes he has counted, and consults the Consolan tables for his bearing. Consolan bearings are not dependent on the compass, on steering, or on an antenna, and can be picked up farther out than regular radio bearings (up to approximately 800 miles.) Information on Consolan is published in HO 117, Radio Navigational Aids.

HOW TO
Compute a Course

BY THE PRINCIPLES
OF MERCATOR SAILING

Author's Note: The essentials of this lecture were prepared for use in the Junior Navigator class of Brooklyn Power Squadron, a unit of the United States Power Squadrons. In view of the diminishing emphasis upon the sailings in standard works, it is hoped that this material, which is partly original in its arrangement, may be of interest to readers outside the class for which it was at first intended.

Course and distance can be plotted on a mercator chart (above). The same results can be achieved, with greater accuracy, by computation, using formulae of mercator sailing

Above: The Mercator Sailing Triangle—a plane right triangle on the surface of the mercator projection.

AB is the rhumb line from one position to another.

D.Lo. is the difference of longitude (in minutes) measured on the parallel of the destination, between it and the meridian of the starting point. One minute = one meridional part.

m is the length of the meridian of A, between A and the parallel of B, and is found from Table 5, Bowditch. It is expressed in meridional parts.

C is the course angle, measured clockwise or counterclockwise as the case may be, from the meridian of the starting point to the rhumb line.

A COMPLETE treatment of all the sailings is no longer found in standard textbooks of navigation. De-emphasis on certain sailings, which are methods of interrelating the elements of travel over the earth's surface by computation rather than by plotting, is understandable. Nevertheless, mercator sailing is valuable background material in the education of a navigator, and also retains much practical importance, for there are still many occasions when it is more desirable to compute the results one would get by making a perfect mercator plot than it is to attempt the making of it. Computation of that sort is accomplished by mercator sailing.

This sailing differs from other sailings in that it is the application of trigonometry to the plane surface of the mercator projection, rather than to the spherical surface of the globe, whereas parallel sailing, middle latitude sailing, and great circle sailing are applications of mathematics directly to the globe. One must therefore briefly review the idea of the mercator projection in order to be prepared to comprehend the sailing. In mercator work plotting and computation are not only two means to the same end, but are actually identical in underlying method.

The mercator projection is a representation of the earth's surface upon a plane whereon the meridians of longitude appear as parallel straight lines, and the parallels of lattitude are placed *accordingly*. The raison d'etre of the projection is simply a determination to have a chart upon which meridians are drawn as parallel straight lines. It results that a rhumb may also be drawn as a straight line and its direction may be readily ascertained on this projection. Since a ship maintaining any true course sails a rhumb, it is obviously these features in a chart which were most to be desired, and they explain why we have mercator charts and use them so often.

One begins to construct the mercator chart, therefore, by the simple expedient of placing the meridians on the paper as parallel straight lines, choosing some quantum of linear measure to represent a minute of longitude. One now has the desired features, but at the cost of introducing an East-West expansion of areas. On the globe the meridians are not parallel to one another but converge and meet at the poles. The meridians, having been straightened out in being transferred from the globe to the projection, must next be stretched. That is to say: in order to preserve the shapes of areas on the chart, a North-South expansion quantitatively the same as the East-West expansion is called for. The quantity is deducible from Table 5, Bowditch, which tells us how much North-South expansion is involved. There we find tabulated the total lengths of the meridians on the mercator projection, from the equator to various latitudes, in terms of the length of a minute of longitude on the projection. Table 5 is known as the table of meridional parts. In working problems by mercator sailing the length of lines drawn or imagined to be drawn on the projection can be expressed in meridional parts only—it is unnecessary to deal with linear measure in working problems, although we would have to deal with it if we were going to construct a chart or plotting sheet.

The East-West expansion resulting from the straightening of the meridians as they are drawn on the projection is a function of the latitude. The higher the latitude, the more expansion there is. The expansion ranges from zero at the equator, where the meridians are naturally parallel to one another, to infinity at the poles, where the meridians are naturally not separated at all. As a result of the East-West expansion, each parallel of latitude on the mercator projection is equal in linear measure to the equator itself. One may demonstrate generally (through parallel sailing) that the ratio of the natural length of any parallel of latitude to the natural length of the equator equals the cosine of the latitude in question. We see, then, that the East-West expansion along any parallel amounts to the difference between the natural length of the parallel and such natural length multiplied by the secant of the latitude in question. (This follows from what has just been stated. If the ratio of x to y equals cosine of the latitude, then x multiplied by secant of the latitude equals y).

The net result of all the foregoing is that, on the mercator projection, the amount of East-West expansion resulting from the straightening out of the meridians can be ascertained by comparing the natural length of any parallel with such natural length multiplied by the secant of the latitude concerned.

Parallels Shift Poleward

IT IS a reasonable guess that any parallel of latitude, when placed on the mercator projection, is shifted poleward from its natural position by an amount which is the same as the amount of East-West expansion in the latitude of that parallel. In that way, the shapes of areas may be preserved. Consider the thirtieth parallel, over a span of 10° of longitude. Using parallel sailing, one may find the natural length of that parallel over 10° of longitude to be 519.6 miles. This is a quantum of linear measure equal to the natural length of 519.6 minutes of arc on the equator. But on the mercator projection the same arc of the thirtieth parallel is expanded to equal the length, on the projection, of 10° of the equator—it is expanded to a length of 600 meridional parts. Therefore the quantity of East-West expansion is 80.4 meridional parts.

Now, the natural length of any meridian from the equator to the thirtieth parallel is 1800 minutes of arc or 1800 sea miles (60 minutes per degree of latitude). Were there no North-South expansion on the projection, we would draw in the thirtieth parallel 1800 meridional parts from the equator. (A minute of arc on a meridian being equal in length, except for refinements, to a minute of arc on the equator, one meridional part may represent each). But in view of what has already been said it is a reasonable guess that the thirtieth parallel should be drawn in 1880.4 parts from the equator. (1800 meridional parts for natural length, and 80.4 for North-South expansion). In point of fact one finds that Table 5, Bowditch, shows the meridional parts for latitude 30° to be 1876.7. The discrepancy from 1880.4 can be ascribed to the facts that Table 5 reflects the earth's imperfect shape, and is calculated by refined methods.

Having now reviewed the idea of the mercator projection, we may take up mercator sailing. Any line either actually or imaginatively drawn on the mercator projector is measurable in meridional parts, since both parallels and meridians are placed on the projection by admeasurement employing meridional parts. To be specific, the parallels are placed by Table 5 and the meridians are placed according to a fixed scale which determines the linear value of the tabulations in Table 5; hence any line drawn on the projection is measurable in meridional parts.

Computing the Course

THE COURSE triangle on the plane surface of the mercator projection is shown in the illustration. It consists of the meridian of the starting place A, the parallel of the destination B, and the rhumb from A to B. The interior angle of the triangle at A is the course angle. Referring to it as angle C,

$$\text{Tan } C = \frac{D. Lo.}{m}$$

D. Lo. is the number of minutes of longitude separating the meridians of A and B, and hence is the number of meridional parts in the parallel of B between B and the meridian of A. The difference according to Table 5 between the meridional parts for A and those for B is the number of meridional parts in the meridian of A between A and the parallel of B, and this value is called m. The first number of meridional parts over the second is a ratio equal to the tangent of the course angle, as may be seen from the figure.

Should A and B lie on opposite sides of the equator, M_1 (the meridional parts for A's latitude) and M_2 (the meridional parts for B's latitude) must be added together to obtain the above "difference," since what is sought is the length of the meridian between A and B. The "difference" is an algebraic difference.

The formula is rearranged in the form D. Lo. = m tan C if the course angle is known and the difference of longitude is sought. In this case, if the course made good over the ground is near 90° the sailing may be inadvisable because the tangents of angles near 90° vary rapidly. As a result, any error in the value assigned to the course made good over the ground would produce a disproportionately large error in the computed D. Lo. Middle latitude sailing, which is well suited to this particular situation, may be used instead.

Computing the Distance

HAVING now seen how to compute the course angle indicating the direction from one position to another by means of a knowledge of the two positions and the use of Table 5 we pass to a consideration of the distance, that is, the mileage represented by the number of meridional parts in AB, the hypotenuse of the course triangle on the plane surface of the mercator projection.

By trigonometry, the length of AB in meridional parts is equal to m sec C. (Because AB/m equals sec C.) Also, where 1 is the difference of latitude between A and B in minutes, and m is the difference in meridional parts mentioned earlier, the ratio 1/m expresses the average quantum of mileage represented by one meridional part along the rhumb AB, or indeed along any straight line drawn on the projection between the parallels of A and B. In view of these two facts, 1/m times m sec C, or $\dfrac{1 \text{ m sec } C}{m}$ expresses the mileage represented by the length of the rhumb AB. Because m cancels out, the distance becomes 1 sec C.

The two formulas, $\text{Tan } C = \dfrac{D. Lo.}{m}$ and d = 1 sec C are used in conjunction, to compute the direction and distance along the rhumb line from one position to another. With a knowledge of the two positions and access to Table 5, one may find the mercator course and distance from one place to another. The formulas are simple, and are quickly worked by means of the tables of logarithms of numbers and logarithms of functions contained in Bowditch. A reconsideration of the comparative ease of solving the formulae and of the comparative difficulty of making extremely accurate measurements of direction and distance on a mercator chart of small scale will lead to the conclusion that intelligent use of mercator sailing, as a means of computing the results that would be had from a perfect mercator plot, is and will continue to be a most valuable device in the practice of the navigator's art.

A NAVIGATION CALCULATOR

ABOUT THE AUTHOR — Until 1950, though he had crewed on small sailboats, the author had never owned a boat. Then he bought a 31-foot Chris-Craft and started immediately to cruise extensively, getting both practical experience and a knowledge of principles at the same time by studying Piloting, Seamanship and Small Boat Handling. *The first year, with his 9-year old son and wife as crew, he cruised Lake Erie from Detroit to the Niagara River. The second year, his brother took the boat to Boston and the author brought it back, again with his wife and son. Later, the same crew made a cruise to Georgian Bay, Little Current, McGregor Bay, Killarney, Collins Inlet and many other interesting places. During those years he has never gotten lost or had any serious mishap. Finding an airplane calculator of inestimable value on his cruises, Mr. Veinott decided to work out a calculator expressly for the yachtsman so that anyone could readily solve time-speed-distance-fuel consumption-cruising range problems simply by inspection, without mathematics. This article is the outcome of his work on such a calculator, the use of which he describes by means of practical examples.—*EDITOR

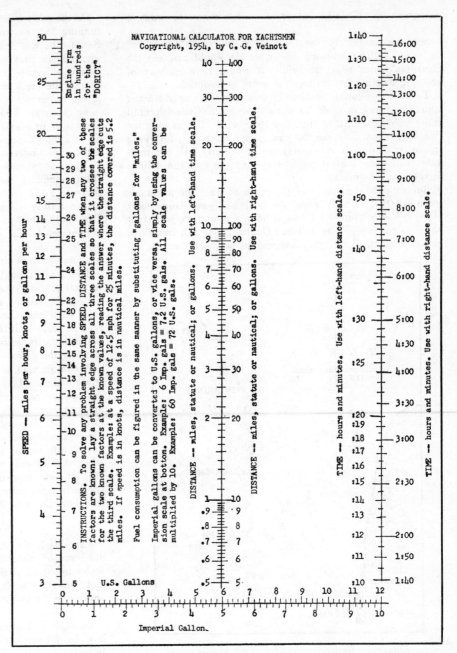

Figure 2—With the calculator, distance run, speed and time can be determined without mathematics. Engine rpm relate to Doricy only but can be calculated for any boat. It was designed by Cyril G. Veinott, 3654 Townley Road, Shaker Heights, Ohio.

AN accurate knowledge of distance covered can be of invaluable assistance to the navigator of the small boat in piloting his craft, particularly in strange waters, and especially when the visibility is limited. Distance-finding seems to be overlooked by many yachtsmen as a valuable aid in piloting. This neglect may be partly due to ignorance of its value as a tool, but a more probable explanation is that the inconvenience of the arithmetical computations involved discourages the average yachtsman, who is out for pleasure, and not to see how much arithmetic he can do. Distance-finding without arithmetic is made possible by a new navigational calculator, developed by the author, and discussed in this article.

How valuable a knowledge of dis-

tance run can be is graphically illustrated in Fig. 1, which is a chart of the southern end of Lake Huron. Suppose one is going from the lightship "Huron" to Goderich, a distance of 57 miles, course 36°; suppose further that the navigator has never made this cruise before and is completely unfamiliar with landmarks. To add to his troubles, the visibility is limited to one or two miles, as he approaches the Canadian shore.

Now, suppose the navigator leaves the Huron, setting his course for what he thinks is 36° (true), and decides to run his course until he sees the Canadian shore. If he did run an ab-

solutely true course, he would sail right into Goderich harbor; but this is an unlikely possibility under the conditions assumed. It is more probable that he is either north or south of the true course, but does not know which.

Suppose he were 10° north, that is, on course 26°; if he runs this course until he sees the Canadian shore, ignoring distance run, he will run into Clark Point Reef; here, he could pile up even before he saw the shore. If he were even slightly farther to the north and continued to the shore, he would go well over a hundred miles—if his gas held out—before he saw shore. He would not know where he was,

438a

nor which way to go to the nearest port, nor how far away it was.

Suppose he ran 10° south, that is, course 46° from the lightship, without knowing his error. He would first see the Canadian shore near Bayfield, but would have no way of knowing whether he was north or south of Goderich.

To solve a piloting problem of this nature, there are many who would say to steer for a point south of Goderich until shore was sighted, then turn and steer north. Let us examine this suggestion. Suppose the course is set for 46°, following the latter advice, if the course run is actually 46°, the navigator will come out all right except that he will run a little farther than necessary.

But suppose the course is 10° south of what the navigator intended, that is, 56°. Then, the boat will pass dangerously close to Kettle Point Reef and, if he misses that, he will sight shore at St. Joseph; he will find Goderich but will run extra miles doing it. If his error happens to be more than 10° to

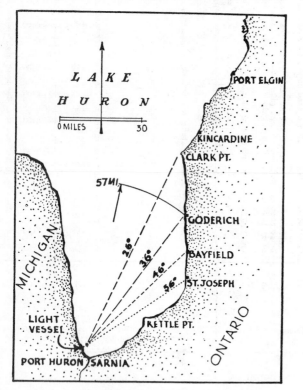

Figure 1—Reproduction of a chart of the southern end of Lake Huron, showing how valuable a knowledge of distance run can be on a cruise to Goderich, particularly when the visibility is poor

the north, he would miss Goderich, for he would sight the shore north of it and continue north, so that he never would see Goderich. His first knowledge of his error would be when he ran aground on Clark Point Reef.

Now, if distance-finding were a part of the repertoire of the navigator, how would it help? The yachtsman would set his speed at a known figure, say 12 miles per hour; he would calculate how long it would take to make the 57-mile run, finding it to be 4 hours, 45 minutes. He would record leaving the Huron at 8:05, noting that he should reach Goderich at 12:50. At that time, at least, he would be 57 miles from the lightship. If his course happened to be true, he would run into Goderich at 12:50, with the certainty that it was Goderich because he was arriving there at the right time.

If, however, at 12:50 no land were in sight, he would know that he was *north* of his course, somewhere on the circle of 57-mile radius, shown in Fig. 1. Therefore, he would turn 90° to the right and run directly into Goderich. The amount of his northerly error would be of little importance, because Goderich would be dead abeam. unless his error was greatly in excess of 10°.

On the other hand if he ran a course of 46°, thinking he was running 36°, he would make a landfall at Bayfield at 12:10. Because he was reaching shore 40 minutes ahead of time, he would know that he was south of where he wanted to be and would, of course, turn north. So, whichever way he was off course, the clock would tell him of his error, and which way to run to correct it.

An accurate knowledge of distance run is also of great assistance in identifying landmarks on an unfamiliar shore, or picking up buoys in a fog. At best, compass errors are not always understood; the deviation may be changed if iron or steel is placed too close to the compass inadvertently. Distance-finding also permits the navigator to run farther off shore to avoid reefs; a knowledge of distance run tells him with certainty when to turn shoreward to make his objective. The real value of distance-finding becomes greatest when needed most. The navigational calculator described in this article makes this method easy to use by the average small boat navigator without arithmetical calculations.

The Navigational Calculator, shown in Fig. 2, has three vertical scales: SPEED, DISTANCE, and TIME. The divisions are not equally spaced, as they have to be logarithmically spaced to serve their purpose. If one is not familiar with reading this type of scale, a little practice may be required; working out the illustrative examples will give one practice while he is learning the various uses to which the device can be put.

A straightedge, preferably transparent, is needed. When the straightedge is laid across the three scales, the three factors are always correctly related. Hence, when any two factors are known, the third is always given by the reading on the third scale. A word of caution may be desirable here: both the DISTANCE and TIME scales have markings on both sides, in order to extend the range of usefulness of the calculator; when the left-side markings of one of these scales is used, the left-side markings of the other should also be used, similarly right sides should also be used together. Use of this calculator is best illustrated by means of typical examples.

Calculation of Distance Run

Example 1. You cruise at 12.5 mph for 25 minutes; how far did you go? Solution: lay the straightedge across all three scales in such a position that it crosses the SPEED scale at 12.5 and the TIME scale at :25 (left-side markings); read the answer on the DISTANCE scale, using left-hand markings, which is 5.2 miles.

Example 2. You cruise at 12.5 mph for 3 hours, 45 minutes; how far did you cruise? The procedure is exactly the same as followed in example 1, except that you use the right-side markings of the TIME and DISTANCE scales. Another difference is that it is necessary to estimate positions between marks; there is no 3:45 mark, but there are markings at 3:40 and 3:50, hence, for 3:45, use a position halfway between the 3:40 and 3:50 marks. The straightedge, cutting the SPEED scale at 12.5 and the TIME scale at 3:45, is found to intersect the DISTANCE scale halfway between the marks 46 and 48; so the distance run is 47 miles, the answer sought.

Example 3. How long does it take to cover 57 miles at a speed of 16 mph? Solution: lay the straightedge across all three scales so that it cuts the SPEED scale at 16, the DISTANCE scale at 57, and read the time, 3:34 (estimating the "4"), on the TIME scale.

Example 4. You are cautiously picking your way through fog at 4.3 knots, passing a known buoy; by measurements on the chart, you have determined that it is 1.45 nautical miles to the next buoy; how long should it take to reach that buoy? Solution: lay the straightedge across all three scales, cutting the SPEED scale at 4.3, the DISTANCE scale at 1.45; the answer, read on the TIME scale, is 20.2 minutes.

Example 5. You cover a distance of 14 miles in 1 hour, 22 minutes; how fast were you cruising? Solution: lay the straightedge across all three scales, cutting the TIME scale at 1:22, and the DISTANCE scale at 14; read the average speed where the SPEED scale is cut, that is the 10.2 mph point.

Example 6. You would like to know the speed of the current in the river up which you are cruising. You know, from engine rpm, that your speed in slack water is 12.0 mph. From landmarks on shore, you observed that you covered 8.2 miles over the bottom in 57 minutes. How fast is the river current? Solution: first, use the calculator to compute your speed over the bottom, which you find to be 8.6 mph; then the strength of the river current must be 12.0 — 8.6 = 3.4 mph.

Rate of fuel consumption, if checked periodically, can afford valuable clues as to the health of the engine. Hence, checking it frequently can give advance warning when a tune-up is needed. The calculator is useful for this purpose: the following examples show how.

Example 7. You start the day's cruise with a full tank and cruise at the same speed for 6 hours and 30 minutes. It takes 48 gallons to refill the tank. What is your rate of fuel consumption? Solution: lay the straightedge across 6:30 on the TIME scale and 48 on the DISTANCE (gallons) scale; the straightedge then cuts the SPEED (fuel-consumption) scale at 7.4, your fuel consumption in gallons per hour.

Example 8. Your tank holds 100 gallons; how long could you cruise on a tankful? At the cruising speed of example 7, the fuel consumption was 7.4 gallons per hour. so, lay the straightedge across the three scales, cutting SPEED at 7.4, and DISTANCE at 100; maximum cruising time is read on the TIME scale—13:30. (Don't plan on reaching destination with an empty tank!)

Example 9. In example 7, you determine, by chart measurements, that the distance covered was 68 miles; what is your cruising radius? Solution: first, lay the straightedge across 6:30 on the TIME scale and 68 on the DISTANCE scale, and read your average cruising speed on the SPEED scale—10.5 mph. From example 8, you learned that your maximum cruising time on a tankful was 13 hours, 30 minutes. Therefore, lay the straightedge across 10.5 on the SPEED scale and 13:30 on the TIME scale, and read the miles on the DISTANCE scale—141, your maximum cruising radius. Your *safe* cruising radius is, of course, less than this.

Problems Involving Canadian Gallons

Example 10. You want to fill your tank at a Canadian port. Your measuring stick shows that you need 56 U. S. gallons; how many Canadian gallons do you need? Solution: use the horizontal scale at the bottom of the calculator, multiplying all scale readings by 10; opposite 5.6 (for (56) on the U. S. gallons side, read 4.65 (for 46.5) gallons on the Imperial gallons side.

In order to compute distance run from the elapsed time, it is, of course, necessary to know the speed of the boat at different engine speeds. This is best determined over a course of known distance. To do this, select two points about a mile apart. The distance between these points needs to be carefully measured on a large-scale chart. Distances shorter than a mile may be difficult to time accurately enough at high speeds, and distances materially greater require too much time for running the test, particularly at the slow speeds. The two points selected should be in water deep enough for the boat to pass close by in order to tell accurately when they are dead abeam. A day should be selected when the water is reasonably calm, but a flat calm is not necessary. To simplify the discussion, let's refer to these points simply as A and B; also let's assume that A is practically due west of B. A stopwatch would be a convenience in these tests, but any watch with a second hand large enough to be read to the nearest second will do well enough. The basic formula from which speed can be calculated is

$$\text{m.p.h.} = \frac{(\text{distance run, in miles}) \times (3600)}{\text{elapsed time, in seconds}}$$

The procedure will be illustrated. Measure the distance on the chart between points A and B; say that this is $6\frac{1}{8}''$, to the nearest 1/64th. Measure the distance on the scale of miles representing one mile; say that this is $6\frac{3}{8}''$, to the nearest 1/64th. Then, the distance between point A and B is 6.125/6.375 = 0.961 miles. For this course only, then

$$\text{mph } \frac{0.961 \times 3600}{\text{seconds}} = \frac{3460}{\text{secs.}}$$

To run the speed tests, proceed to a point about 100 yards or so west of A where A and B are in line; set the engine speed at 1000 rpm and head for A and B, just clearing A. The helmsman should not attempt to do any more than steer his course and hold engine rpm "right on the button" at 1000 rpm. Tave another person use some sighting device aimed squarely abeam; this can be a bulkhead or any part of the boat which is perpendicular with the keel; or, the pelorus can be used. This observer calls "time" when A is dead abeam and again when B is dead abeam; if he has a stopwatch, he can operate the stopwatch. If no stopwatch is used, it is much better to have a third observer ιo read time and record the readings; it is difficult to sight points A and B while reading the watch simultaneously. The course should be immediately rerun in the opposite direction, at the same engine speed, to average out the effect of wind and current. A second pair of runs is made at an increased engine speed, and so on, up to the maximum sustained engine speed. These readings can be recorded in a table like the following:

Direction run	RPM (engine)	Time min:sec	Secs.	MPH	Ave. mph
E	1000	10:28	628	5.50	5.65
W	1000	9:57	597	5.80	
E	1400	7:47	467	7.40	7.48
W	1400	7:38	453	7.56	

Note that the speed is figured for each direction, then these two speeds are averaged. (Do not average the time, as this can lead to appreciable errors, particularly when the time differences are great.)

Now, if these readings are plotted on a sheet of graph paper, a smooth curve can be drawn which has the double advantage of smoothing out observational errors and giving the m.p.h. for intermediate engine speeds; hence, if the readings are plotted on graph paper, fewer readings are actually required. If no curve paper is available, the course should be run once in each direction at intervals of each hundred rpm. Do not neglect the lower speeds; you may need to do distance-finding in a fog when you are running at a low speed.

An alternative way to determine speed vs. r.p.m. would be to make longer runs, using the navigational calculator to compute the speed. In such a case, the distances should be great enough to require about a 30-minute run between points.

You can save time by adding engine rpm for your craft right on the SPEED scale of the navigational calculator. Make a mark, at each hundred rpm on the right side of the SPEED scale, purposely left blank for this purpose; each mark goes opposite the mph your boat makes at that engine speed In Fig. 2, such markings have been added for the author's cruiser Doricy, a 31-foot Chris-Craft. It was found on speed trials, taken as described in this article, that Doricy operated as a displacement boat up to an engine speed of 2300 rpm, above which speed it planed. This change is evidenced in the illustration of the calculator by the sudden increase in distance between hundred-rpm marks above 2300.

With rpm marks on the speed scale, it is not necessary to know the speed; distance run in a given time, or time required to run a given distance, can be calculated by locating the point on the SPEED scale from the engine rpm markings. Also, this single speed scale serves as a permanent record of mph vs. engine rpm, so that a curve of these quantities is not necessary. It should be remembered, however, that the added rpm markings apply only to the one boat, under conditions similar to those when the speed trials were run.

The Radiotelephone—Safety Aid to Piloting

(See also data on Citizens' Band Radio, page 461)

YOUR marine radiotelephone set is a valuable instrument for promoting safety at sea and for keeping in touch with other boats and the shore. It can give you all its potential advantages only when it is properly installed, maintained and operated. Let only competent, authorized personnel work on it. Have your dealer or service man go over it with you. Study it—understand its functions—use it wisely.

The Radio Technical Commission for Marine Services has drafted basic educational data with which every yachtsman should be familiar, and has published this in pamphlet form, from which the following material has been extracted. (Copies of this pamphlet, Marine Radio Telephony, may be purchased from the Radio Technical Commission for Marine Services, % F. C. C., Washington 25, D. C. It includes a summary of the most significant rules with which the licensers and operators of voluntarily installed ship radiotelephone stations should be familiar.)

Get Your Licenses

For the ship station—as soon as you have your set, apply to the Federal Communications Commission, Washington 25, D. C., for a license. Use Form 501. Your dealer or service man will be glad to help you, particularly in describing your equipment. Operate your set only when you have a valid station license. Keep your license posted on your boat.

For the operator—apply to the local office of the Federal Communications Commission for a Restricted Radiotelephone Operator Permit. Use Form 753. Operate your set only when you have a valid permit with you.

What You Have at Your Service

The marine safety and communications system utilizes a number of radio frequencies, each of which has its specific use or uses. They may be divided into three general groups:

1. The International Calling and Distress frequency 2182 kc— Its primary purpose is to provide a means of summoning aid in an emergency. All ship radiotelephone stations in this service, most public shore stations, and most United States Coast Guard stations maintain a watch on this frequency. Thus you have at your command many avenues to secure help when needed.

2. The frequencies for direct ship-to-ship communication—Their use is limited to safety communications, or the operational and business needs of boats.

3. The frequencies for public correspondence—Over them you may talk via a public shore station with any telephone on land.

Before You Sail

Be sure you have on board your station license, operator's permit, Part 8 of the FCC Rules and log sheets in readiness to make the necessary entries (for the latter, see Section 8.368 in your copy of the Rules).

Be sure your set is in proper working order and the power supply on your boat is adequate.

Be sure to advise the company operating the shore station of local ship-shore circuits if you plan to use its shore station so that the necessary data for handling calls can be posted on the company's records.

Maintain Your Watch

While your set is turned on, keep a receiver tuned to 2182 kc and listen so that you will be in a position to help others. They are doing the same thing for you. This watch may be interrupted when you are communicating with another boat or with a shore station; listening to weather or other marine information bulletins; listening for a brief period to receive a scheduled call; waiting for the completion of a call placed or about to be received from a shore station; standing by to place a call through a shore station after the operator has asked you to wait your turn; using your receiver to receive direction finding signals.

It is strongly urged that if you contemplate communicating with a public shore station, you get a separate receiver to meet the watch-keeping requirements. In that way your regular receiver may be kept tuned to a working frequency of the nearby shore station to receive calls from land, thus making 2182 kc more readily available for emergency use.

Using Your Set

Marine radio frequencies in the 2 Mcs band are few in number in comparison with the number of boats equipped. When you use one of them you are using a gigantic party line. Cooperation is necessary so that all may have equal opportunity to make and receive calls. In particular—

Always give precedence to distress or other urgent calls.

Limit your conversation to the essentials. Others are waiting.

Your transmitter is on the air only when the button on your hand-set or microphone is depressed. Only then can others hear you. Your receiver is connected only when the button is released. Only then can you hear others. Remember: PUSH TO TALK. RELEASE TO LISTEN.

How to Make a Call

Listen carefully to make sure the frequency or frequency pair you want to use is not busy. If it is busy, you will hear voices or, from most public shore stations, an intermittent busy tone on your listening frequency of the pair. Except in a safety emergency don't interrupt.

When the conversation is to take place on a ship-to-ship frequency: Unless you have reached an agreement in advance as to the time you will call another boat, establish communications on 2182 kc and then shift immediately to the agreed upon ship-to-ship frequency. When the conversation is to take place through a commercial shore station: Make your initial contact on a working frequency of that station. This will speed your call.

Both of these practices are designed to relieve the load on 2182 kc so that its utility for safety purposes will not be jeopardized.

Steps to Follow in Making a Call
(other than a Distress, Urgency, or Safety Call)

Intership calls.—Listen to make sure 2182 kc/s is not busy. If it is free, put your transmitter on the air and say—

"(Station called) This is (call sign and name of your vessel) Over."

[If necessary, the identification of the station called, and your call sign and the name of your vessel may each be repeated not more than three times; but the entire calling transmission must not last longer than 30 seconds]

Listen for a reply. If no contact is made, repeat after an interval of at least two minutes. After establishing contact, switch to the agreed upon intership channel. One exchange of communications shall not exceed 3 minutes after establishing contact. After conversation is completed say—

"This is (call sign and name of your vessel) out."

You shall not establish contact thereafter with the same vessel until 10 minutes has elapsed.

Ship to shore calls for Public Telephone Service.—Listen to make sure the working channel you wish to use is not busy. If it is clear put your transmitter on the air and say—

"(Coast station desired) Marine Operator."

"This is (call sign and name of your vessel) over"

Listen for a reply. If no contact is made, repeat after an interval of at least two minutes.

When the Marine Operator answers say—

"This is (call sign and name of your vessel) Calling (telephone number desired). Over"

After conversation is completed say—

"This is (call sign and name of your vessel) Out."

How to Receive a Call

Your vessel can be reached only when your receiver is turned on and tuned to the frequency over which you expect to receive calls. The receiver you use to maintain watch on 2182 kc/s will assure that you get calls addressed to you by other ships for conversation over a ship-to-ship frequency. For calls from public shore stations, keep a receiver tuned to a working frequency of such station in your area. It is urged that you have one receiver for watch-keeping and a second one to insure that you can be reached by a public shore station over a working channel. This will help to keep 2182 kc/s free for its primary purpose of securing help.

When you hear your boat being called respond by giving your vessel's name and call sign not more than three times. After completion of the conversation sign off by announcing the name and call sign of your vessel.

Steps to Follow in Receiving a Call

Intership calls.—When you hear your vessel called, put your transmitter on the air and say—

"(Name of vessel which called) This is (call sign and name of your vessel). Over."

Switch to the agreed upon intership channel. After conversation is completed say—

"This is (call sign and name of your vessel) Out."

Shore to ship calls.—When you hear the name of your vessel called, put your transmitter on the air on the proper frequency and say—

"(Name of station which called) This is (call sign and name of your vessel). Over."

After conversation is completed say—

"This is (call sign and name of your vessel) Out."

Test Transmissions

Always remember, when making tests, to take every precaution not to cause interference. Reduce power, and if feasible suppress radiation entirely (by use of a dummy antenna).

Listen, before testing, to make sure that the frequency on which you intend to make the test is not busy; if so you must obtain their consent first. If it is free, put your transmitter on the air and say—
"This is (call sign and name of your vessel) Test."

If you hear no station tell you to "wait," you may proceed, saying "testing" followed by a number count or other phraseology which will not confuse listeners.

The test signals must be brief—not more than 10 seconds.

At the end of the test, announce the call sign and name of your vessel and the general location of your ship at the time the test is made.

Tests shall not be repeated on 2182 kc/s until after a wait of at least 5 minutes; on other frequencies, a wait of at least 1 minute is sufficient.

Weather Reports

When aboard your craft, you can keep up to date on weather and other marine information by listening to the working frequencies of public or U.S. Government shore stations. Coast Guard stations transmit weather and other marine information on 2670 kc/s after a preliminary announcement on 2182 kc/s, and in some areas, Standard Broadcast Stations transmit special marine information broadcast for the benefit of boat owners. Don't take chances—the weather report is there—get it.

Distress, Urgency, and Safety

In an emergency as a part of this marine safety and communication system, you have help on 2182 kc/s at your fingertips wherever you may be.

Only when grave and imminent danger threatens your vessel and immediate help is required, use the distress procedure—radiotelephone alarm signal (if available) and MAYDAY. Announced on 2182 kc/s, it should be heard by nearby boats, as well as by Coast Guard and public shore stations within range. [The distress shall be sent ONLY on the authority of the person responsible for the ship. This law is important and easy to follow on large vessels. But in the case of a small craft where the sole person responsible is lost and those remaining are passengers—common sense will have to prevail as to who shall assume charge.]

For less serious situations than warrant the distress procedure, the urgency signal "PAN" or the safety signal "SECURITY," as appropriate, should be used. You can talk with a nearby boat, with the Coast Guard, or in most cases, with any agency on land via a public shore station.

Communications preceded by a distress "MAYDAY," urgency "PAN," or safety "SECURITY" signal must be given precedence, and in that order. When you hear one of these signals, it is your obligation to terminate any transmission you may be making which would interfere with such communications, and to render assistance if needed and possible.

The Distress Procedure—"Mayday"—2182 kc/s

The distress communications include the following actions:
1. The RADIOTELEPHONE ALARM SIGNAL (whenever possible) followed by—
2. The DISTRESS SIGNAL "MAYDAY."
3. The DISTRESS MESSAGE.
4. Acknowledgment of Receipt of Distress Message.
5. Further Distress Messages and other communications.
6. Transmission of the DISTRESS PROCEDURE by a VESSEL or SHORE STATION not itself in Distress.
7. TERMINATION OF DISTRESS.

The RADIOTELEPHONE ALARM SIGNAL consists of two audio tones, of different pitch, transmitted alternately.

The purpose of this signal is to attract the attention of persons on watch or to actuate automatic devices giving an alarm. It shall only be used to announce that a distress call or message is about to follow.

Exception: It may be used with the Urgency Signal in two instances, see pamphlet.

The DISTRESS CALL consists of:
—the distress signal MAYDAY, spoken three times;
—the word THIS IS;
—the call sign or the name (if no call sign is assigned yet) of the vessel in distress, spoken three times.

The DISTRESS MESSAGE follows immediately and consists of:
—the distress signal MAYDAY;
—the call sign and name of the vessel in distress.
—particulars of its position (latitude and longitude, or true bearing and distance in miles from a known geographical position);
—the nature of the distress and kind of assistance desired;
—any other information which might facilitate the rescue; especially a description of the vessel: length, color, type, etc.; and the number of persons on board. OVER.

Example of the Distress Procedure for the first three important steps

"Alarm Signal (if available) (for approximately one minute). MAYDAY MAYDAY MAYDAY THIS IS WZ 6789 THE YACHT BLUE DUCK, WZ 6789 THE YACHT BLUE DUCK, WZ 6789 THE YACHT BLUE DUCK;

MAYDAY WZ 6789 THE YACHT BLUE DUCK 133 DEGREES TRUE 12 MILES OFF MONTAUK POINT, STRUCK SUBMERGED OBJECT, TAKING WATER FAST, ENGINE DISABLED, ESTIMATE CANNOT STAY AFLOAT MORE THAN ONE HOUR. FOUR PERSONS ON-BOARD, BLUE DUCK IS 26 FOOT CABIN CRUISER, WHITE HULL. MAINTAINING CONTINUOUS WATCH ON 2182 kc/s. THIS IS THE WZ 6789 THE YACHT BLUE DUCK, OVER."

The pamphlet *Marine Radio Telephony* also goes into detail to explain how and when to acknowledge receipt of a distress message; further distress messages and other communications; transmission of the distress procedure by a vessel or shore station not itself in distress; termination of distress; the urgency signal PAN; and the safety signal SECURITY. Readers are urged to familiarize themselves with all of this.

General Rules for Distress

With your life at stake, you have a far better chance by following correct procedure as given in detail in the pamphlet *Marine Radio Telephony;* but the provisions of the International radio regulations do not prevent a vessel in distress to use *any means* at its disposal to attract attention, make known its position, and obtain help.

Stay on 2182 kc/s; but when no answer to a distress is received; you may repeat it on any other available frequency on which attention might be attracted.

Speak slowly and distinctly. Use phonetics when necessary, especially when giving the letters of your call sign.

You may be requested to transmit suitable signals followed by your call sign and name to permit direction finding stations to determine your position.

If you have to abandon ship, the radio transmitter should be locked on the air, if considered necessary and circumstances permit. The purpose of this is to locate you by radio direction-finding bearings. If you have already been visually located, you should not lock the transmitter as this signal would interfere with rescue operations.

All vessels having knowledge of distress traffic, and which cannot themselves assist, are FORBIDDEN to transmit on the frequency of the distress traffic; but they should follow such traffic until it is evident that assistance is being provided. Always listen before transmitting. It is UNLAWFUL for any radio operator to WILLFULLY or MALICIOUSLY INTERFERE WITH or cause interference to ANY RADIO COMMUNICATION or SIGNAL. And no person shall knowingly transmit, or cause to be transmitted, any FALSE or FRAUDULENT SIGNAL of DISTRESS or COMMUNICATION relating thereto.

NOTE:—Since June 1, 1963 no new station licenses or renewals for marine radiotelephones have been issued by the FCC unless the sets are "type-accepted," meaning that specifications have been okayed as conforming to certain standards. As of the same deadline, the FCC requires that radio transmitters aboard vessels carrying more than 6 passengers for hire must have a power output of at least 25 watts.

Important changes affecting radio operation on boats went into effect October 1, 1962. With respect to log-keeping, simplified rules now require that (1) the time the set is in operation must be logged and (2) all distress calls in which the radio-equipped boat plays any part must be logged completely. A serviceman who makes changes in a radio transmitter must note the work in your log, including his name and address. It is the responsibility of the boat owner or operator to see that the log is properly kept.

Formerly transmitters were required to have at least three channels but under a new regulation transmitters and receivers having only the 2182KC frequency can now be licensed. This should appeal to boatmen interested in the radio solely as a safety measure. VHF (VERY HIGH FREQUENCY). Use of VHF is expected to become increasingly popular, and its applicability and availability should be checked by those contemplating purchase of a radio set. Range is about 20 miles between boats and 25-50 miles for ship-to-shore communication where the shore station has a high antenna. Lack of static and low interference from other stations should be attractive features. VHF has an international calling frequency of 156.8 megacycles, monitored by many Coast Guard stations and coastal harbor telephone stations. The frequency of 156.45 mc is available for use between boats and also for the use of shore stations owned by yacht clubs and marinas having mooring and anchoring facilities. Installation of VHF is simpler, requiring a shorter antenna (five feet) and no ground plate. At present, equipment is relatively more costly. In time it should relieve congestion on the air.

SEAMANSHIP IN BREAKING INLETS

CHAPTER XXVIII

ILLUSTRATED BY LESTER FAGANS

FOR a motor boat to proceed in safety at sea and to carry its passengers and crew in security and comfort from port to port along the coast, such a craft must possess certain hull characteristics. These are:

1. Stability   3. Propulsion   5. Strength
2. Buoyancy   4. Steering   6. Endurance

In the modern well-designed motor boat all of these six items of construction characteristics were designed and inbuilt into the craft by its creators when its lines were laid down on the drafting board. The elastic limits of safety in each case have been mathematically and accurately computed and are known with a proven degree of exactitude by test. Knowing that the boat would roll and might even capsize in violent sea conditions when immersed in her native element, her creators placed within her hull an invisible but powerful mechanical servant —her righting arm. Sufficient length and weight were given to this physical force to insure that the boat would return to an even keel in her struggles to constantly stabilize herself at sea and to withstand the ordinary rigors of wave formations, consideration having been given to the individual motor boat's size.

In these articles we are not concerned with ordinary wave conditions of the so-called trochoidal type met commonly off shore and far at sea but rather with the confused maelstrom found during a summer on-shore gale or strong wind before any breaking coastal inlet. The deceiving appearance of these seas, from an off-shore aspect, might overwhelm the unwary, the novice or the careless should he enter them in his boat unprepared or inexperienced. Under these conditions and upon entry into such surf, should a single one of the elements of boat construction enumerated above fail or become destroyed as a result of poor seamanship or inexperience, it is almost axiomatic that the destruction of the remaining five elements will rapidly follow and the boat and its crew may be lost.

The characteristics listed above are set down in order of importance as related to surf running in broken water and it becomes obvious, upon inspection, that the first requisite for a motor boat's safe passage through a breaking inlet is the *preservation of the boat's stability*. In other words, the boat must be handled with that degree of seamanship, as she drives through the racing inlet, that will insure that she will remain in an upright position.

Little that is comprehensive and authentic as to collective detail covering the many and varied phases of this subject's widely scattered components has been written. An effective treatise of all of them would be material for volumes. In our consideration of the subject as a whole we must keep in mind that all inlet conditions vary greatly and the speed, shape, cadence, and height

A MASTER SURFMAN DISCUSSES

THE TECHNIQUE OF HANDLING

MOTOR BOATS IN BREAKING SEAS

with which the seas crash onward to the land in violent crescendo are largely governed by the great compressive influence of bottom contour, bottom declivity and bottom channels.

It is difficult, therefore, to set down didactic direction for the guidance of the seaman when he enters broken water before a coastal inlet with his motor boat. The manufacturing of a norm of explanation must be approached with caution on account of the ever-changing wave behavior encountered in the field's dissimilar scope and the seamanship requirements and surf practices that are required by the many varied types of motor boat hull construction and speeds. The truth is that there is no norm. Safety and success in running broken surf depends almost wholly on the individual motor boat captain's brand of seamanship as suited to the particular hull under him.

In order to correctly evaluate most of the known components of adequate seamanship in breaking inlets, in relation to our research, we are forced to use applicable portions of the knowledge and experience of the master surfman, the naval architect and the engineer. Such a combination of human avocations fertilized in the brain of one individual during a single lifetime is rare indeed. No scientific studies, of record, of wave formations, heights, velocities, currents and counter-currents in any breaking inlet have ever been made.

We do know, however, from the collective experience of those who have spent their lives in surf, that as these great trochoids approach the beach from the sea, owing to the influence of bottom declivity, friction and compression are initiated and the sea wave rushing along at some 40 knots starts to decelerate but that its crest starts to climb and may reach a height of 50 to 60 feet with a crest speed of 25 to 30 or more knots, in some cases.

Imagine, then, in an ordinary on-shore gale, the difficulty of safe passage that confronts the motor boat captain as he lies before a breaking coastal inlet contemplating the cadence of the seas. Heaving in the trough in a hull whose water-planes, projected rudder area and shaft torque were designed for maximum efficiency at some 15 knots in the long and regular swells at sea, he now reflects, as he watches, that the ability of the same boat to now turn Mr. Hyde and carry him through the racing white mass off there to leeward, rests with his skill as a seaman, the strength and endurance of his boat and the integrity of his power and gear under stress.

Sensitive to the realization that when his boat was built her designers created her to go to sea and that it was not intended that she should cruise in steep, short seas whose height of crest might attain some 50 feet and roar along at a speed of 30 to 35 knots, he realizes that his boat was built as a compromise of naval architecture. He knows that the hiatus of difference between the required characteristics of the motor cruiser and those of the professional surf-boat were too great for the engineer's art to successfully bridge.

One of the illustrations shows a motor surf boat used commonly on both European and American coasts. It is impossible, in breaking surf, to destroy this motor boat's stability or impair her buoyancy—provided she is not holed. The illustration demonstrates her general hull lines; a future illustration will show the extent of her water-tight integrity—she is self-bailing and self-righting. Should sea water in any tonnage enter the motor boat in either of her open compartments that are exposed to the sea (passenger space forward and cockpit aft) these compartments would immediately free themselves through

When heavy seas are breaking on an inlet bar, the thing to avoid at all costs is a broach.
Here a sea has caught the boat on the port quarter and she is starting to go into a broach.

With nothing to hold her stern up to the sea, the boat illustrated on the previous page is shown here swinging broadside into broach. In this position, water will start to pour over the deck and coaming into the cockpit. When necessary to enter an inlet through heavy seas, it is imperative to keep the boat square before the seas, and avoid braking crests

freeing ports that are provided along her sides in the way of these spaces. Her deck under these compartments is water-tight and extremely strong. There is one case of record in which one of these boats, crossing a bad bar in extremely boisterous weather and bad surf conditions, rolled over three times and yet brought her crew through, hurt but alive.

In her short 36 feet of length she has six transverse bulkheads and two longitudinal ones. She has tremendous strength and weight (12 tons) in comparison with the ordinary motor boat of similar dimensions. She has a bar keel made up of two tons of cast lead. The boat has generous beam, 10 feet 8 inches. She is rather deeper than similar motor boats of her length, 5 feet 6 inch draft; she has moderate power for her size, 100 h.p., direct connected internal combustion engine. Her oak ribs are about half the distance on center as are those of the ordinary motor boat's frames and about 100 percent larger in size. Through heavy cypress planking she is put together with wood screws and her cost of construction with gear is in excess of $30,000—quite a price for a 36-foot boat with a speed of 9 knots. There is no boat in the world that is her equal or her better in surf, breaking or surging. She is sharp on both ends and her controls are water-tight.

Her items of equipment are simply but efficiently arranged and it is pertinent to note that her twin drogue pawls are mounted *on the center line aft;* more will be heard of this arrangement later. The boat has positive stability under any sea conditions and even though, with inexpert handling, she may turn over, she most surely will come back to an upright position as a result of the placement of her heavy bar keel and consequent low center of gravity. Her entire bottom is completely water-tight with the exception of her machinery space and she has buoyancy voids even above the water line, a cross section of which will be shown later on. To sink her she would have to be holed through about 80 percent of her bottom.

For the motor boat yachtsman or small boat operator it is obvious that it is neither desirable or possible to own or attempt to build a motor boat of the type described above. The cost of construction alone is prohibitive and the boat's ability to perform successfully in surf has been obtained by great sacrifice of other important seagoing qualities that are commonly found in comfortable and able boats of similar dimensions. Considerations of weight, economy, maneuverability, speed and leg-room would prohibit ownership of such a craft either as a yacht or workboat. Further than this, the boat is extremely lively at sea owing to her rapid and whip-like gyrations from one roll to another since the low and concentrated placement of her heavy keel results in an unnaturally low center of hull gravity which produces an extremely short rolling period.

For the average motor boat owner the designer is put to the task of creating a motor boat whose stability, while not the equal of the motor surf-boat, or positive under all of the conditions met in broken surf, is sufficient to insure the safety of the boat at sea under all wave conditions, provided she is handled with a reasonably good degree of seamanship, and will successfully cope with unfavorable wave conditions and even dangerous ones for a reasonable period of time.

It becomes apparent now that the motor boat owner who may, through emergency or other uncontrollable circumstance at sea, be forced to attempt passage of a breaking inlet in his boat, should understand something of, or sufficient of, the nature of the stability in the craft under him since his boat's stability plays so great a part in her performance the moment she enters the outer edge of the breakers.

Consider now the diagram illustrating the stern view of a motor boat rolling freely, easily and deeply in a seaway—actually the boat's action simulates that of a pendulum. Like the pendulum her hull has been set in motion by some exterior force. In this case the physical energy that is stored up in the sea waves has spent a portion of its force against the sides and bottom of her hull and precipitated motion in the form of rotation similar to that of the pendulum.

In the case of the pendulum the mechanical couple of force that is stored up between the suspended weight and the pivoted pendulum (which is capable of oscillation) has produced rotation, when an exterior force, such as the touch of a finger, has initiated motion. Now in a motor boat hull there exists a similar couple of forces which also produce rotation, the result and manifestation of which is rolling, the degree of the roll being controlled by the boat's center of gravity in relation to the boat's center of buoyancy.

Referring again to the diagram (right) of a boat rolling freely in a seaway, B is the center of buoyancy if the boat were in an upright position and immersed in still water. B' represents the boat's new center of buoyancy as related to the new position she assumed in a deep starboard roll from her original vertical state. CG is the center of gravity of the boat's mass. CG-M is called the motor boat's meta-centric height and is a measure of her initial stability or safety against capsizing. The higher M is above CG the greater will be the value of the righting arm and consequently the greater will be the tendency of the boat to right herself. GZ is the righting arm and the greater the length of this line, the greater will be the couple of forces tending to right or capsize the boat. Arrow W pointing downward through CG is the thrust of gravity tending to force the boat back to an even keel. Arrow W' pointing upward through B' is the center of the force of buoyancy and tends to lift the boat back to even keel—the force of buoyancy lift being centered through B'.

Now it is axiomatic that as long as the vertical line drawn through B' intersects the line BM above CG, the center of gravity, the boat is in a stable condition and will return to an even keel. Since the force of gravity acting through the arrow W is downward and the lift of buoyancy concentrated through the point B' is upward, a mechanical couple of forces is set up and will produce rotation in the direction of the arrow above the sketch at D. If, however, the vertical through B' should intersect the line B-CG below CG, the couple will produce rotation in the opposite direction than shown in the diagram at D, and the boat will capsize or, in surf, will go into a broach. This is clearly illustrated in the diagram showing the boat on her beam ends.

Preserve the Stability

It is apparent from the foregoing that the motor boat captain entering a coastal inlet where white crests are seen to be breaking must first *know what he is trying to accomplish* if he is to bring his boat and crew through it safely. His first consideration, then, in this direction, is the *preservation of the stability of his boat*. In the accomplishment of this, his personal skill as an able seaman is so intertwined and bound up with his boat's construction characteristics and her resultant behavior in boisterous surf that it is extremely difficult, or impossible, to separate the two.

That the boat must be kept squarely before the seas now as she approaches the outer breakers is an obvious mandate of good seamanship—that both of her bilges must rest squarely immersed on the back of the sea that will carry

her through the inlet is an imperative necessity for insurance that her rudder will act instantly and that her propeller will not beat the air. That her bulwarks must not dip into the spume so that she takes sea water aboard which would immediately affect her *stability* and buoyancy is a consideration of major import.

Her speed must now be carefully gauged. The boat must not be allowed to approach a crest, for once she

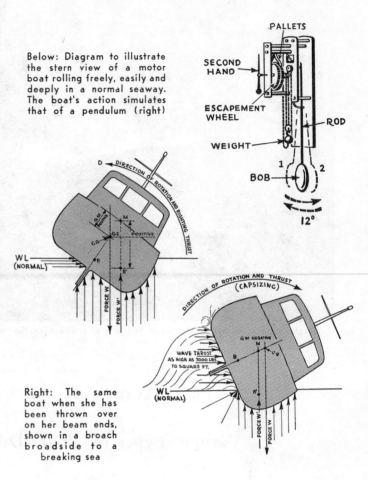

Below: Diagram to illustrate the stern view of a motor boat rolling freely, easily and deeply in a normal seaway. The boat's action simulates that of a pendulum (right)

Right: The same boat when she has been thrown over on her beam ends, shown in a broach broadside to a breaking sea

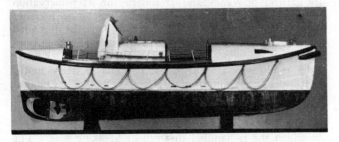

A modern motor surf boat. Unless she is holed, it is impossible to destroy her stability or impair her buoyancy

climbs near one of these racing tufts of scud there is no power on earth that will stop her run—neither must she be allowed to slowly slide downwards towards the slatch or hollows—if she should be overwhelmed in the trough the forces of hundreds of tons of sea water might tear her apart—the seas must be kept breaking ahead and astern of her at all costs.

The above are all considerations of the master seaman in broken surf. They are closely allied to all effort to preserve the motor boat's stability in a breaking inlet. Yet there are other important construction characteristics in-built into motor boats, the effect of which bears considerably on the performance of the small boat in surf. These effects must be explored fully before further considering methods of inlet seamanship. A concise understanding of all of the collective purpose of these details must be had in order that the dictates of good seamanship in breaking inlets may be more readily applied at the proper time.

Buoyancy! The submarine chasers of World War I withstood the incredible pounding of the short steep seas of the English Channel

A Discussion of the Differences in Handling

Various Types of Boat, Depending on Their Design

And the Speeds At Which They Can Be Driven

BUOYANCY is defined, according to Webster, as the resultant upward pressure of a fluid on an immersed object floating on the surface of a still liquid. When 35 cubic feet of water are displaced by any motor boat hull floating in salt water, sufficient buoyancy exists under the boat to support one ton of weight. Boats of generous beam and draft, with bottom area distributed over a large area of water, are usually found to be not only the most stable boats but also the buoyant ones.

The modern motor boat, therefore, with a good turn of speed, comes into its own in breaking surf in this respect and among the motor boats of the work boat class probably the Jersey beach fishing skiff from 18 to 40 feet in length, when properly handled, has no peer in breaking inlets. What this type of hull might lack in length of water planes underway it gains in freeboard and beam, the fullness of which, in most cases, is carried from the hull's point of entry of wetted surface, in operation, in almost a straight line to the stern.

Beyond this, these motor boats are powered with high horsepower for their size and tonnage which, transmitted to the propeller shaft, results in the production of tre-

mendous shaft torque. This becomes a large stabilizing influence in an open surf-boat which depends largely on its natural buoyancy and freeboard for its preservation in breaking seas, where safe and stable flotation together with sufficient fairness of hull contour must be depended upon to cope with the high wave speeds that are encountered at the entrance of coastal inlets in moderate on-shore gales. The upward thrust of buoyancy in these motor boat hulls at an immersion of 3 feet is roughly 192 pounds to the immersed square foot.

Now the location of the position of the center of buoyancy in any hull has a great influence on the manner in which she is handled in steep or breaking seas. The position of this center is largely controlled by the motor boat's designed water planes underway, the location and extent of her hull weights (machinery, equipment, etc.), her general dimensions, hull contour and shaft torque. There are other considerations affecting the location of her center of buoyancy but these are the main ones that concern us here.

Notice, now, the illustration showing a longitudinal section of the ordinary round-bilged surf boat whose dimen-

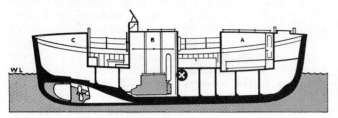

Longitudinal section of the ordinary round-bilged surf boat. The center of buoyancy is about where spotted. Numerous watertight compartments would serve to localize any threat to buoyancy by the entrance of water

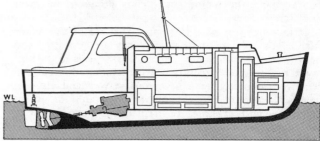

Above: Section of a conventional round-bilge slow-speed cruiser (10 knots). In steep seas she is handled like the surf boat (left, above) but, because she has no watertight compartmentation, great care must be exercised to prevent entrance of sea water into hull

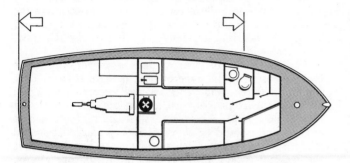

Center of buoyancy, longitudinally and transversely, falls about at point X, somewhat abaft of amidships when underway

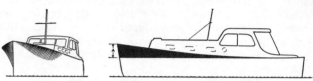

Much of the reserve buoyancy forward in newer, faster semi-displacement types of hull is gained by flare (shaded area, above, left) and sheer (black area "A", above right). Buoyancy aft is great due to extreme beam at the transom. Note, in the plan at left and drawing below, how her water planes underway differ from those of slower types of hull. The slow and fast types call for different methods of handling

sions are roughly 36 feet by 10 feet 6 inches by 5 feet 6 inches. Compare this with the illustration showing a typical section of the conventionally arranged and designed motor boat hull of similar dimensions with the exception of somewhat smaller beam and slightly less draft. Each hull is equipped with about 100 h.p. at 1000 r.p.m. motors. In both of these motor boats the center of buoyancy is in about the same locational plane and since the power and speed of both hulls are about equal (9-10 knots), it is evident that in steep seas both motor boats should be handled with about the same method of sea-

manship, due allowance being made for the great strength of the professional motor surf boat.

It is mandatory, for safe seamanship, that each boat of the type described should have the full length of its water planes in immersion at all times, regardless of sea condition, so that the center of buoyancy of each will remain as near as possible to its designed location. The center of buoyancy in all motor boats of the type described is approximately about the midship section, transversely and longitudinally, and your hull's greatest flotation effort therefore is centered through her midship section aided by the reserve

The faster type of modern cruiser, due to its design and speed, must be handled differently from the surf boat

buoyancy on the motor boat's ends produced by sheer and flare.

It is worthy of note in passing that all of the motor surf boat's areas of natural buoyancy are profusely and heavily compartmented. This, of course, gives to the hull great rigidity and strength in withstanding the crushing strains encountered in a boisterous seaway and also enhances the motor boat's ability to withstand for an indefinite length of time the tremendous pounding with which cycloidal seas will punish a small motor boat. She will wear out her crew before she tires herself.

The great boon, however, of this profuse compartmentation is her security from the hazard of free surface should a leak develop in any portion of her bottom. In this case, such an entering volume of seawater, that would otherwise surge at will over her bilges creating a hazard to her buoyancy and a threat to her stability through its rapidly shifting weight, is immediately localized by the water-tight compartments constructed within her bilges. If half of her bottom were ripped out she would still float on her water-tight decks with the aid of her secured reserve buoyancy from the water line to the top of her deck erections.

Should her passenger well forward and her cockpit aft become filled by a sweeping sea she would immediately free herself, for both spaces are self-bailing. No sea water can enter her bilges through any topside source since all her deck erections are water-tight against 100 pounds pressure and any apertures in her deck structures are secured by heavy dogs setting her hatch door knife-edges deeply in heavy rubber. There are no deck transoms or skylights installed. Any hatches are made of heavy bronze screwed into heavy recess rings installed in her deck. This motor boat was designed and built to steam *out of* a breaking inlet and into the face of seas that may reach 40 feet in height whose crest speed might exceed 30 knots. She is homely as a hedge fence but she is perfection in buoyancy, stability and security; even with lubberly hand-ling she is practically indestructible as she waddles her way through the breakers.

Look for a moment at the illustration of the motor boat with no watertight compartmentation. In the event that a cross sea either ripped her skylight open or tore the hatches from their coamings on either her trunk cabin or cockpit deck and three or four tons of sea water entered the hull, disaster would surely follow in the violence of the breakers. With the first roll that the boat took this uncontrolled mass of seawater, surging about the interior of the hull, would immediately seek the lowest level of the hull's depression, the boat would be hove down on its beam ends, and the chances are that the boat would never again be able to rise since her propeller would be jerked out of the water, her rudder control totally lost, her buoyancy invaded and her stability destroyed, which would insure her capsize. She has, of course, no bilge compartmentation and in the case of an uncontrollable leak developing in steep or broken seas the seawater would course through the entire length and breadth of her interior, rendering her, to say the least, uncontrollable.

The moral is, of course, that whenever you enter broken seas with this type of boat be sure that all deck hatches, transoms and vents are well secured and tight; all deck appurtenances such as anchors, life buoys and deck boxes should be securely lashed and no loose line or ends of lines should be above decks *any place*. It should all be stowed securely below—any loose line left about the decks or cockpit might end up in one of your screws. Any loose gear that might come adrift might go through your transom.

Extreme care and judgment as to the time of entry into the breakers should be used with these round-bilged slow boats. In an inlet that is breaking white across its entire width such an entry should only be made in the most pressing emergency and then only if the motor boat is equipped with an efficiently built drogue. Never attempt

Do not allow your boat to get close to the top of a crest. She might be hurled over the crest and pitch-poled into the trough below

to tow swamped dinghies or the ends of unsecured lines over the stern of your boat—you may not be able to get rid of the dink when you anticipated you should and it may be that the tender might board your boat and either kill some one or so damage the gear of your boat that you might lose control of her. This has actually happened.

A heavy or light line towed over the stern will always float and most certainly will find its way into your propeller in heavy surf. It is impossible either to see or anticipate what an unsecured bight of line hanging over your stern will do next or what direction it may take. It is also impossible to keep a strain on such a line for the reason that you are constantly engaged in the rapid manipulation of your throttle, to keep the seas breaking either ahead or astern of her and you are using radical and frequently large degrees of rudder angle in an attempt to keep her squarely before the seas.

Seas Have a Regular Cadence

It is true that all breaking seas before a coastal inlet during a strong onshore breeze have a regular cadence and, as the bottom slope starts to slow down the great ocean trochoids and build up their crests, smaller waves form after the passage of the large ones. Usually the smaller seas form in well defined locations and appear in regular cadence after several large seas have passed. If you are going to enter the surf you should do so at a time when you are sure of operating and maneuvering your way through the inlet in an area of seas of this type, keeping a close eye on the color of the water ahead of you and attempting, as best you can, to keep your boat in the darkest green of the water and measuring the break of the crests both ahead and astern of you.

The sea crests must be kept breaking ahead and astern of your boat for if you allow a sea to break aboard your motor boat, she might survive one such break if she were extremely well constructed and did not fill but it is difficult to imagine she would live through the second one to come aboard. Do not allow your boat to gather speed that might become uncontrollable. In this respect you must keep a close watch on the vertical movement of your bow and stern. Should your stern start to rise under you and your bow begin to descend, slow down your motor and let the sea roll under the total length of your immersed water planes and let it break ahead of you.

Do not try to ride the back of a sea with a full bilged boat; your hull was not designed to be efficient at the wave speed with which the sea is travelling and your torque is too low in value to give you much effective rudder control. If your stern begins to descend rapidly and your bow starts to rise, increase your r.p.m. and do so radically immediately; this is a sure sign that you are falling back into the trough and should your boat be sucked into the counter-current *travelling in the opposite direction than that of the crests* a sea may break on your boat at any time. Such counter-currents exist in the hollows of these steep seas and more will be heard of them later.

Using the Drogue As a Brake

Should your boat begin to run and you feel that you cannot stop her by closing the throttle, do not attempt to reverse her if seas are very bad; you may kite your stern around to port in an instant and hopelessly broach her. Use your drogue to break her. Keep your drogue lines clear and free and when you give the word to set the drogue keep everyone clear of the stern except the drogue tender. When your drogue "roots," its towline will straighten out like an iron bar and sing like a bow-string. Your boat will immediately start to slow down and you may find that by keeping your drogue rooted (set) and blasting your power wide open you have better control of her.

If you do not find this to be so, trip your drogue by simply releasing the tow line and the drogue will spill the instant it feels the touch of the trip line on its apex. Do not allow your boat to get close to the top of any crest; wave speed in this type of cycloidal sea is highest just before the crest is reached and in this position not even a drogue will stop her. Your boat might be hurled over the crest and pitch-poled (see the illustration) into the trough below. When you arrive in less boisterous water, slow down your boat and get your drogue aboard by slacking out on your tow line and heaving in on your trip line while you are going slowly ahead.

Remember that all of the foregoing are the usual tactics applied in breaking surf by experienced surfmen in *full displacement, round bilged* and normally slow boats. You could not apply this practice successfully to modern, well designed semi-displacement and fairly fast types of hull; all surf running in broken seas simply amounts to keeping a motor boat's center of buoyancy somewhere near its designed position in an attempt to preserve her stability and this is accomplished by keeping the boat, while she is maneuvering through breaking surf, on her designed water planes underway. The designed wetted surfaces of the modern motor cruiser differ greatly from those of the slow round-bilged boat in respect to length, breadth, contour and depth.

Handling the Modern Motor Boat

Now let us consider the modern type of motor boat. From simple inspection of the illustration of this type, it immediately becomes apparent that to attempt to handle boats of this type in breaking seas in a similar manner to those boats of the slow round-bilged types which we have discussed would be only to tempt fate. We first note that as a result of carrying out her lines of flotation in almost a straight line from her widest breadth somewhat forward of amidships to the stern her center of buoyancy underway has been shifted from the amidships section and falls somewhere abaft of the center section of the boat, somewhere about the point X. From an inspection of the illustrations, we note that the length of the modern boat's immersed water-planes is considerably shorter but that she has relatively greater beam than her slower type sister. We see that much of the reserve buoyancy in the newer type of hull forward is gained by deck sheer, flare and contour; her buoyancy aft is very great on account of her extreme beam at the transom. The exact length of her designed and operational water-planes underway is governed primarily by her trim and amount of shaft torque applied at her strut or struts.

It is well to remember here that, when you are about to enter breaking seas with your semi-displacement type hull, this is not the time to start monkeying with your normal trim. This statement is made *all books and articles on the subject to the contrary notwithstanding.* As you have found your boat's trim to be correct at sea under normal conditions—so it should remain when you start through a breaking inlet. Do not go shifting weights to the stern; by so doing you might slow down your boat at a time when all of the speed you can possibly get out of the hull might be the only requisite for a safe passage through the inlet. Once your correct trim has been established both by design and your own experience with your boat, let the boat alone. There are very definite reasons for the foregoing statement as applied to the modern semi-displacement type motor boat.

Throttle the Key to Control

The one variable over which you have direct and manual control, which will determine whether or not you shall keep your boat immersed fairly on its designed water-planes during your passage through the inlet is the *amount of shaft torque* (turning effort) that is applied to your shaft through the manipulation of your engine throttle. Your degree of judgment in the handling of your throttle and your dexterity and sensitivity to the urge of your helm are now the factors that are going to see you safely through the tumbling seas about you. Remember that your stern controls your bow and that your rudder's greatest point of efficiency is reached only as the highest shaft torque is applied to your screw and your rudder is fed a literal wall of hydraulic pressure surrounding both sides of its vertical surfaces against which its motion becomes effective at the instantaneous touch of your hand.

Again you must watch the seas closely and patiently before you attempt to enter the area of breakers. Judge, if you can, the speed of the slowest of the seas and make a decision as to whether or not you can handle your hull at the speed that the smallest groups of waves to leeward are traveling. You know from past experience with your hull, before a following sea, just about how much of a run your boat will take before she starts to become unmanageable. If you should decide that there is any element of doubt as to your ability to handle your craft at the speed with which the inlet seas are crashing onward to the land do not, under any conditions, attempt to enter the inlet. It is by far better to go to sea and spend a miserable night hove to than risk loss of life. Ordinarily, a hull whose designed full power is produced between 12 and 16 knots will stand a run in a seaway of about 17 to 22 knots before she starts to become difficult to control, provided she is not pounding. Twin screw boats will do somewhat better than this in steep seas that are traveling from astern.

When you have decided to enter the breakers, have streamed

your drogue, and selected your point of entry on the back (seaward side) of one of the smallest and slowest of the seas, approach the surf as near as possible at the speed of the sea that is going to take you through the inlet. Your drogue tow line should be secured over the center line of your transom; your trip line can be made fast to any cleat or samson post about the quarter—it does not matter as long as your lines have no chance of fouling. Mentally measure the length of the sea you are about to ride and so manipulate your throttle and rudder that your eventual position upon it will place you squarely on its horizontal center with your stern directly before the following seas.

Keep Clear of Breaking Crests

Watch her now and note her behavior as you gather speed; there is a possibility that you might ride the sea, if you have made a selection in the right group of seas, clear through the inlet without it showing any tendency to break. Should the sea show a proclivity to gather sufficient speed and accelerate itself to the point of breaking keep its crest well ahead of your bows. Take a quick glance astern now and then and note your position with respect to the sea that is breaking over your quarter. Should you find your boat uncomfortably close to the one that is breaking astern open your throttles immediately—don't wait until you can feel the suction of the slatch (undertow) pulling your hull back into the yawning hollow that lays just beyond your stern. Remember that that suction is travelling in a reverse direction to your own forward motion and there is a possibility that you might lose rudder control if you allow your boat to slide down the back of the sea and too close to this hollow vortex.

As you gather speed on your opened throttles and regain your correct and safe position on the sea's back, attempt to synchronize your speed to that of the sea as you race through; should your hull show a tendency to dip either gunwale or become tender at the quarters to the sea action racing from the direction of the stern slow her down again and straighten her up with your helm immediately. When she straightens up again and regains her normal position gun her again and keep her scudding along resting squarely on the full length of her normal water planes.

Breaking a Run

When she is out before it again and should she show a tendency to run and you feel that she might get out of control due to the great speed which you are now making, set your drogue immediately by simply releasing the trip line; by manipulation of your throttles, in bursts if necessary, keep sufficient torque applied to your shafts to guarantee you steerage in attempting to keep her squarely before the seas. As the drogue breaks her run and pulls you back from the crest, cautiously open your throttles without tripping the drogue. You may find that you have better control of her by keeping your drogue set and blasting the full discharge of her fast-turning screws into her rudders. In twin screw installations this is often found to be the case for your keel, held in the vise-like mechanical center of the slip-streams of both screws, now resists any tendency of the flying seas to broach her.

As she roars along, approaching the quiet water which can now be seen on the other side of the breakers, her speed seems to increase—20 . . . 21 . . . 22 knots the speed indicator clocks, her motors thundering under you, while the drogue digs a valley in the breakers astern and the tow rope sings in the spume. This is a thrill supreme. Its only equal in the world perhaps is the performance of the beach boys *riding the forward face* of the steeply breaking surf before the Waikiki Beach Hotel. Like the surfboard of the aborigine some of these modern hulls, intelligently handled and properly powered, are marvels in breaking surf.

Secure the Dinghy Aboard

Before closing this part of the discussion, it may be well to mention a word of caution regarding the towing of tenders upon the entrance to a coastal inlet under the conditions previously described. If the tender cannot be taken aboard and lashed down securely, bottom up, it is by far safer to cast the tender adrift and lose it rather than to attempt to tow it through the breakers. Once you enter the breakers you have no control over its gyrations whatsoever; your attention is necessarily bent in the direction of keeping your boat in a stable condition and it is impossible for a crew member to exercise any control of it at all while your boat is charging through the surf. A towed tender may capsize, interfere with your drogue lines or actually come aboard of your boat. There is a case of record in which a fisherman (200 tons and 92 feet in length) towing a heavy seine boat, in which a large seine was being carried, while crossing a badly breaking bar on the southeastern coast of the United States, was broached and beached with a loss of six of her crew. This happened as a result of the seine boat boarding the ship, due to the unequal speeds of the two craft in the breakers, killing the engineer and two of the crew members on deck, while the seine fouled the vessel's screw and the ship became helpless in heavily breaking seas. She was beached ultimately with the loss of three more of her crew from the decks.

Should the tender capsize, it would immediately act as a stern anchor as a result of which your motor boat would be immediately swept by a sea and the water-tight integrity of your hull would be instantly invaded, to say the least. If it should foul your drogue lines it might take charge of the operation of the drogue and set it at a time when such an occurrence might result in disastrous disadvantage to your motor boat, laboring in the breakers, or, vice-versa, it might release the drogue at a time when operation advantage might require that the drogue be set and deeply rooted. A tender, therefore, should either be brought aboard and securely lashed bottom side up to the deck or if this is impractical the tender should be cast adrift.

The modern fast sea skiff is among the ablest of small boats in breaking inlets

439i

How Waves Are Generated—The Trochoidal Type

Of the Open Sea and the Breaking Cycloid in Shallow

Water on the Coastal Shelf and at Inlet Bars

AS a motor boat skipper, you are not likely to get into difficulty with your craft in steep, following seas until the speed of those seas approaches and exceeds the speed of your boat.

Sea speed and wave height in breaking inlets depend largely on the depth of breaking, depth to the bottom, rapidity and degree of bottom compression, depth and disposition of bottom obstructions, and state of the tide and currents. Sea contour and shape, in conjunction with the foregoing, are in the main controlled by direction and force of the winds; angular approach of the swells to the inlet bars; and the direction and positional relation of bars (when a number of them are present) to the

are present or where multiple bars extend in divergent directions. To go back to the beginning, sea waves, in general, are creatures begot from the winds over the oceans. Their speed and direction at sea are directly dependent upon the speed and direction of the winds. In a Western Ocean winter gale, as a result of the wind's blowing heavily in one direction for several days, storm waves of over 1,000 feet in length with wave speeds of 71.6 feet per second (about 42.5 to 43 knots) are commonly met by large express passenger vessels. Progress of even the largest and most powerful of these ships is seriously hampered, if not stopped, by these graybacks— trochoidal seas.

The cycloidal type of wave breaking on a bar. Hitting it obliquely, it starts to break where it first feels the effect of shoaling. Note especially the steepness of the crest

others. plus the direction and dimensions of bottom channels.

Knowing the speed of the wind and with an intimate knowledge of local bottom conditions, the type of breaker, approximate wave height and wave speed can be predicted with a fair degree of accuracy in individual localities. However, the statement contained in Part One of this series regarding the futility of attempting to prescribe didactic directions for the motor boat man about to enter breaking seas before a shallow coastal inlet is still true. The bottom approach to every inlet varies widely as to depth, declivity, bottom contour, number of bars and their position in relation to each other and bottom obstructions.

The most difficult of these coastal inlets to run before steeply peaked seas are those where outer and inner bars

It is a common occurrence for these great ships to be forced to heave to in the heavy gusts and the largest of the seas. Hull strains encountered in storm waves reaching heights of 37 to 44 feet are such that even the largest of these powerful vessels might suffer severe damage if not navigated with caution. A ship is but an extended steel girder and it *is* possible to bend it.

The waves of such a storm area at sea travel rapidly out of the locality of the gale and approach the land after a passage of many hundreds of miles in the form of swells. That these swells travel great distances in a relatively short time can be attested by any boatman who has observed the heavy swells outside of the breaker line and surf pounding on the Jersey beaches 650 to 1,000 miles in advance of a tropical hurricane the center of which might be located in the West Indies, a couple of days previous to the actual arrival of the gale itself.

Where such a storm changes its direction, the tendency of these trochoidal swells, as they advance toward the beach, is to decrease both in length and height. As they arrive at the outer inlet coastal bars in rapid succession, even with no storm winds driving them onward, their speed and volume are still considerable and thus, even in fine cruising weather beyond the breaker line, extremely heavy surf may be seen pounding the beaches while high, confused breakers assault the inlet jetties. Should the storm continue in the direction in which the swells have approached the land, such inlets become impassable except to the professional surf-boat.

Basically, then, breaking seas in coastal inlets are precipitated by winds either of the local area variety or may be caused by those of some distant storm area. The characteristics, contour, speed and condition of wave heights before a breaking coastal inlet, however, are another matter.

For his own safety the cruising motor boat man should learn to identify the two primary classes into which sea waves fall. See illustrations. The storm sea that we described in the first part of this series, racing at 30 or more knots beyond the 90-fathom curve and attaining

are met at sea as well as before breaking inlets. These are creatures of wide shoal water areas where shoalness exercises a great effect in the steepening of wave crests and the shortening of seas into vicious cycloids as the result of the wind's blowing over the sea for a prolonged period in one direction. Southern reaches of the North Sea and the westerly portion of the English Channel are world famous for their creation of breakers of this type for sustained periods. Such waves, like their inlet cousins (of the breaker type) are dangerous to small boats. Equally, they constitute a hazard to large ocean freighters. Owing to the length of these vessels, they may be forced to straddle three to four such seas, thereby setting up within hull structures severe sagging and hogging strains under which their collective girder strength might buckle.

With regard to the above, in passing, it is interesting to note the record of the American submarine chaser of World War I in those tumultuous breakers in the English Channel and North Sea during the winters of 1917 and '18. The chaser itself was probably an accident of birth—she was never meant to be a surf boat—but she acquitted herself in those distant and seething breakers as probably the greatest motor surf-boat of all time.

Deep-sea wind waves, as they advance to the shore,

In steep seas, the boat must be kept away from the crests. With sufficient
power, this skiff can ride the back of one sea right through the inlet

wave heights of over 40 feet, are generated from swells of the trochoidal type as a result of wind pressure in some distant or local area. They attain great lengths but seldom break except under the influence of storm winds and become confused only as a result of winds of hurricane force; in gusts or squalls, they become dangerous to large ships. It is possible to find these trochoidal type swells present in a delightful cruising area, beyond the beach line, where no wind is apparent. Should you find such a situation you had best watch your barometer for these swells may easily portend difficulty for your boat upon return to your inlet if such return is to be delayed more than three to six hours. Slopes approaching the peaks of such sea waves are long and gradual.

In the second or cycloidal type of sea wave, with which we are mainly concerned, it is well to know that these

do not progress landward as phalanxes of motional regularity or in consistent direction. In the course of their travel, they may either lose or gain some of the speed of transmission, and they may approach the beach from divergent directions. Since they advance over great distances from the locality of their origin they may travel either in the same direction in which the winds were moving that generated them or, having passed through areas where swells advancing from other localities were met, they may take on a new direction. It is entirely possible, therefore, that an observer on the beach may, at times, behold heavy breakers crashing into an inlet entrance against the prevailing local winds. In other words the direction of the prevailing off-shore winds in the locality in which the motor boat captain might be cruising offers no assurance that he will not be confronted

Coast Guardsmen are experienced in the handling of boats in heavy weather.
At Yaquina Bay, Ore., this 52' motor lifeboat goes out on routine winter patrol

Two-hundred-foot sea waves (typical of a mid-August blow in northern latitudes) approach the inlet bars at a speed of about 20 knots and with a shortened wave period of about 6.2 seconds. In the case of the 1,000-foot wave pounding into any coastal inlet bar at a wave speed of 42 knots such a confused sea and steep breakers would result as to definitely preclude inlet navigation to small boats. The inlet would be impassable. Were it possible to place a 35-foot motor boat on the back (seaward side) of one of these roaring cycloids, its captain would find that his bow had risen some 45 to 50 degrees from its normal horizontal plane. The motor boat would probably go into a reverse pitchpole and upend backwards as a result of its fore and aft stability being destroyed. Of course, it would be entirely unmanageable as a result of the excess of wave speed over that of its own top hull speed.

In the latter case, considering the breaking effect of the 200-foot wave, depending on bottom depths, number and related positions of inlet bars, bottom declivity and channel contour, the inlet would very likely be passable, but extremely dangerous. Such seas are fast enough to produce breakers of the so-called plunging type which, owing to their speed, height, shortness of wave period and steepness, are capable of producing chaotic conditions to confront the small boat operator contemplating entrance through them.

Even sea waves of 100 feet in length with a surface speed of 13.4 knots and a wave period of 4.4 seconds, passing over a bar whose submerged depth is 15 feet, have been known to produce a plunging type breaker with a height of 14 feet, almost equal to the depth. Now a 15-foot breaker with another one 4.4 seconds behind it is a dangerous proposition to the small boat captain who finds himself scudding before it. If he ever needs that old propeller torque blasting its solid and uninterrupted stream of water down onto his rudder surfaces, he

with badly breaking inlet conditions upon his return to his particular inlet.

Ordinarily, any motor boat operator who must return to his home port through any coastal inlet should keep himself generally informed as to over-all weather conditions, even those existing far at sea, as a hedge against what he can expect for inlet sea conditions between the time of his departure from the jetties and the time of his return. Lacking such knowledge, he should consult his barometer frequently and should any deviation from its ordinary height be observed he must view this occurrence as a cause for caution.

From storm areas trochoidal seas and swells move in the direction of the land in groups or, as some observers have put it, in trains of swells. Deep-water waves advancing on the land from any wind area are not uniform as to wave height, wave period or speed. As they approach and pass over the coastal shelf their entire complexion as to contour and characteristic rapidly changes to that of the shorter-period steep cycloid, owing to the influence of rapid bottom shoaling and other various bottom conditions and obstructions peculiar to the locality.

A 1,000-foot storm wave, for instance, after it crosses the 100-fathom curve, begins a rapid process of slow-down mainly owing to bottom friction and the compression of declivity but it starts to build up in height and steepness, as a result of decreased depth and compression, from a wave speed of some 42.4 knots and a wave period of 14.0 seconds (passing of two successive crests by a fixed point) until it finally crashes into the outer bar of a coastal inlet perhaps reduced in length to some 400 to 600 feet and slowed down to a speed of 26.8 to 32.7 knots. The wave period has now been shortened to, roughly, 11 seconds. A lot can happen in a period of 11 seconds to a motor boat operating in breakers — you have little time to change your mind.

Confused inlet conditions are created when seas strike a bar at several angles. In some cases it is impossible to keep a boat squarely before the sea

needs it now! Should you consider this statement slightly extravagant, just go up to the gutters on your roof and visualize what would happen to a 5- or 6-ton mass of wooden construction, capable of being moved in four directions at once but advancing at a speed of 15 to 20 knots over the ground, should it be hurled down from such a height. Do not forget in a situation of this type that, unless your boat is expertly handled, you may have a portion or all of the speed of translation here to contend with (speed of the wave plus the speed of the boat).

Factors Affecting Breaker Height

Breaker height, it has now been seen, depends on the height of deep water waves approaching the coast, the depth of the water over bars which they must pass before coursing into an inlet, the strength of local winds (at times), and general bottom topography. Tides, state of the tide and currents also affect their height in a contributory sense. Practically the same components govern their speed with the exception that influence of currents and the state of tide has a more pronounced effect on the speeds of breakers *before inlets* than they do on height. The *depth* of breaking also influences their speed. Any or all of these components might operate in conjunction before inlets whose contour and general topography or bar condition produces them all. On the other hand, but a single one or two of them might be present and yet produce the greatest of breaker confusion.

Direction and contour of the breakers meeting bottom bars from the sea are often governed largely by the angular approach of the ocean waves to such bars as they meet before inlets. Should the swells arrive in an oblique direction to that of the submarine bars, that end of the swell which makes first contact with these obstructions will break sharply over the bar end and the remaining portion of the wave may swing about the bar, in a wide turn, refracting as it breaks against the remaining length of bar. We have already seen that bottom channels, the shape of submarine shelves and bottom obstructions such as ledges and heavy boulders lying in diverse directions also contribute their influence to the contour of inlet breakers.

Effect of Outer and Inner Bars

Now knowing all of the foregoing it would seem reasonable to conclude that the most hazardous inlet conditions that the entering motor boat captain might expect to meet will be encountered before inlets where outer and inner bars are present on the ocean's floor. A submerged outer bar lying at a depth of 35 to 40 feet upon impact of such seas immediately slows down the first portion of the on-rushing trochoid to a speed of probably 20 to 22 knots and at the same time bottom compression deflects a large portion of its volume upwards and the wave "breaks" upon the surface of the sea. When it peaks up to the point that its top becomes unstable, the wind whips off its crest and the wall of solid water, now risen to a height of 18 to 20 feet, crashes into the trough.

Its crest having been formed and its contour well defined, the breaker, driven on by the remainder of its initial sea-speed, now roars across the intervening space of sea until it again begins to feel the shoaling over the inner bar and the compression of its shallower declivity. As a result of this further compression or squeeze and the wave's meeting the inner bar at a different angle of approach and contact, a perfect welter of confusion now exists on the surface of the sea and it may well be possible that the observing motor boat man offshore would not be able to find *any safe path* or channel through such confused breakers before the inlet jetties.

Where Channels Are Oblique to the Sea

Jones Inlet, hard by Fire Island on the south shore of Long Island, is a notorious example of this type of breaker confusion, resulting, in a driving southeaster, from the presence of outer bars lying on the ocean's floor in divergent directions, thus forcing the seas to meet them at different angles of approach. Even in quite mild weather where ocean swells are present and are rolling in here at speeds varying between 12 and 15 knots, passage of such an inlet channel might be difficult and even hazardous. No small boat operator should enter such an area without a reliable local pilot unless he possesses an intimate knowledge of the bottom contour of the vicinity in which he proposes to operate in breakers. Low-powered motor boats, small boats with hydroplane-type bottoms, outboard-driven boats with low freeboard and flat bottom sections, and small sailboats should use extreme caution in attempting to

navigate in such areas. Their operators should be watchful of weather conditions and cognizant of local forecasts. It should be pointed out here that where a winding and angular channel presents itself as the only navigable path through confused breakers, high freeboard in motor boat construction is a prime essential, high propeller torque is a vital necessity, and instantly responsive engine power in large amounts must be available. Almost any type of sailboat in breakers is a bad risk.

Breaker cadence before such inlets as Jones Inlet is entirely unrecognizable during the times of a heavy on-shore blow. The changing direction of the channel and the presence of the outer bar in angular relation to the inner obstruction (bar) simply destroy the contour and recognizable profiles of any wave trains between the two bars under the influence of heavy, onshore winds.

Breaker Cadence Destroyed

The entrance to Scituate Harbor on the coast of Massachusetts is a similar locality in which breaker cadence disappears and becomes unrecognizable in any wind that is blowing hard from the eastward, onshore. The same effect that is produced before Jones Inlet in relation to the destruction of well-defined breaker and swell cadences is repeated before the jetties at Scituate, however, from differing bottom conditions. Though the channel before the jetties at Scituate runs in lengths that are fairly straight, the bottom that surrounds this pathway through the gradually rising ocean floor is strewn with giant boulders and long and irregular bottom ledges lying close to the channel edges, scattered in all directions in a wide area of open sea before the inlet. These ledges are barely submerged, during periods of low water, and under the influence of a driving easterly, across the full sweep of Massachusetts Bay, a mass of breaking and white confusion is produced that may easily awe even the hardiest local professionals.

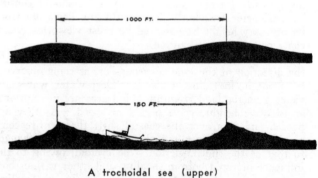

A trochoidal sea (upper)
and cycloidal type (lower)

Look at the height of the sea (breaker) that has assaulted Minots light that stands like a sentinel before its entrance. This lighthouse structure lacks but three feet of stretching its warning finger 100 feet into the heavens. Two previous structures were destroyed by the strength of the breakers, and the breaker that you see in the second of the sketches has reached its height of breaking (about 30 feet). The breaker seen in the first sketch is a coastal breaker but in the process of development crashing against the base structure of the same light; its height at the time of meeting the base structure of the light is about 10 feet. Note the steepness of the angular approach to the breaker's crest (nearly 45 degrees). Even a 10-foot breaker can offer difficulties to the small motor boat man who may be uninitiated or unwary.

Watch Surface Swells

So—get out your chart, irrespective of the direction of the local wind as you lie before a breaking inlet—watching. Remember: the breakers hold their secrets well, and the winds that blow before these breaking inlets are fickle indeed. During the summer months on the Atlantic seaboard they have been recorded as changing as many as twenty times in twenty-four hours. So, when you lie around fishing before one of these inlets, keep one eye peeled on the nature of the surface swells as they lazily roll in from over the horizon, and the other on your barometer. Don't wait "until it starts to get rough." An inspection of your bottom chart may assist you in making the correct decision, right now.

(Use the chart for all the information it can give you, but remember that channels and shoals shift so fast at many inlets that buoys cannot be indicated on the chart, and buoys at times may not mark the best water.—Ed.)

Leaving the "I-love-you" (1—4—3) flash of lonely Minot's over the quarter and picking up the long, piercing fingers of the Highland about a point off the starboard bow and coursing it down until we bring it abaft the beam a few degrees, we turn west and south down past the booming beaches of the southerly side of Cape Cod—the natives call it "the back side." Down over the shoals we run, wind northwest, force 2, and picking up a little, barometer slowly rising. She's making good time—getting a little push from the light northwester and rolling easily in the swells that seems to be coming from a general northerly direction. We cross the gulley (Hudson River Canyon) and seem to lose some of the swell. In the early hours of the morning Atlantic City Light stabs through the loom of the half-twilight in staccato sweepings and gleams, between periods, in friendly beckoning. Swell rising somewhat now, as we roll along over the coastal shelf.

Use Judgment Before Entering

The beach line into which Atlantic City Inlet cuts its long length of passage runs roughly in a north-northeast and south-southwest direction. Ordinarily therefore, a northwester, even though it may be blowing force 3 to 4, may not compel the small boat captain to seek shelter on any course to the northward provided he just clears the seaward end of the fish trap stakes in his progress up the beach. Should he mistakenly reason, however, that *since the wind is off the beach* either Atlantic City or Manasquan would offer convenient shelter in the event of the wind's hardening, he will be well warned to inspect bar conditions off both inlets before attempting entrance. In a moderately fresh offshore breeze, where strong flooding tides or currents run heavily against the wind, breaker heights and speeds build up in certain long inlets that, at times, may preclude passage of such channels even to the professional surf-boat man. Under such weather conditions, even in the upper reaches of Atlantic City Inlet, half a mile from the entrance and well inside, breakers clear and solid may be observed going over the railroad structure.

In spite of assurances by local professionals and beach captains that this popular inlet is never impassable to those who possess an intimate knowledge of local bar conditions, this simply is not so. The inlet is a long and dangerous one and, owing to the duration of time that the motor boat captain must spend traversing its extended

length through the short steep breakers, his boat may take a severe drubbing before she rides her last sea on through the other side of the bridge structure. In this inlet one must make the correct decision first; you cannot turn around when you are half way through it, should you decide you cannot control your boat in the steepness and speed with which the breakers are roaring up the inlet, or as you see the light buoy dip its lantern. The beach over there on the westerly side of the inlet is very hard and you have a long way to go to find a worse spot to be in, if you attempt to turn the bow of your boat into the breakers.

Where the Beach Is Steep

A few miles up the beach, to the northward, lies another artful Charybdis jutting her jettied fingers out into the surf—Manasquan. An ebb tide and the arrival of heavy sea swells off the inlet bar here simply create a havoc of white confusion; heavy wind need not be present. However, as opposed to the bottom topography off Scituate, which destroys the cadence and natural contour of sea swells on their arrival over the shoals, before Manasquan the average motor boat man can recognize the swells arriving in their trains and groups even in moderately boisterous weather. Beach declivity here is steep, and high-speed breakers start to build up in height about the 30-foot curve. From that point shoreward the wedge of rapidly shoaling bottom accelerates their tendency to climb until, at less than $\frac{1}{8}$ mile to seaward of the jetties, breakers of 8 to 10 feet in height have been observed with speeds over the bottom of about 14 to 15 knots in weather off the beach that might be considered moderately good cruising weather, offshore. Even if you were able to pass successfully through these seas, with a period of less than 5 seconds and a degree of steepness that would probably put the bows of your boat at an angle of about 35 to 40 degrees from her normal horizontal plane, the seas as they pass over the 16-foot shelf crossing the mouth of the inlet drop abruptly down into 7 feet of channel depth between the jetties and roar up the alley formed by the stone buttresses, their hollows sometimes exposing the bottom of the inlet between crests. Any boat, if she did not become unmanageable before her nose got inside the stone breakers, would be smashed here, on contact with the bottom, in seas like this.

If you intend to do any inlet running in bad weather, look to your gear. Confidence in the craft under you is the supreme requisite.

Sailboats and auxiliaries, as a rule, should be kept out of breaking inlets. The Friendship sloop (above) does fairly well in breakers up to five or six feet in height

Approaching the bar, look for the dark water, indicating the best depth, and keep out of the white water of the breakers

Some Thoughts on Bottom Design;

Effect of Currents on Breakers;

Use of Oil and the Drogue;

Handling a Skiff in the Breakers;

Suggestions for Sailing Craft

Much information has been made available to the motor boat man, both scientific and practical, concerning static surf conditions on open beaches and procedures for safe landing through them. Men have made professions of the surf's mastery and many texts are replete with knowledge of such tactics. Not so the inlet, however. Breakers, both of the coastal variety and those surging before a coastal inlet, offer difficult situations for the procurement of exact scientific data, since this is attended by considerable risk.

The motor boat captain must not confuse recommended practices for landing through beach surf with the running of coastal inlets before which white water is surging. Static surf conditions on open beaches are widely dissimilar to the almost organized confusion of wild breakers coursing over an inlet bar. Neither is the regularity of surf or the cadence of its swells affected by so many unseen but compelling components of force, and factors of form, speed, height and direction, as is the inlet breaker.

Never attempt to back your boat into a breaking inlet. Were you to try this in a modern semi-displacement hull, your quarter would be seized by the seas and you would be broached long before your beam was parallel to them. Should you escape this situation and ultimately find your bows facing the breakers, you would immediately lose steering control; if you attempted to gun your motor to give you sufficient rudder effect to hold her head up to the breakers, you would either plunge her nose under a breaker or stave in your bows.

Oil, before a badly breaking inlet, is valueless. The action of bottom declivity in forcing seas to break at such precipitous heights allows the wind to get under their crests and scatter the crest spume in all directions. The shortness of the breaker period continuously breaks the hold of the oil's viscosity upon the surface and scatters the oil with the spume in all directions. The use of oil in breakers on the coastal shelf is another matter and has much to recommend it, since the breaker period is much longer. This is particularly true where towing operations are imminent or in progress. Placing a tow line aboard a disabled boat or taking the crew off a distressed craft is often facilitated by using an oil slick to windward. If you think, however, that the condition of the breaking inlet is so bad as to warrant the use of oil, stay out of it if possible. Go to sea and heave her to, if necessary, for there never was a boat built, that was capable of keeping the sea, that will not heave to on some quarter and in some direction.

Do not attempt to tow another boat (especially a sailboat) through a breaking inlet. Collision is almost a certainty.

The use of a surf line as an aid in entering a breaking inlet is attended with danger to those who might be tending the line. Should you attempt to hold your boat's head up with such an arrangement you might jerk the samson post out of her or shatter the bow section. Cross seas or current might fling the stern of your boat across the jetties, for you have no control of her at the end of a line. Unlike beach surf, the direction of breaking seas before a coastal inlet is by no means constant. Remember that high surf on open beaches is influenced and precipitated to a much greater degree than are the breakers before a coastal inlet by the local direction of the winds. Surf in beach localities is usually at its greatest height during the course of an on-shore gale or high wind. The steepness of these beach breakers is ordinarily governed by declivity, the length of the swell train as it arrives on the beach from the ocean, and the length of time the wind has been blowing in force in one direction. The cadence of such beach surf is usually much more regular and discernible.

We have discussed elsewhere the proclivity of Manasquan to break with no wind present in its viciny or with the wind blowing off the beach, yet precipitating breakers before its entrance of such short period and height as to preclude safe passage through it in an ordinary motor boat. Likewise, before Atlantic City, combinations of bottom topography, channel contour, tides, currents and obstructions produce collateral effects on breakers that the surfman operating on an open beach may never meet.

A three or four-knot current flowing in heavy volume out of a narrow inlet and funneled into a restricted opening will bore into the base of a concaved on-rushing breaker and all but stop the turbulent water there. At the same time it tends to force the crest higher while the residual speed of the breaker drives that crest on over its stalled hollow, which may have reversed its direction now in obedience to the current's influence. Rising in great height to the point of instability, it crashes down into the trough—this, every 4.5 seconds. Add to this the natural flow of recession—for the pounding breakers ascending the bar must find their way back to the sea—and you can see why counter-currents in the trough may travel in a direction directly opposite to that of the breaker's crest.

In surf on open beaches where such currents exist in lesser extent it is called undertow. You can feel it seething about your ankles as your feet sink into the beach sands. As the current flows back in recession to the sea, it undermines the sand that bears the weight of your body. Should you advance too close to the breaker zone the undertow might seize your body and draw it into the vortex of the pounding surf.

In heavy breakers before a coastal inlet you can feel that current clutching at your boat's bottom. The laboring exhaust will warn you as it changes its note. With one eye watching the seas over the side you can see her slow down and feel a tension peak in the hull vibrating under you. Naturally, therefore, the best position for your boat as you enter the breaker zone is about the horizontal center of the sea's broad back. Should you ever sense the clutch of that counter-current, *open your throttle wide, instantly*. You understand, now, why we said that plenty of power *must* be available at the touch of your finger tips.

If you have a drogue set, trip it right now. Every drogueman that knows his business always carries a sharp, heavy knife or has an axe within reach. She may labor a little in the twenty seconds (that seem an hour) it takes to claw her way clear, but keep forcing her. As she shakes herself free and you feel the tension on her hull slacken a bit, be careful to close the throttle some. If you approach the top of the crest where the speed of the breaker is highest, you risk being hurled over in a pitchpole.

In inlet areas where the range of the tide may vary between 6 and 12 or more feet the state of the tide exerts a strong influence on the breakers. Here, between the two extremes of tide, there exists a varied condition of sea contour, speed and height. This may be due to differing degrees of beach declivity being presented to the breakers between the two tide depths or to the increased or lessened effect of bottom obstructions before the inlet. In approaches to those inlets where the bottom has no submerged obstructions such as bars, ledges or both scattered about and where the degree of beach declivity is almost pleateau-like, breakers of less steepness can usually be expected at low water than at higher states of the tide. Scituate and Manasquan are both affected by rapid rise of the ocean floor at high stages of the tide. Before Scituate, though, this characteristic is complicated by the presence of large ledges and huge boulders, lying all over the bottom.

The effect on an inlet breaker's wave period and its height produced by currents flowing into it, across it or in a direction oblique to it is always greatest when the current is at its maximum strength in either direction. No general rules can be laid down for the guidance of the motor boatman confronted with the confusion of white water created where steep breakers and cross seas tear about the inlet's mouth as a result of such

The sketch below illustrates how waves of the open sea, encountering shallow water on bars at the entrance to inlets, may form breakers which must be avoided at all costs by the boatman running an inlet. At A and B, at the crests, the velocity is the highest—in this case, 22 knots for waves that are advancing with a speed, at C and D, of 15 knots. At E a swell is shown starting to peak up as it feels the effect of the beach declivity, G. At F, the direction of currents of recession and the undertow is reversed, with a speed of 2 to 3 knots. The boat is shown with drogue set, the tow line attached to a bridle at the large end. The trip line to the smaller aft end is slack, and if the boat must gain speed to escape a breaker astern, the trip line will be hauled in to upset the drogue

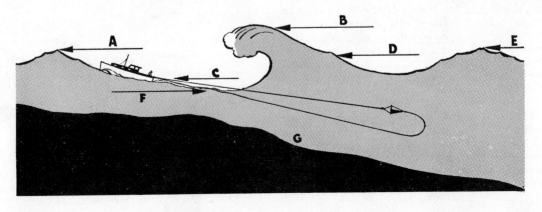

bottom topography, current and tidal effects. Safe passage of the inlet *must* take all of these considerations into account. It is mandatory to enter the breakers at a time when the wave period is at its greatest length and the lessened wave heights are at their lowest value of steepness. This period occurs about twenty minutes before reversal of the tides in either direction. We cannot separate the effect of any single one of these varied components on inlet breakers. We must consider them collectively, since we are dealing with a complicated collateral result on a fluid substance that moves in all directions at the whim of winds, tides and currents. Wave cadence, in most cases at this time, seems to be more regular and discernible.

It is of interest to record here a few impact pressures of inlet breakers accurately obtained as a result of dynamometer tests in shoal water areas, in pounds per square foot.

Height of breaker	Pressure per sq. foot (pounds)
4-foot	406 lbs.
6 "	3,000 "
10 "	4,562 "
20 "	6,083 "

The height of one of the highest cycloidal type breakers was recorded in the North Sea—43 feet. Sea trochoids will *also* break under the lash of prolonged winds of gale force or the hurricane. Bars they meet far off shore will produce breaking seas. The Pacific probably produces the highest of such breakers for over the long reaches or fetch of that ocean, winds blow for thousands of miles in one direction for protracted periods, commonly building up crest lengths of over 1,000 feet during the winter period. The Columbia River bar, during periods of high on-shore winds or protracted gales in the same direction, commonly produces breakers of between 55 and 60 feet in height. These prohibit the passage of 10,000-ton ships. Green water descending on a ship of this size in such tonnage as a breaker that high would produce would tear apart any assembled structure similar to a ship floating on the ocean's surface, with the exception of a sphere—*contour* again.

The highest sea trochoid, whose height was ever accurately computed, was observed by the navigating officer of the USS Ramapo during a protracted gale in the North Pacific during the winter season of 1933. The method of computation and circumstances under which the observation was made were recorded in Naval Institute Proceedings some years ago. In the English Channel strong currents alone have been known to produce breakers some 25 feet in height and about 250-270 feet in length. They can give the staunchest steel ship an astonishing punishment. A series of unending breakers of such dimensions assaulting the hull structure of a ship or boat about its forward flat keel sections with trip-hammer blows, delivering a wallop of about 4,500 pounds per square foot every 7.7 seconds, has been a fatal test for many a ship at sea, of either wooden or steel construction.

Looking back at the table showing the force of breakers crashing against any flat surface at an angle of 90 degrees, one marvels that any kind of vessel can withstand the impact of such blows. The answer lies in the designer's dexterity to fashion hull contour so it will deflect such blows and distribute the force of impact, or divert it from the hull. Sturdiness of hull structure is also paramount. Demands for speed and comfort tend to interfere, at times, with the accomplishment of such a purpose. Often the designer, as a result, has been forced to compromise, and to deviate from the age-old principle of the strongest type of construction ever known—spherical or ring-type.

The frigate United States, built about 1800, is an example of this kind of construction. Were she to be placed in a drydock and you viewed her from astern you could trace around her stern section a perfect circle. Her bulwarks were given tumble-home; even the vital sections of her decks were heavily cambered, thus completing a connected circle. Her broad stern sections (transom) and her bows show pronounced curvature. Her transom was curved outboard to break the force of following seas and to prevent her from being pooped in high breakers or seas. Her bows were fined up only enough to give her deflective entrance to the impact of waves. Ships of such construction as this made a tremendous fuss as they swept through the seas. Their bulbous underbodies set up large areas of submerged frictional resistance end eddy currents. They were exasperatingly slow in light airs and threw stern waves as high as a house when driven by the gale. All this is granted, but they cruised the seven seas both in high latitudes and low; few, if any, were ever lost as a result of destruction by sea waves.

A wooden ship of this type of ring construction even circumnavigated the Polar ice pack—around the top of the world. Her entire hull structure was forced above the surface of the sea time and again by the crushing action of the heaviest ice known to man. Yet she lived to *sail* her intrepid crew home in safety. There was not one inch of area about the weather surfaces of these old veterans that the full force of a breaker could clutch at to obtain leverage to start an opening as a lever to

In the sketch above, drawn to scale, the bottom lines of a World War I subchaser are shown. There was no flat spot anywhere in the hulls of these remarkably able boats

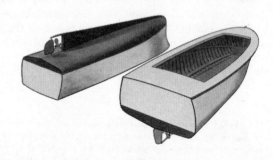

Two views of the hull of a comparatively modern type of semi-displacement motor boat, showing the flared bow sections forward and the underbody aft designed for good cruising speeds

An older type of full displacement cruiser, showing the roundness of lines, both in profile and section. The dotted lines show how nearly her midship section approaches a semicircle

weaken her hull structure. Unlike their more modern sisters with sweeping, graceful speed lines, their bottoms were of such contour as to make them sufficiently stable in high seas and give enormous strength in breakers. They were built about the postulate that they *must* weather any gale in any ocean.

Those were strong ships but their manner of construction could not be applied with success to modern motor boats nor could their "system" of curvature cope with demands for speed in present day motor-driven craft. About the only relic of this example of floating construction left in modern motor boat building may be observed under the turtle deck of the modern motor surf boat. Here speed has necessarily been sacrificed. You cannot have both, and your brand of seamanship plus your ability to utilize to advantage the highly contoured surfaces of your craft in breakers must take the place of the great strength of connected ring construction. Remember that the professional motor surf boat was built to steam out of any breaking inlet where she can find sufficient depth for her propeller, and for effective steering. Your pleasure boat was never designed to do this, so look over inlet conditions before you go to sea.. You can always get authentic reports on bar conditions—don't take a chance and "try it."

Perhaps the most successful compromise of modern motor boat construction in respect to contour-build and retained ring strength was, again, the little American chaser of World War I. Coupled with these qualities was the dependable placement of continuous high torque and its position under her quarter. There was not a flat spot in her entire hull structure (see illustration of the chaser's bottom); she had a modified degree of flare forward and her deck, to complete the connected circle of ring construction, was cambered.

Yet she possessed considerable speed. The placement of her balanced rudder was so expert in relation to her screws that there was no possible position she might assume in the breakers that could deprive her of effective rudder control. Her enormous delivery of torque was available on her shafts 2.5 seconds after the demand for it was rung down. So great was the effect of her high torque on rudder surfaces that the unwary quartermaster was often shocked to attention by having the helm jerked from his hands, when either of her two wing motors were started, despite the fact that her rudder operating linkage passed through a system of gearing.

Some Aspects of Bottom Design

Now of the various resistances which oppose a motor boat's progress through the water, those of greatest detriment and ever-present obstruction to the designer are frictional resistance and wave-making. To the motor boat captain, struggling in steep breakers, where either of these twin elements is present in exaggerated degree, both work as a double-edged hindrance to safe passage through breaking seas. The frictional wake which is the result of the confluence of the two is usually greater in velocity in full displacement type hulls about the center section of the boat; it may be defined as water having forward motion in the direction in which your craft is traveling. Where it is observed at the stern of your boat, surging about in high turbulence, your propellers are being forced to deliver their power in water that already has forward motion. This results in high slip and propeller thrust losses. Since it interferes with instantaneous delivery of high torque in breakers the designer has resorted to streamlining of bottom sections. Any abrupt termination of hull contour or poorly faired bottom sections handicap you in breakers. In part, the designer is relying on your knowledge of seamanship and good sense in the handling of your craft in breakers in his admonishment of *never pounding* any of your streamlined bottom sections. Such contour has been necessary to produce the speed that *you* demanded.

In the evolution of boat contour, the designer has evolved a hull form whose bottom section, limits of wetted surface (underway), and stern profiles are highly streamlined. These are aimed at decreasing the length of frictional resistance and minimizing effects of frictional wake. Thus additional speed is gained for less weight of horsepower. Greater comfort, extra stability athwartship, and roominess aft also result from carrying out much of the boat's full beam almost to the stern. To the extent that a design is intended for greater speed, a higher caliber of seamanship is called for when handling the boat in rough, breaking seas.

As we study the modern motor boat's underbody (see illustration) we note that the patterned ends of her wide quarter are somewhat flatter in section than the steeper curves of her runs forward. Viewing her forward, from the forefoot knuckle to the top of her stem post, the graceful curves of her bow flares are pleasing. By the stern we note her broad transom is brought in at the bilge in a sharp but graceful turn. Her rudders look small for the job but the propellers just ahead of the rudder post look business-like. Many elements of her design reveal a similarity to the famous Jersey beach skiff which, intelligently handled, is one of the most able of modern boats in inlet or beach breakers.

Handling a Skiff

The skiffman well realizes the necessity of keeping his stern squarely before the break of the seas when he enters the breakers. He learned the hard way and he knows that if his boat should become tender at the quarters as a result of inattention or lack of realization of his position, as he roars along on the back of a sea, the submerged portion of his transom and waterline section of his planking aft will instantly produce rudder effect. Since the projected area in friction against the sea in that portion of his hull is far greater than that of his rudders, he can only expect the breakers to seize that portion of his hull and throw him into a broach.

He is deeply conscious of the presence and force of the pressure wave surging along at his bottom's entrance to the sea just forward of his 'midship section and he uses his controls to keep the force of that pressure wave constant and surging evenly down over the outer surfaces of his bottom planking *in a fore and aft direction. He never pounds it.* To do so would immediately destroy the continuity of the stabilizing effect of his high and continuous torque; in exaggeration it might even fracture a plank. It's risky, and *bad* seamanship.

He can feel the force of that pressure wave through the soles of his shoes and he can judge its degree by the vibrations of his hull as his reflexes tell him to move his throttle ahead slightly when they decrease and to ease it back a bit if the rumblings beneath him become excessive.

He rarely uses his drogue for he is not the fool to get caught out there when the breakers are high before the inlet. But, should his boat start to run, its pretty to see his "drugman" go to work and break her out of it. He knows his boat is so constructed aft that she'll stand the whipping strain of that shattering jerk of the drogueline as the drogueman spins off the turns of the trip and the tow-line's red markers fly in the spume—ripping out of the sea as his 2-inch drogueline takes the entire load of his roaring motor's output plus the speed of the breaker's advance.

His skiff now broken out of her run, the Jerseyman knows he cannot ease off and allow a following sea to assault the broad face of his transom. His racing hull now being in a high state of tension, a breaker packing a two-ton wallop reaching his transom might demolish the whole after section of his boat. The chaser's transom was concaved outboard; a sea just couldn't hit it a solid jolt. Not so his skiff, however—so he runs from the breaker and holds her where the tumbling sea cannot reach him.

Dodge the Cross Seas

Contour construction in small boats in breaking inlets is a mighty important element of design for none better than the Jerseyman realizes those sweeping sections of bow flare forward become flat when faced with the impact of the sea as it attempts to pound them. Should he see a cross sea tearing across his course he'll slow her down or dodge it if he senses that his bows are on a collision bearing with it, for you might as well hit the jetty full tilt as collide with that breaker.

Such cross seas are grave risks to motor boats with bow cockpits, whether or not these are supposed to be self-bailing.

It will be gleaned, as the reader follows through the text, that drogues and their use assume an important stature at times of emergency in breakers. Reference to the *details* of their use and the manner of *adaptation* of the different types of drogues to specific types of hulls have been left unexplained—largely for the reason that pages of explanation might divert the attention of the reader from the subject at hand. Limitations of space might not do that field of seamanship full justice in a discussion where so many elements of boat construction and sea condition are fused together and must be separated in part and then placed back together again for the purposes of full understanding. The amateur boatman has a long voyage to make on the course we have set here. It must not be complicated any more than necessary. Use of drogues and their adaptation is simply another field of seamanship.

In these days ot great, responsive and dependable power, able and staunch motor craft and rapid, accurate, reliable weather and bar forecasts, the use of a drogue in breakers is all but a lost art. Only a few of the older beach denizens are left now who were expert in their use. Yet it is a great comfort to have one aboard suited to your own particular boat both in inlet breakers and for the purpose of lying to it in bad weather at sea.

Forward Cockpits

Before leaving the subject of handling modern motor boats in breaking seas, perhaps a word should be said concerning the vulnerability of open forward cockpits. It is not meant to infer that motor boats of such construction must always be restricted from entrance to the breakers before a coastal inlet. However it seems rather a contradiction of good seagoing sense to otherwise construct a boat whose strength, hull contour, and power are equal to the challenge of the breakers and then to vitiate these good qualities by placing in vulnerable ends a deep, open compartment capable (if filled) of throwing the craft into an immediate broach. Rarely do forward cockpits have adequate means of freeing themselves as fast as demands of safe operation in breakers press upon such a craft. Remember that breaking seas may be encountered in other waters than those of coastal inlets. They may occur at any place on the coastal shelf where the force of wind, depth of water, and combinaton or strength of currents are conducive to their formation.

Flat Surfaces Vulnerable

Looking back over the taffrail, we have also noted the vulnerability of flat-surfaced structures exposed to waves and weather. We know something of the force *in tons* that assaults these non-contoured weather surfaces. Therefore, if you plan a cruise along the coast, see to it that you have a stout hatch that can be battened down over your forward cockpit—or at least carry aboard materials from which you can quickly construct a suitable cover, if conditions necessitate your bringing the boat's head into heavy seas.

Among the modern materials that have found increasing use in boat construction is flat sheet plywood. Primarily, of course, it is used in the hulls of small craft that are not expected to run breaking inlets. It also lends itself to use in bulkheads, interior joiner work, etc. Properly framed, it has tremendous strength—as in decks, which can often be made stronger than those planked in the conventional manner. But it certainly should not be expected, in either hulls or superstructure, to be able to withstand the full impact of breaking seas, if used in the form of flat surfaces with inadequate framing to back it.

Remember—if you are confronted with the necessity of running breakers before a coastal inlet—every portion of the weather surfaces of your ship becomes a strength member. Collectively, they must be tied into your main framing in a secure and rigid fashion—your deck carlins, cabin sides and bulwarks, weather bulkheads and transoms—flat deckhouse structures, even your cabin and cockpit decks all bear their proportion of the sea-load in the breaker. The breakers will *always* attack the weakest link in the construction chain of your motor boat *first*.

Fast Boat Runs Bahia Honda

We have mentioned that the amount of punishment some of these well built modern high-speed motor boats will take in breakers is little short of amazing when handled with confidence and the certainty of experience. As a case in point, it might be recalled that some years ago, running the inlet off Bahia Honda with an injured sailor aboard, in one of the more modern, strong, high-speed motor boats a little over 38 feet in length and capable of a speed of about 28 knots with her two big engines full out, on her passage through the inlet she turned completely over in a period of (as near as could be calculated) 2.5 seconds. She righted herself inside the breakers on the inlet side of the bar and came up with her crew in the cockpit and with her port motor still pounding out its 3200 r.p.m. Her two-man crew had been lashed on short bights to her cockpit stanchions previous to her entry into the breakers. The injured sailor had been lashed to the cabin floor.

It looked like only a 50-50 chance, as her crew watched on the seaward side of the breaker line, and from what could be seen of the breakers in the darkness through the flying spume of the gale, the inlet breakers appeared to be about seven to eight feet in height but their period was extremely short. The sailor's life was at stake

and the chance had to be taken. If the boat had a drogue aboard and set when she laid down on her port side and started to run, her mad speed might have been broken and stopped but, like the Dutchman's anchor, old faithful Charlie wasn't there that time. This boat was capable of an honest 28 knots. Her engines, at the time she entered the outer breakers, were not quite full out and she was being handled by a sailor who had spent many years of his life in small boats in the breakers. You can imagine the speed those inlet seas were making!

A few days later the boat was hauled out—the couplings connecting both engines to the tailshafts were checked for alignment, both machines carefully gone over, holding down bolts and all framing in the way of her power plant was checked. Except for three of her six tailshaft flange bolts on the starboard coupling that were found to have slacked up and were only hand-tight, there was nothing amiss with her power plant. A tight wire was run over her hull and she was carefully trammed by two experts both in her center section and at her ends. Her hull was as fair as the day she first met the sea. The only evidence of the mauling she took and damage sustained in her wild passage through Honda was the tearing from their flanges of two 1¼-inch pipe stanchions that supported and stiffened her cabin top. These two were badly twisted. She had no forward cockpit.

The Auxiliary in Breakers

The difficulties in breakers of the sail boat with auxiliary engine are complicated by the general contour of both its submerged and exposed body plan, its rigging and lofty sparring. In any coastal inlet where breakers are present over three feet in height in conjunction with strong winds blowing on the land, a breaker length of roughly 100 feet and wave periods of less than five seconds, entrance may be attended with extreme difficulty and should only be attempted in extreme emergency, with the auxiliary type of boat. Unless such a boat, contemplating the entrance of a coastal inlet where breakers are seething across its mouth, is extremely high-powered, has a body and topside form that will easily assimilate a sea speed in excess of 15 knots, has very short ends and is very moderately sparred, she should not attempt any such entrance. Rather she should be taken to sea and hove to even in the face of worsening weather; her chance for survival is far better.

It should be borne in mind that the inlet breaker is no respecter of size and great length of hull. A 90-foot Gloucesterman, probably one of the most able types of small sailing vessels afloat, in consideration of its heavy power installation, rig and hull contour, excepting perhaps the world famous Ramsgate trawler and Dutch Pilot boat, found this out one night in a roaring southeaster and a snowstorm while attempting to enter Cold Spring Inlet on the Jersey coast. With the wind almost dead astern, force 5, and approaching the narrow entrance to the inlet under power and bare poles, excepting a rag of riding trysail set flying on the main, she took a heavy squall just off the entrance to the jetties. A cross sea struck her under the flare of her port bow and forced her bows to starboard and slowed her down; she was then pooped by a following breaker, losing her dog-house over the wheel box. Her starboard nest of dories went by the board across the deck and demolished her fish pens as they went, tearing loose from the chain-plates her forward, port side, mainmast shroud. The vessel now being in a deep port roll, the wind from astern, driving at her lofty spars and rigging, simply took charge of her steering arrangements and directed her course squarely at 90 degrees to the direction of the gale (while the ship was making an estimated speed of better than 15 knots) into the immovable bulk of the north jetty. She rode clear to the top of the jetty before the cold stone stopped her mad run.

Auxiliaries Need Sea Room

Many qualified and authoritative persons have written, in a general sense, of the hazards connected with the driving of such auxiliary craft before high following seas and winds of gale force from astern. Every experienced captain of such motor-sail boats senses this danger. The wise sailor, therefore, even though he may be entirely uninitiated or have no conception whatever of the forces at work aloft and those acting on his hull, will watch his chance and, using his power if necessary, will bring his bows to the seas at the earliest opportunity before he dismasts his vessel or she is hopelessly pooped or broached. This can only be done where sea room is available. It cannot be accomplished where the captain of such a boat is threatened with loss of control of his ship in a breaking inlet.

Maneuvering through a breaking coastal inlet the captain of the strictly motor-driven craft has none of these problems to deal with. A clear understanding, however, of the effect of the elements of construction, general contour of hull form and the possibilities of lofty rig leverages must be possessed by the operator of an auxiliary. He should realize how these components are so closely connected with the difficulties of handling his straining hull in breakers before high winds, and, in particular, when his hull is cramped for sea room and maneuvering space when an attempt is made to force her through the narrow channel of a breaking inlet.

Now as the size and lateral plane of auxiliary craft are reduced, the general ratio of the combined qualities of weatherliness, in such types, falls off in almost direct proportion to the degree in size to which the boat is reduced. In other words, it does not necessarily follow, because a big auxiliary might be an able craft in breakers on the coastal shelf, that a smaller vessel of similar design will retain her ability to keep the sea and handle reliably under identical sea conditions.

How Size Affects Craft of Similar Design

In moderate weather and reasonably smooth going, an exact counterpart of the larger craft but only half her size might possibly outclass her larger sister in ability to work to windward under sail, would probably be fast in stays and possess the general rapid response to her helm which the overall design of her larger counterpart makes possible. However, when the smaller version is brought before heavy seas, alternately breaking, or where it is necessary to bring her bows head to the seas in an attempt to heave her to—the abilities of the larger auxiliary and her diminutive counterpart part company.

To begin with, the righting moments of such small craft when heeled at any angle of inclination near the crest of a breaker are far less than when such a boat is making headway on her normal water planes. Consequently, this factor of tenderness augmented by the gyrations of lofty rigging weights, reeling aloft under the influence of high windage, creates a situation where extreme watchfullness, in heavy breakers, becomes the pass-word of safety. Despite their other attributes of speed, grace and quick response to rudder motion in moderate weather, there is no heaving-to of these ships, with the wheel hard down in a becket, and going below to a pinochle game. By reason of their short keels and resultant quickness in stays, they are also quick under boisterous sea conditions and must be constantly "handled." Resorting to the use of power, before high following breakers, is liable to complicate the situation and in most cases combinations of motor and canvas should only be used when such boats are riding head-to or just off the seas, or to aid in bringing them head to the seas. Despite all of the above (since such motor-sail craft must always be "handled") they must have sea-room, and the forcing of one of these sensitive craft into the tumultuous confines of a breaking inlet channel is fraught with danger to the boat and its crew.

The Underbody Design

Answering the constant demands for speed, speed and more speed out of such motor auxiliaries particularly on windward legs and in stays, the designer has constantly cut away at the bottom sections of these boats until in some cases there is little evidence of such a boat's keel sections left, and the forefoot has all but disappeared. This has to be done in the interest of reducing the amount of frictional area in contact with the sea, an elimination of frictional wake and eddy-making, and, where a boat's forefoot has disappeared, a lessening of the slowing effects of lee bow surge and rapidity of motion in stays. That the designer has achieved his objective there is not the least doubt, but such success has been bought at the cost of creating a craft whose action under power in almost any type of cycloid, unless handled with extreme care, does not emulate, in any sense, the predictable action of a modern motor boat in heavy following breakers before high winds.

There are few boats of any type devoid of forefoot or forefoot gripe, that will "hang on" when hove to or lie without fretfulness to the end of a drogue line in heavy cycloids. This applies equally to both motor and sailing vessels, and combinations of the two. Boats of such construction all evince a tendency to pivot on the after sections of their keel while their bows are at the whim of

surface forces of the sea and are shoved higher and yon by them, making the boat uncomfortable when stemming breakers and resulting in the necessity of having to "sail" such craft constantly. Before the breakers and running, this tendency is exaggerated in the opposite direction, for now the boat's stern, which is the first portion of the ship's bulk to feel the force and direction of the waves from astern, seems to want to proceed off in one direction unmindful of the fact that it might be pushing the overhanging and lightly displaced bows off in another direction. There are several components of hull shape, sectional displacement and rigging plan that are responsible for this alarming tendency of such craft before steep breakers and high winds from astern. They are difficult to separate.

Tendency to Broach

Auxiliary craft whose straight keel section is but a third or less of their waterline length seem to be more prone to this yawing proclivity before heavy breaking seas and are more likely to be thrown into a broach than are their long, straight-keeled and extended-forefoot sisters. As a result of their deep draft aft and the pulling aft of concentrated keel weights (aft of designed centers of buoyancy) to offset the tendency of their sail plans to depress shallow bows, the inertia built up in that section of the vessel where displacement is greatest and weights are heaviest tends to follow the natural physical law of proceeding in a straight line. Unfortunately, this submerged section of the ship about the keel knuckle and slightly forward of it, feels the violence of the breakers least while the exposed topsides (transom) of the vessel, directly above the keel knuckle, are first to meet the onslaught of breakers and to be attacked from diverse directions. At sea, such forces tearing at the hull produce wild twisting strains. In the narrow confines of an inlet channel, if the breakers are more than four feet high, her actions are likely to be so unpredictable as to make the passage difficult, if not hazardous. You just could not get power enough in her to control her and, under power alone, she could never hope to approach the performance of the modern motor boat in breakers. The inlet just is no place for her.

In my opinion, about the ablest thing in a small auxiliary that has been produced in this country that will stay with you in breakers of up to about six feet in height is the Friendship sloop. Her keel, though sloping, runs her full length; she has short ends, and she'll waddle through small breakers like the professional surfboat. There are sailboats in the world that will run breakers—the planing type sailboats of the South Sea natives which, like the modern semi-displacement motor boat, has none of the foregoing complications of contour to beset them in the breakers. These native craft attain speeds of 15 knots and higher sailing against the wind.

Keep the Auxiliary Out of Breaking Inlets

When you attempt to make a motor boat out of the average auxiliary, and take her through a badly breaking inlet, you are forcing your vessel into a situation which her creators never intended she should be pushed into. If you want to run breakers, tell your architect. What he designs for you will have few of the characteristics of the auxiliary.

We have pointed out the restlessness of this type of ship when you attempt to heave it to in breakers on the coastal shelf. She *will* heave to and she *will* lay to a drogue line, but you can't put the gyro-pilot on her when the wind is force 6 and the seas are 5 and breaking. She won't do the thinking, for that lies in the department of your seamanship and good judgment.

Many sailboat rudders are relatively inefficient. Under sail, the bottom third of such rudders is the position where their greatest projected area should be placed. That section of the rudder, however, is often cut away to preserve contour and reduce eddy-making. Under power, it is the vertical center section of the rudder directly abaft the discharge from your wheel where such rudders should be given their greatest lateral area. But here steering control has been reduced by the cutting away of the rudder blade to make room for the propeller. If you run your shaft out through either of the bilges you are faced with a worse situation in the breakers for then you have the directional effect of your wheel to fight and you do not have the influence of high shaft torque to mitigate the effect of any of these constructional deficiencies. Your power, of necessity, is low. She just doesn't belong in breaking inlets.

CHAPTER XXIX

• # River Piloting

Piloting on Our Fresh-Water Inland Waterways Can

Be a Rewarding Experience—a Pleasant Change,

for the Salt-Water Boatman, from Coastal Cruising.

LEGEND

▬▬▬ IMPROVED INTRACOASTAL WATERWAY
●●● OPEN BAY WATER
■■■ AUTHORIZED FOR IMPROVEMENT
▬▬▬ PRINCIPAL IMPROVED CONNECTING WATERWAYS

Chart of the principal navigable waterways in the eastern half of the United States. The Mississippi River System, including its tributaries, constitutes a network of more than 12,000 miles navigable by pleasure craft.

From Booklet "The Gulf Intracoastal Waterway"

A typical river scene on the Ohio, made from the Kentucky side below Louisville. Deep water favors the outside of the bend.

FOR the cruising yachtsman who has never laid his course inland, there are surprises in store. Many a coastal boatman is likely to regard the inland waterways as little better than glorified "canals" to be used only as links between large bodies of salt water. Cruising them for their own sake might never occur to him, and canalling, in his mind, is synonymous with "ditch-crawling."

As a matter of fact, some of the finest cruising this country affords can be found on the vast network of interconnected rivers and lakes which give access to areas far removed from tidal waters. Throughout the United States there are nearly 30,000 miles of improved inland waterways. The Mississippi River system alone embraces more than 12,000 miles of waterways navigable by small craft —the largest network of navigable inland waterways, in fact, in all the world. Of these 12,000 miles, the greater part provides depths of better than 6 feet. Using the Mississippi, the Great Lakes, the New York State Barge Canal and other waterways linking these with the Atlantic and Gulf Intracoastal Waterways, the boatman can circumnavigate the entire eastern portion of the United States, a cruise of more than 5,000 miles. Only a comparatively small portion of this would be in the open sea, although the Great Lakes, of course, are sizable bodies of water, comparable to the ocean insofar as small boat cruising is concerned.

While rivers as a rule seldom offer great open expanses common to the coast where the usual techniques of piloting are called into play, they do demand unique piloting skills. On the rivers, local lore often outweighs some of the fundamental piloting principles which are the coastal pilot's law. Ever-changing conditions on the rivers put a premium on local knowledge and elevate river navigation to the status of an art.

One of the first things to impress the salt water boatman on his cruise inland is the perpetual change of scenery as he threads mile after scenic mile of sinuous cross-country course—over hills, into the valleys, through farmlands, forests and cities. Basically the transition is one from salt water to fresh, from tidal to nontidal waters. "Fresh" water does not necessarily imply clear, pure water. In the Missouri, river water is freighted with silt that clogs water strainers and wears out strut bearings and shafts. But in Lake Champlain, you can stop in mid-lake and top off your fresh water tanks.

Because inland water may be designated as non-tidal, it does not follow that there are no fluctuations in level. On the coast we are accustomed to daily changes in height —normally two highs and two lows each day. Inland, the variation in rivers is more apt to be of a seasonal nature, as spring freshets, loaded with debris, flood down from the headwaters, overflow banks, and course down to the sea at surprising velocities. At St. Louis, the seasonal fluctuation in river level from flood conditions in the late winter and early spring to normal levels in the late summer and fall may range from 40 to 50 feet. And in some of the navigable streams, sudden hard rains may raise the level several feet in a matter of hours.

In the passes at the mouth of the Mississippi, there is generally one high and one low water in 24 hours, with a range of about 18 inches. At New Orleans the diurnal range of the tide during low water stages averages about

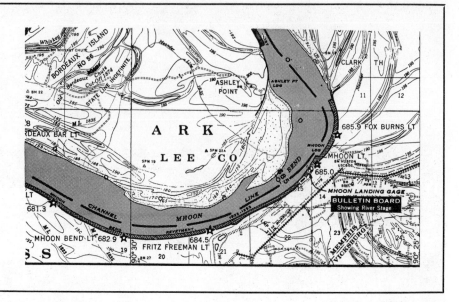

Section of a typical Mississippi River chart. On the original, the shaded areas appear in blue tint. Channel lines, lights and mileages are printed in red. River stages, or heights, are given on the bulletin boards, locations of which are indicated on the chart in red. Note the revetment which Army Engineers have constructed on the outside of the bend to protect the bank from erosion. Small circles are 1 statute mile apart. Parallels of latitude and meridians of longitude appear, but no compass rose, as used on coastal charts.

9 inches, with no periodic tide at high river stages. Current in this area is negligible from a piloting standpoint. High water stages occur around April, low in October, with extreme differences in level up to 21 feet.

In the larger lakes, a strong wind will lower levels to windward and pile up the water to leeward. Lake levels vary from year to year and show a seasonal rise and fall as well, low in the winter, high in the summer. Barometric pressure also exerts an influence on lake levels, sometimes causing a sudden temporary oscillation of consider-

able magnitude. This lake phenomenon is called a seiche.

Usually the cruise inland from the coast does mean a change from exposed to sheltered waters. That, however, is purely relative. While it is true that you can cruise hundreds of miles continuously on streams where shelter from bad weather is seldom more distant than the nearest bank, the larger lakes must be treated with respect. Lake Superior, for example, is the largest body of fresh water in the world. Deep, with rock-ribbed coasts and subject to storm and fog as well, it presents a challenge to even

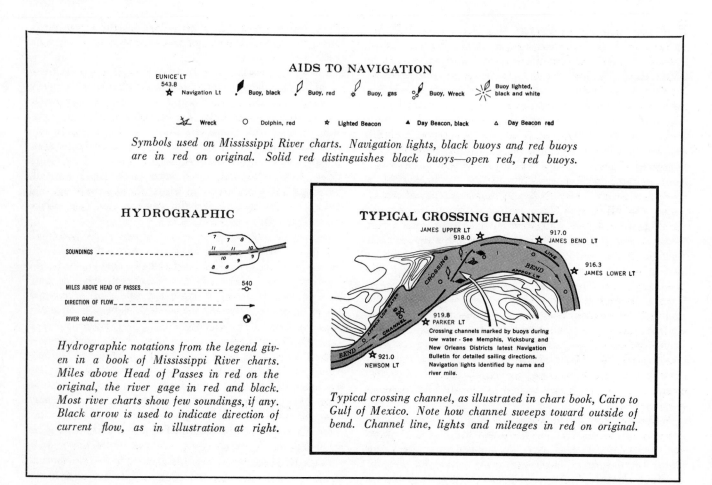

AIDS TO NAVIGATION

EUNICE LT 543.8 ★ Navigation Lt · Buoy, black · Buoy, red · Buoy, gas ○· Buoy, Wreck ☀ Buoy lighted, black and white

⚓ Wreck ○ Dolphin, red ☆ Lighted Beacon ▲ Day Beacon, black △ Day Beacon red

Symbols used on Mississippi River charts. Navigation lights, black buoys and red buoys are in red on original. Solid red distinguishes black buoys—open red, red buoys.

HYDROGRAPHIC

SOUNDINGS

MILES ABOVE HEAD OF PASSES — 540○

DIRECTION OF FLOW — →

RIVER GAGE — 🌐

Hydrographic notations from the legend given in a book of Mississippi River charts. Miles above Head of Passes in red on the original, the river gage in red and black. Most river charts show few soundings, if any. Black arrow is used to indicate direction of current flow, as in illustration at right.

TYPICAL CROSSING CHANNEL

JAMES UPPER LT 918.0 ☆
917.0 ☆ JAMES BEND LT
916.3 ☆ JAMES LOWER LT
919.8 ☆ PARKER LT
921.0 ☆ NEWSOM LT

Crossing channels marked by buoys during low water · See Memphis, Vicksburg and New Orleans Districts latest Navigation Bulletin for detailed sailing directions. Navigation lights identified by name and river mile.

Typical crossing channel, as illustrated in chart book, Cairo to Gulf of Mexico. Note how channel sweeps toward outside of bend. Channel line, lights and mileages in red on original.

440b

Photograph from T.V.A., Knoxville

Locks and dams make rivers navigable by changing levels in successive stages. Here a group of cruisers on the Tennessee ascend to a higher level, as they pass through Wilson Dam Lock in Alabama. Coiling lines, the crew make ready to sail out of the lock.

the saltiest pilot. Lake Erie, though smaller than Superior, is comparatively shallow. In a gale of wind, seas cannot shape up in the normal pattern of ocean waves. Consequently, they are short and steep, frequently breaking in heavy squalls. Even New York's Lake Oneida, only 20 miles in length, can build up seas that will test the ability of an offshore boat.

Broadly speaking, river currents, though they may fluctuate in velocity, will trend always in one direction—from headwaters to mouth. Despite this, tidal rivers connecting with the sea may feel the effect of tidal conditions at the mouth, backing the water up so that the cruiser can take advantage of a favorable current going upstream when tidal conditions are right. On the Hudson, for example, a 10-mile cruiser, starting at The Battery at the beginning of the flood, can carry a favorable current all the way to Albany, 150 miles inland. Tides, here, even this far inland, may range in excess of 6 feet, yet at Newburgh and West Point far down the river, the mean range will be only half that.

Shoaling is a serious problem in most rivers. Spring floods build up current velocities, stir up silt in river bottoms, wash more down from the banks, and carry this load in suspension to be deposited in the form of mud flats and sand bars that present navigational hazards by closing off channels. The Connecticut River on the East Coast is a good example of this, where heavy expenditures are required annually to keep channels dredged to project depths. In the Mississippi, a jellied mass of muck called flocculation is deposited as a sediment on the river bed to a depth of 10 or 15 feet. Deep-draft vessels plow through

it, and high water stages of the river flush it out into the Gulf so Army Engineers do not bother to dredge it at low water stages.

Often where a river discharges into a bay or sound, current velocities are no longer sufficient to hold the silt in suspension and a bar or shoal is built up across the river mouth, much as creeks and streams behave when they flow into the ocean, creating an obstacle against free passage into open water, unless a channel is dredged and protected by breakwaters. On bars of this kind, bad seas may build up in strong currents opposed by the wind. As a matter of fact, at the confluence of some rivers, disturbed surface conditions may be encountered, even where there is seemingly no wind to account for it.

River currents have been the subject of extensive studies and their vagaries are of utmost importance to the masters of deep-draft commercial craft. The surface current acting on a small pleasure boat may in fact be actually contrary to that which grips the keel of a large ship near the river bottom. Even with respect to surface currents alone, there is a variation from bank to mid-stream. Friction of the banks and bottom retards velocity. The skipper of the commercial boat—where fuel costs and hours of operation are of vital import—knows this as he carries the strength of a mid-river current downstream with him. Returning he runs close under the bank to escape the strength of flow opposing him—even turning slightly into coves behind points to take advantage of the counter-current that tends opposite to the trend of the river's flow.

Perhaps the factors which the professional pilot weighs so carefully are less significant to the small boatman.

440c

A lone cruiser passes out of one of the highest lift locks in the nation, having been raised 80 feet at Fort Loudon Lock as she proceeds up the Tennessee toward Knoxville, Tenn.

Nevertheless, the pleasure boatman can profitably take a leaf from the river pilot's log and cut his running time and fuel bills merely by running courses that make elemental factors work for him, rather than against him.

Again, speaking broadly, unless there is something in the bottom contour or man-made structures to alter them, river channels have a natural trend somewhat akin to the configurations in creeks along the marshes of our coasts, where the flow of water tends to carry across the stream on the outside of bends, scouring out a natural channel at the outside while depositing a bar on the points.

Study a river chart which gives the depths (those of the Coast & Geodetic Survey do) and notice the trend. Then when you are piloting a river where the navigational "maps" give no clue to depths (as in the Ohio and Mississippi) you can begin to develop an instinct with regard to interpretation of the river's natural course. Try to visualize the whole picture, if you can, as it would appear to you if you were looking down on the river *and* your boat from a plane. This way you will be less likely to run straight courses from buoy to buoy, cutting corners, with obvious risk of piling up on a point. You will appreciate better the problems of the agency which buoys the waterway, where a pair of buoys are used to mark a point and the channel edge opposite, with a similar pair abreast of the next point. Between the two points the river may be taking a natural curve and a mid-channel course would be represented, not by a straight line between the two pairs of buoys, but by a curved line conforming roughly to the trend of the river as a whole.

Gradually developing this sense of perspective, you'll be more acutely conscious of the actual track you make good over the bottom relative to nearby shoals and side limits of the channels. Where currents do occasionally flow diagonally across your

Corps of Engineers, U. S. Army

Two big tows pass on the Mississippi at Vicksburg bridge.

course, you will allow for them instinctively and look astern frequently to help maintain that sense of position.

As you glance astern in unfamiliar waters, your wake will provide a clue to the safety of your course. When the natural sequence of waves in your wake is broken, there must be something to disturb it. As it rolls off into shallow water, the smooth undulation will give way to a sharper formation, even cresting on the flats in miniature "breakers." When they encounter a reef or flooded area where submerged stumps lie close to the surface, the wake will show the difference. But when that short peaked unnatural wake closes up toward your stern, sheer off . . . . fast!—away from the side where the telltale wake builds up.

On some river charts, even the curves showing the topography ashore supply clues to what may be expected in the river itself. Frequently contour curves crowded close together on land at the water's edge indicate a cliff rising sheer from the surface, with prospects of good depths close under such a bank. The cliff or hill, as the case may be, may at the same time provide a prominent landmark as a guide to steer by.

Piloting the rivers and canals, encountering bridges, locks and guard gates in rapid succession, you will soon acquire a new awareness of controlling vertical and horizontal clearances. On tidewater you were, no doubt, acutely conscious of depths as a critical consideration. Navigating a waterway where you normally could be assured a 6-foot depth, you automatically exercised extra caution around inlets where rapid shifting of the

Cruiser entering Kentucky Dam Lock. Note striping on wall.

shoals might cut your controlling depth to a couple of feet. On the rivers, you will have the clearance overhead on your mind. There may be places on some streams where a fixed bridge will arbitrarily determine your "head of navigation." Beyond that point, your cruising may be restricted to an exploratory trip in the dinghy.

On some of our principal waterways—the New York State Barge Canal System, for example—overhead clearance is restricted to 15½ feet. Masts on auxiliaries must be unstepped and carried on deck, and outriggers and radiotelephone antennas hinged down out of the way. Commercial craft are built with regard for limiting clearance under bridges and in locks. Superstructures are kept low and pilot houses may even be made retractable, to lower for passage under bridges. Fixed overhead power cables are generally high enough to provide clearance for masted vessels, and this clearance is noted on the chart. High water stages on the rivers naturally cut overhead clearances under bridges by the amount of rise above normal pool levels. Chart books for the Ohio give examples of how to calculate existing clearances at open river stages from the vertical clearances at normal pool stage, and at 1936 high water stage, shown on the charts.

Signals for the opening of drawbridges, lift bridges, etc., are not uniform in all waters so it will be necessary to consult local regulations. For the Great Lakes area, for example, they

The wandering Ohio from the campus of Hanover College

Five cruisers, bound upstream, leave Pickwick Dam Lock located in southern Tennessee. Note the long guide wall.

are covered in detail in the Great Lakes Pilot. Elsewhere, as on the Illinois Waterway, information may be had from Army Engineer District Offices. On the New York Barge Canal, the signal is three short distinct blasts of the whistle.

Before the days of locks and dams, many of our rivers were unnavigable. Water coursing down valleys at the land's natural gradient, dropping perhaps hundreds of feet in a score of miles, runs too fast and encounters too many natural obstacles. To overcome them, engineers dam the natural waterways at strategic spots, creating a series of "pools" or levels that may be likened to a stairway. Good examples of how closely these can resemble a flight of stairs will be found at places like Waterford, N. Y., and the Rideau Canal at Ottawa, where vessels descend or ascend a series of locks in quick succession.

To a river pilot, the term "pool stage" indicates the height of water in a pool at any given time with reference to the datum for that pool. On the rivers pool stages are posted on conspicuous bulletin boards along the river banks so as to be easily read from passing vessels. Locations of the bulletin boards are given on the river charts. On the Ohio, gage readings are displayed at the powerhouses of the dams. These indicate depths of the pool impounded by the dam next below. A depth of 9 feet is uniformly taken to indicate the pool at normal elevation. A reading of 8.7 feet would indicate that the lower pool at the dam is 0.3 foot below normal elevation. These readings are preceded by the letters NP (normal pool) in white on a green background.

Locks and Dams, and the Part They Play in Making Rivers
Navigable. The Proper Handling of Pleasure Craft in Passing
Through Locks, and Some Special Problems of Meeting and Passing
Commercial Traffic in Narrow Canals and Congested Waterways.

Photograph from Corps of Engineers, U. S. Army

A fleet of pleasure craft, locking through together, almost fill all of the available space in a lock chamber of the Inner Harbor Navigation Canal Lock in New Orleans, as they head east on the Gulf Intracoastal Waterway. Gates recess into the lock walls.

DAMS on our inland waterways, without locks, would restrict river cruising to the individual pools and prevent through navigation except to small craft light enough to be portaged around the dams. Locks, in conjunction with the dams, provide the means for watercraft to move from level to level. Locks vary in size but since they must invariably handle commercial traffic, their limiting dimensions offer no restriction to the movement of pleasure craft. On the New York State Barge Canal, a tanker will almost fill a lock, with little space to spare.

Locks are practically water-tight chambers with gates at each end. Valves are provided to admit water as re-

quired. When a vessel is about to be locked upstream to a higher level, the upstream gate is closed, the downstream gate opened, and the water stands at the lower level. The vessel enters the lock through the open gates at the lower end, the gates close behind her and water is valved in until the chamber is full to the upstream level. Now the upstream gate is opened, and the boat is free to resume her course upstream. Locking down is naturally the reverse of this procedure.

Signals are provided for vessels approaching a lock (commonly a long and a short blast) answered by signals from the lock tender. The river boatman should familiarize himself with the special signals applicable to the particular waterway he is using. The Army Engineers at Pittsburgh publish an informative little illustrated leaflet entitled "Locking Through," which sets forth, in a nutshell, the main essentials as they apply to the Ohio.

On the Ohio, vessels sound a long and short blast on the whistle from a distance of not more than one mile from the lock. (On the New York State Barge Canal, they signal with three distinct blasts.) When approaching a lock, boats must wait for the lockmaster's signal before entering. When bound downstream, stay in the clear at least 400 feet upstream from the end of the guide wall leading along the bank into the lock. Approach through the buoyed channel directly toward the lock and keep clear of spillway sections of the dam. Be particularly careful not to obstruct the movement of any large commercial craft that may be leaving the lock. When bound upstream, keep well clear of the turbulent water invariably found below a dam.

On the Mississippi, signs are painted on the river face of the guide wall warning small craft not to pass a given point until signalled by the lock attendant. Near this sign a signal cord is placed. Small craft may use this to alert lock attendants, in lieu of signals used on other waters.

Traffic signal lights at the Ohio locks resemble those you find on the highway—red, amber and green, vertically arranged. Flashing red warns: do not enter, stand clear. Flashing amber signifies: approach, but under full control. Flashing green gives you the all-clear signal to enter. (On N. Y. State Canals, a fixed green light gives clearance to enter; fixed red requires the vessel to wait. U. S. and commercial vessels take precedence; pleasure boats may be locked through with commercial craft if a safe distance may be maintained between them.)

Where locks are in pairs (landward and riverward) the lockmaster on the Ohio may also use an air horn, the significance of his blasts as follows: 1 long, enter landward lock; 2 long, enter riverward lock; 1 short, leave landward lock; 2 short, leave riverward lock.

The Secretary of the Army has established an order of priority with respect to the handling of traffic at locks, giving precedence in this order: 1, U. S. military craft; 2, mail boats; 3, commercial passenger craft; 4, commercial tows; 5, commercial fishermen; and 6, pleasure boats. This means that small pleasure craft may sometimes have to wait to be locked through with other vessels. In deciding on an order of precedence, the lockmaster also takes into account whether vessels of the same class are arriving at landward or riverward locks, and whether they are bound upstream or downstream.

The concrete walls of locks are usually rough and dirty. Consequently a boat will need adequate fender protection. Ordinary cylindrical fenders will pick up dirt and roll on the wall to smear the topsides. Fender boards, consisting of a plank (2-by-6 perhaps, several feet long) suspended horizontally outside the usual fenders, work well amidships or aft where sides are reasonably straight. Bags of hay have the same objection as cylindrical fenders, except

A view of the wickets at one of the Ohio River movable dams. Wickets are held in an upright position during low water stages of the river. At high water, they can be lowered, creating a navigable pass which river boats use without locking.

Photograph from J. M. Wallace

Photograph from Corps of Engineers, U. S. Army

At Mile 633 on the Mississippi, Army Engineers' equipment works on bank protection. Such floating equipment should be passed with caution. Day signal (extreme right) is a black-and-white vertically striped ball over a red ball; at night, equipment of this kind will show three red lights in vertical line.

440g

A westbound tug and barge (pushed ahead) enter the empty Erie Canal Lock No. 4, where they will be raised 34½ feet to the upper level. Propellers on large commercial craft throw a lot of water astern—something for small craft to watch.

on heavily flared bows at the edge of deck where they flatten down and work pretty well. Auto tires wrapped with burlap would be ideal except that their use is illegal in some canals. As you can't be sure which side of a lock you'll be using, it's wise to fender both sides.

Another essential in locking is adequate line. How heavy it is to be depends on the size of boat; how long depends on the depth of the locks. Good ½″ manila is generally adequate for average sized cruisers. In general, each line (bow and stern) will have to be at least twice as long as the depth of lock. The object of this is to permit your running the bight of a line around a bollard on the top of the lock wall, using it double. Then, on the lower level, when you're read to cast off, you can haul the line in without assistance from above. At Little Falls, N. Y., the drop is roughly 40 feet, so 100 feet is not too much for

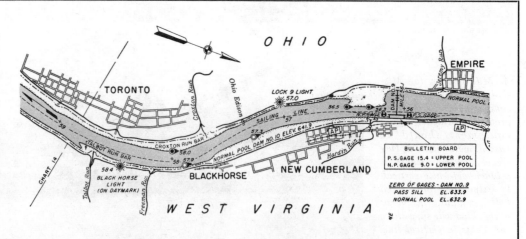

Reproduction of a portion of an Ohio River chart. Arrow (top) indicates true north, seldom at top of chart. Arrow at left indicates direction of river flow. Note symbols for cans and nuns (see legend, next page). Location of bulletin board showing river gages is shown on chart.

the length of each of the two lock lines in such cases.

Ladders are often recessed into lock walls and on some canals small craft by choice will follow the ladder up, rung by rung, with boat hook or lock lines. On the Ohio, this is frowned upon and boats are requested not to use the ladders. In addition to big bollards along the top of the lock wall, some locks have other recessed posts at intervals in the walls in vertical line. Locking up, lines can be cleared successively from lower posts and transferred to higher ones within reach. In other locks, floating mooring hooks move up and down to follow the pool levels.

Rising or falling, stand by your lock lines at all times and tend them carefully. This requires a hand forward and another aft, though with only two aboard the helmsman could handle the after line. One of the most dangerous practices is to make fast to a bollard above and then secure to a bitt or cleat on deck. If the level drops, your craft is "hung," with risk of serious damage.

Entering and leaving locks, it's always imperative to throttle down and keep the boat under complete control. This is especially true when locking through with other boats. Sometimes, on fleet cruises, it will be necessary to tie up two abreast at each lock wall. This is entirely feasible as long as all boats are intelligently handled. On sailaway cruises to New York from the plant of a western New York State boatbuilder, fleets of twenty or more were handled successfully without damage to any.

Occasionally one hears cautions concerning the possibility of a boat's being tossed about as water boils into locks from the open valves. Actually, lock tenders on our inland waters are careful to control this flow, and there is little cause for apprehension on this score. With a light craft, however, some thought should be given to placement in a lock when passing through with large commercial craft. A light hull, directly astern of a powerful tug, can take quite a tossing around when her big wheel starts to throw the water astern.

There are various kinds of locks, all of which accomplish the same end of effecting a change of level. Gates may swing or roll back and in cases are hoisted in vertical lift, permitting traffic to pass through under the gate. Such is the case at Little Falls, N. Y. On the Trent Waterway in Canada, a hydraulic lock lifts the boat in a water-filled chamber and in another instance a marine railway actually hauls the boat out to get her up over a hill. Through passage on a waterway like the Trent, then, is obviously

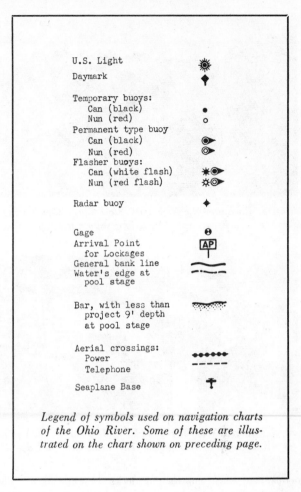

Legend of symbols used on navigation charts of the Ohio River. Some of these are illustrated on the chart shown on preceding page.

limited to craft within the capacity of the ways to haul. At Troy, N. Y., a Federally operated time lock opens only at stated intervals—on the hour—occasionally causing a slight delay in lockage.

Lock permits, obtainable without charge from the Superintendent of Operation and Maintenance, State Department of Public Works, Albany, N. Y., are required to navigate the New York State Barge Canal. On Western Rivers, no special permission or clearance is required for passage through the locks. There are regulations to be observed, however, and copies of these should be obtained from Army Engineer Offices at Chicago or St. Louis.

The point made by Army Engineers as to the necessity

Longest vessels in the world are not the big ocean liners but the tows on Western Rivers made up of barges propelled by a towboat at the stern. Length often exceeds 1000 feet. They should always be passed with great care, especially at bends.

440i

West of Rochester the New York State Barge Canal passes through a rock cut. Speed limit is 6 statute miles per hour.

At Lockport, New York, lock tenders open the gates for craft ready to lock down. The locks here are double.

for caution when approaching locks is well taken. They emphasize the importance of following the buoyed channel closely. Some years ago, a cruiser bound down the Hudson missed the lock at Troy, which lies far over on the east bank, and went *over* the dam. By rare good fortune, she was able to continue her cruise to New York under her own power. Looking down the river from above the dam, it's virtually impossible to see any break in the water's surface, yet there's no excuse for such an occurrence if one pays attention to the buoys as indicated on the chart.

Actually, there are times and places when it is proper to go *over* a dam, strange as that may sound. On the Ohio, they use a movable type of dam having a lock chamber on one side and "bear traps" on the other. In the middle, between them, there are movable wickets which can be held in an upright position during low water stages and lowered at times of high water. When the wickets are up, traffic necessarily passes through the lock. With the wickets down, at high water, boats run through the navigable pass, over the dam, without locking. By day, it is important to watch the bulletin boards at the locks to know whether the lock or the navigable pass is to be used. By night, distinguishing lights are used on the guide walls. When the navigable pass is being used, the gage reading on the powerhouse bulletin board shows the depth of water over the pass sill at the dam. The reading is in white on a scarlet background, and is preceded by the word PASS.

One point that needs careful watching is the strong current set when bear traps are open. These bear traps are devices used to regulate pool levels within certain limits without having to lower the wickets in the navigable pass. In your passage downstream, while waiting for a lock to open, the set may tend to draw you away from the lock approach toward the dam.

One other caution—approach each lock with care and heed the signals at every one. The fact that the navigable pass is in use at one dam is no assurance that it will be at the next.

Be on guard against current set anywhere near a spillway.

Not all waterways are merely improved versions of natural rivers and lakes. Artificial land cuts are often used to connect navigable waterways and provide continuous passage between major bodies of water. Lake Champlain is accessible from the upper reaches of the Hudson only because of a 24-mile land cut connecting the two. A dredged land cut is also encountered at the western end of the Erie Canal to connect Lake Erie with mid-state rivers.

Narrow cuts of this kind pose problems of their own. A typical earth section of dredged canal might have a bottom width of only 75 feet, at the surface perhaps 125 feet, and a depth, let's say, of 12 feet. If normal cruising speeds were maintained through such sections, the bank would be quickly washed down into the channel and maintenance problems would be aggravated. Consequently in such artificial waterways, speed limits are rigidly enforced. In New York canals, the limit is 6 statute mph in the land lines, 10 mph in canalized rivers and lake sections. It's wise to heed the regulations as lock keepers use their phone connections between locks to check on running times.

Some of the land lines are cut through solid rock, perhaps only 100 feet or less in width. This makes a virtual trough with ragged walls of blasted rock. Anyone who has ever run in company with other craft in a confined channel like this knows full well how the wakes of a group of boats may synchronize at times and build up out of all proportion to that of a single craft running alone. Unless serious thought is given to maintenance of moderate speed, regardless of legal limits, small craft can get out of control under such conditions and yaw exactly as they would in a steep swell over an inlet bar. We've seen it happen, with damage to the boat, when the boat's run was ultimately checked by the rock walls.

Most of our inland waterways handle considerable commercial traffic. In a narrow dredged cut a big tug or tanker requires the better part of the channel. As she approaches, you'll see a sizable bow wave built up, practically running ahead of her, and the water drawn away by suction to lower the level at both her sides amidships. Give such traffic as wide a berth as safety with respect to channel widths permits.

Tugs with tows astern in narrow waterways present a real problem to approaching small craft. Fortunately, most of the "towing" today is done by pushing scows and barges ahead of the tug. This keeps the whole tow under better control as a single unit. In times past we have, however, seen a single file of a dozen or more pleasure boats following the right hand edge of a channel, start to pass a tug with tow astern at a bend. The first boats would get through nicely with

A pleasure steamer locking through one of the TVA locks.

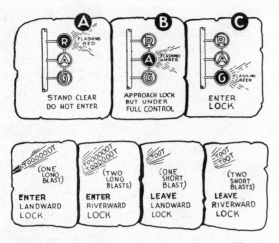

Signal lights and air horn signals used on the Western Rivers to control traffic at locks. (From "Locking Through," prepared by Army Engineers, St. Louis.)

ample passing room but the swinging barges would gradually cut down the passing room to starboard to such an extent that boats bringing up the rear would be forced to pass to port. Even with the tow ahead, this swinging effect must be taken into account at narrow bends so it's generally wise to pass on the inside of the bends.

Big rafts of barges bunched together on the Mississippi in one vast tow may cover many acres in extent. The prudent pleasure boat pilot will appreciate the problems of handling such colossal floats and never jeopardize their activities, regardless of any considerations of right of way. Integrated tows are often made up of a bowpiece, a group of square-ended barges, and a towboat (at the stern) lashed together in one streamlined unit 1000 feet or more in length. At night, to an observer in a small boat, the towboat's lights may be more conspicuous than those on the tow far out ahead. Consequently, special caution is indicated when attempting to run the rivers at night, even though the river itself be so well lighted as to make this feasible. When commercial traffic is using powerful searchlights their blinding beams may make it impossible for the small boatman to see anything at all. Shore lights add to the difficulty, because of reflections in the water. Then, too, in some rivers, especially in flood, there's the hazard of floating and partially submerged debris.

On all the rivers, recreational craft should give commercial tows a wide berth. In particular they should stay away from the front of tows when under way. If you happen to stall in such a spot, it might be impossible for the tow to stop or steer clear. With the way she carries, a commercial tow may at times travel half a mile or more before she can come to a full stop.

The need for keeping a boat under control on approach to locks has already been mentioned. The same applies to bridges, especially when strong currents tend to sweep a boat down toward the bridge structure. This takes on increased significance when vessels must wait to allow a bridge to open after signalling. Unless care is exercised the current may carry a boat down and put her in a position from which it may be virtually impossible to extricate her without twin-screw power. It is on this principle that Western River Rules grant right of way to a "descending" vessel (one proceeding downstream) since the "ascending" vessel is under far better control. Difficulty of maneuvering is aggravated when vessels are trying to handle tows.

River currents sometimes attain such speed that navigation upstream is unfeasible though capably handled boats may safely be taken down. Such is the case in the Galop Rapids of the St. Lawrence where the velocity may run around 12-13 mph. Some river boats have power enough to ascend certain rapids. As a general rule, it is best to avoid them by using canals and locks that by-pass them, unless the skipper has local knowledge or engages the services of a local pilot.

From Kodachrome by Wm. H. Koelbel

A guard gate on the Champlain Canal. Gates of this kind can be lowered when work is being done on the locks below.

440k

Guntersville (Ala.) Yacht Club on TVA's Guntersville Lake.

Finding an Anchorage or Mooring

for Overnight Stops on the Rivers.

River Charts and How They Differ

from Those of Coastal Waters.

Local Knowledge for Boatmen

Running the Mississippi River.

PROBLEMS of where to tie up or anchor for the night are always with us when cruising, whether on coastal or inland waters. On coastal waters, it may be essentially a matter of finding a sheltered cove or basin to avoid risk of a rough night in an exposed anchorage. As a rule on the rivers, shelter from blows is closer at hand, yet there are areas great enough in expanse to work up sizable seas, especially with the wind opposing the current. Then too, there is the matter of finding protection in narrow waterways from passing river traffic and the wake it throws. Finally, there's always the question of personal preference as to whether one seeks the seclusion of quiet anchorages off the beaten track or prefers the activity usually associated with cities and centers of population.

The development in recent years of new marinas on some of the inland waterways—the TVA, for example—has been of great help in this respect. Not only do they provide a place to tie up for the night, but fuel supplies and other necessities are generally available at the marina or near at hand.

On the Tennessee River, safety harbors and landings have been provided for use in case of bad weather, mechanical failure or other contingencies. Their locations are shown on the charts. Safety harbors are usually coves off the navigable channel. Direction boards on shore define the entrance, and cross boards mark the upper limits.

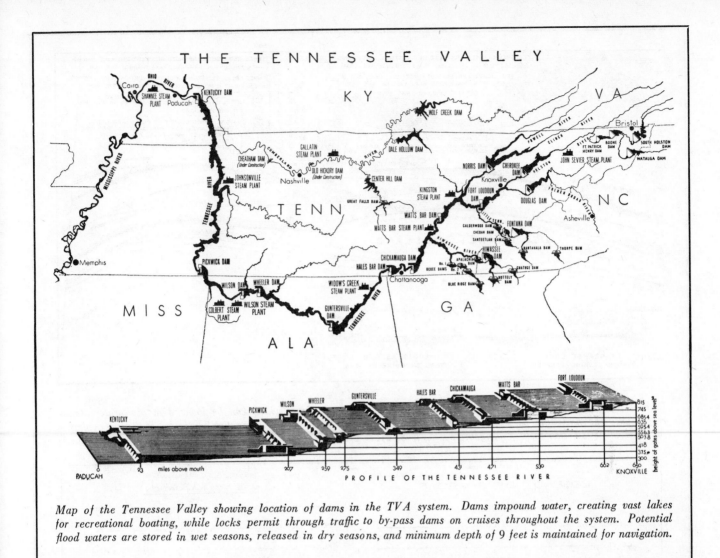

THE TENNESSEE VALLEY

Map of the Tennessee Valley showing location of dams in the TVA system. Dams impound water, creating vast lakes for recreational boating, while locks permit through traffic to by-pass dams on cruises throughout the system. Potential flood waters are stored in wet seasons, released in dry seasons, and minimum depth of 9 feet is maintained for navigation.

Safety landings are areas where banks have been cleared of stumps, boulders and snags, so vessels may land safely. Upper and lower limits are marked by direction boards—white if a 9' depth is available at all pool stages; orange if the depth is 9' at all except low water stages of the river.

The New York State Barge Canal provides terminals at intervals along the route, though these may be occupied by commercial craft. Of concrete, the terminals require adequate fendering when used by small pleasure craft. In order to allow for the seasonal range in levels, or stages, on Western rivers, most yacht clubs are afloat,

on strings of barges, necessitating a long climb up the river bank at low-water stages to get to town.

Frequently a glance at the chart (or navigational map) will reveal a likely place to anchor for the night. A widening of the river may offer an opportunity to get out of the reach of traffic, a small tributary or slough may invite exploration (with caution, sounding as you go), or the natural configuration of river banks and bars may provide a natural harbor with complete protection. Islands in mid-river frequently leave a secondary channel fine for small craft of easy draft, while heavy-draft commercial

The Illinois Waterway provides a navigable connecting waterway between the Great Lakes at Chicago on Lake Michigan to Grafton, Ill., on the Mississippi by way of the Chicago, Des Plaines and Illinois Rivers. View at left shows a tow passing through bridges at Joliet, Illinois.

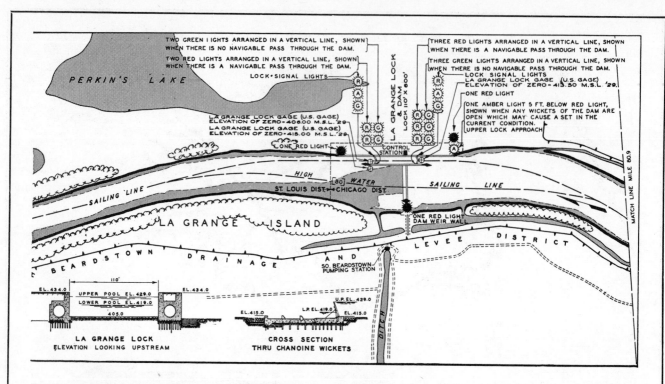

Extract from one of the Illinois Waterway charts. With wicket-type dams which can be lowered at high-water stages, traffic uses the navigable pass through the dam, indicated by "high water sailing line." System of lights, explained on chart, shows whether lock or navigable pass is to be used. Below, the symbols. Lights and nun buoys in red on original.

LEGEND OF SYMBOLS

GENERAL

SHORE LINE	▬▬▬
LEVEE	⊢⊣⊢⊣
9-FOOT CONTOUR	-------
MILES FROM GRAFTON	[50]
VERTICAL BRIDGE CLEARANCE FOR 80 FOOT HORIZONTAL CLEARANCE	⊙
MOVABLE TYPE BRIDGE, NO OPERATING MACHINERY INSTALLED	•
U.S. GAGE	⊕

AIDS TO NAVIGATION

FLASHING POST LIGHT IN PEORIA LAKE	⊛
POST LIGHT	✳
FLOAT LIGHT	◉◁
DAYMARK	◈
BLACK (CAN) BUOY	•◆
RED (NUN) BUOY	•◇
BRIDGE CLEARANCE GAGE	◐
FLASHING SIGNAL LIGHTS ON BRIDGE	•

traffic is confined to the main channel. When a river cuts a channel behind a section of bank, a "towhead" is formed. Sometimes these are filled in at the upper end by river deposits, forming a natural protected anchorage in the lower end. At times you can get behind a pile dike, a type of structure used on rivers to protect banks from washing away. The dike juts out into the river and, by tying up to one of the piles just inside the outer end, on the downstream side, you have protection not only from passing traffic but from floating debris as well. When entering sloughs between islands in search of an anchorage, beware of submerged wing dams at the upstream end. To be safe, enter and leave from the downstream end.

In some cases sufficient protection for an overnight anchorage can be obtained behind a mid-river bar. Occasionally one can find a tiny cove (like Partridge Harbor on Lake Champlain) where there's room for only a few boats, and no room to swing at anchor, so you anchor the

bow off and run a stern line to the nearest tree ashore.

One trick they use on Western rivers is the so-called river hitch. To tie up to a bank for the night, the boat's bow is held up to the bank with power while a line is run to a nearby tree. Then a sapling is cut, 15 to 20 feet long, and lashed from bank to stern to hold the stern off. Another line ashore holds the stern in.

As a rule when tying up for the night on inland rivers, lines need not be laid with allowance for the tidal range common on the coasts. On tidal rivers, it is of course a factor (6-foot range at Albany) and even on the inland rivers there's always the chance of a change in level with hard rainstorms, etc. It pays to observe the practices of local craft and to be guided accordingly. Tied to a barge or float which will itself rise and fall with changing levels, the boatman need provide only such slack in lines as may be required for comfort if a passing craft happens to throw a disturbing wake.

The character of the bottom varies widely on inland waterways. Especially in their lower courses, river bottoms are often soft mud, pointing to the desirability of carrying, in your complement of ground tackle, at least one anchor with broad flukes of a design that will dig down till it reaches good holding bottom. In such spots, the anchor with spidery arms and flukes will cut through and provide no holding power at all, whereas on a hard bottom the same anchor might be highly efficient. When you get into rocky bottoms or areas infested with roots and snags, you will want to resort to one of the tricks for being prepared to recover the anchor if fouled. One easy way is to use a light line from the anchor crown long enough to reach the surface, where the end of line is buoyed. If the anchor snags, pick up the buoy and raise the anchor with the trip line, crown first. Some anchors are provided with slip rings, shear pins or other device to make them snag-proof.

On the subject of anchoring, there's a point to bear in mind when piloting in bodies of water like Lake Champlain. Along some shores, which may be particularly inviting because of their scenic attractions, you may find a depth of a couple of hundred feet running up to sheer cliff shores. If your power fails, your anchor would be of little use in such depths, and if the breeze is toward those cliffs you're on a bad lee shore.

When anchoring on the big rivers near a sand bar or island, or, for that matter, when beaching the boat to go ashore in such a place, a good rule to follow is to pick the downstream rather than the upper end. If an anchor drags or if for any reason you get aground on the upstream end, it's practically like being on a lee shore except that in this case the current, instead of the wind, is constantly working to drive you harder aground. Water at the downstream end is likely to be quieter and the eddies encountered there may help to free a grounded boat. Grounding hard on the rivers may be more troublesome than it is on tidewater, where the next rising tide will generally free a craft without any other assistance.

One of the points likely to strike the tidewater boatman most forcefully when he takes to the Western rivers is the radical difference between river charts and the Coast and Geodetic Survey charts to which he is accustomed. River charts are commonly in the form of books of "navigational maps," each page covering successive short stretches of the river in strip form. A typical example is the bound volume prepared by the Mississippi River Commission, Vicksburg, Miss., to cover the Mississippi from Cairo, Ill., to the Gulf of Mexico. This is on a scale of 1:62,500 (approximately 1 inch to the mile). All of the soundings (with a few exceptions) and detailed positions of rocks, reefs, ledges and shoals so familiar on

A view of the upstream side of Alton Lock and Dam No. 26 on the Mississippi River above St. Louis, Missouri. Note the double locks (extreme left). The landward lock of the pair is considerably larger than the riverward lock. Signals indicate which to use.

SYMBOLS

⊙	Light	⊿	Wreck above water
⊘	Lighted buoy	⊣⊢	Wreck below water
!	Unlighted buoy	*Wreck*	Wreck below water, depth shown
△	White beacon, white reflector	△	Triangulation station
⋯⋯	6 Foot contour	⊙	Landmarks
⋯⋯	12 Foot contour	●	Tanks
⋯⋯	18 Foot contour	⋯⋯	Aerial cable
•	Piles above water	*Pipeline*	Submerged pipe
○	Piles below water	∿∿	Submerged cable
*	Rocks awash	═╪═	Fixed bridge
+	Rocks below water	⇌ ⇋	Bascule bridge
□	Cribs above water	⇌ ◖ ⇋	Draw bridge
∷	Cribs below water		
⑤	State route	④	U.S. Route

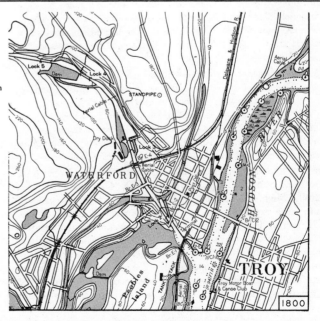

Right: New York State Canal chart at junction of Erie Canal and Hudson River. State buoys are white to port, red to starboard, ascending river. Federal buoys used below Troy. On original chart and symbols (above), lighted aids are shown by orange discs instead of the circles indicated.

coastal charts are omitted. In their place the course of the river is traced in blue tint between heavy black lines which delineate the banks. A broken red line is used to indicate the channel line. Navigation lights are denoted by a red star with white dot in the center together with a number which designates its distance upstream above a fixed reference point—in this case A.H.P., "Above the Head of Passes." The Head of Passes is the point not far above the mouth where the river splits into separate channels leading through the delta into the Gulf. Mileages are given in red every five miles, with red circles at one-mile intervals. Mileages above and below the Head of Passes are printed in red. A detailed table is given in the book, listing in alphabetical order all towns, cities, bridges, mouths of rivers, and other important features adjacent to the main channel, with distances (AHP) in miles and map numbers on which the features appear.

Before starting a cruise on the lower Mississippi, the pilot should make a careful study of the legend which appears on the inside front cover of the chart book. Symbols used to designate the various aids to navigation are given, with abbreviations, topographic and hydrographic features, and an illustration of a typical crossing channel (the latter marked by buoys during periods of low water). Charts are on the polyconic projection and elevations refer to mean level.

On the Illinois Waterway

The book of charts for the Illinois Waterway is prepared by the Chicago District of the Army Engineers. A page of general information in this volume covers practically everything the pilot needs to know in navigating the waterway as he follows his charts. Attention should be paid to the legend of symbols, which differ in some respects from those found on coastal charts. The main channel is shown in white, shoal areas in blue tint. The "sailing line" is indicated by a broken line, the miles from Grafton in brackets in black. Scale is 1 inch to 1000 feet.

Aids to navigation include post lights or range lights with fixed white lights, and some flashing lights. Daymarks are white diamonds on posts without lights. Red nuns are found on the left edge of the channel, black cans on the right edge, proceeding downstream. Detailed information on the operation and lighting of bridges and locks and locking regulations are all given in the Illinois Waterway chart book.

Charts for the Middle and Upper Mississippi from Cairo to Minneapolis (also prepared by the Chicago District of the Army Engineers) resemble those for the lower river except that they are done in black and white with no color to help distinguish significant features. Mileages are reckoned above Cairo. A separate book is available for the Mississippi from Cairo at the mouth of the Ohio to Grafton at the mouth of the Illinois Waterway.

A small booklet of charts for Navigation Pools 25 and 26 of the Mississippi River and Illinois Waterway (published by the St. Louis Engineer Office) is distinguished primarily by the fact that it shows hazard areas (under 6-foot depth) in bright red shading, harbors or anchorage areas with an anchor symbol, and the availability of fuel, water, railways, launching ramps, repairs and docking facilities at specified locations.

When the salt water pilot turns to the book of charts of New York State Canals (published by the U. S. Lake Survey, Detroit, Mich.) he finds himself on more familiar ground. Land areas are tinted a light buff, channels in white, depths of 12 feet or less in a light blue tint with dotted depth curves for 1 and 2 fathoms and distinct black lines delineating the banks. Here, too, are the buoy symbols (diamond and dot) with orange disc signifying lights. Buoys and other aids on shore have their identifying numbers given and rough scattered soundings appear to give the pilot a good idea as to whether he dare venture out of the channel to seek an anchorage in some bend behind an island. Buoy symbols appear in white

to port and red to starboard, entering from seaward, to correspond with the white and red lights they carry at night. Even rocks and wrecks are indicated with symbols similar to those used on coastal charts. The scale in this series of charts, with a few exceptions, is 1:21,120 (3 inches to the mile). Reference plane is normal pool level. Arrows indicating direction of current flow, used on other river charts, do not appear on those of New York waterways.

Tennessee Easy to Navigate

Commercial towboat pilots consider the Tennessee River channel to be one of the best marked and easiest to navigate of all the inland waterways. The Tennessee itself is navigable for cruisers for 650 continuous miles from Paducah, Kentucky, to Knoxville, Tenn. The channel is marked with buoys, lights and dayboards so that it can be navigated both day and night. Locks in each of the nine main stream dams are open 24 hours a day every day and may be used without charge. Pleasure boats are locked through with commercial tows when there is room, or are entitled to separate lockage at the end of each hour. In addition to the main navigation channels, there are about 225 miles of feeder channels, marked by buoys and dayboards, which are used by recreational craft.

Navigation charts are available in two sizes for the entire length of the Tennessee, as well as navigation maps for the thirteen major tributary reservoirs, from the Tennessee Valley Authority, Knoxville, Tenn. The charts, on scales of 1 inch to the mile, and 1 inch to the half-mile, are multi-colored, showing sailing lines and aids to navigation, including buoys, lights, daymarks, safety harbors, hazards, and depths of water at all reservoir pool stages. Other important features are highways, railroads, bridges, wire crossings, terminals, docks, piers, landings and towns. Many private boat docks offering a variety of services and accommodations are scattered along the 10,000 miles of TVA shoreline. A survey of these is available in a folder from the TVA Information Office at Knoxville. Bound sets of charts of the Tennessee are also available from District Engineers at Cincinnati, Nashville and Louisville.

Charts of the Ohio River, in the form of bound sets of continuous multilith charts, are available from District Engineers at Pittsburgh, Huntington and Louisville. There are three sets—Pittsburgh to Powhatan Point, Ohio; Powhatan Point to Aberdeen, Ohio; and Aberdeen to Cairo, Ill. On a scale of one inch to 2000 feet, they show sailing lines, lights, daymarks, arrival point markers for locks, normal pool elevations, mouths of tributary systems, location of bars, channel buoys, bridges, aerial crossings, seaplane bases, docks, terminals, landings, and navigation structures. No soundings are given. Mileages zero at Pittsburgh.

Corps of Engineers, U. S. Army

At River Mile 775 AHP in Tennessee on the Mississippi a towboat with 23 barges passes a channel dredge. Small craft are advised to pass such dredges with caution and to avoid areas upstream from the dredge and floating discharge pipe line which usually extends several hundreds of feet.

440p

In addition to these, there is also a set of photolithographic charts of the Ohio from Pittsburgh to the mouth in 281 sheets, on a scale of one inch to 600 feet. These show topographic features, sailing lines, 5-foot contours, high water, low water, normal pool lines, bench marks, etc.

A detailed list of all charts of the Ohio and its navigable tributaries—the Allegheny, Big Sandy, Cumberland, Green, Barren, Nolin, Rough, Kanawha, Kentucky, White and Eel—is available from the Division Engineer, Ohio River Division, in Cincinnati. This list is in the form of a mimeographed Division Bulletin and contains much other valuable data on navigation of the Ohio.

Missing from the river map is the compass rose of coastal charts which enables the pilot to lay a compass course and determine true and magnetic bearings and courses. River charts generally show instead a simple arrow to indicate true north, and on strip charts north may not necessarily be at the top of the page. On charts of the Lower Mississippi, parallels of latitude and meridians of longitude are given. The compass is little used on river boats and the binoculars take its place to aid the pilot in sighting from one navigational aid to the next. In fog, this means that pleasure boat traffic comes pretty much to a standstill, though the big commercial craft carry on using radar for their eyes. This is not to imply that the compass can be dispensed with on all rivers and lakes. In the lower reaches of larger tidal rivers, like the Connecticut, compass courses are occasionally laid in fog, and on the Great Lakes where straight-line courses of 100 miles or more are not unusual, the compass is an indispensable accessory.

Charts of the Great Lakes

Piloting problems on the Great Lakes are much the same as they are along the coast because of the great expanse of water involved. Charts of the Great Lakes, published by the U. S. Lake Survey, are excellent, covering features of the navigable waters in great detail. They show depths of water (the lesser depths in blue tint), safe channels, submerged reefs and shoals, aids to navigation, adjacent shorelines with topographic features and landmarks, types of bottom, and much additional related information. Scales of the charts vary from as large as 1:2,500 to 1:20,000 for harbor charts and insets, down to 1:80,000 to 1:130,000 for coast charts, and 1:400,000 or 500,000 for general charts of individual lakes. Smallest scale used is the general chart of all the Great Lakes, at 1:1,200,000. For close work on the rivers, the scale varies from 1:15,000 to 1:40,000.

On Lake charts, the familiar compass rose is available, showing in orange tint both true and magnetic directions, with the variation stated. In parts of the Lakes, variation reduces to zero, where, except for deviation, which is always with us, magnetic and true courses are alike. Elsewhere on the Lakes, great deposits of iron ore in the earth produce a strong local attraction, most pronounced along the north shore of Lake Superior where variation has been observed to change from 26° to 7° in a distance of 650 feet.

Most Lake charts are on the polyconic projection and show some of the principal courses between ports, giving the course in both degrees true and points, with the distances in statute miles. Comparative elevations are referred to mean tide at New York.

To supplement the information available on Lake charts, cruising boatmen should have a copy of the Great Lakes Pilot (published by the U. S. Lake Survey, Detroit). Corresponding to the Coast Pilots used on coastal waters, it provides detailed information which cannot be given on the charts. Included are full descriptions of the waters charted, laws and regulations governing navigation, bridge clearances, signals for locks and bridges, dimensions and capacities of marine railways, and weather information. Purchasers of the Pilot get, free, seven monthly supplements (May-November) to keep the Pilot up to date.

The Army Engineers at Vicksburg, Miss., publish an informative pamphlet, "Mississippi River Navigation," which contains not only a great deal of interesting background information on navigation of the Mississippi, but also a few pages with explicit instructions "For Part-Time Pilots," the pleasure boatmen who are using the great river in increasing numbers.

Among other things, the Engineers caution against regarding the Mississippi with insufficient respect. The lower river, they point out, is very large, with low-water widths of ½ mile and bankfull widths up to 9000 feet. These bankfull stages generally occur between December and July, most frequently in March or April. Low-water stages occur in the fall months, October and November.

Lake Pepin typifies the kind of exposed area that may be encountered even on the upper river. This lake, a broadening of the river proper, is 21 miles long and up to 2½ miles in width. Sizable seas build up in such areas. Current velocities on the Mississippi average 4 to 6 mph. At extreme high stages of the river, velocities may be even greater in the narrower sections. At low and medium stages velocities range from 2 to 2½ mph.

River Engineers call special attention to the many kinds of floating equipment constantly at work on construction and maintenance projects along the river. Hydraulic pipeline dredges may have long lengths of floating pipeline which must be avoided. Bank protection equipment carried on barges may extend several hundred feet from shore into the stream, frequently in the swiftest part of the current. Small craft should keep well clear of all such equipment because of the hazard of being swept under it. As a matter of fact, on all waters, river traffic should exercise caution and consideration when passing dredges and similar equipment, slowing down to avoid doing damage with the wake. Army Engineers have prepared regulations governing lights and day signals displayed by all types of craft working on river projects, and the passing of such equipment by other vessels. These will be found in full detail in one section of the Pilot Rules for Western Rivers.

Though in some areas small craft do tie up to the river banks, the Engineers urge caution here, too. Avoid, they advise, vertical banks which may be in a stage of active caving. Exposed tree roots in the banks should be viewed with suspicion as a possible evidence of recent erosion. Such areas obviously are places to avoid when seeking a place to tie up along the bank. Rock riprap can be rough on a boat's bottom.

As for navigation of the river itself, the Engineers point out, too, that sand bars encountered during periods of low water may be quite unstable. Consequently, caution should be exercised in using them for camping or swimming. Floating and partially submerged debris, such as tree trunks and branches, constitute a navigational hazard for small craft, requiring a sharp lookout at all times. The same applies to piloting in the shallower areas, to avoid submerged stumps and snags. Floating debris is generally at its worst in the spring months under flood conditions, when high water and drifting logs may also shift buoys from their charted locations.

River currents sometimes flow so fast that buoys are towed under, leaving only a V-shaped eddy on the surface to reveal their location. Coastal boatmen have sometimes experienced this condition at inlets. Sometimes the top of the buoy will be visible to a boat bound upstream, or the wake of a passing boat may expose it momentarily.

The V-shaped surface eddy left by a buoy partially or totally submerged in a strong current will necessarily point upstream, as the wake divides downstream from the buoy. Any surface wake like this is to be mistrusted, as a submerged obstacle may lurk beneath. This is not to be confused with the condition where two currents meet at the downstream end of a middle bar where converging surface eddies may also show as a V shape, pointing downstream.

Photograph from Corps of Engineers

One of the major aids to navigation along the Mississippi is the light on shore. In this view, illustrating the position of a typical light used for marking bends and upper and lower ends of crossings, the steamer Mississippi approaches Four Mile Bayou Light, River Mile 728 A.H.P. Number board visible just above the light shows the mileage on the river side.

Piloting on the Mississippi River. Aids to Navigation on the Rivers.

Light Lists and Other Publications of Interest to the River Boatman.

Some Special Rules of the Road Applicable to River Cruising.

ON its meandering way to the Gulf, the Mississippi winds and twists and bends in a sinuous course that adds many miles to the airline distance. The river is eternally changing, and Army Engineers are everlastingly at work to maintain and improve the navigable channels. Sometimes, a single loop in the river will necessitate a 10-mile run to gain one mile on the route south.

At some of the bends, when the river goes on a rampage under flood conditions, it will cut a channel across the narrow neck of land, forming what is called a chute and creating an island from what was once a peninsula. With-

out local knowledge it is usually wise to avoid the chutes and stick to the main channel. To save distance and straighten navigable channels, the Army Engineers have dredged cut-offs, like the chutes, and these become the new navigable channel.

This constant changing of the Mississippi's course, both by nature and by dredging, has left old channels as dead-end arms of the new, and elsewhere, by closing them off, has created horseshoe-shaped ("oxbow") lakes with no connection with the new channel. River piloting always demands close attention to the chart to avoid being shunted

Extract from the Mississippi River Light List, showing some of the lights and daymarks on the Illinois Waterway. Distances are given in statute miles, above Grafton. These agree with mileages given on aids to navigation. Note the data given on visibility of directional lights.

Name of aid Character and period of light	Number of miles from Grafton	Bank or side of channel	Remarks
GRIST ISLAND BEND DAYMARK	258.9	Left	
Grist Island Light Fl. W., 2 sec.	258.8	Right	Visible 360° with 3° directional light oriented downstream.
Barry Island Light Fl. W., 2 sec.	256.0	Right	Visible 360° with 3° directional light oriented upstream.
Heule Light Fl. W., 2 sec.	255.1	Right	3° directional light oriented downstream; daymark.
C., R. I. & P. Ry Bridge, vertical lift. Clearances: Horizontal, 141 feet; vertical, closed 19.9 feet, open 47.5 feet, above pool stage.	254.1		
ROCK ISLAND BRIDGE DAYMARK	254.1	Left	Painted on bridge pier.

into one of the unnavigable arms, or a dead-end heading.

On the Mississippi, as on most rivers, the deepest water and the fastest current are usually found on the outside of bends, at the end of dikes and along the steep banks. As a rule, gently shelving shores should be given a wide berth. Always be wary of unusual surface conditions, especially at high water. A smooth slick or a line or broken water may reveal the presence of a submerged dike or wing dam, used to control the direction of flow of river current. As these wing dams are often submerged even at normal river stages, they constitute a real hazard unless close attention is paid to the chart.

No flat statement can be made as to the relative depth of water indicated by certain sets of surface conditions. This requires a river sense the pilot must develop with experience. On the one hand, where there is a chop in the channel there may be areas of relatively smooth slicks over the bars, especially if there is any weed growth present. As against this, there will be combinations of wind-current conditions where the channel will be comparatively smooth with ripples to reveal the bars. In some narrow river channels, with wind against the current, a small sea builds up in which the larger waves disclose the deeper water, growing progressively smaller until there is no sea at all on the bars at channel's edge. But under any given set of conditions, the boatman with an eye peeled for natural signs will, with the aid of his chart and the buoys, quickly learn to read the signs the river has for those eager to understand its secrets.

Boatmen running the rivers bring back widely conflicting reports of hazards encountered, or the absence of them. Perhaps this may be attributed to the fact that one made his cruise in the early spring, encountering high water, flood conditions, racing currents and drifting trees pos-

ing a constant threat to propellers, even to hulls. Another, no doubt, has made his trip under ideal conditions in September or October, possibly as the first leg of a cruise down to the Gulf and Florida for the winter season. With water levels at a low stage and currents at reasonable velocities, no obstacles have been encountered on the entire cruise from Lakes to Gulf. There is that much difference in seasonal conditions. River navigation at extreme flood stages, as a rule, is not to be recommended without the services of an experienced pilot.

A typical example of this conflict in reports of conditions observed is the story of "sand boils" in the Mississippi caused by sand piling up on the river bed. One reports these whirlpool-like disturbances so violent that they practically throw the boat out of control. Others, in more favorable months, find them no worse than surface eddies felt at the helm, but certainly with no element of danger for a boat. (For a swimmer, it might be otherwise.)

Some river boatmen have reported underwater bearings ruined, jackets filled with silt, and water pump gears worn out at the end of one river run. Others have observed no difficulty whatever on this score. As a general rule, as in all other places where waters are laden with silt, the logical course is to provide, in advance, what protection is available in the form of effective water strainers, fresh water cooling systems, cutless type underwater bearings, and pump impellers of a type that will handle mud and sand better than bronze gears.

Discounting all the stories of violent current disturbances, the fact remains, of course, that current is a real factor to be reckoned with on the rivers. When one stream of some velocity flows out into another, a small boat crossing the current at the mouth will feel the effect of this set and will probably have to allow

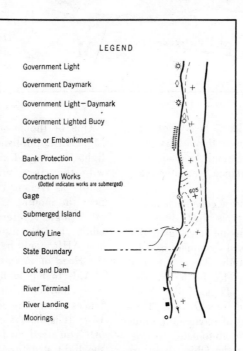

LEGEND

Government Light
Government Daymark
Government Light—Daymark
Government Lighted Buoy
Levee or Embankment
Bank Protection
Contraction Works
(Dotted indicates works are submerged)
Gage
Submerged Island
County Line
State Boundary
Lock and Dam
River Terminal
River Landing
Moorings

Symbols used on charts of the Middle and Upper Mississippi River—Cairo to Minneapolis—all in black and white, no distinguishing colors.

A fleet of pleasure craft heading downstream on the Mississippi River after leaving the lock chamber at Harvey Lock, on the west bank at New Orleans. About two dozen craft have passed through at one time in a single locking. Note the towboats standing by waiting their turn to enter lock. Gate (lower right corner) is closed; other (center) is open.

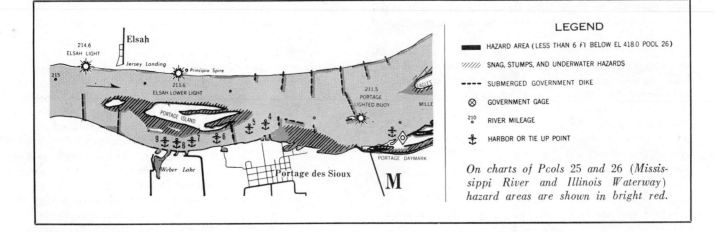

LEGEND

▬ HAZARD AREA (LESS THAN 6 FT BELOW EL 418.0 POOL 26)

/////// SNAG, STUMPS, AND UNDERWATER HAZARDS

---- SUBMERGED GOVERNMENT DIKE

⊗ GOVERNMENT GAGE

²¹⁰ RIVER MILEAGE

⚓ HARBOR OR TIE UP POINT

On charts of Pools 25 and 26 (Mississippi River and Illinois Waterway) hazard areas are shown in bright red.

somewhat by heading up into it. Pilots of heavy commercial craft are keenly aware of the way they carry with the current under their vessel. To the small boat operator it's a factor of relatively less importance, yet significant enough to be remembered at all times.

Since conditions on the river are in a constant state of flux, with channels changing and levels fluctuating, the river boatman should keep posted on the latest available data at all times. Just as the coastal boatman has his *Notices to Mariners* to turn to for authoritative information, so, too, the river boatman can refer to the *Navigation Bulletins* issued by the district offices of the Army Engineers at Memphis, Vicksburg and New Orleans. They show latest sailing directions, locations of navigational aids such as lights, buoys, etc., and similar up-to-date information required by the river pilot. For the Ohio, there are *Notices to Navigation Interests,* available from the Engineer Office at Pittsburgh.

Detailed information on rules and regulations applicable to the Mississippi may always be obtained from the Commander of the 2nd Coast Guard District at St. Louis.

One of the most helpful aids to the river pilot is the Light List, published by the U.S. Coast Guard. In it all lights, buoys and aids to navigation are tabulated, together with the river mileage (in statute miles to the nearest tenth) as reckoned from a zero point which may be at or near the mouth, as in the case of the Mississippi, or some other logical reference point, such as Pittsburgh on the Ohio. For the Lower Mississippi, a designation of Mile 104 AHP would be interpreted as 104 statute miles "Above the Head of Passes."

Aids to navigation along the river banks are conspicuously marked with mileages which correspond to the distances from the zero reference tabulated in the Light List. It is always an easy matter, therefore, to get a "fix." All you need do is read the mileage as posted on one of the light structures ashore, and compare with the mileage figures given on the chart. These lighted aids, of various shapes, are painted white and have names which appear on the charts and in the Light Lists as well. The mileage figures take the place of the odd and even numbers that are characteristic of buoys on coastal waters. They are a

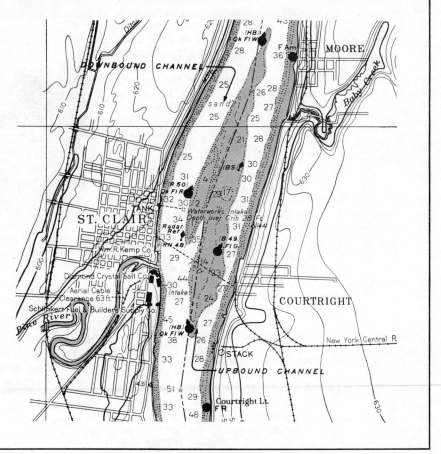

Portion of U.S. Lake Survey Chart No. 43 (Saint Claire River) scale 1:40,000, drawn on the polyconic projection, in which distortion is very small and relative sizes are correctly preserved. Depths are referred to the sloping surface of the river at specified lake levels above mean tide at New York. Note the International Boundary, in mid-stream, and separate channels around the flats for traffic upstream and downstream. River traffic here is heavy. Illustration is to the same scale as the chart itself.

A light and mileage board, showing the river mile. Note the wake of the strong river current flowing past the piles of the dike. Currents are a factor to be reckoned with in river piloting.

distinct convenience in computing boat speeds and figuring the total day's run from the log.

In the larger rivers, it is usually feasible to run close to shore to identify the aid from the Light List, then head for the next, picking it up with binoculars if necessary. In closer work on some narrower rivers, as previously cautioned, it may be wise to ease around bends to follow the channel trend as delineated by the buoys rather than running straight from aid to aid. With no aids to serve as guides, the safest practice usually is to favor the center, keeping at least one-quarter of the river's width off the bank.

Designation of the banks of a river may at first be confusing. Left and right banks are named relative to your course *downstream*. The left bank, in river terminology, is the left bank as you face downstream; the right bank to your right facing downstream. On the New York State Barge Canal, however, when regulations refer to the "starboard" side of the canal, they mean the right hand side entering from Waterford. Thus the starboard side of the Champlain Canal is the east side; but on the

Erie Canal, the north side becomes the starboard side.

Most lights on the Mississippi River System show through 360°—visible, that is, all around the horizon. In some cases, however, directional aids project the light in one direction only. Some of these directional aids suplement the power of a 360° light by increasing the candlepower in one direction only. The arc through which the directional beam is visible varies with the navigational need of the locality. A concentrated beam may be used in a long narrow reach, but a wider spread in a more open area where conditions are less critical.

Generally speaking, lights on the Western Rivers are placed strategically at the upper and lower ends of crossings as marks to steer by, with additional lights between as required by conditions. Where there are no crossings, lights are used along the banks as passing lights. Reference to the chart will indicate how the light is to be used.

Daymarks on the Mississippi are usually white diamond shapes with number board at the top to designate the mileage. In the center, a red triangle is used for left bank aids (descending the river) and a vertical black rectangle for right (descending) bank aids. Daymarks have a reflector at each of the four corners, red on the left bank, white on the right bank. Daymarks among the trees on shore may take the form of two white boards crossed in the form of an X.

The coastal boatman will have no difficulty whatever with buoyage systems on the rivers. In the main, they will follow the same basic principle which puts black can-type buoys to port and red nun-type buoys to starboard when entering from seaward. Sometimes, as on the Mississippi, buoys will be topped with white for improved visibility, to show up against shore backgrounds.

Buoys on the Mississippi carry reflectors similar to those used on shore aids—red on the left bank, white on the right bank. Buoys marking wrecks show a quick flashing light, white or red on the left (descending) side of the channel, white or green on the right (descending) side. On buoys marking channel junctions or obstructions, the light characteristic is an interrupted quick flash (5 flashes 10 times a minute). Generally in mid-channel these lights will be white; red if toward the left side of the channel; and green if toward the right. As on the coast, the red-and-black horizontally banded buoy is used to mark junctions and obstructions. If found near the edge of a channel, it should be passed with caution, taking soundings to determine which is the proper side.

In all cases, buoys should be followed with reference to whatever charts or navigational maps may be available, as deviations from the conventional system of buoyage will be found in some rivers. On the New York State Barge Canal, for example, buoys are alike in shape on both sides of the channel. Entering from seaward, red buoys with red lights are on the starboard hand, but white buoys with white lights are found on the port hand. When craft are anchored at night along the side of the canal marked by red navigation lights, New York state authorities require the use of a red, rather than white, anchor light.

The chart, invariably, will prevent confusion and misunderstanding in following any system of buoyage. Symbols for can and nun buoys on Ohio River charts will seem particularly strange to coastal boatmen (See illustration, Part Two, from the legend.) In the Great Lakes Light List, Canadian buoys are specially identified by the letter C. Except for minor differences in design, the system of buoyage used in Canadian waters is in agreement with that adopted by the United States.

On some of the rivers, notably the Hudson and the Connecticut, where channels through flats in the river are stabilized and maintained by dredging, ranges on shore marked by conspicuous squares and diamonds are of great aid to the pilot in staying inside the limits of a narrow channel. Aligning the front and rear ranges, the pilot can hold his course in mid-channel, despite even heavy cross winds that might otherwise tend to set him off on the shoal to leeward.

Special River Rules

If the coastal boatman cruises far inland, his course will inevitably lead him into waters where Pilot Rules for traffic afloat—the Rules of the Road—differ from those to which he is accustomed. Consequently he should study in detail the rules applicable to the particular waters he uses.

On the coast, vessels operate mainly under two sets of rules—the International Rules when outside the boundaries prescribed for the high seas (even though this be just outside the inlet or off the beach), and the Inland Rules for waters inside these boundaries, with certain exceptions. It is these exceptions which require attention. For example, on the Great Lakes and their connecting and tributary waters as far east as Montreal, and the St. Marys River, vessels are subject to the Great Lakes Rules. On the Mississippi River system, with its tributaries, between its source and the Huey P. Long Bridge, ten miles above New Orleans (including part of the Atchafalaya River), and the Red River of the North, they are subject to the Pilot Rules for Western Rivers.

Elsewhere, the specific differences in rules under the four jurisdictions have been treated at length (see "How Pilot Rules Differ," *Piloting, Seamanship and Small Boat Handling,* Chapter IV). It is outside the scope of this series to repeat them here. In broad principle, Western River Rules are largely in general agreement with International Rules. However, it is interesting to point up a few of the outstanding differences encountered on the rivers.

We have already called attention to one Western River rule for vessels meeting in narrow channels, which gives right of

A typical Mississippi river bank riprapped with cement to protect banks against erosion. Boatmen must use care near such banks due to risk of damage to the boat's bottom.

way to a vessel bound downstream. Here is an example of a special rule having particular significance to the river pilot. The ascending (burdened) vessel, bound upstream, must sound the first passing signal, but vessels pass on the side determined by the (privileged) descending vessel.

Ascending vessels, on the Western Rivers, stop if necessary below the entrance of narrow channels to allow descending vessels to pass through. At the confluence of two rivers, the vessel having the other to port gives the first signal.

Bends in rivers, insofar as floating traffic is concerned, may be compared with blind corners on the road. Western River Rules provide that when a vessel could not be seen at a distance of 600 yards, three distinct blasts are to be sounded on the whistle. This warning signal must be answered by any approaching vessel within hearing around the bend, and the vessels exchange the usual passing signals only when they come within sight of each other. (On waters other than Western Rivers, the warning signal at a bend is a long, or prolonged, blast.)

Commercial craft on Western Rivers use a special amber visual signal synchronized with their passing whistle signal blasts. Motorboats are exempt from this rule. On both the Western Rivers and Great Lakes passing whistle signals are given in all weathers, regardless of visibility.

The fog signal for power-driven vessels under way on the Rivers is 3 distinct blasts every minute (2 of equal length, followed by a longer one). Sailing vessels give the same fog signals prescribed for power-driven vessels, but use the fog horn.

When towing, power-driven vessels sound 3 distinct blasts of equal length, at intervals of not more than 1 minute. Steamers lying to during fog or thick weather, when another vessel is heard approaching, give 1 tap on the bell if lying at the right bank, 2 taps if lying at the left bank, at 1-minute intervals.

One other fundamental difference, peculiar to Western River rules, requires a privileged vessel to hold her course, but not her speed. When risk of collision exists, all power-driven vessels reduce speed or stop if necessary.

If in cruising the Great Lakes and northern rivers, you should cross the International Boundary into Canada, bear in mind that there are customs and immigration regulations to be observed.

For detailed information on rules of the road, right of way, whistle signals, fog signals, lights for all types of craft and other pertinent regulations, the boatman is referred to the Pilot Rules, available free from Coast Guard Marine Inspection Offices in principal ports, or the Commandant (CHS), U.S. Coast Guard, Washington, D.C.

PUBLICATIONS OF INTEREST TO RIVER PILOTS

One of the best single sources of information concerning charts of inland waters and other publications on river piloting is the Mississippi River Commission, Corps of Engineers, U. S. Army, P.O. Box 80, Vicksburg, Miss. They publish a comprehensive mimeographed list of offices which issue charts of the various sections of the Mississippi, Missouri, Ohio and other tributaries, the Illinois Waterway, Great Lakes, etc. This list also includes mention of many publications of the Coast Guard and other government agencies. A Division Bulletin listing in detail all charts of the Ohio and its tributaries is prepared by the Division Engineer, Ohio River Division, P.O. Box 1159, Cincinnati 1, Ohio.

RIVER CHARTS, as well as the indispensable **NAVIGATION BULLETINS** and **NOTICES TO NAVIGATION INTERESTS** are distributed by the various offices of the Corps of Engineers, U. S. Army. in the areas over which they have jurisdiction. They are located at:

Memphis District—P.O. Box 97, Memphis 1, Tenn.
Vicksburg District—P.O. Box 60, Vicksburg, Miss.
New Orleans District—Foot of Prytania Street, New Orleans, La.
St. Louis District—420 Locust St., St. Louis 2, Mo.
Rock Island District—Clock Tower Building, Rock Island, Ill.
St. Paul District—U. S. Post Office & Customhouse, 180 E. Kellogg Blvd., St. Paul 1, Minn.
Missouri River Division—Farm Credit Bldg., 206 So. 19th St., Omaha 1, Neb.
Chicago District—475 Merchandise Mart, Merchandise Mart Plaza, Chicago 54, Ill.
North Central Division—536 So. Clark St., Chicago 5, Ill.
Ohio River Division—P.O. Box 1159, Cincinnati 1, Ohio.
Pittsburgh District—925 New Federal Bldg., Pittsburgh, Pa.
Huntington District—237 Fourth Ave., P.O. Box 2127, Huntington 18, W. Va.
Louisville District—830 West Broadway, P.O. Box 59, Louisville 1, Ky.
Nashville District—306 Federal Office Bldg., P.O. Box 1070, Nashville 1, Tenn.
Southwestern Division—1114 Commerce St., Dallas 2, Texas.
Galveston District—606 Santa Fe Bldg., Galveston, Texas.
Mobile District—2301 Grant St., Mobile 7, Ala.

CHARTS—Tennessee River—Available from the Tennessee Valley Authority, Maps and Engineering Records Section, 102A Union Building, Knoxville, Tennessee. Bound sets available from District Engineers at Cincinnati, Nashville and Louisville.

CHARTS—Great Lakes and connecting rivers, Lake Champlain, New York Canals and Minnesota-Ontario Border Lakes (including some Canadian waters). U. S. Lake Survey, Corps of Engineers, U. S. Army, 630 Federal Building, Detroit 26, Mich.

CHARTS—Canadian Waters. Hydrographic Chart Distribution, Canadian Hydrographic Service, Department of Mines and Technical Surveys, 615 Booth St., Ottawa, Canada.

CHARTS—Coastal Waters and Intracoastal Waterway, New York to Florida. Also Coast Pilots, Tide Tables and Current Tables, all for coastal waters. U. S. Coast & Geodetic Survey, Washington 25, D. C. (The Coast Pilot for the Gulf Coast contains much valuable data on the Mississippi River System.)

NOTICE TO MARINERS—Data for up-to-date corrections to coastal charts, Coast Pilots, etc. U. S. Oceanographic Office, Navy Department, Washington, D. C. (Local daily notices available from Commanders of the various Coast Guard Districts. For the Mississippi, from St. Louis and New Orleans offices.)

LIGHT LISTS—Separate volumes for Mississippi River System, Great Lakes, and coastal waters. Superintendent of Documents, Government Printing Office, Washington 25, D. C., and local Coast Guard offices at St. Louis and New Orleans.

GREAT LAKES PILOT—U. S. Lake Survey, Corps of Engineers, U. S. Army, 630 Federal Building, Detroit 26, Mich.

YACHTSMAN'S GUIDE TO THE GREAT LAKES—Seaport Publishing Co., 843 Delray Ave., S.E., Grand Rapids 6, Mich.

RULES OF THE ROAD—Separate volumes for Inland Waters of Atlantic and Pacific Coasts and Gulf of Mexico; Great Lakes; and Western Rivers. U. S. Coast Guard Headquarters, Washington 25, D. C. For Western Rivers, available also from local Coast Guard offices at St. Louis and New Orleans.

REGULATIONS to Govern the Use, Administration and Navigation of the Ohio River, Mississippi River above Cairo, Ill. and Their Tributaries—District Engineer, St. Louis, Mo. (Also available at any lock.)

RULES AND REGULATIONS to Govern the Operation of Drawbridges Crossing the Mississippi River and All Its Tributaries and Outlets—District Engineer, Chicago, Ill.

RULES AND REGULATIONS Governing Navigation and Use of the New York State Canal System—Superintendent of Operation and Maintenance, State Department of Public Works, Albany, N. Y.

NEW YORK STATE CANALS AND WATERWAYS—Official map, with condensed information on canal system, navigational aids, pleasure boat regulations, data on locks, etc. Superintendent of Operation and Maintenance, State Department of Public Works, Albany, N. Y.

CRUISING GUIDE BOOK for the New York State Barge Canal System and Connecting Navigable Canadian Lakes, Rivers and Waterways—Cruising Guidebook, 146 Sheridan Ave., Albany, N. Y.

MISSISSIPPI RIVER NAVIGATION—Division Engineer, Lower Mississippi Valley Division, Corps of Engineers, U. S. Army, P. O. Box 80, Vicksburg, Miss.

LOCKING THROUGH—Things you should know if you use navigation locks, District Engineer, St. Louis, Mo. Also available from other District Engineers.

OHIO RIVER HANDBOOK—Piloting information, statistics, lore and legend pertaining to the Ohio and its tributaries. Young & Klein, Inc., 1351 Spring Lawn Ave., Cincinnati 23, Ohio.

YOUR OHIO—Pamphlet of general interest. Corps of Engineers, Ohio Division.

RADIO AIDS TO NAVIGATION, GREAT LAKES—U. S. Coast Guard, 9th District, Main Post Office Building, Cleveland 13, Ohio.

INLAND WATERWAY GUIDE, Great Lakes Edition—Inland Waterway Guide, Inc., 101 North Andrews Ave., Fort Lauderdale, Fla.

RECREATION IN TVA LAKES—Tabulates boat docks and related services, with map. Information Office, Tennessee Valley Authority, Knoxville, Tenn.

BOATING AND FISHING GUIDE to the Great Lakes of the South—The Nashville Tennessean, Nashville, Tenn.

MAP, PRINCIPAL WATERWAYS OF THE UNITED STATES—Chief of Engineers, Department of the Army, Operations Division, Civil Works, Washington 25, D. C.

CHARTING THE GREAT LAKES—The story of the United States Lake Survey, United States Lake Survey, 630 Federal Bldg., Detroit 26, Mich.

CRUISING GUIDES AND CHARTS AND HARBOR BOOKLETS—Several of the large oil companies offer useful publications dealing with the inland waterways. Texaco Waterways Service, 135 E. 42nd St., New York 17, N. Y.; Gulf Tourgide Bureau, Box 8056, Philadelphia 1, Pa. (east of Mississippi); Mobil Touring Service, Mobil Oil Co., 150 E. 42nd St., New York, N. Y.; Esso Touring Service, 15 W. 51st St., New York 19, N. Y.

NAVIGATION LOCKS AND DAMS, MISSISSIPPI RIVER—District Engineer, St. Louis, Mo.

TIPS ON RIVER SAFETY—District Engineer, St. Louis, Mo.

MISSISSIPPI RIVER, CHAIN OF ROCKS CANAL AND LOCKS—District Engineer, St. Louis, Mo.

THE GULF INTRACOASTAL WATERWAY—District Engineer, Vicksburg, Miss. (Charts from same source.) More complete pamphlet available from Superintendent of Documents, Washington 25, D. C.

YOUR KEY TO THE LOCK—U. S. Army Engineer District, Corps of Engineers, Room 322, Federal Building, P. O. Box 991, Albany 1, N. Y. Pamphlet prepared for the guidance of yachtsmen passing through the Federal Lock at Troy, N. Y.

From "Your Key to the Lock"

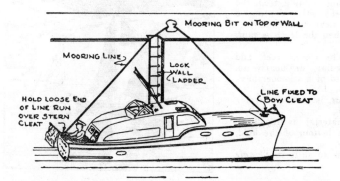

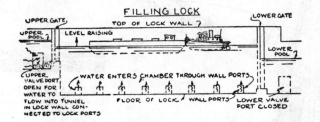

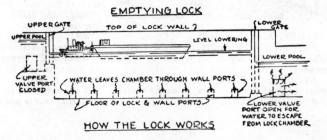

HOW THE LOCK WORKS

CHAPTER XXX

NAUTICAL DICTIONARY

Illustrations by Meredith A. Scott

A

ABACK. The position of the sails when the wind presses their surface toward the mast, tending to force the vessel astern.

ABAFT. Toward the stern.

ABEAM. On the side of the vessel, amidships, or at right angles.

ABOARD. Within, on board the vessel.

ABOUT. To go on the opposite tack.

ABREAST. Alongside of. Side by side.

A-COCK-BILL. The position of the yards of a ship when they are topped up at an angle with the deck. The position of an anchor when it hangs to the cathead.

ADRIFT. Broken from moorings or fasts.

AFLOAT. Resting on the surface of the water.

AFORE. Forward. The opposite of abaft.

AFT. Near the stern.

AGROUND. Touching the bottom.

AHEAD. In the direction of the vessel's bow. *Wind ahead* is from the direction toward which the vessel's head points.

AHULL. When a vessel lies with her sails furled and her helm lashed alee.

ALEE. When the helm is in the opposite direction from that in which the wind blows.

ALL-ABACK. When all the sails are aback. (See *Aback.*)

ALL HANDS. The entire crew.

ALL IN THE WIND. When all the sails are shaking.

ALOFT. Above the deck.

AMIDSHIPS. In the centre of the vessel; either with reference to her length or to her breadth.

ANCHOR. An iron instrument which, when dropped to the bottom, holds the vessel.

ANCHOR-WATCH. (See *Watch.*)

APEAK. When the cable is hove taut so as to bring the vessel over her anchor.

APRON. A timber fixed behind the lower part of the stem above the fore end of the keel.

ARM. YARD-ARM. The extremity of a yard. Also, the lower part of an anchor, crossing the shank, and terminating in the flukes.

ARMING. A piece of tallow put in the cavity and over the bottom of a lead-line.

ASTERN. In the direction of the stern. The opposite of ahead.

ATHWART. Across.

Athwart-ships. Across the line of the vessel's keel.

Athwart-hawse. Across the direction of a vessel's head. Across her cable.

ATHWART-SHIPS. Across the length of a vessel. The opposite to fore-and-aft.

ATRIP. The position of the anchor when it is raised clear of the ground.

AVAST. To stop; "Avast heaving!"

AWEATHER. When the helm is put in the direction from which the wind blows.

AWEIGH. The same as atrip.

AWNING. A covering of canvas over a vessel's deck, or over a boat, to keep off sun or rain.

AYE. Yes; and is always used in lieu therefor at sea, as "Aye, aye, sir," meaning "I understand."

B

BACK. To back an anchor, is to carry out a smaller one ahead of the one by which the vessel rides, to take off some of the strain.

To back a sail, is to throw it aback. (See *Aback.*)

To back and fill, is to alternately back and fill the sails.

To back water, is to push on the oars, to give a boat sternway.

BACKSTAYS. Rigging running from the masthead to the vessel's side, slanting a little aft, or to the deck near the stern.

BAG. A sail bags when the leech is taut, and the canvas slack.

BALANCE-REEF. The closest reef, and makes the sail triangular, or nearly so.

BALD-HEADED. Said of a schooner having no topmasts.

BAIL. To bail a boat, is to throw water out of her. (Also *bale.*)

BALLAST. Heavy material, as iron, lead, or stone, placed in the bottom of the hold, to keep a vessel steady.

To freshen ballast, is to shift it. *Shingle ballast is coarse gravel.*

BALLOON JIB. A large triangular headsail used in light and moderate weather, with a free wind.

BANK. A boat is *double banked* when two oars, one opposite the other, are pulled by men seated on the same thwart.

BAR. A bank or shoal. *Capstan-bars* are heavy pieces of wood by which the capstan is worked.

BARE-POLES. The condition of a vessel when she has no sail set.

BARGE. A large double-banked boat, usually used by the commander of a vessel in the navy.

BARK, OR BARQUE. A three-masted vessel, having her fore and main masts rigged like a ship's, and her mizzen mast like the main mast of a schooner, with no sail upon it but a spanker, and gaff topsail.

BARNACLE. A shell-fish often found on a vessel's bottom.

BATTENS. Thin strips of wood put around the hatches, to keep the tarpaulin down. Also, put upon rigging to keep it from chafing. A large batten widened at the end, and put upon rigging, is called a *scotchman*. Battens are often used on yachts on the leech of a mainsail to make it set flat.

BEACON. A post or buoy placed over a shoal or bank to warn vessels of danger. Also a signalmark on land.

BEAMS. Strong pieces of timber stretching across the vessel, to support the decks.

On the weather or lee beam, is in a direction to windward or leeward, at right angles with the keel.

On beam-ends. The situation of a vessel when turned over so that her beams are inclined toward the vertical.

BEAR. An object *bears* so and so, when it is in such direction from the person looking.

To bear down upon a vessel, is to approach her from the windward.

To bear a hand. To make haste.

BEARING. The direction of an object from the person looking. The *bearings* of a vessel are the widest part of her below the plank-sheer. That part of her hull which is on the water-line when she is at anchor and in her proper trim.

BEATING. Going toward the direction of the wind, by alternate tacks.

BECALM. To intercept the wind. A vessel

to windward is said to *becalm* another. So one sail *becalms* another. A highland has the same effect. (See blanket.)

BECKET. A piece of rope placed so as to confine a spar or another rope. A handle made of rope, in the form of a circle; the handle of a chest is called a *becket*.

BEES. Pieces of plank bolted to the outer end of the bowsprit, to reeve the foretopmast stays through.

BEFORE THE WIND. Said of a sailing vessel when the wind is coming from aft, over the stern.

BELAY. To make a rope or line fast by turns around a pin or coil, without hitching or seizing it.

BELOW. Beneath, or under, the deck. One *goes below* when going down into the cabin.

BEND. To make fast.

To bend a sail, is to make it fast to the spar.

To bend a cable, is to make it fast to the anchor.

A bend, is a knot by which one rope is made fast to another.

BENDS. The strongest part of a vessel's side, to which the beams, knees, and foothooks are bolted. The part between the water's edge and the bulwarks.

BERTH. The place where a vessel lies. The place in which a person sleeps.

BETWEEN DECKS. The space between any two decks of a ship.

BIBBS. Pieces of timber bolted to the hounds of a mast, to support the trestle-trees.

BIGHT. The double part of a rope when it is folded. Any part of a rope may be called the bight, except the ends. Also, a bend in the shore, making a small bay or inlet.

———— • ————

The language of the sea is spiced with terms and phrases so trenchant and vigorous that "salty talk" is no idle figure of speech. Our nautical terminology of today has been handed down from an era of "iron men and wooden ships," when wind-bellied canvas drove tall-sparred vessels to the ends of the *Seven Seas*. Often the boatman using nautical terms as they are commonly applied today, fails to grasp the significance of their original derivations. While the barbed expletives and commands that flew so freely across the decks of ancient windjammers would scarcely be appropriate aboard a modern yacht (and quickly be recognized as affectations when so used), an understanding of the jargon of the sea is certainly an aid to fuller appreciation of its literature. If this nautical dictionary aids in such an understanding, and helps the reader to add a dash of salt to his nautical talk, while avoiding such affectation, it will have served its purpose well. The definitions are necessarily brief; all could be amplified if space permitted.

BILGE. That part of the floor of a ship upon which she would rest if aground; being the part near the keel which is more in a horizontal than a perpendicular line.

Bilge ways. Pieces of timber bolted together and placed under the bilge, in launching.

Bilged. When the bilge is broken in.

Bilge Water. Water which settles in the bilge.

Bilge. The largest circumference of a cask.

BILGEWAYS. Timbers placed beneath a vessel when building.

BILL. The point at the extremity of a fluke of an anchor.

BINNACLE. A receptable placed near the helm, containing the compass, etc.

BITTS. Perpendicular pieces of timber going through the deck, to secure ropes to. The cables are fastened to them, if there is no windlass. There are also *bitts* to secure the windlass, and on each side of the heel of the bowsprit.

BITTER, OR BITTER-END. The inboard end of an anchor cable secured to the bitt, or below decks to some strong structural member.

BLADE. The flat part of an oar which goes into the water.

BLANKET. A vessel to windward of another is said to blanket the leeward vessel when she takes the wind from the latter's sails, due to their relative positions.

BLOCK. A piece of wood with sheaves, or wheels, through which the running rigging passes, to add to the purchase.

BLUFF. A vessel which is full and square forward.

BOARD. The stretch a vessel makes upon one tack, when she is beating.

Stern-board. When a vessel goes stern foremost.

By the board. When the masts of a vessel fall over the side.

BOAT-HOOK. An iron hook with a long staff.

BOATSWAIN. A ship's officer who has charge of the rigging and who calls the crew to duty.

BOBSTAYS. Used to confine the bowsprit to the stem or cutwater.

BOLSTERS. Pieces of soft wood, covered with canvas, placed on the trestle-trees, for the eyes of the rigging to rest upon.

BOLTS. Cylindrical bars of iron, copper, or composition, used to secure the different parts of a vessel.

BOLT-ROPE. The rope which goes round a sail, and to which the canvas is sewed.

BONNET. An additional piece of canvas attached to the foot of a jib by lacings.

BOOBY HATCH. A raised small hatch.

BOOM. A spar used to extend the foot of a fore-and-aft sail or studdingsail.

Boom-horse. A curved metal fitting made into the boom band, on which a sheet-block travels.

Boom-irons. Iron rings on the yards, through which the studdingsail booms traverse.

BOOMKIN. A short spar projecting from the stern, to which a sheet block is secured, for an overhanging boom.

BOTTOMRY. A term in marine law referring to mortgaging on ships.

BOUND. Refers to destination or condition of vessel. (Outward bound, fogbound.)

BOW. The rounded part of a vessel, forward.

BOWER. A working anchor, the cable of which is bent and reeved through the hawsehole.

Best bower is the larger of the two bowers.

BOWLINE. A rope leading forward from the leech of a square sail, to keep the leech well out when sailing close-hauled. A vessel is said to be *on a bowline*, or *on a taut bowline*, when she is close-hauled. Also a knot tied in the end of a line to form a loop that will not slip.

Bowline-bird. The span on the leech of the sail to which the bowline is toggled.

BOWSE. To pull upon a tackle.

BOWSPRIT. A large, strong spar, standing from the bows of a vessel.

BOX-HAULING. Wearing a vessel by backing the head sails.

BOX. *To box the compass*, is to repeat the thirty-two points of the compass in order.

BRACE. A rope by which a yard is turned about.

To brace a yard, is to turn it about horizontally.

To brace up, is to lay the yard more fore-and-aft.

To brace in, is to lay it nearer square.

To brace to, is to brace the head yards a little aback, in tacking or wearing.

BRACKISH. Said of a mixture of fresh water and salt sea water.

BRAILS. Ropes by which the foot or lower corners of fore-and-aft sails are hauled up.

BRAKE. The handle of a ship's pump.

BREAK. *To break bulk*, is to begin to unload.

To break ground, is to lift the anchor from the bottom.

To break shear, is when a vessel, at anchor, in tending, is forced the wrong way by the wind or current, so that she does not lie well to keep clear of her anchor.

BREAKER. A small cask containing water.

Breakers. Waves broken by ledges or shoals.

BREAST-FAST. A rope used to confine a vessel broadside to a wharf, or to some other vessel.

BREAST-HOOKS. Knees in the forward part of a vessel, across the stem, to secure the bows.

BREAST-ROPE. A rope passed round a man in the chains, while sounding.

BREECH. The outside angle of a knee-timber. The after end of a gun.

BREECHING. A strong rope used to secure the breech of a gun to the ship's side.

BRIDLE. Spans of rope attached to the leeches of square sails to which the bowlines are made fast. *Bridle-port.* The foremost port, used for stowing the anchors.

BRIG. A square-rigged vessel, with two masts. An *hermaphrodite brig* is rigged on the foremast like a brig and on the mainmast like a schooner.

BRING TO. The act of stopping a sailing vessel by bringing her head up into the wind.

BROACH-TO. To slew round when running before the wind.

BROADSIDE. The whole side of a vessel.

BROKEN-BACK. When a vessel is so strained as to droop at each end.

BUCKLERS. Blocks of wood made to fit in the hawse-holes, or holes in the half-ports, when at sea. Those in the hawse-holes are sometimes called *hawse-blocks*.

BULK. The whole cargo when stowed. *Stowed in bulk,* is when goods are stowed loose, instead of being stowed in casks or bags.

BUNK. Bed on board ship.

BULKHEAD. Strong partitions in the hold of a vessel at regular lengths, to prevent water filling all parts of the vessel in case of accident.

Temporary partitions of boards to separate different parts of a vessel.

BULL. A sailor's term for a small keg, holding a gallon or two.

BULLS EYE. A small piece of stout wood with a hole in the centre for a stay or rope to reeve through, without a sheave, and with a groove round it for the strap, which is usually of iron. Also, a piece of thick glass inserted in the deck to let in light.

BULWARKS. Wood work around a vessel above deck, fastened to stanchions.

BUM-BOATS. Boats which lie alongside a vessel in port with provisions, fruit, etc., to sell.

BUMPKIN. Pieces of timber projecting from the vessel to board the fore tack to; also from each quarter, for the main brace-blocks.

BUNT. The middle of a sail.

BUNTING. Thin woolen stuff of which flags are made.

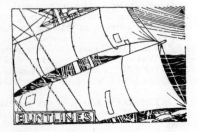

BUNTLINES. Ropes used for hauling up the body of a sail.

BUOY. A floating cask, or piece of wood, attached by a rope to an anchor, to show its position. Also, floated over a shoal, or other dangerous place as a beacon.

To stream a buoy, is dropping it into the water before letting go the anchor.

A buoy is said to *watch,* when it floats upon the surface of the water.

BURGEE. A small flag, either pointed or swallowtail.

BURTON. A tackle, rove in a particular manner.

A single Spanish burton has three single blocks, or two single blocks and a hook in the bight of one of the running parts.

A double Spanish burton has three double blocks.

BUSH. The center piece of a wooden sheave in a block.

BUTT. The end of a plank where it unites with the end of another.

Scuttle-butt. A cask with a hole cut in its bilge, and kept on deck to hold water.

BUTTOCK. That part of the convexity of a vessel abaft, under the stern, contained between the counter above and the after part of the bilge below, and between the quarter on the side and the stern-post.

BY. *By the Head.* When the head of a vessel is lower in the water than her stern. If her stern is lower, she is *by the stern. By the Wind.* Close-hauled.

C

CABLE. A large, strong rope, made fast by the anchor, by which the vessel is secured. A cable is usually 120 fathoms in length.

CABOOSE. A house on deck, where the cooking is done. Commonly called the *Galley.*

CALL. Bos'n's call used for piping orders.

CAMBER. A curvature upwards.

CAN-HOOKS. Slings with flat hooks at each end, used for hoisting barrels or light casks, the hooks being placed round the chimes, and the purchase hooked to the centre of the slings.

CANT-TIMBERS. Timbers at both ends of a vessel, raised obliquely from the keel.

Lower Half Cants. Those parts of frames situated forward and abaft the square frames or the floor timbers which cross the keel.

CANVAS. The cloth of which sails are made.

CAP. A thick, strong block of wood with two holes through it, one square and the other round, used to confine together the head of one mast and the lower part of the mast next above it.

CAPSIZE. To overturn.

CAPSTAN. A machine placed perpendicularly on the deck, used for heaving or hoisting.

CARDINAL POINTS. The four main points of the compass.

CAREEN. To heave a vessel down upon her side. To lie over, when sailing on the wind.

CARLINGS. Pieces of timber running between the beams.

CARRICK-BEND. A kind of knot. *Carrick bitts* are the windlass bitts.

CARRY-AWAY. To break a spar, or part a rope.

CARRY ON. To carry all sail possible.

CARVEL. Smooth-planked, as distinguished from lapstrake.

CAST. To pay a vessel's head off, in getting under way, on the tack she is to start upon.

To *cast off* a line is to let it go.

CAT. The tackle used to hoist the anchor up to the cat-head. *Cat-block,* the block of this tackle.

CAT BOAT. A sailboat having one mast, well forward, and no headsails.

CAT-HARPIN. An iron leg used to confine the upper part of the rigging to the mast.

CAT-HEAD. Large timbers projecting from the vessel's side, to which the anchor is secured.

CAT'S-PAW. A kind of hitch made in a rope. A light current of air on the surface of the water.

CAULK. To fill the seams of a vessel with oakum or caulking cotton.

CEILING. The inside sheathing of a vessel.

CENTERBOARD. A pivoted board or metal plate, housed in a trunk, which can be lowered to reduce a sailboat's tendency to make leeway when tacking.

CHAFE. To rub the surface. *Chafing-gear* is the stuff put upon rigging and spars to prevent chafing.

CHAINS. Strong links or plates of iron, the lower ends of which are bolted through the ship's side to the timbers. Their upper ends are secured to the bottom of the dead-eyes in the channels. The chain cable of a vessel is called familiarly her *chain*.

Rudder-chains lead from the outer and upper end of the rudder to the quarters.

CHAIN-PLATES. Plates of iron bolted to the side of a ship, to which the chains and dead-eyes of the lower rigging are connected.

CHAMFER. To take off the edge, or bevel the plank.

CHANNELS. Broad pieces of plank bolted edgewise to the outside of a vessel. Used in narrow vessels for spreading the lower rigging.

CHARTER PARTY. A contract in marine law.

CHECK. To stop or impede, as to check the cable from paying out.

CHEEKS. The projections on each side of a mast, upon which the trestle-trees rest. The sides of the shell of a block.

CHINE LOG. Longitudinal member used at the intersection of sides and bottom of flat or V-bottom boats.

CHINSE. To drive oakum into seams.

CHIPS. Nickname for ship's carpenter.

CHOCKS. Wedges used to secure anything with, or to rest upon. The long boat rests upon two *chocks*, when it is stowed. *Chock-a-block*. When the lower block of a tackle is run close up to the upper one, so that you can hoist no higher. This is also called *two-blocks*.

CISTERN. An apartment in the hold of a vessel, having a pipe leading out through the side, with a sea-cock, by which water may be let in.

CLAMPS. Thick planks on the inside of vessels, to support the ends of beams.

CLAWING OFF. To work off close-hauled from lee shore.

CLEAR. A vessel clears from a port when necessary papers are put in order at the custom house, preparatory to sailing. Lines or rigging are cleared when tangled gear is straightened out. Land is cleared when left as a vessel sails. The bilge is cleared when pumped out.

CLEAT. A piece of wood used in different parts of a vessel to belay ropes to.

CLEW. The lower corner of square sails, and the after corner of fore-and-aft sails.

CLEWLINE. A rope that hauls up the clew of a square sail.

CLINCH. A half-hitch, stopped to its own part.

CLINKER. Lapstrake planking, in which planks overlap at the edges, as distinguished from carvel (smooth).

CLOSE-HAULED. When a vessel is sailing as close to the wind as she will go.

CLOSE-REEFED. When all the reefs are taken in.

CLOVE-HITCH. Two half-hitches round a spar or other rope.

CLOVE-HOOK. An iron clasp, in two parts, moving upon the same pivot, and overlapping.

CLUBBING. Drifting down a current with an anchor out.

COAL TAR. Tar made from bituminous coal.

COAMINGS. Raised work around the hatches, to prevent water going into the hold.

COAT. *Mast-coat* is a piece of canvas, tarred or painted, placed around a mast or

COLLIER

bowsprit, where it enters the deck to keep out water.

COCK-BILL. To cock-bill a yard or anchor. (See *A-cock-bill*.)

COCKPIT. An apartment in a vessel of war, used by the surgeon during an action. A space or well, sunken below the sheer line. Usually aft, but small *forward cockpits* are also in common use on motor cruisers.

CODE SIGNALS. Flag signals for speaking at sea.

CODLINE. An eighteen thread line.

COIL. To lay a rope up in a circle, with one turn or fake over another.

A coil is a quantity of rope laid up in this manner.

COLLAR. An eye in the end or bight of a shroud or stay, to go over the mast-head.

COLLIER. A vessel used in coal trade.

COMPANION. A wooden covering over the staircase to a cabin.

Companion-way, the staircase to the cabin. *Companion ladder*. Leading from the poop to the main deck.

COMPASS. The instrument which shows the course of a vessel.

COMPOSITE. A vessel with iron or metal frame and wooden skin.

CONNING, or CUNNING. Directing the helmsman in steering a vessel.

CORINTHIAN. Amateur.

COUNTER. That part of a vessel between the bottom of the stern and the wing-transom and buttock. *Counter-timbers* are short timbers put in to strengthen the counter.

COURSES. The common term for the sails that hang from a ship's lower yards. The foresail is called the *fore course* and the mainsail the *main course*.

COXSWAIN. The person who steers a boat and has charge of her.

CRAB. To catch a crab is to catch the oar in the water by feathering it too soon.

CRADLE

CRADLE. A frame to hold a vessel upright when hauling her up.

CRAFT. A general term applied to any collection of small vessels.

CRANES. Pieces of iron or timber at the vessel's sides, used to stow boats or spars upon. A machine used for hoisting.

CRANK. A vessel which is inclined to lean over a great deal and cannot bear much sail.

CRANSE IRON. A cap or ring at end of bowsprit.

CREEPER. An iron instrument, with four claws, used for dragging the bottom of a harbor or river.

CRINGLE. A short piece of rope with each end spliced into the bolt-rope of a sail confining an iron ring or thimble.

CROSS-BARS. Round bars of iron, bent at each end, used to turn the shank of an anchor.

CROSS-JACK. The cross-jack yard is the lower yard on the mizzen mast.

CROSS-PAWL. Pieces of timber that keep a vessel together while in frame.

CROSS-PIECE. A piece of timber connecting two bitts.

CROSS-SPALES. Pieces of timber placed across a vessel, and nailed to the frames, to keep the sides together until the knees are bolted.

CROSS-TREES. Pieces of oak supported by the cheeks and trestle-trees at the mast-heads, to sustain the tops on the lower mast, and to spread the rigging at the topmast-head.

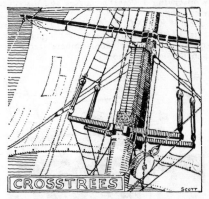

CROSSTREES

CROW-FOOT. A number of small lines rove through the euvrou to suspend an awning by.

CROWN of an anchor, is the place where the arms are joined to the shank.

To crown a knot, is to pass the strands over and under each other above the knot.

CRUTCH. A knee or piece of knee-timber, placed inside of a vessel to secure the heels of the cant-timbers abaft. Also the chock upon which the spanker-boom rests when the sail is not set.

CUCKOLD'S NECK. A knot by which a rope is secured to a spar, the two parts of the rope crossing each other, and seized together.

CUDDY. A cabin in the fore part of a boat.

CUT-WATER. The foremost part of a vessel's bow, which projects forward of the bows.

CUTTER. A small boat. Also, a kind of sloop.

CUTTER

D

DAVY JONES. The Spirit of the sea. Davy Jones' Locker is the bottom of the sea.

DAVITS. Pieces of timber or iron, with sheaves or blocks at their ends, projecting over a vessel's sides or stern, to hoist up boats. Also, a spar with a roller or sheave at its end, used for fishing the anchor, called a fish-davit.

DEAD EYE. A circular block of wood, with holes through it, for the lanyards of rigging to reeve through, without sheaves, and with a groove round it for an iron strap.

DEAD-LIGHTS. Ports placed in the cabin windows.

DEAD RECKONING. A reckoning kept by observing a vessel's courses and distances by the log.

DEAD-RISING, or RISING-LINE. Those parts of a vessel's floor, throughout her length, where the floor-timbers terminate upon the lower futtock.

DAVITS

DEAD-WATER. The eddy under a vessel's counter when in motion.

DEAD-WOOD. Blocks of timber, laid upon each end of the keel, where the vessel narrows.

DECK. The planked floor of a vessel, resting upon the beams.

DECK-STOPPER. A stopper used for securing the cable forward of the windlass or capstan, while it is being overhauled.

DEEP-SEA-LEAD. The lead used in sounding at great depths.

DEPARTURE. The easting or westing made by a vessel. The bearing of an object on the coast from which a vessel commences dead reckoning.

DERELICT. A vessel forsaken on the high seas.

DERRICK. A single spar, supported by stays and guys, to which a purchase is attached, used to unload vessels, and for hoisting heavy objects.

DINGHY. A small open boat.

DISPLACEMENT. The weight of water displaced by any vessel.

DOG. A short iron bar, with a fang or teeth at one end, and a ring at the other. Used for a purchase, the fang being placed against a beam or knee, and the block of a tackle hooked to the ring.

DOG-VANE. A small vane, usually made of bunting, to show the direction of the wind.

DOG-WATCHES. Half watches of two hours each, from 4 to 6 and 6 to 8 P.M.

DOLPHIN. A rope or strap around a mast to support the puddening, where the lower yards rest in the slings. Also, a spar or buoy, to which vessels may bend their cables.

DOLPHIN - STRIKER. The martingale boom, a spar projecting down from the bowsprit cap to spread the martingale stays which run out to the jib boom and counteract the strain of head stays.

DOUSE. To lower suddenly.

DOWNHAUL. A rope used to haul down jibs, staysails, and studdingsails.

DRAFT. The depth of water which a vessel requires to float her.

DRAG. A machine with a bag net, used for dragging on the bottom for anything lost. A sea anchor to keep the head of the vessel to the wind, in bad weather.

DRAW. A sail draws when it is filled by the wind.

DRIFTS. Pieces in the sheer-draught where the rails are cut off.

DRIVE. To scud before a gale, or to drift in a current.

DRIVER. The fifth mast of a six-masted schooner. Also the small fore-and-aft spanker sail set at the stern of a full-rigged ship.

DROP. The depth of a sail, from head to foot, amidships.

DRUM-HEAD. The top of the capstan.

DUB. To reduce the end of a timber.

DUCK. A kind of cloth, lighter and finer than canvas; used for small sails.

DOLPHIN STRIKER

DUNNAGE. Loose material, placed on the bottom of the hold, above the ballast, to stow cargo.

E

EARING. A rope attached to the cringle of a sail, by which it is bent or reefed.

EBB. The reflux of the tide.

EDDY. A circular motion in the water caused by the meeting of opposite currents.

ELBOW. Two crosses in a hawse.

ENSIGN. The flag carried by a ship as the insignia of her nationality.

EQUINOX. The time the sun crosses the equator.

EVEN-KEEL. The position of a vessel when she is so trimmed that the sits evenly upon the water, neither end being down more than the other.

EUVROU. A piece of wood, by which the legs of the crow-foot to an awning are extended.

EYE. The circular part of a shroud or stay, where it goes over a mast.

Eye-bolt. A long iron bar, having an eye at one end, driven through a vessel's deck or side into a timber or beam, with the eye remaining out, to hook a tackle to. If there is a ring through this eye, it is called a ring-bolt.

ENSIGN

An Eye-splice is a kind of splice made with the end of a rope.

Eyelet-hole. A hole made in a sail for cringle or roband to go through.

The Eyes of a vessel. The extreme forward part.

F

FACE-PIECES. Pieces of wood wrought on the fore part of the knee of the head.

FACING. Letting one piece of timber into another with a rabbet.

FAG. A rope is fagged when the end is untwisted.

FAIR-LEADER. A strip of board or plank or metal, with holes in it, for running rigging to lead through. Also, a block or thimble used for the same purpose.

FAKE. A turn of rope in a coil. To fake (or flake) down is to coil a line down with ends overlapping so it will run freely without fouling.

FALL. That part of a tackle to which the power is applied in hoisting.

FALSE KEEL. A supplementary keel, bolted to the main keel on the outside, to give a vessel more draft.

FANCY-LINE. A line rove through a block at the jaws of a gaff, used as a downhaul. Also, a line used for cross-hauling the lee topping-lift.

FASHION-PIECES. The aftermost timbers, forming the shape of the stern.

STERN FASTS

FAST. A rope by which a vessel is secured. There are *bow*, *breast*, *quarter*, and *stern* fasts.

FATHOM. Six feet.

FEATHER. To *feather an oar* in rowing, is to turn the blade horizontally with the top forward as it comes out of the water, so as not to take the wind or dip up water.

FEATHER-EDGED. Planks which have one edge thicker than another.

FENDERS. Pieces of rope or wood hung over the side of a vessel or boat, to protect it from chafing. The fenders of small boats and yachts are usually made of canvas and stuffed with cork.

FID. A block of wood or iron, placed through the hole in the heel of a mast, and resting on the trestle-trees of the mast below. This supports the mast. Also, a wooden pin, tapered, used in splicing rigging, etc.

FIDDLE-BLOCK. A long shell, with one sheave over the other, the lower smaller than the upper.

FIFE-RAIL. The rail around a mast.

FIGURE-HEAD. A carved head or full-length figure, over the cut-water.

FISH. To raise the flukes of an anchor upon the gunwale. Also, to strengthen a spar when sprung or weakened, by fastening on other pieces.

FISH-DAVIT. The davit used for fishing an anchor.

FISH-HOOK. A hook with a pennant, to the end of which the fish-tackle is hooked.

FISH-TACKLE. The tackle used for fishing an anchor.

FLARE. When a vessel's sides go out from the perpendicular. The opposite to *tumbling-in*.

FLAT. A sheet is said to be hauled *flat*, when it is hauled down close.

Flat-aback, when a sail is blown with its after surface toward the stern.

FLAW. A gust of wind.

FLEET. To come up on a tackle and draw the blocks apart, for another pull, after they have been hauled *two-blocks*.

Also, to shift the position of a block or fall, so as to haul to more advantage.

FLEMISH-HORSE. An additional foot-rope at the ends of top-sail yards.

FLOOR. The bottom of a vessel, on each side of the keelson.

FIGUREHEAD

FLOOR TIMBERS. Timbers of a vessel placed across the keel.

FLOWING SHEET. When a vessel has the wind free, and the sheets are eased off.

FLUKES. The broad triangular plates at the extremity of the arms of an anchor, terminating in a point called the *bill*.

FLUSH. Level with.

FLY. That part of a flag which extends from the Union to the extreme end.

FOOT. The lower end of a mast or sail.

FOOT-ROPE. A rope upon which to stand when reefing or furling sail.

FOOT-WALING. The inside planks or lining of a vessel, over the floor-timbers.

FORE. Used to distinguish the forward part of a vessel, or things forward of amid-ships: as *fore mast, fore hatch*. The opposite to *aft* or *after*.

FORE-AND-AFT. Lengthwise with the vessel. The opposite to *athwartships*.

FORECASTLE. That part of the upper deck forward of the foremast; or, forward of the after part of the fore channels. Also, the forward part of the vessel, under the deck, where the sailors live.

FORE-FOOT. A piece of timber at the forward extremity of the keel, upon which the lower end of the stem rests.

FORE-LOCK. A flat piece of iron, driven through the end of a bolt, to prevent its drawing.

FORE MAST. The forward mast of a vessel.

FORE-REACH. To shoot ahead, as when going in stays.

FORE-RUNNER. A piece of rag, terminating the stray-line of the log-line.

FORGE. To *forge ahead*, to shoot ahead; as, in coming to anchor, or when going in stays.

FORWARD. In front of.

FOTHER OR FODDER. To draw a sail,

filled with oakum, under a vessel's bottom, to stop a leak.

FOUL. The opposite of clear.

FOUL ANCHOR. When the cable has a turn around the anchor.

FOUL HAWSE. When the two cables are crossed or twisted, beyond the stem.

FOUNDER. When a vessel fills with water and sinks.

FOX. Made by twisting together two or more ropeyarns.

A *Spanish fox* is made by untwisting a single warn and laying it up the contrary way.

FRAME. Skeleton of a vessel.

FRAP. To pass ropes around a sail to keep it from blowing loose. Also, to draw ropes around a vessel which is weakened, to keep her together.

FLOWING SHEET

FREE. A vessel is going *free*, when she has a fair wind. A vessel is *free*, when the water has been pumped out of her.

FREEBOARD. That portion of a vessel out of water.

FRESHEN. To relieve a rope, by moving its place; as, to *freshen the nip* of a stay, is to shift it so as to prevent its chafing through. To *freshen ballast*, is to alter its position.

FRENCH-FAKE. To coil a rope with each fake outside of the other, beginning in the middle. If there are to be riding fakes, they begin outside and go in. This is a *Flemish coil*.

FOOTROPES

FULL-AND-BY. Sailing close-hauled on a wind. The order given to keep the sails full and at the same time close to the wind.

FURL. To roll a sail up snugly on a yard or boom, and secure it.

FUTTOCK-PLATES. Iron plates crossing the sides of the toprim perpendicularly. The dead-eyes of the topmast rigging are fitted to their upper ends, and the futtock-shrouds to their lower ends.

FUTTOCK-SHROUDS. Short shrouds, leading from the lower ends of the futtock-plates to the bend around the lower mast, just below the top.

FUTTOCK-STAFF. A short piece of wood or iron, seized across the upper part of the rigging, to which the cat-harpin legs are secured.

FUTTOCK-TIMBERS. Timbers between the floor and navel timbers, and the top-timbers. There are two—the *lower*, which is over the floor, and the *middle*, which is over the navel timber. The navel timber is sometimes called the *ground futtock*.

FULL AND BY STAR B'D TACK

GAFF TOPSAIL

G

GAFF. A spar, to which the head of a fore-and-aft sail is bent.

GAFF-TOPSAIL. A light sail set over a gaff, the foot being spread by it.

GAGE. The depth of water of a vessel. Also, the position as to another vessel, as having the *weather* or *lee gage*.

GALLEY. The place where the cooking is done.

GALLOWS-BITTS. A strong frame raised amidships, to support spare spars, etc.

GAMMONING. The lashing by which the bowsprit is secured to the cutwater.

GANG CASKS. Small casks, used for bringing water on board in boats.

GANGWAY. That part of a vessel's side, amidships, where people pass in and out of the vessel.

GARBOARD-STRAKE. The planks next the keel, on each side.'

GARLAND. A large rope, strap or grommet, lashed to a spar when hoisting it on board.

GARNET. A purchase on the mainstay, for hoisting.

GASKETS. Ropes or piece of canvas, used to secure a sail when it is furled.

GEAR. A general term, meaning rigging.

GIG. Usually, the officers' boat.

GIMBALS. The brass ring in which a compass sets to keep it level.

GIMBLET. To turn an anchor around by its stock. To turn anything around on its end.

GIRTLINE. A rope rove through a single block aloft, making a whip purchase. (Also known as a gantline.)

GIVE WAY! An order to men in a boat to pull with more force, or to begin pulling. The same as, *Lay out on your oars!* or *Lay out!*

GOB-LINE or **GAUB-LINE.** A rope leading from the martingale inboard. The same as *back-rope.*

GOOSE-NECK. An iron ring fitted to the end of a yard or boom.

GORES. The angles at one or both ends of cloths that increase the breadth or depth of a sail.

GORING-CLOTHS. Pieces cut obliquely and put in to add to the breadth of a sail.

GRAFTING. Covering a rope by weaving yarns together.

GRAINS. An iron with four or more barbed points, used for striking small fish.

GRANNY KNOT. A square knot improperly tied.

GRAPNEL. A small anchor with several claws.

GRAPPLING IRONS. Crooked irons, used to seize and hold vessels fast.

GRATING. Open lattice work of wood. Used principally to cover hatches in good weather; also to let in light and air.

GREAVE. To clean a ship's bottom by burning.

GRIPE. The outside timber of the forefoot, under water, fastened to the lower stem-piece. A vessel *gripes* when she tends to come up into the wind.

GRIPES. Bars of iron, with lanyards, rings, and clews, by which a boat is lashed to the ring-bolts of the deck. Those for a quarter-boat are made of long strips of canvas, going round her and set taut by a lanyard.

GROMMET. A ring formed of rope, by laying around a single strand.

GROUND TACKLE. General term for anchors, cables, warps, springs, etc.; anything used in securing a vessel at anchor.

GUN-TACKLE PURCHASE. A purchase made by two single blocks.

GUNWALE. The upper rail of a boat or vessel.

GUY. A rope attached to anything to steady it, and bear it one way or another in hoisting.

GYBE. To change the position of the sails of a fore-and-aft vessel from one side to the other without going in stays.

H

HAIL. To speak or call to another vessel, or to men in a different part of the ship.

HALYARDS. Ropes or tackles used for hoisting and lowering yards, gaffs, and sails.

HALYARD

HAMMOCK. A piece of canvas, suspended by each end, in which seamen sleep.

HAND. To *hand* a sail is to *furl* it. *Beara-hand;* make haste. *Lend-a-hand;* assist. *Hand-over-hand:* hauling rapidly on a rope, by putting one hand before the other alternately.

HAND-LEAD. A small lead, used for sounding in rivers and harbors.

HANDSOMELY. Slowly, carefully. As "Lower handsomely!"

HANDSPIKE. A long wooden bar, used for heaving at the windlass.

HANDY BILLY. A watch-tackle.

HANKS. Rings or hoops of wood, rope, or iron, around a stay.

HARPINGS. The fore part of the wales, which encompass the bows of a vessel, and are fastened to the stem.

HARPOON. A spear used for striking whales and other fish.

HATCH, or **HATCHWAY.** An opening in the deck to afford a passage up and down. The coverings over these openings are called *hatches.*

HATCH-BAR. An iron bar going across the hatches to keep them down.

HAUL. *Haul her wind,* when a vessel comes up close upon the wind.

HAWSE-HOLE. The hole in the bows through which the anchor cable runs.

HAWSE-PIECES. Timbers through which the hawse-holes are cut.

HARPOON

HAWSE-BLOCK. A block of wood fitted into a hawse-hole when at sea.

HAWSER. A large rope used for various purposes, as warping, for a spring, etc.

HAWSER-LAID, or **CABLE-LAID** rope, is rope laid, with nine strands, against the sun.

HAWSE HOLE

HAZE. Punishing a man by keeping him unnecessarily at some disagreeable work.

HEAD. The work at the prow of a vessel. If it is a carved figure, it is called a *figurehead;* if simple carved work, bending over and out, a *billet-head;* and if bending in, like the head of a violin, a *fiddle-head.* Also, the upper end of a mast, called the *mast-head.* On pleasure boats, the toilet compartment is referred to as the head.

HEAD-SAILS. All sails that set forward of the fore-mast.

HEART. A block of wood in the shape of a heart, for stays to reeve through.

HEART-YARNS. The center yarns of a strand.

HEAVE SHORT. To heave in on the cable until the vessel is nearly over her anchor.

HEAVE-TO. To put a vessel in the position of lying-to.

HEAVE IN STAYS. To go about, tacking.

HEAVER. A short wooden bar, tapering at each end, used as a purchase.

HEEL. The after part of the keel. The lower end of the mast or boom. Also, the lower end of the stern-post. *To heel,* is to careen on one side.

HEELING. The square part of the lower end of a mast, through which the fid-hole is made.

HELM. The machinery by which a vessel is steered, including the rudder, tiller, wheel, etc.

HELM-PORT. The hole in the counter through which the rudder head passes.

HIGH AND DRY. The situation of a vessel when she is aground, above water mark.

HITCH. The manner of fastening ropes.

HOG. A flat, rough broom, used for scrubbing the bottom of a vessel.

HOGGED. Said of a vessel which, as a result of strain, droops at each end.

HOLD. The interior of a vessel, where the cargo is stowed.

HOLD WATER. To stop the progress of a boat by keeping the oar-blades in the water.

HOLY-STONE. A large stone, used for cleaning a ship's decks.

LABOR

HOME. The sheets of a sail are said to be *home*, when the clews are hauled chock out to the sheave-holes. An anchor *comes home* when it is loosened from the ground and is hove in.

HEAD SAILS

HOOD. A covering for a companion hatch, skylight, etc.

HOOD-ENDS or **HOODING-ENDS.** The ends of the planks which fit into the rabbets of the stem or stern-post.

HOOK-AND-BUTT. The scarfing, or laying the ends of timbers over each other.

HORNS. The jaws and booms and gaffs. Also, the ends of crosstrees.

HOUNDS. Projections at the mast-head serving as shoulders for the trestle-trees to rest upon.

HOUSE. *To house* a mast, is to lower it about half its length, and secure it by lashing its heels to the mast below. *To house a gun*, is to run it in clear of the port and secure it.

HOUSING, or **HOUSE-LINE.** A small rope made of three small yarns, and used for seizings.

HULL. The body of a vessel.

I

IRONS. A ship is *in irons*, when, in tacking, she will not bear away one way or the other.

J

JACK. A common term for the *jack-cross-trees*.

JACK-BLOCK. A block used in sending topgallant masts up and down.

JACK-CROSS-TREES. Iron cross-trees at the head of the long topgallant masts.

JACK-STAFF. A short staff, raised at the bowsprit cap, upon which the Union Jack is hoisted.

JACK-STAYS. Ropes stretched taut along a yard to bend the head of the sail to. Also, long strips of wood or iron, used for the same purpose.

JACK-SCREW. A purchase, used for stowing cotton.

JACOB'S LADDER. A ladder made of rope, with wooden steps.

JAWS. The inner ends of booms or gaffs, hollowed to go around the mast.

JEWEL-BLOCKS. Single blocks at the yard-arms, through which the studdingsail halyards lead.

JIB. A triangular sail set on a stay, forward. *The Flying-jib* sets outside of the jib.

JIB-BOOM. The boom, rigged out beyond the bowsprit, to which the tack of the jib is lashed.

JIGGER. A small tackle, used about decks or aloft. Small sail set aft on yawls and ketches. Gaff sail on fourth mast of large schooners.

HELM

JOLLY-BOAT. A small boat, usually hoisted at the stern, on coasting vessels.

JURY-MAST. A temporary mast, rigged at sea, in place of one lost.

K

KECKLING. Old rope wound around cables, to keep them from chafing.

KEDGE. A small anchor, used for warping. *To kedge*, is to warp a vessel ahead.

KEEL. The lowest and principal timber of a vessel, running fore-and-aft the entire length, and supporting the frame. It is composed of several pieces, placed lengthwise, scarfed and bolted together.

KEEL-HAUL. To haul a man under a vessel's bottom, by ropes at the yard-arms on each side. Formerly practised as a punishment in ships of war.

KEELSON. A timber placed over the keel on the floor-timbers, and running parallel with it.

KENTLEDGE. Pig-iron ballast, laid each side of the keelson.

KEVEL, or **CAVIL.** A piece of wood, bolted to a timber or stanchion, used for belaying ropes to.

KEVEL-HEADS. Timber-heads, used as kevels.

KINK. A twist in a rope.

KNEES. Crooked pieces of timber, having two arms, used to connect the beams of a vessel with her timbers.

KNIGHT-HEADS. The timbers next the stem on each side, and continued high enough to form a support for the bowsprit.

KNITTLES, or **NETTLES.** The halves of two adjoining yarns in a rope, twisted together, for pointing or grafting. Also, small line used for seizings and for hammock clews.

KNOT. A division on the log-line, answering to a mile of distance. A nautical mile is 6,080 feet; a land mile is 5,280 feet.

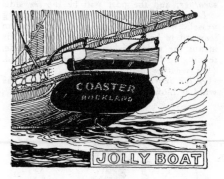

COASTER
ROCKLAND

JOLLY BOAT

L

LABOR. A vessel is said to labor when she rolls or pitches heavily.

LACING. Rope used to lash a sail to a spar, or bonnet to a sail.

LAND-FALL. Making land. *A good land-fall*, is when a vessel makes the land as intended.

LAND HO! The cry used when land is first seen when coming from sea.

LANYARDS. Ropes rove through dead-eyes for setting up rigging. Also a rope made fast to anything to secure it.

LARBOARD. The old term for the port or left-hand side of a vessel.

LATCHINGS. Loops on the head rope of a bonnet, by which it is laced to the foot of the sail.

LATITUDE. Distance north or south of the equator.

LAUNCH. A large boat. The *Long-boat*.

LAY. To come or to go; as, *Lay aloft! Lay forward! Lay aft!* Also, the direction in which the strands of a rope are twisted; as, from left to right, or from right to left.

LEACH LINE. A rope used for hauling up the leach of a sail.

LEAD. A piece of lead, in the shape of a cone or pyramid, with a small hole at the base, and a line attached to the upper end, used for sounding. The hole in the base is greased so as to get at the formation of the bottom.

LEADING-WIND. A fair wind. Applied to a wind abeam or quartering.

LEDGES. Small pieces of timber placed athwart-ships under the decks, between the beams.

LEADING WIND

LEE-BOARD

LEE. The side opposite to that from which the wind blows; if a vessel has the wind on her starboard side, that will be the *weather*, and the port will be the *lee* side. *Lee helm* is the condition, in a sailing vessel, when the helm must be kept to leeward to hold a boat on her course. This means the rudder is on the windward side, tending to bring the bow up into the wind. (See weather helm.)

A lee shore is the shore upon which the wind is blowing.

LIE-TO

Under the lee of anything, is when you have that between you and the wind.

By the lee. A vessel, going free, when she has fallen off so much as to bring the wind around her stern, and to take her sails aback on the other side.

LEE-BOARD. A board fitted to the lee side of flat-bottomed crafts, to prevent their drifting to leeward.

LUG SAIL

LEEWAY. What a vessel loses by drifting to leeward. When sailing close-hauled with all sail set, there should be little leeway.

LEECH, or **LEACH.** The border or edge of a square sail, at the sides. In a fore and aft sail, the after edge.

LEEWARD. The lee side. In a direction opposite to that from which the wind blows, which is called *windward*. The opposite of *lee* is *weather,* and of *leeward* is *windward*.

LIBERTY. Leave to go ashore.

LIE-TO, is to stop the progress of a vessel at sea, either by counter-bracing the yards, or by reducing sail so that she will make little or no headway, but will merely come to and fall off by the counteraction of the sails and helm.

LIFE-LINES. Ropes carried along yards, booms, etc., or at any part of the vessel, to hold on by.

LIFT. A rope or tackle, going from the yard-arms to the mast-head, to support and move the yard. Also, a term applied to the sails when the wind strikes them on the leeches and raises them slightly.

LIGHTER. A craft, used in loading and unloading vessels.

LIMBERS, or **LIMBERHOLES.** Holes cut in the lower part of the floor-timbers, each side of the keel, so as to allow water to flow fore-and-aft. *Limber-boards* are placed over the limbers to keep dirt from choking the limber-holes, and are movable. *Limber-chain.* A chain or small wire-rope rove fore-and-aft through the limbers, to clear them if necessary. *Limber-streak.* The streak of foot-waling nearest the keelson.

LIST. The inclination of a vessel to one side; as, a *list* to port, or a *list* to starboard.

LOCKER. A chest or box, to stow things in. *Chain-locker.* Where the chain cables are kept. *Boatswain's locker.* Where tools and small stuff for working upon rigging are kept.

LOG-BOOK. A journal kept by the chief officer, in which the position of the vessel, winds, weather, courses, distances, and everything of importance that occurs, is noted down.

LOG. An instrument for determining the speed of a vessel.

LONG BOAT. The largest boat in a merchant vessel.

LONGITUDE. Distance east or west of meridian of Greenwich.

LOOF. That part of a vessel where the planks begin to bend as they approach the stern.

LOOM. That part of an oar which is within the row-lock. Also, to appear above the surface of the water; to appear larger than natural, as in a fog.

LOOSE-FOOTED. A sail (fore and aft) not secured along the foot to a boom.

LUBBER. A greenhorn aboard a ship. *Lubber Line,* the fore-and-aft line of a compass.

LUFF. To put the helm so as to bring the ship up nearer the wind. Also, the round part of a vessel's bow. The forward leech of fore-and-aft sails. *Keep your luff!* etc. Order to luff.

LUFF-TACKLE. A purchase composed of a double and single block. *Luff-upon-luff.* A luff-tackle applied to the fall of another.

LUGGER. A small vessel carrying lug-sails.

LUG-SAIL. A sail used in boats and small vessels, bent to a yard which hangs obliquely to the mast.

LURCH. The sudden rolling of a vessel to one side.

MARKS

M

MADE. A *made mast* or *block* is one composed of different pieces. A ship's lower mast is usually a made spar, her topmast is a whole spar.

MAIN. In all vessels it applies to the principal mast and sail.

MAKE. To *make sail* is to set it. To *make fast* is to secure a line to a bitt, cleat, etc.

MALLET. A small maul, made of wood; as, *caulking-mallet;* also, *serving-mallet,* used in putting service on a rope.

MANILLA. A fibre grown in the Philippines.

MAN-ROPES. Ropes used in going up and down a vessel's side.

MARCONI RIG. Uses tall triangular jib-headed sails, as distinguished from the gaff rig.

MARKS. The markings of a lead line to show depths at a glance or by feeling.

MARL. To wind or twist a small line or rope around another.

MARLINE. Small two-stranded stuff, used for marling. A finer kind of spunyarn.

MARLING-HITCH. A hitch used in marling.

MARLINGSPIKE. An iron pin, sharpened at one end, and having a hole in the other for a lanyard.

MARRY. To join ropes together by a worming over both.

MARTINGALE. A short, perpendicular spar, under the bowsprit end, used for guying the head-stays. Sometimes called a dolphin striker.

MAST. A spar set upright from the deck, to support rigging, yards, and sails.

MASTER. The commander of a vessel.

MAT. Made of strands of old rope, and used to prevent chafing.

MATE. An officer ranking next to the master.

MATTHEW WALKER. A stopper knot which takes its name from the originator.

MESSENGER. A rope used for heaving in a cable by the capstan.

MIDSHIPS. The timbers at the broadest part of the vessel.

MILE. A nautical mile is 1-60 of a degree of latitude, generally 6,080 feet.

MISS-STAYS. To fail of going about from one tack to another.

MIZZEN-MAST. The aftermost mast of a ship. The spanker is sometimes called the *mizzen.*

NEAP TIDES

MONKEY BLOCK. A small single block strapped with a swivel.

MOON-SAIL. A small sail sometimes carried in light winds, above a skysail.

MOORING. Commonly, the anchor, chain, buoy, pennant, etc., by which a boat is permanently anchored in one location.

MOP. A cloth broom used on board vessels.

MOULDS. The patterns by which the frames of a vessel are worked out.

MOUSE. To put turns of rope-yarn or spunyarn around the end of a hook and its standing part when it is hooked to anything, so as to prevent its slipping out.

MOUSING. A knot or puddening, made of yarns, and placed on the outside of a rope.

MUFFLE. Oars are muffled by putting mats or canvas around their looms in the row-locks.

N

NAVIGATION. The art of conducting a ship from port to port.

NEAP TIDES. Low tides, occurring at the middle of the moon's second and fourth quarters.

NEAPED. The situation of a vessel when she is aground at the height of the spring tides.

NEAR. Close to the wind.

NEST. Dories, or small boats, are nested when stowed one inside the other.

NETTING. Network of rope or small lines. Used for stowing away sails or hammocks.

NIP. A short turn in a rope.

NOCK. The forward upper end of a sail that sets with a boom.

NUN-BUOY. A buoy tapering at each end.

NUT. Projections on each side of the shank of an anchor, to secure the stock to its place.

O

OAKUM. Stuff made by picking rope-yarns to pieces. Used for caulking, and other purposes.

OAR. A long wooden instrument with a flat blade at one end, used for propelling boats.

NUN BUOY

OFF-AND-ON. To stand on different tacks towards and from the land.

OFF THE WIND. Said of a boat sailing with sheets eased (slacked off.) She is *on the wind* when close-hauled.

OFFING. Distance from the shore.

OUT-HAUL. A rope used for hauling out the clew of a sail.

OUT-RIGGER. A spar rigged out to windward from the tops or cross-trees, to spread the breast-backstays.

OVERHAUL. To overhaul a tackle, is to let go the fall and pull on the leading parts so as to separate the blocks. *To overhaul a rope,* is generally to pull a part through a block so as to make slack. *To overhaul rigging,* is to examine it.

P

PAINTER. A rope attached to the bows of a boat, used for making her fast.

PALM. A piece of leather fitted over the hand, with an iron for the head of a needle to press against in sewing canvas. Also, the fluke of an anchor.

PARBUCKLE. To hoist or lower a spar or cask by single ropes passed around it.

PENNANT

PARCEL. To wind tarred canvas around a rope (called *parcelling.*)

PARRAL. The rope by which a yard is confined to the mast at its center.

PART. To break a rope or chain.

PARTNERS. A frame-work of short timber fitted to the hole in a deck to receive the lower end of a mast or pump, etc.

PAZAREE. A rope attached to the clew of the foresail and rove through a block on the swinging boom. Used for guying the clews out when before the wind.

PAUNCH MAT. A thick mat, placed at the slings of a yard or elsewhere.

PAWL. A short bar of iron, which prevents the capstan or windlass from turning back.

PAY-OFF. When a vessel's head falls off from the wind. *To pay.* To cover over with tar or pitch. *To pay out.* To slack up a cable or rope, and let it run out.

PEAK. The upper outer corner of a sail attached to a gaff.

PENDANT OR PENNANT. A long narrow piece of bunting, carried at the masthead. *Broad pennant,* is a square piece, carried in the same way, in a commodore's vessel. *Pennant.* A rope to which a purchase is hooked. A long strap fitted at one end to a yard or masthead, with a hook or block at the other end, for a brace to reeve through, or to hook a tackle to.

PILLOW. A block which supports the inner end of the bowsprit.

PIN. The axis on which a sheave turns. Also, a short piece of wood or iron to belay ropes to.

PINCH. To hold a sailboat so close to the wind that sails shiver.

OFFING

PINK-STERN. When a vessel has a high, narrow stern, pointed at the end.

PINNACE. A boat, in size between a launch and the cutter.

PINTLE. A metal bolt, used for hanging a rudder.

PITCH. A resin taken from pine, and used for filling up the seams of a vessel.

PLANKS. Thick, strong boards, used for covering the sides and decks of vessels.

PLUG. A piece of wood, fitted into a hole in a vessel or boat, so as to let in or keep out water.

PINK STERN

POINT. To take the end of a rope and work it over with knittles.

POLE. Applied to the highest mast of a ship, as *sky-sail pole.*

POOP. A deck raised over the after part of the spar deck.

POPPETS. Perpendicular pieces of timber fixed to the fore-and-aft part of the bilge-ways when launching.

PORT. The left side of a vessel as you look forward.

PORT OR PORT-HOLE. Holes in the side of a vessel. Also, holes in the bow of a vessel by which to load and unload large timber, etc., too long to go through the hatches.

PORTOISE. The gunwale. The yards are *a-portoise* when they rest on the gunwale.

PRAYER BOOK. A small, flat holystone used in narrow places.

PREVENTER. An additional rope or spar, used as a support.

PRICKER. A small marling spike, used in sail-making, rigging, etc.

PUDDENING. A quantity of yarns, matting, or oakum, used to prevent chafing.

PUMP-BRAKE. The handle to the pump.

PURCHASE. A mechanical power which increases the force applied.

Q

QUADRANT. An instrument used in navigation.

QUARTER. The part of a vessel's side between the after part of the main chains and the stern. The *quarter* of a yard is between the slings and the yard-arm.

QUARTER-BLOCK. A block fitted under the quarters of a yard on each side of the slings, for the clewlines and sheets to reeve through.

QUARTER-DECK. That part of the upper deck abaft the mainmast.

QUARTER-MASTER. A petty officer, who attends the helm and binnacle, watches for signals, etc.

QUICK-WORK. That part of a vessel's side which is above the chainwales and decks.

QUILTING. A coating about a vessel, outside, formed of ropes woven together.

QUOIN. A wooden wedge for the breach of a gun to rest upon.

RAKE

R

RABBET. A grove to receive the edge of a plank in ship building.

RACE. A strong, rippling tide.

RACK. To seize two ropes together, with cross-turns. Also, a *fair-leader* for running rigging.

RACK-BLOCK. A course of blocks made from one piece of wood, for fair-leaders.

RAIL. Top of the bulwarks (topsides above the deck).

RAKE. The inclination of a mast from the perpendicular.

RAMLINE. A line used in mast-making to get a straight middle line on a spar.

RANGE OF CABLE. A quantity of cable, ready for letting go the anchor or paying out.

In piloting, a *range* consists of two objects in line, used as an aid in steering a course. *Range of tide* is the amount of its rise and fall.

RATLINES. Lines running across the shrouds, horizontally, and used, in going aloft, as a ladder.

RATTLE-DOWN RIGGING. To put ratlines upon rigging. It is still called rattling

RATLINES

down, though rigging is now rattled *up,* beginning at the lowest.

RAZEE. A vessel of war which has had one deck cut down.

REACH. A sailing vessel reaches when the wind is, roughly, abeam. With the wind on the quarter, it is a *broad reach.* It is a *close reach* when the wind is just forward of the beam, but the vessel is not close-hauled.

READY ABOUT. The order to stand by to tack ship.

REEF

REEF. To reduce a sail by taking in upon its head, if a square sail, and its foot, if a fore-and-aft sail.

REEF-BAND. A band of stout canvas sewed on the sail across, with points in it, and earrings at each end for reefing.

REEF-TACKLE. A tackle used on a square sail to haul the middle of each leech up toward the yard, so that the sail may be easily reefed. Also, on fore-and-aft vessels, to haul out the foot of the sail.

REEVE. To pass the end of a rope through a block, or an aperture.

RELIEVING TACKLE. A tackle hooked to the tiller, to steer by in case of accident to the wheel or tiller-ropes.

RENDER. To pass a rope through a place. A rope is said to *render* or not, as it goes freely.

RIB-BANDS. Long, narrow, flexible pieces of timber nailed to the outside of the ribs so as to encompass the vessel lengthwise.

RIBS. The timbers of a vessel.

RIDE AT ANCHOR

RIDE AT ANCHOR. To lie at anchor. Also, to bend or bear down by main strength and weight.

RIDERS. Interior timbers placed occasionally opposite the principal ones, to which they are bolted, reaching from the keelson to the beams of the lower deck. Also, casks forming the second tier in a vessel's hold.

RIGGING. The general term for all the ropes of a vessel. Also, the common term for the shrouds with their ratlines; as, the *main rigging, mizzen rigging,* etc.

RIGHT. To *right* the helm, is to put it amidships.

RING. The iron ring at the upper end of an anchor, to which the cable is bent.

RING-BOLT. An eye-bolt with a ring through the eye.

RING-TAIL. A small sail, shaped like a jib, set abaft the spanker in light winds.

ROACH. A curve in the foot of a square sail, by which the clews are brought below the middle of the foot. The *roach* of a fore-and-aft sail is in its forward leech.

ROAD, or *ROADSTEAD.* An anchorage at a distance from the shore.

ROLLING TACKLE. Tackles used to steady the yards in a heavy sea. Also, used on smoke stacks of steamers to keep them steady.

ROPE. Generally speaking, rope is cordage of greater than one-inch circumference. The term has often been abused, as a piece of rope when put to use on a vessel becomes a line, in most cases. Among the relatively few ropes, properly speaking, are bolt ropes, foot ropes, bell ropes, bucket ropes, man ropes, yard ropes, back ropes, and top ropes.

ROPE-YARN. A thread of hemp, or other stuff, of which a rope is made.

ROUGH-TREE. An unfinished spar.

ROUND IN. To haul in on a rope.

ROUND UP. To haul up on a tackle.

ROUNDING. A service of rope, hove around a spar or larger rope.

ROWLOCKS. The receptacles for the oars in rowing.

ROYAL. A light sail next above a top-gallant sail.

ROLLING TACKLE

ROYAL YARD. The yard from which the royal is set. The fourth from the deck.

RUBBER. A small instrument used to rub or flatten down the seams of a sail in sail-making.

RUDDER. That by which a vessel or boat is steered, attached to the stern-post.

RULES OF THE ROAD. The international regulations for preventing collisions at sea.

RUN. The after part of a vessel's bottom, which rises and narrows in approaching the stern-post. *By the run.* To let go *by the run,* is to let go altogether, instead of gradually.

RUNG-HEADS. The upper ends of the floor-timbers.

RUNNER. A rope to increase the power of a tackle. It is rove through a single block, and a tackle is hooked to each end, or to one end, the other being fast.

RUNNING RIGGING. The ropes that reeve through blocks, and are pulled and hauled, such as braces, halyards, etc.; in contrast to the *standing rigging,* the ends of which are securely seized, such as stays, shrouds, etc.

S

SADDLES. Pieces of wood hollowed out to fit on the yards to which they are nailed, having a hollow in the upper part for the boom to rest in.

SAG. To *sag to leeward,* is to drift off bodily to leeward.

SAILS are of two kinds: *square. sails,* which hang from yards, their foot lying across the line of the keel, as the courses, topsails, etc.; and *fore-and-aft-sails,* which set upon gaffs, booms, etc., their foot running with the line of the keel.

SAILS FORE and AFT and SQUARE

SAIL HO! The cry used when a sail is discovered at sea.

SAMSON POST. A single bitt in the bow of a small boat.

SAVE-ALL. A small sail sometimes set under the foot of a lower sail, often called a *catch-all.*

SCANTLING. A term applied to any piece of timber, with regard to its breadth and thickness, when reduced to the standard size.

SCARF. To join pieces of timber at their ends by shaving them down and overlapping them.

SCHOONER. A vessel with two or more masts. A *fore-and-aft* schooner has only fore-and-aft sails. *A topsail schooner* carries a square fore topsail, and frequently, top-gallant sail and royal schooners are now built with two, three, four, and many with five masts.

SCORE. A groove in a block or dead-eye.

SCOTCHMAN. A large batten placed over the turnings-in of rigging, to prevent chafing.

SCRAPER. A small, triangular iron instrument, with a handle fitted to its centre, used for scraping decks, masts, etc.

SCROWL. A piece of timber bolted to the knees of the head, in place of a figure-head.

SCUD. To drive before a gale, with no sail, or only enough to steady the vessel.

SCHOONER

Also, low, thin, clouds that fly swiftly before the wind.

SCULL. A short oar. *To scull,* is to impel a boat by one oar at the stern.

SCUPPERS. Holes cut in the water-ways for the water to run from the decks.

SCUTTLE. A hole cut in a vessel's deck, as, a hatchway. Also, a hole cut in any part of a vessel. *To scuttle,* is to cut or bore holes in a vessel to make her sink.

SEA. Waves (collectively) caused by wind blowing at the time and place of observation. (See *swell.*)

SEAMS. The intervals between planks in a vessel's deck or side.

SEIZE. To fasten ropes together by turns of small stuff, to secure hooks, etc.

SEIZINGS. The fastenings of ropes that are seized together.

SELVAGEE. A skein of rope-yarns or spunyarn, marled together. Used as a neat strap.

SENNIT, or *SINNIT.* A braid, formed by plaiting rope-yarns or spunyarn together.

SERVE. To wind small stuff, as rope-yarns, spunyarn, etc., around a rope, to keep it from chafing. It is wound and hove round taut by a serving-board or mallet.

SET. To *set up rigging,* is to tighten it.

SEXTANT. The instrument used in determining altitudes of heavenly bodies.

SHACKLES. Links in a chain cable fitted with a movable bolt so that the chain can be separated.

SHANK. The main piece in an anchor; the stock is made fast at one end, and the arms at the other.

SHANK-PAINTER. A strong rope by which the lower part of the shank of an anchor is secured to the ship's side.

SHARP UP. Yards when braced as near fore-and-aft as possible.

SHEATHING. A casing or covering on the bottom of a vessel.

SHEARS. Two or more spars, raised at angles and lashed together near their upper ends, used for lowering or hoisting heavy objects.

SHEAR HULK. An old vessel fitted with shears, etc., and used for taking out and putting in the spars of other vessels.

SHEAVE. The wheel in a block upon which the rope runs. *Sheave-hole,* the place cut in a block for the ropes to reeve through.

SHEEP-SHANK. A hitch or bend, used to shorten a rope temporarily.

SHEEPSHANK

SHEER, or *SHEER-STRAKE.* The line of plank on a vessel's side, running fore-and-aft under the gunwale. Also, a vessel's position when riding by a single anchor.

SHEETS. Ropes used in working a sail, to keep the clew down to its place. With square sails, the sheets run through each yard-arm. With boom sails, they haul the sails to the desired positions.

SHEET ANCHOR. A vessel's largest anchor.

SHELL. The case of a block.

SHIP. A vessel with three or four masts, with tops and yards. To enter on board a vessel. To fix anything in its proper place, such as *ship* shape.

SEXTANT

SHIVER. To shake the wind out of a sail by bracing it so that the wind strikes upon the leech.

SHOE. A piece of wood used for the bill of an anchor to rest upon. Also, for the heels of shears, etc. Also added to a vessel's keel to give her more draft.

SHOE-BLOCK. A block with two sheaves, one above the other, the one horizontal and the other perpendicular.

SHORE. A prop or stanchion, placed under a beam. To *shore,* to prop up.

SHORT BOARD. Same as a short tack or leg. A long board is a long tack.

SHORTEN. One shortens sail when he takes in canvas to reduce the area of sail set.

SHROUDS. Ropes on each side of a vessel, reaching from the mast-heads to the vessel's sides, to support the masts.

SILLS. Pieces of timber put in horizontally between the frames to form and secure openings.

SISTER BLOCK. A long piece of wood with two sheaves in it, one above the other, with a score between them for a seizing, and a groove around the block, lengthwise. Two blocks of same size attached to a ring usually used for jib-halyards, etc.

SKEG. Timbers used to deepen the after part of a keel, or a metal or wood extension of the keel protecting the propeller, and often supporting the rudder.

SHIP

SPINNAKER

SPARS. The general term for masts, yards, booms, gaffs, etc.

SPEAK. One speaks a vessel when communicating with her at sea.

SPEAKING TRUMPET. A trumpet for conveying orders on board a vessel.

SPELL. The common term for a portion of time given to any work. To spell, is to relieve another.

SPENCER. A fore-and-aft sail, set with a gaff and no boom, and hoisting from a small mast called a spencer-mast, just abaft the fore and main masts.

SPILL. To shake the wind out of a sail.

SPILLING LINE. A rope used for spilling a sail. Used in bad weather.

SPLICE. To join two ropes together by interweaving their strands.

SPINNAKER. A light sail of great spread used on yachts when running before the wind.

SPIRIT COMPASS. The modern style of compass.

SPOON-DRIFT. Water swept from the tops of the waves by the violence of the wind, and driven along before it, covering the surface of the sea.

SPRAY. An occasional sprinkling dashed from the top of a wave by the wind.

SPREADERS. Arms of metal or wood used to spread shrouds or stays and give better support to a mast.

SPRING. To crack or split a mast. To spring a leak, is to begin to leak. To spring a luff, is to force a vessel close to the wind, in sailing.

A spring line is one used at a dock to keep a vessel from moving ahead or astern.

SPRING-STAY. A horizontal stay running between mastheads of a schooner.

SPRING TIDES. The highest and lowest course of tides, occurring every new and full moon.

SPRIT. A small boom or gaff, used with sails in small boats. The lower end rests in a becket or snotter by the foot of the mast, and the other end spreads and raises the outer upper corner of the sail, crossing it diagonally. A sail so rigged is called a sprit-sail.

SPRIT-SAIL-YARD. A yard lashed across the bowsprit or knightheads, and used to spread the guys of the jib and flying jibboom.

SPUNYARN. A rope formed by twisting together two or three rope-yarns.

SPURLING LINE. A line communicating between the tiller and tell-tale.

SPURS. Pieces of timber fixed on the bilge-ways, their upper ends being bolted to the vessel's sides above the water. Also, curved pieces of timber, serving as half beams, to support the decks where the whole beams cannot be placed.

SPUR-SHOES. Large pieces of timber that come abaft the pump-well.

SQUARE. Yards are squared when they are horizontal and at right angles with the

SKIN. The part of a sail which is outside and covers the rest when it is furled. Also, the sides of the hold; as, an article is said to be stowed next to the skin.

SKYSAIL. A light sail next above the royal.

SKY-SCRAPER. A skysail when it is triangular.

SLABLINE. A small line used to haul up the foot of a course.

SLACK. The part of a rope or sail that hangs down loose. Slack in stays, is sail of a vessel when she works slowly in tacking.

SLEEPERS. The knees that connect the transoms to the after timbers on the ship's quarter.

SLING. To set in ropes, so as to put on a tackle to hoist or lower it.

SLINGS. The ropes used for securing the centre of a yard to the mast. Also, a large rope fitted so as to go around anything which is to be hoisted or lowered.

SLIP. To let go a cable and stand out to sea. To slip the anchor.

SLIP-ROPE. A rope bent to the cable outside the hawse-hole, and brought in on the weather quarter, when ready to slip the anchor.

SLOPS. A name given to ready-made clothing supplied by the captain.

SLOOP. A small vessel with one mast.

SLOOP OF WAR. A vessel of any rig, mounting between 18 and 32 guns.

SMALL STUFF. Spun-yarn, marline, and the smallest kinds of rope, such as ratline, etc.

SNAKE. To pass small stuff across a seizing, with marling hitches at the outer turns.

SNATCH-BLOCK. A single block, with an opening in its side below the sheave, or at the bottom, to receive the bight of a rope.

SNOTTER. A rope going over a yard-arm, with an eye, to bend a tripping-line to in sending down topgallant and royal yards, and other spars.

SNUB. To check a rope suddenly.

SNYING. A curved plank edgewise, to work in the bows of a vessel.

SO! An order to stop hauling upon anything when it has come to its right position.

SOLE. A piece of timber fastened to the foot of the rudder, to make it level with the false keel.

SOUND. To get the depth of water by a lead and line. The pumps are sounded by an iron sounding rod, marked with a scale of feet and inches.

SPAN. A rope with both ends made fast, so a purchase can be hooked to its bight.

SPANKER. The after sail of a ship or bark.

SQUARE

keel. Squaring by the lifts makes them horizontal; and by the braces, makes them at right angles with the vessel's line. *To square a yard*, means to bring it in square by the braces.

SQUARE-SAIL. A temporary sail, set at the fore-mast of a schooner or the main-mast of a sloop, when going before the wind.

STAFF. A pole or mast, used to hoist flags upon.

STABILITY. Stiffness of a vessel.

STANCHIONS. Upright posts of wood or iron, placed so as to support the beams of a vessel. Also, upright pieces of timber, placed at intervals along the sides of a vessel, to support the bulwarks and rail, reaching down to the bends, by the side of the timbers, to which they are bolted. Also, any fixed, upright support.

STAND. The interval during which the tide is neither rising nor falling.

STAND BY! To be prepared to act at once.

STANDING. The *standing part* of a rope is that which is fast, the opposite to the

STARBOARD

hauling part. The *standing part* of a tackle is that part which is made fast to the blocks and between that and the next sheave, the opposite to the hauling and leading parts.

STANDING RIGGING. That part of a vessel's rigging which is made fast to the sides.

STARBOARD. The right side of a vessel, looking forward.

STEEVE

START. A sheet is started when it is eased off.

STATION BILL. A list showing the station of every man, in case of accident.

STAY. To tack a vessel, or put her about, so that the wind, from being on one side, is brought upon the other, around the vessel's head. *To stay a mast,* is to incline it forward or aft, or to one side or the other, by the stays and backstays. A mast is said to be *stayed* too much forward or aft, or too much to port, etc.

STAYS. Large ropes, used to support masts, and leading from the head of one mast down to another, or to some part of the vessel. Those which lead forward are called *fore-and-aft stays;* and those which lead down to the vessel's sides, *back-stays.*

In stays or *hove in stays,* a vessel when she is *staying,* or going from one tack to the other.

STAYSAIL. A triangular fore-and-aft sail set from a stay.

STEADY! To keep the helm as it is.

STEERAGE. That part of the between-decks which is just forward of the cabin.

STEEVE. A bowsprit *steeves* more or less, as it is raised more or less from the horizontal. The *steeve* is the angle it makes with the horizon. Also, a long, heavy spar, with a place to fit a block at one end, and used in stowing cargo, which need be stowed close.

STEM. A piece of timber reaching from the forward end of the keel, to which it is scarfed, up to the bowsprit and to which the two sides of the vessel are secured.

STEP. A block of wood secured to the keel, into which the heel of the mast is placed.

STERN. The after end of a vessel.

STERNWAY. The motion of a vessel when going stern foremost.

STERN-FRAME. The frame composed of the stern-post transom and the fashion-pieces.

STERN-POST. The aftermost timber in a vessel, reaching from the after end of the keel to the deck. The stem and stern-post are the two extremes of a vessel's frame. The rudder is attached to the stern-post.

STERN-SHEETS. The after part of a boat, abaft the rowers, where the passengers sit.

STEVEDORE. A man who loads and unloads cargoes of vessels.

STIFF. The quality of a vessel which enables her to carry a great deal of sail without lying over much on her side. The opposite to *crank.*

STIRRUPS. Ropes with thimbles at their ends, through which the foot-ropes are rove, and by which they are kept up towards the yards.

STERN

STOCK. A beam of wood or a bar of iron, secured to the upper end of the shank of an anchor, at right angles with the arms. An iron stock usually goes with a key, and unships.

STOCKS. The frame upon which a vessel is built.

STOOLS. Small channels for the dead-eyes of the backstays.

STOPPER. A stout rope with a knot at one end, and sometimes a hook at the other, used for various purposes about decks; as, making fast a cable, so as to overhaul.

STOPPER BOLTS. Ring-bolts to which the deck stoppers are secured.

STOP. A fastening of small stuff. Also, small projections on the outside of the checks of a lower mast, at the upper parts of the hounds.

STOPWATER. A soft wood dowel driven in a hole bored through the joint between the keel and an adjoining timber, such as the stern to prevent leakage.

STOVE. A vessel is stove when her hull is smashed in from the outside.

STOW. To pack the cargo.

STRAND. A number of rope-yarns twisted together. Three, four, or nine strands twisted together form a rope. A rope is *stranded* when one of its strands is parted or broken. A vessel is *stranded* when she is driven on shore.

STRAP. Rope or iron around a block to keep its parts together.

STREAK, or **STRAKE.** Planks running fore and aft on the outside of a vessel.

STREAM. The *stream anchor* is one used for warping, etc., and sometimes as a lighter anchor to moor by, with a hawser. It is smaller than the *bowers,* and larger than the *kedges.*

STRETCHERS. Pieces of wood placed across a boat's bottom, inside, for the oars-

STUDDING SAILS

men to press their feet against, when rowing. Also, cross pieces placed between a boat's sides to keep them apart when hoisted up and griped.

STRIKE. To lower sail or colors.

STRIP. To dismantle.

STUDDINGSAILS. Light sails set outside the square sails, on booms rigged out for that purpose. They are only carried with a fair wind and in moderate weather.

SUED, or *SEWED*. The condition of a ship when she is high and dry on shore.

SUPPORTERS. The knee-timbers under the cat-heads.

SURF. The breaking of the sea upon the shore.

SURGE. A large, swelling wave. To *surge* a rope or cable, is to slack it up suddenly where it renders around a pin, or around the windlass or capstan.

SWAB. A mop, formed of old rope, used for cleaning and drying decks.

SWAY. To hoist up.

SWEEP. To drag the bottom. Also, large oars, used in small vessels to force them ahead.

SWELL. Wave movements caused by wind blowing at some point remote from that of observation, or by winds which have blown at the point of observation previous to the time of observation. (See *sea*.)

SWIFT. To bring two shrouds or stays close together by ropes.

SWIFTER. The forward shroud to a lower mast. Also, ropes used to confine the capstan bars to their places when shipped.

SWIG. The mode of hauling upon the bight of a rope when its lower end is fast.

SWIVEL. A long link of iron, used in chain cables, made so as to turn upon an axis intended to keep the turns out of a chain.

SYPHERING. Lapping the edges of planks over each other for a bulk-head.

T

TABLING. Letting one beam-piece into another. Also, the broad hem on the borders of sails, to which the bolt-rope is sewed.

TACK. To put a ship about, so that from having the wind on one side it is brought around on the other by the way of her head. The opposite of *wearing*.

A vessel is on the *starboard tack,* or has her *starboard tacks on board,* when she has the wind on her starboard side.

The rope or tackle by which the weather clew of a course is hauled forward and down.

The *tack* of a fore-and-aft sail is the rope that keeps down the lower forward clew; and of a studdingsail, the lower outer clew. The tack of the lower studdingsail is called the *outhaul*. Also, that part of a sail to which the tack is attached.

TACKLE. A purchase; formed by a rope rove through one or more blocks.

TAFFRAIL. The rail around a ship's stern.

TAIL. A rope spliced into the end of a block and used for making it fast to rigging or spars is called a *tail-block*. A ship is said to *tail* up or down stream, when at anchor, according as her stern swings up or down with the tide; the opposite to *heading* one way or another.

TAIL-TACKLE. A watch-tackle.

SURGE

TAIL ON! To take hold of a rope and pull.

TAR. A liquid gum, taken from pine and fir trees, and used for caulking, and to put upon yarns in rope-making, and upon standing rigging, to protect it from the weather.

TAIL ON

TARPAULIN. A piece of canvas, covered with tar, used for covering hatches, boats, etc. Also, the name commonly given to a sailor's hat when made of tarred or painted cloth.

TAUT. Tight, snug.

TELL-TALE. A compass hanging from the beams of the cabin, by which the heading of a vessel may be known at any time. Also, an instrument connected with the steering apparatus, and traversing so that the position of the rudder can be determined.

TEND. To watch a vessel at anchor at the turn of tides, and cast her by the helm, and some sail, if necessary, so as to keep turns out of the cables.

TENDER. A top-heavy vessel, with insufficient stability, is said to be tender.

TENON. The heel of a mast, made to fit into the step.

THICK-AND-THIN BLOCK. A block having one sheave larger than the other. Sometimes used for quarter-blocks.

THIMBLE. An iron ring, having its rim concave on the outside for a rope or strap to fit snugly.

THOLE-PINS. Pins in the gunwale of a boat, between which an oar is held when pulling.

THROAT. The inner end of a gaff, where it widens and hollows in to fit the mast. Also, the hollow part of a knee. The *throat* brails, halyards, etc., are those that hoist or haul up the gaff or sail near the throat. Also, the angle where the arm of an anchor is joined to the shank.

THRUM. To stick short strands of yarn through a mat or canvas, to make a rough surface.

THWARTS. The seats going across a boat, upon which the oarsmen sit.

TIDE. To *tide up or down* a river or harbor, is to work up or down with a fair tide and head wind or calm, coming to anchor when the tide turns.

TIDE RODE. When a vessel, at anchor, swings by the force of the tide. Opposite to *wind-rode*.

TIER. A range of casks. Also, the range of the fakes of a cable or hawser.

The *cable tier* is the place in a hold or between decks where the cables are stowed.

TILLER. A bar of wood or iron, put into the head of the rudder, by which it is moved.

TILLER

TIMBER. A general term for all large pieces of wood used in ship-building. Also, more particularly, long pieces of wood in a curved form, bending outward, and running from the keel up, on each side, forming the *ribs* of a vessel. The keel, stem, stern-posts and timbers form a vessel's outer frame.

TIMBER-HEADS. The ends of the timbers that come above the deck. Used for belaying hawsers and large ropes.

TOGGLE. A pin placed through the bight or eye of a rope, block-strap, or bolt, to keep it in its place, or to put the bight or eye of another rope upon, securing them together.

TOMPION. A bung or plug placed in the mouth of a cannon.

TOP. A platform placed over the head of a lower mast, resting on the trestle-trees, to spread the rigging, and for the convenience of men aloft. To *top* up a yard or boom, is to raise up one end of it by hoisting on the lift.

TOP-BLOCK. A large iron-bound block, hooked into a bolt under the lower cap, and used for the top-rope to reeve through in sending up and down topmasts.

TOP-LIGHT. A signal lantern carried to the top.

TOP-LINING. Lining on the after part of sails, to prevent chafing against the top-rim.

TOPMAST. The second mast above the deck. Next above the lower mast.

TOPGALLANT MAST. The third mast above the deck.

TOP-ROPE. The rope used for sending topmasts up and down.

TOPSAIL. The second sail above the deck.

TOPGALLANT SAIL. The third sail above the deck.

TOPSIDES. Sides of a vessel between the water line and the rail.

TOPPING LIFT. A lift used for topping up the end of a boom.

TOP-TIMBERS. The highest timbers on a vessel's side, being above the futtocks.

TOSS. To throw an oar out of the row-lock, and raise it perpendicularly on its end, and lay it down in the boat, with its blade forward.

TOUCH. A sail is said to *touch,* when the wind strikes the leech so as to shake it a little.

Luff and touch her! To bring the vessel up and see how near she will go to the wind.

TOW. To draw a vessel along in the water.

TRAIN-TACKLE. The tackle used for running guns in and out.

TRANSOMS. Pieces of timber going across the stern-post, to which they are bolted. Raised platforms in small vessels and yachts, used for seats, etc.

TRANSOM-KNEES. Knees bolted to the transoms and after timbers.

TRAVELLER. An iron ring, fitted so as to slip up and down rigging.

TREENAILS, or *TRUNNELS.* Long wooden pins, used for nailing a plank to a timber.

TREND. The lower end of the shank of an anchor, being the same distance on the shank from the throat that the arm measures from the throat to the bill.

TRESTLE-TREES. Two strong pieces of timber, placed horizontally and fore-and-aft on opposite sides of a mast-head, to support the cross-trees and top, and for the fid of the mast above to rest upon.

TRIATIC STAY. A rope secured at each end to the heads of the fore and main masts, with thimbles spliced into its bight, to hook the stay tackles to.

TRICE. To haul up by means of a rope.

TRICK. The time allotted to a man to stand at the helm. A *trick* at the wheel.

TRIM. The conditions of a vessel, with reference to her cargo and ballast. A vessel is *trimmed* by the head or by the stern. *In ballast trim,* is when she has only ballast on board. Also, to arrange the sails with reference to the wind.

TRIP. To raise an anchor clear of the bottom.

TRIPPING LINE. A line used for tripping a spar in sending it down.

TROUGH. A vessel lies *in the trough* of the sea when down in the hollow between crests.

TRUCK. A circular piece of wood, placed at the head of the masts of a vessel. It has small holes or sheaves in it for signal halyards to be rove through. Also, the wheel of a gun-carriage.

TRUNNIONS. The arms on each side of a cannon by which it rests upon the carriage, and on which, as an axis, it is elevated or depressed.

TRUSS. The rope by which the centre of a lower yard is kept in toward the mast.

TRYSAIL. A fore-and-aft sail, set with a boom and gaff, and hoisting on a small mast abaft the lower mast, called a *trysail-mast.* This name is generally confined to the sail so carried at the mainmast of a full-rigged brig; those carried at the foremast and at the mainmast of a ship or bark being called *spencers,* and those that are at the mizzenmast of a ship or bark, *spankers.*

TUMBLING HOME. A ship's sides when they fall in above the bends. The opposite of *wall-sided.*

TURK'S HEAD. An ornamental knot.

TURN. Passing a rope around a pin or kevel, to keep it fast. Also, two crosses in a cable. *To turn in* or *turn out,* nautical terms for going to rest in a berth or hammock, and getting up. *Turn up!* The order given to send the men up from between decks.

TYE. A rope connected with a yard, to the other end of which a tackle is attached for hoisting.

TYPHOON. A hurricane in the Eastern seas.

U

UNBEND. To cast off or to untie.

UNION. The upper inner corner of an ensign. The rest of the flag is called the *fly.* The *union* of the U. S. ensign is a blue field with white stars and the *fly* is composed of alternate white and red stripes.

Union-down. The situation of a flag when it is hoisted upside down, bringing the union down instead of up. Used as a signal of distress.

Union-jack. A small flag, containing only the union, without the fly, usually hoisted at the bowsprit-cap.

UNMOOR. To heave up one anchor so that the vessel may ride at a single anchor.

V

VANE. A fly at the mast-head, revolving on a spindle, to show the direction of the wind.

VANG. A rope leading from the peak of the gaff of a fore-and-aft sail to the rail on each side, used for steadying the gaff.

VEER. The wind when it changes. Also, to slack a cable and let it run out.

To veer and haul, is to haul and slack alternately, until the vessel gets headway.

VIOL. A larger messenger sometimes used in weighing an anchor by a capstan. Also, the block through which the messenger passes.

W

WAIST. That part of the upper deck between the quarter-deck and forecastle.

Waisters. Green hands, or broken-down seamen, placed in the waist of a man-of-war.

WAKE. The track or path a vessel leaves behind her when sailing.

WALES. Strong planks in a vessel's sides, running her entire length fore-and-aft.

WALL. A knot put on the end of a rope.

WALL-SIDED. A vessel is *wall-sided* when her sides run up perpendicularly from the bends. The opposite to *tumbling home* or *flaring out.*

WARD-ROOM. The room in a vessel of war in which the commissioned officers live.

WARE, or *WEAR.* To turn a vessel around, so that, from having the wind on one side, the wind will be on the other side, carrying her stern around by the wind. In *tacking,* the same result is produced by carrying a vessel's head around by the wind.

WARP. To move a vessel from one place to another by means of a rope made fast to some fixed object, or to a kedge. A *warp* is a rope used for warping. If the warp is bent to a kedge which is let go, and the vessel is hove ahead by the capstan or windlass, it would be called *kedging.*

WASH-BOARD. Light pieces of board placed above the gunwale of a boat.

WATCH. A division of time on board ship. There are seven watches in a day reckoning from 12 M. round through the 24 hours, five of them being of four hours each, and the two others, called *dog watches,* of two hours each, viz., from 4 to 6, and from 6 to 8 P. M. Also, a certain portion of ship's company, appointed to stand a given length of time. In the merchant service all hands are divided into two watches, port and starboard, with a mate to command each. A *buoy* is said to *watch* when it floats on the surface.

WATCH-AND-WATCH. The arrangement by which the watches are alternated every other four hours. In distinction from keeping all hands during one or more watches.

Anchor watch, a small watch of one or two men, kept while in port.

WATCH HO! WATCH! The cry of the man that heaves the deep-sea-lead.

WATCH-TACKLE. A small luff purchase with a short fall, the double block having a tail to it and the single one a hook. Used about deck.

WATER SAIL. A *save-all,* set under the swinging-boom.

WATER-WAYS. Long pieces of timber, running fore-and-aft on both sides, connecting the deck with the vessel's sides. The scuppers run through them to let the water off.

WAY. Movement of a vessel through the water. Technically, she is *under way* when not at anchor, aground, or made fast to the shore, but commonly way is interpreted as progress through the water—*headway,* when going forward; and *sternway* when going astern, backward. To clarify terms often confused, it might be said that one *weighs anchor* preparatory to getting *under way.*

WEAR. To bring a vessel on the other tack by swinging her around before the wind.

WEATHER. In the direction from which the wind blows.

A ship carries a *weather helm* when she tends to come up into the wind.

Weather gage. A vessel has the *weather gage* of another when she is to windward of her.

A weatherly ship, is one that works well to windward, making but little leeway.

WEATHER-BITT. To take an additional turn with a cable round the windlass-end.

WEATHER ROLL. The roll which a ship makes to windward.

WEIGH. To lift up, as, to weigh an anchor or a mast.

WELL FOUND. A vessel is well found when well equipped.

WHEEL. The instrument attached to the rudder by which a vessel is steered.

WHIP. A purchase formed by a rope rove through a single block. *To whip,* is to hoist by a whip. Also to secure the end of a rope from fagging by seizing of twine. *Whip-upon-whip.* One whip applied to the fall of another.

WHISKERS. The cross-trees to a bowsprit.

WINCH. A purchase formed by a horizontal spindle or shaft with a wheel or crank at the end.

WINDLASS. The machine used to weigh the anchor.

WIND-RODE. The situation of a vessel at anchor when she swings and rides by the force of the wind, instead of by the tide or current.

WINDWARD. The direction from which the wind blows, as distinguished from leeward. The weather side of a ship is the windward side.

WING. That part of the hold or between-decks which is next the side.

WINGERS. Casks stowed in the wings of a vessel.

WING-AND-WING. The situation of a fore-and-aft vessel when she is going dead before the wind, with her foresail on one side and her mainsail on the other.

WITHE or *WYTHE.* An iron band fitted on the end of a boom or mast, with a ring or eye to it, through which another boom or mast or rigging is made fast.

WOOLD. To wind a piece of rope around a spar.

WORK. A vessel works when otherwise rigid members of the construction loosen up. She *works to windward* when gaining ground against the wind by successive tacks.

WORK UP. To draw the yarns from old rigging and make them into spunyarn, foxes, sennit, etc. Also, a phrase for keeping a crew constantly at work upon the needless matters, and in all weathers, and beyond their usual hours, for punishment.

WORM. To fill up between the lays of a rope with small stuff wound around spirally. Stuff so wound round is called *worming.*

WRING. To bend or strain a mast by setting the rigging up too taut.

WRING-BOLTS. Bolts that secure the planks to the timbers.

WRING-STAVES. Strong pieces of plank used with the wring-bolts.

Y

YACHT. A vessel of pleasure or state.

YARD. A long piece of timber, tapering slightly toward the ends, and hung by the centre to a mast, to spread the square sails upon.

YARD-ARM. The extremities of a yard.

YARD-ARM AND YARD-ARM. The situation of two vessels, lying alongside each other so that their yard-arms cross or touch.

YAW. The motion of a vessel when she goes off her course.

YAWL. A vessel with two masts, the small one aft, stepped abaft the rudder post.

YELLOW FLAG. Signifies vessels in quarantine.

YEOMAN. A man employed in a vessel of war to take charge of a store-room; as, boatswain's yeoman the man that has charge of the stores, of rigging, etc.

YOKE. A piece of wood placed across the head of a boat's rudder with a rope attached to each end, by which the boat is steered.

OUTBOARD SEAMANSHIP

As in any workable partnership, it is essential that the components—in this case, boat and motor—can get along together. Within that boundary the boatman must determine 1) what he needs from 2) what is available within his budget.

For the new boatman especially, it is a deranging problem to sift the bag of brightly colored, boldly worded, attention-grabbing brochures, flyers, throw-aways; to disengage himself from the pouring of claims; to stand beyond the flood of "bigger and better," "mostest." and "fastest"; to de-

CHAPTER XXXI

PART ONE

cide what he wants a boat for and, on the basis of competent knowledge, what he wants in a boat.

Now, if it is speed you want—and certainly the sensation of a planing hull streaking over the water is one of outboarding's pleasures—be sure to acquire the boat, motor and combina-

Proper trim is important. In illustration above, boat lists heavily to port. Weight should be distributed to keep boat on even keel, as shown below.

tion thereof that will give you maximum safe performance even at high speed ranges. Too heavy a motor—too heavy, that is, for the particular boat—will cause the boat to squat at the stern and keep the bow pointed acutely celestial. Too light a motor, conversely, will cause the boat to perform sluggishly.

Bear in mind when determining horsepower that a boat which makes 15 mph with a 7½-hp motor won't necessarily make 30 with a 15. The better boats are designed for certain speeds with certain power; exceed that plan and you will perhaps do no more than burn fuel and dangerously overload your craft's transom.

Apart from consulting with competent dealers and others with experience, you can obtain reliable advice from the Outboard Boating Club of America's (OBC) "capacity recommendation plate" affixed to the hulls of some outboard boats. It gives the maximum horsepower and load the boat is designed to take.

If your boat lacks such a plate, ask the dealer for recommendations, or request them directly from the builder. Following these limitations will help avoid two common causes of accidents: over-powering and overloading!

TYPES OF BOATS

There is a wide array of boats from which to choose, from 4-hp car-top prams to buxom cruisers able to take two of the highest horsepower motors available. There are dinghies, skiffs, canoes, runabouts and utilities. There are special rigs like Sea Sleds, modified motor-catamarans and outboard-powered houseboats.

Your first question: What are you going to use your outboard boat for. Fishing? Family cruising? Skiing? Beach picnics? Skindiving? Photography? Speed? Combinations of any of these? Narrow your choice and you've practically decided on your type boat. A fisherman doesn't want to troll in a hydroplane designed to zoom at 50 mph!

Your second question: In what kind of water are you going to use the boat? Salt or fresh? Large, open bays and lakes, or shallow, sheltered rivers? The shoal-draft boat you drive on placid ponds may not stand you in good stead on open, rough waters.

Here is a brief rundown on the types of outboards available. Hulls break down into two basics: displacement and planing. Displacement boats cruise *through* the water, planing hulls lift and skim *over* the surface.

Often it is difficult to make a sharp distinction between "displacement" and "planing" types of hulls. Planing hulls receive a large part of their support at speed from the dynamic reaction of the water against the bottom, and part from buoyancy which diminishes with increased speed, but never quite disappears at any speed. Generally, planing begins when the water breaks cleanly away at the chines and transom. In these days of high horsepower, many cruisers are actually planing hulls. Practically all runabouts plane, of course.

Flat bottom (displacement type) hulls. Usually rowboats or skiffs 14' to 18'; used for fishing or utility purposes on shallow streams and small, protected lakes. They are not fast, are generally heavy and roomy. (Some light, flat bottom boats plane and are fast.)

Round bottom (displacement) hulls. Dinghies, tenders, car-top craft, occasionally runabouts 12' to 18'. These hulls at low speeds are often more easily driven and maneuvered than the flat-bottom craft. (Many fast, light, round bottom boats will also plane.)

Hydroplane (planing) hulls. Generally used for racing. Bottom, which is flat, may be "stepped," i.e., divided into two levels, about amidships. The resultant notch reduces wetted surface, increasing speed.

Vee-bottom hulls. Commonly used for runabouts, utilities and cruisers when speed is a factor. Forward undersection is usually deep "V" in shape. Bottom flattens toward amidships, until at the stern it becomes broad and flat.

A utility and a runabout, in effect, are practically interchangeable terms. Both craft function about the same, are

about the same size, take about the same horsepower, etc. The runabout, however, is generally considered to be a bit faster and more luxuriously equipped than a utility of comparable size.

Now, if you've made your choice, here are a couple of tips before actually buying. Take the boat and motor for a trial spin to see how they operate together and in various water conditions. Never buy a boat, especially a used boat, when it is in the water without first having her hauled. Check to see that bottom, frames, planking and fastenings are sound. If you are inexperienced, have a competent person examine the rig.

UNDER THE LAW

Be sure you and your boat comply with federal, state and local boating laws. You will have to check the laws of your community yourself (OBC publishes a round-up of state laws; federal laws are obtainable from the Coast Guard).

Determine if your boat must be numbered. Under the Federal Boating Act of 1958, all boats regardless of length (but not documented) that carry an engine of *more* than 10 hp, and are used on navigable (federal) waters, must be numbered. Some states, enacting legislation under the federal act but varying from the hp specification, require that all boats carrying *any* propulsive machinery be numbered. Where states have not assumed the numbering function, the Coast Guard is doing the job, following the "more-than-10-hp" guide.

FITTING HER OUT

Begin by installing the motor properly—manufacturer's diagrams will

Heavy 22-foot runabout above can safely carry two large (60 hp here) motors. Even one of these would overpower small outboard below.

Photographs from Mercury Outboard Motors

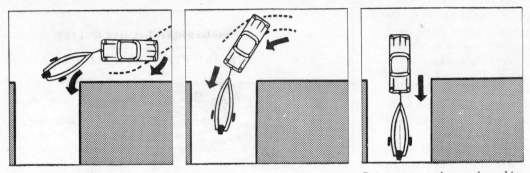

Remember, trailer always backs in direction opposite to that of car. Driver swings close to launching ramp (left), then cuts car away from ramp, placing trailer at angle to ramp and driveway, cuts wheels of car to left (center), backs slowly into ramp, as trailer moves to right. Driver straightens wheel after "jackknifing" car-and-trailer until both are in line, then backs slowly down ramp.

help here. Generally the task is to seat the motor squarely on the center of the transom and to securely tighten the bracket screws (motor angle will be discussed later). Some motor makes provide special transom plates for mounting, and you may prefer using a transom pad beneath the clamps to reduce vibration and prevent the wood from being marred. A length of chain through the motor bracket and around a transom knee will prevent the motor from being lost overboard.

Next, let's buy our required equipment. The skipper has much leeway as to brand and type of equipment he'll carry in this category, provided it meets legal requirements. For life-saving devices, for example, he can purchase cushions or jackets or ring buoys—provided each is Coast Guard approved. He must, of course, have one such device for each person aboard. OBC strongly recommends life jackets for children and non-swimmers. and that these persons wear them at all times when aboard.

Make sure your passengers know where the life-saving devices are—keep them accessible!—and how they are used, before you get under way. A buoyant cushion, incidentally, is used by slipping the left arm through one of the loops and the right leg through the other (reverse this for left-handers). The wearer then holds the cushion against his chest with the bridled arm, keeping the other arm and both legs free for swimming.

If your hull is even partially enclosed, the law requires that you carry a fire extinguisher. Place it where it can be grabbed quickly! Extinguishers of the vaporizing liquid type, particularly carbon tetrachloride, can no longer be installed on boats. Those manufactured before December, 1958, however, and already installed and serviceable, can be used until January 1962.

Even if you plan absolutely never to use your boat at night, you should install the lights prescribed for your class boat. Engine trouble, fuel problems or unexpectedly fine fishing may keep you out longer than you intended. Two lights are required (Inland Rules) for outboards up to 26′: a combination red and green light on the bow, and a white stern light, visible all around the horizon (360°) for at least two miles.

Outboards between 16 and 26 feet must carry a horn, or a hand-, mouth- or power-whistle audible for at least ½ mile. This device can be used both for passing whistle signals and fog signals.

The equipment required by law does not cover all that is required by boating's exigencies. The law, for instance, says nothing about carrying an extra propeller, but if your motor should slam into some hefty debris, disabling the propeller, the situation would demand a spare. An anchor with enough line (at least ⅜″ nylon or ½″ manilla for most outboards), a compass, enough fuel, a well-equipped tool box, a first-aid kit, flashlight, distress flares and smoke signals, are some of the items a prudent skipper will demand. The accompanying equipment list gives a complete rundown.

Don't pass over an oar, or paddle, on your list, even if it presents a stowage problem. An oar may turn out to be all you have for motive power at one time or another, and can be used to swing the bow around should you go aground. Not infrequently, an extended oar handle is used to help a person who has fallen overboard to get back to the boat.

ON THE ROAD

Trailers, like boats and motors, come in many varieties. They are produced variously equipped with electric winches, adjustable keel rollers, finger-tip controls for loading and launching, etc. Your problem, as before, is to get the right combination—this time the right trailer for your boat and motor.

You must have a trailer able to

Although this runabout demonstrates great carrying capacity, she should never carry so many passengers. Overloading is dangerous practice in small craft. No one should be permitted on forward deck while under way.

carry the weight of your motor(s), the boat, *and the gear stowed in the boat.* This last factor is too often overlooked in making calculations. That done, check the prospective trailer's load capacity, found usually on a plate affixed to the trailer. If the load to be carried (some builders underestimate the weight of their boats, so check carefully) is within 100 pounds of the trailer's listed weight capacity, buy the *next larger* model! Don't mislead yourself here, though, and purchase a huge trailer for a modest-size boat. The trailer must fit the hull!

Remember, a trailer, like any dryland cradle, is an unnatural place for a boat, so you must baby the craft all you can. Make the trailer bed as comfortable as possible. See that it fits the contours of the hull (special trailers are made for the modified catamaran type of outboard). Plenty of padding and bracing may be needed. Treat the boat right on the trailer and you'll get sought-for results in the water. There must not be a "sag" in the hull or a "hook" (in the stern, from too short a trailer). Such things may change the shape of your boat permanently, affecting your speed in the water and handling of the boat.

One type of trailer—often referred to as the full-keel support type—rests the boat on a boom or series of adjustable rollers. Another kind supports the boat with cradles, usually one forward and one aft. A boat kept too long on such a cradle, though, as for winter storage, tends to sag.

If you trailer the boat with the motor clamped to the transom, be sure the clamps are tight and the lower unit is secured to the transom or to the trailer frame, this last step to prevent the motor from tilting forward during sudden stops.

Be sure, too, that your trailer is adequately supporting the weight of the motor. In some instances it may be necessary to relocate trailer wheels closer to the rear, thus providing more direct support and at the same time keeping the load weight heavier—by 50 to 60 pounds—at the trailer front.

With the center of gravity located somewhat forward, towing will be smoother. Also, when you disconnect the trailer from the car you will be able to walk away with it—even when the trailer's loaded!

A bumper hitch will serve if you are trailering a light rig. For the heavier jobs, though, use a hitch that

EQUIPMENT CHECK LIST

FOR SKIPPER, CREW AND BOAT

POWER:
Two outboard motors, one with generator
Set of engine controls
Two propellers
Tachometer with throw-switch
Two 12-volt batteries
Two battery boxes

NAVIGATION:
Charts • Light list • Log book
Pair of lucite parallel rules
Pair of dividers
Pair of 7 x 50 binoculars
Lead line
Coast Pilots
USPS textbook: Piloting, Seamanship and Small Boat Handling
Inland Waterway Guide
Oil company cruising charts
Compass
Plenty of paper, pens and pencils
Watch with second hand

GROUND TACKLE:
8-pound standard Danforth anchor
12-pound Hi-Tensile Danforth
Two 100-foot lengths of 3/8" nylon
Two 5-foot lengths of 1/4" galvanized chain
Four 1/4" galvanized shackles
Four 3/8" galvanized thimbles

REQUIRED:
Freon-type air horn with refill
2½-pound dry chemical fire extinguisher
Four approved life jackets
Four Coast Guard-approved buoyant cushions
Properly functioning running lights with spare bulbs, fuses
State registration certificate
State numbers properly mounted

SAFETY EQUIPMENT:
First-aid kit
Flares, day and night
Electric bilge pump
Manual bilge pump
12-foot oar • Boat hook
Portable radio
Two spare propellers
Cotter pins for propeller hubs
Hand flashlight

Hand lantern
Two extra spark plugs

MOORING:
Four 25-foot lengths of 3/8" nylon
One 50-foot length of 3/8" nylon
Three plastic-foam fenders
Six fender locks

CLOTHING:
Two pair of foul-weather suits
Two pair of boating shoes
Two ski parkas
Sun glasses • Towels • Warm socks
Chinos • Bathing suits • Underwear
Sweaters • Caps • Gloves
Shirts, warm and summery
Set of thermal underwear

SLEEPING:
Sheets • Pillows • Warm blankets
Alarm clock

TOOLS:
Fiberglass tool-tackle box
Several sharp pen knives
Set of regular screwdrivers
Set of Phillips screwdrivers
Interchangeable-headed hammer
Pliers, regular and long-nosed
Boat tape
Spark plug remover and gauge
Sandpaper and emery cloth
Various types of oil and graphite
Assortment of screws and bolts with nuts and washers
Wrenches, socket and open end
Wood filler
Waterproof sealer
Extra fuses
Extra "keys" for tanks

GALLEY:
Stainless steel ice pick
Alcohol
Cigarettes • Matches • Lighter fluid
Copper wool • Soap • Soap dish
Assorted pots and pans
Spice containers
Plastic plates and cups
Stainless-steel eating utensils
Aluminum foil
Can and bottle openers
Stainless steel cleaner

HEAD:
Toilet paper • Comb
Sun tan lotion • Insect repellent
Tooth brush • Tooth paste

MISCELLANEOUS:
Swab • Bucket • Sponges
Camera • Plastic wrap • Film
Bilge cleaner • Ash trays

ALL THE EQUIPMENT LISTED ABOVE IS CARRIED ABOARD ONE PARTICULAR BOAT, A 22-FOOT EXPRESS CRUISER POWERED BY TWO OUTBOARD MOTORS. BECAUSE THE BOAT IS REPRESENTATIVE OF A GREAT MANY CRAFT IN USE TODAY, THE LIST SERVES AS AN EXCELLENT REFERENCE FOR THOSE SEEKING AN EQUIPMENT GUIDE.

fits directly to the car's frame—a frame hitch. It's a good idea, too, to cover the motor while trailering to keep dust out. Remove the cover at journey's end so condensation does not cause damage.

Keep trailer tires correctly inflated.

Keep trailer lights and reflectors working properly.

Make sure your insurance covers your boat and motor while being trailered.

Know and comply with the trailer laws that obtain in the areas you use. Often, these laws vary from state to state.

For launching, you'll probably use one of the many hard-topped ramps available. Occasionally, you may launch from a natural site. In this case, choose an area with a gently sloping shore but with ground hard enough to give ample tire traction. You can increase traction by slightly deflating the tires—but remember this when you start homeward. Stop at the first place for air.

Maneuvering your trailered boat into the water takes practice: beginners often come to a stalemate when car and trailer are "V"-ed before the water. Have someone shout instructions while you back onto the launching ramp at a 90° angle to the water.

Remember that in backing if you want the trailer to go to the right, you turn the steering wheel to the left, and vice versa.

Don't back the trailer into the water immediately. When in position on the ramp, stop and 1) release any tie downs and 2) tilt the motor so it doesn't hit any obstacle. Now back the trailer slowly, making sure the water doesn't reach the car's hubcaps.

Unlock the bow winch and secure a line to the bow. Push the boat off the trailer into the water, always holding the bow line so the boat does not float away. Unlock the trailer winch cable and with the bow line ease the boat into position for boarding.

GETTING ABOARD

If you are boarding from a beach, climb in over the bow when practical. When boarding from a float or low pier, step aboard as nearly amidships as possible. Bend so your weight is kept low, thus helping to keep the boat stable. Grasp the gunwale (the boat's side rails) for balance. In a small outboard, do not step on a gunwale or you'll flip the craft.

Do not carry bulky supplies while boarding. If you are alone, place the supplies where you can get at them from aboard. Or have someone hand them to you.

FUELING

A half pint of gasoline has the destructive power of five sticks of dynamite. When you fuel, you deal with at least several gallons of gasoline. So take every precaution—take nothing for granted!

It is wise, for instance, to remove portable fuel tanks from the boat when possible and take them ashore to fill. Extinguish all flames and close all electrical circuits. Warn everyone aboard and everyone about that there'll be no smoking.

Make sure the gas pump hose nozzle is in contact with the rim of the fill tank opening to prevent generating a spark of static electricity, which might ignite the gas.

Watch your fuel mixture now, both as to gas-oil ratio and the physical mixing of the two. Both are important to the smooth operation of the motors. Afterwards, make sure the lid of the tank is on tight to prevent leakage.

If your outboard carries fuel tanks which would be impractical to remove for fueling—anything larger than a 6-gallon tank would probably be impractical to remove—or permanently installed fuel tanks, your fueling procedures closely follow those for inboards. Before taking on fuel, close all doors, hatches, windows, etc., to keep gasoline vapors from

getting below. After fueling, open all doors, hatches, etc., and allow enough time for ventilation to clear these areas before starting the motors.

The mixing of gasoline and oil for large portable tanks and for permanently installed tanks can be done in several ways—all of which are time-consuming but, outboard motor engineers agree, extremely important, even more so than getting the exact gas-oil ratio.

One method is to use a metal (for grounding gas hose nozzle) funnel, preferably with a screen filter, which is inserted into the fill pipe or tank and into which can be poured the gas and oil at the same time, apportioning the oil at a slow rate and allowing the stream of gasoline to thoroughly blend with the oil.

A second method is to mix the gasoline and oil in a separate 5- or 6-gallon can (with pouring spout) and then pour from this into your fuel tanks.

Some gasoline companies are supplying their marinas with outboard pumps that serve up fuel already mixed. A dial regulates the ratio, according to your needs.

Do not, as should already be clear, pour the oil directly into the tank—it will not mix!

Check the fuel system now for leakage. Moreover, if you've spilled any gasoline, carefully wipe the area with a rag (which should then be disposed of) and hose down with fresh water, when possible.

Remember to thoroughly ventilate the boat before starting the motor. It is essential that you be alert for gasoline vapors. These vapors, heavier than air, crawl into the lower portions of the boat and wait, stubbornly and menacingly! A bilge blower, especially on an outboard cruiser, may be a prudent investment.

MOTOR ANGLE

For best motor performance, the drive of the propeller should be in a line parallel to the keel of the boat and parallel to the flat surface of the water. This means you must set your motor at a 90° angle (or very close to it) to the water, straight up and down. If the propeller is tilted away from the stern—assuming a vertical transom—the bow of the boat tends to rise too high while the stern squats. If the propeller is tilted toward the stern, pushing it up, the bow tends to nose too deep, plowing its way unnecessarily.

TRIM

The number of seats in a boat is no indication of the number of persons she can carry safely. Overloading, as has been pointed out, is a frequent cause of boating accidents. One of the best ways to avoid overloading is by planning how many people you will take—within the limits of your boat's capacity—and inviting *just so many*, no more!

Before discussing trim it would be well for readers to realize that the factors involved become more critical as boat size and weight decrease.

Have all weight evenly distributed (passengers seated toward the centerline of the boat and not hanging over the gunwales) so the boat will trim properly—slightly down by the stern; never down at the bow—and perform as she was designed to do. If the load is concentrated forward or aft, the boat will needlessly plow or drag, respectively, reducing your safety margin and increasing your fuel consumption.

Trim your boat as well as possible before getting under way. It is dangerous for passengers to change places or move around in a boat (except in a large outboard cruiser) that is scooting along briskly. If such movement becomes essential, stop or slow the craft first, remembering in rough weather to keep enough momentum to retain steerage control and to keep the boat headed into waves and wind. Have the person who must move keep low and near the boat's centerline.

Part One of this series dealt with such preliminary matters as choosing the outboard boat, motor and trailer, and fitting out the craft. Now we're ready to take the outboarder for a spin—the real test of the things he has bought and the things he should know.

PART TWO

YOUR boat gets its directional "orders" from the stern. That outboard motor at the transom does more than provide propulsion: it acts as a rudder, pushing the transom in the direction of the drive and thus pointing the bow the opposite way. Remote control steering, however, that is, a steering wheel generally near the bow with cable installation aft to the motor, permits you to steer your boat in the manner of an automobile: turn the wheel to starboard (right) and your boat will head to starboard, turn to port and it will go to port. But let the boat-automobile simile end there. The pivoting action of a boat is not like the turning action of a car, and leaving or getting into a slip or float will quickly point up the distinctions.

Make a final check before getting under way. Do you have enough fuel? Are your passengers seated properly? Have you told them about the life-saving devices, their location and their use? Is the way ahead or astern, as the case may be, clear?

Getting under way with an electric starting motor is as easy as pressing a button or turning a key. Once the motor is running, allow enough time for it to warm up before casting off. Listen carefully now, and from now on, to the running motor. Familiarity with that sound so that you detect even slight changes in it will enable you to pick up faults which may develop, such as worn plugs, improperly adjusted carburetor, wrong size propeller for the particular load or job, insufficient or contaminated fuel, and so on.

When the motor is running smoothly and the lines are free, ease the shift into gear and proceed slowly. Remember this about speed: the slower your boat is going the less room it needs to turn or stop, but your boat must be in gear—forward or reverse—for you to have steerage way. Guide your throttle accordingly.

UNDER WAY

Exercise your knowledge of the Rules of the Road now, tempered by good sense, right of way or no! Small craft should stand off as far as possible from large yachts and commercial ships. Watch their wakes with vigilant care. Don't count on such ships to look out

---

A BOAT HAS NO BRAKES

Many persons who have not handled a boat have the misconception that one can be maneuvered and stopped as easily as an automobile. But a boat has no brakes. The new boat owner should practice landings and leaving of docks as often as possible. Work on steering too.

1   2   3

4   5   6

for you; they need more room to stop, are more difficult to turn, and sometimes have "blind spots"—areas which are obscure or entirely blocked to the helmsman. Never assume the pilot of a vessel sees you: stay clear.

It is courteous and incumbent, too, to tend to your own wake and wash so as not to cause damage to other craft. You are legally responsible for the damage caused by your wake or waves.

Should you come upon a tow in the bend of a river. or a tow maneuvering near shore, note whether the tow is swinging to port or starboard, and give it the room it needs.

You should not bring your boat near a moored vessel. If circumstances make it necessary to do so, be exceedingly wary. Strong river currents moving under a moored barge can pull a boat under. Moreover, cross currents, that is, a current that is running at about a right angle to your course, require great caution. When you get into such a situation, give any object, floating or made fast, an extra wide berth.

WATCH THE WEATHER

Keep your mind on your course and boat handling but keep an eye on the weather. even if this morning's weathercast was for blue skies. Learn to recognize threatening cloud formations. Train yourself to be sensitive to shifts in wind direction; a shift in the wind often presages a change in the weather. And know and observe official storm warnings.

CARRY AN ANCHOR

In boating be prepared to do things you may not have planned to do. Anchoring, for instance. Always carry an anchor aboard, properly rigged with plenty of line and accessibly stowed.

In rough waters, anchoring will generally hold your bow into the wind or waves, a desirable effect to stay safest and driest, provided your boat is properly trimmed. A boat down at the bow while at anchor will not head into the wind. (We use "wind" here as a convenience. Actually, the direction and force of the current may have more effect on the position the boat will take at anchor than the wind alone. Experience along these lines is the best teacher.)

One auxiliary use of an anchor is to help get your boat clear should you run it aground. If a small boat is available or if the nearby water is sufficiently shallow so that you can wade, carry the anchor as far out as the line will permit—the farther the better—either from the bow or from the stern, wherever the deeper water is. A strong pull on the anchor line now will usually get the boat free.

Always check the water's depth, by chart, line or paddle, before letting go the anchor. Anchoring in relatively

Important part of your job in deriving peak performance from boat is getting right propeller for job. Number of blades, diameter and pitch are factors to consider. Here outboarder uses dial device on variable pitch propeller to change pitch to one most suitable for boat's load and planned activity this time out. Check propeller frequently for nicks, dents and out-of-pitch blades. These should be corrected as speed, fuel consumption and smoothness of operation are affected by propeller's action.

APPROACHING AND LEAVING A FLOAT WITH AN OUTBOARD

The outboard boat has true "power steering" in that the direction of thrust of the motor, and not a ruddder, guides the boat. As a result. outboard craft are exceptionally maneuverable. They handle easily in reverse because the boat follows the motor, making especially easy the maneuvers for approaching and leaving a float. With twin engines, one can be driven ahead and the other astern to provide an efficient means of turning in restricted waters. The technique of handling a single-screw outboard when approaching (Figures 1-4) and leaving (Figures 5-8) is illustrated here.

1. *Float is approached at an angle, with crew member ready to get bow line ashore. Fenders should be out.*

2. *Crewman takes line ashore and makes it fast to cleat on float.*

3. *Driver puts motor into reverse, turning his wheel to bring stern in.*

4. *Forward line will hold fast as motor brings it dockside. Stern line is then made fast to another cleat.*

5. *In leaving float when it is not practical to steer dead ahead, stern line is taken in while bow line is still fast to float. Motor is reversed and turned away from float.*

6. *Crewman releases bow line and steps aboard while taking in line.*

7. *As bow line is cast off, driver brings his wheel about to straighten boat, continuing in reverse until well clear.*

8. *With both lines in, driver switches gear to forward and pulls ahead, making certain stern is safe in case he should swing to port.*

7   8

deep water is inefficient; don't do it except in emergencies.

The type of anchor—or anchors, for a spare, heavier "hook" is worth springing for—you carry depends on the size of your boat, the kind of bottom in which you will generally anchor, and various other conditions. Coil the anchor rode (line) neatly for running, before you lower the anchor, and keep your feet out of the coils. Secure the bitter (inboard) end of the rode to a cleat, this apart from the hitch you make to stop the rode from running out (and check that the anchor is fast to the rode).

Don't throw the anchor overboard; lower it, and slowly so it doesn't arc into your hull. Don't lower it, however, until the boat's headway is stopped. Come up into the wind or current, whichever is strongest. Wait until the bow is over the spot where you want the anchor to lie. Then, when all headway is off and just before the boat makes sternway (drifts backwards), lower the anchor until the crown hits the bottom. You'll feel the gentle thud.

With the anchor on the bottom and the boat reversing slowly, let out the rode. As a general rule, pay out a scope of approximately six or seven times the depth of water. The longer the scope the better the anchor's holding power. Be sure, though, that you have room enough to swing around the amount of feet you've payed out.

You won't want to anchor too close to another craft. Privacy and safety are comforts skippers cherish.

In heavy weather you'll want to let out as much scope as possible. The length of the anchor rode is even more important in holding power than the weight of the anchor. A lightweight anchor with a long rode will hold in many cases where a heavy anchor with a short scope will drag.

CAUSES OF ACCIDENTS

Various studies have shown the following to be major causes of accidents:

1) Overloading, overpowering and improper trim.

2) High speed turns, particularly in rough water.

3) Failure to keep a sharp lookout for obstructions.

4) Going out in bad weather.

5) Standing in a moving boat.

6) Having too much weight too high on the boat, as when someone sits on the deck of a small outboard.

7) Leaks in the fuel system.

8) Going too far off shore.

Each of these factors—and others not listed here—can and should be avoided. A carefully matched boat, motor, propeller, etc., operated in accordance with the law and with courtesy, will go a long way toward eliminating accidents and even distressing moments. But some possibility always remains. You should be prepared to act in an emergency.

One of the leading causes of death in boating accidents is drowning. Many

Top: Boat at left is burdened vessel. She slows, yields right of way and goes astern of boat on right (privileged vessel).

Left center: To use a cushion as a life preserver, slip one leg through a strap, opposite arm through other strap. Right center: In water, wearer floats face up.

Left: Outboarders no less than other boatmen should have working knowledge of various piloting aids used on our waterways. Familiarity with charts, with system used to buoy various waters, with navigational instruments, etc., will apart from increasing safety aboard provide much added range for boating activities.

of these fatalities result from people falling overboard. As the skipper of your boat you have a responsibility to *know how* to rescue such a person. You should practice the maneuvers involved in accomplishing this. A ring buoy with line attached can be used as a simulated victim. Practice enough so you'll be able to act almost instinctively should the need arise; the minutes saved can be a life saved.

The Outboard Boating Club of America suggests that you adopt the following rescue procedure:

As soon as someone falls overboard, maneuver the boat's stern away from him. Shift into neutral (cut the motor if you do not have a gearshift) and throw a ring buoy or buoyant cushion near him . . . *near* him, don't conk him with it. See that you are clear of the overboard person now before engaging the propeller.

Circle around quickly, selecting the course that will allow you to get to the person while the boat heads into the wind or waves. Approach him slowly, now, taking care to come alongside and not over the victim. Stop the motor before attempting to take him aboard.

When alongside, extend a paddle or boat hook to him, or toss him one end of a line. Lead him around to the stern, where freeboard is lowest, if there is enough space at the transom for him to get aboard without injuring himself on the motor. On many outboards the transom is cramped with motor, fuel tanks, junction boxes, etc., so that it would be necessary to help the victim aboard over the side, as far aft as possible. In either case, the use of a boarding ladder will help matters. To avoid capsize when he is boarding, passengers should help trim the boat by shifting their weight.

On very small outboards without remote controls, it may be practical to remove the motor and take the man-overboard in over the transom. When helping a person aboard, hold him under the armpits and lift.

If the person has sunk from sight, probe gently beneath the surface with a paddle. Dive for him only if you are an experienced swimmer, and then just as a last resort.

OTHER EMERGENCIES

Stay with the boat if it capsizes! Almost invariably the temptation is to swim to shore, and almost invariably the shore is farther than it appears. Many outboard boats will float, even if filled with water. Aluminum and fiberglass boats usually have built-in flotation tanks. (Flotation tanks of wood or metal must be watertight, or they become a hazard. Sailboats with such tanks sometimes test them during the season by "sinking" the craft.) Some boats are fitted with materials like Styrofoam to give reserve buoyancy. And life jackets for persons in the water, of course, will provide much safety.

If your boat gets caught in a squall or in heavy seas, slow down immediately, maintaining only enough power to head the boat into or at a slight angle to the wind and waves. Have everyone don life preservers, yourself included. Don't try to smash your boat through the waves at high speed in an attempt to get home; you're inviting disaster. Rather, take the seas as gently as possible on the bow. The hull may pound, and the waves may toss up a lot of spray, but you'll have your best point of control over the boat. Should the craft get caught broadside in a trough, you run the risk of capsize.

If you find it difficult to keep the boat headed into the seas, or if the motor quits, some kind of drag, like a heavy anchor or a bucket, payed out with a long scope from the bow, may help in keeping the boat from falling into a trough. Some boats, though relatively few, carry sea anchors for this purpose, but opinions as to their effectiveness vary. As a rule, one would expect to use such a rig only in a storm at sea where there is plenty of sea room—not a situation the outboarder is likely to encounter. In heavy weather and where the motor can be idled, it is best to keep the motor going so it can be used instantly to keep the boat under control. Idling it will minimize fuel consumption.

Keep enough weight at the stern in stormy weather to hold the propeller in the water. Because the motor, as was pointed out earlier, serves as a rudder apart from providing propulsive power, you will have no helm control when the propeller leaves the water.

Whenever safely possible, of course, get to a protected harbor rather than attempt to ride out a storm. But don't let your haste disturb your judgment. Try to avoid taking large

waves on the stern; they can swamp the craft, though self-bailing wells aft reduce this potential. There's risk, too, of pitchpoling (turning end over end) in a heavy following sea, by being driven too fast before it. You may have to use reverse to check your speed.

If you must turn in a heavy sea watch for a lull in the wave formations in which to do it, so you won't get caught broadside in a trough by an approaching wave.

Always cross a large wave, or wake, at about a right angle. This lets you retain the best possible control over your boat.

Should your fuel supply run out—manually choking the motor will get the last few drops from the fuel tank—or should you be in need of other assistance, there are several distress signals that can be used. These include waving a white flag (a shirt or towel will serve), shooting smoke or flare signals, sending repeated blasts on a horn or whistle, lowering and raising both arms over your head and down to your sides, or flying an ensign upside down.

Photograph from Mercury Outboard Motors

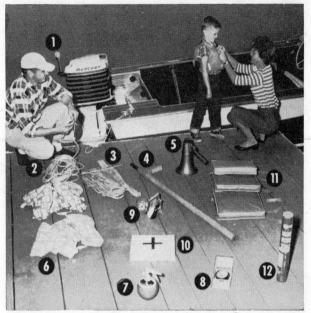

As a starter your equipment should include at least these dozen items: 1) proper running lights; 2) 50 feet of extra line; 3) anchor and line; 4) bilge pump; 5) horn; 6) life jacket for each passenger aboard; 7) fire extinguisher; 8) compass; 9) hand lantern; 10) first-aid kit; 11) buoyant cushions, and 12) safety flares. You'll add to these later.

MOORING AND DOCKING

You've made a short, practice run now and are ready to return. When making a landing, proceed slowly. Your wake won't disturb other moored vessels; you'll be better able to gauge the effects of wind, wave or current upon your boat; you can easily avoid mooring buoys, frequently found in berthing areas; and, if your motor is of the gearshift type, the throttle will be closed enough for shifting gears.

If the water is shoal in your landing area, put the motor on "release" so it will kick up if anything is hit, or, lacking such a device, have someone stand by the motor, ready to tilt it up at your command.

In landing at natural areas, try to select a sandy beach with little surf breaking. What from the boat appears to be a gentle, undulating surf may from the beach be a boiling tempest breaking over an acute land slope.

Close the beach (bring the boat in) at a right angle. Tilt up the motor before it strikes bottom, and haul the boat up the beach as far as possible—allowing for tide—so it will not be battered nor broached by waves.

In bringing your boat alongside a pier or up to a mooring,

watch the wind. Do not land on the weather side of the pier unless necessary. A crowded gas dock, though, often makes it necessary. Bear in mind, in such a situation, that the wind will be nudging your craft into the pier, so maneuver and use your reverse gear as needed to keep your boat clear. Also, come into the pier at an angle that will permit you to lie alongside at least a boat length away, permitting the wind to move you next to the pier. See that your boat is properly fendered before you come up to the pier, and don't cut your motor(s) until you're safely secured.

When making a preferable landing, on the lee side of a pier, head your boat into the wind or current, thus retaining better control.

From whichever side you approach, turn the craft before it reaches the pier so that it comes parallel to the structure. If you have a gearshift, use reverse to stop headway, then shift to neutral and make the landing with the motor still running.

If you do not have a gearshift, throttle down to a low speed, pivot the motor 180° (which gives you the equivalent of reverse), and get a bow line to the pier. Using this as a spring, the stern can be brought in, if necessary, by going forward slowly with the propeller turned *away* from the pier. Once the boat is alongside, secure a stern line.

MAKING FAST

An eye spliced into one end of each dock line makes it easy to quickly throw them over a bollard or around a cleat. In other situations, a couple of fast and handy knots to know and use are the clove hitch and bowline.

Generally you'll want to use at least a bow and stern line to make fast. Under certain conditions of wind and current, it may be desirable to tie with a bow line only, allowing your boat to float away from the pier; but if the boat's going to

be left untended, put out a stern anchor. A change in the wind or current may bring your boat bumping into the pier.

In tidal waters, allow enough line for rise and fall. You may otherwise return to find your boat lynched unceremoniously out of the water, if the cleats have not let go.

A block (pulley) and weight arrangement, a shackle and cable setup on pilings, etc., will allow the lines and thus the boat to ride the tide. Where such an arrangement is lacking, run the bow and stern lines several bollards (or equivalent) away from the boat so that the lines are at about 45° angles to the boat. This allows considerable flexibility for tidal variation.

IN GENERAL

Keep your boat's speed under control at all times. Don't show off. Respect the rights, and comforts, of others afloat: slow down not only when your boat's in danger but when it's a matter of courtesy to others. When passing other craft in the same or opposite direction, give them a wide berth. Never attempt to "hose-down" those aboard another boat. When passing by or through an anchorage, throttle down to your lowest speed and keep an acutely alert lookout for moorings, swimmers, debris, etc.

If you are going off shore or for a relatively long cruise even on inland waters, make those at home familiar with your plans, in as much detail as possible. Should trouble develop, you'll find the Coast Guard most welcomely cooperative, ready to render assistance. The more they know about your plans and boat, the more help they can be.

Your actions on the water can do much to fight against the restricting legislation that inevitably will be proposed from time to time concerning boats and boatmen. And remember, your speed may be prima facie evidence of your guilt.

Mercury Outboard Motors

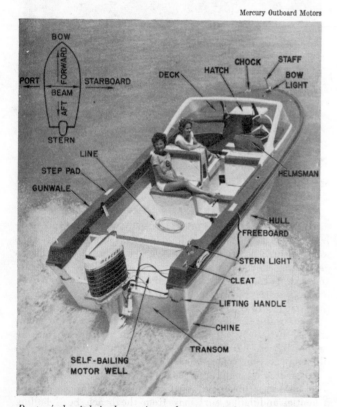

Part of the job in becoming a boatman is learning the language inherent to the sport. Illustration above gives many of the commonly used terms you'll want to know and use.

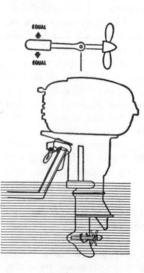

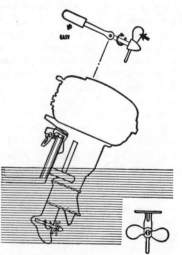

Below: If motor is tilted with lower unit toward transom, effective blade pitch on port side is practically zero, but increased on starboard side. Result easier steering to starboard and harder turning to port. With thrust not parallel to water line, stern will rise and bow will trim too low. Opposite effect results when motor is tilted aft.

Above: For easy steering and proper trim, adjust the motor vertically on the transom with cavitation plate parallel to the water flow, as illustrated. In this position, propeller blades take an equal bite on the water on each side of the center line.

To insure safety, check your boat and motor against these curves and formulas, designed to prevent over-powering and overloading. A check list to use for trouble-shooting the motor; thoughts on propeller choice and additional miscellaneous equipment; safety suggestions; and a quiz to test your outboarding knowledge.

Photograph from Scott Outboard Motors

Twin-motor installation, *increasingly popular on today's outboards, provides plenty of power and safety margin besides: if one motor quits the other will get boat in. Tachometer is helpful instrument to keep motors synchronized for most efficient operation.*

PART THREE

THIS series on outboarding, readers may recall, placed much emphasis on the matching of boat and motor. If the boat doesn't have an OBC (Outboard Boating Club of America) plate listing the hull's load and power limits, part one pointed out, it was suggested that you get sound advice on the matter. Here now is a way for you to determine those limits yourself.

For horsepower, simple multiplication and a look at the graph (right) will render the *maximum* horsepower that can be safely used on the boat in question. This horsepower can be derived from a single engine or as a total from a twin installation. Either way, it is an uppermost limit, a sort of safety belt that all boatmen are encouraged to use.

THE HORSEPOWER CURVE

The first step, the simple arithmetic we talked about, is to multiply the hull's overall length by its maximum width *at the stern.* Length is measured from the stem to the transom on a straight line parallel to the keel. Don't include extensions like outboard brackets, fins, etc., in the measurement.

The second step is to take the product of the length-times-width problem (if fractions are involved use the nearest integer, or whole number) and find this figure along the vertical axis (left

edge) of the graph. Enter here and follow the horizontal line to where it intersects the curve. Now follow down to the bottom. The figure you reach at the bottom scale is the maximum horsepower for that particular hull.

If the intersection falls between figures, the one at the right is taken as the maximum horsepower for the hull.

Example: The length-width product of a 14½-foot hull with a maximum transom width of 5 feet is 72.5. Enter

the side of the graph at 73 and follow the horizontal line to its intersection with the curve. Reading this point of intersection along the bottom of the graph gives us a figure somewhere between 55 and 60. Because it is between ratings, we take the figure to the right of the intersection, so that 60 is our answer. The *maximum* power then that we can use on our 14½-footer is 60 horsepower, in the form of either a single 60-hp engine or two 30s.

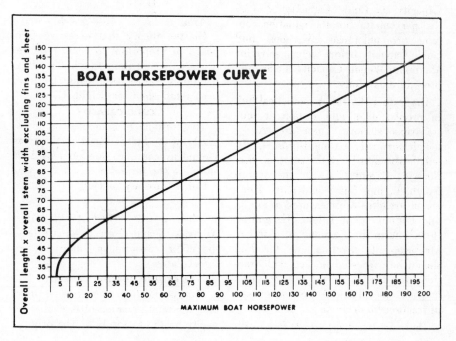

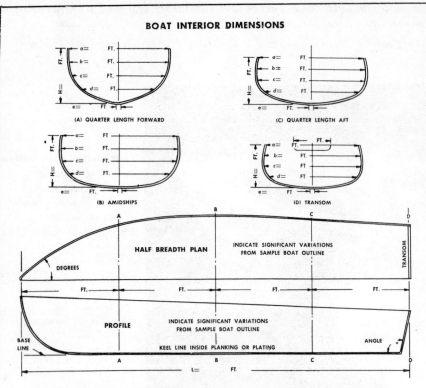

BOAT INTERIOR DIMENSIONS

(A) QUARTER LENGTH FORWARD

(C) QUARTER LENGTH AFT

(B) AMIDSHIPS

(D) TRANSOM

HALF BREADTH PLAN

INDICATE SIGNIFICANT VARIATIONS FROM SAMPLE BOAT OUTLINE

DEGREES

PROFILE

INDICATE SIGNIFICANT VARIATIONS FROM SAMPLE BOAT OUTLINE

KEEL LINE INSIDE PLANKING OR PLATING

BASE LINE

ANGLE

TRANSOM

Diagram 1 shows hypothetical hull in profile, plan, and section at four transverse stations: A, B, C and D. Horizontal breadths are noted a, b, c, d and e; H is symbol for height. Measurements taken inside hull should be expressed in feet, with fractions of a foot converted to three-place decimals (table is included in text).

For full information on boat horsepower and weight capacities, flotation, standardized dimension of outboard boats and motors, ventilation, fuel systems, steering systems, lighting for small boats, safety equipment, trailer facts, fire protection standards and many other details of recommended practices for outboards, readers may consult the Engineering Manual published by the Outboard Industry Associations, 307 North Michigan Ave., Chicago 1, Illinois.

★ ★ ★

TROUBLE SHOOTING THE OUTBOARD

MOTOR WON'T START:
Fuel tank empty
Fuel line closed
Fuel tank air vent closed
Motor not primed or choked
Low speed carburetor needle valve needs adjusting
Spark plug improperly gapped, cracked, fouled or lose
Magneto points improperly gapped; coil or condenser weak
Improper fuel mixture

MOTOR MISSES:
Pinched or kinked fuel line
Fouled spark plugs
Carburetor needs adjustment and/ or cleaning
Fuel filter needs cleaning
Improper fuel mixture
Frayed lead wire insulation

MOTOR LOSES POWER:
Carburetor needs adjustment
Fuel line not clear
Wrong type spark plugs
Motor overheating, check cooling system

EXCESSIVE VIBRATION:
Carburetor needs adjustment
Propeller bent, broken or fouled
Spark plug not firing
Clamp screws or other device loose

MOTOR OVERHEATS:
Water pump defective
Water intake clogged

★ ★ ★

A SAFE LOAD

Determining the load limit—that is, the *maximum* combined weight of passengers, engine and miscellaneous equipment a given hull can safely carry —is not quite so simple. The OBC, it is true, has provided us with a formula for the job, namely Maximum Weight Capacity = Cubic Capacity × 12.5 lbs. per cu. ft., but the equation contains *two* unknowns. We must find Cubic Capacity before we can solve for Maximum Weight Capacity. Follow the procedure carefully.

Diagram 1 shows a hypothetical hull in profile, plan, and section at four transverse stations. These are: A, ¼ length forward; B, amidships; C, ¼ length aft; and D, at the transom. Sections A, B and C divide the overall length, L, into four equal parts. Horizontal breadths are measured at top, a, and bottom, e, of height, H, and at three intermediate points: b, c and d. Measurements taken inside the hull should be expressed in feet, with fractions of a foot converted to three-place decimals (see Table A for conversions of fractions to decimals).

There are two steps now before work-ing out the final equation. These are 1) computing areas of sections which will permit us to 2) compute cubic capacity.

AREAS OF SECTIONS

Areas of Sections A, B and C are each found separately by using the formula:

$$\text{Area} = \frac{H}{12}(a+4b+2c+4d+e).$$

On the theory that excessive free-board in proportion to beam does not necessarily contribute to a hull's safety, maximum values (see Table B) have been established for height, H.

CUBIC CAPACITY

The formula to compute Cubic Capacity of the hull is based on the areas (found in step one) for Sections A, B and C in the formula:

Cubic Capacity of Hull =

$$\frac{L}{12}(4A+2B+4C).$$

Areas A, B and C are in square feet; the cubic capacity in cubic feet, to three places.

MAXIMUM WEIGHT CAPACITY

This is the final step, and requires only the multiplication of the cubic capacity by the factor 12.5. The original equation, you'll perhaps remember, is:

Maximum Weight Capacity = Cubic Capacity × 12.5 lbs. per cu. ft. The result is an overall total in pounds, expressing to the nearest integer the safe maximum weight capacity of a given hull. But remember, a boat safely loaded and safely powered still has its limits, which is where seamanship and competent boat handling come into use.

ADDED FLOTATION

Still another step can be taken to assure the safety of your passengers and your boating rig: built-in flotation. This can take the form of air chambers or of the addition of some buoyant material, in either case, of sufficient quantity to support the weight even if the boat is entirely submerged.

A note to the OBC, 307 North Michigan Ave., Chicago, Ill., will bring you information on how you can determine the amount of flotation you need for your craft. First, however, you might try writing directly to your boatbuilder; he may already have done the computation involved.

WHAT PROP?

Your outboard motor, carefully selected under the foregoing considerations discussed in this series, may or may not come with a propeller. Either way, you want to be sure to turn the right wheel for the job your boat and motor must do.

Propeller manufacturers, and some outboard motor manufacturers, make a wide range of wheels for you to choose from. Ask their advice before buying. The choice, say, for a 16′ to

TABLE A
Conversion of Inches to Decimals in Feet

Inches (or fractions)	Decimals in Feet	Inches (or fractions)	Decimals in Feet
1/8″	.010′	3″	.250′
1/4″	.021′	4″	.333′
3/8″	.031′	5″	.417′
1/2″	.042′	6″	.500′
5/8″	.052′	7″	.583′
3/4″	.062′	8″	.667′
7/8″	.073′	9″	.750′
1″	.083′	10″	.833′
2″	.167′	11″	.917′

18′ runabout might go from a 2-bladed propeller with a pitch ratio (pitch divided by diameter) of 1.3 for a high-speed, lightweight rig to a 3- or 4-bladed propeller with a pitch ratio of .8 for a heavily loaded, slow speed craft. Fuel economy and boat performance will be markedly affected by propeller selection.

ELECTRONIC EQUIPMENT

Much of the electronic equipment previously held to be suitable only for yachts and their kin is now designed and produced for use in the smaller boat, including the outboard. Chief items in this equipment are the radiotelephone, depth finder and direction finder. Their price, bulk and weight have all been put into a range that will appeal to the outboarder, especially in the light of the equipments' various uses.

MISCELLANEOUS EQUIPMENT

Many of the points to be made here, readers will observe, have been dealt with in preceding parts. They are repeated, briefly, because of their significance.

The fire extinguisher(s) you use aboard the boat must be of a Coast Guard-approved type. If there's any doubt as to the approval status of the particular extinguisher, check with your local Coast Guard Inspection Office.

Of the approved types now on the market you'd do well to buy a carbon dioxide, dry chemical or foam extinguisher. The vaporizing liquid type, both those that must be pumped and those with stored pressure, will not be accepted as approved after January 1, 1962.

Check your extinguisher regularly, and recharge or refill as needed.

Lifesaving devices too must be of an approved type. The choice ranges from preservers and cushions to ring buoys and vests. The buoyant materials used in these devices include kapok, cork, balsawood, and vinyl-covered fibrous glass.

Take care that you have enough of these devices (one for each person aboard) and that their location and use is common knowledge—*before* you get under way!

Fire prevention of course is the responsibility of everyone

aboard but it is the special province of the skipper. In that capacity you must insist upon certain rules—and see to it that they are followed. You must, for instance, see that all cigarettes are out when approaching a gas dock. And you must see that none of your passengers forgets the smoking moratorium during the fueling process.

Most outboards are equipped with portable tanks. If they are of six-gallons or less in capacity, remove them from the craft for fueling. And see that they are made secure when in the boat. Ventilation, leakage and spill, of course, are all things you'll have to watch vigilantly.

Outboards with permanent fuel tanks should conform with approved inboard practice, running fill pipes to decks outside the coaming and venting outside the hull. Fill pipes should extend almost to the bottom of the tank, and not terminate at the top of the tank.

Permanent or portable, ground the gas hose nozzle to the fill pipe when fueling. This prevents static electricity from generating a spark which, in turn, might ignite gasoline fumes and blast boat and passengers out of the running.

IN CASE OF AN ACCIDENT

If you are involved in a boating accident on the navigable waters of the United States you are required by law to stop and give whatever help you can, without seriously endangering your boat or passengers. You must also identify yourself and your boat to any person injured or to the owner of any property damaged.

You must file a written accident report if there is 1) loss

TABLE B
Maximum Allowable Height for a Transverse Section

Beam of Section	Max. Height	Beam of Section	Max. Height
Up to 4.042′	1.583′	5.710′ to 6.042′	2.083′
4.043′ to 4.375′	1.667′	6.043′ to 6.375′	2.167′
4.376′ to 4.709′	1.750′	6.376′ to 6.709′	2.250′
4.710′ to 5.042′	1.833′	6.710′ to 7.042′	2.333′
5.043′ to 5.375′	1.917′	7.043′ to 7.375′	2.417′
5.376′ to 5.709′	2.000′	7.376′ to 7.709′	2.500′

NOTE:—The maximum allowable height (H) is based on **width** (a) for that section on the Interior Dimensions. If the actual height of the section is **less** than the maximum allowable height, use the **actual height**. If the actual height of the section is **more** than the maximum allowable height, use the **maximum allowable height**.

of life, 2) injury causing a person to remain incapacitated for more than 72 hours, or 3) physical damage to property (including vessels) in excess of $100. If in doubt, report!

If you're in trouble while afloat, you'll find the Coast Guard, other boatmen and professional seamen ready to do what they can. To help the Guard assist you, the following steps are recommended:

1) Let somebody know your plans for the day including destination, intended stops en route, and estimated time of return. At the first opportunity notify those concerned of any change in plans.

2) Don't use MAYDAY in voice radio distress communications unless immediate assistance is required.

To get help when it's needed, of course, you'll want to know and carry some of the recognized distress signals. Apart from the radiotelephone, perhaps the most valuable distress aid available, there are a host of other devices. Flares, a continuous sounding with a whistle or horn, the raising and lowering of outstretched arms to each side, and so on, are some examples.

YOUR RESPONSIBILITIES

When you are admonished to know the Rules of the Road you should be aware that there are four different sets of such rules in effect according to your boating locality. These are: 1) Inland, 2) Great Lakes, 3) Western Rivers and 4) International. Copies of the rules you're interested in can be secured from your local Coast Guard office.

Hints on understanding the Inland Rules appear in the CG booklet *Recreational Boating Guide,* for sale by the Superintendent of Documents, U.S. Government Printing Office, Washington 25, D.C., at 40 cents a copy. The section is worth quoting here:

"Note that in these rules, 'steam vessel' includes *any* vessel propelled by machinery.

"If you are equipped with both machinery and sail, the *only* time you are considered as a sailing vessel under the rules is when you are propelled by sail alone. (Note: If you carry an engine of more than 10 hp—or less where states have so specified—you are required to have a registration number.)

"Risk of collision can, when circumstances permit, be ascertained by carefully watching the compass bearing of an approaching vessel. If the bearing does not appreciably change, such risk should be deemed to exist.

"The law says that in obeying and construing these rules due regard shall be had to all dangers of navigation and collision and to any special circumstances which may render a departure from the rules necessary in order to avoid immediate danger.

"The rules of the road apply alike to the small pleasure craft and large commercial ships such as ocean liners or freighters. However, the large vessel with her great length and tremendous weight requires a great deal more room to maneuver; because her turning circle is large, her stopping distance is relatively great, and often her deep draft restricts her to little variance from channel courses. Common sense dictates that operating a small pleasure craft too close to the large oceangoing vessel or a tug with tow may be dangerous."

QUIZ FOR OUTBOARD BOATMEN

1) Outboard boats on federal waterways are not required to follow the same Rules of the Road that apply to large commercial steamers.

2) A tacking sailboat always has right of way over an outboard boat.

3) Outboarders may disregard federal regulations that concern "steam vessels."

4) Outboard boats under way on federal waters must carry their registration certificates aboard.

5) Outboard boats powered by engines of 10 hp or less when used on federal waters are always required to be registered.

6) Money paid for boat registration fees is deductible from federal income taxes.

7) Sailboats with auxiliary outboard motors, used on federal waters, always must be registered.

8) Sailboats propelled by sail alone and used on federal waters are never required to be registered.

9) Outboard boats are required by law to have sufficient flotation to keep the boat afloat should it fill with water.

10) The proper propeller for a particular hull, motor and job helps achieve best boat performance.

11) Depth sounders are not suitable for use on outboard boats.

12) Life-saving equipment, like cushions, used on an outboard boat need not be Coast Guard-approved.

13) Liquid-type fire extinguishers will be CG-approved after January 1, 1962.

14) Fire extinguishers on an outboard boat should be kept in some remote place aboard, well out of the way of wind and water which may come aboard.

15) Portable fuel tanks should never be removed from the boat for filling.

16) You are not responsible for any damage caused by your boat's wake or waves.

17) In case of capsize, promptly swim as far from the boat as possible.

18) Only one set of Rules of the Road is in effect in the United States.

19) If your outboard boat is equipped with sail also, it is under the Rules considered a sailing vessel only when you are propelled by sail alone.

20) If you use both an outboard motor and a sail to propel your boat you are under the Rules considered a sailing vessel.

21) The Rules invariably require a large commercial vessel to keep clear of an outboard craft.

22) A boat propelled by oars must keep clear of an outboard boat.

23) You may anchor your outboard in a channel to fish, providing you keep clear of traffic.

24) A boating accident in which no one is killed need not be reported.

25) Any outboard hull is suited for the highest-powered stock outboard motor.

26) High-powered outboard motors on small, light hulls provide greatest speed and safety.

27) When under way at high speed give *all* your attention to your own safety.

28) Maintain your course and speed when passing another vessel close aboard.

29) Under all circumstances, maintain your course and speed when you have the right of way.

30) When an outboard boat turns, its stern swings in a direction opposite to the desired change in course.

31) Once your anchor is "holding bottom" the length of the anchor rode payed out is unimportant.

32) Wise practice to help assure proper anchor holding is to pay out anchor rode at least five times the depth of the water.

33) If you run aground you should attempt to get the anchor into deep water as far from the boat as possible.

34) The outboard motor(s) serves as a rudder on an outboard boat.

35) Maneuvering an outboard boat is relatively more difficult with two motors than with one.

36) The Coast Guard themselves can impose no penalty for the reckless operation of a boat on federal waters.

37) A bow line about 8 feet long and a stern line about 6 feet long, both made ready for landings, are always of sufficient size.

38) The bitter end of your anchor rode should be made fast when anchoring.

39) When anchoring, throw the anchor as far from the boat as possible.

40) Lower the anchor into the water, don't drop it.

41) Give the boat sternway after the anchor sets to test the anchor's holding power.

42) When attempting to get a person into the boat from the water, the boat's engine(s) should be kept running.

43) In a squall give the boat plenty of speed through the water.

44) When in a storm and heavy sea, stop your boat's engine(s) and drift.

45) Usually try to cross a large wave at about a right angle.

46) Because an unexpected delay might change your schedule, don't tell friends or relatives what your estimated time of arrival is, especially when making lengthy cruises or going off shore.

47) Don't equip your boat with running lights if you don't expect to run at night.

48) A compass is not required by federal law to be aboard an outboard boat.

49) Some states now issue boat registration numbers.

50) Some states now have jurisdiction over the federal waters within their state boundaries, concerning the equipment carried by and the inspection of boats operated upon those waters.

51) Boats exempted from their state's federally approved numbering provisions must apply to the Coast Guard for a number.

52) All violations of the Federal Motorboat Act of 1940 are punishable by a fine of not more than $2000.

53) Fog horns should not be used in place of a whistle.

54) The permanent seats in your new boat are an indication of how many persons that boat may safely carry.

55) It is preferable for safety's sake to have your outboard boat trim slightly by the stern rather than by the bow, when underway.

56) When adjusting trim underway by the relocation of passengers, never slow boat speed.

57) Your boat's freeboard is not a factor in determining the number of passengers you can safely carry.

58) The buoyancy of Coast Guard-approved kapok cushions remains unaffected when sat upon frequently.

59) It is desirable to paint the underbody of a boat moored in salt water with an anti-fouling paint, whether the boat is wood, fiberglass or metal.

60) At open throttle a 2-cycle outboard motor of 20 horsepower will consume less fuel than a 4-cycle inboard engine of 20 horsepower.

61) The improper mixing of oil and gasoline is apt to cause spark plug fouling on an outboard motor.

62) Gasoline spilled in a wet bilge, because it mixes with bilge water, loses its explosion potential.

63) Federal law requires U.S. pleasure boats underway to display the U.S. flag.

64) Speed limits posted on the water by the U.S. Corps of Army Engineers must be obeyed by boatmen.

65) A hull that makes 15 mph with a 7½-hp outboard motor will make 30 mph with a 15-hp outboard motor.

66) It is wise to carry a paddle or pair of oars of sufficient length (relative to the size of the boat) aboard an outboard boat.

67) Federal law requires all boat trailers to exhibit back-up lights.

68) Federal law specifies no minimum age for boat operators on federal waters.

69) A siren may be substituted for the whistle required by Pilot Rules for fog signals given by "steam vessels."

70) To insure sufficient ventilation when filling the permanent fuel tanks on your outboard boat, open all windows, hatches and doors.

ANSWERS TO QUIZ QUESTIONS

Compare your answers with these:
Questions 4, 6, 10, 19, 30, 32, 33, 34, 38, 40, 41, 45, 48, 49, 53, 55, 59, 61, 64, 66, 68 and 69 are true. All others are false.

CHAPTER XXXII

Court Interpretations of Marine Law

Comments on recent decisions by admiralty and other courts of interest to yachtsmen, because yachts or other pleasure boats themselves were involved, or because the law laid down by the court would be applicable to situations in which yachtsmen might find themselves, or because the facts of the case suggest warnings which pleasure-boat skippers should heed in matters of equipment or operation. The citation of each case mentioned is given so that any person interested can readily examine it in detail. The reference "A.M.C." means American Maritime Cases and this citation is used for decisions not yet officially reported and for any decision where the A.M.C. report is thought to be better adapted to use by readers who want to read it in full. No attempt is made to state the law completely on any point involved in any of the decisions.

THE rules of the road provide that the vessel with the right of way, called the privileged vessel, must hold her course and speed, except for unavoidable changes such as a reduction in speed when approaching a slip or dock, and that the other vessel, called the burdened vessel, must keep clear of her. In a situation where collision will result unless the burdened vessel keeps clear, it is a grave fault for the burdened vessel to cross the signal given by the privileged vessel by blowing a one whistle signal in answer to a two whistle signal by the privileged vessel, and normally the burdened vessel will be held liable for a collision. *Robert Wright-Lackawanna*, 1936 A.M.C. 533. It has been held, also, to be negligence not to blow a danger signal when an approaching vessel is giving signals obviously wrong, due to the palpable confusion of her master. *Dixon-King*, 1936 A.M.C. 891.

ON most small motor boats, the helmsman cannot hear whistle signals given by other similar boats when his own engine is running, because of the engine noise. If for any reason it is not practicable to deaden or muffle that noise so that whistle signals can be heard, or if a bow watch cannot be maintained entirely free from it, then common sense dictates that in thick weather the engine should be stopped for at least two minutes at frequent intervals in order that such signals may be heard. Failure to take this precaution may impose liability for collision damage. *City of Dalhart*, 1936 A.M.C. 125.

SUPREME command must be exercised on a motor boat under way for the same reason that it must be exercised on an ocean liner. Lives and property values are at stake in each case, the difference being one of degree and not one of kind. The skipper of a small motor boat with volunteer workers and guests on board should be tactful, in fact he must be if he wants companions on subsequent trips, but he should nevertheless be able to make correct decisions promptly and to see that nothing interferes with the execution of his orders. One of the most important decisions to be made concerns the number of persons whom he will permit to be on board, because the owner of a motor boat who overloads it with guests is liable for the death of any one of them if the boat capsizes.

Speedboats, because of their construction, are peculiarly subject to the risk of capsizing if they become unseaworthy through overloading. No expert knowledge of metacentric heights is needed; just plain common sense will suffice. Not so long ago, an owner of a 28 foot speedboat, with a beam of 7 feet, 2 inches and a draft of 2 feet, 1 inch, permitted 17 guests to climb aboard, of whom 7 perched on the engine hatch and other deck spaces. The rated capacity of the boat was 10 persons, and thus his overload was almost 100 per cent. He then ran out into the open sea. With so light a boat, having so small a draft and so little freeboard, the presence of 18 persons seriously affected the stability, the boat cap-

sized, and about half of the guests were drowned. The accident may have been caused by an unusual or unexpected wave, but a sudden shifting of the helm at a speed of 40 miles per hour would have been enough to capsize the boat. *Calanchini v. Bliss*, 1937 A.M.C. 203.

RECONDITIONING work on a motor boat hauled out for the winter and securely shored up in a boat or ship yard has a fire hazard which should not be ignored. An example is furnished in *International Mercantile Marine S.S. Co. v. W. & A. Fletcher Co.*, 296 Fed. 855. Varnish was being removed from woodwork by the use of a volatile liquid varnish remover. Cotton waste soaked with benzine was used to wipe off the varnish remover and then thrown on the deck. Others nearby were removing paint with an open-flame torch and a serious fire was started in the cotton waste. More than ordinary care should be exercised in circumstances such as these. An unusual explosion was reported in *International Marine Co. v. Fels*, 164 Fed. 337. In that case a quantity of naphtha soap, securely wrapped, was stowed in an enclosed compartment. Vapor given off by the soap, despite the wrappings, became mixed with air and formed a highly explosive gas and this was touched off by a spark caused probably by faulty insulation.

WIRING installation on a motorboat should be made with the Marine Rules of the American Institute of Electrical Engineers as minimum requirements for safety. Those rules specify that feeders of every description should be run with a view to avoiding a space where heat and gases may be encountered, such as an engine room, a fire room, and a galley, and spaces where damage may occur, such as the exposed side of a deck house. Lead and armored cable is generally regarded as more satisfactory for vessels than an iron pipe conduit system because there is a tendency for moisture to condense in an iron pipe and to cause the rubber insulation on the wire to deteriorate. A fire starting from defective wiring is usually a slowly smoldering one easily extinguished, but it will not be that type if it starts in a space with little or no ventilation and surrounded by tanks of explosive gas. Sparks not infrequently result when a short circuit occurs if there is a loose connection or if the insulation has become worn. The *Doris Kellogg*, 1937 A.M.C. 254 is a good example of an avoidable fire.

DINGHY problems are not confined to the settlement of such question as whether to tow or carry the troublesome but indispensable little adjunct on davits or deck, or whether to equip it with an outboard or sails. A most important problem, usually not thought of at all, is how to light it when under way at night. The Pilot Rules are specific in prescribing that "rowing boats under oars shall have ready at hand a lantern showing a white light which shall be temporarily exhibited in sufficient time to prevent collision," but it is probable that this rule is more honored in the breach than in the observance. A recent tragedy in the Ohio River near Louisville illustrates the danger of being without a light. *Feige, Adm. v. Hurley*, 89 Fed. (2nd) 575.

Canoes technically are not covered by this Pilot Rule but courts have stated that the rule indicates a standard of care which canoe parties should observe. In the case cited, a 15 foot speed boat capable of 35 miles per hour but running at about 23 crashed into an unlighted 16 foot canoe and caused the death of one of its occupants. The court condemned the speed boat operator for running through the darkness at such a speed that he was unable to see the canoe until he was within 10 or 15 feet of it and stated that "This was more than negligence; it showed a reckless disregard for the rights of others on the river." Nevertheless, the speed boat was exonerated from liability because the canoeists were negligent in that they should have anticipated the presence of other craft and foreseen the danger of collision; had they looked they could have seen the speed boat's lights or had they listened they could have heard its motor; and they had failed to display a light in accordance with the Pilot Rules upon seeing or hearing the approach of the other boat.

NARROW channels necessitate strict observance of the rules of the road. Each of two excursion steamers meeting in the entrance to Rye Beach, N. Y., was held at fault for a collision, one for keeping to her port hand in violation of the narrow channel rule and the other for swinging across her course. One steamer was leaving and the other was approaching the dock at the beach. The one leaving was improperly on the port side of the channel and apparently she insisted on keeping to that side. She blew two blasts and then when this signal was not answered she blew two blasts a second time. Thereupon the in-coming steamer blew one blast and the out-going one blew three and went astern, but too late to avoid collision. The court held that the latter was at fault for not immediately blowing the alarm signal and going astern full speed when her request for a starboard to starboard passing was not agreed to. The incoming steamer was held at fault for unduly insisting upon her rights, the court quoting with approval the opinion in the *Quoque* case, 47 Fed. (2nd) 873, to the effect that however great the temptation to refuse to give way to a vessel wantonly insisting on crossing one's bow, duty clearly requires a skipper to stop and reverse instead of obstinately insisting on his rights. *Islander Steamboat Company, Inc., v. Steamer Americana*, 1938 A.M.C. 147.

NARROW channels sometimes cannot be avoided and it is well to remember that three blasts must be blown when one's engines are put at full speed astern even though headway has not been entirely lost. This is especially important if there is a nearby boat astern. The court stated, in *Western Shore Steamboat Company v. S.S. Jean*, 1937 A.M.C. 589: "I know of no case which denies that there is an obligation to look both astern and forward in passing down a channel." One should not rely solely on the rule that the overtaking boat is the burdened vessel, especially when the overtaking craft is a commercial steamer. When a motor boat is the privileged vessel in such a situation, her skipper should decide which side of the channel the overtaking vessel will probably want and then pull over to the other side to get out of the way. It is not safe to wait for the commercial vessel to blow a signal to indicate on which hand she asks permission to pass, especially in crowded waters like Hell Gate, N. Y., where tugs with floats, excursion boats, passenger steamers, freighters, and all sorts of commercial craft are busily plying their trades.

IN *Edwards v. American Steamship Catalina*, 1937 A.M.C. 401, a steamer proceeding at 16 knots, which was practically at full speed, through a patchy fog was held solely at fault for collisions with a yacht proceeding at a reduced speed of 6 knots. It is a rule that a lookout should have no other duty. In this case the lookout on the yacht occasionally wiped spray from the pilot-house window in front of the wheel, but the court held that giving this additional duty to the lookout did not constitute negligence on the part of the yacht's skipper. The court computed the steamer's speed by multiplying the pitch of the propeller, 17 feet, by the 112 revolutions per minute which her engine room log showed she was making, and reducing the total by 15 per cent for slip. $112 \times 17 = 1904$, which reduced by 15 per cent = 1618.4 feet per minute or 97,104 feet per hour. Dividing this by 6,000, the approximate number of feet in a nautical mile, showed the steamer's speed to be somewhat more than 16 knots.

FOG plays many tricks in the conveyance of sounds from whistles, bells, and other producers of warning signals. The Circuit Court of Appeals in *Wilmington Transportation Company v. Edwards*, 95 Fed. (2nd) 283, made this comment which should be part of the mental equipment of every motor boat skipper: "The deflection of whistles in a fog so that they are heard at a greater distance but not nearby is too frequent a phenomenon for us to hold that the *Catalina* has sustained her burden of proof that this was not the reason her whistle was not heard on the *Arbutus*." In this decision the court on appeal affirmed the decree of the lower court digested above. The *Catalina* was a 300 foot steamer running from Catalina to San Pedro (Los Angeles) and she was unharmed by a collision in fog which demolished the *Arbutus*, a 77 foot motor boat. The steamer was held solely responsible. An interesting feature of this decision was the court's holding that a lookout on a small boat with low freeboard was properly placed outside the pilot house where there was a stanchion to which he could hold, notwithstanding the fact that he was 23 feet aft of the stem. It would not have been practicable to post the lookout further forward, because even at moderate speed an ordinary swell might cross over her bow.

STEAMER lanes are good places for pleasure craft to keep out of, and especially to get out of if fog comes. A motor boat drawing three or four feet does not require a sixteen or twenty foot channel and a chart, corrected to the date of use, will usually disclose safe water adjacent to it not actually within the channels used by steamers. Incidentally, such a chart is invaluable for showing good holding bottoms in the event that emergency anchoring becomes necessary. A steamer is required by law to proceed at reduced speed in a fog, but steamers have been known to take chances by proceeding at full speed in order to maintain schedules. If one is so proceeding, there is slight chance of escape for a motor boat which happens to lie in the steamer's course.

FOGBOUND vessels at anchor in a channel must be careful to ring their bells at the intervals prescribed by whatever rules apply to the place of anchorage. In *Pyman Bros., Ltd., v. S.S. Cherokee and Cherokee-Seminole S.S. Corpn.*, 1937 A.M.C. 737, a collision occurred in the St. Johns River, Fla., 23 miles to seaward from Jacksonville. A freight steamer was anchored in a fog in the narrowest part of the channel although her master thought he was outside of it. She was hit by a passenger steamer proceeding upstream at 14 knots. The freighter was held at fault for anchoring there when she had had sufficient warning of the fog to enable her to anchor in a harbor which she had passed, and when she could have proceeded to sea despite the fog. But she was held at fault chiefly for ringing her bell at two minute intervals instead of at the one minute intervals prescribed by the Inland Rules. The passenger steamer was held partly at fault for steaming at an excessive speed.

FOG is no respecter of persons or the size of boats, and thus yachtsmen have a problem in common with their professional brethren when anchoring or proceeding in a fog. As reported in *Quirigua-Southern Cross*, 1936 A.M.C. 1555, the *Southern Cross* anchored in a fairway or channel in a fog and thus exposed herself to collision, although a nearby anchorage was available. She was struck by the *Quirigua*, but the latter was held also at fault for proceeding at 5 knots over the bottom (6½ knots through the water). This speed was deemed excessive because she could not stop within the distance at which another vessel could be seen. In the case of another collision a few hundred feet away from and two hours prior to this one, a speed of 4 knots over the bottom (6 knots through the water) was judicially determined as excessive (*Tai Ping v. Jean*, 1935 A.M.C. 219). A small motor boat under control can always proceed to a nearby anchorage by feeling her way with the lead, taking care to allow for tidal changes in depth after anchoring. There can be no excuse for not having on board an up-to-the-minute chart and tide and current tables.

FOG requires the observance of several special rules, but perhaps the most important one is that a vessel must proceed at a speed which will enable her to stop well within the limits of visibility. Another rule is that a vessel in a heavy fog should anchor when an anchorage is readily available. *Eastern Steamship Lines v. Steamship West Mahwah*, 1938 A. M. C. 54. This concerned a collision in Hampton Roads between the *Robert E. Lee* and the *West Mahwah*. An incidental point was that the failure of one of the steamers to stand by the other after the collision or even to answer the other's calls raises presumptions against her.

A PORTION of the *Silver Line* decision (1937 A.M.C. 1427) dealt with navigating in a clear atmosphere but along the edge of a fog bank. A vessel in that situation must maintain a moderate speed just as if she herself were in the fog, because she would not be visible to a vessel in it. This especially is true if the fog bank is being blown across the vessel's course. One of the long established principles of law in maritime navigation is that a vessel shall not proceed in a fog at a speed at which she cannot be stopped dead in the water in one-half the visibility before her. Vessels in a fog so dense that in order to comply with this rule they must proceed so slowly that they lose their steerage way, are required to stop from time to time to maintain their proper speed. This rule of moderate speed in a fog may be violated, although the vessel is dead in the water at the moment of impact if she has crossed more than her allowable portion of visibility.

OVERTAKING vessels must anticipate reasonable maneuvers by privileged vessels ahead. In *Spentonbush Fuel Transport Service v. Diesel Tanker Almo*, 1937 A.M.C. 1177, a collision occurred in daylight with the wind light and no fog. Two small tankers, each having a Diesel engine operated from the pilot house, were proceeding in the same direction against an ebb tide. One passed through the east draw of a bridge and the other through the west draw at about the same time, but one was definitely an overtaking vessel. When they had passed through the draws, both captains saw considerable fog ahead. The overtaking vessel, rounding-to to avoid entering the fog bank, rammed the privileged vessel ahead which was engaged in a similar maneuver. The court held that the overtaking, or burdened, vessel should have foreseen this maneuver by the vessel ahead and avoided the collision.

OVERTAKING vessels must guard against normal and forseeable changes of course on the part of the leading vessel, but no duty exists to guard against the results of improper navigation by the vessel ahead. Thus one must foresee a change in course which will be necessitated by a known current into which the leading vessel is certain to run. Incidentally a court will not attempt to ascertain exactly the relative positions of vessels running practically abreast, in order to apply to one of them these rules as to overtaking vessels. These principles were applied in *Emery v. Steamship Carisco, Thames River Line*, 1938 A.M.C. 119, which arose out of a collision in the East River, New York, off Hallett's Point near Mill Rock, Hell Gate.

RUNNING lights which are lighted seem to be a pretty obvious safety requirement and yet instances are reported with surprising frequency where this simple precaution is neglected. The neglect may be due to failure to see that the lights are in working order, or to oversight in not turning them on, or to a thrifty desire not to use them until in the skipper's judgment it is sufficiently dark. There is no excuse, of course, for any of these alibis, and especially none for the last one because the Rules require lights after sunset, which means the almanac time of sunset without regard to twilight. In *Evans v. Ferry Boat Miss Constance*, 1937 A.M.C. 1422, a 57 foot motor boat without running lights was run down in January, 1937, by a ferry boat half an hour after sunset at Solomon's Island Harbor, Maryland. The motor boat was held solely liable because of her failure to display lights. The ferry had a lookout in the pilot house, eight feet above the deck and 15 feet aft of the stem, but none on the bow. The court ruled that the failure to have a bow watch did not contribute to the collision. The court was unwilling to adopt an inflexible rule to the effect that blame attaches to a ferryboat plying in a relatively small inland harbor because of failure, *per se*, to have a bow lookout.

RUNNING lights are not mere mathematical points but the lamps have diameters and thus there always is a sector where both lights can be seen by each of two opposing vessels. It is true that subdivisions (b) and (c) of Inland Rule 2 require that running lights shall throw their lights from right ahead to two points abaft the beam and that subdivision (d) requires that running lights be fitted with inboard screens, projecting at least three feet forward from the lights so as to prevent them from being seen across the bow. But this requirement must not be taken too literally, because there always is an angle between a line from the center of the light to the end of the screen and the fore and aft line of the boat. If that angle is as large as seven degrees, it follows that at a distance of a quarter of a mile there will be a sector approximately 300 feet wide in which both lights are visible. In fact, the existence of such a sector is recognized by Inland Rule 1. Thus care must be exercised, when both running lights are observed, to determine whether the approach is head-on or at an angle sufficient for safety, and in this determination the range lights are designed to play an important part. Neither range lights nor running lights should be obstructed in any way. *Seaboard Shipping Corpn. v. Globe Oil Delivery Corpn., et al.*, 1937 A.M.C. 1607.

SWELL damage often is actionable and motor boat owners should more frequently proceed against offenders, partly to help break up the practice of running at excessive speed through waters where boats are anchored or otherwise subject to damage. The case of *Behringer v. Ferryboat Columbia*, 1937 A.M.C. 881, is of interest to all pleasure boat owners. The ferryboat, proceeding from Sheepshead Bay toward Rockaway Point, at from 6½ to 9 knots, was held liable for injuries sustained by the wife of the owner of a 30 foot motor boat properly moored at the regular mooring place of the Sheepshead Bay Yacht Club, when the ferryboat's unusually large swells caused the wife to fall in the galley and be burned by boiling water from an upset kettle in which potatoes were being cooked on the stove. She suffered also from bruises, contusions and shock, and $20 worth of cups, glasses, and dishes were broken, not to mention the loss of bottles of wine. The ferryboat proceeded through the channel without slowing down and passed the motor boat within 150 feet. The court held that the fact that the ferryboat was pursuing her usual and customary course was no defense to the action for swell damage. She should have proceeded at such a rate of speed that no danger would result from her swell, of which she was bound to know the effect. A vessel is not an insurer against swell damage but is liable unless it was not in her power to prevent the injury by any practicable precaution such as slowing down or keeping further off.

A recent application of the rule that a vessel is responsible for damage caused by swells due to excessive speed is found in *Loughlin v. Tanker J. A. Martin, et al.*, 1938 A.M.C. 149. In that case, a tanker passing along Newtown Creek, N. Y., at four miles per hour, was held liable for damage caused by her swells to barges which were being shifted by hand. The tanker passed the barges about fifteen feet off; how often does a motor boat pass one moored or at anchor within that distance at a speed two or three times as great? Such an offender can be held liable for the damage he causes.

ASSIGNMENTS of wages made by paid captains or other members of a paid crew and attachments of them made by their creditors should be recognized by a motor boat owner only upon advice by the owner's attorney. An owner should stand firmly by this decision no matter how insistent or how threatening the demands made on him by creditors or assignees may be, because if he pays on an illegal assignment or attachment he may have to pay the same amount a second time to his employee. A Federal statute (46 U.S.C.A. 601) provides that "No wages due or accruing to any seaman or apprentice shall be subject to attachment or arrestment from any court" and such wages cannot legally be assigned, except by the making of certain allotments authorized by this statute. This section applies also to fishermen employed on fishing vessels. In *Nessen Transportation Co. v. Larsen*, 7 N.E. (2nd) 765, an Illinois court discusses many decisions construing the word "seaman" and holds that it includes the master of a vessel. Other decisions have held that it includes a stevedore. It is not safe for a layman boat owner to pay wages to anyone other than the employee to whom they are due, unless he receives competent legal advice approving the payment.

YACHT crews are not entitled to liens in admiralty for services rendered on yachts out of commission and laid up in their home ports. *Burdine v. Walden*, 91 Fed. (2nd) 321. Such services are regarded as those of a watchman. The claim in this case was made by a paid captain on a 58 foot cruiser laid up at Miami, her home port. He was not entitled to recover wages in a proceeding *in rem* against the vessel, although he might have succeeded in another type of action.

INSURANCE policies should be read and, if possible, understood. A person unused to reading documents of that sort finds it difficult to extract a connected and complete account of what the policy covers because one of two things is apt to happen to him. Either he will fail to concentrate and his attention will be so dispersed that he will find himself reading words and missing ideas, or he will over-concentrate and fail to note connections among details, not seeing the forest because of the trees. His difficulty is not lessened when his policy carries numerous riders. The unnecessary use of riders brought forth the following caustic comment in *Conners Marine Company, Inc. v. Northwestern Fire & Marine Ins. Co.*, 1937 A.M.C. 344: "This litigation illustrates once more the likelihood of controversy when underwriters pursue their inveterate and abominable practice of using an inappropriate printed form and attaching thereto a typewritten rider which describes elliptically the real terms of the insurance contract and contradicts nearly everything in the printed form."

LONGSHOREMEN'S and Harbor Workers' Compensation Act (33 U.S. Code 901) excludes from its provisions a master or member of a crew of any vessel, and frequently the courts have to classify an injured employee as either a seaman or a harbor worker. This distinction might be of real value to a motorboat owner when an accident occurs while his boat is being towed or is tied up and not under way. In *Diomede v. Lowe, et al.*, 87 Fed. (2nd) 296, the court discusses the meaning of master and member of a crew. In that decision, the court refused to classify as a master the captain of a scow, without means of self-propulsion, and with no crew. "A master without men to command, without a ship to navigate, and subject to the orders of the tug captain when the scow is in tow, is a notion difficult to accept." Nor was he a member of a crew. In an earlier decision, *Seneca Washed Gravel Corp. v. McManigal*, 65 Fed. (2nd) 779, the court defined crew as "a company of seamen belonging to the vessel, usually including the officers. It is the 'ship's company' . . . those who are on board and aiding in the navigation without reference to the nature of the arrangement under which they are on board."

SHAKESPEARE'S admonition that one should neither a borrower nor a lender be, sometimes is ignored when a competent friend urges a boat owner to lend his boat. The owner is reminded of it when his friend's guests sue him for damages. The *Pegreen* was a 36 foot cruiser with a modern 8 cylinder engine, both boat and engine being in excellent condition. The owner permitted a friend, who was a licensed small boat operator, to use the boat, without charge of any sort, for a day's trip. The friend took seven guests with him but the owner did not accompany them. Due to some carelessness, the exact nature of which could not be ascertained, an explosion occurred, and the boat sank. The guests promptly sued the owner, who theretofore had never seen or heard of any of them, but the court exonerated him. The lending was a gratuitous bailment and the owner, as bailor, was under duty only to disclose defects in the boat or engine of which he was aware. He was aware of none because there were none. *Pegreen*, 14 Fed. Supp. 748.

A BAILMENT situation is created also when one leaves his boat at a shipyard for repairs. If the boat is damaged while in the custody of the yard, the yard owner, as bailee, has the burden of showing that he exercised reasonable care, first to prevent the damage, and then to minimize it. *Guard*, 79 Fed. (2nd) 802; *Patience-Dorothy*, 1936 A.M.C. 343; *Dupont (Ex Saelme)*, 14 Fed. Supp. 193. When a boat is chartered under an agreement that no claims or liens are to be entered against her, the charter being for the sole benefit of the charterer, a shipyard at which the charterer ordered repairs and supplies cannot hold the owner personally, although the boat itself may be liable through a proceeding *in rem*. *Lizzie Burt*, 16 Fed. Supp. 67.

DRAWBRIDGES are hazards which must be respected, especially by motor boats which lie so low on the water that they are not as clearly visible to draw tenders as are large vessels. Further, motor boat skippers must never forget that bridges of any sort are designed primarily to convey land vehicles and pedestrians across the water spanned and that drawbridges should not be kept open longer than necessary to permit the expeditious passage of water craft. The recent decision in *Steel All Welded Boat Co. v. City of Boston*, 1937 A.M.C. 802 illustrates the danger of not passing promptly through a draw which has been opened.

East Boston is connected to Chelsea by a drawbridge which has a central pier dividing the Chelsea River into northerly and southerly channels. This bridge is maintained and operated by the City of Boston. The *Mary L. Connelly*, a 54 foot boat with 9 feet beam and powered with a Diesel engine, was proceeding down stream in daylight and she gave the proper signal for an open bridge. She chose the northerly channel to avoid three tugs, coming up stream, which were making for the southerly channel. For some reason, the *Connelly* did not proceed at the moment when the draw was sufficiently open but delayed for some minutes and then started through at full speed. The draw had started to close and before it could be stopped it broke the *Connelly's* mast and damaged her afterhouse. The Court held that the *Connelly* was at fault for not proceeding with due diligence to go through the draw when it was open and for failing to watch the movement of the draw after it had started to close. The City of Boston was held equally at fault for negligence in its operation of the bridge.

NEGLIGENCE which is customary is no defense. The fact that other persons regularly and customarily are negligent or otherwise violate the law is no defense for a wrongdoer who causes damage and is detected in it. It appears to be the custom for tugs in the New York Barge Canal to slide their tows along the boomlog fenders at approaches to locks while waiting for the locks to open. These boomlogs were intended to provide places at which tugs and tows could stop, but it is negligence to slide the tows along them. It is no excuse to an offender that other tug captains follow the same practice. *Ford Motor Company v. Barge Manhattan No. 50*, 1938 A.M.C. 136.

INEVITABLE accident is apt to be the first defense to occur to one who has been unfortunate enough to be a party to a collision. In *Ben Franklin Transportation Co. v. Scow Charles H. Sells*, 1937 A.M.C. 774, the court gave an enlightening explanation of the doctrine of inevitable accident. In that case a vessel moored at the outside of a pier in Yonkers, N.Y., on the Hudson River, suddenly broke adrift, and damaged other vessels. It was held that she could be exonerated only if she had made a proper display of nautical skill. Inevitable accident is not always an excuse for what otherwise would be a wrong. This phrase does not cover ascertainable exculpating occasions. It means no more than that the vessel must show herself free from fault in the ordinary sense. The legal standard is the function of three variables: the actuarial possibility that the event will occur; the gravity of the damage which will result if it does occur; the expense and effort necessary to prevent occurrence. When a safe berth is readily available, it requires but a slight probability of breaking adrift to charge a vessel which remains in the more exposed position.

HIGH freeboard exposed to the wind causes maneuvering trouble for large steamers as well as for motor boats. A collision in the 300 foot Erie, Pa., channel was due in the first instance to this cause. *P. E. Crowley-Arcturus*, 1937 A.M.C. 125. The ship was unable to turn to enter a basin. She dropped an anchor as a drag and then began to swing, whereupon the anchor held her, with her engines going ahead. About 150 feet of her stern lay across the channel and she was struck by another steamer which took a sudden sheer due to currents set up by the freighter's propellers. The freighter was held solely at fault. She was not anchored but under way because her engines were shoving her forward and her purpose was not to come to rest. She could have moved by letting out more anchor chain. She set up currents which caused the other vessel to sheer. If she was helpless, she should have given adequate warning. If she was at anchor, she violated the rule against unnecessarily anchoring in and blocking a navigable channel.

SHAVING pier heads is a dangerous practice. In *Grymes Engineering Corp. v. Ferryboat Chicago, Penn. R. R. Co.*, 1937 A.M.C. 840, a ferryboat leaving her slip at Atlantic Avenue, Brooklyn, N. Y., on a clear day with a light wind was hit by a tanker proceeding at a good speed within 25 feet of the pier head. The tanker was held responsible because she could have taken a course much farther off the pier. "Had she done so," said the court, "the two vessels would have been visible to each other at a time which doubtless would have enabled them to avoid collision." The *reductio ad absurdum* is doing it with a row boat, which was the case in *Governor Moore-Row Boat*, 1936 A.M.C. 1550. The electric ferry *Governor Moore* leaving her slip at Weehawken, N. J., hit a row boat manned by the plaintiff who was attempting to cross the mouth of the ferry slip. In this instance the plaintiff was ill advised as to the selection of a forum in which to bring his suit. He sued at common law for damages but the court dismissed his complaint because it found him guilty of contributory negligence. If one must row across the mouth of a ferry slip, he should plan to bring his subsequent action for damages in admiralty where he might recover some amount if he could prove negligence on the part of the ferry boat which hits him.

USE OF CITIZENS' BAND RADIO CHANNELS BY BOATMEN

(This supplements data on radiotelephones, page 438d)

THE article on the radiotelephone, pages 438d, 439, deals with the channels assigned for marine communications in the 2-3 mc band, which form the Marine Safety System.

There are also available to boatmen channels in the Citizens Radio Service (CRS) which can be useful in supplementing the facilities in the 2-3 mc band. Of the four classes available (see Part 19 of the FCC Rules), Class D is the one most likely to be of use to boatmen. A total of 23 specified frequencies in the 26-27 mc band have been assigned for use. Operators' licenses are not required but it is necessary to obtain a station license for each of the stations which will communicate as a group. Forms for applying for a Station license are usually furnished with a set when it is sold. Station licenses good for 5 years are usually issued for two or more units to form a private communications system. The Citizens Band may be of great value on a cruise or for communication to a yacht club or marina which has been equipped with a set working on the channel used by a boat or group of boats.

Difficulty may be avoided by making sure that equipment which has been "Type Accepted" by the FCC is purchased. Local coordination may be necessary to make sure that sets which are to work together are arranged to work on the same frequency. They may be used in private communication systems for any legal personal or business activity. Communication must be limited to the local ground wave coverage area, which with proper antenna and equipment is normally about 10-15 miles. Sets may not be used for "Ham" purposes nor for calling outside the normal working area.

The sets are compact and light in weight. A quarter-wave whip antenna suitable for use with this type of set is a little over 8 feet in length. Transmitters are usually crystal-controlled, while receivers may be either tunable or crystal-controlled. A set for single channel operation may cost as little as about $65 for the complete transmitting and receiving unit, while sets for operation on two or more channels will be considerably higher in price.

It should be kept in mind that in the Citizens Radio Service no provision has been made for priority calls and that during periods of normal operation no protection can be afforded to the communications of any station in the Citizens Radio Service from interference which may be caused by the operation of other authorized stations, even when the protection of life and property may be involved. In other words, the Citizens Radio Service is not a part of the Marine Safety System.

Your Responsibility in Receiving Aid

EARLY one morning some years ago, the steamer Evangeline was slowly feeling her way into Yarmouth through a heavy fog when it was discovered that her port propeller had picked up a six-ton buoy and a lot of its chain. Her captain radioed the line's local agent to have a tug at the dock. She proceeded without assistance to a point near the dock where the channel narrowed to 400 feet. From that point on through docking, tugs assisted her, although she was in no immediate danger and she probably could have docked without help. But she was justified in procuring paid assistance because of her size, the narrowness of the winding channel, the set of the tide, and the possibility of damage from the dragging chain. The tugs demanded $25,000 salvage. Upon the company's refusal to pay, a Canadian admiralty court held that the service rendered was salvage but very slight, and awarded the tugs $500.[1]

When does towing service become salvage service, how could there be the enormous spread between $500 and $25,000, and what is salvage? These are pertinent questions because most salvage claims arise out of the towing of disabled vessels, there is no standard by which the amount of compensation or reward can be fixed, and the meaning of salvage is not commonly understood. The word is used, as in the preceding paragraph, to denote either reward or service; in insurance parlance, it sometimes means property saved, or salved.

What Salvage Is

Answering the last question first, salvage, meaning a reward, is "compensation given by the maritime law for services rendered in saving property or rescuing it from impending peril on the sea, or, in the United States, on a public navigable river or lake, where interstate or foreign commerce is carried on."[2] Salvage, meaning service, "may be described sufficiently for practical purposes, as a service which saves or helps to save maritime property . . . or lives of persons belonging to any vessel, when in danger, either at sea, or on the shore of the sea, or in tidal waters, or on the shore of tidal waters, if and so far as the rendering of such service is voluntary, and attributable neither to legal obligation, nor to the interest of self-preservation, nor to the stress of official duty."[3]

The fact that services were performed pursuant to an agreement or contract has no bearing on the question whether they were salvage services; unless the contract specifies that payment is to be made regardless of success.[4] In that event, a claim can be made for the compensation specified in the contract but not for salvage, because, as explained below, success is an element in a salvage claim. A common type of salvage contract is the "no cure, no pay" form in which the reward is contingent upon success. A contract not on this contingent basis made in an hour of danger may be modified by a court if its terms are inequitable.

The right to salvage usually arises without agreement or contract, but regardless of whether a contract exists certain factors discussed herein are always taken into account in determining whether an award should be given to the salvor. First, there must have been danger to the property salved; in the second place, the salvor must have acted voluntarily; and, lastly, subject to many qualifications, the attempt to salve must have been successful.

Danger One of the Requisites

As to the first factor, "It is not necessary that there should be absolute danger in order to constitute a salvage service; it is sufficient if there is a state of difficulty and reasonable apprehension."[5] But the danger must not be merely fanciful or vaguely possible; it must be so reasonably apprehended that no reasonably prudent or skilful seaman would refuse help if offered on condition that he pay for it on a salvage basis. The danger may, in a sense, be subjective; ignorance or inefficiency may constitute a real danger to a master although there would be none to one more skilful. Signalling for or accepting assistance is admissible but not conclusive evidence to prove the existence of the type of danger necessary to establish a case of salvage. On the other hand, the fact that service was requested would not convert what otherwise would be salvage into a contractual service.[6] The court, in determining the existence

A Discussion of Salvage—What the Motor Boatman Should Know About It, and How It May Enter into Situations Where Assistance Has Been Volunteered and Accepted

of danger, will not speculate, for example, as to whether a vessel stranded on a jetty would have come off with a turn of the tide, and if so whether she would have been picked up by some craft other than the salvor before stranding again.[7] In cases of towing, only towing fees are allowed for service which merely accelerates the speed of the vessel. But salvage for towing, a higher rate of compensation, is allowed when there has been some damage or accident which affects or may affect either the safety of the ship or the difficulty of towing her.

For example, pulling on a stranded tug and barge in fair, easy weather, with the assistance of the Coast Guard and without risk, was held not to be salvage but high towage, for which $25 per hour was allowed. In this case, the tug owner was reproved by the court for trying to create a claim for salvage.[8] A situation of slight salvage occurred on the Ohio River. A steamer was towing barges down the river in fair, clear weather, when, in midafternoon, the barges broke away. A tug coming up-stream landed her own barges and picked up the drifting ones in response to a distress signal. The master and crew of the tug refused to claim salvage because of the general custom among river captains to assist one another, but the owner of the tug brought suit. The court felt that this was little more than ordinary towing, for which the usual charge was $20 per hour, but awarded the owner $300 and gave the mate $10 and each of the seven seamen $5. The salving tug was never in danger and the salvage operation required a little less than three hours.[9]

Cases Where Towing Constituted Salvage

Towing was held to constitute salvage in two recent cases. In one of them, a ship with a full cargo of gasoline ran aground, was unable to free herself, and called for assistance. Tugs pulled on her on three successive high tides without success; they got her off on the fourth high tide but only after about 1/7 of her cargo had been removed. The tugs were in real danger from heavy weather and from the possibility of ignition of the gasoline by sparks.[10] In the other case, a tug had become wedged under the span of a railroad bridge at Savannah and about half of her pilot house had been crushed. The tide was rising and the tug was in danger of being sunk. A larger tug pulled her clear in fifteen minutes with slight risk and very little labor. The court held that this service was meritorious and important and that it constituted salvage.[11]

Since danger is a necessary element, when the danger ceases there can be no further salvage. In one instance, a ship aground had to slip both her anchors and chains to enable a salvor to pull her off. After she had been towed to a place of safety, other volunteers recovered her anchors and chains. Their service was not salvage because the ship was in no danger at the time the service was rendered.[12] In another situation a steamer broke her rudder chain in a hurricane area and sent out an S.O.S. A salvor ship towed her into quiet water where she repaired the chain and stated that no further assistance was needed. Nevertheless, the salvor ship convoyed her to port. The court held that this convoying was an unnecessary and unsolicited service which did not constitute salvage.[13]

Service Must Be Voluntary

The second element of salvage service is that the salvor must have acted voluntarily. This is a principle peculiar to admiralty law. A voluntary benefit rendered ashore creates no claim. Over 135 years ago, Chief Justice Marshall of the United States wrote that if property on land be in peril and be saved, for example if valuable goods be rescued from a house in flames, no right to reward exists even though life may have been risked. "Let precisely the same serv-

462

ice, at precisely the same hazard, be rendered at sea, and a very ample reward will be bestowed in the courts of justice."[14] The reason for this difference is public policy. The right to salvage is more than a private right. Salvage awards are allowed as encouragements in the public interest because of the perils at sea and for the promotion and advantage of commerce. They are not allowed primarily as compensation for work and labor, nor are their amounts fixed primarily with reference to benefits received.

The requirement that the service be voluntary automatically excludes everyone who is under any duty to render service. Thus there can be no salvage service by the officers or crew of the ship, by the agent of the line which owns the ship, by the owner or crew of a tug engaged in ordinary towing, by officers and men in the government service, or by passengers. A passenger is excluded for the reason that all persons on board have a common duty in self-interest to assist because in saving the ship they may save themselves.

But the persons listed in the preceding paragraph are excluded only while actually acting in their respective capacities. Thus, a passenger, although entitled to no reward for manning a pump, may become a salvor by extraordinary conduct; for example, if he remains on board to help although offered an opportunity to leave the ship, or if he is competent and takes command when all officers have become incapacitated, or if he devises a means of steering when the ship's steering gear is out of commission. And members of the crew may act as salvors after they have been discharged by the master, or after the ship has been abandoned in good faith by the master's orders.

Abandonment of the Vessel

There obviously was no abandonment in the case of a 65-foot fishing boat which began to sink while making a California port. All members of the crew except the captain and one hand were put in the life boat and towed. The fishing boat's engines kept running but the steering finally had to be done from the top of the pilot house. The member of the crew who remained on board with the captain was denied a salvage award because he was merely doing his duty in preserving the vessel.[15] Two other cases presented closer questions. In one, a vessel either hit a mine or was torpedoed, and the crew were ordered into the boats. The captain's boat stood by for half an hour when he concluded his vessel would remain afloat. He and some volunteers went back aboard and they took the ship into port. One member of the crew asked for salvage but it was denied because it was his duty to render all possible assistance. The court held that the vessel had not been abandoned without hope of return and that the crew had not been discharged.[16] This decision closely follows an English case, in which the court stated that the fact of calling for volunteers instead of ordering the crew to return had no bearing on the matter.[17] "Let the ship be imperilled and their (the crew's) duty to save it increases with the peril."[18] In the other case, a freight steamer in ballast was badly damaged by a troop ship which ran into her. The master put his crew aboard the troop ship but later he decided that salvage was feasible and he returned to his vessel with his officers and a few crew members who had volunteered. The ship was saved but salvage was denied on the ground that the ship had not been abandoned without hope of return. The court explained that crew members are denied salvage "not only because it is their duty to save both ship and cargo, if it is in their power, but because it would be unwise to tempt them to get the ship and cargo into a position of danger in order that by extreme exertion they might claim salvage compensation."[19]

Generally speaking, a service to be rendered voluntarily must be rendered personally. Officers and crew who do not participate in any way in a salvage operation by their vessel are usually not entitled to share in the award. But officers and members of the crew of a salving vessel who remain on board under orders when other officers and men have left her on a salvage mission are entitled to share because they must perform extra labor and incur extra risks arising from their being shorthanded. Also, the owners of the salving vessel regularly receive a portion of the award, although they personally did not participate in the salvage work, whenever their interests were affected or in risk of being affected by the use of their property or employees. Even when salvage is denied, they may be given compensation for the use of their equipment. Some of the risks which owners may incur are liabilities to shippers and passengers for delay, loss of insurance through deviation, and loss of profitable trade.

Salvage Operation Must Be Successful

The third requirement is that the salvage operation must have been successful because a salvage award is for service rendered, not for service attempted. Certainly, efforts to save are not compensable if the vessel in danger is in no better position after the effort than before it, nor if the efforts caused more damage than would have resulted if the well meaning salvor had kept away. But mistake, negligence, or misconduct on the salvor's part, when not flagrant, which causes some damage or expense does not completely bar an award but merely reduces the amount of it. And a salvor who has contributed to a successful result is entitled to a share in the award, although his work by itself would not have accomplished the result.

An example of a salvor who contributes to but does not complete a salvage is that of a salving vessel from which some special assistance has been requested by the ship in distress; for instance, a vessel that is asked to stand by, or to steam to a port and bring out an anchor. If the service is rendered but the ship is saved through some other agency or circumstance, such as a rising tide or a change in the weather, or the ship attempts to discharge the salvor before the requested service has been completed, the assisting vessel is entitled to share in the award although it may have contributed little if anything to the success of the salvage operation.

To justify a salvage claim, property must have been salved which can form a fund from which the salvage can be paid, except for the statutory deviation from this general rule which allows salvage for the saving of life. The property to be salved includes not only the vessel but also all tackle, furniture, stores, fittings, and other removable equipment in ordinary use aboard the vessel at the time of salvage. These are as much a part of the vessel as her hull, engines, or life boats.[20] Of course a contract can be made for services to be paid for regardless of result, but such a contract would create only a right to sue on it for the specified compensation and no claim for salvage, as such, would arise. The salvor is given a lien on the ship, the cargo, or the money earned or to be earned for the transportation of cargo or passengers, and his usual remedy is a proceeding in rem to have the salvage property sold if necessary. But he may have also a claim personally against an owner who has benefited or who requested the service.[21] But a charterer ordinarily is not personally liable unless he personally requested the service. The mere fact that the vessel was in use by him does not place him in the position of the owner.[22] Salvage service must not be rendered contrary to specific and reasonable prohibitions by the salved vessel, because a salvage operation must not be made "merely an opportunity for officious interlopers; a vessel in distress is not to be killed by kindness, particularly that of interested friends."[23]

Examples of Salvage Services

The range of possible salvage services is so great that only the most commonly found situations can be listed. Towing a disabled vessel probably is the service most frequently rendered. Similar to it is the piloting or navigation of a ship in distress into a safe position. Salvage may be claimed for preventing an impending collision, for clearing a ship from a wreck or from another ship which has fouled her, for extinguishing a fire or rescuing a ship, cargo, or persons from it, for getting a stranded ship afloat, for standing by to aid, for bringing assistance to the ship, for landing, transshipping, or otherwise saving cargo or persons from the ship or from her life boats, and for supplying officers or men to man a ship which is short handed because of disease or other calamity. Then there are the unusual situations of extricating a ship from an ice floe, of raising a sunken ship or cargo, and of saving a derelict or wreck. Neither the common law on shore nor the law of the sea compels active benevolence to a stranger whose plight one has neither caused nor aggravated.[24] Although there may be a tendency toward more liberal views,[25] courts are slow to lay down a new principle not in harmony with the generally accepted views of the great maritime nations. The International Salvage Treaty of 1910 bound the United States to enact a law requiring the master of a ship to render assistance and such a statute was enacted.[26] But that statute merely makes failure to render assistance a crime on the part of the master. In this country, imputed crime is practically unknown and neither the owner nor the ship can be punished or made financially responsible.

Of especial interest to the owners and operators of small motor boats was the brutal disregard of human life, about thirteen years ago, by the captain of an Italian steamer. Two men set out in a small motor boat for an hour's run near Coney Island, N. Y. It didn't occur to them to have either fresh water or food on board. Their engine broke down, they didn't know how or were unable to signal for assistance, and they drifted to sea. After drifting for six days without water, food, or shelter, they were sighted by the steamer which saw but ignored their frantic signals, although the steamer could have rescued them without the slightest risk. They drifted for two more days before a Coast Guard cutter picked them up. One of the men survived long enough to sue the owners of the steamer, but the court found no way of holding the owners financially responsible for their captain's atrocity.[27]

By statute today, salvors of human life who have participated in a salvage operation are entitled to a fair share of the remuneration awarded to the salvors of the vessel or her cargo. [28] Salvors of human life have no direct award but are entitled merely to share in the award for salving property. This led, a few years ago, to a shocking contest in inhumanity. Two tug boat captains argued for twenty minutes as to which should leave his salvage work on a burning steamer in order to take ashore an injured seaman who at that time was bleeding to death. Finally, one of them lost the argument and took the dying man ashore. But the court allowed him to share in the award to his brethren who had kept their eyes on the main chance and had refused to be diverted from the salvage of property.[29]

Fixing the Amount of Salvage

Finally, there comes the difficulty of fixing the amount of the award. The United States Supreme Court has stated the factors in this way: "(1) The labor expended by the salvors in rendering the salvage service. (2) The promptitude, skill and energy displayed in rendering the service and saving the property. (3) The value of the property employed by the salvors in rendering the service, and the danger to which such property was exposed. (4) The risk incurred by the salvors in securing the property from impending peril. (5) The value of the property saved. (6) The degree of danger from which the property was rescued."[30] The Brussels International Convention stated the factors to be: "Firstly, the success achieved, the efforts and merits of the salvors, the danger run by the salved vessel and her cargo, and by the salvors and their vessel, also the expenses incurred and damage suffered by the salvors, due regard being had to any appropriation of the salvor's vessel for salvage purposes; secondly, the value of the property saved and of the salvor's vessel."

Naturally, courts and arbitrators differ widely in their applications of these general rules. The maximum salvage award in the most meritorious case cannot be expected to exceed one moiety, which means one-half of the value of the property saved. To warrant that amount, there must be unusual effort and perseverance, if not actual heroism. If the peril to the salvors is not great, the award is not apt to be more than 10 per cent of the salvaged value. It is almost certain to be less than that in cases of harbor salvage when the operation can be completed in a short time with no real risk to the salvors. In determining value, some courts take the market value at the time the salvage was completed. Others take the cost of reproduction less sustained depreciation. Earlier in this article, it was pointed out that the danger to the vessel in distress may be subjective in that it merely exists, reasonably, in her master's mind. In the same way, the danger to the salvor may be subjective and not real, but if it reasonably exists in the mind of her master, it will be given full weight in fixing his award. If the risk to the salvor is no more than moderate, the award may be based chiefly on the time, labor, and expense involved. It is customary for the court which fixes the award to specify how it shall be divided among the salvors; for example, 4/5 to the ship and 1/5 to the crew, the allowance to the ship being given to her owners, or 2/3 to the ship, 1/9 to the master, and 2/9 to the crew, or 1/3 to the ship and 2/3 to the master and crew.

Some Salvage Awards

A salvage award is not merely compensation based on the ordinary value of ordinary services but it is in the nature of a bounty offered from motives of public policy. In fixing the amount, no stated percentage of the value of the property saved can be used because that would be too high when large values are rescued and too low when the rescued values are small. Also, such a rule would ignore the other essential elements, such as risk to the salvor, his efforts,

and his loss due to his engaging in the salvage operation instead of attending to his own business. Because the value of property salved is one of the elements, the salvage of very small craft such as skiffs, canoes, and row boats is apt to be a losing venture. Court proceedings are out of the question because their cost would exceed any possible award. In such cases, the owner often waits to claim his boat until the finder has spent time and money on it, and then he may refuse to pay more than a nominal amount for the reconditioning. The editor of the Boating-Fishing column in the Miami News, who signs himself as "Salty," took a realistic view when he wrote in his issue of April 30, 1944; "In the future, this skipper is going to let drifting skiffs drift."

In the prior edition of this article in the October 1935 issue, earlier decisions dealing with the amounts of awards were digested. The following are a few of the recent ones. An 80-foot sardine fishing vessel 16 miles out from the Golden Gate in California on a calm September night received a call for help from a similar vessel which had capsized. The crew of the latter were found in a skiff and were taken aboard. A radio message was sent to the Coast Guard who directed the vessel to stand by, which it did for six hours, during which it was in no danger at any time. The service rendered was slight and it required no particular skill. The value of the vessel salved was $15,000 but the award was only $201.86.[31] In the case of the Diesel Tug Egbert H. described above, the tug wedged under the bridge span, the salved tug was valued at $25,000, her actual repairs cost $975, if she had sunk the cost of raising and repairing her would have been about $15,000, and the salvor tug was valued at $120,000. The award for that 15 minute work was $3,000.[32] In the Caliche case described above, the gasoline steamer pulled off the reef, the value of the salved vessel and cargo was $603,000, her repairs cost $14,248, and the total value of the four rescuing tugs was $505,000. The award was $16,000.[33]

Salvage is of interest to owners of boats large or small because the need for salvage help can arise in the most unexpected ways. There is a widespread spirit of helpfulness among skippers of motor boats and of sail boats and salvage questions do not often arise unless commercial craft are called upon or involved. But those who go down to the sea in ships for pleasure should be intelligent about their rights and obligations. They should know that liability for salvage can be included in collision damages.[34] They should know that it is dangerous legally, as well as unjustifiable morally, to destroy evidence after mistakes have been made.[35] They should be able to recognize overcharges by greedy commercial captains and owners, who sometimes think (often incorrectly) that one who owns a pleasure craft has money enough to pay exorbitant claims. They should not attempt to be sea lawyers, but they should be cautious in the light of recorded experience.

Citations

1. Evangeline, 1934 A.M.C. 146
2. Freedom, 1932 A.M.C. 933
3. *The Law of Civil Salvage*, A. R. Kennedy (2nd ed.)
4. Freedom, 1932 A.M.C. 933
5. The Phantom, L.R. 1 A. & E. 58
6. Atlantic Towing Co. et al v. M/V Caliche et al., 1942 A.M.C. 1635
7. Wahkeena, 56 Fed. (2d) 836
8. R. R. Stone v. M/T Pejepscott, 1939 A.M.C. 316
9. Costanzo Transp. Co. v. American Barge Line, 1940 A.M.C. 1382
10. Atlantic Towing Co. et al, v. M/V Caliche et al., 1942 A.M.C. 1635
11. Atlantic Towing Co. et al. v. Diesel Tug Egbert H., 1942 A.M.C. 443
12. The Endeavor, 6 Moore P. C. 334
13. West Harshaw-Ansaldo San Giorgio Secondo, 69 Fed. (2d) 521
14. Mason v. Ship Blaireau, 2 Cranch 240
15. Walter Brown v. Diesel Boat Mary M., et al., 1938 A.M.C. 1237
16. Drevas v. United States of America et al., 1945 A.M.C. 254
17. The Portreath, L.R. Probate Div. 155 (1923)
18. Robinson on *Admiralty*, page 724
19. Frank J. Elrod et al. v. Luckenbach S.S. Co., Inc., 1945 A.M.C. 1100
20. Tashmoo, 48 Fed. Supp 808
21. G. L. 40, 66 Fed. (2d) 764
22. Tony Lauro v. Pennsylvania R.R. Co. et al., 1946 A.M.C. 125
23. William Rockefeller, 55 Fed. (2d) 904
24. Amer. Law Institute Restatement of Torts, Sec. 314
25. *Paradoxes of Legal Science*, Cardozo, page 25
26. U. S. Code, Title 46, Shipping, Chapter 19, Section 728
27. Conte Biancamano, 71 Fed. (2d) 146
28. U. S. Code, Title 46, Shipping, Chapter 19, Section 729
29. William Rockefeller, 55 Fed. (2d) 904
30. Blackwell, 77 U. S. 1, 14
31. North Star—Frigidland, 1940 A.M.C. 1017
32. Atlantic Towing Co. et al. v. Diesel Tug Egbert H., 1942 A.M.C. 443
33. Atlantic Towing Co. et al. v. M/V Caliche et al., 1942 A.M.C. 1635
34. Integrity-Raritan, 54 Fed. (2d) 978; Childs-Mills, 1934 A.M.C. 1511
35. Samson-John and Frederick, 1935 A.M.C. 489

CHAPTER XXXIII

Navigation and Piloting Hints

When piloting, try to visualize from the chart how landmarks, channels, obstructions, and navigational aids will appear when you pick them up.

+

Do you have difficulty with the identification of buoys? Remember the letters BPOE—*b*lack buoys, on the *p*ort side, with *o*dd numbers, *e*ntering harbors.

+

Entering strange inlets, use the buoys with caution. Bars shift continually. Breakers reveal the shoal spots.

+

If you are running a compass course, corrected for predetermined deviation, be sure that all principal iron and steel objects are in the position they occupied when the deviation was calculated.

+

Know your speed on a measured course. Estimated speeds are invariably flattering . . . and unreliable in piloting.

+

Your outboard boat, if it was designed primarily as an outboard, must carry the equipment specified by law, like any other motor boat. The fact that it may be shorter than sixteen feet does not excuse it.

+

Check your side-light screens to see that they do not shine across the bow. Red must be visible only on the port side, green to starboard.

+

Too much emphasis cannot be placed on the value of ranges in navigating difficult waterways. If there are no established marks to serve as guides, pick natural landmarks with the aid of the chart.

+

Aside from the possibility of being stopped by some watchful inspector, sea-going ethics prescribe that whistle signals be answered, promptly.

+

Blind corners, where a river or creek makes a sharp bend, call for caution. Best to throttle down and sound a long warning whistle blast.

+

Stern lights are often mounted on the aft end of the canopy top. Under way, the stern settles and the light is obscured to approaching boats at close range. A foot of brass pipe will raise it high enough to be visible all around, as the law requires.

+

A well used chart adds much to the satisfaction of cruising. Thorough study of the one showing your local waters may reveal a good many interesting features that would escape the keenest observer.

+

To steer a straight course, when stuck without a compass, tow a sinker or weight from a light line made fast amidships. Any deviation from a straight course will show as the line moves away from a center point on the taffrail.

Coming to anchor in a strange harbor, it's always good practice to check your position by reference to buoys or landmarks on the chart.

+

If another boat approaches your course from any point in the area covered by your green light (dead ahead to two points abaft the starboard beam) give way to her. She has the right of way.

+

When the inboard scupper of a self-bailing cockpit runs below the water line, permitting water to back in, push a thin stick through the hole until it projects outside the planking. Vacuum behind the stick will draw the water out.

+

If your compass is electrically lighted, be sure that the wires are twisted around each other. Current flowing through straight wires might be the source of a large compass error.

+

An anchor frequently gets such a bite that a man cannot break it. When that happens, heave up short on the line till it stands straight up and down and take a turn around the bitt. Then go ahead with the power a few yards.

+

Surface rips will often be produced by deep-lying reefs or obstructions. If they are of consequence to boatmen, the chart or Coast Pilot will give necessary information.

+

Running at night, keep a lookout astern. Helps a lot in keeping your bearings under certain conditions of visibility.

+

Small or illegible numbers will not pass Government inspection. See that they are at least three inches high and keep on the right side of the law.

+

Boats with right hand propellers frequently have a slight tendency to run to port when going ahead with the rudder set for a straight course. This is caused by a difference in thrust exerted by the upper and lower blades.

+

Ripples, eddies and surface colors tell a story of their own. Watch them in channels you know and you'll profit by them in strange waterways.

+

Twin-screw engine installations are most effective when the motors turn in opposite directions. Maneuvering qualities are best when the tops of the propeller blades turn outward from the center.

+

Before making fast to a tidewater dock, consider the stage and range of the tide. Then make due allowance so the boat isn't hung or swamped with the rise and fall.

Docking a boat with right hand wheel is facilitated if she is brought up port side to dock or float. The propeller, reversing, throws the stern toward the dock, instead of away from it.

+

The essence of good seamanship is preparedness. The ablest skipper, like an adept at chess, anticipates the next move and is ready to meet it.

+

New boats occasionally suffer a temporary loss of speed shortly after launching. Bottom planks swelling as they absorb water squeeze out seam fillers, leaving ridges which create resistance. Smoothing the seams will correct this condition.

+

In case of grounding, quick action with the reverse often saves the day. Chances are she'll back off as the wake rolls under the boat.

+

Blisters on paint jobs are caused by moisture in the wood. The sun, in drawing out the water, takes the paint with it. To avoid this, paint only on thoroughly dry surfaces.

+

Night running develops confidence. And tests your powers of observation. Limited range of vision alters the perspective.

+

When dinghies and other equipment are carried on deck, they should be lashed securely, even in smooth water. The wash of a fast boat can create as much disturbance as a good sized sea.

+

A small amount of canvas on a motor boat will steady her a lot offshore in a beam sea.

+

Water will stop an alcohol blaze—but not gasoline. Keep your extinguishers freshly filled and know how to use them. That will take all the hazard out of fire.

+

A drag, like a bucket or sea anchor, towed astern, is useful in a bad following sea. Helps to prevent broaching to.

+

Shoal water affects a boat's speed and control—even though the keel doesn't actually strike bottom.

+

In waters littered with drift, reasonable attention to the course ahead will often save a haulout to repair a crippled wheel.

+

Running a doubtful channel on a windy day, favor the windward side. In case of grounding, it might be hard to work off a leeward shoal.

+

If you ever carry "paying guests," remember that you are then operating the boat for hire and require a license. It is awarded without cost.

Bucking a heavy head sea, it's often helpful to meet the waves quartering somewhat on the bow. Depends, of course, on the boat and the sea.

+

There's a thrill in spectacular landings —but a bill if your reverse gear lets you down.

+

A wise boatman will observe, and glean bits of experience from all sources. A large part of that skill you admire in men who have a way with the helm of a yacht, has been picked up among the fishermen.

+

Visibility varies with atmospheric conditions. Sometimes it is possible to see clearly objects normally below the horizon. Refraction of light rays causes this.

+

Never leave poles or boat hooks on deck where they may be stepped on. Rolling under foot, they might give some one a ducking.

+

River sailing is intriguing. One always wonders what lies just around the bend ahead.

+

Grass and weed can be thrown from an anchor line before getting it on deck. Swish the line up and down before the grass is clear of the water.

+

When laying up for the winter, frame the cover if possible to keep it away from the hull. Complete circulation of air, inside and out, will promote a sweet, clean condition through the winter months.

+

Blocking under a boat shored up out of water should be so placed as to simulate conditions as nearly as possible when the hull is waterborne. Stresses concentrated at certain points should be avoided.

+

Riding out a gale at anchor or towing under strenuous conditions, it's not a bad idea to wrap canvas around lines where they rub on chocks or rails. The chafing gear will take the wear and save the rope.

+

Making fast to a cleat, let the strain of the line come on the cleat first, rather than on the last turn of rope. Otherwise, it might be hard to free with a heavy strain on it.

+

Ring buoys are sometimes lashed too well. When needed, they are wanted quick. Light lashings or hooks will hold them in place, yet leave them free for instant use.

+

In selecting equipment, utility is a more vital consideration than beauty or finish. A chromium plated pump that won't pump isn't a pump.

+

Have a spare tiller aboard, so arranged that the boat can be handled with it direct—irrespective of any failure in any part of the regular steering mechanism.

Wet lines in closed lockers are a prolific source of trouble. Dry them thoroughly before stowing whenever possible.

+

In a pinch, ordinary soap will temporarily seal a gas line leak.

+

Lines should always be neatly coiled down. Aside from ship-shape appearance, it's desirable that they always be ready for immediate use.

+

A strainer in the gas line will trap more dirt than a carburetor can swallow.

+

Getting under way, be sure you haven't left a line trailing overboard. Propellers have a strange attraction for them.

+

Water pump suction sometimes collapses the intake hose and stops circulation. A short length is enough to stop vibration, and the walls should be strong.

+

Old plugs in a motor spell poor economy. A good fat spark from a clean new plug with the right gap will cut down fuel cost and improve engine performance.

+

If you haven't been able to locate the source of that persistent vibration, or if you suspect your motor of inefficiency, have your propeller checked for pitch. A bent blade could be responsible . . . and it's easily fixed.

+

Anchoring on a foul bottom, attach a short buoyed trip line to the crown. A pull on it will release the flukes if caught under a rock or ledge.

+

Dock lines require renewal just as much as other rope used aboard. It takes a stout line to withstand the surge created by a passing boat or the strain of a violent gale of wind.

+

Electrolytic action destroys iron used near brass or bronze in salt water. Zinc in contact with the iron will take the action and save the iron.

+

Don't run with a slipping clutch. Simple adjustments are always provided and taking up a notch or two will save the gear.

+

In changing wheels, remember that propellers may be right-handed or left-handed. Looking forward at the driving face of the blades from aft, a right-handed wheel swings clockwise.

+

A few minutes are well spent occasionally in going over all nuts and bolts on the engine with a wrench. Lag screws holding the motor down are particularly prone to loosen up with vibration.

+

Some engines suffer more from over-overhauling than from neglect. Modern engines don't have to be pulled down every year. Keep your motor clean and leave it alone when it's running right.

There is a happy medium in the choice of anchor line. Given strength enough, thin lines will hold better in deep water than thick, buoyant ones.

+

Thin ice will often damage a hull more than a thick coating. "Window-pane" ice, an eighth of an inch thick, cuts cedar like a sharp chisel. Sheet copper at the water line will protect the hull.

+

If you foul your propeller with grass or other debris, it's not always necessary to go overboard or haul the boat out to clear it. Reversing will often do the trick.

+

A hull afloat soaks up an amazing weight of water. With cruisers, that's not so vital. But if you own a fast runabout, and want to take home the silverware from regattas, hoist the hull clear of the water whenever it's not in service.

+

When the soft purr of the exhaust suddenly takes on a dry, hollow note, check up on the water circulation. It's likely that the water has failed.

+

It is not regarded as good form to fly the burgees of more than one club at a time, even though you may be a member of each.

+

Neglect will ruin a storage battery. Add enough distilled water occasionally to keep the plates covered with liquid at all times.

+

In general practice, boat steering wheels turn with the boat's head, as in automobiles. The opposite method is likely to be confusing, except to some old tug skippers.

+

Before letting an anchor go, make sure the line is clear and ready to run without fouling. One foot caught in the coils might create an embarrassing situation.

+

In heaving a line, hold it in such a manner that the end uncoils itself naturally from the outside. Otherwise it's likely to snarl up and fall short.

+

Colors should be flown from eight in the morning till sundown. Club burgee at the forward staff, owner's private signal at the masthead, and ensign aft.

+

Boarding ladders are all right over-side at anchor. But they ought to be stowed when the boat is under way.

+

Gasoline tanks should be provided with tight fillers to the deck.

+

Motors run best with the switch on. Just before the expiring battery gives its last gasp from futile cranking, check up on this small, but important, detail.

+

As a rough basis of estimating, the height of sea waves, in feet, is generally reckoned at half the velocity of the wind in miles per hour.

New lines have a mean habit of twisting themselves into hard kinks. They can be worked out by towing the line astern, one end made fast to the after bitt.

+

In greater numbers every year, boatmen are keeping their craft in commission all winter. If you do, keep jackets and water lines drained to prevent bursting from the expansion caused by freezing.

+

When using a compass with considerable deviation and it is desired to steer a compass course to make good a certain magnetic course, an appreciable error will be introduced if the deviation is taken from the usual table under compass heading of ship; several interpolations are necessary to eliminate this error.

+

In taking vertical sextant angles where large tidal ranges exist, it is well to remember that the height of lighthouses above high water, as stated in the Light List, should be corrected for tide.

+

The taking of bearings of distant objects which have been sighted by binoculars will be greatly facilitated by noting cloud formations directly over or near the object observed.

+

On a rocky coast it should be borne in mind that the lead of the surveying vessel may have missed a rising head. Except where surveys have been made in great detail, only a survey with a wire drag is sure to have caught every rock.

+

In taking vertical sextant angles the object observed should be close to the shore line for the best results. The sextant angle will be in error if the object is situated far inland from the shore.

+

A vessel with an object one point on the bow will pass it abeam at about one-fifth of the distance away at the time of the first bearing.

+

A check on the patent log may be obtained occasionally when spar buoys are standing upright, denoting little or no current.

+

A sounding taken at the same time as an observation for a line of position will, under certain conditions, prove of great value in giving an approximate position on the line.

+

At times of distant haze a better horizon is often secured by reducing the height of eye.

+

In planning to enter a strange port, the mariner should give careful previous study to the chart, sailing directions, and tide tables; and should select the most suitable marks for use, providing substitutes in case those selected can not be recognized with absolute certainty.

To prevent kinks in the patent log line when hauling it in, pass the inboard end across the deck and stream it as the line comes in.

+

Never be too positive as to your ship's position, for overconfidence has led many an experienced and skillful navigator into distressing disaster.

+

Where available, ranges should be marked on the chart to be used either to lead clear of dangers or to check the deviation of the compass.

+

A single line of position will at times furnish the mariner with valuable information. For instance, if it points toward the coast, it marks the bearing of a definite point on the shore; or if it parallels the coast, it clearly indicates the distance off.

+

When determining a ship's position by cross bearings, objects should be selected with not less than 30° nor more than 150° between them. Near objects are preferable to those at a distance, keeping in mind the disadvantage of very near landmarks which may change rapidly in bearing.

+

When plotting the position of a ship with three correctly observed cross bearings an intersection will not result if the compass error used is incorrect. The ship's true position is within the triangle formed by bearings only when she is within the triangle formed by the objects themselves, otherwise her position lies outside the triangle formed by the bearings.

+

A vessel's run from a point with an object bearing 26½° forward of the beam until it bears 26½° abaft the beam is equal to the distance from the object when abeam.

+

A vessel's distance from an object abeam is five times the distance run between its bearing 1 point forward of the beam and its bearing abeam, current excepted.

+

An excellent substitute for the three-armed protractor (station pointer), with which to lay off horizontal sextant angles for position, will be found in a piece of fairly stiff transparent paper. Place the paper over the chart compass rose and lay off the angles from the center of rose and then use in the same way as the protractor.

+

There are three methods by which, without obtaining the precise position, the navigator may assure himself that he is clear of any particular danger. They are: (1) By following a range. (2) By using the danger angle. (3) By using the danger bearing.

When piloting during thick weather it is often desirable to estimate the vessel's position by echo from a bold shore or echo board. A convenient approximation is to point off one place in the number of seconds elapsed from sounding of ship's whistle until echo is heard. This will be the distance off in miles and tenths of miles.

+

In taking a bearing on the tangent of an island or point, an error will be introduced if the shore is shelving and the tide is above the chart datum. What may appear as a long point at low water disappears with the rise of tide. This error is emphasized where there is a great tidal range.

+

When steaming along a well-charted coast in overcast weather, the error of the compass may be obtained by fixing the position by sextant angles between three suitable objects. Another observer at the same moment should carefully note the compass bearing of a distant, well-defined, and charted object. With the position plotted with a three-armed protractor (station pointer) or tracing paper, the true bearing of the distant object is readily taken from the chart, and when compared with the compass bearing furnishes the error. Lights may be used at night.

+

If a vessel, with an object at a certain bearing on the bow, steams until the angle of the bearing is doubled, the distance run during the doubling of the angle is the distance off at the last bearing. Thus, if the angle is 30° and a vessel runs until the object bears 60° on the bow, covering 10 miles, she is 10 miles from the object when it bears 60°; current excepted.

+

The distance at which a light will be passed when abeam may be ascertained at the time it first appears on the horizon by the use of Table 3, Bowditch, using the light's bearing from the bow as a course and its visibility, corrected for height of eye, as the distance. In the departure column will be found the distance off when abeam. The distance to be run until light is abeam will be found in the latitude column. It is assumed that the course is made good and that weather conditions render visibility normal.

+

The distance from any object of a known height may be ascertained by multiplying the height in feet by 0.565 and dividing the result by the number of minutes in the vertical sextant angle of the object. The quotient will be the distance off in nautical miles and decimals of a mile.

+

Navigators may ascertain the distance they will pass a charted object abeam by use of the following bearing combinations. The bearings are from the bow. The distance run between them is the distance the object will be passed abeam, current excepted:
22°—34°, 27°—46°, 32°—59°. 40°—79°

When locating a ship's position by sextant angles, using three charted objects, a condition arises where this method fails. A circle can always be drawn through three points, and when the ship happens to be on this circle, the position is indeterminate and another object must be selected.

+

Radio bearings near sunrise or sunset are not always reliable.

+

Compass deviations can be conveniently and reliably checked when at anchor, or when steaming along a coast, by taking bearings of a range consisting of two conspicuous well-charted objects. The distance between the objects should be greater than the ship's distance from the nearer object.

+

In piloting, the vessel's position should be fixed at all times, even when entering ports considered safe and easy of access, and should be constantly checked, using those marks whose identity has been established beyond doubt.

+

A change in engine rpm does not always necessarily mean engine trouble. Check the depth of water. You may be crossing a shoal. Sometimes boat speed will be reduced, the trim changed and rpm affected, even though the keel is not in fact touching bottom.

+

Mariners are cautioned when plotting bearings received from a radiocompass station to use the position of the receiver ashore, and when plotting bearings obtained by a direction finder aboard ship to use the position of the transmitter of the sending station. In some cases the transmitter and the receiver are a considerable distance from each other.

+

When a vessel sights a known light her distance off in miles, when abeam, may be anticipated approximately by multiplying the number of degrees the light bears on the bow by the visibility (corrected for height of eye), and dividing this product by 60.

+

In determining accurately the distance off a light by any method where two bearings of one object with the run between are taken and when current or heavy wind exists, the course made good and the distance over the bottom must be known and used.

+

Radiobeacons are operated continuously during thick and foggy weather. Vessels approaching port from seaward or steaming along a coast may infer that the visibility conditions ahead are poor if, by listening in, the beacon in that quarter is found to be working. This should be done at a time other than its scheduled clear-weather operating period, and they sometimes operate upon request for tests. Certain stations pause during thick weather to listen in. (See H. O. No. 205 for schedules.)

Fog at sea is principally caused by three conditions, namely, (1) by calm or comparatively still air which fosters the radiation fogs, (2) by warm or moist winds blowing over a cold sea surface, and (3) by cold winds, either wet or dry, blowing over the warm sea surface.

A temperature fall of 2° F. is often sufficient to produce a fog; a corresponding rise, to dispel it.

+

On approaching land during a fog the nearest radiocompass station should be requested to furnish bearings.

+

In light fog or drizzling rain an iceberg may be visible 1 to 3 miles; in dense fog it can not be seen more than 100 yards ahead of the ship. On a clear, starlit night a lookout will not pick up an iceberg at a distance greater than one-fourth of a mile, unless its position is definitely known.

+

In a light fog it may be assumed that a man aloft will sight an iceberg sooner than one on deck; in a dense fog, however, the latter will probably catch the first evidence of a berg by the breaking of the sea at its base or by growlers and fragments of ice from it.

+

Radio bearings crossing intervening land should be mistrusted.

+

Near the lee side of lofty islands the weather is generally clear as far as fog, mist and low clouds are concerned. Therefore in making a landfall in thick weather better visibility may be experienced if approach is made from leeward.

+

Moderate speed in a fog is held by the courts to be: "Such a rate of speed as will enable a vessel, after discovering another vessel meeting her, to stop and reverse her engines in sufficient time to prevent any collision from taking place."

+

Entire dependence can never be placed on fog signals, because with no apparent reason large zones of silence often occur at varying directions and different distances from the origin of sound.

+

Set of current is the direction toward which it flows; the direction of wind from whence it blows.

+

The flood tide may be running in a harbor and the water falling at the piers; conversely, the ebb may be running in the stream and the water rising at the piers.

+

A vessel proceeding against the tide, especially the ebb, in a tidal river will gain an advantage by favoring the bank.

+

Current arrows on pilot charts indicate averages; actual currents may be encountered that differ widely, even opposite to the charted arrows.

In estimating current when vessel is in ballast, leeway should be carefully allowed for.

+

The mariner is enabled to note the set of the current at night by the establishment of riding lights on the forestays of lightships.

+

A vessel in light trim may not encounter the same current as a deep-draft vessels. The current is usually greater on the surface than at the bottom. The flood in the Hudson River off New York has its greatest velocity at mid-depth.

+

In navigating the lower reaches of tidal rivers the ebb near the surface will be found to be stronger and will last longer than the flood; near the bottom the duration of flood and ebb become approximately equal. Wind, barometric pressure, and recent rains over regions contiguous to the upper river, all affect flow and duration of tidal current.

+

In a bay with a narrow entrance through which great quantities of tidal water must pass each tide, the maximum velocity at the entrance may be expected at about high and low water. The flood and ebb current at such points is found to begin about 3 hours after low water and high water, respectively.

+

When the water is fairly homogeneous and the depth is great, the surface movement is deflected about 45° to the right of the wind's direction of travel in the Northern Hemisphere, and 45° to the left in the Southern Hemisphere.

+

The best water of a river or natural channel may be expected in the center of the stream of the straight reaches and at the outside of the bends; the swiftest current will usually be found along the line of the best water.

+

After currents are generated, in the Northern Hemisphere, the conformation of the bottom tends to deflect them to the right around islands and shoals and to the left around basins and deeps.

+

The flood tide in an estuary makes earlier at the bottom than at the surface. This variation is more marked in midstream than at the sides. Hence a deep-draft vessel will probably swing to the flood before a light-draft vessel does in the same vicinity. The ebb makes at about the same time at the surface as at the bottom.

+

When a large-scale harbor chart is not available, a workable substitute may be constructed from the information given on a small-scale chart. Divide the desired harbor area of the small-scale chart into a convenient number of equal squares and transfer the shoreline, as an enlargement, to a plain sheet of desirable size likewise ruled in similar squares. Add soundings, contours, landmarks, etc., in their relative positions. Check the accuracy of the plan by bearings and distances and construct a scale of distances.

A liquid compass should be shielded from the sun, especially when in the Tropics.

+

If a compass is unshipped for any purpose, check the lubber's line upon replacement, to be sure it is on the fore-and-aft line.

+

It is advisable to keep chronometers away from positions where severe shocks are liable to occur, such as the constant slamming of a door.

+

A watch officer obliged to look at a chart on a dark night may, with advantage, close one eye when the light is turned on and when again in darkness open the closed eye. The vision will be improved by this expedient, which lessens the temporary blindness caused by the light.

+

When adjusting compasses or ascertaining deviation by known bearings of terrestrial objects, distant objects are preferable to those near at hand.

+

Excessive rolling or pitching due to synchronism may be checked by changing the course or speed, at times very slightly.

+

Swells are waves propagated by wind at a distance, or may be caused by a wind that previously was blowing in the locality; while the waves set up by wind prevailing are called, collectively, sea.

+

Wind blowing over smooth water has less wave-producing power than when blowing over water already in motion.

+

Any marked change from diurnal variation in the barometer readings within the Tropics is a sign indicative of an atmospheric disturbance; caution should be exercised during the hurricane season.

+

The velocity of the wind is dependent upon the steepness of the barometric gradient rather than on the reading of the barometer; that is, there may be little or no wind with a reading of 29.00 inches, yet on another occasion a wind of hurricane force may be blowing with a reading of 29.70 inches. The distance between the isobars controls the wind force; the closer they are the steeper the gradient and the stronger the wind.

If the wind shifts to the right in the Northern Hemisphere the vessel is in the right-hand or dangerous semicircle of the depression; to the left, she is in the left-hand or navigable semicircle.

+

According to the Buys Ballot's law, when facing the wind, the barometer will be lower on the right hand than on the left in the Northern, and vice versa in the Southern Hemisphere.

+

If the wind does not shift, but continues to blow steadily with increasing force, and with a falling barometer, it may be assumed that the vessel is on or near a storm track.

+

Waves reach their greatest development in the rear quadrant of the dangerous or right semicircle of the Northern and the left semicircle of the Southern Hemisphere.

+

When in front of a hurricane but not very near the center, the vortex bears with an average of 10 points to the right when facing the wind in the Northern Hemisphere, but a larger allowance must be made when in the rear quadrants. When directly in front of a hurricane the wind does not change in direction.

+

Vessels anchored or moored under high land should be prepared for sudden and violent squalls which sweep down the mountains. The cold, heavy air of the heights seeks the lower levels with destructive force in many ports of the world.

+

Oil has the greatest modifying effect on deep-water waves.

+

Changes in wave formation may be an indication of shoaling water for waves close up and heighten when running from deep into shoal water. A deeply laden vessel in heavy weather would be safer in avoiding, if possible, the position of abrupt changes in depths, as the seas running from deeper water feel the bottom, rise and become sharper.

+

The length of waves due to wind increases with the distance from the weather shore (fetch). The longest fetch is in the waters of the higher latitudes of the Southern Hemisphere, hence in that region are experienced the longest seas.

Wreckage and floating objects which eventually sink beneath the surface through loss of buoyancy will continue to the bottom, regardless of the greater density and pressure, at increasing depths, so long as their weight exceeds the weight of water they displace.

+

A vessel's draft in salt water is roughly one-quarter of an inch per foot less than in fresh water.

+

The area of a vessel's waterplane in square feet (that is, the area of a deck everywhere flush with the water line) divided by 420 will give roughly the number of tons required to increase the mean draft 1 inch.

+

Sound travels at about 1,132 feet per second in air, at 68½° F.; about 4,794 feet per second through water, at 66° F.

+

Icebergs in the North Atlantic float with about one-ninth of their mass out of water.

+

The earth moves left-handed around the sun; that is, toward the right when facing that body in the southern sky. As a result the sun seems to work correspondingly eastward among the fixed stars as a background, and at sunset new constellations appear in the east from month to month and the old ones disappear in the west.

+

When the declination of the sun is 0° (on the Equator) the days and nights are of equal length (12 hours) the world over, except in extreme polar regions.

+

When the sun is 0° declination about March 21 and September 22, it rises in true east and sets in true west throughout the world, except in the polar regions.

+

About June 21 the sun reaches its highest point of northern declination, 23° 27'. This is the longest day of the year for the Northern Hemisphere. At the North Pole this day the sun's path is everywhere parallel to the horizon and 23° 27' in altitude.

+

When the star Mizar of the Great Bear and the star Ruchbah of Cassiopeia, which are in line with Polaris, are either above or below that star, the latter is bearing north true, and the error of the compass may be easily obtained.

SHIP'S BELL TIME

SHIP'S bell time originated in sailing ship days, when the crew of a vessel was divided into Port and Starboard Watches, each on duty four hours, then off four hours.

One stroke on the ship's bell indicates the first half hour of the watch. Then an additional bell is struck for each succeeding half hour. Thus 8 bells indicates the end of a four-hour watch. This is repeated each watch. When the time calls for two or more strokes, they are sounded in groups of two.

The first five watches are as follows: First Watch, 8:00 P. M. to Midnight; Middle Watch, Midnight to 4:00 A. M.; Morning Watch, 4:00 to 8:00 A. M.; Forenoon Watch, 8:00 A. M. to Noon; and Afternoon Watch, Noon to 4:00 P. M.

The next 4 hours are divided into two Dog Watches—the First Dog Watch, 4:00 to 6:00 P. M.; and the Second Dog Watch, 6:00 to 8:00 P. M. By means of the Dog Watches, the watches can be changed every day, so that each watch gets a turn of eight hours rest at night. Otherwise each member of the crew would be on duty the same hours every day.

*In the Second Dog Watch, to indicate that a new watch has taken over, the sequence of bells is varied as follows: *1* Bell, 6:30 P. M.; *2* Bells, 7:00 P. M.; *3* Bells, 7:30 P. M.; *8* Bells, 8:00 P. M. The ship's clock of course repeats the sequence of 1 to 8 bells every four hours day and night without variation.

Bells, and How Struck	First Watch	Middle Watch	Morning Watch	Forenoon Watch	Afternoon Watch	First Dog Watch	Second Dog Watch
1 Bell (.)	8:30 P.M.	12:30 A.M.	4:30 A.M.	8:30 A.M.	12:30 P.M.	4:30 P.M.	—
2 Bells (..)	9:00	1:00	5:00	9:00	1:00	5:00	—
3 Bells (. . .)	9:30	1:30	5:30	9:30	1:30	5:30	—
4 Bells (. . . .)	10:00	2:00	6:00	10:00	2:00	6:00 P.M.	—
5 Bells (. . . . .)	10:30	2:30	6:30	10:30	2:30	—	*6:30 P.M.
6 Bells (. . . . . .)	11:00	3:00	7:00	11:00	3:00	—	*7:00
7 Bells (. . . . . . .)	11:30	3:30	7:30	11:30	3:30	—	*7:30
8 Bells (. . . . .)	12:00 Midnight	4:00 A.M.	8:00 A.M.	12:00 Noon	4:00 P.M.	—	*8:00 P.M.

* See text for sequence of bells in Second Dog Watch.

SCALES OF VISIBILITY AND SEA CONDITIONS AS USED BY THE NAVY

Numeral	Prominent Objects Not Visible At
0.	500 yards
.1 to .9	100 to 900 "
1.	1,000 "
2.	2,000 "
50.	50,000 "
51.	over 50,000 "

(Numerals to be used in recording visibility in thousands of yards. Range finder readings of known landmarks should be used as scale.)

Code Fig.	Approx. Height of Sea in Feet	Description
0	0	Calm
1	1	Smooth
2	1– 3	Slight
3	3– 5	Moderate
4	5– 8	Rough
5	8–12	Very rough
6	12–20	High
7	20–40	Very high
8	40+	Mountainous
9	Note: Qualifying condition applicable to the previous conditions, e.g. (5–9) a very rough, confused sea.	

(This sea scale in the revised edition of the Navy log is a slight modification of the Douglas Sea Scale. Direction from which the sea moves to be recorded in numeral points.)

GUN SALUTES AS MILITARY HONORS

(See also page 371)

Rank	Guns at Arrival	Guns at Departure	Ruffles and Flourishes
President	21	21	4
President of foreign republic or a foreign sovereign	21	21	4
Member of a royal family	21	21	4
Former President	21	21	4
Vice-President		19	4
Secretary of State on board a vessel of the Navy representing the President		19	4
Ambassador		19	4
Secretary of the Navy	19	19	4
Secretary of War	19	19	4
Assistant Secretary of the Navy	17	17	4
Cabinet Officer		19	4
Chief Justice		17	4
Governor General, United States Islands		19	4
Governor of state, territory or United States Islands		19	4
President pro tempore of the Senate		19	4
Speaker of the House of Representatives		17	4

Rank	Guns at Arrival	Guns at Departure	Ruffles and Flourishes
Committee of Congress		17	4
Envoy Extraordinary		15	3
Assistant Secretary of War		15	3
Minister resident or "diplomatic representative"		13	2
Charge d'affairs		11	1.
Consul general		11	..
Consul		7	..
Vice-consul or consular agent (where he is the only representative of the United States)		5	..
Admiral		17	4
General		17	4
Vice-admiral		15	3
Lieutenant general		15	3
Rear Admiral		13	2
Major General (Army or Marine Corps)		13	2
Commandant of the Coast Guard		13	2
Commodore		11	1
Brigadier general (Army or Marine Corps)		11	1

ATLANTIC COAST
PERPETUAL TIDE CHART

"Two tides every day — Flow into our bay
The moon in the Sky — Tells when they'll be high."

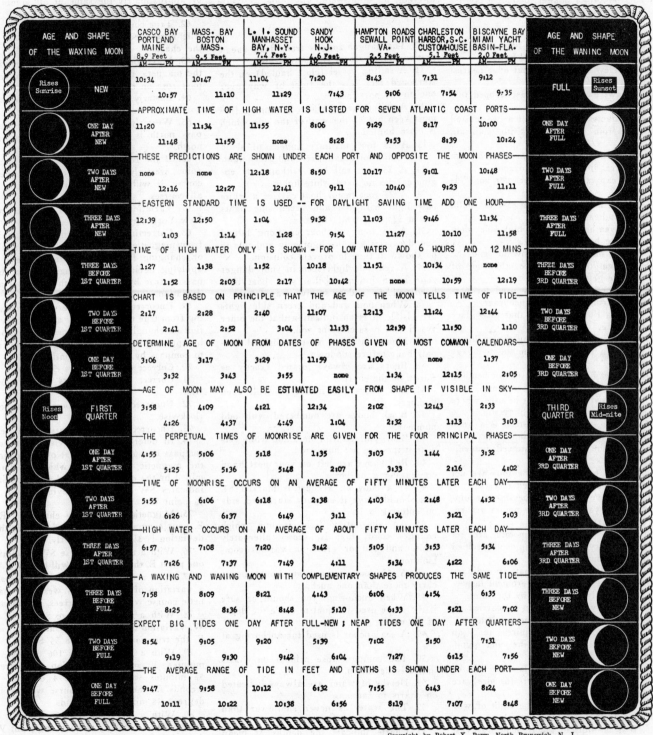

AGE AND SHAPE OF THE WAXING MOON	CASCO BAY PORTLAND MAINE 8.9 Feet		MASS. BAY BOSTON MASS. 9.5 Feet		L.I. SOUND MANHASSET BAY, N.Y. 7.4 Feet		SANDY HOOK N.J. 4.6 Feet		HAMPTON ROADS SEWALL POINT VA. 2.5 Feet		CHARLESTON HARBOR, S.C. CUSTOMHOUSE 5.1 Feet		BISCAYNE BAY MIAMI YACHT BASIN-FLA. 2.0 Feet		AGE AND SHAPE OF THE WANING MOON
	AM	PM	AM	PM	AM	PM	AM	PM	AM	PM	AM	PM	AM	PM	
NEW (Rises Sunrise)	10:34	10:57	10:47	11:10	11:04	11:29	7:20	7:43	8:43	9:06	7:31	7:54	9:12	9:35	FULL (Rises Sunset)
ONE DAY AFTER NEW	11:20	11:48	11:34	11:59	11:55	none	8:06	8:28	9:29	9:53	8:17	8:39	10:00	10:24	ONE DAY AFTER FULL
TWO DAYS AFTER NEW	none	12:16	none	12:27	12:18	12:41	8:50	9:11	10:17	10:40	9:01	9:23	10:48	11:11	TWO DAYS AFTER FULL
THREE DAYS AFTER NEW	12:39	1:03	12:50	1:14	1:04	1:28	9:32	9:54	11:03	11:27	9:46	10:10	11:34	11:58	THREE DAYS AFTER FULL
THREE DAYS BEFORE 1ST QUARTER	1:27	1:52	1:38	2:03	1:52	2:17	10:18	10:42	11:51	none	10:34	10:59	none	12:19	THREE DAYS BEFORE 3RD QUARTER
TWO DAYS BEFORE 1ST QUARTER	2:17	2:41	2:28	2:52	2:40	3:04	11:07	11:33	12:13	12:39	11:24	11:50	12:44	1:10	TWO DAYS BEFORE 3RD QUARTER
ONE DAY BEFORE 1ST QUARTER	3:06	3:32	3:17	3:43	3:29	3:55	11:59	none	1:06	1:34	none	12:15	1:37	2:05	ONE DAY BEFORE 3RD QUARTER
FIRST QUARTER (Rises Noon)	3:58	4:26	4:09	4:37	4:21	4:49	12:34	1:04	2:02	2:32	12:43	1:13	2:33	3:03	THIRD QUARTER (Rises Mid-nite)
ONE DAY AFTER 1ST QUARTER	4:55	5:25	5:06	5:36	5:18	5:48	1:35	2:07	3:03	3:33	1:44	2:16	3:32	4:02	ONE DAY AFTER 3RD QUARTER
TWO DAYS AFTER 1ST QUARTER	5:55	6:26	6:06	6:37	6:18	6:49	2:38	3:11	4:03	4:34	2:48	3:21	4:32	5:03	TWO DAYS AFTER 3RD QUARTER
THREE DAYS AFTER 1ST QUARTER	6:57	7:26	7:08	7:37	7:20	7:49	3:42	4:11	5:05	5:34	3:53	4:22	5:34	6:06	THREE DAYS AFTER 3RD QUARTER
THREE DAYS BEFORE FULL	7:58	8:25	8:09	8:36	8:21	8:48	4:43	5:10	6:06	6:33	4:54	5:21	6:35	7:02	THREE DAYS BEFORE NEW
TWO DAYS BEFORE FULL	8:54	9:19	9:05	9:30	9:20	9:42	5:39	6:04	7:02	7:27	5:50	6:15	7:31	7:56	TWO DAYS BEFORE NEW
ONE DAY BEFORE FULL	9:47	10:11	9:58	10:22	10:12	10:38	6:32	6:56	7:55	8:19	6:43	7:07	8:24	8:48	ONE DAY BEFORE NEW

Instructional lines interspersed between the rows of the chart:

- APPROXIMATE TIME OF HIGH WATER IS LISTED FOR SEVEN ATLANTIC COAST PORTS
- THESE PREDICTIONS ARE SHOWN UNDER EACH PORT AND OPPOSITE THE MOON PHASES
- EASTERN STANDARD TIME IS USED -- FOR DAYLIGHT SAVING TIME ADD ONE HOUR
- TIME OF HIGH WATER ONLY IS SHOWN - FOR LOW WATER ADD 6 HOURS AND 12 MINS
- CHART IS BASED ON PRINCIPLE THAT THE AGE OF THE MOON TELLS TIME OF TIDE
- DETERMINE AGE OF MOON FROM DATES OF PHASES GIVEN ON MOST COMMON CALENDARS
- AGE OF MOON MAY ALSO BE ESTIMATED EASILY FROM SHAPE IF VISIBLE IN SKY
- THE PERPETUAL TIMES OF MOONRISE ARE GIVEN FOR THE FOUR PRINCIPAL PHASES
- TIME OF MOONRISE OCCURS ON AN AVERAGE OF FIFTY MINUTES LATER EACH DAY
- HIGH WATER OCCURS ON AN AVERAGE OF ABOUT FIFTY MINUTES LATER EACH DAY
- A WAXING AND WANING MOON WITH COMPLEMENTARY SHAPES PRODUCES THE SAME TIDE
- EXPECT BIG TIDES ONE DAY AFTER FULL-NEW; NEAP TIDES ONE DAY AFTER QUARTERS
- THE AVERAGE RANGE OF TIDE IN FEET AND TENTHS IS SHOWN UNDER EACH PORT

From this chart one can estimate the time of high water at any of the seven key ports for any day, any year, simply by knowing the phase of the moon at that time, that is, the number of days before or after new, first quarter, full, or last quarter—usually indicated on most calendars. For adjacent coastal ports the times differ only by minutes, except on rivers, bays, and inland tributaries. For these exceptions, consult the U. S. Coast and Geodetic Survey Tide Tables. It will be found that for many of such inland places the times of high water will approximate those at one of the key locations listed in the chart above. For example, the time of high water at Essex, on the Connecticut River, is the same as the time of high water at Boston.

CHAPTER XXXIV—Right or Wrong?

The following quiz was used originally during the war to qualify students of the Seamanship Training Corp for seamanship certificates. Test yourself, marking the statements true or false, and compare with answers on page 471. Credit for each correct answer, 7 points. For each incorrect answer, deduct 4 points. No credit for unanswered questions. Passing grade 700 points.

1. Broad on the starboard bow means the same as 4 points on starboard bow.

2. The clew of a sail is that edge nearest mast.

3. A yawl has her mainmast stepped forward of the rudder post.

4. The names of the sails of a two masted schooner from forward are: jib, mainsail, mizzen.

5. The names of the sails of a ketch from forward are: jib, mainsail, mizzen.

6. The expression "10 knots per hour" is correct.

7. The wind backed from east to south, through southeast.

8. The weather side is the high side when sailing close hauled.

9. When one sails downwind and he wishes to get the sail on the other side of the boat, he generally jibes.

10. Grapnels are generally used for permanent moorings at a club anchorage.

11. Spring tides are those that take place in the Spring.

12. A fix refers to repairing the engine.

13. Hard a lee is the command to heave the anchor.

14. A sheet bend may be used for bending two lines together for towing purposes.

15. The bowline should not be used where there is danger that the loop may slip.

16. Towing a new line astern is a good method of taking the kinks out of it.

17. Wet line should be stowed immediately.

18. Yachts of less than 300 tons are not required to carry any licensed officers.

19. The government specifies what equipment sailing yachts without motors are required to carry.

20. Sailing yachts with motors are required to carry certain equipment specified by the government.

21. For a 30-foot motor boat, an ordinary mouth whistle will pass government inspection as the whistle required by the rules.

22. A dinghy towed astern or carried on deck will pass as life-saving equipment.

23. The government requires that an anchor, compass, anchor line and pump must be carried on board.

24. Motor or sailing vessels of 16 tons or more (not carrying passengers for hire) are required to be documented.

25. The boat which has the right of way is known as the privileged vessel.

26. It is the duty of the right of way vessel to hold her course and speed.

27. The burdened vessel should always keep clear of the privileged vessel.

28. Answering one blast of the whistle with one blast is known as giving a cross signal.

29. In case of collision between two vessels, there is no obligation for them to stand by each other to render assistance.

30. The danger zone is from dead ahead to two points aft of the port beam.

31. A sailing vessel (close hauled) on the starboard tack has the right of way over one on the port tack.

32. A sailing vessel which is running free must keep out of the way of the one which is close hauled.

33. A 25 foot auxiliary under sail alone carries only a combination red-and-green light.

34. A 25 foot sail boat without any engine carries no fixed white lights.

35. A 25 foot motor boat carries a white bow light with red and green side lights and a 32 point white light.

36. A 16 foot sail boat on Long Island Sound carries a white light only and this to be shown in time to prevent collision.

37. A red side light seen in your danger zone is an indication that your boat is a burdened one and must give way.

38. When both red and green side lights are visible, it is an indication that the other vessel will pass clear of you.

39. Lights on boats must be lighted one-half hour before sundown.

40. Buoys are always located exactly as shown on the chart.

41. Red buoys are numbered with even numbers.

42. Black buoys are numbered with odd numbers.

43. Buoys painted with black and white vertical stripes are not numbered.

44. Red buoys are left on your port hand on leaving a harbor.

45. If a buoy on a chart is marked S4, you should leave it on your starboard side on entering a harbor.

46. An alternating light is one which changes color, that is, shows alternately white and red or green in various combinations.

47. A 45 foot motor boat should never carry more than one anchor.

48. When anchoring, you should be safe if the scope used is equal to twice the depth of the water.

49. A sea anchor is used for anchoring at sea.

50. The compass rose printed on charts indicates deviation.

51. Depths of water are always indicated on charts in fathoms.

52. The water is never shallower than that indicated on the chart.

53. Charts indicate the depths at mean high water.

54. The direction of an arrow shown on the chart indicates the best possible course.

55. The North Pole of the compass points toward geographic north.

56. The compass card is divided into 360 points.

57. The cardinal points are N, NE, E, SE, S, SW, W, NW.

58. The reverse course of 315 degrees is 45 degrees.

59. Deviation is the angular difference between true north and a free needle suspended at the point in question.

60. Variation is determined by referring to the compass rose on the chart.

61. The amount of variation is the same or approximately the same at all points on the earth's surface.

62. True courses are those referred to the true north or to the true compass rose on the chart.

63. Magnetic courses are those referred to the magnetic north or to the magnetic compass rose on the chart.

64. Easterly variation is when magnetic north is to the east of the true North.

65. Westerly deviation is when the compass north is to the west of the magnetic north.

66. If the compass on one's boat has one point westerly deviation on a northerly course, it will have the same deviation on all courses.

67. Variation at Portland, Maine, and New York City is 15 degrees westerly.

68. Correcting a course means changing from magnetic to true by applying variation or changing from compass to magnetic by applying deviation, or changing from compass to true by applying both variation and deviation.

69. Uncorrecting a course means changing from true to magnetic by applying deviation or changing from magnetic to compass by applying deviation or changing from true to compass by applying variation.

70. Correct easterly errors clockwise.

71. Correct westerly errors counter-clockwise.

72. Uncorrect westerly errors counterclockwise.

73. Uncorrect easterly errors clockwise.

74. In determining the deviation of your compass by putting your boat over a course, the magnetic direction of which as determined by the chart is SW and your compass indicates SW ¼ W, the deviation will be ¼ point W.

75. Magnetic direction by chart is NE x E, your compass indicates N x E ½ E, then deviation is 3½ points westerly.

76. With a magnetic course SW, variation one point E, the true course will be SW x W.

77. With a true course of 225 degrees and a variation of 11¼ degrees west, the magnetic course will be 236 degrees, 15 minutes.

78. With a magnetic course SW x W ½ W, variation one point E, deviation ½ point E, the true course is W x S ½ S.

79. With a true course of 106 degrees, 52 minutes, 30 seconds; variation 10 degrees, 56 minutes west; deviation 4 degrees, 06 seconds E; the magnetic course will be 117 degrees, 48 minutes, 30 seconds.

80. With a true course of 70 degrees, 18 minutes, 45 seconds; variation one point W; deviation ¾ point W; the compass course will be E.

81. Rudder is as effective when boat is going astern as it is when going ahead.

82. With rudder hard right, single right hand screw, when starting to back, the boat will generally back to starboard.

83. In turning, the bow swings the greater amount.

84. If a boat is drifting with wind or current, a course may be directed by her rudder.

85. In turning around in a narrow canal, where it is not possible to make a complete turn in one swing, it is better to turn to starboard when going ahead.

86. The painter of the dinghy towed astern should be given no attention upon making a landing.

87. As a general rule in a single screw boat, the bow tends to swing to port.

88. Most modern small sailing craft are gaff rigged.

89. Both the centerboard and keel of a sail boat tend to give it leeway.

90. A lee helm is preferable to a weather helm on a sailing craft.

91. The CE should be located slightly forward of C L P.

92. A boat with a lee helm tends to swing up into the wind more readily than one with weather helm.

93. If your sailing vessel were heading into the wind and you should hear two blasts on the fog horn ahead of you, you would know that a sailing vessel on the port tack might be crossing your bow from your port to your starboard.

94. In a fog, if you heard a rapid ringing of a bell, you would know that it was a boat at anchor or aground.

95. In a fog, if you heard one long blast followed by two short blasts on a whistle, it would indicate a vessel with a tow or one not under control.

96. A motor boat gives her fog signal on a fog horn.

97. Two strips of leather on the lead line indicates two fathoms.

98. Five strips of leather on a lead line indicates five fathoms.

99. Ten fathoms on the lead line is marked by a red rag.

100. Fathoms which correspond with the depths marked on the lead line are called marks.

101. The intermediate fathoms which do not correspond with the depths marked on the lead line are called deeps.

102. The patent log always indicates distance in nautical miles.

103. The time of high water at Sandy Hook may be determined from the Tide Tables.

104. The characteristics of Execution Light should be obtained from the Coast Pilot.

105. Piloting is defined as a science of navigation without the use of physical landmarks.

106. In dead reckoning, the position of buoys and lighthouses is made use of at frequent intervals.

107. Two of the more common methods of locating one's position or determining a fix, are: cross bearings, and two bearings and a run between.

108. If a light bears 4 points off the bow at 10 A.M. and is abeam at 10:45 A.M. and the speed of the boat is 12 m.p.h., the boat will be 9 miles off the light at 10:45 A.M.

109. Course SE, bearing of light at 8:00 P.M. E; at 9:00 P.M. NE; speed of boat 10 m.p.h., then the boat will be 9 miles off the light at 9.00 P.M.

110. If an object is 26½° off the bow at noon and 45° at 12:30 P.M. with a speed of 8 knots, then the object will be 4 miles off when abeam.

111. The International Flag Code consists of 26 flags representing letters, 10 flags representing numerals, 3 repeater flags and an answering pennant.

112. Time is signaled by four numeral pennants preceded by and joined with the letter T.

113. Numbers are signaled by the pennants and require no further signal to indicate that they represent numbers.

114. The N flag means yes in the International Code.

115. The C flag means no.

116. The International flag signal of distress is the code flags N. C.

117. The first repeater always repeats the first flag, reading from the top down, of that class of flag that immediately precedes the repeater.

118. The code flag over E means that the letters that follow are spelling.

119. The code flag over G means that the spelling is completed.

120. The U. S. ships' calls begin with the N flag, the K flag or the W flag.

121. The Z flag is used to call shore stations.

122. The Coast Guard indicates to you that this is the best place to land, by a man on shore beckoning in the day time and two torches burning close together at night.

123. One black ball shown from a steamer indicates that she is taking explosives aboard.

124. The signal for a submarine in distress is a red smoke bomb.

125. Upon seeing a red smoke bomb, it should be reported to the Coast Guard without delay.

126. The NE storm warning signal is two square red flags with black square centers.

127. The day mark for a fishing vessel is a basket in the rigging displayed in the direction from the anchor ball towards nets or gear.

128. Ship's bell time strikes 8 bells at 12, 3 and 8 o'clock.

129. Storms which develop in the southwest are usually quickly followed by clearing.

130. To expect clearing weather, the wind should veer.

131. The forces of the wind are expressed by the Beaufort scale, numbers 0 to 12.

132. A spring line is used for towing in heavy weather.

133. If you suspected local attraction as the cause of your compass error, you would check this in the Coast Pilot.

134. Range is a term having to do with all of the following: (1) The alignment of navigation lights to indicate a channel, (2) Measurement of the vertical movement of tide between high and low water, (3) The white lights on a vessel's masts which indicate her course, (4) Running out all anchor cable for cleaning. (Only one T. or F. for answer required.)

135. You see a vessel sailing with the wind abeam. She is sailing full and by.

136. Because of the gravitational influence of the moon and sun, acting on the earth, every locality along the Coast has two high and two low tides every 24 hours.

137. A Lyle gun is used by the Coast Guard in life saving.

138. In heavy weather, it is preferable to find shelter under a windward shore rather than under a lee shore.

139. A sea painter is a line used on vessels when handling life boats.

140. Drift refers to the velocity of a tidal current.

141. The U. S. flag and Yacht Club burgee should be flown during daylight, that is, from dawn to dusk.

142. No penalty can be imposed for personal injury or property damage caused by operating a boat recklessly.

143. Going through a yacht anchorage at high speed or close to a boat at anchor or underway indicates that you are a good seaman. (Credit 6 points.)

(Answers below)

Answers to True-or-False Quiz

1. True	17. False	33. False	49. False	65. True	81. False	97. True	113. True	129. True
2. False	18. True	34. False	50. False	66. False	82. False	98. False	114. False	130. True
3. True	19. False	35. False	51. False	67. False	83. False	99. False	115. False	131. True
4. False	20. True	36. False	52. False	68. True	84. False	100. True	116. True	132. False
5. True	21. False	37. True	53. False	69. False	85. True	101. True	117. True	133. True
6. False	22. False	38. False	54. False	70. False	86. False	102. False	118. True	134. True
7. False	23. False	39. False	55. False	71. True	87. True	103. True	119. True	135. False
8. True	24. False	40. False	56. False	72. False	88. False	104. False	120. True	136. False
9. True	25. True	41. True	57. False	73. False	89. False	105. True	121. True	137. True
10. False	26. True	42. True	58. False	74. True	90. False	106. False	122. False	138. True
11. False	27. True	43. True	59. False	75. False	91. True	107. True	123. False	139. True
12. False	28. False	44. True	60. True	76. True	92. False	108. True	124. True	140. True
13. False	29. False	45. True	61. False	77. True	93. True	109. False	125. True	141. False
14. True	30. False	46. True	62. True	78. True	94. True	110. True	126. True	142. False
15. False	31. True	47. False	63. True	79. True	95. True	111. True	127. True	143. False
16. True	32. True	48. False	64. True	80. True	96. False	112. True	128. False	

UNITED STATES

COAST GUARD

AUXILIARY

STUDY COURSE

The U. S. Coast Guard Auxiliary has recommended the use of this book, Piloting, Seamanship and Small Boat Handling, both by individuals preparing themselves for Auxiliary membership and by Auxiliary units in organized instruction classes. Below are listed the Auxiliary recommendations.

Further information may be obtained from the local director of the Coast Guard Auxiliary.

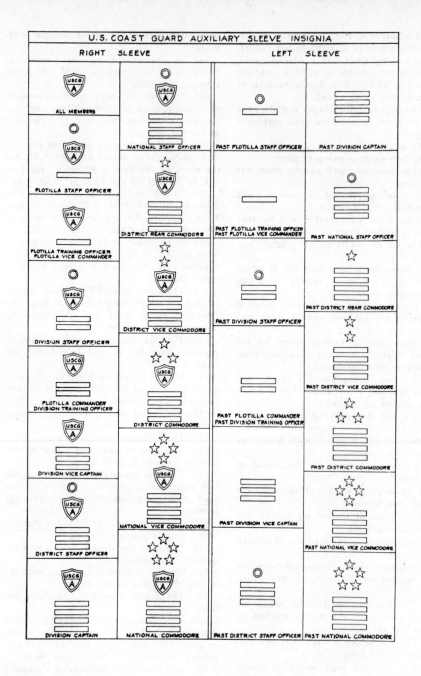

U. S. COAST GUARD AUXILIARY SLEEVE INSIGNIA

RIGHT SLEEVE — LEFT SLEEVE

ALL MEMBERS — NATIONAL STAFF OFFICER — PAST FLOTILLA STAFF OFFICER — PAST DIVISION CAPTAIN

FLOTILLA STAFF OFFICER — DISTRICT REAR COMMODORE — PAST FLOTILLA TRAINING OFFICER / PAST FLOTILLA VICE COMMANDER — PAST NATIONAL STAFF OFFICER

FLOTILLA TRAINING OFFICER / FLOTILLA VICE COMMANDER — DISTRICT VICE COMMODORE — PAST DIVISION STAFF OFFICER — PAST DISTRICT REAR COMMODORE

DIVISION STAFF OFFICER — DISTRICT COMMODORE — PAST FLOTILLA COMMANDER / PAST DIVISION TRAINING OFFICER — PAST DISTRICT VICE COMMODORE

FLOTILLA COMMANDER / DIVISION TRAINING OFFICER — NATIONAL VICE COMMODORE — PAST DIVISION VICE CAPTAIN — PAST DISTRICT COMMODORE

DIVISION VICE CAPTAIN — NATIONAL COMMODORE — PAST DISTRICT STAFF OFFICER — PAST NATIONAL VICE COMMODORE

DISTRICT STAFF OFFICER — DIVISION CAPTAIN — PAST NATIONAL COMMODORE

REQUIREMENTS OF U.S.P.S. INSTRUCTION COURSES

●

In addition to the above references in this book, there are references to Bowditch, Dutton, the Light List, HO 205, HO 206 and USC & GS Chart #1210.

SUGGESTIONS OFFERED BY THE COAST GUARD
TO PROMOTE SAFETY AT SEA

A RECENT issue of the Federal Register (Vol. 25—No. 190) was devoted largely to regulations dealing with small passenger vessels. One of its subparts, concerned with "preparations for emergencies" was drafted primarily with the safety of passengers in mind. Supplementing specific instructions to cover emergency situations, the Coast Guard included condensed "recommended emergency checkoff lists" which might well be a part of the basic understanding of seamanship essential to every boatman who puts to sea.

PREPARATIONS FOR EMERGENCIES
a) Rough weather at sea or crossing bars.

1) Close all watertight and weathertight doors, hatches, and airports to prevent taking water aboard.

2) Keep bilges dry to prevent loss of stability.

3) Keep passengers seated and evenly distributed.

4) Have passengers put on life preservers if the going becomes very rough or you are about to cross a bar.

5) Never abandon a vessel (particularly a wooden boat) unless actually forced to do so.

6) If assistance is needed use the International Distress call over radiotelephone or call Coast Guard at once.

7) Prepare life floats for launching.

b) Man overboard.

1) Throw a ring buoy overboard close to the person.

2) Post a lookout to keep the person overboard in sight.

3) Maneuver the vessel to pick up the person.

4) Have crew member put on life jacket, attach a safety line to him and have him stand by to jump into the water to assist the person overboard if necessary.

5) If person is not immediately located notify Coast Guard and other vessels in vicinity by radiotelephone.

6) Continue search until released by Coast Guard.

c) Fire at sea.

1) Cut off air supply to fire; close hatches, ports, doors, ventilators, etc.

2) Immediately use portable fire extinguishers at base of flames for inflammable liquid or grease fires, or water for fires in ordinary combustible materials.

3) If fire is in machinery spaces shut off fuel supply and ventilation and discharge fixed CO_2, if installed.

4) Maneuver vessel to minimize effect of wind on fire.

5) If unable to control fire, immediately notify the Coast Guard and other boats in the vicinity by radiotelephone.

6) Move passengers away from fire, have them put on life preservers and, if necessary, prepare to abandon ship.

WHEN YOU'RE ON WATCH

IN LINE with one of its primary aims of promoting safety at sea, the U.S. Coast Guard has requested a digest of standing orders in use aboard various ships at sea. These are reprinted from time to time in the Coast Guard's *Proceedings of the Merchant Marine Council*.

Responding to the request, Moore-McCormack submitted a copy of Standing Orders originated by one of their experienced Masters. Parts of this are so directly applicable to good seamanship practice on yachts making coastal and ocean cruises or races, that we reprint extracts below, taking the liberty of making minor modifications to better adapt them to pleasure craft requirements.

The orders are given in Night Order Books prepared by the Master for the guidance of Watch Officers, by whom they must be signed each night the vessel is at sea.

Keep a good lookout: as a Watch Officer of this vessel you are expected to keep a good lookout, first, last, and all the time, and to see that those placed under you do the same. Do not stay in the Chart Room for long periods. CALL ME AT ANY TIME FOR ANY REASON: whenever you are in doubt.

Come on watch five minutes early: study the chart, the light lists, the tide tables and the Radio Aids to Navigation, the contour of the bottom, and the trend of the coast line. Memorize facts that will help you during the watch.

After being relieved remain on the bridge for a few minutes until the officer who relieved you has the feel of things, and his eyes have become accustomed to the darkness. Give him a quick synopsis of happenings during your watch.

Take an interest in navigation of the vessel, remembering that you as watch officers of today are the Masters of tomorrow, and that part of your compensation here is the valuable experience acquired. Never take it for granted that because the Master set the course it is a guarantee that the vessel cannot get into trouble during the four hours you are in charge on the bridge. KEEP ON YOUR TOES.

Thick weather, heavy rain, snow or low visibility: sound your whistle or siren, reduce speed if necessary, or stop. Reassure yourself that lookouts are at their stations.

Soundings with the depth sounder: when on soundings, take frequent soundings, noting the results in the log, also the time that you crossed depth curves shown on the chart. Watch for persistent strays.

Radio direction finder bearings: must be taken at frequent intervals whenever you are within range of beacons; enter results in the log.

Meeting or passing other vessels: give them a wide berth, and never try to bluff another vessel out of her right of way. Make a study of trade routes, because a knowledge of where the other vessel is bound will often save you long detours. Watch out for small craft and fishermen; many of them do not carry lights, and others show them only when you are upon them.

During heavy weather: close all ports and openings through which water may be shipped. Secure loose gear that may come adrift. In sailing craft, shift to heavy sheets and guys.

Keep your eyes and ears open while on watch: be alert, and should you hear a door slamming below as the ship rolls, have it secured. If it rains or a heavy dew forms, take in any gear that might be damaged if left on deck. Have ports secured, and open them again after the rain passes.

These orders shall state the 8 PM position, the courses to be steered (with compass error and leeway used); the speed to be made by engine and estimated speed over the ground; the lights or other aids to navigation it is expected to sight; the anticipated time of sighting; the expected bearing, and the characteristics of each; the proximity of land, derelicts, ice, shoals or any other known dangers; the proximity of banks over which soundings might be obtained and instructions for use of the depth sounder; instructions for use of the radio direction finder; warning as to traffic which may be met; and any other instructions necessary for safe navigation.

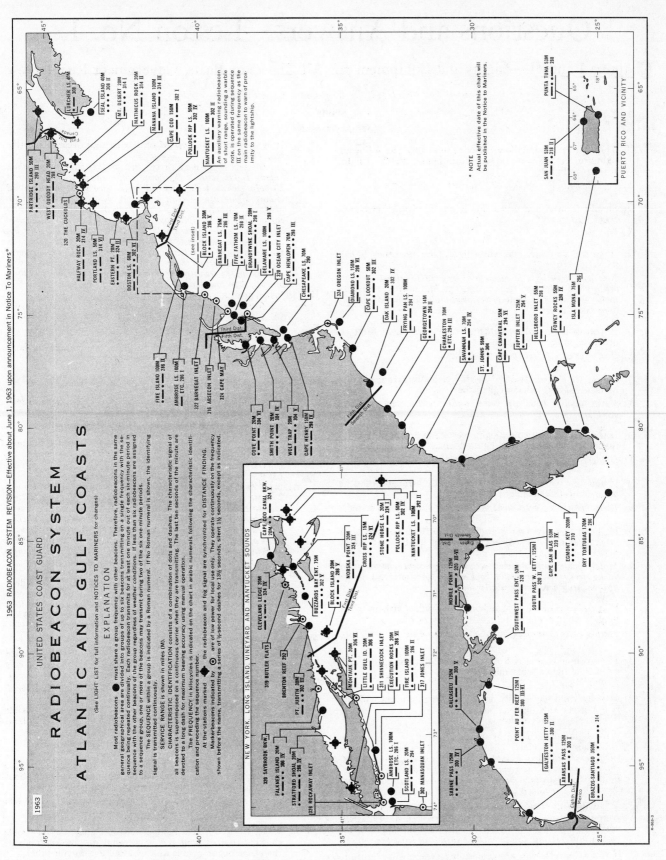

Radiobeacon charts like the one illustrated above are published in the Light Lists

Distance of Visibility at Sea

Elevation of Eye (Feet)	0.8	3	7	12	19	27	49	76
Horizon Distance (Nautical Miles)	1	2	3	4	5	6	8	10

Questions and Answers—Lesson No. 1

Chapters I and II—Lights and Equipment for All Classes of Boats, Government Regulations

(Lesson No. 100, U. S. P. S. Piloting Course Reference Sheet)

Lights

(See pages 28-46)

1. Q: Through or around how many points may the following lights on vessels show? (a) White light. (b) Red light. (c) Green light.
   A: *(a) 12, 20, 32. (b) 10, 32. (c) 10.*

2. Q: Should the red and green side lights be visible across the bow? Are they?
   A: *No; yes.*

3. Q: If at sea you saw one white light (and no other light), what might it be?
   A: *Range or stern light of motor boat any class, inland steamer, ocean-going steamer, ocean-going yacht, sailing vessel or motor boat under sail and power, boat under 150 feet at anchor; open boat lantern.*

4. Q: If you saw two white lights vertically arranged (and no other light), what might it be?
   A: *Boat of over 150 feet in length at anchor.*

5. Q: If you should see two red lights vertically arranged (and no other lights), what might it be?
   A: *Vessel totally disabled; vessel under partial control being overtaken.*

6. Q: If you should see two red lights vertically arranged in addition to one or more white lights near by, what might it be?
   A: *Dredge; vessel made fast to or moored over a wreck.*

7. Q: If you saw two white lights horizontally arranged (and no other light), what might it be?
   A: *Ferry boat being overtaken; ocean-going barges being towed.*

8. Q: If at sea you saw two white lights (vertical, horizontal or otherwise) and one red and one green light, what might it be?
   A: *Motor boat, inland steamer, ocean-going steamer, ocean-going yacht, ferry boat or motor boat under both sail and power approaching head on or nearly so.*

9. Q: If at sea you saw one red and one green light (without white lights), what might it be?
   A: *Sailing vessel approaching head on or nearly so.*

10. Q: If you should see a red over a white light, but no red and green side lights, what might it be?
    A: *Fishing vessel.*

11. Q: If you should see a white light over a red light but with no red or green side lights, what might it be?
    A. *Pilot vessel on her station at anchor.*

12. Q. What lights are carried by motor vessels?
    (a) Classes A and 1. (b) Class 2. (c) Class 3.
    A. *(a) Classes and 1 combination bow light and 32-point stern showing through the required arc. (b) Class 2 white bow light, port and starboard lights and stern lights showing through the required arc. (c) Class 3 same as Class 2.*

13. Q: What does the law say about the visibility of lights?
    A: *Side lights (Class 2 and Class 3) must be screened so they will not shine across the bow. Colored lights must be visible at least 1 mile. White lights must be visible at least two miles.*

14. Q. If you are overtaking an ocean-going vessel, what light or lights do you see?
    A: *12-point taffrail light.*

15. Q: Do vessels under sail only show any white lights?
    A: *Yes. Under regulations effective August 14, 1958, vessels not otherwise required to show a light visible from aft, must carry a fixed white 12-pt. stern light (excepting only small boats in bad weather, which may show an electric torch or lighted lantern to overtaking vessels.)*

16. Q: How do the lights on ocean and inland steamers differ?
    A: *After range light on ocean-going steamer shows 20 points. After range light on inland steamer shows through 32 points. On the high seas, a 12-point white stern light is now mandatory.*

17. Q: How do the lights carried on harbor and ocean-going tow boats differ?
    A: *Harbor tow boats may carry (two or three) 20-point white towing lights with a 32-point white range light aft, or a 20-point white light forward with (two or three) 32-point towing lights aft. Ocean-going tow boats must carry (two or three) 20-point towing lights forward. A 20-point white range light aft is optional. All carry red and green side lights and may show a small light aft for the tow to steer by. Two lights on the inland tow boat indicate tow is alongside; on the ocean-going boat, two lights mean one vessel in tow astern. Three white lights on the inland tow boat mean tow is on hawser astern; on the ocean-going boat, three lights indicate more than one vessel in tow, length of tow exceeding 600 feet.*

18. Q: When are the side lights carried on
    (a) Motor boats. (b) Pilot vessels. (c) Ferry boats. (d) Disabled boats. (e) Ocean steamers. (f) Fishing vessels. (g) Cable vessels.
    A: *When underway.*

19. Q: How should the aft range light (32 point) on a motor boat always be placed relative to the bow light?
    A: *Higher than bow light.*

20. Q: Should a tug boat when towing carry a single 20-point bow light?
    A: *Yes. If, under Inland Rules, she is carrying 32-point towing lights aft. This makes a central range.*

21. Q: What lights do the following vessels being towed carry?
    (a) Ocean barges towed tandem.
    (b) Barges and canal boats on Hudson River towed tandem, with intermediate hawser.
    (c) Barges and canal boats on Hudson River towed in tiers.
    (d) Car floats.
    A: *(a) Side lights and the last barge in the string will show 2 white lights horizontally arranged; 12-point steering light is also carried. (b) Show a white light bow and stern and 2 horizontal white lights at stern of last barge. (c) A white light at the bow of each outside boat in the first tier and at the stern of every barge. (d) Car floats show a white light at the outboard corners of the outboard barge. In case of a single barge, lights are carried on the side away from the tug.*

22. Q: When may an inland tug carry
    (a) One 32-point light? (b) Two 32-point lights? (c) Three 32-point lights?
    A: *(a) When she has no tow, or when she carries 20-point towing lights forward. (b) When tow is alongside. (c) When tow is on hawser astern.*

Note: In questions 23–33, assume your boat to be a motor vessel.

23. Q: When a red side light on a vessel is visible showing toward your red light, what do you know about the other boat's course and what action do you take?
    A: *Perfect safety; go ahead. Both boats hold course and speed.*

24. Q: When the red side light of a vessel underway is visible showing toward your green light, what do you know about the other boat's course and what action do you take?
    A: *Other boat has right of way; you should give way.*

25. Q: When the green side light of a vessel underway is visible showing toward your green light, what do you know about the other boat's course and what action do you take?
    A: *Perfect safety; go ahead. Both boats should hold course and speed.*

26. Q: When the green side light of a vessel underway is visible showing toward your red light, what do you know about the other boat's course and what action do you take?
    A: *You have right of way; other boat must keep clear.*

27. Q: When both red and green side lights are visible, what is your action?
    A: *Boats approaching head on or nearly so. Your action should be guided by position of range lights. Give way to the right if possible.*

28. Q: When a side light is visible on your starboard bow and the upper (range) white light is to the right of the lower white light, what does it indicate to you and what is your action?
    A: *The other boat's course is approaching your course, danger of collision exists, other boat has right of way and should hold course and speed; you should keep clear.*

29. Q: When a side light is visible on your port side and the upper white (range) light is to the right of the lower white light, what does it indicate and what is your action?
A: *Other boat has or will clear your course; hold your course and speed.*

30. Q: When a side light is visible on your port bow and the upper (range) white light is to the left of the lower white light, what does it indicate and what is your action?
A: *The other boat's course is approaching your course, danger of collision exists, your boat has right of way and should hold course and speed; other boat must keep clear.*

31. Q: When a side light is visible on your starboard bow and the upper (range) white light is to the left of the lower white light, what does it indicate and what is your action?
A: *Other boat has or will clear your course; hold your course and speed.*

32. Q: When both green and red lights are visible ahead and the two white lights are becoming nearer and nearer vertical, what does it signify and what is your action?
A: *Other boat's course is approaching yours; danger of collision is becoming more acute; navigate with caution.*

33. Q: When both green and red lights are visible ahead and the two white lights are separating more and more from the vertical, what does it signify and what is your action?
A: *Other boat's course is diverging from yours; danger of collision is becoming less acute.*

34. Q: What lights are carried by a row boat?
A: *A white light kept ready at hand to show when necessary.*

35. Q: Between what hours are lights carried?
A: *From sunset to sunrise.*

Equipment and Government Regulations
(*See pages 11-27*)

1. Q: What motor boats fall in Class A?
A: *Under 16 feet.*

2. Q: What motor boats fall in Class 1?
A: *16 to 26 feet.*

3. Q: What motor boats fall in Class 2?
A: *26 to 40 feet.*

4. Q: What motor boats fall in Class 3?
A: *40 to 65 feet.*

5. Q: What Government equipment is to be carried on Class A?
A: *Combination red-and-green lantern, fire extinguisher capable of extinguishing gasoline fire, one life preserver for each person on board, certificate of award of number. At anchor, white light visible at least 1 mile.*

6. Q: Does Class 1 equipment differ from Class A?
A: *Yes. In addition to that mentioned for Class A, Class 1 boats must carry an efficient whistle.*

7. Q: What equipment is required by law for Classes 2 and 3?
A: *Separate white bow light, red port side light, green starboard side light (side lights screened), white stern light, sufficient fire extinguishers, life preservers for each person aboard, efficient whistle, efficient bell, and certificate of award of number.*

8. Q: What additional or different equipment must be carried on motor boats of not more than 65 feet in length carrying passengers for hire?
A: *Regulation life preservers approved by the Coast Guard. (Cushions and life rings not suitable.) Also an additional 10% suitable for children.*

9. Q: To whom does one desiring to obtain a license to operate a boat carrying passengers for hire make application?
A: *The U. S. Coast Guard.*

10. Q: What credentials, letters or statement of qualifications must the applicant (Question No. 9) present?
A: *Letters from reputable citizens advising of acquaintance with the necessary reputation of applicant. Also documentary evidence of at least one year's experience in operating motorboats.*

11. Q: Is an examination required to obtain a license to operate a motor boat carrying passengers for hire?
A: *Yes. An oral one.*

12. Q: Will an ordinary mouth whistle pass Government inspection as the whistle required on a motor boat?
A: *On Class 1 only.*

13. Q: Will the various forms of electric horns pass Government requirements for the whistle specified for motor boats?
A: *Yes, if they are "efficient."*

14. Q: Will a buoyant cushion pass as a life preserver on motor boats not carrying passengers for hire?
A: *Only on boats up to 40 feet.*

15. Q: Will a buoyant cushion pass as a life preserver on boats carrying passengers for hire?
A: *No.*

16. Q: What may be substituted for life preservers, buoyant cushions, buoyant vests, etc., on motor boats not carrying passengers for hire?
A: *Ring buoys.*

17. Q: Does a dinghy pass as life-saving equipment?
A: *No.*

18. Q: Will fog horns pass Government requirements for the whistle specified for motor boats?
A: *No.*

19. Q: Are motor boats over 15 tons, carrying passengers for hire, subject to inspection?
A: *Yes.*

20. Q: Are motor boats under 15 tons, carrying passengers for hire, subject to inspection?
A: *Yes, if they carry more than six passengers.*

21. Q: What Government officials have charge of the inspection of those motor boats carrying passengers for hire which are subject to inspection?
A: *The U. S. Coast Guard.*

22. Q: Are motor boats or motor yachts of any size, not carrying passengers for hire, subject to inspection?
A: *Only those of more than 300 gross tons.*

23. Q: Motor boats of what size (not carrying passengers for hire) may be documented?
A: *5 net tons and over.*

24. Q: Is a motor boat on shore required to have Government equipment on board?
A: *No.*

25. Q: Must a motor boat have been seen underway or known to have been underway by an inspector before he can board that boat for the purpose of inspecting the equipment?
A: *Yes.*

26. Q: What flags must be flown by a boat authorized to make the Government inspection for equipment?
A: *U. S. Coast Guard.*

27. Q: Does the Government require that the owner or operator of a motor boat of any size, not carrying passengers for hire, know anything about his boat, its operation, navigation, etc.
A: *No.*

28. Q: Does the Government require any of the following equipment to be carried on board: an anchor, a compass, an anchor line, a pump, a dinghy and provisions?
A. *No.*

29. Q: From whom may copies of the Pilot Rules be obtained?
A: *Offices of the U. S. Coast Guard or any of the agencies handling Government publications.*

30. Q: Are licensed officers required on yachts or pleasure motor boats (not carrying passengers for hire) of any size?
A: *Only on seagoing motor vessels of 300 gross tons and over.*

31. Q: What boats must be numbered?
A: *All undocumented boats (see question on "exceptions" below) equipped with propellent machinery of 10 horsepower or more, in states where Coast Guard administers numbering program; where states are doing the numbering, boatmen must consult particular state's regulations to find what boats must be numbered.*

32. Q: What boats are not required to be numbered?
A: *The Federal Boating Act of 1958 provides exceptions from its numbering provisions for the following craft: Foreign vessels temporarily using the navigable waters of the U.S., its territories, etc.; public vessels of the U.S.; state and municipal vessels; ships' lifeboats; certain vessels specifically designated by the Secretary of the Treasury as being exempt; undocumented vessels used exclusively for racing; and undocumented vessels operating under valid temporary certificates of number.*

33. Q: Who gives the examination for licensed officers required to be carried on documented boats other than yachts and pleasure motor boats?
A: *Officer in Charge, Marine Inspection, U. S. Coast Guard.*

34. Q: Do licensing and safety regulations apply to motor boats operated on navigable waters by summer camps, schools, individuals or organizations for recreation and instruction?
A: *Yes. If expense of their operation is defrayed by charges, assessments or tuitions, they are construed to be carrying passengers for hire, and must be licensed by the Coast Guard. They must carry approved life preservers and fire extinguishers and otherwise comply with the Motorboat Act.*

Documenting

1. Q: What is a documented vessel?

A: *A documented vessel is one which has been issued a register, enrollment and license, or license under the laws of the United States. Such a vessel is also properly referred to as a "vessel of the United States."*

2. Q: Where are documents issued?

A: *Documents are issued by the collector or deputy collector of customs at any one of the approximately 124 ports of documentation located in the United States and in certain territories, districts, and possessions thereof.*

3. Q: Are documented vessels subject to the requirements for numbering as motorboats?

A: *No. A vessel which is documented is not required to be numbered and in fact may not be numbered.*

4. Q: What size vessel may be documented?

A: *Any American-built vessel of 5 net tons or over owned by a citizen may be documented upon compliance with the applicable requirements. Foreign-built vessels of similar size and ownership may be documented for foreign trade or as yachts upon compliance with special requirements and with the approval of the Commissioner of Customs.*

5. Q: What are the principal privileges extended to documented vessels which are not extended to others?

A: *Such vessels may (1) fly the yacht ensign; (2) proceed to a foreign port without clearing; (3) if of 15 gross tons or less, return from a foreign voyage without entering; (4) have bills of sale, mortgages, and certain other title instruments recorded and be the subject of a preferred mortgage.*

6. Q: Is the documentation of any vessel as a yacht required?

A: *The documentation of vessels as yachts is not mandatory but discretionary with the owner. However, if the vessel is not documented it may be required to be numbered as a motorboat.*

7. Q: Is there a charge for documentation?

A: *There is no charge for documentation but nominal fees are charged for recording instruments of title and, if the vessel is outside a port of entry or a customs station at the time of measurement, certain charges are made to cover cost.*

8. Q: May a documented yacht be used in the transportation of passengers or freight?

A: *No. A vessel documented as a yacht may be used only for pleasure purposes. Severe penalties may be incurred if used otherwise. It is immaterial whether the transportation is or is not for hire.*

9. Q: If the owner of a documented yacht takes friends and acquaintances on a cruise, is that a transportation of passengers?

A: *No. A cruise in a documented yacht with friends and acquaintances, for pleasure purposes and without charge, is not a transportation of passengers.*

10. Q: What is the hailing port of a vessel?

A: *The hailing port may be either the port where the vessel is permanently documented (that is, the home port) or the place in the same customs collection district where the vessel was built or where one or more of the owners reside.*

11. Q: What are the requirements for showing the name and the hailing port on a yacht?

A: *The name and hailing port of a yacht are required to be marked upon some conspicuous part of the hull. (It has been ruled that to paint the name and port on a board which is screwed or attached to the transom or other part of the hull does not fulfill the requirements of the law. It has also been held that the marking of a name and hailing or home port on the hull of a vessel by the use of individual roman letters of suitable size and color which have been cut, carved, or stamped from aluminum or other metal or from masonite, plywood, plastic, or other similar material firmly secured in place by means of screws or nails is an acceptable form of marking under the law. A decalcomania transfer properly applied and covered over with four or five coats of clear varnish is also regarded as suitable. However, the use of cut or carved letters joined in one continuous piece, the use of individual letters not firmly secured in place, or the use of decalcomania transfers not applied in such a manner as to be as secure against wear and weather as painted names is not acceptable in compliance with the requirements.)*

12: Q: Are the requirements in this regard the same for commercial vessels?

A: *No. The name of every documented vessel, other than a yacht, is required to be marked upon each bow and upon the stern, and the hailing port is also required to be marked upon the stern. Documented steam vessels must also have the name on each side of the pilot house and, if the vessel has side wheels, on the outer side of each wheel house.*

13. Q: What pleasure vessels are required to report their arrival from a foreign port?

A: *Every pleasure vessel arriving in the United States from a foreign port or place must come into a port of entry and within 24 hours thereafter the master must report to the customhouse at that port. In addition, every foreign pleasure vessel must report to the customs house upon its arrival at every port or place in the United States from another such port or place. No person, other than the one reporting the vessel's arrival, should leave the vessel and no person should remove any baggage or merchandise, except upon instructions from the customs officer receiving the report.*

14. Q: What American pleasure vessels are exempted from entry and clearance?

A: *Licensed American yachts and undocumented American pleasure vessels, regardless of tonnage, which are not engaged in trade, have not violated any customs or navigation laws, and have not visited a hovering vessel.*

15. Q: Is regular tonnage tax assessed against a pleasure vessel?

A: *No. Regular tonnage tax is charged only against a vessel which is engaged in trade.*

16. Q: What vessels must pay special tonnage tax and light money upon entry?

A: *All undocumented vessels of 5 net tons and over which are engaged in trade must pay special tonnage tax and light money upon entry from a foreign port or place. However, an exemption from such tax is afforded to any vessel which is documented as a vessel of the United States prior to its departure from the port of first arrival.*

Notice of Arrival on Coastwise Cruises

There is a little-known law on the statute books (C.F.R. Title 33, Chapter I, Part 124, Section 124.10) which requires foreign vessels and documented vessels of the United States (not numbered boats) navigating the "high seas" on coastwise cruises to give 24 hours' notice of their time of arrival to the Captain of the Port at their next intended port of call.

Bodies of water like Long Island Sound and Chesapeake Bay are excluded from the act's definition of "high seas" but waters of the open sea below the low-water mark (as, for example, offshore along the Jersey beach) are included.

This is basically a safety and security measure to control entrance of commercial vessels into U.S. ports. For a time, the law was invoked occasionally against documented yachts, but now they are specifically exempted (Fed. Reg. Document 60-7063, July 29, 1960) in an amendment which exempts, among several types of vessels, "United States yachts, arriving at a United States port or place from a port or place outside the United States, or destined from one port or place in the United States to another port or place in the United States."

NOTE: The regulations discussed on pages 20 and 474 dealing with documentation are basic and are based on maritime statutes. However, it has been found that interpretations differ in the various districts. As so often happens, local administration conforms to local conditions, e.g., the port limits of Port "A" may not only include City "A" but also Cities "B" and "C" while Port "L" harbor limits may follow strictly the city limits of City "L." In the first case Government boarding officers may be called to perform duties 20 or 30 miles from their station and yet within the port limits whereas in the 2d case a short travel distance may be outside the Port Limits. Again, admeasurement services may be available at all times in one port while at another nearby port the admeasurer is a travelling admeasurer and service would be at very irregular intervals. Different conditions exist at Border ports and Seaboard ports.

Questions and Answers—Lesson No. 2

Chapter III—Rules of the Road, Right of Way, Whistle Signals

(Lesson No. 101, U. S. P. S. Piloting Course Reference Sheet)

See pages 47-60

1. Q: What are the objects of the rules of the road?
   A: *To prevent collisions at sea or on the water.*
2. Q: When do the rules of the road apply?
   A: *To all types of vessels when underway.*
3. Q: When is a boat underway?
   A: *When she is not at anchor, aground or made fast to the shore.*
4. Q: Is a boat adrift subject to the rules?
   A: *Yes.*
5. Q: Is a boat not under control subject to the rules?
   A: *Yes.*
6. Q: To what type of boats or vessels do the rules apply?
   A: *To all types, to all forms of floating craft.*
7. Q: If there is doubt as to whether the rules apply in any particular case, should you consider that they do?
   A: *Yes.*
8. Q: What is the boat called which has the right of way?
   A: *Privileged vessel.*
9. Q: What is the boat called which does not have the right of way?
   A: *Burdened vessel.*
10. Q: What is the duty of the right-of-way boat?
    A: *Hold her course and speed.*
11. Q: What is the duty of the burdened vessel?
    A: *Adopt every known means to keep out of the way of the privileged vessel.*
12. Q: (a) Is a departure from the rules ever allowed?
    (b) When? (Give an example in your own words.)
    A: (a) *Yes.*
    (b) *In bad weather or any condition leading to a collision. When the burdened vessel alone cannot prevent a collision, the privileged vessel should change her course.*
13. Q: Is there any special burden placed upon motor boats when there is danger of collision with a large commercial boat? Explain.
    A: *Yes, as they are small and readily maneuvered.*
14. Q: What is your idea about the proper speed of motor boats?
    A: *Reasonable speed with reference to the place and time. She should be able to readily change course from headway to sternway.*
15. Q: What are the rights of fishing vessels?
    A: *All boats when underway must keep out of the way of fishing vessels and must not disturb them with their wash. They, however, cannot fish in channels or fairways.*
16. Q: When should whistle signals be given?
    A: *When danger of collision exists.*
17. Q: When should whistle signals not be given?
    A: *Never give them in fog, heavy snow or rain and not to sailing vessels.*
18. Q: What should passing signals be given on?
    A: *Whistle.*
19. Q: Must a whistle signal be answered?
    A: *Yes.*
20. Q: When is a signal of one blast given?
    A: *When you intend to pass the other vessel on your own port side—1 blast in answer to 1 blast.*
21. Q: When is a signal of two blasts given?
    A: *When you intend to pass the other vessel on your own starboard side—2 blasts in answer to 2 blasts.*
22. Q: When is a signal of three blasts given?
    A: *Three blasts when you are backing.*
23. Q: When is a signal of four blasts given?
    A: *Four blasts means danger.*
24. Q: What do you do if you do not understand a whistle signal?
    A: *Stop, reverse, blow 4 blasts and do not proceed, until signals are understood.*
25. Q: What is a cross signal?
    A: *One blast answered with two or two blasts with one.*

26. Q: What do you do if a cross signal is given?
    A: *Give danger signal, stop and straighten out signals.*
27. Q: Are a vessel's rights altered by whistle signals?
    A: *No.*
28. Q: (a) If a boat gives you a signal which is in violation of your rights, what do you do?
    (b) What should the other boat do?
    A: (a) *Give danger signal and stop, or answer her signal and give her permission to proceed.*
    (b) *If you have given permission she can proceed—otherwise, if you have given danger signal, she must stop, and signals must be given and understood.*
29. Q: What whistle signals and action are proper for boats?
    (a) Meeting head on?
    (b) Crossing obliquely?
    (c) Courses in opposite direction but parallel?
    (d) Courses in same direction but parallel?
    (e) Overtaking?
    (f) Both crossing and overtaking?
    (g) Boats backing?
    (h) Boats coming out of slip?
    (i) Boats meeting in winding channel?
    (j) Motor boat meeting sail boat?
    A: (a) *One blast—port side to port side.*
    (b) *One blast—privileged boat to hold her course and speed and burdened boat slow down and pass astern.*
    (c) *Courses parallel and boats far enough to starboard of each other to pass clear. Two blasts answered by two blasts. Both boats hold course and speed.*
    (d) *Keep out of way unless one boat desires to cross other's course, then give proper signals.*
    (e) *Overtaking vessel is burdened vessel and she must ask permission—one blast to starboard and two to port.*
    (f) *Same as (e).*
    (g) *Three blasts—and then signals are same as going ahead—stern considered bow for the time being.*
    (h) *One long blast.*
    (i) *One long blast and boat going upstream should stop and wait for other boat to pass.*
    (j) *No signals—motor boat must keep clear.*
30. Q: What special precaution is to be taken when a boat is operated by both sail and power at the same time?
    (a) In the day time?   (b) At night?
    A: (a) *Same status as motor boat and should give signals accordingly. Must not take any action that might confuse an approaching boat.*
    (b) *At night, the status of a motor boat with respect to rights, whistle signals, etc., even though she carries only the colored side lights of a sailing vessel.*
31. Q: What are the rights and duties of tow boats with a tow?
    A: *Boats with tow considered one boat and rules apply to it—however, being very awkward to handle motor boats should keep out of the way and not insist on right of way.*
32. Q: What is one's duty in case of collision?
    A: *Stand by and give every assistance without endangering boat and crew and if involved in collision, give name, port and so forth. If accident is of serious nature, report to the U. S. Coast Guard.*
33. Q: Should whistle signals be given when there is no danger of collision?   A: *No.*
34. Q: What is the danger zone—where is it—what should a boat do that is in your danger zone?
    A: *Danger zone is your starboard bow from dead ahead to two points aft your starboard beam. She should hold her course and speed.*
35. Q: Do war vessels have any special rights?
    A: *War vessels, strictly speaking, have no special rights; however, motor boats should not attempt to force their right of way on them.*

The questions and answers given in this chapter are an important part of the subject matter of this book. The reader will find them useful in checking his knowledge of the various phases of piloting.

Questions and Answers—Lesson No. 3

Chapters V, VI, VII and VIII—Seamanship, Boat Handling, Anchoring, Nautical Terms, Rigs of Sailing Vessels

(Lesson No. 102, U. S. P. S. Piloting Course Reference Sheet)

See pages 79-176

1. Q: Which is the weather side of the boat?
   A: *The side toward the wind.*
2. Q: Which is the leeward side of the boat?
   A: *The sheltered or opposite side of the boat toward which the wind blows.*
3. Q: What is meant by off the wind?
   A: *Sailing with the wind abaft the beam.*
4. Q: What is meant by down the wind?
   A: *Sailing with the wind coming over the taffrail.*
5. Q: What is meant by windward?
   A: *The direction from which the wind is coming.*
6. Q: What is a beam wind?
   A: *One which is blowing from the side or at right angles to the ship's keel.*
7. Q: If the rudder is put to port, which way does the stern swing?
   A: *To the right, or starboard.*
8. Q: If the rudder is put to starboard, which way does the stern swing?
   A: *To the left, or port.*
9. Q: As a general rule, which way does the bow tend to swing due to the action of the propeller?
   A: *Right-hand wheel swings the bow to port, left-hand wheel to starboard.*
10. Q: In making a landing, as a general rule, is it preferable to run the port or starboard side of the boat alongside of the float when winds, currents, etc., are not a factor?
    A: *The port side.*
11. Q: Are the terms port helm and starboard helm correct according to current usage?
    A: *No. Say right rudder and left rudder.*
12. Q: In turning around in narrow quarters, or in restricted quarters, is it better to turn to port or to starboard?
    A: *To port with a right-hand wheel. However, if necessary to back, plan to back to port.*
13. Q: In backing, does the bow tend to swing toward the port or starboard?
    A: *To starboard.*
14. Q: When it is necessary to back in restricted quarters, is it better to plan to back so that the bow will swing to port or to starboard?
    A: *To starboard.*

    In the questions numbered 15 to 22, which follow, the assumption is that the offshore side of the float bears north-south. The other two sides bear east-west. while the inshore side or westerly edge is inaccessible.

15. Q: A raised deck cruiser is made fast to a float and is heading due north, the wind is blowing from the north, turning quarters are limited, but the course which the boat is to take is due south. Describe the best method to get away from the float and get on one's course.
    A: *Cast off the bow line and hold fast on the stern. Reverse slightly and allow the bow to swing to starboard. The wind will then act on the port bow and side, causing the boat to swing about. When nearly completely about cast off stern line and proceed in the desired direction.*
16. Q: A raised deck cruiser is made fast to a float and is heading due north, the wind is blowing from the northeast, turning quarters are limited, but the course which the boat is to take is due south. Describe the best method to get away from the float and get on one's course.
    A: *Cast off bow line and hold fast on the stern, as before, allowing a greater length of line which should be fastened to the southerly end of the wharf. Reverse, and as the boat backs the stern line will check its way and permit the bow to swing to starboard, the stern entering the space to the south of the wharf and the boat swinging so that the bow will shortly take the wind on the port side. When the hull has swung sufficiently, come ahead with right rudder and assume the southerly course desired.*
17. Q: A raised deck cruiser is made fast to a float and is heading due north, the wind is blowing from the east, turning quarters are limited, but the course which the boat is to take is due south. Describe the best method to get away from the float and get on one's course.
    A: *The procedure in this case will be in general similar to the answer given in question 16. It will be necessary to secure the stern line on the port side aft of midships. Back up slowly with left rudder and see that the hull clears the southeast corner of the wharf. Hold the line until the boat heads east and then come ahead, as before, and assume the southerly course desired.*

18. Q: A raised deck cruiser is made fast to a float and is heading due north, the wind is blowing from the southeast, turning quarters are limited, but the course which the boat is to take is due south. Describe the best method to get away from the float and get on one's course.
    A: *Cast off the stern line and hold a bow line. With left rudder, come ahead slowly and allow the stern to swing to starboard. As the hull swings, the wind will blow stronger on the port side and help the boat around. When it heads about southwest, reverse and cast off the bow line. When clear of the wharf come ahead and assume the desired course.*
19. Q: A raised deck cruiser is made fast to a float and is heading due north, the wind is blowing from the south, turning quarters are limited, but the course which the boat is to take is due south. Describe the best method to get away from the float and get on one's course.
    A: *The procedure in this case will be in general similar to the answer given in question 18. Hold the bow line and come ahead slowly with left rudder. The hull will swing out, since the wind is south. As the boat begins to head southwest, cast off the bow line, reverse and come ahead on the desired course when clear.*
20. Q: A raised deck cruiser is made fast to a float and is heading due north, the wind is blowing from the southwest, turning quarters are limited, but the course which the boat is to take is due south. Describe the best method to get away from the float and get on one's course.
    A: *In this case it will be merely necessary to cast off the stern line and allow the wind to do the work of turning the hull. When the boat is heading directly into the southwest wind, the bow line can be cast off and by coming ahead slowly with left rudder the boat will swing to the south and assume the desired course.*
21. Q: A raised deck cruiser is made fast to a float and is heading due north, the wind is blowing from the west, turning quarters are limited, but the course which the boat is to take is due south. Describe the best method to get away from the float and get on one's course.
    A: *Cast off the stern line and hold the bow line, which can be fastened further aft than the bow bitts, if possible. Permit the wind to swing the hull until it heads west or south of west. Cast off this line, reverse slightly, and when clear come ahead with left rudder.*
22. Q: A raised deck cruiser is made fast to a float and is heading due north, the wind is blowing from the northwest, turning quarters are limited, but the course which the boat is to take is due south. Describe the best method to get away from the float and get on one's course.
    A: *Cast off the bow line and hold fast with a line outside of the hull, on the starboard side, under the stern. The wind will swing the bow and the hull will head southeast. When almost on a southeasterly course, come ahead and straighten out as desired.*
23. Q: It is desired to land at a float having three sides free to land against. The east side is the offshore side and bears north-south and the other two sides bear east-west. Assuming that there is plenty of room to maneuver, describe how you would land at this float, on which side of the float and with which side of the boat when coming from the south with the wind blowing from the north. (No current.)
    A: *Approach the east face on northerly course and when sufficiently close to secure a bow line, do so and make it fast. A stern line can then be made fast and the stern hauled in to the required distance from the float.*
24. Q: In question 23, describe landing with the wind from the northeast.
    A: *Approach with the intention of landing the port side of of the boat to the east side of the float. Allow sufficient clearance, check the headway, and as the wind will drive the boat toward the float, secure the bow and stern lines when sufficiently close.*
25. Q: In question 23, describe landing with the wind from the east.
    A: *There is a choice of landing against the northerly or southerly faces of the float as desired, against the wind. It will be necessary to swing completely around so as to head into the wind on the desired side and run in on an easterly course parallel to the edge of the float. Check the speed and when abreast of the required position*

secure bow and stern lines, making the bow line fast first.

26. Q: In question 23, describe landing with the wind from the southeast.

A: *In this case it is possible to approach the float by circling about so as to approach on a southerly or an easterly course, with the intention of landing the starboard side on the easterly, or the port side on the southerly faces. When sufficiently close to the float, check the headway and permit the wind to drive the boat against the float and secure bow and stern lines.*

27. Q: In question 23, describe landing with the wind from the south.

A: *It will be necessary to proceed past the float and reverse the course of the boat so as to approach the float on a southerly course. Land with the starboard side against the easterly face of the float and in this case it will be merely necessary to check the headway when abreast of the desired position and secure bow and stern lines, making the bow line fast first.*

28. Q: In question 23, describe landing with the wind from the southwest.

A: *In this case it is best to head in on a westerly course parallel to the edge of this float. Check the headway and permit the wind to force the hull sideways to the float, when lines can be secured at the bow and stern.*

29. Q: In question 23, describe landing with the wind from the west.

A: *There is a choice of landing with the starboard side against the southerly face of the float, or with port side against the northerly face. Approach on a westerly course parallel to the selected face of the float and run abreast of the desired position. Check the headway and secure the boat, making the bow line fast first.*

30. Q: In question 23, describe landing with the wind from the northwest.

A: *Approach the float on a northwesterly course. Land with the port side of the boat against the northerly face of the float and run abreast of the desired position. Check the headway and secure the boat, making the bow line fast first.*

31. Q: In question 23, assuming that there is no wind, but that the current is flowing from the north, describe how you would land when coming up from the south.

A: *Approach the wharf on a northerly course parallel to the east face of the float. Check the headway of the boat with the bow into the current. Secure a bow line and then the stern line.*

32. Q: In question 23, assuming that there is no wind, but that the current is flowing from the south, describe how you would land when coming up from the south.

A: *It will first be necessary to proceed past the float and approach it on a southerly course against the current. The landing will then be made exactly the same as described for question 31.*

33. Q: Assuming you desire to pick up a mooring on the Hudson River with the tide flowing ebb and your boat coming down the river, describe how you would do it.

A: *Circle completely about in the stream so that the boat will be heading against the ebb current. Approach the mooring buoy against the current and slow down with the boat heading directly into the stream. Do not permit the bow to swing out of the line of the current. When sufficiently close to the buoy pick it up at the bow or, if single-handed, approach it so that it comes directly alongside of the steering position. With the headway checked, the lines can be picked up and as the boat begins to drift with the current the line can be secured at the bow.*

34. Q: If you should desire to come to anchor in a southerly wind, which way should your boat be heading before throwing over your anchor (assuming no current)?

A: *Heading south into the wind.*

35. Q: If your anchor became fast in rocks or other obstruction on the bottom so that you could not readily haul it on board, what action would you take?

A: *The general method would be to pay out a long length of cable and then circle about the anchor on the end of this cable. This will probably break it loose in some other direction. Another option would be to haul in tight on the anchor cable with a winch, and then try to break it out by main force. This may result in a broken or bent anchor or a parted cable. Another option would be to buoy the cable and pass another line in a loop around it. Maneuver the loop down the cable so that it engages the flukes of the anchor and then endeavor to raise it, flukes first.*

36. Q: If you ran aground what means would you take to get off bottom?

A: *The answer to this question will vary according to the nature of the bottom on which the boat finds itself. If in tidal waters and on a rocky bottom, it might be best to wait for the tide to raise the boat clear, rather than to drag it over the rocks to deeper water. If in ordinary sand or mud bottom, the best practice would be to get an anchor out over the stern on a very long cable as promptly as possible. Haul in tight on this cable, with a winch if possible, and reverse the engine, bringing all live weights in the boat to the stern, assuming that the grounding occurs on the forward portion of the hull. If possible secure the assistance of another boat to help drag the unfortunate one into deeper water. If these methods fail, there is no choice but to wait for the rising tide to do the work.*

37. Q: With a tide having an average range of 12 feet and the chart showing a depth of 6 fathoms at mean low water, which on the particular day in question occurs at noon, how deep would you expect the water to be at 1 P.M.?

A: *Six fathoms and one foot, or 37 feet.*

Rigs of Sailing Vessels

(See pages 83-84)

1. Q: Describe the rig of a cat boat.
   A: *One mast and one sail.*
2. Q: Describe the rig of a yawl.
   A: *Mainmast forward, short mizzen mast aft of the after waterline, fore and aft rigged.*
3. Q: Describe the rig of a sloop.
   A: *Single mast, headsail, mainsail and sometimes topsail, fore and aft rigged.*
4. Q: Describe the rig of a ketch.
   A: *Mainmast forward, mizzen stepped forward of after water-line. Fore and aft rigged.*
5. Q: Describe the rig of a brig.
   A: *Two masts, square sails on both masts.*
6. Q: Describe the rig of a brigantine.
   A: *Two masts, square sails on foremast and fore and aft sails on mainmast.*
7. Q: Describe the rig of a schooner.
   A: *Two or more masts all fore and aft rigged.*
8. Q: Describe the rig of a bark.
   A: *Three or more masts all square rigged except aftermast which is fore and aft rigged.*
9. Q: How does a yawl differ from a ketch?
   A: *The mizzen of a yawl is stepped abast of the after water-line; the mizzen of a ketch is stepped forward of the after waterline.*

Questions and Answers—Lesson No. 4

Chapters IX, X, XI and XII—Safety at Sea, Knots, Weather, Fog Signals, Distress Signals and Day Marks

(Lesson No. 103, U. S. P. S. Piloting Course Reference Sheet)

See pages 177-248

Safety at Sea

(See pages 182-196)

1. Q: What are the requirements as to speed in fog?
   A: *Extreme caution. Must be able to stop vessel within a distance of one-half the limits of visibility.*
2. Q: On hearing "Man overboard," what is the first thing to do?
   A: *Stop propellers, then heave a ring buoy.*
3. Q: What is the fastest way of getting to a person who has fallen overboard?
   A: *In a motor boat (single screw), full left rudder. Turn with wind on a twin screw boat. Under sail, jibe usually.*
4. Q: Where should gasoline filler pipes be located?
   A: *On outside decks, so spillage goes overboard.*
5. Q: What ventilation should be provided for engine rooms?
   A: *At least two ducts to the bilge with cowls on deck.*
6. Q: What precautions should be taken when filling gas tanks?
   A: *Close hatches, doors and ports; extinguish open flames, cigarettes, galley fires, etc.; stop all motors, except explosion-proof blowers.*
7. Q: Where will dangerous concentrations of fumes lie, if present?
   A: *Lowest part of the bilge, being heavier than air.*
8. Q: What fire fighting equipment might be useful, other than extinguishers?
   A: *Fire pump, hose, buckets, axe.*
9. Q: What are the advantages of foam type extinguishers?
   A: *Smothers fire. Harmless to those using it.*
10. Q: Why is carbon tetrachloride not approved as fire extinguishing equipment on boats?
    A: *Fumes may be dangerous in closed spaces.*
11. Q: What is the principle of the fixed carbon dioxide extinguishing system?
    A: *Carbon dioxide gas in tanks under pressure piped to spaces to be protected. Discharged through nozzles either automatically or manually. Smothers fire.*

Knots

(See pages 200-210)

12. Q: Name four of the most useful knots.
    A: *Clove hitch, bowline, fisherman's bend, square knot.*
13. Q: How would you make fast to a spile?
    A: *Use a clove hitch or a bowline.*
14. Q: Describe one method of bending lines together for towing.
    A: *Use a sheet bend and stop down the free ends.*

Weather

(See pages 211-248)

15. Q: What is the small craft warning?
    A: *One red pennant (red light over white light at night) indicating winds up to 38 mph (33 knots).*
16. Q: What is the difference between the gale warning and the whole gale warning?
    A: *The gale warning is two red pennants (white light over red at night) to indicate winds from 39 to 54 mph (34 to 48 knots). The whole gale warning is a single square red flag with black center (two red lights at night) indicating winds from 55 to 73 mph (48 to 63 knots).*
17. Q: What may be expected when two square red flags with black square centers are seen by day or a white light between two red lights at night?
    A: *A hurricane, with winds above 74 mph (64 knots).*

Fog Signals

(See pages 177-180)

18. Q: If you were heading into the wind and should hear 2 blasts on the fog horn ahead of you, what type of boat would you know was crossing your bow and from what direction?
    A: *A sailing vessel on port tack crossing your bow from your port to your starboard.*

19. Q: In the fog if you heard the rapid ringing of a bell, what would it indicate to you?
    A: *A boat at anchor or aground.*
20. Q: On the high seas if you heard 2 blasts of a steam whistle in succession at intervals of not over 2 minutes, what would it indicate to you and what would be your action?
    A: *A vessel underway but having no way on her. Navigate carefully and stop if in doubt about other boat's position. Give proper fog signals.*
21. Q: On the coastwise waters in the fog if you heard 1 blast of a whistle, what would it indicate to you and what would be your action?
    A: *A steam or motor vessel underway. Navigate with caution and give proper fog signals. Stop if in doubt.*
22. Q: On the Great Lakes in a fog if you heard a siren, what would it indicate to you and what would be your action?
    A: *A vessel towing a raft. Navigate with caution. Give proper fog signals.*
23. Q: In a fog if you heard 1 long blast followed by 2 short blasts on a whistle, what would it indicate to you and what would be your action?
    A: *A vessel with a tow or one not under control. Navigate with caution. Give the proper fog signals. Stop if in doubt.*
24. Q: In a fog, on coastal waters, if you heard 1 long blast followed by 2 short blasts on a fog horn, what would it indicate to you and what would be your action?
    A: *A vessel being towed. Proceed carefully, giving the proper fog signals.*
25. Q: May a motor boat use a fog horn?
    A: *When being towed, when in distress, when under sail alone in a fog. She is not required to carry one.*
26. Q: A motor boat or other power vessel aground in a fog gives what fog signal?
    A: *Rapid ringing of bell for five seconds at one-minute intervals.*
27. Q: What caution ought always to be remembered about fog signals in reference to the carrying power and direction of sound in a fog?
    A: *Neither sound nor direction can be absolutely relied upon.*
28. Q: Should you assume that a fog signal is not being sounded or that you are not near a danger if you do not hear the fog signal?
    A: *No.*

Distress Signals, Day Marks

(See pages 67, 69, 78, 177, 181)

29. Q: How does a Coast Guardsman indicate to you that "This is the best place to land"?
    A: *By day, vertical motion of a white flag or the arms. By night, vertical motion of a white light or flare.*
30. Q: How does the Coast Guard indicate to you "Landing here is dangerous"?
    A: *By day, horizontal motion of a white flag or arms extended horizontally. By night, horizontal motion of a white light or flare.*
31. Q: What does the American ensign when set Union down indicate?
    A: *Vessel is in distress (though this is not one of the distress signals prescribed by the rules).*
32. Q: One black ball shown from a steamer indicates what?
    A: *Proceeding under sail alone. If no sails are set, it indicates a vessel of more than 65 feet in length at anchor in a fairway.*
33. Q: How does a motor boat on inland waters indicate that she is in distress at night?
    A: *Continuous sounding of any fog signal apparatus, firing a gun, or flames from a burning tar or oil barrel.*
34. Q: If you noticed a vessel flying the code flag "G" with a code pennant over it, what would you know this vessel desired?
    A: *A pilot.*

Questions and Answers—Lesson No. 5

Chapters XIII and XIV—The Compass, Variation, Deviation, Applying Compass Error

(Lesson No. 104, U. S. P. S. Piloting Course Reference Sheet)

See pages 249-281

1 Q: How should a compass be placed on a boat in reference to the keel line?
A: *Imaginary line drawn through center of compass and lubber lines should be over keel line or parallel to keel line.*

2 Q: How do you determine whether the compass on a boat is correctly placed?
A: *Draw long line on deck which if continued would pass through center of compass and lubber line. Ascertain whether this line is along center line of boat or parallel to keel line.*

3. Q: Does the North Pole of the compass point towards magnetic north or geographic north?
A: *Approximately magnetic.*

4. Q: What liquid is used in the compass?
A: *Generally water and alcohol. Sometimes oil. Sometimes kerosene. Sometimes gasoline.*

5. Q: What is the object of the liquid used in the compass?
A: *To help buoy the card and to prevent freezing and to steady the card and to prevent moving on account of boat's vibration.*

6. Q: Into how many points is the compass card divided?
A: 32.

7. Q: Into how many degrees is the compass card divided?
A: 360.

8. Q: How many degrees in one point? **A:** 11¼.

9. Q: Name the cardinal points. *A: N, E, S, W.*

10. Q: Name the intercardinal points. *A: NE, SE, SW, NW*

11. Q: Name the quarter points which have two names.
A:

New Method	Old Method	New Method	Old Method
NNE ¼ E	NE x N ¾ N	SSW ¼ W	SW x S ¾ S
NNE ½ E	NE x N ½ N	SSW ½ W	SW x S ½ S
NNE ¾ E	NE x N ¼ N	SSW ¾ W	SW x S ¼ S
ENE ¼ E	E x N ¾ N	WSW ¼ W	W x S ¾ S
ENE ½ E	E x N ½ N	WSW ½ W	W x S ½ S
ENE ¾ E	E x N ¼ N	WSW¾ W	W x S ¼ S
ESE ¾ E	E x S ¼ S	WNW ¾ W	W x N ¼ N
ESE ½ E	E x S ½ S	WNW ½ W	W x N ½ N
ESE ¼ E	E x S ¾ S	WNW ¼ W	W x N ¾ N
SSE ¾ E	SE x S ¼ S	NNW ¾ W	NW x N ¼ N
SSE ½ E	SE x S ½ S	NNW ½ W	NW x N ½ N
SSE ¼ E	SE x S ¾ S	NNW ¼ W	NW x N ¾ N

12. Q: Give the two methods of naming by degrees the following points:
NE. **A:** *N 45° E; 45°.*

13. Q: SE. **A:** *S 45° E; 135°.*

14. Q: SW. **A:** *S 45° W; 225°.*

15. Q: W. **A:** *270°.*

16. Q: NW.
A: *N 45° W; 315°.*

17. Q: W x S¾ S.
A: *S 70° 18' 45" W; 250° 18' 45".*

18. Q: WSW ¼ W. **A:** *S 70° 18' 45" W; 250° 18' 45".*

19. Q: What would be the name of the point equivalent to 42° 11' 15"? **A:** *NE ¼ N.*

20. Q: What would be the name of the point equivalent to N 56° 15' E? **A:** *NE x E.*

21. Q: What would be the name of the point equivalent to 92° 48' 45"? **A:** *E ¼ S.*

22. Q: What would be the name of the point equivalent to S 87° 11' 15" E? **A:** *E ¼ S.*

23. Q: What would be the name of the point equivalent to 146° 15'? **A:** *SE x S.*

24. Q: What would be the name of the point equivalent to S 33° 45" E? **A:** *SE x S.*

25. Q: What would be the name of the point equivalent to 303° 45"? **A:** *NW x W.*

26. Q: What would be the name of the point equivalent to N 56° 15" W? **A:** *NW x W.*

27. Q: Name all the four point courses.
A: *NE; SE; SW; NW.*

28. Q: Name the reverse course of SW x W ¼ W.
A: *NE x E ¼ E.*

29. Q: Name the reverse course of 315°. **A:** *135°.*

30. Q: Name the reverse course of SW x S ¼ S.
A: *NE x N ¼ N.*

31. Q: Name the reverse course of SSW ¾ W.
A: *NNE ¾ E.*

32. Q: What is variation?
A: *Variation is the angular difference between true N. and a free needle suspended at the point in question.*

33. Q: What is deviation?
A: *Deviation is the angular difference between that direction shown by the ship's compass and a free needle suspended at the point in question.*

34. Q: How do you determine the amount of variation for a particular locality?
A: *From charts and other Government publications.*

35. Q: Describe briefly one method of determining the deviation of a compass.
Q: *By reciprocal bearings taken from the boat and shore at the same time.*

36. Q: What is local attraction?
A: *Local attraction is that effect on a boat's compass caused by magnetic influences not on the ship itself other than the magnetic North Pole.*

37. Q: How would you determine the local attraction for any particular locality?
A: *It is stated on charts, and in Coast Pilots and Government publications.*

38. Q: What is a true course?
A: *True courses are those referred to the true north or true compass rose of the chart.*

39. Q: What is a magnetic course?
A: *Magnetic courses are those referred to the magnetic north or the magnetic compass rose on the chart.*

40. Q: What is a compass course?
A: *Compass courses are those shown by the compass on a particular boat for a particular heading of the boat.*

41. Q: What kind of course (true, magnetic or compass) do you prefer to work with on a motor boat when sailing short distances?
A: *Magnetic courses.*

42. Q: What is meant by easterly variation?
A: *When the magnetic North is to the East of the true North; when magnetic directions are to the right of true directions.*

43. Q: What is meant by westerly variation?
A: *When the magnetic North is to the West of the true North; when magnetic directions are to the left of true directions.*

44. Q: What is meant by easterly deviation?
A: *When the compass north is to the East of the magnetic North; when the compass directions are to the right of magnetic directions.*

45. Q: What is meant by westerly deviation?
A: *When the compass North is to the West of the magnetic North; when the compass directions are to the left of magnetic directions.*

46. Q: If the variation at Portland Me., is 15° westerly, is it necessarily the same at New York City?
A: *No.*

47. Q: If the deviation on a particular boat is one point westerly when sailing NE, will it likely be the same when heading SE?
A: *No.*

48. Q: If you have a westerly deviation, do you steer to the right or left of the magnetic course by your compass?
A: *Right.*

49. Q: If you have an easterly deviation, is the correct magnetic course to the right or left of the course indicated by your compass?
A: *Right.*

50. Q: When sailing in localities where the variation is westerly with zero deviation, do you steer to the right or left of the true course?
A: *Right.*

51. Q: Will a true course be to the right or left of the compass course when sailing in localities with easterly variation and zero deviation?
A: *Right.*

52. Q: What is the net error which must be accounted for to convert a true course to a compass course with two points westerly variation and one point easterly deviation?
A: *One point W.*

53. Q: What is the net error which must be accounted for to convert a true course to a compass course with two points westerly variation and ½ point westerly deviation?
A: *2½ points W.*

54. Q: What is the net error which must be accounted for to convert a magnetic course to a compass course with two points westerly variation and one point easterly deviation?
A: *One point E.*

55. Q: What is the net error which must be accounted for to convert a magnetic course to a compass course with two points westerly variation and ½ point westerly deviation?
A: *½ point W.*

56. Q: What is the net error which must be accounted for to convert a magnetic course to a true course with two points westerly variation and one point easterly deviation?
A: *2 points W.*

57. Q: What is the net error which must be accounted for to convert a magnetic course to a true course with two points westerly variation and ½ point westerly deviation?
A: *2 points W.*

58. Q: In which direction should the error mentioned in question No. 52 be applied?
A: *To the right.*

59. Q: In which direction should the error mentioned in question No. 53 be applied?
A: *To the right.*

60. Q: In which direction should the error mentioned in No. 54 be applied?
A: *To the left.*

61. Q: In which direction should the error mentioned in No. 55 be applied?
A: *To the right.*

62. Q: In which direction should the error mentioned in No. 56 be applied?
A: *To the left.*

63. Q: In which direction should the error mentioned in No. 57 be applied?   A: *To the left.*

64. Q: In changing from true to magnetic courses, or vice versa, should variation, deviation, or both, be allowed for?
A: *Variation only.*

65. Q: In changing from magnetic to compass courses, or vice versa, should variation, deviation, or both, be allowed for?   A: *Deviation only.*

66. Q: In changing from true to compass courses, or vice versa, should variation, deviation, or both, be allowed for?
A: *Both variation and deviation.*

67. Q: The variation off the Florida coast is 0. Off the coast of Maine 1½ points westerly. If the true course to go from Maine to Florida is SW ½ S off the coast of Maine, what will be the true direction of the same course off the coast of Florida?
A: *SW ½ S; same true course as off the coast of Maine.*

68. Q: The variation off the Florida coast is 0. Off the coast of Maine 1½ points westerly. If the magnetic course to go from Maine to Florida is SW x W off the coast of Maine what will the same magnetic course be off the Coast fo Florida?
A: *SW ½ S.*

69. Q: In determining the deviation of your compass by putting your boat over a course the magnetic direction of which as determined by the chart is NE x N and your compass indicates NE ¾ N what is the deviation?
A: *¼ point W.*

70. Q: In determining the deviation of your compass by putting your boat over a course the magnetic direction of which as determined by the chart is NE x E and your compass indicates N x E½E what is the deviation?
A: *3½ points E.*

71. Q: In determining the deviation of your compass by putting your boat over a course the magnetic direction of which as determined by the chart is E and your compass indicates E ½ S what is the deviation?
A: *½ point W.*

72. Q: In determining the deviation of your compass by putting your boat over a course the magnetic direction of which as determined by the chart is S x E and your compass indicates S x E what is the deviation?
A: *0 deviation.*

73. Q: In determining the deviation of your compass by putting your boat over a course the magnetic direction of which as determined by the chart is SW and your compass indicates SW¼W what is the deviation?
A: *¼ point W.*

74. Q: In determining the deviation of your compass by putting your boat over a course the magnetic direction of which as determined by the chart is WSW and your compass indicates WSW½W what is the deviation?
A: *½ point W.*

75. Q: In determining the deviation of your compass by putting your boat over a course the magnetic direction of which as determined by the chart is WNW and your compass indicates NW x W¼W what is the deviation?
A: *¾ point W.*

76. Q: In determining the deviation of your compass by putting your boat over a course the magnetic direction of which as determined by the chart is NW x N and your compass indicates NW x N½N what is the deviation?
A: *½ point W.*

77. Q: True course NE variation one point E. Find magnetic course.
A: *NE x N.*

78. Q: True course NE variation 1 point E deviation ½ point W. Find compass course.
A: *NE ½ N.*

79. Q: Magnetic course SE deviation 1 point E. Find compass course.
A: *SE x E.*

80. Q: Compass course NW deviation ½ point W. Find magnetic course.
A: *NW ½ W.*

81. Q: Compass course NW deviation ½ point E, variation 1 point E. Find true course.
A: *NW x N ½ N; or N 28° 7′ 30″ W; or NNW ½ W; or 331°, 52′ 30″.*

82. Q: Magnetic course SW, variation 1 point E. Find true course.
A: *SW x W; or 236° 15′ or S 56° 15′ W.*

83. Q: True course 225°, variation 11¼° W. Find magnetic course in degrees.
A: *236° 15′ or S 56° 15′ W.*

84. Q: True course S 45° W, deviation 5⅝ E. Find compass course in degrees.
A: *Can't be answered without knowing amount of variation. Assuming 0 variation answer is SW ½ S; 219° 22′ 30″; or S 39° 22′ 30″ W.*

85. Q: True course S 45° W, variation 11¼° W, deviation 5⅝° E. Find compass course in points.
A: *SW ½ W.*

86. Q: Magnetic course 135°, deviation 5⅝° E. Find compass course in degrees.
A: *129⅜° or 129° 22′ 30″; or S 50° 37′ 30″ E. Answer if given in points should be SE ½ E.*

87. Q: Compass course S 45° E, deviation 5⅝° E, variation 11¼° W. Find true course in degrees.
A: *S 50⅝° E or S 50° 37′ 30″ E or 129° 22′ 30″.*

88. Q: Magnetic course N 45° E, variation 5° 37′ 30″ W. Find true course.
A: *N 39° 22′ 30″ E; or 39° 22′ 30″; or NE ½ N.*

89. Q: True course NE x E ¼ E, variation 1 point W, deviation 1 point E. Find compass course.
A: *NE x E ¼ E.*

90. Q: Magnetic course SW x W ½ W, variation 1 point E, deviation ½ point E. Find true course.
A: *W x S ½ S; or WSW ½ W; or 253° 7′ 30″; or S 73° 7′ 30″.*

91. Q: Compass course E x S, deviation ½ point W, variation ¼ point E. Find magnetic course.
A: *E ½ S.*

92. Q: Magnetic course E ¾ S, variation 10° 26′ E. Find true course.
A: *108° 52′ 15″*

93. Q: Compass course NE, deviation ⅝ point E. Find magnetic course.
A: *NE ⅝ E.*

94. Q: Magnetic course 45°, variation 11° E, deviation 17° W. Find compass course.
A: *62°.*

95. Q: True course 106° 52′ 30″, variation 10° 56′ W, deviation 4° 06″ E. Find magnetic course.
A: *117° 48′ 30″.*

96. Q: True course ENE ¼ E variation 1 point W, deviation ¾ point W. Find compass course.
A: *E.*

97. Q: True course E x N, ¾ N, variation 1 point W, deviation ¾ point W. Find compass course.
A: *E.*

98. Q: True course 70° 18′ 45″, variation 1 point W, deviation ¾ point W. Find compass course.
A: *E.*

99. Q: True course N 70° 18′ 45″ E, variation 1 point W. deviation ¾ point W. Find compass course.

100. Q: Suggest any other compass question which you think has been overlooked and answer it.

Questions and Answers—Lesson No. 6

Chapters XV, XVI and XVII—Buoys, Lights and Other Aids, Government Publications

(Lesson No. 105, U. S. P. S. Piloting Course Reference Sheet)

Buoys *(See pages 291-299)*

1. Q: Should it be taken for granted that buoys are always where they should be, or where the chart shows they are located?
A: *No.*

2. Q: How may spar buoys be colored?
A: *Red, black, red and black horizontal stripes, black and white vertical stripes, yellow, white, green (special colorings may also be used on private buoys authorized by proper authorities).*

3. Q: How may can buoys be colored?
A: *Usually black, black and white vertical stripes, white, yellow; or black and red horizontal stripes.*

4. Q: How may nun buoys be colored?
A: *Red, red and black horizontal stripes; black and white vertical stripes.*

5. Q: How are red buoys numbered?
A. *Even numbers.*

6. Q: How are black buoys numbered?
A: *Odd numbers.*

7. Q: Are buoys painted red and black numbered?
A: *No.*

8. Q: Are buoys painted black and white numbered?
A: *No.*

9. Q: What colors are used on an obstruction buoy?
A: *Red and black horizontal stripes.*

10. Q: What colors are used on a mid-channel buoy?
A: *Black and white vertical stripes.*

11. Q: On which side are red buoys left when entering a port or harbor?
A: *On your starboard hand.*

12. Q: On which side are red buoys left on leaving a port or harbor?
A: *On your port hand.*

13. Q: On which side are black buoys left when entering a port or harbor?
A: *On your port hand.*

14. Q: On which side are black buoys left on leaving a port or harbor?
A: *On your starboard hand.*

15. Q: When entering a port or harbor on which side do you leave buoys with even numbers?
A: *On your starboard hand.*

16. Q: When leaving a port or harbor on which side do you leave buoys with odd numbers?
A: *On your starboard hand.*

17. Q: Do you pass close to or far away from a buoy colored with black and white vertical stripes?
A: *Close to.*

18. Q: Do you pass close to or far away from a buoy colored with red and black horizontal stripes?
A: *Far away from.*

19. Q: When off shore, going from Maine toward Florida on which side do you pass red buoys?
A: *On your starboard hand.*

20. Q: If on the chart you saw a buoy marked S4, what kind and color of a buoy would you look for and on which side would you pass it when entering a harbor?
A: *Red spar buoy No. 4; pass on your starboard side.*

21. Q: If on the chart you saw a buoy marked N6, what kind and color of a buoy would you look for and on which side would you pass it when leaving a harbor?
A: *Red nun buoy No. 6; pass on your port hand.*

22. Q: If on the chart you saw a buoy marked C5, what kind and color of a buoy would you look for and on which side would you pass it when at sea, running from Cape Hatteras to Cape Charles?
A: *Black can buoy No. 5; pass on your starboard hand.*

23. **Q:** Show by means of a rough sketch how a buoy which is used to indicate the center of a channel is shown on the chart.
A: *(Cut of black and white vertical stripe buoy.)*

24. **Q:** Show by means of a rough sketch how a buoy which is used to mark a rock or isolated danger is shown on the chart.
A: *(Cut of red and black horizontal stripe buoy.)*

25. **Q:** Show by means of a rough sketch how a light buoy is indicated on the chart.
A: *(Cut of light buoy.)*

26. **Q:** Show by means of a sketch how a black can buoy is shown on the chart (give it an odd or even number as would be proper).
A: *(Cut of black buoy with odd number and the letter "C".)*

27. **Q:** Show by means of a rough sketch how a bell buoy is shown on the chart.
A: *(Cut of buoy with the word bell.)*

28. **Q:** Show by means of a rough sketch how a buoy which is both a bell buoy and a light buoy is indicated on the chart.
A: *(Cut of combination bell and light buoy.)*

29. Q: Describe the light characteristics of an occulting light buoy.
A: *A steady light suddenly and totally eclipsed, with the period of the eclipse less than or equal to the period of light.*

30. Q: Describe the light characteristics of a flashing light buoy
A: *A light suddenly and totally eclipsed, with the period of eclipse greater than the period of light.*

31. Q: A buoy on the Hudson River is marked FL. GN. EV. 3 SEC. Describe this light.
A: *A flashing green light flashing once every three seconds.*

32. Q: A buoy on the chart is marked FL. W WHISTLE. Describe the characteristics of this buoy
A: *A combination light and whistle buoy, the light is a flashing white.*

33. Q: If you are in doubt on which side a buoy should be passed how do you determine it?
A: *Stop, consult chart, do not proceed until you are sure.*

34. Q: What Government publication gives you complete information about all buoys?
A: *Light List.*

35. Q: If you find a buoy which is not in its proper location or light buoy whose light is extinguished at night, to whom do you report this?
A: *To the nearest District Commander of the Coast Guard.*

36. Q: In what depth are many buoys commonly placed?
A: *On the 3-fathom or 18-foot contour.*

NOTE:—Some of the symbols found on the newest charts may not be identical with those sketched in questions 23-28. Symbols and abbreviations are gradually being brought into conformity with a standard system, for details of which see pages 324-328.

Government Navigation Lights

(See pages 282-293)

1. Q: Describe a fixed light.
A: *A continuous steady light.*

2. Q: Describe a flashing light.
A: *A single flash at regular intervals. (Note: a flash is usually shorter than the duration of an eclipse.)*

3. Q: Describe occulting light.
A: *A steady light suddenly and totally eclipsed at regular intervals. The period of light must be greater than, or equal to, the period of darkness.*

4. Q: Describe fixed and flashing light.
A: *A fixed light varied at regular intervals by a single flash of greater brilliancy.*

5. Q: Describe group flashing light.
A: *Showing at regular intervals groups of flashes.*

6. Q: Describe group occulting light.
A: *Steady light suddenly and totally eclipsed by a group of two or more eclipses at regular intervals.*

7. Q: What is an alternating light?
A: *Lights which change color, i.e., show alternately white and red or green in various combinations.*

8. Q: The Light List describes New London Ledge light as follows: Gp. Fl. W. Alt. R; Fl. 30 sec.; 3 W., 1 R, flashes. Tell briefly in your own language how this light would appear to you.
A: *Three white flashes followed by one red flash; this combination being repeated every thirty seconds.*

481

9. Q: The Light List describes Smyrna light on the Delaware River as follows:
Smyrna Front
Smyrna Rear
Fl. R., 1 sec. U.
Occ. W., 4 sec. U.
Tell briefly in your own language how these lights would appear to you and how used.

A: *The front range flashes red every second. The rear is eclipsed every four seconds. The lights are unwatched. When on the proper course to enter Smyrna Harbor the lights are brought into line.*

10. Q: What is a red sector and what does it usually indicate?

A: *A light which shows red over a certain designated sector and another characteristic over the remainder of the 360 degree arc. The portion showing red usually covers waters where navigation is dangerous or sections to which it is desired to call the mariner's attention on account of local reasons.*

11. Q: If a fixed white light suddenly became visible ahead of you, how would you determine whether it was a vessel's light or a government lighthouse?

A: *Lower the eyes some six or ten feet. If a navigation light, it will disappear from view. If a sailing light, it will probably remain in view.*

12. Q: How far would a lighthouse 100 feet high be visible from a point on deck 9 feet above water?

A: *About 13 nautical miles.*

13. Q: From your Light List describe the appearance of the structure, and the light characteristics of, some lighthouse in your vicinity, such as Navesink, Montauk Point, etc.

A: *Depends on lighthouse selected.*

14. Q: From your Light List describe the appearance of some lightship in your locality, the characteristics of its light, its fog signal, and its international code signal.

A: *Depends on ship selected.*

15. Q: If you noticed a navigational light which was extinguished or not showing the proper light, to whom would you report the fact?

A: *The nearest District Commander of the Coast Guard.*

Government Publications
(*See pages 300-306*)

1. Q: What Government publications should be carried on any motor boat?

A: *Tide tables, current tables, light lists, notice to mariners, Coast Pilot and chart catalog.*

2. Q: From whom do you obtain the above publications?

A: *Offices of the Coast and Geodetic Survey, U. S. Coast Guard, Oceanographic Office, and Government agencies.*

3. Q: If you wish to sail from Sandy Hook to Philadelphia, how would you know what charts you required, their price, and from whom to purchase them?

A: *Refer to Government catalog of charts, etc.*

4. Q: What charts (state numbers) would be required if you wished to sail from Sandy Hook to Philadelphia?

A: *1215, 1216, 1217, 1218, 294, 295.*

5. Q: Where would you look for detailed information on aids to navigation in Nantucket Sound?

A: *Light List, North Atlantic Coast.*

6. Q: What is the Notice to Mariners? (When and by whom published? What information does it give?)

A: *A weekly publication issued by Oceanographic Office; gives information relative to all changes in aids to navigation, new aids, new Government publications, charts, etc. Distributed every week by Oceanographic Office, Washington, D. C.*

*7. Q: What time is it high water at New London, Connecticut, on the morning of July 15? (Do not omit this question—get a copy of the Government Atlantic Coast Tide Tables and learn to use it.)

*8. Q: What time is it high water at Yonkers, Hudson River, New York, on the morning of July 15?

*9. Q: If you should go aground on the Delaware River near Philadelphia on August 11, what day during that week would your prospects be best to be floated by the tide?

10. Q: How much earlier does maximum flood occur in Plum Gut than in The Race? (See Current Tables.)

A: *One hour and fifteen minutes.*

*11. Q: When are the best moonlight nights during the month of August at New York? (See Atlantic Coast Tide Tables.)

12. Q: What are the chances of getting fuel and supplies at Port Washington, Long Island, New York? (This information may be had from Section B, Coast Pilot.)

A: *Fuel and supplies will be obtained at Port Washington.*

13. Q: In going from New York to Florida in a motor boat, what harbors may be safely entered between Beaufort, North Carolina, and Southport?

A: *(This information may be had from the Inside Route Pilot from New York to Key West.)*

14. Q: What lights are specified by the Rules of the Road to be carried on a vessel moored or anchored and engaged in laying pipe or operating on submarine construction or excavation?

A: *Three red lights carried on a vertical line not less than 3 ft. or more than 6 ft. apart and not less than 15 ft. above the deck and in such a position as may best be seen from all directions.*

15. Q: When on account of bad weather the side lights cannot be kept in place, what action is permitted by the Rules of the Road on boats of less than 10 gross tons?

A: *May be kept inboard at hand to be shown when occasion requires.*

16. Q: On steam vessels how much higher must the after white range light be than the forward white light?

A: *At least 15 ft.*

17. Q: What do the Rules of the Road specify about the use of searchlights?

A: *Must not be flashed in the pilot house of any passing vessel or used to hinder the navigation of another vessel.*

18. Q: How much later does high water occur in Albany than at New York City?

A: *9 hours, 34 minutes.*

19. Q: Albany is 140 miles from New York. With a ten-mile an hour boat, how much before or after the time of low water at New York should such a boat leave New York to carry a favorable current up the Hudson?

A: *Two or three hours after low water at New York.*

* NOTE:—Use the Tide Tables for the current year. Answers depend on the year of the tables.

1. Q: What characteristics of the bottom are shown on charts?

A: *Characteristics depend upon scale of chart to some extent. Characteristics shown include some or all of the following: Channels, contour curves, shoals, obstructions to navigation, quality of the bottom such as mud, sand, gravel, shells, pebbles, specks, clay, stones, coral; color of the bottom such as Black, White, Red, Yellow, Gray, Blue, dark, light, Green, Brown, consistency of the bottom such as hard, soft, fine, coarse, rocky, sticky, broken, large, small, steep, decayed, rotten, spreckled, flinty, gritty, ground, streaky, volcanic; wrecks, cables, eel grass.*

2. Q: What characteristics of the land are shown on charts?

A: *Wharves, buildings, streets, conspicuous objects, ranges, outlines of shore and land, magnetic and true directions, cities and towns, latitude and longitude, variations of the compass, broken water, bridges, coast guard stations, dams, hills, bluffs, sand dunes, levee, marshes, woods. (Note—charts also show visibility of lights, buoys-type, number and color, aids to navigation, characteristics of aids to navigation, depths of water, ferries, dykes, tide rips, etc.)*

3. Q: Name the three methods of showing depths of water on a chart.

A: *Fathoms, feet, feet and fathoms.*

4. Q: How would one know whether the figures on charts indicating depths mean fathoms, feet and fathoms or feet?

A: *By referring to a note on the chart which always indicates how depths are shown.*

5. Q: Do figures printed on the clear portion of a chart always indicate depths or fathoms?

A: *No.*

6. Q: Do figures printed on the shaded portions of charts always indicate depths in feet?

A: *Refer to note on chart.*

7. Q: What is a ten fathom curve?

A: *Is a line passing through all points having a depth of ten fathoms.*

8. Q: Do the figures shown on charts indicate depths at high or low water?

A: *Mean low water.*

9. Q: Is the water ever shallower than indicated on the chart?

A: *Yes.*

10. Q: How does one determine for any particular time and place whether the water is likely to be shallower than indicated on the chart?

A: *By referring to the Tide Tables published by the U. S. Coast & Geodetic Survey.*

11. Q: Can a general coastwise chart be safely used for inshore navigation?

A: *No.*

12. Q: Are all aids to navigation shown on all charts?

A: *No.*

13. Q: How does one know whether there is published a chart of any particular locality?

A: *By reference to chart catalogs published by the U. S. Coast and Geodetic Survey; the Corps of Engineers, War Department, U. S. Lake Survey; Mississippi River Commission; Oceanographic Office, Navy Department.*

14. Q: How does one know the number of the chart of a particular locality?

A: *By reference to chart catalogs published by the U. S. Coast and Geodetic Survey; the Corps of Engineers, War Department, U. S. Lake Survey; Mississippi River Commission; Oceanographic Office, Navy Department.*

15. Q: How may one determine where to purchase charts?

A. *By reference to the first issue of each half-year of the Notice to Mariners or by application to the director of the U. S. Coast & Geodetic Survey, Washington, D. C.; or the Lake Survey, War Department, Old Customs House, Detroit, Michigan; Mississippi River Commission, St. Louis, Mo.; Oceanographic Office, Navy Department, Washington, D. C.*

16. Q: What branch of our Government publishes the charts of coastwise waters?

A: *U. S. Coast & Geodetic Survey, Department of Commerce, Washington.*

17. Q: What branch of our Government publishes the charts of the Great Lakes and St. Lawrence River?

A: *Corps of Engineers, Lake Survey.*

18. Q: What branch of our Government publishes charts of foreign waters?

A: *Oceanographic Office, Navy Dept., Washington, D. C.*

19. Q: If the principal characteristics of a light are not given on a chart how does one determine same?

A: *By reference to the light list published by the U. S. Coast Guard.*

20. Q: How should one determine the day appearance of a lighthouse shown on the chart?

A: *By reference to the light list published by the U. S. Coast Guard.*

21. Q: What does the direction of an arrow shown on the chart indicate?

A: *The direction of a current, tidal or otherwise.*

22. Q: What does an arrow with tail feathers indicate?

A: *A flood current.*

Give the meaning of the following markings shown on the chart:

23. ⎯⎯ ⚓ L.S.S. (T)

23.A: *Life Saving Station. "T" indicates telegraphic connection.*

24. ⎯⎯⎯⎯ ✺

24.A: *Light or lights of any kind.*

25. ⎯⎯⎯⎯ •

25.A: *Light on a small scale chart.*

26. ⎯⎯⎯⎯ ⚓

26.A: *Light vessel of any kind.*

27. ⎯⎯⎯ ⚓ ⚓ ⚓

27.A: *Light vessel showing number of masts.*

28. ⎯⎯⎯ ⊛ •

28.A: *A light with wireless.*

29 ⎯⎯⎯ ⊕

29.A: *A light vessel with wireless.*

30. ⎯⎯⎯ ⚓ ⚓

30.A: *A light with a submarine bell.*

31. ⎯⎯⎯ ⚓

31.A: *A light vessel with a submarine bell.*

32. ⎯⎯⎯ ⊛ ⚓

32.A: *Light with submarine bell and wireless.*

33. ⎯⎯⎯ ⊕

33.A: *Light vessel with submarine bell and wireless.*

34. ⎯⎯⎯⎯ ✳ ✿

34.A: *A lighted Beacon.*

35. Bna ⚲⚲⚲⚲⚲⚲

35.A: *An unlighted Beacon with characteristics indicated.*

36. ⎯⎯⎯⎯ ⚲

36.A: *Black Buoy.*

37 ⎯⎯⎯⎯ ⚲

37.A: *Obstruction Buoy with horizontal stripes.*

38. ⎯⎯⎯⎯ ⚲

38.A: *Channel buoy with Black and White vertical stripes.*

39. ⎯⎯⎯⎯ ⚲

39.A: *Checkered Buoy.*

40. ⎯⎯⎯⎯ ⚲⚲⚲⚲

40.A: *Buoy with perch & square.*

41. ⎯⎯⎯⎯ ⚲⚲⚲⚲

41.A: *Buoy with perch and ball.*

42. ⎯⎯⎯⎯ ⚲⚲⚲⚲

42.A: *Whistling buoy.*

43. ⎯⎯⎯⎯ ⚲⚲⚲⚲

43.A: *Bell buoy.*

44. ⎯⎯⎯⎯ ⚲

44.A: *Lighted buoy.*

45. ⎯⎯⎯⎯ ⚓

45.A: *Spindle or stake.*

46. ⎯⎯⎯⎯ ⚓

46.A: *Anchorage for large vessels.*

47. ⎯⎯⎯⎯ ⚓

47.A: *Anchorage for small vessels.*

48. ⎯⎯⎯⎯ ⚓

48.A: *Mooring buoy.*

49. Q: What does an arrow without tail feathers indicate?
A: *Ebb*.
50. Q: What do the figures printed alongside of an arrow indicate?
A: *Strength or velocity or current, expressed in knots*.
51. Q: How does one tell whether certain figures printed on the chart indicate depth of water or the number of a buoy?
A: *The number of a buoy is indicated by Italic type and depth by Roman type*.
Give the meaning of the following markings shown on a chart:
52. Q: rky. A: *Rocky*. 53. Q: stk. A: *Sticky*.
54. Q: hrd. A: *Hard*. 55. Q: sft. A: *Soft*.
56. Q: bu M, brk Sh. A: *Blue mud, broken shells*.
57. Q: hrd S. A: *Hard sand*.
58. Q: crs yl S bk Sp. A: *Coarse yellow sand with black specks*.
59. Q: fne dk gy S M. A: *Fine dark gray sand with mud*.

60. Q: gy S, bu M, brk Sh. A: *Gray sand, blue mud, broken shells*.
61. Q: fne yl gy S. A: *Fine yellow gray sand*.
62. Q: C1. A: *Can buoy No. 1*.
63. Q: N2. A: *Nun buoy No. 2*.
64. Q: S15. A: *Spar buoy No. 15*.
What is the method of indicating on the chart the following qualities of the bottom:
65. Q: mud. A: *"M."* 66. Q: specks. A: *"Sp."*
67. Q: shells. A: *"Sh."* 68. Q: pebbles. A: *"P."*
69. Q: gravel. A: *"G."* 70. Q: Sand. A: *"S."*
71. Q: How do you determine the scale of a chart?
71. A: *By reference to the note and the scale on the chart*.
72. Q: If one wished to know the direction and force of the prevailing winds east of Bermuda which chart would give one this information?
72. A: *Pilot chart of the North Atlantic Ocean, published by the Oceanographic office, Navy Department, Washington, D. C.*

NOTE:—*Some of the symbols shown in questions 23-48 are being replaced on newer editions of charts as they are brought into conformity with a standard system. For a complete survey of this new system, see pages 324-328.*

RULES FOR SMALL PASSENGER VESSELS

(*See also pages 15 and 20*)

Rules and regulations for small passenger vessels were prescribed under the Act of May 10, 1956, (Public Law 519) and their provisions made effective as of June 1, 1958. (Copies of the new rules and regulations (CG-323) may be purchased from U. S. Coast Guard Headquarters, Washington 25, D. C.)

Under this act a "passenger-carrying vessel" means any vessel which carries *more than six passengers* and which is:

(1) Propelled in whole or in part by steam or by any form of mechanical or electrical power and is of 15 gross tons or less; or

(2) Propelled in whole or in part by steam or by any form of mechanical or electrical power and is of more than 15 gross tons and less than 100 gross tons and not more than 65 feet in length measured from end to end over the deck excluding sheer; or

(3) Propelled by sail and is of 700 gross tons or less; or

(4) Non self-propelled and is of 100 gross tons or less.

A few exceptions are made, including: certain foreign vessels; vessels operating on non-navigable waters of the United States; vessels laid up and out of commission; public vessels; and lifeboats.

Vessels subject to the act must be inspected by the Officer in Charge, Marine Inspection, U. S. Coast Guard, from whom applications for inspection are obtained.

Certificates of inspection are valid for three years. They describe the area in which the vessel may operate; minimum crew required; maximum number of passengers; minimum lifesaving and firefighting equipment required, etc.

Effective June 1, 1959, no person holding only a "motorboat operator's license" is permitted to operate vessels subject to this law. The scope of licenses issued under the act varies according to the waters plied. For offshore waters, an "ocean operator's license" is issued. Within the coastline and on the Great Lakes, the license is an "operator's license" (illustrated herewith). Licenses are valid for 5 years; application is to be made on Coast Guard Form CG-866, to the nearest U. S. Coast Guard Officer in Charge, Marine Inspection.

Of particular interest to yachtsmen and boatmen who use their craft exclusively for pleasure is the definition, in the regulations, of a passenger. "A passenger is every person other than the master and the members of the crew or other persons employed or engaged in any capacity on board a vessel in the business of that vessel." (There are, however, certain exceptions, for example: aboard vessels on international voyages, children under one year of age; the owner or his representative; members of a paid crew; employees of the owner or charterer; and persons aboard tugs and towboats not over 50 gross tons who have not contributed for their carriage.) Most important exception, insofar as the yachtsman is concerned, is the following: *"any guest on board a vessel which is being used exclusively for pleasure purposes who has not contributed any consideration, directly or indirectly, for his carriage."*

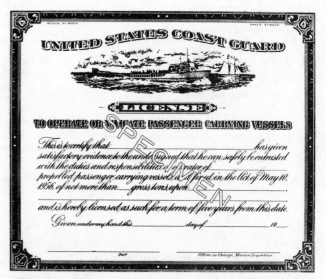

The type of license now issued by the Coast Guard to operators of small passenger vessels (carrying more than six passengers) within the coastline and on the Great Lakes

Questions and Answers—Lesson No. 7 (Cont.)

Chapter XIX—Piloting Instruments, The Log and Log Line, The Lead and Lead Line, The Chronometer, Course Protractor, etc.

(Lesson No. 106, U. S. P. S. Piloting Course Reference Sheet)

See pages 329-334

1. Q: What navigating instruments should be carried aboard a small cruiser?

   A: *Compass, celluloid course protractor, dividers (bronze), pelorus or bearing finder, patent log and log line, lead and lead line, good timepiece, deviation card, log book, charts, coast pilot, lake survey bulletin, tide table, current table, light list.*

2. Q: How is the depth corresponding to two fathoms marked on the lead-line?

   A: *Two strips of leather.*

3. Q: How is the depth corresponding to three fathoms marked on the lead-line?

   A: *Three strips of leather.*

4. Q: How is the depth corresponding to five fathoms marked on the lead-line?

   A: *White rag.*

5. Q: How is the depth corresponding to seven fathoms marked on the lead-line?

   A: *Red rag.*

6. Q: How is the depth corresponding to ten fathoms marked on the lead-line?

   A: *Leather with hole in it.*

7. Q: What depths are indicated by three strips of leather?

   A: *Three fathoms, Thirteen fathoms.*

8. Q: What depths are indicated by a white rag?

   A: *Five fathoms, Fifteen fathoms.*

9. Q: What depths are indicated by a red rag?

   A: *Seven fathoms, Seventeen fathoms.*

10. Q: What depth is indicated by two knots?

    A: *Twenty fathoms.*

11. Q: What depth is indicated by three knots?

    A: *Thirty fathoms.*

12. Q: What depth is indicated by four knots?

    A: *Forty fathoms.*

13. Q: What depths are indicated by one knot?

    A: *Twenty-five fathoms.*

14. Q: What is meant by "marks"?

    A: *Fathoms which correspond with the depths marked are called "Marks."*

15. Q: What is meant by "deeps"?

    A: *The intermediate fathoms which do not correspond with the depths marked are called "Deeps."*

16. Q: What is meant by "arming the lead"?

    A: *Filling the hollow in the base of the lead with tallow or other sticky substance so that particles of the bottom will adhere to it.*

17. Q: Does the patent log indicate distances in Statute or Nautical miles?

    A: *Some indicate Statute miles and some indicate Nautical miles. One must be careful to ascertain by a marking on the patent log whether the log indicates distance in Statute or Nautical miles.*

18. Q: In using the Chip log, if 73-1/3 feet of line flow over the taffrail in five seconds, what is the speed of the boat through the water?

    A: *Ten miles an hour.*

19. Q: If, when using the ground log, 88 feet of the line pass over the taffrail in five seconds, what is the speed of the boat over the bottom?

    A: *Twelve miles an hour.*

20. Q: If the observations mentioned in questions 18 and 19 were taken simultaneously, what would be the speed of the current?

    A: *Two miles an hour.*

21. Q: Would the current mentioned in example number 20 be fair or head?

    A: *Fair.*

22. Q: An observation taken with a pelorus which is set with the boat's compass which has a deviation of one point west shows SW. What is the magnetic bearing?

    A: *SW x S*

23. Q: If the bearing of an observation taken by the pelorus which is set with the boat's compass which has a one point east deviation is NE by E, what is the true bearing in the location where the variation is ½ point west?

    A: *NE x E ½ E*

24. Q: A patent log shows the following readings: 10 A. M. 2.75, 10.30 A. M. 5.25. What is the speed of the boat?

    A: *Five miles per hour.*

25. Q: A patent log shows that it requires 7½ minutes to cover one mile. What is the speed of the boat?

    A: *Eight miles per hour.*

26. Q: Are patent logs absolutely accurate?

    A: *No.*

27. Q: What care must be taken in the use of patent logs in reference to the distance which the rotator should be towed from the stern of the boat?

    A: *Keep rotator at sufficient distance astern so that it will not be in boat's wake or influenced by propeller action.*

28. Q: What conditions are likely to cause patent logs to give inaccurate readings?

    A: *Slow speed of boat, waves and abnormal sea, drifting sea-weed, fouled rotator, etc.*

29. Q: What is a chronometer?
    A: *An accurate time-piece.*

30. Q: What is meant by the chronometer rate?

    A: *The amount in seconds or fractions thereof which the Chronometer gains or loses each day.*

31. Q: New York City is located in longitude 74 degrees west— Peoria, Illinois, in 89 degrees west. When it is noon by suntime in New York City, what time is the suntime in Peoria? (Omit any considerations of the equation of time.)

    A: *11 A. M.*

32. Q: Portland, Maine, and New Bedford, Mass., are both located in approximately 70 degrees west longitude. However, the latitude of Portland is 43 degrees north and the latitude of New Bedford is 41 degrees north. Is there any difference in suntime between these two cities?

    A: *Approximately none.*

Chapter XX—Piloting Problems, Chart Work, Laying Courses and Determining Position

(Lesson No. 106, U. S. P. S. Piloting Course Reference Sheet)

See pages 335-342

1. Q: A light bears 4 points off bow at 10 A. M. and is abeam at 10.45 A. M. Speed of boat 12 miles an hour. How far off is light at 10.45 A. M.?
   A: *Nine miles.*

2. Q: Course SE, bearing of light at 8 P. M. East, at 9 P. M. North East, speed of boat 10 miles an hour. How far off is the light at 9 P. M.?
   A: *Ten miles.*

3. Q: Course E bearing of light ENE at 8 P. M., North East at 8.30 P. M. Speed of boat 10 miles an hour. What is distance from light at 8:30 P. 'M.?
   A: *Five miles.*

4. Q: In question No. 3 how far off is light when abeam?
   A: *3½ miles.*

5. Q: In question No. 3 what time will light be abeam?
   A: *8.51 P. M.*

6. Q: An object 2½ points off bow at noon and abeam at 1.30 P. M. Speed of boat 8 knots. How far off is object when abeam?
   A: *6½ miles.*

7. Q: Object is 6 points off bow at noon, log reads 10.5, is abeam at 12.30 P. M. with log reading of 15.5. How far off is object at 12.30?
   A: *Twelve miles.*

8. Q: In question No. 7 what is speed of the boat?
   A: *Ten miles.*

9. Q: Using the chart reproduced below, lay a course (or courses) from buoy B to Q (do not pass over Jackson Shoal or Duryee Middle Ground). Describe course or courses which you would lay off and follow for a night run.
   Answer: Starting from Buoy B, I would head for the light buoy on The Cows, which course I would hold until light buoy E, off Matinicock Point, was abeam. I would then change my course and head directly for the light on Eaton's Neck, which course would just clear the southerly point of Duryee Middle Grounds. When I reached this point, which would be determined by cross bearings on Matinicock Point light buoy and Great Captain's Island light, I would change my course again and head directly for point Q, inasmuch as the chart shows no obstructions and plenty of water from Duryee Middle Ground to point Q. I would endeavor to check my position by the buoy off Lloyd's Neck which, although not a light buoy, should be passed close enough abeam to be seen on the average night. Point Q would be located by cross bearings taken on Lloyd's Harbor light and Green's Ledge light. This would also be checked by a 90-degree bearing on Eaton's Neck light.
   (Note: Questions 10-25 refer to Question 9 and its answer.)

10. Q: State magnetic courses you would follow.
    A: *72°; 98°; 90°.*

11. Q: State compass courses you would follow (deviation 6° W.).
    A: *78°; 104°; 96°.*

12. Q: State true courses you would follow (variation 11° W.).
    A: *61°; 87°; 79°.*

13. Q: State length of each leg or course.
    A: *2 miles; 3.7 miles; 8.4 miles.*

14. Q: State total distance from B. to Q.
    A: *14.1 miles (approximately).*

15. Q: State time to hold each course with a 10-mile boat (no current).
    A: *12 minutes; 22⅕ minutes; 50⅖ minutes.*

16. Q: State total time to complete distance from B. to Q. (10-mile boat).
    A: *1 hour 24⅗ minutes.*

17. Q: State magnetic directions of cross bearings taken at end of second leg on Matinicock Point light and Great Captain's Island light.
    A: *234°; 335°.*

18. Q: State compass directions of cross bearings taken at end of second leg on Matinicock Point Light and Great Captain's Island light (deviation 6° W.).
    A: *240°; 341°.*

19. Q: State time when the light on The Cows will be 4 points off the Bow (10-mile speed).
    A: *37⅘ minutes from start.*

20. Q: State time when the light on The Cows will be abeam (10-mile speed).
    A: *54⅗ minutes from start.*

21. Q: State distance off the light on The Cows when abeam.
    A: *2.9 miles.*

22. Q: State time Lloyds Neck buoy should be abeam.
    A: *One hour 1⅘ minutes after start.*

23. Q: State time Eaton's Neck light should be 2 points off bow.
    A: *One hour 7⅘ minutes after start.*

24. Q: State time Eaton's Neck light should be 4 points off bow.
    A: *One hour 18 minutes after start.*

25. Q: State distance off Eaton's Neck light when it is 4 points off bow.
    A: *1¾ miles.*

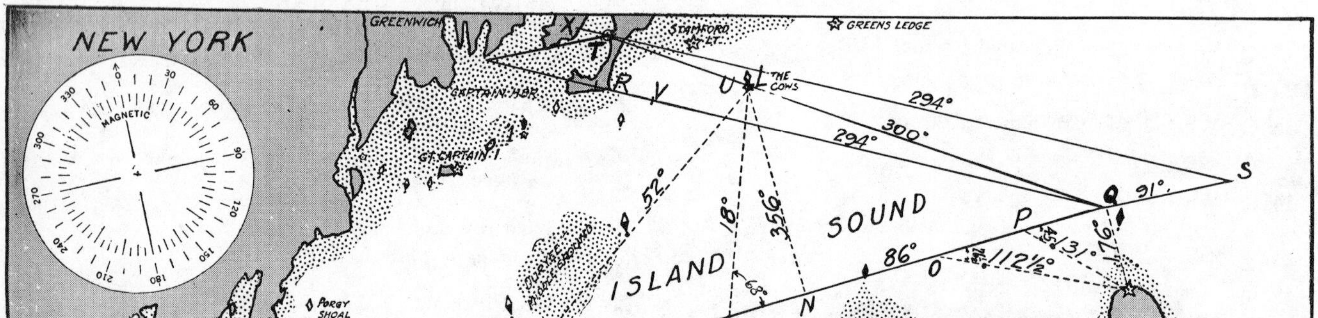

Illustration to be used in connection with problems Nos. 9 to 25 above.

Questions and Answers—Lesson No. 7 (Cont.)

Chapter XXI—Allowances for Tides and Currents, Short Cuts in Piloting

(Lesson No. 106, U. S. P. S. Piloting Course Reference Sheet)

See pages 345-354

1. Q: Speed of boat 10 miles per hour, speed of current 2 miles per hour, boat sails upstream 5 miles and back to starting point. How long will be required to make the round trip?

   A: *1 hour and 2½ minutes.*

2. Q: In question No. 1, what is the average speed of boat over the bottom for round trip?

   A: *9.6 miles per hour.*

3. Q: In question No. 1, what is the speed of the boat over the bottom while going upstream against the current?

   A: *8 miles per hour.*

4. Q: In question No. 1, what is the speed of the boat over the bottom when going downstream with the current?

   A: *12 miles per hour.*

5. Q: Course to go from A to B is North, distance 10 miles, speed of boat 10 miles per hour; direction of current toward East, speed of current 2 miles per hour. Find course to be steered.

   A: *Approximately N x W.*

6. Q: In question No. 5, how long will be required to go from A to B?

   A: *1 hour 1½ minutes.*

7. Q: In question No. 5, what is the speed of the boat over the bottom?

   A: *9.76 miles per hour.*

8. Q: Course to go from A to B is North, distance is 10 miles, speed of boat 10 miles per hour; direction of current toward Northeast, speed of current 2 miles per hour. Find course to steer.

   A: *N ¾ W.*

9. Q: In question No. 8, how long will be required to go from A to B?

   A: *53½ minutes.*

10. Q: In question No. 8, what is the speed of the boat over the bottom?

    A: *11¼ miles per hour.*

11. Q: Course to go from A to B is North, distance is 10 miles, speed of boat 10 miles per hour; direction of current is toward SE, speed of current 2 miles per hour. Find course to steer.

    A: *N ¾ W.*

12. Q: In question No. 11, how long will be required to go from A to B?

    A: *1 hour 8½ minutes.*

13. Q: In question No. 11, what is the speed of the boat over the bottom?

    A: *8¾ miles per hour.*

14. Q: The course to go from A to B is North, distance between points is 10 miles, speed of boat is 10 miles per hour; current is flowing toward North; speed of current 5 miles per hour. How long will be required to go from A to B?

    A: *40 minutes.*

15. Q: In reference to No. 14, what is the speed of the boat over the bottom?

    A: *15 miles per hour.*

16. Q: In reference to No. 14, what is the proper compass course to steer, deviation 1 point West?

    A: *N x E.*

17. Q: Course to go from A to B is North, speed of boat 10 miles per hour; distance is 10 miles; current is flowing toward South at a speed of 5 miles per hour. How long will be required to go from A to B?

    A: *2 hours.*

18. Q: In reference to No. 17, what is the speed of the boat over the bottom?

    A: *5 miles per hour.*

19. Q: In question No. 17, what is the true direction which must be steered, variation ½ point E?

    A: *N ½ W.*

20. Q: Speed of boat 16 miles per hour; speed of current 4 miles per hour; current is 2 points off direct course. What allowance must be made in course for the current (see Fig. 228, next page)?

    A: *6 degrees.*

21. Q: Speed of boat 20 miles per hour, speed of current 6 miles per hour; course to be made good NE, current setting N x E. What course must be steered (use Fig. 228)?

    A: *Allow 10 degrees (Steer NE x E).*

22. Q: Distance to be run 20 miles, estimated drift or leeway 4 miles. What allowance in course must be made (use Fig. 229)?

    A: *One point (see Fig. 228, next page).*

23. Q: Starting from Buoy A, (see chart on next page), speed of boat 10 knots; current setting 266° at 2 knots; (a) sail for 15 minutes 86°; then (b) sail 40°, 14¼ minutes; then (c) sail 86° for 4 nautical miles (over bottom); then (d) sail 135° true (variation 6° E), 28½ minutes; then (e) steer proper course to make good a course of 40° for five miles; then (f) engine breaks down for 45 minutes and you drift (no wind); then (g) steer 220° for 16 minutes. (h) What should be the direction of the next course to reach point Q, and the distance? (All directions are magnetic unless otherwise stated, distances and speed are expressed in nautical miles, zero deviation, use nearest degree. By the Course "sailed" is meant the course "made good," *not* "steered.")

    A: *87°; 7.1 miles.*

24. Q: In question No. 23a, what is the distance covered over the bottom?

    A: *2 miles.*

25. Q: In question No. 23b, what magnetic course is steered?
    A: 48°.

26. Q: In question No. 23b, what distance over the bottom is covered?

    A: *2 miles.*

27. Q: In question No. 23c, how long is this course held?
    A: *30 minutes.*

28. Q: In question 23c, what magnetic course is steered?
    A: 86°.

29. Q: In question No. 23d, what magnetic course is sailed?
    A: 129°.

30. Q: In question No. 23d, what magnetic course is steered?
    A: 121°.

31. Q: In question No. 23d, what true course is steered?
    A: 127°.

32. Q: In question No. 23e, what magnetic course is steered?
    A: 48°.

33. Q: In question No. 23e, how long is this course held?
    A: *35¼ minutes.*

34. Q: In question No. 23f, in what direction does the boat drift?
    A: *266°.*

35. Q: In question No. 23f, how far does the boat drift over the bottom?

    A: *1½ miles.*

36. Q: In question No. 23g, what is the magnetic course made good?

    A: *227°.*

37. Q: In question No. 23g, what is the distance made good over the bottom?

    A: *3 miles.*

38. Q: In question No. 23h, what time will be required to reach point Q?

    A: *53¼ minutes.*

39. Q: What will be the course to be steered to reach point V from point Q (see chart on next page) when the current is flowing west (270°) 2 miles per hour with a boat having a speed of 8 miles per hour?

    A: *300°.*

40. Q: In question No. 39, what time will be required to run from point Q to point V?

    A: *45¼ minutes.*

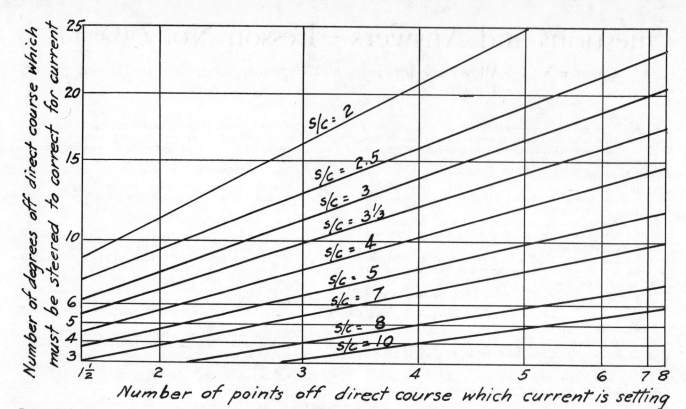

Number of points off direct course which current is setting

Figure 228, Above. Diagram for Rapidly Estimating the Amount Which Must Be Allowed for a Current Which Is Meeting the Boat's Course at Any Angle.

The amount which must be allowed in one's compass course for an oblique current depends upon two factors, in addition to the direction of the current. These two factors are the speed of the boat through the water and the speed of the current, which we will call the Speed-Current Ratio and the value of which is determined by dividing the speed of the boat expressed in miles per hour by the flow of the current expressed in miles per hour. The amount which must be allowed for a given Speed-Current Ratio depends only upon the angle at which the current meets the boat's course. For example: Suppose we have a current which is meeting the boat's course at an angle of 45 degrees or 4 points, then the amount which must be allowed for this current will be the same for an 8 mile boat with a 4 mile current as it would be for a 10 mile boat with a 5 mile current, or for

a 12 mile boat with a 6 mile current. In other words there would be the same allowance for all boats whose Speed-Current Ratio was 2 when the current meets at a 4 point angle.

A Speed-Current Ratio of 3 would result from such combinations as a 9 mile boat in a 3 mile current; 12 mile boat in a 4 mile current; 15 mile boat in a 5 mile current, etc. The allowance which would have to be made with conditions of this kind would be the same, that is, if the current were meeting the boat's course at an angle of 6 points, the allowance in one's heading which would have to be made to take care of this angle would be the same for all conditions where the Speed-Current Ratio was 3.

A Speed-Current Ratio of 10 would result from such combinations as a 10 mile boat speed in a 1 mile current; a 15

(Continued on page 490)

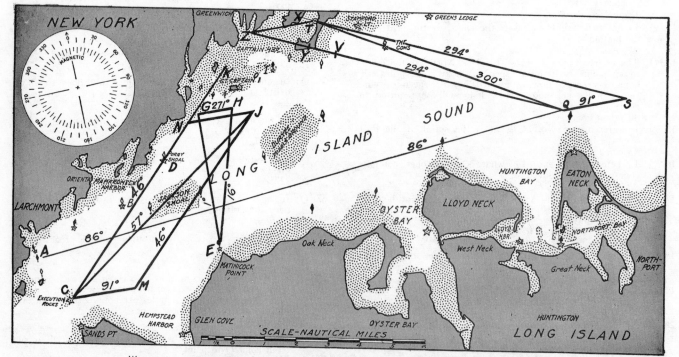

Illustration to be used in answering questions 23 to 39 in Lesson No. 7, Chapter XXI.

Questions and Answers—Lesson No. 8

Chapters XXII, XXIII and XXIV—Flags, Yachting Etiquette and Customs, Clothing

(Lesson No. 107, U. S. P. S. Piloting Course Reference Sheet)

Flag Etiquette *(See pages 355-366)*

1. Q: Describe the Yacht ensign.
   A: *Rectangular flag, 13 horizontal stripes, alternate red and white, top and bottom stripes being red. Blue field containing white fouled anchor, and thirteen stars around same.*

2. Q: Describe the American ensign.
   A: *Rectangular flag, 13 horizontal stripes, alternate red and white, top stripes being red. Blue field containing 48 white stars.*

3. Q: What is the shape of the Club Burgee?
   A: *Triangular.*

4. Q: What is generally the shape of the owner's private signal?
   A: *Swallow tail.*

5. Q: What is the shape of a flag officer's flag?
   A: *Rectangular.*

6. Q: Describe the owner's absent flag.
   A: *A blue rectangular flag.*

7. Q: Describe the guest flag.
   A: *A blue rectangular flag with a white diagonal stripe.*

8. Q: What time are colors hoisted?
   A: *8 A.M.*

9. Q: What time are colors taken in?
   A: *Sundown.*

10. Q: From whom is the time to hoist or lower colors taken?
    A: *A naval vessel if one is present, a naval station if near one; from the senior flag officer present, if any; or from the senior member present.*

11. Q: When is owner's absent flag flown?
    A: *During daylight when the owner or guests are not on board.*

12. Q: When is the guest flag shown?
    A: *During daylight when the owner is not on board, but his guests are.*

13. Q: If one belongs to more than one Yacht Club should he display more than one Club Burgee at a time?
    A: *No.*

14. Q: If one belongs to more than one Yacht Club, which Club Burgee should be flown?
    A: *If he is in the anchorage of a club he is a member of, or with a fleet of a club he is a member of, he should fly the club burgee of that club. On other occasions the owner may choose which club burgee.*

15. Q: When is the United States Jack flown?
    A: *On Sundays, holidays, or special occasions when at anchor, only.*

16. Q: During what hours is a flag officer's flag flown?
    A: *Day and night when the yacht is in commission.*

17. Q: Does a person who is a flag officer fly his officer's flag or his private signal or both?
    A: *His flag officer's flag.*

18. Q: If one who is a flag officer of a club is cruising with or at the anchorage of another club of which he is a member but not an officer, should he fly his private signal or his officer's flag?
    A: *His private signal.*

19. Q: It is proper to ever fly two flags from the same hoist?
    A: *No.*

20. Q: Is it ever permissible to fly a flag with a name spelled out thereon?
    A: *No.*

21. Q: An open boat having only bow and stern staffs, flies what flags?
    A: *The ensign aft and the club burgee forward, both underway and at anchor, 8 A.M. to sundown.*

22. Q: Where is a flag officer's flag displayed on an open boat?
    A: *It may be flown from a special staff placed forward of the cockpit.*

23. Q: A boat having bow and stern staffs and signal mast displays what flags and from where?
    A: *Club burgee forward; ensign aft; private signal or officer's flag from the signal masthead; absent, guest or owner's meal flag starboard yardarm; crews meal pennant from port yardarm.*

24. Q: Where is the owner's absent flag flown?
    A: *Starboard yardarm on single masted vessels; main starboard yardarm, two masted vessels.*

25. Q: Where is the guest flag flown?
    A: *Same as No. 24.*

26. Q: Where is the owner's meal flag flown?
    A: *Same as No. 24.*

27. Q: Where is the crew's meal pennant flown?
    A: *Port yardarm on single masted vessels; and fore port yardarm on two masted vessels.*

28. Q: Is it ever permissible to fly a flag before 8 A.M. or after sundown with the exception of the flag officer's flag?
    A: *When leaving or entering harbor early or late.*

29. Q: A boat with two masts flies what flags and where?
    A: *Jack from jackstaff when at anchor only on Sundays or holidays; club burgee from fore masthead; officer's flag or private signal from main masthead; crew's meal pennant from fore port yardarm; absent, guest, and owner's meal flag from main starboard yardarm; ensign aft.*

30. Q: Should a U. S. Government Vessel or a commercial craft fly the Yacht ensign?
    A: *No.*

31. Q: What flags are flown by a club tender?
    A: *Ensign aft; yacht club burgee forward. Club burgee replaced by flag officer's flag when flag officer is aboard.*

32. Q: What flag is flown by a boat in a race?
    A: *Racing flag only.*

33. Q: Where is the ensign flown on a sailing craft underway?
    A: *At the peak.*

34. Q: Where is the ensign flown on a sailing craft at anchor?
    A: *From a staff, aft.*

35. Q: Where is the ensign flown on an auxiliary yawl?
    A: *At the mizzen peak.*

36. Q: What flag is half-masted to indicate the death of a citizen of national importance?
    A: *The ensign.*

37. Q: What flag is half-masted to indicate the death of a club member?
    A: *The club burgee.*

38. Q: What is the proper procedure in destroying or disposing of a national ensign which has become worn out?
    A: *Burn it with reverence, in private.*

39. Q: What is the proper method of exchanging salutes?
    A: *Dipping the ensign once.*

40. Q: What is the procedure in half-masting flags or hauling down flags from a half-masted position?
    A: *In half-masting flags, they should be mastheaded before placing them at half mast. In hauling down flags from half-masted position, they should first be mastheaded.*

Manners and Customs
(See pages 367-371)

1. Q: When you join a fleet, what vessel should you salute?
   A: *The vessel of the senior officer present.*
2. Q: At a rendezvous, should the junior or senior make the first call?
   A: *The junior.*
3. Q: If you are participating in a club cruise, should you leave without permission?
   A: *No. Request permission from the commodore.*
4. Q: When sailing yachts are racing, is it courteous to pass to windward of them?
   A: *No. Keep to leeward and keep well clear.*
5. Q: What courtesy should be exercised near motor boat race courses?
   A: *Do not get on the course and stay within the limits prescribed for the spectator fleet. If necessary and permissible to get under way, be sure your wake does not disturb the racing craft.*
6. Q: What should you do when passing other vessels?
   A: *Slow down enough to be sure that your wash does not cause any damage or inconvenience.*
7. Q: What special precautions should be observed in anchorages with respect to speed?
   A: *Same as 6A.*
8. Q: Is a vessel responsible legally for damage caused by her wash?
   A: *Yes.*
9. Q: When entering an anchorage, how would you obtain a mooring?
   A: *Make a request to the person in charge of the anchorage.*
10. Q: How should refuse be disposed of afloat?
    A: *At sea or in facilities provided at an anchorage, never over the side in a harbor. Puncture top and bottom of cans when disposing of them, to make them sink.*
11. Q: Should the whistle ever be used for saluting?
    A: *No.*
12. Q: When juniors and seniors enter and leave boats, what procedure is prescribed?
    A: *The junior enters first and leaves last.*
13. Q: What practice is recommended in connection with boat booms at night?
    A: *Rig them in at night whenever possible. Otherwise show a white light at the end.*

Clothing
(See pages 372-375)

1. Q: What kind of footwear is desirable aboard yachts?
   A: *Soles and heels should be non-skid on wet decks and of a type that will not scratch or leave marks on decks.*
2. Q: What cap insignia distinguishes a commodore?
   A: *Three gold stars with the club emblem at the intersection of crossed fouled anchors in gold.*
3. Q: What cap insignia is worn by a vice commodore?
   A: *Same as 2A, but with two stars.*
4. Q: What cap insignia is worn by a rear commodore?
   A: *Same as 2A, but with one star.*
5. Q: What cap insignia is worn by a yacht club member who does not own a boat?
   A: *The club emblem on a single fouled anchor, placed vertically.*
6. Q: What is the cap insignia of a U.S.P.S. member, who holds no office?
   A: *An enamelled disc bearing the U.S.P.S. ensign, in the center of an eight-spoked ship's wheel in gold.*
7. Q: What is the distinction between the cap insignia of a U.S.P.S. chief commander and the commander of a local unit?
   A: *The chief has three crossed gold tridents with the U.S.P.S. cap device superimposed at the intersection. The local commander rates three tridents but they are not crossed; one is above, and one each side of the cap device.*
8. Q: What is the sleeve insignia of the commodore of a yacht club?
   A: *Five stripes of black mohair braid on blue uniforms (white stripes on white) the upper stripe finished in a trefoil, with gilt star in each loop of the trefoil.*
9. Q: Is the trefoil used on U.S.P.S. sleeve insignia?
   A: *No. Stripes of varying width designate the rank.*
10. Q: Should the insignia of a yacht club member and those of a U.S.P.S. member ever be worn at the same time?
    A: *No. One or the other.*
11. Q: Should any insignia ever be worn to which a yachtsman is not entitled by rank?
    A: *No.*
12. Q: Does the trefoil ever appear on the sleeve of a paid member of a crew?
    A: *No.*
13. Q: What does a rope or circle of gold bullion in the cap device indicate?
    A: *A paid hand.*

(Continued from page 488)

mile boat speed in a 1½ mile current; 20 mile boat speed in a 2 mile current, etc.

The diagram above shows the allowance which must be made for a current meeting the boat's course at various angles from 0 to 90 degrees, bow or stern and with various Speed-Current Ratios. The figures along the bottom of the diagram indicate the number of points off the direct course which the current is setting or meets the boat's course. The figures at the left indicate the allowance in degrees which must be made to counteract for the effects of a current. For example: If we desire to sail between two points and the direct course between these two points is North and we have a current which is setting Northeast which is 4 points from North, with a 10 mile an hour boat and a 2 mile current, which would give us a Speed-Current Ratio of 5: we would follow along the bottom until it meets the diagonal line marked $\frac{S}{C} = 5$ and then horizontally to the left we would see it would meet the left hand margin at a point equivalent to approximately 8 degrees. Therefore, the allowance which would have to be made in this case would be 8 degrees. Now as the current is flowing Northeast which would tend to carry the boat to the right of North, we must therefore, apply our 8 degrees to the left of North and steer North 8 degrees West or approximately N ¾ W in order to make good our northerly course.

If we had a case where the current was setting at right angles to our course which is 8 points, such as sailing directly across the Hudson River, in which there was an ebb tide of 3.2 miles an hour setting down stream and our boat had a normal speed in still water of 8 miles an hour, the Speed-Current Ratio would then be 2.5. Therefore, to use the diagram we would follow along the vertical line marked 8 until we came to the diagonal line $\frac{S}{C} = 2.5$ which would be opposite 20 degrees at the left. Therefore, an allowance of 20 degrees or approximately 1 ¾ points would have to be made in one's compass course to sail across the Hudson River under these conditions. If the course across the Hudson was due West then we would have to steer 1 ¾ points North of West or W x N ¾ N.

It makes no difference in the method of calculating the course whether the current is meeting the boat's course from a direction forward of the beam or aft of the beam, as the method of determining the allowance would be the same in both cases. For example: The course which would have to be steered to allow for a current 6 points off the bow would have the same allowance which would be made for a current 6 points from the stern. However, the time required to cover a given distance would be different depending upon whether the current was forward of the beam which would retard the boat or aft of the beam which would assist the boat. The methods of calculating these times are described in figures 223 and 224.

490

How Well Do You Know
the Rules of the Road?

TRY THESE QUESTIONS

ASKED BY

THE COAST GUARD

WHEN RENEWING LICENSES

FOR DECK OFFICERS

RECOGNIZING that a solid understanding of rules of the road governing traffic afloat is essential to hold collisions to a minimum, the Coast Guard has modified requirements for renewal of deck officers' licenses.

When such officers have not seen active service for three years, they must pass an examination. Those who have been in active service or have held a position closely associated with ship operation during that three-year period must submit an affidavit that they have, within the preceding three months, read the Rules of the Road, and must demonstrate their knowledge of how to apply them.

This "demonstration of knowledge" takes the form of an "exercise," not an examination, in which the officer answers multiple-choice questions, published in the Coast Guard's Navigation and Vessel Inspection Circular No. 7-60. When answering, the officer may refer to published Rules of the Road. There is no minimum passing grade, but each question must be answered correctly before the license will be renewed. This may necessitate re-checking with the Rules where incorrect answers have been given.

There are four groups of questions, covering the separate jurisdictions —International, Inland, Great Lakes, and Western Rivers. The applicant is tested only on rules applicable to the waters he sails.

Because the rules are of equal importance to pleasure boatmen, even though they need no license, extracts from the several sets of questions are published on pages 490a-490f, in four parts. Those given below (Part I) are based on the Inland Rules. In lieu of answers, the Coast Guard cites in each case the appropriate rule to be found in *Rules of the Road, International, Inland—CG 169.*

PART ONE—INLAND RULES

The day signal sketched indicates that the vessel is:
(a) Handling buoys, (b) Anchored, (c) Dredging, (d) Engaged in hydrographic survey.
(See Pilot Rule 80.25)

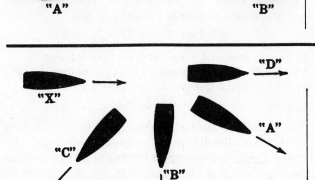

If you were in charge of navigation of "A", you should:
(a) Blow one blast, (b) Blow two blasts, (c) Hold course and speed, letting "B" take avoiding action, (d) Stop in all cases.
(See Article 18, Rule 1)

At different times, vessel "X" was navigated with respect to the four vessels sketched. Which one was she obligated to give way to?
(a) "A" ("A" is overtaking "X"), (b) "B", (c) "C", (d) "D" ("X" is overtaking "D").

(See Article 24)

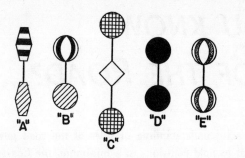

"A"   "B"   "C"   "D"   "E"

Match the signals sketched above with the class of vessel denoted:

(a) Suction dredge underway and engaged in dredging *(See Pilot Rule 80.21)*, (b) Engaged in hydrographic survey *(See Pilot Rule 80.33)*, (c) Towing a submerged object *(See Pilot Rule 80.18)*, (d) Handling navigation aid *(See Pilot Rule 80.33a)*, (e) Laying cables or pipes *(See Pilot Rule 80.22)*.

Whistle signals to indicate course changes have a duration of:

(a) One second, (b) Two seconds, (c) Three seconds, (d) Four seconds.

(See Pilot Rule 80.03)

The Rule of Special Circumstance would apply when meeting *all but one* of the following—To which one would it *not* apply?

(a) When meeting several vessels at one time, (b) When meeting a tug with tow bound downstream in a heavy current, (c) When meeting a vessel unable to maneuver in accordance with the Rules, (d) When encountering a vessel engaged in laying cable, (e) When meeting a vessel end on or nearly end on.

(See Article 27)

LEGEND

WHITE   BLACK   RED   GREEN   ORANGE

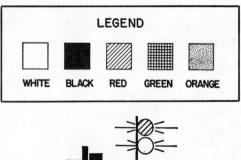

The vessel with lights shown as sketched above seen in inland waters would be:

(a) Dredging, (b) Laying mats, (c) Fishing, (d) Not under command, (e) A pilot vessel.

(See Article 9)

The vessel showing lights as sketched above would be:

(a) Towing a submerged object, (b) Not under command, (c) A self-propelled suction dredge, (d) Laying telegraph cable.

(See Pilot Rule 80.21)

Moderate speed in fog is generally interpreted to mean ability to stop within which of the following fractions of the range of visibility:

(a) One-fourth, (b) One-half, (c) Two-thirds, (d) Three-fourths.

A steam vessel under way in fog but stopped and having no way upon her blows on her whistle:

(a) One prolonged blast every two minutes, (b) Two prolonged blasts every two minutes, (c) One prolonged blast every minute, (d) One short blast every minute.

(See Article 15)

On overtaking another vessel, before passing her on her port side you must:

(a) Blow one short blast and be answered by one short blast, (b) Blow two short blasts and be answered by two short blasts, (c) Blow one short blast, (d) Blow two short blasts.

(See Article 18, Rule VIII)

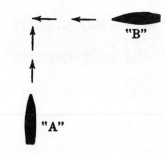

If you were in charge of navigation of "A" (above) you should *not:*

(a) Go under stern of "B", (b) Back down on engines, (c) Stop, (d) Cross ahead of "B".

(See Article 22)

If you were in charge of navigation of "B", *(sketch above)* you should:

(a) Go under stern of "A", (b) Back down on engines, (c) Stop, (d) Hold course and speed.

(See Article 21)

When collision cannot be avoided by "A" alone *(sketch above)* "B" must:

(a) Cross under "A"'s stern, (b) Back down, (c) Hold course and speed under all circumstances, (d) Take such action as will best aid to avert collision.

(See Article 27)

Rowing boats under sail or oars must show:

(a) Side lights, (b) Mast lights, (c) Stern light, (d) A white light in time to prevent collision.

(See Article 7)

In fog, an anchored vessel must ring the bell every:

(a) Minute for five seconds, (b) Two minutes for five seconds, (c) Three minutes for ten seconds.

(See Article 15)

Risk of collision can best be determined by:

(a) Checking the distance of an approaching vessel, (b) Carefully watching the compass bearing of an approaching vessel, (c) Watching the other vessel for any signals he may give, (d) Observing the range of the approaching vessel's masts or mast lights.

(See Preliminary to Steering & Sailing Rules)

Match the fog signals listed with the class of vessel denoted:

(a) A prolonged blast of the whistle every minute, (b) A blast of the fog horn every minute, (c) A rapid ringing of the bell for 5 seconds every minute, (d) Two blasts of the fog horn every minute, (e) Three blasts of the fog horn, (f) One prolonged blast followed by two short blasts.

A. a steam vessel towing, B. a sailing vessel on the starboard tack, C. a sailing vessel on the port tack, D. a sailing vessel with the wind abaft the beam, E. a steam vessel under way, F. a vessel at anchor.

(See Article 15)

Nearing a bend where the channel around the bend is obscured a vessel should blow on the whistle:

(a) A short blast, (b) A long blast, (c) Two long blasts, (d) Three long blasts.

(See Article 18, Rule 5)

A vessel signifies intention to pass a dredge by blowing:

(a) One short blast, (b) Two short blasts, (c) Three short blasts, (d) One long blast.

(See Pilot Rule 80.26)

"My engines are going full speed astern" is indicated on the whistle by:

(a) One short blast, (b) Two short blasts, (c) Three short blasts, (d) Four short blasts.

(See Article 28)

PART TWO

INTERNATIONAL RULES

Part One was concerned only with Inland Rules of the Road. Officers navigating the high seas would be given questions from the International Rules, similar to those below. (Refer to *Rules of the Road—CG 169*.)

Vessel "A":
(a) Can continue on course and speed, (b) Must alter course to left, (c) Must alter course to right, (d) Must back down.

(See Rule 18 (a))

At different times, vessel "X" was navigated with respect to the vessels sketched. Which one was she obligated to give way to?

(a) "A" ("A" has overtaken "X"), (b) "B", (c) "C", (d) "D" ("X" is overtaking "D")

Striped balls indicate RED color

Match the day signals sketched with the class of vessel denoted:

(a) Trawler *(See Rule 9)*, (b) Vessel aground *(See Rule 11)*, (c) Vessel at anchor *(See Rule 11)*, (d) Vessel not under command *(See Rule 4)*, (e) Vessel tending a navigational aid *(See Rule 4)*.

At different times, vessel "X" was navigated with respect to the vessels sketched. Which one was she obligated to give way to?

(a) "A", (b) "B" ("B" is overtaking "X"), (c) "C" ("C" is overtaking "X"), (d) "D".

In fog, a bell forward and a gong aft must be sounded by anchored vessels whose length is over:
(a) 200 feet, (b) 250 feet, (c) 300 feet, (d) 350 feet.
(See Rule 15)

Vessels towed make fog signals on:
(a) Fog horn or whistle, (b) Whistle only, (c) Fog horn only, (d) Bell, (e) Gong.
(See Rule 15)

Match each fog signal with the vessel which would sound it:
Signals: (a) One prolonged blast on whistle, (b) A blast consisting of a series of several alternate notes of higher and lower pitch, (c) Three blasts on the fog-horn, (d) Two prolonged blasts on the whistle, (e) One prolonged and three short blasts on the whistle, (f) One prolonged and two short blasts on the whistle.
Ships: A. Vessel towing, B. Fishing vessel, C. Sailing vessel, wind abaft the beam, D. Power driven vessel underway, E. Vessel towed, F. Power driven vessel underway but stopped and making no way through the water.
(See Rule 15)

Match each fog signal with the vessel which would sound it:
Signals: (a) Two blasts on the fog-horn, (b) One prolonged and two short blasts on the whistle, (c) A rapid ringing of a bell following by the sounding of a gong, (d) One blast on the whistle followed by the ringing of a bell, (e) One blast on the fog-horn, (f) A rapid ringing of the bell preceded and followed by three strokes on the bell.
Ships: A. A sailing vessel on the starboard tack, B. A fishing vessel of 20 tons or upward, C. A vessel aground, D. An anchored vessel over 350' in length, E. A vessel picking up a navigation mark, F. A sailing vessel on the port tack.
(See Rule 15)

Match each of the sound signals given with its proper meaning:
Sound Signal: (a) One short blast on the whistle, (b) Two short blasts on the whistle, (c) Three short blasts on the whistle, (d) Five or more short and rapid blasts on the whistle.
Meaning: A. I am altering course to port, B. My engines are going astern, C. I am altering course to starboard, D. I am in doubt whether you are taking sufficient action to avert collision.
(See Rule 28)

If, at night, you sighted the towboat sketched you should see looking from abeam:
(a) Two white lights in a vertical line and a red side light, (b) Three white lights in a vertical line, (c) A red side light, (d) Three white lights in a vertical line and a red side light.
(See Rule 3)

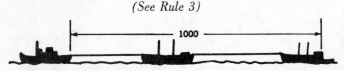

A vessel is under way when she is:
(a) At anchor, (b) Aground, (c) Made fast to shore, (d) None of the above.
(See Rule 1)

One of the following statements is correct if A and B (below) are in sight of one another:
(a) "A" and "B" should each alter course to the right, each blowing one short blast on the whistle, (b) "A" and "B" should each alter course to the right. No whistle signals need be sounded, (c) "A" or "B" should blow one blast and wait for a response before altering course.
(See Rule 18 and Rule 28)

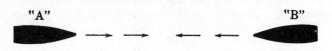

The day signal of a basket is displayed by:
(a) Dredges, (b) Trawlers, (c) Cable-layers, (d) Boats tending divers.
(See Rule 9)

A sailing vessel of 20 tons or upward under way makes her fog signal on a:
(a) Bell, (b) Gong, (c) Whistle, (d) Fog horn.
(See Rule 15)

In a narrow channel, power-driven vessels shall whenever possible:
(a) Stay in the middle, (b) Keep to the left, (c) Keep to the right.
(See Rule 25)

Match the lights sketched below with the class of vessel denoted:
(a) Cable layer *(See Rule 4)*, (b) Power driven Pilot vessel *(See Rule 8)*, (c) Fishing vessel *(See Rule 9)*, (d) Not under command *(See Rule 4)*.

"A"	"B"	"C"	"D"

Solid black disc indicates RED light

Approaching an anchorage in fog, you hear one short, one prolonged, and one short blast in that sequence on a ship's whistle. This indicates a vessel:
(a) Towing, (b) Not under command, (c) Anchored, and warning you of her position, (d) Just getting underway from the anchorage, (e) Stopped.
(See Rule 15)

In fog, a power-driven vessel, hearing forward of the beam another vessel which cannot be seen, must wherever possible:
(a) Put the engines on standby, (b) Reduce to one-half speed, (c) Reduce to slow speed, (d) Stop her engines.
(See Rule 16)

Whistle signals to denote course changes must be sounded:
(a) In fog, (b) When vessels are in sight of one another, (c) When you can be reasonably sure of hearing the other vessel's acknowledgement, (d) Every time you alter course.
(See Rule 28)

Match the signal to be used between pilot and engineer with its meaning:
(a) 1 bell, (b) 2 bells, (c) 3 bells, (d) 4 bells.
A. all right, B. check, C. back, D. stop.
(See Pilot Rule 90.15 (d))

On overtaking another vessel, before passing her on her port side you must:
(a) Blow one distinct blast and be answered by one distinct blast, (b) Blow two distinct blasts and be answered by two distinct blasts, (c) Blow one distinct blast, (d) Blow two distinct blasts.
(See Pilot Rule 90.8)

A steam vessel hearing, apparently not more than four points from right ahead, the fog signal of another vessel shall at once reduce her speed to:
(a) Slow ahead, (b) Zero, (c) Bare steerageway.
(See Rule 15)

A sailing vessel under way makes her fog signal on:
(a) Bell, (b) Gong, (c) Whistle, (d) Fog horn.
(See Rule 14)

Approaching a bend where the channel around the bend is obscured a steam vessel should blow on the whistle:
(a) One distinct blast, (b) Several short and rapid blasts, not less than five, (c) One blast of at least 8 seconds duration, (d) Three long blasts.
(See Pilot Rule 90.6)

Match the vessel with the fog signal.
(a) Four bells at intervals of one minute, sounded in the same manner in which four bells are struck in indicating time, (b) One blast on the fog horn every minute, (c) At intervals of not more than 2 minutes a rapid ringing of the bell for from 3 to 5 seconds and, in addition, at intervals of not more than 3 minutes one short blast, two long blasts, and one short blast in quick succession on the whistle, (d) A screeching or Modoc whistle for from 3 to 5 seconds every minute, (e) Three distinct blasts of the whistle every minute.
A. a steam vessel underway, B. a steamer with a raft in tow, C. a sailing vessel on the starboard tack, D. a steam vessel aground in or near a channel or fairway, E. a vessel in tow.
(See Rule 14)

Incorrectly answering a two blast signal with one blast, or incorrectly answering a one blast signal with two blasts is known as:
(a) Reverse signals, (b) Reciprocal signals, (c) Cross signals, (d) Danger signals.
(See Pilot Rule 90.3)

When passing within 200 feet of a Coast Guard vessel servicing an aid to navigation, maximum speed is:
(a) 1 mph, (b) 3 mph, (c) 5 mph, (d) 7 mph.
(See Pilot Rule 90.15a)

A vessel of 600 feet in length is at anchor. She must display in addition to four anchor lights, a white light at least every ——— feet along the deck:
(a) 50, (b) 75, (c) 100, (d) 125.
(See Rule 9)

The passing signal when two steam vessels are meeting in a narrow channel with a current should first be sounded by:
(a) The ascending steamer, (b) The descending steamer, (c) Either vessel, (d) The faster steamer.
(See Rule 24 Pilot Rule 90.5)

In fog, a steam vessel underway, excepting only a steam vessel with raft in tow, shall sound at intervals of not more than ——— minute(s) ——— distinct blast(s) of her whistle:
(a) one, one; (b) two, one; (c) one, two; (d) one, three.
(See Rule 14)

Two red lights in a vertical line one over the other indicate a vessel that is:
(a) Not under command, (b) In distress, (c) Fishing, (d) Servicing aids to navigation.
(See Rule 30)

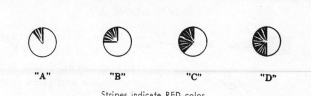

Stripes indicate RED color

Which of the circles shown has a *red* sector which best shows the arc of visibility of the red side light?

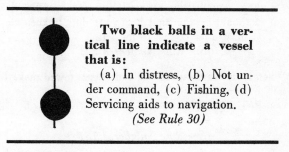

Two black balls in a vertical line indicate a vessel that is:
(a) In distress, (b) Not under command, (c) Fishing, (d) Servicing aids to navigation.
(See Rule 30)

In the situation sketched, one distinct blast by "B" means:
(a) I am directing my course to starboard, (b) I intend to hold course and speed and cross your bow, (c) I intend to go under your stern, (d) You should direct your course to starboard.
(See Pilot Rule 90.10)

Which of the circles sketched below has a *white* sector which best represents the arc of visibility of the foremast light?
(See Rule 3 (a))

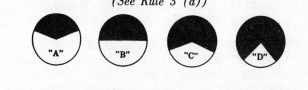

HOW WELL DO YOU KNOW THE RULES OF THE ROAD?

Part Four — WESTERN RIVERS

In previous installments, specimen questions were published from the Inland, International and Great Lakes rules of the road as used by the U.S. Coast Guard when renewing licenses for deck officers. We conclude, below, with questions from the Western River Rules. No operator's licenses are required on boats used exclusively for pleasure but these questions serve as a refresher to test your familiarity with the rules. Where appropriate citations are given in italics, see publication Rules of the Road, Western Rivers (U.S.C.G. 184).

If an overtaking vessel blows two distinct blasts and you think it dangerous for her to pass you:

(a) Blow one short blast, (b) Blow two short blasts, (c) Blow four or more short and rapid blasts, (d) Do not answer.

(See Rule Numbered 22)

If in overtaking another vessel as sketched at left you occasionally saw her mast lights and green side lights:

(a) The other vessel must keep clear of you, (b) You and the other vessel share equally the responsibility for keeping clear, (c) You should assume that it is your duty to keep clear, (d) You must alter course to the left.

(See Rule Numbered 22)

When underway, sail vessels and vessels towed make fog signals on the:

(a) Bell, (b) Whistle or fog horn, (c) Whistle, (d) Fog horn.

(See Rule Numbered 15)

In fog, an anchored vessel must ring the bell every:

(a) Minute for five seconds, (b) Two minutes for three seconds, (c) Three minutes for ten seconds, (d) Four minutes for five seconds.

(See Rule Numbered 15)

The two white lights displayed, as sketched at right, would indicate at night that the vessel is:

(a) Not under command, (b) Over 150 feet in length and is at anchor, (c) Under 150 feet in length and is at anchor, (d) A pilot vessel.

(See Rule Numbered 13)

Passing within 200 feet of floating plants in channels, maximum speed is:

(a) 3 mph, (b) 4 mph, (c) 5 mph, (d) 6 mph.

(See Western Rivers Pilot Rule 95.61)

If an ascending steamer makes no signal by the time a descending, approaching steamer is within one-half mile, the descending steamer blows first:

(a) One distinct blast, (b) Two distinct blasts, (c) Four or more short and rapid blasts, (d) One long blast.

(See Rule Numbered 18)

If the pilot of a descending steam vessel deems it unsafe to take the side indicated by a two blast signal given by an approaching, ascending steam vessel, he shall immediately signify that fact by sounding:

(a) One distinct blast, (b) Two distinct blasts, (c) Three distinct blasts, (d) Four or more short and rapid blasts.

(See Rule Numbered 18)

The two vessels sketched above, are governed by which of the following rules:

(a) Overtaking, (b) Meeting end on, (c) Crossing, (d) Approaching.

(See Rule Numbered 19)

When temporarily moored to the right bank in fog, a steamer hears a fog signal of an approaching vessel. The temporarily moored vessel should sound at intervals not to exceed one minute:

(a) One blast of the whistle, (b) Two blasts of the whistle, (c) One tap of the bell, (d) Two taps of the bell.

(See Rule Numbered 15)

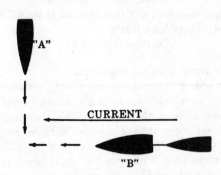

Steam vessel "B" (above) towing with the current has the right of way, and intends to cross the bow of "A." "B" should blow:

(a) One distinct blast of her whistle, (b) Two distinct blasts of her whistle, (c) Three distinct blasts of her whistle, (d) Four short and rapid blasts of her whistle.

(See Rule Numbered 19)

In fog, a steam vessel underway *without* a tow sounds at intervals not more than one minute:

(a) One long blast, (b) Three distinct blasts, (c) Two blasts of equal length, followed by a longer blast, (d) A longer blast followed by two blasts of equal length.

(See Rule Numbered 15)

In fog, a steam vessel underway and *towing* another vessel or vessels sounds at intervals of not more than one minute:

(a) One distinct blast of the whistle, (b) Two distinct blasts of the whistle, (c) Three distinct blasts of the whistle, (d) Four short and rapid blasts of the whistle.

(See Rule Numbered 15)

A vessel intending to pass a dredge first blows:

(a) One distinct blast, (b) Three distinct blasts, (c) Four short and rapid blasts, (d) One long blast.

(See Western Rivers Pilot Rule 95.60)

Where To Obtain Charts, Cruising Information, And Other Publications

CHARTS OF VARIOUS WATERWAYS

Charts, U. S. Coastal Waters—Charts of coastal waters such as the Atlantic, Pacific and Gulf Coasts, the Hudson River as far north as Troy, and the Atlantic and Gulf Intracoastal Waterways, are published by the United States Coast & Geodetic Survey, Washington 25, D. C., and are available from them, their district offices, or any of their sales agents, listed in their catalog, and semi-annually in the Hydrographic Office Notice to Mariners.

Charts, Great Lakes—Charts of the Great Lakes and connecting rivers, Lake Champlain, New York State Canals, Lake of the Woods, and Rainy Lake are available from the U. S. Lake Survey, 630 Federal Bldg., Detroit 26, Michigan. They also publish a catalog of charts issued by that office.

Charts, New York State Canals—A bound booklet of charts of the New York State canals (Champlain, Erie, Oswego, and Cayuga-Seneca), east of Lyons, is available from the U. S. Lake Survey, 630 Federal Building, Detroit, Mich.

Charts, Mississippi River and Tributaries—(*Middle & Upper Mississippi River; Cairo, Ill. to Minneapolis, Minn.*)
(*Middle Mississippi River; Cairo, Ill. to Grafton, Ill.*)
(*Mississippi River from Cairo, Ill. to Gulf of Mexico*)
(*Small Boat Navigation Chart; Alton, Ill. to Clarksville on the Mississippi River and Grafton, Ill., to LaGrange, Ill. on the Illinois River*)
U. S. Army Engineer District, 420 Locust Street, St. Louis 2, Missouri.
(*Illinois Waterways; from Grafton, Ill. to Lake Michigan at Chicago and Calumet Harbors*)—U. S. Army Engineer District, 536 So. Clark St., Chicago 5, Ill.
The offices listed below will supply exhaustive lists of available charts, detailing sources, prices, scales, and exact sections covered.
Mississippi River and connecting waterways, north of Ohio River—U. S. Army Engineer Division, North Central, 536 South Clark Street, Chicago 5, Ill.
Mississippi River and tributaries, below Ohio River—U. S. Army Engineer Division, Lower Mississippi Valley, P. O. Box 80, Vicksburg, Miss.
Ohio River and tributaries; Pittsburgh, Pa., to the Mississippi River—Ohio River Division, Corps of Engineers, P. O. Box 1159, Cincinnati 1, Ohio.
Missouri River—U. S. Army Engineers, 6012 U. S. Post Office and Court House, Omaha 2, Neb.
Tennessee River—Tennessee Valley Authority, Maps and Engineering Records Section, 102A Union Building, Knoxville, Tenn.

Charts, Canadian Waters—Charts of Canadian waters are available from Hydrographic Chart Distribution, Canadian Hydrographic Service, Department of Mines and Technical Surveys, 615 Booth St., Ottawa, Canada. These include charts of Canadian coastal waters; Canadian sections of the Great Lakes including Georgian Bay; the St. Lawrence River; Richelieu River; Ottawa River; The Rideau Waterway; and other Canadian lakes, canals, etc.
A chart catalog is available from Hydrographic Chart Distribution, at the address given above.

Charts, Foreign Waters—These are published by the U. S. Naval Oceanographic Office, Washington 25, D. C., and are available through any of the sales agents listed twice a year in Notice to Mariners, published by the U. S. Naval Oceanographic Office. A general catalog and ten regional catalogs are available.

NOTICE TO MARINERS

Notice to Mariners—This is a weekly pamphlet published by the U. S. Naval Oceanographic Office, Washington, D. C. It is issued so mariners may keep nautical charts and Coast Pilots up to date. Twice a year the Notices contain lists of Branch Oceanographic offices; U. S. Coast Guard District offices; U. S. Coast & Geodetic Survey District offices; U. S. Engineer offices; agents for the sale of Oceanographic Office charts and publications; data on all publications of the Oceanographic Office; data on the various Coast Pilots, Tide Tables, Current Tables and Tidal Current Charts sold by the U. S. Coast & Geodetic Survey; data on U. S. Coast Guard Light Lists; and a list of agents for the sale of Coast and Geodetic Survey and Coast Guard publications.
Local Notices, of interest primarily within the limits of each of the Coast Guard Districts, are issued by Commanders of the respective districts, and are available from their district offices.

COAST PILOTS

Coast Pilots—For coastal waters, and the Atlantic and Gulf Intracoastal Waterways, these are published by the U. S. Coast and Geodetic Survey, Washington 25, D. C., and are available from them, their district offices, or any of their sales agents in principal ports, as listed semi-annually in Notice to Mariners. These volumes supplement the information given on charts, with detailed descriptions of routes, courses, distances, depths, harbors, sources of supplies, tides, currents, weather, list of yacht clubs, facilities for repairs, etc.
For the Great Lakes and other waters covered by U. S. Lake Survey charts, the publication corresponding to the Coast Pilot is called the Great Lakes Pilot. This is an annual publication, kept up-to-date during the navigation season by seven monthly supplements issued from May to November. It is obtained from the U. S. Lake Survey, 630 Federal Bldg., Detroit 26, Michigan.
For Canadian waters—available from Hydrographic Chart Distribution, Canadian Hydrographic Office, Dept. of Mines and Technical Surveys, 615 Booth St., Ottawa, Canada. Details are given in the Coastal and Inland Waters Catalog available from Hydrographic Chart Distribution at the address given above. A descriptive list of Pilots and Sailing Directions is also available.

LIGHT LISTS

Light Lists—These are published by the U. S. Coast Guard and are for sale by the Superintendent of Documents, Washington 25, D. C., or any of the Coast Guard sales agents listed semi-annually in the Oceanographic Office Notice to Mariners. They describe lighted aids, radio beacons, fog signals, unlighted buoys, and daymarks. Vol. I covers Atlantic Coast from St. Croix River, Me., to Little River, S. C. Vol. II, Atlantic and Gulf Coasts from Little River, S. C., to Rio Grande River, Tex., and the Antilles. Vol. III, Pacific Coast and Islands. Vol. IV, Great Lakes. Vol. V, Mississippi River system.

TIDE AND CURRENT TABLES

Tide Tables, Current Tables and Tidal Current Charts—These are also publications of the U. S. Coast & Geodetic Survey, Washington 25, D. C., and may be obtained from them, their district offices, or from any of the sales agents listed semi-annually in Notice to Mariners.

Tides and Currents in Long Island and Block Island Sounds—Special publication No. 174 (1932). Superintendent of Documents, Government Printing Office, Washington 25, D. C.

RULES OF THE ROAD

Rules of the Road—Rules of the Road are published for three areas, namely: C.G. No. 169—Certain inland waters of the Atlantic and Pacific coasts and of the coast of the Gulf of Mexico; C.G. No. 172—The Great Lakes and their connecting and tributary waters and the St. Mary's River; and C.G. No. 184—The Western Rivers and the Red River of the North. They are published by the U. S. Coast Guard and copies may be obtained from Coast Guard Marine Inspection Offices in principal ports, or the Commandant (CHS), U. S. Coast Guard, Washington, D. C.

NEW YORK STATE CANALS

Rules and Regulations Covering Navigation and Use of the New York State Canal System—A booklet by this title is published by and is available from New York State Dept. of Public Works, Division of Operation and Maintenance, Albany 1, N. Y. It contains a description of the New York Canal System, and regulations pertaining to use of the canal. Applications for free season permits to use the canals should be made to the same office. (Information on the book of charts of the New York State Canal System, published by the U. S. Lake Survey, is given above.)

Canal Guide Book for the New York State Barge Canal System and Connecting Navigable Waterways—A booklet of great value in cruising the Hudson River, Lake Champlain, New York State canals, and connecting Canadian waterways, including the St. Lawrence River and parts of Lake Erie and Lake Ontario. Lists sources of supplies such as fuel, oil, engine repairs, fresh water, provisions, anchorage and dockage. Available from Cruising Guide Book, 146 Sheridan Avenue, Albany 10, N. Y.

INTRACOASTAL WATERWAYS

Inland Waterway Guide—A publication detailing for the yachtsman a vast amount of information concerning the inland waterways. The Northern Edition covers the coast from Maine to New York; the Middle Atlantic Edition from New York to Sea Island, Ga.; the Southern Edition from Sea Island, Ga., to Florida and Gulf Coast to New Orleans; the Great Lakes Edition from New York to the Great Lakes with connecting Canadian canals and rivers. Available from Inland Waterway Guide, Inc., 101 North Andrews Ave., Fort Lauderdale, Florida.

Intracoastal Waterway Booklets—Comprehensive descriptions of the Intracoastal Waterway, with data on navigation, charts, distances, etc. Prepared by Corps of Engineers, U. S. Army, and sold by Superintendent of Documents, Washington 25, D. C. In two sections: (1) Atlantic Section, Boston to Key West, (2) Gulf Section, Key West to Brownsville, Tex.

Intracoastal Waterway Bulletins—Frequent bulletins giving latest information on the condition of the Intracoastal Waterway are published by the Corps of Engineers. These are available from the following District Offices of the Army Engineers: Norfolk, Va.—Ft. of Front St.; Wilmington, N. C.—308 Custom House; Charleston, S. C.—Municipal Marina; Savannah, Ga.— 200 East St. Julian St.; Jacksonville, Fla.—575 Riverside Ave.; Galveston, Tex.—P. O. Box 1229; Mobile, Ala.—Box 1169.

OTHER CRUISING PUBLICATIONS

Cruising Charts, Guides and Booklets—Some of the large oil companies provide free cruising services for yachtsmen. These companies will go to considerable length to provide such items as cruising charts from which the itinerary can be planned, harbor booklets showing the facilities available in all the principal ports, mimeographed outlines of various cruises containing a digest of up-to-date information on the waterways involved, etc. Sources for this kind of material include: Texaco Waterways Service, 135 E. 42nd St., New York 17, N. Y.; Gulf Tourgide Bureau, Box 8056, Philadelphia 1, Pa. (east of Mississippi); Mobil Touring Service, Mobil Oil Co., 150 E. 42nd St., New York 17, N. Y.; Esso Touring Service, 15 W. 51st St., New York 19, N. Y.

Cruising Guide to the New England Coast—Descriptions of harbors, anchorages, and waterways by Fessenden Blanchard. Includes Hudson River, Long Island Sound and the New Brunswick coast. Available from Sailing Book Service, 31 E. 10th St., New York 3, N. Y.

Yachtsman's Guide to Northern Harbors—Harbors, boat basins and services around Long Island, and seacoast of New England. Seaport Publishing Co., 843 Delray Ave., S.E., Grand Rapids 6, Mich.

Guide for Cruising Maryland Waters—Prepared by Maryland Dept. of Tidewater Fisheries. Twenty full-color charts, with more than 200 courses and distances plotted. Maryland Board of Natural Resources, State Office Bldg., Annapolis, Md. Available from the same address is the pilot edition of Maryland Marine Facilities.

Chesapeake Bay Country—With map in color of Chesapeake Bay country and tributaries, indexed marine facilities, and fishing grounds, Dept. of Tidewater Fisheries, Annapolis, Md.

Florida Boating—Pamphlet giving data on waterways, charts, Florida boat registration, and water safety regulations, fishing licenses, area maps and information, plus a directory of marine facilities throughout the state. Available from Florida Development Commission, Carlton Bldg., Tallahassee, Fla.

Yachtsman's Guide to the Great Lakes—Harbors, services, supplies on the Great Lakes, St. Lawrence River, Richelieu River, Lake Champlain, and New York State Barge Canal. Seaport Publishing Co., 843 Delray Ave., S. E., Grand Rapids 6, Mich.

Cruising the Georgian Bay—Cruising information, with 23 pages of Ontario Government Aerial Survey Maps and tabulations of services and facilities at ports. British Book Service (Canada) Ltd., Kingswood House, 1068 Broadview Ave., Toronto 6, Can.

Cruising the North Channel—Covers the waterway between Manitoulin Island and the north shore of Lake Huron. British Book Service, see address above.

Cruising the Trent-Severn Waterway—A cruising guide, including rules and regulations, supply points and services, mileages and general data. British Book Service, see address above.

Trent Severn Waterway Guide—All the data you need to cruise the Trent, including tables of mileages, general information, and index map of charts required. Gillis Adv. Service, 252½ Charlotte St., Peterborough, Ont., Can.

Trailer Boating Where the North Begins—Written especially for the small boatman, and includes the Muskoka, Parry Sound, and Lake-of-Bays areas of Ontario. British Book Service, see address above.

Harbor Guide to the Upper Mississippi River—From St. Paul to Davenport, including St. Croix River. Covers harbors (services and location), cities and towns (population, transportation, shopping centers, tourist interest), locks and dams, mileage charts, source of navigation charts, history of river. Available from Quimby, 322½ Brady, Davenport, Iowa.

Yachtsman's Guide to the Bahamas—A complete guide book for a cruise in the Bahamas. The data it contains is much like the information found in Coast Pilots. The Customs and Immigration information will be found especially valuable to those who have never cruised to foreign waters. Available from Tropic Isle Publishers, Inc., P. O. Box 34-613, Coral Gables, Fla.

The Alluring Antilles—This cruising guide provides accurate, precise and ample information about every island in the West Indies. D. Van Nostrand Co., Inc., 120 Alexander St., Princeton, N. J.

Virgin Islands—Eggleston's descriptions of islands, harbors, people, history, passages, and facilities. Illustrated. Sailing Book Service, 31 E. 10th St., New York 3, N. Y.

U. S. COAST GUARD PUBLICATIONS

Recreational Boating Guide—CG-340. 77 pp. Information on boat numbering; legal minimum equipment requirements; other equipment you should carry; responsibilities when operating; aids to navigation; hints on safety afloat; emergency procedures; and U. S. Coast Guard Auxiliary services. Contains copies of Federal Boating Act of 1958, and the Motorboat Act of April 25, 1940; sample of Application for Number form; Boating Accident Report; and Radio Distress Information Sheet. Superintendent of Documents, Government Printing Office, Washington 25, D. C.

Pleasure Craft—CG-290. Digest of boating laws and regulations. Numbering. Boating accidents. Sales to aliens. Law enforcement. Documentation. C. G. approved equipment. Equipment requirements. Suggestions for safety.

Aids to Marine Navigation of the United States—U. S. Coast Guard publication CG-193. Illustrated. 32 pages. Treasury Department, U. S. Coast Guard, Washington 25, D. C. Basic principles underlying the marking of coasts and waterways with lighthouses, lightships, fog signals, radiobeacons, loran, and buoys. Treats primarily of the manner in which the physical characteristics of various aids to navigation serve the mariner.

Marine Radiobeacons—U. S. Coast Guard. 16 pp. Obtainable from U. S. Coast Guard, Washington, D. C. Instructional pamphlet for the beginner studying navigation.

Ocean Electronic Navigational Aids—U. S. Coast Guard pamphlet CG 157-1. 73 pp. Loran, radiobeacon and radarbeacon systems; and loran, radio direction finder and radar ship equipment. United States Coast Guard, Washington 25, D. C. Available from Superintendent of Documents, Washington 25, D. C.

Rules and Regulations for Uninspected Vessels—U. S. Coast Guard. 16 pages. Copies may be obtained from District Coast Guard Offices. Requirements for all vessels not subject to inspection, including those subject to the Motorboat Act of April 25, 1940. Every motorboat owner should obtain a copy. Refer to CG-258.

Rules and Regulations for Numbering Undocumented Vessels—U. S. Coast Guard publication CG-267. Available from District Coast Guard Offices or the Commandant (CHS), U. S. Coast Guard, Washington, D. C.

Rules and Regulations for Small Passenger Vessels—U. S. Coast Guard publication CG-323. Requirements for vessels carrying more than six passengers. Available from District Coast Guard Offices, or the Commandant, U. S. Coast Guard, Washington 25, D. C.

Manual for Lifeboatmen and Able Seamen—Illustrated. 63 pages. Obtainable from the U. S. Coast Guard, Washington, D. C. Lifeboats, life rafts, life floats, buoyant apparatus, davits, and releasing gear are described. Refer to C.G. 175.

GASOLINE TAX REFUNDS

Gasoline Tax Refunds—The Federal government and some states allow a refund, in whole or in part, of the gasoline tax when the fuel is used for boat purposes. However, the regulations differ greatly and it would be well for the yachtsman to become familiar with these regulations in advance. The Texaco Waterways Service, 135 E. 42nd Street, New York 17, N. Y.; and Mobil Oil Co., Inc., Marine Retail Dept., 150 E. 42nd St., New York 17, N. Y., issue Bulletins describing these regulations.

Rules of the Nautical Road—U. S. Naval Institute, Annapolis, Md. Revised edition by Lt. Alfred Prunski, U.S.C.G., of the textbook by Captain Raymond F. Farwell, U.S.N.R., designed to show new changes in International Rules which took effect January 1, 1954. Gives comparison with up-to-date Inland Rules and Pilot Rules. Includes interpretations of rules by courts.

The American Nautical Almanac—United States Naval Observatory. Copies purchased from the Superintendent of Documents. A compact publication containing all the ephemeris material essential to the solution of problems of navigational position. Contains a Star Chart which shows the position of the stars used in navigation. Instructions for its use are included. The Star Chart may be purchased separately. (Star Chart in larger form may be purchased from Oceanographic Office sales agents.)

Tide and Current Investigations of the Coast and Geodetic Survey—U. S. Department of Commerce, Coast and Geodetic Survey. Illustrated. 50 pages. Types and forms of tides, earthquake waves, tidal currents, and wind currents.

First Aid—Supt. of Documents, Washington, D. C. Illustrated. 160 pages. This is one of the best first aid manuals obtainable. Only first aid instruction is given.

Miscellaneous Publication No. 9. The Ship's Medicine Chest and First Aid at Sea—United States Public Health Service. Illustrated. 498 pages. Prepared especially for seafaring people. An excellent treatise. Sections included give special instruction for emergency treatment, and First Aid by Radio. (Superintendent of Documents, Washington 25, D. C.)

Magnetic Poles and the Compass—U. S. Coast and Geodetic Survey. Superintendent of Documents, Washington, D. C.

MISCELLANEOUS PUBLICATIONS
OF THE OCEANOGRAPHIC OFFICE

The Oceanographic Office produces charts and Sailing Directions (Pilots) and lists of lights of all oceans and seas, and of foreign coasts and islands and harbors, but only general charts of the coasts of the United States.

Information on Oceanographic Office Charts and Publications. H. O. Pub. 1-N. Catalog listing some of the more popular index charts, world charts, general nautical charts, magnetic charts, pilot charts, bathymetric charts, special charts, plotting charts, oceanographic and bottom sediment charts, aeronautical charts, loran charts, published by the U. S. Navy Oceanographic Office, with information on H. O. nautical, aeronautical and oceanographic publications. Free Introduction, Part I, is a general listing.

Sailing Directions are books supplementing the nautical charts issued by the Oceanographic Office. They contain descriptions of coast lines, harbors, dangers, aids, port facilities, and other data which cannot be conveniently shown on charts.

Notice to Mariners containing corrections to nautical charts and publications are issued weekly by the Oceanographic Office, Branch Oceanographic Offices, and United States Consulates.

Daily Memorandum carries a synopsis of the latest information relating to dangers and aids to navigation, including reports of drifting buoys, wreckage, and other hazards together with advance items that will appear in the Notice to Mariners. The Daily Memorandum is issued locally by the Branch Oceanographic Offices and the most urgent of the reports are also broadcast by radio under the title, Government Hydro All Ships and Stations, and rebroadcast locally.

Pilot Charts of the North Atlantic Ocean, North Pacific Ocean are issued monthly. These present information on average winds and currents, percentages of gales and calms, and other hydrographic data of a varied nature.

H.O. Pilot Charts

#576 Atlas of Pilot Charts—South Atlantic Ocean and Central American Waters.

#577 Atlas of Pilot Charts—South Pacific, Indian Oceans.

#1400 Pilot Chart of the North Atlantic Ocean (Monthly).

#1401 Pilot Chart of the North Pacific Ocean (Monthly).

H.O. Lists of Lights and Fog Signals

Light Lists published by the Oceanographic Office give detailed descriptions of navigational lights and fog signals, and mention signals of various kinds operated at lighthouses.

Vol. I covers the Coast of North and South America (only the seacoast lights of the United States), the West Indies, and the Hawaiian Islands.

Vol. II covers islands of the Pacific and Indian Oceans, Australia, Asia, and the East Coast of Africa.

Vol. III covers the West Coasts of Europe and Africa, the Mediterranean Sea, Black Sea, and the Sea of Azov.

Vol. IV covers the British Islands, English Channel, and North Sea.

Vol. V covers Norway, Iceland, and Arctic Ocean.

Vol. VI covers the Baltic Sea with Kattegat, Belts and Sound, and Gulf of Bothnia.

Volumes I, II, III, are revised and reissued annually and Volumes IV, V, VI at less frequent intervals. Volumes IV, V, VI are corrected by annual supplements containing changes that have taken place during the year or years since the books were published. These supplements are mailed free of charge to purchasers of the books. Weekly corrections to the Light Lists are published in the section, Corrections to H.O. Light Lists, at the end of the Notice to Mariners. This section includes minor corrections not appearing in the main body of the Notice.

Other H. O. Publications of the Oceanographic Office

Chart #1—Nautical Chart Symbols and Abbreviations.

#9 American Practical Navigator. Originally by Nathaniel Bowditch, LL.D. etc. Revised (Including the Useful Tables.)

#234 Breakers and Surf; Principles in Forecasting.

#601 Wind, Sea, and Swell: Theory of Relations in Forecasting.

#602 Wind Waves at Sea, Breakers and Surf.

#103 International Code of Signals, Vol. I, Visual Signals.

#104 International Code of Signals, Vol. II, Radio Signals.

#117 Radio Navigational Aids. Marine Direction-Finding Stations, Radiobeacons, Time Signals, Navigational Warnings, Distress Signals, Medical Advice and Quarantine Stations, Loran, Consol, and Regulations Governing the Use of Radio in Territorial Waters.

#118 Radio Weather Aids. General weather information, broadcast schedules, international index numbers with locations of stations, key groups, and call signs.

#151 Tables of Distances Between Ports.

#2100 World Star Chart.

#2102D Star Finder and Identifier (AN Type).

#226 Handbook of Magnetic Compass Adjustment and Compensation.

WEATHER

Weather Forecasting—U. S. Department of Commerce, Weather Bureau. Illustrated. 40 pages. Generally accepted facts and theories of meteorology and some of the principles of weather forecasting, in popular style. Atmospheric Pressure, Circulation of the Atmosphere, Weather Forecasting, and An Atmospheric Survey, concerning the gathering of information by the Weather Bureau stations for weather maps. Superintendent of Documents, Washington 25, D. C.

The Hurricane—United States Department of Commerce, Weather Bureau. Illustrated. 22 pages. An interesting paper dealing solely with the hurricane. The general information contained in this publication should be known by all who go to sea. Superintendent of Documents, Washington 25, D. C.

Circular R. W. B. 1151 Preparation and Use of Weather Maps at Sea—U. S. Department of Commerce, Weather Bureau. Illustrated. 100 pages. The Ship's weather observation, Radio weather message and its uses, Radio weather bulletins, Preparation of weather maps, Weather types, Tropical storms. Drawing inferences from weather map.

Florida Hurricanes—United States Department of Commerce, Weather Bureau. Illustrated. 3 pages. Discusses frequency, time, and initial starting point of Florida hurricanes. The eight great hurricanes that reached the Florida coast in the last fifty years are described. Wind velocities, damage by hurricanes to buildings, and other property are additional items of interest.

Circular F. Barometers and the Measurement of Atmospheric Pressure—U. S. Department of Commerce, Weather Bureau. Illustrated. 3 pages. A treatise on different kinds of barometers.

The Daily Weather Map—United States Department of Commerce, Weather Bureau. Five weather maps of the United States are included, data for which are prepared from observations taken daily at hundreds of stations throughout North America. A complete explanation of the maps, including all symbols and tables used in plotting the data appears on the reverse side of the Sunday map only. Superintendent of Documents, Washington 25, D. C.

Manual of Cloud Forms and Codes for States of Sky—United States Department of Commerce, Weather Bureau Circular S. Illustrated. 43 pages. Definitions and descriptions of cloud forms, specifications of cloud codes, etc.

EQUIPMENT CARRIED BY U.S. COAST GUARD AUXILIARY FACILITIES

*Special requirements regarding equipment applicable to boats enrolled in the
Coast Guard Auxiliary, flying the Auxiliary flag—the boats used by Auxiliary
members in making courtesy examinations preliminary to award of a decalcomania*

As THE guiding thought behind all United States Coast Guard Auxiliary operations is safety, it is only logical that standards set for equipment of C.G.A. vessel facilities are even higher than requirements for award of a decalcomania to a pleasure boat operator.

An Auxiliary vessel must be one of the safest boats afloat. To this end, in its Vessel Examiners Guide (CG-289), the Coast Guard outlines certain minimum requirements for different types of craft flying the Auxiliary flag.

Auxiliary facilities of the conventional pleasure boat type, for example, must carry at least two *anchors* and *lines*—a medium weight anchor for service conditions and a heavier one for use in emergencies. Length and diameter of anchor lines will depend on a number of variables such as the length and weight of boat, normal depths of water, the type of fiber used, etc.

For signaling they must carry a *distress flare* and the means of producing a *flashing light* at night. *Bilge pumps* must be in good order. Class 2 and 3 boats must have at least two means of pumping bilges.

Storage batteries must be secured against shifting, and covered to minimize danger from sparks should a tool or metal object be accidentally dropped across terminals. Terminals must be soldered lug type, and additional recommendations are given as to location of batteries for safety.

High standards are set for the installation of *wiring* and electrical connections, *fuel systems, auxiliary generators, stoves* and *heaters*. Gasoline is not acceptable as fuel in stoves in any Auxiliary facility.

The items noted above are those specifically mentioned as applicable to all Auxiliary facilities of the pleasure motorboat type. Beyond that, an additional list of equipment is required; this varies, naturally, with the type and size of boat and its location. The Director of Auxiliary in each District advises Examiners which items must be carried by vessels in his particular District.

A typical listing of such additional (mandatory) equipment is given below, as it applies to Auxiliary boats enrolled in the Third Coast Guard District, Southern Area. Pleasure boatmen in general will find it helpful as a guide.

Equipment Req—Required NR—Not required Opt—Optional	Sailboats of open design (used primarily for racing)	Class A and Class I (open boats)	Class I and II (except Class I open boats)	Class III and Facilities over 65' in length	Equipment Req—Required NR—Not required Opt—Optional	Sailboats of open design (used primarily for racing)	Class A and Class I (open boats)	Class I and II (except Class I open boats)	Class III and Facilities over 65' in length
1. Charts	Opt	Opt	*	*	14. Fenders	Opt	Opt	Opt	Opt
2. Light List	NR	NR	NR	NR	15. Boathook	Req	Req	Req	Req
3. Lake Survey Bulletin	NR	NR	NR	NR	16. Water lights	NR	NR	Opt	Opt
4. Coast or River Pilot (Sandy Hook to Cape Henry)	NR	NR	Req	Req	17. Searchlight	Opt	Opt	Opt	Opt
5. Deviation table	NR	NR	Req	Req	18. Hand lead and lines	Opt	Opt	Req	Req
6. RPM table (except outboard)	NR	NR	Req	Req	19. Mooring lines	Req	Req	Req	Req
7. First aid kit	Req	Req	Req	Req	20. Heaving lines	Opt	Opt	Req	Req
8. Means of taking bearing	NR	NR	Req	Req	21. Tools	Req	Req	Req	Req
9. Auxiliary ensign	Preferable if a regular member				22. Extra oil lamp or flashlight	Req	Req	Req	Req
10. National ensign	Opt	Opt	Opt	Opt	23. Spare running light bulbs	Req	Req	Req	Req
11. Compass	NR	NR	Req	Req	24. Course protractor or parallel rules	NR	NR	Req	Req
12. Dividers	NR	NR	Req	Req	25. Aircraft emergency procedure	Req	Req	Req	Req
13. Ring buoy (or one spare approved buoyant cushion)	NR	NR	Req	Req	* Local and coast charts				

494

PILOTING, SEAMANSHIP AND SMALL BOAT HANDLING

1964–65 Edition

MoToR BoatinG's Ideal Series — Volume V

GENERAL INDEX

(See Definitions of Nautical Terms, Pages 440x, 441-456 and Contents, Pages vii and viii)

NOTE:—Page numbers in the 1964–65 edition of this book remain the same as in earlier editions. Additional new material is folioed by the use of letters, a, b, c, etc.

* NOTE:—Although this page is numbered "504," yet by actual count it is in reality page No. "624." This difference is due to the fact that many pages are numbered, such as 27, 27a, 27b, 27c, etc. Altogether in this edition there are 120 pages so numbered. The reason for this is that, as new material is added to new editions, such new pages are given folio numbers corresponding to those of the existing allied subjects plus letters. By this method the basic page numbers remain unchanged and reference in student outlines, etc., do not go out-of-date.